HANDBOOK OF CHILD PSYCHOLOGY

HANDBOOK OF CHILD PSYCHOLOGY

Formerly CARMICHAEL'S MANUAL
OF CHILD PSYCHOLOGY

PAUL H. MUSSEN EDITOR

FOURTH EDITION

Volume I
HISTORY, THEORY, AND METHODS

William Kessen
VOLUME EDITOR

JOHN WILEY & SONS
NEW YORK   CHICHESTER   BRISBANE   TORONTO   SINGAPORE

Library of Congress Cataloging in Publication Data
Main entry under title:

History, theory, and methods.

   (Handbook of child psychology; v. 1)
   Includes bibliographies and index.
   1. Child psychology—History. 2. Child psychology—
Methodology. I. Kessen, William. II. Series.
[DNLM: 1. Child psychology. WS 105 H2354 (P)]
BF721.H242 1983 vol. 1 155.4s [155.4'09]   83-6517
ISBN 0-471-09057-3

Printed in the United States of America

10 9 8 7 6 5 4 3

65, 128

PREFACE TO THE FOURTH EDITION

The *Handbook of Child Psychology* is a direct descendant of three editions of the *Manual of Child Psychology*. The first and second editions, edited by Leonard Carmichael, were published in 1946 and 1954, the third, called *Carmichael's Manual of Child Psychology*, which I edited, was published in 1970. Each of these editions attempted to provide a definitive account of the state of knowledge of child psychology at the time of its publication.

In the 13 years since the publication of the third edition of *Carmichael's Manual*, child psychology has been an extraordinarily lively and productive discipline, expanding in many directions and at a rapid rate. Only a few of the most important of the countless changes will be reviewed here. The volume of the research activity and the annual output of research articles and books have accelerated enormously. As more information accumulates, new questions are generated, new research approaches are invented and older ones are applied in new versions, established theories are challenged and revised, novel theories are proposed, concepts are redefined, and specialized fields of interest and investigation evolve. These changes are closely intertwined and consequently have an impact on one another. Investigation of a new issue (or a revised version of an older one) often requires novel research techniques and approaches. New research findings may evoke questions about the conclusions derived from earlier studies and about underlying theories, and these questions, in turn, lead to further research. These cycles of events are repeated, progress in the field is continuous, and the amount of accumulated data snowballs. Consequently, even an authoritative 1970 publication cannot give an adequate picture of the field in the 1980s. A brand new source book is needed and the present volumes are intended to satisfy this need.

This *Handbook* attempts to reflect the changes in child psychology that have occurred since 1970 and to present as comprehensive, balanced, and accurate a survey of the contem-porary field as possible. It is twice the size of the earlier two-volume work and differs from it in many ways. The coverage is broader and more topics are included, discussed in greater depth, and organized according to different principles. Discussions of topics of enduring interest that were presented in chapters in the last edition of *Carmichael's Manual*—for example, Piaget's theory, learning, language, thinking, aggression, sex-typing, socialization in the family and peer group—are reconceptualized and brought up to date in chapters in this *Handbook*.

The reader may get a clearer understanding of the structure and contents of the *Handbook* by noting some of the most significant contrasts between it and the last edition of *Carmichael's Manual*. The *Handbook* includes more chapters on theories and fundamental approaches to research in child psychology (Volume I). The chapter by Piaget on his own theory has been retained. In addition, there are chapters on information processing and systems theories—previously applied to issues in perception, learning, cognition, and social organization—which have proven useful in integrating a substantial body of the data of developmental psychology and in stimulating research. Cross-cultural and field studies have become very fruitful in the last 20 years and these too are discussed in separate chapters, as are the latest advances in general research methodology and assessment. And, as the discipline has matured, there is heightened (or renewed) interest in its philosophical and historical antecedents, so two chapters of Volume I are centered on these issues.

Developmental psychologists have always been interested in the *origins* of behavior, and the factors involved in very early development have become more prominent foci of research attention in the last 10 or 15 years. The psychological study of infants has burgeoned, while advances in research methodology in physiology, ethology, genetics, and neurology have made possible more refined and penetrating explorations of the biological bases of behavior. These research emphases are examined in Volume II of this *Handbook*.

The content area of greatest activity since 1970 has been cognitive development and the results of this activity are apparent in Volume III. For example, the third edition of *Carmichael's Manual* contained one chapter on language development and it dealt almost exclusively with the acquisition of grammar. In contrast, the *Handbook* has separate chapters on grammar, meaning, and communication. Much of the recent research in cognitive development confirms and extends Piaget's conclusions, but the results of other studies challenge aspects of Piagetian theory. Both kinds of findings are included in chapters in Volume III.

Several research areas that were new in 1970 have become well established, vigorous, and fruitful. Among these are social cognitive development, moral reasoning, and prosocial behavior; each of these is the topic of a chapter in this *Handbook*. In addition a number of traditional issues that had been somewhat neglected until recently have become more prominent in the literature of developmental psychology. For example, this *Handbook* contains chapters on representation, on logical thinking, play, the self, and on the school as an agent of socialization. None of these topics was discussed in the 1970 edition of *Carmichael's Manual*.

In response to social needs, developmental psychologists in increasing numbers conduct research on practical problems and attempt to apply their research findings to the solution of urgent problems, spelling out the implications of basic data for such areas as educational practice and social policy (see particularly the chapters on intervention and on risk factors in development in Volume II, on learning, memory, and comprehension in Volume III, and on treatment of children with emotional problems in Volume IV). The results of these activities are highly salutary for advancing the field of child psychology, for they extend the definitions of concepts investigated, test the findings of laboratory research in real-life settings, and illuminate the limitations of available data and theory.

The volume editors (William Kessen of Yale University, Marshall Haith and Joseph Campos of the University of Denver, John Flavell and Ellen Markman of Stanford, and E. Mavis Hetherington of the University of Virginia) and I met to plan and organize this *Handbook* over five years ago. Our objective was clear and straightforward: to prepare a source book that would present as complete, accurate, balanced, and up-to-date view of the field as possible.

Although there is no entirely satisfactory way of subdividing and organizing all of the vast body of theory, methods, and data in a field as large, varied, and ever-changing as developmental psychology, we constructed a table of contents that in our opinion included all the key topics—that is, all the topics that are currently receiving substantial amounts of research and theoretical attention. It soon became obvious that four volumes would be required, and we decided to arrange the material in accordance with the four predominent divisions of the field—theory and methods, biological bases of behavior and infancy, cognitive development, and social and personality development.

Comprehensive coverage was not our only aim; integrative summaries were to be accompanied by new perspectives and insights, critical analyses, and explications of deficiencies in existing data and theoretical orientations. We hoped to produce more than an encyclopedic review of accumulated knowledge; our goal was a source book that would encourage sophisticated thinking about fundamental issues, formulation of questions and hypotheses, and, ultimately, more good research.

We selected and invited a group of distinguished authorities in developmental psychology and related fields who were highly qualified to contribute chapters that would accomplish these goals. Almost all of our invitations were accepted and the assignments were carried out with extraordinary diligence, care, and thoughtfulness. Each working outline, preliminary draft, and final manuscript was reviewed by the volume editor, the general editor, and another authority on the subject, and suggestions for revision were communicated to the author. Although three of the chapters included in the original plan are missing, all the key chapters are included. We are therefore convinced that the *Handbook* provides the most comprehensive picture of contemporary child psychology that exists in one place.

If the objectives of the *Handbook* have been achieved, it is due primarily to the painstaking work, dedication, and creativity of the contributors and the volume editors. The lion's share of the basic work—preparation of scholarly, integrative, and critical chapters—was done by the authors. The contribution of the volume editors was indispensable; in their difficult roles of critic, advisor, and guardian of high standards, they were infinitely wise, patient, and persistent. My debts to all these individuals are incalculable.

PAUL H. MUSSEN

PREFACE TO VOLUME I

From the beginning, children were part and parcel of American psychology, although not everyone who helped make psychology an academic discipline proved friendly to research with the young. In fact, the legendary founders of American psychology were a mixed lot, and, in the proper way of legends, they have become more distinct from one another and more mythic in form as the years pass. James the polymath, Ladd the clerical oldtimer, Titchener the bringer of the New German Psychology—as well as Hall, Baldwin, Dewey, Cattell, each with his own distinctive personality and contribution—have all been carved oversize and put in niches made to shape them. But myths are not wholly false; legends do have their reasons. Indeed, we may understand better the growth of child psychology if we look back for a moment at our origins. James, Ladd, and Titchener had no professional interest in children; Titchener, like his mentor Wundt, thought an experimental psychology of children impossible. But the four other men in this short list shared the creation of developmental study in America and each, planfully or not, staked out a distinctive working strategy toward children and toward research with children that can be seen still in the divisions of contemporary child psychology.

G. Stanley Hall, as he did in his lifetime, slips out of any simple mold; whether we praise his breadth or regret his shallowness, child psychologists owe Hall for the institutionalization of professional interest in children. We also owe him, perhaps less gladly, for the strategy that can best be called *child study,* a sometimes undisciplined but always enthusiastic interest in all the doings of children. Child study was, after Hall, not a regular or comfortable part of the academic study of children; rather, the strategy was worked out in isolated pockets until the establishment of the great longitudinal studies of the Thirties gave child study both an institutional definition and a somewhat systematic mode of study.

In contrast, child science—the hardheaded study of children, calling on classical research models and emphasizing its rigor and epistemological correctness—was early on and continuously connected with American colleges and universities. The spokesman for child science between 1855 and 1905 was James Mark Baldwin, who scarcely veiled his opinion of President Hall and child study in a little book that he wrote for laymen in 1898.

''Child study'' has become a fad to be pursued by parents and teachers who know little about the principles of scientific method, and where influential educators have enlisted so-called ''observers'' in taking indiscriminate notes on the doings of children with no definite problem in view, and with no criticism of their procedure.

Because Baldwin cared about social psychology and because his later work on genetic epistemology has put him retrospectively in the line that led to Piaget, we tend to forget that he was also the fiery defender of the laboratory experimental study of ''reflex movements, . . . sensation, . . . discrimination and preference, the origin of right- and left-handedness, . . . the meaning of imitation, the acquisition of speech . . . , the growth of the child's sense of personality and of his social consciousness, and the laws of physical growth.'' Given this listing of approved topics, one can easily see Watson as Baldwin's successor in preserving a strategy toward children that valued sound method, laboratory manipulation, strong theory, and the education of expert child scientists.

A third line of strategy toward children in the first years of American psychology was suggested in the early years of John Dewey's career and increasingly became a central theme of his massive work—*child as social construction.* In his *Psychology* (1887, 1889), Dewey sketched an image of the mind that was radically different from Hall's and that of the early Baldwin.

The mind grows, not by keeping unchanged within itself fair or unconscious copies of its original experiences, but by assimilating something from each experience, so that the next time it acts it has a more definite mode of activity to bring to bear.

Together with G. H. Mead, Dewey elaborated the social constructionist strategy into a philosophy, a pedagogy, a social and a cognitive psychology. For reasons not fully documented but surely related to the institutional tension between pedagogy and psychology, Dewey's influence on the study of the child flowed through educational rather than psychological channels. Through much of the century, his vision of the child was protected in academic settings more by Europeans than by Americans.

James McK. Cattell, the longtime survivor of the founding, takes his place in the pantheon as the strategist of *child as measurable.* He, with Jastrow, established the psychometric line that has persisted, in child psychology and in the field at large, with such stamina and stability for almost a hundred years.

This *Handbook,* which descends in noble lineage from Murchison's *Handbook* of 1931—and especially this first volume—represents a coming into touch of the four main strategic strands in the history of child psychology as epitomized by the work of Hall, Baldwin, Dewey, and Cattell. More than their Murchison and Carmichael predecessors, the chapters that follow are sensitive to the high cost of maintaining these separate strategies in isolation from one another and, at the same time, sensitive to the high promise of winding them together. If there is a singular theme that can be heard throughout *History, Theory, and Methods,* it is the theme of *contextual child psychology.* The chapters on history are explicitly and necessarily concerned with the place of children and child research in the cultural context of their times. The chapters on theories, though they show less vividly the agitation of a contextual psychology, clearly recognize the rootedness of children in their individual places and moments, and emphasize the centrality of their caretakers. And the chapters on methods are,

without exception, essays on the new ways we must devise in order to understand the life of children in the context of their families, their social surroundings, and their cultures.

The most joyful reading in this volume are the passages that attempt to conjoin—and, at the same time, to preserve—the openness and humanity of Hall, the rigor of Baldwin, the social sensitivity of Dewey, and the metrical hopes of Cattell in our study of children. In these pages, the mythic forms are in conversation. Even without so euphoric a reading, this volume, with its companions, presents an accurate portrait of child psychology in the latter years of the twentieth century—still a field of inquiry pursuing empirical study, still seeking theoretical guidance, still searching for revealing methods—but in tones different from those of 1946 or 1954 or 1970: child psychology, as this volume reveals, now confronts frankly the complexity of the child's life and takes more intellectual risks in trying to understand the child in context. I am convinced that, of all the ancestors of Volume I of the *Handbook,* John Dewey has most reason to smile broadly at the general acceptance given his special legacy.

If the rank of Hero-Author were in the Editor's gift, I would award it to each of the people who have labored, each in his own way and each at his own pace, to construct the present volume. The rewards for the authors were largely the rewards of duty done and responsibility accepted; the tasks accepted, as you will see, were Herculean. Throughout the several years that the volume has been growing, all of its contributors have remained committed, thoughtful, and concerned; I am grateful to them in my own voice and for the community of child psychologists. Of course, editors of volumes have somewhat ambiguous conceptions of their role—ranging from that of a shrewish nudge who natters constantly all the way to that of a Michaelangelo who helps a masterpiece to emerge from stone. But perhaps the most accurate metaphor for the Editor is caretaker of reluctant coccoons. He knows that the butterflies, colorful and high-flying, are there somewhere in the dark; and like the caretaker, he can only wait, as patiently as he can, for the metamorphosis to be completed.

Two butterflies are missing from this collection. The Editors had hoped to have a new chapter from Jean Piaget but he chose, in 1978, not to prepare another contribution. Our further hope, that one of the members of the Geneva group would either comment on and extend Piaget's 1970 chapter or write a new piece, was also disappointed. The absence of a new chapter on Piaget has been repaired in large measure by the decision to reprint, with minor editorial changes, the fine statement that he prepared for the *Manual of Child Psychology* just over a decade ago. The second absence is more glar-

ing. The Editors felt that the *Manual* should contain an original commentary on present-day psychoanalytic views of child development. Unfortunately, such a chapter could not be completed in time to join its companions here.

For the rest, the chapters that follow will speak in their own voices and with their own authority. The children you will meet in the minds of child psychologists in 1983 are subtly and valuably different from the ones you met in the *Manual* of 1970. The transformations are benign; they measure the liveliness, the openness, and the variety of child psychology in our time.

WILLIAM KESSEN

New Haven, Connecticut

CONTENTS

CHILDREN BEFORE PSYCHOLOGY: IDEAS ABOUT CHILDREN FROM ANTIQUITY TO THE LATE 1800s | 1

LLOYD J. BORSTELMANN, *Duke University*

CHAPTER CONTENTS

The present survey is concerned with ideological conceptions of the child from antiquity to the late nineteenth century, with the premise that perspectives on children are cultural inventions: beliefs about the nature, development, and socialization of children constructed and sustained in the service of a society's beliefs about human nature, the social order, and the cosmos. In this study, ideologies refer to ideas concerning observed events, especially those of social life that are commonly shared among persons of particular groups and that serve as articles of faith. As historians, child specialists, or citizens, we should neither ignore nor deny our own inventions; nor should we derogate those of others, but instead seek to understand each vision in the context of persons, places, and times. Polyani is no doubt correct that all knowledge is personal; yet any conclusions we agree to accept as scientifically established must accord with acknowledged rules of evidence. But we must also recognize that science thrives and develops more often than not through discord than accord, and consensual acceptance may mask more than reveal understanding. Yet faith and hope in the destiny of ourselves and our children, which are essential to the enterprise of childrearing, necessitate conceptions about the child appropriate to our total pattern of beliefs about life and death. To convey some sense of this story in times past is the intention of the present inquiry.

Our task of grasping the whole sweep of Western civilization's variegated notions about children has only begun. Those of us who seek such understanding can offer at this time only mere sketches for a landscape, glimpses into the murky domestic scenes of the past. Until quite recently, the intellectual discipline of history has shown little interest in the ubiquitously ordinary, mundane matters of the household, save for the private lives of important public persons. Certain newer trends in historical scholarship have contributed to and defined a recent upsurge of investigations into children of times past. Although some historians pioneered early in this century (Earle, 1915; Payne, 1916) by inquiring into ideas about the nature of children and conceptions of childrearing, not until after World War II did cultural historians begin broader and more intensive investigations of these subjects. Some were interested in the American Progressive reform movement of the late nineteenth and early twentieth centuries, wherein concern with the child as the salvation of society and also as a displaced person seems to have been a central theme (Takanishi, 1978). Perry Miller's classic studies of the New England mind and temperament had already stimulated Edward Morgan's excellent study of *The Puritan Family* (1944). David Potter gave historical credence to psychological inquiry into issues of national character with his *People of Plenty* (1954).

Another trend leading to historical study of the family and child has been the resurgence of interest in psychoanalytic formulations of emotional and interpersonal development. During the 1920s the advent of Freudian ideas into general intellectual thought had offered historical biographers a more formal theoretical alternative to their traditional intuitive approach. Although some historians then embraced psychoanalytic ideas enthusiastically, others dismissed them disdainfully as mysticism or mere balderdash. Among cultural historians, however, psychoanalytic insights into the human condition have had an indirect and more significant impact through stimulation of interest in the child and family by social scientists, especially in the fields of child development and anthropology (Sears, 1975). The scientific children of Darwin and Freud began peering inquisitively into the nursery, the schoolroom, the ghetto, and the homes of city, countryside, and jungle. Margaret Mead sailed off to Samoa and explored the cultural relevance of adolescence. Erik Erikson discovered the Freudian child in Vienna of the 1930s, brought him along to the States with a more psychosocial life in *The Child and Society* (1950), and later found him contributing to the Protestant revolution in *Young Man Luther* (1958). In the process of disciplinary development among the social sciences, certain conventions of intellectual ownership with respect to family and child life became established. The child belonged to Psychology, the family to Sociology, the tribe to Anthropology, and the school to Education. All of this social science enterprise relating to matters concerning the child and family began to provide historians with perspectives to encourage and enhance their latent interest in domestic matters.

A third recent development contributing to more historical interest in the family has been computerized demographic research, which reemphasized the ageless differentiation between ideas and actions, between the acutely perceived and felt distinctions that bifurcate the partisans of intellectual history from those of social history. This split reflected tensions between the discipline's traditional affiliation with the humanities of academe and its newer strivings as a social science. Intellectual historians deal with ideas as set forth in documented sources of literary expression. For purposes of domestic inquiry, such materials are abundant, for example, in colonial New England the self-conscious Puritans were prone to discourse at every anticipation of sin. Social historians have found new veins of inquiry in the statistics of domestic affairs (births, deaths, marriages, etc.). However, because our forefathers were generally negligent in recording their private domestic actions for posterity, social historians have been less fortunate with respect to behavioral evidence of family relationships and childrearing. Thus, the differential preference for ideations or for actions as data bases takes on at times the character of an old guard versus new frontierpersons in terms of style and substance. The more traditional attentiveness to precise and eloquent expression of intuitive insight is pitted against the presumably more solid records of communally related actions. But, as Brinton (1963) reminds us, the task of the intellectual historians "is to try and find the relations between the ideas of the philosophers, the intellectuals, the thinkers, and the actual way of life of the millions who carry the tasks of civilization" (p. 4).

The paucity of domestic behavioral records has led some historians to assume that parental actions were accurately represented in the literature of advice about proper childrearing. In a cautionary commentary on this tendency, Mechling (1975) suggests that the only proper use of such advice-literature is for the study of the advisors themselves. Indeed, to know the advice may be merely to know the advisor, yet surely considerations of communality, diversity, and transition therein are part of the essence of cultural ideologies about children. To know the advisors in terms of evidence about the sources of their ideas and the relations of these to relevant other ideologies of the times is to understand the advice given in a context larger than the writers. This position makes no necessary assumptions about causative relations, such as that parents are influenced by and behave in accordance with published child-care advice. Instead, one may reasonably argue that writers on childrearing are responding to and seeking to relate themselves to evident concerns of parents and other caretakers of the young. In this sense, such advisors may actually follow rather than lead the parent, addressing themselves to transitional concerns that have already begun to resolve themselves in ways not yet clear. Ideas and actions about children are interactive, though in more complex ways than we might prefer.

In seeking to understand times past, we are prone to search for ourselves, for earlier signs of the persons we have become. This is the task of biographers, historical or clinical. Historians are wary of the post hoc reasoning process involved in the process and strive to view the person in the context of his or her times as both adult and child. The present survey of our ancestral ideologies about the child has sought to set aside our contemporary concerns and ideas about children and their caretaking in favor of taking them on their own terms as diligent historical scholars have found them. Yet we are often fascinated when encountering in the past strong shades of our own ideologies about the nature, development, and requisite caretaking of the child. Whether we are thereby merely reading ourselves into the past is a question of the validity of sources and inferences, always a matter of continuing debate among historians, only to be clarified or resolved by further inquiry.

Here, the review of conceptions of the child through time reflects the interests of the writer and the sources available to him in presenting the course of inquiry into the children of Western civilization and in particular the American scene. Beginning with the children of Antiquity in the Mediterranean basin, especially of Greece and Rome, the account proceeds through the Christian era of the Middle Ages, first into the onset and continuance of the modern cosmology of the Enlightenment philosophy, then into the more recent era of Darwinian science. Though the presentation in terms of successive emergence of major intellectual ideologies may at times seem to indicate complete conquest of older views by newer ones, the reader should keep in mind the reality of increasing pluralism of multiple conceptions about the child, each recycling through time rather than simply being submerged by newer ideas. A further caution is that the ingredients of any tale are necessarily a function of its narrator's sources and interpretations of them. The reader is subject to processes of selectivity compounded—of the sources in terms of both their interest choices and inferences therefrom, and of the same processes in the narrator. In his searches, this narrator has accumulated a considerable body of literature; and in the accompanying reference list, a fair sampling of basic titles on the history of ideas about children is given.

A final introductory note on historical interest among scholars of child development must be added. In its first century of disciplinary existence, psychology has been often neglectful or indifferent to historical perspectives, though perhaps no more so than science in general. This ahistorical tendency may be more particular to American science and to American culture in general. But is not a lack of historical perspective more surprising in the instance of developmental scholars? Surely scholars concerned with the course and processes of lives through time would be expected to be interested in their own professional history. Yet two considerations may have been counterindicative. First, we had to fashion a past in order to reflect on it. Thus, those among us who have initiated reflections on our disci-

plinary history were themselves among the early contributors to the field—Gardner Murphy (1949), John Anderson (1956), Lawrence Frank (1962), Wayne Dennis (1972), Robert Sears (1975), Milton Senn (1975). The other consideration is that the very preference of American culture for science and the future has focused our national attention more on *pre*diction than *post*diction. In this sense, science and history point in opposite temporal directions. Indeed, the history of science is an attempt to mesh these divergent perspectives in order to enhance our understanding of science as an ongoing human enterprise, both culture bound and ever seeking to be culture free.

CHILDREN OF ANTIQUITY

The cultures of Western European civilization all pay homage to their heritage from the ancient Greeks in the study of philosophy, political systems, mythology, the arts, education, and even—at times—the family. Yet studies of the family and education in antiquity have been structured in institutional terms that provide little sense of conceptions about children as expressed or experienced by their caretakers (Beck, 1964; Lacey, 1968). Curiously, those youngsters of long ago have been receiving recently a particular kind of attention reflective of our contemporary societal consciousness about child abuse. DeMause, for instance, has documented (1974) from relevant source materials numerous incidents of violence against the young by abandonment, sexual abuse, disfigurement, infanticide, and so forth. Yet all of the woesome detail is presented outside any context of cultural values and mores. No doubt incidents of child victimization were plentiful in ancient times, as they are today, but we may wonder whether such actions were directed selectively toward children and not toward adults of the times as well. The issue must be considered as a question of whether child abuse may be notable in ancient times, as today, in terms of violations against prevailing special considerations of the child, rather than as culturally condoned actions. The answer lies in a careful study of beliefs about children in a cultural context, rather than in simply viewing with alarm actions in Antiquity that would be condemned in present-day terms. A more useful beginning for such purposes is French's search of the sources on ancient Mediterranean civilizations for evidence of the child's influence on others (1977).

In all cultures of the eastern Mediterranean during the millennium preceding the Christian era, children were generally seen as helpless and incapable of directing their own affairs, as having special physical needs in terms of feeding and mobility, as needing and desiring to play. A pervasive emphasis on school discipline implies a view of the child as lacking in sufficient self-control, prone to disorder, unable or unwilling to pay attention or to sit still. The importance attributed to children is clear, and there are many expressions of tenderness and affection toward children. In Egypt, there is an abundance of paintings that include children in family and ceremonial groups and also depicts them at play with balls and dolls and in jumping games. The Egyptians had large families and seemed to have sought to raise all of their offspring. Hammurabi's code included specific provisions for child maintenance. In Carthage, filicide seems to have occurred as an act of ritual sacrifice, the people handing over to the gods their most precious possessions as atonement or supplication (French, 1977).

The Child of Biblical Times

The Old Testament of the Bible covers three broad historical periods extending over a thousand years. Within these wide-ranging and various histories of the peoples of ancient Israel, incidents centering on children are rare. In the few references that exist on their nature, children are characterized as lacking in understanding, self-willed, prone to naughtiness, and in much need of discipline. There is little indication that the individuality of children was prized, that the idea of childish innocence existed, or that any mythology of a divine child prevailed. From birth, human beings are depicted as caught in a struggle with guilt and punishment that can only be resolved by the grace of God. The principal components of the social structure in ancient Israel were the family group, kindred, and the tribe, in which relations between parents and their progeny had central importance. The whole tribe was deemed to be the special children of God; their survival depended on fulfilling certain responsibilities to the deity and receiving his reciprocal protection and favor in return. Children were viewed as God's gift, with barrenness an indication of his displeasure, fruitfulness an indication of his favor. For their parents, children represented honor, pride (Ps. 144.12) and a notable help, male descendants being of particular value. The educative task of both parents was instruction and discipline. Responsibility for children rested primarily with the mother in the early years until the baby was weaned, which might not be until the third year. After that time, the mother devoted herself especially to the daughter. The son was

well advised to observe the teachings of his mother as well as those of his father (Prov. 1.8f; 6.20; Friedrich, 1967).

The father's role grew in importance with the age of the child. Because a son normally followed his father's vocation, his upbringing and his training for vocation resided in the same hands. Young persons were expected to learn to live with varying weather, with changing seasons and times, with the laws and with suffering, and with God, as expressed in the collection of proverbs preserved in stories and in the Psalms. There are frequent accounts of fathers informing their sons by telling of their own experiences in life. An essential means of education was to show the consequences of an act, the connections between what a man does and what befalls him. The necessity of correcting the foolishness of the young by firm discipline is expressed in Proverbs (29.15), "The rod and reproof give wisdom, but a child left to himself brings shame to his mother."* Also stressed is the importance of parental discipline as necessary to the child's welfare. "Do not withhold discipline from a child; if you beat him with a rod, he will not die. You beat him with the rod but you save his life from Sheol [the world of the dead]" (Prov. 23.13f; Wolff, 1975).

The Old Testament talks with extraordinary frequency of the sins of the fathers, particularly from Jeremiah onwards. God is the ultimate source of wisdom and salvation, rather than parents; sons may even have the duty of disobedience. "And I said to their children in the wilderness, do not walk in the statutes of your fathers, nor observe their ordinances, nor defile yourselves with their idols" (Ezek. 20.18). Yet sons are by no means faultless, "A fool despises his father's instruction, but he who heeds admonition is prudent." "He who throws warnings to the winds casts his life away, but he who heeds admonition gains understanding" (Prov. 15.5, 32). When parents get old, the central issue becomes not one of obedience, but rather of considerate care by their children (Wolff, 1975).

The New Testament of the Bible is a quite different history; it deals with the brief span of years in the first century A.D. of Jesus and the Apostles and reflects both Judaic and Greek influences. The character and behavior of Jesus is depicted as radically deviant from the cultural mores of his contemporaries, notably in his attentions to people of little

---

*All Biblical quotes are from *The Holy Bible*, (Harold Lindsell, ed.). Revised standard version 1946–52; second edition of the New Testament, 1971. Grand Rapids, Mich.: Zondervan Bible Publishers.

status—the poor, social outcasts, women, and children. There are many positive references to children as symbols for regeneration of the spirit, unspoiled, humble creatures of God whose very dependency on others makes them open to receiving the fatherly love of the deity. "Unless you turn and become like children, you will never enter the kingdom of heaven. Whoever humbles himself like this child, he is the greatest in the kingdom of heaven" (Matt. 18.3). "Let the children come to me, and do not hinder them; for to such belongs the kingdom of heaven" (Matt. 19.14). The innocence of children refers not to some quality of innate purity, but to their trusting, dependent attitude toward adults as representative of the necessary attitude of adults to the deity as children of God. "Whoever receives child in my name receives me; and whoever receives me, receives not me but him who sent me" (Mark 9.37; Friedrich, 1967).

The human potential for destructive impulses and the susceptibility of the young to negative influences is expressed by Paul. "We all once lived in the passions of our flesh, following the desires of body and mind, and so we were by nature children of wrath, like the rest of mankind" (Eph. 2.3). "So that we may no longer be children, tossed to and fro, and carried about with every kind of doctrine, by the cunning of man, by their craftiness in deceitful wiles" (Eph. 4.14). Childhood functioning was quite different from that of adults and less desirable. "When I was a child, I spoke like a child, I thought like a child, I reasoned like a child; when I became a man, I gave up childish ways" (1 Cor. 13.11). Parents bore great responsibility for this transition, and children must respect and follow the guidance of their parents. The authority of parents was strong, but it must be used wisely. "Children, obey your parents in the Lord, for this is right. Honor your father and mother. . . Fathers, do not provoke your children to anger, but bring them up in the discipline and instruction of the Lord" (Eph. 6.1f/4; Friedrich, 1967).

The Child of Ancient Greece

Just as the origins of Western culture, philosophy, science, and medicine are centered in the classical period of pre-Christian Greece, so also the conceptions of the child that are evident over the subsequent millennia are also found there. Our sources of information about ancient Greek children are Athenian. Written by men of social status, these sources are concerned with well-born children; thus they express nothing of the harsh severity of Spartan discipline, nor of the lives of slave children. Affection for children and concern about proper discipline in the service of societal interests were hardly inventions of the Greeks, since these themes are manifested throughout recorded time and probably before. But the Athenians' philosophical concerns about the nature and development of humans, their relationship to their gods, to their social order, and to the cosmos, led the Athenians to be more attentive to the particular characteristics, needs, and training of the young. As in earlier Near Eastern civilizations, the Greeks viewed children as objects of affection, important family members, and symbols of their society's future. They placed much more stress on very early training to mold and shape children to cultural interests and took particular cognizance of age and individual differences. Although infanticide was both legally and culturally approved, there was considerable unease about such action and expression of compassion for abandoned newborns. Once accepted into a family, an infant's safety and place were secure; the child was usually seen as important and loved, as providing pleasure to the parents. The importance of children is frequently expressed in drama, as witness Medea's terrible revenge on her husband Jason by depriving him of their children and Oedipus's compassion for his ill-begotten daughters (French, 1977).

Artistic conventions visually represented children as small adults, but literary descriptions clearly show recognition of physical differences other than mere size, for example, their plasticity of limbs required protection and molding by swaddling. Children were seen as typically more unformed, helpless, fearful, cheerful, affectionate, playful, unruly, imitative, and innocent than adults. A basic belief that children can be well trained in mind and body underlies the Greeks' emphasis on education. Lack of knowledge made children both impressionable and gullible. Throughout Greek society, there was great concern with discipline and control, implying that the child was deemed unwilling or unable to sit still and pay attention. The difference between the Greek and the Biblical stress on discipline was in the need children have to be closely supervised in their proper development rather than in the need to be punished for their evildoing. Athenian fathers are warned not to be too harsh or austere. The special needs of children for protection, affection, and play are commonly noted. Plutarch both recognizes and encourages his daughter's imaginative pretense in her play. He also strongly advises mothers to nurse their children, as the process makes them more kindly disposed to the child. Always a physically demonstrative people, the Greeks were so with their young-sters (French, 1977).

Plato's *Laws* and Aristotle's *Politics* both take note of developmental age characteristics and care-taking demands related to them. Plato comments on swaddling, rocking, and crooning infants, on the formation of character in early years with the need for protection from pain, fear, grief, corruption. During preschool years, the young child engages in peer play and requires only mild discipline. At age 6, children are to be sexually segregated for common education. Aristotle accords good bodily develop-ment in infancy as basically important, with free use of limbs and acclimation to endurance of cold, with plenty of milk but no wine. For the preschool years, he stresses bodily exercise, play as preparatory for adult roles, and protection from base influences. Un-til starting school at age 7, children are to be kept at home and sheltered from improper sights and talk, including lampoons and comedies. Rigorous train-ing does not begin until puberty. Awareness of indi-vidual differences in natural gifts is given particular note in Plutarch's biographies (French, 1977).

Both Plato and Aristotle were concerned about corruption in politics and sought to devise ways of childrearing and education that would assure selec-tion of better governing officials. Plato was con-vinced that the citizens of Athens were incapable of making wise leadership choices, that many had suc-cumbed to moral decadence of the society and, thus, were unfit to rear young children. Therefore, he de-cided that all children should be separated from their parents early in life, to be reared and trained under state control. By stringent selective screening only the most capable would become rulers after the age of 50. His ideal society was to be a meritocracy, wherein each person's place would be decided by objectively determined abilities. Each infant was to have equal opportunity regardless of family back-ground or sex. As a program of childrearing advice, the *Republic* provides a dramatic instance of Mech-ling's caution about inference of actual child training from advice literature; for no one has ever put Plato's recommendations into effect. Although girls and boys were to have the same basic education, boys required more carefully arranged and stringent instruction.

> Now of all wild young things a boy is the most difficult to handle. Just because he more than any other has a fount of intelligence in him which has not yet 'run clear,' he is the craftiest, most mis-chievous, and unruliest of brutes. (*Laws,* Bk. 7, 808)

> [Self-control] is the aim of our control of chil-dren, our not leaving them free before we have established, so to speak, a constitutional govern-ment within them and, by fostering the best ele-ment in them with the aid of the like in ourselves, have set up in its place a similar guardian and ruler of the child, and then, and then only, we leave it free. (*Republic,* Bk. 9, 591)*

Plato struggled with the problem of how self-control can be instilled in children without damage to indi-viduality and initiative in the process.

> While spoiling of children makes their tempers fretful, peevish, and easily upset by mere trifles, the contrary treatment, the severe and un-qualified tyranny which makes its victims spirit-less, servile, and sullen, renders them unfit for the intercourse of domestic and civic life. (*Laws,* Bk. 7, 791; Biehler, 1976)

Aristotle agreed that Athens needed a state-con-trolled educational system, but only for the most capable individuals who would become the city-state's leaders. "The citizen should be molded to suit the form of government in which he lives" (*Pol-itics,* Bk. 8, 1). He wanted most citizens to have freedom of opportunity for individual liberty and privacy, and considered the family as essential to personal and social stability. The privacy of home life should be encouraged and protected, the varia-tions of childrearing in the home being considered advantageous because no particular and single ap-proach would likely be effective with all children. Where Plato saw undesirable incongruities, Aristo-tle saw desirable individuality. "It would seem then that a study of individual characters is the best way of making education perfect, for then each has a better chance of receiving the treatment that suits him" (*Nicomachean Ethics,* Bk. 10, Ch. 9, 1180).†

Aristotle seems to have been attuned to the need for adapting child training to the particular natures of the young.

> Now some think that we are made good by na-ture, others by habituation, others by teaching. Nature's part evidently does not depend on us, but as a result of some divine causes is present in

those who are truly fortunate; while argument and teaching, we may suspect, are not powerful with all men. . . . (*Nicomachean Ethics*, Bk. 10, Ch. 9)

His concern with fostering family life for children led him to separate education for females, who must devote themselves to childrearing and domesticity.

Aristotle's interest in the nature of the mind included an inquiry into how children acquire ideas about things, anticipating in his conclusions that the child's mind may be considered as a blank slate.

Mind is in a sense potentially whatever is thinkable, though actually it is nothing until it has thought. What it thinks must be in it just as characters may be said to be on a writing tablet on which as yet nothing stands written: that is exactly what happens with the mind. (*De Anima*, Bk. 3, Ch. 4, 430; Biehler, 1976)

The Child of Rome

Just as Roman society assimilated much of the literature, philosophy, science, and art of Greek society, so it assimilated many of the Greeks' conceptions of childhood. But there were two distinctively Roman aspects of the context in which children were raised: the absolute power and control of the Roman father over his children and family, and the continual struggle of the Roman society to replenish itself over a millennium. Fathers retained legal power of life and death over their children even as adults. Not until late in the fourth century A.D. was infant exposure banned by imperial edict. That children were important to the Romans seems clear from the many oaths and appeals that included references to one's children, the ceremonies and rituals attending birth, and the existence of a goddess of childrearing, Rumilia. The continual disinclination of upper-class and perhaps other Romans to have large families is puzzling, given the manpower demands of a militaristic society (French, 1977).

Many characteristics more particular to children are noted in the Roman literature. Most generally noted were their unformed nature, creatures who were moldable, teachable, ignorant, unaware, even witless, and corruptible. Latin sources make more references than the Greek to the unruly, angry, deceitful, jealous character of children, while giving less attention to weakness, helplessness, and fearfulness. Also, children are considered playful, cheerful, affectionate, lovable, innocent, imitative, competitive (boys), curious, retentive in memory. In

training the young, good example is deemed essential to the development of good character, the stress is laid upon shielding them from corruption. Quintilian, the famous teacher of oration, in his *Institutio Oratoria* (first century A.D.) presents a quite positive view of children and their ability to learn. Romans, like parents of all times, sought a proper balance between love and discipline of the child. Harsh abuse of children was considered undesirable. Physical punishment was common, though Quintilian and others deplored the practice (French, 1977).

As did the Greeks, the Romans observed the stages of growth in their children and differences among them. The Romans had a rather consistent view of stages of development with writers such as Quintilian, St. Augustine, and Macrobius presenting detailed accounts. These schemes roughly delineate three periods of development: infancy, young childhood, and adolescence. Quintilian was keenly aware of variations in native abilities and advised tailoring a boy's program of instruction to his abilities and needs.

The skillful teacher will make it his first care, as soon as a boy is entrusted to him, to ascertain his ability and character . . . the teacher must next consider what treatment is to be applied to the mind of his pupil. There are some boys who are slack, unless pressed on; others again are impatient of control; some are amenable to fear, while others are paralyzed by it; in some cases the mind requires continued application to form it, in others this result is best obtained by rapid concentration. (French, 1977)

In summary, all of the ancient cultures of the Mediterranean valued the child as of future importance to the society. The common practice of infanticide through exposure of the newborn seems to have been selective to those of evident birth defects and excess progeny, especially females. The ancients simply did not place on individual life the high value that has become a cornerstone of modern cultural beliefs. None of these civilizations romanticized the child; the idea of an innocent child of inherent goodness in opposition to a corrupt society never occurred to them. The child was meant to serve the interests of the gods through his family and society; he had no status independent of such considerations. Discipline was typically authoritarian and often harsh, as was the life of adults. The Greeks of Athens with their democratic social order, with their humanistic, philosophical, scientific, and artistic interests, introduced articulated ideas of care and attention to understanding and training of the young. More than any other ancient people, they gave consideration to a more gentle shaping and guidance of the young, but they also imposed strict discipline because of the child's lack of self-control.

MEDIEVAL CHILDREN

A prominent and widely promulgated thesis about the Middle Ages is Aries's contention that there was no concept of childhood in the sense of recognizing the nature of children as distinct from adults.

> In medieval society the idea of childhood did not exist; this is not to suggest that children were neglected, forsaken, or despised. The idea of childhood is not to be confused with affection for children; it corresponds to an awareness of the particular nature of childhood, that particular nature which distinguishes the child from the adult, even the young adult. In medieval society this awareness was lacking. That is why, as soon as the child could live without the constant solicitude of his mother, his nanny, or his cradle-rocker, he belonged to adult society. (Aries, 1962, p. 128)

Aries's work is an important landmark of the recent surge of interest in families and children of times past among cultural historians and social scientists. As one of the first significant publications of contemporary analysis, the book has been widely read in academia and beyond. The enthusiastic reception of his thesis by social scientists and their students may be due in some degree to an unstated a priori conviction on our part that children have only been discovered in modern times, rescued from the dark ages of ignorant, indifferent, and cruel custodians. Historians have been less sanguine and more critical of Aries's analysis, as is their wont and responsibility.

Aries argues that until the Renaissance the separateness of the nuclear family did not exist, being subordinate to and permeated by extended kinship networks. Only when the family became a protective, sheltered enclave could the idea of childhood as distinct and separate from adulthood emerge. As Kroll (1977) points out, Aries's reasoning is oddly circular.

> If we accept his premise that it is the emotional closeness of relationships within the nuclear family today that defines the concept of childhood, and if we agree that this emotionally close nuclear family did not exist in medieval times, then

we would expect as a matter of fact and logic that the nature of childhood was viewed differently then. Therefore, if we look for a modern western concept of childhood, we should not be surprised when we do not find it. It is more likely that children then were viewed differently than children now, but still viewed as children. (Kroll, p. 384)

Today relationships tend to be based on and defined more by personal feelings, whereas in earlier times they were defined in terms of rules, obligations, and expectations. Perhaps emotional closeness and attachment were not ordinary components of parent-child relationships, nor of any for that matter. Yet medical, legal, and religious sources of the Middle Ages provide clear evidence that there was a realization of and accommodation to the specialness of childhood, derived from and consistent with their world views and therefore, of necessity, different from our own in many ways (Kroll, 1977).

The dark ages of the decline of Western civilization that followed the collapse of the Roman Empire under the invasion of the barbarian tribes were no doubt times of widespread turmoil, terror, and superstition. Yet this period was also encompassed by the flowering of Christianity and the preservation of knowledge in monastic enclaves. The church fathers of the Patristic Age (ca. A.D. 400–800) did proclaim a more compassionate attitude about the child in that they had souls, were important to God, educable, and not to be abused. The radical asceticism of early Christianity was softened with Jerome to allow concern for children; children were not evil but potential recruits for the desired spread of the new faith. John Chrysostom, addressing parents in Antioch (388) on the right way to bring up children, sounded the themes of the malleable nature of children and the need for balanced discipline:

> If good precepts are impressed on the soul while it is yet tender, no man will be able to destroy them when they have set firm, even as does a waxen seal. The child is still trembling and fearful and afraid in look and speech and in all else. Make use of the beginning of his life as thou shouldest.

A child is born with the capacity for growth, and sound training is a father's responsibility. Chrysostom advised a father to

> punish him, now with a stern look, now with incisive, now with reproachful, words: at other times win him with gentleness and prom-

ises . . . Let him rather at all times fear blows but not receive them. . . . our human nature has some need for forebearance. (Lyman, 1974, p. 87)

Early in the fifth century, Augustine crystalized the Christian attitude about the infant and child as being under God's special protection. He was evidently a close observer of the infant and its needs. *The Confessions* presents a vivid recollection of early childhood, impressive for his understanding of the trials and tribulations of the young. Though he frequently idealizes the role of the mother, he considered the true family as not the natural one, but the family of Christ. Augustine depicts the child as educable and relatively guiltless, but not truly innocent in that the child is by nature self-centered and grasping; the child merely has had little opportunity to sin (Lyman, 1974).

The medieval church showed awareness of the special nature of childhood in both chronicles and monastic rules. In the eleventh century Lanfranc, the ecclesiastical architect of the Anglo-Norman kingdom, wrote a revised set of rules for monastic life with descriptions of daily duties and included many special provisions for resident children. Accounts of the monastic life give evidence both of great severity and of great gentleness in treating children. Some of this difference followed from a particular abbott's position on the continuing controversy of whether children were basically innocent or sinful. St. Anselm (1100) is represented in a discussion with a pious abbott:

> Even as a weak or a strong body hath each his own proper good, so also strong and weak souls have their different measures of nourishment . . . the weakling soul, yet tender to the service of God, had need of mild, that is, of loving kindness from others, of gentleness, mercy, cheerful address, charitable patience, and many such-like comforts. (Kroll, 1977, p. 390)

The Church was caught in its own doctrinal ambivalence. On the one hand, the newborn child was sweet, pure, innocent, the symbol of God's wonder; yet, at the same time, that newborn bore the burden of Original Sin, living evidence of parental sin. This ambivalence extended to the view of the child as simultaneously vulnerable and powerful: vulnerable to the wiles of Satan, to wrong-headed parenting, and to the ills of the flesh; powerful as a portent of the future, as significant of God's will, and as threatening in its grasping willfulness. Children were at times exalted, feared, abused, but ever special. The church both promoted and founded refuges for the

protection of abandoned and orphaned children (Kroll, 1977; McLaughlin, 1974).

Evidence from medical treatises of the Middle Ages provides further insights into conceptions of childhood. Medieval medicine was laced with philosophical-theological considerations, as the worlds of the secular and the sacred, of nature and spirit, were not as yet split apart. Medical practice encompassed an unbroken tradition of empiricism from Hippocrates and Galen as well as a mixture of pagan and Christian ritual and dogma. Yet the written works were remarkably naturalistic and free of theological reasonings. Christianity did not seem to have any influence on the basic principles of infant care. These reflected a view of the infant and young child as vulnerable and fragile; the newborn was not considered to have health as a positive and present factor. There were set forth a series of procedures to help nature; for example, to overcome the newborn's inherent weakness the limbs were swaddled to prevent them from becoming twisted or deformed because of their evident plasticity (Kroll, 1977).

In the late Middle Ages, an increasing number of encyclopedias, compendiums of general knowledge, incorporated medical works that included attention to the physical care and training of young children. One of the earliest and most influential was compiled by Bartholomew of England (ca. 1230), who described the physical constitution, emotional qualities, and habits of children. Early childhood was viewed as a carefree, playful time. Young boys, though innocent in the sense of sexual immaturity, needed careful discipline and teaching to restrain their tendencies to guile and deceit. Little girls were considered more disciplined, careful, modest, timid, and graceful. Vincent of Beauvais, a zealous encyclopedist, drew upon contemporary knowledge in the development of ideas and showed a genuine concern for the needs and abilities of children at different ages. He repeats the ancient authority of Soranus, the most influential medical authority through the Middle Ages, on the care of infants: frequent baths, careful feeding, ample playtime. Vincent carries forth the precepts of St. Anselm on moderation in discipline and teaching. To teach without beating was the stated ideal, though he suggests that discipline requires distinctions between child temperaments, some requiring physical coercion and others not. Yet many writers warned against indulgence of children (Kroll, 1977; McLaughlin, 1974).

Legal codes recognized both the vulnerability and potential of children. Though the law did not protect the life and well-being of children as we might deem fit today, neither were there well-developed concepts of the individual rights of anyone. Laws were intended principally to settle property disputes, including at times protection of the rights of women and children, not to define individual status. There were many laws recognizing the minority status of children in various barbarian codes and in the Byzantine codes of the late Roman Empire. The child was a commodity in the sense that his particular needs were subordinated to the interests of his overlords, which reflected the governing principle in all feudal relationships. In the later medieval period in England, certain rights of children were asserted in the Magna Carta with respect to the property rights of minor heirs and more generally through the establishment of English common law, wherein the settled law of the king's court applied to all free men. Special status was given to those of particular disabilities, including lunatics, lepers, and infants. All of these exceptional persons were judged legally incompetent for varying reasons, but all because of a special status conferred by God. Lunatics and children were believed to be lacking in reason, yet closer to God. Concepts of adult premeditation and responsibility did not apply to them (Kroll, 1977).

Over the millennium of the barbarian invasions and medieval times, changes in ideas with respect to the child were more in terms of increasing attention to the role of the nurturant mother as natural with expectations of gentleness and tender care. This increasing emphasis on the importance of the maternal role may be attributed in part to the emergent idolatrous imagery of Christianity: the child Jesus and his kind, loving mother assumed a central role. The general portrait of well-born women in the late Middle Ages depicted them as efficient household administrators, prudent yet generous, and charitable to the poor; they were noted for piety, devoted to the physical and spiritual welfare of their children, and actively concerned with their education. All of this is imagery contained in literary sources, reflective of prominent ideologies but not necessarily of operative realities. There are no descriptions of actual family life that indicate the daily concerns of domestic intimacy. Accounts of childhood are provided by adult men in recollections of their personal early experiences. These often indicate that mothers were capable of inspiring enduring devotion, even in the case of felt rejection. But the reciprocal accounts of the childrearing experiences of the mothers are lacking; the mothers themselves remain silent (Lyman, 1974; McLaughlin, 1974).

Throughout the Middle Ages, the Church was active in fostering more humane ideals and protective care of displaced children, all in the service of a concept of the child as an object of theological importance, a soul to be saved for the glory of God. By fostering their children's welfare, especially their moral character, parents would serve the Lord. But there was probably a great gap between such fine ideals and the day-to-day realities of parental practice. Prohibitions by civil and religious authorities of the period seem to have had little effect on abortion, infanticide, child abandonment, and sale. The onset and flowering of Christianity did not save the children from the grim and brutal lives of the times, no more than it did the adults. Children shared the lives, deaths, and night terrors of their elders. The child remained the possession and property of the parent, especially the father, and thus subject to the particular kinship networks, values, characters, and personal dispositions of their elders. There was little note of children as such aside from religious, medical, and legal considerations. Even the term "child" was not limited to prepubescent persons, as has since become the custom, but was used widely in reference to adults in accordance with social roles and literary conventions.

Everywhere over the domestic scene hung the heavy pall of maternal and infant mortality. Estimates of death during the first year of life suggest that one, and sometimes two, of every three children born died within their first postnatal year, a figure that did not change much until after the middle of the 1700s. Many historians, especially of the English and early American scenes, have inferred maternal indifference to young children as a self-protective mechanism by mothers threatened with loss of their little ones. We should note that such scholars are all male, presumably given to more objective distantiation not only in their professional roles but also as fathers. In all this discourse one misses the softer sounds of women. If there is any validity to Bowlby's thesis of reciprocal infant-mother attachment as a universal psychobiological process, the proposition that mothers of high infant-mortality times avoided this mutual attachment process by anticipatory rejection seems highly questionable. That mothers commonly suffered emotional trauma through loss of young children would seem probable, but the power of religious faith in God's inscrutable will as consolation must have been great. Today we may have difficulty in grasping that transcendent experience, preferring the more modern secular faith in intrapsychic, psychodynamic mechanisms of defense.

Finally, foreshadowing the subsequent rise of the modern ideology of individuality, and its consequences in a more enlightened awareness of the child as a being important in his or her own right, there were indications of a rising self-awareness after about 1000. The search for greater self-knowledge as the path of God appears to have been a prominent theme in the commentaries and autobiographies of churchmen during the twelveth century. Confession became universal instead of occasional, and increased emphasis was placed on intention as the criterion of sinfulness. An increasing awareness of the self also made itself felt in portraiture, which came more and more to seek expression of an individual's character as well as his or her social position (Morris, 1972).

RENAISSANCE-TUDOR CHILDREN

The three centuries from the fourteenth to the seventeenth were long years of major political, economic, and religious transitions that moved Western Europe from the shades of the Middle Ages into the dawn of the modern era. The complex, interwoven patterns of powerful cultural change were to cause dramatic alterations in the societal structure of nations, communities, and families and to produce accompanying ideologies of lasting significance for our subsequent conceptions of the child. Before the fourteenth century the English economy had been agricultural with a feudal social order of a few wealthy landowners, a large mass of peasant farmworkers, along with village artisans, the clergy, and military mercenaries. After 1300, the agricultural economy began to change in favor of sheep over crops because of the great demand of Continental weavers for English wool. The impact of this transition over the next centuries was to have enduring consequences for the lives of families and children. The booming wool trade led to enclosure of their fields by landowners for more effective care of sheep, and in the process peasants were driven off the land and into the towns. The displaced and deteriorated status of the poor became matters of state concern and management in Tudor times. The wool trade, and later the more widespread trade in other commodities by the British seafarers, also resulted in the emergence of a middle class of merchants and professionals. This development of a bourgeoisie was further augmented by the establishment of a highly organized state bureaucracy during the Tudor reign of the sixteenth century. Prior to that dynasty, educated men of letters were primarily the clergy, who were schooled to the service of their theological and political lords. During the Tudor regime, the English Protestant Reformation (a political rather than a theological upheaval) resulted in the marked decline of the Church's material, religious, and political power throughout the realm. State demands for an educated civil service, as well as increased international trade, led sons of the newer middle class increasingly to seek access to economic and political status through education. Even the aristocracy shifted from a derogatory attitude about learning to a standard expectation of educated sons. Though neither Henry VIII nor his Anglican clergy sought substantive religious change, other than national control, the reforming religious zeal of the dissenters from Catholicism, especially the Puritans, was to have lasting impact on the state, the family, and children.

All of these major forces contributed to the transformation of English society and patterns of family life. As Stone (1977) has pointed out, the history of childhood, or of women, is necessarily the history of the family. To consider trends through time about children in isolation from family patterns and the larger context of particular societies at given times, is to engage in empty polemics, however passionate. Historians as well as social scientists have often failed to consider that they too, like parents and their advisors, seek to capture, contain, and control "the child" in the service of their particular ideologies. "The child" is always, however, a cultural invention, a powerful symbol of how adults view themselves and the world in which they live.

Let us then consider the character of family life in transition from medieval to modern times as formulated by Aries in his *Centuries of Childhood* (1962) and more recently in a major study by Stone, *The Family, Sex and Marriage in England, 1500–1800* (1977). The traditional family structure of the Middle Ages was one of open lineage, permeable to outside influences, but with a strong loyalty to ancestors and kinship networks; neither individuality nor privacy were valued. Aries's thesis is that a conception of childhood as a separate world, different from the adult sphere, was not possible until nuclear family boundaries became quite distinct from kinship networks, not until the domestic enclave became more isolated and fearful of the child's inherent corruptibility. The latter emphasis he attributes to increasing clerical concern about protection of child innocence. This new pattern led to repressive severity of the child at home and to the great expansion of schooling under church auspices. There is about Aries's interpretation a rather sentimental aura to the Middle Ages as an era of free sociability for the child, with a pessimistic perspective on the more nuclear family as one of inhibiting restraint. Though he is diffusely vague in his temporal and geographical references, Aries gives major attention to the development of French schools. He views education—because it inspired birth control—as the most significant force affecting both interior family life and demographic change (Stone, 1974).

Stone (1977), focusing on the English scene, argues that declining primary allegiances to kin, patrons, and community, in favor of more universalistic ties to church and state during the sixteenth century initiated a growing isolation of the nuclear family. In the process, both church and state reinforced the patriarchal ideology of the medieval aristocracy by providing a microcosm of national and theological patterns of paternalistic power and social controls. The state intentionally weakened kinship ties as antithetical to national allegiance and began to institutionalize traditional familial functions, thereby enhancing the nurturant and socializing functions of the infant and young child. The effect was to isolate the child more protectively and to place more stress on direct and personal emotional ties among family members. Aries and Stone agree that the impact of a more enclosed domestic scene and the strong Calvinistic influence on containing innate sinfulness combined to produce a devastatingly negative effect on child training and thereby established a repressive regime that was unshackled only as Enlightenment philosophy began to champion individual human freedom.

What, then, of the children? Despite indications of a more humane consideration of the child by some noted clerics of the Middle Ages, children were generally deemed of little importance, not worthy of record once born. Infancy (the first five to seven years) was but a biologically necessary prelude to the sociologically important business of the adult world. Children lacked wit, strength, cunning, profit. Popular proverbs of the times likened children to senile old men, foolish women, drunks, and churls. They were forgetful and not trustworthy, as in the old adage, "A man should not trust on a broken sword, nor on a fool, nor on a child, nor on a wraith, nor on a drunkard" (Tucker, 1974). Insofar as Aries maintained that children did not dwell in a world separate from adults, he seems quite correct. The marvelously kaleidoscopic portraits of peasant communal life by Pieter Bruegel the Elder (ca. 1525–1569) depict children playing adult games and joining in the midst of joyous celebrations and raucous revelry. Nursery rhymes that we now consider standard children's fare were originally folk jingles of social and political commentary; for example, "Sing-a-Song-of Sixpence" told the story of

Henry's love for Anne Boleyn and the English Reformation (Opie, 1957). Children of all social classes were put to work as soon as they were capable of simple tasks. Aristocratic families sent their sons at about age 7 to kinsmen or patrons to serve as household pages. Children of peasants worked in the fields or were put to apprenticeship at crafts or trades. Work was considered a moral activity; idleness sinful, as the devil would always find work for idle hands (Tucker, 1974).

The Christian ambivalence about the theological status of the child as both symbol of innocence and bearer of the human taint of inherent sinfulness gained a certain intensity in the Tudor Age. On the side of the angels, the humanistic educators such as Erasmus stressed the malleable innocence of children. Also, there was great fascination with the Christ child and his loving, nurturant mother, a symbol of the child as innocent of both sexuality and the ways of adult evil, abundantly expressed in iconography by Flemish and Italian paintings. On the darker side was the Puritans' concern to contain and control rigorously the pridefulness in themselves and their offspring. Nonetheless, there did seem to be increasing expression in the delights of children, and even references to the child as a good luck sign (Tucker, 1974).

During the sixteenth century increasing interest in the welfare of the child was also evident in the increased attention given to the physical care of children. The first English volume of pediatrics by Thomas Phayre was published in 1545. The recent invention of the printing press had begun to revolutionize the availability of literary materials, including manuals on the care of infants and children. So children were important enough to write about, including awareness that careful attention to infants was critical to their survival in the face of dire expectations of mortality. Henry VIII was meticulously demanding of hygiene in the care of his long-awaited son Edward. At the same time, old superstitions about pregnancy, childbirth, and wet nursing persisted. Swaddling of infants remained the order of the day to prevent misshapen development of naturally weak limbs; freedom from containment for infant, child, and man awaited the startling impact of Rousseau. Mother's milk was considered best for moral as well as physical nutriment, but wet nursing continued to be common practice with careful scrutiny of the moral character behind the breast; redheads were automatically suspect. And more humane ideals had not appreciably affected the practice of infanticide (Tucker, 1974).

Education in the sixteenth century underwent a

quantitative if not qualitative change. More grammar schools became established with the increasing demand for learning in order to gain economic and political advantage. One of the effects of more organized schools was to prolong the period that children were withheld from the adult world; another was to foster the idea that childhood is a formative phase. But the teaching style remained oppressively authoritarian, mostly rote learning of classical curricula in this age of imitating the ancients. And young scholars were administered large doses of moralism with their letters. The object was to train for gentility, respect and reverence for all authority, and the task required a strict disciplining of naturally unruly material. Common usage followed the Biblical adage of spoiling the child by sparing the rod. In the next century John Locke was to take this whole regime severely to task not only as tediously boring but as actually counterproductive. Yet there were clear indications of more child-sensitive ideas among some eminent people. Sir Thomas More was keenly interested in childhood and a loving, nurturant father to his three daughters and son (Tucker, 1974).

While middle-class sons were going to school, poor men's sons were being put to work by the Crown. The dispossessed peasant poor that accumulated in towns were seen as an increasing threat to the economic and social order of the kingdom. Tudor policy held the belief that poverty, delinquency, and vagrancy could be eradicated by training schemes and penalties for those deviating from the ideal of self-support. The Protestant ethic of middle-class consciousness associated moral rectitude with a social and economic, as well as spiritual, salvation. Pinchbeck and Hewitt (1969) maintain that this ideology was a necessary precondition to the emergence of a new consciousness of family and domestic intimacy with child nurturance as a focal responsibility. The Poor Relief Act of 1598 required each parish to assume responsibility for gathering together the footloose, idle youngsters and putting them to productive work. This state management of a young labor pool failed because of waning enthusiasm, and at last the administrative means to implement it were destroyed after the Stuart monarchy was restored in 1660. Puritans and other evangelicals asserted that poverty and wickedness were closely linked, a view that reinforced the conviction that statutory provisions for the poor should be minimal and punitive. Promotion of individual and national wealth, rather than welfare, had become the prevailing ideology. Child labor for the poor, instead of education, became both doctrine and practice from the days of cottage industries into mecha-

nized industrialization of the late 1700s. Locke, as Commissioner of the Board of Trade, reiterated the theme in a 1697 report on Poor Law reform: "Children of the labouring people are an ordinary burden to the parish, and are usually maintained in idleness, so that their labour is also generally lost to the public, till they are twelve or fourteen years old." He proposed work schools for them starting at age 3 (Pinchbeck & Hewitt, 1969; Tucker, 1974).

Shakespeare, a man for all ages in perceptive awareness of human dilemmas, was very much a man of his own age in his lack of attention to children as beings in their own right. The many references to a child or children in his works define either generational status or qualities of foolishness, emotionality, innocence, impotence, and the need for discipline in adults. In *The Merchant of Venice,* Shylock's servant Launcelot, on meeting his old poor-sighted father on the street, teases him by feigned nonrecognition. "Nay, indeed if you had eyes you might fail of the knowing me; it is a wise father that knows his own child" (2.02.70). Mistress Page in *The Merry Wives of Windsor,* while concocting a sport with old Falstaff that includes the children, notes that "the children must be practiced well to this, or they'll ne'er do't" (4.04.65). In his well-known statement of the classical seven developmental stages of life as delivered by Jacques in *As You Like It,* Shakespeare gives short shrift to childhood.

> All the world's a stage,
> And all the men and women merely players;
> They have their exits and their entrances,
> And one man in his time plays many parts,
> His acts being seven ages. At first, the infant,
> Mewling and puking in the nurse's arms.
> Then the whining schoolboy, with his satchel
> And shining morning face, creeping like
> snail . . .
>   Last scene of all,
> That ends this strange eventful history,
> Is second childishness and mere oblivion,
> Sans teeth, sans eyes, sans taste, sans
> everything.

CHILDREN OF THE NEW WORLD

In the course of Western civilization the seventeenth century was remarkable because not one, but two new worlds—one located on the western shores of the great ocean sea and the other in the very nature of man himself—emerged. Both new worlds had primary roots in the religious, political, and economic soil of England. The implantation of European colonies on the Atlantic shores of North America during the 1600s brought a long-established Christian view of man to trial and justification in the wilderness. The radical new view of man and the social order that characterized Enlightenment philosophy was not to be imported to the new land in any significance until the middle of the next century. Meanwhile, from New England to Virginia and the Carolinas permanent settlements were established for commercial, religious, and political purposes.

Among the tools for creating a new life carried by those doughty passengers across the broad sea were the customs and expectations for social orders, religious practices, family life, and childrearing derived from their experiences in their lands of origin. All of their anticipations were to be put to the test by the demands of the wilderness environments, transformed in the process, and evolved over time into a core of shared commitments that have been characterized by Gabriel (1956) as the basic tenets of the American democratic faith—the freedom and dignity of the individual, the premise of fundamental moral principles, and the special mission of the nation to promote universal freedom and humane living. In this new world of changed and uncertain circumstances, the care and training of the young necessarily became even more the particular responsibility of the nuclear family; for extended families and established communities were nonexistent. Our knowledge of the colonists' ideas about family life and children is largely limited to the Bible Commonwealths of Puritan New England. Since they were especially concerned with the interlocking relationships between family, community, and religion, they discoursed and legislated frequently on such matters. Over the past century we seem to have become ambivalent toward our Puritan heritage: we honor the Protestant ethic of productive work as having the moral value that the Puritans themselves so strongly epitomized; yet we castigate morally righteous censorship and repression as "Puritan." The latter has been pejoratively extended to the assumption that Puritan children were treated with harshly repressive authoritarianism by sober, sternly demanding parents. Studies by historians of the colonial family in recent decades do not support such a dour, limiting view of our Puritan forebearers.

The Puritan Child

The Puritans' ideas about the nature and requisite training of the child provide a clear demonstration of the proposition that childhood is a cultural invention tailored to fit a society's basic shared beliefs and value orientations. We are prone to view the colonial child of Massachusetts through the myopic lens of Rockwellian sentimentalism about Thanksgiving Day or as the victim of child abuse in the terrifying hell-fire repressive regimes of their elders. The most quoted admonition of the latter perspective is no doubt that of John Robinson, minister of the Plymouth colonists in 1618.

> And surely there is in all children, though not alike, a stubbornness, and stoutness of mind arising from natural pride, which must, in the first place, be broken and beaten down.

Indeed, this out-of-context statement would indicate to the modern reader a ruthless, brutal lack of understanding about the child. Yet Sommerville (1978) argues from evidence of materials written for children by English Puritans in the 1600s that they were more sensitive to the importance of children and to readings appropriate to their ages than were their contemporaries of the prevailing Anglican persuasion. The strong devotion to and love for their children by Puritan parents demanded that children be prepared for salvation through a firm adherence to God's will by first learning absolute obedience to parental will.

English Puritanism on both sides of the Atlantic was a militant religious expression of the English Protestant Reformation, a direct and articulate challenge to the power, wealth, and Papism of the established Anglican religious authority. Puritans were fundamentalists in their strict adherence to Biblical scriptures and in their opposition to a priesthood intervening between any communicant and the words of God. Most Puritan congregations sought to reform the church from within, while separatists abandoned such hope and sought refuge elsewhere. The Plymouth colonists migrated originally to Holland and subsequently turned westward across the ocean to establish a visible kingdom of God, a society of conduct according to His laws, in family, church, and state. They saw themselves as the new Israelites, heirs of both Adam and Abraham, born with the stamp of Adam's fall from Grace by disobedience of the Lord, but granted a Covenant of Grace by the promise of abiding faith and a sanctified life. Only faith in Christ could bring about salvation, yet that faith remained a free gift from God and could not be won by human effort. Although good behavior could not bring about salvation, it might be evidence of that sainted state, though no guarantee of it. On the other hand, an uncivil life was a certain sign of damnation. The Covenant played a central role in the Puritans' world view; it united family, church, and state in a closely coordinated commitment to the deity. By entering freely and jointly into this contract, members of the community of saints committed themselves to assurance of a sanctified life for all members of the family and community. The duty to enforce good behavior in the family thus became the basis of all political and ecclesiastical authority. Incessant vigilance was essential to assure that no sin went unpunished, or all might suffer from Godly retribution. In addition, a zealous enforcement of moral behavior by others might be another possible evidence of the enforcers' true faith (Morgan, 1944).

For the Puritans, the laws of God covered all human actions and were set forth in the Scriptures. Consequently, knowledge of the scriptures was a necessity for all potential saints; hence all must be able to read. Because subordination to the deity was fundamental—the very soul of order—it defined all patterns of relationships in terms of superior and inferior: husband and wife, parents and children, master and servant. Pious households were the cornerstone of the Puritan community. All individuals were required by law to live in family groups. Laws were established and maintained to assure that families carried out their Christian responsibilities. Any sin was a violation of order, and only Grace could restore order. Yet no one could be forced into the community of saints, the covenant with the Lord. Free consent was essential to enter the covenant, but freedom consisted of the opportunity to obey the will of God (Morgan, 1944).

Given the Puritans' conceptions about the moral nature of man, his relationship to the deity, and the social order requisite to both, their ideas about children and the education of saints were articulate, logical, and reasonable. They took for granted that children were born both ignorant and sinful, but also that ignorance could be enlightened and evil propensities restrained. Pious parents were faced with two tasks, instruction and discipline. They had to fill their children's minds with knowledge, and their children had to apply this knowledge in right action. There was no question of developing children's personalities, of drawing out or nourishing any desirable inherent qualities in them. They had to receive all good from outside themselves, from education and, ultimately, from the Holy Spirit. The Puritans sought knowledge because salvation was impossible without it. They retained throughout the seventeenth century a sublime confidence that the chief enemy of humankind was ignorance, especially ignorance of the Scriptures. The main business of education was to prepare children for conversion by teaching them the doctrines and moral precepts of Christianity. For a people who believed in predestination and the absolute sovereignty of God, the Puritans ascribed an extraordinary power to education (Morgan, 1944).

The problem of discipline was to make an evil-natured, but at least partly rational, creature act against its nature and according to reason. When Puritan children had been catechized at home, taught at school, and exhorted at church, they were doubtless well filled with sound doctrine; however, being of an evil nature, they were not likely to choose the right way simply because they knew it to be right. Neither instruction nor good parental example were sufficient; forceful restraint was also necessary. Parents had to decide individually on the proper method of discipline for their child. Although the Puritans no doubt often resorted to the birch rod, as did other contemporary parents, there is no proof that they did so more freely than their twentieth-century counterparts. In fact, ministers who wrote and spoke on the subject almost always counseled their readers and listeners to win children to holiness by kindness rather than by efforts to force them to it by severity. In reading Puritan praises of the rod, it is necessary to remember that they regarded it as a last resort, reserved for intransigent disobedience or stubbornness, the cardinal sin of pride. Highest approval was given to methods of discipline that evoked a special attitude in children and evidenced a thoughtful understanding by parents of a child's particular disposition. Puritan children were always taught to revere their parents, to feel ashamed of their faults, to fear loss of parental favor or of falling short of parental expectations. But reverence was more than fear and awe; it was also a matter of love. Parents were cautioned not to meet their children on equal ground, not to display too great visible affection.

Granted its purposes and assumptions, Puritan education was intelligently planned. The relationship between parent and child envisaged was not one of harshness and severity but of tenderness and sympathy. A parent in order to educate his children properly had to know them well, to understand their particular characters, and to treat them accordingly. If in practice some parents failed to do so, they failed, by so much, to be good Puritans. (Morgan, 1944, p. 61)

The Quaker Child

The pervasive Calvinistic image of the colonial child as innately sinful justified firm and absolute parental authority over the child, the necessity of strict and strong child control being taken for granted in all religious persuasions. So it was with the Quakers. The Society of Friends shared the dilemma of all Christians, how to reform society while keeping aloof from worldly ways. They gave great emphasis to sheltering the young from the evils of the world, to eradicating any natural inclinations to evil, which otherwise could become so hardened as to preclude the grace of God from reaching the inner light. Therefore, because Quaker parents were expected to exercise strict control over the life of a child, the child was duly subordinated to parental expectations. The best way of evangelizing children within the home was by good example; pious parents would have religious children. The authority of parents was founded on natural right and scriptural prescription. The Friends often cited instances of dire punishment suffered by disobedient children. The child was to be loved but not pampered; proper care required tenderness but not softness. The authority of the father was to be applied gently for unnecessary severity would turn the child against both parent and religion. On the other hand, Friends were wary of indulgence as turning children into little tyrants (Frost, 1973).

The religious status of the Quaker infant was quite different from that of the Calvinist infant. For Friends, the occurrence of sin required the existence of the moral sense. Until a person could distinguish right from wrong, the person's actions were not considered as sinful. The child had to have reached the age of reason and to have deliberately chosen to do what he or she knew was wrong, usually considered to occur between the ages of 4 and 8 years when the child began school. Children were subjected to a plain style of life from infancy and had to learn to keep their places in due humility. Quaker catechisms indicate significant change in attitudes towards children after about 1760 to a more sentimental view of child innocence. Although Quakers did not forget the world's harsh realities, they now deemed them as incompatible with the sweetness and innocence of children. Along with this newer focus there emerged a conception of children as displaying distinct personalities that were evident in infancy. More attention was given to the happiness of the child; less emphasis was placed on early conversion to the way of Christ. (Frost, 1973).

Other Colonial Children

The Puritan conception of the child tends to dominate our view of the colonial child and obscure important differences that were evident by the turn of the eighteenth century. Historians have not as yet delineated other versions of American colonial ideas about childhood, but some indication is provided by

Greven's recent study, *The Protestant Temperament* (1977), wherein he sets forth a typology of three distinctive patterns of feeling, thought, and sensibility that shape different forms of the self. He characterizes these patterns as Evangelical, Moderate, and Genteel modes. These styles of Protestant temperament differ in ways of regarding the self, the family, life situation, and fate in God's scheme of things. The Evangelicals are familiar to us in Puritan pietism, though not limited to that particular religious denomination, in their stress on human depravity; the only hope resides in absolute submission to the deity. As sober, demanding parents, Evangelicals were constantly engaged in battle against the inherently prideful nature of their children. Their constant vigilance against sinfulness in themselves and others expressed itself in various manifestations of self-denial. Their children grew up to be men and women of exacting conscience. Memories in the later years of childhood and youth were painful and embarrassing for Evangelicals to recall, since they cataloged the sins of disobedience and rebelliousness; of playfulness, worldliness, and sensuality; of pride and self-confidence. Obsessed with ideas of depravity, they also became vigorous, inspired disciples. Jonathan Edwards is presented as the prototypical Evangelical.

Another colonial type that Greven characterizes as authoritative were families more moderate in bringing up their children. They, too, fully accepted the reality of sinfulness, but they placed higher value on the power of reason; for they believed that the young could be taught good judgment and control over their sinful tendencies, that parental love and reason were more persuasive than threat of hellfire. John Winthrop and the Adams family, prototypes of this mode, believed in a process of negotiation with their children. Moderates were more inclined to view their offspring as innocents deserving of love and a gentle but firm guidance. They saw virtue as each child's inheritance, vice as the world's bequest to all, and a favorable balance of the two as the best one might hope for in this life. They exhorted, persuaded, cajoled, worried about, and at times spoiled their children, but remained ever hopeful and optimistic about the outcome as being in accord with community standards. The pattern of childrearing indicated by Greven for the Moderates is more in accord with Locke's precepts; indeed, as a prevalent mode in the American colonies, it was closer to Locke than the pattern prevalent in England itself (Illick, 1974).

The third style of Protestant temperament depicted by Greven, the Genteel, was quite self-assured, independent enough to tolerate the raising of children without concern about the community, the church, or the deity. Greven sees in the Genteel mode the emergence of a native American gentry, of families whose wealth, eminence, and power made them close knit but aloof from the world. They taught their children to be decorous, self-assured, and aware of their distinctness from others. Many became Tories in the emerging struggle for political independence. Governor Thomas Hutchinson of Massachusetts is seen as a prototype. The Genteel families were indifferent to most of the issues that concerned those of the other temperaments, taking a state of grace for granted along with their own superiority.

Greven acknowledges that the distribution of such variants among colonial families may be closely related to socioeconomic circumstances: the Genteels enjoyed the greatest affluence, the Moderates, the more middling, and the Evangelicals, the least; but this linkage is yet to receive full and careful study. Also, it may be that the distinctions he draws are geographically linked, with proportionally more Evangelicals in New England, more Moderates in the middle Atlantic states, and more Genteels in the southern plantation societies.

Toward a New Cosmology

Ideas about the nature and training of children can be shown to reflect the cosmology of culture and societies—prevalent beliefs of people about themselves, the social order, and the universe. To be sure, cognitive dissonance theory gives credence to the propositions of social historians that changing social, economic, and political conditions will necessitate change in belief systems to accommodate the altered realities of life situations. And, indeed, we find such transitions both in the reshaping of Puritan policy to fit the development of New England communities during the colonial period and in the present-day waning of the conviction that the mother is the essential and constant caretaker of the young, a change that fits the new life styles of many educated women, who are moving away from exclusive domesticity. Whatever the sources, and they were no doubt multiple, interactive, and accumulative, there emerged among the intellectuals of Western Europe during the seventeenth and eighteenth centuries a dramatically different view of mankind, one that came to be designated as the Enlightenment. Protestantism had destroyed the working unity of Christianity and medieval authority. By 1700 there existed many writings favoring the tolerance of religious differences, the separation of Church and State, and especially the freedom of individuals to decide for themselves matters of religious belief. This movement toward a direct personal relation between human beings and the deity was more significant as an advance in individual freedom of choice than as a challenge to basic tenets of Christian belief. Protestants of the seventeenth century still believed in the sinful nature of themselves, the power of a supernatural entity, and the inspiration of the Bible. Secularization of humanity's beliefs about itself came about through the force of the Rationalists, who not only banished the supernatural from their universe, but began to place all of humankind wholly within the framework of nature and the material universe. The growing prestige of Rationalism owed much to the achievements of natural science (Brinton, 1963).

Two major figures of seventeenth-century thought, Newton and Locke, brought to a focus the core elements of the new image of human beings. Newton's work seemed to contemporaries to explain all natural phenomena, or at least to show that all things of nature, including the behavior of human beings, could be so explained. By taking the methods of clear, simple reasoning out of the bewilderment of metaphysics, Locke seemed to make them a nice extension of common sense. Newton and Locke set forth those great clusters of ideas, Nature and Reason, to function as the basic principles of the Enlightenment in much the same way as two other great clusters of ideas, grace and salvation, had functioned in traditional Christianity. The Newtonian-Lockean concept of Nature was that of the orderly, untroubled, and beautifully simple working of a universe properly understood. Once this Nature was seen at work in human affairs, human beings would simply regulate their actions accordingly and thereby abolish unnatural behaviors (Brinton, 1963). Yet neither Newton nor Locke considered their ideas as displacing the Christian deity. Newton was an ardent student of the Bible; at times, he also believed in superstitions such as numerology.

The new cosmology as popularly conceived by most educated people of the eighteenth century was an inseparable mix of Rationalism and Romanticism. The natural man of the simpler followers of the Enlightenment was both innately virtuous and inherently reasonable; his heart and head were both sound. Romanticism became a revolt from Rationalism by giving more emphasis to heart than head, but both held that a person's life on earth could be almost infinitely improved, that the good life could be attained by making certain environmental changes. In the latter part of the eighteenth century, the heart came into its own against the head; sentiment and feeling were then perceived as the working principles that would tell us how to build a new world. The dramatic shift in the attitudes of Western man toward the universe and everything in it, a change from adherence to a Christian supernatural heaven after death to a rationalist natural heaven on this earth, led inevitably to the optimistic doctrine of progress, a faith that the spread of reason would enable people to control their environments. Here we find clearly the historic association of scientific and technological improvement with the idea of moral and cultural progress. By the middle of the eighteenth century there was sufficient evidence of material progress to justify and support the belief in the potential contributions of science. The faith in progress involves a theory of morals and metaphysics: progress will inevitably lead human beings to a state in which all are happy, and everywhere evil will disappear (Brinton, 1963).

Before that outcome is reached, all the faithful of the new religion of Reason must contend with the problem of evil, and without the help of the Christian God. For the enlightened person, evil is equated with the environment and good with something innate in human beings, with ''human nature'' as persons who absorbed Rousseau's writings believed. The way to reform individuals is thus to reform society. The juxtaposition between environment and heredity may be seen in the continuing conflict between Christian and Enlightenment conceptions of the moral nature of mankind. The peoples of Western civilization have mostly agreed on the broad outlines of what is good and what is evil; where they differ is in their explanation for the persistence of evil. The tradition of the Enlightenment continues to hold that we only need to work out the right arrangements—laws, institutions, education—and we will get along closer to the good life. The Christian tradition leans more to explanation in terms of inherent human wickedness, which must be tempered and controlled. The doctrine of natural goodness is a fundamental heresy to the traditional Christian (Brinton, 1963).

CHILDREN OF THE ENLIGHTENMENT

Two children of the Enlightenment, the conceptions of Locke and Rousseau, were notably precocious and have had an enduring influence on subsequent thinking about the nature and training of the young. Each was a well-articulated representa-

tion of his father's philosophy; both proved to be sturdy youngsters in their own right; and their breed still thrives in the nurseries, schoolrooms, and psychology research laboratories of our own times. We need to consider carefully the attributes of each, including their ideological origins and bequests to later eras.

John Locke is best known in the history of Western intellectual history for his classic essays on civil government and human knowledge, both published in 1690. The former, in part a justification for the assumption of the British crown by William and Mary in 1688, became the basis for the American Declaration of Independence. The *Essay Concerning Human Understanding* was set forth as a refutation of the Cartesian proposition of innate concepts of knowledge and quickly became a cornerstone of empiricism. Locke's predilection for metaphors to drive home the basic theme that the contents of all knowledge accrues through perceptual experience has made famous the idea of a newborn's mind as a blank slate, a tabula rasa. Less well known is his treatise on childrearing, *Some Thoughts Concerning Education,* published in 1693, wherein he not only applies himself to the educational implementation of his philosophical position regarding the acquisition of knowledge but also gives much detailed counsel and advice on the physical and psychological training of children.

In order to understand Locke's ideas about children in the context of his times, we must cast ourselves backward into the turbulent years of seventeenth-century England. Locke was born into a west country Puritan family in 1632, the decade preceding the political revolution of Parliament. He attended Westminster School in his late teens and resented the rigid pedantic instruction in the classics. During the time Cromwell headed the Commonwealth Locke went to Oxford to study philosophy, but he found himself fruitlessly mired in the muddle of scholastic metaphysics and turned to the study of medicine and science, then emerging in the work of Boyle, Sydenham, and others. His fifteen years at Oxford extended into the period of the Stuart Restoration. The succeeding twenty years, his more public life as a civil servant and member of Lord Ashley's entourage, concluded with the political stabilization of 1688. Locke was an intimate of the small group of new scientists represented in the recently founded Royal Society. He was both ideationally and personally familiar with many Continental intellectuals, having been abroad for four years because of poor health and as a political exile in Holland from 1685–1688. During the latter period, the material for the education essay was set down in a series of letters in response to a kinsman's request for advice on raising his young son (Aaron, 1963).

Locke considered the character and behavior of an individual to be more essential than any particulars of knowledge. This very focus of his ideas about education was especially pertinent to the times. The educational needs of the emerging merchantile economy of England—a greatly increased demand for literacy and for knowledge relating to international affairs—were in conflict with the traditional classically oriented educational model. Many contemporary writers were critical of existing education and made recommendations similar to Locke's. His ideas were unique in basing such proposals on a careful philosophical analysis of human understanding and on a comprehensive view of the human organism. Locke realized more fully than others before him that children were individuals with their own particular needs, abilities, and patterns of development. Also novel was his perceptive awareness of the child's point of view. From his scientific training and life-long status as a bachelor, one might expect a certain degree of objectivity, yet his evident empathy with children suggests some continuing personal involvements with the young. And, indeed, we find from his biographers that he greatly loved children, appointing himself guardian of all of his friends' children. And at various periods he had more formal tutorial responsibilities with Lord Ashley's family (Aaron, 1963; Axtell, 1968).

In reading Locke's ideas on education today, one is struck by the familiarity of so many psychological insights about children and precepts of child training. His thinking has become so thoroughly absorbed into the mainstream of ideas about the young over the past two centuries that attribution to Locke has been lost in the process. Until the past decade, when some attention to the history of childhood became obligatory in textbooks on developmental psychology, references to his treatise and the ideas contained in it were not to be found in the literature of the field. Even in the context of the current nod to historical roots, references to Locke acknowledge his philosophical empiricism but not of his program of child training. Therefore, some detailed attention to his understanding and precepts seem warranted in a survey of ideas about children. We must keep in mind that Locke's ideas were expressed in terms of practical advice to a father about raising his son. Because he is careful to explain both the premises

and reasoning for his management advice, *Thoughts* is one of the more psychologically sophisticated and popular childrearing manuals of all time.

Locke on Child Training

Locke begins by giving quite explicit instructions on physical care, including apparently the first attention to toilet training in the literature. In accordance with his basic emphasis on establishing firm habits of body and mind at the earliest possible age, he strongly recommends putting the infant on the pot at regular times as soon as he is able to sit erect. In summing up this section, Locke states that bodily care

> reduces itself to these few and easy observable rules: plenty of open air, exercise, and sleep, plain diet, no wine or strong drink, and very little or no physic, not too warm and strait clothing, especially the head and feet kept cold . . .*

The principles are quite clear, to harden the physical self to endure a rugged climate, to avoid appetite indulgence. Probably the counsel most startling to eighteenth-century English readers was his proposal to immerse the child's feet in cold water every day; people of that era never immersed the body in the way that we are accustomed to bathe.

Locke then proceeds to state his general principles of early education in the home: the foundations of good character are laid down in infancy; the growth of character is corrupted by parental indulgence; right values are needed in the home; habits of violence, vanity, dishonesty, and intemperance are to be shunned. Here he emphasizes the now familiar themes of the long-term impact of early experience and of parents bearing the responsibility for the outcome of character formation.

> The great mistake I have observed in people's breeding their children . . . that the mind has not been made obedient to discipline and pliant to reason when it was most tender, most easy to be bowed.

> Parents, being wisely ordained by nature to love their children, are very apt . . . to let it run to fondness. They love their little ones and it is their

*All quotes of Locke are from *Some Thoughts on Education*, abridged and edited by F. W. Garforth. Woodbury, N.Y.: Barron's Education Series, 1964.

duty; but they often, with them, cherish their faults too.

The child's submission to reasonable authority and to discipline by parents is the primary goal of early child training. Because reason is deemed the essential mechanism of self-control, only by exposure to a model of reasoned external control will the child be able to internalize the process.

> He that is not used to submit his will to the reason of others when he is young, will scarce hearken to submit to his own reason when he is of an age to make use of it.

Locke considers both authority and friendship as essential to the pattern, and a balance of relations between parents and children is needed

> for the setting of your [parental] authority over your children in general. Fear and awe ought to give you the first power over their minds, and love and friendship in riper years to hold it.

Though Locke places great stress on clear establishment of absolute authority over the young child, he views this as necessary to prevent the child from being controlled by his own impulses while the process of self-governance develops.

> I think [authority] should be relaxed as fast as their age, discretion, and good behaviour could allow it . . . The sooner you treat him as a man, the sooner he will begin to be one.

Locke shows keen awareness of developmental changes and marked individual differences among children. His stated goal is that parent-child relationships should move over time from a pattern of authority-submission to one of equalitarian friendship.

> Would you have him open his heart to you and ask you advice? You must begin to do so with him first and by your carriage beget that confidence. But whatever he consults you about . . . be sure you advise only as a friend of more experience; but with your advice mingle nothing of command or authority. You must not expect his inclination should be just as yours nor that at twenty he should have the same thoughts you have at fifty.

Repeatedly the apostle of empiricism stresses

differences among children in temperament and style that must be taken into account in dealing with them.

> There are not more differences in men's faces and . . . bodies than there are in the makes and tempers of their minds; . . . the peculiar physiognomy of the mind is most discernible in children . . .

> Begin therefore betimes nicely to observe your son's temper . . . See what are his predominant passions and prevailing inclinations . . . for as these are different in him, so are your methods to be different.

Reading Locke on disciplining a child with rewards and punishments is a bit like scanning Baumrind's (1971) files of interviews with authoritative parents. Both search for a pattern of directive guidance that encourages responsible instrumental competence. Repeatedly Locke stresses a firmly moderate approach between the excesses of punitiveness and of indulgence if a child is to learn to master impulse by exercising its own reason.

> He that has not a mastery over his inclinations, he that knows not how to resist the importunity of present pleasure or pain for the sake of what reason tells him is fit to be done, wants the true principle of virtue and industry and is [in] danger never to be good for anything.

> If the mind be curbed and humbled too much in children, if their spirits be abased and broken much by too strict a hand over them, they lose all their vigour and industry and are in a worse state than the former.

> To avoid the danger that is on either hand is the great art; and he that has found a way how to keep up a child's spirit easy, active and free, and yet at the same time to restrain him from many things he has a mind to and to draw him to things that are uneasy to him . . . has, in my opinion, got the true secret of education.

This idea of an equitable balance in child training between freedom and authority seems to capture the core of American parental aspirations of the past two centuries.

The theme of sustaining the natural free and easy spirit of children again points up Locke's astute observations of the young and his respect for the functional value of childish characteristics.

For all their innocent folly, playing and childish actions are to be left perfectly free and unrestrained, as far as they can consist with the respect due to those that are present, and that with the greatest allowance. If these faults of their age, rather than of the children themselves, were, as they should be, left only to time and imitation and riper years to cure, children would escape a great deal of misapplied and useless correction . . . this gamesome humour, which is wisely adapted by nature to their age and temper, should rather be encouraged to keep up their spirits and improve their strength and health than curbed and restrained.

Whilst they are very young, any carelessness is to be borne with in children that carries not with it the marks of pride or ill nature; but those, whenever they appear in any action, are to be corrected immediately.

Not for Locke the authoritarian control of children that demands submissive obedience for obedience's sake. Instead, there is consistent encouragement of the child's motivations for independent understanding and responsible self-management. As might be expected from his Puritan heritage, the only behaviors completely unacceptable were those giving evidence of obstinancy and willfull disobedience, the sin of pride. Always preeminent for Locke was the development of the child's powers of reasoning, even from an early age.

It will perhaps be wondered that I mention reasoning with children; and yet I cannot but think that the true way of dealing with them. They understand it as early as they do language . . . they love to be treated as rational creatures sooner than is imagined.

And the importance of parental models must not be neglected:

You should make them sensible by the mildness of your carriage and the composure even in your correction of them that what you do is reasonable in you and useful and necessary for them.

Once again we find Locke's sensitivity to dealing with children in words and explanations appropriate to their age.

It must be by such reasons as their age and understanding are capable of, and those proposed always in very few and plain words.

Much less are children capable of reasonings from remote principles. The reasons that move them must be obvious and level to their thoughts, and such as may be felt and touched.

Because in recent decades we have had considerable investigative inquiry into the effects of punishment upon children; it is instructive to hear Locke on the matter. Corporal punishment

contributes not at all to the mastery of our natural propensity to indulge corporal and present pleasure and to avoid pain . . . but rather encourages it and thereby strengthens that in us which is the root from whence spring all vicious actions and the irregularities of life.

And he sets forth the reasons why physical punishment is ineffective, starting with the importance of internalized conscience.

I cannot think any correction useful to a child, where the shame of suffering for having done amiss does not work more upon him than the pain.
(2) This sort of correction naturally breeds an aversion to that which 'tis the tutor's business to create a liking to.
(3) Such a sort of slavish discipline makes a slavish temper.
(4) Or if severity carried to the highest pitch does prevail . . . it often brings a worse and more dangerous disease by breaking the mind.

Locke furthermore has no use for nagging a child.

I think frequent and especially passionate chiding of almost as ill consequence. It lessens the authority of the parents and the respect of the child.

Thus, dismissing punitiveness, physical or verbal, Locke again emphasizes the internalized psychological control of parental authority.

Shame of doing amiss and deserving chastisement is the only true restraint belonging to virtue.

And, again, he stresses the necessity of that authority being maintained.

Whatever particular action you bid him to do or forebear, you must be sure to see yourself obeyed; . . . for when once it comes to a trial of

will, a context for mastery betwixt you . . . you
must be sure to carry it . . . unless, forever after,
you intend to live in obedience to your son.

But, again, he cautions that such confrontation
should be avoided, save as a last resort to stubbornness or obstinate disobedience.

> This requires care, attention, observation and a
> nice study of children's tempers and weighing
> their faults well before we come to this sort of
> punishment . . . that has not weight with them
> that appears sedately to come from their parents'
> reason.

In addition to admonishing his readers about the
ill effect of physical punishment, he also warns them
about the harm of indulgent rewards.

> To flatter children by rewards of things that are
> pleasant to them is as carefully to be avoided. I
> would have their lives made as pleasant and
> agreeable to them as may be, in a plentiful enjoy-
> ment of whatsoever might innocently delight
> them; provided it be with this caution, that they
> have those enjoyments only as the consequences
> of the state of esteem and acceptation they are in
> with their parents and governors; but they should
> never be offered or bestowed on them as the re-
> wards of this or that particular performance.

> Esteem and disgrace are, of all others, the most
> powerful incentives to the mind, when once it is
> brought to relish them. Children are very sensible
> of praise and commendation. They find a plea-
> sure in being esteemed and valued, especially by
> their parents and those whom they depend upon.

In accordance with the general belief of the times,
Locke adds a cautionary word about the folly and
perverseness of servants: "the caresses of those
foolish flatterers."

Locke on the Educational Process

Because Locke sets forth his ideas on education
in the context of an assumed tutorial arrangement,
they have often been ignored as elitist; yet there is
much of general application that is now familiar to us
in child-centered or progressive doctrine. With regard to methods of training, he maintains that children learn not by rules and precepts but by the practice of doing, setting habits that then operate of
themselves easily and naturally. The teacher must

observe a child closely to determine aptitudes and
limits; for no child can be shaped in ways contrary to
his or her nature. Good example is important, since
children are prone to emulate what they see; for they
aspire to adult status. Do not, Locke advises, inhibit
initiative by restrictive prohibition; instead, provide
opportunity to exercise potentials and use gentle persuasion of good example.

> The great work of a governor is to fashion the
> carriage and form the mind; to settle in his pupil
> good habits and the principle of virtue and
> wisdom; to give him little by little a view of
> mankind, and work him into a love and imitation
> of what is excellent and praiseworthy; and, in the
> prosecution of it, to give him vigour, activity and
> industry.

Locke shows a very practical, utilitarian slant to
education.

> And since it cannot be hoped he should have time
> and strength to learn all things, most pains should
> be taken about that which is most necessary, and
> that principally looked after which will be of
> most and frequentest use to him in the world.

The primacy of proper character development is
clearly stated in Locke's ordering of educational
aims: virtue, wisdom, breeding, and learning. Virtue must be laid in religious teaching and obser-
vance, in habits of honesty, and in love and respect
for others. Wisdom means managing one's affairs in
the world, preparation for which lies in training for
honesty, self-discipline, reflection, and high ideals.
Breeding refers to self-esteem, respect for others,
appropriate behaviors according to social custom;
manners will emerge from love and respect. Learning should never be burdensome nor required of children when they are not so inclined, but their minds
must be trained to direct attention at will to the self or
others. Children learn better when work is linked to
interest and play; Locke rejects "that rough discipline of the rod." Finally, the program of studies
Locke proposes are the basic subjects of today: the
three Rs, composition, history, geography, languages, science, manual crafts, physical pursuits,
and leisure activities. He emphasizes the use of the
vernacular, clear expression, and practice.

Locke's Influence and Heritage

The writings of John Locke portray the spirit of
his age. In them we find that balanced and toler-

ant attitude to life which characterized late seventeenth century England at its best. The prevailing love of cool, disciplined reflection and the careful avoidance of excess are mirrored with fidelity on every page. (Aaron, 1963, p. 1)

Locke, however, was born into a quite different age, a turbulent period of bitter conflict and narrow zeal, where people's emotions and behaviors were excessive and reason forgotten; or so it seemed to those of Locke's generation. Lady Masham, Locke's hostess and patroness of his later years, tells us

His father used a conduct towards him when young that he often spoke of afterwards with great approbation. It was the being severe to him by keeping him in much awe and at a distance when he was a boy, but relaxing still by degrees of that severity as he grew to be a man, till, he being capable of it, he lived perfectly with him as a friend.

As a child, Locke was trained to the sobriety and industry of a Puritan household, made to love simplicity and to avoid ostentation. Locke was ever a prudent man, as revealed in his works—modest, simple, unaffected, sincerely seeking for truth, catholic in his interests (Aaron, 1963).

Locke's ideas dominated English, French, and American thought in the first half of the eighteenth century and became part of the common sense of political and intellectual thought. Although his *Thoughts on Education* was reprinted only once in the United States between 1783 and 1861, the book is in many old library lists in New England and among the scant volumes belonging to persons who had but a single bookshelf. Abstracts and transpositions of his precepts appeared in almanacs, the most universally studied of all eighteenth-century books save the Bible. Locke's views on religious tolerance, rationalist theology, and the plasticity of human nature were very appealing to leaders of the American Enlightenment. Both Benjamin Franklin and Joseph Priestley quoted him favorably for his emphasis on the importance of a sound body and mind, of wisdom in the management of one's affairs, of sensory training, and of reason rather than authority. The idea of individual persons as the products of their experience was basic to democratic ideals. Pedagogical guides during the first half of the eighteenth century were partial to his stress on character training. His works were widely used in private academies and by those who favored tutorial education. The common school advocates of the 1830s avoided direct use of Locke's work as aristocratic

and antithetical to their interests. They were much more oriented to Germany where a public school system was already well established. Yet they freely borrowed from Continental writers those ideas of Locke fitting their needs (Curti, 1955; Earle, 1915).

Rousseau on Child Training

The child of the English Enlightenment, incubated, nurtured, and brought to articulation by John Locke, rapidly became the ideal resident offspring of many middle-class, educated households. This child was a comfortable charge whose unwarranted impulses were properly contained by reason and self-restraint, a being that was in respectful awe of reasonable authority, one trained to virtue, wisdom, and behaviors appropriate to his or her station. The eighteenth century produced another child, more dramatic and revolutionary, the *enfant terrible* of Jean-Jacques Rousseau, who might be designated as the democratic child. This startling mental offspring has continued for the ensuing two centuries to both enchant and dismay the minds and tempers of persons in Western civilization. Not surprisingly perhaps, the two most influential eighteenth-century conceptions of the child were provided by two of that century's preeminent political philosophers. Both were centrally concerned with the balance between freedom and authority; both tried to cope with the potential for evil inherent in natural impulses. Each sought to state the form of political order necessary to both authority and freedom and to make it work by creating citizens to fit that order.

As Rousseau was ever controversial in his time and seemed to thrive on this status, so he has remained controversial in his person as well as his ideas. Biographers have ranged from enraged to ecstatic about him; on the other hand, several intellectual historians, Gay (1964), Cassirer (1954), and Crocker (1968–1973), have provided us with less impassioned but more helpful insights into the man and his ideas. In an essay setting forth a blueprint for a biography, Gay characterizes Rousseau in a series of paradoxes: the lifelong adolescent, the modern ancient, the cosmopolitan Genevan, the practical Utopian, the isolated philosopher, the innocent penitent, and the nostalgic prophet. Rousseau's one great principle was

that man is good, that society makes him bad, but that only society, the agent of perdition, can be the agent of salvation. . . . The contradictions between freedom and authority were to be resolved in a society of Emiles who want for themselves only the things that are good for society as a whole. (Gay, 1964, pp. 259–260)

Rousseau assigns two basic attributes to the child: consuming impulse, infinite adaptability. The first is Rousseau's constant concern; the second provides the basis for a solution of the central dilemma of how imperious human impulse can be brought into line with a moral social order. His vision of the child as infinitely perfectible was based on a construction of the child as the interactive product of the child's own impulses and environmental demands, that each stage of development involved a restructuring to effect a workable compromise between passion and reality. The associated propositions of childhood as natural and worthwhile in its own right, and the child as actively engaging the world to his own purposes and understanding, revolutionized thinking about the child and have been continuing issues of debate. But the child was not deemed capable of solving the problems of adaptation on his own, contrary to the Romantic interpretations. For Rousseau, both child development and the social order required the unseen hand of a tutor, a father figure, a lawgiver (Kessen, 1978).

Through the course of Rousseau's pedagogical writings (the *Second Discourse, Julie, Emile* and the *Government of Poland*), he set forth ideological and psychological principles that together created a radically new vision of children. Following and extending Locke, Rousseau saw all knowledge as based on early acquisition through experience.

We are born capable of learning, but knowing nothing, perceiving nothing.

Man's education begins at birth; before he can speak or understand he is learning. Experience precedes instruction; when he recognizes his nurse he has learnt much.

If all human knowledge were divided into two parts, one common to all, the other peculiar to the learned, the latter would seem very small compared with the former. But we scarcely heed this general experience, because it is acquired before the age of reason.*

Sensation and associated affect are considered the basis of infant learning.

*All quotes of Rousseau are from *Emile, or On Education* (trans. Barbara Foxley). London: Dent, 1911.

The child's first mental experiences are purely affective, he is only aware of pleasure and pain.

Rousseau is often cited as the apostle of parental permissiveness, letting the natural positive forces in children emerge without restraint. The proposition that human beings have an innate moral status that is inherently good is the Romantic idealist's misinterpretation of Rousseau and a common assumption about his view of children. Rousseau, ever given to a flamboyant style of resounding phrases, expresses the theme of healthy nature versus ill society as, "God makes all things good; man meddles with them and they become evil." Certainly a fundamental premise of Rousseau was that children must gain knowledge by the force of their encounters with experience rather than by authoritative precept. But he also maintained the necessity of firm control by tutors in structuring those experiences to which children are exposed. The key phrase is "well-regulated liberty."

Do not undertake to bring up a child if you cannot guide him merely by the laws of what can or cannot be. The limits of the possible and the impossible are alike unknown to him, so they can be extended or contracted around him at your will.

Give him no orders at all, absolutely none. Do not even let him think that you claim authority over him. Let him only know that he is weak and you are strong, that his condition and yours puts him at your mercy.

Yet he seeks to avoid the conflict of interpersonal dominance between child and caretaker by making adult authority impersonal, a function of knowledge instead of will. Here we see the clear hand of Rousseau as the manipulative behavioral engineer.

Let him find this necessity in things, not in the caprices of man; let the curb be force, not authority. If there is something he should not do, do not forbid him, but prevent him without explanation or reasoning; what you give him, give it at his first word . . . without conditions.

Moreover, there is no middle course; you must either make no demands on him at all, or else you must fashion him to perfect obedience.

Rousseau, the eternal rebel, seems to have enjoyed raising hackles as well as eyebrows by taking positions outrageous in that they were diametrically opposed to usual practices. Thus,

> Give your scholar no verbal lessons; he should be taught by experience alone; never punish him, for he does not know what it is to do wrong; . . . Wholly unmoral in his actions, he can do nothing morally wrong.

> The mind should be left undisturbed till its faculties have developed.

> Reverse the usual practice and you will almost always do right. Fathers and teachers who want to make the child, not a child but a man of learning, think it never too soon to scold, correct, reprove, threaten, bribe, teach, and reason. Do better than they; be reasonable and do not reason with your pupil. Exercise his body, his limbs, his senses, his strength, but keep his mind idle as long as you can.

Rousseau was obviously intrigued and impressed with Locke's ideas on the nature and training of the child—the importance of physical training for a sturdy bodily constitution, sensory experience as the basis of all knowledge, the necessity of fitting a tutorial program to the particular character of a child, the dismissal of existing pedagogy as contradictory to and interfering with the children's learning. He cites Locke's rules and reasons on bodily training as excellent.

Children are considered by Rousseau as incapable of true reasoning until they are about age 12. Until the onset of the age of reason, they receive only images, not ideas; sensations are passive processes, while ideas require active judgment. Because children lack the powers of judgment, they have no true memory and do not retain ideas about relations. Thus, symbols are of no value without a tangible idea of what is represented. Children cannot be taught geography by maps since they will learn only maps, not the true nature of the world. The first reasonings of children must be based on direct sensory experience, for they are capable of reasoning well enough about matters concerned with their actual well-being. From this perspective, learning from books is useless, since they teach children to use the reasoning of others, to believe much and know little. Because the senses are the first faculties to mature, children must be trained to calculate the effects of all their actions and to correct by experience.

The task of a tutor is not to teach a child many things, but never to let her or him form inaccurate or confused ideas. Reason and judgment come slowly, while prejudices flock in on us. The fundamental principle of all good education is to give children a taste for knowledge and the methods of learning. "It matters little what he learns, it does matter that he should do nothing against his will." Answers to the questions of children should be only enough to whet their curiosity, but not enough to satisfy it. Do not become a slave to questions. Consider the motives behind them rather than the words themselves. For Rousseau the critical time for tutorial guidance is the short span between the onset of reason and of adolescent passions.

Rousseau did not seem to be concerned with impulses in children so long as they are not misguided by others. But the passions of adolescents bring on tumultuous change; youngsters now become deaf to the voice that they used to obey, distrust their keepers, and refuse to be controlled. Rousseau's ambivalence about impulses is evident in his formulations. On the one hand, he sees passions as essential to self-preservation, the basis of freedom. The only inborn and eternal passion is self-love, always good. The child becomes attached to the nurse because the nurse contributes to the child's welfare. Children achieve love of others from self-love by discovering that others desire to be helpful to them. On the other hand, inevitable conflict resides in this very self-focus.

> Self-love, which concerns itself only with ourselves, is content to satisfy our own needs; but selfishness, which is always comparing self with others, is never satisfied and never can be; for this feeling, which prefers ourselves to others, requires that they should prefer us to themselves, which is impossible. Thus, the tender, gentle passions spring from self-love; the hateful and angry passions spring from selfishness.

Rousseau was constantly obsessed with the destructive passions in human beings. Whenever individuals require the help of others, human society inevitably declines; for vanity, scorn, shame, and envy become more and more dominant. He struggled through his series of pedagogical writings to find a solution to the corruptive force of negative passions with variations on his principle of human adaptability. In order to prevent the development of destructive impulses in a child and to contain them when the powerful natural forces of adolescence surge forth, Rousseau required the unseen hand of a tutor, father, lawgiver. The guiding hand of a master was deemed necessary to create the moral child and the moral society. Inevitably, perhaps, the need for imposed constraints on individuals and society led Rousseau in *The Government of Poland* to propose a totalitarian regime with education as its foundation. Children raised by the state will learn never to want anything except what society wants. Freedom for Rousseau came to mean the submission to a strict and inviolable law that the individual erects for himself (Kessen, 1978).

Rousseau ultimately abandoned faith in the power of individual reason and knowledge to contain selfishness in the interests of a social group. But in the process of seeking a solution to the problem of individual freedom within a moral society, he developed a new and radical vision of children. The behavior of a child is neither incomplete nor preadult but right and appropriate in thought and action for a particular stage of development. Child development is an ongoing process of reconstruction to effect a compromise between a child's own needs and the requirements of the world. By placing children center stage as beings worthy in their own right, Rousseau expressed his constant concerns with the tension between reason and impulse, gave to the revolutionary forces of his time a vision of the democratic child and adult, and dramatically affected future thinking about childhood.

Rousseau's Influence and Heritage

The most fascinating child of Rousseau may be Jean-Jacques himself. A flamboyant, impassioned man, much given to stirring aphorisms in his writings, he seems to have been a charismatic enigma in his time and has continued to be so. Granted that an era of significant cultural transition produces individuals symbolic of the changes then occurring, Rousseau surely qualifies as a candidate for the transitional man of the eighteenth century. Heir to the theocracy of Calvin in Geneva and the rationalism of the early Enlightenment, he became the secular philosopher of the democratic revolutions and the embodiment of Romantic sentiment. His writings—widely translated, quoted, imitated, praised, and attacked—created a great stir in the late eighteenth century. The radical character of his pedagogy was lauded as visionary and scorned as eccentric. Another Swiss, J. H. Pestalozzi, carried, for a time, the Rousseau banner of pedagogical reform and even kept his own son from books until age 12, but he seems to have seriously misread the master and soon disclaimed him as an impractical dreamer. Pestalozzi and others have drawn from Rousseau

what they sought, the Romantic impetus for attacking society and idealizing nature. In the process, Rousseau appears to have become more symbol than substance, often cited but rarely read. Perhaps the revolutionary fervor of Rousseau's vision of individuality, ''Man is born free and is everywhere in chains,'' had obscured his more anguished concern with the moral duality of individualism. One of his lasting contributions is clearly the legitimatizing of human impulses, counterposing the force of sentiment to the force of rationalism. While Locke was ever wary of impulse, Rousseau put human urges center stage and glorified the positive affects while struggling with negative, destructive inclinations. In a world of rampant industrialization, the British Romantic movement of Wordsworth and Blake needed a child of inherent innocence and purity as symbol of artistic sensibility to nature. It is odd that in the Age of Jackson, Americans, who were celebrating the common man and believed in an optimistic view of the child's potential (though they were acutely attuned to his sinful nature), seemed to be unaware of or indifferent to Rousseau's ideas. The Enlightenment thinkers of the Independence generation found Locke's ideas more to their temper, even though education in American generally continued to be Calvinistic in manner and style. When pedagogical reform came to the States in the nineteenth century, along with the common school movement, Pestalozzi and Froebel became the important figures. The new vision of the child as the redeemer of moral purpose took the text of Wordsworth rather than that of Rousseau (Kessen, 1978).

CHILDREN OF THE REPUBLIC

> Ever since the Enlightenment in the mid-eighteenth century, philosophers and psychologists have been developing ''modern views'' on the nature of childhood and child development. . . being ''modern'' about the child has consistently involved two conflicting themes: vindicating the claims of the child against tradition and authority, while at the same time trying to find rational sanctions for limits on his freedom. (Wishy, 1968, p. vii)

Throughout the century and a half of colonial experience, American parents assumed as their major childrearing responsibility the development of moral character in their children. Greven (1977) suggests that the severity of that burden was borne with varying degrees of intensity, reflective of concerns of parents about their own moral character—

the evangelical Calvinists, as a hair shirt; more moderate religionists, as a protective armor; and the more affluently genteel society, as a grand raiment of self-assurance. By the time of the founding of the Republic, the pervasively predominant Calvinist conception of the child began to be seriously challenged by differing views of the child's moral status and development. The first half-century of the new republic is significant in the development of ideas about children. At that time there emerged into the arena of public discourse alternative formulations about innate moral status and requisite training of the young: first by the new intellectual influence of the Scottish Enlightenment in the 1780s, later by the Romantic movement of the 1830s (Slater, 1977).

The Calvinist rationale of domestic education was given most frequent public expression in the late 1700s by Congregational and Presbyterian ministers of New England, though all religious denominations (save the Unitarians) agreed on basic premises. The primary function of parents was to prepare the child for a heavenly home by facilitating the requisite conversion experience. Both God and the safety of society required that the child become enlisted among the saints. The task of the parent was to pour into the child's mind knowledge of the evangelical scheme and thus prepare the way for the reception of the Lord's grace. Parents must restrain the child from the natural inclination to sin. Seventeenth-century Puritans had struggled with dualistic conceptions about the child. They believed both in innate depravity and in some good natural inclinations, that the infant mind was blank but also had innate knowledge of God. Such ambivalence seems to have been based on the need to prevent fatalistic attitudes by parents, to encourage a conviction that the task of salvation for the young was possible. The original belief in the automatic sanctity of children who are born into a community of saints was badly shaken by evidence of how sinful children can be. The significance of baptism thus shifted from the sealing of an inner covenant to that of parental vows for moral training of the child, to an external covenant (Slater, 1977).

By the early 1800s, there was widespread dismay about the moral fiber of the new nation and pessimism about child religious training. Ministers cited the spread of Deism and the Enlightenment rationale, along with general depravity, as reasons for decline of the family. Exhortations to improvement in childrearing had begun to be connected with the millennium theme, the triumph of old values over vice and infidelity. Moralization and Christianization of the child would bring about the Kingdom of God on earth. This theme of the child as savior of a wayward society was to become increasingly prominent throughout the nineteenth century and to be continued in more secular form in the present century (Slater, 1977).

The Enlightenment rationale of domestic education, as represented in the writings of Locke, Kames, the Edgeworths, and Priestley, rejected the Calvinistic assumption of infant depravity. The child was viewed as having an essentially neutral moral status, though Kames and Hitchcock modified Locke to attribute innate knowledge of the deity and other desirable qualities. These writers vacillated between complete sensationalism and adherence to some innate moral sense. They held to the purpose of molding a moral being, more secular than theological, and considered the development of virtue as sufficient to salvation, eschewing the conversion experience. By the late 1700s, Calvinist writers had begun to incorporate much of Locke's methods of childrearing, though limiting the tabula-rasa proposition to a child's rational facilities; for depravity still lurked in the children's hearts. The Romantic writers of the 1830s (Alcott, Child) adhered to the necessity of regeneration through grace as essential to salvation, but they assumed that the basis resided in the latent, positive natural forces within children. Alcott and the Transcendentalists were concerned with the force and vision of direct spiritual experiences. The Age of Jackson that celebrated common wisdom and goodness might have favored the Romantic conception of the child, yet the parents had been raised with Calvinistic religious training and many were educated with Enlightenment ideas (Slater, 1977).

Though proceeding from divergent conceptions of innate moral status, Calvinist and Enlightenment writers were surprisingly in agreement on the methods of childrearing. They stressed the need for parental authority and for strict obedience by children; sinfulness was to be restrained through punishment. Most recognized the diversity of individual temperaments and set forth general tactics to be modified for a particular child. In a child's early years, no attention was given to sex differences. Parental consistency was deemed vital, with any lapse from discipline considered seriously subversive to moral training. Because the child's earliest impressions were considered as fundamental, early and complete parental authority was widely accepted. Though mothers were seen as the more central parental figure, with fathers as supportive, mothers were also seen as reluctant to impose punishment when required. There was common and constant concern about leniency that led to neglect of punishment. Natural parental affection was a danger to which mothers were particularly susceptible. Yet parents were advised to temper their absolute authority with gentleness, affection, tenderness, and sympathy. So long as parental dignity was maintained, children were to be granted their innocent, harmless, reasonable desires. Punishment was necessary, but only as a last resort for such children's offenses as stubbornness and lying. Calvinists depicted depravity as contained not only by divine grace but also by parental correction. Physical punishment was most prominently discussed and disputed, with the caution that the child should not be disciplined in anger. Enlightenment writers were particularly concerned about emotionality in parent and child as evidence of lack of reason. Yet the Edgeworths argued that the rod was an effective constraint with young children (Slater, 1977).

Certain psychological principles were commonly shared and accepted in training children. Great emphasis was given to parental examples of appropriate behaviors, since children were viewed as very prone to imitate. Few of the writers saw association between thought and action, but instead emphasized utilitarianism, the child's functioning so as to maximize pleasure and to reduce pain. The Calvinists emphasized repetition of instruction; the Enlightenment writers did not. All sought as the principal goal the inculcation of self-control in the child. Tension between habits and principles, between behavior and character, was due to the conflict between idealistic emphasis on beliefs and utilitarian stress on behaviors. For the Calvinists, rational meant the acceptance of revealed truth, while Enlightenment writers emphasized the autonomy of reasoning with mechanistic conditioning. The Romantic authors gave most focus to feelings and sensibilities as the basis for good moral character (Slater, 1977).

The Child Redeemable (1830–1860)

By the 1830s a substantial body of childrearing literature existed for the first time in parent and family magazines, medical and religious books, biographies, travel accounts, stories, children's books, and advertisements. These publications offered advice ranging from practical infant care to elaborate theories of moral training. Fifty years after the American Independence, national life was widely viewed as betraying the heritage of an Olympian age. A great public debate on child nurture began with a call to citizens to save their children from the sins and errors undermining the Republic. Though the popula-

tion was still located largely in rural settings, part of the blame was placed on disruption of established patterns of family life by the impact of recent trends of industrialization and urbanization. Both fathers and mothers were seen as failing in their responsibilities for proper, upright child training; fathers were neglecting their duties while mothers were merely *inexpert* at theirs. The writers on nurturance gave major emphasis to the mother's role as being central to the task of producing moral, honest, religious, independent citizens. Childrearing was generally viewed as a rational process with certain results from definite methods. Yet, because no body of facts about physical and psychological development existed, advice about child training tended to be abstract and exhortative (Sunley, 1955; Wishy, 1968).

For a supposedly practical and antireflective people, Americans have been extraordinarily concerned with moral and religious justifications of their actions to themselves and to the world. We have been constantly preoccupied with the conflict between our desires and our ideals, between our intense coarser ambitions and our Utopian aspirations. In the debates about the child before the Civil War, Americans began to argue that harmony between the child and society, success and sanctity, was possible without sacrificing either the child's individuality or the adult's fixed principles. However monumental the job of creating an America both fully powerful in will and perfectly pure in spirit, the nurture writers of the time called on parents to perform just such work. By 1800, Calvinist views of the child and of human destiny under God's stern judgment had demonstrated remarkable staying power. The experts on nurturance had to suggest a way to develop the child's will that would do justice to American ideals of individualism while at the same time saving that freed will from yielding to the corruptions plaguing American society (Wishy, 1968).

Horace Bushnell's *Views of Christian Nurture* (1847) set forth the new idea of a more wholesome guided growth of the child's moral life. Kindness, love, and tender care by a mother who herself exemplified all the virtues would prepare the child for salvation and a life of moral responsibility. Both traditionalist and enlightened writers envisioned the child as a potential servant of some universal moral imperative, usually an absolute moral law ordained by God. All writers agreed that the child was to be trained consciously and carefully to develop both well-defined ideas and the will to live by them. For this purpose mothers were cast in the central role as the best mentor of character development, with the early years as most crucial. Thus mothers were deemed responsible for the future of the social order and human destiny (Greven, 1973; Slater, 1977; Wishy, 1968).

Increasing attention was being given to the direct experience of the child as the most effective source of education. If the child turned out badly, the blame was laid on the parent rather than proof of the child's essential depravity. Obedience was still the goal—to parents, elders, conscience, God, ''just government,'' the Golden Rule—without breaking the will. Both orthodox and the more benign nurture enthusiasts stressed the importance of proper environment and carefully formed habits. Spontaneity, joy, affection slowly moved to a higher status than singleminded piety. The new realism in nurture was first envisioned as a more effective means of fulfilling the child's destiny of obedience to the laws of God and the rules of moral righteousness; authoritarian regimes simply were not doing the job. The most striking feature across the range of child-rearing advice was the emphasis on the connection between daily tactics and moral strategy. Nursing of the infant followed nature's pattern and was thus essential. Milk from the breast might even supply the child with the mother's moral virtues. Wet nurses were inadvisable and, if required, should be carefully scrutinized for their moral character, to avoid exposing the child to corrupting influences. The diet of the child was to be simplified for moral purposes. Similarly, freedom of the body was encouraged along with plenty of exercise to strengthen both body and mind. Moral virtues were associated with cleanliness, order, and regularity of habits. Physicians stressed the earliest possible rigorous toilet training, though weaning should be gradual to preserve the child's temper. Yet even with the most intimate matters of child care, there began to appear a less moralistic, more matter-of-fact tone. However, masturbation was considered a serious problem leading to disease, insanity, and death. Erotic play was no doubt induced by servants, slaves, and depraved peers. The problem was how to discourage sexual interest without inciting curiosity (Rogers, 1980; Sunley, 1955; Wishy, 1968).

With child obedience to external authority and to internal dictates of conscience as a central concern, disobedience and bad conduct were vexing problems to morally zealous parents. Many writers opposed corporal punishment as detrimental to a regime of love and gentleness; it was to be employed only as a last resort when all other methods failed. Whatever the punishment, it was to be used with proper understanding of the child as a being capable of moral improvement. Love and gentleness, when combined with appeals to conscience and reason, persuasion, precept, good examples, firm and consistent treatment, and especially reminders of the pain that wickedness caused others, would guarantee that conscience would control the child and the adult (Wishy, 1968).

The preeminent concern that children learn clear moral lessons is apparent in children's literature of the period. While parents were urged to become more realistic about the child's needs and to abandon moralistic preaching, the children themselves were not allowed any freedom from moralism in their books. Most books on conduct had the same basic theme, the fulfillment of the individual by accepting unquestioned truths of morality and religion. This happy goal could be reached only if the child began by giving complete obedience and love to parents in thought as well as deed. Jacob Abbott's popular books for children used most of the themes that dominated even the most imaginative literature. Life was a trial and the world a place of temptation in which one must make right prevail. Every material and spiritual success could be attained if the child improved himself by shunning bad companions and by remembering that sure and just punishment follows immoral or improper conduct. The major educational journals, textbooks, and school reports of the period present a struggle between partisans of religious and secular education, between defenders of strict or enlightened pedagogical methods (Wishy, 1968).

During this middle third of the nineteenth century, nurture writers were urging responsibilities for the moral redemption of American society on the schools as well as the family. The reforming tendency toward more tenderness about the child was coming into conflict with another reform trend of systematizing socialization of work values in children. Locke's constant emphasis on early establishment of firm habits of diligence, self-control, and restraint had become absorbed into the fabric of moral education as expressed in literature for parents, teachers, and children. This faith in dutiful self-denying industry is perhaps strange in an age of expansive entrepreneural capitalism that would reward adventuresomeness, and seemed to reflect anxieties about evident currents of social change related to increasing industrialization, urbanization, and immigration. The resultant tension between sentiment and rigorous demands was later resolved in favor of an increasingly Romantic vision of the child as expressed through pedagogical revolt against academic rigidity and a shift in children's fiction to melodramatic stories of individual heroic endeavors prevailing over the unsavory world. The child's moral energies and will were to be engaged and strengthened through tenderness and supportive regimes of caretaking. However, there were no doubt discordant messages to the child as both schools and families are more resistant to change than the trendsetters would like to assume (Rogers, 1980).

The Child as Future Redeemer (1860–1890)

There was a child went forth every day
And the first object he looked upon,
    that object he became.
And that object became part of him for
    the day, or a certain
part of the day, or for many years,
    or stretching cycles of years . . .
(Walt Whitman, 1819–1892)

The theme of the future of American society as inherent in the child was hardly a novel conception in the later half of the nineteenth century. For the Puritans of the seventeenth century the future as represented in the child was a matter of intense theological concern. The fulfillment and continuance of their community of saints required that their biological and social heirs honor their spiritual legacy. Yet the fulfillment of the Puritans' covenant with God necessitated the suppression and continual containment of inherent negative qualities of the child. Over the next two centuries, the Calvinistic premise of the child as inherently depraved, the heir of Adam's sin of pride and disobedience of the Lord, was to come into increasing conflict with the evolving American values of independence, individualism, and self-sufficiency that were required and encouraged for the development of the ever-expanding frontier. In this context parents were faced early on with the realization that the future as represented in their children was to be somewhere else.

British travelers to the United States in the 1800s were generally appalled with American children as impertinent and disrespectful and blamed this sorry state of affairs on parental indulgence, the refusal of parents to discipline their children properly. Foreign visitors seem to have been troubled by the familiarity and intimacy of parent-child relations, the lack of reverence essential to an aristocratic society. European authority and traditionalism had proved inappropriate for the New World. By 1750 the typical American family pattern had become an isolated nuclear group dispersed from extended families, marriage a contract of equals, individual achievement more important than ascribed status due to family

lineage. The child had become a democratic experiment, a sturdy republican impatient of parental authority—saucy, self-reliant, wild, spontaneous, immodest, independent, demanding, and irreverent. The conversion of the Calvinistic child to the democratic cause dissipated the intensity of Puritan theological concerns but did not lessen the pervasively continuing preoccupation of parental advisors with the development of the moral child in an increasingly uncertain and materialistic world. Obedience to parents was still emphasized as important to learning the absolute truths of morality and religion, but assumptions about the nature of children had become more optimistic: they were capable of salvation, if given proper models and encouraged in supportive rather than dominating ways (Bailyn, 1960; Rapson, 1971; Wishy, 1968).

In the decades following the mid-1800s, the democratic moral child was joined in the American family with various siblings—the scientific child of Darwin, the child as victim of societal disruption, and the child as redeemer of a corrupt society. An increasingly powerful vision of the child, as evident in popular childrearing manuals, was the sentimental notion that purity and innocence as represented in the child could save the world. However, there was also increasing fear that the world might be too much for even this marvelous creature of superior energy, purity, and magical qualities. This idealization of the child called for more optimistically nurturant ways of childrearing as represented in Jacob Abbott's *Gentle Measures in the Management and Training of the Young* (1871). His principal themes were authority without violence or anger and development in accordance with the nature of the juvenile mind. The evolutionary perspective on the child had already begun to be employed in support of the vision of the child as redeemer of adult failures. There was no doubt that the child did develop and change in response to the potentials of his or her native endowment playing against the limitations of the child's environment. Along with the new fascination with growth of the child was Abbott's awareness of the difficult moral issues confronting both parents and children. The development of morality was clearly seen as influenced more by the qualities of the person the child sought to emulate than by instruction or proscription. The parent needed to be tolerant, patient, and sympathetic, focusing on naturally emergent virtues rather than seeming faults, emphasizing the positive rather than the negative (Wishy, 1968).

The manuals and journals on home life and child training show how rapidly the study of children came under professional scrutiny and control. Early academic advocates of child study, especially G. Stanley Hall, reached out to the general public, and popular writers were alertly responsive to the usefulness of science in understanding the child. The Darwinian propositions of a struggle for survival, natural selection, and survival of the fittest seemed to point toward a definitive naturalistic cosmology, appealing to both scientists and laymen searching for a viable model of the child. The success of science and technology in medicine and engineering had given substance to a long-standing belief in childrearing as a rational process with certain results from definite methods. Surely science would discover and show the way for producing the Utopian child. Child-study clubs of middle-class women sprang up in several American communities and rapidly extended into a national movement. By the 1890s special journals of child study were begun (Schlossman, 1976; Sears, 1975; Wishy, 1968).

The mass of materials published about the child after 1880 encompassed a broad range and diversity of ideas, yet there were certain central problem themes, among them the question of nature versus supernature in the development of the child, reflective of the confrontation of Darwinian evolution with Christian creation. To face fully and honestly the importance of evolutionary naturalism was to reject the belief in any permanent transcendent essence of human beings. To accept evolutionary naturalism also meant that morals had no sanction beyond their value to particular people, and that the fate of humankind's best ideals was ever in doubt. Yet most experts on the child were not pessimistic nor converted to moral relativism. Instead, the idea of human evolution was incorporated into meliorist melanges of science and faith that passed off successfully as Christianity. By 1900 the notion of infant depravity had mostly disappeared from theological discourses about the child's essence; God had become the rational and loving father. And evolutionary naturalism had broadened sufficiently to recognize the importance of humane ideals, intelligent minds, and the stubbornly resisting will (Wishy, 1968).

Before the Civil War period, nurture writers had begun to grant greater neutrality or even dignity to the natural impulses of the child. They were more concerned with capturing these impulses for ideals; impulses were still viewed predominantly as intrinsically moral or immoral. By 1900 psychologists such as James, Thorndike, and Dewey were seeking to demonstrate that functions such as will, instinct, desires, energy, imagination, temperament were to be viewed as phenomena without any necessary moral connotations. Nor was the child to be romanticized as innately divine or innocent; his essence simply consisted of raw powers to be used to best advantage. Yet another problem of parental uncertainty had been created by the proposition of evolutionary development. With each new child a link in the continuous process of human evolution, one whose potentials were set by the limits of inherited endowment, what were the implications for the child and the race? Since one could never know just what a child inherited, most popular writers on nurture contributed to a growing optimistic activism (Wishy, 1968).

Mothers of the new child-study group were eagerly seeking the new ideas, but now more from the new experts on children instead of from popular writers. They were still like earlier generations in emphasizing general moral goals over specific techniques and in their lack of sensitivity to great individual differences among children. The child had become a home laboratory experiment for which they required the best scientific advice. The right kind of children were to be happy as well as dutiful. Could parents serve both high moral ideas and the spontaneous pleasures of childhood? The most persistent criticism of the calls for more freedom for the child came from people deeply troubled by the weakening of religion in the family. Though the nationally printed nurture literature had become more humane and secular, millions of homes adhered to more old-fashioned ideas of strict, absolutistic morality and of child obedience. Perhaps the most serious challenge to the optimistic, humanistic belief in the salvation of every child was "the boy problem," a dramatic increase in reports of juvenile crime. Yet this problem was attributed by the nurture writers, and even in scientific journals, to a degenerative process in drunken families exacerbated by bad environment, a morbid deviation from normality. The answer lay in surrogate parentage by social workers who would save the slum child from the degeneracy, ignorance, poverty, and the foreign habits of the un-American home (Wishy, 1968).

New Education for Old Ideals

Education for literacy as essential to a democratic society had its roots in the Puritans' theological conviction that personal salvation and enrollment in the community of saints required direct personal knowledge of the Biblical texts. During the first two centuries of the American experiment, religious groups fostered and maintained denominational schools as necessary to perpetuate and extend their theological domains. Bailyn (1960) argues that the transformation of inherited English linear authority in family and community under the challenges of the wilderness environment heightened the sensitivity to educational processes as the family's traditional effectiveness declined. Increasing attention was given to formal, nonfamilial education as institutions of cultural transmission as well as vocational training. Although the establishment of the Republic secularized the state by abolishing governmental support of particular religious denominations and by legalizing freedom for individual religious conscience, the implementation of the democratic ideal of common literacy through free public educational schools was not realized until the Jacksonian period of the 1830s. By the 1880s, a nationwide network of public schools had become firmly established and had already experienced much public concern about their inadequacies, expressive of anxieties about the unpredictable future of the American child in drastically changing times. As transcendent sanctions for the old Christian-republican code became increasingly challenged by industrialization and science, a new scientifically based education seemed to guarantee that the schools had found a way of saving traditional ideals of character and faith (Wishy, 1968).

The ideas of post-Darwinian education are represented in the philosophy of John Dewey. His belief in the power of science to illuminate educational thought and his humanistic perspective satisfied philanthropic sentiments and the need to make education useful to democracy. Dewey linked current ideas about the child to pragmatic philosophy and the growing demand for social reform. The established pedagogy of the times was still based on classroom passivity of the child, authoritarian teacher control, and rote learning. Ironically, the British travelers of the period who deplored the lack of firm family discipline were most impressed with the orderly control of the child in the schools. The strength of the new education was the freshness of method in trying to utilize the interests of the child, to make use of the need for activity, to involve teachers with a better sense of the child's nature, to develop the child's expression as well as the ability to learn, to establish pedagogical rules that require the teacher to avoid arbitrary authority (Hofstadter, 1962; Rapson, 1971).

Dewey was truly a child of Darwin, born in the year of the publication of *The Origin of Species* (1859) and reared during the flowering of evolutionary science. In devising a theory of education consistent with Darwinism, he began thinking of the individual learner as using the mind instrumentally to solve various problems presented in the environment and went on to a conception of education as the growth of the learner. Education must abandon the traditional view that knowledge is the contemplation of fixed verities in order to meet the requirements of the new age of democracy, science, and industrialization. For Dewey, the distinction between knowledge and action was artificial; knowledge is a form of action, and action is an important way by which knowledge is acquired and used. Dewey was seeking to find the educational correlates of a democratic, progressive society. He saw education as a major force in social reconstruction insofar as schools could provide means for the child to cultivate capacities and learn how to improve the social order, rather than merely to reproduce it in himself. Because social reform must look to the regenerative contribution of the child, the child must be placed at the center of school focus; the child's developing interests and abilities must displace the rigid authority of teachers and the traditional weight of curricula. To mobilize the developing processes in the child under gentle adult guidance would facilitate learning and form a character and mind suitable to the work of social reform (Hofstadter, 1962).

Hofstadter cites an address by the state superintendent of public instruction in Georgia, ''What manner of child shall this be?,'' delivered to the National Education Association in 1900 as illustrative of the prevalent conditions of the new educational thinking: Christian fervor and benevolence, the central place of the child in the modern world, democracy and opportunity as criteria of educational achievement, concern with the dull child, optimism about educational research and child study, education defined essentially as growth, and the faith that self-realization of the individual child will automatically work toward the fulfillment and salvation of democratic society.

The conception of the child formed by Dewey and his contemporaries was more romantic and primitivist than it was post-Darwinian, in the sense that these pedagogical reformers set up an antithesis between the development of the individual and the imperatives of the social order. The child is at once natural and divine, a merger of post-Darwinian naturalism with the Romantic heritage. The natural pattern of the child's needs and instincts become an imperative that it is profane for educators to violate. Dewey referred respectfully to Rousseau, Pestalozzi, Froebel, and Emerson, whose essay ''Culture'' anticipated many of his ideas. In this juxtaposition of the natural child against artificial society, the child came into the world trailing clouds of glory, and it was the holy office of the teacher to see that the child remain free, instead of imposing alien codes on him or her. The United States seems to have both produced and been unusually receptive to this new view of education, out of longtime concern with preparing the child of the future, the relative fluidity of the educational system, and the evangelical fervor of the country. Even so secular a thinker as Dewey in 1897 believed that the good teacher would usher in ''the true kingdom of God.'' The new progressives in education were on the side of the older angels. Dewey always had deep and continuing ties with a humanistic individualism and the traditional moral virtues of the old American character. The humane beliefs in the potentials of the individual child and in the boundless powers of education to move the child toward social capacity and service, the emphasis on the need for expert advice, intelligence, patience, and love in handling the impressionable creature, were all ideas that linked Dewey with the large body of child nurture writers of the time (Hofstadter, 1962; Wishy, 1968).

The new education as scientifically based on the study of the child was vigorously championed by G. Stanley Hall. In his 1901 article, ''The Ideal School as Based on Child Study,'' Hall proclaimed a complete break from all pedagogical traditions in favor of education that would be based solely on a fresh and comprehensive view of the nature and needs of children. The school was to stand for health, growth, and heredity, ''a pound of which is worth a ton of instruction.'' Every invasion of his time, every demand of the curriculum must be conclusively justified before subjecting the child to the regime. This belief in a natural and normal course of child development as the touchstone of education states the essential core of the new education. Hall's hopes were admittedly Utopian, but he had every confidence in both the child and the new science of child study (Hofstadter, 1962; Ross, 1972).

In *Democracy and Education,* Dewey argues that education is growth, that growth is life, that life is development. Attempting to provide ends for education is meaningless, since it has no possible further end but more education. ''The aim of education is to enable individuals to continue their education.'' The idea of growth as a biological metaphor and an individualistic conception had the effect of turning away from the social to the personal function of education. The child-centered focus invited educational thinkers to set up an invidious contrast between self-determining, self-directing growth from within, which was good, and molding from without, which was bad. Dewey himself did not accept this antithesis because he hoped to achieve a harmonious balance of the two. Yet the historical effect of the concept of education as growth was to exalt the child and dismiss the problem of society. Dewey never argued for a directionless education. He often wrote that the child himself, unguided, is not capable of selecting the proper content of his education. The teacher must somehow, without undue imposition, guide, direct, and develop the positive forces within the child. But this left the teachers without any clear directional guidelines. Thus, Dewey struggled with the old problem of an equitable balance between freedom and authority in his conception of education as a central force in social reform. By freeing children to develop their inherently positive forces for growth, which would necessarily benefit society, Dewey was very much in the vein of the ''child-as-the-redeemer'' theme prevalent in much of contemporary writings about the child. But along with this hope for redemption through the child, there was emerging a profound uneasiness about the powers of this marvelous creature in a world hostile to innocence. By 1900 there existed a powerful fantasy that the corrupt complexity of the new polygot civilization might be rejected as too costly in terms of character and faith. This revolt against pluralism in America at the end of the century is quite as remarkable as the revolt against formalism of the progressive intellectuals (Hofstadter, 1962; Wishy, 1968).

The Child of Science

As set forth by Locke and Rousseau, the child of the Enlightenment was expressive of the central concepts of nature and reason and the optimistic corollary of inevitable progress. Locke and Rousseau gave cognizance to both concepts as essential attributes of the child and of pedagogy; although Locke placed more emphasis on reasoning as controlling the natural impulses, Rousseau gave center stage to the natural powers of the child. For Locke, the development of reasoning in the child required procedures of tutorial modeling and precept; for Rousseau, understanding and reasoning would develop from the interaction of the child's natural impetus with the force of necessary limits and restraints. Both gave the child a central role in the evolutionary process of social progress and sought to free the child from the limiting confinements of traditional authority in order to fulfill that destiny. In proclaiming the child as a natural creature of interest in his or her own right, Rousseau foreshadowed both the child of evolutionary doctrine and the child as a symbol of romanticized individualism. These themes were to be conjointly expressed a century later in the early conception of the scientific child as proclaimed by Hall.

The child as an object of scientific interest is linked to the post-Darwinian period of general intellectual enthusiasm about evolutionary theory in the sense of a pervasive and continuing impact on our conceptions of the child. But we should note that the origins of normal child psychology in terms of systematic study may be traced to Tiedemann's recorded observations of his own son over the first two and a half years of life that were published in German in 1787. For the first time in human history, someone thought it worthwhile to record and publish a description of the behavioral development of a normal child. Dennis (1972) notes that the report was a careful naturalistic description, unprejudiced by theoretical bias. Many aspects of early child behavior presented by Tiedemann are familiar to present-day researchers: common sequences and differential rates of behavioral development, the effect of experience on feeding, transition of the grasp reflex into precise and intentional prehension, the significance of stimuli variability and novelty, the increase of crying by reinforcement, the animistic and anthropomorphic nature of the child's thoughts, and a range of behaviors that have become standard items in infant developmental scales.

Also to be noted is that Darwin's recorded observations of his own son Doddy were made in 1840–1841, after his famous voyage on the *H. M. S. Beagle* but probably before his ideas of evolutionary theory were clearly formulated. The seeds of his search for common links between organismically based behaviors of humans and other species, including the notion of the inheritance of acquired characteristics, are evident both in the foci of his infant observations and the inferences drawn from them. Darwin's observations of his children served not only as the basis for the published biographical sketch of an infant, but were drawn on extensively for his comparative behavioral analysis in *The Expression of the Emotions in Man and Animals* (1872). Many eminent psychologists have studied their own children and have found therein the progeny of their theories. Just as Doddy Darwin was the child of evolutionary affects, so Binet's daughters exemplified individual differences in mental and personal styles, Watson's children were proper behaviorist products, Piaget's infants were active constructionists, and Skinner's daughter dwelt happily in the baby box. Thus, children of behavioral scientists are not only their fathers' biological progeny but their cultural inventions.

The idea of a human being developing was a quite ancient notion and a major proposition of the Enlightenment philosophy. The importance of Darwin to our subsequent conceptions of the child was that he gave a scientific basis to the Enlightenment proposition of humans as part of the natural order of the universe, that he placed them within the spectrum of biological species and thereby denied them the Christian status of special creation. The possible implications of this new scientific conception of humankind were uncertain; they permitted both positive and negative interpretations of the future of society and humanity. Darwin himself took no position on the outcome; he presented the forces of nature as blind agents of selection either favoring or reducing the probability that a species would survive. The intellectual and cultural climate of the times favored an optimistic interpretation: society had evolved from savagery to Victorian sensibility; humans had evolved from simple organisms to rational beings; individual persons continued to evolve from the ineptly dependent infants to the independently competent adults with social responsibilities. Darwinism provided members of the Establishment in an era of rampant economic individualism with justification for their achieved status, and the progressive social reform movement with the potentials for a different social order. Yet latent in all of this prevailing euphoria was the fear of the negative, destructive impulses of humans that was to surface in Freud's revival of the demonic child, a conception that offended the late Victorian sentimentalism about the child as innocent and innately pure.

Darwin's ideas led to the establishment of anthropology, comparative psychology, and to a conception of the child as a natural museum of human phylogeny and history. In the late 1800s, parallels between animals and children, primitive societies and the early history of humans were rampant. "Ontogeny recapitulates phylogeny" became a slogan of the times. As Cairns discusses in this Handbook (*vol. I, chap. 2*), the concept of individual and species development tended to be used interchangeably and confusingly. Despite the eager naïveté of such speculations, the search for phylogenetic and societal shades in children marked the beginning of the science of child behavior by the proposition that humans are to be understood by a study of their origins in nature and in the child. This was in marked contrast to the prevailing orientation of Wundtian psychology that humans are to be understood by analysis of their adult functioning. The field of child study became established as distinct from and not really part of general psychology until the 1950s (Kessen, 1965; White, 1970).

The impact of the theory of evolution on Western intellectual thinking about the nature and development of humankind was immediate, dramatic, and pervasive. All of the seminal contributors to the scientific study of the child were immediate heirs of Darwin. In 1859, when *The Origin of Species* was published, Preyer was 17, Hall 13, Freud 3, Binet 2, Dewey was born, and Baldwin was born two years later. The second generation of major contributors—Terman, Watson, Thorndike, and Gesell—were born in the decade of the 1870s, when Darwin's more psychological volumes were published and evolutionary enthusiasm was in full flower. Indicative of the full force of evolutionary concepts about the child is the realization that the broad spectrum of interests and theories among this diversity of thinkers all bear the mark of Darwinian origins.

CONCLUDING COMMENTARY

The foregoing survey has presented ideas about the nature of children and their requisite training as set forth by writers from antiquity to the late nineteenth century. The most striking pattern over the millennia is the consistent concern with the child's inherent moral, philosophical, or psychological status—those characteristics that require constraint or enhancement—and with the socialization processes deemed necessary to ensure that the person immanent in the child will become a responsible cultural heir and fulfill the destiny envisioned for him or her by the family and the society. In this concluding section some of the major themes of these concerns will be noted, along with their variations through time, and various suggestions will be made about how these themes are expressed in twentieth-century America.

The theme of the culturally embedded context of conceptions about the child is basic to all others. The ideas that any society holds about its progeny express broader cultural beliefs about economic, social, political, and religious issues, about the future prospects of the society itself. Children have ever been viewed and handled as beings in the service of the parent, the family, the community, and the "great chain of being." The contrary proposition—that the environment should be in the service of children—may well be an ancient child fantasy, but only

since the last century, and most particularly in America, has this belief been taken seriously as a philosophical position. Such a transposition of adult/child status relationships may follow from a vision of irremediable failure in adult management of society, from a disillusionment in the modern faith of inevitable individual and societal progress; or perhaps it may represent merely the maintenance of that belief by transferring the faith from environmental manipulation of the child to a belief in the benevolence of the child's inherent potentialities. This transition was expressed at the turn of our own century by the moral reformers in the millennial theme of the child as the redeemer of a corrupt society and by the new professional childsavers as the innocent child warped by the evils of an industrialized urban environment. The underlying belief in the inherent (or at least potential) goodness of the child, and in the vulnerability of the child to environmental badness (including inept parentage), has pervaded our assumptions about children through the past hundred years, an ideology that most generally captures the child of science. Perhaps this is in part why we have always lived uncomfortably with the Freudian child, who clearly carries the demon within. Rousseau placed the child firmly center stage, yet his steady belief in the demonic aspect of man's nature rendered impossible his wish for society's salvation through the general will. In the end, his belief led him to require the impersonal, dispassionately controlling hand of the child tutor and the societal manager. The child is a cultural invention as well as a cultural product.

The basic perspective about the child as serving the adult world yields a conception of the child as an incomplete, inadequate adult, in need of special attention and controls in order to be rid of the deficiencies as rapidly as feasible. Early psychological science was concerned primarily with the functioning of the adult mind and not much interested in the child as worthy of study. The child as worthy of study was vigorously promoted by Hall, but usually found a home in academic departments of education or home economics, or in separate institutes. Developmental psychology did not become fully incorporated into academic psychology departments until the 1950s, led by a postwar generation seeking to escape the limitations of both learning and psychoanalytic theories.

The ancient cultures of the eastern Mediterranean were not only aware of but actively promulgated ideas about socialization training that have engaged our own attention. The Greeks believed that early training was important for development of both bodily and mental discipline, that the mind was impressionable from infancy, that both age and individual differences called for caretaking and instructional adaptations, that a central goal was to instill internalized monitoring and control, and that example was as important as precept. By age 7 the child was expected to begin the active assumption of adult responsibilities of vocational and citizenship roles, at home, in school, and in the fields or marketplace. Save for lacking the physical capacity for engaging in procreational or military activities, the child was in most respects already launched on the path of adulthood. Adult authority over children was unquestioned, as was child obedience to it, but that authority carried grave responsibility and was not to be used severely nor rendered austerely. Athenian parents were encouraged to maintain an equitable balance of love and discipline, favoring an ideal of shaping through gently administered control. The widespread practice of infant abandonment seems to have been authorized and practiced as a means of population control, disposing of excessive or evidently defective newborns. Once accepted into the household the child became a treasured possession.

Conquest of the Western world by Christianity, a slow development over a millennium, brought into the soul and mind of humans a discordant conception of themselves as both special creatures of a loving, forgiving God and earthy beings of residual sinful heritage, whereby they became acutely wary of prideful disobedience of the deity's expectations and demands. The principle of absolute authority of the deity was carried forth from the Old Testament and became enhanced by the Church in obedience to all God's agents as personified in the authority of Pope, king, and father. The wariness of unauthorized, unacceptable impulses focused more attention on the selfish character of the child, a natural quality that required reshaping and/or containment. The child was deemed to be peculiarly susceptible to indulgence and to bad company that would foster the child's sinful nature. Yet the Christian conception of human nature also embraced the child as inherently good, the symbol of God's wonder. This continuing ambivalence about the moral status of the child was reflected in the vacillation between harsh and gentle treatment, strictures against indulgence as encouraging selfish motivations and undermining the rule of warranted authority, either external or internal. Mothers were considered especially susceptible to affectionate indulgence, owing to their natural fondness for the young. An antipathy became established between parental control of and affection for the child that has persisted to the present day, though our

studies of parent behaviors clearly indicate an orthogonal relationship.

Our American culture, that exquisitely anguished heir of the Protestant rebirth of the Christian moral dilemma, has been probably the most moralistic of nations in the need to justify even our most pragmatic, materialistic actions in moral terms. Even in the secularized versions, the Christian morality drama is as much a part of our heritage as the Enlightenment faith in reason and progress. And we have shared this heritage freely with our children. The field of child development was conceived from the marriage of Darwinian naturalism with moral reform of the social order, gestated during an uneasy marital alliance, born with the help of European specialists, weaned abruptly from the Victorian sentimentalized indulgence by the Watsonians, developed studiously by the Gesellians, and adopted as the wondrously secular charge of an ever-expanding family of investigative caretakers. Hartshorne and May made the terrible discovery that the schoolchild lacked any coherent moral gyroscope, and Piaget gave it back. The Europeans never seem to have abandoned so completely the organismic, cognitive child as did the Americans. Moral concerns on this side of the Atlantic were more often addressed to the environment than to the organism. As we have more recently become somewhat disenchanted with environmentalism, we have once again readmitted to the household the unruly but engaging organismic child of conscience.

Displacing the pagan gods of antiquity, Christianity relegated them to the status of childish myths and old wives' tales and created in their place a homocentric world, a world in which human beings are the special dominant creatures of the universe. The modern cosmology of the Enlightenment unseated religious man from his world throne by returning him to the natural order; and, in the very process of this decentration, created a newer secularized homocentric vision of humankind as the measure of all things, as the creator of a kingdom of heaven in this earthy life through the inevitability of reason and scientific progress. By divesting themselves of divine souls and placing themselves within the natural order, human beings accepted kinship with other biological beings and invested their progeny with the symbolic potency of both past and future destiny of humankind. Humans became masters of their own fate and their children the measure of their accomplishments toward ameliorative or Utopian ideals. A parent was no longer simply the delegate of the reigning deity, someone preparing a child for salvation through acceptance of that holy allegiance; now people became the creators of their own god, involving a faith in the positive potentialities of naturalism rediscovered, a faith in the power of the mind and heart to master that uncertain nature. Nature versus nurture, heredity versus environment became and remained key concepts of pragmatic and moral significance.

Human beings did not thereby free themselves of the moral struggle between the forces of good and evil; the descent of these forces from the heavens to this earthly and subterranean world made the balance among them more uncertain. The signs of human destiny could no longer be read in the rituals of sacrifice or in the worship of the deity; the totality of human behavior provided the text—and the outcome. Sin became deviations from consensual codes; innocence and guilt became defined in terms of the existence of individual moral sense and intentional violation. Persons lacking in moral sensibility—children, mental defectives, insane—were not sinners. They simply lacked any moral sensibility. They required protective restraint because of their special vulnerability to undue influence. The innocence of children reflected their insufficient knowledge and experience, but these fortunately were remediable. Literacy and education became matters of intense moral as well as vocational concern and effort. All aspects of child training were imbued with moral significance, from breast to Bible, from weaning to wooing, from external to internal regulation. As humans became creators of their own universe, they became creators of their own private domestic kingdom, the isolated nuclear family a product of change in ideological as well as political and economic forces. Now endowed with the status of domestic monarchs, parents were heavily burdened with the responsibility not only for their immediate household charges, but the future of the family, community, state, and world. This has proved to be an awesomely anxious assignment, one requiring increasing assistance from knowledgeable experts in an age of scientific reason. Throughout our long past and short history, the field of child development has responded to such needs of the society by studying evident foci of caretaking concern, and in turn sharing our knowledge and understanding with the public in varying degrees of caution and certainty. Thus have we shared in and contributed to our cultural inventions of the child (Kessen, 1979).

Locke and Rousseau are figures of continuing central significance to childrearing and the study of child development as they were magnificently articulate spokesmen of their times and therefore of our own era. Concepts such as habit training, love versus material discipline, training attuned to child interests and motivations, child play being natural and necessary, conformity achieved through the exercise of reason can hardly be thought of without acknowledging Locke's formulations. Likewise, Rousseau's major concerns with the equitable balance of individual freedom and duty in a moral social order, with childhood as a psychological world different from and worthy of respectful understanding by adults, with the child as a reconstructionist of sequential stages, with learning as operative at birth yet dependent on organismic development, and with the positive and negative consequences of the child as preoccupied with inevitable infantile self-love are all issues and concepts that have demanded our attention ever since. The reader can readily trace our own conceptual lineage from such distinguished progenitors.

Two issues relating to our heritage of Enlightenment philosophy and the democratic experiment are particularly notable: One bears on our assumptions about basic human motivations; the other, on our uncertainty about the proper status relationships of parent and child. Locke was much concerned with issues of child motivation in childrearing and education. He gave special emphasis to the principles of pleasure and pain as primary motivators, but distinguished carefully between appetitive and psychological levels of approach and avoidance and argued that esteem and disgrace are powerfully productive motivational forces in the child. Locke considered these psychological reinforcers as necessary for adult control of potentially negative impulses and essential to the inculcation of internalized habits of reasoned self-control. Save for the innate powers of intelligent reasoning, Locke had little confidence in the benevolence of human nature. Although Rousseau extolled, on the other hand, the natural child, he was centrally concerned with the ambivalent consequences of self-serving motivations. He had no confidence in the direct authoritative tutoring of Locke; instead, he believed in the impersonalizing control of the child through manipulation of the environment. No doubt Rousseau would be impressed with the techniques of behavior modification as devised by his disciples of the "impersonalized controlling tutor," yet he might well be perturbed by their apparent indifference to his concerns about establishing a moral social order.

In the American arena of scientific discourse about the child, we have operated more in the vein of Darwin and Freud than Locke by reducing the infant and child to seekers of bodily pleasure and avoiders of pain and by attempting to derive more psychological motivations therefrom. Both psychoanalytic and learning theories have given more attention to deprivation than to enhancement, to anxiety than to serenity, to fear and hate than to trust and love, to antisocial than to prosocial behaviors and motivations. Cultural childrearing fashions have cycled from sentimentalized love to austerity to indulgent love and later to more disciplined affection. More recently, favor has shifted from the basically organismic child of survival motivations to the cognitively constructed child of various temperaments, to the child who is seeking his or her own competent grasp of the world. We seem to have become both more Lockean and Rousseauan in emphasizing authoritative, affectionate parenting as well as the positive potentialities of the child.

The democratic experiment of the child, which is most clearly exemplified in the American household, has sought to free the child from arbitrary authority, to encourage independent self-sufficiency, and, at the same time, to instill a sense of duty and responsibility to the community and its values. This issue of tension between freedom and authority remains a basic political, economic, social, and personal issue for our own age. Just as conceptions of the child have ever been cultural inventions, so Rousseau's born-free/enslaved individual became embodied in the Romantic view of the innocent child besieged by a malevolent or misguided world, the pure but vulnerable youngster frustrated and thwarted by the evils of society. This image, which became a potent social force with the childsavers of the Progressive reform movement, was nurtured in the programmed permissiveness of early childhood education, was revived for the culturally disadvantaged of the 1960s, and is now fostered in much of the child advocacy movement, where it is most dramatically projected in the immediately salient social problem of child abuse. All this romanticism about the child has produced negative parental images that seriously erode the idea of the child as a family prerogative and heighten the idea of the child as the responsibility of a presumably benevolent bureaucracy. While the conservative moralists decry both the decay of the family and governmental intrusion therein, a more moderate movement has emerged to support, strengthen, and enhance the family as a viable childrearing institution, whatever the composition of persons within the household. For, as a society we continue to seek, as individuals and as communities, to provide productively supportive child-care arrangements for all our children. They are indeed the embodiment of our past and symbols of our visions of the future.

REFERENCES

Aaron, R. I. *John Locke.* Oxford: Clarendon Press, 1963.

Anderson, J. Child development: Historical perspective. *Child Development,* 1956, *27,* 181–196.

Aries, P. *Centuries of childhood.* London: Cape, 1962.

Axtell, J. L. *The educational writings of John Locke.* Cambridge, England: University Press, 1968.

Bailyn, B. *Education in the forming of American society.* Chapel Hill, N.C.: University of North Carolina Press, 1960.

Baumrind, D. Current patterns of parental authority. *Developmental Psychology Monograph,* 1971, *4* (no. 1, part 2).

Beck, A. G. *Greek education 450–350 B.C.* London: Metheun, 1964.

Biehler, R. F. *Child development: An introduction.* Boston: Houghton Mifflin, 1976.

Bremner, R. H., et al. (Eds.). *Children and youth in America: Vol. 1, 1600–1865.* Cambridge: Harvard University Press, 1970.

Brinton, C. *The shaping of modern thought.* Englewood Cliffs, N.J.: Prentice-Hall, 1963.

Calhoun, A. W. *A social history of the American family from colonial times to the present* (3 vols.). Cleveland: Clark, 1917–1919.

Cassirer, E. *The question of Jean-Jacques Rousseau* (Peter Gay, Trans.). Bloomington: Indiana University Press, 1963.

Cleverley, J., & Phillips, D. C. *From Locke to Spock: Influential models of the child in modern western thought.* Melbourne: University Press, 1976.

Coveney, P. *The image of childhood.* Baltimore, Penguin Books, 1967.

Cranston, M. *John Locke.* London: Longmans, 1957.

Crocker, L. G. *Jean-Jacques Rousseau* (2 vols.). New York: Macmillan, 1968–1973.

Curti, M. The great Mr. Locke, America's philosopher, 1783–1861. *Probing our past.* New York: Harper, 1955.

deMause, L. The evolution of childhood. In L. deMause (Ed.), *The history of childhood.* New York: Psychohistory Press, 1974.

deMause, L. (Ed.). *The new psychohistory.* New York: Psychohistory Press, 1975.

Demos, J. *A little commonwealth: Family life in Plymouth Colony.* New York: Oxford University Press, 1970.

Dennis, W. Historical beginnings of child psychology. *Psychological Bulletin*, 1949, *46*, 224–235.

Dennis, W. (Ed.). *Historical readings in developmental psychology*. New York: Appleton-Century-Crofts, 1972.

Earle, A. *Child-life in colonial days*. New York: Macmillan, 1915.

Frank, L. K. Beginnings of child development and family life education in the twentieth century. *Merrill-Palmer Quarterly*, 1962, *8*, 207–227.

Fraser, A. *A history of toys*. London: Weidenfeld and Nicolson, 1966.

French, V. History of the child's influence: Ancient Mediterranean civilizations. In R. Q. Bell & L. V. Harper, *Child effects on adults*. Hillsdale, N.J.: Erlbaum, 1977.

Friedrich, G. (Ed.). *Theological dictionary of the New Testament* (Vol. 5) (G. W. Bromily, Trans.). Grand Rapids, Mich.: Eerdmans, 1967, 636–654.

Frost, J. W. *The Quaker family in colonial America*. New York: St. Martin's Press, 1973.

Gabriel, R. *The course of American democratic thought*. New York: Ronald Press, 1956.

Gadlin, H. Child discipline and the pursuit of self: An historical interpretation. In H. W. Reese & L. P. Lipsett (Eds.), *Advances in child development and behavior* (Vol. 12). New York: Academic Press, 1978.

Gay, P. Reading about Rousseau: A blueprint for a biography. *The party of humanity: Essays in the French Enlightenment*. New York: Knopf, 1964.

Gordon, M. (Ed.). *The American family in social-historical perspective*. New York: St. Martin's Press, 1973.

Greven, P. J., Jr. *Child-rearing concepts, 1628–1861: Historical sources*. Itasca, Ill.: Peacock, 1973.

Greven, P. J., Jr. *The protestant temperament: Patterns of child-rearing, religious experience, and the self in early America*. New York: Knopf, 1977.

Hechinger, F. M., & Hechinger, G. *Growing up in America*. New York: McGraw-Hill, 1975.

Hofstadter, R. *Anti-intellectualism in American life*. New York: Knopf, 1962.

Illick, J. E. Child-rearing in seventeenth century England and America. In L. deMause (Ed.), *The history of childhood*. New York: Psychohistory Press, 1974.

Kessen, W. *The child*. New York: Wiley, 1965.

Kessen, W. Rousseau's children. *Deadalus*, 1978, *107*, 155–166.

Kessen, W. The American child and other cultural inventions. *American Psychologist*, 1979, *34*, 815–820.

Kett, J. F. *Rites of passage: Adolescence in America, 1790 to the present*. New York: Basic Books, 1977.

Kroll, J. The concept of childhood in the Middle Ages. *Journal of the History of the Behavioral Sciences*, 1977, *13*, 384–393.

Lacey, W. K. *The family in classical Greece*. Ithaca: Cornell University Press, 1968.

Locke, J. *Some thoughts concerning education* (abridged and edited by F. W. Garforth). Woodbury, N.Y.: Barron's Educational Series, 1964.

Lowry, R. *The evolution of psychological theory: 1650 to the present*. Chicago: Aldine, 1971.

Lyman, R. B., Jr. Barbarism and religion: Late Roman and early Medieval childhood. In L. deMause (Ed.), *The history of childhood*. New York: Psychohistory Press, 1974.

McGiffert, M. (Ed.). *The character of Americans* (Rev. ed.). Homewood, Ill.: Dorsey, 1970.

McLaughlin, M. M. Survivors and surrogates: Children and parents from the ninth to the thirteenth centuries. In L. deMausse (Ed.), *The history of childhood*. New York: Psychohistory Press, 1974.

Mechling, J. Advice to historians on advice to mothers. *Journal of Social History*, 1975, *9*, 44–63.

Morgan, E. *The Puritan family*. Boston: Public Library, 1944. New York: Harper & Row, 1966.

Morris, C. *The discovery of the individual, 1050–1200*. New York: Harper & Row, 1972.

Murphy, G. *An historical introduction to modern psychology*. London: Routledge & Kegan Paul, 1949.

Newson, J., & Newson, E. Cultural aspects of child-rearing in the English-speaking world. In M. P. M. Richards (Ed.), *The integration of a child into a social world*. Cambridge, England: University Press, 1974.

Opie, I., & Opie, P. Nursery rhymes. In W. Targ (Ed.), *Bibliophile in the nursery*. Cleveland: World, 1957.

Opie, I., & Opie, P. *The lore and language of school-children*. Oxford: Clarendon Press, 1960.

Payne, G. H. *The child in human progress*. New York: Putnam, 1916.

Pinchbeck, I., & Hewitt, M. *Children in English society: Vol. 1, From Tudor times to the eighteenth century*. London: Routledge & Kegan Paul, 1969.

Plumb, J. H. *In the light of history*. Boston:

Houghton Mifflin, 1973.

Potter, D. *People of plenty*. Chicago: University of Chicago Press, 1954.

Rabb, T. K., & Rotberg, R. I. (Eds.). *The family in history: Interdisciplinary essays*. New York: Harper & Row, 1971.

Rapson, R. L. The American child as seen by British travelers, 1845–1935. In R. L. Rapson (Ed.), *The cult of youth in middle-class America*. Lexington, Mass.: Heath, 1971.

Rogers, D. T. Socializing middle-class children: Institutions, fables, and work values in nineteenth century America. *Journal of Social History*, 1980, *13*, 354–367.

Ross, D. G. *Stanley Hall: The psychologist as prophet*. Chicago: University of Chicago Press, 1972.

Rousseau, J. -J. *Emile, or on education* (Barbara Foxley, Trans.). London: Dent, 1911.

Schlossman, S. L. Before home start: Notes toward a history of parent education in America, 1897–1929. *Harvard Educational Review*, 1976, *46*, 436–467.

Sears, R. R. Your ancients revisited: A history of child development. In E. M. Hetherington (Ed.), *Review of research in child development* (Vol. 5). Chicago: University of Chicago Press, 1975.

Senn, M. J. E. Insights on the child development movement in the United States. *Monographs of the Society for Research in Child Development*, 1975, No. 161, *40*, (3–4).

Skolnick, A. The limits of childhood: Conceptions of child development and social context. *Law and Contemporary Problems*, 1975, *39*, 38–77.

Slater, P. G. *Children in the New England mind: In death and in life*. Hamden, Conn.: Shoe String Press, 1977.

Sommerville, C. J. Toward a history of childhood and youth. *The Journal of Interdisciplinary History*, 1971, *2*, 439–447.

Sommerville, C. J. English Puritans and children: A social-cultural explanation. *The Journal of Psychohistory*, 1978, *6*, 113–137.

Stewart, A. J., Winter, D. G., & Jones, A. D. Coding categories for the study of child-rearing from historical sources. *Journal of Interdisciplinary History*, 1975, *4*, 687–701.

Stone, L. The massacre of the innocents. *The New York Review of Books*, November 13, 1974, 25–31.

Stone, L. *The family, sex and marriage in England 1500–1800*. New York: Harper & Row, 1977.

Sunley, R. Early nineteenth century American literature on childrearing. In M. Mead & M. Wolfenstein (Eds.), *Childhood in contemporary cultures*. Chicago: University of Chicago Press, 1955.

Takanishi, R. Childhood as a social issue: Historical roots of contemporary child advocacy movements. *Journal of Social Issues*, 1978, *34*, 8–16.

Tucker, M. J. The child as beginning and end: Fifteenth and sixteenth century English childhood. In L. deMause (Ed.), *The history of childhood*. New York: Psychohistory Press, 1974.

White, S. The learning theory approach. In P. Mussen (Ed.), *Carmichael's manual of child psychology*, vol. I, 657–702. New York: Wiley, 1970.

Wishy, R. *The child and the Republic: The dawn of modern American child nurture*. Philadelphia: University of Pennsylvania Press, 1968.

Wolff, H. W. *Anthropology of the Old Testament* (M. Kohl, Trans.). Philadelphia: Fortress Press, 1975.

THE EMERGENCE OF DEVELOPMENTAL PSYCHOLOGY* | 2

ROBERT B. CAIRNS, *University of North Carolina*

CHAPTER CONTENTS

*Some ideas and phrasing in this chapter were taken from an earlier one written in collaboration with Peter A. Ornstein (Cairns & Ornstein, 1979), with the kind permission of the publisher, Lawrence Erlbaum. Beverley D. Cairns collaborated in writing parts of this chapter, and in preparing its references. I am deeply grateful to Robert R. Sears for his detailed critique of an earlier, much longer version of this chapter, and to William Kessen for having proposed that the work be undertaken in the first place. Ronald W. Oppenheim, Alice Smuts, and Lloyd Borstelmann also offered valuable suggestions and criticisms, and I wish to thank them for their help. Preparation of this chapter was made possible by NICHD support (HD 14648–02).

This chapter, which is concerned with the recent history of developmental psychology, spans the hundred year period that began in the early 1880s when Wilhelm Preyer wrote *Die Seele des Kindes* in Jena and G. Stanley Hall initiated his Saturday lectures on child study in Boston. To recount the main events of a century of scientific thought can be a sober and dusty task unless some focus prevails. Accordingly, one of the aims in this chapter will be to identify the issues that have proved to be central for the science over a significant period of its history. A second aim follows from the first. It is to examine the most significant attempts to deal with these issues and the possible reasons why they worked or failed.

Looking backward, it seemed almost inevitable that the study of behavioral development should have emerged as the focal problem for the new science of psychology. Several of the founders of the discipline approached the subject matter of psychology from a developmental perspective, and the genetic theme dominated influential areas of philosophical and biological thought in the late nineteenth century. Alfred Binet in France, Wilhelm Preyer in Germany, Herbert Spencer and George J. Romanes in England, and several American psychologists from G. Stanley Hall and John Dewey to James Mark Baldwin and John B. Watson agreed on the fundamental viewpoint of development, if little else. What is this fundamental viewpoint? Watson, who is often wrongly depicted as an opponent of the developmental approach, summarized it as requiring the continuous observation and analysis "of the stream of activity beginning when the egg is fertilized and ever becoming more complex as age increases" (1926, p. 33). For Watson, the developmental approach constituted the "fundamental point of view of the behaviorist—viz. that in order to understand man you have to understand the life history of his activities. It shows, too, most convincingly, that psychology is a natural science—a definite part of biology" (p. 34). Nor was the kernel idea of development a new one for biological science or for psychology. It had guided the work and thinking of biologist Karl von Baer (1828) and those who followed his early lead in the establishment of modern embryology. It was also a nuclear theme in the earliest systematic statements of psychology by J. N. Tetens (1777) and F. A. Carus (1808) in German and Herbert Spencer (1855) in English.

But not all of the founders of the new science subscribed to the developmental perspective. Some of the most influential workers—including Wilhelm Wundt, founder of the first productive laboratory of experimental psychology—had a different view. Noting the difficulties that one encounters in efforts to study young children in experimental settings, Wundt argued that "it is an error to hold, as is sometimes held, that the mental life of adults can never be fully understood except through the analysis of the child's mind. The exact opposite is the case" (1907, p. 336). Even the "father" of child psychology in America, G. Stanley Hall, relegated developmental concerns to second-class status. In his inaugural lectures at Johns Hopkins, Hall (1885a) indicated that psychology could be divided into three areas: experimental psychology, historical psychology, and the study of instinct. The study of children and adolescents was assigned to historical psychology, which included as well the study of primitive people and folk beliefs. Instinct psychology dealt with those processes and behaviors that were considered innate, thus encompassing much of what is today called comparative and evolutionary psychology. Of the three divisions, Hall considered experimental psychology to be the "more central, and reduced to far more exact methods" (p. 123). These methods included the use of reaction time, psychophysical procedures, and introspection to examine the relations between sensation and perception. Historical and instinct psychology necessarily relied upon observational and correlational methods, hence were seen as less likely to yield general and enduring principles.

The division between experimental and developmental psychology proved to be surprisingly durable, and it continues to influence both areas. But that is getting ahead of the story. The main point is that developmental issues could have been nuclear concerns for the new science, but they did not become so (see Boring, 1929, 1950).

Developmental psychologists have not been especially mindful of the persons and ideas in their past. It is mildly ironic that an area that is committed to the study of the origins of behavior and consciousness should have shown so little interest in its own origins. Yet it is also understandable. If progress is to be made in empirical research, it will probably be won by those who look forward, not backward. Granted the validity of this commitment to the present, at least some developmental investigators have nonetheless believed that a better understanding of the ideas and accomplishments of their predecessors might contribute to future growth. In any case, significant contributions to the history of developmental thought have appeared in recent years, both from within psychology and from related areas (e.g., embryology, evolutionary biology). The present chapter has been facilitated in multiple ways by this re-birth of interest in the background of developmental study, and a large debt is owed to those who have led the way in its investigation.[1]

Developmental psychology as a scientific area of study was established only within the last century, yet its precursors in biology and philosophy extend backward at least one additional century. It was then that questions on the origin of life, species trans-mutation, and individual development began to be considered to be solvable problems and open to em-pirical investigation.[2] In our focus on the activities and ideas of the past 100 years, we can divide the century into three main phases: a formative period (1882–1912), a period of development and frag-mentation (1913–1946), and a period of modern growth and expansion (1947–1982). These time di-visions are for convenience, but they are also modestly justified by the nature of the events that occurred within them.

THE FORMATIVE PERIOD (1882–1912): PRECURSORS AND PIONEERS

The "birth" of a science is usually established in retrospect, after particular lines of investigation and thought have been shown to be productive and others have not. In this vein, the year 1979—one century after Wilhelm Wundt established a psychology lab-oratory at the University of Leipzig—became acknowledged as the official centennial of modern experimental psychology (Hearst, 1979). The as-signment involves a modest fiction. Even a casual reading of the literature then available in English and German indicates that by 1879 the enterprise of modern psychology was already well under way in the laboratories of Helmholtz, Fechner, Weber, James, Galton, and Wundt (Littman, 1979).

What about developmental psychology and its founding? The question must be raised because, as we have seen, the study of behavioral and mental development was not simply an outgrowth of work initiated by experimental psychologists. Indeed, de-velopmental studies flourished despite the influence of traditional experimental psychology laboratories rather than because of it. For whatever reasons, the study of behavioral and mental development was going full steam in the 1890s. By mid-decade, ge-netic or developmental psychology had its own sci-entific journal (*Pedagogical Seminary*, 1891, later to be renamed the *Journal of Genetic Psychology*), research institutes (Sorbonne, 1893; Clark Univer-sity, 1890), influential textbooks (e.g., *Die Seele des Kindes*, 1882; *L'évolution intellectuelle et mor-*

ale de l'enfant, 1893; *Mental Development in the Child and the Race*, 1895), professional organiza-tions (e.g., Child Study Section of the National Edu-cation Association, 1893; Société Libre pour l'Étude Psychologique de l'Enfant, 1899), and a psycholog-ical clinic (University of Pennsylvania, 1896). There was also a respectable and rapidly expanding empirical literature in both human and nonhuman development (Romanes, 1884, 1894). As early as 1888, G. Stanley Hall was able to refer to the "near-ly fourscore studies of young children printed by careful empirical and often thoroughly scientific ob-servers" (Hall, 1888, p. xxiii). The field had ad-vanced so far that it was christened with a name—Paidoskopie—to emphasize its newly won scientific independence (Compayré, 1893, p. 5). Happily, the activity survived the name.

There remains, as yet, no strong consensus on which year should serve as an anchor for develop-mental psychology's centennial. The problem is that the area is now sufficiently diverse so that one can point to several landmark dates, depending on which movement or which pioneer one wishes to honor. The founding of the child development research in-stitute at Clark and the establishment of the journal, *Pedagogical Seminary*, by G. Stanley Hall were clearly of signal importance for the area. But to cele-brate Hall's contributions over those of Alfred Binet can hardly be justified. Binet, at almost the same time, was laying the empirical foundations for mod-ern developmental psychology at the Sorbonne and establishing *L'Année Psychologique* as a prime source for developmental publications. Perhaps the dilemma may be eased by recognizing that these major advances were themselves beneficiaries of a zeitgeist that seems to have begun about 1880, and which gained significant momentum with the pub-lication of Wilhelm Preyer's volume (*Die Seele des Kindes*, 1882; trans. *The Mind of the Child*, 1888–1889). This volume has been called "the first work of modern child psychology" (Stern, 1914a, p. 4) and provided "the greatest stimulation for the development of modern ontogenetic psychology" (Munn, 1965). Not everyone agrees with these high evaluations of Preyer's work or of its originality (see, for instance, Debesse, 1970; Kessen, 1965; and below). Nonetheless, Preyer's book served as a powerful catalyst for the further study of develop-ment in psychology and in biology, and 1882 seems to be a reasonable date for us to begin this story of the development of modern developmental psychology. In addition to Hall and Binet, two other persons—James Mark Baldwin and Sigmund Freud—contrib-uted much to the molding of the area. The nature and extent of their contributions will be the main focus of this section.

Wilhelm Preyer (1841–1897)—Psychobiologist and Behavioral Embryologist

When *The Mind of the Child* was published, Preyer intended it to be only the first installment of a more comprehensive study of the nature of development. He completed the project four years later in the book, *Specielle Physiologie des Embryo* (1885) [*The Special Physiology of the Embryo*]. That these two contributions were not translated together and studied as a unit is a pity, for, in Preyer's mind, the issues to which they were addressed were mutually dependent and complementary. Preyer's strong assumption was that the methods and concepts applicable to embryological study could be applied with advantage to behavioral study, and that investigations of the one would support and complement investigations of the other. Why then two books? As Preyer explains it:

> I proposed to myself a number of years ago, the task of studying the child, both before birth and in the period immediately following, from the physiological point of view, with the object of arriving at an explanation of the origin of separate vital processes. It was soon apparent to me that a division of the work would be advantageous to its prosecution. For life in the embryo is so essentially different a thing from life beyond it, that a separation must make it easier both for the investigator to do his work and for the reader to follow the exposition of its results. I have, therefore, discussed by itself, life before birth, the "Physiology of the Embryo." (*The Mind of the Child*, p. ix)

To Preyer's credit, he completed work on both phases of the project, embryogenesis and postnatal development, in a significant number of species (including human beings). It is almost true that the feat has yet to be matched by a single investigator.

What drew Preyer to the study of development in the first place? That question cannot be answered definitively for Preyer (or for anyone else), but we do know that he was trained in physiology in Germany and, with others of his generation, came under the spell of Ernst Haeckel's vision of the unity of science and the centrality of development in evolution and life. Preyer recognized that the scientific program of modern biology would be incomplete without a careful analysis of human development

from conception through maturity, and that such a program would necessarily be interdisciplinary. As he put it, detailed observations "are necessary, from the physiological, the psychological, the linguistic, and the pedagogic point of view, and nothing can supply their place" (1889, pp. 186–187). Beyond Preyer's appreciation that intellectual and scholarly breadth were required for the productive study of children, he established methodological standards for the enterprise. The procedures that he endorsed, and followed, belied the proposition that children, even immature and unborn ones, could not be studied objectively and with profit.

Preyer was not the first person to undertake detailed observations of his offspring for scientific purposes. A professor of Greek and philosophy at the University of Marburg, Dietrich Tiedemann (1748–1803), had earlier employed the method, and Tiedemann's monograph, *Beobachtungen über die Entwickelung der Seelenfähigkeiten bei Kindern* (1787) [*Observations on the Development of Mental Capabilities in Children*] seems to have been the first known published psychological diary of longitudinal development in children. In the hundred years between Tiedemann and Preyer, several more studies appeared, many of which were sufficiently free of parental bias and distortion from other sources to be considered useful scientific contributions.[3]

The methodological standards that Preyer established for himself are admirable even by today's criteria. He reports that he "adhered strictly, without exception," to the following rules:

1. Only direct observations are cited by the investigator, and compared for accuracy with observations of others.

2. "Every observation must *immediately* be entered in writing," regardless of whether the details seem uninteresting or "meaningless articulations."

3. To the extent possible, observations are to be unobtrusive and "every artificial strain upon the child" avoided.

4. Insofar as possible, specific training of "such tricks as children are taught" is prevented. This included, in the first and second years, the elimination of "learning by heart of songs, etc., which he was not capable of understanding."

5. "Every interruption of one's observation for more than a day demands the substitution of another observer, and, after taking up the work again, a verification of what has been perceived and noted down in the interval."

6. "Three times, at least, every day the same

child is to be observed, and everything incidentally noticed is to be put upon paper, no less than that which is methodically ascertained with reference to definite questions.'' (*The Mind of the Child*, vol. 2, pp. 187–188.)

In brief, most problems of observation and categorization were anticipated by Preyer, including those of reliability and observer agreement.

How Preyer chose to organize his findings is almost as interesting as his methods and findings. For Preyer, the mind of the child, like Gaul, can be divided into three parts: Senses, Will, and Intellect. His knowledge about the comparative development of vision, hearing, taste, smell, touch, and temperature perception was surprisingly broad, so many of Preyer's generalizations on the ''Development of Senses'' were on target. But not all, and a few of his statements were demonstrably wrong. For instance, he wrote ''the normal human being at birth hears nothing'' (1888, p. 96). Preyer arrived at an opposite (and correct) set of conclusions on the capabilities of various nonhuman species to hear at birth. In the light of the care and precision of most of the observations, it is puzzling that Preyer made such an elementary error. In retrospect, we may speculate that a primary flaw was theoretical rather than methodological. Preyer's conclusions on neonatal incompetence were partly colored by his general assumption that human beings are less mature at birth than are species ancestral to them (i.e., *neoteny*). This was not the first time, nor the last, that strongly held hypotheses about the nature of children led to erroneous conclusions, despite disconfirming empirical evidence.

The ''Development of the Will'' provided an informative and informed analysis of the onset of such patterns as sitting, grabbing, pointing, standing, and other motoric acts. But Preyer was looking for more than a behavioral inventory; he hoped to find out *how* the pattern arose. For instance, ''deliberate'' pointing seemed to arise from an early action, that of abortive ''seizing'' or ''grabbing,'' and only at about 9 months did ''pointing'' gain the capacity to signal to others the child's wants and needs. Among other things, he concludes ''The first deliberate movements occur only after the close of the first three months'' (1888, p. 332). Preyer thus found in the study of the development of movement patterns, reflexes, and other actions a possible clue to the systematic analysis of the onset of intentionality.

The third part of *The Mind of the Child*, ''Development of Intellect,'' includes the consideration of language comprehension and production as well as the development of social cognition, including the concept of the self. Preyer's discussion proceeds with uncommon good sense, from a description of onset of landmarks of language development to an attempt to determine when the concept of ''ego'' or the notion of ''I'' develops. When is that? For Preyer, it occurs when the child can recognize ''as belonging to him the parts of his body that he can feel and see'' (1889, p. 189). Whatever the other merits of that proposal, it did permit Preyer to undertake a series of observations and mini-experiments on the matter. One section deals with the ability of children to respond to their reflections in a mirror; another with the uses and misuses of personal pronouns by young children. Both methods are still employed, with electronic assistance (see Lewis & Brooks-Gunn, 1979).

In addition to his study of infancy and early childhood, Preyer left another legacy to modern developmentalists, *Specielle Physiologie des Embryo* (1885). To complete his analysis of the ''origin of separate vital processes,'' Preyer conducted experiments and made observations on the embryos of invertebrates, amphibians, birds, and various mammals. Some of these observations—on the prenatal development of sensory and motor functions—have only recently been confirmed and extended using modern techniques. In line with recent interpretations of early development, Preyer concluded that (1) integrated, spontaneous motor activity is antecedent to the development of responsiveness to sensory stimulation, and (2) motor activity may provide the substrate for later mental, emotional, and linguistic performance (see Oppenheim, 1982, for an excellent discussion of the significance of this work). Because of Preyer's pioneering studies, he is acknowledged to be the father of behavioral embryology (Gottlieb, 1973).

Preyer has sometimes been depicted as the prototypical methodologist—careful, precise, compulsive, and pedestrian.[4] On this score, Karl Bühler (1918) writes that *The Mind of the Child* is ''a noteworthy book full of interesting and conscientious observations and—deficient in ideas'' (trans. Reinert, 1979, p. 49). Others have remarked that Preyer's ''book was more like a developmental psychophysiology than a developmental psychology'' (Reinert, 1979). Has Preyer's empirical reputation outrun his theoretical contribution to developmental psychology? The answer depends in part on what aspects of theory one chooses to focus upon. Preyer's main concern in preparing both *Mind* and *Special Physiology* was the clarification of a basic issue of development; namely, the relations between ontogeny and phylogeny of behavior and how these two processes influence each other. His categorization of the dates of onset was *not* an end in itself, to develop a behavioral timetable. Rather, his aim was to establish the lawful sequence of development of sensory and cognitive systems so that meaningful generalizations could be drawn between species and among systems in development.

Hence for Preyer, one key theoretical issue was how to reconcile competing claims of the "nativists" and the "empiricists" in the origin and perfection of the "vital processes" of behavior and thought. As far as human vision was concerned (and other sensory processes), he concludes that "my observations show that . . . *both parties are right*" (1888, p. 35, my emphasis). He speculates that "The brain comes into the world provided with a great number of impressions upon it. Some of these are quite obscure, some few are distinct" (1889, p. 211). Through experience, some of the pathways are obliterated, and others are deepened.

Lest Preyer be written off as a naive nativist, it should be added that his position was closer to the bidirectional approach of modern developmental psychology than to the innate ideas of Immanuel Kant. Drawing upon studies of the comparative anatomy of the brain as well as cross-species comparisons of behavior, he concludes that there is a feedback between experience and normal structural development in the brain. He offers a foresightful statement of the bidirectional structure/function hypothesis, reaching the conclusion that "*The brain grows through its own activity*" (1889, p. 98, my emphasis). How then does the individual contribute to his own development? Preyer's answer was clearly speculative, but it followed the same line of reasoning that is reflected in the structure/function bidirectional proposals offered in the next century by developmental psychobiologists Z.-Y. Kuo (1967) and T. C. Schneirla (1966).

The theoretical import of Preyer's behavioral timetable comes into focus when viewed in the context of Haeckel's biogenetic law. Its key assumption is that human maturation is *accelerated* with respect to ancestral species. That is, humans are presumed to pass through the several stages of development more rapidly than the species from which they were derived, so that evolutionary "novelties" and distinctively human characteristics appear at maturity, not infancy. To be tested, the view required precise information about the relative rates of maturation, hence the need for exactness in plotting the onset of particular behaviors. But Preyer was not a biogenetic apologist. He offered the compelling hypothesis

that human maturation rate was *retarded* relative to ancestral species, an idea that ran counter to the accepted version of recapitulation. In other words, human beings should enjoy a longer (not shorter) period of immaturity than their closest phyletic relatives. Accordingly, in most "vital processes" and behavior, there should be relatively greater plasticity in development and opportunities for learning for children than for nonhuman animals (1888, pp. 70–71). This is essentially an early statement of behavioral neoteny: that the relatively slower rate of maturation should be an advantage in making for an extended period of curiosity, flexibility, and adaptability in human beings. Echoes of his theoretical interpretations can be found in modern studies of ontogenetic/phylogenetic relations (e.g., Mason, 1980) and the bidirectionality of structure/function relations (Gottlieb, 1976).

Tracing the heritage that Preyer left for developmental study, we find that he set high standards for scientific observations of behavioral development. Though not unflawed, his observations were carefully recorded and sanely written. For those who followed him, Preyer embedded the study of children in the framework of biological science, and demonstrated how interdisciplinary techniques could be employed. Beyond the methodological message, there was a theoretical one. Preyer was a man of his times, evolutionary in outlook and committed to the clarification of the relations between ontogeny and phylogeny, between nature and nurture. Surprisingly, he was perhaps as influential in embryology as in developmental psychology. Through his work, talented young men and women were recruited to experimental embryology (including Hans Spemann, who identified "critical periods" and "organizers" in embryological development). Perhaps most important, Preyer demonstrated, by his successful integration of experimental studies of human and nonhuman young, that the investigation of behavioral development could be as much a scientific enterprise as a social, humanistic movement. Happily, some of his North American colleagues understood the message, at least the part about children.

Alfred Binet (1857–1911)—Experimentalist and Personalist

Statements about historical priority and influence are delicate matters, but there seems no serious debate over the claim that Alfred Binet was France's first significant experimental psychologist.[5] Moreover, as Jenkins and Paterson observed (1961),

"Probably no psychological innovation has had more impact on the societies of the Western world than the development of the Binet-Simon scales" (p. 81). Given the influence of this procedure identified with Binet's name, it is understandable yet regrettable that his other contributions to developmental psychology have gained so little attention. As it turns out, it has taken experimental child psychology 70 years or so to catch up with some of Binet's insights on cognition and the organization of memory.

Throughout his career, Binet was characterized by an independence of thought and action, starting with his introduction to psychology. It was his third choice in careers, after he had dropped out of law school and medical training (Wolf, 1973). In 1879–1880 Binet began independent reading in psychology at the Bibliothèque Nationale in Paris. Curiously, he selectively avoided experimental psychology, Wundtian version, by reading little or no German, and he took no trips to Leipzig. Shortly after he began work in psychology, he published his first paper, a useful discussion of experiential contributions to the psychophysics of two-point tactile discrimination. For research training, Binet affiliated himself with the distinguished neurologist, Jean Martin Charcot, at the Salpêtrière (the noted Paris hospital). Over a period of 7 years, Binet collaborated with Charcot and Charles Féré (1888) in studies of hypnotism and its expression in normal persons and the patient population. Binet's introduction to "experimental methods" thus was some distance removed from the then-acceptable laboratory procedures. His apprenticeship in research led to some spectacular controversies, with young Binet in the middle of the fray. The problem was that certain of the phenomena reported by the Salpêtrière group defied credibility—such as the report that the effects of hypnotic suggestion migrate from one side of the body to the other by virtue of electromagnetic influences. They used a very large magnet in demonstrations.[6] Attempts to replicate the phenomena elsewhere proved unrewarding. As it turned out, the research procedures followed by Binet and Féré were remarkably casual, and they gave scant attention to the possible suggestibility of their subjects, or of themselves.

While he was at the Salpêtrière, Binet's research skills were stimultaneously being sharpened in the embryological laboratory of E. G. Balbiani. He became acquainted firsthand with the rigorous procedures of biological research and the then-current concepts of evolution, development, and genetics.[7] This work culminated in 1894 with his being awarded a doctorate in natural science from the Sorbonne and his being appointed Director of the Laboratory of Physiological Psychology at the same institution. In that year, Binet also founded and edited *L'Année Psychologique*, coauthored two books (one dealing with the determinants of the extraordinary memory feats of chessmasters and calculators; the other, a critical treatment of the methods and approaches of experimental psychology), and published 15 articles. Among the articles were studies of the psychology of aesthetics, suggestibility, the nervous system of invertebrates, perception in children, and studies on the development of memory. Only a *single* year's work? No, because some of the studies had been ongoing over the previous 2 or 3 years; yes, because his publication list was just as impressive in 1895 as it was in 1894. He maintained this pattern until his death in 1911, except that later in his career he also wrote and supervised several plays that were produced in Paris and London.

Prolificacy can be embarrassing if one does not have much to write about. That seems not to have been a problem for Binet, due in large measure to his "very open, curious, and searching" mind.[8] Although he began his research training in the library, he soon became committed to the task of expanding the empirical foundations of the area in ways that seemed novel if not heretical. He early rejected the conventional methods of experimental psychology, as they had been practiced in Leipzig and Baltimore, as being narrow and misleading. On psychophysical experiments, he wrote in his *Introduction to Experimental Psychology:*

> Subjects go into a little room, respond by electrical signals, and leave without so much as a word to the experimenter. . . . With the three choices only—"equal," "greater," or "less"—they often seem to set up the results of the experiments in advance. . . . Their aim is simplicity, but it is only a factitious one, artificial, produced by the suppression of all troublesome complications. (Binet, Phillippe, Courtier, & Henri, 1894, pp. 28–30; trans. T. H. Wolf, 1973)

Nor was Binet impressed by the large-scale studies of Hall and his students who used the questionnaire methodology. On the latter, he wrote: "The American authors, who love to do things big, often publish experiments made on hundreds or even thousands of persons; they believe that the conclusive value of a study is proportional to the number of observations. That is only an illusion" (1903, p. 299).

What Binet had to offer psychology was a pragmatic, multimethod, multipopulation approach to the problems of behavior, instead of relying merely upon introspection and psychophysiological experimentation. Binet thoroughly dissected behavioral phenomena. To explore memory, for instance, he varied the nature of the stimuli (memory for figures and for linguistic material; memory for meaningful sentences vs. individual words), the subjects tested (chessmasters and superior "calculators" who performed on the stage; normal children and retarded children), measures employed (free recall, recognition, physiological measures of blood pressure and electrical activity), type of design (large group samples, individual analysis over long-term periods), and statistics employed. Through it all, Binet selected designs, procedures, and subjects with a purpose, not merely because they were available. To investigate imagination and creativity, he studied gifted playwrights and explored new techniques (inkblots, word association, and case-history information).

Such methodological catholicism is not without pitfalls. He was open not only to new discoveries but to new sources of error. In his day, he received high praise and devastating criticism for his work, and both were earned. The early studies were vulnerable: Binet was in the process of learning a trade for which there were no masters. He came out on the short end of a devastating exchange on the "magnetic" nature of hypnotism (see Wolf, 1973), and there was equally justified criticism by H. S. Jennings (1898–1899) on Binet's interpretations of his studies on the psychic life of the lower beasts. Further, S. Franz (1898), a student of J. M. Cattell, took him to task for the quality of his statistical presentation in a series of studies on the relation between cognition and physical measures in children. Florence Mateer (1918) doubtless had Binet in mind when she commented that "The French write brilliantly and convincingly but their technique is apt to be at fault" (p. 24).[9] Such errors—and the attitudes they fed—unfortunately masked the fundamental brilliance of Binet's work. Though shy in personal demeanor, Binet as a scientist was not a timid man; he judged the gains as worth the risks, and he published.

Experimental Studies of Cognition in Children

In 1890, Binet reported demonstrational studies of memory and perception that he had conducted with his two young daughters. The work was extended in succeeding years not only with his children (through adolescence) but with diverse subjects and areas of memory. Along with his collaborators, notably Victor Henri, the work was extended to persons who were extraordinarily talented or extraordinarily retarded. Through it all, Binet operated on the working assumption that the study of normal processes was the key to understanding special talents or deficits, so his laboratory also made a major investment in the analysis of memory in normal children, adolescents, and adults. Binet was highly sensitive to the need for convergent analyses that intersect on a common problem. He argued in 1903 that "our psychology is not yet so advanced" that we can limit our analyses to information obtained in the laboratory; instead, complex intellectual functions are best understood in studies of persons "whom we know intimately, to relatives and friends" (Binet, 1903).

Binet did not, however, disdain large-scale research designs; he simply believed that they were insufficient *in themselves* to tell the full story about the nature of memory processes. Accordingly, in collaboration with Henri, he conducted a remarkable series of studies on memory development that involved several hundred children.

In one of their analyses, Binet and Henri (1894) found that the children reconstructed material into chunks of information that were meaningful to them. It should be noted that this idea of active reorganization has now returned to occupy the attention of "modern" views of memory and recall (e.g., Paris, 1978). In the words of Binet and Henri:

> The children have a tendency to replace a word from the spoken text when the word appears in a rather lofty style, with another word with which they are better acquainted, and which they encounter more often in their own conversation. Their act of memory is accompanied by an act of translation. (Trans. Thieman & Brewer, 1978, p. 256)

How Binet and his colleagues chose to follow up this experimental work is instructive. Noting that other researchers might do things differently, Binet embarked on the intensive study of "superior functions" in relatives (viz., his two adolescent daughters) and friends. Binet did not give up on experimental designs so much as he extended their boundaries by conducting experiments on persons whose histories and characteristics were known intimately to him. For Binet, the key to unlocking the secrets of intelligence involved not only mapping its outline in large-scale studies but also a detailed tracing of its internal features in individual analysis.

This movement back and forth from a focus on individuals to a focus on large samples, then back to individuals, was a distinctive and deliberate research strategy.

Individual Differences in Cognitive Functioning

Attention to two or three children, rather than to a single individual or to large samples, inevitably leads one to a focus on the differences among them. So it was with Binet. He was not the first psychologist, of course, to be curious about differences among persons and their assessment and explanation. Following A. Quetelet (1835) in Belgium, Francis Galton (1883) had earlier used sensory discrimination tests to assess differences in basic abilities. The rationale for such tests was stated succinctly by Galton: "The only information that reaches us concerning outward events appears to pass through the avenue of our senses; and the more perceptive the senses are of difference, the larger is the field upon which our judgment and intelligence can act" (1883, p. 27). In other words, modest differences at the level of sensation would be directly reflected in "complex" cognitive functioning, or would be multiplied. A similar rationale and research strategy was recommended by the American psychologist, James McKeen Cattell, in an article entitled "Mental Tests and Measurement" (1890). Specifically, Cattell proposed that mental measurement should employ several tests of "basic" sensory and motor abilities, including assessments of color discrimination, reaction time, and other standard psychophysical procedures. Other experimental psychologists—including Joseph Jastrow at Wisconsin, Hugo Münsterberg at Freiberg, and J. M. Gilbert at Yale and Iowa (1894, 1897)—concurred.

Characteristically, Binet and Henri (1895) took a radically different approach from their American and German colleagues. It was, however, wholly consistent with the conclusions they had arrived at in their earlier studies of memory development; namely, it was absurd to focus on elementary units of memory as opposed to a recall for ideas and meaning. Furthermore, from Binet's studies of individuals, it seemed clear that great differences could be observed among persons in terms of "higher" mental functions, including language skills, suggestibility, common-sense judgments, and imagination. Binet and Henri (1895) thus argued for a methodological strategy that was precisely opposite to that of Galton and Cattell:

The higher and more complex a process is, the more it varies in individuals; sensations vary from one individual to another, but less so than memory; memory of sensations varies less than memories of ideas, etc. The result is that if one wishes to study the differences between two individuals, it is necessary to begin with the most intellectual and complex processes, and it is only secondarily necessary to the simple and elementary processes. (Binet & Henri, 1895, p. 417)

Although "complex processes" are more difficult to measure than simple ones, less precision is required because individual differences in complex functions are much greater than in elementary ones. Whether that assumption is correct remains to be demonstrated. The more fundamental problem, it seems, was another one that Binet and Henri identified; namely, the nature of the relationship between individual differences in simple processes and individual differences in complex ones. That is, the more puzzling issues arise not in the initial assessment of sensory elements but in determining how they should be *combined* to predict intellectual performance. How should the components be appropriately weighted, and what is the nature of the process by which sensations are translated into cognitions? The solution that Binet and Henri offered was a wholly pragmatic one: Bypass the recombination problem and assess the complex functions directly. Given this simplifying solution, Binet and Henri outlined a programmatic approach to the assessment of individual differences that was completed 10 years later.

The child study movement in France directly contributed to the eventual development of workable mental tests. Soon after the formation of the Société Libre pour l'Étude Psychologique de l'Enfant [Society for the Psychological Study of the Child], Binet was invited to become a member and he shortly became a leading voice in its activities and publications. Not only did this society prod the Ministry of Public Instruction to think constructively about the needs of retarded children but it was influential in having a commission appointed to set up special classes. Binet, as a leader of the society, was appointed to the commission. It was not entirely coincidental, then, that he was invited to develop tests for identifying children who could benefit from special instruction, and the results of the work were reported in a series of articles in *L'Année Psychologique* in 1905 (Binet & Simon, 1905a, 1905b, 1905c), later to be extended (Binet & Simon, 1908; Binet, 1911). Although they offered guides for the assessment in each of the three areas (medical, educational, psychological), their greatest attention was given to psychological tests. The 30 tests of the 1905 scale followed the outline offered by Binet and Henri (1895) almost 10 years earlier, except some procedures—including the suggested use of inkblots to study imagination—were omitted and new techniques were borrowed from other investigators—including Ebbinghaus's incomplete sentence technique (1897) and Jacobs' (1887) "memory for digits" test.

Although most of the basic concepts of intelligence test construction were reflected in the initial scale (e.g., multiple tests arranged in order of difficulty, various areas of competence tested, age standardization, and external validation), the refinement of the scale so it could be used productively with normal children required extensive further revision. The task was begun by Binet & Simon (1908) and completed by American developmental psychologists, notably Goddard (1911) and Terman (1916). Despite the magnitude of their achievement, Binet and Simon (1905c) were fully aware of the limitations of the technique as well as its promise. They wrote in conclusion:

> We have wished simply to show that it is possible to determine in a precise and truly scientific way the mental level of an intelligence, to compare this level with a normal level, and consequently to determine by how many years a child is retarded. Despite the inevitable errors of a first work, which is of a groping character, we believe that we have demonstrated this possibility. (p. 336)

They had indeed.

Developmental Theorist

Binet eschewed identification as a theorist, even declining initially to offer a definition of intelligence, "a problem of fearful complexity." "Some psychologists affirm that intelligence can be measured. Others affirm that intelligence cannot be measured. But there are still others, better informed, who ignore these theoretical discussions and apply themselves to the actual solving of the problem" (Binet & Simon, 1908, p. 1).[10]

Despite his disinclination to define intelligence, Binet was not hesitant to take a strong stand on the nature of intellectual functioning and its determinants. The design of the tests themselves reflect the assumption that the aim was to diagnose different levels of functioning, not to assess the child's "faculty" for thought. Consistent with this functional

view of cognitive processing, Binet argued that one of the test's primary virtues would be to identify children who needed to "learn to learn." For Binet, intellectual adaptation reflected dynamic, ever-changing processes that underwent constant modification and reorganization. Hence his focus on the ways that these processes become organized over time, and their "plasticity and extendibility" (1909, pp. 127–128). On this score, he proposed a program of "mental orthopedics" that should be followed to enhance cognitive functioning. In *Les idées modernes sur les enfants* (1909), Binet specifically deplores the notion that "the intelligence of the individual is a fixed quantity" and protests the idea as "brutal pessimism" (p. 126). Ironically, it is exactly the opposite assumption that fueled the enthusiasm of most American translators for the test, along with the conviction that this "fixed quantity" is hereditarily determined.

Binet's Legacy

In summary, what can we say about Binet's primary contributions to understanding development? Beyond his specific insights on psychological phenomena, three fundamental advances may be attributed to this remarkable scientist. The first concerns the insight that the assessment of reliable individual differences in higher-order cognition requires a molar rather than a molecular strategy. In retrospect, the idea seems to make a good deal of sense, but it was embraced by American psychology only after the research of Binet and Simon made the conclusion inescapable. After all, it seems intuitively obvious that precise, microanalytic experimental methods *should* be superior to imprecise ones in predicting everyday behavior. The idea dies slowly, and it is alive and well today in the study of social development. As with cognition, recent molecular analyses of social interactions appear to fare less well in prediction and classification than do molar assessments of the same phenomena. Exactly why molar techniques have an advantage continues to be a matter of debate, and Binet's analysis may still be the key.

A second contribution is related to the first. For Binet, the "two sciences of psychology" described by Cronbach (1957) were both essential. Binet pioneered both experimental child psychology and the study of individual differences. His stance on the matter is embodied in the methodological credo: "To observe and experiment, to experiment and observe, this is the only method that can obtain for us a particle of truth" (Binet, 1904, trans. Wolf, 1973, p. 293). As Binet saw it, problems inevitably arise when the two basic methodologies are divorced. If questions are raised that cannot be settled by experimentation, then they should be dismissed "since they are not susceptible to the sole criterion of certainty" that modern psychology can accept.

One other, more general legacy requires comment. Beyond the other pioneers in the field, Binet was the first to provide convincing evidence for the proposition that a *science* of human development was possible. He understood not only the complexity of the problem, but he persevered in the attempt to help developmental psychology "become a science of great social utility" (Binet & Simon, 1908, p. 94). Binet demonstrated that an empirical science of behavioral development in humans was within grasp, if the investigator maintained a profound respect for the information yielded from the dual methods of observation and experimentation.

G. Stanley Hall (1844–1924)—Teacher, Founder, and Catalyst

In the business of organizing the new science of psychology and the child study movement in America, G. Stanley Hall had no peer. In his long career, he proved to be an effective and durable spokesman and recruiter for the area. Among his other accomplishments, he was:

- the first American PhD in psychology (Harvard, 1878, under the direction of William James and physiologist H. P. Bowditch);
- the first American student in Wundt's laboratory (1879);
- the first American researcher to employ the questionnaire method with children (1880);
- the founder of the first laboratory of experimental psychology in America (1883; a claim, however, disputed by his mentor, William James);
- the first person to be named to a chair of psychology in North America (Johns Hopkins University, 1884);
- the founder and first editor of a major psychological journal in the United States (*American Journal of Psychology*, 1887);
- the first president of Clark University (1888);
- the founder and first editor of a developmental journal in English (*Pedagogical Seminary*, 1891);
- the founder of a child study institute at Clark University (1891);
- the first president of the American Psychological Association (1892);
- the first president of the Child Study Section of the National Educational Association (1893);
- the author of the first textbook on adolescence (1904);
- the author of the first American textbook on aging (1922).

The story of Hall's career has been expertly told by D. Ross (1972), and the details need not be repeated here. Born in Massachusetts, Hall was a minister, professor of philosophy, experimental psychologist, child psychologist, educational psychologist, and university president. But Hall did not change careers, he cumulated them. The product was a visionary and influential spokesman for psychology, evolution, and child study. Hall enjoyed great enthusiasm and tolerance for ideas, and he was a master at conveying his enthusiasm to others.[11]

Hall's introduction to developmental psychology occurred in 1880, when he returned to America from postdoctoral study in Europe with Wundt. He brought with him the "questionnaire method" that had been employed by K. Lange in 1879 in Germany to investigate "the contents of children's minds." The method was initially aimed at helping teachers learn what concepts children had available at the time that they entered school. Accordingly, the procedure involved asking children brief questions about their experiences and about the meaning of words—for example, "Have you ever seen a cow?" or "Where are your ribs?" The answers were scored right or wrong, and the percentage correct was used to describe groups of children, not individuals. So rural children were compared with city ones, boys with girls, black children with white ones, and so on. Accordingly, the "questionnaire method" was a precursor of later general aptitude tests of general information and vocabulary, at least in terms of the kind of questions asked. In Hall's core investigation, children just entering school in Boston were asked some 134 questions, such as those given above. Data collection was ambitious but haphazard; about half of the protocols from the 400 children tested had to be eliminated. Nonetheless, educators were impressed, if not by the conclusions themselves then by Hall's vision of how scientific research had the potential to revolutionize educational practices (Hall, 1883, 1885b).

Hall's chance to shape the direction of psychology in America came when he was offered the first professorship in psychology in the United States, at Johns Hopkins University in 1884. Following the general model established by Wundt at Leipzig, Hall set up a teaching laboratory at Hopkins and recruited to it several young persons who were later to play a formative role in the development of the science. In the first laboratory course, the students included John Dewey, James McKeen Cattell, Joseph Jastrow, and E. H. Hartwell. With the support and encouragement of President D. Gilman of Johns Hopkins, Hall also established the first psychological journal in the United States, the *American Journal of Psychology*. On the basis of his success at Johns Hopkins, Hall was offered in 1889 the opportunity of shaping a university himself by serving as first president of Clark University. Hall remained at Clark until his death in 1924, and established there a tradition of developmental study. Although many of the students who worked with Hall at Clark entered education, two of them—Lewis Terman and Arnold Gesell—were to play extraordinarily influential roles in developmental psychology in the twentieth century.

During the latter half of Hall's life, development and evolution displaced experimental psychology as the major theme around which he organized his work and thinking. In the spirit of *Naturphilosophie* and Ernst Haeckel, Hall applied the biogenetic law that "ontogeny recapitulates phylogeny" to all phenomena of mind and life as a universal explanation for the course of development and evolution. For Hall, the implications for the education, rearing, and religious instruction of children were manifold. With former student John Dewey, he warned about the hazards of "unnatural" and "artificial" constraints on learning and early development, and expressed disdain for parents and teachers who attempt to instruct children rather than permit their natures to unfold. Why? According to the psychological recapitulation argument, behaviors, like morphological structures, follow an invariant course of development that has been determined by ancestral evolutionary progression. Interference with that "natural" process would be detrimental, and likely to bring about a stunting of growth or "developmental arrest."

Hall's biogenetic framework also led him to a focus on the phenomena of adolescent development. For recapitulationist Hall, adolescence was the point where the fast-forward replay of ancestral psychological characteristics ended, and where the individual became free to superimpose distinctive and individual talents on the predetermined phyletic structure. Hence it should be the developmental stage of greatest plasticity and possibility for change. As Hall puts it: "While adolescence is the great revealer of the past of the race, its earlier stages must be ever surer and safer and the later pos-

sibilities ever greater and more prolonged, for it, and not maturity as now defined, is the only point of departure for the superanthropoid that man is to become" (1904, vol. 2, p. 94).[12]

Fueled by his conviction that the adolescent period was the nuclear one for the fulfillment of human potential, Hall (1904) prepared his masterwork, a two-volume compendium entitled *Adolescence: Its Psychology and its Relations to Physiology, Anthropology, Sociology, Sex, Crime, Religion, and Education*. The textbook tackled all of these topics and more, with a broad sweep of citations from philosophical, physiological, anthropological, religious, and, of course, psychological sources. Where the data fell short, as they usually did, Hall offered speculative evolutionary and moral interpretations. The product was a discursive but often informative view of adolescence.

Some of the insights and discussion appear remarkably modern in content if not in tone. On social cognition and developmental changes in attitudes, Hall writes:

Children's attitude toward punishment . . . tested by 2,536 children (ages 6–16) showed also a marked pubescent increase in the sense of the need of the remedial function of punishment as distinct from the view of it as vindictive, or getting even, common in earlier years. There is also a marked increase in discriminating the kinds and degrees of offenses; in taking account of mitigating circumstances, the inconvenience caused others, the involuntary nature of the offense and the purpose of the culprit. All this continues to increase up to sixteen. (vol. 2, pp. 394–395)

Similarly, in a discussion of moral reasoning, Hall concludes that "Thus with puberty comes a change of view-point from judging actions by results to judging by motives" (vol. 2, p. 394). The statement was also based on empirical data using a reformed version of the questionnaire method. In this context, Hall cites Schallenberger's study (1894) on the development of moral judgments:

From one thousand boys and one thousand girls of each age from six to sixteen[13] who answered the question as to what should be done to a girl with a new box of paints who beautified the parlor chairs with them with a wish to please her mother, the following conclusion was drawn. Most of the younger children would whip the girl, but from fourteen on the number declines very rapidly. Few of the young children suggest explaining why it was wrong, while at twelve, 181, and at sixteen, 751 would explain. The motive of the younger children in punishment is revenge; with the older ones that of preventing a repetition of the act comes in; and higher and later comes the purpose of reform. With age comes also a marked distinction between the act and its motive and a sense of the girl's ignorance. (vol. 2, pp. 393–394)

Adolescence thus is "the stage when life pivots from an autocentric to an heterocentric basis" (vol. 2, p. 301).

So far, so good, except Hall had the misfortune of discovering the biogenetic law at about the time that the new generation of biologists was discarding it. Problems arose when Hall's explanations became grandly speculative, unimpeded by empirical data. Here, for example, is his account of the origins of "athletic sports and games":

Why is it, this writer asks, that a city man so loves to sit all day and fish? It is because this interest dates back to time immemorial. We are sons of fishermen and early life was by the water's side, and this is our food supply. This explains why certain exercises are more interesting than others. It is because they touch and revive the deep emotions of the race. Thus we see that play is not doing things to be useful later, but it is rehearsing racial history. . . . Just as psychic states must be lived out up through the grades, so the physical activity must be played off, each in its own time. The best exercise for the young should thus be more directed to develop the basal powers old to the race than those peculiar to the individual, and it should enforce those psychoneural and muscular forms which race habit has handed down rather than insist on those arbitrarily designed to develop our ideas of symmetry regardless of heredity. (vol. 1, p. 207)

Hall does not explain why some people do not like to fish; presumably it can be accounted for in terms of their aberrant upbringing. Or because they are female.

If evolution and recapitulation ranked high on Hall's psychological priorities, then morality and religion ran a close second. The linkages came about in ways that were not always immediately obvious, but seemed to represent his faith in the psychic "continuity throughout the universe" (vol. 2, p. 208). For Hall, religious conversion should occur in adolescence because it is "a natural, normal, universal, and necessary process" (vol. 2, p. 301). Nonetheless, the adolescent is especially vulnerable to particular diseases and psychic disorders. Masturbation, for instance, is "one of the very saddest of all the aspects of human weaknesses and sin" (vol. 1, p. 432). The negative consequences are both immediate and delayed. On the one hand, masturbation can bring about the "phenomena of arrest. Growth, especially in the moral and intellectual regions, is dwarfed and stunted. . . . The masturbator's heart, so often discussed, is weak like his voice" (vol. 1, pp. 443–444). Furthermore, the delayed effects are likely to show up in the offspring of "the masturbator, in a persistent infantilism or overripeness of children" (p. 444). Hall's psychology of adolescence thus was broad enough to encompass evolution and pantheism and narrow enough to damn masturbation and promiscuity.

How does one evaluate Hall's contributions to developmental psychology? It is almost true to say that they were unique. Kessen (1965) provides a perceptive and succinct summary: "There have been diggers in the sand pile of child study since him, but in a sense, Hall has had no descendants—only heirs" (p. 151). Few influential persons in child development have stepped forward to claim him as their intellectual guide—even his students Terman and Gesell chose tó complete their dissertations with persons other than Hall. Nonetheless, Hall was extraordinarily effective in recruiting others to the study of children and stimulating interest in and support for the activity. By forging linkages between the study of development and the everyday questions that concern parents and teachers, he expanded the boundaries of the academic discipline, and stimulated fresh approaches to it. Of special importance was his pivotal role in the organization and support of the activities of the child study movement in America, including the Child Study Section of the National Education Association. His success inspired the founding of parallel organizations in other countries and one, Société Libre pour l'Étude Psychologique de l'Enfant, provided the forum and framework for Alfred Binet's later developmental investigations.

In his scientific role, Hall was more an importer and translator of ideas than he was a creator of them, and during his era there were plenty of ideas to import. In addition to the questionnaire method and the biogenetic law, Hall helped to bring to America Wundtian experimental procedures and Preyer's volume on *The Mind of the Child*. (Hall wrote the foreword to the American translation.) He also helped change the face of American psychology when, in 1909, he arranged a meeting between Sigmund Freud and his lieutenants (C. G. Jung, A. A. Brill, E. Jones, S. Ferenczi) and the most prominent psychologists in North America. This meeting was held to commemorate the twentieth anniversary of the founding of Clark University, and it is generally viewed as a key event in the acceptance of psychoanalysis in North America at a time when Freud felt ostracized by the European scientific establishment. At first blush, Hall's version of child/adolescent development and Freud's psychoanalysis would seem to be an odd couple. A closer look at the assumptions and aims that they shared, however, suggests some basic affinities. The concepts of developmental arrest, developmental stages, and recapitulation figure importantly in both approaches, and Hall was as convinced as Freud of the key role of sexuality in development, but on a different timetable. Throughout his career, Hall remained open to new and controversial approaches, and to psychology's need to make itself more useful and relevant to society.

To assess Hall's direct scientific contributions, it is perhaps fairest to measure his accomplishments against those of his contemporaries. On this score, Hall and Alfred Binet stood apart from most research psychologists in holding that the discipline had a responsibility to share in the solution of applied problems, especially those of education. But Hall's scientific work, in contrast with Binet's, was more a victim of his applied concern than a beneficiary. To supply "scientific" answers to pressing social concerns when relevant data were meager, Hall rationalized the then-current social attitudes with the modest empirical data at hand. Research was employed by him to demonstrate relationships, not to discover them. Hence his otherwise puzzling casualness about research design, and his ability to absorb information selectively, ignoring contradictory empirical findings. The larger problem is that loose but plausible formulations such as Hall's not only competed successfully in the short run with substantive research and theoretical gains; worse, they tended to submerge and distort them. Progress became not only difficult to achieve, but more difficult to recognize once it had been achieved.

Hall was a remarkable teacher, organizer, and catalyst for the field. Some of the most significant current areas of developmental study—mental testing, child study, early education, adolescence, lifespan psychology, evolutionary influences on development—were directly stimulated by Hall himself or by persons who at one time had been his students. His life's work illustrates that persons who are effective in providing impetus and activity in a science are

not always suited for making substantive theoretical and empirical contributions to it.

James Mark Baldwin (1861–1934)—Developmental Theorist

As a young professor at Princeton, James Mark Baldwin established himself as a brilliant developmental theorist with the publication of companion volumes on cognitive development (*Mental Development in the Child and the Race*, 1895) and social development (*Social and Ethical Interpretations in Mental Development*, 1897). The books, which won immediate acclaim, were translated into several languages. The honors also came. He was elected fourth president of the American Psychological Association, awarded an honorary Doctorate of Science from Oxford University, and won the Gold Medal of the Royal Academy of Denmark. Over the next decade, he published influential works in biology (on the relationship between behavioral ontogeny and behavioral phylogeny), in philosophy (a dictionary of philosophy and psychology), and in the history of psychology. With James McKeen Cattell, Baldwin cofounded and served as coeditor of the *Psychological Review* and its offspring, the *Psychological Bulletin* and *Psychological Monographs*. During the period from 1894 to 1910, Baldwin was almost as prolific in creating and writing on developmental theory as Alfred Binet was in creating and writing on developmental research.[14]

The rest of Baldwin's academic life is something of a tragedy, rivaling that of another innovator in psychology's early years, Charles Saunders Peirce. Because of a personal scandal, Baldwin was forced from his professorship at Johns Hopkins in 1909 and from the presidency of the 1913 International Congress of Psychology. He also left the United States, living briefly in Mexico City (where he helped reorganize the National University of Mexico) and permanently in Paris (where he was active in lobbying for American intervention into World War I). Although politically visible, he lapsed into professional obscurity. So did, temporarily, many of his ideas.

The major themes of Baldwin's work were enunciated early. In the introduction to *Mental Development in the Child and the Race* (1895), Baldwin wrote that his aim was to outline a "system of genetic psychology" that would attempt to achieve a "synthesis of the current biological theory of organic adaptation with the doctrine of the infant's development" (p. vii). That aim proved to be the theme of his professional life. His work was guided by the key question: "How can development of the mental order of phenomena—or that of any other truly genetic order, involving progress—be fruitfully investigated?" (Baldwin, 1930, p. 7). His answer was that mechanistic or atomistic methods will not do the job because:

Life and mind alike become eviscerated of all their richer meaning. Every genetic change ushers in a real advance, a progression on the part of nature to a higher mode of reality. Actually new things—novelties—are daily achieved in life, mind, and society; results which we cannot interpret in terms of the mere composition of the elements involved. (1930, p. 86)

In development, the whole is not only greater than the sum of its parts, it is also richer, more complex, and better adapted.

While aiming toward a synthetic theory, Baldwin extended developmental analyses in three areas: cognitive development in children, the social and cognitive foundations of personality, and the relations between behavioral ontogeny and behavioral phylogeny. Although we will consider these contributions under separate headings, in Baldwin's theory they were inextricably woven together.

Genetic Epistemology and Cognitive Development

The initial outline of Baldwin's theory of cognitive development was provided in *Mental Development in the Child and the Race* (1895). This book addressed the problem of how consciousness and thought develop in children and in evolution. According to Baldwin, mental development proceeds from infancy to adulthood through epochs or stages, beginning with a reflexive or physiological process, continuing through sensorimotor and ideomotor stages, and progressing to symbolic and ideational transformations. Baldwin thus conceived of consciousness emerging in stages, in both the individual and the species. Beyond emergence, there were more advanced stages, whereby "prelogical, logical, and hyper-logical designate well-characterized stages in mental development." Only in the most advanced epochs do "syllogistic forms come to have an independent or a priori force, and pure thought emerges—thought, that is, which thinks of anything or nothing. The subject of thought has fallen out, leaving the shell of form" (1930, p. 23). This is, of course, "formal" thinking.

What are the essential mechanisms of individual growth? According to Baldwin, the young child must accommodate to the stimulating environment through "oppositions" and "assimilations," in a "dialectic of personal growth." In the absence of a suitable mechanism of learning, Baldwin invented one: the circular reaction. Accordingly, feedback-produced repetition ("circular action") provided the conditions for both the establishment of habits as well as the basis for new accommodations. The feedback principle was seen as operating not only in fundamental sensory adaptations but also in the more complex learning experiences of children (broadly labeled by Baldwin as "imitation"). Circular reactions early in life in sensorimotor accommodations give rise to mental representations of the activities, or cognitive "schemes."[15] Hence the concept was employed to account for not only simple habit formation but also the process whereby motor actions are translated into cognitive ones. But it was not a one-way street: Cognitive and voluntary patterns can themselves become "semi-conscious" and "automatic." How? In the initial stages of cognitive learning, voluntary attention facilitates the occurrence of appropriate circular reactions. With the consolidation or acquisition of the pattern, attention becomes less necessary and the actions can be performed even in the absence of self-monitoring.

How did Baldwin arrive at these concepts of cognitive development? In part, from the observation of his own children, following the model of Preyer.

It was with the birth of the first child, Helen (the "H" of the books on mental development), that interest in the problems of genesis—origin, development, evolution—became prominent; the interest which was to show itself in all the subsequent years. "H" became (with, later on, her sister "E") from her extreme infancy, the focus through which all the problems of general biology and psychology presented themselves. The series of experiments recorded in the book, *Mental Development in the Child and the Race* opened the way to the correlation of data with those of biology. (Baldwin, 1930, p. 4)

Sound familiar? Most of the ideas that Baldwin discussed remain in one form or another in contemporary models of cognitive development, and so do many of the terms. The central concepts of age/stage progression and possible analogues between mental accommodation and biological adaptation illustrate the continuity. It would be a mistake, however, to assume that a given term necessarily had the same meaning for Baldwin as it has today. He had a tendency to employ concepts in ways that mystified his contemporaries. Nonetheless, there is enough common ground in terms and in ideas to conclude that Baldwin's views influenced present-day theories, directly and indirectly (Kohlberg, 1969; Mueller, 1976).[16]

Social and Personality Development

The new experimental science of psychology seemed less concerned with the study of social behavior and personality than with the analysis of consciousness and the mind. In recognizing the oversight, Baldwin had this to say about it in his first volume on development:

And it is equally true, though it has never been adequately realized, that it is in genetic theory that social or collective psychology must find both its root and its ripe fruitage. We have no social psychology, because we have had no doctrine of the *socius*. We have had theories of the *ego* and the *alter;* but that they did not reveal the *socius* is just their condemnation. So the theorist of society and institutions has floundered in seas of metaphysics and biology, and no psychologist has brought him a life-preserver, nor even heard his cry for help. (1895, p. ix)

Baldwin heard, and responded with an outline for "social psychology" that remains useful today. Indeed, Baldwin's contributions to the analysis of social interactions and the genesis of personality must rank alongside his seminal contributions to understanding cognitive development.

In *Social and Ethical Interpretations in Mental Development: A Study in Social Psychology,* Baldwin outlines the implications of his genetic theory for social and moral development. This volume, which is apparently the first work in English to bear the title "social psychology," was addressed to the problems of social development, social organization, and the origins of self. The major theme of this work was that the child is a "social outcome, not a social unit." In Baldwin's view, the child experiences a *dialectic of personal growth* progressing from an egocentric receptive stage to a subjective one and, finally, achieving an empathic social self. Accordingly, "the development of the child's personality could not go on at all without the constant modification of his sense of himself by suggestions from others. So he himself, at every stage, is really in part someone else, even in his own thought of himself" (Baldwin, 1906, p. 30).

The child's sense of self and others ("alter") is determined both by the "social nexus" in which the child is embedded and by the stage of mental development of the child. In considering the problem of motivational development, Baldwin (1906) argues that the child's "wants are not at all consistent. They are in every case the outcome of the social situation; and it is absurd to endeavor to express the entire body of his wants as a fixed quantity under such a term of description as 'selfish,' or 'generous,' or other, which has reference to one class only of the varied situations of his life" (p. 31). So much for personality types.

Nor are personality dispositions irreversibly fixed by early experience. In Baldwin's view, "personality remains after all a progressive, developing, never-to-be-exhausted thing" (1906, p. 338). The dialectic of personal growth—whereby the self becomes accommodated to others and the traditions of society in a continuing "give-and-take"—persists from birth to maturity. From each relationship there emerges a refined sense of oneself and of others, and "the only thing that remains more or less stable is a growing sense of self which includes both terms, the ego and alter" (1906, p. 30).

Just as "circular reaction" and "imitation" were key terms in Baldwin's account of mental development, so were they central to his theory of social and personality development. As they are employed by Baldwin, the concepts refer to the bidirectional feedback that social acts produce for children. The notions of mutuality and circularity underlie Baldwin's concept of imitation, and the concept refers to a dynamic and interactive process that occurs in the context of social interchanges. On this score, the concept both encompasses and transcends contemporary usage of "imitation" and "modeling." Accordingly, the child not only learns from others but they, in turn, are influenced by the child. Hence the child's behaviors and attitudes become formed by the dominant social influences to which he is exposed in a given social system. The child becomes both a factor and a product of the social organization.

Baldwin's views on the nature of human nature and the self seem to have been influential, though not in psychology. Sociologist Charles H. Cooley seems to have owed a debt to Baldwin in his concepts of "primary group" and the "looking-glass self." Similarly, the major tenets of symbolic interactionism were entirely compatible with Baldwin's original statements (e.g., Cottrell, 1942, 1969; Mead, 1934). The concepts of interactional analysis were reintroduced to psychology from sociology by Robert R. Sears (1951) in his classic paper on the need for an interactional foundation for the study of personality and social processes. J. M. Baldwin had made a similar plea to psychologists over a half-century before, but his arguments were for the most part ignored. So were those of Sears, at least initially.

Ontogeny and Phylogeny

For Baldwin, the question of origin was not limited to the study of individuals. In its broadest and most intellectually challenging form, the problem of the development encompassed both the person and the species. As Baldwin put the matter:

It is clear that we are led to two relatively distinct questions: questions which are now familiar to us when put in terms covered by the words, "phylogenesis" and "ontogenesis." First, how has the development of organic life proceeded, showing constantly, as it does, forms of greater complexity and higher adaptation? This is the phylogenetic question. . . . But the second question, the ontogenetic question, is of equal importance: the question, How does the individual organism manage to adjust itself better and better to its environment? . . . This later problem is the most urgent, difficult, and neglected question of the new genetic psychology. (Baldwin, 1895, pp. 180–181)

In addition to the separate questions, there was the issue of how they fit together; namely, the futile "antithesis between 'heredity and environment.'" Baldwin argued that this either/or contrast "supposes that these two agencies are opposed forces" and that it fails to entertain the possibility that "most of man's equipment is due to both causes working together" (1895, p. 77). In other words, evolutionary adaptations and developmental accommodations both reflect the impact of environmental selection, although over vastly different time intervals. They typically collaborate, not compete, in bringing about unique adaptations.

Expanding on the theme of the interrelation between ontogeny and phylogeny, Baldwin offered a counterproposal to the biogenetic law that ontogeny was merely the recapitulation of phylogeny. He proposed, in effect, that the relationship may be the other way around, and that changes in ontogeny may precede and shape subsequent changes in phylogeny. How? More specifically, how might ontogeny guide phylogeny without assuming that accommodations acquired in the course of a lifetime are directly transmitted to one's offspring? Consistent with the rest of Baldwin's genetic theory, he proposed that in the course of individual development there was a "natural selection" of behavior patterns by a process that he labeled "organic selection." In effect, the patterns that are most beneficial are retained (via circular reactions), thus securing the accommodation of the organism to the peculiar circumstances of its life. Now the problem arises as to how the effects of organic selection can be transmitted to the next generation. On this matter, Baldwin was not entirely clear, except that he implied that individuals who have experienced common adaptations in development would be more likely to mate than those who have not shared common experiences. Such biases in the reproductive process should be sufficient to "guide" natural selection and make it appear that there was an inheritance of acquired characteristics without the assumption of the "Lamarckian" factor.

The prominent American biologist H. S. Jennings (the same one who criticized Binet) devoted considerable attention to "organic selection" in his classic *Behavior of Lower Organisms* (1906). Although the "Baldwin effect" is still discussed in biology, sometimes in the context of Waddington's similar concept of "genetic assimilation," it has not yet played a major role in evolutionary accounts of behavior (but see Gottlieb, 1979, and Piaget, 1978, for discussions of this point). In any case, the relationship between ontogeny and phylogeny—and the specific problem of how ontogenetic variations contribute to evolutionary modifications—remains a significant issue for contemporaneous discussion and debate in biology and developmental psychology.

Developmental Theory

Although he clearly appreciated and recognized the value of empirical investigations, Baldwin's principal contributions were neither experimental nor observational. On this point, Baldwin wrote:

And as for "experiment," greater still is the need. Many a thing a child is said to do, a little judicious experimenting—a little arrangement of the essential requirements of the act in question—shows it is altogether incapable of doing. But to do this we must have our theories, and have our critical moulds arranged beforehand. That most vicious and Philistine attempt in some quarters to put science in the straight-jacket of barren observation, to draw the life-blood of all science—speculative advance into the secrets of things—this ultrapositivistic cry has come here as everywhere else, and put a ban upon theory. On the contrary, give us theories, theories, always theories! Let every man who has a theory pronounce his theory! (1895, pp. 37–38)

After his initial volume on development, Baldwin's work became increasingly removed from confrontations with data. The second developmental book—*Social and Ethical Interpretations*—was written with few references to supporting or disconfirming experimental or observational evidence. The further Baldwin moved his theoretical analyses beyond the stage of infancy, the more speculative and distant from empirical findings he became. American psychology was going in precisely the opposite direction, and leading the way were two younger colleagues whom Baldwin had brought to Johns Hopkins (J. B. Watson and Knight Dunlap).

The upshot was that the empirical assessment of Baldwin's key cognitive and ethical concepts, and their refinement, had to await the efforts of subsequent workers, notably Jean Piaget and Lawrence Kohlberg. Other aspects of Baldwin's thought have just begun to be investigated, including his developmental theory of the self (e.g., Lewis & Brooks-Gunn, 1979) and social development (Selman Yando, 1980). Still other areas have yet to be explored. The second half of Baldwin's productive career was devoted to the expansion of his "genetic epistemology," which appears in a series of volumes under the general title, *Thought and Things: A Study of the Development and Meaning of Thought or Genetic Logic* (1906–1911, 3 vols.). In these volumes, Baldwin went beyond the boundaries that psychology had set for itself (then and now) to consider the limits of human knowledge and its relationship to aesthetics and the ultimate ideal of Beauty. William Kessen has judged the volumes to be "brilliant, and one of the few truly original statements in psychology, crowded with invented words and all the apparatus of a philosophical system" (1965, p. 165). For Baldwin, the line between a developmental theory of psychology and a genetic theory of philosophy became fuzzy if not wholly imaginary. Baldwin's summary volume, *Genetic Theory of Reality* (1915), provides not only a statement of his views on genetic epistemology but an expansion of his metaphysical orientation that was subsumed by the "very indefinite category known to some under the phase 'Ethical or Spiritual Idealism'" (1895, p. xi). The linkages to the neoidealistic statements of Schelling and Fichte seem unmistakable. Small wonder that the work caused little stir among psychologists who were just learning from Binet and Watson that there could be an empirical science of child cognition and behavior.

Baldwin's Contributions

Why was Baldwin's influence so short-lived? Or was it? One could make a strong case for the proposition that his impact on modern thought has been enormous, although mostly unrecognized and indirect. On matters of science, Baldwin was clearly less of a methodologist and researcher than he was a theorist and writer. He seemed unwilling (or unable) to link his provocative ideas on the nature of development to empirical test and verification. In addition, Baldwin fares best with sympathetic readers. His use of concepts was not always consistent, and terms such as "circular reaction," "organic selection," and "accommodation" evolved in their meaning. Other terms, such as "social heredity," mean exactly the opposite of what they first bring to mind. He used social heredity to refer to the traditions and enduring organizations of the society that facilitated cross-generational transfer, and he did *not* mean the direct inheritance of social patterns from parents to children. "Race" was used by Baldwin in a special sense to refer to the species, not ethnic groups, so *Mental Development in the Child and the Race* is an evolutionary title, not a racist one.[17]

Recent evaluations of Baldwin's views promise to set his contributions in a balanced perspective. Even when one resists the temptation to *eject* (another Baldwin term) contemporary ideas into his system, most of the primary concepts endure and some still bear the labels that Baldwin christened them with. Baldwin clearly grasped the need for psychology to produce a systematic theory of individual development that could complement and extend the Wallace-Darwin theory of species evolution. Beyond this recognition, he made remarkable progress toward creating a system of developmental psychology: a genetic model that encompassed cognition, the self, and the social order. Looking backward, perhaps the most ironic aspect of psychology's eventual incorporation of Baldwin's ideas is that they gained acceptance only by penetrating the field from elsewhere: from Geneva, from sociology and symbolic interactionism, and from developmental biology. The field had to mature and so, apparently, did the ideas.

Sigmund Freud (1856–1939)—Psychoanalyst and Child Psychopathologist

Sigmund Freud stood in curious relationship to the founding of developmental psychology. Unlike the other investigators covered in this section, Freud published no empirical research on behavioral development per se: He observed few children in a clinical setting, and none in a traditional experimental design. Yet psychoanalysis has emerged as one of the more important influences—if not the most important—for developmental psychology in the twentieth century. Further, the early acceptance of psychoanalysis in the United States and elsewhere was due in large measure to the enthusiasm of G. Stanley Hall. Freud himself has described the emergence of the psychoanalytic movement:

> In 1909 Freud and Jung were invited to the United States by G. Stanley Hall to deliver a series of lectures on psychoanalysis at Clark University, Worcester, Mass. From that time forward interest in Europe grew rapidly; it showed itself, however, in a forcible rejection of the new teachings, characterized by an emotional colouring which sometimes bordered upon the unscientific. (1926, 1972, p. 720)

Hall recognized a novel developmental idea when he saw one. His promotion of psychoanalysis occurred at a time when it was suffering rejection in Europe and obscurity in North America. Freud's lectures at Clark, published in Hall's *American Journal of Psychology*, in 1910, provide one of the most lucid early presentations of psychoanalysis by its founder.

Born in Moravia and raised in Vienna, Freud as a student showed the catholicity of interests that was to appear in his mature work. Although anatomy and physiology were his primary areas of concentration, he was greatly impressed by the work of Darwin and Haeckel, on the one hand, and by the ideas of British associationist John Stuart Mill, on the other. After completing medical studies, Freud engaged in neurobiological research for several years, initiating, among other things, a phyletic/ontogenetic analysis of the fetal brain and the mapping of sensory neural tracts. Freud's early physiological publications were well received, and he achieved international recognition as a highly promising researcher and methodologist.

The mid-1880s constituted a turning point in his career when he decided to practice neurology, in part for economic considerations, according to Jones (1953). To further his training in this specialty, Freud won a fellowship to study in Paris with the renowned neurologist, J. M. Charcot. From October 1885 until late February 1886, Freud thus worked in the facilities at the *Salpêtrière* and, presumably, shared some of the same interests as Alfred Binet

(and some of the same ideas; see fn. 19). Apparently both young men were attracted by Charcot's demonstrations of the interrelations between physical symptoms and the mind, including the use of hypnotism in the remission of hysteric symptoms and in probing the "unconscious" mind. Returning to Vienna, Freud began his neurological practice, leading to a collaboration with Josef Breuer in the writing of *Studien über Hysterie* (1895). When Freud substituted free association and dream analysis for hypnotism in reaching the unconscious, psychoanalysis was invented.

As Freud (1926/1972) has pointed out, psychoanalysis "in the course of time came to have two meanings: (1) a particular method of treating nervous disorders and (2) the science of unconscious mental processes, which has also been appropriately described as 'depth psychology' " (p. 720). Psychoanalysis, the theory, involves strong assumptions about the development and evolution of personality that psychoanalysis, the method and therapy, does not. Why, then, did psychoanalysis-as-theory emerge as a developmental one? One answer would be that it was demanded by the data. Accordingly, the roles of, say, infant sexuality and the primacy of early experiences would be seen as having been revealed by the use of psychoanalysis-as-method. A second possibility, not incompatible with the first, is that Freud may have been intellectually prepared to focus on the formative nature of ontogenetic events by virtue of his research training and experience in neurobiology. Recall that Freud had, in his physiological work, undertaken analyses of embryogenesis. Finally, broader intellectual-scientific forces appear to have been at work. As Gould (1977) and others have noted, parallels to the then-contemporary evolutionary/developmental assumptions seem to be liberally represented throughout psychoanalytic thought.

That Freud should draw on biological approaches in the formulation of his theory of personality and psychopathology seems entirely reasonable in the light of his scientific training in the area. Contrary to the view that Freud employed physics as the basic model for psychoanalysis, the theory seems more analogous to the biological thought of the day than to either "physical" or even "medical" models. Hence certain psychoanalytic propositions appear to be immediately parallel to Darwinian-Haeckelian proposals on development and evolution. These include (1) the never-ceasing intrapsychic struggle and competition among instincts for survival and expression; (2) the psychoanalytic focus on two immanent motivational forces that figure importantly in evolution—instincts that bring about reproduction (sexual, Eros), and instincts that bring about selection and destruction (aggression, Thanatos); (3) the assumed preestablished progression of the stages of ontogenesis that parallel the stages of phylogenesis, hence the appearance of sexual expression in human infancy; and (4) the notion of developmental arrest or fixation, an idea introduced into recapitulation theory to account for fetal teratology, whereby "monsters" would be produced if the ancestral stages of phyletic evolution were not permitted to be sequentially produced in individual development. Later, in *Moses and Monotheism* (1939), Freud makes his debt to the biogenetic law explicit. As we have already seen, the primary American psychological recapitulationist, G. Stanley Hall recognized the fundamental harmony of his ideas on development and evolution with those of psychoanalysis.

The methodological legacy of psychoanalysis requires comment. Freud's main endeavor in life, according to Freud himself, was "to infer or to guess how the mental apparatus is constructed and what forces interplay and counteract it" (Jones, 1953, vol. 1, p. 45). The inferences on development and infantile experiences were colored, in large measure, by statements and reconstructed memories of his adult neurotic patients. It was a narrow data base, hardly adequate to construct a theory of normal development. But Freud had an advantage that most other theorists of his day (and these days) did not have; he, like Preyer and Binet, was permitted the opportunity to study complex processes in "persons whom we know intimately." Psychoanalysis thus evolved from the exhaustive observation of single individuals over a long-term period, including Freud's own self-analysis. Theory construction and its evaluation thus proceeded on an idiographic basis, following a research strategy not unlike the method he found effective in his earlier physiological studies.

If the contributions of investigators who employed the idiographic method are any indication—Preyer, Binet, Baldwin, Lewin, Piaget—then the procedure seems not wholly without merits. But there are pitfalls. While Binet argued that it was necessary to work back and forth—verifying and testing one's hypotheses at both levels of analysis—Freud eventually expressed a disdain for systematic experimental work, and the validity of the results it produced. For instance, in response to what seemed to be the experimental demonstration of repression in the laboratory, Freud observed: "I cannot put much value on these confirmations because the wealth of reliable observations on which these assertions rest makes them independent of experimental verification" (cited in Shakow & Rapaport, 1964, p. 129).[18] In time, the validity of psychoanalytic assertions came to be evaluated by dogma, not by data. That is a pity on two counts. First, the history of developmental research indicates that Freud was correct in holding that idiographic methods are no less "scientific" than are nomothetic ones, though the more enduring advances have occurred when the two methods have been coupled. Second, the scientific status of the entire area was compromised when it became permissible to denigrate the value of a conclusive empirical observation or experiment if it happened to be in conflict with kernel hypotheses.

In any case, psychoanalysis has thrived in one form or another for over 80 years in science and society. At both levels, its impact cannot be overestimated. As a scientific orientation, the breadth of its roots in the evolutionary/developmental thought of Darwin and Haeckel, on the one hand, and the psychological associationism of Mills and British empiricism, on the other, made it especially susceptible to hybridization. Psychoanalysis-as-theory was as readily married to the hypotheticodeductive behavioral model of C. L. Hull as it was to the ethological theory of K. Lorenz and N. Tinbergen. Both syntheses—social learning theory and attachment theory—have proved to be exceedingly influential in developmental research, a matter to which we return later.

Other Pioneers

The preceding coverage of significant contributions and persons is clearly incomplete, even for an abbreviated overview of the period. In Europe and elsewhere, child psychology was thriving by 1900. Given the impetus provided by Preyer, developmental work in German-speaking countries expanded, with William Stern (e.g., 1911, 1914a) taking the lead in the publication of several influential volumes on general development and individual diagnosis. Although Stern is most often remembered in American psychology for his proposal that the age-level score could be converted into an intellectual quotient by a simple mathematical transformation, his role in German developmental psychology was far more important. In France, developmental work progressed in brilliant leaps in education and became bogged down in the universities. Binet himself was rejected in his three attempts to secure an academic appointment as chairs became open at the Sorbonne and the Collège de France; he died without having been named to a professorship in France despite his preeminent role in establishing psychology as an empirical science. Binet's founding of a laboratory for the experimental study of educational problems in Paris seems to have inspired the founding of the J.-J. Rousseau Institute in Geneva by E. Claparède (Claparède, 1930).

In England, James Sully (1896) and William Drummond (1907) produced influential textbooks on psychology and on development, although there was relatively little novel research being conducted on children (but see McDougall, 1906–1908). In this regard, Mateer (1918) observed that "on the whole English contributions to child study, in so far as it deals with the child of preschool age, have been imitative rather than original and very scanty in number" (p. 28). Additionally, the contributions of G. Stanley Hall were being brought back to Europe whence they had originated. The British Child Study Association, in England, and the Society for the Psychological Study of the Child, in France, were two of the more influential groups modeled after Hall's American association. Comparable developments were occurring elsewhere, in Italy, Russia, Denmark, and Portugal, but these events were relatively remote from the mainstream of ongoing developmental work and thinking. They soon were to become less remote with the importation of N. Krasnogorski's method for the study of conditioning in infants and children by Mateer (1918).

From 1890 onward, North America was undoubtedly the center for scientific interest in child development. Millicent Shinn's "Notes on the Development of a Child" appeared in 1893 and led to a renewed interest in individual studies. At the time, her replication and extension of Preyer's method was considered to be a "masterpiece" (Mateer, 1918). Hall gathered a cadre of highly talented students at Clark who were bright enough to recognize the limitations of his evolutionary framework but who nonetheless remained committed to the study of development.

Beyond the contributions identified as falling within the range of child psychology, two additional areas of advance demand attention. One was the direct study of childhood psychopathology and disturbance. The first psychological clinic in the United States was opened in 1896 at the University of Pennsylvania under the direction of Lightner Witmer, former student of Wundt and Cattell. The aim of Witmer's work was to assist in the diagnosis and treatment of children with school problems and to apply the principles of the newly established science to everyday concerns. What were those principles? In Witmer's view, the study of children required a multidisciplinary approach, and from the beginning he brought together different professions, including social workers, physicians, and practicing psychologists. In the absence of a treatment model, he created one. Although the clinic was essentially a local Philadelphia operation, it grew and prospered under Witmer's leadership, and a journal, the *Psychological Clinic,* was founded to describe its activities. The concept of an applied as well as clinical psychology caught on, and one of the clinical students from Witmer's group at Pennsylvania, Morris Vitales, led the way in the establishment of industrial psychology in America.

The second area of advance that occurred during the period was of utmost importance for the establishment of the scientific status of developmental psychology. Recall that the second theme of Preyer's work was the study of development of behavior in nonhuman organisms, and the identification of the significant prenatal and postnatal influences that directed and determined development. He was not the only investigator who had been inspired by the evolutionary revolution to undertake comparative studies of development. In England, Douglas Spalding (1873) reported the remarkable effects of early experience in establishing filial preferences in newly hatched chicks. His experimental demonstrations seemed to confirm that phyletic and ontogenetic influences must operate in tandem, that the young animal was predisposed to form preferences during a period of high sensitivity shortly after hatching, and that the experiences that occurred then were especially effective in the rapid establishment of preferences.

George John Romanes, a young protégé of C. R. Darwin, was impressed by Spalding's demonstrations and, with him, emphasized the early formation and plasticity of behavior despite its basic evolutionary foundations. More generally, Romanes's analysis of the stage-paced development of sexuality and cognition served as a basic text for the two most important theorists in developmental psychology, Sigmund Freud and James Mark Baldwin. *Mental Evolution in Man* (Romanes, 1889) was one of the most annotated books in Freud's library, according to R. Oppenheim (personal communication). Oppenheim suggests that it provided inspiration for Freud's later emphasis on the early appearance of infantile sexuality. In accord with recapitulation theory, Romanes had placed the onset of human sexuality at 7 weeks. J. M. Baldwin (1895), for his part, gives explicit credit to Romanes and Spencer as providing inspiration and direction to the work embodied in *Mental Development in the Child and the*

Race. It should also be observed that Romanes, whose aim was to clarify the evolution of the mind and consciousness, is also regarded as the father of comparative psychology (Gottlieb, 1979; Klopfer & Hailman, 1967).

Studies of behavioral development in nonhumans were rapidly becoming a focal concern in North America. Wesley Mills, the Canadian physiologist, offered an especially clear statement of the need for developmental studies in a *Psychological Review* paper that appeared in 1899. In this article Mills took E. L. Thorndike (1898) to task for his narrow view of how experimental analyses can contribute to understanding animal learning and intelligence. Mills concluded, "In making experiments on animals it is especially important that they should be placed under conditions as natural as possible. The neglect of this is a fatal objection to the work of [Thorndike]" (p. 274). For Mills, the notions of ecological validity and biological constraints on learning would not be unfamiliar ideas. What, then, would be the method that he could endorse as being likely to yield up the secrets of social behavior and cognition? In a remarkable passage, Mills outlines a research strategy that captures the essential ideas of a thoroughly modern research approach to behavioral development (1899, p. 273). However convincing Mills's proposals may appear in retrospect, E. L. Thorndike completed the work, and brief experimental methods won the battle of the day and, for the most part, the war of the century. By the next generation, experimental studies of learning in animals and children were dominated by Thorndikian short-term, nondevelopmental experimental designs, at least in the United States.

A Summary of Themes and Concerns

The emergence of modern developmental psychology in the late nineteenth and early twentieth centuries was hardly a coherent, systematic enterprise. But it was vigorous, contentious, fresh, and, in some instances, brilliant. Despite the lack of unanimity in method and theory, certain ideas and goals captured the attention and guided the work of these early developmental investigators. Seven themes of special import concerned (1) the ontogeny of consciousness and intelligence, (2) intentionality and how it arises, (3) moral development, (4) relations between evolution and development, (5) the relative contributions of nature and nurture, (6) the effects of early experience, and (7) how science may contribute to society. A few comments on each is in order.

Development of Knowledge and Consciousness

The origins of consciousness and the development of knowledge were the major empirical concerns of this formative period for both comparative and developmental investigators. In the view of Romanes (1884), the main business of comparative psychology was to investigate the continuity of consciousness and intelligence from animals to man. To establish the linkage, it was necessary to undertake studies of animal consciousness and their apparent "intelligent" adaptations to the varied circumstances of life. Why continuity? For Romanes, continuity would demonstrate that human beings could not be set apart from nonhuman beings in the evolutionary scheme, as A. R. Wallace had seemingly done in his version of evolution. The strategy was anthropomorphic. Using information brought to him from varied and informal sources, Romanes collected anecdotes on how various beasts (dogs, chickens, spiders, cats) demonstrated high levels of intelligence in their adaptations. The reliance on anecdotes and the assumption of higher order cognitive processes when simpler ones might do the job led to an elegant retort by Lloyd Morgan (1896). Nonetheless, Romanes's work inspired "objective" analyses of the biophysical, chemical, and mechanical controls of animal behavior (e.g., Jennings, 1906; Loeb, 1912) and comparative studies of "animal intelligence" (e.g., Thorndike, 1898). This scientific movement in biology and psychology led immediately to the "behavioristic revolution" and, ironically, the denial of consciousness.

The origin of knowledge was also the central empirical problem for developmentalists. Not only were child psychologists concerned with "the content of children's minds" (Hall, 1891), but with how the contents got into the mind. Hence Preyer gave primary attention to the establishment of the senses, language, and cognition, and Binet and Baldwin early focused on experimental studies of childhood perception, discrimination, and memory. Baldwin's (1895, 1915) developmental theory on the origins of knowledge arose in part from an admixture of the speculations of the post-Kantians and the evolutionary views of Herbert Spencer and G. J. Romanes on stages in consciousness and cognition. At its root, however, were observations of infants that provided empirical substance to the ideas of "reflexive," "sensorimotor," and "ideomotor" adaptations. Unfortunately, the Binet-Simon advances in the study of complex processes did not appear until after Baldwin's mature theory of "genetic epistemology" had been formulated, hence it was based mostly on brilliant intuition and the framework that had been established by predecessors in philosophy and biology.

Development of Volition and Intentionality

Although the problem of consciousness was the major theme for developmentalists, questions of motivation and volition lagged not far behind. At what point in ontogeny do "willful" acts arise, and what is the relationship between intention and action at any stage of development? These related questions were explored by virtually all early developmental investigators, but, again, with different emphases and different conclusions. Binet and Freud, in part because of their experience with hypnotism and exposure to the work of Charcot, were concerned with the role of unconscious processes in the direction and control of behavior, both normal and pathological. Binet's (1892) studies of alterations of personality dealt with the effects of unconscious forces, and Breuer and Freud (1895) made motivation and unconscious control the central theme of psychoanalytic theory.[19] Similarly, Baldwin (1897) considered how conscious acts with practice and time become unconscious, and how awareness and intentionality develop in step with cognitive development. Nonetheless, the study of "intentionality" posed formidable methodological problems that were not solved (although Preyer launched an early assault on the problem in his studies of infants).

Morality and the Perfectibility of Man

The concern with intentionality and willfulness can be viewed as part of a broader question of ethics, namely: How can science help understand how human perfectibility may be achieved and imperfections avoided? This core issue was clearly pervasive in the moral psychologies of Tetens and Carus, and it was also a matter of no little import for Spencer, Hall, Baldwin, and several others of the era. A goal shared by many of them was to formulate a developmental science, which, in its highest application, would supplement—or supplant—religion.

By 1900, the key empirical finding that stages existed in the "development of moral judgments" had been established, in that older children gave greater weight to the motivation and intentions of a transgressor than did younger children. Similarly, striking age/developmental differences were obtained in the level of abstraction of the "moral judgments," and in the extent to which older children as opposed to younger ones (12 to 16 vs. 6 to 10) took the point of view of the offender. These generaliza-

tions were drawn from voluminous questionnaire studies, based on the responses of hundreds of children at each age level (e.g., Hall, 1904; Schallenberger, 1894). The methodology, but not the conclusions, was severely criticized at home and abroad. On matters of moral conduct, J. M. Baldwin (1897) adumbrated the arguments later to be employed by Hartshorne and May (1928–1930) on the specificity and social context of moral conduct.

Relations Between Ontogeny and Phylogeny

Developmental psychology was born in the wake of the biological revolution created by the formulation and widespread adoption of the Darwin–Wallace theory of species origins. The challenge to produce a similarly powerful theory of individual genesis was felt by biologists and psychologists alike. The initially popular candidates for such a general developmental theory were unfortunately limited. Doubtless the most influential developmental theory was the "biogenetic law." Virtually all early important developmental writers were recapitulationists of one sort or another: evangelical (e.g., Hall), enthusiastic (e.g., Preyer, Freud, the young Binet), or agnostic (e.g., Baldwin). Adoption of the recapitulation perspective did not, however, preclude consideration of alternative or supplementary views. On this score, the delayed maturation hypothesis of Preyer and the Baldwin-Morgan-Osborne proposal on organic selection represented efforts to solve the puzzle of how development could contribute to evolution, as opposed to the reverse. Both of these proposals have contemporary versions (e.g., Piaget, 1978; Waddington, 1939).

The initial evolutionary/behavioral hypothesis collapsed shortly after the turn of the century when the cornerstone assumption of recapitulation was discredited in biology. Embryological studies indicated that morphological steps in development could not be simply accounted for in terms of ancestral analogues. Even in embryogenesis, morphology was adaptive to the special conditions that prevailed and, as K. E. von Baer had earlier argued, development was appropriately described in terms of early differentiation of structures in ways that became increasingly distinctive for the species. In psychology, E. L. Thorndike (1913), among others, pointed out the problems in Hall's behavioral extrapolations of the recapitulation doctrine. The upshot was that evolutionary accounts of development were discredited, but the problem that gave rise to the explanations was not solved. It was merely submerged, to be revived in various forms over the rest of the century. During the formative period, the recapitulation proposal met the need for a general theory of development that would complement the Darwin-Wallace theory of evolution. Its collapse left the embryonic discipline without a theoretical substructure to guide and integrate its activities.

Heredity and Environment

A related but separable matter concerns the attempt to account for the extent to which an individual's behavior and propensities reflect the operation of his or her own experiences as opposed to an inborn, heritable potential. The "nature-versus-nurture" problem continued to tease and beguile the most brilliant developmental writers. Positions on this matter then were as diverse as they are today. Virtually all writers of this early period paid at least lip service to the proposal that it was not an "either/or" proposition but a question of how the two influences were fused in the course of development. Hall, for instance, took the developmental stance that individual experience played a major role in adolescence and beyond. (Prior to adolescence, evolutionary forces were presumed by Hall to predominate.) But there was little consensus on what roles should be assigned to which factors, and when.

A variety of methods were employed for the study of "natural" influences on behavior. Preyer, for instance, assumed that the actions that develop in the absence of training must reflect the operation of innate factors in the infancy of an individual child. Galton, in a nomothetic approach, emphasized the information to be obtained from pedigree studies, familial and twin comparisons, and selective breeding in animals. Along with Karl Pearson, he developed new statistical tools for the evaluation of covariation and correlation, and these fit neatly with the metric scale of intelligence.

Enduring Effects of Early Experience

Emphasis on the effects of early experience came then, as now, from two sources: the ontogenetic study of animals, and the origins of psychopathology in children. In animal behavior, D. Spalding (1873) reported an informative series of experiments on the early formation of filial attachment in birds, and G. J. Romanes (1884) expanded on this theme and proposed the primacy and critical effects of early experience. Others, including Wesley Mills (1898, 1899), urged programmatic longitudinal studies be undertaken that involve the observational and experimental analyses of behavioral ontogeny.

In human development, there was little agreement on the weight that should be assigned to early experiences in accounting for later behavior. Baldwin, for instance, considered personality development to be a continuing, never-to-be-exhausted thing, while others considered earlier stages to be especially formative (e.g., infancy for Freud, adolescence for Hall). Except for clinical retrospective reports, the evidence for the enduring effects of early experience on later personality and motivation was meager, or based on biological analogues. The necessary studies of continuity and longitudinal development had not been completed, not even for animals.

Application and Politicalization of Developmental Psychology

The application of developmental psychology to the needs of society presented both opportunities and problems. To promote the application of "scientific" principles to rearing and educating children, child study movements arose in America, and similar efforts were initiated on the continent and in England. The problem was that scientific principles were in short supply. On this point, William James noted in *Talks to Teachers on Psychology* (1900) that "all the useful facts from that discipline could be held in the palm of one hand." Not everyone, including Binet and Hall, agreed with James. Then, as now, the temptation was great to go beyond empirical findings and common-sense beliefs in writing about children.

The ideas and claims of some early developmentalists had political ramifications as well. One of the darker outcomes was the establishment and rapid growth of the eugenics movement, with Francis Galton as its intellectual leader and the protection of superior genes as its goal. Another byproduct of "Social Darwinism" was the importance attached to the newly devised metric scale of intelligence and the belief that it would permit rapid identification of innate, stable differences in talent.

There was, of course, a much brighter side to the application of developmental principles and ideas that we have not discussed (see Sears, 1975). Persons concerned with the science tended to act as child advocates, lending their prestige to the passage of child labor laws, the revision of elementary and secondary school curricula, and the promulgation of child-centered rearing and control practices. The discipline may not have directly benefited from these efforts, but the welfare of children did. Happily, the field moved ahead to consolidate its claim to be an empirical science as well as a progressive social movement.

Comments on the Formative Period

In overview, the modern study of behavioral development had an auspicious beginning as a vigorous, multidisciplinary undertaking, pregnant with new ideas, fresh approaches, and novel developmental methods. To the founders, the resolution of the basic problems of development seemed within grasp. Perhaps they were, but that early promise was not to be fulfilled, at least not for another half-century.

THE MIDDLE PERIOD (1913–1946): INSTITUTIONALIZATION AND FRAGMENTATION

The third of a century from 1913 to 1946 encompassed two world wars, an economic depression of unprecedented depth and duration, the rise to world power of two new politicoeconomic systems, and an unspeakable attempt to eliminate a whole class of human beings through genocide. These events affected the course of all intellectual and scientific work undertaken during the period, and developmental psychology was no exception. Paradoxically, some of the events that had tragic worldwide consequences served to enrich and broaden the discipline in the United States. World War I brought attention to the advantages and potential of psychological assessment, particularly intelligence testing, and World War II saw the establishment of psychology as a profession as well as a science. The American prosperity enjoyed in the 1920s was directly translated into liberal support for the discipline by private foundations and state funds. Likewise, the depression of the 1930s and early 1940s saw a massive withdrawal of funds and, concomitantly, a drop in the level of research activity on developmental problems.

Beyond societal and political influences, there was much to be accomplished within the area. There was an immediate need to extend the methodological boundaries of the discipline in order to permit systematic investigation of the several issues claimed by its investigators and theorists. Hence the formulation of ways to translate ideas into research operations remained a first task for the area. Virtually all substantive issues required attention, from social, cognitive, and sensorimotor analyses to the study of language, moral development, and psychobiological changes. With the widespread granting of funds in the 1920s that were specifically assigned to support studies of children, there was an explosive increase in empirical research.

In the establishment of its empirical foundations,

the enterprise of child and developmental psychology became segregated into separate subareas, topics, and theories. No single model, not even behaviorism, was broad enough to encompass and provide direction for the activities of researchers. This fragmentation stimulated efforts to put the field back together again through the publication of handbooks (which served to summarize the diverse investigations) and the founding of development-centered journals and scientific societies. But in the absence of a compelling and coherent general theory of development, the subareas of developmental investigation and thought evolved along separate trajectories. The story of the main events and ideas of this period is perhaps best told by recounting the progress made in the several areas of inquiry; from mental testing and moral development to language and thought and developmental psychobiology. That will be the strategy adopted in this section, beginning with some comments on the institutionalization of American developmental psychology and ending with a brief review of some major theoretical ideas of this period.

The Institutionalization of Developmental Psychology

The child study movement led by G. Stanley Hall in the 1880s and 1890s came to maturity some 20 years later. Child study associations had been established in one form or another in all regions of the country. Collectively, they formed a potent movement for child advocacy. In 1906, an Iowa housewife and mother, Cora Bussey Hillis, proposed that a research station be established for the study and improvement of childrearing (Sears, 1975). Her argument was simple but compelling: If research could improve corn and hogs, why could it not improve the rearing of children? The campaign to establish a Child Welfare Research Station at the University of Iowa was eventually successful. The Iowa unit was established in 1917 and its research-laboratory school opened in 1921. The Iowa facility—along with a comparable research unit that opened shortly afterwards at the Merrill-Palmer Institute in Detroit—became models for child development institutes that were to spring up across the United States and Canada in the 1920s and 1930s. Since one of the main functions of the institutes was dissemination of information about children, various publications were established, ranging from university monograph series (at Iowa, Columbia, Minnesota, Toronto, Berkeley) and journals (*Child Development, Child Development Monographs*) to handbooks (Murchison, 1931, 1933) and magazines

(*Child Study, Parent's Magazine*). Most of the institutes also awarded advanced degrees and, thereby, helped create a new professional work force. The graduates found placements in university teaching and research positions as well as in a wide range of applied settings. An interdisciplinary organization, the Society for Research in Child Development, was established in 1933 to provide a forum and framework for scientific contributors to the discipline (Frank, 1935).

The story of this "golden age" for the study of children in America has been recently told expertly by two of its participants (Sears, 1975; Senn, 1975), so that only an overview is required here. New funds from diverse private and governmental sources were made available to researchers in child development. Among the more notable contributors were the individual sponsors of the Fels and Merrill-Palmer child study institutes, along with various special mission projects (i.e., Terman's study of gifted children by the Commonwealth Fund, the study of the effects of motion pictures on children by the Payne Foundation, and the study of the causes of morality by the Institute for Religious and Social Education). But in terms of sheer impact on the field, the Laura Spelman Rockefeller Memorial Fund must be acknowledged as having the greatest influence. Through the Rockefeller funds, major centers for research were established at four universities (California, Columbia, Minnesota, and Yale), substantial support was awarded to the existing institutes at Yale and Iowa, and smaller-scale research centers were created at the University of Michigan and Washington University (St. Louis). Studies of personality and child development at Vassar, Sarah Lawrence, and Teacher's College, Columbia, also shared in the Rockefeller support.[20] This liberal support for child study provided stimulation for ongoing work at Stanford, Harvard, and Cornell. All in all, the effect was to confirm Binet's earlier observation that Americans like to do things big.

To attempt to summarize in detail the specific activities and accomplishments of these institutes from 1920 to 1940 is beyond the scope of this review. At midstream, Goodenough (1929–1930) provided an informative coverage of the work and accomplishments during a period of great activity. Each institute soon evolved its own "personality" in terms of methods employed and problems addressed. The issues that they tackled should illustrate the point.

Intellectual Development

Virtually all of the institutes were committed, at some level, to clarifying the problems of intelligence assessment and how individual differences in test performance came about. By the late 1930s, studies at Iowa on the effects of enrichment on intelligence test performance had appeared, and work on the stability and change of IQ had been completed at Fels and California. At Minnesota, Anderson (1939) offered a provocative theory of the continuity of intellectual functions, which was based on the extent to which early tests assessed functions that overlapped with those assessed in later tests.

Longitudinal Study

Most thoughtful developmental psychologists recognized the need for gaining adequate information about behavior and development over a significant portion of the lifespan, and two of the institutes—Berkeley and Fels—launched systematic longitudinal investigations. The work complemented the study already initiated by Terman at Stanford (see *Mental Testing* below).

Behavioral and Emotional Development

The study of children's fears and how they arise was undertaken at Columbia, Johns Hopkins, Minnesota, California, and Washington University. This work was essentially an extension of the projects launched by Watson and his collaborators at Johns Hopkins (see "Behaviorism and Learning" below), and dealt with the problems of how emotions arise in ontogeny and fears are learned and unlearned (Jersild, Markey, & Jersild, 1933; M. C. Jones, 1931).

Growth and Physical Maturation

The early work of the Iowa group was concerned with the study of children's physical development, including the care and feeding of children (Baldwin & Stecher, 1924). Similarly, Arnold Gesell's Yale institute led the way in establishing graphs of normal development so as to be useful in identifying instances of aberrant behavior or developmental disorders (see "Maturation and Growth" below). The Fels Institute early established a tradition for clarifying the relations between physical and behavioral development, which led, among other things, to significant advances in the assessment and diagnosis of psychosomatic relations.

Research Methods in Child Study

John Anderson and Florence Goodenough at Minnesota, Dorothy S. Thomas at Columbia, and H. McM. Bott at Toronto recognized the need for more adequate observational research methods (see Anderson, 1931; Bott, 1934; Goodenough, 1929; Thomas, 1929). But the methodological work was not limited to observational techniques. Good-enough (1930a) continued to explore alternative and flexible methods for personality and intellectual assessment (including her Draw-a-Person test), and these workers led the way in ensuring that high levels of statistical sophistication would be employed in research design and analysis. Dorothy McCarthy at Minnesota and Jean Piaget at the J.-J. Rousseau Institute began their influential studies of the origins of children's language and thought (see *Development of Language and Thought* below).

This is a mere sampling of the major concerns and issues. Without detracting from the high intellectual and scientific quality of the work completed, it should be noted that few major theorists were associated with the newly founded institutes. There were some notable exceptions to this generalization, including Jean Piaget at the Rousseau Institute and, in the 1940s, Kurt Lewin and Robert Sears at Iowa. For the most part, the institutes were devoted to the pragmatic problem that Mrs. Hollis had identified, "How can we improve the way that children are reared?" The area soon learned that it had neither methods nor theories adequate to the task. The institutes focused on devising more adequate methods and left the primary theoretical work to others.

Mental Testing

In the eyes of many developmentalists in the 1920s and 1930s, the major obstacle to establishing a credible science of child psychology was not theoretical so much as it was methodological. Given Binet's insights into and career-long devotion to the matter, it seems altogether fitting that he, along with his collaborators, engineered the most significant methodological advance of the first half-century of the science. Whatever may be the flaws and shortcomings of the Binet-Simon method of intellectual assessment, it provided the tool that was required for the precise study of children's development, and for the translation of cognitive events into quantifiable units. The test opened the door for comparisons on significant psychological dimensions across ontogeny, and for the analysis of individual differences among persons. It also provided a reliable method for addressing the major themes that had been identified during the first era of work in the field, including the problems of nature/nurture, early experience, continuity of consciousness, and the predictability of behavior and cognition.

Although Goodard (1911) deserves credit for having been the first to bring the Binet-Simon scale to America, Lewis M. Terman was the major force in extending the testing movement worldwide. Like other students of G. S. Hall who gravitated toward educational psychology, Terman's initial academic appointment was in the School of Education (at Stanford University). Formerly a school principal, Terman had a long-standing interest in the problems of individual difference in the classroom. He selected as his dissertation project the comparison of seven bright and seven dull boys on various measures (Terman, 1906). He had been acquainted with Binet's work since his undergraduate thesis at Indiana University, and given his background and the Barnes-associated tradition at Stanford for large-scale study, it seemed entirely in character that Terman should attempt an extensive standardization of the Binet-Simon scales (on some 1,000 California school children; Terman, 1916). Among other improvements to the scale, Terman adopted a suggestion by William Stern (1914b) that any child's performance could be expressed in terms of an Intelligence Quotient (IQ). In his commitment to observation and standardization, Terman proved to be a worthy successor to Binet. The Americanized version of the test was an almost immediate success. The method was widely adopted and modified to meet the needs of the military (in screening recruits for World War I) and the schools (to sort out highly gifted or retarded children).

This is not the place to attempt a comprehensive account of the testing movement; useful histories of mental testing, through 1925, can be found in Peterson (1925) and Young (1924), and more recent accounts can be found in Carroll (1978) and Tuddenham (1962). Three comments on mental testing and its relation to developmental psychology are in order, however.

First, the method paved the way for systematic comparisons across time, across persons, and across conditions. This was a necessary step toward the conduct of longitudinal studies of human behavior. It also provided the tool for comparing persons of different backgrounds, races, and environmental experiences, thereby permitting the researcher to address anew the problems of heredity and environmental influence. The study of the effects of early experience on IQ was explored by Sherman and Key (1932), Wheeler (1942), and by an Iowa group (Skeels, Updegraff, Wellman, & Williams, 1938; also Skeels, 1966). In addition, the procedure was applied in ways not anticipated by its innovators. For instance, Kamin (1974) has documented how the tests were used as a screening device to determine the "fitness" of immigrants to the United States, a practice that was hardly appropriate given the diverse backgrounds of the persons being tested and the conditions of assessment. The device proved to be an exceedingly powerful tool for prediction, for categorization, and for discrimination.

The second comment concerns the relation of the testing movement to the rest of psychology, especially the rest of developmental psychology. Interest in the use of the procedure as a research device initially rode a wave of enthusiasm, followed by a period of neglect. When experimental studies of how children's performance on intelligence tests could be modified were conducted in the 1930s, it became clear that increments of one or more standard deviations (e.g., 10 to 20 IQ points) were not uncommon and could be brought about in a relatively brief period (4 to 16 weeks) (see H. E. Jones, 1954, for an excellent review of this work). In addition, Sherman and Key (1932) demonstrated that a negative correlation was obtained between IQ and age among children living in culturally deprived Appalachia. Such outcomes raised questions about the environmental contributions to IQ scores, and generated much debate about the nature and meaning of the findings (see McNemar, 1940). A parallel controversy arose over the interpretation of data on twins, and the implications of findings from the tests of monozygotic twins, dizygotic twins, and siblings for the inheritance of intelligence. The issues subsided, without clear resolution, in the late 1930s; they again came to the forefront some 30 years later.

Third, the method of intelligence testing did not give rise to a coherent theory of the development of intelligence. The theoretical debates centered mostly around matters of test structure and statistical analysis (e.g., whether a single factor could account for the variance or whether two or multiple factors were required) and whether the results of the experimental tests were being properly interpreted. There was a significant gap between the emerging theories of cognition (following the model of Baldwin-Piaget) and the methods of assessment being employed. The gap was not unprecedented: A parallel problem could be found between the methods of social interactional assessment and theories of personality and learning social patterns (see *Social and Personality Development* below). But the test procedures proved their worth in education and in the marketplace, even though they could not be readily integrated into the existing body of psychological theory. Hence the testing movement evolved and prospered outside the mainstream of developmental psychology.

Longitudinal Studies and Lifespan Development

According to Wesley Mills (1899), the discipline needed (1) longitudinal studies of individual organisms from birth to maturity, and (2) systematic experimental manipulations of the long-term conditions for development. Without that information, one could scarcely hope to achieve a firm grasp of the processes of development, whether nonhuman or human. Since the major hypotheses about development were concerned at their root with these processes, one would have thought that longitudinal studies would have been given the highest priority in the new discipline. They were not. Perhaps the practical difficulties in mounting lifespan projects in humans seemed too formidable, or the investment and risks seemed too great. For whatever reasons, the information available about longitudinal development by the end of the first period of the area's history was either sketchy (e.g., Binet's study of his two daughters) or subjective and retrospective (e.g., psychoanalytic interviews). But it was on this fragmentary information that the most influential psychoanalytic and behavioristic theories of cognitive and personality development were formulated, and few data were available to assess their implications or correct their shortcomings.

As indicated in the preceding section on mental testing, one of the obstacles for longitudinal study—that of measurement—seemed to be solved by the development of a reliable device for the metric assessment of cognitive abilities. That advance was sufficient for Lewis Terman, who both perfected the instrument and pioneered the first large-scale longitudinal study of behavioral/cognitive characteristics in 1921. He selected 952 boys and girls in California from 2 to 14 years of age who achieved a test score of 140 IQ or above. This group comprised the brightest children (in terms of test performance) who could be found in a population of about a quarter-million (Terman, 1925). His initial aim seems to have been the planning of educational procedures for gifted children. As it turned out, the sample provided the core group for follow-up studies that have continued through most of the twentieth century. At several stages in childhood and early adulthood, these "gifted" children-becoming-adults were reassessed, with the behavioral net widened to include personality characteristics, life accomplishments, and social adaptations. Later, their spouses and children were included in the study, with the persons being followed through their sixtieth year of life (Sears, 1975). Despite shortcomings in the original design (e.g., absence of matched nongifted control or comparison group), the data provided a rich yield of development through the lifespan. Overall the work constitutes one of the major achievements of the science in its first century, incorporating the efforts of three of its most influential figures (Binet, Terman, Sears).

Another factor (in addition to method) that had

inhibited longitudinal studies was the need for research institutes that would survive as long as their
subjects. That problem was solved in the 1920s by
formation of the several child research institutes
across the United States. Soon afterward, longitudinal projects were initiated at Berkeley, Fels Institute, Minnesota, and Harvard. Initially, smaller
short-term projects were undertaken to investigate
particular issues. Mary Shirley (1931, 1933a,
1933b), for instance, completed a two-year-long investigation of the motor, emotional, and social development of infants. In contrast to the cross-sectional studies of Gesell, her longitudinal work
permitted her to identify particular sequences in
growth and change. Experimental intervention studies of the sort that Mills (1899) had called for in
animals were undertaken with children. Myrtle
McGraw's work with twins (*Jimmy and Johnny*,
1935), who were given different training experiences, is one of the better instances of the use of what
Gesell called the "co-twin" control procedure. By
providing "enrichment" experiences prior to the
normal onset of basic motor functions, McGraw was
able to demonstrate that experiences can indeed facilitate the appearance and consolidation of climbing
and other movement patterns. The "enriched" twin
continued to show a modest advantage over the control twin, even though age and associated growth
greatly diminished the apparent gains. Along with
these well-known works, a large number of lesser-
known investigations were addressed to the same
issues, using short-term longitudinal interventions
to influence intelligence test performance (e.g., Hilgard, 1933), and motor skills (e.g., Jersild, 1932).

These studies of longitudinal development were
limited to children, at least in the initial stages. What
about development beyond childhood? Since the
early investigations of Quetelet, there had been few
attempts to address directly the problems of developmental change during maturity. The exceptions are
noteworthy, because they provide part of the foundation for contemporary emphasis on the study of
development over the entire lifespan of human experience. One of the first texts on aging was produced
by G. Stanley Hall (1922), shortly before his death.
Later in the same decade, Hollingworth (1927) published a text on development over the whole life-
span, and some 12 years later, Pressey, Janney, and
Kuhlen (1939) extended the coverage. Baltes (1979)
recently commented that the basic theoretical orientation of these writers "is amazingly similar to what
the current trends in developmental psychology appear to be" (p. 261). These include an emphasis on
the dynamic nature of developmental change
through ontogeny and not merely in its initial stages,
a concern with the adaptability and reversibility of

behavior as circumstances and structures change,
and a focus on the essential bidirectionality between
psychobiology and behavior and cognitive patterns.
On this matter Hall wrote that "we all really live not
one but a succession of lives" (1922, p. 319).

The data base for these extensions to developmental issues over the lifespan beyond childhood
was not great. Surprisingly little research on behavioral development in adolescence was stimulated by
Hall's major work; perhaps, it gave the appearance
that all the important questions were already answered. One of the more interesting studies of this
age group was reported by Bühler (1926), in which
she analyzed the diaries of approximately 100 adolescents from Germany, Austria, America, Czecho-
slovakia, Sweden, and Hungary. Despite the cross-
cultural sampling, some remarkable similarities appeared in the themes covered by the diaries, especially among the girls. Romantic concerns seem,
for instance, to become highly salient, at least for the
young women who write diaries. Partly on the basis
of these data, Bühler proposed that there is a "negative phase" in adolescence, lasting about 2 to 6
months. There were of course hazards in using such
self-report material, in that it may be susceptible to
dissimulation and misinterpretation. Even Sigmund
Freud was fooled on the authenticity of one of the
diaries (Burt, 1920–1921).[21] Despite the pitfalls,
the rich self- and social-cognitions derived from this
source seemed worth the risk.

Given the amount of time, effort, and funding
required for these longitudinal studies, what could
be said about their payoffs by mid-century? Were
they worth the investment? The early returns indicated that the greatest immediate payoffs in predictability were obtained when the assessment procedures had previously established reliability and
utility (i.e., intelligence and physiological measures). In social and personality characteristics,
however, individual differences appear to be demonstrably less stable over time. Because the longitudinal work was for the most part atheoretical, except for an implicit belief in the long-term stability of
human characteristics, the early findings posed serious problems for interpretation. Were the methods
or the assumptions at fault? The question continued
to perplex researchers through the next scientific
era.

Behaviorism and Learning

At about the time that World War I began in
Europe, American psychology underwent an internal upheaval of its own. John B. Watson
(1878–1957) called behaviorism a "purely American production" (1914, p. ix). Its essential message

was of fundamental importance—that the study of man, animals, and children required the objective methods of natural science—but it was hardly novel. Others close to Watson, including his mentors in behavioral biology (Jacques Loeb and H. S. Jennings) and colleagues in psychology (e.g., K. Dunlap) had expressed similar ideas. But none had presented the argument with the persuasiveness and flair that Watson did in person and in print. As Watson put it:

> Psychology as the behaviorist views it is a purely objective experimental branch of natural science. Its theoretical goal is the prediction and control of behavior. Introspection forms no essential part of its methods, nor is the scientific value of its data dependent upon the readiness with which they lend themselves to interpretation in terms of consciousness. The behaviorist attempts to get a unitary scheme of animal response. He recognizes no dividing line between man and brute. The behavior of man, with all of its refinement and complexity, forms only a part of his total field of investigation. (1914, p. 1)

For Watson, there was an essential unity in animal and human psychology. The methodological differences that trifurcated the discipline for Hall and divided it for Wundt were not valid; the study of children, animals, and adult human beings could be reduced to the same behavioral, noncognitive techniques. Moreover, Watson called for a pragmatic psychology, one that could be applied in society and useful in everyday affairs. Watson liberalized psychology by holding, in effect, that the science could apply itself to *any* problem of life and behavior.

The story of behaviorism and of Watson's life has been told elsewhere (e.g., Cohen, 1979; Hearst, 1979), and it will not be repeated here except as it helps to clarify the emergence of developmental ideas. In this regard, Watson's contributions to development evolved through two stages, empirical and theoretical.

Consider first his methodological and research contributions to developmental study. Consistent with his vision, Watson set about to demonstrate the relevance of purely behavioral procedures to the study of human behavior. He began his work with newborn infants and the analysis of the conditioning of emotional reactions (Watson & Morgan, 1917; Watson & Rayner, 1920). Watson was well prepared for the task, for by mid-career he had been recognized as one of America's leading researchers in comparative and physiological psychology.

Why did Watson then choose to work with infants? Given the methodological outline of behaviorism, would it not have been as appropriate to begin with adolescents or adults? Watson provides the answer himself in his "life chart" of human development where he asserted that "to understand man," one must begin with the history of his behavior (1926). He saw personality as being shaped by learning experiences from birth onward. Though innate reflexes and inherent emotions provided the substrate, conditioning and learning mechanisms permitted the elaboration of emotions and behavior in development. Personality thus was the outcome of an organization of increasing complexity (p. 33). The conditioning of early emotions—love, fear, or rage—provided the foundation for all that followed. In his stress on emotions and early experience, Watson seems to have been influenced directly by Freud (as Watson suggested in his autobiographical statement, 1936), as well as by other views of personality current in the day (including McDougall's, 1926, theory of sentiments). In any case, the study of emotional development in infancy became the focus for Watson's experimental and observational work from 1916–1920. Because of his work, Watson (along with E. L. Thorndike) was credited in the first *Handbook of Child Psychology* as having initiated experimental child psychology (Anderson, 1931, p. 3), a conclusion that, surprisingly, overlooked Binet's earlier work.

The infant work was conducted in the laboratories and newborn nursery at Johns Hopkins Hospital from 1916 through 1920, being interrupted by Watson's service in World War I and terminated by his being fired from Hopkins in 1920. The series involved controlled observation of stimuli which elicit emotional reactions in infants (Watson & Morgan, 1917), the systematic attempt to catalogue the behavior responses present at birth and shortly afterward (Watson, 1926), and the experimental conditioning and manipulation of fear reactions (Watson & Rayner, 1920).

Although Watson's conditioning studies were only demonstrational and would hardly deserve publication on their methodological merit, they proved to be enormously influential. Following the lead of the more extensive and careful work of Mateer (1918) and of Krasnogorski (1909), who had reported the conditioning of motor responses in children, Watson and Rayner (1920) boldly attacked the problem of the conditioning of emotions in infancy in the "case of Albert." What was impressive about this work was the conclusion that fear was conditioned and, once established, resisted extinction and readily generalized. As M. C. Jones (1931) pointed out, "conditioned emotional responses" differ from earlier demonstrations of reflexive conditioning in that there was one obvious discrepancy: "Whereas the conditioned reflex is extremely unstable, emotional responses are often acquired as the result of one traumatic experience and are pertinacious even in the absence of reinforcement" (p. 87). According to Watson, "guts can learn" (1928), and they seemed to have excellent memories. He wrote, "This proof of the conditioned origin of a fear response puts us on a natural science grounds in our study of emotional behavior. It yields an explanatory principle which will account for the enormous complexity in the emotional behavior of adults" (1928, p. 202). Conditioned emotional responses, whether in the form of the "CER" of Estes and Skinner (1941), the "two-factor theory of anxiety" of Solomon and Wynne (1953), or the "learned helplessness" concept of Maier, Seligman, and Solomon (1969), have continued to play a significant if enigmatic role in neobehavioral accounts of personality and development.

Although Watson himself completed no further scientific investigations, his experimental studies with infants were taken up by students and colleagues through the 1920s and early 1930s (see M. C. Jones, 1931). Mary Cover Jones (1924) explored the problem of the extinction of emotional reactions, demonstrating how experimentally produced fears could be "undone." H. E. Jones (1930) clarified the short-term stability of the response (not great after 2 months). Later, experimental psychologists investigated the possibility of neonatal (e.g., Marquis, 1931; Wickens & Wickens, 1940) and fetal (Spelt, 1938) conditioning, along with extensive studies of early motor learning (e.g., McGraw, 1935). Watson's work also stimulated the development of observational methods to assess children's behaviors, on the one hand, and the establishment of the family of behavioristic theories of learning, on the other (e.g., Guthrie, 1935; Hull, 1943; Skinner, 1938; Tolman, 1932).

This brings us to Watson's theory of psychological development, which grew both more extreme and more expansive the further he became removed from data in time and space. As Watson's ideas on child development became elaborated, it seemed clear that he considered all emotions—not merely fear and rage—to be obstacles for adaptive behavior and a happy life. Among other things, he campaigned in his influential bestseller, *Psychological Care of Infant and Child* (1928), against too much mother love because the child would become "honeycombed" with affection and, eventually, a social "invalid" wholly dependent on the attention and responses of others. Love, like fear, can make one sick to the stomach.

Despite such rhetoric, Watson's books carried a deadly serious message for the 1920s and 1930s. Science could lead to improved and efficient ways to rear children, and if mothers and children could be liberated from each other early in the child's life, the potential of both would be enhanced. This "modern" view of childrearing was predictably controversial, attracting both staunch converts and scathing critics. Along with his emotionally cool view of personality, Watson became increasingly extreme in his environmentalism. Although he was developmental in his approach, Watson downplayed the role of psychobiological factors in personality after birth; he considered learning to be the key mechanism for the pacing and stabilizing of behavior development from birth to maturity. Biology was important, of course, but only as it established potential for learning. In the absence of evidence on the long-term effects of early experience or longitudinal studies of human development, Watson was skating on extremely thin ice. To his credit, he said so (1926, p. 10). But Watson was in no position to obtain corrective or confirming data; except for occasional part-time teaching at the New School and a lecture series at Clark University, he had dropped out of academics and out of scientific research in 1920.

Watson nonetheless became a symbol for a "modern" scientific approach to childrearing of the 1920s and 1930s through his popular magazine articles. His views extended into education, pediatrics, psychiatry, and child study, where the stress on the acquisition of habits and avoidance of emotions became translated into prescriptions for behavioristic childrearing. A cursory review of these materials reveals virtually no empirical citations, except for references to the demonstrational studies that Watson conducted or loosely supervised. It should be noted, however, that Watson's advice for mothers to adopt a psychologically antiseptic approach toward their children had not been original with him. In physician Emmet Holt's *The Care and Feeding of Children*, a bestseller since its first edition in 1894, rather the same guidance had been given. On the evils of kissing children ("Tuberculosis, diphtheria, syphilis, and many other grave diseases may be communicated in this way"; Holt, 1916, p. 174) or playing with babies ("They are made nervous and irritable"; Holt, 1916, p. 171), Watson did not offer fresh guidance so much as new reasons.

What might have happened if Watson had remained involved in empirical research? We can only guess that his statements would have been more closely tied to facts than to speculations and that his views about childrearing would have become less idiosyncratic and less extreme. But, as we have indicated elsewhere, certain problems remained at the heart of his system (Cairns & Ornstein, 1979). Beyond the behavioristic model of an emotionless and consciousless child, perhaps the most salient weakness in Watson's view was the assumption that development was a mechanistic process that could be reduced to fundamental units of learning. Seemingly all behavior was learned, from birth onward, with the earliest experiences being the most basic. This was a peculiar and unnecessary position for a behaviorist to take. Although Watson claimed psychology was ''a definite part of biology,'' his view of development was nonbiological and nonorganismic. Learning is an essential process in development, but it is not the only process.

Experimental studies of learning in children did not begin and end with Watson, of course. Another influential line of research followed the lead of E. L. Thorndike in studies of verbal learning and in the analysis of the effect of different reward and punishment contingencies (see Peterson, 1931, for a review of relevant studies). The work followed not only the laboratory analogues used by Thorndike (following Binet & Henri, 1895, and Ebbinghaus, 1897), but also within-classroom manipulations of the efficacy of different kinds of reward/punishment feedback (e.g., Hurlock, 1924). The studies of learning and memory were for the most part divorced from conditioning research in infants and animals, studies of mental testing, and investigations of language and thought. Areas of inquiry that might be seen as potentially fitting together to form a developmental view of cognition instead evolved separately, each toward its own distinctive methodology, concepts, and discipline affiliation. It would be another 50 years before serious attempts were made to bring them back together (see Carroll & Horn, 1981; Ornstein, 1978).

Maturation and Growth

While Watson served as the spokesman for behaviorism and environmentalism in child development, Arnold Gesell was gaining stature as an advocate of the role of growth and maturation in behavior. Trained at Clark University in the early 1900s, Gesell absorbed G. S. Hall's vision of the significance of child study, the importance of bio-

logical controls in behavior, and the practical implications of child research, particularly for education. Gesell worked initially in the field of schools and curriculum following his PhD (as did most of the Clark graduates in developmental psychology during that period). He returned at mid-career to complete an MD degree at Yale, then founded a child study laboratory in 1911 which permitted him to extend the tradition of W. Preyer and M. Shinn. Gesell (1931, 1933) early demonstrated himself to be an innovative and careful methodologist, being one of the first to make extensive use of motion pictures in behavioral analysis and to explore the advantages of using twins as controls in experimental studies (i.e., one twin is subjected to the experimental manipulation, the other serves as a maturational control).

In 1928, Gesell published *Infancy and Human Growth*, a remarkable report on several years of study on the characteristics of infancy. According to Gesell, one of his aims was to provide ''objective expression to the course, the pattern, and the rate of mental growth in normal and exceptional children'' (p. viii). The other aim was theoretical, and the last section of the book takes on ''the broad problem of heredity in relation to early mental growth and personality formation . . . and the significance of human infancy'' (p. ix). Gesell (1928) was characteristically thorough in dealing with both problems, and his normative tables and descriptions of how *Baby Two* (2 months old) differs from *Baby Three* and *Baby Nine* ring true to the contemporary reader. On basic characteristics of physical, motor, and perceptual development, children showed reasonably constant growth and age-differentiation. If the infants selected did not, as in a couple of instances, they may be substituted for by more ''representative'' ones. All in all, the business of establishing appropriate norms was seen as an essential part of his medical practice and the practical issues of diagnosis. As Gesell later described it, his clinical practice

has always been conducted in close correlation with a systematic study of normal child development. One interest has reinforced the other. Observations of normal behavior threw light on maldevelopment; and the deviations of development in turn helped to expose what lay beneath a deceptive layer of ''obviousness'' in normal infancy. (Gesell & Amatruda, 1941, p. v)

In any case, Gesell and his associates established definitive norms for growth and behavioral change in the first 5 years of life in a series of exhaustive and detailed reports (e.g., Gesell & Amatruda, 1941; Gesell & Thompson, 1934; Gesell & Thompson, 1938).

Few nowadays regard Gesell as a theorist. That is a pity, for his contributions might have provided a useful stabilizing influence during a period that became only nominally committed to "developmental" study. "Growth" was a key concept for Gesell. But what did he mean by growth? Horticultural terms have long been popular in describing children (a classic example being Froebel's coining of "kindergarten"). But Gesell was too astute to become trapped in a botanical analogue; he recognized human behavioral and mental growth as having distinctive properties of its own. He writes:

Mental growth is a constant process of transformation, of reconstruction. The past is not retained with the same completeness as in the tree. The past is sloughed as well as projected, it is displaced and even transmuted to a degree which the anatomy of the tree does not suggest. There are stages, and phases, and a perpetuating knitting together of what happens and happened. Mental growth is a process of constant incorporation, revision, reorganization, and progressive hierarchal inhibition. The reorganization is so pervading that the past almost loses its identity. (1928, p. 22)

What does this lead to? For Gesell, to a new perspective on the relations between heredity and environment. Similar to what Preyer had written some 50 years before, Gesell concludes:

The supreme genetic law appears to be this: All present growth hinges on past growth. Growth is not a simple function neatly determined by X units of inheritance plus Y units of environment, but is an historical complex which reflects at every stage the past which it incorporates. In other words we are led astray by an artificial dualism of heredity and environment, if it blinds us to the fact that growth is a continuous self-conditioning process, rather than a drama controlled, *ex machina,* by two forces. (1928, p. 357)

These are not the only similarities with the interpretations offered by earlier students of infant development. Recall Preyer's analysis of infancy, and the functions of the extended immaturity of children

for the plasticity of behavior. The concept of neoteny is elegantly restated by Gesell, along with a fresh idea on the social responsiveness that is unique to humans:

The preeminence of human infancy lies in the prolongation and deepening of plasticity. There is specific maturation of behavior patterns as in subhuman creatures; but this proceeds less rigidly and the total behavior complex is suspended in a state of greater formativeness. This increased modifiability is extremely sensitive to the social milieu and is constantly transforming the context to adaptive behavior. In the impersonal aspects of adaptive behavior of the nonlanguage type (general practical intelligence) there is a high degree of early correspondence between man and other primates. This correspondence may prove to be so consistent in some of its elements as to suggest evolutionary and even recapitulatory explanations. But transcending, pervading, and dynamically altering that strand of similarity is a generalized conditionability and a responsiveness to other personalities, to which man is special heir. This preeminent sociality exists even through the prelanguage period, long before the child has framed a single word. Herein lies his humanity. (1928, p. 354)

As a rule, Gesell stayed close to his data. When he ventured away, he was drawn irresistibly back to the facts that had been meticulously collected, sifted, and plotted. He felt strongly that the understanding of the properties of growth *qua* growth would be the key to unlocking the central dilemmas of the area. The same year that Watson offered his polemic on the role of early stimulation in childrearing, Gesell offered the counterposition on the invulnerability of the infant to experience. He wrote:

All things considered, the inevitableness and surety of maturation are the most impressive characteristics of early development. It is the hereditary ballast which conserves and stabilizes the growth of each individual infant. It is indigenous in its impulsion; but we may well be grateful for this degree of determinism. If it did not exist the infant would be a victim of a flaccid malleability which is sometimes romantically ascribed to him. His mind, his spirit, his personality would fall a ready prey to disease, to starvation, to malnutrition, and worst of all to misguided management. As it is, the inborn tendency toward optimum development is so inveterate that he benefits liberally from what is good in our practice, and suffers less than he logically should from our unenlightenment. Only if we give respect to this inner core of inheritance can we respect the important individual differences which distinguish infants as well as men. (1928, p. 378)

The infant is more robust than he appears, in that he is buffered by psychobiological fail-safe systems and driven by an ''inborn tendency toward optimum development.'' The message is a general one, issued by one who observed the remarkable similarities among infants as they developed from the stage of the neonate to the first year and beyond.

Does this inborn determinism apply to all features of infant growth—to mental development as well as personality and social development? On this matter, Gesell drew a distinction between the mechanisms that control cognitive and social growth. In the latter instance—social growth—the essential determinants were the social matrix present in the ''web of life'' and the ''conditioned system of adaptation to the whole human family.'' Sound Watsonian? Not really, for Gesell is closer to the transactional views of James Mark Baldwin than to the unidirectional ones of behaviorism and its emphasis on the parental shaping of children. Gesell writes:

All children are thus, through correlation, adapted to their parents and to each other. Even the maladjustments between parent and child are adaptations in a psycho-biological sense and can only be comprehended if we view them as lawfully conditioned modes of adaptation. Growth is again the key concept. For better or for worse, children and their elders must grow up with each other, which means in interrelation one to the other. The roots of the growth of the infant's personality reach into other human beings. (1928, p. 375)

In effect, maturational changes demand interactional ones, and the nature of the resolution reached between child and others at each stage is the stuff out of which personality is built. Gesell offers here the outline for a psychobiological theory of social development. Where did the theory go? Not very far, for it remained in a bare outline form, with scant data to back it up. Like Baldwin before him, Gesell did not have the methods (or perhaps the desire) to continue to explore the dynamic message implicit in this psychobiological view of social interactions. That is doubly unfortunate, for his views on social development were at least as reasonable and no more speculative than those of Watson. If enunciated more fully, they may have provided explicit guides for his next-door colleagues in the Institute of Human Relations when they set about to fabricate the first version of social learning theory.

Other investigators recognized, of course, the role of age-related biological changes in the development of behavior, and their relations to the occurrence of basic changes in emotional, cognitive, and social patterns. For example, M. C. Jones (1931), in discussing the development of emotions, remarks that a wariness or fear of unfamiliar persons tends to emerge in the second half of the first year of life (from 20 weeks to 40 weeks; see Bayley, 1932, and Washburn, 1929). M. C. Jones notes that this phenomenon appears in the absence of any apparent pairing of the stranger with some external noxious stimulus, hence it would not fit very well with the Watsonian view of the conditioned elaboration of fear, or of love. Other developmental mechanisms must be at work. Why, then, the relative popularity of experimental demonstrations of fear and its conditioning and extinction as opposed to careful longitudinal studies of the development of the phenomena subsumed by fear? Jones's (1931) answer was probably correct, in that she suggested that ''Because training and practice are more readily subject to laboratory proof, we have at times minimized the importance of the less accessible intraorganismic factors'' (p. 78).

The availability of funding and staffing for the major child development institutes permitted the support of significant studies of maturation and growth at Teacher's College (Columbia), Berkeley, Iowa, Minnesota, and Fels Institute. Among the more notable studies was that of M. M. Shirley at the University of Minnesota. To extend Gesell's cross-sectional observations, Shirley conducted a longitudinal investigation of motor, emotional, and personality development over the first 2 years of life with 25 infants, publishing the results in a comprehensive three-volume work (Shirley, 1931, 1933a, 1933b). Similarly, the Shermans at Washington University (St. Louis), McGraw (1935) at Teacher's College, and Bridges at Montreal completed useful studies of growth-related changes in infants and young children.

Social and Personality Development

In a review of studies of social behavior in children, Charlotte Bühler (1931) gave the American Will S. Monroe credit for having completed the first studies of "the social consciousness of children." Monroe's work, published in German (1899), reported a number of questionnaire studies dealing with various aspects of social development. For instance, children were asked what sort of "chum" they preferred, what kinds of moral qualities they found in friends, and what their attitudes were about punishment, responsibility, and discipline. Monroe's work was not, however, the first published set of studies on these matters. Earl Barnes of Stanford (who had been Monroe's teacher) had earlier edited a two-volume work (*Studies in Education;* 1896–1897, 1902–1903) that had covered the same ground, reporting a reasonably comprehensive set of questionnaire studies of social disposition. Margaret Schallenberger (1894), for instance, had been at Stanford and a student of Barnes at the time she completed the report discussed above on age-related changes in the social judgments of children. In the 1890s, questionnaires were being circulated throughout the country to teachers through the various state child study associations (in Illinois, South Carolina, Massachusetts), and literally thousands of children were being asked brief questions about their social attitudes, morals, and friendships. G. Stanley Hall from time to time would include questionnaires in the *Pedagogical Seminary,* asking readers to submit the results to him.

Because of the shortcomings in the method, ranging from the haphazard sampling procedures to problems in nonstandard administration and scoring of questions, the questionnaire studies were hardly models of scientific research. Nonetheless, certain age-related phenomena were sufficiently robust to appear despite the methodological slippage. A case in point was Schallenberger's (1894) conclusion that young children relied upon concrete forms of punishment, with reasoning and empathy playing roles of increasing importance in early adolescence. These findings were given wide circulation in Hall's *Adolescence,* and provided the empirical substrate for some of the more useful sections of that work. In time, the criticisms took effect, and after about 10 to 15 years of questionnaire studies, the method was no longer a procedure of choice. As Bühler notes, "little was done in the decade after Monroe made this first start in the direction of developmental social psychology," and, she concludes, the studies failed because of "the lack of a systematic point of view" (1931, p. 392).

Following a hiatus in work on social development, another method was introduced for studying the social behavior of infants and children in the mid-1920s. It was essentially an extension of the "objective" or "behavioral" procedures that had been used in the investigation of individual infants and young animals. Almost simultaneously, reports of behavioral studies appeared in child study institutes in Vienna, Columbia, Minnesota, and Toronto. Somewhat earlier, Jean Piaget had recorded the naturalistic verbal exchanges among young children (Piaget, 1923, 1926). Five of the first eight *Child Development Monographs* from Teacher's College of Columbia University were concerned with the methods and outcomes obtained by the behavioral assessments of social patterns (Arrington, 1932; Barker, 1930; Beaver, 1930; Loomis, 1931; Thomas, 1929). Dorothy S. Thomas, co-author with sociologist W. I. Thomas of *The Child in America* (1928), seems to have spearheaded this attempt to apply "the methodological scheme of *experimental sociology* to children." In addition to the work of Thomas and her colleagues, insightful methodological papers on the procedure were published by Goodenough (1929, 1930) at Minnesota and Bott (1934) at Toronto. Charlotte Bühler (1927) should herself be credited with having pioneered the method, and she seems to have been one of the first, if not the first, investigator to have completed an "experimental study of children's social attitudes in the first and second year of life" (Bühler, 1931).

Observational studies from 1927–1937 generated almost as much enthusiasm as earlier questionnaire studies. They were based on the assumption that the stream of behavior could be classified into particular behavior units, and that these units could be submitted to the statistical analyses previously developed for the treatment of experimental and test data. Careful attention was given to issues of observation, including observer agreement, code reliability, stability of measures, various facets of validity and generality, and statistical evaluation. The problems addressed by the method ranged from the mere descriptive and demographic—including size and sex composition of groups as a function of age (Parten, 1933) and nature of play activities (Challman, 1932)—to studies of the natural occurrence of aggression (e.g., Goodenough, 1931) and reciprocal patterns of interchange (Bott, 1934). By 1931, Bühler was able to cite some 173 articles, many of which dealt directly with the observation of children's social behavior patterns. In the following 5 to 10 years, an equal number of studies was reported, some of which are now recognized as having laid the foundation for work taken up again in the 1970s (e.g., Murphy, 1937). In terms of method, the reports were on par with the current generation of observational analysis of social interchange.

What theoretical ideas were associated with these behavioral methods and to what extent was there a "systematic" point of view? There was, as it turns out, as little theoretical guidance for this work as for the earlier questionnaire studies. The work was behavioral, but it was not concerned with developmental processes, either learning or psychobiological. J. M. Baldwin had virtually been forgotten (save for some exceptions, e.g., Piaget, 1923, 1924). Given the aims and background of D. S. Thomas (1929), it is mildly surprising that the procedures at Columbia were not more intimately linked to the sociological models of Cooley, Mead, and Baldwin. Perhaps that conceptual extension was part of the general scheme, but it failed to materialize, either in the work completed at Teacher's College or in that of the other child institutes. As it turned out, the research focused on the immediate determinants of the actions and interactions of children, but scant information was gained about their relationship to how interactions are learned, modified, or what they mean for long-term personality development.

If there were any theoretical underpinnings for the research on interactions and social development, the model seems to have been drawn either from a belief in the importance of growth and maturation, on the one hand, or a commitment to the enduring nature of personality types, as determined by genetic, constitutional, or early experience factors. In this regard, Bühler (1929, 1931) classified infants into three types, depending on their reactions to social stimulation. "These types were called the *socially blind, the socially dependent, and the socially independent* behavior" (1931, p. 411). Socially blind children do not pay much attention to the actions and reactions of other persons; instead they take toys, play, and move about without regard for the other child. The socially dependent child, on the other hand, is "deeply impressed by other's presence and activities; . . . he observes the effect of his behavior on the other and carefully watches the other's reactions." The socially independent child "is one who—though aware of the other's presence and responsive to his behavior—yet does not seem dependent on him, is neither intimidated nor inspired" (1931, p. 411). Bühler sees these dispositions as being independent of home and rearing conditions, hence a *"primary disposition."* Retests of the children (who were 6–18 months of age) suggested to Bühler that these types were relatively stable, but she adds the caveat, "it remains to be seen, of course, whether these pioneer observations will be confirmed by other authors" (1931, p. 411). The matter is still being debated (Ainsworth, 1969).

In retrospect, the interactional studies were estranged from the issues being debated by the dominant theories of the day—psychoanalytic, learning, cognitive—and few seemed willing to attempt to bridge the theoretical or empirical gaps. As it turned out, the data did find a useful service in the practical areas of nursery school management and in the training of young teachers. Because the findings were either ignored or deemed irrelevant by those concerned with major psychological theories of development, the method and its concerns passed from the scene, temporarily.

Moral Development

Recall that the perfectibility of man and the establishment of a higher moral order had been a continuing concern for developmentalists. Although questionnaires on children's beliefs and attitudes toward transgressions and punishments were useful, they had obvious shortcomings as scientific instruments. In the 1920s and 1930s, work on these issues continued, but with an appreciation of the limits of the techniques that were available. Nonetheless, there were substantive issues to be addressed and real-life problems to be solved, and it seemed entirely reasonable to expect that the investigators of moral development would be ingenious enough to meet the challenge (see V. Jones, 1933). Out of this need arose three major advances in the study of moral development: the use of short-term experimental manipulations in the assessment of honesty and prosocial behaviors; the employment of observations of naturally occurring rule-making and moral judgments; and the refinement of attitudinal questionnaires that might be employed in the assessment of particular experiences.

Moral Conduct and Its Assessment

The demonstration of the utility of short-term experimental procedures with school-age children has an unusual background, at least in what the sponsors had hoped to learn and what they actually got. Hugh Hartshorne was a professor in the School of Religion at the University of Southern California, and Mark May was a psychologist at Syracuse University when they were recruited by the Institute of Social and Religious Research to conduct a multi-year project on how Sunday schools, churches, and religious youth groups could better do their job. If physical science could create problems for the society, why could not behavioral science help solve some of the moral and ethical issues that had arisen? The project was an ambitious one: to analyze the effects of various institutions of the society upon moral behaviors, and to determine how the institutions could improve their performance. At the outset, Hartshorne and May recognized that they must solve the problem of the assessment of moral and ethical behaviors. Following a critique of then-available questionnaire and rating procedures, Hartshorne and May concluded that a fresh approach to the study of values and character was required. They wrote: "Although recognizing the importance of attitude and motive for both social welfare and individual character, as ordinarily understood, we realized that in any objective approach to ethical conduct we must begin with the *facts of conduct*" (1928–1930, vol. 2, p. 361). Accordingly, the investigators developed a battery of tests and experimental settings designed to yield information about honesty, helpfulness and cooperation, inhibition, and persistence. The best-known measures are the brief experimental assessments of deceit (permitting the misuse of answer sheets, peeping, and other forms of cheating, all of which were monitored in sly ways by the experimenter). They also devised various sociometric techniques, including a "Guess Who" procedure to assess peer reputation. The results of this work and the authors' interpretation on the relative specificity of moral conduct have been widely discussed. For our purposes, it is sufficient to note that this was one of the first studies to be conducted of short-term experimental manipulations of social behavior in school-age children. In addition, the authors offered a courageous if premature theoretical statement on how ethical conduct is acquired (via Thorndikian learning principles).[22]

Attitude Assessment

Although questionnaire procedures were generally in disfavor by the 1920s, the essential problem of how to quantify attitudes remained. L. L. Thurstone, a pioneering quantitative psychologist at the University of Chicago, was recruited by the Payne Foundation to determine the effects that moviegoing had upon the social attitudes and prejudices of children. The assignment provided Thurstone the opportunity to develop a new technology for the assessment of moral and ethnic attitudes. In a series of studies, Thurstone and his colleague R. C. Peterson (Thurstone & Peterson, 1933) introduced new methodologies for gauging the effects of specific motion pictures on attitudes toward national and ethnic groups. They used a pre- and posttest design, coupled with a 5-month follow-up test (post-post). Although these studies are today rarely cited, Thurstone (1952) considered them to have been

highly influential for the development of his attitude-assessment methodology. Moreover, the work provided a wholly convincing demonstration of the strong effects that certain films had in decreasing, or increasing, racial or national prejudice. In the case of some films (such as the antiblack *Birth of a Nation*), the unfavorable attitudes induced by the film observation were detected 5 months later. This study was an admirable forerunner to the research of the 1960s and 1970s concerned with the effects of television (see also, V. Jones, 1933).

Moral Reasoning

Another major advance was pioneered by Jean Piaget in his assessments of moral reasoning (Piaget, 1931, 1932). Piaget's clinical method—that of observing individual children and carefully recording their actions—permitted him to identify changes in the children's employment of rules and their origins. Although the procedure shared the self-report properties of questionnaires, his observations and direct inquiries permitted a more precise identification of the ethical standards being invoked idiosyncratically by the children.

Development of Language and Thought

From 1924 onward, the problem of how language and thought develop attracted the attention of the brightest talents of the discipline. Some of them—including Jean Piaget and L. S. Vigotsky—were concerned with language as a vehicle for understanding how thought patterns develop in the child. Others focused on language as a phenomenon in itself, with attention given to the "amazingly rapid acquisition of an extremely complex system of symbolic habits by young children" (McCarthy, 1954).

The comprehensive review articles by D. McCarthy that span this period provide an excellent overview of the era (McCarthy, 1931, 1933, 1946, 1954). At one time or another, virtually all major developmental investigators have been drawn to the study of language development, and so were some nondevelopmental ones as well. The intimate relationship which exists between language and thought was brought brilliantly to the attention of psychologists by Jean Piaget in a small book that he published to report the results of his new functional approach to the study of language development. Piaget's study of language breathed fresh life into one of the oldest questions of the area: How do thought, logic, and consciousness develop? For Piaget, language is a mirror to the mind, something to be used to reflect the nature and structure of the mental schemata which give rise to verbal expressions. In this work, Piaget seems to have been explicitly guided by J. M. Baldwin's view that the young child proceeds in his thought to progressively discriminate himself from nonself. The major empirical marker for this shift in thinking is movement from egocentric speech to socialized speech. He writes:

> "Egocentric" functions are the more immature functions, and tend to dominate the verbal productions of children 3–7 years of age, and, to a lesser extent, children 7–12 years. In this form of speech, a child does not bother to know to whom he is speaking nor whether he is being listened to. He talks either for himself or for the pleasure of associating anyone who happens to be there with the activity of the moment. This talk is egocentric, partly because the child speaks only about himself, but chiefly because he does not attempt to place himself at the point of view of his hearer. Anyone who happens to be there will serve as an audience. (Piaget, 1932, p. 9)

Socialized speech, where the child "really exchanges his thoughts with others, either by telling his hearer something that will interest him and influence his actions, or by an actual interchange of ideas by argument or even by collaboration in pursuit of a common aim," does not emerge until about age 7–8, and the process is not complete until 11–12 years of age. Later in the same volume, Piaget linked egocentricism to the child's tendency to personalize thought. Without the ability to "objectify" one's thinking,

> the mind tends to project intentions into everything, or connect everything together by means of relations not based on observation . . . the more the ego is made the centre of interests, the less will the mind be able to depersonalize its thought, and to get rid of the idea that in all things are intentions either favourable or hostile (animism, artificialism, etc.). . . . Ego-centricism is therefore obedient to the self's good pleasure and not to the dictates of impersonal logic. It is also an indirect obstacle, because only the habits of discussion and social life will lead to the logical point of view, and ego-centricism is precisely what renders these habits impossible. (1932, pp. 237–238)

In other words, Piaget shares with both Baldwin and Freud the assumption that the child's concept of reality and logic develops from contact with the external world, emerging from an amorphous sense of the self and the omnipotent ego. On this count, it is not insignificant that in the foreword to *The Language and Thought of the Child*, Piaget writes, "I have also been deeply impressed by the social psychology of M. C. Blondel and Professor J. M. Baldwin. It will likewise be apparent how much I owe to psychoanalysis, which in my opinion has revolutionized the psychology of primitive thought" (pp. xx–xxi).

The method employed by Piaget and the concepts that he embraced stimulated almost immediate worldwide attention and controversy. In McCarthy's thorough reviews of the empirical data that bore on the question (including her own), she (1931, 1933, 1946, 1954) traced the evolution of a huge literature on the matter. Strict interpretation of Piaget's categories suggested that, over a wide variety of populations and settings in which young children were observed, seldom did the proportion of egocentric remarks exceed 6% to 8%. Moreover, the negative evidence came not merely from studies of children in the United States; an equally convincing set of disconfirming investigations were reported from studies of Chinese (Kuo, 1937), Japanese (Ohwaki, 1933, cited in McCarthy, 1943), Russians (Vigotsky & Luria, 1929), and Germans (Bühler, 1931). After identifying what was meant by the concept of egocentric as opposed to socialized speech, C. Bühler wrote:

> It is agreed, however, among other authors— e.g., William Stern and David and Rosa Katz— that this result is due to the special conditions of life in the "maison des petits" in Geneva, where Piaget's work was done. *The Katzes (1927) emphasize, in opposition to Piaget, that even the special relationship of the child to each of the different members of the household is distinctly reflected in the respective conversations.* This is surely true of all the dialogues they published. (Bühler, 1931, p. 400; my emphasis)

This point was a key one for Bühler, who had just spent several years of her life demonstrating the quality and nature of the social patterns of children in infancy and early childhood. She had conclusively shown the truly "social" nature of their behaviors. Note that Bühler attributes the discrepant findings to the contextual-relational specificity of the initial Piaget observations.[23] Another explanation, favored by McCarthy (1933, 1954), is that the problem resides in the ambiguity of the classification system employed by Piaget. For whatever reason, there have been notably few confirmations of Piaget's assertion that young children are predominantly egocentric in their speech. The controversy extended into the 1970s (see, e.g., Garvey & Hogan, 1973; Mueller, 1972) and included replications of the earlier disconfirmations of Piaget's report.

The issue was a significant one for the area because it had implications for the understanding of virtually all psychological aspects of development, whether cognitive, linguistic, social, or moral. Beyond the issue of whether egocentric speech was 6% or 40% or 60%, there was agreement that this form of communication tended to decrease as a function of the child's age. Why? Piaget's answer—one that seemed compatible with the earlier formulations of Baldwin and Freud—was that egocentric communication directly reflected young children's "personalized" mode of thinking and that as children became more objective in their views of themselves and of reality, the transition to socialized speech occurred. It became dysfunctional and was discarded. A counterproposal by the Russian psychologist L. S. Vigotsky (1939) constituted a serious challenge to the Piagetian interpretation. The key to Vigotsky's proposal is that, at maturity, there exist two speech systems: inner speech and socialized speech. For Vigotsky,

The relation of thought to word is first of all not a thing, but a process; it is a proceeding from thought to word and, conversely, from word to thought . . . every thought moves, grows and develops, each fulfills a function and solves a given problem. This flow of thought occurs as an inner movement through a series of planes. The first step in the analysis of the relationship between thoughts and words is the investigation of the different phases and planes through which the thought passes before it is embodied in words. (1939, p. 33)

Herein lies the need for a developmental investigation of speech functions, for it may provide us with an answer as to how thought and speech are interrelated. This investigation

reveals, in the first place, two different planes in speech. There is an inner, meaningful semantic aspect of speech and there is the external, acoustic, phonic aspect. These two aspects although forming a true unity, have their own particular laws of movement. . . . A number of facts in the development of children's speech reveal the exis-

tence of independent movement in the phonic and the semantic aspects of speech. (1939, p. 33)

How does Vigotsky interpret the role of egocentric speech, and how does his interpretation differ from Piaget's? While egocentric speech has no apparent function of its own in Piaget's formulation—merely reflecting the child's egocentric thinking and thereby doomed to disappear with the child's cognitive growth—it assumes great functional importance for Vigotsky. Egocentric speech constitutes, in effect, a way station in development, "a stage which precedes the development of inner speech" (1939, p. 38). It is a form of speech that aids in the young child's thought processes but, rather than waning in childhood and becoming dysfunctional, egocentric speech undergoes an evolution with "inner speech" and thought as its end product. Vigotsky writes:

To consider the dropping of the coefficient of egocentric speech to zero as a symptom of decline of this speech would be like saying that the child stops to count at the moment when he ceases to use his fingers and starts to do the calculations in his mind. In reality, behind the symptoms of dissolution lies a progressive development, lies the formation of a new speech form. (1939, p. 40)

Vigotsky then took a significant step forward in the analysis both of speech functions and their relation to thought by conducting some ingenious experiments on the nature of egocentric speech. He went beyond the controversial naturalistic observations to manipulate theoretically relevant dimensions. He determined, for instance, that the incidence of egocentric speech decreased sharply when children were placed in the company of others who could not possibly understand them—a group of deaf and dumb children, or a group of children speaking a foreign language. Vigotsky reports that the coefficient of egocentric speech "sank rapidly, reaching zero in the majority of cases and in the rest diminished eight times on the average." While these findings seem "paradoxical" for Piaget's view, they were consistent with the idea that "the true source of egocentric speech is the lack of differentiation of speech for oneself from speech for others; it can function only in connection with social speech" (1939, p. 41).

To summarize the rest of Vigotsky's argument and experimental work would take us beyond the limits of this overview (see McCarthy, 1954). The general point is that (1) Piaget's ideas were exceedingly important in this period, and (2) the results and their interpretation were critically challenged. Obviously the story did not end in the 1930s; many of the same concerns and proposals reappeared in the 1960s and 1970s. Unfortunately, the brilliant Vigotsky—who was born the same year as Piaget—died in 1934 at the age of 38. His developmental views were brought forward to contemporary psychology by his colleague and collaborator, A. R. Luria.

The functional analysis of language development, although most intriguing on theoretical grounds, constitutes only a portion of the total research effort devoted to language. Researchers have focused, in addition, on developmental stages in language expression (e.g., prelinguistic utterances, phonetic development, the growth of vocabulary, changes in syntactic complexity as a function of age) and individual differences in language development and how they arise (through experience, schooling, early exposure, etc.). The literature on these matters is such that, by the end of the period, no child development text could be prepared without a significant section given to the report and summary of these findings. The mass of data seemed to outrun the ability of theorists to organize it in terms of meaningful models.

Developmental Psychobiology and Ethology

The Gesellian emphasis on growth and maturation was part of a broader attempt within developmental psychology and developmental biology to unlock the secrets of ontogeny (see McGraw, 1946). In biology, the study of genetic transmission (from parents to offspring) seemed to be progressing more rapidly than the study of ontogenetic succession (development in the life of the individual). On this count, the understanding of the mechanisms of genetic transfer was significantly advanced by the rediscovery of the work of Mendel, on the one hand, and the revolutionary discoveries by Morgan and his students on the loci of units of chromosomal transmission. But these discoveries raised a significant question for developmentalists. If all somatic cells have the same genetic code, how does differentiation occur in development and why do cells at maturity have distinctly different functions and properties? Where is the "master plan" for development, and how can particular cells be induced to perform their unique and special services for the organism?

Among the embryologists who addressed these issues, Hans Spemann (1938) provided a provocative suggestion following his discoveries that cellu-

lar tissues can be successfully transplanted from one area of presumptive growth to another. If the transplantation occurs at the appropriate time in development, tissues from the presumptive area of the neural plate of amphibia can be successfully transplanted to areas where limbs would otherwise arise. The transplanted tissue then develops in accord with its surrounds, taking on the characteristics of skin or muscle, not those of the brain. On the basis of these experiments, Spemann proposed that extranuclear or contextual forces serve to "organize" the development of cellular materials in the course of ontogeny. Once organization has occurred, during the period that is critical for the formation of its form and function, then the effects are irreversible or highly resistant to change (see Waddington, 1939).

Such demonstrations provided the substantive empirical demonstrations for the formulation of a view on development that has come to be known as "organismic" theory or "system" theory of biological development (von Bertalanffy, 1933). In its initial form, organismic theory was concerned with the question "What directs development?" The answer, simply stated, is the organism. Development is directed by the constraints inherent in the relationship among elements of the living system as they act upon themselves and upon each other. These elements can be either cells, clusters of cells, or entire subsystems, such as those formed by hormonal processes. The kernel idea is that the several features of the organism—including its behavior—depend on the whole of the reciprocating system of which they form parts. The mutual regulation among components permits the possible feedback to the original source, and self-regulation.

Organismic theory is thus compatible with the Darwinian perspective of evolution as a dynamic, adaptive process. Development is equally dynamic. It required only a modest conceptual leap to consider *behavior* to be an essential component of the organismic system, and behavioral development to be understood in terms of biological and social features of the system. Hence the "system" in which the organism developed was not merely under the skin. The concept of "organization" would be broadened to include feedback from other organisms and from the social network in which development occurred. Two developmental/comparative psychologists, T. C. Schneirla and Zing-Yang Kuo, led the way in the early 1930s for the application of such an organismic perspective to the problems of behavioral ontogeny.

The problem that Schneirla tackled was to unravel the complex social structure of army ants, who despite their lack of grey matter, were highly coordinated in virtually all phases of their adaptation. Wilson (1975) considers the species as a prototypical "truly social" one. How is the high level of social organization accomplished? Schneirla (1933) attacked the problem by undertaking a series of comprehensive field investigations in the Panama and laboratory studies in his facilities at the American Museum of Natural History. He tested the assumption that colony organization does not arise from some single internal source; rather, the complex social system arises as an outcome of the interdependence of events in the brood, workers, queen, and the contextual environmental constraints.

Schneirla identified the pattern of empirical relationships that provided elegant support for his developmental analysis of social organization. He discovered, for instance, that a primary trigger for migration and foraging raids in the colony is the heightened activity produced by the developing larvae. When the larvae emerge from the quiescent phase of development, their activity stimulates the rest of the colony to action, keying both foraging raids and migration. When the activity of the larval brood diminishes as a consequence of growth-related changes, the raids cease and the nomadic phase ends. The surplus food that then becomes available in the colony (due to decreased needs of the young) fattens the queen and serves to trigger a new ovulatory cycle, thus recreating the conditions for reproduction. Looking backward on this work, Schneirla (1957) concluded "The cyclic pattern thus is self-rearoused in a feedback fashion, the product of a reciprocal relationship between queen and colony functions, not of a timing mechanism endogenous to the queen."

Z.-Y. Kuo, a Chinese psychologist who completed his doctoral training with E. C. Tolman at Berkeley before returning to work in China, came to similar conclusions at about the same time. Kuo was originally motivated by J. B. Watson's extravagant claims about the malleability of behavior. He went beyond Watson and collected relevant data. In a series of provocative studies, where he produced novel environments for the young animals to grow up in, Kuo demonstrated how key features of social patterns can be changed, and "neophenotypes" created. Cats, for instance, can be made to "love" rats, not kill them, if the kittens are raised together with rodents from infancy onward (Kuo, 1930). Beyond behavioral plasticity, Kuo addressed the fundamental problem of behavioral origins: when and how key behavior patterns arise in the course of ontogeny.

In his study of the origin of "instinctive" behaviors, such as pecking, vocalization, and movement patterns in birds, Kuo assumed that these characteristics arise in development because of necessary feedback relationships between central nervous system, physiological, and behavioral functions. Pushing the organismic proposition on the self-stimulative role of behavior to its limits, Kuo offered the proposal that the behavior of the embryo itself provides feedback that helps to direct its subsequent development. While Preyer (1888) had earlier suggested the possibility of such feedback effects in development, there were scant data relevant to the proposal.

The story of how Kuo explored these ideas can be found in a series of papers that he published during the 1930s, and summarized in his later volume on behavioral development (e.g., Kuo, 1939, 1967). He first had to solve the problem of how to keep embryos alive while viewing their development (he invented a way to produce a "window" by removing the external shell but keeping the embryo and the membranes surrounding it intact). Kuo was then able to plot, from the onset of development to hatching, the movement patterns in the egg, including the presumptive initial stages of heart activity, breathing, limb movement, and pecking. On the basis of these observations, he concluded that the activity of the organism itself is influential in determining the direction of development, including leg coordination and pecking. The first reports of these observations met initial skepticism (e.g., Carmichael, 1933), and for good reason. Some of Kuo's speculations have not been upheld because he did not give sufficient weight to the effects of spontaneous central nervous system innervation in producing cycles of activity and inactivity (Oppenheim, 1973, 1982). But his more general assumption that behavioral feedback functions can contribute to embryonic development has in some instances been strikingly confirmed. For example, inhibition of leg movement in the chick embryo has been found to be associated with ossification of the joints and difficulty in posthatching mobility (Drachman & Coulombre, 1962). Moreover, self-produced vocal calls by the embryo facilitate the development of posthatching species-typical preferences (Gottlieb, 1976).

As powerful as were Schneirla's and Kuo's demonstrations of the utility of a developmental approach to behavior, they had little immediate effect upon child psychology (although Kuo's work was discussed at length by Carmichael, 1933, in the revised *Handbook of Child Psychology*, and Schneirla was a reviewer for the same volume). It was not until the next generation that their essential message was heard and understood in both comparative and developmental psychology.

Another psychobiological researcher had greater immediate success and visibility. Leonard Carmichael carried the psychological tradition of Wilhelm Preyer into the 1930s. His *Handbook* chapters (Carmichael, 1933, 1946) provided a scholarly reminder of the unsolved problems of the relations between biological development and behavioral establishment. Carmichael also brought to the attention of child psychologists the impressive body of literature concerned with the analysis of early biological and behavioral development. The *Manual* chapter by M. B. McGraw (1946) provided an excellent critical overview of the basic issues of developmental psychobiology.

In Europe, the study of the "biology of behavior," or ethology, experienced a rebirth in Konrad Lorenz's article, "Der Kumpan in der Umwelt des Vogels" (1935; trans. & pub. in English, 1937). In this paper, Lorenz reasserted the contribution of evolutionary forces in the determination of behavior and reminded biologists and psychologists of the importance of early experience and its possible irreversibility. Building on the foundation laid by American C. O. Whitman (1899) and German O. Heinroth (1910), Lorenz offered a convincing argument for studying instinct and the evolutionary bases of behavior. Taking American behaviorists head on, Lorenz argued that the effects of experiences in the "critical period" could not be accounted for in then-available principles of learning and association. Specifically, he distinguished the phenomenon of imprinting (the establishment of filial preferences and species identification in precocial birds) from "association learning" on four counts: (1) imprinting occurs only during an early critical period; (2) it is irreversible in later development; (3) it is supraorganismic in its effects (not limited to the imprinted object but to the species of which the object is a member); and (4) it takes place prior to the developmental appearance of the response that is "conditioned" (e.g., sexual preferences are influenced, even though they are not present in infancy). Virtually no immediate notice was taken of ethological work by developmental psychologists; the gulf between disciplines and World War II combined to delay the introduction of these ideas into the mainstream of psychological and developmental thought.

Theoretical Trends

What theoretical activity took place over this third of a century? A great deal, for each of the major developmental models established in the previous period underwent revision, modification, and extension. Behaviorism was liberalized and enlivened by a marriage with psychoanalysis. Psychoanalysis itself was split into three recognizable subdivisions (Munroe, 1955): classical psychoanalysis, postpsychoanalytic theory, and neopsychoanalytic theory. Similarly, the Baldwinian approach to cognitive and social development was partitioned and extended: toward the theory of mental development now associated with Jean Piaget and toward the symbolic interactionism movement in sociology, anthropology, and psychiatry. Nor was behavioral Darwinism overlooked. The foundations for modern ethology had been laid by Whitman and Heinroth, and extended by Lorenz and Tinbergen. The "organismic" approach affected theories in biology and psychology. Most immediately related to developmental concerns were the developmental psychobiological theory of Schneirla and Kuo and the gestalt principles of Wertheimer, Koffka, and Lewin. At first blush, it seemed as if Baldwin's vision that "every man have his theory" had been fulfilled.

Except for some intrafamilial squabbles, there were few direct confrontations or face-offs between the major theories. It was not so much mutual respect as it was selective inattention. As A. Baldwin (1966, 1980) observed, these developmental theories tended to talk past each other rather than at each other; they had different aims, were concerned with different issues, employed different methods, and were challenged by different findings. In due course, as the interests and concerns of the discipline shifted, each of the general orientations was to experience its day in the sun.

A few comments on three major theoretical systems of the period that have not yet been singled out for attention seem in order: social learning theory, psychoanalysis and its derivatives, and Lewinian "field theory."

Social Neobehaviorism

The family of theories called "social learning" descended from a wedding of the general behavioral models of the 1930s and psychoanalytic ideas of personality. During the heyday of general behavioral systems, four models of learning emerged as especially influential: the behavior system of C. L. Hull (1943), the contiguity learning model of E. R. Guthrie (1935), the purposive behaviorism of E. C. Tolman (1932), and the operant learning theory of B. F. Skinner (1938, 1953). Despite differences in language and assumptions about the nature of learning, the models share the belief that the basic principles of learning are universal, transcending differences in species, age, and circumstances.

Beyond a faith in the universality of the basic principles of behavior, there was a need to specify the implications of these theories for distinctly human problems, including the acquisition of personality patterns and social dispositions. J. B. Watson had earlier led the way in offering bold speculations about the learning and unlearning of fears and loves. The challenge to the writers of the 1930s was to provide a more systematic, and yet equally convincing, case for the learning of significant human behaviors. To this end, a group of able young scientists at Yale University set about to put the study of personality processes on a solid empirical and behavioral basis. This group attempted to link certain concepts of psychoanalysis with assumptions drawn from the general behavioral theory of C. L. Hull. The upshot was a remarkably influential set of concepts that were to dominate theoretical formulations in child psychology for the next 2 to 3 decades.

The first major collaborative effort was directed at the analysis of the controls of aggressive patterns, as viewed from a psychoanalytic/behavioral perspective. The product of this collaboration, a slim volume entitled *Frustration and Aggression*, appeared on the eve of World War II and gained immediate attention and influence (Dollard, Miller, Doob, Mowrer, & Sears, with others, 1939). Although the basic hypothesis that "aggression is always a consequence of frustration" (p. 27) was soon amended by the authors themselves (see Miller, et al., 1941), the idea behind the work was enthusiastically endorsed. The associationistic assumptions of psychoanalysis were neatly melded with the stimulus-drive assumptions of Hullian theory.

The direct application of concepts of learning and imitation to children was soon made by Miller and Dollard (1941) in their book *Social Learning and Imitation*. This was not the first such extension; Sears's study of infant frustration (cited in Dollard et al., 1939), and Mowrer's study of enuresis (1938) had already shown that social learning principles can be readily applied to problems of child development. After World War II, the full impact of the social learning perspective was to be felt by child psychology.

Psychoanalysis

By the 1930s, the enterprise of psychoanalysis had undergone multiple divisions and had exercised a significant impact upon the study of behavioral development. The most obvious influence was direct, through the teachings of Sigmund Freud himself and those who remained faithful to the orthodox theory. But equally powerful influences were indirect, mediated through the theories of those who—like J. B. Watson, J. Piaget, and R. R. Sears—had been impressed by particular features of psychoanalytic theory. In between were the so-called "post-Freudians" (those who extended psychoanalytic theory within the constraints established by Freud himself) and "neo-Freudians" (those psychoanalysts who challenged key assumptions, such as the emphasis on infantile sexuality and the primacy of early experience). These various themes have been expertly traced in discussions of psychoanalytic theory (e.g., Hall & Lindzey, 1957; Munroe, 1955). For our present purposes, some comments on the relation between psychoanalysis and the study of behavioral development are in order.

By the late 1930s, psychoanalysis appeared to many child psychologists to be the answer to their search for a unifying theory of development. One of the more influential writers on the matter was Freud's daughter, Anna Freud. Her view on the adequacy of the theory for understanding personality development—indeed, all features of development—was unambiguous and uncompromising. In the chapter that she prepared for the first *Handbook of Child Psychology*, A. Freud wrote:

> Psychoanalysis does not permit itself to be ranged with other conceptions: it refuses to be put on an equal basis with them. The universal validity which psychoanalysis postulates for its theories makes impossible its limitation to any special sphere such as the conception of the neurotic child or even the sexual development of the child. Psychoanalysis goes beyond these boundaries, within which it might even have been granted the right of judgment, and encroaches upon domains which, as demonstrated by the table of contents of this book, other specialists consider their own. (1931, p. 561)

Psychoanalysis would settle for nothing less than the whole pie of developmental psychology, and, in the 1940s, it came close to getting it.

It seemed inevitable that empirically minded American psychologists would attempt to put some of the key propositions of the theory to experimental test; indeed, the enterprise attracted some of the best young scientists in psychology (see *Social Neobehaviorism* above). What did they find? In summing up the then-available results of the experimental assessments of fixation, regression, projection, and other psychoanalytic mechanisms, Sears (1944) wrote:

> One is driven to the conclusion that experimental psychology has not yet made a major contribution to these problems. . . . It seems doubtful whether the sheer testing of psychoanalytical theory is an appropriate task for experimental psychology. Instead of trying to ride on the tail of a kite that was never meant to carry such a load, experimentalists would probably be wise to get all the hunches, intuitions, and experience possible from psychoanalysis and then, for themselves, start the laborious task of constructing a systematic psychology of personality, but a system based on behavioral rather than experiential data. (p. 329)

All this is to say that the experimental testing of psychoanalytic proposals was not a profitable enterprise. Sears was to follow his own advice, as we shall see, and thereby pave the way for the modern generations of social learning theory.

Despite the equivocal returns on the scientific analysis of the theory, its influence gained, not lost, during the 1930s and 1940s (Maher & Maher, 1979). Virtually every major theoretical system concerned with human behavior—save those that dealt with purely physiological, motor, or sensory phenomena—was accommodated to psychoanalytic theory. Behaviorism (whether "radical" Watsonianism or "conventional" Hullian theory) and Piagetian cognitive theory alike were significantly influenced in that era, just as ethology and social learning theory are influenced in the present one. The immediate effects on childrearing practices were as great, if not greater, than the earlier ones associated with Holt and Watson. With the publication of the first edition of Benjamin Spock's bestselling manual on infant care in 1945, the American public was encouraged to adopt practices not inconsistent with psychoanalytic thinking. The rapid growth of professional clinical psychology—as World War II demanded specialists in diagnosis and therapy—also underscored the need for a theory of assessment and treatment. The major tools available for the task included projective tests (which were typically congruent with psychoanalytic assumptions) and methods of psychotherapy (which were derived, directly or indirectly, from the psychoanalytic interview). Psychology as a professsion and a science became increasingly indebted to psychoanalytic theory and practice.

But psychoanalysts themselves proved to be an intellectually heterogeneous lot, and the theory could hardly be viewed as a static, unchanging view of personality. Among the more prominent revisionists were Carl G. Jung, Alfred Adler, Karen Horney, Eric Fromm, and Harry Stack Sullivan. The last three writers shared in common an emphasis on the interpersonal implications of dynamic theory, as these are expressed in the family system and in interpersonal exchanges of later childhood and maturity. With this focus on "object relations," there was a concomitant deemphasis on the importance of infantile sexuality and the irreversibility of very early experiences (see Munroe, 1955). Horney (1937) and Sullivan led the way in the neo-Freudian theory of interpersonal relations. In 1940, in a lengthy article in *Psychiatry*, Sullivan outlined a rapprochement between theories of symbolic interaction from sociology and anthropology and a neoanalytic interpersonal theory of psychopathology. Sullivan's position was that the "self dynamism" arises from "the recurrent interpersonal situations of life." Ideas about the self-dynamism (which is not an entity but a process) are derived by the interpersonal settings of life and depend, in large measure, on the "consensual validation" of the views of "significant others" with whom one interacts. Because of the continuing impact of the social system on one's behavior and one's thought of oneself, the development of personality is a continuing, ongoing process. Sullivan's views had a significant impact on subsequent sociological (Cottrell, 1942, 1869), psychiatric (Bateson, Jackson, Hayley, & Weakland, 1956; Jackson, 1968a, 1968b), and psychological models of social interaction.

Field Theory and Ecological Psychology

When Kurt Lewin immigrated to the United States in the early 1930s, he had already established himself as a distinguished child psychologist in Germany. American readers were first introduced to his powerful theory of "behavior and development as a function of the total situation" in two articles that appeared in English in 1931. In his classic theoretical paper, "Conflict between Aristotelian and Galilean Modes of Thought in Psychology" (1931a), Lewin offered an elegant defense for studying individual children in the actual, concrete, total situation of which they are a part. He argued that the dynamics of behavior—the study of the forces that exercise momentary control over the direction and form of actions—cannot be clarified by the use of standard statistical methods. Averages that are obtained by combining the results of large numbers of children in a "standard" environment are bound to obscure the precise dynamic controls of behavior, not clarify them. Hence, "An inference from the average to the concrete particular case is . . . impossible. The concepts of the average child and of the average situation are abstractions that have no utility whatever for the investigation of dynamics" (Lewin, 1931b, p. 95). Lewin provided a rationale for the conclusion that had been arrived at intuitively by some of his most insightful predecessors (including Preyer, Binet, Freud, and Piaget). The conclusion stood in sharp contrast to that arrived at by Galton and by most American psychologists.

Lewin's ideas about method were consistent with his theoretical position on the contextual relativity of psychological experience and action. In the second paper published in 1931, "Environmental Forces in Child Behavior and Development," Lewin outlined his field theory of behavior and perception. A key element in Lewin's theorizing was his emphasis on the *psychological* environment as opposed to the physical or objectively determined concrete environment. Lewin observed, "All these things and events are defined for the child partly by their 'appearance' but above all by their 'functional possibilities' (the 'Wirkwelt' in v. Uexküll's sense)" (Lewin, 1931b, p. 100). In endorsing animal behaviorist J. von Uexküll's emphasis on the individual's reconstructed inner space (the *Umwelt* and the *Innenwelt*) as opposed to the objective mechanical forces of the external world, he captured an idea whose implications have yet to be fully realized. Lewin formulated his psychological field theory in keeping with the gestalt and system theoretic approaches. Although behavior is seen as a function of both the person and the environment, these two major variables "are mutually dependent upon each other. In other words, to understand or to predict behavior, the person and his environment have to be considered as *one* constellation of interdependent factors. We call the totality of these factors the life space (*LSp*) of that individual" (Lewin, 1954, p. 919). Lewin's theory is basically a model of action, to account for the directionality of behavior in terms of the forces present in a given psychological environment. But the effective forces belong neither to the person nor to the field alone; actions can be understood only in the totality of forces as they are merged to determine behavior.

In his work in the United States in the 1930s and 1940s, Lewin extended this theoretical model to diverse social and developmental phenomena, including the analysis of conflict, social influence, level of aspiration, and goal setting, as well as the effects of autocratic and democratic social environments. Beyond their influence on specific research programs,

Lewin's principles of behavior and development became incorporated into the discipline without being identified with his particular school of thought. For instance, his "field theory" demanded attention to the context in which behavior occurs and, particularly, the individual's personal response to that setting. The "environment" is not only the physical and social context but also a child's perception of that setting. Thus, one and the same "objective" environment may be perceived differently, according to the needs of a child and the forces that operate upon her or him; conversely, seemingly identical responses may reflect the operation of quite different psychological forces. There is a contextual relativity to both stimuli and responses, and neither should be divorced from the social-environmental matrix in which they are embedded.

This overview does not permit an account of Lewin's developmental and social theory (excellent summaries may be found in A. Baldwin, 1980, and in Estes, 1954). It should be noted that Lewin and the Lewinians pioneered in the study of conflict resolution (Lewin, 1935), level of aspiration (Lewin, Dembo, Festinger, & Sears, 1944), small group processes (Lewin, Lippitt, & White, 1939), and the effects of interruption and frustration (Barker, Dembo, & Lewin, 1942; Zeigarnik, 1927). Furthermore, students inspired by Lewin (including D. Cartwright, M. Deutsch, L. Festinger, H. Kelley, S. Schachter, and J. Thibaut) virtually sculpted the face of modern social psychology. What did Lewin not cover? Criticisms of field theory note that relatively little attention is given to the processes of enduring change; namely, those of learning. Also, field theory gives only modest attention to how such developmental changes may be integrated with modifications in psychological forces. Hence the model is exceedingly convincing as a descriptive model, but it is less clear how it may be critically tested, modified, and falsified. Lewin's emphasis aroused psychology from its behavioristic slumbers by pointing out that the idea of a context-free, objective "stimulus" may be illusionary. The implications for methodology and theory, especially for the study of social development and social psychology, were enormous.

Comments on the Middle Period

It seems ironic that the most notable development in child psychology during this period was brought about initially by social and economic forces instead of scientific advances. We refer to the founding of child research institutes throughout the United States which, once established, became enormously influential in the science and remained so throughout the better part of the twentieth century. Behind the foundations and governmental/university agencies that provided the actual financial support for the institutes, there was a broad national coalition of concerned teachers and parents who pressed for more attention, scientific and otherwise, to the needs of children. This was the same sociopolitical "movement" that had been given early form and direction by G. Stanley Hall in the 1880s and 1890s. But the establishment of study centers did not a science make, and investigators were immediately challenged to develop more adequate procedures in virtually every sector of child research. Each area of study—intelligence, honesty, emotionality, language, thinking, perception, growth, predictability—presented its own problems of methodology and analysis, and each had to be solved in its own terms. The upshot was an inevitable fragmentation of developmental study.

What were the empirical advances in the period? To attempt to answer that question would be tantamount to compressing the information contained in the three compendia edited by C. Murchison (1931, 1933) and L. Carmichael (1946). Beyond the demonstration that almost all aspects of child behavior and cognition could be profitably studied by empirical procedures—something that had been promised but not demonstrated in the earlier period—we find substantive findings that perplexed the researchers themselves and seemed to defy integration with earlier concepts of the child. These phenomena included the specificity of honesty, the rapid conditionability of fear in infants, the egocentricism of children, the physical normality (or superiority) of bright children, and the modest predictability of behavior over time and space. Spectacular controversies were ignited by studies of early experience that purported to show that children's basic intellectual adaptations could be influenced by especially stimulating or deprived early care. Perhaps more important for the science than controversy were the less dramatic yet critical advances in describing the "normal" (i.e., species-typical) course of sensorimotor, cognitive, and social behavioral development.

Theoretical activity in this period proceeded at two "levels," specific and general. The empirical advances—methodological and substantive—produced information that demanded attention and integration. Hence Hartshorne and May (1928–1930) offered the "specificity" proposal on altruism and honesty, C. Bühler an account of "negativism" in adolescence, F. Goodenough (1931) an explanation for the development of anger and quarrels, J. Anderson (1939) the overlap hypothesis for continuity in individual differences, and so on. These data-based hypotheses constituted a necessary step between empirical outcomes of child study and the overarching theoretical conceptions that stimulated the research in the first place.

On the second level of theoretical activity, attempts were made to fill the void left by the collapse of the recapitulation hypothesis as the integrative theory of development. For every general developmental theory that vied for hegemony in the 1920s and 1930s, a direct line may be drawn to antecedent models of the 1880s and 1890s. The cognitive-developmental proposals of J. Piaget were immediately linked to prior concepts of J. M. Baldwin; the organismic theories of Z.-Y. Kuo, T. C. Schneirla, and L. von Bertalanffy followed from prior conceptual advances in embryology; the maturational model of A. Gesell constituted in several key respects a restatement and extension of the developmental views of W. Preyer; and the neopsychoanalytic positions retained much of the parental theory.

Despite obvious differences among the above models, they shared a family similarity in that they were, in a basic sense, developmental. Differences among them arose on assumptions about how developmental processes might be most adequately described and how behavioral phenomena might be most appropriately conceptualized. These assumptions, in turn, reflected the behavioral or cognitive phenomena that were addressed by the theory. Although psychoanalysis gained a clear edge in popular recognition and in professional support, organismic models became quietly influential in the research of psychobiological and cognitive investigators. But none of the models achieved clear dominance, and the science could not claim as its own a unifying theory of behavioral development that might complement or extend the theory of biological evolution. Indeed, the very advances in identifying the contextual events that determined actions and learning also raised questions on whether a general theory of behavioral development was possible, or necessary.

THE MODERN ERA (1947–1982): EXPANSION AND MATURATION

Following a general depression in research activity during World War II, work on behavioral development began in the postwar period an upward trajectory that did not begin to level off until the late 1970s. We saw a new "golden age" for the discipline that surpassed those of the two previous ones of 1895–1905 and of 1925–1935. New techniques and approaches were introduced in rapid succession, stimulated in part by advances in electronic recording, coding, and computer analysis. The effective life span of research methods—from new projective procedures to questionnaires on authoritarianism or brief experimental procedures for studying children's learning—appeared to have shortened from about 15 to 10 years. Promising ideas—on test anxiety, social reinforcement satiation, impulsivity, modeling—came rapidly to dominate the area, then faded away, often without a decent postmortem or obituary. In large measure the quickened pace of research activity and analysis could be attributed to great increases in federal support for empirical research and the opening of new teaching and research positions. There were more hands to do the work and more minds to criticize it. The summary picture of this period is one of expansion, invention, and criticism, with new discoveries in virtually all areas of developmental research and application.

Perhaps the most visible early theoretical trend in this period was the rise, domination, and passing of general learning theories. Until their grip began to fail in the early 1960s, behavioral models of learning were hegemonous in American psychology, and developmental psychology was no exception. To enter the theoretical mainstream, research in the several areas of child study from language acquisition and cognitive learning to social behavior and childrearing had to be couched in learning terms. Behaviors did not develop, they were acquired. Despite their austere and parsimonious construction, learning models appeared to be remarkably adaptable for developmental psychologists. But not adaptive enough. By the mid-1960s, the area began to identify flaws in the general learning model and to rediscover the dynamic developmental models upon which the field had been established. Hence many of the ideas and problems that had been pursued over the first half-century came again to the forefront, from the study of developmentally paced changes in thought and language to the effects of interactions upon social and personality development.

This section of developmental history overlaps with contemporary events, including those covered in depth in other chapters of this revision of the *Handbook*. Hence we will stop short of a full 100-year coverage, leaving the final 20 years for those who survey the contemporary scene.

The Rise, Hegemony, and Decline of Social Learning Theories

Contrary to general impressions, there is no single "social learning theory;" there are several. The plurality came about initially because there was only a modest consensus on which principles of learning

are universal. Over the past 40 years, a number of social learning theories have evolved, each with its own distinctive emphasis and adherents. It has been a complex and often misunderstood endeavor, and we comment here only on certain of the historical highlights.

The beginning is easy, because Robert R. Sears can be recognized as the person whose influence was pervasive in the introduction of the psychoanalytic/learning synthesis to the study of children. One of the original members of the Yale group, Sears was a pivotal influence for students and colleagues at the Iowa Child Welfare Research Station, Harvard University, and Stanford University. With his colleagues at these institutions, many of whom went on to develop influential revisions of social learning (including E. E. Maccoby, J. Whiting, V. Nowlis, J. Gewirtz, L. Rau Ferguson, R. Alpert, R. Walters, A. Bandura, and R. R. Sears's wife, Pauline Snedden Sears), Sears was instrumental in bringing about major changes in the scope and concerns of developmental psychology.

In the first major publication to come from this group (Sears, Whiting, Nowlis, & Sears, 1953), "aggression" and "dependency" were seen as motives that are learned early in the life history of the child. How are they learned? The answer was not an easy one, at least not for Hullians, since the theory of conditioned drives had not been elaborated by C. Hull (1951) and had been only vaguely outlined by Freud. Drawing from both of these views, Sears and his colleagues argued that these key social motives are acquired as a universal consequence of the early rearing experiences of the child. Moreover, variations in the strength of the drives and in their expression are produced by differences in the quality of the parent/child relationship, as indexed by the rewards, punishments, and frustrations that occur in the mother/child interaction. This social learning theory was extended to account for the development of gender role-typing (through internalization of parental values and self-reinforcement) and conscience (through nurturance and the withdrawal of love by the mother). The original statement underwent revisions, both modest (e.g., Sears, Maccoby, & Levin, 1957; Sears, Rau, & Alpert, 1965) and major (e.g., Bandura & Walters, 1959; Whiting & Whiting, 1975), in attempts to extend it and correct its shortcomings.

What were its shortcomings? Many of them were identified by the investigators themselves in three large-scale studies of childrearing conducted in Iowa, Massachusetts, and California. Employing lengthy in-depth interviews with parents as a primary research technique, these studies attempted to relate childrearing practices with assessment of children's social behavior and personality patterns. The assessments of children capitalized upon advances that had been made in observational methodology, and in child-appropriate "projective test" measures. Instead of using inkblots or semistructured pictures, the investigators used dolls and dollhouses to permit the preschool child to reconstruct the nuclear family (Bach, 1946). The interview and observational procedures provided the model for a wide range of cross-cultural and cross-age studies (e.g., Whiting & Whiting, 1975). When the results of the 20-year research effort were compiled and analyzed, the outcomes provided only modest support for the theory that had inspired the work. The problem was that there were few reliable correlates between variations in child-rearing practice and the children's social behavior and personality patterns. Not all of the outcomes were negative, nor were all unreliable. But the overall pattern of the findings provided scant support for the ideas that had stimulated the effort. What was to blame—the theory or the methods employed to test it? The methods could be criticized, and were (see the incisive critique of Yarrow, Campbell, & Burton, 1968). In retrospect, it seemed less painful to blame the techniques and to preserve the theory.

Two other noteworthy contributions by Sears and his colleagues require mention. In a presidential address to the American Psychological Association, Sears (1951) brought renewed attention to the theoretical concept of social interaction and the bidirectionality of familial relations. Although the research methods employed by the Sears group made it difficult to study interactional phenomena directly, interactional concepts figured importantly in the conceptions that were offered in each of his major subsequent publications. They provided the impetus for renewed attention to the issues that had been initially raised by James Mark Baldwin and were then represented in the work of H. S. Sullivan (1940, 1953) and L. S. Cottrell (1942).

The second contribution was the reintegration of child development research into the mainstream of psychology, a position that it had not held for most of the previous half-century. By linking the study of children to the then-current theoretical systems of psychology, the door was opened for a fresh generation of psychologists to enter the field. The gains were not without cost, however, in that much of the earlier developmental work was set aside or ignored by the new generation. Traditional developmental studies, as embodied in the chapters of successive editions of the Carmichael *Manual*, were seen as irrelevant for the basic issues of social learning and behavior modification. Instead of *descriptions* of developmental change, this generation of developmentalists was concerned with *explanations* of change in terms of the "new" concepts of social reinforcement, imitation, dyadic analysis, dependency, aggression, and conscience. Overlooked in the social learning revolution was the fact that most of these ideas had been represented in the formative period, and most of the phenomena to which the concepts refer had been extensively researched in the middle period.

Coming back to the evolution of social learning theories, we find that in the early 1960s, the movement was split into two major divisions, each of which was in intellectual debt to the parental movement and to the reinforcement concepts of B. F. Skinner (1953). In one division, J. Gewirtz, S. Bijou, and D. Baer (Bijou & Baer, 1961; Gewirtz, 1961) followed Skinner's lead in applying the ideas and concepts of operant conditioning to analyses of behavior modification in normal and retarded children. But there were theoretical problems in the application. Just as the concept of "conditioned" or "learned motivation" had presented difficulties for the initial generation of social learning theories, the notion of "conditioned" or "social reinforcement" proved to be an enigmatic concept for the operant revision (see Gewirtz & Baer, 1958; Parton & Ross, 1965).

The other major division was headed by A. Bandura and R. H. Walters (1963) who reinstituted "imitation" to the position of importance that it had occupied in J. M. Baldwin's original "social psychology." For Bandura and Walters, imitation (or modeling) was employed to explain the establishment (acquisition) of behavior patterns, a matter that had been for the most part overlooked by social learning theories of development.

The next modification in social learning views came shortly afterward. The need for further revision arose when it became clear that the short-term studies of social learning were open to alternative, cognitive interpretations. For instance, careful examination of the determinants and outcomes of social reinforcement processes in children indicated that they did not behave in a fashion that was analogous to reinforcement processes in animals. Marked variations in reinforcer effectiveness could be induced by instructions or other cognitive manipulations, leading to the interpretation that "social reinforcement" in children may more appropriately be viewed in terms of information transmission processes than in terms of primary reinforcement processes (see Stevenson, 1965). Other "information" interpretations of punishment, dependency, and conscience appeared. A similar revision was made in the interpretation of imitation and modeling, for parallel reasons (Bandura, 1969). The cognitive reformulation of social learning theories continues to the present, guided at least in part by the early ideas of J. Rotter (1954). A continuing problem for the orientation has been to clarify the relations between the earlier noncognitive usage of such key ideas as "social reinforcement" and "modeling" with the new cognitive interpretations. It is ironic to find that the social cognition/learning reformulations have now come to embrace not only J. M. Baldwin's concept of imitation but also his concept of the self as a central organizing theme (see Bandura, 1977; Lewis & Brooks-Gunn, 1979).

But some characteristics of behaviorist models remained unchanged in social learning theories. Social learning researchers as a group have maintained a curious stance toward the concept of development. From Watson onward, learning theories have been developmental in the sense that they have shared the "fundamental point" that man's activities should be studied historically. But social learning views have been reluctant to consider processes of development other than learning. The implicit assumption has persisted that the incremental changes produced by learning are sufficient to account for the major phenomena of social development (see Baldwin, 1980).

Not all of the researchers of this period were converted to social learning principles. Indeed, some of the most influential contributions were made by investigators who followed the functional tradition established by C. Bühler, D. Thomas, and K. Lewin. Under the guidance of Alfred and Clara Baldwin, Roger Barker, Lois Murphy, Marion Radke-Yarrow, and Harriet Rheingold, social development research with young children regained its earlier momentum. Although field theory per se did not become a dominant force in this work, some key Lewinian principles did, including the need for ecological study and the analysis of the individual's actions in the concrete social and physical context in which they occur. The functional background of the researchers also made a difference in the nature of the variables explored and the outcomes studied. The virtues of life—kindness, empathy, charity, helpfulness—tended to get short shrift by the psychoanalytically inspired themes of conflict and aggression that were embedded in social learning views. The functional tradition helped to balance the coverage by refocusing attention on the "prosocial" and "altruistic" patterns of early development.

Recent Activity (1962–1982)

A consideration of the past two decades carries us beyond history and into the contemporary scene. It is not within the scope of a single chapter—whose aim has been to highlight a century of developmental thought and work—to integrate the several lines of investigation that are currently underway. That is the task of the authors of the remaining chapters in this *Handbook*. For our present purposes, it may suffice to observe that the themes initiated in the early 1960s continued to dominate developmental research through the present. We close with a brief comment on the onset of these themes.

The reemergence of the cognitive/developmental theory of Piaget as a central focus for thinking and research was doubtless the most visible development in the field. Stimulated in part by a national reexamination of the educational process (e.g., Bruner, 1960), in part by influential volumes on Piaget's theory (Hunt, 1961; Flavell, 1963), and in part by the fading vigor of social learning approaches, the problem of how mental development occurs became a dominant concern for developmental researchers. Virtually all aspects of the field were touched by the cognitive revolution. Investigations of language development, thinking, sensation, and information processing in children flourished as they had in no earlier era. Even hardcore behavioristic models proved to be vulnerable to cognitive modifications, with the new directions on "mediational mechanisms" being provided by H. H. and T. S. Kendler (Kendler & Kendler, 1962) and M. R. Kuenne (1949). Given the thrust of the movement, it seemed inevitable that the barriers between social development and cognitive development should be transcended.

Another rapprochement, that between animal and child investigations, provided the opening for a fresh look at the major issues of psychobiological and behavioral development. These included the effects of early experience and whether the infant is especially "sensitive" or invulnerable, the bidirectional influences between structure and function in prenatal and postnatal development, and, more broadly, the interrelations between animal and human behavioral development, and between ontogenetic and phyletic processes. These constituted some of the major unresolved matters from the earliest period of the science. Among those working in animal behavior, the contributions of H. F. Harlow, J. P. Scott, T. C. Schneirla, and Z.-Y. Kuo and the cadre of investigators whom they influenced proved to be of special importance. Harlow's studies of "mother love" and the role of affectional relations between the rhesus monkey infant and others yielded perhaps the most influential developmental findings of the period (Harlow, 1958; Harlow & Harlow, 1965). Evolutionary concerns were brought forward in the work of the classical ethologists (K. Lorenz, 1937; N. Tinbergen, 1951), neoethologists (R. Hinde, 1970; P. Bateson, 1966; J. Crook, 1970), and sociobiologists (W. Hamilton, 1964; E. O. Wilson, 1975; J. Maynard Smith, 1974; R. Dawkins, 1976). A most important synthesis was produced when psychoanalytic concepts of personality development were wedded to ethological theory by J. Bowlby (1958, 1969) and extended by M. D. S. Ainsworth (1969) in studies of mother/child social attachment.

Concomitant with this surge of interest in early development, a handful of investigators led by H. L. Rheingold, N. Bayley, and E. Gibson (1969) reopened the study of infancy. In the past decade, virtually all aspects of infant development—social, sensory, motor, cognitive—have been vigorously investigated. The concept of the infant as an adaptive and adapting organism was rediscovered, accompanied by precise accounts of the competencies of the infant and how they emerged. This "organismic" concept of development is to be found not only in investigations of infants but in studies of persons across the lifespan; it provides a linkage among the diverse areas of psychology that deal with the dynamics of cognitive and social adaptation (Baltes, Reese, & Nesselroade, 1977).

TOWARD A SCIENCE OF BEHAVIORAL DEVELOPMENT

In the light of the continued fragmentation of the area these days, it may have seemed premature, even presumptuous, to attempt to write a history of the *science* of behavioral development. Doubtless the story of the past 100 years would have been more orderly if there had been greater consensus on which lines of work had yielded the greatest returns in solving the problems of behavioral establishment, maintenance, and change. Nonetheless, an overview of the past suggests that today's investigators are as much determined by history as they are makers of it. The major issues of the present appear to be, in large measure, the same ones that thoughtful contributors to the science had addressed in the past. This is true even for the most central matter of all. One finds in

the work of Wesley Mills, Wilhelm Preyer, and James Mark Baldwin eloquent statements of the need for an integrated, organismic perspective on behavioral development. Essentially the same idea has been advanced in successive generations by key figures of the enterprise, from Arnold Gesell to Jean Piaget. Writing on the place and role of a science of behavioral development, T. C. Schneirla (1966) stated the need succinctly:

> Behavioral ontogenesis is the backbone of comparative psychology. Shortcomings in its study inevitably handicap other lines of investigation from behavioral evolution and psychogenetics to the study of individual and group behavior. (p. 283)

In short, studies of behavioral development are as important for psychology as studies of evolution and genetics have been for biology, and for similar reasons.

Perhaps the most important difference between Schneirla's statement of 1966 and Preyer's of 1882 is that, at the conclusion of the current era, there is much empirical evidence to support the accuracy of the essential message. The centrality of behavioral development is no longer merely a matter of perspective or faith: it is an empirical conclusion. Moreover, recent developmental investigations of behavior seem to be converging, however obliquely, upon organismic models that promise to integrate information about the adapting organism over its lifespan. But a formidable scientific task remains. The problem is twofold: (1) to state the models with greater precision than has been done up to this point; and (2) to determine their limits in integrating (and predicting) the diverse features of sensory, cognitive, and social development. The completion of the task is a suitable goal—perhaps a reachable one— for the field in the era that is now beginning.

NOTES

1. The sources that were of particular value in the preparation of this chapter include Wolf's (1973) biography of A. Binet, Ross's (1972) biography of G. S. Hall, Reinert's (1979) and Baltes's (1979) histories of lifespan psychology, and the histories of child psychology by Kessen (1965), Sears (1975), and Senn (1975). Other useful references included Gottlieb (1979), Gould (1977), Klopfer and Hailman (1967), Oppenheim (1982), White (1970), and the several chapters in Lerner (1982).

2. The focus of this chapter does not permit an excursion into 19th-century biology and philosophy,

where one should properly search for the roots of contemporary approaches to behavioral development (see Reinert, 1979, and Oppenheim, 1982).

3. According to available sources, it appears that the earliest records of observations of young children were made by Pestalozzi during the year 1774 (see Mateer, 1918; Reinert, 1979). However, Pestalozzi himself chose not to publish the diary. Following Tiedemann, the most noteworthy studies were those by American E. Willard (1835; the first in English), B. Sigismund (1856), H. Taine (1876), C. Darwin (1877), and B. Perez (1878). The article by Charles Darwin played a curious role in stimulating further interest in the endeavor. It appeared in the new psychological journal *Mind* in 1877, having been triggered by the appearance of a translation of Taine's parallel observations in the immediately preceding issue two months earlier. (Publication lags were shorter in those days, at least when Darwin was the author.) Darwin's article was based on 37-year-old notes of the first two years of one of his sons. Although inferior to the other reports in terms of care of observation and depth of reporting, Darwin's contribution served to legitimize the method and promoted research with children.

4. Cultural stereotypes also have played a role in the evaluation of *The Mind of the Child*. For instance, Compayré (1893) called the book a "monument of German assiduousness." Later, comparing Frenchman Perez's "logical, brilliant style" with that of Preyer, Mateer (1918) remarked that

the French write brilliantly and convincingly but their technique is apt to be at fault. They seem to hit intuitively upon right premises and conclusions, although their data may be unconvincing or scanty. The German work is more solid, more convincing in its facts but less inspiring in application. (pp. 24–25)

Finally, on the general issue of Germanic devotion to detail, Wilhelm James (1890) wrote, in typical Jamesian fashion, that experimental psychology "could hardly have arisen in a country whose natives could be bored." For the record, Wilhelm Preyer was born in England.

5. But not France's first child psychologist. Recall that Perez (1878) published his *The First Three Years of the Child* some four years before Preyer's *The Mind of the Child* (1882). The two authors covered the same ground, but as Reinert (1979) indicates, Perez was generally considered to be the more imaginative and Preyer the more methodical.

6. An absurd idea, of course. But lest we feel too superior (or embarrassed by the naïveté of Binet and

Féré), it should be noted that Féré shortly afterward (1888) became the first investigator to discover that emotional changes were correlated with electrical changes in the human body.

7. The collaboration with Balbiani must have been close. Binet published a summary of his lectures and married his daughter.

8. Binet was so described when, prior to completing his doctorate, he was named lauréat by the Moral and Political Academy of the Institute of France (Wolf, 1973).

9. Lest we overemphasize national and methodological chauvinism among early psychologists, it should be noted that Binet had strong supporters in American psychology, including James Mark Baldwin.

10. It was in a footnote to this passage that Binet provided an elegant statement of his view on what should be the appropriate relationship between empirical research and theoretical speculation.

We have sometimes been accused of being opposed, with blind infatuation to all theory and to the a priori method. It is an unjust reproach. We admit the use of theory before the experimental researches, for preparation, and, afterwards, for interpretation. What we strongly reject are theoretical discussions that are intended to take the place of an exploration of empirical facts or that are established upon obscure, equivocal and legendary reports, such as are gathered from books, for this is what certain people call observing; it is reading. In our opinion, the ideal of the scientific method must be a combination of theory and of experimentation. Such a combination is well defined in the following formula: prolonged meditation upon facts gathered at first hand. (p. 1)

11. On this score, the U.S. Commissioner of Education, W. T. Harris, wrote in 1896 that "The present widespread study of the child in school and in the family is due, more than to anyone else, to the enthusiastic efforts of Dr. G. Stanley Hall" (Harris, 1896, p. vi).

12. His designation of adolescence as the time that the child begins a fresh set of tracks was optional. Other recapitulation theories proposed that the adding on of unique features occurs in the early postnatal period, or even prenatally (see Gould, 1977, for an informed discussion of the matter).

13. Twenty-two thousand subjects? Not really. Schallenberger (1894) actually reported the responses of 3,434 girls and boys who were 6 to 16 years of age. The misinterpretation arose because Schallenberger transformed their responses to pro-

portional scores, then multiplied by 1,000, to permit comparisons between age/sex groups.

14. In the *Psychological Index* (forerunner of *Psychological Abstracts*) for the year 1897, Binet and Baldwin held first and second place in the sheer frequency of articles published. The box score read 17 for Binet, 11 for Baldwin, and the rest of the world behind. Beyond this similarity in productivity and influence, there were direct linkages between the two men. Baldwin admired Binet's work, and he was responsible for the translation of Binet's *Alterations of Consciousness* (1896) into English. Helen Baldwin translated the text, and J. M. Baldwin wrote editorial notes. It seems likely that it was because of Baldwin that Binet was appointed the only foreign consulting editor to the *Psychological Review*. Binet held the position for the next 10 years despite his low regard for American research in general and for J. McK. Cattell's views of mental testing in particular.

15. Baldwin employs the concepts of *schema* or *schematic* to refer to hypotheses in the logical stage, in accord with the Kant-Fichte-Schelling doctrine of the "schema" as an image lying between imagination and judgment. The problem of whether images were required for thought was a matter of considerable controversy, and the notion of "schema" remains with us.

16. A clue as to the nature of the effects is provided by Jean Piaget, who wrote in personal correspondence: "Unfortunately I did not know Baldwin personally, but his works had a great influence on me. Furthermore, Pierre Janet, whose courses I took in Paris, cited him constantly and had been equally very influenced by him" (cited in Mueller, 1976).

17. At a personal level, Baldwin seems to have attracted few students who could fill the gaps left in his theoretical statements, or who would tackle their empirical analysis. Apparently no one completed a doctorate in psychology in the 6-year period that Baldwin was at Johns Hopkins. When he was forced to resign from the university and chose to leave North America, only loyal friends (including Howard C. Warren at Princeton and William James at Harvard) were left behind, and no students. His name seems to have been selectively ignored by the next generation of psychologists, and forgotten by the next.

18. Ironically, Freud had earlier held that the rejection of psychoanalytic teachings had been for "emotional" and "unscientific" reasons. Here the suggestion appears to be that they should be accepted on the same grounds.

19. Might not Binet's concepts of the unconscious have contributed to the psychoanalytic movement? In a remarkable passage in Breuer and Freud (1895, 1936), we find:

> The continuation of the hysterical symptoms which originated in the hypnoid state, during the normal state, agrees perfectly with our experiences concerning post-hypnotic suggestions. But this also implies that complexes of ideas incapable of consciousness co-exist with groups of ideas which function consciously; that is to say, there is a *splitting of the psyche*. [p. 170] It seems certain that this too can originate without hypnoidism from an abundance of rejected ideas which were repressed, but not suppressed from consciousness. In this or that way there develops a sphere of psychic existence, which is now ideationally impoverished and rudimentary, and now more or less equal to the waking thoughts, for the cognition of which we are indebted above all to Binet and Janet. (Breuer & Freud, 1936, p. 188)

One reason that the Binet-Freud linkage has been heretofore overlooked may be that A. A. Brill failed to include this section in his earlier English translation of *Studies in Hysteria* (i.e., before 1936).

20. And that's not all. Under the general direction of Lawrence Frank, the Rockefeller funds provided support for individual research projects (including C. Bühler's pioneering investigations) and made possible the establishment of the national Child Study Association (see vols. 1–3, *Child Study*).

21. Cyril Burt's exposure of the bogus autobiography seems ironic in the light of questions that have been raised about his own research reports (Kamin, 1974).

22. It was not exactly what the sponsoring agency had expected, or wanted. The Executive Secretary of the sponsoring Institute of Social and Religious Research wrote apologetically in the foreword:

> To lay minds this volume, at first glance, may seen overloaded with matter that has little to do with moral and religious education—a medley of tests and statistics and a paucity of clear directions as to building character. Such readers might profitably reflect that these preliminary processes are inevitable if character education is ever to emerge from guesswork into a science. Medical and surgical science had to follow a similar road to advance from magic and quackery. (Hartshorne & May, 1928–1930, Vol. 2, p. v)

Hartshorne and May had concluded that traditional religious and moral instruction have little, if any, relationship to the results of experimental tests of honesty and service to others.

23. Piaget seemed to accept that explanation, at least in 1930. In the foreword to the second edition of *The Language and Thought of the Child,* he wrote:

> Our original enquiries dealt only with the language of children among themselves as observed in the very special scholastic conditions of Maison des Petits de l'Institut Rousseau. Now, Mlles. M. Muchow, M. D. Katz, Messrs. Galli and Maso, and M. A. Lora [Luria], after studying from the same point of view children with different scholastic environments in Germany, Spain, and Russia, and especially after studying children's conversations in their families, have reached results which, on certain points, differ considerably from ours. Thus, while the little pupils show in their conversations coefficients of ego-centricism more or less analogous to those we have observed, M. Katz's children, talking among themselves or with their parents, behave quite differently. (Piaget, 1930, 1932, pp. xxiii–xxiv)

REFERENCES

Ainsworth, M. D. S. Object relations, dependency, and attachment: A theoretical review of the infant-mother relationship. *Child Development,* 1969, *40,* 969–1025.

Anderson, J. E. The methods of child psychology. In C. Murchison (Ed.), *A handbook of child psychology.* Worcester, Mass.: Clark University Press, 1931.

Anderson, J. E. The limitations of infant and preschool test in the measurement of intelligence. *Journal of Psychology,* 1939, *8,* 351–379.

Arrington, R. E. Interrelations in the behavior of young children. *Child Development Monographs* (No. 8). New York: Teachers College, Columbia University, 1932.

Bach, G. R. Father fantasies and father-typing in father-separated children. *Child Development,* 1946, *17,* 63–80.

Baer, K. E. von. *Über Entwickelungsgeschichte der Thiere: Beobachtung und Reflexion* (2 vols.). Königsberg: Bornträger, 1828.

Baldwin, A. *Theories of child development.* New York: Wiley, 1967. (Rev. ed., 1980)

Baldwin, B. T., & Stecher, L. I. *The psychology of the preschool child.* New York: Appleton, 1924.

Baldwin, J. M. *Mental development in the child and the race: Methods and processes.* New York: Macmillan, 1895.

Baldwin, J. M. *Social and ethical interpretations in mental development: A study in social psychology* (4th ed.). New York: Macmillan, 1906. (1st ed., 1897)

Baldwin, J. M. *Thought and things: A study of the development and meaning of thought or genetic logic* (3 vols.). London: Sonnenschein, 1906–1911.

Baldwin, J. M. *History of psychology: A sketch and an interpretation* (2 vols.). New York: Putnam, 1913.

Baldwin, J. M. *Genetic theory of reality, being the outcome of genetic logic, as issuing in the aesthetic theory of reality called pancalism.* New York: Putnam, 1915.

Baldwin, J. M. [Autobiography.] In C. Murchison (Ed.), *A history of psychology in autibiography* (Vol. 1). Worcester, Mass.: Clark University Press, 1930.

Baltes, P. B. Life-span developmental psychology: Some converging observations on history and theory. In P. B. Baltes & O. G. Brim, Jr. (Eds.), *Life-span development and behavior* (Vol. 2). New York: Academic Press, 1979.

Baltes, P. B., Reese, H. W., & Nesselroade, J. R. *Life-span developmental psychology: Introduction to research methods.* Monterey, Calif.: Brooks/Cole, 1977.

Bandura, A. *Principles of behavior modification.* New York: Holt, Rinehart & Winston, 1969.

Bandura, A. *Social learning theory.* Englewood Cliffs, N.J.: Prentice-Hall, 1977.

Bandura, A., & Walters, R. H. *Adolescent aggression.* New York: Ronald Press, 1959.

Bandura, A., & Walters, R. H. *Social learning and personality development.* New York: Holt, Rinehart & Winston, 1963.

Barker, M. A technique for studying the social-material activities of young children. *Child Development Monographs* (No. 3). New York: Columbia University Press, 1930.

Barker, R. G. (Ed.). *The stream of behavior: Explorations of its structure and content.* New York: Appleton-Century-Crofts, 1963.

Barker, R., Dembo, T., & Lewin, K. Frustration and regression: An experiment with young children. *University of Iowa Studies in Child Welfare,* 1941, *18,* No. 1.

Barnes, E. *Studies in education* (2 vols.). Philadelphia: Author, 1896–1897, 1902–1903.

Barnes, E. *The psychology of childhood and youth.* New York: Huebsch, 1914.

Bateson, G., Jackson, D. D., Hayley, J., & Weakland, J. H. Toward a theory of schizophrenia. *Behavioral Science,* 1956, *1,* 251–264.

Bateson, P. P. G. The characteristics and context of imprinting. *Biological Reviews,* 1966, *41,* 177–220.

Bayley, N. A study of crying of infants during mental and physical tests. *Journal of Genetic Psychology,* 1932, *40,* 306–329.

Beaver, A. P. The initiation of social contacts by preschool children. *Child Development Monographs* (No. 7). New York: Columbia University Press, 1930.

Bertalanffy, L. v. *Modern theories of development: An introduction to theoretical biology* (J. H. Woodger, Trans.). London: Oxford University Press, 1933.

Bijou, S. W., & Baer, D. M. *Child development.* New York: Appleton-Century-Crofts, 1961.

Binet, A. Perceptions d'enfants. *Revue Philosophique,* 1890, *30,* 582–611.

Binet, A. *Les altérations de la personnalité.* Paris: Alcan, 1892.

Binet, A. *Alterations of personality* (Helen Green Baldwin, Trans.; notes and a preface by J. Mark Baldwin). New York: Appleton, 1896.

Binet, A. *L'étude experimentale de l'intelligence.* Paris: Schleicher, 1903.

Binet, A. Nos commission de travail. *Bulletin de la Société libre pour l'étude psychologique de l'enfant,* 1904, No. 14, 337–346. [Cited from Wolf, T. H., *Alfred Binet.* Chicago: University of Chicago Press, 1973.]

Binet, A. *Les idées modernes sur les enfants.* Paris: Schleicher, 1909. [Reprinted edition referred to here: Paris: Flammarion, 1978.]

Binet, A. Nouvelles recherches sur la mesure du niveau intellectuel chez les enfants d'école. *L'Année Psychologique,* 1911, *17,* 145–201.

Binet, A., & Henri, V. La mémoire des phrases (mémoire des idées). *L'Année Psychologique,* 1894, *1,* 24–59.

Binet, A., & Henri, V. La psychologie individuelle. *L'Année Psychologique,* 1895, *2,* 411–465.

Binet, A., Phillippe, J., Courtier, J., & Henri, V. *Introduction à la psychologie expérimentale.* Paris: Alcan, 1894.

Binet, A., & Simon, T. Sur la necessité d'établir un diagnostic scientifique des états inférieurs de l'intelligence. *L'Année Psychologique,* 1905, *11,* 163–190. (a)

Binet, A., & Simon, T. Méthodes nouvelles pour le diagnostic du niveau intellectuel des anormaux. *L'Année Psychologique,* 1905, *11,* 191–244. (b)

Binet, A., & Simon, T. Application des méthodes nouvelles au diagnostic du niveau intellectuel chez des enfants normaux et anormaux d'hospice et d'école primaire. *L'Année Psychologique,* 1905, *11,* 245–336. (c)

Binet, A., & Simon, T. Le développement de l'intelligence chez les enfants. *L'Année Psychologique,* 1908, *14,* 1–94.

Boring, E. G. *A history of experimental psychology.* New York: Century, 1929. (Rev. ed., 1950)

Borstelmann, L. J. Children before psychology: Ideas about children from Antiquity to the late 1800s. (Chapter 1)

Bott, H. McM. *Personality development in young children.* Toronto: University of Toronto Press, 1934.

Bowlby, J. The nature of the child's tie to his mother. *International Journal of Psychoanalysis,* 1958, *39,* 350–373.

Bowlby, J. *Attachment and loss. Vol. 1: Attachment.* New York: Basic Books, 1969.

Breuer, J., & Freud, S. *Studies in hysteria* (A. A. Brill, Trans.). New York: Nervous and Mental Disease Publishing Co., 1936. (Originally published, 1895.)

Bridges, K. M. B. Emotional development in early infancy. *Child Development,* 1932, *3,* 324–341.

Bruner, J. S. *The process of education.* Cambridge, Mass.: Harvard University Press, 1960.

Bühler, C. Die ersten sozialen Verhaltungsweisen des Kindes. In C. Bühler, H. Hetzer, & B. Tudor-Hart, *Soziologische und psychologische Studien über das erste Lebensjahr.* Jena: Fischer, 1927.

Bühler, C. Personality types based on experiments with children. *Proceedings and Papers of the 9th International Congress of Psychology,* 1929, 100–112.

Bühler, C. The social behavior of the child. In C. Murchison (Ed.), *A handbook of child psychology.* Worcester, Mass.: Clark University Press, 1931.

Bühler, C. The social behavior of children. In C. Murchison (Ed.), *A handbook of child psychology* (2nd ed.). Worcester, Mass.: Clark University Press, 1933.

Bühler, C., & Hetzer, H. Zur Geschichte der Kinderpsychologie. In E. Brunswik, C. Bühler, H. Hetzer, L. Kardos, J. Krug, & A. Willwoll (Eds.), *Beitrage zue Problemgeschichte der Psychologie: Festschrift zu Karl Bühlers 50*

Geburtstage. Jena: Fischer, 1929.

Bühler, K. *Die geistige Entwicklung des Kindes*. Jena: Fischer, 1918.

Burt, C. A young girl's diary. *British Journal of Psychology: Medical Section*, 1920–1921, *1*, 353–357.

Cairns, R. B., & Ornstein, P. A. Developmental psychology. In E. Hearst (Ed.), *The first century of experimental psychology*. Hillsdale, N.J.: Erlbaum, 1979.

Carmichael, L. A further study of the development of behavior in vertebrates experimentally removed from the influence of external stimulation. *Psychological Review*, 1927, *34*, 34–47.

Carmichael, L. Origin and prenatal growth of behavior. In C. Murchison (Ed.), *A handbook of child psychology* (2nd ed.). Worcester, Mass.: Clark University Press, 1933.

Carmichael, L. (Ed.). *Manual of child psychology*. New York: Wiley, 1946.

Carroll, J. B. On the theory-practice interface in the measurement of intellectual abilities. In P. Suppes (Ed.), *Impact of research on education: Some case studies*. Washington, D.C.: National Academy of Education, 1978.

Carroll, J. B., & Horn, J. L. On the scientific basis of ability testing. *American Psychologist*, 1981, *36*, 1012–1020.

Carus, F. A. *Psychologie* (Q. Te.: *Specialpsychologie*). Leipzig: Barth & Kummer, 1808.

Cattell, J. Mental tests and measurements. *Mind*, 1890, *15*, 373–381.

Challman, R. C. Factors influencing friendships among preschool children. *Child Development*, 1932, *3*, 146–158.

Claparède, E. [Autobiography.] In C. Murchison (Ed.), *A history of psychology in autobiography* (Vol. 1). Worcester, Mass.: Clark University Press, 1930.

Cohen, D. *J. B. Watson: The founder of behaviourism. A biography*. London: Routledge & Kegan Paul, 1979.

Compayré, G. *L'évolution intellectuelle et morale de l'enfant*. Paris: Hachette, 1893. [*The intellectual and moral development of the child*. 2 vols. M. E. Wilson, Trans. New York: Appleton, 1896, 1902.]

Cottrell, L. S. The analysis of situational fields in social psychology. *American Sociological Review*, 1942, *7*, 370–382.

Cottrell, L. S., Jr. Interpersonal interaction and the development of the self. In D. A. Goslin (Ed.), *Handbook of socialization theory and research*.

Chicago: Rand McNally, 1969.

Cronbach, L. J. The two disciplines of scientific psychology. *American Psychologist*, 1957, *12*, 671–784.

Crook, J. H. Social organization and the environment. Aspects of contemporary social ethology. *Animal Behaviour*, 1970, *18*, 197–209.

Dahlstrom, W. G. The development of psychological testing. In G. A. Kimble & K. Schlesinger (Eds.), *A history of modern psychology*. New York: Wiley, 1982.

Darwin, C. Biographical sketch of an infant. *Mind*, 1877, *2*, 285–294.

Dawkins, R. *The selfish gene*. Oxford: Oxford University Press, 1976.

de Beer, G. *Embryos and ancestors* (3rd ed.). London: Oxford University Press, 1958.

Debesse, M. L'enfance dans l'histoire de la psychologie. In H. Gratiot-Alphandéry & R. Zazzo (Eds.), *Traité de psychologie de l'enfant* (Vol. 1: *Histoire et généralités*). Paris: Presses universitaires de France, 1970.

Dollard, J., Miller, N. E., Doob, L. W., Mowrer, O. H., Sears, R. R. (with Ford, C. S., Hovland, C. I., & Sollenberger, R. T.). *Frustration and aggresssion*. New Haven, Conn.: Yale University Press, 1939.

Drachman, D. B., & Coulombre, A. J. Experimental clubfoot and arthrogryposis multiplex congenita. *Lancet*, 1962, *283*, 523–526.

Drummond, W. B. *An introduction to child study*. London: Arnold, 1907.

Ebbinghaus, H. Über eine neue Methode zur Prüfung geistiger Fähigkeiten und ihre Anwedung bei Schulkindern. *Zeitschrift für angewandte Psychologie*, 1897, *13*, 401–459.

Estes, W. Kurt Lewin. In W. Estes, S. Koch, K. MacCorquodale, P. Meehl, C. Mueller, Jr., W. Schoenfeld, & W. Verplanck (Eds.), *Modern learning theory*. New York: Appleton-Century-Crofts, 1954.

Estes, W. K., & Skinner, B. F. Some quantitative properties of anxiety. *Journal of Experimental Psychology*, 1941, *29*, 390–400.

Féré, C. Note sur les modifications de la résistance électrique sous l'influence des excitations sensorielles et des émotions. *Comptes Rendus de la Société de Biologie*, 1888, *40*, 217–219.

Flavell, J. H. *The developmental psychology of Jean Piaget*. Princeton, N.J.: Van Nostrand, 1963.

Frank, L. The problem of child development. *Child Development*, 1935, *6*, 7–18.

Franz, S. I. Review of *L'Année Psychologique*, 1898, Vol. 4. [*Psychological Review*, 1898, *5*,

665. Specifically the series of articles by A. Binet and N. Vaschide.]

Freud, A. Psychoanalysis of the child. In C. Murchison (Ed.), *A handbook of child psychology.* Worcester, Mass.: Clark University Press, 1931.

Freud, S. The origin and development of psychoanalysis. *American Journal of Psychology,* 1910, *21,* 181–218.

Freud, S. Psychoanalysis: Fundamentals. *Encyclopaedia Britannica,* vol. 18, 1972, 721–722. [Article first appeared in the 1926 edition of *Encyclopaedia Britannica.*]

Freud, S. *Moses and monotheism.* New York: Random House, 1939.

Gadlin, H. Child discipline and the pursuit of self: An historical interpretation. In H. W. Reese & L. P. Lipsitt (Eds.), *Advances in Child Development and Behavior,* 1978, *12,* 231–265.

Galton, F. *Inquiries into human faculty and its development.* London: MacMillan, 1883.

Garvey, C., & Hogan, R. Social speech and social interaction: Egocentrism revisited. *Child Development,* 1973, *44,* 562–568.

Gesell, A. L. *Infancy and human growth.* New York: MacMillan, 1928.

Gesell, A. The developmental psychology of twins. In C. Murchison (Ed.), *A handbook of child psychology.* Worcester, Mass.: Clark University Press, 1931.

Gesell, A. Maturation and the patterning of behavior. In C. Murchison (Ed.), *A handbook of child psychology.* Worcester, Mass.: Clark University Press, 1933.

Gesell, A., & Amatruda, C. S. *Developmental diagnosis: Normal and abnormal child development.* New York: Hoeber, 1941.

Gesell, A., & Thompson, H. (assisted by C. S. Amatruda). *Infant behavior: Its genesis and growth.* New York; McGraw-Hill, 1934.

Gesell, A., & Thompson, H. *The psychology of early growth.* New York: Macmillan, 1938.

Gewirtz, J. L. A learning analysis of the effects of normal stimulation, privation, and deprivation on the acquisition of social motivation and attachment. In B. M. Foss (Ed.), *Determinants of infant behavior.* New York: Wiley, 1961.

Gewirtz, J., & Baer, D. The effect of brief social deprivation on behaviors for a social reinforcer. *Journal of Abnormal and Social Psychology,* 1958, *56,* 49–56.

Gibson, E. J. *Principles of perceptual learning and development.* New York: Appleton-Century-Crofts, 1969.

Gilbert, J. A. Researches on the mental and physical development of school children. *Studies of the Yale Psychology Laboratories,* 1894, *2,* 40–100.

Gilbert, J. A. Researches upon school children and college students. *University of Iowa Studies: Studies in Psychology,* 1897, *1,* 1–39.

Goddard, H. H. Two thousand normal children measured by the Binet measuring scale of intelligence. *Pedagogical Seminary,* 1911, *18,* 232–259.

Goodenough, F. L. The emotional behavior of young children during mental tests. *Journal of Juvenile Research,* 1929, *13,* 204–219.

Goodenough, F. L. Work of child development research centers: A survey. *Child Study,* 1929–1930, *4,* 292–302.

Goodenough, F. L. Interrelationships in the behavior of young children. *Child Development,* 1930, *1,* 29–47.

Goodenough, F. L. *Anger in young children.* Minneapolis: University of Minnesota Press, 1931.

Gottlieb, G. Dedication to W. Preyer (1841–1897). In G. Gottlieb (Ed.), *Behavioral embryology.* New York: Academic Press, 1973.

Gottlieb, G. The roles of experience in the development of behavior and the nervous system. In G. Gottlieb (Ed.), *Neural and behavioral specificity.* New York: Academic Press, 1976.

Gottlieb, G. Comparative psychology and ethology. In E. Hearst (Ed.), *The first century of experimental psychology.* Hillsdale, N.J.: Erlbaum, 1979.

Gould, S. J. *Ontogeny and phylogeny.* Cambridge: Belknap Press of Harvard University Press, 1977.

Guthrie, E. R. *The psychology of learning.* New York: Harper, 1935.

Hall, C. S., & Lindzey, G. *Theories of personality.* New York: Wiley, 1957.

Hall, G. S. The contents of children's minds. *Princeton Review,* 1883, *2,* 249–272.

Hall, G. S. The new psychology. *Andover Review,* 1885, *3,* 120–135, 239–248. (a)

Hall, G. S. New departures in education. *North American Review,* 1885, *140,* 144–152. (b)

Hall, G. S. Foreword. In W. Preyer, *The mind of the child* (Vol. 1). New York: Appleton, 1888–1889.

Hall, G. S. The contents of children's minds on entering school. *Pedagogical Seminary,* 1891, *1,* 139–173.

Hall, G. S. *Adolescence: Its psychology and its rela-*

tions to physiology, anthropology, sociology, sex, crime, religion, and education (2 vols.). New York: Appleton, 1904.

Hall, G. S. Senescence, the last half of life. New York: Appleton, 1922.

Hamilton, W. D. The genetical theory of social behavior, I, II. Journal of theoretical biology, 1964, 7, 1–52.

Harlow, H. F. The nature of love. American Psychologist, 1958, 13, 673–685.

Harlow, H. F., & Harlow, M. K. The affectional systems. In A. M. Schrier, H. F. Harlow, F. Stollnitz (Eds.), Behavior of nonhuman primates: Modern research trends (Vol. 2). New York: Academic, 1965.

Harris, W. T. Editor's preface. In G. Compayré, The intellectual and moral development of the child. New York: Appleton, 1896.

Hartshorne, H., & May, M. S. Studies in the nature of character (3 vols.). New York: Macmillan, 1928–1930.

Hearst, E. (Ed.). The first century of experimental psychology. Hillsdale, N.J.: Erlbaum, 1979.

Heinroth, O. Beiträge zur Biologie, namentlich Ethologie und Psychologie der Anatiden. Verhandlungen der IV. Internationale Ornithologisches Kongress (Berlin, 1910), 1911, 5, 589–702.

Hilgard, J. The effect of early and delayed practice on memory and motor performances studied by the method of co-twin control. Genetic Psychology Monographs, 1933, 14, 493–567.

Hinde, R. A. Animal Behaviour: A synthesis of ethology and comparative psychology (2nd ed.). New York: McGraw-Hill, 1970.

Hollingworth, H. L. Mental growth and decline: A survey of developmental psychology. New York: Appleton, 1927.

Holt, L. E. The care and feeding of children: A catechism for the use of mothers and children's nurses (8th ed., rev.). New York: Appleton, 1916. (1st ed., 1894.)

Horney, K. The neurotic personality of our time. New York: Norton, 1937.

Hull, C. L. Principles of behavior. New York: Appleton-Century-Crofts, 1943.

Hull, C. L. Essentials of behavior. New Haven: Yale University Press, 1951.

Hunt, J. McV. Intelligence and experience. New York: Ronald Press, 1961.

Hurlock, E. B. The value of praise and reproof as incentives for children. Archives of Psychology, 1924, No. 71.

Jackson, D. D. (Ed.). Communication, family, and marriage. Palo Alto, Calif.: Science & Behavior Books, 1968. (a)

Jackson, D. D. (Ed.). Therapy, communication, and change. Palo Alto, Calif.: Science & Behavior Books. 1968. (b)

Jacobs, J. Experiments on "prehension." Mind, 1887, 12, 75–79.

James, W. The principles of psychology (Vol. 1). New York: Macmillan, 1890.

James, W. Talks to teachers on psychology: And to students on some of life's ideals. New York: Holt, 1900.

Jenkins, J. J., & Paterson, D. G. (Eds.). Studies in individual differences: The search for intelligence. New York: Appleton-Century-Crofts, 1961.

Jennings, H. S. The psychology of a protozoan. American Journal of Psychology, 1898–1899, 10, 503–515.

Jennings, H. S. Behavior of the lower organisms. New York: Macmillan, 1906.

Jensen, D. D. Foreword to the reprinted edition. In H. S. Jennings, Behavior of the lower organisms. Bloomington: Indiana University Press, 1962.

Jersild, A. T. Training and growth in the development of children: A study of the relative influence of learning and maturation. Child Development Monographs (No. 10). New York: Teachers College, Columbia University, 1932.

Jersild, A. T., Markey, F. V., & Jersild, C. L. Children's fears, dreams, wishes, daydreams, likes, dislikes, pleasant and unpleasant memories: A study by the interview method of 400 children aged 5 to 12. Child Development Monographs (No. 12). New York: Teachers College, Columbia University, 1933.

Jones, E. The life and work of Sigmund Freud (Vol. 1). New York: Basic Books, 1953.

Jones, H. E. The galvanic skin reflex in infancy. Child Development, 1930, 1, 106–110.

Jones, H. E. The environment and mental development. In L. Carmichael (Ed.), Manual of child psychology (2nd ed.). New York: Wiley, 1954.

Jones, M. C. A laboratory study of fear: The case of Peter. Pedagogical Seminary, 1924, 31, 308–315.

Jones, M. C. The conditioning of children's emotions. In C. Murchison (Ed.), A handbook of child psychology. Worcester, Mass.: Clark University Press, 1931.

Jones, V. Children's morals. In C. Murchison (Ed.),

A handbook of child psychology (2nd ed.). Worcester, Mass.: Clark University Press, 1933.

Kamin, L. J. *The science and politics of I.Q.* Hillsdale, N.J.: Erlbaum, 1974.

Katz, D., & Katz, R. *Gespräche mit Kindern: Untersuchungen zur Sozialpsychologie und Pädagogik.* Berlin: Springer, 1927.

Kendler, H. H., & Kendler, T. S. Vertical and horizontal processes in problem solving. *Psychological Review,* 1962, *69,* 1–16.

Kessen, W. *The child.* New York: Wiley, 1965.

Klopfer, P. H., & Hailman, J. P. *An introduction to animal behavior: Ethology's first century.* Englewood Cliffs, N.J.: Prentice-Hall, 1967.

Kohlberg, L. Stage and sequence: The cognitive-developmental approach to socialization. In D. A. Goslin (Ed.), *Handbook of socialization theory and research.* Chicago: Rand McNally, 1969.

Krasnogorski, N. Über die Bedingungsreflexe im Kindesalter. *Jahrbuch für Kinderheilkunde und physische Erziehung,* 1909, *19*(series 3).

Kuenne, M. R. Experimental investigation of the relation of language to transposition behavior in young children. *Journal of Experimental Psychology,* 1946, *36,* 471–490.

Kuo, H. H. [A study of the language development of Chinese children.] *Chinese Journal of Psychology,* 1937, *1,* 334–364. (English abstract, 363–364.)

Kuo, Z.-Y. The genesis of the cat's response to the rat. *Journal of Comparative Psychology,* 1930, *11,* 1–35.

Kuo, Z.-Y. Studies in the physiology of the embryonic nervous system: IV. Development of acetylcholine in the chick embryo. *Journal of Neurophysiology,* 1939, *2,* 488–493.

Kuo, Z.-Y. *The dynamics of behavior development.* New York: Random House, 1967.

Lerner, R. M. *Developmental psychology: History of philosophy and philosophy of history.* Hillsdale, N.J.: Erlbaum, in press.

Lewin, K. Conflict between Aristotelian and Galilean modes of thought in psychology. *Journal of General Psychology,* 1931, *5,* 141–177. (a)

Lewin, K. Environmental forces in child behavior and development. In C. Murchison (Ed.), *A handbook of child psychology.* Worcester, Mass.: Clark University Press, 1931. (b)

Lewin, K. *A dynamic theory of personality.* New York: McGraw-Hill, 1935.

Lewin, K. Behavior and development as a function of the total situation. In L. Carmichael (Ed.), *Manual of child psychology* (2nd ed.). New York: Wiley, 1954.

Lewin, K., Dembo, T., Festinger, L., & Sears, P. Level of aspiration. In J. McV. Hunt (Ed.), *Handbook of personality and the behavior disorders.* New York: Ronald Press, 1944.

Lewin, K., Lippitt, R., & White, R. Patterns of aggressive behavior in experimentally created "social climates." *Journal of Social Psychology,* 1939, *10,* 271–299.

Lewis, M., & Brooks-Gunn, J. *Social cognition and the acquisition of self.* New York: Plenum, 1979.

Littman, R. A. Social and intellectual origins of experimental psychology. In E. Hearst (Ed.), *The first century of experimental psychology.* Hillsdale, N.J.: Erlbaum, 1979.

Loeb, J. *The mechanistic conception of life.* Cambridge, Mass.: Harvard University Press, 1964. (Originally published, 1912.)

Loomis, A. M. A technique for observing the social behavior of nursery school children. *Child Development Monographs* (No. 5). New York: Teachers College, Columbia University Press, 1931.

Lorenz, K. Z. Der Kumpan in der Umwelt des Vogels. *Journal für Ornithologie,* 1935, *83,* 137–213; 289–413.

Maher, B. A., & Maher, W. B. Psychopathology. In E. Hearst (Ed.), *The first century of experimental psychology.* Hillsdale, N. J.: Erlbaum, 1979.

Maier, S. F., Seligman, M. E. P., & Solomon, R. L. Pavlovian fear conditioning and learned helplessness. In R. Church & B. Campbell (Eds.), *Aversive conditioning and learning.* New York: Appleton-Century-Crofts, 1969.

Marquis, D. B. Can conditioned responses be established in the newborn infant? *Journal of Genetic Psychology,* 1931, *39,* 479–492.

Mason, W. A. Social ontogeny. In P. Marler & J. G. Vandenbergh (Eds.), *Social behavior and communication.* New York: Plenum Press, 1980.

Mateer, F. *Child behavior: A critical and experimental study of young children by the method of conditioned reflexes.* Boston: Badger, 1918.

Maynard Smith, J. The theory of games and the evolution of animal conflict. *Journal of Theoretical Biology,* 1974, *47,* 202–221.

McCarthy, D. Language development. In C. Murchison (Ed.), *A handbook of child psychology.* Worcester, Mass.: Clark University Press, 1931.

McCarthy, D. Language development in children. In C. Murchison (Ed.), *A handbook of child psychology* (2nd ed.). Worcester Mass.: Clark University Press, 1933.

McCarthy, D. Language development in children. In L. Carmichael (Ed.), *Manual of child psychology*. New York: Wiley, 1946.

McCarthy, D. Language development in children. In L. Carmichael (Ed.), *Manual of child psychology* (2nd ed.). New York: Wiley, 1954.

McDougall, W. An investigation of the colour sense of two infants. *British Journal of Psychology*, 1906–1908, *2*, 338–352.

McDougall, W. *An introduction to social psychology* (Rev. ed.). Boston: Luce, 1926.

McGraw, M. *Growth: A study of Jimmy and Johnny*. New York: Appleton-Century-Crofts, 1935.

McGraw, M. B. Maturation of behavior. In L. Carmichael (Ed.), *Manual of child psychology*. New York: Wiley, 1946.

McNemar, Q. A critical examination of the University of Iowa studies of environmental influences upon the IQ. *Psychological Bulletin*, 1940, *37*, 63–92.

Mead, G. H. *Mind, self and society*. Chicago: University of Chicago Press, 1934.

Miller, N. E., & Dollard, J. *Social learning and imitation*. New York: McGraw-Hill, 1941.

Miller, N. E., Sears, R. R., Mowrer, O. H., Doob, L. W., & Dollard, J. I. The frustration-aggression hypothesis. *Psychological Review*, 1941, *48*, 337–342.

Mills, W. *The nature and development of animal intelligence*. London: Unwin, 1898.

Mills, W. The nature of animal intelligence and the methods of investigating it. *Psychological Review*, 1899, *6*, 262–274.

Monroe, W. S. *Die Entwicklung des sozialen Bewusstseins der Kinder*. Berlin: Reuther & Reichard, 1899.

Morgan, C. L. *Habit and instinct*. London: Arnold, 1896.

Mowrer, O. H. Apparatus for the study and treatment of enuresis. *American Journal of Psychology*, 1938, *51*, 163–168.

Mueller, E. The maintenance of verbal exchanges between young children. *Child Development*, 1972, *43*, 930–938.

Mueller, R. H. A chapter in the history of the relationship between psychology and sociology in America: James Mark Baldwin. *Journal of the History of the Behavioral Sciences*, 1976, *12*, 240–253.

Munn, N. L. *The evolution and growth of human behavior* (2nd ed.). Boston: Houghton Mifflin, 1965.

Munroe, R. L. *Schools of psychoanalytic thought*. New York: Dryden Press, 1955.

Murchison, C. (Ed.). *A handbook of child psychology*. Worcester, Mass.: Clark University Press, 1931.

Murchison, C. (Ed.). *A handbook of child psychology* (2nd ed.). Worcester, Mass.: Clark University Press, 1933.

Murchison, C., & Langer, S. Tiedemann's observations on the development of the mental faculties of children. *Journal of Genetic Psychology*, 1927, *34*, 205–230.

Murphy, L. B. *Social behavior and child personality: An exploratory study of some roots of sympathy*. New York: Columbia University Press, 1937.

Oppenheim, R. W. Prehatching and hatching behavior: Comparative and physiological consideration. In G. Gottlieb (Ed.), *Behavioral embryology*. New York: Academic Press, 1973.

Oppenheim, R. W. Preformation and epigenesis in the origins of the nervous system and behavior: Issues, concepts, and their history. In P. P. G. Bateson & P. H. Klopfer (Eds.), *Perspectives in ethology*. (Vol. 6). New York: Plenum, 1982.

Ornstein, P. A. (Ed.). *Memory development in children*. Hillsdale, N.J.: Erlbaum, 1978.

Overton, W. F. Historical and contemporary perspectives of development. In I. Sigel & D. Brodzinsky (Eds.), *Developmental psychology*. New York: Holt, Rinehart and Winston, in press.

Ovsiankina, M. Die Wiederaufrahme von unterbrochener Handlungen. *Psychologique Forschung*, 1928, *11*, 302–379.

Paris, S. G. Coordination of means and goals in the development of mnemonic skills. In P. A. Ornstein (Ed.), *Memory development in children*. Hillsdale, N.J.: Erlbaum, 1978.

Parten, M. B. Social play among preschool children. *Journal of Abnormal and Social Psychology*, 1933, *28*, 136–147.

Parton, D. A., & Ross, A. O. Social reinforcement of children's motor behavior: A review. *Psychological Bulletin*, 1965, *64*, 65–73.

Patterson, G. R. A performance theory for coercive family interaction. In R. B. Cairns (Ed.), *The analysis of social interactions: Methods, issues, and illustrations*. Hillsdale, N.J.: Erlbaum, 1979.

Perez, B. *La psychologie de l'enfant: Les trois premières années*. Paris: Alcan, 1878. [A. M. Christie, Ed. and Trans., *The first three years of childhood*. Chicago: Marquis, 1885.]

Peterson, J. *Early conceptions and tests of intelligence*. Yonkers-on-Hudson, N.Y.: World Book, 1925.

Peterson, J. Learning in children. In C. Murchison (Ed.), *A handbook of child psychology*. Worcester, Mass.: Clark University Press, 1931.

Piaget, J. *Le langage et la pensée chez l'enfant*. Neuchâtel: Delachaux & Niestlé, 1923, 1930. [*The language and thought of the child*. New York: Harcourt, Brace, 1926, 1932. The 1932 edition is cited here.]

Piaget, J. *Le jugement et le raisonnement chez l'enfant*. Neuchâtel: Delachaux & Niestlé, 1924. [*Judgment and reasoning in the child*. New York: Harcourt, Brace, 1928.]

Piaget, J. Children's philosophies. In C. Murchison (Ed.), *A handbook of child psychology*. Worcester, Mass.: Clark University Press, 1931.

Piaget, J. [Autobiography.] In E. G. Boring et al. (Eds.), *A history of psychology in autobiography* (Vol. 4). Worcester, Mass.: Clark University Press, 1952.

Piaget, J. *Le jugement moral chez l'enfant* (4th ed.). Paris: Presses universitaires de France, 1973. (Originally published, 1932.)

Piaget, J. *Behavior and evolution*. New York: Pantheon Books, 1978.

Pressey, S. L., Janney, J. E., & Kuhlen, J. E. *Life: A psychological survey*. New York: Harper, 1939.

Preyer, W. *Die Seele des Kindes*. Leipzig: Fernan, 1882. [*The mind of the child* (2 vols.). New York: Appleton, 1888–1889.]

Preyer, W. *Specielle Physiologie des Embryo. Untersuchungen über die Lebenserscheinungen vor der Geburt*. Leipzig: Grieben, 1885.

Quetelet, A. *Sur l'homme et le développement de ses facultés, ou essai de physique sociale*. Paris: Bachelier, 1835.

Reinert, G. Prolegomena to a history of life-span developmental psychology. In P. B. Baltes & O. G. Brim (Eds.), *Life-span development and behavior* (Vol. 2). New York: Academic Press, 1979.

Rheingold, H. L. A comparative psychology of development. In H. W. Stevenson, E. K. Hess, & H. L. Rheingold (Eds.), *Early behavior: Comparative and developmental approaches*. New York: Wiley, 1967.

Romanes, G. J. *Mental evolution in animals*. New York: Appleton, 1884.

Romanes, G. J. *Mental evolution in man: Origin of human faculty*. New York: Appleton, 1889.

Ross, B. M., & Kerst, S. M. Developmental memory theories: Baldwin and Piaget. In H. W. Reese & L. P. Lipsitt (Eds.), *Advances in Child Development and Behavior*, 1978, *12*, 184–230.

Ross, D. *G. Stanley Hall: The psychologist as prophet*. Chicago: University of Chicago Press, 1972.

Rotter, J. B. *Social learning and clinical psychology*. Englewood Cliffs, N.J.: Prentice-Hall, 1954.

Schallenberger, M. E. A study of children's rights, as seen by themselves. *Pedagogical Seminary*, 1894, *3*, 87–96.

Schneirla, T. C. Studies on army ants in Panama. *Journal of Comparative Psychology*, 1933, *15*, 267–299.

Schneirla, T. C. Theoretical consideration of cyclic processes in Doryline ants. *Proceedings of the American Philosophical Society*, 1957, *101*, 106–133.

Schneirla, T. C. Behavioral development and comparative psychology. *Quarterly Review of Biology*, 1966, *41*, 283–302.

Scott, J. P. *Aggression*. Chicago: University of Chicago Press, 1958.

Sears, R. R. Experimental analysis of psychoanalytic phenomena. In J. McV. Hunt (Ed.), *Personality and the behavior disorders* (Vol. 1). New York: Ronald Press, 1944.

Sears, R. R. A theoretical framework for personality and social behavior. *American Psychologist*, 1951, *6*, 476–483.

Sears, R. R. Your ancients revisited: A history of child development. In E. M. Hetherington (Ed.), *Review of child development research* (Vol. 5). Chicago: University of Chicago Press, 1975.

Sears, R. R., Maccoby, E. E., & Levin, H. *Patterns of child rearing*. Evanston, Ill.: Row, Peterson, 1957.

Sears, R. R., Rau, L., & Alpert, R. *Identification and child rearing*. Stanford, Calif.: Stanford University Press, 1965.

Sears, R. R., Whiting, J. W. M., Nowlis, V., & Sears, P. S. Some child-rearing antecedents of aggression and dependency in young children. *Genetic Psychology Monographs*, 1953, *47*, 135–234.

Selman, R. L., & Yando, R. *Clinical-developmental psychology*. San Francisco: Jossey-Bass, 1980.

Senn, M. J. E. Insights on the child development movement in the United States. *Monographs of the Society for Research in Child Development*, 1975, *40*(Serial No. 161).

Shakow, D., & Rapaport, D. *The influence of Freud on American psychology*. New York: International Universities Press, 1964.

Sherman, M., & Key, C. B. The intelligence of

isolated mountain children. *Child Development*, 1932, *3*, 279–290.

Shinn, M. Notes on the development of a child. *University of California Publications*, 1893–1899, *1*.

Shinn, M. *Biography of a baby*. Boston: Houghton Mifflin, 1900.

Shirley, M. M. *The first two years. A study of twenty-five babies* (Vol. I. *Postural and locomotor development*). Minneapolis: University of Minnesota Press, 1931.

Shirley, M. M. *The first two years, a study of twenty-five babies* (Vol. II. *Intellectual development*). Minneapolis: University of Minnesota Press, 1933. (a)

Shirley, M. M. *The first two years, a study of twenty-five babies* (Vol. III. *Personality manifestations*). Minneapolis: University of Minnesota Press, 1933. (b)

Sigismund, B. *Kind und Welt: Vatern, Müttern und Kinderfreuden gewidmet*. Braunschweig: Vieweg, 1856.

Skeels, H. M. Adult status of children with contrasting early life experiences. *Monographs of the Society for Research in Child Development*, 1966, *31*(3, Whole No. 105).

Skeels, H. M., Updegraff, R., Wellman, B. L., & Williams, H. M. A study of environmental stimulation: An orphanage preschool project. *University of Iowa Studies in Child Welfare*, 1938, *15*(No. 4).

Skinner, B. F. *The behavior of organisms: An experimental analysis*. New York: Appleton-Century-Crofts, 1938.

Skinner, B. F. *Science and human behavior*. New York: Macmillan, 1953.

Solomon, R. L., & Wynne, L. C. Traumatic avoidance learning: Acquisition in normal dogs. *Psychological Monographs*, 1953, *67*(No. 354).

Spalding, D. A. Instinct: With original observations in young animals. *Macmillan's Magazine*, 1873, *27*, 282–293.

Spelt, D. K. Conditioned responses in the human fetus *in utero*. *Psychological Bulletin*, 1938, *35*, 712–713.

Spemann, H. *Embryonic development and induction*. New Haven, Conn.: Yale University Press, 1938.

Spencer, H. *Principles of psychology* (2 vols.). New York: Appleton, 1855.

Stern, W. *Die differentielle Psychologie in ihren methodischen Grundlagen*. Leipzig: Barth, 1911.´

Stern, W. *Psychologie der frühen Kindheit bis zum sechsten Lebensjahre*. Leipzig: Quelle & Meyer, 1914. (a)

Stern, W. *The psychological methods of testing intelligence* (F. M. Whipple, Trans.). Baltimore Md.: Warwick & York, 1914. (b)

Stevenson, H. W. Social reinforcement with children. In L. P. Lipsitt & C. C. Spiker (Eds.), *Advances in child development and behavior* (Vol. 2). New York: Academic Press, 1965.

Sullivan, H. S. Some conceptions of modern psychiatry. *Psychiatry*, 1940, *3*, 1–117.

Sullivan, H. S. *The interpersonal theory of psychiatry*. New York: Norton, 1953.

Sully, J. *Studies of childhood*. New York: Appleton, 1896.

Taine, H. Note sur l'acquisition du langage chez les enfants et dans l'espèce humaine. *Revue Philosophique*, 1876, *1*, 3–23.

Terman, L. M. Genius and stupidity. *Pedagogical Seminary*, 1906, *13*, 307–313.

Terman, L. M. *The measurement of intelligence*. Boston: Houghton Mifflin, 1916.

Terman, L. M., assisted by B. T. Baldwin, E. Bronson, J. C. De Voss, F. Fuller, F. L. Goodenough, T. L. Kelley, M. Lima, H. Marshall, A. S. Raubenheimer, G. M. Ruch, R. L. Willoughby, J. B. Wyman, & D. H. Yates. *Genetic studies of genius* (Vol. I. *Mental and physical traits of a thousand gifted children*). Stanford, Calif.: Stanford University Press, 1925.

Tetens, J. N. *Philosophische Versuche über die menschliche Natur und ihre Entwicklung*. Leipzig: Weidmanns Erben and Reich, 1777.

Thieman, T. J., & Brewer, W. F. Alfred Binet on memory for ideas. *Genetic Psychology Monographs*, 1978, *97*, 243–264.

Thomas, A., Chess, S., & Birch, H. G. *Temperament and behavior disorders in children*. New York: New York University Press, 1968.

Thomas, D. S. Some new techniques for studying social behavior. *Child Development Monographs* (No. 1). New York: Teachers College, Columbia University, 1929.

Thomas, D. S., Loomis, A. M., Arrington, R. E., with E. C. Isbell. *Observational studies of social behavior*. New Haven, Conn.: Institute for Human Relations, Yale University, 1933.

Thomas, W. I., & Thomas, D. S. *The child in America: Behavior problems and programs*. New York: Knopf, 1928.

Thorndike, E. L. Animal intelligence: An experimental study of the associative processes in animals. *Psychological Monographs*, 1898, *2*(Whole No. 8).

Thorndike, E. L. *Educational psychology: The original nature of man.* New York: Teachers College, Columbia University, 1913.

Thurstone, L. L. [Autobiography.] *History of Psychology in Autobiography,* 1952, *5,* 295–331.

Thurstone, L. L., & Peterson, R. C. Motion pictures and the social attitudes of children. In W. W. Charters (Ed.), *Motion pictures and youth.* New York: Macmillan, 1933.

Tiedemann, D. *Beobachtungen über die Entwickelung der Seelenfähigkeiten bei Kindern.* (First published in 1787. Altenburg Bonde, 1897. See C. Murchison & S. Langer, 1927.)

Tinbergen, N. *The study of instinct.* Oxford: Clarendon Press, 1951.

Tolman, E. C. *Purposive behavior in animals and men.* New York: Appleton-Century, 1932.

Tuddenham, R. D. The nature and measurement of intelligence. In L. Postman (Ed.), *Psychology in the making.* New York: Knopf, 1962.

Vigotsky, L. S. Thought and speech. *Psychiatry,* 1939, *2,* 29–54.

Vigotsky, L. S., & Luria, A. R. The function and fate of egocentric speech. *Proceedings and Papers of the 9th International Congress of Psychology,* 1929, 464–465.

Waddington, C. H. *An introduction to modern genetics.* New York: Macmillan, 1939.

Warren, H. C. Review of Binet's *L'introduction à la psychologie expérimentale. Psychological Review,* 1894, *1,* 530–531.

Washburn, R. W. A study of the smiling and laughing of infants in the first year of life. *Genetic Psychology Monographs,* 1929, *6,* 397–537.

Watson, J. B. *Behavior: An introduction to comparative psychology.* New York: Holt, 1914.

Watson, J. B. What the nursery has to say about instincts. In C. Murchison (Ed.), *Psychologies of 1925.* Worcester, Mass.: Clark University Press, 1926.

Watson, J. B. *Psychological care of infant and child.* New York: Norton, 1928.

Watson, J. B. [Autobiography.] *History of Psychology in Autobiography,* 1936, *3,* 271–281.

Watson, J. B., & Morgan, J. J. B. Emotional reactions and psychological experimentation. *American Journal of Psychology,* 1917, *28,* 163–174.

Watson, J. B., & Rayner, R. A. Conditional emotional reactions. *Journal of Experimental Psychology,* 1920, *3,* 1–14.

Werner, H. *Comparative psychology of mental development.* New York: Harper, 1940. (Rev. ed., Chicago: Follett, 1948.)

Wheeler, L. R. A comparative study of East Tennessee mountain children. *Journal of Educational Psychology,* 1942, *33,* 321–334.

White, S. H. The learning theory tradition and child psychology. In P. Mussen (Ed.), *Carmichael's manual of child psychology.* New York: Wiley, 1970.

Whiting, B. B., & Whiting, J. W. M. *Children of six cultures: A psycho-cultural analysis.* Cambridge: Harvard University Press, 1975.

Whitman, C. O. Animal behavior. In E. B. Wilson, *Biological lectures from the Marine Biological Laboratory, Wood's Hole, Massachusetts, 1898.* Boston: Ginn, 1899.

Wickens, D. D., & Wickens, C. D. A study of conditioning in the neonate. *Journal of Experimental Psychology,* 1940, *26,* 94–102.

Willard, E. Observations upon an infant during its first year by a mother. In N. de Saussure (Ed.), *Progressive education.* Boston: Ticknor, 1835.

Wilson, E. O. *Sociobiology: The new synthesis.* Cambridge: Harvard University Press, 1975.

Wolf, T. H. *Alfred Binet.* Chicago: University of Chicago Press, 1973.

Wundt, W. *Outlines of psychology* (C. H. Judd, Trans.). New York: Stechert, 1907.

Wynne, L. C., & Solomon, R. L. Traumatic avoidance learning: Acquisition and extinction in dogs deprived of normal peripheral autonomic function. *Genetic Psychology Monographs,* 1955, *52,* 241–284.

Yarrow, M. R., Campbell, J. D., & Burton, R. V. *Child rearing: An inquiry into research and methods.* San Francisco: Jossey-Bass, 1968.

Young, K. The history of mental testing. *Pedagogical Seminary,* 1924, *31,* 1–48.

Zeigarnik, B. Über das Behalten von erledigten und unerledigten Handlungen. *Psychologie Forschung,* 1927, *9,* 1–85.

PIAGET'S THEORY* | 3

JEAN PIAGET†

CHAPTER CONTENTS

The following theory of development, which is particularly concerned with the development of cognitive functions, is impossible to understand if one does not begin by analyzing in detail the biological presuppositions from which it stems and the epistemological consequences in which it ends. Indeed, the fundamental postulate that is the basis of the ideas summarized here is that the same problems and the same types of explanations can be found in the three following processes:

a. The adaptation of an organism to its environment during its growth, together with the interactions and autoregulations that characterize the development of the "epigenetic system." (Epigenesis in its embryological sense is always determined both internally and externally.)

b. The adaptation of intelligence in the course of the construction of its own structures, which depends as much on progressive internal coordinations as on information acquired through experience.

c. The establishment of cognitive or, more generally, epistemological relations, which consist neither of a simple copy of external objects nor of a mere unfolding of structures preformed inside the subject, but rather involve a set of structures progressively constructed by continuous interaction between the subject and the external world.

We begin with the last point, on which our theory is furthest removed both from the ideas of the majority of psychologists and from "common sense."

THE RELATION BETWEEN SUBJECT AND OBJECT

1. In the common view, the external world is entirely separate from the subject, although it encloses the subject's own body. Any objective knowledge, then, appears to be simply the result of a set of perceptive recordings, motor associations, verbal descriptions, and the like, which all participate in producing a sort of figurative copy or "functional copy" (in Hull's terminology) of objects and the connections between them. The only function of intelligence is systematically to file, correct, and so on these various sets of information; in this process, the more faithful the critical copies, the more consistent the final system will be. In such an empiricist prospect, the content of intelligence comes from outside, and the coordinations that organize it are only the consequences of language and symbolic instruments.

*[Professor Piaget wrote this chapter in French and Dr. Guy Gellerier of the University of Geneva and Professor Jonas Langer of the University of California at Berkeley translated it, with kind assistance from Professors Bärbel Inhelder and Hermione Sinclair, into English. It first appeared in *Carmichael's Manual of Child Psychology* (1970). The editors of *Mussen's Handbook of Child Psychology* are proud to reproduce here (with only a few minor, mechanical changes) this chapter as published originally in *Carmichael's Manual.*]

†The present chapter is, in part, the expansion of an article on my conceptions of development published in *Journal International de Psychologie*, a summary of previous publications, but it also takes into account recent or still unpublished work by the author or his collaborators and colleagues. As a matter of fact, "Piaget's theory" is not completed at this date and the author of these pages has always considered himself one of the chief "revisionists of Piaget." (Author's note)

But this passive interpretation of the act of knowledge is in fact contradicted at all levels of development and, particularly, at the sensorimotor and prelinguistic levels of cognitive adaptation and intelligence. Actually, in order to know objects, the subject must act upon them, and therefore transform them: he must displace, connect, combine, take apart, and reassemble them.

From the most elementary sensorimotor actions (such as pushing and pulling) to the most sophisticated intellectual operations, which are interiorized actions, carried out mentally (e.g., joining together, putting in order, putting into one-to-one correspondence), knowledge is constantly linked with actions or operations, that is, with *transformations*.

Hence the limit between subject and objects is in no way determined beforehand, and, what is more important, it is not stable. Indeed, in every action the subject and the objects are fused. The subject needs objective information to become aware of his own actions, of course, but he also needs many subjective components. Without long practice or the construction of refined instruments of analysis and coordination, it will be impossible for him to know what belongs to the object, what belongs to himself as an active subject, and what belongs to the action itself taken as the transformation of an initial state into a final one. Knowledge, then, at its origin, neither arises from objects nor from the subject, but from interactions—at first inextricable—between the subject and those objects.

Even these primitive interactions are so close-knit and inextricable that, as J. M. Baldwin noted, the mental attitudes of the infant are probably "adualistical." This means they lack any differentiation between an external world, which would be composed of objects independent of the subject, and an internal or subjective world.

Therefore the problem of knowledge, the so-called epistemological problem, cannot be considered separately from the problem of the development of intelligence. It reduces to analyzing how the subject becomes progressively able to know objects adequately, that is, how he becomes capable of objectivity. Indeed, objectivity is in no way an initial property, as the empiricists would have it, and its conquest involves a series of successive constructs which approximates it more and more closely.

2. This leads us to a second idea central to the theory, that of *construction,* which is the natural consequence of the interactions we have just mentioned. Since objective knowledge is not acquired by a mere recording of external information but has its origin in interactions between the subject and ob-

jects, it necessarily implies two types of activity— on the one hand, the coordination of actions themselves, and on the other, the introduction of interrelations between the objects. These two activities are interdependent because it is only through action that these relations originate. It follows that objective knowledge is always subordinate to certain structures of action. But those structures are the result of a *construction* and are not given in the objects, since they are dependent on action, nor in the subject, since the subject must learn how to coordinate his actions (which are not generally hereditarily programmed except in the case of reflexes or instincts).

An early example of these constructions (which begin as early as the first year) is the one that enables the 9- to 12-month-old child to discover the permanence of objects, initially relying on their position in his perceptual field, and later independent of any actual perception. During the first months of existence, there are no permanent objects, but only perceptual pictures that appear, dissolve, and sometimes reappear. The "permanence" of an object begins with the action of looking for it when it has disappeared at a certain point A of the visual field (e.g., if a part of the object remains visible, or if it makes a bump under a cloth). But, when the object later disappears at B, it often happens that the child will look for it again at A. This very instructive behavior supplies evidence for the existence of the primitive interactions between the subject and the object that we mentioned earlier (¶1). At this stage, the child still believes that objects depend on this action and that, where an action has succeeded a first time, it must succeed again. One real example is an 11-month-old child who was playing with a ball. He had previously retrieved it from under an armchair when it had rolled there before. A moment later, the ball went under a low sofa. He could not find it under this sofa, so he came back to the other part of the room and looked for it under the armchair, where this course of action had already been successful.

For the scheme* of a permanent object that does not depend on the subject's own actions to become

---

*Throughout the term *scheme* (plural, *schemes*) is used to refer to *operational* activities, whereas *schema* (plural, *schemata*) refers to the figurative aspects of thought—attempts to represent reality without attempting to transform it (imagery, perception, and memory). Later in this paper the author says, ". . . images . . . , however schematic, are not schemes. We shall therefore use the term schemata to designate them. A schema is a simplified image (e.g., the map of a town), whereas a scheme represents what can be repeated and generalized in an action (for example, the scheme is what is common in the actions of 'pushing' an object with a stick or any other instrument)."

established, a new structure has to be constructed. This is the structure of the ''group of translations'' in the geometrical sense: (a) the translation $AB + BC = AC$; (b) the translations $AB + BA = O$; (c) $AB + O = AB$; (d) $AC + CD = AB + BD$. The psychological equivalent of this group is the possibility of behaviors that involve returning to an initial position, or detouring around an obstacle (a and d). As soon as this organization is achieved—and it is not at all given at the beginning of development but must be constructed by a succession of new coordinations— an objective structuration of the movements of the object and of those of the subject's own body becomes possible. The object becomes an independent entity, whose position can be traced as a function of its translations and successive positions. At this juncture the subject's body, instead of being considered the center of the world, becomes an object like any other, the translations and positions of which are correlative to those of the objects themselves.

The group of translations is an instance of the construction of a structure, attributable simultaneously to progressive coordination of the subject's actions and to information provided by physical experience, which finally constitutes a fundamental instrument for the organization of the external world. It is also a cognitive instrument so important that it contributes to the veritable ''Copernican revolution'' babies accomplish in 12 to 18 months. Whereas before he had evolved this new structure the child would consider himself (unconsciously) the motionless center of the universe, he becomes, because of this organization of permanent objects and space (which entails moreover a parallel organization of temporal sequences and causality), only one particular member of the set of the other mobile objects that compose his universe.

3. We can now see that even in the study of the infant at sensorimotor levels it is not possible to follow a psychogenetic line of research without evolving an implicit epistemology, which is also genetic, but which raises all the main issues in the theory of knowledge. Thus the construction of the group of translations obviously involves physical experience and empirical information. But it also involves more, since it also depends on the coordinations of the subject's action. These coordinations are not a product of experience only, but are also controlled by factors such as maturation and voluntary exercise, and, what is more important, by continuous and active autoregulation. The main point in a theory of development is not to neglect the activities of the subject, in the epistemological sense of the term. This is even more essential in this latter sense

because the epistemological sense has a deep biological significance. The living organism itself is not a mere mirror image of the properties of its environment. It evolves a *structure* that is constructed step by step in the course of epigenesis and that is not entirely preformed.

What is already true for the sensorimotor stage appears again in all stages of development and in scientific thought itself but at levels in which the primitive actions have been transformed into *operations*. These operations are interiorized actions (e.g., addition, which can be performed either physically or mentally) that are reversible (addition acquires an inverse in subtraction) and constitute set-theoretical structures (such as the logical additive ''grouping'' or algebraic groups).

A striking instance of these operational structurations dependent on the subject's activity, which often occurs even before an experimental method has been evolved, is *atomism*, invented by the Greeks long before it could be justified experimentally. The same process can be observed in the child between 4 to 5 and 11 to 12 years of age in a situation where it is obvious that experience is not sufficient to explain the emergence of the structure and that its construction implies an additive composition dependent on the activities of the subject. The experiment involves the dissolution of lumps of sugar in a glass of water. The child can be questioned about the conservation of the matter dissolved and about the conservation of its weight and volume. Before age 7 to 8 the dissolved sugar is presumed destroyed and its taste vanished. Around this age sugar is considered as preserving its substance in the form of very small and invisible grains, but it has neither weight nor volume. At age 9 to 10 each grain keeps its weight and the sum of all these elementary weights is equivalent to the weight of the sugar itself before dissolution. At age 11 to 12 this applies to volume (the child predicts that after the sugar has melted, the level of the water in' the container will remain at its same initial height).

We can now see that this spontaneous atomism, although it is suggested by the visible grains becoming gradually smaller during their dissolution, goes far beyond what can be seen by the subject and involves a step-by-step construction correlative to that of additive operations. We thus have a new instance of the origin of knowledge lying neither in the object alone nor in the subject, but rather in an inextricable interaction between both of them, such that what is given physically is integrated in a logicomathematical structure involving the coordination of the subject's actions. The decomposition of a whole into its parts (invisible here) and the recomposition of these parts into a whole are in fact the result of logical or logicomathematical constructions and not only of physical experiments. The whole considered here is not a perceptual "gestalt" (whose character is precisely that of *non*additive composition, as Köhler rightly insisted) but a sum (additive), and as such it is produced by operations and not by observations.

4. There can be no theoretical discontinuity between thought as it appears in children and adult scientific thinking; this is the reason for our extention of developmental psychology to genetic epistemology. This is particularly clear in the field of logicomathematical structures considered in themselves and not (as in ¶2 and ¶3) as instruments for the structuration of physical data. These structures essentially involve relations of inclusion, order, and correspondence. Such relations are certainly of biological origin, for they already exist in the genetic (DNA) programming of embryological development as well as in the physiological organization of the mature organism before they appear and are reconstructed at the different levels of behavior itself. They then become fundamental structures of behavior and of intelligence in its very early development before they appear in the field of spontaneous thought and later of reflection. They provide the foundations of these progressively more abstract axiomatizations we call logic and mathematics. Indeed, if logic and mathematics are so-called "abstract" sciences, the psychologist must ask: Abstracted from what? We have seen their origin is not in objects alone. It lies, in small part only, in language, but language itself is a construct of intelligence. Chomsky even ascribes it to innate intellectual structures. Therefore the origin of these logicomathematical structures should be sought in the activities of the subject, that is, in the most general forms of coordinations of his actions, and, finally, in his organic structures themselves. This is the reason why there are fundamental relations among the biological theory of adaptation by self-regulation, developmental psychology, and genetic epistemology. This relation is so fundamental that if it is overlooked, no general theory of the development of intelligence can be established.

ASSIMILATION AND ACCOMMODATION

5. The psychological meaning of our previous points (¶1 to 4) is that the fundamental psychogenetic connections generated in the course of development cannot be considered as reducible to empirical "associations"; rather, they consist of *assimilations*, both in the biological and intellectual sense.

From a biological point of view, assimilation is the integration of external elements into evolving or completed structures of an organism. In its usual connotation, the assimilation of food consists of a chemical transformation that incorporates it into the substance of the organism. Chlorophyllian assimilation consists of the integration of radiation energy in the metabolic cycle of a plant. Waddington's "genetic assimilation" consists of a hereditary fixation by selection on phenotypes (phenotypic variations being regarded, in this case, as the genetic system's "answer" to stresses produced by the environment). Thus all the organism's reactions involve an assimilation process which can be represented in symbolic form as follows:

$$(T + I) \rightarrow AT + E \qquad (1)$$

where T is a structure, I the integrated substances or energies, E the eliminated substances or energies, and A a coefficient > 1 expressing the strengthening of this structure in the form of an increase of material or of efficiency in operation.* Put in this form it becomes obvious that the general concept of assimilation also applies to behavior and not only to organic life. Indeed, no behavior, even if it is new to the individual, constitutes an absolute beginning. It is always grafted onto previous schemes and therefore amounts to assimilating new elements to already constructed structures (innate, as reflexes are, or previously acquired). Even Harlow's "stimulus hunger" cannot be reduced simply to subordination to the environment but must rather be interpreted as a search for "functional input" (*"éléments fonctionnels"*) that can be assimilated to the schemes or structures actually providing the responses.

At this point it is appropriate to note how inadequate the well-known "stimulus-response" theory appears, in this context, as a general formulation of behavior. It is obvious that a stimulus can elicit a response only if the organism is first sensitized to this stimulus (or possesses the necessary reactive

---

*For example, take T to be an already established classification on a set of objects, O, which divides it into two distinct subclasses. I is a set of new objects that are added to the original ones and to which the classification T must be extended. When this is done (I has been assimilated to T), it turns out that there are say two new subclasses (the whole structure is now AT) and some properties of the new objects I (e.g., the number of elements in I, or their shape, size or color) have been neglected in the process. We now have $T + I \rightarrow AT + E$, where T = the two original subclasses, I = the new elements, AT = the four subclasses, and E = the irrelevant properties of the new elements, that is, the properties which are not used as criteria for classifying in this specific instance.

"competence" as Waddington characterizes genetic sensitization to specific inducers).

When we say an organism or a subject is sensitized to a stimulus and able to make a response to it, we imply it already possesses a scheme or a structure to which this stimulus is assimilated (in the sense of incorporated or integrated, as defined previously). This scheme consists precisely of a capacity to respond. Hence the original stimulus-response scheme should not have been written in the unilateral $S \rightarrow R$ form, but in the form:

$$S \rightleftarrows R \text{ or } S \rightarrow (AT) \rightarrow R \qquad (2)$$

where AT is the assimilation of the stimulus S to the structure T.

We thus return to the equation $T + I \rightarrow AT + E$ where, in this case, T is the structure, I the stimulus, AT the result of the assimilation of I to T, that is the response to the stimulus, and E is whatever in the stimulus situation is excluded in the structure.

6. If assimilation alone were involved in development, there would be no variations in the child's structures. Therefore he would not acquire new content and would not develop further. Assimilation is necessary in that it assures the continuity of structures and the integration of new elements to these structures. Without it an organism would be in a similar situation to that of chemical compounds, A, B, which, in interaction, give rise to new compounds C and D. (The equation would then be $A + B \rightarrow C + D$ and not $T \rightarrow AT$).

Biological assimilation itself, however, is never present without its counterpart, accommodation. During its embryological development, for instance, a phenotype assimilates the substances necessary to the conservation of its structures as specified by its genotype. But, depending on whether these substances are plentiful or rare or whether the usual substances are replaced by other slightly different ones, nonhereditary variations (often called "accommodates") such as changes in shape or height may occur. These variations are specific to some external conditions. Similarly, in the field of behavior we shall call accommodation any modification of assimilatory scheme or structure by the elements it assimilates. For example, the infant who assimilates his thumb to the sucking schema will, when sucking his thumb make different movements from those he uses in suckling his mother's breast. Similarly, an 8-year-old who is assimilating the dissolution of sugar in water to the notion that substance is conserved must make accommodations to invisible particles different from those he would make if they were still visible.

Hence cognitive adaptation, like its biological counterpart, consists of an equilibrium between assimilation and accommodation. As has just been shown, there is no assimilation without accommodation. But we must strongly emphasize the fact that accommodation does not exist without simultaneous assimilation either. From a biological point of view, this fact is verified by the existence of what modern geneticists call "reaction norms"—a genotype may offer a more or less broad range of possible accommodations, but all of them are within a certain statistically defined "norm." In the same way, cognitively speaking, the subject is capable of various accommodations, but only within certain limits imposed by the necessity of preserving the corresponding assimilatory structure. In Equation 1 the term A in AT specifies precisely this limitation on accommodations.

The concept of "association," which the various forms of associationism from Hume to Pavlov and Hull have used and abused, has thus only been obtained by artificially isolating one part of the general process defined by the equilibrium between assimilation and accommodation. Pavlov's dog is said to associate a sound to food, which elicits its salivation reflex. If, however, the sound is never again followed by food, the conditioned response, or temporary link, will disappear; it has no intrinsic stability. The conditioning persists as a function of the need for food, that is, it persists only if it is part of an assimilatory scheme and its satisfaction, hence of a certain accommodation to the situation. In fact, an "association" is always accompanied by an assimilation to previous structures, and this is a first factor that must not be overlooked. On the other hand, insofar as the "association" incorporates some new information, this represents an active accommodation and not a mere passive recording. This accommodatory activity, which is dependent on the assimilation scheme, is a second necessary factor that must not be neglected.

7. If accommodation and assimilation are present in all activity, their ratio may vary, and only the more or less stable equilibrium which may exist between them (though it is always mobile) characterizes a complete act of intelligence.

When assimilation *outweighs* accommodation (i.e., when the characteristics of the object are not taken into account except insofar as they are consitent with the subject's momentary interests) thought evolves in an egocentric or even autistic direction. The most common form of this situation in the play of the child is the "symbolic games" or fiction games, in which objects at his command are used only to represent what is imagined.* This form of game which is most frequent at the beginning of representation (between 1½ and 3 years of age), then evolves toward constructive games in which accommodation to objects becomes more and more precise until there is no longer any difference between play and spontaneous cognitive or instrumental activities.

Conversely, when accommodation prevails over assimilation to the point where it faithfully reproduces the forms and movements of the objects or persons which are its models at that time, representation (and the sensorimotor behaviors which are its precursors and which also give rise to exercise games that develop much earlier than symbolic games) evolves in the direction of imitation. Imitation through action, an accommodation to models that are present, gradually extends to deferred imitation and finally to interiorized imitation. In this last form it constitutes the origin of mental imagery and of the figurative as opposed to the operative aspects of thought.

But as long as assimilation and accommodation are in equilibrium (i.e., insofar as assimilation is still subordinate to the properties of the objects, or, in other words, subordinate to the situation with the accommodations it entails; and accommodation itself is subordinate to the already existing structures to which the situation must be assimilated), we can speak of cognitive behavior as opposed to play, im-

itation, or mental imagery, and we are back in the proper domain of intelligence. But this fundamental equilibrium between assimilation and accommodation is more or less difficult to attain and to maintain depending on the level of intellectual development and the new problems encountered. However, such an equilibrium exists at all levels, in the early development of intelligence in the child as well as in scientific thought.

It is obvious that any physical or biological theory assimilates objective phenomena to a restricted number of models that are not drawn exclusively from these phenomena. These models involve in addition a certain number of logicomathematical coordinations that are the operational activities of the subject himself. It would be very superficial to reduce these coordinations to a mere "language" (though this is the position of logical positivism) because, properly speaking, they are an instrument for structuration. For example, Poincaré narrowly missed discovering relativity because he thought there was no difference between expressing (or translating) phenomena in the "language" of Euclidian or of Riemannian geometry. Einstein was able to construct his theory by using Riemannian space as an instrument of *structuration*, to "understand" the relations between space, speed, and time. If physics proceeds by assimilating reality to logicomathematical models, then it must unceasingly accommodate them to new experimental results. It cannot dispense with accommodation because its models would then remain subjective and arbitrary. However, every new accommodation is conditioned by existing assimilations. The significance of an experiment does not derive from a mere perceptive recording (the "*Protokollsätze*" of the first "logical empiricists"); it cannot be dissociated from an *interpretation*.

8. In the development of intelligence in the child, there are many types of equilibrium between assimilation and accommodation that vary with the levels of development and the problems to be solved. At sensorimotor levels (before 1½ to 2 years of age) these are only practical problems involving immediate space, and as early as the second year, sensorimotor intelligence reaches a remarkable state of equilibrium (e.g., instrumental behaviors, group of displacements; see ¶2). But this equilibrium is difficult to attain because, during the first months, the infant's universe is centered on his own body and actions, and because the distortions owing to assimilation are not yet balanced by adequate accommodations.

---

*The categories of play defined by Piaget (in *Play, Dreams and Imitation*, 1951, for example) are the following:

a. *Exercise Games*. These consist of any behavior without new structuration but with a new functional finality. For example, the repetition of an action such as swinging an object, if its aim is to understand or to practice the movement, is *not* a game. But the same behavior, if its aim is functional pleasure, pleasure in the activity in itself, or the pleasure of "causing" some phenomenon, becomes a game. Examples of this are the vocalizatons of infants and the games of adults with a new car, radio, etc.

b. *Symbolic games*. These consist of behaviors with a new structuration, that of representing realities that are out of the present perceptual field. Examples are the fiction games where the child enacts a meal with pebbles standing for bread, grass for vegetables, etc. The symbols used here are individual and specific to each child.

c. *Rule Games*. These are behaviors with a new structuration involving the intervention of more than one person. The rules of this new structure are defined by social interaction. This type of game ranges over the whole scale of activities, starting with simple sensorimotor games with set rules (the many varieties of marble games, for instance) and ending with abstract games like chess. The symbols here are stabilized by convention and can become purely arbitrary in the more abstract games. That is, they bear no more relation (analogy) with what they represent. (Translator's note)

The beginning of thought creates multiple problems of representation (which must extend to distant space and can no longer be restricted to near space) as well as the problem of adaptation no longer measured by practical success alone; thus intelligence goes through a new phase of assimilatory distortion. This is because objects and events are assimilated to the subject's own action and viewpoint and possible accommodations still consist only of fixations on figural aspects of reality (hence on states as opposed to transformations). For these two reasons—egocentric assimilation and incomplete accommodation—equilibrium is not reached. On the other hand, from the age of 7 to 8 the emergence of reversible operations ensures a stable harmony between assimilation and accommodation since both can now act on transformations as well as on states.

Generally speaking, the progressive equilibrium between assimilation and accommodation is an instance of a fundamental process in cognitive development which can be expressed in terms of centration and decentration. The systematically distorting assimilations of sensorimotor or initial representative stages, which distort because they are not accompanied by adequate accommodations, mean that the subject remains centered on his own actions and his own viewpoint. On the other hand, the gradually emerging equilibrium between assimilation and accommodation is the result of successive decentrations, which make it possible for the subject to take the points of view of other subjects or objects themselves. We formerly described this process merely in terms of egocentrism and socialization. But it is far more general and more fundamental to knowledge in all its forms. For cognitive progress is not only assimilation of information; it entails a systematic decentration process which is a necessary condition of objectivity itself.

THE THEORY OF STAGES

9. We have seen that there exist structures which belong only to the subject (¶1), that they are built (¶2), and that this is a step-by-step process (¶7). We must therefore conclude there exist stages of development. Even authors who agree with this idea may use different criteria and interpretations of stage development. It therefore becomes a problem that requires discussion in its own right. The Freudian stages, for instance, are only distinct from each other in that they differ in one dominant character (oral, anal, etc.) but this character is also present in the previous—or following—stages, so that its "domi-

nance" may well remain arbitrary. Gesell's stages are based on the hypothesis of the quasi-exclusive role of maturation, so that they guarantee a constant order of succession but may neglect the factor of progressive construction. To characterize the stages of cognitive development we therefore need to integrate two necessary conditions without introducing any contradictions. These conditions for stages are (a) that they must be defined to guarantee a constant order of succession, and (b) that the definition allow for progressive construction without entailing total preformation. These two conditions are necessary because knowledge obviously involves learning by experience, which means an external contribution in addition to that involving internal structures, and the structures seem to evolve in a way that is not entirely predetermined.

The problem of stages in developmental psychology is analogous to that of stages in embryogenesis. The question that arises in the field is also that of making allowance for both genetic preformation and an eventual "epigenesis" in the sense of construction by interactions between the genome and the environment. It is for this reason that Waddington introduces the concept of "epigenetic system" and also a distinction between the genotype and the "epigenotype." The main characteristics of such an epigenetic development are not only the well-known and obvious ones of succession in sequential order and of progressive integration (segmentation followed by determination controlled by specific "competence" and finally "reintegration") but also some less obvious ones pointed out by Waddington. These are the existence of "creodes," or necessary developmental sequences, each with its own "time tally," or schedule, and the intervention of a sort of evolutionary regulation, or "homeorhesis." Homeorhesis acts in such a way that if an external influence causes the developing organism to deviate from one of its creodes, there ensues a homeorhetical reaction, which tends to channel it back to the normal sequence or, if this fails, switches it to a new creode as similar as possible to the original one.

Each of the preceding characteristics can be observed in cognitive development if we carefully differentiate the construction of the structures themselves and the acquisition of specific procedures through learning (e.g., learning to read at one age rather than another). The question will naturally be whether development can be reduced to an addition of procedures learned one by one or whether learning itself depends on developmental laws that are autonomous. This question can only be answered experimentally, but we shall discuss it further in the section entitled. *The Relations Between Development and Learning.* Whatever the answer is, it remains possible to distinguish between major structures, such as the operational "grouping," and particular acquisitions. It then becomes proper to inquire whether the construction of these major structures can be defined in terms of stages. If this were so, it would then become possible to determine their relations to developmental laws of learning.

10. If we restrict ourselves to major structures, it is strikingly obvious that cognitive stages have a sequential property, that is, they appear in a fixed order of succession because each one of them is necessary for the formation of the following one.

If we now consider only the principal periods of development, one can enumerate three of them:

a. A sensorimotor period lasts until approximately 1½ years of age with a first subperiod of centration on the subject's own body (lasting about 7 to 9 months) followed by a second one of objectivization and spatialization of the schemes of practical intelligence.

b. A period of representative intelligence leads to concrete operations (classes, relations, and numbers bound to objects) with a first preoperational subperiod (there is no reversibility or conservation, but the beginnings of directional functions and qualitative identities), which begins around 1½ to 2 years of age with the formation of semiotic processes such as language and mental imagery. This is followed by a second subperiod (at about 7 to 8 years) characterized by the beginnings of operational groupings in their various concrete forms and with their various types of conservation.

c. Finally, there is the period of propositional or formal operations. This also begins with a subperiod of organization (11 to 13 years old) and is followed by a subperiod of achievement of the general combinatory and the group INRC of the two kinds of reversibilities. (See ¶ 28 and the accompanying footnote.)

If we now consider the preceding sequence, it is easy to observe that each one of these periods or subperiods is necessary to the constitution of its successor. As a first example, why do language and the semiotic function emerge only at the end of a long sensorimotor period where the only significates are indexes and signals, and where there are no symbols or signs? (If the acquisition of language were only dependent on an accumulation of associations, as is sometimes claimed, then it could occur much earlier.*) It has been shown that the acquisition of language requires that at least two conditions be satisfied. First, there must exist a general context of imitation allowing for interpersonal exchange, and second, the diverse structural characters that constitute the one basic unit of Chomsky's (1957) transformational grammars must be present. For the first of these conditions to be met means that in addition to the motor techniques of imitation (and this is by no means an easy task), the object, spatiotemporal, and causal decentrations of the second sensorimotor subperiod must have been mastered. For the second requirement, our collaborator H. Sinclair, who specializes in psycholinguistics, has shown that Chomsky's transformational structures are facilitated by the previous operation of the sensorimotor schemes, and thus that their origin is neither in an innate neurophysiological program (as Chomsky himself would have it) nor in an operant or other conditioning "learning" process [as Chomsky (1959) has shown conclusively].

A second example of the sequential character of our periods and subperiods is the subperiod of ages 2 to 7, which itself results from the sensorimotor schemes elaborated in the ninth and tenth months and which prepares the concrete operations of ages 7 to 10. This subperiod is characterized by some negative aspects (lack of reversibility and absence of the concept of conservation), but it also evolves some positive achievements such as the directional functions [*fonctions orientées*—mappings where $y = f(x)$ with unity of the value $f(x)$ for any (x) and the qualitative identity $a = a$]. In fact, these functions already play an extensive role in preoperational thought. Their one-way orientation explains the general primacy of the concept of order at this level, with its adequate aspects, but this also is the source of systematic distortions (e.g., "longer" understood as "going farther"; estimation of a quantity of water by taking only its level into account). The elementary functions are nothing other than the con-

---

*The contention is that there already exists symbol manipulation, that is, storage and computation, on indexes and signals during the sensorimotor stage. Therefore the absence of language cannot be attributed to the lack of such functions, and conditioning (classical or operant) should be possible at least on the input side. At this stage the child can discriminate between sounds, and he should be able to respond selectively, verbally or otherwise, to phonetic inputs on a purely associative basis. It is claimed that this is impossible for more than a finite (and very limited) set of inputs because of the absence of the most essential linguistic structure (monoid) that would permit the generation and storage of rules allowing for the analysis and recognition of an unlimited set of organized sequences of sounds. (Translator's note)

nections inherent in the schemes of action (which, before they become operational, are always oriented toward a goal) and therefore originate in the sensorimotor schemes themselves. Qualitative identity (the type of identity expressed by the child when he says: "It is the same water," even if the quantity of water changes) has its origin in the concept of permanent object, and in the notion that the subject's own body (as well as those of other subjects) maintains its identity both in time and in space; and these are three achievements of the sensorimotor stage. On the other hand, the one-way, directional functions and the identities they involve constitute the necessary condition for future operations. Thus we can see that the stages between 2 and 7 years are simultaneously an extension of the sensorimotor stages and the basis of the future concrete operations.

The propositional operations that appear between ages 11 and 15 with the INRC group and general combinatorial structures, all consist of applying operations to operations and transformations to transformations. It is therefore obvious that the existence of this last stage necessarily involves the acquisitions of the previous one (concrete operations, or operations to the first power).

11. Thus defined, the stages always appear in the same order of succession. This might lead us to assume that some biological factor such as maturation is at work. But it is certainly not comparable to the hereditary neurophysiological programming of instincts. Biological maturation does nothing more than open the way to possible constructions (or explain transient impossibilities). It remains for the subject to actualize them. This actualization, when it is regular, obeys the law of creodes, that is, of constant and necessary progress such that the endogenous reactions find support in the environment and in experience. It would therefore be a mistake to consider the succession of these stages as the result of an innate predetermination, because there is a continual construction of novelty during the whole sequence.

The two best proofs of this point are the possibilities of deviations from the norm (with regulation by homeorhesis) and of variations in the time tally with the possibility of accelerations or delays. Deviations may be brought about by unforeseen experiences encountered by the activity of the child himself as well as by adult pedagogical interventions. Some pedagogical interventions can, of course, accelerate and complete spontaneous development; but they cannot change the order of the constructions. For example, educational programs

rightly introduce the concept of metric proportions a long time after the elementary arithmetical operations, although a proportion seems to consist only of an equivalence between two divisions, as in 4:2 = 6:3. But there also exist untimely pedagogical interventions, such as those of parents who teach their children to count up to 20 or 50 before they can have any concept of number. In many cases, such premature acquisitions in no way affect the creode specific to the construction of integers. for instance, when two lines of m and n elements ($m = n$), respectively, are first put into visual one-to-one correspondence and their lengths changed by changing the spacing of the elements, the fact that the child of a certain age can count will not prevent him from saying that the longer line has more elements. On the other hand, when a pedagogical intervention has been successful or when the child obtains by himself a partial conquest in a specific operatory domain, the problem of the interactions between the various creodes remains still unsolved. In the case of classes or relations, for example, are the additive and multiplicative operations always synchronic (as they often seem to be), or can one follow the other—and in that event does the final synthesis remain unchanged (as is probably the case)?

12. In considering the problem of duration or rate of succession of the stages, we can readily observe that accelerations or delays in the average chronological age of performance depend on specific environments (e.g., abundance or scarcity of possible activities and spontaneous experiences, educational or cultural environment), but the order of succession will remain constant. Some authors even believe unbounded acceleration would be possible and desirable. Bruner (1960) went so far as to assert that if one tackles it the right way, one can teach anything to children of any age, but he does not seem to believe this any longer. On this point, however, we can quote two situations investigated by Gruber. The first is that of developing kittens. It has been shown that they go through the same stages as infants in acquiring the "concept" of permanent object, and further that they achieve in 3 months what the infant does in 9. However, they do not progress any further and one may wonder whether the child's slower rate of development does not, in this case, make for greater progress ultimately. The second study by Gruber concerns the remarkable tardiness with which some of Darwin's main concepts appeared to him, although they were logical consequences of his previous ideas. Is this remarkably slow speed of invention one of the conditions of fruitfulness or only a deplorable accident? These are major problems in

cognitive psychology that are not yet solved. Nevertheless, we would like to put forward a plausible hypothesis. For a specific subject the speed of transition from one stage to the following one has an *optimal rate*. That is, the stability and even the fruitfulness of a new organization (or structurization) depends on connections that cannot be instantaneous but cannot be indefinitely postponed either since they would then lose their power of internal combination.

THE RELATIONS BETWEEN DEVELOPMENT AND LEARNING

13. If we give the name *learning* to every form of cognitive acquisition, it is obvious that development only consists of a sum or a succession of learning situations. Generally, though, the term is restricted to denote essentially exogenous acquisitions, where either the subject repeats responses, parallel to the repetition of external sequences (as in conditioning), or the subject discovers a repeatable response by using the regular sequences generated by some device, without having to structure or reorganize them himself through a constructive step-by-step activity (instrumental learning). If we accept this definition of learning, the question arises whether development is merely a succession of learned acquisitions (which would imply a systematic dependency of the subject on the objects), or whether learning and development constitute two distinct and separate sources of knowledge. Finally, there is, of course, the possibility that every acquisition through learning represents, in fact, only a sector or a phase of development itself, arbitrarily provided by the environment (which entails the possibility of a local deviation from the "normal" creodes) but remaining subject to the general constraints of the current developmental stage.

Before we examine the experimental facts, we would like to mention a talented behaviorist's attempt to reduce our theory to Hull's theory of learning. To effect this reduction, however, Berlyne (1960) was obliged to introduce two new concepts into Hull's theory. The first is stimulus-response generalization, which Hull foresaw but did not use. The second and more fundamental is the concept of "transformational responses," which are not restricted to repetitions but are amenable to reversible transformations in the same way as "operations." In discussing equilibration and regulation, Berlyne extends the concept of external reinforcements, introducing the possibility of "internal reinforcements" such as feelings of surprise, incoherence, or coherence. Though these modifications of Hull's

theory change its structure fundamentally, it is not certain that they are sufficient. The main question remains, indeed, whether the "transformational responses" are simple copies of observable external transformations of the objects or whether the subject himself transforms the objects by acting on them. The main point of our theory is that knowledge results from *interactions* between the subject and the object, which are *richer* than what the objects can provide by themselves. Learning theories like Hull's, on the other hand, reduce knowledge to direct "functional copies" which do not enrich reality. The problem we must solve, in order to explain cognitive development, is that of *invention* and not of mere copying. And neither stimulus-response generalization nor the introduction of transformational responses can explain novelty or invention. By contrast, the concepts of assimilation and accommodation and of operational structures (which are created, not merely discovered, as a result of the subject's activities) are oriented toward this inventive construction, which characterizes all living thought.

To close this theoretical introduction to the problem of learning and development we would like to point out how peculiar it is that so many American and Soviet psychologists, citizens of great nations, which intend to change the world, have produced learning theories that reduce knowledge to a passive copy of external reality (Hull, Pavlov, etc.), whereas human thought always transforms and transcends reality. Outstanding sectors of mathematics (e.g., those that involve the continuum hypothesis) have no counterpart in physical reality, and all mathematical techniques result in new combinations that enrich reality. To present an adequate notion of learning, one first must explain how the subject manages to construct and invent, not merely how he repeats and copies.

14. A few years ago the International Center of Genetic Epistemology investigated two problems:

a. Under what conditions can logical structures be learned, and are these conditions identical to those for learning empirical sequences?

b. And, even in this last case (probabilistic or even arbitrary sequences), does learning imply a logic analogous, for example, to the logic of the coordinators of action, the existence of which can be observed as early as during the organization of sensorimotor schemes?

On the first point, studies such as those of Greco (1959) and of Morf and Smedslund (1959) have shown that in order to learn how to construct and master a logical structure, the subject must start from another, more elementary logical structure, which he will differentiate and complete. In other words, learning is no more than a sector of cognitive development that is facilitated or accelerated by experience. By contrast, learning under external reinforcement (e.g., permitting the subject to observe the results of the deduction that he should have made or informing him verbally) produces either very little change in logical thinking or a striking momentary change with no real comprehension.

For example, Smedslund found that it was easy to make children learn the conservation of weight with pieces of clay whose shape was modified and whose constant weight could be read by the child on a pair of scales, because in this case mere repetition of these observations facilitates generalization. The same processes of reinforcement by observation are not at all sufficient to induce the acquisition of transitivity in the weight equivalences: $A = C$ if $A = B$ and $B = C$. In other words, the logical structure of conservation (and Smedslund has checked the correlation between transitivity and operational conservation) is not acquired in the same way as the physical contents of this conservation.

Morf observed the same phenomenon in the learning of the quantification of inclusion: $A < B$ if $B = A + A'$. The spontaneous tendency of the child is to compare part A to the complementary part A' whenever his attention is called to the parts of the whole B and B ceases to be preserved as a whole.

By contrast, previous training on the intersection of classes facilitates learning of inclusion. It is true that the Dutch psychologist Kohnstamm (1956) has tried to show that it is possible to teach young subjects the quantitative dominance of the whole over the part ($B > A$) by purely didactic and verbal methods. Hence educational psychologists who believe that educational methods make it possible to teach anything at any age are considered optimistic and the psychologists of the Geneva school who assert that only an adequate spontaneous development makes understanding possible under any circumstances are considered pessimistic. However, the checks on Kohnstamm's experiment now being made in Montreal by Laurendeau and Pinard show that things are not as simple as they appear (verbally trained children make a great many mistakes on the relations between A and A'). One can easily understand that teachers of the traditional school will call anyone who believes in their methods an optimist, but, in our opinion, genuine optimism would consist of believing in the child's capacities for invention. Re-

member also that each time one prematurely teaches a child something he could have discovered for himself, that child is kept from inventing it and consequently from understanding it completely. This obviously does not mean the teacher should not devise experimental situations to facilitate the pupil's invention.

To turn to the second problem we mentioned, Apostel has shown that all learning, even empiricist learning, involves logic. This is true in the sense of an organization of the subject's action as opposed to immediate perception of the external data; moreover, Apostel has started to analyze the algebra of the learning process and its necessary basic operations.

15. Following these investigations at the International Center of Genetic Epistemology, Inhelder in Geneva, with her colleagues Bovet and Sinclair (1967), and later Laurendeau (1966) in Montreal, with her colleagues Fournier-Choninard and Carbonneau, have carried out more detailed experiments. The aim of their inquiries was to isolate the various factors that may facilitate an operational acquisition, and to establish the possible relations with the factors involved in the "natural" constructions of the same concepts (e.g., conservation in the course of spontaneous development).

As an example, one of Inhelder, Bovet, and Sinclair's experiments (with Fot) is performed by showing the child transparent jars filled with the same quantities of liquid. Instead of pouring in the usual manner, these jars empty through taps in their bases into glass jars of various shapes, which in turn empty into more jars on other levels. The heights and widths of successive jars vary at each level, but at the bottom of the sequence are jars identical to the ones at the top. This arrangement should lead the child to perform both dimensional and quantitative comparisons and eventually to understand the reason for the equality of the quantities at the starting point and at the end point.

It was discovered in this experiment that the results vary very significantly as a function of the initial cognitive levels of the children, which were classified according to the available schemes of assimilation. No child starting at a preoperational level succeeded in learning the logical operations underlying the elementary concepts of the conservation of physical quantities. The great majority (87.5%) did not even show any real progress, while a minority (12.5%) moved up to an intermediate level characterized by frequent oscillations where conservation would be alternatively asserted or denied. This uncertainty is ascribable to the fact that the coordina-

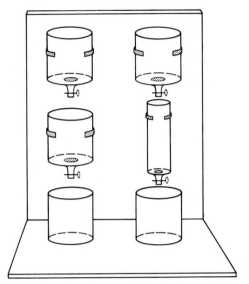

Figure 1. Experimental apparatus for learning the concept of conservation of quantity.

tion of the centrations or successive isolated states or their variations were still partial and transient. Clearly, it is one thing to observe that in a closed system of physical transformations nothing is created and nothing destroyed, and quite another to infer from this a principle of conservation. The situation is different with children who initially were already at this intermediate level. In this case only 23% did not achieve conservation, while 77% benefited in various degrees from the exercise and achieved a conservation based on a genuinely operatory structure. It is true that for about half of them (38.5%), this result involved only an extension of a structuration already started at the time of the pretest, whereas for the other half the gradual construction of the conservation principle was easy to observe during the experiment. Subsequently their reasoning acquired a real stability (there were no regressions in the first and the second posttests). In addition, they were able to generalize conservation, extending the concept to include the transformations of a plasticine ball in a context that outwardly only remotely resembled the previous learning situation. However, in comparing the arguments for conservation given by subjects who had acquired it by the much slower "spontaneous" process, it was observed that they were not entirely identical. The former had constructed a structure that did not make use of all the possibilities of operational mobility, which in its complete form entails general reversibility. In fact, they gave a majority of arguments by identity and compensation,

which had been evolved in the experimental situation, and very few arguments by reversibility based on cancellation.

On the other hand, progress in the experimental situation was more general and complete in the cases of children who were initially at an elementary operational level (characterized by the acquisition of conservation of quantity during the experiment) but who had not yet acquired the more complex concept of conservation of weight, which, during spontaneous development, generally appears 2 or 3 years later. In this case progress is genuine when the experimental situation does not restrict the child to passive observation but involves a series of operational exercises (e.g., establishing equality of weight for objects of different sizes, and regardless of position on the scales, and, more essentially, comparing the weights of collections of different objects and establishing their equivalence or nonequivalence). After being subjected to this type of training sequence, 86% of the subjects achieved conservation (in three sessions). Among them, 64% were able to use the transitive properties of order or equality in weight and, using arguments based on total reversibility, showed that they felt these properties were logically evident. These kinds of acquisition are therefore clearly distinct from the pragmatic solution given by children who, at a preoperational level, were subjected (as in Smedslund's experiment) only to empirical evidence.

Essentially what this experiment shows is that learning is subordinate to the subjects' levels of development. If they are close to the operational level, that is, if they are able to understand quantitative relations, the comparisons they make during the experiment are enough to lead them to compensation and conservation. But the farther they are from the possibility of operational quantification, the less they are likely to use the learning sequence to arrive at a concept of conservation.

An experiment carried out by Laurendeau consists of trying to induce progressive decentration and equilibration, and comparing the results thus obtained to those obtained by Skinner-type operant learning with external reinforcement. One group of subjects is asked to predict the level a liquid will reach when it is poured from one container to another of a different shape. The subjects are then shown the level reached when the liquid is actually poured so that they may see whether their prediction was correct. The subjects are then questioned about conservation, and when they deny it, they are asked to add the quantity necessary to make the levels equal. This is repeated with containers whose shape is more and more different, until one is very wide and low and the other very high and thin, and it becomes obvious that equal levels do not produce equal quantities of liquid. In this third part of the experiment 12 gradually higher and thinner containers are used, the median ones (6 and 7) being equal; these are filled by the subject with quantities of liquid he judges to be equal. They are then poured into containers 5 and 8, respectively; the operation is then repeated and 6 and 7 are poured into 4 and 9, etc. With children between 5 and 6 a definite improvement in performance can be observed, and this is corroborated by the posttests given 1 week and 3 months later.

Subjects in a second group are asked to make the same prediction, but then they are asked only questions (some 20 in all) about conservation; correct answers are suitably rewarded. In fact, the child is very quickly able to give only correct answers and can still do this 2 or 3 days later, but posttests show that learning is much more limited and less stable.

To summarize, learning appears to depend on the mechanisms of development and to become stable only insofar as it utilizes certain aspects of these mechanisms, the instruments of quantification themselves, which would have evolved in the course of spontaneous development.

THE OPERATIVE AND FIGURATIVE ASPECTS OF COGNITIVE FUNCTIONS

16. The stages described in the section labeled *The Theory of Stages* are only those concerning the development of intelligence, and the apects of learning considered in the subsequent section are only relevant to these stages.

If we wish to obtain a complete picture of mental development, we must not only consider the operative aspect of the cognitive functions but also their figurative aspect. We will call *operative* the activities of the subject that attempt to transform reality: (*a*) the set of all actions (except those that, like imitation or drawing, are purely accommodatory in intent) and (*b*) the operations themselves. "Operative" is thus a broader term than "operational," which is only related to the operators. In contrast, we shall call *figurative* the activities that attempt only to represent reality as it appears, without seeking to transform it: (*a*) perception, (*b*) imitation, in a broad sense (including graphic imitation or drawing), and (*c*) pictorial representations in mental imagery.

Before discussing these figurative aspects and their relations with the operative aspects of knowledge, we must briefly analyze their relations with the semiotic function (generally called symbolic function). In considering semiotic functions, Peirce introduced a distinction between "indexes" (perceptions), "icons" (images), and symbols, in which he included language. We prefer de Saussure's terminology, which is more widely used in linguistics, and which is characterized psychologically in the following way:

a. Indexes are signifiers that are not differentiated from their significants since they are part of them or a causal result; for example, for an infant, hearing a voice is an index of someone's presence.

b. Symbols are signifiers that are differentiated from their significants, but they retain a measure of similarity with them; for example, in a symbolic game representing bread by a white stone and vegetables by grass.

c. Signs are signifiers that are also differentiated from their signifiers but are conventional and thus more or less "arbitrary"; the sign is always social, whereas the symbol can have a purely individual origin as in symbolic games or in dreams.

We shall thus call the semiotic function (or symbolic function, but semiotic has a broader meaning) the ability, acquired by the child in the course of his second year, to represent an object that is absent or an event that is not perceived by means of symbols or signs (i.e., of signifiers differentiated form their significants). Thus the semiotic function includes in addition to language, symbolic games, mental and graphic images (drawings), and deferred imitation (beginning in the absence of its model), which appears nearly at the same time (except for drawing, which appears slightly later), whereas indexes (including the "signals" involved in conditioning) already play a role during the first weeks. The transition from indexes to symbols and signs—in other words the beginning of the differentiation that characterizes the semiotic function—is definitely related to the progress of imitation, which at the sensorimotor level, is a sort of representation through actual actions. As imitation becomes differentiated and interiorized in images, it also becomes the source of symbols and the instrument of communicative exchange that makes possible the acquisition of language.

Thus defined, the semiotic function partially includes the figurative activities of knowledge, which in their turn partially include the semiotic function. There thus exists an intersection between their respective domains, but not equivalence or inclusion. In effect, perception is a figurative activity, but it does not belong to the semiotic function since it uses only indexes and no representative signifiers. Language belongs to the semiotic function, but it is only partly figurative (mainly when the child is young, or less so with increased age, especially with the onset of formal operations). In contrast, imitation, mental imagery, and drawing are both figurative and semiotic.

17. The discussion of perception here is very brief; Seagrim's excellent translation of the author's *Perceptual Mechanisms* (1961) will be published in the near future. However, it is relevant to note here that, during our study of the development of perception in the child, we have been led to distinguish between "field effects" (field being understood here as field of visual motor centration, *not* as field in the sense of Gestalt theory) and the perceptual activities of exploration such as visual transports, relating, and visually placing in reference (as far as position or direction are concerned).

Field effects quantitatively decrease with age (this is the case for the primary opticogeometrical illustrations such as Müller Lyer's), but they retain their qualitative characteristics. Consequently, their evolution with age does not yield a succession of stages. For instance, based on the concept of visual centrations (studied with Vinh-Bang in ocular movements), we have been able to construct a probabilistic model of "encounters" and "couplings" (through successive centrations) which gives a general law for the plane primary illusions and can be used to compute for each one its theoretical positive and negative maximum point. These points have been checked experimentally and remain the same at every age, though the quantitative amount of the illusion decreases.

In contrast, perceptual activities are modified with age and roughly approximate stages can be distinguished. For example, if one exposes the same subject to 20 or 30 presentations of the Müller-Lyer or lozenge illusion (underestimation of the main diagonal), one observes an effect of learning that increases with age after 7 years. Noelting and Gonheim were able to show that it did not appear before 7. This perceptual learning (which is dependent on autoregulations or spontaneous equilibrations) is not reinforced, since the subject does not know the error in his estimate; this error is the result of perceptual activities that become more efficient with age.

Moreover, while studying the way in which children perceptually estimate the horizontality of a line (e.g., in a tilted triangle), we found (with Dadsetan) a real improvement toward 9 to 10 years, which is in direct correlation with the corresponding spatial operations. Here, as in all the cases in which we could study the relations between perception and intelligence, it is intelligence that directs the movements—naturally not by experimenting with the perceptual mechanisms but by indicating what must be looked at and which indexes are useful in making a good perceptual estimate.

18. We have studied mental images extensively with Inhelder (1966) and many other colleagues, especially considering their relations to intelligence (e.g., by asking subjects to imagine the result of pouring a liquid into a different container in a conservation experiment, before they have actually seen the result). Our first conclusion is that the image does not come from perception (it only appears at approximately 1½ years together with the semiotic function) and that it obeys completely different laws. It is probably the result of an interiorization of imitation. This hypothesis seems corroborated in the domain of symbolic games in their initial stages (fiction or imagination games, which show all the transitions between imitative symbols by gestures and actions and interiorized imitation or images).

Further, if one distinguishes "reproductive" images (to imagine an object or an event that is known but is not actually perceived at the time) and "anticipatory" images (to imagine the result of a new combination), our results have shown the following:

a. Before 7 years, one can find only reproductive images, and all of them are quite static. For example, the subjects experience systematic difficulty in imagining the intermediate positions between the initial vertical and final horizontal position of a falling stick.

b. After 7 to 8 years, anticipatory images appear, but they are not only applied to new combinations. They also seem to be necessary for the representation of any transformation even if it is known, as if such representations always entailed a new anticipation.

But this research has shown above all the strict interdependency between the evolution of mental images and the evolution of operations. Anticipatory images are possible only when the corresponding operations exist. In our experiments concerning conservation of liquids the younger subjects go through a stage of "pseudo-conservation" where they imagine that in a narrow container the level of the liquid would be the same as in a wide one (and it is only when they see that it is not the same level that they deny conservation). About 23% of the subjects know the level will rise, but this knowledge is contained in a reproductive image (founded on experience) and they conclude that there will be no conservation (when asked to pour the ''same quantity'' in the two containers, they pour liquid up to the same levels).

In short, while mental images can sometimes facilitate operations, they do not constitute their origin. On the contrary, mental imagery is generally controlled by the operations gradually as they appear (and one can follow their construction stage by stage).

19. The study of mental imagery led us to investigate the development of memory. Memory has two very different aspects. On the one hand, it is cognitive (entailing knowledge of the past), and in this respect it uses the schemes of intelligence, as we shall show shortly in an example. On the other hand, imagery is not abstract knowledge and bears a particular and concrete relation to objects or events. In this respect such symbols as mental images and, more specifically, ''memory images'' are necessary to its operation. Images themselves can be schematized, but in an entirely different sense, for images in themselves, however schematic, are not schemes. We shall therefore use the term schemata to designate them. A *schema* is a simplified image (for example, the map of a town), whereas a *scheme* represents what can be repeated and generalized in an action (e.g., the scheme is what is common in the actions of ''pushing'' an object with a stick or any other instrument).

The main result of our research has been, in this context, to show not the generality but the possibility that progress in memory is influenced by improvements in the operational schemes of intelligence. For example, we showed (with Sinclair and others) 3- to 8-year-old children an array of 10 wooden bars varying in length between 9 and 16 cm arranged according to their length, and we merely asked the subjects to look at the array. A week (and then a month) later they were asked to draw the array from memory.

The first interesting result is that, after 1 week, the younger children do not remember the sequence of well-ordered elements, but reconstruct it by assimilating it to the schemes corresponding to their operational level: (*a*) a few equal elements, (*b*) short ones and long ones, (*c*) groups of short, medium, and long ones, (*d*) a correct sequence, but too short, (*e*) a complete seriation. The second remarkable result is that after 6 months (without any new presentation, memory was improved in 75% of the cases. Those who were at level *a* moved up to *b*. Many at level *b* moved up to *c* or even *d*. The *c*'s moved up to

d or *e*, and so on. The results, naturally, are not as spectacular in other experiments, and there is less progress as the model is less schematizable (in the sense of being made schematic, and not being assimilated to a scheme). The existence of such facts shows that the structure of memory appears to be partly dependent on the structure of the operations.

THE CLASSICAL FACTORS OF DEVELOPMENT

20. We have seen that there exist laws of development and that development follows a sequential order such that each of its stages is necessary to the construction of the next. But this fundamental fact remains to be explained. The three classical factors of development are maturation, experience of the physical environment, and the action of the social environment. The two last cannot account for the sequential character of development, and the first one is not sufficient by itself because the development of intelligence does not include a hereditary programming factor like the ones underlying instincts. We shall therefore have to add a fourth factor (which is in fact necessary to the coordination of the three others—equilibration, or self-regulation (*auto régulation*).

It is clear that maturation must have a part in the development of intelligence, although we know very little about the relations between the intellectual operations and the brain. In particular, the sequential character of the stages is an important clue to their partly biological nature and thus argues in favor of the constant role of the genotype and epigenesis. But this does not mean we can assume there exists a hereditary program underlying the development of human intelligence: there are no ''innate ideas'' (in spite of what Lorenz maintained about the a priori nature of human thought). Even logic is not innate and only gives rise to a progressive epigenetic construction. Thus the effects of maturation consist essentially of opening new possibilities for development, that is, giving access to structures that could not be evolved before these possibilities were offered. But between possibility and actualization, there must intervene a set of other factors such as exercise, experience, and social interaction.

A good example of the gap that exists between the hereditary possibilities and their actualization in an intellectual structure can be provided by an inspection of the Boolean and logical structures discovered by Pitts and McCulloch (1947) in the neural connections. In this context the neurons appear as operators that process information according to rules analogous to those of the logic of propositions. But the logic of propositions only appears on the level of thought at around 12 to 15 years of age. Thus there is no direct relation between the "logic of the neurons" and that of thought. In this particular case, as in many others, the process must be conceived of not as progressive maturation but as a sequence of constructions, each of which partly repeats its immediate predecessor but at a very different level and on a scope that goes far beyond it. What makes possible the logic of neurons is initially exclusively a nervous activity. But this activity makes possible in its turn a sensorimotor organization at the level of behavior. However, this organization, while retaining certain structures of the nervous activity, and consequently being partially isomorphic to it, results at first in a set of connections between behaviors which is much simpler than that of the nervous activity itself because these behaviors have to correlate actions and objects and are no longer limited to exclusively internal transmissions. Further, the sensorimotor organization makes possible the constitution of thought and its symbolic instruments, which imply the construction of a new logic, partially isomorphic to the previous ones, but which is confronted with new problems, and the cycle repeats. The propositional logic that is constructed between 12 and 15 years is thus by no means the immediate consequence of the logic of neurons, but it is the result of a sequence of successive constructions that are not preformed in the hereditary nervous structure but are made possible by this initial structure. So we are now very far from a model of continuous maturation that would explain everything by preformed mechanisms. For this purely endogenous model, there must be substituted a series of actual constructions, the sequential order of which does not imply a simple predetermination but involves much more than this.

21. A second factor traditionally invoked to explain cognitive development is *experience* acquired through contact with the external physical environment. This factor is essentially heterogeneous, and there are at least three categories and meanings of experience, among which we shall distinguish two opposite poles.

a. The first is simple *exercise,* which naturally involves the presence of objects on which action is exerted but does not necessarily imply that any knowledge will be extracted from these objects. In fact, it has been observed that exercise has a positive effect in the consolidation of a reflex or of a group of complex reflexes such as sucking, which noticeably improves with repetition during the first days of life. This is also true of the exercise of intellectual opera-

tions that can be applied to objects, although these operations are not derived from the objects. In contrast, the exercise of an exploratory perceptual activity or of an experiment can provide new exogenous information while consolidating the subject's activity. We can thus distinguish two opposite poles of activity in exercise itself: a pole of accommodation to the object, which is then the only source of the acquisitions based on the object's properties; and a pole of functional assimilation, that is, of consolidation by active repetition. In this second perspective, exercise is predominantly a factor of equilibration or autoregulation, that is, it has to do with structurations dependent on the subject's activity more than with an increase in the knowledge of the external environment.

As regards experience proper in the sense of acquisition of new knowledge through manipulations of objects (and no longer through simple exercise), we must again distinguish two opposite poles, which will correspond to categories (*b*) and (*c*).

b. There is what we call *physical experience,* which consists of extracting information from the objects themselves through a simple process of abstraction. This abstraction reduces to dissociating one newly discovered property from the others and disregarding the latter. Thus it is physical experience that allows the child to discover weight while disregarding an object's color, and so on, or to discover that with objects of the same nature, their weight is greater as their volume increases, and so forth.

c. In addition to physical experience (*b*) and to simple exercise (*a*), there is a third fundamental category, which strangely practically never has been mentioned in this context. This is what we call *logicomathematical experience.* It plays an important part at all levels of cognitive development where logical deduction or computation are still impossible, and it also appears whenever the subject is confronted with problems in which he has to discover new deductive instruments. This type of experience also involves acting upon objects, for there can be no experience without action at its source, whether real or imagined, because its absence would mean there would be no contact with the external world. However, the knowledge derived from it is not based on the physical properties of these objects but on properties of the actions that are exerted on them, which is not at all the same thing. This knowledge seems to be derived from the objects because it consists of discovering by manipulating objects, properties introduced by action which did not belong to the objects before these actions. For example, if a child, when he is counting pebbles, happens to put them in a row and to make the astonishing discovery that when he counts them from the right to the left he finds the same number as when he counts from the left to the right, and again the same when he puts them in a circle, etc., he has thus discovered experimentally that the sum is independent of order. But this is a logicomathematical experiment and not a physical one, because neither the order nor even the sum was in the pebbles before he arranged them in a certain manner (i.e., ordered them) and joined them together in a whole. What he has discovered is a relation, new to him, between the action of putting in order and the action of joining together (hence, between the two future operations), and not, or *not only*, a property belonging to pebbles.

Thus we see that the factor of acquired experience is, in fact, complex and always involves two poles: acquisitions derived from the objects and constructive activities of the subject. Even physical experience (*b*) is never pure, since it always implies a logicomathematical setting, however elementary (as in the geometrical gestalts of perception). This amounts to saying that any particular action such as "weighing" that results in physical knowledge is never independent of more general coordinations of action (such as ordering, joining together, etc.) which are a source of logicomathematical knowledge.

22. The third classical factor of development is the influence of the social environment. Its importance is immediately verified if we consider the fact that the stages we mentioned in the section titled *The Theory of Stages* are accelerated or retarded in their average chronological ages according to the child's cultural and educational environment. But the very fact that the stages follow the same sequential order in *any* environment is enough to show that the social environment cannot account for everything. This constant order of succession cannot be ascribed to the environment.

In fact, both social or educational influences and physical experience are on the same footing in this respect; they can have some effect on the subject only if he is capable of assimilating them, and he can do this only if he already possesses the adequate instruments or structures (or their primitive forms). In fact, what is taught, for instance, is effectively assimilated only when it gives rise to an active reconstruction or even reinvention by the child.

An excellent example of this complex situation is provided by the difficult problem of the relations between language and thought. Many authors have maintained not only that language is the essential factor in the constitution of representation or thought, which raises a first question, but also that language is the origin of the logical operations themselves (e.g., classification, order, propositional operations), which raises a second question.

With respect to the first question, it is doubtless true that language plays a major part in the interiorization of action into representation and thought. But this linguistic factor is not the only one at work. We must refer to the symbolic or semiotic function as a whole—and language is only a part of this. The other instruments of representation are deferred imitation, mental imagery (which is an interiorized imitation and not a mere extension of perception), symbolic games (or games of imagination), drawing (or graphical imitation), and so forth; and it is certainly imitation in the general sense which constitutes the transition between the sensorimotor and semiotic functions. Thus it is in the general context of the semiotic function that language must be considered, however important its part may be. The study of deaf-mutes, for example, shows how far the other symbolic instruments can reach when the development of articulate language is disturbed.

Turning to the question of the relations between language and logical operations, we have always maintained that the origin of logical operations is both deeper than and genetically prior to language; that is, it lies in the laws of the general coordinations of action, which control all activities including language itself.

An elementary logic already exists in the coordination of the sensorimotor schemes (see *The Relation Between Subject and Object:* the group of translations, the conservation of the objects, etc.). It exists in a form of intelligence which is yet neither verbal nor symbolic. But there still remains to establish more precisely the relations between language and the logical operations on the level of interiorized thought.

This has recently been done by Sinclair in a set of experiments at the psychological and linguistic level, which are most instructive. She studied two groups of 5- to 7-year-old children, one clearly at a preoperational stage and unable to attain the concept of conservation, whereas the other possessed all the instruments that lead to conservation. She was then able to show that their language is on the average noticeably different when one examines them on subjects other than conservation, for instance, when one asks them to compare two or more objects such as a long, thin pencil and a short, thick one. The preoperational group uses mainly the nonrelational terms of a scale: "This one is long, this one is short, this one is thick, and this one is thin." The operational group, in contrast, uses mainly "vectors": "This one is smaller and thicker," and so on. There is thus a clear relation between linguistic and operational level (and this is also true in other situations). But in which direction? To establish this, Sinclair then taught a group of younger subjects to use the verbal forms used by the older ones. Once this was done, she again investigated their operational level and discovered that only approximately 10% had improved; this very small proportion could even represent intermediate cases, or cases who were already very near the operational threshold. We can thus observe that language does not seem to be the motor of operational evolution but rather an instrument in the service of intelligence itself (see Sinclair De Zwart, 1967).

To conclude ¶ 20, 21, and 22, it appears that the traditional factors (maturation, experience, social environment) are not sufficient to explain development. We must therefore appeal to a fourth factor, *equilibration,* and we must do this for two reasons. The first is that these three heterogeneous factors cannot explain a sequential development if they are not in some relation of mutual equilibrium, and that there must therefore exist a fourth organizing factor to coordinate them in a consistent, noncontradictory totality. The second reason is that any biological development is, as we now know, self-regulatory, and that self-regulating processes are even more common at the level of behavior and the constitution of the cognitive functions. We must thus consider this factor separately.

EQUILIBRATION AND COGNITIVE STRUCTURES

23. The main aim of a theory of development is to explain the constitution of the *operational* structures of the integrated whole or totality (*structure opératoire d'ensemble*); and we believe only the hypothesis of progressive equilibration can account for it. To understand this we must first briefly consider the operational structures themselves.

The concept of structure became classical in psychology when it was introduced by gestalt theory to combat association and its atomistic habits of thought. But the gestaltists conceived of only one type of structure as applicable to the whole of psychology, from perception to intelligence. They did not distinguish two characters, which in reality are quite different. The first is common to all structures; they all possess holistic laws derived from the fact that they form a system, and these laws are distinct from the properties of the elements in the totality.

The second character is nonadditive composition, that is, the whole is quantitatively different from the sum of the parts (as in Oppel's perceptual illusion). But in the field of intelligence, there exist structures that verify the first characteristic and not the second; the set of integers, for instance, has holistic properties as such ("group," "ring," etc.), but composition in it is strictly additive—$2 + 2 = 4$, no more, no less.

We have therefore attempted to define and analyze the structures specific to intelligence, and they are structures involving operations, that is, involving interiorized and reversible actions such as addition, set-theoretic union, logical multiplication, or, in other words, composition of a multiplicity of classes or relations "considered simultaneously." These structures have a very natural and spontaneous development in the child's thought: to seriate, for instance (i.e., to order objects according to their increasing size), to classify, to put into one-to-one or one-to-many correspondence, to establish the multiplicative matrix—these are all structures that appear between ages 7 and 11 at the level of what we call "concrete operations" which deal directly with objects. After 11 to 12 other structures appear, such as the four-group and combinatorial processes, which we shall describe later.

To investigate the properties of these concrete operational structures, and to establish their laws, we need to use the language of the logic of classes and relations, but this does not mean we are leaving the field of psychology. When a psychologist computes the variance of a sample or uses the formulas of factor analysis, it does not mean his field has become statistics and not psychology. To analyze structures we must do the same, but, since we are not dealing with quantities, we must simply resort to more general mathematical instruments such as abstract algebra or logic. But they are only instruments that will allow us to reach genuinely psychological entities such as operations, considered as interiorized actions or general coordinations of actions.

A totality structure such as a classification has the following properties, which characterize, simply, the operations that are actually present in the subject's action.

a. He can combine one class A with another A', to obtain class B, denoted $A + A' = B$ (he can then go on to perform $B + B' = C$, etc.).

b. He can dissociate A or A' from B, denoted $B - A' = A$, which constitutes the inverse operation. Notice this reversibility is necessary to the understanding of the relation $A < B$, and we know that until 7 or 8, the child does not grasp easily the idea that if he is given 10 primroses A, and 10 other flowers A', then there are more flowers B than primroses A, because to be able to compare the whole B to the part A, one must be able to combine the two operations $A + A' = B$ and $A = B - A'$, otherwise the whole B is not preserved, and A is then only compared to A'.

c. He will understand that $A - A = 0$, and $A + 0 = A$.

d. Finally, he will be able to associate $(A + A') + B' = A + (A' + B') = C$, while $(A + A) - A = 0$ is not equal to $A + (A - A) = A$.

We have called *groupements* these elementary groupings* (*structures de groupoïdes*), which are more primitive than mathematical groups, but which are also much more limited structures and less elegant ones, in that composition is defined only between neighboring elements without general combinatorial properties and shows restricted associativity.† We have often been criticized for having thus only constructed structures that have no psychological reality. But such structures actually exist,

---

*A grouping can be considered as a lattice that has been made reversible. In a lattice, if $A + A' = B$, where B is an upper bound of A and A', A can be recovered by operating on B: $B - A' = A$. But the more general case is where C is an upper bound of A and A', for example, and $A \pm D - C'$. In other words, the operation $A + A'$ can only be ''reversed'' between contiguous elements such as A and A', in the sense that in the 3-tuple A, A', B any two elements uniquely determine the third (Fig. 2a).

This is not the case for A, C', D, where $A + C' = D - D' - B' - A'$. Here we consider a grouping as a group where composition is restricted to contiguous elements only ($A + C'$, for example, is not defined without special conditions) and by the special identities $A + A = A$, $A + B = B$. A grouping is therefore only defined as a sequence of nested elements, such as a classification (Fig. 2b). It consists of (*a*) a direct operation: (*b*) an inverse operation: (*c*) an identity operation O: and (*d*) special identities:

$$A + A' = B$$
$$B - A' = A$$
$$A + O = A; \qquad A - A = O$$
$$A + A = A; \qquad -A - A = -A;$$
$$A + B = B$$

†Associativity is limited by the fact that the grouping only combines contiguous elements. $A + C'$ can only be constructed by operating step-by-step on the nearest contiguous classes A, A', B', up to D, the first class containing both A and C', then $A + C' = D - B' - A'$. Similarly, $A - C'$ only gives rise to the tautology $A - C' = (D - C' - B' - A') - C'$ where $(D - C' - B' - A') = A$. The consequence of these restrictions is that associativity is not verified before the elements in parentheses have first been ''reduced'': $(A + A') + B' = B + B' = C$, but $A + (A' + B')$ has no meaning since $(A' + B')$ contains A. (For further details of the reduction rules, cf. Piaget, 1959). In contrast, on the group of the integers under addition, any number can be immediately added to or subtracted from any other because an integer can be completely freed from its successors that ''contain'' it. (Translator's note)

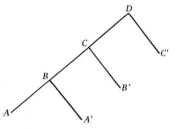

Figure 2a.

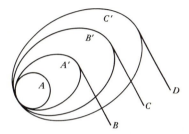

Figure 2b.

primarily because they describe simply what happens in a classification, a seriation, and so on, all of which are quite contemporaneous behaviors. Moreover, they can be recognized on the psychological level by the more general characters that reveal the existence of a totality structure, such as transitivity (e.g., in a seriation $A < C$ if $A < B$ and $B < C$) and the constitution of conservation concepts (conservation of a whole B when the arrangement of its parts A and A' is modified, conservation of length, quantity, etc.).

24. The problem then becomes that of understanding how the fundamental structures of intelligence can appear and evolve with all those that later derive from them. Since they are not innate, they cannot be explained by maturation alone. Logical structures are not a simple product of physical experience; in seriation, classification, one-to-one correspondence, the subject's activities add new relations such as order and totality to the objects. Logicomathematical experience derives its information from the subject's own actions (as we saw in ¶ 21), which implies an autoregulation of these actions. It could be alleged that these structures are the result of social or educational transmission. But as we saw (¶ 22), the child must still understand what is transmitted, and to do this the structures are necessary. Moreover, the social explanation only displaces the problem: How did the members of the social group acquire the structures in the first place?

But on all levels of development actions are coordinated in ways that already involve some properties of order, inclusion, and correspondence, and also foreshadow such structures (e.g., seriation for order, classification for inclusion, multiplicative structures for correspondence). What is more important though, is that coordination of actions involves correction and self-regulation; in fact, we know regulatory mechanisms characterize all levels of organic life. (This is true for the genetic pool as well as for behavior.) But regulation is a process of retroaction (negative feedback), which implies a beginning of reversibility; and the relationship between regulation (which is correction of error with semireversibility in the retroaction) and operation, whose full reversibility allows for precorrection of errors (i.e., for ''perfect'' regulation in the cybernetic sense) becomes apparent.

Thus it seems highly probable that the construction of structures is mainly the work of equilibration, defined not by balance between opposite forces but by self-regulation; that is, equilibration is a set of active reactions of the subject to external disturbances, which can be effective, or anticipated, to varying degrees. Equilibrium thus becomes identical with reversibility, but when one objects (as Bruner does, for example) that equilibrium therefore becomes superfluous, because reversibility is sufficient in itself, one forgets that it is not only the final state of equilibrium that must be considered, but that *equilibration* is essential as the self-regulating process leading to this final state and thus to the reversibility that characterizes the structures that must be explained.

25. Equilibration has explanatory value because it is founded on a process with increasing sequential probabilities. We can understand this better through an example. How can we explain the fact that when a spherical lump of clay is changed into the shape of a sausage in front of him, a child will begin by denying that the quantity of clay is preserved under this transformation, and end by asserting the logical necessity of this conservation? To do this we must define four stages, each of which *becomes more probable*, not a priori, but as a function of the present situation or of the one immediately preceding it.

a. Initially the child considers only one dimension, for instance, length (say 8 times out of 10). He then says the sausage contains more matter because it is longer. Sometimes (say 2 times out of 10) he says it is thinner, but forgetting its greater length, he concludes the quantity of matter has decreased. Why does he reason thus? Simply because the probability of considering one dimension only is greater. If the probability for length is .8 and that for width is .2, that for length *and* width is .16, because they are independent occurrences as long as compensation is not understood.

b. If the sausage is made longer and longer, or if the child becomes weary of repeating the same argument, the probability of his noticing the other dimension *becomes* greater (though it was not initially), and he will fluctuate between the two.

c. If there is oscillation, the probability of the subject's noticing some correlation between the two variations (the sausage becoming longer as it becomes thinner) *becomes* greater (third stage). But as soon as this feeling of the solidarity existing between variables appears, his reasoning has acquired a new property: it does not rest solely on *configurations* any more but begins to be concerned with *transformations:* the sausage is not simply ''long''; it can ''lengthen,'' and so on.

d. As soon as the subject's thought takes transformations into account, the next stage *becomes* more probable in which he understands (alternately or simultaneously) that a transformation can be reversed, or that the two simultaneous transformations of length and width compensate, because of the solidarity he has glimpsed [see stage (c)].

We can thus see that progressive equilibration has effective explanatory value. Stage (a) (which all those who checked our research have found) is not an equilibrium point because the child has noticed only one dimension: in this case the algebraic sum of the virtual components of work (to quote d'Alembert's principle on physical systems) is not zero since one of them, which consists of noticing the other dimension, has not been completed yet and will be sooner or later. The transition from one stage to another is therefore an equilibration in the most classical sense of the word. But since these displacements of the system are activities of the subject, and since each of these activities consists of correcting the one immediately preceding it, equilibration becomes a sequence of self-regulations whose retroactive processes finally result in operational reversibility. The latter then goes beyond simple probability to attain logical necessity.

What we have just said about an instance of operational conservation could be repeated about the construction of every operational structure. Seriation $A < B < C$, for example, when it becomes operational, is the result of coordinating the relations $<$ and $>$ (each new element in E in the ordered sequence having the property of being both $> D, C, B, A$, and $< F, G, H, \ldots$ and this coordination is again the result of an equilibration process of increasing sequential probabilities of the kind we have described. Similarly for inclusion of classes, $A < B$ if $B = A + A'$ and $A' > O$ is obtained by an equilibration of the same type.

It is not therefore an exaggeration to say that equilibration is the fundamental factor of development, and that it is even necessary for the coordination of the three other factors.

THE LOGICOMATHEMATICAL ASPECTS OF STRUCTURES

26. The "concrete" operational structures we have just mentioned all presuppose the construction of certain quantities: extension of classes for classification (which explains the difficulty of quantifying the inclusion of classes), size of the differences for seriation, quantitative conservations, and so forth. But even before these quantitative structures are constructed, some partial and qualitative structures may be observed at the preoperational levels. These levels are of great interest because they constitute the first half, so to speak, of the logic of reversible operations. These are the directional functions (one-way functions that do not have inverses, which would imply reversibility) and the qualitative identities (see ¶ 10).

The functions, we remember, are "mappings" in the mathematical sense, which have no inverses because, as we saw, they are psychologically related to the schemes of action, which are goal directed. Suppose, for instance, we have a piece of string b, part a of which is at right angles to the rest (a') and can slide on a nail when a weight is connected with a' and a is held back by a spring. All children between 4 and 7 understand that if one pulls b, a grows shorter as a' grows longer. But they do not yet have conservation of the length of the whole b ($b = a + a'$), and what they perform is not a quantified operation but simply a qualitative or ordinal equation (longer = farther).

Similarly for identity, all children (or nearly all) agree, as we saw, that when a ball of clay is changed into a sausage, it is the "same" lump of clay even if quantity is not preserved. These identities are acquired early and the scheme of permanent objects we mentioned in ¶ 2 is one of them. In a recent book, Bruner considers them the origin of quantitative conservations. This is true in a sense (they are a necessary condition, but not a sufficient one), but a central difference remains: qualities (on which qualitative identity is founded) can be established perceptually, whereas quantity involves a lengthy structural elaboration whose complexity we have just seen (¶ 23 to 26).

In fact, functions and qualitative identity constitute only that half of a logic which is both preoperational and qualitative and leads to the logic of reversible and quantitative operations but is not powerful enough to account for this other half.

27. This quantification of concrete operations, as opposed to the qualitative nature of preoperational functions and identities, is revealed in particular by the construction, around 7 or 8, of the operations related to number and measure, which are partly isomorphic to one another but have very different content. The construction of cardinal numbers cannot be explained, as was believed by Russell and Whitehead, simply by one-to-one correspondence between equivalent classes, because the correspondence they used, by abstraction of qualities (in contrast with qualified correspondence between individual objects with the same properties), implicitly introduced unity and therefore number, which made their reasoning circular. In fact, when we deal with finite sets, cardinal numbers cannot be dissociated from ordinal numbers and are subject to the three following conditions:

a. Abstraction from qualities, which makes all singular objects equivalent and therefore $1 = 1 = 1$.

b. The intervention of order: $1 \rightarrow 1 \rightarrow 1 \ldots$, which is necessary to distinguish the objects from one another—otherwise $1 + 1 = 1$ would be true.

c. An inclusion of (1) in (1 + 1), then of (1 + 1) in (1 + 1 + 1), etc.

The integers thus result from synthesis of order (seriation) and inclusion or nested sets (classification), which is made necessary by the abstraction from qualities. Hence the integers are built up from purely logical elements (seriation and classification), but they are rearranged in a new synthesis that allows for their quantification by an iterative process: $1 + 1 = 2$, etc.

Similarly, measurement in a continuum (e.g., a line, a surface) implies (a) its partition into segments one of which is then chosen as unity and made equivalent to others by congruence $a = a = a \ldots$, (b) its translation in a certain order, $a \rightarrow a \rightarrow a$, and so on, to make it congruent to others, and (c) the units settling into its additive compositions, thus a into ($a + a$) and ($a + a$) into ($a + a + a$). This synthesis of partition with nested segments and order in the translations of unity is thus isomorphic to the synthesis of order and inclusion which characterizes number, and this makes it possible to apply number to measurement.

It is thus clear that without having recourse to

anything other than the synthesis of elementary "groupings" of inclusion or order relations, the subject attains a numerical or metrical quantification whose power by far surpasses the elementary quantification (relations from part to whole) of the extension of classes or of seriation based on differences evaluated simply by "more" or "less."

28. After the concrete operational structures mentioned in ¶ 23, two other new structures are constructed between ages 11 and 15 that make possible the manipulation of such propositional operations as implications ($p > q$), incompatibilities ($p \mid q$), and disjunctions ($p \vee q$), and so on. These two new structures are the four-group and combinatorial operations. Combinatorial activity at this stage consists of classifying all possible classifications (just as permutations are a seriation of seriations) aa, ab, ac, bc, bb, cc, etc., and this does not therefore constitute an entirely new operation but an operation on other operations. Similarly, the four-group $INCR$* results from connecting in a whole the inversions N and reciprocities R (thus the inverse of the reciprocal $NR = C$ appears, as well as the identity operation $I = NCR$). But inversion already exists in the groupments of classes, under the form $A - A = O$, and reciprocity exists under the form $A = B$ therefore $B = A$ in the groupments of relations. The $INCR$

group is thus again an operational structure bearing on prior operations. As for the propositional operations, $p > q$, etc., which involve both combinatorial activity and the $INRC$ group, they are new in their form, but in their content they deal with connections between classes, relations, or numbers, and so on, and are therefore again operations on operations.

In general, the operations belonging to the third period of development (see ¶ 10, period c for ages 11 to 12) have their roots in concrete operations (subperiod b II, between 7 and 11) and enrich them, just as the source of concrete operations is in the sensorimotor schemes (period a, until about 2), which they also considerably modify and enrich. The sequential character of the stages (which we sufficiently stressed in ¶ 10) thus corresponds, from the point of view of the construction of structures, to a mechanism which we must now analyze, because it is too important for us to merely call it a sequential or progressive equilibration process. We must still understand how the constructions that bring about novelty occur, and this is a well-known problem in the development of mathematical structures.

29. We saw (¶ 21c) that before the level at which logicomathematical operations are constructed and thus become a deductive system, we can speak of logicomathematical experiments, which extract in-

---

*The $INRC$ group is a set of operations that act on the operations or elements of some other algebraic structure which has an involutive operation (an operation that is its own inverse: $N^2 + I$). An example of an involutive operation is the duality (de Morgan) law of Boolean algebra: $\overline{p \cup q} = \bar{p} \wedge \bar{q}$, which we can write $N(p \vee q) = \bar{p} \cup \bar{q}$ (N for negative). If we define C (correlative) to be the rule that acts on the connectives, changing $\wedge$ into $\vee$ and conversely, and R (reciprocal) to be the rule that acts on the sign of the variables, changing p into $\bar{p}$ and conversely, then by using C and R in succession [on, say $(p \cup q)$], we get the same result as by using N. The following "state diagram" shows the relations between N, R, and C acting on $(p \vee q)$

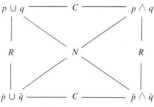

Identity I can now be defined as the rule that changes any formula into itself, and the following properties can easily be verified by "chasing around the diagram."

a. $RC = N$, $RN = C$, $CN = R$, and all couples are commutative— $RC = CR$, etc.

b. $C^2 = N^2 = R^2 = I$ (all transformations are involutive, i.e., each element has an inverse).

c. $RNC = I$.

From this we can show the set $[I, N, R, C]$ together with the operation of composition (in the usual sense of applying one transformation on the result of another) forms a noncyclic group of four elements (known as the Klein four-group).

The $INRC$ group can also be defined on physical systems that have the proper structure (i.e., an involutive transformation that can be "decomposed" into two other involutive transformations). In one of his experiments on double reference-systems Piaget uses a snail, which can move from left to right and conversely on a small board, which can itself be moved both ways on a table. We can define C to be the rule that reverses the movement of the snail: C (L, L) = (R, L), for example [where (R, L) means the snail (first coordinate) is moving right, and the board moving left]. Then we can define R to be the rule that reverses the second coordinate, for example, R (L, L) = (L, R) (this reverses the movement of the board). The "state diagram" has the same structure as before, and N (N reverses both movements) is the product of R and C.

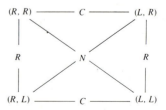

(Translator's note)

formation from the properties of actions applied to objects, and not from the objects themselves—which is quite another matter. We thus have, in contrast with abstraction proper, a new type of abstraction that we shall call *reflective abstraction* and that is the key to our problem. To abstract a property from an action or an operation, it is not enough to dissociate it from those that will be disregarded (e.g., a dissociation between the "form" to be retained and the "content" to be disregarded); the property or form thus retained must in addition be transferred somewhere, that is, on a different plane of action or operation. In the case of abstraction proper this question does not appear since we are dealing with a property of an object, which is assimilated by the subject. In the case of reflective abstraction, however, when the subject extracts a property or a form from actions or operations on a plane P_1, he must then transfer it to a higher plane P_2, and this is thus a reflection in quasi-physical sense (as in the reflection of a light beam). But for this form or property to be assimilated on this new plane P_2, it must be reconstructed on this new plane and therefore subjected to a new thought process that will this time mean "reflection" in a cognitive sense. Thus it is in both senses of the word that we must understand "reflective abstraction."

But if a new cognitive processing is necessary on plane P_2 to assimilate the properties or forms abstracted from plane P_1, this means new operations or actions on plane P_2 will be added to those of plane P_1 from which the required information was abstracted. Consequently, reflective abstraction is necessarily *constructive* and *enriches* with new elements the structures drawn from plane P_1, which amounts to saying it constructs new structures. This explains why the concrete operations based on sensorimotor schemes are richer than they were and why the same is true of propositional or formal operations, which are themselves based on concrete operations. As operations *on* operations, they add new modes of composition (combinatorial ones, etc.).

But reflective abstraction is the general constructive process of mathematics: it has served, for example, to evolve algebra out of arithmetic, as a set of operations on operations. Cantor constructed transfinite arithmetic in the same manner; he put into one-to-one correspondence the sequence $1, 2, 3, 4, \ldots$, with the sequence $2, 4, 6, 8. \ldots$. This generates a new number $(\aleph_0)$ which expresses the "power (a number) of the denumerable," but is an element of neither sequence. Present function theory constructs "morphisms" and "categories," and so forth, in

the same manner, and this is also true for the Bourbaki with the "mother structures" and their derivatives.

It is thus a remarkable fact that the process of the construction of structures we observe in the sequential stages of development in children and in the mechanisms of equilibration through self-regulation (which result in this self-regulation through feedback of a higher order, which is a reversible operation) coincides with the constant constructive process used by mathematics in their indefinitely fruitful development. This solution to the problem of development reduces to neither an empirical process of discovery of a "ready-made" external reality nor to a process of preformation or predetermination (a priori), which would also mean believing that everything is ready-made from the beginning. We believe truth lies between these two extremes, that is, in a constructivism that expresses the manner in which new structures are constantly being elaborated.

CONCLUSION: FROM PSYCHOLOGY TO GENETIC EPISTEMOLOGY

30. The theory we have outlined is necessarily interdisciplinary, and it involves, in addition to psychological elements, components belonging to biology, sociology, linguistics, logic, and epistemology. The relations with biology are obvious, since the development of cognitive functions is a part of the epigenesis that leads from the first embryological stages to the adult state. From biology we essentially retain the three following points:

a. There can be no transformation of the organism or of behavior without endogenous organizational factors, because the phenotype, although it is constructed in interaction with the environment, is the genome's "response" (or a response of the entire population's genetic pool, the individual genome being a cross section of the gene pool) to environmental "stresses."

b. Conversely, there is no epigenetic or phenotypic transformation independent of interaction with environmental influences.

c. These interactions involve continuous processes of equilibration or self-regulation, of which the equilibrium between assimilation and accommodation is an early instance. This also appears in sensorimotor, representative, and preoperational self-regulations, and even in operations themselves, since they are anticipatory self-regulations and corrections of error which do not rely any more on the feedback from an error that has already happened.

The relations with sociology are also self-evident, because even if the origin of cognitive structures is in the general coordinations of action, they are also interpersonal or social as well as individual, since the coordination of the actions of individuals obeys the same laws as intraindividual coordination. This is not true of social processes involving constraint or authority, which lead to a sociocentrism closely akin to egocentrism, but it is true of situations of cooperation, which are in reality "co-operations." One of the fundamental processes of cognition is that of decentration relative to subjective illusion (see ¶ 8), and this process has dimensions that are social or interpersonal as well as rational.

The relations with linguistics would have very little meaning if linguistics were still defending positions like Bloomfield's, with its naïve antimentalism. But we can adopt, in G. A. Miller's words, a position of "subjective behaviorism," and in linguistics proper, the contemporary work of Chomsky and his group on transformational grammars is not very far from our own operational perspectives and psychogenetic constructivism. But Chomsky believes in the hereditary basis of his linguistic structures, whereas it will probably be possible to show that the necessary and sufficient conditions for the construction of the basic units on which are founded the linguistic structures are satisfied by the development of sensorimotor schemes, and this is what Sinclair is working on at the present time.

The relations with logic are more complex. Modern symbolic logic is a "logic without a subject," whereas psychologically there exists no "subject without a logic." The subject's logic is undeniably poor and the groupment structures in particular are of little algebraic interest, except for the fact that related elementary structures do seem to arouse the mathematician's interest. But we must note that in studying the subject's logic we were able to formulate the laws of the four-group of propositional transformations *INRC* in 1949, that is, even before logicians themselves began to look into it. On the other hand, present work on the limits of formalization, initiated with Gödel's proof, will, more or less necessarily, orient logic toward a kind of constructivism, and in this light the parallel with psychogenetic construction has some interest. Generally speaking, logic is an axiomatic system, and in our context we must ask: An axiomatization of what? It is certainly not an axiomatization of the subject's conscious thought processes, because they are inconsistent and incomplete. But behind conscious thought are the "natural" operatory structures, and it is obvious that, even though it can indefinitely surpass them (because the productivity of axiomatics has no formal limit), they became the basis of logical axiomatization through a process of "reflective abstraction."

31. Finally, there remains the great problem of the relations between the theory of the development of cognitive functions and epistemology. When one adopts a static rather than a psychogenetic point of view and when one studies, for example, the intelligence of an adult or of subjects considered at a single level, it is easy to distinguish psychological problems (how intelligence functions or what are its performances) from epistemological problems (what are the relations between the subject and the objects, and whether or not knowledge of the former adequately attains the latter). But when one adopts a psychogenetic point of view, the situation is completely different because one is then concerned with the formation or the development of knowledge, and it is essential to consider the roles of objects or of the activities of the subject (i.e., those issues that necessarily raise all the epistemological problems). In fact, those who attribute the formation of knowledge exclusively to experience, in the sense of physical experience, and those who introduce the activities of the subject, in the sense of necessary organization, will orient toward different epistemologies. To distinguish, as we have done (¶ 21), between two types of experience—one physical with abstraction beginning from objects and the other logicomathematical with reflective abstraction—is to make a psychological analysis, but one whose epistemological consequences are clear.

There are authors who fail to appreciate the interconnections between genetic psychology and epistemology, but this only indicates that they are choosing one epistemology among other possible ones and that they believe their own epistemology is evident. For example, when Bruner tries to explain conservations by means of identities and symbolization based upon language and imagery, believing himself able to avoid operations and all epistemology, he is actually taking the point of view of empirical epistemology. At the same time he invokes an operation of identity without noticing that it implies others. In giving conservations a more operational explanation, and in supposing that quantities call for a complex construction and not simply a perceptual activity, we *de facto* remove ourselves from empiricism in the direction of a constructivism, which is another epistemology; moreover, it is much closer to present biological trends, which underscore the necessity of constructive autoregulations.

If we turn now to the epistemological side, we

discover that *its* trends also differ noticeably, according to whether it adopts a static or a historical and genetical point of view as is its natural internal tendency. When epistemology simply asks itself what knowledge is in general, it believes itself able to make abstractions without recourse to psychology, because, in fact, when knowledge is achieved, the subject retires from the scene. But, in reality, this is a great illusion, for all epistemology, even when it tries to bring down to *a minimum* the activities of the subject, makes implicit appeal to psychological interpretations. For example, logical empiricism attempts to reduce physical knowledge to perceptual states and logicomathematical knowledge to laws of an ideal language (with its syntax, its semantics, and its pragmatics, but without reference to transformational actions). Now, these are two highly conflicting hypotheses: first, because physical experience rests on actions and not only on perceptions and always supposes a logicomathematical framework drawn from the general coordination of actions (of such kind that the operationalism of Bridgman must be completed by that of Piaget!). Second, logicomathematical knowledge is not tautological but constitutes a structural organization drawn from reflective abstraction of the general coordination between our actions and our operations.

But, most importantly, it is impossible that epistemology is static in point of view, because all scientific knowledge is in perpetual evolution, including mathematics and logic itself (of which the constructivist aspect has become evident since the theorems of Gödel have shown the impossibility of a theory to be self-sufficient [complete]—therefore, the necessity of always constructing "stronger" ones; from whence finally the inevitable limits of formalization!). As Natorp said in 1910:

> science evolves continually. The progression, the method is everything . . . as a consequence, the *fact* of science can only be understood as *hope*. Only the *hope* is the fact. All being (or object) that science attempts to fix must again dissolve in the current of becoming. It is in the furthest removes of this becoming, and there only, that one has the right to say, It is (fact). Therefore, that which can and must be sought is "the law of this process." (p. 15)

32. These incontestable declarations are tantamount to stating the principle of our "genetic epistemology," that in order to resolve the problem of what is knowledge (or its diversity of forms) it is necessary to formulate it in the following terms: How does knowledge grow? By what process does

one pass from knowledge judged to be ultimately insufficient to knowledge judged to be better (considered from the point of view of science)? It is this that the proponents of the historicocritical method have well understood (see among others the works of A. Koyré and T. Kuhn). These critics, to understand the epistemological nature of a notion or a structure, look to see first how they were formed themselves.

If one takes a dynamic rather than a static point of view, it is impossible to maintain the traditional barriers between epistemology and the psychogenesis of cognitive functions. If epistemology is defined as the study of the formation of valid knowledge, it presupposes questions of validity, which are dependent on logic and on particular sciences, but also questions of fact, for the problem is not only formal but equally real: How, in *reality*, is science possible? In fact, all epistemology is therefore obliged to invoke psychological presuppositions, and this is true of logical positivism (perception and language) as well as of Plato (reminiscence) or of Husserl (intuition, intentions, significations, etc.). The only question is to know if it is better to content oneself with a speculative psychology or whether it is more useful to have recourse to a verifiable psychology!

This is why, as all our efforts lead to epistemological conclusions (this was moreover their initial goal), we have founded an International Center for Genetic Epistemology, so that psychologists, logicians, cyberneticists, epistemologists, linguists, mathematicians, physicists, and others, may collaborate there, depending on the problems being considered. This center, which has already published 22 volumes (and several others are in press), has therefore had as its goal, from the beginning, to study a certain number of epistemological problems seeking to analyze experimentally the psychological data necessary for the other aspects of the problem.

We have thus studied the interrelations of logical structures from the double point of view of their psychological genesis and their formal genealogy (with several colleagues), which has permitted us to find a certain covergence between the two methods. We have examined the problem with what the great logician Quine ironically called the "dogma" of logical empiricism, that is to say, the absolute distinction between the analytic and the synthetic: after having declared that all these authors, being occupied with that question, have had recourse to *factual* data, we have put the distinction under experimental control and have declared that numerous intermediaries exist between these two sorts of relationships incorrectly judged as irreducible.

We have also studied the problems of the development of the notions of number, space, time, speed, function, identity, and so on, and have been able to bring to all these questions new psychogenetic data, while completely removing from their regard epistemological conclusions, which are as far removed from the a priori as from the empirical, and suggesting a systematic constructivism. With regard to empiricism, we have above all analyzed the conditions for an adequate interpretation of experience and have added to this result what a mathematician-philosopher has summed up in these terms: "Empirical study of experience refutes empiricism!" We have seen previously (¶ 14) several of our studies on the role of learning.

In a word, the psychological theory of the development of cognitive functions seems to us to establish a direct, and even quite intimate, relationship centered on (*a*) the biological notions of interactions between endogenous factors and the environment and (*b*) the epistemological notions of necessary interactions between the subject and the objects. The synthesis of the notions of structure and of genesis which determines psychogenetic study finds its justification in the biological ideas of autoregulation and organization, and touches on an epistemological constructivism that seems to be in line with all contemporary scientific work; in particular, with that which concerns the agreement between logico-mathematical constructions and physical experience.

REFERENCES

Apostel, L. *Etudes d'Epistémologie Génétique II: Logique et équilibre.* Paris: Presses universitaires de France, 1957.

Berlyne, D., & Piaget, J. *Etudes d'Epistémologie Génétique XII: Théorie du comportement et opérations.* Paris: Presses universitaires de France, 1960.

Bruner, J. *The process of education.* Cambridge, Mass.: Harvard University Press, 1960.

Chomsky, N. *Syntactic structures.* The Hague: Mouton, 1957.

Chomsky, N. Review of B. F. Skinner. *Verbal Behavior in Language,* 1959, *35* (1), 26–58.

Greco, P., & Piaget, J. *Etudes d'Epistemologie Génétique VII: Apprentissage et connaissance, ler et IIième parties.* Paris: Presses universitaires de France, 1959.

Inhelder, B., Bovet, M., & Sinclair, H. In *Revue suisse de psychologie,* 1967.

Kohnstamm, G. A. La méthode génétique en psychologie. *Psychologie française,* No. 10, 1956.

Laurendeau, M., & Pinard, A. *Psychologie et épistémologie génétique.* Paris: Dunod, 1966.

Morf, A., Smedslund, J., Vinh-Bang, & Wohlwill, J. *Etudes d'Epistémologie Génétique IX: L'Apprentissage des structures logiques.* Paris: Presses universitaires de France, 1959.

Natorp, P. *Die logischen Grundlagen der exakten Wissenschaften.* Berlin: Tuebner, 1910.

Piaget, J. *Traité de logique.* Paris: Colin, 1959.

Piaget, J. *The mechanisms of perception* (Trans. by G. N. Seagrim). New York, Basic Books, 1969.

Piaget, J., & Inhelder, B. *L'image mental chez l'enfant.* Paris: Presses universitaires de France, 1966.

Pitts, W., & McCulloch, W. S. How we know universals: The perception of auditory and visual forms. *Bulletin of Mathematical Biophysics,* 1947, *9,* 127–147.

Waddington, C. H. *The strategy of the genes.* New York: Macmillan, 1957.

De Zwart, H. Sinclair. *Acquisition du langage et développement de la pensée.* Paris: Dunod, 1967.

INFORMATION PROCESSING APPROACHES TO DEVELOPMENT* 4

ROBERT S. SIEGLER, *Carnegie-Mellon University*

CHAPTER CONTENTS

INTRODUCTION

In the 1970 edition of this *Handbook,* information processing was the primary topic in none of the 29 chapters. The subject index included only two references to it. Thirteen years later, the information processing approach is arguably *the* leading strategy for the study of cognitive development. I would be surprised if the subject index of the current *Handbook* included fewer than 100 references to it. How can this growth be explained?

One source of the approach's appeal is its general perspective on human beings. Seen from this perspective, people are in essence limited capacity manipulators of symbols. The symbol manipulation process takes place on multiple levels. People orga-

nize elementary information processes, whose execution takes less than one-tenth of a second, into hierarchies of goals and subgoals. Using such goal hierarchies, they can accomplish great cognitive feats. However, a variety of processing limitations can prevent people from attaining their goals: limitations on the number of symbols that they can manipulate simultaneously, on the speed with which they can manipulate symbols, on the depth to which they can search memory, and on their resistance to interference, to name but four. To overcome these processing limitations, people use a variety of strategies. Mnemonic strategies such as rehearsal, elaboration, and organization can augment short-term memory. External memory aids such as books and other reference materials can combine information from many sources to overcome limitations of the knowledge base. Problem-solving strategies such as means-ends analysis can overcome limitations connected with decision making. The tensions among the setting of goals, the processing limitations that hinder their attainment, and the strategies developed to overcome the processing limitations

*This work was supported in part by NICHHD Grants HD-15285 and HD-16578 and also by a grant from the Spencer Foundation. Thanks for careful readings and useful comments on earlier versions of the manuscript go to Patricia Carpenter, Margaret Clark, William Kessen, Catherine Sophian, and Bob Sternberg.

create an appealing, even dramatic, metaphor for humankind's effort to know the world.

A second reason that information processing approaches have been accepted is the usefulness of their languages for characterizing cognition. General notions such as scripts and frames provide means for describing the ways in which knowledge might be organized. More tangible representations such as flow diagrams and decision trees have proved valuable for representing hypotheses about the temporal course of cognition. Very precise computer languages such as production systems have encouraged hypotheses about the internal manipulation of symbols that gives rise to behavior. These languages have improved our capacity to formulate and express ideas about the workings of the "black box." Compared either to standard written language or to alternative formalisms such as stochastic models or the propositional calculus, information processing languages strike a happy balance among precision, flexibility, and intuitive appropriateness for characterizing cognitive activity.

A third reason for the growth of the information processing approach is its arsenal of powerful methodologies. Chronometric methods utilize patterns of reaction times to evaluate models of the time course of information processing. Protocol analyses rely on people's verbalizations to indicate the strategies that they used to solve problems. Error analyses emphasize patterns of correct answers and errors to reveal children's conceptual understanding. Eye-movement analyses examine eye fixations to determine how people process visual information. These information processing methodologies have in common several characteristics. Each is oriented toward testing models of cognition, rather than simply indicating which variables affect performance. Each utilizes a relatively rich data base, in which many pieces of data are produced each minute. In each approach, the *pattern* of data is of the greatest importance, rather than the percentage of correct answers or the absolute speed of performance.

The information processing approach also has attracted adherents because of the issues that it addresses. These issues focus on the way that information is represented and the processes by which it is manipulated. Many of the questions have long been of interest in psychology. Do people think in terms of verbal statements, spatial images, or in some amodal form that can be translated into both verbal and spatial codes? Are mental manipulations performed serially or in parallel? Is there a difference between knowing how and knowing that? Information processing theories have provided new conceptual frameworks within which to consider these

questions; information processing languages have provided new ways of phrasing the questions; and information processing methodologies have provided new tools for gathering data relevant to them.

It is difficult to define the difference between information processing and noninformation processing approaches. Viewing the information processing approach as a family resemblance concept may be more profitable. The same features that were cited to explain the approach's popularity may be used to characterize it informally. Information processing approaches are the ones that view human beings as manipulators of symbols. They strive to produce real time models of cognitive activity. They use languages such as scripts, frames, flow charts, tree diagrams, and production systems to represent cognitive activity. They use chronometric, eye-movement, verbal protocol, and error-pattern data to establish whether people's behavior corresponds to hypothesized models. Finally, they focus on how people represent information and what processes they apply to it. The more of these criteria an investigator's work meets, the more likely that she will view her work as falling within the information processing category.

This chapter is divided into two sections. The first is an overview of what is known about the information processing system (IPS). After considering some of the historical developments leading to the information processing approach, we examine two types of theories that have been influential: theories that focus on the IPS as such, and theories that focus on the interaction between the IPS and the task environment. Following this, we examine information processing languages for representing knowledge. This section includes descriptions of semantic networks, production systems, and scripts. Next, we consider several commonly used methodologies for studying the IPS: chronometric methods, protocol analyses, eye-movement analyses, and error analyses. Finally, we discuss several issues about the nature of the IPS, among them serial versus parallel processing and exhaustive versus self-terminating processing.

A large percentage of the work cited in this first section is not explicitly developmental. Some of the work involves empirical studies of adults; other parts are theoretical and are intended to apply equally to people of all ages. At first glance, such investigations might not seem to be relevant to the study of development. I believe, though, that they are entirely relevant. Many aspects of the information processing system would not be expected to change with age: If adults have separate sensory registers, short-term memories, and long-term memories, so almost certainly do children; if adults perform serially most processing beyond the sensory level, so almost certainly do children; if adults represent all information amodally, so almost certainly do children; and so on. In those aspects of the information processing system where developmental change would be expected, knowledge about the adult system also is useful. Development is much easier to understand when we know where it is going. Finally, the information processing approach has been used widely in studying adult cognition for more than 20 years; developmentalists may benefit both from what has been learned and from what seems to be unlearnable. Therefore, the first main section, roughly the first half of the chapter, provides an overview of what is known about the IPS in general.

The second half of the chapter focuses on the development of the IPS. The first two parts within this section correspond to the two types of information processing theories already described: theories emphasizing the development of the IPS as such, and theories emphasizing the development of interactions between the IPS and task environments of interest. The section on the development of the IPS as such is organized around four frequently cited explanations for cognitive development: the growth of basic processes, strategies, metacognition, and the knowledge base. The section on the development of interactions between IPS and task environment is organized around task environments of special interest. Among these are classical reasoning problems, Piagetian problems, and academic tasks. Next, the focus turns to mechanisms of development: Through what processes does the IPS develop? The chapter concludes with a number of predictions about the future of information processing approaches to development. Figure 1 illustrates schematically the chapter's organization.

AN OVERVIEW OF THE INFORMATION PROCESSING SYSTEM

Historical Antecedents of the Information Processing Approach

The information processing approach did not rise out of a vacuum. It has roots in several disciplines—communications theory, computer science, and linguistics among them. Examination of the approach's historical origins renders more understandable its current form (cf. Lachman, Lachman, & Butterfield, 1979, for a more detailed discussion of the history of information processing psychology).

In the 1940s, a small group of scientists and mathematicians (e.g., Shannon, von Neumann, Wiener) developed a theory of communications.

Within their analysis, the essential characteristic of communications systems was the transmission of information from one station to another. They described transmitters and receivers in terms of capacity limitations, that is, limits on the messages that could pass through a communications channel in a unit of time. Within information processing psychology, the notions of limited capacity sensory buffers and short-term memory stores stem directly from this notion of limited channel capacity (e.g., Broadbent, 1954).

Communications theory also gave rise to the concepts of serial and parallel processing. The issue was whether two messages could be communicated simultaneously without any loss of information (parallel processing) or whether the messages needed to be attended to one at a time for reception to be perfect (serial processing).

Another communications theory concept that influenced information processing approaches is coding. Coding and the related concept of representation refer to the rules by which stimuli in one form are converted into another form. For example, rules can be formulated for converting a written word into phonemes, Morse code, or machine language. The issue of which external world properties are preserved in people's internal representations and the rules for translating external input into internal representations have commanded continuing attention from information processing psychologists.

Many of the scientists and mathematicians who formulated communications theory also helped bring into being computer science and cybernetics. The first response to these fields by psychologists was to relate information-theoretic measures to human performance. For example, Hick (1952) examined the relations between reaction time and the amount of information, measured in bits, contained in the response. These direct applications of cybernetic notions soon reached a dead end. The analyses of uncertainty could be applied to only a limited range of tasks, and even where they could be applied, the objective amount of uncertainty was a mediocre predictor of performance (Garner & Clements, 1963).

Later incorporations of ideas from cybernetics and computer science have been considerably more successful. One contribution is the idea that both men and computers can be thought of as symbol-manipulating devices. Newell and Simon (1972) phrased this insight in the following way:

> With a model of an information processing system [a computer], it becomes meaningful to try to represent in some detail a particular man at work

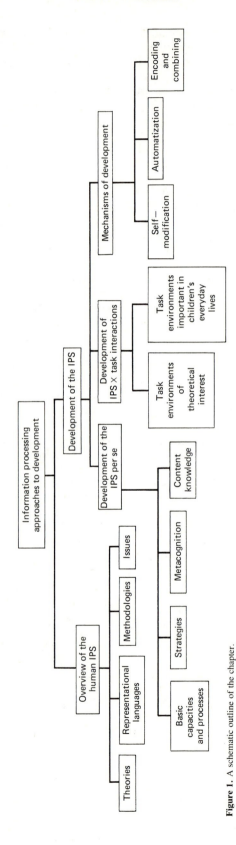

Figure 1. A schematic outline of the chapter.

on a particular problem. Such a representation is no metaphor, but a precise symbolic model on the basis of which pertinent specific aspects of the man's problem-solving behavior can be calculated. This model of symbol manipulation remains very much an approximation, of course, hypothesizing in an extreme form the neatness of discrete symbols and a small set of elementary processes, each with precisely defined and limited behavior. This abstraction, though possibly severe, does provide a grip on symbolic behavior that was not available heretofore (p. 5).

Newell and Simon's claim is not that men and computers are generally similar. Rather, they view both men and computers as symbol manipulators, with the complexity necessary to solve difficult problems. Because computers and computer programs are man-made, we are in a better position to understand their symbol manipulation processes. If we can program computers to mimic human behavior, we may obtain insights into how men as well as machines produce the behavior. Also, because computers only do what they are told, they force simulators to be specific about the symbols that are manipulated and the processes that do the manipulating. This constraint has been part of the motivation for using computer languages to characterize human cognition.

At a more specific level, computer science has contributed a huge number of issues for psychologists to consider. Does the IPS include separate storage and processing units? How does the system know what program to use? Does it search its data base in a self-terminating or in an exhaustive fashion? How is information added to the system and how is it lost from it? Computers may well perform these functions differently from the way people do. Some have argued, however, that there may be very few ways in which symbol manipulators can produce intelligent behavior (e.g., Anderson, 1976). At a minimum, computer science has forced consideration of "black box" issues, has offered to psychology precise languages for describing symbol manipulations, and has suggested resolutions for a number of important issues in human cognition.

Although the contributions of linguistics are more difficult to characterize than are those of computer science or communications theory, they are substantial nonetheless. Chomsky's (1959) review of Skinner's (1957) book on language was especially influential. The review challenged not just the particulars of Skinner's operant analysis but whether behavioristic accounts could ever explain language.

The ability of language users to produce and comprehend novel utterances was identified as a central problem; how could reinforcement explain the production of appropriate responses that had never been reinforced? Nor was it clear how reinforcement could account for people's skills in paraphrasing or how it could account for the entire phenomenon of grammar.

Chomsky's critique identified several aspects of language that any comprehensive theory would have to explain: its generativity, its recursiveness, and its grammatical structure. These goals have been accepted as crucial by information processing psychologists. His criticism also was influential in legitimizing complex cognitive skills (e.g., language) as appropriate targets of inquiry. Before Chomsky's review, experimental psychologists focused on simple, arbitrary learning tasks; after the review, they began to investigate a wider range of cognitive activities. Reaction to Chomsky's alternative to behaviorism, transformational grammar, has been more complex. For a time, research on the psychological implications of Chomsky's theory dominated the field of psycholinguistics. This research persuaded most psycholinguists that transformational grammars are not viable psychological models of language comprehension and production. On the other hand, transformational grammars' emphasis on rules as the basic unit of analysis for complex behavior has become an integral part of the information processing approach. The goal of formulating grammars also has been retained, as recent work on story grammars demonstrates (e.g., Stein & Glenn, 1979; Thorndyke, 1977). Finally, Chomsky's work on transformational grammar greatly stimulated psychologists' interest in syntax; after an initial spate of enthusiasm and a later decrease in interest, psycholinguists' attention to syntax again seems to be growing (e.g., Maratsos & Chalkley, 1981; Morgan & Newport, 1981).

The contributions of computer science and communications theory to the information processing approach were evident in the earliest information processing theory—Broadbent's (1954, 1958) theory of attention. Broadbent's theory was motivated by findings on dichotic listening tasks. On such tasks, people are presented simultaneously pairs of digits, one in each ear, and later asked to recall them. People might hear "2" in the left ear and "5" in the right ear, followed by "4" in the left ear and "1" in the right ear, followed by "8" in the left ear and "7" in the right ear. This task is rather easy if people first can repeat all of the digits presented to one ear and then all of the digits presented to the other ear (e.g., 2,4,8,5,1,7). However, they find it much more difficult to integrate the lists presented to the two ears so as to match the actual sequence of presentation (e.g., 2,5,4,1,8,7).

Broadbent's explanation of these results is illustrated in Figure 2. It is a theory of the entire information processing system as well as of performance on the dichotic listening task. Information passes through the senses to a buffer, called the short-term store, where it can be retained for a few seconds. Then it goes to the selective filter, which attends to part of the information. The selective filter chooses information to attend to on the basis of physical characteristics, such as which ear the information entered. The attended information is sent to a limited capacity perceptual system that extracts its meaning. Then the information is sent to long-term memory and used to respond.

Broadbent accounted for performance on the dichotic listening task by hypothesizing a speed constraint on the selective filter's switching of attention from ear to ear. Because of this constraint on switching speed, people would attend to the information entering one ear, retain the other ear's information temporarily in the short-term store, and then switch attention to the previously unattended ear's information. This theory clearly reflects the influence of communications theory and computer science. (Note the flow chart representation and the use of such concepts as limited capacity channels, buffers, serial processing, filters, and information overload.)

All contemporary information processing theories have followed Broadbent's lead in certain respects: they postulate sensory apparatuses, a long-term storage system, and limited attentional capacity. However, the contemporary models have diverged into two classes: those that focus on the information processing system (IPS) per se, and those that focus on the interaction between the IPS and the task environment. Theories of the first type are the more direct descendants of Broadbent's model. They represent attempts to study processes in pure form, as abstracted as possible from the contexts in which processing occurs. Thus, researchers choose tasks on which to study retrieval from long-term memory (LTM), scanning of short-term memory (STM), and rehearsal of serially presented lists not because of the inherent interest of the tasks but because the tasks possess no obvious idiosyncratic features that would detract from their representativeness. By contrast, in theories of the second type, the task environment is emphasized; cognitive activity is viewed as the person's efforts to adapt to it. What is represented and processed is viewed as depending crucially on the task that is given. Below, we examine in depth one prominent example of each type of theory. Atkinson and Shiffrin's (1968) theory of memory will be used to exemplify approaches that focus on the IPS per se. Newell and Simon's (1972) theory of problem solving will be used to exemplify theories that focus on the interaction between IPS and task environment.

The fact that a theory of memory was chosen to illustrate the first approach and a theory of problem solving to illustrate the second is not coincidental. Theories of memory traditionally have focused on people's mental activities in the abstract, whereas theories of problem solving have focused more on how those activities are applied to particular tasks. Although the colinearity between the psychological

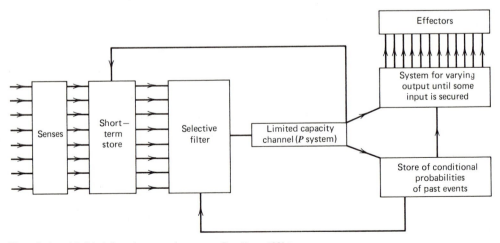

Figure 2. A model of the information processing system. (Broadbent, 1958.)

domain and the type of theory is high, it is not perfect. For example, investigations of how the knowledge base influences recall fall within the area of memory, but such studies often emphasize the interaction between the IPS and the material being remembered (Chase & Ericsson, 1983). In addition, although most information processing research on memory (and also on perception and language) has emphasized the IPS as such, the trend in these areas is toward research focusing on the interaction between the IPS and the task environment. This is especially the case in developmental research. For these reasons, the theme that information processing theories can be divided into those that focus on the IPS per se and those that focus on the IPS X task environment interaction will recur in this chapter.

Contemporary Information Processing Theories

A Theory That Focuses on the IPS Per Se

Atkinson and Shiffrin's (1968) model exemplifies one dominant type of theory of the IPS, the stores approach. This type of theory is based on an explicit analogy between human minds and digital computers. Computers include input units that register information from the environment, central processing units that manipulate information, and long-term storage units that hold on an enduring basis programs and data. Each of these units can be characterized in terms of its capacity, coding, and temporal limits. On how much information can the unit operate at any one time? In what forms can information enter, and in what forms can it be held? How fast can the unit perform its basic processes? Store models of memory suggest similar questions about the human information processing system.

Atkinson and Shiffrin's model began with a distinction between structural features of memory and control processes. First consider structural features. These features were viewed as inborn, inflexible, and constant across individuals. They include the basic architecture of memory and the fixed operating characteristics of each system within it. Atkinson and Shiffrin's hypothesized memory architecture included three stores: the sensory store (also called the sensory register), the short-term store, and the long-term store. Each of these stores could be divided further according to the code of the entering information; thus the system might include a visual sensory register, an auditory sensory register, a visual short-term store, an auditory short-term store, and so on. All three stores were believed to be limited in the speed with which basic processes could be performed. Sensory and short-term stores were believed also to be limited in their capacity and in the durability of entering traces.

Now consider control processes. These differed from structural features of memory in being learnable, flexible, and variable across individuals. They were thought to influence the workings of all three stores subject to each store's structural limitations. Coding, rehearsal, and search strategies were included under the central process heading.

Figure 3 illustrates Atkinson and Shiffrin's model of the memory system. Information enters the system through the appropriate sensory register. When Atkinson and Shiffrin formulated their model, only the characteristics of the visual register were established. Much of the evidence came from an elegant experiment by Sperling (1960). Sperling presented college students a 3 × 4 matrix of letters for 50 milliseconds (msec). When asked immediately after the presentation to name as many letters as they could, students typically listed four or five, about 40% of the list. Then Sperling changed the procedure in a small but important way. Rather than having students recall all of the letters, he asked them to recall only the letters in one row. Since students could not anticipate the identity of the row, they needed to process all 12 letters, just as in the original format. However, requiring them to recite the contents of only one row eliminated the need to retain the information during the recitation period.

Sperling found that when the experimenter indicated which row to recall immediately after stimulus offset, subjects recalled 80% of the letters in the row. When the row's identity was indicated 300 msec after stimulus offset, recall declined to 55%, and when it was indicated 1 sec. after, performance declined to the original 40%. Sperling's interpretation was that a 50 msec exposure was sufficient for letters to create a visual icon, but that the icon was largely dissipated within 300 msec, and completely gone by 1 sec. Averbach and Coriell (1961), using a quite different methodology, reached a similar conclusion not only about the existence of a visual sensory register but about its temporal characteristics; they too hypothesized that the icon was largely dissipated within 300 msec.

Masking studies have revealed several processes by which the visual sensory register operates. In such studies, people are shown in close temporal proximity a target display, such as a matrix of letters, and an interfering stimulus, such as a bright light or pattern. Bright light is most disruptive of recall when the light is presented concurrently with the display of letters. Its effects fall off symmetrically when it is presented shortly before or

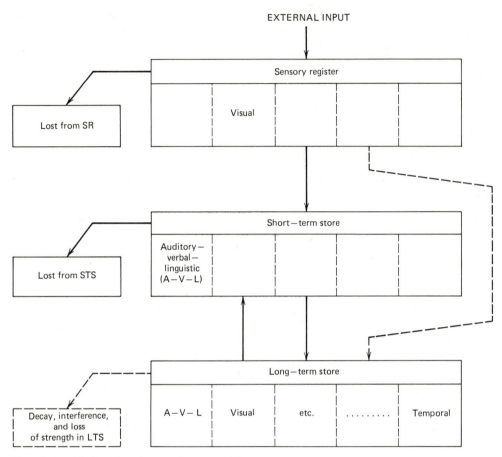

Figure 3. A model of the information processing system. (Atkinson & Schiffrin, 1969.)

shortly after the letters. This suggests that it disrupts the process of icon formation (Eriksen, 1966). Patterns, on the other hand, are maximally disruptive when presented 100 msec *after* the display is presented. They seem to exert their effects by interfering with the reading of the already formed icon. Thus, the visual sensory register seems to subsume at least two separable processes: icon formation and icon readout.

Atkinson and Shiffrin contended that control processes, as well as structural characteristics, influence the functioning of the sensory register. They cited data that people can control which sensory register they attend to; they can screen out information from sensory modalities other than the one they believe will be important. The investigators also pointed out that within a given sensory modality, people can heighten their attention to some information and attenuate it to other parts.

After information is processed in the sensory store, it moves to the short-term store. This short-term store is the central processing unit. It is here that information from the immediate environment and information from long-term memory are combined to perform whatever calculations are necessary. Atkinson and Shiffrin also conceived of the short-term store as the conscious part of memory. People are not aware of the workings of either the sensory register or the long-term store, but they are conscious of the short-term store's activities. Finally, they conceived of the short-term store as limited in capacity; it can retain simultaneously only a few elements. The capacity constraint is a function of the number of meaningful units (chunks) rather than the number of physical units; the rate of decay from STM of three unrelated letters is identical to that of three unrelated words, each having three letters (Murdock, 1961).

Atkinson and Shiffrin focused on the auditory (or more precisely the auditory-verbal-linguistic (a-v-l)) code within the short-term store. The reason was the same one that motivated them to concentrate on the visual code in the sensory register. Although Atkinson and Shiffrin believed that other types of codes could enter the short-term store, they had no evidence to support their intuition. In addition, Conrad (1964) reported that even for visually presented letters, subjects' errors were predominantly auditory in nature. Intrusion errors sounded like the correct letters rather than looking like them. Thus, it seemed possible that before entering the short-term store, all information was converted to the a-v-l code.

Atkinson and Shiffrin hypothesized several types of limits on the operations of the short-term store. One of these involved its capacity, the number of symbols it could include at one time. Following Miller (1956), they proposed a slot model in which short-term memory had approximately seven locations that could hold chunks of information. Additional information either would not enter the system or would push out existing information.

The rate of decay of information also was hypothesized to limit the short-term store. Material in the store ordinarily would be lost within 15 to 30 sec. However, rehearsal could maintain it for a longer time, and the longer the rehearsal period, the greater the probability that the information would be transferred to the long-term store.

Atkinson and Shiffrin emphasized the influence of three control processes on the short-term store's functioning: search and retrieval strategies; rehearsal; and information transfer between long- and short-term memory. Search and retrieval strategies embodied such decisions as whether to search short-term memory contents exhaustively or in a self-terminating fashion. Rehearsal involved decisions about which new information to attend to and which information to allow to decay. Transfer of information between stores again reflected decisions about the importance of retaining information; to achieve such transfer, people could chunk, group, organize, or recode material.

The long-term store constituted the third main unit in Atkinson's and Shiffrin's model. They said relatively little about the structural features of this store except that the memory trace was not in all-or-none form. They cited data about the tip-of-the-tongue phenomenon to support this conclusion, as well as data demonstrating that when people recalled a fact incorrectly, their second guesses were much better than chance. They also concluded that memory traces were permanent. Inability to recall was due either to structural interference from other contents of the long-term store or to difficulties in accessing the material.

Atkinson and Shiffrin contended that control processes dominate the activities of the long-term store. They noted that natural language mediators, elaborative imagery, and adaptive search strategies greatly enhance long-term retention. Although they believed that control processes played some role in the functioning of the sensory register, and a large role in the functioning of the short-term store, they thought they played an especially significant role in the functioning of the long-term store.

Developments in the past 15 years can be classified into three groups with regard to Atkinson and Shiffrin's model of the IPS: those that support it; those that extend it; and those that contradict it or suggest alternatives. Below, brief and selective accounts of these developments will be given; many important developments will be omitted because of limitations of space.

Developments Supporting, Extending, and Challenging Store Models of Memory

Perhaps the two most notable features of Atkinson and Shiffrin's model were the division of memory into separate structures and the emphasis placed on control processes. Much evidence consistent with each of these emphases has been collected in the past 15 years. A small portion of this evidence is cited below.

Craik (1970) provided particularly compelling evidence for the separation between short- and long-term memory. His experiment had two parts. First, Craik presented college students with 10 lists, each having 10 words; after each list, students were to recall the 10 words. Then the experimenter did something unexpected; he asked the students to recall all 100 of the words that had been presented. This changed the task from a test of short-term memory to a test of long-term memory, since the list presentation period had lasted several minutes.

In the first part of the experiment, involving recall of the individual lists, Craik observed standard serial position effects, with recall somewhat elevated at the beginning of each list (primacy effect) and considerably elevated at the end of each list (recency effect). In the second part, the primacy effect remained but the recency effect disappeared. The probability of recall actually was lower for the last position in each list than for any other of the 10 positions. These results suggested that serial position effects are due to separable short- and long-term memory influences. Primacy effects reflect long-term memory processes, whereas recency effects reflect short-term memory ones.

Atkinson and Shiffrin's emphasis on control processes also has received support. The method of loci, rehearsal, elaboration, and semantic organization all have been given considerable attention (Bower, 1972; Bower & Clark, 1969; Delin, 1969; Drozdal & Flavell, 1975). The effects of qualitative and quantitative variations in the use of these strategies, and the conditions under which each method is most effective, have been among the most frequent themes of research on control processes.

Atkinson and Shiffrin's model also has been extended in several ways. For all three memory stores, people have been found to use codes corresponding to more than one sensory modality. An auditory analog to the visual sensory register has been found, in which a large amount of relatively unanalyzed auditory information is held briefly (Darwin, Turvey & Crowder, 1972; Effron, 1970). Evidence that visual information as well as a-v-l information is utilized in the short-term store (Brooks, 1968; Kroll, 1972) and in the long-term store (Shepherd & Podgorny, 1978) also has been forthcoming.

Another extension has been in the direction of characterizing the nature of the bottleneck in short-term memory. Some types of processing do not seem to be affected by STM limitations in the same way as others. Treisman and Gelade (1980) provided evidence for seemingly unlimited capacity processing of single visual features but limited processing of conjunctions of features. Duncan (1980) and Taylor (1978) characterized the nature of the bottleneck differently; information can be processed up to the level of item identification in a way unlimited by capacity constraints, but meaning can be extracted only by a slow, serial process. At present, the bulk of the evidence seems to support the Duncan and Taylor characterization, but the question still is open.

Other investigators have examined issues that were not addressed directly by the Atkinson and Shiffrin model. Much work has been done on the organization of long-term memory. Atkinson and Shiffrin said little about the workings of long-term memory, save that control processes greatly influenced them. Since then, several ideas have been proposed concerning intra- and interconcept relations in long-term memory. One of the most prominent has involved propositional network (also known as semantic network) models.

Propositional networks depict memory as a set of node-link relations. Such links as ''isa,'' ''hasa,'' ''becauseof,'' and ''madefrom'' relate concepts to their properties and to other concepts. When people attempt to answer questions or recall facts, their searches for the relevant information proceed along the node-link pathways. Many computer simulations of long-term memory use the propositional network representation (Anderson & Bower, 1973; Collins & Loftus, 1975; Norman, Rumelhart, & LNR, 1975; Quillian, 1969). This formalism will be discussed in more depth in the representational languages section of this chapter; indeed, the salutary effect of semantic networks on understanding of long-term memory is a prime example of how innovative representational languages can spark theoretical progress.

These extensions go beyond Atkinson and Shiffrin's model but are not at odds with it. A variety of other data, however, call into question the entire stores approach to memory. If separable stores exist, their quantitative parameters are elusive. Estimates of trace duration in the auditory sensory register range from 130 msec (Efron, 1970) to 5 sec. (Glucksberg & Cowan, 1972). Estimates of trace duration in the visual sensory store vary from 250 msec (Averbach & Coriell, 1961) to 25 sec. (Kroll, Parks, Parkinson, Bieber, & Johnson, 1970). Estimates of the capacity of the short-term store range from 2–4 chunks (Glanzer, 1972) to 20 chunks (Hunt & Love, 1972). Estimates of the rate of forgetting from the short-term store range from complete forgetting within 15 sec. (Peterson & Peterson, 1959) to no forgetting within 15 sec. (Shiffrin, 1973). Nor can the stores easily be distinguished by the codes that they accept. Visual, a-v-l, and semantic variables influence the workings of each of the stores (Brooks, 1968; Posner & Boies, 1971; Shulman, 1972; Treisman, 1964).

Investigators have reacted to these data in two ways. Some have continued to distinguish among memory stores but to change the particular distinctions. Some theorists distinguish between the sensory store and the rest of memory (Anderson, 1976; Collins & Loftus, 1975; Schneider & Shiffrin, 1977); others distinguish between primary memory, including the sensory and short-term stores, and secondary memory, including the long-term store (Craik & Levy, 1976); still others hypothesize that many distinguishable stores exist (Baddeley & Hitch, 1974). The second approach has been to move away from the stores framework entirely, adopting alternatives such as the levels of processing approach (Craik & Lockhart, 1972; Craik & Tulving, 1975) or the encoding specificity approach (Thomson & Tulving, 1970). These alternatives emphasize the way in which information is processed and the intended purpose of processing rather than the limits imposed by fixed stores.

Despite these challenges, most investigators

probably continue to work within some sadder-but-wiser variant of Atkinson and Shiffrin's stores framework. Whatever its faults, it is straightforward, it identities sets of phenomena that hang together reasonably well, and nothing clearly superior has arisen to take its place. Even those who have formulated alternative models, such as Anderson (e.g., 1976) and Craik (e.g., Craik & Levy, 1976) have maintained the fundamental distinction between short- and long-term memory. In addition, Atkinson and Shiffrin's emphasis on control processes, quite novel when they formulated the model, has worn well.

The largest shortcoming of the stores' approach is not unique to it but rather is shared by all approaches that focus on hardware to the exclusion of content. People process information flexibly. They use this flexibility to adapt to the demands of myriad task environments. What they already know about a content domain and how they represent the knowledge substantially influences their subsequent reasoning. For these reasons, information processing researchers have devoted increasing amounts of effort to analyzing the content about which people reason.

A Theory that Focuses on the Interaction Between IPS and Task Environment

Easily the most influential theory of this type is Newell and Simon's theory of problem solving. Newell and Simon (1972) summarized their theory in four propositions:

1. A few, and only a few, gross characteristics of the human IPS are invariant over task and problem solver.
2. These characteristics are sufficient to determine that a task environment is represented (in the IPS) as a problem space and that problem solving takes place in a problem space.
3. The structure of the task environment determines the possible structures of the problem space.
4. The structure of the problem space determines the possible programs that can be used in problem solving. (pp. 788–789)

These propositions identify three constructs as central—the information processing system, the task environment, and the problem space produced by the interaction between the IPS and the task environment. The present discussion of Newell and Simon's theory is organized around these three constructs.

The IPS.   Newell and Simon's model of the IPS closely resembles Atkinson and Shiffrin's model. Both postulated sensory buffers, a short-term mem-

ory, and a long-term memory. The quantitative parameters in Newell and Simon's model also were similar to those suggested by Atkinson and Shiffrin, as was the emphasis on control processes. Newell and Simon went beyond Atkinson and Shiffrin's model, however, in drawing several conclusions about the nature of the processing system. These concern the basic elements of memory, the way these elements are organized, the temporal course of processing, and the organization of programs.

Newell and Simon suggested that the basic element of the IPS is the *symbol*. Symbols can be combined to form *symbol structures* that represent data, processes, and programs. Many organizations of symbols are possible, but Newell and Simon suggested that they are organized, in fact, as lists, structures in which symbols are connected by the single relation ''next.''

An example may help clarify the nature of symbols, symbol structures, and lists. Figure 4 is a representation of the quadratic equation. Note that symbols representing constants, variables, and arithmetic operations are combined to produce the symbol

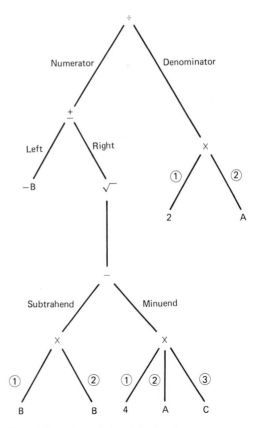

Figure 4. Network model of quadratic formula.

structure. The bottom-up ordering of the hierarchy implies the sequence in which operations are performed. The two "B's" at the bottom are multiplied to produce B^2; 4, A, and C are multiplied to produce 4AC; these two terms are combined to produce B^2-4AC, which in turn is placed under the square root sign; and so on. The only organization of the structure is in terms of *next* relations, making it a list structure. Although mathematical relations are especially easy to represent as list structures, a wide variety of other verbal and visual material can be represented similarly (e.g., Anderson, 1976; Norman et al., 1975).

Newell and Simon argued that the IPS is serial; it can execute only one elementary information process at a time. They postulated considerable parallelism at the physiological level and at the level of memory search (obviously, children's fact retrieval does not slow down as the size of their memory systems increases). However, they claimed that problem solving is basically serial (it takes twice as long to solve two arithmetic problems as one). Thus, for purposes of a theory of problem solving, the IPS can be thought of as strictly serial.

Newell and Simon also postulated that people's problem-solving programs are structured as production systems. As shown in Figure 5, a production system can be thought of as a five-level hierarchy. The production system divides into the production system proper and the short-term memory. The production system proper is made up of individual productions. Each production has a condition side (the symbols to the left of the arrow) and an action side

(the symbols to the right of it). The condition side of production, the action side of productions, and the short-term memory are all composed of symbols.

Proceeding from the bottom of the hierarchy, the condition side of each production lists the symbols that must be in the short-term memory for the production to fire. In a sense, a match between symbols in short-term memory and all of the symbols on the condition side of a production indicates that the production is relevant to the immediate situation. If a production fires, the actions on the right side of its arrow are executed. The firing may add, subtract, or change symbols in the short-term memory and may also produce behavior. Next, the production whose condition side matches the new contents of short-term memory fires, again altering the short-term memory contents. The cycles continue until no production matches the STM contents or until a production fires whose action side includes the command "Stop." Note that unlike many other computer languages the order in which a production system's statements are listed does not imply any particular order of execution. In a production system with 10 elements, the tenth production may fire first. The order of execution depends not on the order of listings but on which production's condition side elements are included among the symbols in short-term memory.

Figure 6 illustrates a very simple production system. In this system, short-term memory can include three elements at any one time. The production system proper includes three productions. P1 says that if you have a circle and a plus, replace them with a

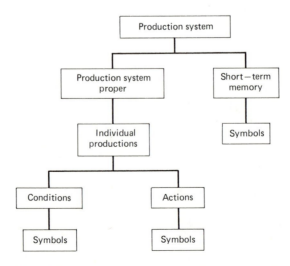

Figure 5. A schematic model of a production system.

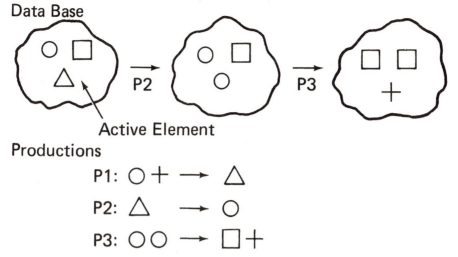

Figure 6. A simple production system. (Siegler & Klahr, 1982.)

triangle. P2 says that if you have a triangle, replace it with a circle. P3 says that if you have two circles, replace them with a square and a plus.

At the outset of the production system's run, short-term memory contains a triangle, a circle, and a square. On the first recognition cycle, only P2 has all of its conditions (the presence of a triangle) matched by the short-term memory contents. It fires, and its action side tags the triangle "old" and adds a circle to the STM contents. Now the STM includes two circles and a square. These STM contents match neither the P1 nor the P2 conditions, but they do match P3's, since STM includes two circles. P3 replaces the two circles with a square and a plus. At this point, the STM contents (two squares and a plus) do not meet any production's conditions, and the system stops.

Newell and Simon noted a number of parallels between the workings of such production systems and the ways that humans solve problems. Both create explicit goals and subgoals and integrate them with other information in memory rather than storing control information separately. Both systems balance stimulus-bound and stimulus-independent aspects; information can enter STM and influence further processing either through sensory detection of events in the external world or through the actions of previous productions. Finally, the distinction between the condition and action sides of the productions allows for parallelism in memory search (matching the condition side) yet seriality in problem-solving activity (reflecting the time necessary to execute each action).

The Task Environment. Although the nature of the IPS imposes some limits on problem solving, the limits are broad. Newell and Simon contended that the task environment constrains problem solving to a much greater degree. They assumed that people's behavior is adaptive, that is, appropriate to the goal of the task. Therefore, in those cases where behavior efficiently accomplishes its goal, we learn more about the structure of the task than about the nature of the IPS. This view implies that to study problem solving, researchers first should analyze the task in order to formulate an optimal performance model and then study departures from optimality for what they might reveal about the IPS.

The Problem Space. The task environment and the IPS combine to create the problem space. Problem spaces are representations of the parts of the task environment that the problem solver thinks essential. The problem-solver's behavior is limited by the elements of the problem space, but the problem space includes other possible behaviors as well. For example, it includes behaviors that are considered but rejected as physically impossible, as contrary to the constraints of the task instructions, or as simply unwise. Effective problem solving depends on the problem space reflecting the essential aspects of the task environment.

What might a problem space look like? Table 1 represents a problem space for the game of number scrabble. In number scrabble, two players take turns choosing from among nine titles. Each tile has on it a different digit from 1 through 9. The goal is to be the first player to get three tiles whose numbers sum to 15.

Table 1A represents the part of the problem space

Table 1. Knowledge Used in the Game of Number Scrabble

A. Symbol Structures for Number Scrabble

player-1 $\xrightarrow{\text{own-pieces}}$ pieces-of-player-1:
 (piece-3 piece-6)
player-2 $\xrightarrow{\text{own-pieces}}$ pieces-of-player-2:
 (piece-5)
unmoved-pieces: (piece-1 piece-2 piece-4
 piece-7 piece-8 piece-9

move piece for player
sum (integer-1, integer-2)
complement (integer)

B. Basic Processes for Number Scrabble

move piece for player:
1. delete piece from unmoved-pieces,
    if fail stop move and report illegal;
2. find own-pieces of player;
3. insert piece on result.

sum (integer-1, integer-2):
1. initialize count to be 0;
2. initialize total to be integer-1;
3. test if count = integer-2,
    if true stop and report total;
4. find next of count ($\Rightarrow$ count);
5. find next of total ($\Rightarrow$ total),
    go to 3.

complement (integer):
1. initialize count to be 0;
2. initialize total to be integer;
3. test if total = 15,
    if true stop and report count;
4. find next of count ($\Rightarrow$ count);
5. find next of total ($\Rightarrow$ total), go to 3.

C. Program for Finding Winning move

make-winning-move for player:
1. generate-pairs own-pieces of player ($\Rightarrow$ (first
    second)):
2. sum (integer of first, integer of second);
3. complement (sum);
4. generate unmoved-pieces:
5. test if integer of unmoved-piece = comple-
    ment, if false continue generation;
6. move unmoved-piece for player, stop
    process.,
    stop and report no move.

(From Newell & Simon, 1972)

that describes the game. It specifies that at any point, players 1 and 2 possess sets of pieces, and a third set of pieces does not belong to either player. It also indicates the existence of nine tiles, each bearing an integer (1 through 9) on it. Relevant information from long-term memory also is included: the list of numbers 0 through 15. Finally, the description includes three processes for approaching the goal: *move*, which deletes a tile from the unchosen pieces and places it in one of the players' piles; *sum*, which adds two integers; and *complement*, which subtracts

an integer from 15 to reveal the number that should be chosen next. Table 1B represents in greater detail the move, sum, and complement subroutines. Table 1C represents the optimal strategy for playing the game: generate the possible pairs of your pieces; compute the sum of the first pair; check whether an unchosen piece is the complement of 15 and that sum; repeat the cycle if necessary with the next pair; and continue until you find a complement or try all pairs. If you have tried all pairs and have not found the complement of any of them, then arbitrarily choose a tile if any are left or stop the game if none are.

The number-scrabble example illustrates several features of problem spaces. They include information about elements of the task, legal operations, and strategies for choosing among legal operations. People construct initial knowledge states from among the elements of the problem space; they solve problems by progressing through one knowledge state after another until they reach the goal. Successive knowledge states are very similar, typically differing in only one respect (in the example, players create a new knowledge state each time they choose a piece). Finally, people use relatively few general problem-solving strategies—working forwards, working backwards, planning, and means-ends analysis are the most common ones—and they choose these on the basis of the structure of the problem space. In the number-scrabble example, the structure of the problem space almost dictates a strategy of means-ends analysis (comparing the existing state with the desired state and seeking to eliminate the differences).

Developments Supporting, Extending, and Challenging Newell and Simon's Model of Problem Solving

Newell and Simon's theory has led to fewer experiments whose data have supported, extended, or challenged their ideas than has Atkinson and Shiffrin's. In part, this is due to cognitive psychologists having emphasized problem solving less than memory. A high percentage of contemporary work on problem solving is influenced by Newell and Simon's theory, but it is a high percentage of a small base. Another reason is the nature of Newell and Simon's theory. Their theory is more a way of viewing the world, a representational language, and a set of worked out examples, than it is a theory in which evidence can disconfirm a central hypothesis.

Most studies of problem solving that touch on Newell and Simon's theory are best classified as extensions. One direction has been an increased emphasis on the role of pattern recognition in problem solving. This emphasis was stimulated by De Groot's (1966) and Chase and Simon's (1973) work on chess. They found that much of the advantage of skilled chess players over novices was that the experts recognized a greater number of patterns of pieces and recognized them more quickly.

A second extension has been to emphasize alternative strategies that people can use to solve problems. Investigators have realized that people choose among multiple problem-solving approaches that entail different advantages and disadvantages. For example, Simon (1975) described four solution strategies for Tower of Hanoi problems: a rote method, in which people memorize all moves; a recursive method, in which people successively reconceptualize the problem of moving N disks to a given peg in terms of the problems of moving N-1 disks to that peg; a perceptual method, in which people always try to move the largest disk that is not yet at the goal peg and in which they develop subgoals if this goal is physically unattainable; and a pattern method, in which people recognize the cyclical nature of the correct pattern of moves and base moves on this recognition. To use some of these strategies demands great memory capacity; to use others requires knowledge of powerful general problem-solving procedures; to use others requires superior pattern recognition. Research determining which strategy people choose under varying conditions has added to understanding of the IPS constraints that shape choices of problem-solving strategies.

A third extension of Newell and Simon's work has been to educationally relevant problems. Early work on the Tower of Hanoi, missionaries and cannibals, and two-strings problems has increasingly been joined by work on problem solving in academic contexts. Greeno (1976) has examined the approaches of high school students to geometry problems; Case (1978) has examined the approaches of elementary school students to arithmetic problems; and Larkin (1978) has examined and compared the approaches of experts and novices to physics problems. All these efforts represent direct applications of ideas from Newell and Simon's theory.

Some criticisms also have been voiced, in particular concerning Newell and Simon's conclusion that the information processing system contains few structural invariants. For example, Posner and McLeod (1982) agreed with Newell and Simon that examination of problem-solving tasks had yielded few invariants, but commented: "The use of the protocol method itself tends to limit analysis to strategies developed by the subject in the execution of problems and is not a very good way for understanding more structural limits on performance" (p. 482).

Both Newell and Simon's and Atkinson and Shiffrin's approaches highlight the need for rich and precise languages to characterize cognition. Many means for representing people's knowledge and mental processes have been developed: semantic networks, production systems, scripts, frames, story grammars, and others. The field of knowledge representation has emerged to examine the properties of these languages.

Representational Languages

Issues in Selecting a Representational Language

Information processing theories are distinguished by their emphasis on knowledge representation. Associationist, Piagetian, gestalt, and psychometrically oriented investigators all have developed cognitive theories, but none have approached information processing researchers in the amount of attention devoted to representing knowledge. Bobrow (1975) graphically depicted the key issue in knowledge representation (Fig. 7). Imagine a freeze-frame image of an environment. This is called the world state. Through some mapping process "M," a symbol manipulator produces a knowledge state that corresponds to this world state. The symbol manipulator then can answer questions about the world state (e.g., how many chairs are in a room) either by directly observing the world or by examining the internal representation. Similarly, he, she, or it can determine the effects of an action either by observing the effects in the world or by thinking about the effects of the corresponding operation on the knowledge state.

Evaluating the adequacy of alternative "M" functions and their attached knowledge states is far from simple. Both the mapping function and the representation are unobservable; they only can be inferred from behavior. Fundamentally different representations often are consistent with the same observations. In light of this difficulty, some investigators have suggested an indirect criterion: people will choose the most cognitively efficient representation (e.g., Hayes-Roth, 1979; Pylyshyn, 1979). Cognitive efficiency has proven to be an elusive concept, however. Representations entail tradeoffs; a representation that is efficient for one purpose almost always is inefficient for others. In addition, the efficiency of a representation for even a single purpose cannot be specified without knowledge of the processes that operate on it (Anderson, 1978). Thus, representational issues usually cannot be resolved on the basis of one representation generally being more efficient than another.

Choosing among representations is a frustrating task; if the issue were not so basic, it likely would have been abandoned years ago. Instead, it has led to some of the most spirited debates in modern cognitive psychology: verbal versus visual representations, discrete versus analog representations, procedural versus declarative representations, single code versus dual code representations, among others. Unfortunately, despite large volumes of research, not one of these issues seems even close to being resolved.

Bobrow (1975) contended that one reason for the inconclusive nature of these debates is that representations differ on many dimensions. Only by contrasting alternatives on each dimension separately, he suggested, can reasonable comparisons be made. The seven dimensions that Bobrow considered can serve as a point of departure for considering the representational languages that researchers have developed in the past decade.

The first of these, *domain and range*, involves which aspects of the world are represented. No representation is complete; even a most comprehensive description of a person in his kitchen would be unlikely to include an explicit statement that his shoes did not need new soles. Models differ in what properties of the world they represent explicitly, what properties they leave inferable from other properties, and what properties they ignore.

Operational correspondence refers to the parallel relation between actions in the world and operations in the model. This relation determines which actions the representation specifies, which it leaves inferable, and which it excludes.

Mapping concerns the specificity of units in the representation and the ways in which values are bound to (substituted for) variables. When we anticipate a visit to the doctor, do we think of it in terms of a visit to a particular doctor, to doctors in that spe-

A. Observations

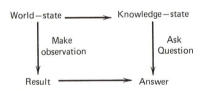

B. Actions

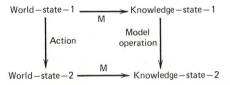

Figure 7. Relationships between world states and knowledge states. (Bobrow, 1975.)

ciality, or doctors in the abstract, to professional people, or to any human being?

Inference deals with the ways in which knowledge can be added to the representation without input from the world. It would be enormously inefficient, and probably impossible, for a system to represent explicitly every fact that it knows (e.g., that a cow breathes). Instead, many properties are inferred from other explicitly noted relations (e.g., that a cow is an animal and that animals breathe).

Access involves the ways in which units in a representation are linked so that they can be called on when needed. Access raises issues of the ways in which integral units are organized (e.g., how are the properties of cows linked to each other?), the ways in which separate units are related (e.g., how are cows linked to other ungulates, to animals, and to living things?), and the mechanisms by which such information is located (e.g., is there some general index like a card catalog in which addresses of information are looked up? How do contextual constraints quicken our access to material? And so on).

Matching involves comparisons among units. A system can use this process to recognize and classify inputs from the environment; it compares an input to already labeled patterns to determine the input's identity. Matching also can be used for decomposition; a sentence may be parsed by matching it to the general passive pattern. Several mechanisms can produce matches: form-matching mechanisms compare physical features; function-matching mechanisms compare purposes; parametric-matching mechanisms compare numerous form and function dimensions to compute general goodness of fit parameters. Representations vary in the types of matches that are sought and in the mechanisms by which matching is done.

Finally, *self-awareness* concerns the explicit knowledge that a system has about its workings and organization. Part of self-awareness involves knowledge of the facts that the system knows and their importance for other aspects of the system's knowledge; such knowledge may be crucial to making inferences. Another part involves knowledge about processes; this may be essential to allocating limited cognitive resources.

Bobrow used these dimensions to compare three representations of a visual stimulus (a 4″ square). The three representations are shown in Figure 8. The MATRIX representation is a two-dimensional imaginal depiction of the square's spatial features. The GRID representation locates the square in the visual display by identifying the location of its bottom left vertex and describing propositionally its shape, ex-

```
0000000000
0000100000
0001110000
0011111000
0111111100
0011111000
0001110000
0000100000
0000000000
```

A. A binary matrix visual representation
(A 1 indicates a light intensity below a certain level)

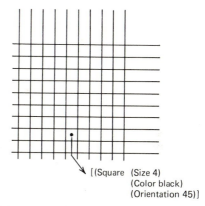

[(Square (Size 4)
         (Color black)
         (Orientation 45)]

B. A Grid—positioned/feature—oriented representation

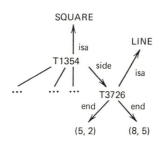

C. A semantic network representation

Figure 8. Three representations of a square. (Bobrow, 1975.)

tent, color, and orientation. The NET representation identifies a physical entity (T1354) as a square and identifies one of its sides as a line with ends having particular spatial coordinates.

These three representations differ in their domain and range—which properties are explicitly stated, which must be inferred, and which are ignored. For example, the area of the square is inferable in MATRIX and NET but is explicit in GRID. The representations also differ in which operations seem most likely to be performed on them (operational correspondence). Consider the operation of rotation. The

MATRIX representation suggests that this operation might be accomplished by a continuous shifting of which spaces have zeroes and which have ones, whereas The NET representation suggests that the square could be rotated by changing the coordinates of the one line whose coordinates are specified. Another way in which the representations differ is in the most obvious access routes. The GRID and MATRIX representations suggest that the units most directly accessible from the square are neighboring objects in space. The NET representation, with its emphasis on semantic relations such as "ISA" and "END" suggests that conceptually similar units such as other squares would be the most accessible. The representational languages do not demand these properties—different representations of the square are possible in each language—but certain representational languages seem to connect naturally with certain processes (cf. Anderson, 1976).

Semantic Networks

Semantic networks, such as the NET representation in Figure 8, are interconnected sets of propositions. Propositions are the simplest entities that have truth values. Ordinary verbal statements often include several propositions; for example, the sentence "The quick red fox jumped over the lazy brown dog" can be decomposed into seven propositions:

1. There was a fox.
2. The fox was quick.
3. The fox was red.
4. The fox jumped over something.
5. The something that was jumped over was a dog.
6. The dog was lazy.
7. The dog was brown.

A semantic network representation of the sentence would include each of these propositions.

Gentner (1975) used semantic networks to model how children learn possessive verbs such as borrow, receive, give, take, buy, and sell. She analyzed each of these terms into its semantic primitives. Semantic primitives express relations that can be used to define many terms. Among Gentner's (and the LNR group's) semantic primitives are POSS (possession), LOC (location), CONTR (a contractual relation), TRANS (transfer), CAUSE, CHANGE, DO, and BECOME. As may be surmised from this list, LNR's semantic networks are verb centered; objects and their properties enter in largely as they relate to the verbs. This is not the case in all semantic network

models; Anderson and Bower's (1973) and Collins and Loftus's (1975) models, for example, are noun centered.

Gentner's representations of the verbs "give" and "sell" are shown in Figure 9. (Readers unfamiliar with semantic networks will find it useful to go back and forth between Figure 9 and the text.) As shown at the top of the network, "give" implies an agent, a recipient, and an object. The agent does something that causes the transfer of the object from its source to some goal. "Sell" also involves an agent and a recipient, but entails two objects and two transfers: an object is transferred from its source (the agent) to its goal (the recipient), and money is transferred from its source (the recipient) to its goal (the agent). In addition, a contractual relation links the two transfers and implies that two parties are involved. Finally, possessives imply a causal sequence; an agent did something that caused the transfer and contract relations to go into effect (e.g., walked into a store and asked whether they had the morning newspaper). Gentner formulated similar analyses for "buy," "take," and a number of other possession verbs.

After generating her analyses, Gentner asked 3- to 8-year-olds to have dolls act out sentences containing the verbs. As she had predicted on the basis of the semantic networks, children understood "give" and "take," which involved one transfer, earlier than "buy" or "sell," which involved two. Also as she had predicted, 3- to 5-year-olds frequently confused "sell" with "give" and "buy" with "take," neglecting the exchange of money between buyer and seller. Finally, children understood "sell" later than "buy;" the similarity of the verbs' representations suggested that this discrepancy was due to the children's greater experience in the buyer than the seller role rather than to any structural difference between the verbs.

Production Systems

Earlier, we discussed a simple production system (Fig. 6). Table 2 illustrates a more interesting one: Klahr and Wallace's (1976) model of how children fail on class inclusion problems.

It frequently is useful to analyze production systems at several levels of detail. In the present case, we will examine the theory underlying Klahr and Wallace's model first. Then we will outline the model's major components. Next we will interpret some individual productions. After that, we will discuss the mechanisms by which productions put symbols into STM and push them out. Finally, we will

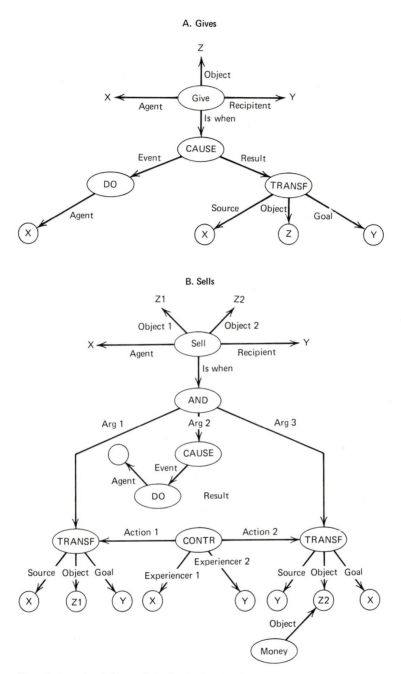

Figure 9. Semantic primitive analysis of ''gives'' and ''sells.''
(Adapted from Gentner, 1975.)

describe the production system's behavior on a class inclusion problem.

First consider the theory underlying Klahr and Wallace's model. The core idea is that children fail on the standard class inclusion task because they encode the two quantifiable properties as having mutually exclusive referents. For example, they would encode the sentence ''are there more square blocks or more red ones'' to mean ''are there more square blocks that are not red than there are red blocks that

Table 2. **Production System Model of How Children Fail on Class Inclusion Problems**

```
00200    PS.QC2 Model for CI failure
01900           Counting by enumeration
02200    PDC.01:((NEW X0)(QS 0) --> (COUNTED**)(0 ===> 1))
02300    PDC.12:((NEW X0)(QS 1) --> (COUNTED**)(1 ===> 2))
02400    PDC.23:((NEW X0)(QS 2) --> (COUNTED**)(2 ===> 3))
02500    PDC.34:((NEW X0)(QS 3) --> (COUNTED**)(3 ===> 4))
02600    PDVS1:((GOAL*COUNT X0)(SEE (OB X0) --> (OB= VS=>SAW)(NEW X0))
02700    PDC1:((GOAL*COUNT X0)(QS 0) --> RELAX.TARGET)
02800    PDC2:((GOAL*COUNT X0)(QS X1) --> SAT (QS===>QS X0))
02900
03000    PSCOUNT:(PDC.01PDC.12PDC.23PDC.34PDVS1 PDC1 PDC2)
03100
03200         Goal Manipulation
03300    PA:((*GOAL)(*GOAL) --> (* ===>%))
03400    PZ:((*GOAL)ABS(%GOAL) --> (% ==> *))
03500
03600         Verbal Encoding
03700    PDV1:((MORE)(WVAL1)(WVAL2) --> (X0 ===>OLDX0)(X1 ====> OLD X1)
03800                               (VALUE(WVAL1 NOT-WVAL2))
03900                               (VALUE(WVAL2 NOT-WVAL1)))
04000
04100         Main productions
04200    P1:((+GOAL MORE)(X0 REL X1) --> (OLD**)(SAY X0)(SAY REL)(SAY X1))
04300    P3:((MORE) --> (MORE ==> *GOAL MORE))
04400    P4:((*GOAL MORE) --> (*GOAL COMPARE))
04500    P5:((+GOAL COMPARE)(%GOAL MORE) --> (% ===>+))
04600    P7:((QS)(QS)(*GOAL COMPARE) -->
04700      (QS ==> OLD QS)(QS===>OLD QS)RELATE)
04800    P6:((*GOAL COMPARE)(XO REL) --> (* ==> +))
04900
05000    P9:((*GOAL COMPARE)(VALUE X0) --> (VALUE ===>OLD VAL)
05100      (*GOAL QUANTIFY X0))
05200    P10:((*GOAL QUANTIFY X0)(QS X0) --> (* ==> +))
05300    P11:((*GOAL QUANTIFY X0) --> (GOAL*COUNT X0)(QS 0)(PS PSCOUNT))
05900
06000    PSEXEC:(PA PDV1P1P3P4P5P7P6P9P10P11PZ)
```

(From Klahr & Wallace, 1976)

are not square?'' The production system chronicles the steps by which this faulty encoding leads to children's errors.

Now consider the major components of the production system proper. The productions fall into four groups: verbal-encoding productions, main productions, counting productions, and goal manipulation productions. The single verbal-encoding production notices the terms ''more,'' ''red,'' and ''square'' and interprets ''red'' and ''square'' as mutually exclusive. The main productions progress down the hierarchy of subgoals (MORE, COMPARE, QUANTIFY, and COUNT) until the system finds a subgoal that it can achieve: counting. The counting productions yield quantitative symbols (numbers) corresponding to the number of objects that are red and the number that are square. The goal manipulation productions keep a single goal directing the system; they interrupt the less recently activated goal if two goals are active and reactivate the most recently interrupted goal if no goal is active.

Next, consider the meaning of some individual productions. PSEXEC (Line 6000) is a special production that indicates the order in which the other productions are to be considered: first PA, next PDV1, and so on. This order determines the resolution of conflicts when two or more productions could fire: the first production in the PSEXEC list that can fire does. Now consider the two goal manipulation productions (Lines 3300–3400). PA indicates that given two active (*) goals, the less recently activated goal (the second one listed) should be interrupted (%). PZ indicates that given no active goal ((* GOAL)ABS) and an interrupted goal, the interrupted goal should be made active. PDV1 (Lines 3700–3900) is the one verbal-encoding production. It indicates that if the system hears the word ''more'' and two value terms (e.g., red and square) it should take two types of actions. The two value terms should be marked ''old'' (this prevents them from influencing the future working of the system), and they should be interpreted as mutually exclusive.

Now we can consider the main productions (Lines 4200–5300). P1 states that if the goal of MORE is satisfied ($+$), and a relation ($>$, $<$, $=$) has been established between variables X0 and X1, then tag ''old'' the satisfied goal and say ''X0 is ($>$, $<$, or $=$) X1.'' This last action constitutes the system's final behavior, its answer to the original question of whether there are more reds or squares. P3 says that if you hear the word ''more,'' adopt a goal of determining which value in the question has more. P4 says that if you have an active goal of finding which is more, add an active goal of comparing. Note that PA always must fire immediately after P4 has, because P4 creates two active goals: finding more and comparing. P5 says that if you have satisfied the goal of comparing and if you earlier interrupted the goal of finding which has more, then relabel the interrupted goal of finding-which-has-more as satisfied. In other words, if you have made a comparison, you know which has more. P7 says that if you have two quantitative symbols and an active goal of comparing, label the two quantitative symbols OLD and determine the relation between them. The reason the quantitative symbols are labeled ''old'' is that otherwise P7 would fire over and over again, since its conditions still would be met. P6 says that if you have an active goal of comparing and you already have a relational symbol, then relabel the goal of comparing as satisfied. Knowing that one number is greater or less than another by definition satisfies the goal of making a comparison. P9 says that if you have an active goal of comparing and you have an element with the tag VALUE (e.g., (VALUE SQUARE)), change VALUE to OLD VALUE and add an active goal of quantifying the value (e.g., *GOAL QUANTIFY SQUARE). Again the purpose of labeling the value as ''old'' is to prevent the production from firing repeatedly. P10 says that if there is an active goal of quantifying a value and you already have a quantitative symbol for the value, label the goal satisfied. P11 says that if you have an active goal of quantifying a value, then establish an active goal of counting the elements that have that value, set the initial value of the quantitative symbol to 0, and go to the counting subroutine.

Now that we have interpreted some of the individual productions, we can consider how produc-

tions enter symbols into STM and what happens when the number of symbols exceeds the STM's capacity. In Klahr and Wallace's model, the first production that fires enters symbols into the left end of STM. The firing of other productions enters new symbols at the left end of STM and pushes rightward the original symbols. Once the number of symbols equals the STM's capacity, addition of new symbols causes the original symbols to exit from the right end of the list.

A production's firing adds elements to the left end of STM in two ways. First, in the production that fired, the elements on the condition side are entered at the left end of STM in the order in which they are listed. The rationale is that the production's firing refreshes those elements so that they can be moved as a unit to the beginning of STM. After the condition side elements have been inserted into STM, the action side elements are added to the left end of STM in the reverse order from that in which they are listed. The rationale is that the actions are executed one at a time in the order listed in the production; the last action executed will be the last to enter STM and therefore will be farthest to the left when all of the production's actions have been taken.

These two symbol manipulation rules are fairly elusive. An illustration may be helpful. Read the first three lines, then predict the STM elements on the fourth line:

If STM includes 5 slots; and
If current STM symbols are A B C D E; and
If the production that fires is C B $\rightarrow$ F G;
Then the new STM contents will be ———.

Successfully predicting that the new STM contents are GFCBA strongly indicates understanding of how productions make symbols enter into and exit from STM.

Traces of production systems' activities, such as the one in Table 3, are useful for learning about how such systems work. They provide an opportunity for readers to test their predictions of what the production system will do, given particular short-term memory contents. They provide two types of feedback: feedback concerning which production will fire, and feedback concerning what symbol manipulations that production's firing will yield. Again, accurate predictions of the trace's contents will signify understanding of the production system.

Now we are ready to examine how Klahr and Wallace's production system performs a class inclusion problem. At the outset of the task, the system is presented two red squares and a red triangle and is asked whether there are more squares or more red

Table 3. **Trace of Class Inclusion Production System**

Production	Short-Term Memory Contents
	((More) (Value(Red)) (Value(Square)))
PDV1	((Value(Red-Not-Square)) (Value(Square-Not-Red)) (Old Value(Square)) (Old Value(Red)) (More)))
P3	
	((*Goal More) (Value(Red-Not-Square)) (Value(Square-Not-Red)) (Old Value(Square)) (Old Value(Red)))
P4	
	((*Goal Compare) (*Goal More) (Value(Red-Not-Square)) (Value(Square-Not-Red)) (Old Value(Square)) (Old Value(Red)))
PA	
	((*Goal Compare) (%Goal More) (Value(Red-Not-Square)) (Value(Square-Not-Red)) (Old Value(Square)) (Old Value(Red)))
P9	
	((*Goal Quantify(Red-Not-Square)) (Old Value (Red-Not-Square) (*Goal Compare) (%Goal More) (Value(Square-Not-Red)) (Old Value(Square)) (Old Value(Red)))
PA	
	((*Goal Quantify(Red-Not-Square)) (%Goal Compare) (Old Value(Red-Not-Square)) (%Goal More) (Value(Square-Not-Red)) (Old Value(Square)) (Old Value(Red)))
P11	
	((QS 0) (*Goal Count(Red-Not-Square)) (*Goal Quantify(Red-Not-Square)) (%Goal Compare) (Old Value(Red-Not-Square)) (%Goal More) (Value(Square-Not-Red)) (Old Value(Square)) (Old Value(Red)))
	((+Goal Count(Square)) ((QS(Square)2) (Counted(New(Square))) (Counted(New(Square))) (*Goal Quantify(Square)) (%Goal Compare) (Old Value(Square-Not-Red)) (+Goal Quantify(Red-Not-Square)) (QS(Red-Not-Square)1) (%Goal More))
P10	
	((+Goal Quantify(Square)) (QS(Square)2) (+Goal Count(Square)) (Counted(New(Square))) (Counted(New(Square))) (%Goal Compare) (Old Value(Square-Not-Red)) (+Goal Quantify(Red-Not-Square)) (QS(Red-Not-Square)1) (%Goal More))

objects. The word "more" and the mention of two value words (red and square) inserts the initial symbols into the short-term memory: more, red, and square. In the production system's first cycle, the presence of these terms triggers the firing of PDV1. The crucial miscoding occurs in this production. The value terms red and square are translated into red-not-square and square-not-red. That is, in this production, (VALUE(WVAL2 NOT WVAL1)) becomes (VALUE(SQUARE-NOT-RED)) and (VALUE(WVAL1 NOT-WVAL2)) becomes (VALUE(RED-NOT-SQUARE)). From the beginning, the system is trying to compare the nonred squares with the nonsquare reds.

After PDV1 fires, the new STM contents lead to P3 firing; P3 would have fired on the first cycle

except that PDV1 fired before P3 was reached (recall that PSEXEC specifies the order in which productions are considered, and that in this system, the first production that can fire does so). P3 creates a goal of finding the set that has "more." The system cannot achieve this goal; therefore, P4 fires, creating a new goal of "compare." Now there are two active goals: "more" and "compare." This triggers PA, whose firing interrupts the less recently activated of the two goals. The system cannot satisfy the compare goal; so, P9 fires, setting up the goal of "quantify." After PA fires and interrupts the goal of comparing, P11 fires, creating the goal of counting, entering an initial quantitative symbol (QS) of 0, and sending the system to the PSCOUNT subprogram at Line 3000.

The next parts of the program will be summa-

Table 3—continued

Production	Short-Term Memory Contents
PZ	
	((*Goal Compare) (+Goal Quantify(Square)) (QS(Square)2) (+Goal Count(Square)) (Counted(New Square))) (Counted (New(Square))) (Old Value(Square-Not-Red)) (+Goal Quantify(Red-Not-Square)) (QS(Red-Not-Square)1) (%Goal More))
P7	
	((Squares More-Than Reds) (Old QS(Red-Not-Square)1) (Old QS(Square)2) (*Goal Compare) (+Goal Quantify(Square)) (+Goal Count(Square)) (Counted(New(Square))) (Counted (New(Square))) (Old Value(Square-Not-Red)) (+Goal Quantify(Red-Not-Square)) (QS(Red-Not-Square)1) (%Goal More))
P6	
	((+Goal Compare) (Squares More-Than Reds) (Old QS(Red-Not-Square)1) (Old QS(Square)2) (+Goal Quantify(Square)) (+Goal Count(Square)) (Counted(New(Square))) (Counted (New (Square))) (Old Value(Square-Not-Red)) (+Goal Quantify(Red-Not-Square)) (QS(Red-Not-Square)1) (%Goal More)
P5	
	((+Goal More) (+Goal Compare) (Squares More-Than Reds) (Old QS(Red-Not-Square)1) (Old QS(Square)2) (+Goal Quantify(Square)) (+Goal Count(Square)) (Counted(New(Square))) (Counted(New(Square))) (Old Value(Square-Not-Red)) (+Goal Quantify(Red-Not-Square)) (QS(Red-Not-Square)1))
P1	
	***"Squares"
	***"More-Than"
	***"Reds"
	((Old(+Goal More) (Squares More-Than Reds) (+Goal Compare) (Old QS (Red-Not-Square)1) (Old QS(Square)2) (+Goal Quantify(Square)) (+Goal Count(Square)) (Counted(New(Square))) (Counted(New(Square))) (Old Value(Square-Not-Red)) (+Goal Quantify(Red-Not-Square)) (QS(Red-Not-Square)1))

rized briefly; the (proverbial) interested reader can work them through. The system counts the number of red-not-squares and finds one. It reactivates the goal of comparing but cannot meet it, since the system only knows one value that would be used in a comparison. Therefore, the goal of quantifying is reactivated, which leads to the activation of the count goal, and the system attempts to count the square-not-reds. None are present: therefore, PDC.1 fires (Line 2700), which relaxes the criterion from square-not-red to simply "square." That is, in the absence of squares-not-reds, the system just counts the squares. In the present case, it counts two squares.

At this point we return to the trace, having established quantitative symbols for both the red-not-squares and the squares. First, P10 fires because the goal is to quantify the squares and we already have a

quantitative symbol for them. P10 labels the quantification goal satisfied. Next, PZ fires because no goal is active; the most recently interrupted goal, comparing, is made active. The combination of two quantitative symbols and a goal of comparing causes P7 to fire. The operator tells the system that $2 > 1$. Next P6 fires, which changes the active goal of comparing to a satisfied goal. Now P5 fires, reflecting the fact that if the goal of comparing is satisfied, then the goal of finding which has more also must be. Finally, P1 fires, announcing the conclusion that there are more squares than reds.

The class inclusion example illustrates several features of production systems (other than that they are complicated). First, recursion emerges as crucial. The system could not begin to solve the problem until it moved down the hierarchy of goals (more, compare, and quantify) to reach the attainable goal of counting. Second, the model points to the large amount of information that must be present in STM for even simple problem-solving to occur; traditional formulations in terms of 7 ± 2 units ignore the control information (goals and subgoals) that seems essential for problem solving and learning. Third, the model makes clear that the difference between adequate and inadequate problem-solving approaches can reside in a very small part of the entire program. Klahr and Wallace's model of correct class inclusion performance differs from Table 2 in only one production (the initial encoding production PDV1). Thus, it is not the case that children who perform in accord with the Table 2 model know nothing about class inclusion. They know something distinct about it which is just not quite right.

Scripts

Scripts, plans, frames, schemata, and story grammars are attempts to capture knowledge of a more amorphous kind than would ordinarily be depicted in production systems or semantic networks. These formalisms are quite similar; the choice of scripts as an illustration is to some degree arbitrary and to some degree due to at least one developmentalist having used the approach.

Schank (1975) defined scripts as predetermined sequences of actions that characterize situations. Less formally, they may be thought of as the way things usually go. Scripts include information about obligatory events and actors, about the range of situations in which the script might apply, about the actors' purposes, and about distinctions between the script and related ones. Scripts also include slots that may be occupied by some range of actors and events. It is acceptable to say that the halfback, fullback, or even tackle ran for the touchdown in a football game, but not acceptable (without considerable explanation) to say that the goalie or desk did.

Schank's script model is based on 11 activities of animate objects that he labeled ACTS. Seven of the ACTS' names directly imply their meanings: PROPEL, MOVE, GRASP, INGEST, EXPEL, SPEAK, and ATTEND. Four others require some explanation: ATRANS involves the transfer of an abstract relation, such as ownership, from one agent to another; PTRANS involves a transfer of the physical location of an object; MTRANS involves a mental transfer of information within someone's memory (remembering, seeing); and MBUILD involves the construction of new information from old (deciding, imagining).

Table 4 is Schank's restaurant script, his representation of the activities involved in eating at a

Table 4. Script for Eating in a Restaurant

Script: restaurant
Roles: customer, waitress, chef, cashier
Reason: hunger for customer, money for others

Part 1: Entering
*PTRANS	(into restaurant)
MBUILD	(where is table)
ATTEND	(find table)
PTRANS	(to table)
MOVE	(sit down)

Part 2: Ordering
ATRANS	(receive menu)
ATTEND	(look at it)
MBUILD	(decide)
MTRANS	(tell waitress)
MTRANS	(waitress tells chef)
DO	(chef prepares food)

Part 3: Eating
ATRANS	(waitress gets food)
*ATRANS	(receive food)
*INGEST	(eat food)

Part 4: Leaving
MTRANS	(ask for check)
ATRANS	(leave tip)
PTRANS	(to cashier)
*ATRANS	(pay bill)
PTRANS	(exit)

*Signifies acts inherent to all restaurants.
(From Schank, 1975)

restaurant. The script is organized into four parts, each of which subsumes several ACTS. For example, in the entering-the-restaurant part, people must physically transport themselves into the restaurant, remember the need to find a table, find a free table, walk over to it, and sit down. Schank noted that this script is specific to restaurants in which people sit down at tables and order food from a waiter; only the asterisked points (entering the restaurant, receiving food, and paying for the food) are inherent to all restaurants. He also noted, however, that other types of restaurants and other activities can be described as combinations of the same 11 ACTs.

Nelson (1978) used the script notion to study young children's understanding of eating situations. She asked 4-year-olds to describe eating at home, at the daycare center they attended, and at McDonald's. The children revealed their understanding in numerous ways. The order in which they recalled the mealtime events closely matched the correct one. Virtually all of the children mentioned those events in Schank's restaurant script that applied to all three eating situations. Events irrelevant to the script but likely to occur rarely were mentioned; children seldom commented on people coming into and leaving McDonald's, though this doubtlessly is part of every visit to the restaurant. Finally, the few inaccurate statements that children made tended to be intrusions from other restaurant scripts. For example, most children said that people paid for their meals at McDonald's after eating rather than before—an accurate description of most restaurants but not of McDonald's. These observations support the view that even young children have general notions, akin to scripts, about what goes on in commonly encountered situations.

Scripts, production systems, and semantic networks differ on numerous dimensions; a reasonable question concerns the domains in which each can be used most profitably. Anderson (1976) suggested that the type of knowledge being represented should be the decisive factor. Semantic networks seem most useful for modeling *declarative knowledge*—facts about the world, such as that there are five pennies in a nickel and five nickels in a quarter. Such facts are used in a variety of circumstances (buying objects, making change, doing arithmetic problems). Therefore, it is desirable that they have many access routes. Semantic networks afford such varied access, since all concepts are linked to all other concepts. Models of long-term memory, which to date have been concerned primarily with declarative knowledge, therefore have found semantic networks a convenient representational language. Among the models that have used semantic networks are Anderson and Bower's (1973) HAM model, Anderson's (1976; 1982) ACT model, Collins and Loftus's (1975) spreading activation model, Kosslyn's (1980) model of imagery, and Norman, Rumelhart, and LNR's (1975) semantic memory model.

Production systems also can be used to model declarative knowledge, but more often have been used to model *procedural knowledge*—knowledge about how to play the piano, ski, look at a Renaissance painting, and so on. People do not seem to have multiple, easy access paths to the components of such knowledge (try for example to recall what note comes after the second C in "Twinkle, twinkle, little star"). On the other hand, they do possess smooth and rapidly executable performance routines (it is not difficult to find the note on the piano). In representing procedural knowledge, therefore, efficient execution seems more important than multiple access routes. Production systems, which place unique conditions on when each production will fire,

seem compatible with this demand. Production system models of procedural knowledge include Newell's (1980) model of speech production, Greeno, Riley, and Gelman's (1982) model of counting, and Rip's (1982) model of formal deductive reasoning. Production systems and semantic networks can be used effectively in conjunction. Anderson's (1976) ACT model for example, represents procedural knowledge via production systems and declarative knowledge via semantic networks.

Both semantic networks and production systems model knowledge at a relatively specific level. Scripts seem most useful for representing event sequences at a more general level. They and the related formalisms of frames, plans, schemata, and story grammars, most often have been used to characterize situations in which procedural and declarative knowledge are both necessary: for example, Rumelhart's (1975), Stein and Glenn's (1979), and Mandler and Johnson's (1977) models of story comprehension; Abelson's (1973) model of cold-war ideologies; and Winograd's (1975) model of how people represent temporal information. At present, the arguments in favor of using scripts and the other high-level languages are largely intuitive. People have high-level knowledge of event sequences; scripts and scriptlike models correspond in some degree to our conscious awareness of this knowledge. I would not be surprised, however, if five years from now a representational language very different from scripts, frames, or schemata superseded them. The problem of how to represent high-level knowledge is an important one, but none of the languages thus far developed has aided theory construction to the same extent as have semantic networks and production systems.

Methodologies for Studying Information Processing

Having examined information processing theories and representational languages, we now can consider methodologies for studying cognitive activity. Among these are chronometric, eye-movement, protocol, and rule-assessment techniques. Although these analytic tools differ in many ways, they share a core similarity: all are intended to test models of what information processors know and how they manipulate symbols.

Chronometric Analyses

Mental processes take time. This assumption may seem uncontroversial today, but it was not always. As late as 1850, J. Müller wrote that the rate of neural conduction could not be measured because it approximated the speed of light. Even today, as Posner (1978) suggested, many people would not believe that adding 4 + 3 takes more time than adding 4 + 2 (Groen and Parkman, 1972).

Chronometric methods subsume at least three types of experimental procedures. The simplest and most common is to measure reaction time, the time that separates two events such as stimulus presentation and response. A related procedure is to measure the duration between presentation of a stimulus and the point at which reaction time to a second stimulus reaches its minimum; this yields an estimate of the time required to encode the initial stimulus (so that it no longer interferes with processing of the second one [cf. Posner & Boies, 1971]). The third procedure is to limit processing time and to observe the errors that arise; this method often is used to study speed/accuracy tradeoffs (cf. Pachella, 1974).

Two primary techniques have emerged for relating chronometric data to models of information processing: the subtractive approach and the additive factors approach. Researchers employ the subtractive approach to estimate the time necessary to perform a process. In the approach's original form, the investigator devised two tasks thought to differ only in the need to perform a single process. The difference between solution times on the tasks was taken as an index of the time necessary to perform the process.

A more recent insight increased the power of the subtractive approach. As long as researchers compared only two tasks, any difference between the tasks might explain the difference in solution times. The additional insight was that if several variants of the task could be devised, requiring one, two, three, or *n* repetitions of the process believed to distinguish the tasks, then a linear slope, reflecting a constant and additive amount of time needed to execute the process, should emerge (S. Sternberg, 1969). Such a linear slope would have fewer explanations than a single difference between the times needed to solve two tasks.

Shepard and Metzler's (1971) model of how people compare objects' spatial orientations exemplifies the subtractive approach. They showed college students pairs of three dimensional figures, one in standard upright position and one rotated to a different orientation, and asked them to determine as quickly as possible whether the objects were the same. The figures differed in the amount of rotation that separated them; thus, to superimpose one figure on the other might require a rotation of 20°, 40°, 60°, and so forth. Shepard and Metzler found that the time required to make ''same'' judgments was a linear

function of the angular disparity between the figures. Their interpretation was that subjects engaged in a kind of mental rotation, similar to a physical process by which objects might be superimposed. This interpretation has been supported in developmental work; here, too, response time is a function of angular disparity. Children rotate figures more slowly, however, about 7 msec/degree of angular disparity for third and fourth graders compared to 4 msec/degree for adults (Kail, Pellegrino, & Carter, 1980).

The subtractive method is elegant, but limited. It often is awkward to apply; many tasks cannot be changed so as to require multiple executions of a process. In addition, the assumption that a difference between tasks affects only one process may be naïve; human thinking is sufficiently flexible that small task changes may result in large strategic changes (cf. Glushko & Cooper, 1978).

To deal with these limitations of the subtractive method, S. Sternberg (1969) devised a companion technique, the additive factors approach. Like the subtractive method, the additive factors approach was designed to test the hypothesis that processing proceeds through independent (additive) serially executed stages. The hypothesis is tested by a different experimental strategy, however. Independent variables that theoretically should influence only a single processing stage are formulated. Dependent variables aimed at measuring the processing at each stage also are devised. If processing is serial and independent, and if the experimental manipulation exercises the expected effect, manipulating the independent variable should influence only those dependent measures that reflect processes occurring in a particular stage.

The additive factors approach is illustrated most easily on the task where it first was applied: S. Sternberg's (1966) memory-scanning task. The experimenter presents the positive set (e.g., the numbers 3, 6, and 8) and then the probe (e.g., 5). The task is to determine whether the probe is included in the positive set. Sternberg found that reaction times (RT) on such problems were a linear function of set size, both on trials where the probe was a member of the positive set and on trials where it was not. Sternberg attributed this pattern to people performing the task in four stages. First they encode the probe number. Then they exhaustively scan the positive set to see if one of its numbers matches the probe. Then they decide whether to answer yes or no. Finally, they respond. Sternberg identified the linear slope of the reaction times with the second (scanning) stage; RT grew with set size because each item in the positive set took a certain amount of time to check (about 40 msec). Encoding, decision, and response stages were thought to contribute to the intercept; these were independent of the positive set's size.

S. Sternberg (1967) used the additive factors method to test the assumption that encoding and scanning are executed serially and independently. After presenting the positive set, he presented the probe digit in either standard or degraded (broken and blurry) form. Degraded stimuli were known to increase encoding time. If people completely encoded the probe before proceeding to the scanning stage, the degrading would be expected to add a constant amount of time to solutions at all set sizes. If they encoded and scanned simultaneously, each comparison of degraded probe and positive set member would take longer than usual. The amount of extra time in the degraded stimulus condition would grow monotonically with the size of the positive set (assuming that encoding was not complete before the last comparison between probe digit and positive set member). Sternberg's data supported the assumption that encoding and scanning were executed serially, at least by well-practiced subjects. Degraded probes added a constant to reaction times independent of set sizes.

Protocol Analysis

The second information processing methodology that we will consider is protocol analysis. The proper use of verbal data has long been controversial. Introspectionists regard such data as the crucial source of evidence about psychological processes; behaviorists proscribe its use altogether; gestaltists view it as useful for generating hypotheses but not for verifying them (Duncker, 1945).

The development of information processing theories and of computer languages for expressing them has led to renewed interest in verbal data. A record of ongoing comments, combined with observations of concurrent nonverbal behaviors, can provide an extremely rich data base. Thus it is not surprising that computer simulators, wishing to achieve a moment-by-moment model of the processes by which behavior is generated, have relied heavily on verbal data.

Protocol analyses are at least as much art as science. However, Newell (1968) described the following rules-of-thumb for performing them. First, the experimenter presents a problem and instructs the subject to say aloud whatever he or she thinks about while solving it. The subject's statements are tape recorded, and along with a record of concurrent nonverbal behavior, they become the raw data of the study. After repeated scrutiny of the data, the investigator formulates an outline of the knowledge states that the problem solver passed through in solving the problem. This outline, known as a problem-behavior graph, is stated at about the level of detail of a flow diagram. Finally, the investigator writes a computer program to characterize the crucial features of the problem-behavior graph and of the original verbal and nonverbal data.

Newell described several steps in proceeding from the problem-behavior graph to the computer simulation (in this case, a production system). The first step is to formulate productions corresponding to the knowledge states in the problem-behavior graph. Each production must create the necessary STM elements for its successor to fire. The next step is to restate as many productions as possible as variants of a few basic ones. This helps to organize the overall production system into a coherent and economical form, much as subroutining does in other computer languages. The final step is to compare the simulation's behavior to the problem-behavior graph and to the original verbal and nonverbal data, and to revise the production system where it does not fit. Note that within this approach, verbal data are treated exactly like chronometric, eye-movement, or error data: as a target behavior for a model to regenerate.

Both within adult and developmental psychology, the validity of verbal data, and therefore its worthiness as a target for simulation, has come under persistent attack (e.g., Braine, 1959; Brainerd, 1978; Nisbett & Wilson, 1977). Verbal data has been criticized for overestimating knowledge, underestimating knowledge, and simply misrepresenting it. In response to these criticisms, Ericsson and Simon (1980) attempted to specify when verbal reports are and are not useful indices of internal states. Their formulation does much to resolve this long-lived controversy.

Ericsson and Simon started with a few, relatively uncontroversial assumptions. They divided memory into short- and long-term components, and suggested that verbal reports reflect current contents of short-term memory. The data that people report can come from STM either directly or through retrieval from LTM into STM. Symbols in STM reflect processes that are fairly long in duration (no shorter than 1 or 2 sec.); processes that occur more rapidly, such as recognition and other highly automated activities, do not produce symbols in STM. A portion of the symbols in STM at any time also enter LTM, but not all of them do.

Two predictions follow from these assumptions. First, if people report information when it initially enters STM, the verbal report will be an accurate though possibly incomplete index of memory contents. Second, if people retrieve information from LTM before reporting it, the verbal report will be a relatively inaccurate index of the cognitive processes that it is supposed to reflect; people will draw inferences, both accurate and inaccurate, to fill in information that no longer is available directly.

Ericsson and Simon presented considerable evidence consistent with these predictions. When people make verbal reports concurrently with problem-solving activity and when the reports concern processes of sufficient duration, they correspond well to other behavioral indices. When the reports are made retrospectively, when they concern very rapid processes, or when the questions concern data that were never in short-term memory (e.g., Why were you able to withstand more pain than other people?), people show little knowledge about their thought processes or about the variables that influence their behavior. Difficulties remain in the interpretation of verbal protocols—in particular, how to evaluate the fit between a simulation model and the protocol on which it was based—but the a priori rejection of such data seems unjustified.

The present discussion has not included illustrations of protocol analyses. This is because of the difficulty of the task. Newell and Simon (1972) spent more than 200 pages describing their protocol analysis of one subject working a single cryptarithmetic problem. Despite the length of that description, it remains the best introduction to how to do a protocol analysis. Other examples of protocol analyses can be found in Rometveit (1965), Klahr and Siegler (1978), and Anzai and Simon (1979).

Analysis of Eye Movements

Eye movements have been used to study visual information processing since the nineteenth century (e.g., Javal, 1878). Then as now, the basic assumption was that the material on which the eye is focusing is also the material on which the mind is focusing. Advances in the last decade in the quality of eye-movement measurement apparatuses and in the precision of psychological theories have allowed increasingly rigorous tests of this eye mind assumption. These tests suggest that there is much truth to it.

To understand analyses of eye movements, it is necessary to know a little about vision. Although the phenomenological impression of vision is of a continuous process, close observation of eye movements indicates a two-stage cycle: stable fixations of fairly long duration separated by brief rapid movements (saccades). The purpose of the saccades is to bring the fovea of the eye, the point of highest acuity, to rest on the material that is desired as the next

input. People use information in the periphery of the eye, as well as context and other cues, to guide the length of the saccades so that new fixations fall on important material. At least in reading, however, the extent of the peripheral information that is used to guide saccades is quite small, subtending no more than 5° of visual angle even for gross physical cues such as word shape (Rayner, 1975). People obtain little if any visual information during saccades; rather, information is obtained during the fixations. The fixations themselves vary greatly in duration, depending on the difficulty of the material fixated, its importance, and numerous other factors.

Now consider how a typical eye-movement apparatus works. The subject looks at text or other visual material on a TV monitor about 2 feet away. An eye-tracking system beams a small light onto the cornea of one eye. The reflection of this light indicates the point of fixation on the TV screen. When the material on the screen is superimposed on the reflection, it is possible to determine the material at which the person is looking. An eye camera takes pictures of this corneal reflection once every 17 msec, allowing rapid tracking of changes in eye position. When the session is over, the data are fed into another computer for analysis. Such automated scoring is crucial to analysis of eye movements; five minutes of average speed reading generate approximately 18,000 eye fixations.

Eye-movement analyses yield two primary types of data—data about the sequence of locations that are examined, and data about the duration of attention at each location. Vurpillot's (1968) analysis of visual scanning illustrates the information that can be yielded by the sequential data alone. Just and Carpenter's (1980) analysis of reading illustrates the utility of duration data.

Vurpillot showed 4- to 8-year-olds pairs of houses, each house having six windows. The task was to determine whether the houses were identical, and if not, where they differed. The implicit model of optimal performance was that children would scan a window in one house, then the corresponding window in the second house, then another window in the first house, then the corresponding window in the second house, and so on. In addition, to minimize memory load, the children would scan windows within each house systematically: from end to end of each column or across each row rather than haphazardly.

Vurpillot found that with age, children scanned more systematically and more exhaustively. They more often looked back and forth between corresponding windows in the two houses and more often proceeded down a column or across a row within a house. They became more likely to scan all of the windows before answering that the houses were identical and focused on a greater number of features in each window. Vurpillot could not have made data-based statements of such detail without the eye-tracking system.

Just and Carpenter (1980) developed a model of reading based largely on durations of eye fixations. Their model rested on two assumptions. The first is that when people fixate a word, they are processing it; thus, fixation length is a direct index of the attention given to the word. The second assumption is that readers interpret every content word as they encounter it; this sometimes leads to inaccurate interpretations, but readers do it nonetheless.

Before examining the reading model itself, it is necessary to discuss two concepts that are central to Just and Carpenter's theory and that have not been focused on previously in this chapter: spreading activation, and case grammars. Following Newell and Simon (1972), Just and Carpenter hypothesized that the cognitive system is organized much like a production system, with no separation of control information from memory. In addition to the serially firing, independent productions that were encountered in Klahr and Wallace's class inclusion model, however, Just and Carpenter's model also included automatic productions that could fire in parallel. They hypothesized that these productions spread activation among related productions. Thus, when productions relevant to kangaroos fire, activation spreads to productions involving Australia, marsupials, jumping, and so on. The spread of activation to a production makes it easier for that production to fire on later cycles. Spreading activation can be used to explain context effects; reading about a topic activates knowledge of associated material, making it more probable that the relevant productions will fire when STM elements match their conditions.

Case grammars were originated by Fillmore (1968) to classify the semantic roles into which words enter—agent, instrument, object, possessive, and so on. Just and Carpenter suggested that a word's case influences how much attention it receives. They also developed a phrase grammar that classified the functions of phrases in the same way that the case grammar classified those of individual words. The phrase grammar's categories included topic, subtopic, cause, consequence, and definition.

With this background, we can examine Just and Carpenter's model of reading. As shown in Figure 10, reading begins with an efferent instruction from the brain for a saccade to secure the next input. The distance of the saccade is determined by the length of the word or two next to the current focus; informa-

tion in the periphery is used to direct the eye to the next meaningful unit. If only the right margin of the text is in the periphery, the eye sweeps leftward toward the beginning of the next line. Because there is little uncertainty about the location of the next stimulus, saccades are rapid; they account for roughly 10% of reading time.

When the eye fixates on the new word, it extracts physical features of the letters and places them in working memory. Perceptual encoding productions take these physical features as their conditions and indicate the word's identity. Activation then spreads to productions corresponding to the word's meaning. The word's case influences the duration of the fixation. Fixations on agents and instruments last almost six times as long as fixations on connectives. The word's familiarity also influences fixation times. Although readers focus on virtually every word, they focus longer on unfamiliar words than on familiar ones, and longer on very unfamiliar words than on relatively unfamiliar ones. Just and Carpenter hypothesized that readers use long fixations on very unfamiliar words to build new representations in long-term memory. Because productions remain at relatively high levels of activation after firing, words require shorter fixations on subsequent presentations than on their initial one. For the same reason, words that are likely on the basis of contextual cues require shorter fixations than words that are unlikely.

The clause and sentence within which a word appears also influence fixation times. Readers focus on words in more central clauses, such as topic and definitional clauses, for longer times than words in less central clauses, such as those presenting details and expansions. These longer fixations on central clauses may reflect time that readers spend integrating information in the central clauses with previously encountered information.

The "end of the sentence wrap-up" exerts an additional effort. The end of a sentence signals the end of a unit of thought. Thus, it is an ideal place to integrate new with old information. The integration process leads to especially long eye fixations. The length of the wrap-up depends on the difficulty of the integration task. In "garden path" sentences, where context and ambiguous cues lead readers to form initial incorrect interpretations, fixations at the end of the sentence often last much longer than would be expected from word and clause considerations alone. For example, the end of the sentence wrap-up would be unusually long for the sentence, "the tear in the dress was still wet."

Just and Carpenter concluded that although reading may seem phenomenologically to be a smooth

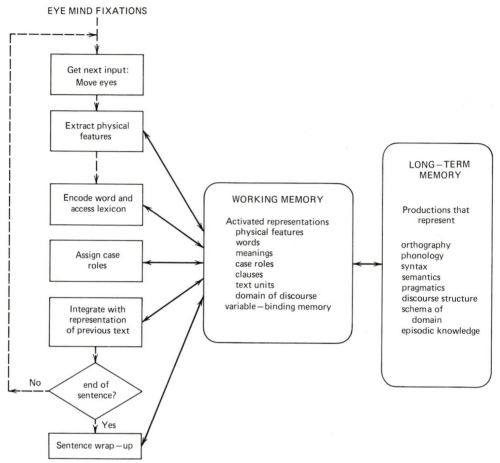

Figure 10. A model of reading. (Just & Carpenter, 1980.)

even process, eye-movement analyses reveal it to be far more eventful. The type of word, the type of clause, the word's place within the sentence, and the sentence's place within the paragraph all influence the duration of eye fixations. The eye-movement data allow a much more precise picture of reading than would be possible without them.

Error Analysis

The final information processing methodology that we will discuss is error analysis. The use of error data is not unique to the information processing approach: Piaget relied heavily on it, and Binet seems to have also (Tuddenham, 1962). Information processing psychologists, however, have extended the method to formulate and test precise models of people's conceptual understanding. I will use my own work to illustrate.

The error-analysis technique that I have used is

the rule-assessment approach. It is based on two assumptions. The first is that children's problem-solving strategies are rule governed, with the rules progressing from less to more sophisticated with age. The second is that hypothesized rule progressions can be tested by creating problem sets in which children who use different rules produce distinct patterns of correct answers and errors.

An example may help illustrate how the rule-assessment approach works. Consider the balance-scale task used in Siegler (1976) and shown in Figure 11. On each side of the fulcrum were four pegs on which metal weights could be placed. The arm of the balance could tip left or right or remain level, depending on how the weights were arranged. However, a lever (not shown in Fig. 11) was set to hold the arm motionless. The task was to predict which (if either) side would go down if the lever were released.

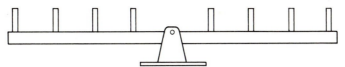

Figure 11. A balance-scale apparatus. (Siegler, 1976.)

Siegler (1976) suggested that children's knowledge about this task could be represented in terms of the four decision trees shown in Figure 12. Children using Rule I consider only the number of weights on each side of the fulcrum. If they are the same, the children predict ''balance''; otherwise, they predict that the side with the greater amount of weight will go down. Children using Rule II rely exclusively on weight if the two sides have different amounts, but if the weights are equal, they also consider the distances of the weights from the fulcrum. Children using Rule III always consider both weight and distance and solve problems consistently correctly if one or both are equal; however, if one side has more weight and the other side has its weight farther from the fulcrum, Rule III children do not know what to do and therefore muddle through or guess. Rule IV represents mature knowledge of the task. Because it includes the torque calculation, children using it always make the correct prediction.

It is possible to determine which, if any, of these rule models accurately characterizes a child's knowledge about the balance scale by examining correct answers and errors on six types of problems (Table 5):

1. *Balance problems:* the same configuration of weights on pegs on each side of the fulcrum.
2. *Weight problems:* unequal amounts of weight equidistant from the fulcrum.
3. *Distance problems:* equal amounts of weight different distances from the fulcrum.
4. *Conflict-weight problems:* one side with more weight, the other side with its weight farther from the fulcrum, and the side with more weight going down.
5. *Conflict-distance problems:* one side with more weight, the other side with ''more distance,'' and the side with more distance going down.
6. *Conflict-balance problems:* the usual conflict between weight and distance cues and the two sides balancing.

As shown in Table 1, children who use different rules produce different response patterns on these problems. Those using Rule I always predict correctly on balance, weight, and conflict-weight problems and never predict correctly on the other three problem-types. Children using Rule II behave similarly except that they also solve distance problems. Those adopting Rule III invariably are correct on all three types of nonconflict problems and perform at a chance level on the three types of conflict problems. Those using Rule IV solve all problems.

To the extent that age correlates with the sophistication of children's rules, these descriptions imply distinct developmental patterns for each of the six types of problems. Most interesting is the predicted developmental decrement on conflict-weight problems. Younger children, using Rules I and II, consistently get these problems right, whereas older children, using Rule III, ''muddle through'' and are correct only one-third of the time. (To the extent that yet older children adopt Rule IV, a U-shaped pattern is produced.) Another prediction is that performance on distance problems shows the most dramatic developmental increment, from below chance for children using Rule I to perfect performance for children using the other three rules.

The rule models predict which error a rule user will make as well as the fact that he or she will make some error. For example, children using Rule II and Rule III both err frequently on conflict-balance problems, but the particular errors differ. All of the Rule II children's errors involve choosing the side with more weight, whereas the Rule III children's errors are distributed evenly between the side with more weight and the side with more distance. Similarly, Rule I children are always incorrect on distance problems, saying ''they will balance,'' but not picking the side with weights closer to the fulcrum. The rule models' prediction of which error will be made greatly reduces the number of rules that are compatible with the data; seen from another perspective, it greatly increases the discriminative power of the problems.

Siegler (1976; Experiment 1) examined 5-, 9-, 13-, and 17-year-olds' existing knowledge about balance scales. The rule models fit the predictions of 90% of children of all ages. Five-year-olds most often used Rule I, 9-year-olds most often used Rule II or III, and 13- and 17-year-olds most often used Rule III. Few children of any age used Rule IV. Children's explanations of how they made their

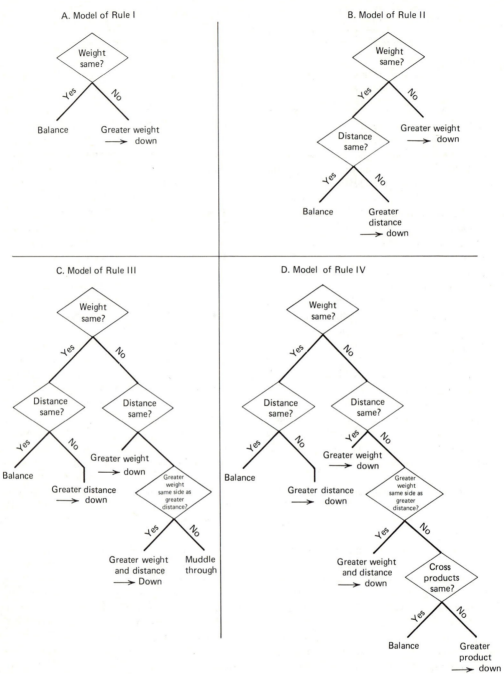

Figure 12. Models of rules for performing the balance-scale task.

choices paralleled their predictions; more than 80% of children were classified as using the same rule on the two measures. The expected patterns of performance on the six problem-types also emerged; for example, the percentage of correct answers declined between ages 5 and 17 on all 6 of the conflict-weight

items but on none of the other 24 items on the test.

These results demonstrate how error analyses can specify individual children's knowledge. The rule-assessment approach has been applied to assessing understanding of 11 other concepts as well: projection of shadows, probability, fullness, time, speed,

Table 5. **Problems Used to Assess Understanding of the Balance Scale**

Problem—type	Rule I	Rule II	Rule III	Rule IV
Balance	100	100	100	100
Weight	100	100	100	100
Distance	0 (Should say "Balance")	100	100	100
Conflict—weight	100	100	33 (Chance Responding)	100
Conflict—Distance	0 (Should say "Right Down")	0 (Should say "Right Down")	33 (Chance responding)	100
Conflict—Balance	0 (Should say "Right Down")	0 (Should say "Right Down")	33 (Chance Responding)	100

(From Siegler, 1976)

distance, life, conservation of liquid quantity, conservation of solid quantity, conservation of number, and the Tower of Hanoi (Klahr & Robinson, 1981; Siegler, 1976; 1978; 1981; Siegler & Richards, 1979; 1983; Siegler & Vago, 1978;). In all cases, the patterns of correct answers and errors have identified partial understandings that children have before they master the concepts.

Issues Concerning the Nature of the IPS

Thus far in this chapter, the information processing approach has been described in terms of theories, representational languages, and methodologies. Another way of viewing the approach is in terms of issues concerning the nature of the IPS. Is process-ing done serially or in parallel? Is it exhaustive or self-terminating? Does it reflect feature extraction or template matching? Is representation visual, verbal, propositional, or multiply coded? Is it analog or discrete? Are representations generated or retrieved? Extended discussion of these issues can be found in the *Handbook of Cognitive Processes* series edited by Estes, the *Psychology of Learning and Motivation* series edited by Bower, and the *Loyola Symposium Series* edited by Solso, among other sources.

In recent years, a small but influential group of investigators has questioned whether these issues ever can be resolved by standard experimental techniques. Newell (1973), Townsend (1974), and Anderson (1976; 1978) have approached the question from different perspectives but have come to the same conclusion.

Newell (1973) observed that much information processing research has proceeded as if the investigators were playing a game of 20 questions with nature. Does forgetting occur through trace decay or through interference? Is learning continuous or all or none? Is there a single memory code, or are there multiple codes? And so on and on. In Newell's view, such formulations often result in elegant experiments and data, but the fundamental issues never seem to be resolved. The more research that is done, the more that answers recede into the distance. As Newell put it: "Thus, far from providing the rungs of a laddar by which psychology gradually climbs to clarity, this form of conceptual structure leads rather to an ever increasing pile of issues, which we weary of or become diverted from, but never really settle" (p. 289).

Newell suggested three strategies for freeing ourselves from this morass. The first was to build complete processing models (i.e., computer simulations) for individual tasks. Simulations must specify representations and processes sufficient to produce a body of data. This sufficiency criterion reduces the degrees of freedom that allow so many models to coexist with the same data. Newell's second suggestion was to analyze more complex tasks. Again, the aim was to reduce the range of possible models consistent with the data, in this case by increasing the amount and variety of data for which the models must account. The third suggested strategy combined the first two: build complete processing models that perform numerous complex tasks.

One response to Newell's suggestions has been to formulate large-scale models of human cognition, implemented at least partially as computer simulations. Perhaps the outstanding example is Anderson's (1976: 1982) ACT model. The stated purpose of this model is no less than to "create a uniform theoretical framework in which to understand the full range of 'higher mental processes': memory, deductive reasoning, language processing, problem solving, and so forth" (Anderson, Kline, & Lewis, 1977, p. 271). The accomplishments of the model are sufficiently impressive to merit extended attention.

Anderson's model divides human cognition into two parts: a data base and a set of rules for operating on the data base. The data base corresponds to the system's declarative knowledge; the rules for operating on it correspond to the system's procedural knowledge. The data base is represented by a semantic network, and the rules for operating on it are represented by a production system.

ACT incorporates a number of assumptions about the nature of the IPS. First consider its assumptions about declarative knowledge. Declarative knowledge is believed to be organized in terms of subjects and predicates. It is viewed as being nonerasable; inability to remember is attributed to retrieval failures rather than to losses of information from the network. Finally, it is assumed to be strategy free; it is separate from control structures, and its storage and retrieval occurs in the same way regardless of the context.

By contrast, ACT assumes that procedural knowledge is organized around conditions and actions. Such knowledge is seen as highly sensitive to context. Its control structure is an integral part of its data base. Finally, it is "data driven"; its working is greatly influenced by the organism's current goals and drives, and also by stimulation from the external environment.

Note that the basic division within ACT mirrors the distinction between the two types of information processing theories discussed above. The semantic network functions in the same way regardless of the task, and it is separate from control strategies. Thus, it corresponds to the "information processing system per se" type of theory. The production system, by contrast, depends heavily on the particulars of the task and the person's strategy. In other words, it attempts to capture the IPS X task interaction. By incorporating the advantages of both types of theories, ACT can simulate people's performance on tasks as diverse as memory scanning, fact retrieval, inference making, and geometry theorem proving.

Large scale computer simulation models such as ACT are the closest present approximation to a comprehensive theory of human information processing. This does not mean that they are a panacea, however. The models depend heavily on a sufficiency criterion and on the assumption that there are very few ways that a system can produce intelligent behavior. The validity of this assumption is unknown. In addition, distinguishing parts of the model that are programming conveniences from parts that reflect substantive assumptions is often difficult and, at times, impossible. This presents a great obstacle to testing the models empirically. Also, to date the models have proved more useful in specifying possible explanations for known phenomena than in predicting new phenomena. These difficulties noted, the promise of large scale simulation models must be reemphasized. Their combination of breadth of scope and precision of detail gives them legitimate claim to the title "the most advanced psychological theories yet devised."

This completes the overview of the information processing approach. Next we will begin the second main section of the paper, the one that focuses on information processing approaches to the study of development.

THE DEVELOPMENT OF THE INFORMATION PROCESSING SYSTEM

In the past 15 years, the information processing approach has changed the way that many people think about development. Before characterizing the approach's contribution in terms of particular concepts and findings, it may be worthwhile to consider some general ways in which it has enriched our understanding. The approach has helped to link research on adults with research on children, has increased the conceptual rigor of developmental research, and has pointed to numerous potentially useful topics for developmental study.

One way in which the information processing approach has contributed to our knowledge of development is through its linking of work on adult and child cognition. Theories of adult information processing can be viewed as first-pass theories of children's information processing. Additions to the theories and differing emphases emerge as development receives intense study, but these differences emerge against the ground of the general theories. At first blush, this might seem to relegate developmental work to an inferior status. This impression is no more accurate, however, than the assumption that studying the Articles of Confederation in light of the Constitution denigrates the importance of the Articles of Confederation. It simply is easier to understand any type of development when we know where the development is going. Indeed, we may be able to isolate the unique aspects of development *only* when we have partialled out the commonalities that unite all developmental periods.

Emphasizing the unities between adults' and childrens' information processing has had several salutary effects. Detailed descriptions of adults' knowledge frequently have suggested what development might involve. Illustratively, R. J. Sternberg (1978) analyzed adults' analogical reasoning into encoding, inference, application, and response components, each of which could be executed in self-terminating or exhaustive fashion. This analysis helped Sternberg and Rifkin (1979) identify the growth of exhaustive encoding as the primary source of development in this domain. At other times, detailed analyses of adults' knowledge have argued against hypothesized aquisition processes. For example, Siegler (1981) found that even adults could not accurately judge the relative amounts of liquid in containers from seeing static arrays. This finding casts doubt on the view that logical multiplication of heights and cross sectional areas leads to liquid quantity conservation. At yet other times, consideration of adult research has placed general characterizations of development in a different perspective. In one such case, Shaklee (1979) questioned Inhelder and Piaget's (1958) characterization of formal operations competence, since it implied much greater rationality than has been revealed in studies of adults' decision making and judgment.

Another contribution of the information processing approach has been to the conceptual rigor of developmental theorizing. Objective indices of conceptual rigor are difficult to find. I can use my own work, however, to illustrate the tendency of the information processing approach to push in the direction of greater conceptual rigor (whatever the absolute level of rigor of the work might be).

In graduate school, I became interested in cognitive development but knew almost nothing about information processing theories and research. In my dissertation on combinatorial reasoning in adolescents and preadolescents (Siegler & Liebert, 1975), I attributed the developmental difference of greatest interest to differences in "foresight." I was unable to extend the analysis deeper than this, probably because my ideas about foresight were only vaguely defined.

After leaving graduate school, I entered an environment in which I was immersed in the information processing approach. This exposure contributed to my decision to represent Piagetian stage description as decision trees. The decision-tree representations helped me notice the need for several conceptual clarifications. In Siegler (1976), for example, it led me to distinguish between two rules that Piaget grouped together as Stage II reasoning on the balance scale. The decision-tree format also helped me to see parallels over many tasks in Piaget's descriptions of children's reasoning (Siegler, 1981).

One criticism of this rule assessment work has been that it does not specify the knowledge that leads children to choose particular rules—for example, their knowledge of weight and distance on the balance scale (Strauss & Stavy, 1982). Partially in response to this criticism, I recently have adopted a more detailed representational language to characterize preschoolers' knowledge of numbers. This format involves task-specific flow diagrams operating on a semantic network; the semantic network includes the types of information that the rule models did not explicitly represent. I have had to revise my models of counting, magnitude comparison, and addition several times after I thought they were complete, because when I formalized the ideas, the models revealed gaps and contradictions (Siegler &

Robinson, 1982). The concreteness of the flow diagrams and semantic networks thus has added to the conceptual rigor of the ideas, forcing me to face vagueness and incompleteness in my thinking that I otherwise might have overlooked.

Information processing theories also have contributed to the study of development by pointing research in useful directions. These directions differ for the two major types of information processing theories. One direction is illustrated by the influence of Atkinson and Shiffrin's (1968) model of the IPS. Recall that this model divided memory into sensory, short-term, and long-term stores, and emphasized the role of control processes. Developmentalists interested in the IPS per se have followed Atkinson and Shiffrin's outlines. The workings of the sensory and short-term stores have been examined under the heading of basic capacities and processes. The characteristics of the long-term store have been examined under the heading of the knowledge base and semantic memory. Perhaps the greatest attention has been given to two control processes: strategies, and metacognitive skills. Each of these four domains—basic processes, strategies, metacognition, and the knowledge base—has been proposed as the principal locus of developmental change.

The second type of information processing theory, focusing on the IPS X task interaction, has exerted a much larger influence on the study of development than on the study of adult cognition. This may be due to the approach's areas of easiest applicability—problem solving and concept acquisition—being especially frequent activities in the lives of children. Brown and DeLoach (1978) referred to young children as "universal novices"; many tasks that are routine for older individuals pose genuine problems for them. It is no accident that so much work on children's problem solving focuses on natural concepts (conservation, torque, morality, etc.), whereas problem-solving research on adults is limited largely to puzzlelike problems (Tower of Hanoi, 9-matchstick problem, 2-strings problem, etc.). Adults' adjustments to many naturally occurring task environments are so successful that the adaptive process fades into the background.

In line with these emphases, the present discussion of the development of information processing skills will be divided into three sections. First, we will consider the development of the IPS per se. This discussion will be organized around the four frequently proposed answers to the question "What develops?" Is it basic capacities, strategies, metacognition, the knowledge base, or any combination of these factors? Next, we will examine the develop-

ing system's adaptations to specific task environments. This discussion will sample task environments of enduring interest: inductive reasoning, deductive reasoning, and academic tasks. Finally, we will describe hypothesized mechanisms of development. This discussion will be organized around specific mechanisms: self-modification, automatization, and encoding and combination.

The Developing System: The Issue of What Develops

Basic Capacities and Processes

One objective of information processing psychologists has been to determine the set of elementary information processes from which complex behavior derives. Numerous researchers have speculated that many, if not all, of these basic processes and representational skills are innate (e.g., Chi, 1976; Haith, 1971; Simon, 1972). This view has special appeal for those interested in simulation. The simulation strategy is to start with a group of primitive processes and to show how they might be used to build complex behaviors. If a certain group of primitive processes can be demonstrated sufficient to account for adult cognition, it is simplest to assume that the same processes may account for cognition in infancy and childhood. In addition, it is far from clear how a cognitive system can develop a basic process that is not present early on. How can a person learn to retrieve facts from long-term memory if retrieval is not a biologically given capability? Experiences that improve the efficiency and speed of these processes are easy to imagine, but how a person can progress from the absence to the presence of a basic process is not.

Two types of studies on basic processes and representational skills have been the most common. The first type demonstrates the early existence of these processes and skills. Recognition, visual scanning, categorical perception, learning, and intersensory integration are among the basic information processes that seem to be present from early in life. The second type of study examines the improvements that basic skills undergo in childhood and adolescence. Examples of each of these types of studies will be reviewed below.

Recognition. If children could not recognize objects, cognitive development would be difficult to imagine. Each experience would be unique, and learning would be precluded. In fact, recognition is strikingly accurate from early in life; Perlmutter and Lange (1978) commented that 2½–year-olds typically are more accurate in recognizing pictures than adults are in recalling them. Recognitory ability also seems to be extremely accurate among people in underdeveloped as well as developed societies (Cole & Scribner, 1974; Sharp, Cole, & Lave, 1979).

Much of what we know about infants' recognition comes from experiments using the habituation paradigm. The first part of this paradigm is the familiarization phase, in which the infant is exposed repeatedly to a stimulus. Then a new stimulus is introduced, either together with the familiar one or alone. Differential attention to the novel stimulus is taken to indicate recognition of the familiar one.

Although recognition is often thought of as a primitive process, several recent theories have divided it into components. The most basic division is between initial encoding of the stimulus and subsequent retention of the encoded information (Anderson & Bower, 1974; Cohen & Gelber, 1975). The encoding component of recognition seems to improve substantially with development, but the retention component is constant or nearly so. Studies that equate the initial encoding of younger and older infants (infant-controlled procedures) consistently have failed to reveal developmental differences (Werner & Perlmutter, 1980). In one representative experiment, Werner and Siqueland (1978) found that even newborn preterm infants retain encoded information sufficiently to habituate to the familiar stimulus.

Thus, some ability to recognize objects appears to be present at birth. Developmental differences in recognitory ability come largely in the range of stimuli that are encoded sufficiently well to be recognized, in the exposure time necessary for recognition, in the range of distractors that interfere with recognition, and, perhaps, in the quality of recognition. The more complex the stimulus, the shorter the exposure period, and the more similar the distractors to the target item, the later the age at which any given level of recognition can be demonstrated. All of these findings are consistent with the view that children start life able to retain encoded information, and that age-related improvements in recognition are due to improvements in the speed, exhaustiveness, and flexibility of encoding.

Visual Scanning.   For children to obtain visual information efficiently, they must scan their environments and focus on the most informative parts. Salapatek (1968) examined newborns' scanning of circles and triangles to see if such selective attention was present from birth. He found that the newborns' eye movements were influenced greatly by the locations and sizes of the figures. Most of their fixations

fell in the area covered by the figures. They fixated more on the vertices and sides of triangles than on their interiors, though the interiors and contours of circles attracted equal attention. These results indicate that from birth, infants attend to objects rather than randomly looking through space, and that in some cases, they differentially attend to the most informative parts of objects.

Some investigators have suggested that infants scan most actively when existing and new information are moderately discrepant. Greenberg (1971) found that younger infants preferred less complex checkerboards than older infants, and concluded that the key was the fit between the infants' overall cognitive level and the complexity of the material. This interpretation must be viewed as tentative, however, since the infants' cognitive level was not measured independently; it was only inferred from their performance on the visual preference task. The problem is a particularly difficult one, since we do not know how to assess infants' general cognitive abilities. All that safely can be concluded at present is that with age, infants prefer increasingly complex stimuli.

Categorical Perception.   The third basic process that we will consider is categorical perception. Many information processing psychologists have argued that people analyze perceptual events into features. In both vision and audition, this ability seems present from early in life. Studies using the habituation paradigm have demonstrated that infants as young as six weeks discriminate between syllables that differ only in voicing (ba and pa), place of articulation (ba and ga), and tongue height and placement (a and i) (Eimas, Siqueland, Juscyk, & Vigorito, 1971; Morse, 1972; Trehub, 1973). Infants also differentiate on the basis of rising or falling intonation and on the basis of accented syllable (Morse, 1972; Spring, 1975). Their discriminative abilities seem especially good for speech sounds (Dale, 1976). Caution is necessary, however, in interpreting this finding as indicative of specific human sensitivity to speech, as chinchillas show similar superior discriminative abilities for speech sounds (Kuhl & Miller, 1975). In any case, infants' ability to discriminate the distinctive features would seem to be useful for acquiring speech.

Similar findings have emerged in the study of vision. Bornstein (1976) presented 4-month-olds with a standard stimulus until they habituated to it. Then a novel stimulus was introduced that differed from the original in spectral wavelength but not in form or size. The novel stimulus' wavelength was a constant number of nanometers removed from the standard; in some cases this involved crossing adults' color boundaries (the standard looked green and the novel stimulus looked blue), and in other cases it did not (the standard and novel stimulus appeared to be different shades of green). Infants showed greater dishabituation when the novel stimulus lay across the color boundaries. They, like adults, seem to classify the spectrum into blue, green, yellow, and red. Bornstein (1978) noted that this early accurate color perception could aid visual development in several ways—by enhancing contrasts, visibility, object evaluation, and visual constancies.

Learning. All information processing theories with which I am familiar view as basic the ability to note correlations among events. A number of studies have shown such learning potential to be present from birth. For example, Siqueland and Lipsitt (1966) presented newborns with a tone and a buzzer. If upon hearing the tone the newborns turned their heads to the right, they received a sweet solution. The same reward was given if they turned their heads to the left upon hearing the buzzer. The infants learned these responses quickly, and almost never confused them once initial learning occurred. The Siqueland and Lipsitt experiment is far from the only one to demonstrate the learning ability of infants; the infancy volume of this *Handbook* provides a good review of this literature.

Intersensory Coordination. Wertheimer (1961) demonstrated that from birth, infants coordinate visual and auditory information. Immediately after a baby was born, Wertheimer entered her delivery room and sounded a clicker on either her left or right side. Wertheimer found that from the first trial, when the clicker was on the left the infant turned her eyes left and when it was on the right she turned them right. It was as if she expected to see something at the location from which the sound came.

Mendelson and Haith (1976) demonstrated in considerably more detail the connections between sight and sound in newborns. They displayed a screen that was blank except for a few lines. Sounds were presented when infants looked at prespecified parts of the display. When the sounds occurred as the infants looked at a vertical line, they centered their attention more on the line and shortened the length of their saccades. Sounds presented from one side caused the infants first to look in the direction of the sound and then in the opposite direction. These observations led Mendelson and Haith to hypothesize that, from birth, infants organize visual and auditory activities in terms of a common spatial framework (cf. McGurk & Lewis, 1974, for a similar suggestion). Coordinating the directions from which

sights and sounds originate is just one of the crossmodal matchings that infants have been found to perform; others include matching of intensities (Lewkowicz & Turkewitz, 1980) and matching of rhythms (Spelke, 1976). The results suggest that from birth, infants may represent auditory and visual input in amodal as well as modality specific forms.

These are some of the basic skills and capacities of infants. Next, the focus will turn to skills and capacities for which development during later periods of childhood has been given the most attention.

Memory Scanning, Retrieval, and Choice Processes. Keating and Bobbitt (1978) examined the development of three processes that have received much attention in adults; short-term memory scanning, retrieval from long-term memory, and choice among response alternatives. They investigated the execution of these processes by average and intellectually gifted 9-, 13-, and 17-year-olds. Keating and Bobbitt found that younger children took more time than older ones to execute the choice and memory retrieval processes, and that intellectually average children took more time than intellectually gifted ones to execute the memory retrieval and memory scanning processes. In addition, scores on the three process measures together accounted for a large percentage of the variance on an intelligence test that the children took. Interestingly, this relation is much stronger than those that have emerged between the same processes and IQ measures in adults (e.g., Hunt, Frost, & Lunneborg, 1973; Hunt, 1976). Keating and Bobbitt suggested that this may be due to the processes being highly efficient in virtually all college students, and thus accounting for little variance, whereas the processes may be developed to a more variable degree, and thus account for more variance, at younger ages.

Integral versus Separable Dimensions. A venerable but largely unsubstantiated claim is that children progress from holistic to differentiated perceptions of multidimensional stimuli (e.g., Bruner, Olver, & Greenfield, 1966; Werner, 1961). Information processing psychologists interested in adults have made a related claim: that people perceive some combinations of dimensions within multidimensional stimuli as integral and others as separable (e.g., Lockhead, 1966; Garner, 1970; 1974). On separable dimensions, such as color and form, variations in one dimension do not interfere with efforts to attend selectively to another. On integral dimensions, such as brightness and saturation, variations in the noncentral dimension do influence efforts to process the central one. One interpretation of this difference is that people represent separable dimensions in terms of a dimensional structure, whereas they represent integral dimensions in terms of an overall similarity structure (Garner, 1974).

Smith and Kemler (1978) found that even on dimensions that are separable for adults (color and size), 5-year-olds performed in a way that was somewhere between the adult separable and integral patterns. They concluded that children progress through three distinct representations for dimensions that are separable for adults. First, there comes integral, nonprimary representations, in which relations of overall similiarity among stimuli are dominant; then, integral, primary representations, in which children rely on overall similarity when possible but use dimensional structures when necessary; and finally, separable dimensions, in which the individual dimensions have an obligatory dominant influence. Smith and Kemler noted that the similarity organization might be especially useful to young children learning the family resemblance concepts common in natural language, whereas the dimensional organization might be most useful in analytic and scientific thinking, more commonly engaged in by adults.

STM Capacity. The last basic process that we will discuss has been the subject of the greatest amount of developmental speculation—short-term memory capacity. Long before the advent of information processing approaches, much of intellectual development was ascribed to increases in memory capacity (e.g., Binet, 1911). Information processing theorists gave impetus to this view by making several conceptual distinctions about memory capacity. First, they divided memory into short- and long-term stores, with only the short-term store subject to capacity constraints (e.g., Broadbent, 1958). Second, they advanced at least three conceptions of STM constraints. The earliest was Miller's (1956) chunks interpretation. Short-term memory was said to allow storage of a limited number of chunks of information. The amount of information in a chunk could vary, but the number of chunks was constant. A second approach was that of Kahneman (1973). Kahneman suggested that the processing bottleneck involved a limited resource of attention. In this view, each task claims a certain amount of processing resources, and when all resources are allocated, the addition of a new task either is impossible or forces inferior performance on the original task. A third view identified information processing speed as the limiting factor. People could execute only a certain number of symbolic manipulations in a unit of time; this limited the tasks they could perform simultaneously.

Developmental claims based on each of these conceptions have been advanced. Pascual-Leone (1970) suggested that the number of slots in working memory increases with age. Manis, Keating, and Morrison (1980) suggested that attention is allocated more efficiently with age. Wickens (1974) and Miller (1969) suggested that speed of information processing increases with age.

These capacity models encounter two types of difficulty. First, they are difficult to distinguish operationally from each other. Excepting physiological evidence, it is unclear how we ever could determine whether central processing capacity is a set of discontinuous slots, a continuous resource that can be allocated, or a limited speed of symbol manipulations. Any behavioral data that could be accounted for by one model could be accounted for equally easily by the others.

The second difficulty is in distinguishing any of the capacity models from models that attribute developmental changes to increased knowledge or improved strategies. Strategies often enter into performance on tasks intended as direct measures of capacity (Baron, 1978; Brown, 1978; Chi, 1978). Performance on tasks that minimize the use of strategies tends to be invariant, or close to invariant, over a broad age range (Brown, 1974; Frank & Rabinovitch, 1974; Hoving, Spencer, Robb, & Schulte, 1978; Morrison, Holmes, & Haith, 1974). In addition, estimated capacity depends on theoretically irrelevant task parameters such as the number of objects to be remembered (Trabasso & Foellinger, 1978). Such evidence has led even proponents of capacity approaches to modify their views; for example, Case (1978) suggested that the underlying capacity of STM may be constant from early in life, but that increases in automaticity may boost its effective capacity.

The fact that we cannot at present demonstrate developmental changes in STM capacity does not mean that no such changes occur. The problem lies in interpreting any particular set of data as demonstrating capacity changes. Thus, the most reasonable reaction to claims concerning such changes may be akin to the Scottish legal verdict "case unproven."

Strategies

The second frequently cited answer to the question "What develops?" is strategies. Atkinson and Shiffrin's and other information processing theorists' emphasis on control processes helped to stimulate developmental research on rehearsal, elaboration, and other non-task-specific mnemonic techniques. Below, a few of the most studied strategies are examined.

Rehearsal. One of the best replicated findings in developmental psychology is that children below 5 or 6 years are less likely than older people to rehearse material that they are trying to memorize. The first investigations of rehearsal examined whether young children's failure to use the strategy was due to their not knowing how or when to rehearse (production deficiency) or to the children not benefiting from rehearsal even if they did use it (mediation deficiency). In one sense, the controversy was settled early in favor of the production deficiency position; 5-year-olds could be taught to rehearse, and when they rehearsed, their recall improved. Even when the young children rehearsed, however, their recall rarely reached the level of older children's. This pair of findings set the stage for a large body of further research on the nature and effects of rehearsal.

First consider some of the evidence that young children rarely rehearse. Among the earliest studies on the development of rehearsal strategies were those conducted by Flavell and his students. Keeney, Canizzo, and Flavell, (1967) presented 5- and 10-year-olds pictures of to-be-remembered objects. Then a space helmet was placed on children's heads; this helmet hid their eyes but allowed the experimenter to see any lip movements that they made. Few 5-year-olds but almost all 10-year-olds moved their lips or said the words aloud in the time between when the pictures were presented and when children were asked to recall them. Children who rehearsed recalled far more objects. When original nonrehearsers were later taught to rehearse, their recall improved substantially.

A second type of evidence involved acoustic confusions. Conrad (1963) observed that in short-term memory experiments, adults recall objects with acoustically similar names less well than objects with acoustically distinct names. He attributed this to the acoustically similar names being more confusable in the a-v-1 rehearsal code. Conrad (1971) found that children under age five did not show this discrepancy; they recalled acoustically similar and dissimilar terms equally often. Conrad concluded that young children do not rehearse and thus are not subject to differential interference effects.

The rehearsal of older and younger children differs in quality as well as in probability of occurrence. Ornstein and his associates described improvements in the quality of elaborative rehearsal that continue well past the age at which children first rehearse. Ornstein, Naus, and Liberty (1975) asked 8-, 11-, and 13-year-olds to rehearse aloud after the presentation of each word in a list. They found that the 8-year-olds typically rehearsed items in isolation—after the item "cat," they would say "cat, cat, cat." The 13-year-olds, by contrast, combined the past few words with the newly presented one—after hearing "cat," they would say "desk, lawn, sky, shirt, cat." The younger children's approach did not yield the primacy effect characteristic of successful use of rehearsal, whereas that of the older ones did. The younger children also recalled fewer words.

Instructing young children to use rehearsal strategies in one situation often is insufficient to persuade them to use it in others, even if the strategy proved effective in the first case. Keeney et al. found that the children they had taught to rehearse abandoned the strategy when they later were given a similar memorization task but no explicit rehearsal instructions. Hagen, Hargrove, and Ross (1973) found that when the experimenter stopped prompting children to rehearse, their recall declined to the level of children who had never been taught the rehearsal strategy. Thus, young children can be taught to rehearse effectively, but they may fail to transfer the strategy to new tasks or to maintain it over time.

Semantic Organization. When the material allows, organizing to-be-memorized words into taxonomic categories aids recall substantially. In semantic organization experiments, people typically are presented a list of words that fall into several taxonomic categories. People can recall the words in any order; of primary interest is whether they group together (cluster) words from the same taxonomic category.

Even very young children's recall is influenced by the semantic relatedness of terms. Goldberg, Perlmutter, and Myers (1974) reported that 2-year-olds' interresponse times for recalling two-item lists are faster for semantically related than for unrelated items. However, the degree of utilization of semantic relations steadily increases from early childhood through college. Young children often use phonemic features, such as rhyming patterns, to link words; older children and adults concentrate more consistently on semantic connections (Bach & Underwood, 1970; Hasher & Clifton, 1974).

Older and younger children also differ in the quality of semantic organizations. Young children tend to use similarity or associative strength as the basis for their organizations; older children and adults more often rely on taxonomic relatedness (Flavell, 1970). Young children also divide lists into a greater number of categories each having fewer members (Worden, 1975). Finally, their categorization schemes are less stable, and considerable reorganization often occurs from one trial to the next

(Moely, 1977).

Lange (1978) questioned whether young children's clustering of related words is best described as an organizational strategy at all. He suggested that their clustering may stem from high interitem associations rather than from taxonomic categorization. When items within a category are not highly associated, preadolescents show little clustering. Similarly, when preadolescents are presented unrelated items, they show little subjective organization (Lawrence, 1963; Ornstein, Hale, & Morgan, 1977). Thus, young children's use of organizational strategies may depend on favorable environmental circumstances. The developmental trend is toward increasing use of such strategies under less hospitable conditions.

Efforts to teach children organizational strategies have yielded similar results to efforts to teach them rehearsal strategies. Children as young as 4 or 5 years can be taught to use organizational strategies (Moely, Olson, Halwes, & Flavell, 1969). Such instruction, however, results in less transfer, less durability over time, and less effective implementation than the same instruction given to older children (Liberty & Ornstein, 1973; Rosner, 1971; Williams & Goulet, 1975). Again, the ability to execute some form of the strategy does not guarantee its effective use.

Elaboration. Elaboration, the third frequently studied memory strategy, might be defined as the imposition of semantic connections in situations where no obvious relations exist. A child who needed to remember his school books, his lunch, and his arithmetic assignment might form an image of a peanut butter and jelly sandwich placed between two pages of a book, with the assignment placed between the peanut butter and the jelly. Such elaborative imagery has been found to facilitate recall in some situations (Delin, 1969).

One feature governing the effectiveness of elaboration is activity. Sentences involving highly active interactions (e.g., the LADY flew on a BROOM on Halloween) facilitate children's recall to a much higher degree than sentences describing more static interactions (e.g., the LADY had a BROOM) (Buckhalt, Mahoney, & Paris, 1976). Similarly, interactive images are more effective than images lacking such interactions (Reese, 1977).

Older and younger children's uses of elaborative strategies differ in a number of ways. Older children are more likely than younger ones to elaborate (Paris & Lindauer, 1976). When they do, their elaborations are more likely to involve active interactions. Finally, older and younger children are differentially influenced by self-generated and experimenter-generated elaborations. Older children benefit more from elaborations that they make up themselves (Reese, 1977), whereas younger ones benefit more from those of the experimenter (Turnure, Buium, & Thurlow, 1976). This may be due to differences in the quality of the elaborations. Older children's elaborations may be particularly meaningful to them, thus leading to superior recall, whereas the elaborations of younger children may be obscure or unmemorable, thus producing inferior recall.

Allocation of Study Time. Children probably employ memory strategies most frequently in deciding how much time to spend studying and how to distribute attention within the material than in any other activity. Flavell, Friedrichs, and Hoyt (1970) examined 4- to 10-year-olds' study strategies. The task involved memorizing pictures that appeared in each of 10 windows. To see the picture in a window, the child needed to press a button that lifted a screen; this provided an objective index of the time each child spent studying each picture. In general, older children spent more time studying than younger ones did. They engaged in a greater variety of subsidiary strategies, such as naming the pictures, rehearsing the names cumulatively, and testing themselves. Each of these activities was associated with greater recall.

Masur, McIntyre, and Flavell (1973) used an identical procedure to examine the study strategies of 7-year-olds, 9-year-olds, and adults after they took a test and received feedback on their performances. Both 9-year-olds and adults spent a greater percentage of time than 7-year-olds focusing on those items they failed to recall on the test. This strategy helped only the adults, however; the 9-year-olds did as well when they studied items that they previously answered correctly as when they studied items that they previously missed. A. L. Brown (1978) suggested an explanation. To succeed on the Masur et al. task, she argued, children needed to identify the missed items, select those items for further study, and maintain the memories of the previously recalled items. She hypothesized that 9-year-olds' maintenance may have been imperfect, thus negating the value of focusing on previously missed items.

With age, children shape study strategies to task demands increasingly precisely. Even preschoolers take some strategic steps when they know they later will be asked to recall material. In particular, they make use of external objects as retrieval cues (Ritter, 1975; Wellman, Ritter, & Flavell, 1975). Older children have available a greater range of strategies and adapt them to finer gradations in task demands. For example, Rogoff, Newcombe, and Kagan (1974) told 4-, 6-, and 8-year-olds that their recognition of 40 pictures would be tested after a few minutes, 1 day, or 7 days. Only the oldest children studied for a longer time when anticipating the longer delays. Similarly, Horowitz and Horowitz (1975) reported that 11-year-olds but not 5-year-olds adopted different strategies when anticipating a test of recall than when anticipating a test of recognition.

Several trends emerge in this discussion of the contributions of memorial strategies to the development of the IPS. The use of such strategies becomes more frequent with age, particularly between ages 5 and 10, and children adjust the strategies increasingly finely to task demands. Children who use the strategies remember more than those who do not. Young children can be taught to use mnemonic strategies, but the instruction often fails to generalize over time and to new tasks. Some investigators (A. L. Brown, 1978; Flavell & Wellman, 1977) have suggested that understanding of one's own memory processes—metamemory—might influence maintenance and generalization of strategies. Thus, by influencing how and when strategies were used, metamemory would account for memory development. Research on this explanation of development is examined in the next section.

Metacognition

Why do people use memory strategies in some situations but not others? One frequently cited possibility is that they do so in response to their knowledge of their own memorial capabilities, the task demands, and the potential effectiveness of the strategies in augmenting their memorial capabilities. Although metacognitive research originally was motivated by issues in the memory area, it now has spread to a large range of cognitive activities. Among the processes that are said to indicate metacognitive knowledge are "predicting, checking, monitoring, reality testing, and coordination and control of deliberate attempts to learn or solve problems" (Brown, 1978, p. 78).

Metacognitive research has been controversial from its inception. Part of the reason is that many researchers distrust measures that demand conscious awareness of internal processes. Another reason is that for some, the metacognitive metaphor summons an image of a homunculus directing the operations of the IPS; how metacognition influences cognitive operations rarely has been specified. A third objection is that the metacognitive construct is superfluous; in this view, metacognitive knowledge follows rather

than precedes appropriate use of memorial processes. These shortcomings, among others, led Cavanaugh and Perlmutter (1982) to conclude: "The concept of metamemory has not yet contributed much to our understanding of memory" (p. 23).

Proponents of metacognitive research have replied to each of these criticisms. Some have designed nonintrospective measures of metacognitive knowledge (e.g., Markman, 1979). Others have shown that entirely mechanistic formalisms, such as productions systems, can use metacognitive knowledge to direct cognitive activities (Greeno et al., 1982; Sacerdoti, 1977). Finally, some investigators have suggested that even though metacognitive knowledge initially may be derived from observations of cognitive functions, it later may aid such functioning (Borkowski, 1980). With these objections and counterarguments in mind, we can consider recent metacognitive research.

Knowledge of Capacity Limitations. One focus of metamnemonic research has been on what children know about their own and other people's memorial limitations. Such knowledge is of interest because it is presumed to help them decide when to use memory strategies. Kreutzer, Leonard, and Flavell (1975) posed children perhaps the most basic question in this domain, "Do you forget?" Almost all children beyond first grade indicated that they at times did forget, but a substantial minority of kindergartners denied that they ever did.

Children's quantitative estimates of their memory capacities also have been of interest. Flavell, Friedrichs, and Hoyt (1970) presented children groups of 10 pictures and asked them how many they thought they could remember. They found that more than half of the nursery schoolers and kindergartners thought they could remember all 10 pictures, whereas very few older children thought they could. (In fact, none of the children could remember this many pictures.) The two younger groups' predictions of the number of pictures they would remember were higher than those of the two older groups, but children in the two older groups actually remembered more.

How does knowledge of capacity limits improve? One plausible explanation is that experience with tasks requiring accurate assessments is essential. The evidence on the point is equivocal, however. Typically, in studies addressing this issue, children are presented alternating trials in which they first estimate how many items they will remember and then see how many items they actually remember. Four- and 5-year-olds have proven surprisingly unresponsive to such experience; many continue to make the same unrealistic estimates after a number of feedback trials (Markman, 1973; Yussen & Levy, 1975), though in some experiments researchers have observed fairly substantial gains (Salatas & Flavell, 1976). Thus, the means by which children develop more accurate estimates of their memorial capabilities remain unclear.

Knowledge about Strategies. Investigators of metamemory also have been interested in the strategies that young children think will be effective in augmenting mnemonic performance. The implicit theory is that knowledge about strategies leads children to choose to use or not to use them. In one study of conscious knowledge about strategies, Kreutzer et al. (1975) asked children what they would do to remember a telephone number. Almost all (95%) of the third and fifth graders but only 40% of the kindergartners indicated that it was wisest to phone quickly, before getting a drink of water. In addition, almost all of the third and fifth graders indicated that they would write down the number, rehearse it, or take some other step to maintain it in memory; only 60% of the kindergartners indicated that they would use any such strategy.

Moynahan (1973) examined children's knowledge of organizational strategies. She asked children to compare the difficulty of learning lists of unrelated or taxonomically related items. The 9- and 10-year-olds were more likely than the 7-year-olds to predict that the taxonomically related items would be easier to recall. This was not attributable to the younger children not knowing the taxonomic relations. Tenney (1975) demonstrated that young children could identify taxonomically related terms, but did not view them as especially easy to remember.

Metamnemonic Knowledge and Memorial Performance. Early investigations of metamemory were fueled by the hope that metamnemonic knowledge and memorial performance would be related directly. This hope has been dashed; some investigators have found no links, and others have found only weak ones (Markman, 1973; Moynahan, 1973; Salatas & Flavell, 1976).

Flavell and Wellman (1977) described several factors that might contribute to the elusive relation between cognitive and metacognitive skills. Consider some factors that might lead a child who knows a strategy not to use it. The child might know the strategy but think that some other strategy was superior in the particular situation. He might know the strategy but judge the task sufficiently simple to do without it. He might know abstractly about the strategy but not be good at executing it; under such circumstances, he might not even try to use it. Finally,

the child might be familiar with the strategy, recognize its utility for the situation, and be skilled in using it, but simply decide that it was not worth the bother. (Flavell and Wellman termed this the "original sin" hypothesis.)

The Knowledge Base

For the same reasons that fish will be the last to discover water, developmental psychologists until recently devoted almost no attention to changes in children's knowledge of specific content as an explanation of development. Such changes are so omnipresent that they seemed uninviting as targets for study. Instead of investigators studying the effects of improved content knowledge, they implicitly dismissed it as a by-product of more basic changes in capacities and strategies. (For purpose of illustration, consider the historic emphasis on learning principles and the lack of emphasis on the material being learned in such areas as concept formation, discrimination learning, and the various mediation paradigms.) Recently, however, several researchers have hypothesized that knowledge of specific content domains is a crucial dimension of development in its own right and that changes in such knowledge may underlie other changes previously attributed to the growth of capacities and strategies.

Research on the knowledge base has an interesting status with regard to the two types of information processing theories distinguished in this chapter. As mentioned above, the type of theory that is dominant is linked to the substantive area being considered. Work on memorial capacities, strategies, and metacognition has emphasized the IPS as such; work on problem solving and conceptual development has emphasized the IPS X task interaction. Research on the knowledge base presents an unusual case in which both types of theories have exerted substantial influence. Many questions that have been asked about the knowledge base are quite removed from any particular task domain. Can changes in knowledge account for apparent changes in capacities and strategies? How is this knowledge reorganized over time? Does a larger knowledge base lead to more inferences being drawn? Other questions depend on the interaction between the IPS and the task. How does knowledge of radiology influence what is recalled about an x-ray? How does knowledge of chess influence the encoding of chess configurations?

Research on the knowledge base has been designed to establish several points. First, prior knowledge influences recall of newly presented material; this phenomenon often is considered under the heading of constructive recall. Second, age-related differences in measures of basic capacities and strategies may be attributable to changes in the knowledge base. Third, under some circumstances, differences in content knowledge outweigh all other age-related differences; knowledgeable children can recall more material in their area of expertise than less knowledgeable adults. Evidence concerning each of these contentions is discussed below.

Constructive Memory. When people are asked to recall a story, they rarely recite the same one that they heard. They leave out some parts, embellish others, and recall yet others that were only implicit. Even adults often fail to distinguish sentences they have heard from sentences whose meaning they inferred (e.g., Bransford & McCarrell, 1974).

One implication of the importance of inference is that as children's knowledge bases grow and become more useful for drawing inferences, they should better integrate incoming with existing information. Analyses of children's intrusion errors support this view. Brown, Smiley, Day, Townsend, and Lawton (1977) presented second, fourth, and sixth-graders a story and then asked them to recall it. They found that although the numbers of intrusion errors were similar for the three age groups, the older children's intrusions more often were relevant to the theme of the story. Brown et al. explained the difference in terms of preexisting knowledge. The older children knew more about the topics of the stories (life among Eskimos and desert Indians) and therefore integrated what they were told with other relevant information. In everyday learning situations, such theme-relevant intrusions, rather than representing errors, would be an encouraging sign that children recognized the relation of the new information to their existing knowledge.

Brown et al.'s research can be contrasted with a study on a similar topic but emphasizing the IPS X task interaction. Spilich, Vesonder, Chiesi, and Voss (1979) examined the mechanisms by which existing knowledge aids recall. They chose baseball as a content area. First, they considered what a person knowledgeable about baseball might know. As shown in Table 6, their analysis stressed setting events that define the immediate situation and goal structures that define a hierarchical ordering of goals ranging from the top level of winning the game to the bottom level of avoiding strikes and accumulating balls. Less and more knowledgeable people were hypothesized to differ primarily in their understanding of these setting events and goal structures.

Spilich et al. compared the recall of college students high and low in baseball knowledge for a prose passage describing a baseball game. As expected,

the knowledgeable students recalled more facts. They were most likely to recall propositions occupying the highest levels within the goal hierarchy and least likely to recall the ones at the lowest levels. By contrast, less knowledgeable students' recall was quite even across levels of the goal hierarchy. The two groups' confusion errors also differed. High-knowledge students often confused players' batting averages; most often, they stated the averages correctly, but assigned them to the wrong players. Low-knowledge students more frequently confused the order and content of actions, often recalling sequences inconsistent with the rules of baseball. They might recall a double play despite no one being on base. These findings support the notion of memory as a constructive process, and indicate some of the mechanisms by which knowledge might exercise its effects: by providing a framework for organizing new information, by serving as a base against which to check the plausibility of recalled sequences, and by facilitating inferences about likely new events.

Content Knowledge as an Explanation for Strategy, Capacity, and Metamemorial Differences. Differences in basic capacities, strategies, and metacognitive knowledge are often used to explain differences in older and younger children's acquisition of specific content. This equation can be reversed; content knowledge may be the causal factor. Chi (1982) examined a 5-year-old learning an alphabetic strategy for retrieving her classmates' names. The child learned the strategy quickly. By contrast, the same child encountered difficulty applying the alphabetic strategy to a set of names of people she did not know. Chi concluded that people may acquire powerful mnemonic strategies only after they thoroughly know the to-be-remembered material.

Huttenlocher and Burke (1976) suggested that age-related changes in digit span, a frequently used measure of memory capacity, could be explained in terms of knowledge-base changes. Previous investigators hypothesized that changes in span were due to development of rehearsal skills (Belmont & Butterfield, 1969; Flavell, 1970). However, Huttenlocher and Burke found that primacy effects, usually interpreted as evidence of rehearsal, were as evident in the performances of 4-year-olds as in those of 11-year-olds. The absolute amounts that children recalled differed, but the shapes of the curves did not. The investigators also cited evidence that instructions to rehearse increased older children's recall by as much as younger children's, a finding that seems unlikely if the source of developmental differences was that older children rehearsed spontaneously and

Table 6. Baseball Knowledge Structure

Setting	
General:	Teams playing, team at bat, team in field, inning, miscellaneous conditions
Specific:	Relevant: teams' records as related to goal structure, players' records as related to goal structure
	Irrelevant: team attributes, player attributes
Enabling:	Batter at bat and pitcher ready to pitch

		Goal structure		
Team at bat	Level	Variables	Values	Team in field
Winning game	1	Game outcome	Win-lose	Winning game
Scoring runs	2	Score	Domain of game scores	Preventing runs from scoring
Getting runners on base and advancing runners	3	Pattern of base runners	Eight possible patterns	Preventing runners from getting on base or advancing by making outs
		Outs	0, 1, 2, 3	
Having "Balls,"	4	"Balls"	0, 1, 2, 3, 4	Getting "Strikes,"
Avoiding "Strikes"		"Strikes"	0, 1, 2, 3	Avoiding "Balls"

(From Spilich, Vesonder, Chiesi, & Voss, 1979)

younger ones did not.

Instead of differential rehearsal accounting for age differences, Huttenlocher and Burke suggested that age differences are due to differences in item identification times. They postulated that people possess a fixed amount of attention that they allocate among tasks, and that young children's shorter spans are due to their knowing less about items and therefore needing to allocate more attention (and more time) to identifying them. Thus, content knowledge influences memory capacity.

Age versus Knowledge. Chi (1978) provided the most dramatic demonstration to date of the impact of the knowledge base. She compared the memorial performance of 10-year-olds and adults on two tasks: a standard digit span task and a chess memory task. The 10-year-olds were skilled chess players, whereas the adults were novices at the game. The primary chess memory task involved displaying on a board for 10 sec. an organized arrangement of pieces (as defined by Chi's analysis of the chess environment). Then the experimenter covered the pieces and asked the child or adult to reproduce the arrangement on a second chess board.

Children's reproductions of the chess boards were more accurate than those of adults (Fig. 13). The finding was not attributable to the children being generally smarter or possessing better memories. On the standard digit span task, adults showed the usual

superiority of recall. Thus, Chi concluded, differences in knowledge can outweigh all other memorial differences between children and adults.

Wagner (1978) made a similar point in a cross-cultural investigation conducted in Morocco. Among the groups that he studied were two of partic-

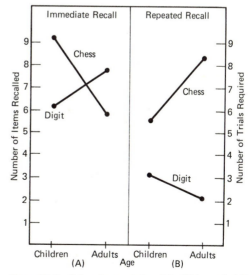

Figure 13. Predictions for repeated recall by children and adults for digits and chess. (Chi, 1978.)

ular interest in the present context: Koranic scholars and rug sellers. The Koranic scholars were well schooled and their schooling involved a great deal of memorization; presumably their general mnemonic skills were developed to a high degree. The rug sellers had little formal education but had expert knowledge about the experimental stimuli—rugs.

The rug sellers proved to be more proficient than the Koranic scholars in recognizing which rugs they had been shown. Wagner hypothesized that the rug sellers' greater knowledge of the stimuli aided them in identifying distinctive features, thus enhancing their recognition. By contrast, the Koranic scholars' expertise appeared to be limited to meaningful verbal material in which serial recall strategies could be used (e.g., the Koran).

Before ending this discussion of the influence of the knowledge base, a word of caution is in order. Research on the topic is still in a preliminary phase. Many of the effects being attributed to differential content knowledge receive this explanation as a default option; the investigator does not know to what else to attribute the effects. Demonstrating that superior content knowledge can outweigh the influence of other capabilities that are acquired with age and experience does not mean that knowledge ordinarily overshadows the other factors. Also, at present we have only vague notions of the mechanisms by which content knowledge influences memory (though see Chi & Koeske, 1983, for a start in this direction). Despite these caveats, I am optimistic about this area of research. We now know that content knowledge can substantially influence memory for new information, and we soon may know more about how it does so.

The Information Processing System as It Interacts with Particular Tasks

In this section, the emphasis switches to the interactions between the developing IPS and several interesting task environments. The particular research programs and experiments that I have chosen to illustrate this approach have been selected on the basis of two criteria: their importance in developmental theory and/or in children's lives, and their illustration of certain themes that have arisen repeatedly in information processing research. First to be examined will be research on transitive inference and on conservation. These tasks have occupied central positions within psychometric and Piagetian theories of intellectual development. Research emphasizing the IPS by task interaction provides more detailed analyses of the requirements of these problems and of children's reasoning strategies on them

than previously were available. Next, the focus turns to tasks of everyday importance: reading, writing, and arithmetic. Siegler and Klahr (1982) noted several benefits to psychologists of focusing on such educationally relevant tasks. First, it helps us formulate questions of enduring interest. These tasks will remain important long after the demise of the theory that motivated the particular study. Second, research on instructionally relevant topics can serve as an index of how well our theories are doing. Possessing a fixed agenda limits our freedom to devise easy tests that our theories can pass. Third, focusing on children's reading, writing, and arithmetic will press us to consider acquisition processes. Over the past 15 years, developmental researchers of many theoretical persuasions have emphasized steady states of knowledge and deemphasized learning (as is discussed at length in the next chapter). The inherent interest of educators in change processes may prove a useful antidote to this trend.

The research that will be described in this section also has been selected to illustrate a number of recurring themes in recent information processing research. One is the centrality of children's representations of tasks for their success in perceiving, remembering, forming concepts, and solving problems. A second is the importance of considering the entire universe of tasks relevant to a concept for formulating theories of conceptual development. A third theme is the complexity of the process by which limited processing resources are allocated on multifaceted tasks. A fourth is the advantage of depicting both representations and processes in describing children's knowledge. These themes arise not only in the research reviewed here but in many other studies that are reviewed in the Cognitive Development volume of this Handbook (*Vol. III*).

Theoretically Motivated Tasks
Transitive Inference.   Transitive inference has been studied by psychometricians, Piagetians, and information processing psychologists alike (Burt, 1919; Guyote & Sternberg, 1981; Piaget, 1921). The problems are usually of the form

$$A > B$$
$$\underline{B < C}$$
$$A > C \text{ (True, false, or can't tell)}$$

Children below age seven rarely solve these problems. Until recently, the most influential explanation for this finding was that advanced by Piaget (1970). Piaget attributed young children's failure to their not understanding the reversible nature of transitive relations (i.e., that A > B implies that B < A).

Trabasso and his coworkers formulated an alternative analysis that focused on the demands of the transitivity task. In their analysis, children needed to memorize the pairwise relations (e.g., A > B), to integrate the pairwise relations into an overall representation, and to draw the appropriate inference from this integrated representation. The analysis suggested that young children's difficulty might be in remembering the original premises rather than in inferring the relations. If this was the case, then insuring that children remembered the premises would lead to appropriate inferences as well.

Bryant and Trabasso (1971) directly tested the memorial-difficulty interpretation. They presented preschoolers with five different-colored sticks of varying length. First, they taught the children which of the sticks in a given pair was longer (e.g., Stick 1 is longer than Stick 2). After children learned these relations, the experimenter presented in random order all four pairs (1 and 2; 2 and 3; 3 and 4; 4 and 5); this procedure continued until the children answered correctly 24 consecutive questions. Finally, the experimenter administered the crucial third phase. Here, children were questioned not only about the original pairs, but also about pairs whose relations they only could infer (e.g., Sticks 2 and 4).

Bryant and Trabasso predicted that children who passed the second step would do well on the untrained inference problems. This prediction proved accurate. Children who memorized the original pairs generally drew appropriate inferences. For example, 13 of 17 4-year-olds performed perfectly in the test phase.

Since this initial experiment, Trabasso and his associates have focused on specifying the representation within which children and adults maintain the premises in memory. The basic model that has emerged is a linear array in which stimuli are ordered from shortest to longest. Given such a representation, drawing the proper inference is straightforward; simply locate the two asked-about stimuli, and choose the one closer to the tall end of the array.

One type of evidence used to support this hypothesized representation involves the order in which premises are memorized (Trabasso, Riley, & Wilson, 1975). Six-year-olds as well as adults build their representations from the outside in; they first master the extreme relations (Stick 1 is longer than Stick 2; Stick 5 is longer than Stick 6), and last the middle one (Stick 3 is longer than Stick 4). This is exactly the pattern that has been observed in studies of linear orders outside of the transitive inference context (e.g., Potts, 1972).

A second type of evidence used to support the idea of a linear representation involved a comparison of subjects' performance in the above-described transitive inference situation with their performance in a visible display condition. In the display condition, children saw six different-colored sticks, ordered from shortest to longest, and were asked the usual inference questions (e.g., whether the red stick was longer than the blue stick). Patterns of both errors and reaction times were almost identical under display and standard conditions (Trabasso et al., 1975). It seemed to make little difference whether the linear array was in the subject's head or in the external environment.

The story until now has had little developmental content; in both representations and processes, young children closely resemble adults. The range of situations under which people of different ages form these representations has proved to differ substantially, however. One differentiating factor involves the linguistic form in which questions are presented during training. Bryant and Trabasso trained children using both marked terms (which stick is shorter) and unmarked ones (which stick is longer). Riley and Trabasso (1974) noted that this procedure departed from the usual transitivity format in which only one linguistic form is used. Therefore, they contrasted the previous training procedure with one that was identical except for using only the marked or only the unmarked form in training. The effectiveness of the two training conditions differed considerably; 87% of the 4-year-olds instructed with both linguistic forms met the training criterion for mastery versus 35% of those given only one. Riley and Trabasso suggested that this was due to young children who were instructed with a single form encoding the relations absolutely (Stick 1 is long; Stick 2 is short) rather than relatively (Stick 1 is longer than Stick 2). Such absolute encoding would produce confusion as Stick 2 eventually was found to be both long and short. One difference between young children and older ones thus may be that older children are more apt to code the premises in relative terms, a view not that different from Piaget's (1970) interpretation cited above.

A second difference between younger and older children involves their rate of memorization of adjacent pairs. Given enough practice, young children memorize all of the pairs, but they are much slower than adults to do so. This slowness may be due to their taking longer to decide on the integrated linear array as the appropriate representation (Falmagne, 1975).

Trabasso's findings concerning the centrality of appropriate representations mirror those of many other investigators who have adopted the IPS X task interaction approach. Young children frequently perform surprisingly competently *if* they adopt an advantageous representation. However, they often adopt less optimal ones (e.g., Chi & Koeske, 1982; Siegler & Robinson, 1982). The finding underlies the value of modeling both representations and processes.

Conservation. Klahr and Wallace's (1973; 1976) production system model of conservation is interesting both as a model of development on the particular concept and as an illustration of the detailed theorizing that can follow from focusing on the range of tasks that correspond to different aspects of a single concept. Before examining the production system itself, consider the analysis of the conservation concept that underlies the model.

The standard conservation situation is familiar. An experimenter transforms one of two identical objects (or sets of objects) in some way that leaves the dimension in question unchanged but that alters some more perceptually salient dimension. The child needs to indicate that the transformed alternative remains the same on the dimension of interest, even though it no longer looks the same.

Klahr and Wallace viewed this standard task as only one within a set of possible conservation tasks. They were particularly interested in three variants. One was identity conservation, in which a single object or row of objects is transformed. The question in such identity procedures is whether the object or row of objects is the same as it was before on the relevant dimension—for example, whether the number of objects in the row remained the same. The second variant was conservation of inequality. Rather than the objects or rows of objects initially being identical on the dimension of interest, they initially can be unequal on it. One row could have four checkers and the other three. Finally, Klahr and Wallace were interested in quantity-altering transformations, involving addition or subtraction, as well as quantity-perserving ones. Instead of simply spreading out a row of checkers, the row could be spread and a checker added.

Klahr and Wallace assigned number conservation a special place in their model. They argued not only that number conservation develops first but also that understanding of the other types of conservation grows out of it. Within the domain of number conservation tasks, they viewed problems involving small numbers of elements as being central. Their hypothesized developmental progression leading to conservation is sufficiently complex that it renders unsurprising the period of years that children take to master all of its steps.

The first step in Klahr and Wallace's developmental sequence was learning to apply quantitative operators to determine the numerousness of a set. That is, the child needed to have some way of finding out that three objects are "three." Klahr and Wallace believed that initially this is done by subitizing, a process by which people rapidly apprehend the numerousness of sets of one to four objects. A child who subitized could note the numerousness of small sets both before and after a transformation. This would allow observations of the form "spreading apart three checkers leaves three checkers," "spreading apart two dimes leaves two dimes," "spreading apart three marbles leaves three marbles," and so on. Klahr and Wallace labeled such observations *specific sequence detections*. After some number of specific sequence detections, the child might infer that "spreading apart two, three, or four objects leaves the number of objects unchanged." They termed this higher level of abstraction *common sequence detection*. Once children possessed it, they would not need to requantify after the transformation on identity conservation tasks; they already would know the answer.

This initial conservation knowledge was hypothesized to spread in several directions. Of special importance in Klahr and Wallace's analysis were extensions to addition and subtraction transformations and to situations of initial inequality between rows. Learning the effects of all of the possible transformations (adding; subtracting; neither adding nor subtracting) on all of the possible initial relations between the rows (A > B; A = B; A < B) yielded the knowledge represented in Table 7.

Children still needed to extend this knowledge to large arrays. This extension required a quantitative operator applicable to sets of all sizes. For conservation of number, counting provides such an operator. Through its use, children could establish that the pattern for large sets was identical to that for small; spreading and contracting left numerousness unchanged, and addition and subtraction changed it. Once this identity was realized at the level of common sequences, counting of the transformed set could be eliminated.

Understanding of another quantitative operator, estimation, was necessary to generalize the knowledge to liquid and solid quantity conservation. Children needed to estimate the initial equality of the objects being compared and also their equality following the pouring or reshaping transformation; neither subitizing nor counting could help them. The development of these types of conservation was more protracted than the development of number conservation for two reasons. First, estimates

Table 7. **Conservation Rules**

Line	Transformation	Relation between x_e and y'_e on Dimension 1	Relation between x_e and y'_e on Dimension 2	Quantitative Relation between x and y'
1	T_p	=	=	=
2	T_p	>	<	=
3	T_p	<	>	=
4	T_+	<	<	<
5	T_+	<	=	<
6	T_+	=	<	<
7	T_+	<	>	<
8	T_+	>	<	<
9	T_-	>	>	>
10	T_-	>	=	>
11	T_-	=	>	>
12	T_-	>	<	>
13	T_-	<	>	>

(From Klahr & Wallace, 1976)

yielded less precise results than counting or subitizing. Second, children's initial estimates were based on values of a single dimension, such as the height of the water in the two containers. Only when this unidimensional approach proved untrustworthy was it abandoned. Children would not note the untrustworthiness for a long time, since the unidimensional strategy works quite well (relative heights correlate highly with relative quantities). When the unidimensional strategy was disconfirmed, and the correct approach adopted, conservation development was complete.

Table 8 illustrates Klahr and Wallace's production system model of how a child with some, but not complete, expertise would perform a number conservation problem. Because of the model's complexity, it is easiest to divide it into parts. The first part is the semantic network (Lines 2200–4500). The semantic network includes knowledge relevant to establishing the conservation program's applicability in particular situations. Lines 2200–2500 indicate values that can be used to describe the two rows of objects: for example, the blue row and the red row. Line 2600 indicates quantifiers that can determine the number of objects in a row. Line 3200 lists quantifiable objects: red dots, for example. Lines 3300 and 3700–4000 mention terms that signal that the initial question concerns quantitative relations. Lines 4200–4500 provide information about transformations, and about equivalence among words describing the same type of transformation.

The next section of the program (Lines 4700–5100) is a subitizing subroutine. It assigns quantitative symbols to small sets. After this is a section on goal manipulation (Lines 5900–6150) similar to that described in the class inclusion production system (Table 2). Next come two verbal encoding productions, again similar to the class inclusion ones except that the first conservation encoding production concerns existing arrangements and the second fires in the presence of a transformed (NEW VI) arrangement.

Conservation rules, equivalent to those in Table 7, are presented in Lines 7200–8700. These solve three types of conservation problems: equivalence, inequivalence, and identity. They also indicate the implications of all three quantitative transformations that can occur with each conservation problem: addition, subtraction, and the null transformation.

The main productions (Lines 9100–10400) resemble in some ways the parallel class inclusion set. One major difference is the possibility of a conservation goal (P2). This refers the program to the conservation rules and constitutes an inherent difference between class inclusion and conservation programs. Another production that should be noted is P11, which limits the production system to arrays that can be subitized. P11 reflects Klahr and Wallace's assumption that at some point in development, conservation understanding is limited to small sets. Programs modeling more sophisticated knowledge would include additional quantifiers.

The hierarchical organization of the program also should be noted. PSEXEC (Line 11800) specifies the order in which productions are considered. After two goal manipulation productions comes PSVS (Line 5600); this specifies the order in which subitizing productions are considered. Next comes

Table 8. **Production System for Performing Inequivalence Conservation**

```
1400   X: (VAR)
1500:  Y: (VAR)
1600
1700          relate simulates (1) relative magnitude determination
1800                         (2) quant. relational attribute
1900   RELATE: (OPR CALL)
1950   SAT: (ACTION (* ==> +))
2000                   Semantic network
2200   WVAL: (CLASS RED BLUE SQUARE ROUND WOOD)
2300   VAL: (CLASS (WVAL) (V1 NOT V2))
2400   V1: (CLASS WVAL)
2500   V2: (CLASS WVAL)
2600   QUANTIFIER: (CLASS SUBIT COUNT ESTIMATE)
3200   XLM: (CLASS XDOT XRED XETC XELM VAL)
3300   REL.WORD: (CLASS MORE LESS LONGER SHORTER BIGGER SMALLER EQUAL SAME)
3400   CS: (CLASS LEFT RIGHT TOP BOTTOM THERE HERE WVAL)
3500   C1: (CLASS CS)
3600   C2: (CLASS CS)
3700   QREL: (CLASS QEQ QLT QGT)
3800   QEQ: (CLASS EQUAL SAME FAIR EQUAL. TO SAME. AS Q=)
3900   QLT: (CLASS FEWER SMALLER LESS LESS. THAN Q<)
4000   QGT: (CLASS MORE MORE. THAN BIGGER GREATER. THAN Q>)
4100
4200   T.PER: (CLASS EXPAND COMPRESS MOVE ROTATE TRANSLATE INVERT)
4300   T.ADD: (CLASS ADD POUR. IN)
4400   T.SUB: (CLASS SUB REMOVE EAT DELETE)
4500   TS: (CLASS T.PER T.SUB T.ADD)
4600
4700   VS. SETUP: (OPR CALL)     Create VSTM In Mid Run
4800   PDVS0: ((GOAL * SUBIT XLM) (SEE XLM) ABS --> VS.SETUP)
4900   PDVS1: ((GOAL * SUBIT XLM) (SEE XLM) (SEE XLM) ABS --> SAT (QS ONE XLM))
5000   PDVS2: ((GOAL * SUBIT XLM) (SEE XLM) (SEE XLM) (SEE XLM) ABS --> SAT (QS TWO XLM))
5100   PDVS3: ((GOAL * SUBIT XLM) (SEE XLM) (SEE XLM) (SEE XLM) (SEE XLM) ABS --> SAT (QS THREE XLM))
5500
5600   PSVS: (PDVS3 PDVS2 PDVS1 PDVS0)
5700
5800                                   goal manipulation
5900   PA: ((* GOAL) (* GOAL) --> (* ===>Z))
6000   PZ: ((* GOAL) ABS (% GOAL) --> (% ==> *))
6150   PQ: ((* GOAL) ABS (% GOAL) ABS --> QUESTION.PLEASE)
6200                                   verbal encoding
6300   PDV1: ((REL.WORD) (V1) (V2) --> (HEARD **)(X ===>HEARD X)(Y ====>HEARD Y)(VALUE (V1))(VALUE (V2))(GOAL GET.REL V1 V2))
```

PS.CON (Line 11600); this indicates the order in which conservation rule productions are considered. Following this is PSM2, which orders the main productions. Finally, if all else fails, PQ fires; this asks the computer operator for a question to start the program.

Now we can examine the production system in action. Suppose that the operator presented a conservation of inequality problem involving three red dots and two blue dots. Given the opening question, "Are there more red dots, more blue dots, or the same number of each?", PDV1 (Line 6300) notices that relational words (more, less, and same) and value words (blue and red) have been used, so it fires. As shown in the Table 9 trace, the production's firing binds blue and red to Value 1 and Value 2 and adds a goal of finding the relation between blue and red. This goal cannot be met, since as yet no comparisons have been made, so P4 fires, adding the goal of comparing the number of objects.

After PA interrupts the older active goal, the system finds that there are no numbers to compare, so P9 fires, and the system inserts a goal of quantifying the number of blue objects. After PA fires, interrupting the compare goal, P11 adds the goal of using the only quantification technique known to this system, subitizing. The subitizing goal directs the system to the PDVS productions, and PDVS2 fires, since there are two objects. PZ reactivates the interrupted goal of quantifying the blues, but since a quantitative symbol now exists, P10 fires and satisfies the quantification goal with the result of the subitizing.

PZ next reactivates the interrupted goal of comparing the number of red and blue objects. Since only the quantitative symbol for the blues is present, P9 adds a goal of quantifying the reds. PA interrupts the goal of comparing the blues and reds and the same sequence as was performed to quantify the blues is followed. This yields a quantitative symbol of three reds. P7 fires, for both blues and reds now

Table 8—continued

```
6600   PDV2: ((REL.WORD) (NEW V1)(V2) --> (HEARD **) (X===>HEARD X) (Y ====> HEARD Y) (VALUE (V1))(VALUE (V2))(*GOAL GET.REL V1 V2))
6800   PSVERB: (PDV1 PDV2)
7000                                                      conservation rules
7100                                              . . . equivalence conservation
7200   PD.CON4: ((* GOAL CON) (OLD (C1 QEQ C2)) (T.PER C2 NEW C2) --> SAT (C1 QEQ NEW C2))
7400   PD.CON5: ((* GOAL CON) (OLD (C1 QEQ C2)) (T.ADD C2 NEW C2) --> SAT (C1 QLT NEW C2))
7500   PD.CON6: ((* GOAL CON) (OLD (C1 QEQ C2)) (T. SUB C2 NEW C2) --> SAT (C1 QGT NEW C2))
7800                                               . . . identity conservation
7900   PD.CON7: ((* GOAL CON) (T.PER C1 NEW C1) --> SAT (C1 Q=NEW C1))
8000   PD.CON8: ((* GOAL CON) (T.ADD C1 NEW C1) --> SAT (C1 Q<NEW C1))
8100   PD.CON9: ((* GOAL CON) (T. SUB C1 NEW C1) --> SAT (C1 Q>NEW C1))
8200                                               . . . inequivalence conservation
8300   PD.CON10: ((* GOAL CON) (OLD (C1 QGT C2)) (T.PER C2 NEW C2) --> SAT (C1 QGT NEW C2))
8400   PD.CON11: ((* GOAL CON) (OLD (C1 QGT C2)) (T.SUB C2 NEW C2) --> SAT (C1 QGT NEW C2))
8500   PD.CON12: ((* GOAL CON) (OLD (C1 QLT C2)) (T.PER C2 NEW C2) --> SAT (C1 QLT NEW C2))
8600   PD.CON13: ((* GOAL CON) (OLD (C1 QLT C2)) (T.ADD C2 NEW C2) --> SAT (C1 QLT NEW C2))
8700   PD.CON.FAIL: ((* GOAL CON) --> (* ==> −))
8800
9000                                                      main productions
9100   P1A: ((* GOAL GET.REL X Y)(X QREL Y) --> SAT (NTC (X QREL))(OLD **) SAY.IT)
9200   P1B: ((* GOAL GET.REL Y X)(X QREL Y) --> SAT (NTC (X QREL))(OLD **) SAY.IT)
9300   P2: ((* GOAL GET.REL)(TS)(− GOAL CON) ABS --> (* GOAL CON))
9400   P4: ((* GOAL GET.REL X Y) --> (* GOAL COMPARE X Y))
9650   P6: ((* GOAL COMPARE) (X QREL Y) --> SAT)
9700   P7: ((* GOAL COMPARE X Y) (OS X) (QS Y) --> RELATE)
10100  P9: ((* GOAL COMPARE) (VALUE X) --> (VALUE ===>OLD VALUE) (* GOAL QUANTIFY X))
10300  P10: ((* GOAL QUANTIFY X) (GOAL + QUANTIFIER X) --> SAT)
10400  P11: ((* GOAL QUANTIFY X) --> (GOAL * SUBIT X))
10500
10900  SAY.IT: (ACTION (SAY X) (SAY QREL) (SAY Y))
11000
11100  QUESTION.PLEASE: (OPR CALL)
11200  SSTMI: (NIL NIL NIL NIL NIL NIL NIL NIL NIL NIL NIL NIL NIL NIL NIL NIL)
11300  VSTMI: (NIL NIL NIL NIL NIL NIL)
11400  INIT.ACT: (QUESTION.PLEASE)
11500
11600  PS.CON: (PD.CON4 PD.CON5 PD.CON6 PD.CON10 PD.CON11 PD.CON12 PD.CON13 PD.CON7 PD.CON8 PD.CON9 PD.CON.FAIL)
11700  PSM2: (P1A P1B P2 P4 P6 P7 P9 P10 P11)
11800  PSEXEC: (PA PZ PSVERB PSVS PS.CON PSM2 PQ)
```

(From Klahr & Wallace, 1976)

have been quantified. The production system has no model of how quantitative symbols are compared, so the human operator must indicate which is greater. P6 then fires, labeling the comparison goal as satisfied. PZ reactivates the original goal of relating the numbers of blues and reds, and the system now can meet this goal. Pla fires and the system says, "There are more reds than blues."

Now the system has certified that the initial configuration contained more reds. It next begins the second part of the conservation procedure. PQ fires and the operator asks, "If someone ate one of the blue ones, which row would have more?" The system's semantic memory recognizes "eat" as a word implying subtraction (Line 4400). Thus PDV2 fires, indicating that the system should determine the quantitative relation between the untouched row and the transformed one. Because there has been a transformation, P2 fires, activating the conservation goal. This directs the system to the list of conserva-

tion transformations. PD.CON11 fires because its conditions of (1) a conservation goal; (2) an original relation of one array being more numerous; and (3) a subtraction transformation involving an object being taken away from the less numerous row are met. The firing of this production satisfies the conservation goal and adds a new relation: the untouched row remains more numerous than the transformed one. PZ reactivates the original goal of relating the numbers of blues and reds, and Pla again states, "More reds than blues." After thus solving the conservation problem, the system rests.

Klahr and Wallace presented little empirical evidence to support their theory. Subsequent work, however, has yielded considerable supportive data. For example, Siegler (1981) found that on the number conservation task, children master addition and subtraction transformations prior to the quantity-preserving one. This difference in age of acquisition supported Klahr and Wallace's emphasis on the dis-

Table 9. **Trace of Production System for Performing Inequivalence Conservation**

n	pd	STM contents after pd fires
Initial state		SSTM: ((BLUE) (RED) (BIGGER) NIL NIL NIL NIL NIL) VSTM: ((RED) (BLUE) (BLUE) (RED) (RED))
1	PDV1	(('GOAL GETREL BLUE RED) (HEARD (BIGGER)) (VALUE RED) (VALUE BLUE) (HEARD BLUE) (HEARD RED) NIL NIL NIL NIL)
2	P4	(('GOAL COMPARE BLUE RED) ('GOAL GETREL BLUE RED) (HEARD (BIGGER)) (VALUE RED) (VALUE BLUE) (HEARD BLUE) (HEARD RED) NIL NIL NIL)
3	PA	(('GOAL COMPARE BLUE RED) (% GOAL GETREL BLUE RED) (HEARD (BIGGER)) (VALUE RED) (VALUE BLUE) (HEARD BLUE) (HEARD RED) NIL NIL NIL)
4	P9	
5	PA	(('GOAL QUANTIFY RED) (% GOAL COMPARE BLUE RED) (OLD VALUE RED) (% GOAL GETREL BLUE RED) (HEARD (BIGGER)) (VALUE BLUE) (HEARD BLUE) (HEARD RED) NIL NIL)
6	P11	((GOAL * SUBIT RED) ('GOAL QUANTIFY RED) (% GOAL COMPARE BLUE RED) (OLD VALUE RED) (% GOAL GETREL BLUE RED) (HEARD (BIGGER)) (VALUE BLUE) (HEARD RED) NIL NIL)
7	PDVS3	((QS THREE RED) (GOAL + SUBIT RED) (' GOAL QUANTIFY RED) (% GOAL COMPARE BLUE RED) (OLD VALUE RED) (% GOAL GETREL BLUE RED) (HEARD (BIGGER)) (VALUE BLUE) (HEARD BLUE) (HEARD RED) NIL)
8	P19, PZ, P9, PA, P11, PDVS2, P10	
15	PZ	(('GOAL COMPARE BLUE RED) (+ GOAL QUANTIFY BLUE) (GOAL + SUBIT BLUE) (QS TWO BLUE) (OLD VALUE BLUE) (+ GOAL QUANTIFY RED) (GOAL + SUBIT RED) (QS THREE RED) (OLD VALUE RED) (% GOAL GETREL BLUE RED) (HEARD (BIGGER)))
16	P7	((RED MORETHAN BLUE)) (' GOAL COMPARE BLUE RED) (QS TWO BLUE) (QS THREE RED) (+ GOAL QUANTIFY BLUE) (GOAL + SUBIT BLUE) (OLD VALUE BLUE) (+ GOAL QUANTIFY RED) (GOAL + SUBIT RED) (OLD VALUE RED) (% GOAL GETREL BLUE RED))
17	P6, PZ, P1B	
		········ "RED MORETHAN BLUE" ········
20	PQ	((EAT BLUE NEW BLUE) (OLD (RED MORETHAN BLUE)) (+ GOAL GETREL BLUE RED) (+ GOAL COMPARE BLUE RED) (QS TWO BLUE) (QS THREE RED) NIL NIL)
21	PQ	(RED BLUE (BIGGER) (EAT BLUE NEW BLUE) (OLD (RED MORETHAN BLUE)) (+ GOAL GETREL BLUE RED) (+ GOAL COMPARE BLUE RED) (QS THREE RED))
22	PDV1	(('GOAL GETREL RED BLUE) (HEARD (BIGGER)) (VALUE BLUE) (VALUE RED) (HEARD RED) (HEARD BLUE) (EAT BLUE NEW BLUE) (OLD (RED MORETHAN BLUE)) (+ GOAL GETREL BLUE RED))
23	P2	(('GOAL CON) (' GOAL GETREL RED BLUE) (EAT BLUE NEW BLUE) (HEARD (BIGGER)) (VALUE BLUE) (VALUE RED) (HEARD RED) (HEARD BLUE) (OLD (RED MORETHAN BLUE)))
24	PA	(('GOAL CON) (% GOAL GETREL RED BLUE) (EAT BLUE NEW BLUE) (HEARD (BIGGER)) (VALUE RED) (HEARD RED) (HEARD BLUE) (OLD (RED MORETHAN BLUE)))
25	PDCON11	((RED MORETHAN NEW BLUE) (+ GOAL CON) (OLD (RED MORETHAN BLUE)) (EAT BLUE NEW BLUE) (% GOAL GETREL RED BLUE) (HEARD (BIGGER)) (VALUE BLUE) (HEARD RED) (HEARD RED))
26	PZ	(('GOAL GETREL RED BLUE) (RED MORETHAN NEW BLUE) (+ GOAL CON) (OLD (RED MORETHAN BLUE)) (EAT BLUE NEW BLUE) (HEARD (BIGGER)) (VALUE RED) (HEARD RED))
27	P1A	((OLD (RED MORETHAN NEW BLUE)) (+ GOAL GETREL RED BLUE) (+ GOAL CON) (OLD (RED MORETHAN BLUE)) (EAT BLUE NEW BLUE) (VALUE RED) (HEARD RED))
		········ "RED MORETHAN BLUE" ········

(From Klahr & Wallace, 1976)

tinctiveness of the three types of transformations. Klahr and Wallace's contention that understanding of number conservation is functionally related to acquisition of other conservations also has received support. Siegler (1981) found that children who answer consistently correctly on number conservation problems first justify their responses as the result of counting or pairing, and only later refer to the transformation. Not until they advance the latter justification do they solve liquid and solid quantity problems. This sequence may be due to the external evidence provided by counting and pairing providing a reliable data base from which children can induce the role of transformations on number problems. Once children discover this role, they may learn more easily about the transformations' roles in other conservation contexts.

Tasks of Everyday Importance

Reading. Perhaps no other task domain has received as much attention from information processing psychologists as reading. In addition to its obvious practical importance, reading offers a rich target for theoretical analyses. It is of particular interest in the present context because it illustrates the multiple levels at which information processing analyses can be performed on a single task and the complexity of allocating processing resources among competing demands.

Consider some of the skills that readers use. They must possess perceptual discrimination skills sufficient to identify letters. They must integrate the letters into a graphemic representation of the word and use this representation or a related phonological one to access the word's meaning. They must integrate the meanings of groups of words into higher order structures. An increasing number of information processing researchers have argued that much processing takes place in parallel (e.g., Just & Carpenter, 1980); reading illustrates this contention particularly clearly.

Even the lowest level process in reading, recognizing and identifying letters, demands complex skills. Many letters in the Roman alphabet are highly confusable. To determine which confusions cause the most difficulty, Gibson, Osser, Schiff, and Smith (1963) briefly showed 4-year-olds a letter, then presented six other letters, and asked which one the children had seen. The most commonly confused pairs were *M* and *W*, *M* and *N*, *Q* and *O*, *E* and *F*, *P* and *R*, and *K* and *X*—in short, the letters with the greatest number of common features.

After (or concurrently with) identifying the letters within a word, readers need to determine the word's phonology. English sound-symbol relations are far from perfectly regular. Letters and letter combinations typically correspond to particular phonemes, but the correspondence is imperfect. Venezky (1970) noted numerous predictors other than the usual sound-symbol correspondences that may help readers decode. One is the graphemic environment of the symbol; for example, *c* typically takes an *s* sound when followed by *i* or *e* but a *k* sound when followed by *a* or *o*. Another is the letter's positions in the word; *gh* typically is silent at the end of words (e.g., although, weigh) but sounds like a hard *g* at the beginning of words (e.g., ghost, ghastly). Yet a third predictor involves morpheme boundaries; distinguishing the *sh* in mishap from the *sh* in meshed is made easier by knowing about the prefix *mis* and the suffix *ed*.

Calfee, Venezky, and Chapman (1969) examined knowledge of these orthographic relations by showing children pseudowords such as "calp" and "cilp" and asking how they would be pronounced. Correlations between pronunciations of pseudowords and reading comprehension were quite high in first and third graders, though the relations were weaker among older children. The finding suggested that decoding may be a larger source of variability in reading skill in the early grades; later, most readers may decode effectively but still vary in ability to extract meaning. The finding parallels Keating and Bobbitt's (1978) result on changes in correlations between efficiency at executing basic processes and IQ test scores.

Before considering the role of meaning in reading, it seems worthwhile to consider another domain where knowledge of sound/symbol correspondence comes into play, spelling. The problems involved in spelling English words are largely the same as those involved in decoding them. Even if children know the most common rules and base their spelling on them, they must cope with considerable irregularity. Rudorf (1965) wrote a computer program to determine the spellings that would result from relying on 200 frequently applicable orthographic rules. He found that the rules produced correct spellings for only one-half of the 17,000 most common English words. Fourth graders spelled better than the computer program on a 50-word test that both were given. Further, the words that the program spelled correctly were words that the children also spelled correctly; thus, instruction in the rules would not likely have helped their performance.

How can we account for fourth-graders' spelling being superior to that of an algorithm incorporating 200 rules? Simon and Simon (1973) suggested that the superiority is due to the children supplementing orthographic rules with recall and recognition of correct letter sequences. Simon and Simon built a computer program, SPEL, to illustrate how the two types of information might interact. The program knows verbatim some letter sequences in words, most often the first few and last few letters. It also possesses a list of phonemes, with each phoneme linked to one or more single letters and/or combinations of letters. If SPEL does not know verbatim the interior of a word, it produces the most common phonemic spelling as a default option.

Simon and Simon found that SPEL's performance resembled that of fourth graders not only in the relative difficulty of words but in the errors that it made. The investigators also suggested means by which children's spelling might be improved. One recommendation was to have children read more. This would help them recognize correct spellings and also would extend their list of letters that might correspond to a given phoneme. Another suggestion was to tell children that with difficult words, they should generate several spellings and then try to recognize the correct one; this would expand the uses of the less error-prone recognition procedure.

Now we can return to reading, in particular the role of meaning in reading. While readers are using their knowledge of symbol/sound relations and their recognitory ability to decode words, they simultaneously are trying to comprehend words, sentences, and larger units. A number of investigators have suggested that decoding and comprehension compete for limited attentional resources. In this view, automatization of decoding frees resources for the task of comprehension (LaBerge & Samuels, 1974).

Wilkinson (1980) applied this reasoning to studying children's reading. He suggested that reading ability is constrained by three limits: decoding limits, comprehension limits, and memory limits. That is, children may encounter difficulty in reading because they cannot decode words, because they cannot understand their meaning even once they decode them, or because they cannot remember the words after they decode and initially understand them.

Wilkinson examined interactions among these processes, in particular the effects of decoding demands on comprehension. Second- through sixth-graders either read material or heard the material read to them. Then they were asked questions, some of which required only memory ("What was the little boy's name?") and some of which required both memory and comprehension ("When the story said, 'He went to the store,' who was the 'he' that the story was talking about?").

Wilkinson found that children recalled more information when questions required only memory than when they required both memory and comprehension and that they remembered more when they listened to material than when they read it themselves. In addition, comprehension and memory questions differed more dramatically under reading than under listening conditions (interactive limitations). That is, when resources were not needed for decoding, more of them could be devoted to comprehending, thus reducing the differences between comprehension and memory questions. Wilkinson also found that for readers of a single age and equal reading ability, comprehension decreased as reading speed increased. Again, this finding indicated an interactive limit, a tradeoff between the processing resource devoted to decoding and those devoted to comprehending.

Despite the effort needed to decode, even beginning readers strive to understand what they are reading. Some of the strongest evidence on this point comes from studies of children's errors. Weber (1970) classified these errors into four types: substitutions of one word for another; omissions of a word; insertions of a word; and scrambles, in which children read words that correspond roughly, if at all, to those printed on the page. Weber found that by far the most frequent type of error made by first graders was substitutions. More than 90% of these substitutions were consistent with the meaning of the sentence. Children were twice as likely to reread sentences when their substitutions led to anomolous meanings as when they led to plausible ones. Thus, both the errors themselves and the rereading patterns indicated sensitivity to meaning from early in the learning-to-read process.

Information processing analyses of reading increasingly have emphasized the reader's purposes and knowledge of the content area as determinants of speed and comprehension. In this view, reading is many tasks rather than just one. Skill in adjusting reading to task demands increases substantially with age. Kobasigawa, Ransom, and Holland (1979) examined one such adjustment that involved skimming a passage to locate a fact. Children of ages 10, 12, and 14 were presented two-paragraph stories. Their task was to find the answer to a question they were posed. Reading of the first sentence of each paragraph, in both cases a clear topic sentence, was sufficient to indicate that the first paragraph was irrelevant to the question and that the second sentence was relevant. The 12- and 14-year-olds progressed through the first paragraph faster under these conditions than under conditions in which they simply were told to read the whole story. However, the 10-year-olds did not. Only under conditions in which the 10-year-olds explicitly were told to search for key words related to the solution of the question did they skim. These results indicate that the younger children were capable of skimming but needed substantial environmental support to do so. Although by most definitions they were skilled readers, they had not mastered all of the tasks involved in reading.

Writing. A venerable sorrow of teachers and other educators is how badly students write. Recent analyses of the composition process reveal some of the reasons for the difficulties and also some ways in which writing can be improved. Of particular interest is Bereiter and Scardemalia's (1982) research on children's compositions. They addressed the issues of why initial writing is difficult, why revisions often are no better than originals, and how writing skills can be taught. As in Wilkinson's work on reading, their analysis of writing highlights the challenges involved in allocating limited processing capacity among the many facets of a complex task.

Why is the initial drafting process so arduous? In Bereiter and Scardemalia's model, writers first must activate relevant material in long-term memory and then, as they write, retrieve material needed to meet immediate goals. Each of these processes poses difficulties. In many cases, people are unable to activate relevant material because they do not possess a file corresponding to the assigned topic (e.g., Why I like winter). Under such conditions, writers must pull together material from diverse parts of their knowledge bases. Meeting immediate goals requires retrieving material that will amuse, convince, inform, or intrigue. Intonations and nonverbal gestures, which might serve these purposes in speech, are unavailable; this makes the search of the activated material in long-term memory all the more critical. In addition, other people's questions and comments in conversations often suggest new goals and paths to pursue. By contrast, writers' feedback ordinarily is limited to their own reactions to what they have written. Thus, writing demands highly autonomous skills.

Bereiter and Scardemalia found that the mechanical demands of writing and its slow rate also contribute to the difficulty of writing. In one study, fourth and sixth graders composed essays under a standard writing condition, a condition in which they dictated their essays at a normal speaking rate into a tape recorder, and a condition in which they dictated their essays to a scribe, thus limiting their dictation to the rate of writing. Children in the standard speaking condition produced essays twice as long as those in the standard writing conditions. (Quality and length of compositions correlated highly.) Children in the slow dictation condition, limited in rate but unburdened by writing mechanics, produced essays of intermediate lengths.

Children's major stumbling block in writing seems to be generating content rather than putting the content into prose. Telling children at the start of their essays to write as much as they can, or instructing them to try to write more when they say that they have written all that they can, doubled their output in one of Bereiter and Scardamalia's experiments. More specific prompts also were found to be helpful. Bereiter and Scardamalia reported giving students a deck of cards with common sentence openings on them: "I think," "For example," "Even though," etc. Such prompts improved elementary schoolers' writing, even though the prompts did not point to particular content.

After people draft essays, they usually must revise them. The difficulty of the revision process is common knowledge. One frequently advanced explanation is that psychological and temporal closeness to the written product interfere with efforts at revision. Writing teachers often advise students to defer revising their work until they can look at it objectively. Such advice may not get to the heart of the problem, though. Bereiter and Scardemalia found that fourth through twelfth graders were no better at revising other people's compositions than at revising their own, except in correcting punctuation and spelling. Nor did the quality of revisions improve when students tried to revise their own work a week after writing rather than immediately. In each case, blind raters were unable to judge accurately which essay was the revision.

The investigators ascribed the difficulties of revision to competition for processing resources, much as Wilkinson did in the reading context. Even in revising a single sentence, people must devote resources to preserving the intended message, to searching for ways to express it, and to resisting the influence of the original wording. The passage of time leaves these difficulties intact; thus, waiting may not improve revisions.

Bereiter and Scardemalia's investigations provide a useful framework for thinking about the writing process, but say little about changes in writing that occur with age and experience. An unusual longitudinal study by Waters (1980) yielded valuable data on how practice at writing contributes to writing skill. Waters analyzed 120 essays written by a second-grade girl (herself) during a school year. All of the essays were written in response to a "class news" assignment; each day, students were to write about that day's events. Waters intensively examined five essays that she had written on consecutive days at the beginning of the year, five in the middle, and five at the end. The analysis indicated large increases in the length and variety of information within her paragraphs. She formulated separate story grammars to describe the essays she produced at the beginning, middle, and end of the year. As shown in Figure 14, story contents at first were limited to the date, weather, and class activities; later they included information about peers, duties, and materials brought to school. The stories also described individual events in greater depth as the year progressed. Whereas the earliest grammar refers to singing happy birthday, the later ones refer not only to the activity but also to the time of day at which it occurred and to the child's response to it. Thus, the content of the essays both broadened and deepened over time. In the terms of Bereiter and Scardemalia's model, the second grader assembled a file of topics useful for satisfying the class news assignment. These files reduced the usual processing demands of the writing task.

Mathematics.   Children's knowledge of mathematics recently has become a "hot topic" (cf. monographs written by Brainerd, 1979, and Gelman & Gallistel, 1978; and volumes edited by Ginsburg, 1982, and Carpenter & Moser, 1982). The content domain is appealing to information processing researchers for at least three reasons. First, mature understanding of mathematics can be modeled precisely. These models of mature understanding provide a clearly defined comparison point against which to assess children's knowledge, thus aiding understanding of development. Second, the research can make a practical contribution. At least one program of research that will be described below has resulted in a product that is being used quite widely to teach teachers how to assess students' mathematical understanding. Third, mathematical understanding is a content domain that almost demands modeling of both representations and processes, a research strategy that is becoming increasingly common among researchers who follow the IPS X task interaction approach.

The first major effort by information processing researchers to study children's mathematical knowledge was performed by Groen and his colleagues.

Groen and Parkman (1972) suggested that both children and adults use a "min" strategy to add. Asked to add $n + m$, they choose the larger number and increment it by one's the number of times indicated by the smaller. Groen and Parkman hypothesized that in the addition context, choosing the larger number takes a constant amount of time, regardless of the numbers involved. Thus, solution times would be a linear function of the size of the smaller number (the number of increments). This chronometric model accounted quite well for both children's and adults' solution times on addition problems with one class of exceptions. Ties, problems with equal augends and addends, were solved much faster than predicted by their minima, and solution times were constant across different tie problems. Groen and Parkman suggested that answers to these problems might be overlearned sufficiently to be retrieved directly from memory rather than being reconstructed via the min process.

Groen and colleagues have extended this approach in a number of directions. They have shown its applicability to subtraction problems (Woods, Resnick, & Groen, 1975), to missing addend problems (Groen & Poll, 1973), and to multiplication problems (Parkman, 1972). In all cases, children used rules similar to the min strategy. Also, Groen and Resnick (1977) investigated how children come to use the min algorithm. They hypothesized that children invent the strategy rather than being taught it. To test this hypothesis, they taught a group of 4-year-olds, who did not yet know how to add, a strategy of counting out a number of blocks corresponding to the augend, counting out a number corresponding to the addend, and then counting all of the blocks. The children practiced this procedure until they were proficient. Then, they were asked to add without the blocks. Examination of their reaction times revealed that half of the children switched to the "min" algorithm. Thus, even after being taught a "sum" approach that yielded consistently correct answers, the children adopted the more efficient min strategy.

Groen's research focused on the way in which children solve simple arithmetic problems. Others have focused on the sources of children's errors on more complex items. Some of the most interesting of this work has culminated in the formulation of BUGGY and DEBUGGY, computer programs for diagnosing error-prone subtraction procedures (Brown & Burton, 1978; Brown & Vanlehn, 1982). Brown and his colleagues first formulated a procedural network model of correct subtraction. They then analyzed children's errors for "bugs" (i.e., rules that

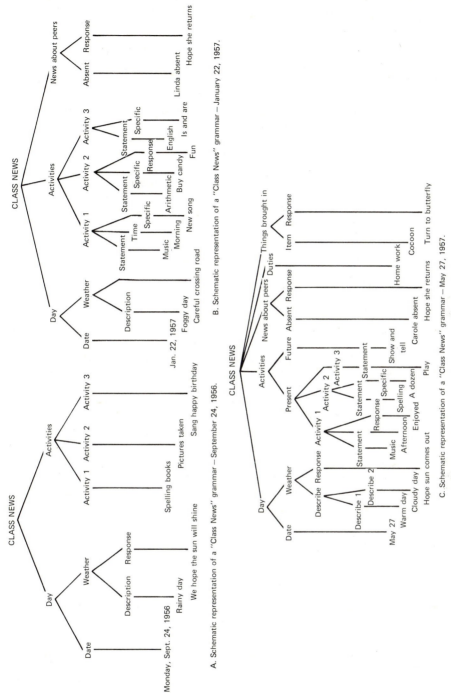

Figure 14. Class news grammars at three points in a second-grade class. (Waters, 1980.)

predicted when each child would answer incorrectly and which error he or she would make). Next they developed an automated system for diagnosing which bug or bugs underlay the errors. Finally, they wrote a computer program to teach teachers to assess bugs in their students' performance and tested the program on groups of future instructors.

Table 10 can be used to illustrate how the bug analysis procedure works. The table indicates the fit of each bug to the student's performance. A "*" indicates that the bug accurately predicted a correct answer, and a "***" indicates a predicted incorrect answer; these are the successes of the hypothesis that the student's performance routine has a particular bug. A "!" means that the bug would give a correct answer but the student gave the wrong one; this is one type of predictive failure that can occur (the others do not arise in Table 10).

No single bug in Table 10A fits the student's performance. By contrast, the interaction of two bugs shown in Table 10B fits quite well. Consider the problem 103 - 64. In accord with the STOPS/BORROW/AT/ZERO bug, the student does not decrement the zero in the second column after borrowing from it. This brings into play the other bug, DIFF/O-N=N, that produces an answer of O − 6 = 6: thus the remainder, 169. The two bugs in tandem account for the student's answer on 13 of the 16 problems. Two of the other three answers can be accounted for by the bug of adding rather than subtracting; the student occasionally may forget which operation to perform.

Brown and Burton applied the BUGGY program to teaching prospective teachers how to detect students' bugs. Their program works in a tutorial fashion. It first displays five problems and a hypothetical student's answers. Teachers are told to indicate when they think they have identified the bug. The next task is for the teachers to generate new problems and to answer them as the bug would. The program gives feedback following each of the teachers' answers. Finally, when the teachers have generated five consecutive correct predictions, BUGGY tests their knowledge by presenting new problems designed to discriminate among bugs. If teachers answer these correctly, the computer congratulates them for perspicacity and insight.

Brown and Burton found that teachers frequently failed to answer correctly BUGGY's test questions. When several bugs were consistent with the original five answers, teachers tended to select new instances that did not discriminate among them. Thus, bugs that were consistent with the previous evidence sometimes proved wrong in the test phase. The investigators intended such surprises when they wrote BUGGY. They hoped to teach teachers to generate alternative algorithms consistent with data patterns and to formulate sets of problems that discriminated among the undisconfirmed ones. Brown and Burton quoted a large number of testimonials from teachers who felt that BUGGY achieved this purpose.

A longstanding criticism of information processing research is that it is particularistic and that it does not cumulate (e.g., Neisser, 1976; Allport, 1975). Newell (1973) was among the first to note this problem; he suggested that in order to overcome it, researchers should integrate numerous task-specific models into a single, encompassing model. Such integrative models would combine detailed analysis of particular problems with breadth.

Siegler and Robinson (1982) adopted this strategy in studying preschoolers' knowledge of numbers. They built separate models of the development of counting, magnitude comparison, addition, and number conservation skills. Then they integrated these models into a single representation that could be operated on by several task-specific processes. The representation was depicted as a semantic network, and the processes as flow diagrams. Separate models were built to characterize 3-, 4-, and 5-year-olds' knowledge.

The model of 4-year-olds' knowledge, Model II, is shown in Figure 15. (Owing to limitations of space, it is the only model that will be described in any detail.) The representation is organized hierarchically: numbers as a class are at the top, then categories of numbers (e.g., small numbers), and then individual numbers (e.g., 6). Numbers as a class can be operated on by a number of processes. They can be counted, their magnitudes can be compared, they can be added and (presumably) subtracted. At the next lower level are categories of numbers, ordered by magnitudes. Both the number conservation data reported in Siegler (1981) and the magnitude comparison data reported by Siegler and Robinson (1982) suggested that these categories possess psychological reality for young children. On these tasks, children treated similarly numbers within the categories but treated differently numbers in separate categories. The lowest level of the hierarchy involves individual numbers. In addition to being tied to the category labels with varying probabilities, the individual numbers also are associated with a variety of properties. For example, 1 is the number that you start counting with; it is the number of heads, bodies, noses, and mouths on a person; and it is the smallest number.

The number conservation process operates on the

Table 10. **Brown and Burton's (1977) Analysis of Bugs in Subtraction Procedures**

A. Initial Bug Comparison Table

8	99	353	633	81	4769	257	6523	103	7315	1039	705	10038	10060	7001
3	79	342	221	17	0	161	1280	64	6536	44	9	4319	98	94
5	20	11	412	64	4769	96	5243	39	779	995	696	5719	9962	6907

Student answers:

—	—	—	—	98	—	418	—	169	738	1095	706	14319	10078	7097

*FORGET/BORROW/OVER/BLANKS:

*	*	*	*	!	*	!	*	139	!	***	***	15719	10062	7007

*STOPS/BORROW/AT/ZERO:

*	*	*	*	!	*	!	*	49	!	***	***	6719	10062	7017

*DIFF/O-N=N:

*	*	*	*	!	*	!	*	!	839	!	!	***	9978	!

*ADD/INSTEADOF/SUB:

11	178	695	854	***	*	***	7803	167	13851	1083	714	14357	10158	7095

B. Multiple Bug Comparison Table

8	99	353	633	81	4769	257	6523	103	7315	1039	705	10038	10060	7001
3	79	342	221	17	0	161	1280	64	6536	44	9	4319	98	94
5	20	11	412	64	4769	96	5243	39	779	995	696	5719	9962	6907

Student answers:

—	—	—	—	98	—	418	—	169	738	1095	706	14319	10078	7097

(*DIFF/O-N=N *STOPS/BORROW/AT/ZERO):

*	*	*	*	!	*	!	*	***	839	***	***	***	***	***

*ADD/INSTEADOF/SUB:

11	178	695	854	***	*	***	7803	167	13851	1083	714	14357	10158	7095

categories of numbers. First it determines whether the problem involves small numbers of objects (perhaps by subitizing). Then, if the problem does, it quantifies the number of objects in each row and compares the quantified values; if not, it chooses the longer row as having more objects.

The counting model is more complex. The process makes use of two parts of the representation: the tagging of the numbers 1–9 as members of the digit repetition list and the tagging of the decade names 20–90 as members of the rule applicability list. The process proceeds as follows. Children are asked to start counting at a particular number (the default value is one), and they first say that number. Then they consider whether a rule applicability list member is part of the number name. If not, children use the "next" connection to recall the succeeding number. This cycle continues until children reach a number that does include a rule applicability list member (e.g., 20). At this point, they operate as shown on the left side of the flow chart. They concatenate the

rule applicability list member with digit list members until they reach the next number with a 9 (e.g., 29). Since 29 in this child's model has a "next" connection to 30, counting continues. At 39, however, no "next" connection exists. The child must either stop or choose arbitrarily a rule applicability list member. This can produce omissions if the number chosen is too far advanced (e.g., 39, 60), repetitions if it is insufficiently advanced (e.g., 39, 20), or, fortuitously, the next number (39, 40). The model predicted 4-year-olds' distributions of stopping points, omissions, repetitions, nonstandard numbers (e.g., 20–10), and counting-on from arbitrary starting points.

The magnitude comparison model is simpler. Children choose a category label associated with each number. If the labels differ, they choose the number associated with the larger label as being greater. If the labels are the same, they choose new labels for the numbers. The probabilities of choosing a given label for each number are shown in the links

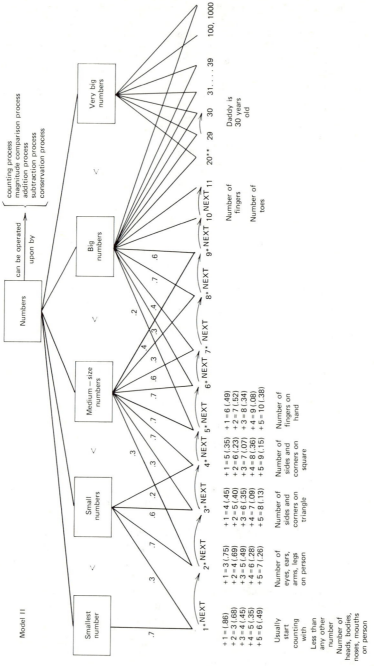

Figure 15. A model of preschoolers' knowledge of numbers. (Siegler & Robinson, 1982.)

B. Processes and the Portion of the Representation Used on Each Task

1. Number Conservation

REPRESENTATION

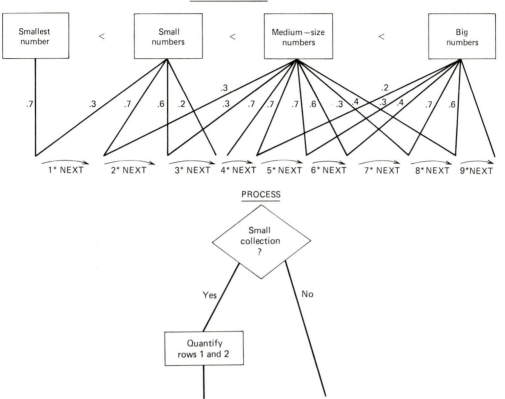

PROCESS

Figure 15—*continued*

2. Counting

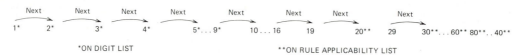

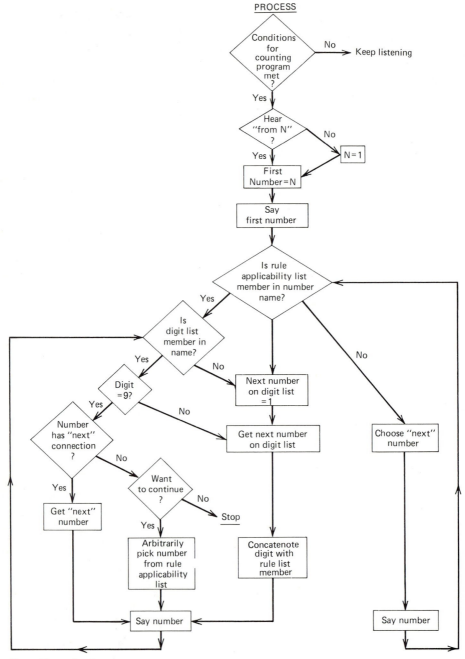

Figure 15—*continued*

3. Magnitude Comparison Process

Representation

Category	Number								
	1	2	3	4	5	6	7	8	9
Smallest	.7								
Small	.2	.72	.61	.22	.06			.06	
Medium	.1	.28	.33	.67	.72	.67	.56	.27	.44
Big			.06	.11	.22	.33	.44	.67	.56

PROCESS

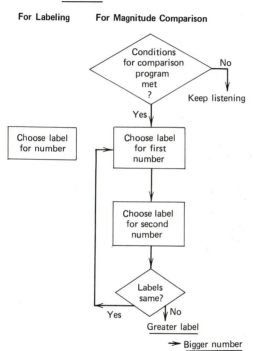

For Labeling   **For Magnitude Comparison**

Figure 15—*continued*

4. Addition Strategy Choice Process

Representation

Sums and (Probability of Recalling Each Sum
with Confidence Beyond Criterion)

Augend	Addend				
	1	2	3	4	5
1	2(.86)	3(.75)	4(.45)	5(.35)	6(.49)
2	3(.68)	4(.69)	5(.49)	6(.28)	7(.26)
3	4(.58)	5(.40)	6(.35)	7(.09)	8(.13)
4	5(.55)	6(.23)	7(.07)	8(.36)	9(.15)
5	6(.68)	7(.52)	8(.34)	9(.08)	10(.38)

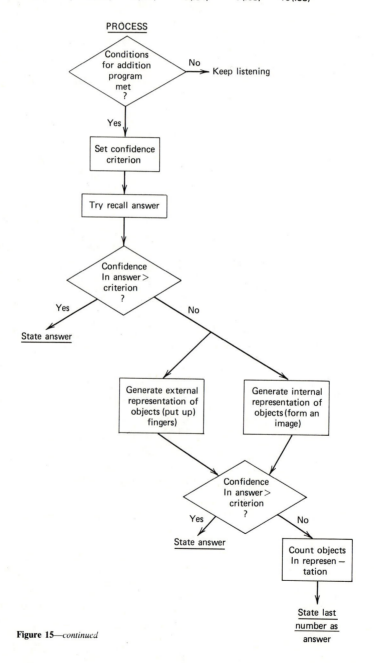

Figure 15—continued

between the categories and the individual numbers; these were derived by asking preschoolers whether each number was "little," "big," or "medium." The model predicted the results of multidimensional scaling and hierarchical clustering analyses of 4-year-olds' performance, the min and split effects, and the results of a training experiment in which 4-year-olds were taught a new labeling framework.

The addition process differs from the others in being a model of strategy choice rather than a model of how any given strategy is executed. First, children set a confidence criterion for how certain of an answer they need to be before they will state it. Then they try to recall the answer to the problem they were posed. If they cannot recall an answer with sufficient confidence, they augment their representation of the augend and addend, either by holding up fingers or by forming a mental image. If their confidence in an answer at this point exceeds their criterion, they state it; otherwise, they count the objects in their representation and give the last number as their answer. This model generated a variety of aspects of 4-year-olds' addition performance: the four approaches that they used (counting fingers, putting up fingers but not counting them, counting without any obvious referent, and no visible strategy); their solution times and accuracy on the 25 problems; and the strong correlation ($r = .91$) between their use of visible or audible strategies and the difficulty of particular problems.

Model II provides a vantage point for considering the more advanced understanding depicted in Model III (the model of 5-year-olds' knowledge) and the less advanced knowledge depicted in Model I (the model of 3-year-olds' knowledge). First, consider some properties that were hypothesized not to change in this age and skill range. The basic hierarchical form of the representation is constant across models. Children have knowledge about numbers in general, about categories of numbers, and about particular numbers. Also constant across models are many particular connections within and across levels of the hierarchy. Even in Model I, the larger numbers more often are associated with the larger categories; even in Model I, "next" connections between digits are present; even in Model I, some facts linking numbers to semantic properties (e.g., people have 2 hands) are known. On the other side of the ledger, changes in the models can be seen both in the representation and in the process. Consider the parts of the model involved in the development of magnitude comparison skills. The shift from chance to above-chance performance, embodied in the move from Model I to Model II, is produced largely by

changes in the process. The shift from above-chance to perfect performance, embodied in the move from Model II to Model III, is produced by changes in the representation. It was not clear how both changes could have been predicted by a model that included only processes or only representations. Thus, modeling both representations and processes seemed to be valuable in accounting for the development of mathematical knowledge.

Mechanisms of Development

Conspicuous by their absence from the above discussion have been insights concerning the mechanisms by which development occurs. Those of us who have adopted the information processing approach have evaded, avoided, and hidden from this issue. We are not alone in this nonconfrontational policy—adherents of other approaches have not done any better—but this is no excuse. The lack of success in identifying mechanisms of development has hindered theoretical progress. It has contributed to the "embarassing fact that the field of cognitive development continues to be much shorter on explicit, testable theories than is the field of adult cognitive psychology" (Flavell, 1978, pp. 99–100).

This chapter will end with a description of several developmental mechanisms that have been proposed. Not coincidentally, each of these mechanisms is embedded in a theory of development; theories demand mechanisms. Thus, this last section also provides a brief survey of current information processing theories of development. I expect that the corresponding section in the next *Handbook* will be both longer and more profound.

Self-Modification

One traditional approach to the issue of how development occurs is to emphasize the system's capacity for self-modification. Piaget's constructs of assimilation and accommodation provide well-known illustrations. The Piagetian constructs never have been defined in sufficient detail to satisfy critics, however; for example, Klahr (1982) commented:

> For 40 years now we have had assimilation and accommodation, the mysterious and shadowy forces of equilibration, the Batman and Robin of the developmental processes. What are they? How do they do their thing? Why is it after all this time, we know no more about them than when they first sprang on the scene? What we need is a way to get beyond vague verbal statements of the nature of the developmental process. (p. 80)

Klahr suggested that production systems might provide a more useful framework for considering self-modification. Productions can be designed to build new productions based on the system's experience. An advantage to considering self-modification within this framework is that the self-modifying productions are distributed among the productions that yield ongoing performance. The system simultaneously performs and develops.

Klahr and Wallace (1976) sketched mechanisms by which a self-modifying production system might operate. The time line—a temporally ordered record within which people preserve their goals, STM contents, and outcomes—provides the data used by the self-modifying productions. Two mechanisms that operate on this data base are consistency detection and redundancy elimination. The consistency detection mechanism notes regular sequences and induces conclusions about them. As shown in Table 11, the workings of the regularity detection mechanism are governed by three factors: (1) the IPS's critical consistency level (CCL), its current sensitivity to new information; (2) the degree of similarity between parts of the time line (D); and (3) the number of similar instances (N). Small letters (ccl: d: n) indicate the current values of these variables.

As Table 11 indicates, consistency detection operates by identifying partial matches in the time line, and considering whether the product of their closeness and their number $(d \times n)$ exceeds the current value required to form a new node (the CCL). The process might be applied to information obtained by looking at birds. Suppose that a child had seen two robins and two cardinals; and suppose that the time line contained a record of all the productions that the child used in visually scanning the birds. The productions used in looking at the two robins might overlap sufficiently to form a new node, corresponding to a visual concept of robins. The "robins" scanning node might eventually have enough commonality with the "cardinals" scanning node to form a common category of "birds," including the productions common to viewing all four birds.

Redundancy elimination involves recasting productions into forms that reduce processing demands; in other words, it involves the search for shortcuts. An example derived from Lewis (1978) aptly illustrates the redundancy elimination process. Lewis demonstrated how a self-modifying production system might fall prey to the einstellung effect (Luchins, 1942). This is the phenomenon whereby practiced subjects are less able than unpracticed ones to find shortcuts for solving problems.

Consider a simple production system (Table 12)

that adds and deletes symbols until it reaches a goal. The production system operates like the ones described above except for one feature. In this system, a production firing removes from the short-term memory the symbols that matched the ones on the production's condition side. This eliminates the need to mark symbols as "old" to keep some productions from firing repeatedly.

The first version of Lewis's production system, PS.1, consists of P1, P2, P3, and P4. As shown under the heading "Initial System," when PS.1 operates on a short-term memory that initially contains the letters A and C, P2 fires, followed by P4, P3, and P1. The sequence of short-term memory states is AC, BC, DE, and GE. During this sequence, four productions fire and four symbol replacements occur. Assume that after much practice on this task, the system notices that the short-term memory contents AC invariably leads to DE. The system therefore forms a new production, P5. The practiced production system achieves its goal with only three productions firing and three symbols being replaced (Table 12). Now suppose an experimenter provides a hint that suggests a shortcut (P6). The effects on both the initial system and the practiced one are shown at the bottom of Table 12. If the hint was provided before practice yielded P5, the production system would take advantage of it to reduce its number of symbol replacements. If practice already had produced P5, however, the system would not generate an intermediate state that would satisfy P6's conditions. The hint would have no impact—thus the einstellung effect.

Several shortcomings of Klahr and Wallace's theory should be mentioned. A large distance separates their reach from their grasp. Although they proclaimed the virtues of self-modifying productions systems as a model of the total cognitive system, their own work was limited to modeling performance on a few Piagetian tasks, and none of their systems was self-modifying. This limits the conclusions that can be drawn about the usefulness of production systems as an inclusive theory of development. The problem is greater than it otherwise might be because almost no other developmentalists have utilized production systems. (The only two exceptions of which I am aware are Baylor and Gascon's (1974) and Young's (1973) models of seriation.)

A second difficulty concerns whether production systems are most appropriately viewed as a theory of cognition or as a language for describing cognition. Newell (1973) characterized production systems as a "theory-laden programming language" (p. 516). He contrasted it with other programming languages

Table 11. Klahr and Wallace's Model of the Time Line

Step 1. Segment time slice using table of partial-match templates under control of *D*.

Step 2. Compute instantaneous values of ccl on current segmentation. ccl $= f(d^* \ n)$.

Step 3. Test: Is ccl = CCL (CCL is cumulative value of critical consistency level)?
    If yes, go to Step 6.

Step 4. Revise CCL downward as function of ccl.

Step 5. Test: Is CCL below minimum level?
    If yes, go to Step 8.
    If no, return to Step 1.

Step 6. Create new node based upon current segmentation.

Step 7. Revise CCL upward as function of ccl.

Step 8. Move to new section of time line: create new time slice. Go to Step 1.

Table 12. A Production System Model of the Einstellung Effect

---

P1: G $\rightarrow$ stop	
P2: A $\rightarrow$ B	initial set
P3: D $\rightarrow$ G	
P4: B,C $\rightarrow$ D,E	
P5: A,C $\rightarrow$ D,E	composite production hint
P6: B $\rightarrow$ G	

Initial system
PS.1: (P1, P2, P3, P4)   ''performance''
Trace: AC $\overset{P2}{\Rightarrow}$ BC $\overset{P4}{\Rightarrow}$ DE $\overset{P3}{\Rightarrow}$ GE $\overset{P1}{\Rightarrow}$ stop   4 cycles; 4 replacements

Practiced system with composite
PS.2: (P1, P2, P3, P4, P5)
Trace: AC $\overset{P5}{\Rightarrow}$ DE $\overset{P3}{\Rightarrow}$ GE $\overset{P1}{\Rightarrow}$ stop   3 cycles; 3 replacements

Hint to initial system
PS.1H: (P1, P2, P3, P4, P6)
Trace: AC $\overset{P2}{\Rightarrow}$ BC $\overset{P6}{\Rightarrow}$ GC $\overset{P1}{\Rightarrow}$ stop   3 cycles; 2 replacements

Hint to practiced system
PS.2H: (P1, P2, P3, P4, P5, P6)
Trace: AC $\overset{P5}{\Rightarrow}$ DE $\overset{P3}{\Rightarrow}$ GE $\overset{P1}{\Rightarrow}$ stop   3 cycles; 3 replacements

---

(From Lewis, 1978)

such as LISP and FORTRAN, which he charac- terized as "theoretically neutral." It is not clear, however, what theoretical positions are implied by production systems that would not already be sub- scribed to by users of other simulation languages or by information processing psychologists who do not simulate.

All of this is not to detract from the potential of self-modifying production systems as a theory of development. Self-modification almost certainly is an important part of development. Production sys- tems represent the clearest explication to date of how self-modification might occur. The fact that produc- tion systems have not been widely used is no reason to assume that they would not be useful. Indeed, their precision, flexibility, and applicability to di- verse domains demand that they be given a more thorough trial than they have thus far.

Automatization

Case (1978) proposed a theory in which the mechanism of automatization played a crucial role. His theory starts with three assertions about cogni- tive development:

1. The sequence of behaviors that emerges may be ascribed to the evolution of qualitatively distinct executive strategies.

2. Progress through any given sequence of exec- utive strategies can be influenced by practice, feed- back, cue highlighting, and strategy modeling.

3. The size of a child's working memory limits the complexity of the strategy he can acquire and utilize, particularly when his only experience is practice or practice with feedback (pp. 44–45).

Case organized his theory around four developmen- tal stages, the role of automatization in the growth of functional memory capacity, and the effects on auto- matization of specific experience, general experi- ence, and maturation.

In many ways, Case's theory resembles Piaget's. Children are said to pass through four developmental stages. The contents of the four stages are charac- terized informally in terms of conditions and ac- tions. Sensorimotor operations take sensory input on the condition side and yield physical movements on the action side. Representational operations also take sensory stimuli as their conditions, but their actions are abstract encodings of the input. Logical operations take abstract encodings of stimuli as their conditions, and their actions involve simple trans- formations of the encoding. Finally, formal opera-

tions take abstractly coded information as their con- ditions, and their actions involve complex (second- order) transformations of the information.

Case proposed that development within each stage depends on the functional size of working memory. The underlying capacity of working mem- ory is said to be constant from birth, or at least from a very early age. However, functional capacity in- creases owing to increases in the automaticity with which operations are executed on the content charac- teristic of the stage. As each operation is executed more efficiently, working memory space is freed for additional operations.

A central issue in Case's analysis of working memory is how to measure a task's memorial de- mands. Table 13 displays his analysis of the de- mands of one task, Noelting's (1975) orange juice problem. Noelting's task involved two sets of tum- blers, each tumbler containing either orange juice or water. Children needed to predict which pitcher would taste more strongly of orange juice if the con- tents of all of the tumblers in one set were poured into one pitcher and the contents of the tumblers in the other set were poured into another.

Case argued that the memory demands of a task are not absolute, but rather depend on the executive strategy adopted to perform it. He described four executive strategies that children used on the orange juice task. Children first judged on the basis of the presence of orange juice. If only one set of tumblers contained orange juice, that set's mixture would taste more strongly of it; if both did, both mixtures would taste more strongly of it. Children next con- sidered the quantity of tumblers with orange juice; the set with the greater quantity would produce a mixture that tasted more like orange juice. Then, they considered both the quantity of orange juice in each set *and* the quantity of water, and they picked the set that had more orange juice than water unless both sets or neither did, in which case they would guess. Finally, they subtracted the number of tum- blers containing water from the number containing orange juice, and chose the side with the greater remainder. Again, if the two sets had the same re- mainder, they thought no judgment was possible. (Note that although these strategies solve more and more problems, none of them are perfect. They model 3- to 10-year-olds' performance, and even 10-year-olds do not adopt the correct ratio rule on this task.)

As shown in Table 13, Case equated the working memory requirements of each executive strategy with the number of elements in memory at the most demanding point in the strategy's execution. For example, at the most demanding point in Strategy 3, children needed to remember the number of orange juice tumblers in Set A, the number in Set B, and the fact of more orange juice than water tumblers in Set A. The most demanding point in Strategy 2 required memory for only the first two of these elements. Progress from Strategy 2 to Strategy 3 depended on each operation becoming more automatized, and thus allowing storage of three rather than two units.

Case noted three factors that could influence the development of automaticity: specific experience with the stimuli involved in the problem, general experience, and maturation. He argued that more than specific experience was likely involved. In a single-subject experiment designed to test this view, he presented a young child with the backward digit span task each day for more than 6 weeks. After two weeks of training, the child's performance improved from two to three digits. Even after a month of additional training, however, the child did not improve further. Case concluded that specific experience had some effect on automaticity, but that general experience and maturation likely exercised a greater effect.

Several criticisms of Case's theory and its use of the automatization construct have been voiced. Flavell (1978) argued that it would be extremely difficult to convince 10 randomly selected psychologists that the working memory demands of any of Noelting's strategies were two, three, four, or n units. The problem is exacerbated because Case has not explicated the principles by which he obtains memory demand estimates. In addition, as Case noted, the automatization construct is more a label than an explanation. We lack an account of how automatization increases functional capacity. On the other hand, as Flavell (1978) also noted, Case's theory is exceptional among information processing approaches to development in its scope and in its attempt to connect basic capacities, strategies, and learning. To the extent that the effort succeeds, it will be a grand achievement.

Encoding and Combining

Why do children not attain advanced conceptual understanding quickly? Why does it take so many years for them to master conservation, seriation, time, and other concepts? Two mechanisms that may limit conceptual development are encoding and combination.

Encoding is the process by which incoming information is segmented and abstracted to build a representation. If the units are not at a useful level of abstraction, or if important information is excluded, conceptual development will be hindered. To appreciate how inadequate encoding can constrain development, consider a composer's description of the history of harmonic forms:

> The entire history of harmonic development shows us a continually changing picture; very slowly, but inevitably, our ears are enabled to assimilate chords of greater complexity and modulations to further off keys. Almost every epoch has its harmonic pioneers: Claudio Monteverdi and Gesualdo in the 17th Century introduced chords that shocked their contemporaries in much the same way that Moussorgsky and Wagner shocked theirs. (Copeland, 1957, p. 52)

The shock to which Copeland referred is a sign of encoding difficulties. Monteverdi's contemporaries probably would have found it difficult to reproduce the novel chords they heard or to relate them to other chords in the piece. Today, the experience of listening to 12-tone music provides many people a similar experience. Once people define the critical features of a stimulus array, greater conceptual progress becomes possible. They can build a coherent representation and note relations among variants of the concept and between the concept and previously understood ones. This analysis is not unique to music. Similar accounts have been advanced to explain the growth of expertise in chess (Chase & Simon, 1973), GO (Reitman, 1976), kinematics (Larkin, McDermott, Simon, & Simon, 1980), and medical diagnosis (Lesgold, Feltovich, Glaser, & Wang, 1981).

In children's cognitive development, encoding skills may play an especially large role. The concepts of musicians and other experts ordinarily are well adapted to their domain of expertise. Such individuals have spent years developing encodings that capture useful features of their task environment. Young children, by contrast, frequently find themselves in task environments about which they know little or nothing. Tasks as diverse as encoding the difference between a Phillips and a standard screwdriver, as distinguishing those typographic features that are of practical importance in reading from those that serve only esthetic purposes, and as reproducing the vowel sounds of foreign languages illustrate the variety of encodings children must acquire.

A second mechanism that governs conceptual progress is combination. Combination subsumes at least two subprocesses: choosing features for inclu-

Table 13. Working Memory Demands for Performing Ratio-of-Orange-Juice Task

Strategy	Steps Involved	Items in Working Memory (i.e., items being attended to)	Memory Demand
I Isolated Centration (3 to 4 years)	*Step 1*—Look for orange juice in A. If it is there, say it will taste of orange juice; if it is not there, say it won't taste of orange juice.	(1) Color of tumblers in array A.	1
	Step 2—Look for orange juice in B. If it is there, say it will taste of orange juice, too. If not, say it won't.	(i) Color of tumblers in Array B.[a]	1
II Unidimensional Comparison (5 to 6 years)	*Step 1*—Count the number of orange juice tumblers to be dumped into A. (Store)	(i) No. of orange juice (A).	1
	Step 2—Count the number of orange juice tumblers to be dumped into B. (Store)	(i) No. of orange juice (A). (ii) No. of orange juice (B).	2
	Step 3—Select larger number and predict that the side with that number will taste stronger. If the two numbers are equal, say they will taste the same.	(i) No. of orange juice (A). (ii) No. of orange juice (B).	2
III Bidimensional Comparison (7 to 8 years)	*Step 1*—Count the number of orange juice tumblers to be dumped into A. (Store)	(i) No. of orange juice (A).	1
	Step 2—Count the number of water tumblers to be dumped into A. (Store)	(i) No. of orange juice (A).[b] (ii) No. of water (A).	2
	Step 3—Notice whether amount of orange juice is more or less than amount of water. (Store)	(i) orange juice $\gtreqless$ water (A).	1
	Step 4—Count number of orange juice tumblers to be dumped into B. (Store)	(i) orange juice $\gtreqless$ water (A).[b] (ii) No. of orange juice (B).	2
	Step 5—Count the number of water tumblers to be dumped into B. (Store)	(i) No. of orange juice $\gtreqless$ water (A).[b] No. of orange juice (B).[b] (ii) No. of water (B). (iii)	3
	Step 6—Notice whether amount of orange juice in B is more, less, or same amount of water in B. (Store)	(i) orange juice $\gtreqless$ water (A).[b] (ii) orange juice $\gtreqless$ water (B).[b]	2

Table 13—continued

Strategy	Steps Involved	Items in Working Memory (i.e., items being attended to)	Memory Demand
	Step 7—**Pick side with more orange juice than water (as more) or side with less orange juice than water (as less). If relative amount on each side is in the same direction, say they have the same.**	(i) orange juice $\geq$ water (A). (ii) orange juice $\geq$ water (B).	2
IV **Bidimensional** **Comparison,** **with Quantification** **(9 to 10 years)**	*Step 1*—**Count orange juice in A. (Store)**	(i) No. of orange juice (A).	1
	Step 2—**Count water in A. (Store)**	(i) No. of orange juice (A).[b] (ii) No. of water (A).	2
	Step 3—**Notice which has more and how much more. (Store)**	(i) orange juice $\geq$ water (A).[b] (ii) difference = X.	2
	Step 4—**Count orange juice in B. (Store)**	(i) orange juice $\geq$ water (A).[b] (ii) difference = X.[b] (iii) No. of orange juice (B).	3
	Step 5—**Count water in B. (Store)**	(i) orange juice $\geq$ water (A).[b] (ii) difference = X^{2b} (iii) No. of orange juice (B).[b] (iv) No. of water (B).	4
	Step 6—**Notice which has more and how much more.**	(i) orange juice $\geq$ water (A). (ii) difference = X. (iii) orange juice $\geq$ water (B). (iv) difference = Y.	4
	Step 7—**Apply same decision rule as in Strategy III, unless relationship is the same on both sides, in which case say equal if difference is equal, or make judgment on basis of greater difference (e.g., if H_2O > OJ by 5 in A, and by 3 in B, pick A as weaker).**		

[a]The reason this is not listed as a second item in working memory is that the first item has already been responded to and no longer needs to be stored.
[b]This item, which was generated in a previous step, must be stored for use in a subsequent step.
(Case, 1978)

sion in concepts, and integrating features into performance rules. Encoding interacts with combination in the first of these; if useful features are not encoded, they cannot be chosen for inclusion into rules. Even if useful features are encoded, however, the two combination processes still must be executed. People must choose from among the features they encode which to include in the concept (e.g., an

encoder might note that dentists' offices always have magazines, but not include magazines in the concept "dentist's office.") They also must establish relations among the features they do include in the concept.

The ways in which encoding and combination contribute to conceptual development can be illustrated with regard to a single problem: the balance-scale task. In one experiment (Siegler, 1976), 5- and 8-year-olds were initially pretested to identify those of each age who used Rule I (the rule that the side with more weight always goes down). Then they were presented feedback problems that discriminated Rule I from the correct multiplicative rule. Despite the children's identical initial rule, 8-year-olds derived great benefits from these feedback problems whereas 5-year-olds derived no benefits from them.

After examining in detail the learning patterns of a few 5- and 8-year-olds, Siegler (1976) hypothesized that younger children's failure to learn rules involving the distance dimension was due to their encoding only information about the amount of weight on the two sides. By contrast, 8-year-olds were hypothesized to encode distance even though they did not use the distance information to predict which side of the balance would go down.

Several sources of evidence supported this encoding hypothesis. First, children's encoding was measured on a reproduction task. An experimenter showed them a balance-scale configuration of weights on pegs for 10 sec. Then the experimenter placed a screen in front of the balance and asked children to reproduce the original configuration on a second, identical balance scale. Eight-year-olds proved quite accurate at putting the correct number of weights on each side and at putting the weights on the correct pegs; thus they encoded both weight and distance. Five-year-olds accurately encoded weight but not distance; they put the correct number of weights on each side but rarely placed the weights on the correct pegs. Following this, new groups of 5- and 8-year-olds were taught to encode both weight and distance. Finally, these children were presented the same feedback problems that previously had not benefited 5-year-olds. Having been taught to encode weight and distance, 70% of the 5-year-olds adopted more advanced rules versus 0% of peers without the encoding training.

The role of combination is exemplified in balance-scale experiments with older children. Siegler (1976) reported that 13- and 17-year-olds did not learn the torque rule (Rule IV) even when they could design unlimited numbers of problems and receive feedback on them. Since even 8-year-olds earlier had been shown capable of encoding both weight and distance dimensions, it seemed likely that the adolescents' difficulty lay in combining the dimensions into a quantitative solution rule. Therefore, 13- and 17-year-olds were presented balance-scale feedback problems along with aids intended to facilitate discovery of the torque rule (cf. Siegler, 1978). One

hint was asking the question in a form intended to emphasize the quantitative nature of the problem; the other was providing schematic representations of all previous problems and their outcomes which could serve as external memory sources. Most 17-year-olds adopted the torque rule given either aid. The 13-year-olds, however, required both aids to formulate it. It was hypothesized that the young adolescents had less experience than the older ones with quantitative rules for solving physical problems, and therefore required more environmental supports to discover the optimum combination rule.

This emphasis on encoding and combination, like the previously described approaches, has several limitations. It does not provide much detail concerning how encoding is done. It does not predict which concepts children will master quickly and which they will understand in terms of partially correct rules for long periods of time. It does not explain why people prefer some combination rules over others. Still, it would be disingenuous of me to appear pessimistic about the approach. It allows us to examine children's existing knowledge and their ability to learn within a single framework. It can help us identify processes that constrain children's acquisition of particular concepts. It has proved applicable to many concepts and over a wide range of ages. Together with work emphasizing automatization and self-modification, it may contribute to future information processing theories of development.

PREDICTIONS OF THE FUTURE

A recent Symposium (R. J. Sternberg, 1979) carried the intriguing title "Intelligence testing in the year 2000." My vision does not extend 20 years into the future, but I can make some predictions about information processing approaches to development in the next 4 or 5 years.

1. Researchers will make greater efforts to identify mechanisms of development. Theoretical progress in development psychology has been slowed by our lack of understanding of the mechanisms by which young children's thinking becomes older children's thinking. In the recent past, we have learned a great deal about what develops. In the near future, we will increase our understanding of how development occurs.

2. Learning will be reemphasized. Through much of psychology's history, learning was the topic of greatest interest. However, information pro-

cessing psychologists never have given the topic much attention, despite its obvious importance and despite the clear applicability of information processing methodologies and representational languages to studying it. This has started to change (e.g., Bereiter & Scardamalia, 1982; Brown, 1982; Case, 1978; Siegler & Klahr, 1982), and I expect it to change further in the next few years. Developmentalists will be in the forefront of this movement because of the inherent connections between learning and development.

3. The trend toward studying educationally important domains will continue. Children spend large portions of their lives learning to read, write, and do arithmetic. Information processing analyses already have enjoyed considerable success in describing more and less-skilled performance in these areas and in identifying the factors that cause children difficulty (Glaser, 1982). Extending the analyses to more advanced skill levels in mathematics, composition, and reading, and using the analyses to prescribe instructional strategies seem to be worthwhile and attainable goals.

4. Researchers increasingly will emphasize how people select strategies. Information processing psychologists have focused on processes involved in strategy execution. However, they rarely have addressed how people choose these strategies from among the approaches that they might use. Advances in the precision of methodologies for identifying people's strategies and in the precision of representational languages for describing them promise to make this a tractable issue. Cooper and Regan (1982), Siegler and Robinson (1982), and Kyllonen, Woltz, and Lohman (unpublished manuscript) provide examples of research in this direction.

5. A number of dichotomies that have divided cognitive psychologists will be resolved along the lines of "you're both right." Recent models of rapidly executed perceptual and linguistic processes have incorporated both serial and parallel aspects (McClelland & Rumelhart, 1981; Hinton & Anderson, 1981; Anderson, Kline, & Beasley, 1979). Representations within a single system are being phrased both in propositional and in imaginal form, depending on the naturalness of the fit to the content domain (Anderson, 1982). Both representations and processes that operate on the representations are being explicitly depicted in order to overcome the indeterminacy of models that focus exclusively on one or the other (Farah & Kosslyn, 1982; Siegler & Robinson, 1982). As the range of domains that are modeled expands, and as the demands on the models increase, ideological purity loses much of its allure.

6. The information processing approach will not prove very helpful in studying social, emotional, and personality development. The omission from this chapter of information processing research on these topics was not an oversight. Relatively few researchers have undertaken this type of research (though the number is growing), and I have not been impressed with the success of those attempts that have been made. People's feelings of love, hate, anger, fear and joy are perhaps the ways in which they differ most from computers. No doubt, all of these emotions involve the manipulation of symbols, but considerably more also is involved. It is difficult to capture this "considerably more" within the information processing framework. Even if this prediction is accurate, it does not seem to be reason for wringing of hands and gnashing of teeth. To provide a coherent framework for considering perception, memory, language, problem solving, and learning, a feat accomplished by the information processing approach, is no small achievement.

7. Increasing attention will be paid to the development of information processing skills between infancy and ages 3 or 4. We have learned a considerable amount about the capabilities of children below age 1, and also about the capabilities of 4- and 5-year-olds. We know very little, however, about 1- and 2-year-olds and not much more about 3-year-olds, except in the area of language development. The capabilities investigated in infancy (mostly perceptual) are discontinuous with those investigated in early childhood (memory, problem solving, and conceptual skills). The methods that are used (visual habituation, heart rate acceleration/deceleration, and high amplitude sucking paradigms versus adult memory, learning, and Piagetian paradigms) also differ radically. The result has been a gap in our knowledge about the growth of representational and processing skills. Children of 1-, 2-, and 3-years are not the easiest subjects to work with—restless and mobile—but the creation of tasks that they find interesting and that we find revealing may expand dramatically our understanding of development. (For starts in this direction, see Myers & Perlmutter's [1978] review of experimental studies of memory, Wellman & Somerville's [1980] review of naturalistic studies of memory, Sophian's [1982] work on search strategies, and Acredolo and Evans's [1980] work on spatial concepts.)

8. Research emphasizing the IPS X task environment interaction will become increasingly prevalent. Human information processing has turned out to be enormously flexible. Few statements can be made about it without specifying the

task environment in which it occurs. Even the comparatively unsophisticated concepts and problem-solving strategies of young children usually incorporate many of the task environment's relevant features. For these reasons, the increasing use of research strategies designed to illuminate the IPS X task environment interaction seems both desirable and likely.

REFERENCES

Abelson, R. P. The structure of belief systems. In R. C. Schank & K. M. Colby, (Eds.), *Computer models of thought and language*. San Francisco: Freeman, 1973.

Acredolo, L. P., & Evans, D. Developmental changes in the effects of landmarks on infant spatial behavior. *Developmental Psychology*, 1980, *16*, 312–318.

Allport, D. P. The state of cognitive psychology. *Quarterly Journal of Experimental Psychology*, 1975, *27*, 141–152.

Anderson, J. R. *Language, memory and thought*. Hillsdale, N.J.: Erlbaum, 1976.

Anderson, J. R. Arguments concerning representations for mental imagery. *Psychological Review*, 1978, *85*, 149–277.

Anderson, J. R. The architecture of cognition. Cambridge, Mass.: Harvard University Press, 1982, in press.

Anderson, J. R., & Bower, G. H. *Human associative memory*. Washington, D.C.: Winston, 1973.

Anderson, J. R., & Bower, G. H. A propositional theory of recognition memory. *Memory and Cognition*, 1974, *26*, 530–541.

Anderson, J. R., Kline, P. J., & Beasley, C. M., Jr. A general learning theory and its application to schema abstraction. In G. Bower (Ed.), *The psychology of learning and motivation* (Vol. 13). New York: Academic Press, 1979.

Anderson, J. R., Kline, P., & Lewis, C. A production system model of language processing. In M. A. Just & P. A. Carpenter (Eds.), *Cognitive processes in comprehension*. Hillsdale, N.J.: Erlbaum, 1977.

Anzai, Y., & Simon, H. A. A theory of learning by doing. *Psychological Review*, 1979, *86*, 124–140.

Atkinson, R. C., & Shiffrin, R. M. Human memory: A proposed system and its control processes. In K. W. Spence & J. T. Spence (Eds.), *Advances in the psychology of learning and motivation*

(Vol. 2). New York: Academic Press, 1968.

Averbach, I., & Coriell, A. S. Short-term memory in vision. *Bell System Technical Journal*, 1961, *40*, 309–328.

Bach, M. J., & Underwood, B. J. Developmental changes in memory attributes. *Journal of Educational Psychology*, 1970, *61*, 292–296.

Baddeley, A. D., & Hitch, G. Working memory. In G. Bower (Ed.), *Recent advances in learning and motivation, 8*. New York: Academic Press, 1974.

Baron, J. Intelligence and general strategies. In G. Underwood (Ed.), *Strategies in information processing*. New York: Academic Press, 1978.

Baylor, G. W., & Gascon, J. An information processing theory of aspects of the development of weight seriation in children. *Cognitive Psychology*, 1974, *6*, 1–40.

Belmont, J. M., & Butterfield, E. C. The relation of short-term memory to development and intelligence. In L. Lipsitt & H. Reese (Eds.), *Advances in child development and behavior* (Vol. 4). New York: Academic Press, 1969.

Bereiter, C., & Scardemalia, M. From conservation to composition: The role of instruction in a developmental process. In R. Glaser (Ed.), *Advances in instructional psychology* (Vol. 2). Hillsdale, N.J.: Erlbaum, 1982.

Binet, A. *Les idées modernes sur les enfants*. Paris: Flammarion, 1911.

Bobrow, D. G. Dimensions of representation. In D. G. Bobrow & A. Collins (Eds.), *Representation and understanding: Studies in cognitive science*. New York: Academic Press, 1975.

Borkowski, J. G. Signs of intelligence: Strategy generalization and metacognition. Paper presented at Gatlinburg Conference on Mental Retardation, Gatlinburg, Tenn., 1980.

Bornstein, M. H. Infants are trichromats. *Journal of Experimental Child Psychology*, 1976, *21*, 425–445.

Bornstein, M. H. Chromatic vision in children. In H. W. Reese & L. P. Lipsitt (Eds.), *Advances in child development and behavior*. New York: Academic Press, 1978.

Bower, G. H. A selective review of organizational factors in memory. In E. Tulving & W. Donaldson (Eds.), *Organization and memory*. New York: Academic Press, 1972.

Bower, G. H., & Clark, M. C. Narrative stories as mediators for serial learning. *Psychonomic Science*, 1969, *14*, 181–182.

Braine, M. D. The ontogeny of certain logical operations: Piaget's formulation examined by nonverbal methods. *Psychological Monographs,* 1959, *73.*

Brainerd, C. J. The stage question in cognitive-developmental theory. *The Behavioral and Brain Sciences,* 1978, *1,* 173–213.

Brainerd, C. J. *The origins of the number concept.* New York: Praeger, 1979.

Bransford, J. D., & McCarrell, N. S. A sketch of a cognitive approach to comprehension: Some thoughts about what it means to comprehend. In W. B. Weimer & D. S. Palermo (Eds.), *Cognition and symbolic processes.* Hillsdale, N.J.: Erlbaum, 1974.

Broadbent, D. E. The role of auditory localization in attention and memory span. *Journal of Experimental Psychology,* 1954, *47,* 191–196.

Broadbent, D. E. *Perception and communication.* London: Pergamon Press, 1958.

Brooks, L. R. Spatial and verbal components in the act of recall. *Canadian Journal of Psychology,* 1968, *22,* 349–368.

Brown, A. L. The role of strategic behavior in retardate behavior. In N. R. Ellis (Ed.), *International review of research in mental retardation* (Vol. 1). New York: Academic Press, 1974.

Brown, A. L. Knowing when, where, and how to remember: A problem of metacognition. In R. Glaser (Ed.), *Advances in instructional psychology.* Hillsdale, N.J.: Erlbaum, 1978.

Brown, A. L. Learning and development: The problems of compatibility, access, and induction. *Human Development,* 1982, *25,* 89–115.

Brown, A. L. & DeLoach, J. S. Skills, plans, and self-regulation. In R. S. Siegler (Ed.), *Children's thinking: What develops?* Hillsdale, N.J.: Erlbaum, 1978.

Brown, A. L., Smiley, S. S., Day, J. D., Townsend, M. A., & Lawton, S. C. Intrusion of a thematic idea in children's comprehension and retention of stories. *Child Development,* 1977, *48,* 1454–1466.

Brown, J. S., & Burton, R. R. Diagnostic models for procedural bugs in basic mathematical skills, *Cognitive Science,* 1978, *2,* 155–192.

Brown, J. S., & Vanlehn, K. Towards a generative theory of "bugs." In T. Romberg, T. Carpenter, & J. Moser (Eds.), *Addition and subtraction: A developmental perspective.* Hillsdale, N.J.: Erlbaum, 1982.

Bruner, J. S. *Beyond the information given: Studies in the psychology of knowing.* New York: Norton, 1973.

Bruner, J. S., Olver, R. R., & Greenfield, P. M. *Studies in cognitive growth.* New York: Wiley, 1966.

Buckhalt, J. A., Mahoney, G. J., & Paris, S. C. Efficiency at self-generated elaborations by EMR and nonretarded children. *American Journal of Mental Deficiency,* 1976, *81,* 93–96.

Burt, C. The development of reasoning in school children. *Journal of Experimental Pedagogy,* 1919, *5,* 68–77.

Bryant, P. E., & Trabasso, T. Transitive inferences and memory in young children. *Nature,* 1971, *232,* 457–459.

Calfee, R. C., Vanezky, R. L., & Chapman, R. S. Pronunciation of synthetic words with predictable and unpredictable letter-sound correspondence. Technical Report No. 71. Wisconsin Research and Development Center of Cognition and Learning, 1969.

Carpenter, P. A., & Just, M. A. Sentence comprehension: A psycholinguistic processing model of verification. *Psychological Review,* 1975, *82,* 45–73.

Carpenter, T. P., & Moser, J. M. The development of addition and subtraction problem solving skills. In T. Romberg, T. Carpenter, & J. Moser (Eds.), *Addition and subtraction: A developmental perspective.* Hillsdale, N.J.: Erlbaum, 1982.

Case, R. Intellectual development from birth to adulthood: A neo-Piagetian approach. In R. S. Siegler, (Ed.), *Children's thinking: What develops?* Hillsdale, N.J.: Erlbaum, 1978.

Case, R. The search for horizontal structure in children's development. Paper presented at the Biennial Meeting of the Society for Research in Child Development. Boston, Mass., April, 1981.

Cavanaugh, J. C., & Perlmutter, M. Metamemory: A critical examination. *Child Development,* 1982, *53,* 11–28.

Chase, W. G., & Ericsson, K. A. Skill and working memory. In G. H. Bower (Ed.), *The psychology of learning and motivation,* 1983, in press.

Chase, W. G. & Simon, H. A. The mind's eye in chess. In W. G. Chase (Ed.), *Visual information processing.* New York: Academic Press, 1973.

Chi, M. T. The representation of knowledge (Review of *Explorations in cognition* by D. A. Norman, D. E. Rumelhart and the LNR Research Group). *Contemporary Psychology,* 1976, *21,* 784–785.

Chi, M. T. Knowledge structures and memory development. In R. S. Siegler (ED.), *Children's thinking: What develops?* Hillsdale, N.J.: Erlbaum, 1978.

Chi, M. T. Knowledge development and memory performance. In M. Friedman, J. P. Das, & N.

O'Connor (Eds.), *Intelligence and learning.* New York: Plenum Press, 1982, in press.

Chi, M. T., & Koeske, R. D. Network representation of a child's dinosaur knowledge. *Developmental Psychology,* 1983, *19,* 29–39.

Chomsky, N. Verbal behavior (Review of *Verbal Behavior* by B. F. Skinner). *Language,* 1959, *35,* 26–58.

Cohen, L. B., & Gelber, E. R. Infant visual memory. In L. Cohen & P. Salapatek (Eds.), *Infant perception: From sensation cognition: Basic visual processes* (Vol. 1). New York: Academic Press, 1975.

Cole, M., & Scribner, S. *Culture and thought.* New York: Wiley, 1974.

Collins, A. M., & Loftus, E. F. A spreading activation theory of semantic processing. *Psychological Review,* 1975, *82,* 407–428.

Conrad, R. Acoustic confusions and memory span in words. *Nature,* 1963, *197,* 1029–1030.

Conrad, R. Acoustic confusions in immediate memory. *British Journal of Psychology,* 1964, *55,* 75–84.

Conrad, R. The effect of vocalizing on comprehension in the prodoundly deaf. *British Journal of Psychology,* 1971, *62,* 147–150.

Cooper, L. A., & Regan, D. Attention, perception, and intelligence. In R. Sternberg (Ed.), *The handbook of human intelligence.* New York: Cambridge University Press, 1982, in press.

Copeland, A. *What to listen for in music.* New York: McGraw-Hill, 1957.

Craik, F. I. M. The fate of primary items in free recall. *Journal of Verbal Learning and Verbal Behavior,* 1970, *9,* 143–148.

Craik, F. I. M., & Levy, B. A. The concept of primary memory. In W. K. Estes (Ed.), *Handbook of learning and cognitive processes* (Vol. 4). Hillsdale, N.J.: Erlbaum, 1976.

Craik, F. I. M., & Lockhart, R. S. Levels of processing: A framework for memory research. *Journal of Verbal Learning and Verbal Behavior,* 1972, *11,* 671–684.

Craik, F. I. M., & Tulving, E. Depth of processing and the retention of words in episodic memory. *Journal of Experimental Psychology: General,* 1975, *104,* 268–294.

Dale, P. S. *Language development: Structure and function.* New York: Holt, Rinehart & Winston, 1976.

Darwin, C. J., Turvey, M. T., & Crowder, R. G. An auditory analogue of the Sperling partial report procedure. *Cognitive Psychology,* 1972, *3,* 255–267.

De Groot, A. D. Perception and memory vs. thought: Some old ideas and recent findings. In B. Kleinmuntz (Ed.), *Problem solving: Research, method, and theory.* New York: Wiley, 1966.

Delin, P. S. Success in recall as a function of success in implementation of mnemonic instructions. *Psychonomic Science,* 1969, *12,* 153–154.

Drozdal, J. G., & Flavell, J. H. A developmental study of logical search behavior. *Child Development,* 1975, *46,* 386–393.

Duncan, J. The locus of interference in the perception of simultaneous stimuli. *Psychological Review,* 1980, *87,* 272–300.

Duncker, K. On problem-solving. *Psychological Monographs,* 1945, *58,* (5, Whole No. 270).

Effron, R. The relationship between the duration of a stimulus and the duration of a perception. *Neuropsychologia,* 1970, *8,* 37–55.

Eimas, P. D., Siqueland, E. R., Juscyk, P., & Vigorito, J. Speech perception in infants. *Science,* 1971, *71,* 303–306.

Ericsson, K. A., & Simon, H. A. Verbal reports as data. *Psychological Review,* 1980, *87,* 215–251.

Eriksen, C. W. Temporal luminance summation effects in backward and forward masking. *Perception and Psychophysics,* 1966, *1,* 87–92.

Falmagne, R. J. *Reasoning: Representation and process.* Hillsdale, N.J.: Erlbaum, 1975.

Farah, M. J., & Kosslyn, S. M. Concept Development. In H. W. Reese & L. P. Lipsitt (Eds.), *Advances in child development and behavior,* New York: Academic Press, 1982.

Fillmore, C. J. The case for case. In E. Bach & R. T. Harms (Eds.), *Universals in linguistic theory.* New York: Holt, Rinehart & Winston, 1968.

Flavell, J. H. Developmental studies of mediated memory. In H. W. Reese & L. P. Lipsitt (Eds.), *Advances in child development and behavior* (Vol. 5). New York: Academic Press, 1970.

Flavell, J. H. Comment. In R. S. Siegler (Ed.), *Children's thinking: What develops?* Hillsdale, N.J.: Erlbaum, 1978.

Flavell, J. H., Friedrichs, A. G., & Hoyt, J. D. Developmental changes in memorization processes. *Cognitive Psychology,* 1970, *1,* 324–340.

Flavell, J. H., & Wellman, H. M. Metamemory. In R. V. Kail, Jr. & J. W. Hagen (Eds.), *Perspectives on the development of memory and cognition.* Hillsdale, N.J.: Erlbaum, 1977.

Frank, H. S. & Rabinovitch, M. S. Auditory short-term memory: Developmental changes in rehearsal. *Child Development,* 1974, *45,*

397–407.

Garner, W. R. The stimulus in information processing. *American Psychologist*, 1970, *25*, 350–358.

Garner, W. R. *The processing of information and structure*. Potomac, Md.: Erlbaum, 1974.

Garner, W. R., & Clements, D. E. Goodness of pattern and pattern uncertainty. *Journal of Verbal Learning and Verbal Behavior*, 1963, *2*, 446–452.

Gelman, R., & Gallistel, C. R. *The child's understanding of number*. Cambridge, Mass.: Harvard University Press, 1978.

Gentner, D. Evidence for the psychological reality of semantic components: The verbs of possession. In D. A. Norman & D. E. Rumelhart (Eds.), *Explorations in cognition*. San Francisco: Freeman, 1975.

Gibson, E. J. *Principles of perceptual learning and development*. Englewood Cliffs, N.J.: Prentice-Hall, Inc., 1969.

Gibson, E. J., Osser, H., Schiff, W., & Smith, J. An analysis of critical features of letters, tested by a confusion matrix. In *Final report on a basic research program on reading*. Cooperative Research Project, No. 639, Cornell University and U.S. Office of Education, 1963.

Ginsburg, H. *The development of children's mathematical thinking*. New York: Academic Press, 1982, in press.

Glanzer, M. Storage mechanisms in free recall. In G. H. Bower (Ed.), *The psychology of learning and motivation: Advances in research and theory* (Vol. 5). New York: Academic Press, 1972.

Glaser, R. *Advances in instructional psychology*. Hillsdale, N.J.: Erlbaum, 1982.

Glucksberg, S., & Cowan, G. N. Memory for nonattended auditory material. *Cognitive Psychology*, 1970, *1*, 149–156.

Glushko, R. J., & Cooper, L. A. Spatial comprehension and comparison processes in verification tasks. *Cognitive Psychology*, 1978, *10*, 391–421.

Goldberg, S., Perlmutter, M., & Myers, N. Recall of related and unrelated lists by two-year-olds. *Journal of Experimental Child Psychology*, 1974, *18*, 1–8.

Greenberg, D. S. Accelerating visual complexity level in the human infant. *Child Development*, 1971, *42*, 905–918.

Greeno, J. G. Cognitive objectives of instruction: Theory of knowledge for solving problems and answering questions. In D. Klahr (Ed.), *Cognition and instruction*. Hillsdale, N.J.: Erlbaum,

1976.

Greeno, J. G., Riley, M. S., & Gelman, R. Young children's counting and understanding of principles. Unpublished manuscript, 1982.

Groen, G. J., & Parkman, J. M. A chronometric analysis of simple addition. *Psychological Review*, 1972, *79*, 329–343.

Groen, G. J., & Poll, M. Subtraction and the solution of open sentence problems. *Journal of Experimental Child Psychology*, 1973, *16*, 292–302.

Groen, G. J., & Resnick, L. B. Can preschool children invent addition algorithms? *Journal of Education Psychology*, 1977, *69*, 645–652.

Guyote, M. J., & Sternberg, R. J. A transitive-chain theory of syllogistic reasoning. *Cognitive Psychology*, 1981, *13*, 461–475.

Hagen, J. W., Hargrove, S., & Ross, W. Prompting and rehearsal in short-term memory. *Child Development*, 1973, *44*, 201–204.

Haith, M. M. Developmental changes in visual information processing and short-term visual memory. *Human Development*, 1971, *14*, 249–261.

Hasher, L. & Clifton, D. A developmental study of attribute encoding in free recall. *Journal of Experimental Child Psychology*, 1974, *7*, 332–346.

Hayes-Roth, F. Distinguishing theories of representation: A critique of Anderson's "Arguments Concerning Mental Imagery." *Psychological Review*, 1979, *86*, 376–382.

Hick, W. E. On the rate of gain of information. *Quarterly Journal of Experimental Psychology*, 1952, *4*, 11–26.

Hinton, G., & Anderson, J. *Parallel models of associative memory*. Hillsdale, N.J.: Erlbaum, 1981.

Horowitz, A. B., & Horowitz, V. A. The effects of task-specific instructions on the encoding activities of children in recall and recognition tasks. Paper presented at the biennial meeting of the Society for Research in Child Development, Denver, April 1975.

Hoving, K. L., Spencer, T., Robb, K., & Schulte, D. Developmental changes in visual information processing. In P. A. Ornstein (Ed.), *Memory development in children*. Hillsdale, N.J.: Erlbaum, 1978.

Hunt, E. Varieties of cognitive power. In L. B. Resnick (Ed.), *The nature of intelligence*. Hillsdale, N.J.: Erlbaum, 1976.

Hunt, E., Frost, N., & Lunneborg, C. Individual differences in cognition. In G. Bower (Ed.), *Advances in learning and motivation* (Vol. VII).

New York: Academic Press, 1973.

Hunt, E., & Love, T. How good can memory be? In A. W. Melton and E. Martin (Eds.), *Coding processes in human memory*. Washington, D.C.: Holt, Rinehart & Winston, 1972.

Huttenlocher, J., & Burke, D. Why does memory span increase with age? *Cognitive Psychology*, 1976, *8*, 1–31.

Inhelder, B., & Piaget, J. *The growth of logical thinking from childhood*. New York: Basic Books, 1958.

Javal, E. Essaie sur la physiologie de la lecture. *Annales d'oculistique*, 1878, *79*, 97.

Just, M. A., & Carpenter, P. A. A theory of reading: From eye fixations to comprehension. *Psychological Review*, 1980, *87*, 329–354.

Kahneman, D. *Attention and effort*. Englewood Cliffs, N.J.: Prentice-Hall, 1973.

Kail, R., Pellegrino, J., & Carter, P. Developmental changes in mental rotation. *Journal of Experimental Child Psychology*, 1980, *29*, 102–116.

Keating, D. P., & Bobbitt, B. L. Individual and developmental differences in cognitive processing components of mental ability. *Child Development*, 1978, *49*, 155–167.

Keeney, T. J., Canizzo, S. R., & Flavell, J. H. Spontaneous and induced verbal rehearsal in a recall task. *Child Development*, 1967, *38*, 953–966.

Klahr, D. Nonmonotone assessment of monotone development: An information processing analysis. In S. Strauss & R. Stavy (Eds.), *U-shaped behavioral growth*, New York: Academic Press, 1982.

Klahr, D., & Robinson, M. Formal assessment of problem-solving and planning processes in preschool children. *Cognitive Psychology*, 1981, *13*, 113–148.

Klahr, D., & Siegler, R. S. The representation of children's knowledge. In H. Reese & L. P. Lipsitt (Eds.), *Advances in child development* (Vol. 12). New York: Academic Press, 1978.

Klahr, D., & Wallace, J. G. The role of qualification operators in the development of conservation of quantity. *Cognitive Psychology*, 1973, *4*, 301–327.

Klahr, D., & Wallace, J. G. *Cognitive development: An information processing view*. Hillsdale, N.J.: Erlbaum, 1976.

Kobasigawa, A., Ransom, C. C., & Holland, C. Children's knowledge about skimming. *Alberta Journal of Educational Research*, 1979.

Kosslyn, S. M. *Image and mind*. Cambridge, Mass.: Harvard University Press, 1980.

Kreutzer, M. A., Leonard, C., & Flavell, J. H. An interview study of children's knowledge about memory. *Monographs of the Society for Research in Child Development*, 1975, *40*. (1, Series No. 159)

Kroll, N. E. A. Short-term memory and the nature of interference from concurrent shadowing. *Quarterly Journal of Experimental Psychology*, 1972, *24*, 414–419.

Kroll, N. E. A., Parks, T., Parkinson, S. R., Bieber, S. L., & Johnson, A. L. Short-term memory while shadowing: Recall of visually and aurally presented letters. *Journal of Experimental Psychology*, 1970, *85*, 220–224.

Kuhl, P. K., & Miller, J. D. Speech perception by the Chinchilla: Voiced-voiceless distinction in alveolar plosive consonants. *Science*, 1975, *190*, 69–72.

Kyllonen, P. C., Woltz, D. J., & Lohman, D. F. Models of strategy and strategy-shifting in spatial visualization performance. Technical Report No. 17. Aptitude Research Project, School of Education, Stanford University, 1981.

LaBerge, D., & Samuels, S. J. Toward a theory of automatic information processing in reading. *Cognitive Psychology*, 1974, *6*, 293–322.

Lachman, R., Lachman, J., & Butterfield, E. C. *Cognitive psychology and information processing: An introduction*. Hillsdale, N.J.: Erlbaum, 1979.

Lange, G. Organization-related processes in children's recall. In P. A. Ornstein (Ed.), *Memory development in children*. Hillsdale, N.J.: Erlbaum, 1978.

Larkin, J. H. Information processing models and science instruction. In J. Lockhead & J. Clement (Eds.), *Cognitive process instruction*. Philadelphia: The Franklin Institute Press, 1978.

Larkin, J. H., McDermott, J., Simon, D. F., & Simon, H. A. Models of competence in solving physics problems. *Cognitive Science*, 1980, *4*, 317–345.

Lawrence, D. H. The nature of a stimulus. In S. Koch (Ed.), *Psychology: A study of a science*. New York: McGraw-Hill, 1963.

Lesgold, A. M., Feltovich, P. J., Glaser, R., & Wang, Y. The acquisition of perceptual diagnostic skill in radiology. Technical Report No. PDS-1, Learning Research and Development Center, University of Pittsburgh, September 1981.

Lewis, C. Production system models of practice effects. Unpublished doctoral dissertation, University of Michigan, Ann Arbor, 1978.

Lewkowicz, D. J., & Turkewitz, G. Cross-modal equivalence in early infancy: Auditory-visual intensity matching. *Developmental Psychology*, 1980, *16*, 597–607.

Liberty, C., & Ornstein, P. A. Age differences in organization and recall: The effects of training in categorization. *Journal of Experimental Child Psychology*, 1973, *15*, 169–186.

Lockhead, G. R. Effects of dimensional redundancy on visual discrimination. *Journal of Experimental Psychology*, 1966, *72*, 95–104.

Luchins, A. S. Mechanization in problem solving. The effect of Einstellung. *Psychology Monograph*, 1942, *54*, No. 248.

Mandler, J. M., & Johnson, N. Remembrance of things parsed: Story structure and recall. *Cognitive Psychology*, 1977, *9*, 111–152.

Manis, F., Keating, D. P., & Morrison, F. J. Developmental differences in the allocation of processing capacity. *Journal of Experimental Child Psychology*, 1980, *29*, 156–169.

Maratsos, M. P., & Chalkley, M. A. The internal language of children's syntax: The nature and ontogenesis of syntactic categories. In K. Nelson, (Ed.), *Children's language* (Vol. II). New York: Gardner Press, 1981.

Markman, E. M. Facilitation of part-whole comparisons by use of the collective noun "family." *Child Development*, 1973, *44*, 837–840.

Markman, E. M. Realizing that you don't understand: Elementary school children's awareness of inconsistencies. *Child Development*, 1979, *50*, 643–655.

Masur, E. F., McIntyre, C. W., & Flavell, J. H. Developmental changes in apportionment of a study time among items in a multitrial free recall task. *Journal of Experimental Child Psychology*, 1973, *15*, 237–246.

McClelland, J. L., & Rumelhart, D. E. An interactive model of the effect of context in perception, part 1. *Psychological Review*, 1981, *88*, 375–407.

McGurk, H., & Lewis, M. Space perception in early infancy: Perception within a common auditory-visual space? *Science*, 1974, *186*, 649–650.

Mendelson, M. J., & Haith, M. M. The relation between audition and vision in the human newborn. *Monographs of the Society for Research in Child Development*, 1976, *41*. (Whole issue)

Miller, G. A. The magical number seven, plus or minus two: Some limits on our capacity for processing information. *Psychological Review*, 1956, *63*, 81–97.

Miller, P. Effects of different amounts of stimulus familiarity on choice reaction time performance in children. *Journal of Experimental Child Psychology*, 1969, *8*, 106–117.

Moely, B. E. Organizational factors in the development of memory. In R. V. Kail & J. W. Hagen (Eds.), *Perspectives on the development of memory and cognition*. Hillsdale, N.J.: Erlbaum, 1977.

Moely, B. E., Olson, F. A., Halwes, T. G., & Flavell, J. H. Production deficiency in young children's clustered recall. *Developmental Psychology*, 1969, *1*, 26–34.

Morgan, J. L., & Newport, E. L. The role of constituent structure in the induction of an artificial language. *Journal of Verbal Learning and Verbal Behavior*, 1981, *20*, 67–85.

Morse, P. A. The discrimination of speech and nonspeech stimuli in early infancy. *Journal of Experimental Child Psychology*, 1972, *14*, 477–492.

Morrison, F. J., Holmes, D. L., & Haith, M. M. A developmental study of the effects of familiarity on short-term visual memory. *Journal of Experimental Child Psychology*, 1974, *18*, 412–425.

Moynahan, E. D. The development of knowledge concerning the effects of categorization upon free recall. *Child Development*, 1973, *44*, 238–246.

Murdock, B. B., Jr. The retention of individual items. *Journal of Experimental Psychology*, 1961, *62*, 618–625.

Myers, N. A., & Perlmutter, M. Memory in the years from two to five. In P. A. Ornstein (Ed.), *Memory development in children*. Hillsdale, N.J.: Erlbaum, 1978.

Neisser, U. General, academic, and artificial intelligence. In L. B. Resnich (Ed.), *The nature of intelligence*. Hillsdale, N.J.: Erlbaum, 1976.

Neisser, U., & Weene, P. Hierarchies in concept attainment, *Journal of Experimental Psychology*, 1962, *64*, 640–645.

Nelson, D. L. Remembering pictures and words: Significance and appearance. In L. S. Cermak & F. I. M. Craik (Eds.), *Levels of processing and human memory*. Hillsdale, N.J.: Erlbaum, 1978.

Newell, A. On the analysis of human problem-solving protocols. In *Calcul et formilisation dans les sciences de l'homme*, Paris: ENRS, 1968.

Newell, A. You can't play 20-questions with nature and win: Projective comments on the papers of this Symposium. In W. G. Chase (Ed.), *Visual information processing*. New York: Academic Press, 1973.

Newell, A. Harpy, production systems, and human

cognition. In R. A. Cole (Ed.), *Perception and production of fluent speech*. Hillsdale, N.J.: Erlbaum, 1980.

Newell, A., & Simon, H. A. *Human problem solving*. Englewood Cliffs, N.J.: Prentice-Hall, 1972.

Nisbett, R. E., & Wilson, T. D. Telling more than we can know: Verbal reports on mental processes. *Psychological Review, 1977, 84,* 231–259.

Noelting, G. Stages and mechanisms in the development of the concept of proportion in the child and adolescent. Paper presented at the 5th Interdisciplinary Seminar on Piagetian Theory and Its Implications for the Helping Professions, University of Southern California, Los Angeles, 1975.

Norman, D. A., Rumelhart, D. E., & the LNR Research Group. *Explorations in cognition*. San Francisco, Calif.: Freeman, 1975.

Ornstein, P. A., Hale, G. A., & Morgan, J. S. Developmental differences in recall and output organization. *Bulletin of the Psychonomic Society, 1977, 9,* 29–32.

Ornstein, P. A., Naus, M. J., & Liberty, C. Rehearsal and organizational processes in children's memory. *Child Development, 1975, 26,* 818–830.

Pachella, R. G. The interpretation of reaction time in information processing research. In B. Kantowitz (Ed.), *Human information processing: Tutorials in performance and cognition*. Hillsdale, N.J.: Erlbaum, 1974.

Paris, S. C., & Lindauer, B. K. The role of inference in children's comprehension and memory for sentences. *Cognitive Psychology, 1976, 8,* 217–227.

Parkman, J. M. Temporal aspects of simple multiplication and comparison. *Journal of Experimental Psychology, 1972, 95,* 437–444.

Pascual-Leone, J. A mathematical model for transition in Piaget's developmental stages. *Acta Psychologica, 1970, 32,* 301–345.

Perlmutter, M., & Lange, G. A developmental analysis of recall-recognition distinctions. In P. A. Ornstein (Ed.), *Memory development in children*. Hillsdale, N.J.: Erlbaum, 1978.

Peterson, L. R., & Peterson, M. J. Short-term retention of individual verbal items. *Journal of Experimental Psychology, 1959, 58,* 193–198.

Piaget, J. Une forme verbal de la comparison chez l'enfant. *Archives de Psychology, 1921,* 141–172.

Piaget, J. *The language and thought of the child.*

London: Routledge and Keegan Paul, 1926.

Piaget, J. *The child's concept of number*. New York: Norton, 1952.

Piaget, J. *The child's concept of movement and speed*. (G. Holloway & M. J. Mackenzie, trans.). New York: Ballantine, 1970.

Piaget, J. Intellectual evolution from adolescence to adulthood. *Human Development, 1972, 15,* 1–12.

Posner, M. I. *Chronometric explorations of mind*. Hillsdale, N.J.: Erlbaum, 1978.

Posner, M. I., & Boies, S. J. Components of attention. *Psychological Review, 1971, 78,* 391–408.

Posner, M. I., & McLeod, P. Information processing models—in search of elementary operations. *Annual Review of Psychology, 1982, 33,* 477–514.

Potts, G. R. Information processing strategies used in encoding linear orderings. *Journal of Verbal Learning and Verbal Behavior, 1972, 11,* 727–740.

Pylyshyn, Z. W. Validating computation models: A critique of Anderson's indeterminacy of representation claim. *Psychological Review, 1979, 86,* 383–394.

Quillian, M. R. The teachable language comprehender: A simulation program and theory of language. *Communications of the ACM, 1969, 12,* 459–476.

Rayner, K. The perceptual span and peripheral cues in reading. *Cognitive Psychology, 1975, 7,* 65–81.

Reese, H. W. Imagery and associative memory. In R. V. Kail Jr. & J. W. Hagen (Eds.), *Perspectives on the development of memory and cognition*. Hillsdale, N.J.: Erlbaum, 1977.

Reitman, J. S. Skilled perception in Go: Deducing memory structures from inter-response times. *Cognitive Psychology, 1976, 8,* 336–356.

Riley, C. A., & Trabasso, T. Comparatives, logical structures, and encoding in a transitive inference task. *Journal of Experimental Child Psychology, 1974, 45,* 972–977.

Ritter, K. Development of production and maintainence of a retrieval cue strategy. Unpublished manuscript, University of Western Ontario, 1975.

Rogoff, B., Newcombe, N., & Kagan, J. Planfulness and recognition memory. *Child Development, 1974, 45,* 972–977.

Rometveit, R. Stages of concept formation, II. Effects of an extra intention to verbalize the concept and stimulus predifferentiation. *Scandinavian Journal of Psychology, 1965, 6,* 59–64.

Rosner, S. The effects of rehearsal and chunking instructions on children's multitrial free recall. *Journal of Experimental Child Psychology*, 1971, *11*, 93–105.

Rudorf, E. H., Jr. The development of an algorithm for American-English spelling (Doctorial dissertation, Stanford University). University Microfilms, 1965, No. 65-6344.

Rumelhart, D. E. Notes on a schema for stories. In D. G. Bobrow & A. M. Collins (Eds.), *Representations and understanding: Studies in cognitive science*. New York: Academic Press, 1975.

Sacerdoti, E. D. *A structure for plans and behaviors*. New York: Elsevier, 1977.

Salapatek, P. Visual scanning of geometric figures by the human newborn. *Journal of Comparative and Physiological Psychology*, 1968, *66*, 247–258.

Salatas, H., & Flavell, J. H. Behavioral and metamnemonic indicators of strategic behaviors under remember instructions in first grade. *Child Development*, 1976, *47*, 81–89.

Schank, R. C. *Conceptual information processing*. New York: Elsevier, 1975.

Schneider, W., & Shiffrin, R. M. Controlled and automatic human information processing: I. Detection, search and attention. *Psychological Review*, 1977, *84*, 1–66.

Shaklee, H. Bounded rationality and cognitive development: Upper limits on growth? *Cognitive Psychology*, 1979, *11*, 327–345.

Sharp, D., Cole, M., & Lave, C. Education and cognitive development: The evidence from experimental research. *Monographs of the Society for Research in Child Development*, 1979, *44*. (Whole issue)

Shepard, R. N., & Podgorny, P. Cognitive processes that resemble perceptual processes. In W. K. Estes (Ed.), *Handbook of learning and cognitive processes*. Hillsdale, N.J.: Erlbaum, 1978.

Shepard, R. N., & Metzler, J. Mental rotation of three-dimensional objects. *Science*, 1971, *171*, 701–703.

Shiffrin, R. M. Information persistence in short-term memory. *Journal of Experimental Psychology*, 1973, *100*, 39–49.

Shulman, H. G. Semantic confusion errors in short-term memory. *Journal of Verbal Learning and Verbal Behavior*, 1972, *11*, 221–227.

Siegler, R. S. Three aspects of cognitive development. *Cognitive Psychology*, 1976, *8*, 481–520.

Siegler, R. S. The origins of scientific reasoning. In R. S. Sielger (Ed.), *Children's thinking: What develops?* Hillsdale, N.J.: Erlbaum, 1978.

Siegler, R. S. Developmental sequences within and between concepts. *Monographs of the Society for Research in Child Development*, 1981, *46* (2, Serial No. 189).

Siegler, R. S., & Klahr, D. When do children learn: The relationship between existing knowledge and the ability to acquire new knowledge. In R. Glaser (Ed.), *Advances in instructional psychology*, Hillsdale, N.J.: Erlbaum, 1982.

Siegler, R. S., & Liebert, R. M. Acquisition of formal scientific reasoning by 10- and 13-year-olds: Designing a factorial experiment. *Developmental Psychology*, 1975, *11*, 401–402.

Siegler, R. S., & Richards, D. Development of time, speed, and distance concepts. *Developmental Psychology*, 1979, *15*, 288–298.

Siegler, R. S., & Richards, D. The development of two concepts. In C. J. Brainerd (Ed.), *Recent advances in cognitive developmental theory*, 1983, in press.

Siegler, R. S., & Robinson, M. The development of numerical understandings. In H. Reese, & L. P. Lipsitt (Eds.), *Advances in child development and behavior* (Vol. 16). New York: Academic Press, 1982.

Siegler, R. S., & Vago, S. The development of a proportionality concept: Judging relative fullness. *Journal of Experimental Child Psychology*, 1978, *25*, 371–395.

Siqueland, E. R., & Lipsitt, L. P. Conditioned head turning in human newborns. *Journal of Experimental Child Psychology*, 1966, *3*, 356–376.

Simon, H. A. On the development of the processor. In S. Farnham-Diggory (Ed.), *Information processing in children*, New York: Academic Press, 1972.

Simon, H. A. The function equivalence of problem-solving skills. *Cognitive Psychology*, 1975, 268–288.

Simon, D. P., & Simon, H. A. Alternative uses of phonemic information in spelling. *Review of Educational Research*, 1973, *43*, 115–137.

Skinner, B. F. *Verbal behavior*. New York: Appleton-Century-Crofts, 1957.

Smith, L. B., & Kemler, D. G. Levels of experienced dimensionality in children and adults. *Cognitive Psychology*, 1978, *10*, 502–532.

Sophian, C. Selectivity and strategy in early search. *Journal of Experimental Child Psychology*, 1982, in press.

Spelke, E. Infant's intermodal perception of events. *Cognitive Psychology*, 1976, *8*, 553–560.

Sperling, G. The information available in brief visual presentations. *Psychological Monographs*,

1960, *74*. (Whole issue)

Spilich, G. J., Vesonder, G. T., Chiesi, H. L., & Voss, J. Test processing of domain-related information for individuals with high and low domain knowledge. *Journal of Verbal Learning and Verbal Behavior,* 1979, *18,* 275–290.

Spring, D. R. Discrimination of linguistic stress location in one-to-four-month-old infants. Unpublished doctoral dissertation, University of Washington, Seattle, 1975.

Stein, N., & Glenn, C. An analysis of story comprehension in elementary school children. In R. Freedle (Ed.), *New directions in discourse processing* (Vol. 2). N.J.: Ablex, 1979.

Sternberg, R. J. Intelligence research at the interface between differential and cognitive psychology. Prospects and Proposals. *Intelligence,* 1978, *2,* 195–222.

Sternberg, R. J. Six authors in search of a character: A play about intelligence tests in the year 2000. *Intelligence,* 1979, *3,* 281–291.

Sternberg, R. J., & Rifkin, B. The development of analogical reasoning processes. *Journal of Experimental Child Psychology,* 1979, *27,* 195–232.

Sternberg, S. High speed scanning in human memory. *Science,* 1966, *153,* 652–654.

Sternberg, S. Two operations in character recognition: Some evidence from reaction-time measurements. *Perception and Psychophysics,* 1967, *2,* 45–53.

Sternberg, S. Memory-scanning: Mental processes revealed by reaction time experiments. *Acta Psychologica,* 1969, *30,* 276–315.

Strauss, S., & Stavy, R. U-shaped behavioral growth: Implications for theories of development. In W. W. Hartup (Ed.), *Review of child development research* (Vol. 6), in press.

Taylor, D. A. Identification and categorization of letters and digits. *Journal of Experimental Psychology: Human Perception Performance,* 1978, *4,* 423–439.

Tenney, Y. J. The child's conception of organization and recall. *Journal of Experimental Child Psychology,* 1975, *19,* 100–114.

Thomson, D. M., & Tulving, E. Associative encoding and retrieval: Weak and strong cues. *Journal of Experimental Psychology,* 1970, *86,* 255–262.

Thorndyke, P. W. Cognitive structures in comprehension and memory of narrative discourse. *Cognitive Psychology,* 1977, *9,* 77–110.

Townsend, J. T. Issues and models concerning the processing of a finite number of inputs. In B. H.

Kantowitz (Ed.), *Human information processing: Tutorials in performance and cognition.* Hillsdale, N.J.: Erlbaum, 1974.

Trabasso, T., & Foellinger, D. B. Information processing capacity in children: A test of Pascual-Leone's model. *Journal of Experimental Child Psychology,* 1978, *26,* 1–17.

Trabasso, T., Riley, C. A., & Wilson, E. G. The representation of linear order and spatial strategies in reasoning: A developmental study. In R. J. Falmagne (Ed.), *Reasoning: Representation and process.* Hillsdale, N.J.: Erlbaum, 1975.

Trehub, S. E. Infant's sensitivity to vowel and tonal contrasts. *Developmental Psychology,* 1973, *31,* 102–107.

Triesman, A. M. Selective attention in man. *British Medical Bulletin,* 1964, *20,* 12–16.

Triesman, A. M. & Gelade, G. A feature integration theory of attention. *Cognitive Psychology,* 1980, *12,* 97–136.

Tuddenham, R. D. The nature and measurement of intelligence. In L. Postman (Ed.), *Psychology in the making,* New York: Knopf, 1962.

Turnure, J., Buium, N., & Thurlow, M. The effectiveness of interrogatives for promoting verbal elaboration productivity in children. *Child Development,* 1976, *47,* 851–855.

Venezky, R. L. *The structure of English orthography.* The Hague: Mouton, 1970.

Vurpillot, E. The development of scanning strategies and their relation to visual differentiation. *Journal of Experimental Child Psychology,* 1968, *6,* 632–650.

Wagner, D. A. Memories of Morrocco: The influence of age, schooling and environment on memory. *Cognitive Psychology,* 1978, *10,* 1–28.

Waters, H. S. "Class news": A single-subject longitudinal study of prose production and schema formation during childhood. *Journal of Verbal Learning and Verbal Behavior,* 1980.

Weber, R. M. First graders' use of grammatical context in reading. In H. Levin & J. P. Williams (Eds.), *Basic studies of reading.* New York: Basic Books, 1970.

Wellman, H. M., Ritter, K., & Flavell, J. H. Deliberate memory behavior in the delay reactions of very young children. *Developmental Psychology,* 1975, *11,* 780–787.

Wellman, H. M., & Somerville, S. C. Quasi-naturalistic tasks in the study of cognition: The memory-related skills of toddlers. *New Directions for Child Development,* 1980, *10,* 33–48.

Werner, H. *Comparative psychology of mental development.* New York: International Universities

Press, 1961.

Werner, J. S., & Perlmutter, M. Development of visual memory in infants. In H. W. Reese & L. P. Lipsitt (Eds.), *Advances in child development and behavior*. Vol. 14. New York: Academic Press, 1980.

Werner, J. S., & Siqueland, E. R. Visual recognition memory in the preterm infant. *Infant Behavior and Development*, 1978, *1*, 79–94.

Wertheimer, M. Psychomotor coordination of auditory-visual space at birth. *Science*, 1961, *134*, 1962.

Wickens, C. D. Temporal limits of human information processing: A developmental study. *Psychological Bulletin*, 1974, *81*, 739–755.

Wilkening, F., Becker, J., & Trabasso, T. *Information integration by children*. Hillsdale, N.J.: Erlbaum, 1980.

Wilkinson, A. C. Children's understanding in reading and listening. *Journal of Educational Psychology*, 1980, *72*, 561–574.

Williams, K. G., & Goulet, L. R. The effects of cuing and constraint instructions on children's free recall performance. *Journal of Experimental Child Psychology*, 1975, *19*, 464–475.

Winograd, T. Frame representations and the declarative-procedural controversy. In D. Bobrow & A. Collins (Eds.), *Representation and understanding: Studies in cognitive science*. New York: Academic Press, 1975.

Woods, S. S., Resnick, L. B., & Groen, G. J. Experimental test of five process models for subtraction. *Journal of Educational Psychology*, 1975, *67*, 17–21.

Worden, P. E. Effects of sorting on subsequent recall of unrelated items: A developmental study. *Child Development*, 1975, *46*, 687–695.

Young, R. M. Children's seriation behavior: A production system analysis. Unpublished doctoral dissertation, Carnegie-Mellon University, 1973.

Yussen, S. R., & Levy, V. M. Jr. Developmental changes in predicting one's own span of short-term memory. *Journal of Experimental Psychology*, 1975, *19*, 502–508.

HOW CHILDREN LEARN—THE QUEST FOR A THEORY $\Big|$ 5

HAROLD STEVENSON, *University of Michigan*

CHAPTER CONTENTS

Theory construction always consists largely of oversimplifying; the attractive theory is merely one that oversimplifies in a palatable manner. (R. C. Bolles, 1975)

In the edition of the *History of Experimental Psychology* published only 30 years ago, E. G. Boring discussed the history of psychology up to 1940 (Boring, 1950). In his index of topics, only two references to child psychology and three to learning can be found. Until we are confronted with such data, we often fail to realize how recently theoretical analyses of children's learning were undertaken. There were studies of animal learning early in the century, and some research on learning in human adults had been reported. However, despite the fact that for centuries parents, educators, and philosophers were interested in how children learn, psychological research on children's learning was slow to develop. The rate of publication remained low until the 1950s, when more than 200 publications of experimental studies appeared (in English) within a 10-year period. In the following decade, the number increased fivefold. More articles dealing with the experimental and theoretical analysis of children's learning were published between 1960 and 1969 than in all earlier decades combined. The amount and quality of this research inspired enthusiasm and confidence about the possibility that sound theoretical positions could be developed. The attractiveness of a theory no longer depended primarily upon the theorist's skill in persuasion; its power could be evaluated through rigorously designed sets of objective experiments.

Surprisingly, the period of exuberant growth was of very short duration. As rapidly as the field had developed, it went into decline. By the mid-1970s, articles on children's learning dwindled to a fraction of the number that had been published in the previous decade, and by 1980 it was necessary to search with diligence to uncover any articles at all. Problems found to be exciting only a few years earlier were considered uninteresting to many child psychologists. Theories languished in untended fashion. Attention had been diverted elsewhere, and no one had to be told that a brief, but active era was over. The discussion of children's learning had been displaced by a newfound interest in cognitive development.

TOWARD THE DEFINITION OF LEARNING

A central theme in the history of philosophy and psychology is the relative importance of subjective experience and overt behavior. In the early days, when psychologists were occupied chiefly with the analysis of sensation and perception, great reliance was placed on reports of subjective experience and the analysis of consciousness. Later, when the first studies were conducted with animals, psychologists were faced with a dilemma. Should they, within themselves, attempt to construct the conscious experience of animals, or should they be satisfied with an analysis of animals' overt responses? The ar-

tificiality of attempting to understand the consciousness of animals led to a choice of the latter alternative. Overt response became the core datum of
animal psychology.

From this background, behaviorism emerged.
Psychology was defined as the study of behavior,
and learning was described in terms of behavioral
attributes. A typical definition of learning within this
point of view is the following:

> Learning refers to the change in the subject's
> behavior to a given situation brought about by his
> repeated experiences in that situation, provided
> that the behavior change cannot be explained on
> the basis of native response tendencies, matura-
> tion, or temporary states of the subject (e.g., fa-
> tigue, drugs, etc.). (Hilgard & Bower, 1975, p.
> 17)

Similar definitions were popular for many years.
No reliance is placed on subjective report, and learning is measured by changes in the probability, vigor,
or latency of response. These are objective variables, capable of being measured reliably. Theories
were constructed and studies were designed with
such definitions in mind. When research interest
turned toward learning in children, the primary data
obtained from the studies were children's overt
motor responses, and efforts to analyse the child's
experiences during the course of learning were
avoided. One wonders how the field would have
differed had the definition of learning been less influenced by the deficits in communication of lower
animals than by the strengths of the human adult.

It did not take long for psychologists to begin to
feel the constraints imposed by this view. With a
growth of interest in problems such as the acquisition of concepts, verbal learning, and learning in
situations with uncertain outcomes, the view
emerged that learning involved the processing of
information and the acquisition of knowledge.
Human learning could not be described convincingly in terms of stimulus and response. There were
inner experiences that could be translated into words
and that could be probed by behavioral measures.
Why was it not possible to penetrate the black box
that stood between stimulus and response, and discuss learning in terms of strategies, hypotheses, and
structured knowledge? Were not these more appropriate in describing learning than intervening variables such as habit strength and fractional anticipatory goal responses, behavioral terms that had
dominated earlier discussions?

The definition of learning changed rather
abruptly. The behavioral definition was replaced by
one that relied on cognitive concepts. The new S-R
psychology became one of structure and rules, rather
than stimulus and response. Computers, rather than
telephone switchboards, became the model of the
human mind. Children, according to this view, were
no longer considered to be receptive creatures, responding passively to the stimuli provided in their
environments, but to be hypothesis-generating individuals, active in constructing the environments in
which they live. The consequences of response were
considered to be influential, not because they acted
to reduce drive or halt behavior as earlier theorists
had postulated, but because they provided information that confirmed the adequacy of the child's
efforts or suggested alternatives that might be tried.
Simple associative learning between stimulus and
response was not denied, but was assumed to be a
special case that occurred only when the generation
of hypotheses was difficult or impossible because
the situation was confusing, obscure, or sterile.

What is learned? Knowledge, says the contemporary cognitive theorist. If this is true, then behavior must be the *result* of learning, rather than that
which itself is learned. "The important innovative
idea in this development," says Greeno, "was the
conceptualization of learning as discrete change between states of knowledge rather than as change in
probability of response" (Greeno, 1980, p. 716).

By this definition, the study of learning becomes
an integral part of cognitive psychology. Surprisingly, however, in the current rush of enthusiasm about
studying cognitive processes, little attention has
been paid to the *acquisition* of cognitive structures.
Whereas a learning approach would concentrate on
rules of acquisition and change, the major effort in
current cognitive studies has been the description of
cognitive structures and operations at particular periods in the child's life. This emphasis has greatly
enriched our understanding of what children know,
but it has not relieved us of the necessity for understanding *how* the knowledge is acquired. The impatience of cognitive psychologists with what they
consider to be mechanistic and simplistic learning
theories has tended to result in their avoiding the
discussion of learning, rather than in providing new,
constructive ideas about how learning occurs. Thus,
despite this major change in paradigms, the problems remain. A major task for cognitive theorists is
to describe both states and transitions; when they
begin to do this, the full power of the cognitive approach may be realized.

What we have experienced in the past decade, then, is a change as great as that which occurred early in the century in the shift from the psychology of introspection to that of behaviorism. Moreover, the change has been rapid, and psychologists trained in the tradition of the behaviorists have been forced either to modify their positions or to be regarded as atavistic remnants of an earlier time in the history of psychology.

My goals in this chapter are to trace the development of the various theoretical positions that have emerged during the past half-century and to describe the ways in which they have influenced our treatment of children. Knowing where we have been may clarify the problems we will face in the future. Such problems will be faced, for we cannot ignore the role played by learning as we pursue our efforts to understand human development. Current inactivity in the field of children's learning is surely a temporary phenomenon, one that will be followed by efforts to construct more robust, comprehensive theories. The current malaise is not due solely to the current popularity of cognitive psychology; of equal significance is the fact that research constructed during the past 10 or 15 years to evaluate the various theoretical positions has produced, instead, some of the most devastating evidence against the positions they were designed to test. The theoretical models proved to be too constricted; they were unable to accommodate the data generated by the experimental studies. We must understand the ways in which theories proved to be inadequate if we are to remedy their deficiencies. The failure of theory to keep up with research data is true not only in the area of children's learning, but in other areas of child psychology as well. For example, Hartup and Yonas, in describing the current status of developmental psychology, point out that the "output in developmental psychology is guided by the aging theories of the past or by no theory at all. The problem for the future is to produce those giant theoretical steps that are needed for an already vigorous and visible field" (1971, p. 378). We will be in a better position to take these steps if we can evaluate the past successes and failures. Although the picture that emerges from this discussion of children's learning is bleak, the overall outcome is a positive one. Scientific investigation of this important area has begun, a large accumulation of useful data is in hand, and refinements in methodology have occurred. We have a much better understanding of what theories of children's learning must encompass than we did even 20 years ago.

Choices obviously had to be made in deciding what this chapter should include. I chose to concentrate on those aspects of the field of human learning that have been of special concern to child psychologists. This means that theories of animal learning and human adult learning were considered only when they had relevance for children. This occurred very seldom, for these theories have not dealt with developmental phenomena, the focus of our concern as child psychologists. There has been no attempt, therefore, to place children's learning within the broader context of theoretical developments in human learning. Nor has there been an attempt to make the chapter international in scope. Other than the conditioning theories of Soviet psychologists and the consideration of modeling by Chinese psychologists, it seems to me that the major theoretical developments in this area of psychology have occurred in the United States. Although there is a research literature in Russian, Japanese, German, French, and other languages as well, it was impossible for me to review these studies in order to evaluate their relevance for theories of children's learning. Therefore, the chapter includes only the various American positions that have dealt specifically with children.

Watson's Behaviorism

Experimental research with children began with the work of John B. Watson (1878–1958), and much of what child psychologists currently are rebelling against is contained in the theoretical position Watson espoused. Watson was a provocative and influential psychologist. He was explicit, confident, and an excellent salesman. He was the first of the child psychologists to reach a large audience with child-rearing advice. Thousands of American mothers bought his books, read his magazine articles, and listened to his talks on the radio. The behaviorism Watson proposed was an applied science, one that sought to bring knowledge of the laboratory to bear on everyday problems of childhood. In the 1920s, such a scientific, pragmatic approach was readily acceptable to Americans, for whom science seemed to have limitless potential.

Behaviorism developed very rapidly. Watson, as an animal psychologist, quickly rejected introspection and consciousness as the method and topic of his studies, realized that the only data available to him were contained in the animals' behavior, and saw his goal to be that of understanding how behavior (responses) was changed as a function of experience (stimuli). Pavlov, the famous Russian physiologist who had been studying animal learning, provided Watson with what appeared to be a simple and effective answer—the modification of behavior occurs through the process of conditioning. A stimulus incapable of producing a particular response can become capable of eliciting the response if it is repeatedly paired with a second stimulus that is effective in producing the response. Associationism, long a traditional philosophical position, was transformed in the twentieth century from the association of ideas to the association of stimulus and response through the process of stimulus substitution. Things fell into place with stunning rapidity.

Watson sought to test the validity of these ideas in his famous study with Rayner of aversive conditioning in the human infant (Watson & Rayner, 1920). In earlier investigations of infants' motor and emotional repertoires, Watson found that among the stimuli leading to emotional response was the sudden appearance of a loud sound. It seemed natural, therefore, to investigate whether this response could be conditioned. Would the emotional response initially made to a loud sound be elicited by another, neutral stimulus that the experimenter paired repeatedly with the sound? Healthy, stolid, 9-month-old Albert, destined to become one of psychology's most famous infants, was chosen as the subject. A white rat was presented to establish Albert's presumed fearlessness in the presence of a white rat. Albert displayed no fear of the rat, nor of a rabbit, dog, monkey, masks, cotton wool, burning newspapers, and other objects. On the other hand, when a steel bar out of Albert's view was struck a sharp blow, the fearless Albert did respond. Conditioning trials began two months later. Each time the rat was presented to Albert, a steel bar was struck with a mallet. After seven paired presentations, Albert recoiled at the sight of the rat, began to cry, and to crawl away. Five days later, and at two still later times, the rat and other similar stimuli produced a negative response, but in muted form.

One study. One subject. This was what Watson relied on to establish the validity of his proposal that the conditioned response was the key to understanding the development of human behavior. We are aghast today to see the uncritical acceptance this study received. Not only was the evidence minimal, but the question has been raised recently whether conditioning was indeed demonstrated in this single case. Harris (1979) and Samelson (1980) have gone back to Watson's correspondence and publications and have concluded that the demonstrations on the successive test trials were neither so clear as Watson described nor so successful as has been believed. Direct evidence about the study was discovered recently, when a copy of a film made of this famous experiment was found (Harris, 1980). Whatever the observer may conclude, it is evident in a single viewing that the conditioned response had only general similarity at best to the previous, unconditioned response. Something other than the direct transfer of a response from one stimulus to another had taken place.

Watson worked later with Mary Cover Jones in studying the elimination of young children's fears, studies that anticipated much of the later work on behavior modification. Jones tried many techniques, including conditioning, disuse, verbal persuasion, repeated presentation of the feared object, distraction, and social imitation (Jones, 1924a). Only social imitation and conditioning were judged effective. The potential usefulness of conditioning was demonstrated in the well-known research with Peter, a 2-year-old who was afraid of a white rat, a rabbit, and the other types of stimuli to which Albert had initially responded so calmly (Jones, 1924b). The first efforts to reduce Peter's fears involved social imitation. Peter and three children who demonstrated no fear of small animals were brought to the laboratory for a play period in which a rabbit was introduced. Peter became increasingly tolerant and eventually showed "tranquil indifference" to the rabbit and was able to pat its back when others set the example. Later, however, Peter and a nurse were attacked by a dog and Peter's fears returned. At this point Jones attempted to reduce Peter's fear of animals by associating a rabbit's appearance with the presence of food. A rabbit was placed in a cage far from Peter as he ate. Day by day the cage was moved closer. Occasionally other children were brought in "to help with the 'unconditioning.'" Peter's fears abated. Can we conclude, however, that this study offers evidence for the transfer of a response from one stimulus to another?

The Watsons also sought to apply conditioning to the rearing of their own children. Cohen (1979), in a recent biography of Watson, describes Rosalie Rayner Watson's unsuccessful efforts to apply the conditioning method as she tried first to toilet train and then to stop nail-biting in their older son. However, these failures did nothing to reduce Watson's confidence in his ability to prescribe how others should rear their children, and in 1928 his famous *Psychological care of infant and child*, an immediate best seller, was published. In this book Watson suggested that:

Since the behaviorists find little that corresponds to instincts in children, failure to bring up a happy child, a well adjusted child—assuming bodily health—falls squarely upon the parents' shoulders. The acceptance of this view makes child-rearing the most important of all social obligations. (p. 7)

By the time the child reaches 3 years of age, Watson asserted that:

The child's whole emotional life plan has been laid down, his emotional disposition set. At that age the parents have already determined for him whether he is to grow into a happy person, wholesome and good-natured, whether he is to be a whining, complaining neurotic, an anger-driven, vindictive, over-bearing slave driver, or one whose every move in life is definitely controlled by fear. (p. 45)

Burdened by the knowledge that the fate of their young children lies nearly totally in their own hands, parents were told that "parenthood, instead of being an instinctive act, is a science, the details of which must be worked out by patient laboratory methods" (p. 12). What were they to do while these studies were being conducted? They need not wait for the details; Watson gave them clear, straightforward rules for childrearing. Two examples in Watson's own words convey his position:

A certain amount of affectionate response is socially necessary but few parents realize how easily they can overtrain the child in this direction. It may tear the heartstrings a bit, this thought of stopping the tender outward demonstration of your love for your children or their love for you. But if you are convinced that this is best for the child, aren't you willing to stifle a few pangs? Mothers just don't know, when they kiss their children and pick them up and rock them, caress them and jiggle them on their knee, that they are slowly building up a human being totally unable to cope with the world it must later live in. (pp. 43–44)

The infant from 8 months of age onward should have a special toilet seat to which he can be safely strapped. The child should be left in the bathroom without toys and with the door closed. Under no circumstances should the door be left open or the mother or nurse stay with the child. This is a rule which seems to be almost universally broken. When broken it leads to dawdling, loud conversation, in general to unsocial and dependent behavior. (pp. 121–122)

It was a long way from Watson's fragmentary experimental evidence to these rules of good parent-ing, yet at the time he gave no indication of understanding how tenuous his position really was. Scientific principles of objectivity, caution, and reliance on data were repeatedly violated in this premature popularization of a few elementary ideas. A few years later in his autobiography, Watson became more critical. His was a book, he wrote, "I feel sorry about—not because of its sketchy form, but because I did not know enough to write the book I wanted to write" (Watson, 1936, p. 28). A revised edition never appeared and Watson published no more research on learning. His career as an academic psychologist came to an abrupt halt when a sensational divorce resulted in his exclusion from academia.

It would seem that Watson's impact should have been short-lived. This was not the case. As Heidbreder (1933) has suggested, Watson's efforts to better humanity through scientific methods had a nearly irresistible appeal for Americans, both laypeople and professionals. His extreme environmentalism offered a hopeful, optimistic, egalitarian view of human behavior. By denying biologically based differences in intelligence and other abilities, and by describing ways in which consistent, objective, and attentive parents could rear bright and independent children, Watson projected an image of a scientific psychology that was of immediate applicability. Childrearing became simply a matter of habit training. Proper habits should and could be instituted at an early age. Good habits of eating, sleeping, and elimination provided a sound basis for a healthy life. In fact, a whole chapter in the 1931 edition of the *Handbook of Child Psychology* was devoted to a description of how these habits could be developed through conditioning (Wooley, 1931).

Psychologists such as Hull and Skinner carried on the tradition of behaviorism where Watson had left off. The legacy of his bold statements about the enduring effects of early experience remains with us, and even now psychologists continue to respond to his overdrawn descriptions of enduring effects of early experiences (e.g., Kagan, 1978). Although others, such as the American pediatrician Thom (1928) had also espoused positions emphasizing long-term influences of early habit training, none has had an impact within the field of psychology comparable to that of Watson.

The 1933 *Handbook of Child Psychology*

Not everyone was convinced of the correctness of the behavioristic view. Some chose to criticize it and others chose to ignore it. Among the harshest critics of the conditioning view was the child psychologist-pediatrician, Arnold Gesell. For Gesell, answers to questions of behavioral development lay in biology. He proposed that the laws of conditioning and the psychology of learning would eventually be reformulated in terms of the "biology and physiology of development." Among the first presentations of his views was a chapter he wrote for the *Handbook of Child Psychology* on "Maturation and the patterning of behavior." The term "maturation," Gesell wrote, "has come into usage as an offset to the extravagant claims which have been made for processes of conditioning and habit formation" (1933, p. 209). Conditioning theories suffer, said Gesell, because they suggest that

the individual is fabricated out of the conditioning process. They do not give due recognition to the inner checks which set metes and bounds to the area of conditioning and which happily prevent abnormal and grotesque consequences which the theories themselves would make too easily possible. (p. 231)

Among those who ignored Watson's work was Peterson, whose chapter on children's learning also appeared in the 1933 *Handbook*. Peterson paid some attention to infant learning and the role of maturation versus training, but for the most part his coverage was of more traditional topics in human learning, such as the acquisition of skill, distribution of practice, associative learning, motivational factors, multiple-choice, and rational learning. This research, and that appearing in America for some years thereafter, offered little insight into distinctive characteristics of children's learning.

Thorndike's Connectionism

A second major American learning theorist proved to be more durable. In over 500 publications, E. L. Thorndike (1874–1949), a professor at Columbia University's Teacher's College, presented his theory of connectionism and its applications. Thorndike was a few years older than Watson, but his research career lasted much longer. His first important book, *Animal intelligence,* was published in 1898, and his final volume, *Selected writings from a connectionist's psychology,* appeared in 1949, over a half-century later. During this period Thorndike became the preeminent theorist of the S-R school. According to Thorndike, learning is a matter of trial-and-error, of selecting and connecting. Responses followed by reward are stamped in, and those that are unsuccessful are stamped out. By proposing that learning occurs through the operation of reward, Thorndike became the first major reinforcement theorist.

Thorndike's area of application was the schoolroom, and he was among the first to seek a scientific basis for educational practice. Perhaps because of this interest in school learning, Thorndike was not an uncompromising behaviorist. Although he sought to devise a theory that was, to use Heidbreder's (1933) terms, as "materialistic, mechanistic, deterministic, and objective" as the approach of the behaviorist, Thorndike always relented a bit and allowed other, mentalistic concepts to enter his thinking. He spoke mainly of forming connections between stimulus and response, but he also recognized other types of learning: connection-forming involving ideas; analysis and abstraction; and selective thinking or reasoning (Thorndike, 1924, p. 138). There is a curious contrast, too, between his consideration of the learner as active—"an individual selects, by action, attention, memory and satisfaction, the features of the environment which are to survive as determinants of his intellect and character" (1924, p. 380)—and the mechanical manner in which he proposed that reward operates on the responses that precede it. A further way in which his views differ from an extreme behaviorism, is in his acknowledgement of sources of influence other than experience on the child's behavior. Genetic endowment, maturation, and "circumstances of life and training" (1924, p. 340) are the forces that shape human behavior. Among these circumstances are the "physiological conditions for the brain's health and growth," and stimuli "to arouse the action of which the brain . . . is capable," and, finally, "the reinforcing or eliminating of these actions through the general law of effect" (1924, p. 394).

These are some of the ideas for which Thorndike became famous. Despite the fact that little of his or his graduate students' research was actually done with children, his theory was influential within the growing field of educational psychology and had an impact on the educational experiences of many American children. His output was prodigious and he enjoyed popular success, but Thorndike was not satisfied with what he had done. He was critical of his own work and suggested that "the connectionist theory of life and learning is doubtless neither adequate nor accurate" (1931, p. 131). Within child psychology, Thorndike's influence has never been great. One wonders, however, if his contributions might not now be more highly valued if reinforcement theory had not become so firmly attached to the name of his successor, B. F. Skinner.

Skinner's Operant Conditioning

The third of the positions to be associated closely with a particular individual is the operant conditioning view of B. F. Skinner (1904–). He, like Thorndike, has had a long career. The book for which he received early fame, *The behavior of organisms,* was published in 1938. In 1980 he attended the meetings of the American Psychological Association, where he could be heard giving an address on ''Selection by consequences'' and in dialogue with a British adversary. Like Thorndike, the major lines of his theory were sketched early, following his work with rats. General laws were formulated and applied unchanged to the rat and pigeon, and to the human infant, child, and adult. Although Skinner considered Thorndike to be a mentalist, he has continued to reiterate his indebtedness to both Thorndike and Pavlov. These were the two persons who provided Skinner with the prototypes for his distinction between two types of learning, those involving *respondents,* responses elicited by particular stimuli, and *operants,* responses by which the individual operates on the environment. Through Pavlovian conditioning, respondents are shifted to new stimuli; and through the law of effect, operants are strengthened.

Sometimes called operant conditioning and sometimes the experimental analysis of behavior, Skinner's views were even more iconoclastic than Watson's. He espoused a radical behaviorism that denies the existence of a mental world and that, in fact, denies the value of theories themselves. Skinner proclaimed that his approach ''is not concerned with testing theories but with directly modifying behavior'' (1969, p. 97). Psychology became to him the study of contingency management, that is, the study of those contingencies between response and reinforcement that would strengthen or weaken responses. Skinner carried reinforcement theory to its extreme. Behavior remained stable when it was maintained by a proper schedule of reinforcement. New responses appeared when the contingencies change, leaving old responses without reinforcement and following new responses with reinforcement. What characterizes a reinforcing stimulus other than its power to strengthen a response never interested Skinner. There were too many other questions to be answered in the discovery of proper schedules and schemes for applying reinforcement

in the maintenance and strengthening of responses. What began as a series of studies of rats pressing levers in barren boxes eventually became a full-fledged technology, involving the application of reinforcement principles in schools, hospitals, and other situations where control of the conditions of reinforcement was possible. I will return to a discussion of these applications later in this chapter.

Skinner and his followers have remained jubilantly enthusiastic about their work and appear not to have felt the pangs of self-doubt that eventually overtook both Watson and Thorndike. Even though the view has been subject to harsh and vigorous criticism (e.g., Chomsky, 1959), Skinner never falters in asserting his confident belief that the solutions of many contemporary problems of the world lie in behavioral science, specifically in the experimental analysis of behavior (Skinner, 1980).

Overview

What we have reviewed thus far are the perspectives of three theorists whose work had great impact on children. Other learning theorists, such as Hull, were also writing at this time, but only through the extension of their work by others did their positions have any influence on child psychology. It is evident that all three of the positions were theories of learning applied to children, not learning theories of development. Nor did the research of this period, nor that appearing in America for some years afterward, offer insight into the ways in which learning might differ at successive developmental levels. Even Watson had failed to consider this matter. His application of the conditioned response differed little, whether the subject was a newborn or a 6-year-old. This was not a necessary consequence of adopting the conditioned response as a model. In the Soviet Union, psychologists during these years were outlining a developmental analysis of the conditioning process (Luria, 1959; Vygotsky, 1962).

It took many years before the complexities of children's thinking and of their behavior became evident to those who were developing theories about how children learn. Perhaps only in the last decade have we fully realized how profound the differences are between lower animals and the human child. Contemporary views offer a radically different assessment of children's capacities from the one on which the stimulus-response theories rested. Children's capacities are not simply quantitatively different from those of lower animals. Children do not learn more effectively because they have the cortical capacity to form more connections, or to generalize a conditioned response to a greater variety of stimuli. Children differ qualitatively from animals. They are capable of transforming stimuli through language in ways that other organisms cannot; and the value, utility, and meaning of stimuli are different for children because children are subject to long periods of socialization. The fact that children are verbal, social animals—as well as being complicated ones—did not escape the attention of the Soviet psychologists, nor of Piaget, but the American stimulus-response psychologists were too imbued with their early experiences in the animal laboratory and too dedicated in their quest to establish an objective psychology to recognize and appreciate these salient facts.

One wonders, in looking back at these early approaches, if the psychology of children's learning would not have been very different today if the initial impetus in the field had come from the research and theory of persons who had visited classrooms, rather than of those who had spent so many hours in the animal laboratory.

RESEARCH WITH CHILDREN

Research with children of the types reviewed by Peterson in 1933 continued in the following years, thereby perpetuating the peculiar split between research with children, which was atheoretical, and theoretical developments, which were occurring outside of child psychology. There were studies of classical Pavlovian conditioning, but the questions were when the infant is susceptible to conditioning (e.g., Wickens & Wickens, 1940) and whether the human fetus can be conditioned (e.g., Spelt, 1948), rather than about possible new principles of conditioning. Studies of operant conditioning were direct replications of animal research, except for a few isolated studies of the experimental manipulation of perceived size of a secondary reinforcer (a poker chip used to obtain candy) by means of reinforcement and its withdrawal (Lambert & Lambert, 1953). Studies which capitalized on the fact that children were used as subjects were not pursued. Rather, child psychologists seemed to be more interested in testing directly with children what had already been found with lower animals. Life-size mazes, enlarged copies of those used with rats, were constructed. Children's performance in these mazes led investigators to favor a trial-and-error rather than an insightful approach to learning (Jones & Batalla, 1944), and to assert that alternation of choice in a single choice-point maze does not occur as frequently in the child as it does in the rat (Wingfield, 1938). A few studies of discrimination learning and problem solving appeared; children were tested in these studies with the kinds of learning-set problems that had been used with monkeys and chimpanzees (e.g., Hayes, Thompson, & Hayes, 1953) or the insight problems that Köhler had investigated with chimpanzees (e.g., Sobel, 1939).

What was the cumulative impact of this research? Munn, in concluding his review of research on children's learning conducted prior to 1954, summarized his impressions in the following way:

So far as discovering anything fundamentally new about the learning process is concerned, the investigations on learning in children have failed. One possible reason for this is that such investigations have from the first been patterned too much after the lines of earlier research with animals and adults in the laboratory. (1954, p. 449)

This was true with a single exception. One set of studies did prove to have an important impact on the field of child psychology. These dealt with transposition. A brief discussion of the background of these studies is useful. Gestalt psychologists, such as K. Koffka and W. Köhler, contended that learning consists, not of strengthening S-R bonds but of developing an understanding of relations that exist among stimuli. Transposition implies the transfer of such a relation from one set of stimuli to another.

Show the child two circles, one larger than the other. Under the larger circle is a small piece of candy. The child will begin to choose this circle consistently. Has the child learned a relation or to choose a specific circle? Do relational or absolute properties of the stimuli guide response? This can be tested by offering a new pair, consisting of the larger circle of the first pair and a still larger circle. If children choose the larger of the two, they are judged to have transposed. Transposition occurs, then, when the child chooses the stimulus in a new set of stimuli that bear the same relation to this set as was held by the correct stimulus in the training set. Gestaltists interpreted positive results from these studies as strong support for their general orientation. But they were faced with a serious obstacle. Transposition typically occurred when the test pair was similar to the training pair. When tests were conducted with more dissimilar stimuli—but ones that still differed only along the dimension by which the first pair differed—children's choices were random. The latter finding perplexed the gestaltists, and the former posed difficulties for the stimulus-response view. Scores of studies by child psychologists were soon to appear on issues related to this topic.

Verbal Mediation

Spence (1937), a leading Hullian and exponent of the stimulus-response approach within animal learning, proposed a theoretical model that seemed to offer a satisfactory account of some of the data obtained from studies of children's learning. The model is of interest here only in broad outline. It contained several assumptions: (1) stimuli are defined by absolute properties expressible in psychophysical units; (2) learning to discriminate among stimuli is a cumulative process in which reward strengthens the tendency to approach a correct stimulus and nonreinforcement increases the tendency to avoid or inhibit response to an incorrect stimulus; (3) both approach and avoidance tendencies generalize to other stimuli; and (4) response to any particular stimulus depends on the differential strength of the tendencies to approach and to avoid responses to that stimulus. If the hypothesized generalization curves are drawn for stimuli varying within a single dimension, it is possible to predict that transposition will occur for pairs of stimuli near the training pair on the psychophysical scale and will drop to a chance level for pairs that are increasingly remote.

It took Margaret Kuenne, a graduate student working with Spence, to make this model relevant for developmental psychology. She did this by asking a question that was ripe for someone to ask: Should predictions be the same for the linguistically sophisticated child as for the rat or the child with only rudiments of language? Spence's model of discrimination learning, like nearly all of those of the era, made no mention of language. However, it was inconceivable that anyone working with Spence could talk about language in anything other than stimulus-response terms. Accepting this requirement, Kuenne's answer to her own question followed naturally. Words must be considered to be stimuli—and responses. Objective stimuli elicit words as responses; words, in turn, can become stimuli effective in eliciting motor responses. Language is thereby conceived to follow the same rules as those governing all other stimuli.

In the transposition problem, words were posited to function in the following manner. The sight of the two circles in our earlier example would lead the child, on the basis of prior experience, to label them, for example, as "big" or "little." When the child says "big" and picks up the larger stimulus, a reward is found. This reward strengthens both the child's tendency to say "big" when confronted with the circles and to pick up the larger circle. This gives the older child an advantage over the younger child, for a new pair of stimuli differing in size leads, through stimulus generalization, to the verbal response "big," which in turn leads the child to choose the larger stimulus. Transposition would occur readily over a broad range of stimuli for these older, "verbal" children. Younger children, deprived of this cue, would show more restricted transfer.

Language, then, acts as a verbal mediator between stimulus and response; it operates according to the same rules that stimulus-response theorists had proposed for motor mediating responses made by nonverbal organisms. Initial research by Kuenne (1946) and others supported her general predictions.

Although Kuenne did not depart from orthodox stimulus-response views, her experiment was a turning point. Subsequent theorists would never be able to return to the simplistic ideas that failed to consider differences between lower animals and the human child. Kuenne's proposals excited interest because her research was a lucid example of how theoretically based research could be conducted with children and because it demonstrated how developmental studies might provide a means of bridging the gap that separated research with lower animals from that conducted with human adults. This kind of research required a knowledge of developmental processes, familiarity with theory, and a willingness to think of new theoretical ideas that considered the changing abilities of the developing child. It was a first effort at a developmental model of learning.

Sixteen years later Kendler and Kendler (1962) published in *Psychological Review* an important paper that outlined their views and presented the results of the first of a large number of subsequent experiments. They, like Kuenne, were students of Spence and operated within what had come to be known as the neobehaviorist framework. The discrimination learning problem they chose as the prototype for their research was a bit more complicated than the transposition problem studied by Kuenne, in that (1) it involved stimuli that differed simultaneously on two dimensions and (2) transfer was tested by making a different value within one dimension correct ("reversal shift") or changing the basis of correct response from one dimension to another ("nonreversal shift"). These slight differences in task required a much more complex theoretical exposition. The general pattern of the Kendlers' position followed that suggested by Kuenne. Young children were assumed to operate in the fashion described in Spence's model. Older children were assumed to go beyond such "single-unit" stimulus-response connections and use mediation. It is not a simple matter to describe the task, nor the predictions made from their theoretical position. Nevertheless, a general understanding of this position is of use, for it involves important issues in the evolution of our thinking about the relation between language development and learning.

I will use an example in which stimuli, say two squares, differ in size and color. Two pairs of these squares (a large blue and a small red square, and a large red and a small blue square) are presented, one pair at a time, to children on a series of trials. For our example, choices of the large square in each pair are arbitrarily deemed to be correct. After the first discrimination is learned, a second, transfer problem is presented. Choices of the small square in each pair suddenly and arbitrarily are correct for half of the children, and choices of the blue square are correct for the other half. The first type of transfer problem was termed a reversal shift ("large" to "small"), and the second a nonreversal shift ("large" to "blue"). Developmental differences in ease of transfer to the two types of shift were predicted. Learning should be more difficult for younger children in a reversal than in a nonreversal shift; for older children a nonreversal shift should be more difficult than a reversal shift. On what bases were these predictions made?

Young children's learning was again explained in terms of strengthening approach and avoidance tendencies through reinforcement and nonreinforcement of overt choice-responses. When the second value on the originally relevant dimension was correct (the reversal from "large" to "small"), young children should encounter difficulty. The choice that had been reinforced consistently had to be replaced by one that had been consistently not reinforced. If a value on the second dimension were correct (nonreversal shift), strengthening the new associations should be more rapid, since values on this dimension would have been reinforced on part of the training trials ("large *blue*" and "large red"). For young, nonmediating children, then, a reversal shift should be more difficult than a nonreversal shift. Different results were predicted for older, mediating children. The nonreversal shift should be more difficult than the reversal shift. In the reversal shift, the dimension initially correct is still relevant, thus the mediating response need not be greatly modified. In the nonreversal shift, however, the child must acquire a new mediating response as well as a new overt response.

Details of this exposition are less important for our purposes than are certain key elements. It is assumed that performance of both mediating and nonmediating children is determined by principles of reinforcement and nonreinforcement. In the case of younger children, the effects are dependent on overt response to absolute characteristics of the stimuli; for older children, reinforcement and nonreinforcement act upon verbal mediators which in turn guide overt responses. Scores of studies were designed over the next several decades to investigate these predictions.

Most aspects of the model are relatively straightforward. However, the central concept in the discussion—mediation—is troublesome. In early definitions (T. S. Kendler, 1963, p. 36), the mediator was conceived of as "a perceptual or verbal response, often overt, which produced cues that elicit overt response." Verbal mediation tended to be emphasized in subsequent discussions. For example, in a study by T. S. Kendler (1964) children were trained during the initial discrimination to say "Black is the winner and white is the loser," thereby presumably providing the children with an explicit verbal mediator. Later, the discussion of mediation became explicitly cognitive. "According to this model," wrote H. H. Kendler and Guenther (1980, p. 339), "there are two distinct modes of learning: a single-unit associative mode in which behavior is controlled by environmental stimuli, and a mediational mode in which behavior is guided by self-generated representational responses that abstract features of the environment." Stimulus-response terminology is not shed entirely, but the inclusion of self-generated representational responses makes the position similar to many that have been proposed recently by cognitive theorists. Whether responses of children, and even infants, ever approximate a single-unit mode of response is vigorously denied by many contemporary researchers. This will be discussed later, but it is important here to discuss briefly the kinds of evidence that necessitated such marked changes in the Kendlers' position.

Many studies revealed that knowledge of a word does not automatically or necessarily result in its use by the child as a means of guiding behavior. Clear evidence was found of a production deficiency, as the failure of the child to produce verbal mediators was termed by Flavell, Beach, and Chinsky (1966). Both children and adults often fail to use words they know very well as spontaneous mnemonic or directive aids. Moreover, even if relevant verbalization occurs, the words sometimes fail to function in the way they should as mediators of overt response. For example, in the study by T. S. Kendler (1964), where the children were trained to instruct themselves about what was the "winner," their self-instructions often were followed by incorrect choices. Failure of a potential mediator to function effectively has been termed a mediational or control deficiency (Reese, 1962).

The presence of production and control deficiencies is not the only argument against the validity of the concept of verbal mediation. Other evidence (e.g., Ash, 1975), indicated that children who are classified as mediating on the basis of their performance in a reversal-shift type of problem are no more adept than those classified as nonmediating when given other learning and memory tasks where mediation would be of value. What are we to make of a mechanism whose appearance and use are so unpredictable?

The verbal-mediation model proved to be a great oversimplification of the complex manner in which language influences children's learning. The concept was persuasive in its apparent simplicity and intuitive appeal. That some type of process intervenes between an environmental event and the occurrence of overt behavior is obvious. That the process operates to transform "incoming stimulation into some internal representation that guides subsequent behavior" (Kendler & Kendler, 1975, p. 203) cannot be denied. But nothing is gained by continuing to refer to this process as verbal mediation.

What was learned from studies related to the verbal-mediation hypothesis? First, the ability to verbalize alternative solutions to a problem involves much more than possessing relevant words. Verbalization is the end product of a long series of activities involved in the solution of such problems. The child must isolate the relevant dimension, develop hypotheses about the relation of the relevant dimension to the solution of the problem, and use these hypotheses when new or modified problems are presented. While doing this, children may or may not code their activities in terms of words, and when asked, may or may not be able to describe in words what has been done. Evidence fails to support a view of learning which considers words as stimuli that mediate between the perception of the stimulus and overt response. Whenever the supplying of words to young children has aided performance, the results can be readily interpreted by assuming that the experimenter's efforts to supply words had the effect of directing the child's attention to relevant aspects of the stimuli. Older children are more facile with language. They are more likely to use language to describe their efforts at learning and to guide their learning. They become adept at responding to the language of other persons as sources of direction and assistance. We find little support for the view that language becomes the mediator of action. Rather, current evidence indicates that language, thought, and action are interdependent, one aided by the other, but capable of developing in a partially independent fashion.

Abandonment of the verbal-mediation hypothesis accompanied a general disillusionment with the neobehavioristic approach. The human child, even in something so simple as discrimination learning, eluded the efforts of the stimulus-response psychologists. Kendler and Kendler, perhaps the most ardent proponents of the neobehavioristic approach in developmental psychology, summarized the changed status of neobehaviorism in the following way:

> Neobehaviorism as originally envisioned by Hull has undergone significant changes: a retreat from the ideals of rigorously derived theoretical deductions, an abandonment of conditioning as the major source of theoretical hypotheses, and a withdrawal from the goal of a general behavior theory to more modest conceptions. (Kendler & Kendler, 1975, p. 239)

These changes in the American view lead us to question, in similar fashion, the tenability of other positions, such as the Soviet conception of the first and second signal systems. Since the time of Pavlov, Soviet investigators have distinguished three types of stimuli that are effective in eliciting responses in human beings. These include (1) unconditioned stimuli that elicit reflexive responses, (2) conditioned stimuli, and (3) language. When a neutral stimulus becomes capable of eliciting a conditioned response, the child is said to be under the control of the first signal system. This system is considered to be the primary basis of learning in lower animals and the first basis of learning in the human being. For the human child, however, sounds develop into words and words develop meanings. Words as conveyors of meaning are assumed to be effective stimuli only with human beings. When this stage of development is reached, the human child is said to come under the control of the second signal system, in which words become capable of eliciting responses. Because the second signal system is dependent on a higher order of activity of the nervous system than is involved in establishing conditioned responses in the first signal system, the second signal system is said to be capable of producing higher-order conditioning. The proposed genesis of the second signal system closely parallels that of the development of verbal mediation, and the Soviet position is therefore susceptible to most of the arguments that have been made against single-unit and mediational theory.

Perceptual Learning

Language was not the only process that was handled inadequately by the S-R position in studying how children learn. Gestalt psychologists persistently charged that behaviorists also ignored perceptual factors. Two brief examples illustrate how a perceptual factor such as the salience of a stimulus may influence learning. The salience of different aspects of stimuli differ greatly for different children. Form, for example, is a salient dimension for some children, while color is more salient for others (Smiley & Weir, 1966). When correct response involves a salient dimension, learning occurs more rapidly than when a nonsalient dimension is correct. Thus, knowledge of what is salient for a child will help predict the child's rate of learning. Again, 3-year-olds may demonstrate concepts found in much older children if they are provided with prior experiences that heighten the salience of these attributes (Caron, 1968).

It is the Gibsons (Gibson & Gibson, 1955; Gibson, 1969; Tighe & Tighe, 1966) who did the most to increase our awareness of how perceptual factors influence learning. The Gibsons' theory of perceptual learning represents an important new approach. Perceptual learning is assumed to involve an increasing sensitivity to characteristics of stimuli that initially are undetected or poorly detected. Learning what occurs when children encounter a new system of writing, like Chinese, is a good example. This is not considered to be a matter of discrimination learning, as had been proposed by such writers as Hull (1920), but of learning the ways in which the characters are the same and the ways they differ. Perceptual learning is considered to be a matter of isolating those features of stimuli that are invariant and those that are distinctive. Although gross features that distinguish Chinese from English are readily perceived, it is only through repeated inspection of Chinese characters that the distinctive features that distinguish individual characters can be isolated. Perceptual learning occurs in the absence of external reinforcement. That is, the child may continue to inspect the Chinese characters, trying to "see what they look like," and not because someone is rewarding the child for doing so. Efforts to differentiate

stimulus characteristics are assumed to occur spontaneously as the individual attempts to resolve the perceptual uncertainty arising from new forms of stimulation.

According to this view, the product of experience is not the acquisition of new responses but of increased perceptual sensitivity. Young children are necessarily less effective in perceptual learning than are older children, for older children have had more experience in differentiating their environments. What were proposed by the behaviorists to be different stages of development during childhood are assumed to be due to differences in degree of prior perceptual learning.

Challenges posed by the perceptual learning view have never been adequately faced by the behaviorists. The tendency to regard stimuli as having absolute characteristics that are essentially the same for all subjects is a misinterpretation of great significance. There is ample evidence that the same "objective" stimuli, however simple, are not necessarily perceived in the same way by different children. Moreover, in problems of the types we have been discussing, learning to make the overt motor response of selecting the appropriate stimulus is a trivial task. Of much greater significance are the perceptual and cognitive problems of isolating the dimensions on which the stimuli differ and determining which dimensions may be important for success.

The theory of perceptual learning played an important role in reducing the dominance of the stimulus-response position. By discarding response and reinforcement as central concepts and by emphasizing the significance of stimulus characteristics, the Gibsons opened new approaches to understanding the learning process. Their work continues to have an important influence in developmental psychology, especially in research on reading (Gibson & Levin, 1975).

An alternative view that interprets perceptual processes within a mediational framework should be mentioned before leaving the discussion of perception and learning. Zeaman and House (1963) gave a central role to attentional phenomena in their discussion of discrimination learning. They assumed that attentional mediation operates at all ages and that an attentional or observing response to the relevant dimension is learned during the early phases of solving a problem. After the attentional response has been learned, the process of attaching a choice-response to one of the cues is rapid. Transfer occurs because other stimuli are capable of activating this attentional response. Although the proposal offered an alternative to verbal mediation and gave an important emphasis to attentional factors, it encountered many of the same difficulties faced by the verbal-mediation hypothesis. It never was clear, for example, what constituted an attentional response to "a broad class of cues having a common discriminative property" (Zeaman & House, 1963, p. 168). By being unable to provide a meaningful analysis of this question in stimulus-response terms, the effort to interpret attention in terms of observing responses met with little eventual success.

Personality and Learning

If the child's learning to choose one of two circles seems a paltry bit of behavior with which to be concerned, we can look at efforts to apply learning principles to the analysis of families and whole cultures. In startling contrast to the types of research typically associated with the stimulus-response approach, several bold efforts were made in the 1950s and 1960s to interpret phenomena of personality through a melding of psychoanalytic theory and behavioristic principles of learning. Whiting and Child (1953) were among the first to do this. They attempted to relate culture and individual behavior by taking the radical step of defining customs in terms of habits learned and displayed by typical members of a culture. Socialization of children occurs in all cultures, but societies differ in factors such as the degree to which a particular type of behavior is rewarded by parents, the age when socialization begins, and the severity of techniques used in socialization.

The strength of habits related to factors such as nursing and weaning, sex training, and independence training, key concepts in psychoanalytic theory, were rated by Whiting and Child from descriptions in field reports of childrearing practices. These ratings were then related, for example, to explanations of illness and to therapies used in various societies. It was assumed that if a particular type of behavior had been strongly rewarded during childhood, the "various responses that make up this system, and the stimuli consistently associated with them, would develop a strong potential for evoking acquired reward" (Whiting & Child, 1953, p. 136). That is, adults' interpretations of therapy in oral, sexual, or dependency terms would depend on the degree to which these systems of behavior had been indulged or rewarded by their parents during childhood. High frustration or punishment associated with a system would lead, on the other hand, to a high potential for anxiety to be displayed about this type of behavior. High anxiety in a particular system of behavior should be used, therefore, as an explanation of the cause of illness. It was assumed that if "lasting anxiety about the oral system was characteristic of members of a particular society, for example, then anxiety about illness might evoke by generalization responses of worrying about oral matters as a possible source of illness" (p. 147). The analysis was admirable in its novelty and venturesomeness, but when it came to testing the results, success was modest. In only a few of the analyses did the relation between variables exceed that which would occur by chance.

Behavior theory also influenced the work of Sears and his colleagues (Sears, Maccoby, & Levin, 1957; Sears, Rau, & Alpert, 1965). Sears had been one of the original group at Yale that attempted to use behavior theory in accounting for social phenomena such as aggression (Dollard, Doob, Miller, Mowrer, & Sears, 1939). A brief illustration of the ways in which learning principles were employed is found in the treatment of dependency by Sears et al. (1957).

The approach was novel in that it considered a system of behavior, such as dependency, in terms of its strength as a habit and as a drive. Accounting for the strength of a habit was not difficult. Dependency was assumed to be a set of habits that are reinforced by nurturant, attention-giving responses of others. The treatment of dependency drive was more unusual. Dependency acting as a drive or motivational system was assumed to develop from the frustration resulting from inconsistent reinforcement. The higher the drive, the greater is the child's tendency to make dependent responses. Several factors were postulated to influence this process. First, the stronger the dependency response becomes, the lower the likelihood that the environment will provide consistent reinforcement. Dependency as a drive is thereby increased. Second, strength of dependency is influenced by parental standards of conduct. Parents with high standards are less likely to reinforce all dependent acts, thereby again producing intermittent reinforcement, with its resulting frustration. A vicious cycle develops. By making dependent responses and receiving inconsistent reinforcement, the strength of the child's dependency drive, and hence the tendency to make further dependent responses, is increased. Other factors are considered, but the important thing for our purposes here is that dependency is considered to be a system of behavior that is learned and follows the general rules by which other systems of behavior are learned.

Many factors stood in the way of success for these ventures. The data were obtained from the analysis of anthropological reports made over periods differing greatly in time, and from parent interviews, observations, and miniature experiments. The reliability of the information, the interrelation of the various indices, and the interpretation of scalar values assigned to the variables were often unclear. The studies were provocative in their analytic approach, but disappointing in their outcomes. They have had little influence on later research. Nevertheless, the efforts to combine the conceptual analysis of psychoanalytic and behavioral approaches were novel attempts at syntheses that excited the imagination of many child psychologists and soon led to what became known as social learning.

Social Learning

Within the context of learning theories, the appearance of theories of *social* learning had a refreshing, immediate appeal, for they acknowledged important human attributes that had been ignored. Children are social creatures, constantly alert to the behavior of others. As parents and teachers know, but the behaviorists were slow to acknowledge, children learn a great deal—whether language, eating habits, or mischief—from observing what others say and do. Observation and imitation are not characteristics of the laboratory animals that psychologists had studied so extensively, and ethologists' studies of animals in natural settings had not yet been undertaken. Whereas it was easy to translate principles of discrimination learning derived from research with rat and monkey to the human child, it was much more difficult for psychologists to find parallels to many social phenomena in the behavior of lower animals. Instead of being able to translate principles directly, learning principles had to be modified and supplemented so they would be more suitable for discussions of children.

Contemporary social learning theory is frequently identified with the writings of Bandura (1977), but many others were important in its early (e.g., Miller & Dollard, 1941; Mowrer, 1950) and later development (e.g., Mischel, 1966). Rather than attempt a broad coverage, this discussion will be restricted to an outline of Bandura's position. Bandura attempts to weave three themes into the fabric of his theory: reinforcement, social processes, and cognition. A major departure from earlier positions is the importance given to vicarious processes. Observing the performance of another person and its consequences is considered to be sufficient for learn-

ing to occur. It is unnecessary for the child to perform a response or to receive personal reinforcement. This zero-trial, nonreinforced type of learning is given a central role in social learning theory.

A linear relation between stimulus-response-reinforcement is abandoned in favor of multidirectional influences between what children think and do and what environmental events precede and follow children's thoughts and actions. Thus, rather than depending primarily on external forces in shaping behavior, reliance is placed on a "continuous, reciprocal interaction between cognitive, behavioral, and environmental determinants" (1977, p. vii).

The concept of reinforcement is loosened so that it no longer is an object or event that strengthens preceding responses, but is a consequence of behavior that provides information and motivates the child to undertake certain actions. Anticipation of reinforcement plays an important role in determining what the child will learn, and informative feedback becomes rewarding only in relation to the performer's standards. The approach differs markedly, therefore, from theories that posit reinforcement of behaviors made in imitation of others as a primary mode of learning (e.g., Gewirtz & Stingle, 1968). What is retained or lost are not responses, but symbolic representations of what was observed. These representations are stored in part in the form of images or words. Cognitive representations! Images! Concepts that were inadmissible to psychological theories only a decade or two earlier were used without apology.

An integral component of social learning theories is modeling. Bandura (1971) appropriately suggests that conditioning and trial-and-error learning are insufficient approaches to learning in everyday life. What kinds of information and skills can be acquired through modeling? "It now seems clear," conclude Hetherington and McIntyre (1975, p. 113) in their review of modeling studies, "that under the right circumstances children will imitate almost anything." Examples run the gamut from facial expressions, commodity preferences, and aggression to moral judgments. Modeling is a broad concept, including verbal and symbolic modeling in addition to the modeling of behavior. With this conclusion one cannot argue. Children can learn from reading, watching television, and being told what to do and how to do it, as well as from observing other persons.

Perhaps the most notable departure from earlier positions is the emphasis given to the concepts of vicarious reward and punishment. Vicarious reinforcement implies that viewing the consequences of another person's behavior is sufficient for learning to occur. That some learning occurs in such situations is obvious. A child is likely to repeat a choice-response that has yielded reward for another child. However, the child must receive personal feedback about the accuracy and effectiveness of his or her efforts when other than simple responses are involved. Only through such feedback is it possible to make changes appropriate to reach a certain type or level of accomplishment. Whether or not some learning occurs independent of personal feedback is not the point. Without such information, proper learning of complicated skills is impossible.

Self-reinforcement is a concept that adds potential power, but it has a hollow ring. It is assumed that reinforcement does not need to be dispensed by someone else; individuals should be able to control their own behavior by providing reinforcement to themselves at appropriate times. Adults may use such tricks and devices to control their own behavior, but the ability to do this is something that is not readily evident during the period of childhood. Children feel pride, joy, and satisfaction in their accomplishments, but this is not what is meant by self-reinforcement. It is through self-reward that "individuals enhance and maintain their own behavior by rewarding themselves with rewards that they control whenever they attain self-prescribed standards" (Bandura, 1977, p. 130). The concept is clear, but is it valid for children? It is easy to demonstrate that children in the laboratory setting can learn to take a certain number of pieces of candy by viewing an adult model do this after making a "correct" response. It is much more difficult to find examples of self-reinforcement by children in everyday life.

The theory is in its early stages of development. It already has influenced learning theories in two powerful ways: first, in calling attention to the fact that learning can occur in many ways other than through performing an act; and, second, in reminding us that in discussing children we are not dealing with the counterpart of a caged rat, but with a sensitive social being. Many questions, however, remain unanswered or with only partial answers. We still have a lot to learn about the ways in which reinforcement operates. When does it have a positive effect and when does it act as a distractor and produce emotional behavior (Miller & Estes, 1961) or reduce motivation to engage in an activity (Lepper, Greene, & Nisbett, 1973)? How is attention directed to certain types of behavior and particular aspects of the environment and not to others? How is what is learned through observation demonstrated in everyday life? Children display but a small part of what

they have learned, and often what they do is not the same as what they have seen. For example, children demonstrate the ability to imitate various lexical items, but this does not necessarily facilitate their spontaneous use of these items (Leonard, Schwartz, Folger, Newhoff, & Wilcox, 1979), and after observing models, children may repeat, not what they hear, but what they already know (Vasta & Teitelbaum, 1976). These are interesting, exciting questions, but it is impossible to go much further in building a theory of social learning until some of them are answered.

CHILD BEHAVIOR AND DEVELOPMENT

Behavioral Analysis

Although B. F. Skinner's name is associated with programmed learning and teaching machines, both of which have been used as means of instructing children, he did nothing to adapt his theoretical position on operant conditioning to encompass variables that would be important in discussing children's behavior. Efforts to do this became the basis of a major project by Bijou and Baer. In 1961 they published the first of what was to be a series of volumes involving a Skinnerian analysis of child behavior and development. General characteristics of the position were described in the first volume (Bijou & Baer, 1961); and in a second volume it was applied to infant development (Bijou & Baer, 1965).

Key constructs were taken directly from Skinner's behavioral analysis. Behavior is described in terms of respondents and operants. The number of reinforcements, acquired reinforcement, schedules of reinforcement—all the variables of behavioral analysis are discussed. Developmental status is considered to influence what the child is able to do, but not to change underlying processes. Bijou and Baer insist that the "descriptive principles . . . can be applied to behavior in general—the behavior of young and old, human and animal, in isolated, social, and laboratory settings" (1961, p. 83).

The view they develop is perhaps the ultimate in reductionism. The child is "conceptualized as an interrelated cluster of responses and stimuli," and psychological development is "made up of progressive changes in the different ways of interacting with the environment" (1961, p. 25). What is presented is the emptiest of black boxes. There is no discussion of motives, thoughts, or feelings. These are considered to be artificial categories, whose ontogenesis, like that of all other psychological attributes, is generated from principles of operant and respondent behavior. The constraints imposed by the use of such a limited number of constructs apparently proved to be an obstacle, for their treatment of child development ended in infancy at the inception of language development.

A second major problem is one faced by all reinforcement theorists: What is meant by reinforcement? It is indeed unfortunate that the concept had its origins in animal psychology. There is a degree of simplicity in the stimuli that can be used as reinforcers with animals, but the entire world, both external and internal, may be the source of potential reinforcement for the human child. As Nuttin (1976, p. 248) has suggested, "almost anything can be either a reward or a punishment to human subjects, according to its motivational and cognitive context." Continuation of a response, disruption of a response, lack of response from another person, the presence of a social response, a change in stimulation, perpetuation of stimulation—all may function as reinforcers, depending upon the state and status of the individual.

Not only the types, but also the mechanism of reinforcement has been questioned. As was suggested earlier, cognitive interpretations have been proposed, ones in which consequences of response are regarded as sources of information. An example from social reinforcement will illustrate the argument. The effectiveness of social stimuli as reinforcers has been assumed to be enhanced by prior deprivation of social stimuli and reduced by prior satiation. Studies have demonstrated this relation (e.g., Gewirtz, 1969), thereby making it appear that social stimuli are subject to the kinds of manipulation possible with food, water, and other primary sources of reinforcement. Could it be, however, that the effect is not due to satiation, but to the failure of the child to comprehend the relation between behavior and reinforcement? Social reinforcement given during pretraining periods typically is delivered according to a random schedule, which may obscure the potential significance of such a relation. Perry and Garrow (1975) provide evidence for this cognitive interpretation. A high frequency of *random* reinforcement during a pretraining period was found to produce deterioration in later performance when social reinforcement occurred, while a high prior frequency of *contingent* reinforcement enhanced the effectiveness of subsequent positive comments. Verbal statements made systematically have meaning; otherwise, they are rapidly disregarded. It is likely, too, that the more frequently comments are made in an erratic manner, the more rapidly their superficiality and irrelevance will be perceived.

If we evaluate a theory in terms of its ability to generate new, testable ideas, we must conclude that Skinnerian behavioral analysis has run its course. There has been little, if any discernible change since Bijou and Baer published their second volume. The view was too limiting, and one suspects that the excessive confidence that was often generated in its adherents served to produce a rigidity in conceptualization that restricted its further development. In the history of psychology, it is possible that its major impact will prove to have been in applied settings.

Behavior Modification

Nowhere in psychology have principles of the laboratory been applied to practical problems with more vigor and zeal than in the area of behavior modification. We associate the names of such contemporary figures as Skinner, Bandura, Wolpe, Lovaas, and Meichenbaum with behavior modification and behavior therapy, but work in this area began many years ago. Mary Cover Jones (1924a,b) anticipated much of the later work on modeling in her early research on the elimination of children's fears. Similarly, the Mowrers (1938), in their discussion of childhood enuresis, were pioneers in using conditioning procedures to treat children's problems. Behavior modification has achieved its greatest popularity, however, during the past 15 years. At its best, it has had a healthy influence in showing how everyday behaviors may be changed by altering environmental events. At its worst, adherents of behavior modification have tended to be fixed in their beliefs and grandiose in their promises. Whatever one's evaluation, the vivid, often dramatic examples of success have led to its widespread adoption with children in institutions, hospitals, and schools.

Best known among the approaches to behavior modification is the reinforcement view of Skinner. In the hands of skilled clinicians this has proved to be a powerful tool. As with so many things that are obvious once demonstrated, Skinner and his advocates have shown with great clarity how the perpetuation and form of a response can be influenced by careful management of contingencies between responses and their outcomes. The basic ideas are not complicated. Change behavior in small steps, give immediate feedback, be consistent, set highly explicit goals, allow adequate rehearsal and practice. These are general, basic principles with which pedagogues and others charged with behavioral change would agree. What Skinner and his followers have done is formulate them in an explicit, systematic manner.

Despite its innovativeness, economy in relation to other forms of therapy, and apparent simplicity, Skinner's approach has not displaced other forms of behavior change, nor does it represent the only effort to use behavior principles in practical settings. Others have introduced cognitive, imagery, modeling, and aversive procedures. In a cognitive approach to behavior modification, (e.g., Meichenbaum, 1973), individuals are led, for example, to think positively, to engage in self-instruction, and to make positive statements about themselves. Attempts are sometimes made to reduce anxiety by asking children to imagine themselves in anxiety-provoking situations. Modeling procedures (e.g., Bandura, Grusec, & Menlove, 1967) involve placing a child in situations where the child can observe other children interacting positively and fearlessly with an object, say, a dog or a snake, or participating in an event, such as swimming or visiting the dentist—objects and events the child has tended to avoid or fear. Aversive therapy has been introduced with children when all other approaches have failed. For example, through the use of electric shock, certain forms of social behavior have been developed in autistic children (Lovaas, Schaeffer, & Simmons, 1966) and self-mutilation by children has been decreased (Lovaas, Freitag, Gold, & Kassorla, 1965).

The confidence of behavior modifiers sometimes rivals that of Watson. For example, the authors of a recent book on behavior therapy suggest that the "availability of a sophisticated technology of learning and behavior change now enables teachers and administrators to design a system to produce just about any kind of person they want" (Lanyon & Lanyon, 1978, p. 128). It is doubtful that many persons, other than loyal adherents to the system, would be quite so confident that the technology is so highly advanced. The challenge is often made that behavior modification produces superficial changes in behavior that are readily reversible, fails to consider many important variables such as motivation and emotional state, and persists in maintaining a causal model of stimulus and response in which factors such as the child's prior history are omitted. If more time were spent in active investigation of the phenomena, behavior modifiers would be in a better position to respond to these and other criticisms.

London (1972) concludes his discussion of behavior modification with a similar point: "We have gotten as much mileage as we are going to out of old principles, even correct ones, but we have barely begun to work the new technology" (p. 919).

Teaching Machines

A second application of learning theory was in the instruction of children in school. Again, it was Skinner and his followers who led the way by introducing the modern teaching machine and programmed instruction. Materials programmed for use in a teaching machine have many advantages. Children can proceed at their own speeds, obtain immediate feedback, and experience success in each of their efforts. Possibilities expanded rapidly with the advent of modern electronic computers, which permitted the construction of programs of incomparably greater sophistication and flexibility than could be obtained with mechanical teaching machines. A technology of computer-assisted instruction began to be developed, and well-known programs in reading, mathematics, logic, and foreign languages were devised (e.g., Atkinson, 1968).

Computer-assisted instruction has never had the popularity that was envisioned in its early days. Perhaps it was because of the expense in purchasing computers, or because teachers trained in older teaching techniques resisted the introduction of computer terminals in the classroom. Nevertheless, the approach has been successful and interest remains high (Bunderson & Faust, 1976). Large computer companies have established their own learning centers, offering assistance to children who experience problems in their schoolwork, and extra opportunities to those who find their schoolwork insufficiently challenging. The prospects for widespread application of computer-assisted instruction increase as the price of small computers declines year after year.

Skinnerians were productive stimulants in this field. What followed in innovative approaches to instruction, however, was much more closely linked with other areas in psychology, such as mathematical learning theory and cognitive psychology. Skinner and other learning theorists have had little further impact on instructional psychology. Rather, contemporary instructional psychology is "largely cognitive; it is concerned with internal mental processes and how their development may be enhanced through instruction" (Resnick, 1981, p. 660).

Developmental Changes in Children

Many of the treatments of children's learning failed to consider developmental changes. Arguments were raised, as we have seen, that the same basic concepts and processes apply to individuals of all ages. Others argued for simple two-stage theories. Both arguments stand in striking contrast to the theoretical treatments of developmental phenomena proposed by cognitive theorists such as Piaget, who found it necessary to posit a complex set of stages to account for cognitive development.

It is evident that learning does change as the child grows older. There are changes in the speed, precision, and generality with which learning occurs. Processes change, too, such as selective attention (e.g., Vurpillot, 1976), development and use of strategies (e.g., Paris, 1978), and self-monitoring of performance (e.g., Flavell & Wellman, 1977). These are important changes, and there are others to which White (1965) directed our attention a number of years ago.

White reviewed changes that had been found between the ages of 5 and 7 years, an interesting period and the one about which we have the most abundant data. White's list included increases in the influence of verbal processes, resistance to conditioning, maintenance of orientation toward invariant dimensions of stimuli in different contexts, growth of inference from past events, and ability to plan ahead for future action. His attempt to account for these and many other changes during this period by proposing two mechanisms of learning, an associative one before 5 and a cognitive one after 7, seems unsatisfactory today, but there are no current efforts to provide a more satisfactory integration.

Other periods in the child's development are also likely to be important as periods of transition. We know little about them, however, because they have been so infrequently studied. Why, then, have satisfactory models for developmental changes in learning not been introduced? Primarily, I believe, because we do not have sufficient information across a wide enough span of ages to know the facts that must be accounted for by such models.

Decline of Experimental Studies

By 1970, experimental child psychology had established itself as an important component of developmental psychology, and prominent among the experimental studies were those dealing with children's learning. Its influence was felt in many ways. For example, 51% of the manuscripts submitted to *Developmental Psychology* in 1968–1969 reported

the results of experimental studies, and 39% were studies of learning and reinforcement effects (McCandless, 1970). Between 1968 and 1973, 8% of the 2,000 submissions were studies of discrimination learning—the fourth highest of all categories—and an additional 6% dealt with memory and verbal learning. Thus, nearly 300 articles on children's learning were submitted during this period to this journal alone. However, a trend of fewer submissions of studies dealing with learning became evident a few years later. Of the submissions to *Child Development* in 1973, only 26% were studies of learning and reinforcement, a one-third decline in only four years (Jeffrey, 1975).

No one would have predicted that within the next several years research on children's learning would have come to a near standstill. The year 1979 was designated as the International Year of the Child, and to celebrate this event a special issue of the *American Psychologist* was published. In the issue, titled "Psychology and children: Current research and practice," brief articles described the current status of major areas of developmental psychology. There was no article devoted to children's learning. In fact, only in a discussion of reading instruction was any mention made of learning at all.

Journals publishing research in child psychology were nearly as barren. Through diligent search, examples could be found of studies of infant conditioning (Stamps & Porges, 1975), operant conditioning (Bloom, 1977; Majorski & Clement, 1977), discrimination learning (Gholson & O'Connor, 1975; Spiker & Cantor, 1977), learning set (Fagen, 1977; Haaf & Smith, 1976), oddity learning (Scott & House, 1978), and imitation and modeling (Ironsmith & Whitehurst, 1978; Oliver, Acker, & Oliver, 1977). For the most part, these and other studies were devoted to tying up loose ends in classical problems rather than to launching new approaches.

A change in paradigms ran throughout all psychology. The human being was no longer looked at as a learner, but as a thinker. Cognitive psychology was in ascendance and learning psychology was in decline. Mind and consciousness reasserted themselves after a forced dormancy of half a century. In addition to the causes of the revolution taking place in general psychology, there were special reasons why child psychologists saw the cognitive approach as an exciting alternative.

First, there were brilliant, charismatic figures such as Piaget and Vygotsky, whose theoretical work had only recently become widely known. Although the careers of both had begun long before, and indeed Vygotsky had died in 1934, the full de-

velopment of their theoretical views had not occurred until much later. These theories had important advantages. Their development occurred within
the field of child psychology and they were based on
the study of children. The earlier trend found in children's learning was reversed; these were not theories
imported and transplanted from work done with
lower animals and college sophomores. As a consequence, the phenomena with which the theories
dealt seemed to be more directly related to children's
lives than did much of learning research. The behaviorists, intent upon studying forms of behavior that
would yield to objective, scientific analysis, had
often used tasks with children that appeared to be
artificial and even trivial. Piaget, Vygotsky, and the
new cognitive psychologists had attempted to devise
tasks for children that would be especially challenging and interesting.

A second reason for the decline in learning studies is that the theories had promised too much and led
to expectations that could not be fulfilled. Child psychology was especially vulnerable, for there always
has been a strong temptation among child psychologists to put current theories into practice in response to the demands of teachers and parents for
ideas about how to educate and rear children. While
few psychologists expected that problems in such
areas as psychopathology and personality development would be readily unraveled, it seemed more
reasonable that learning would be amenable to rapid
analysis. However, flaws in even the fundamental
constructs became apparent. When child psychologists began investigating conditioning, it proved
not to provide the building blocks through which
later behavior could be constructed. Efforts at conditioning were often unsuccessful, and simple distinctions, such as the one between classical and instrumental conditioning turned out to be spurious.
Hearst (1975, p. 218) was led to conclude, for example, that "the tenacity of the classical-instrumental
distinction is as much based on deeply ingrained
philosophical and cultural beliefs as on research and
theory in psychology." Nor did the effort to understand the beginnings of behavior through studying
infants prove to be as simple as had been hoped. This
seemingly simplest of human beings would not yield
to analysis in terms of conditioned response.
Sameroff (1972, p. 170), in his review of infant
learning and adaptation, began with the warning:
"No process found in the young infant has lent itself
to easy explanation. Infant behavior has been found
to be as difficult to study and comprehend as adult
behavior and researchers have been consistently perplexed at making sense of these complexities."

Thus, the combination of disappointment with the
possibility of understanding behavior through the
traditional learning approach, and the refreshing, attractive views of the cognitive psychologists did
much to hasten the transformation of research in
child psychology.

PRESENT TRENDS

In a period of change such as we are now experiencing, it is easy to be pessimistic and to demean
what has been accomplished. This would be a tragic
mistake. It is important to realize that it is *theories*
that have been susceptible to attack, not the *data*
about children's learning. An important aspect of the
behaviorist movement was its emphasis on explicit-
ness in experimental design and interpretation of
data. This emphasis proved to be instrumental in its
own demise. The overthrow of the stimulus-response approach came not only because interesting
alternatives appeared but also because child psychologists discovered solid information that exposed—in glaring fashion—the basic weaknesses of
the propositions that were being tested. Paradoxically, it appears that the enduring contributions of
the laboratory-based, experimentally oriented stimulus-response psychologists are methodological,
rather than theoretical. Sophisticated in experimental design, statistical analysis, and philosophy of science, these psychologists produced methods that
were so powerful and capable of producing clear
results that their theories crumbled as much in the
face of the evidence they produced themselves as
from the criticisms of opposing theorists.

It was more comfortable to write about children's
learning a decade ago (Stevenson, 1970) than it is
now. But the comfort was based in part on ignorance. We have learned a great deal about variables
that influence children's learning. We have less information than we need, but enough to recognize the
inadequacies of the older theories. Oversimplifica-
tions within the theories proved to be excessive; we
look now to approaches that are more palatable.

There are reasons to believe that the current lull
in interest is temporary. Problems do not vanish.
Cognitive theorists have attempted to construct rules
by which cognitive structures operate at particular
periods in the child's life, but they have been deficient in attempting to describe how such structures
and operations are learned. For example, Inhelder,
Sinclair, and Bovet (1974), three of Piaget's most
productive collaborators, approach these problems
in their book, *Learning and the development of cog-*

nition. Among what they consider to be the unsolved problems in understanding cognitive development is that of learning: "The findings of developmental psychology have shown the existence of a succession of stages in cognitive development, but little is as yet known about the mechanisms of transition from one major stage to the next and about the passage between two successive substages" (p. 14). Neither their work nor that of others has shown more than that cognitive structures can be learned through experience. The ingredients of the experience and their manner of operation are not well understood.

Any theory of child development must account for the role of learning and its complex interactions with biological maturation. It seems likely that, released from the constraints in subject matter and procedures that characterized many of their earlier studies, learning psychologists will once again make important contributions. Perhaps we are nearing a time of rapprochement, when cognitive psychologists and learning psychologists will tackle some of the same complicated questions about the acquisition of concepts. Beginnings are evident in the publication of *Cognitive learning in children* (Levin & Allen, 1976), the work of Fowler (1980) on cognitive differentiation and developmental learning, and in Gagne's (1970) efforts to develop a model that posits a hierarchy of learning processes ranging from signal and stimulus-response learning to rule learning and problem solving. Fischer (1980) has discussed the structures of skills that emerge in cognitive development and transformation rules relating these structures to each other. These and several other developments lead one to be optimistic.

The trend toward studying learning in practical settings or in relation to practical problems should have very positive influences. There is a strong current interest in reading, mathematics, and science instruction, and useful advances have been made in understanding the cognitive operations necessary in such domains. However, instructing children also requires an understanding of how these cognitive operations are acquired. Theories of instruction can, in the end, be no more successful than our theories of learning. There also have been applications of traditional learning tasks to practical problems. For example, selective attention has been studied in children with learning disabilities (Pelham, 1979; Tarver, Hallahan, Kauffman, & Ball, 1976), and training programs in self-monitoring strategies have been constructed in an effort to improve the performance of educable, retarded children (Brown, Campione, & Murphy, 1977). Important insights should come from these types of research, for they avoid the problems of artificiality that plagued some of the previous studies of children's learning.

Another important development is achieved in overcoming earlier tendencies to attribute excessive simplicity to the infant and young child. These tendencies had led to several unfortunate consequences. When the model of the child is one that defines behavioral development as proceeding from simple to complex, there is a temptation to describe young children in terms of deficiencies. We tend to emphasize what is lacking, instead of what is present. A different view of development assumes that it is not the degree of complexity that differentiates children of different ages, but the conditions necessary to produce particular kinds of behavior. For example, it was hypothesized that young children do not demonstrate transfer of learning from one context to another because they fail to use verbal mediation. An alternative hypothesis is that young children require different kinds of experience than do older children in order to show such transfer. Learning theorists were willing to talk about a mediational deficiency rather than to attempt to analyse conditions, such as the use of multiple examples, that would enable young children to perform successfully.

Perhaps the most stunning set of discoveries in child psychology during recent years has been the revelation of the remarkable accomplishments of which infants and young children are capable. These accomplishments are not immediately evident, and turn out to be in conflict with predictions from theories such as Piaget's, in which performance is defined by cognitive stages. Preschool children can show transitive inference, class inclusion, conservation, and many more of the operations characterizing later cognitive stages—if they are trained and tested in certain manners (Gelman, 1978). When we know that young children fail transitive inference problems because they fail to remember the components of the problems rather than because they cannot make inferences (Bryant & Trabasso, 1971), and when we realize that young children's failure to solve class inclusion problems is due to a reluctance to count objects more than once rather than to an inability to hold more than one classification in mind at a time (Wilkinson, 1976), we gain important new ideas about how to create optimal conditions for learning. Trying to define these training and testing conditions is a much more positive approach than assuming that performance is impossible because the child is at a certain stage of cognitive development. Studies such as these will yield important information that can be used, not for trying to hasten cognitive development, but for providing more enlightened environments for children's learning.

As is evident from the previous pages, we are far from having a learning theory of development. We have some idea about how changes in knowledge and skills come about through learning, but we do not know how these kinds of change influence the long-term accomplishments that constitute development. Many years ago Vygotsky defined the problem: "learning is not development; however, properly organized learning results in mental development and sets in motion a variety of developmental processes that would be impossible apart from learning" (Vygotsky, 1978, p. 90).

Our task is to begin trying to understand how to go about organizing learning in the proper fashion. A new vision of the human child is emerging and, as is evident in this chapter, boundaries for theoretical developments are beginning to appear. Understanding children's learning is an incredibly complex problem, surely one of the most profound faced by science.

REFERENCES

Ash, M. J. The relation between discrimination shift performance and three related tasks: Some parameters of the Kendler model of the optional shift behavior. *Child Development*, 1975, *46*, 408–415.

Atkinson, R. C. Computerized instruction and the learning process. *American Psychologist*, 1968, *23*, 225–239.

Bandura, A. (Ed.). *Psychological modeling: Conflicting theories*. New York: Aldine, 1971.

Bandura, A. *Social learning theory*. Englewood Cliffs, N.J.: Prentice-Hall, 1977.

Bandura, A., Grusec, J. E., & Menlove, F. L. Vicarious extinction of avoidance behavior. *Journal of Personality and Social Psychology*, 1967, *5*, 16–23.

Bijou, S. W., & Baer, D. M. *Child development* (Vol. 1: *A systematic and empirical theory*). New York: Appleton-Century-Crofts, 1961.

Bijou, S. W., & Baer, D. M. *Child development* (Vol. 2: *Universal stage of infancy*). New York: Appleton-Century-Crofts, 1965.

Bloom, K. Operant baseline procedures suppress infant social behavior. *Journal of Experimental Child Psychology*, 1977, *23*, 128–132.

Bolles, R. C. Learning, motivation, and cognition. In W. K. Estes (Ed.), *Handbook of learning and cognitive processes* (Vol. 1). Hillsdale, N.J.: Erlbaum, 1975.

Boring, E. G. *A history of experimental psychology* (2nd ed.). New York: Appleton-Century-Crofts, 1950.

Brown, A. L., Campione, J. C., & Murphy, M. D. Maintenance and generalization of trained meta-mnemonic awareness in educable retarded children. *Journal of Experimental Child Psychology*, 1977, *24*, 191–211.

Bryant, P. E., & Trabasso, T. Transitive inference and memory in young children. *Nature*, 1971, *232*, 456–458.

Bunderson, C. V., & Faust, G. W. Programmed and computer assisted instruction. In N. L. Gage (Ed.), *The psychology of teaching methods. The seventy-fifth yearbook of the National Society for the Study of Education*. Chicago: University of Chicago Press, 1976.

Caron, A. J. Conceptual transfer in preverbal children as a consequence of dimensional training. *Journal of Experimental Child Psychology*, 1968, *6*, 522–542.

Chomsky, N. Review of Skinner's *Verbal behavior*. *Language*, 1959, *35*, 26–58.

Cohen, D. B. *J. B. Watson: The founder of behaviorism*. London: Routledge & Kegan Paul, 1979.

Dollard, J., Doob, L. W., Miller, N. E., & Sears, R. R. *Frustration and aggression*. New Haven: Yale University Press, 1939.

Fagen, J. W. Interproblem learning in ten-month-old infants. *Child Development*, 1977, *48*, 786–796.

Fischer, K. W. A theory of cognitive development: The control and construction of hierarchies of skills. *Psychological Review*, 1980, *87*, 477–531.

Flavell, J. H. *The developmental psychology of Jean Piaget*. Princeton, N.J.: Van Nostrand, 1963.

Flavell, J. H., Beach, D. R., & Chinsky, J. M. Spontaneous verbal rehearsal in a memory task as a function of age. *Child Development*, 1966, *37*, 283–299.

Flavell, J. H., & Wellman, H. M. Metamemory. In R. V. Kail and J. W. Hagen (Eds.), *Perspectives in the development of memory and cognition*. Hillsdale, N. J.: Erlbaum, 1977.

Fowler, W. Cognitive differentiation and developmental learning. In H. W. Reese & L. P. Lipsitt (Eds.), *Advances in child development and behavior* (Vol. 15). New York: Academic Press, 1980.

Gagne, R. *The conditions of learning* (Rev. Ed.). New York: Holt, Rinehart and Winston, 1970.

Gelman, R. Cognitive development. In M. R. Rosenzweig and L. N. Porter (Eds.), *Annual re-*

view of psychology (Vol. 29). Palo Alto, Calif.: Annual Reviews, 1978.

Gesell, A. Maturation and the patterning of behavior. In C. Murchison (Ed.), *A handbook of child psychology* (2nd ed.). Worcester, Mass.: Clark University Press, 1933.

Gewirtz, J. L. Potency of a social reinforcer as a function of satiation and recovery. *Developmental Psychology, 1,* 1969, 2–13.

Gewirtz, J. L., & Stingle, K. G. Learning of generalized imitation as the basis for identification. *Psychological Review,* 1968, *75,* 374–397.

Gholson, B., & O'Connor, B. Dimensional control of hypothesis sampling during three-choice discrimination learning. *Child Development,* 1976, *46,* 894–903.

Gibson, E. J. *Principles of perceptual learning and development.* New York: Appleton-Century-Crofts, 1969.

Gibson, E. J., & Gibson, J. J. Perceptual learning: Differentiation or enrichment? *Psychological Review,* 1955, *62,* 32–42.

Gibson, E. J., & Levin, H. *The psychology of reading.* Cambridge, Mass.: MIT Press, 1975.

Greeno, J. G. Psychology of learning, 1960–1980. One participant's observations. *American Psychologist,* 1980, *35,* 713–728.

Haaf, R. A., & Smith, J. A. Developmental differences in reinforcer preference value and in learning-set performance under inconsistent reward. *Child Development,* 1976, *47,* 375–379.

Harris, B. Whatever happened to little Albert? *American Psychologist,* 1979, *34,* 151–160.

Harris, B. John B. Watson as film producer and developmental psychologist. Paper presented at the meeting of the American Psychological Association, Montreal, September 1980.

Hartup, W. W., & Yonas, A. Developmental psychology. In P. H. Mussen & M. R. Rosenzweig (Eds.), *Annual Review of Psychology* (Vol. 22). Palo Alto, Calif.: Annual Reviews, 1971.

Hayes, K. J., Thompson, R., & Hayes, C. Discrimination learning in chimpanzees. *Journal of Comparative and Physiological Psychology,* 1953, *46,* 99–104.

Hearst, E. The classical-instrumental distinction: Reflexes, voluntary behavior, and categories of associative learning. In W. K. Estes (Ed.), *Handbook of learning and cognitive processes* (Vol. 2). Hillsdale, N.J.: Erlbaum, 1975.

Heidbreder, E. *Seven psychologies.* New York: Century, 1933.

Hetherington, E. M., & McIntyre, C. W. Developmental psychology. In M. R. Rosenzweig and L. W. Porter (Eds.), *Annual Review of Psychology.*

Palo Alto, Calif.: Annual Reviews, 1975.

Hilgard, E. R., & Bower, G. H. *Theories of learning* (4th ed.). Englewood Cliffs, N.J.: Prentice-Hall, 1975.

Hull, C. L. Quantitative aspects of the evolution of concepts. *Psychological Monographs,* 1920, *28,* No. 123.

Inhelder, B., Sinclair, H., & Bovet, M. *Learning and the development of cognition.* Cambridge, Mass.: Harvard University Press, 1974.

Ironsmith, M., & Whitehurst, G. J. How children learn to listen: The effects of modeling feedback styles on children's performance in referential communication. *Developmental Psychology,* 1978, *14,* 546–554.

Jeffrey, W. E. Editorial. *Child Development,* 1975, *46,* 1–2.

Jones, H. E., & Batalla, M. Transfer in children's maze learning. *Journal of Educational Psychology,* 1944, *35,* 474–484.

Jones, M. C. The elimination of children's fears. *Journal of Experimental Psychology,* 1924, *7,* 382–390. (a)

Jones, M. C. A laboratory study of fear: The case of Peter. *Pedagogical Seminary,* 1924, *31,* 308–315. (b)

Kagan, J. *The growth of the child. Reflections on human development.* New York: Norton, 1978.

Kendler, H. H., & Guenther, K. Developmental changes in classificatory behavior. *Child Development,* 1980, *51,* 339–348.

Kendler, H. H., & Kendler, T. S. Vertical and horizontal processes in problem solving. *Psychological Review,* 1962, *69,* 1–16.

Kendler, H. H., & Kendler, T. S. From discrimination learning to cognitive development: A neobehavioristic odyssey. In W. K. Estes (Ed.), *Handbook of learning and cognitive processes* (Vol. 1). Hillsdale, N.J.: Erlbaum, 1975.

Kendler, T. S. Development of mediating responses in children. In J. C. Wright & J. Kagan (Eds.), *Basic cognitive processes in children. Monographs of the Society for Research in Child Development,* 1963, *28,* Whole No. 2.

Kendler, T. S. Verbalization and optional reversal shifts among kindergarten children. *Journal of Verbal Learning and Verbal Behavior,* 1964, *3,* 428–436.

Kuenne, M. R. Experimental investigations of the relation of language to transposition behavior in young children. *Journal of Experimental Psychology,* 1946, *36,* 471–490.

Lambert, W. M., & Lambert, E. C. Some indirect effects of reward on children's size estimations. *Journal of Abnormal and Social Psychology,*

1953, *48*, 507–510.

Lambert, W. W., Solomon, R. L., & Watson, P. D. Reinforcement and extinction as factors in size estimation. *Journal of Experimental Psychology*, 1949, *39*, 637–641.

Lanyon, R. I., & Lanyon, B. P. *Behavior therapy. A clinical introduction.* Menlo Park, Calif.: Addison-Wesley, 1978.

Leonard, L. L., Schwartz, R. G., Folger, M. K., Newhoff, N., & Wilcox, M. J. Children's imitation of lexical items. *Child Development*, 1979, *50*, 19–27.

Lepper, M. R., Greene, D., & Nisbett, R. Undermining children's intrinsic interest with extrinsic rewards: A test of the 'overjustification' hypothesis. *Journal of Personality and Social Psychology*, 1973, *28*, 129–137.

Levin, J. R., & Allen, V. L. *Cognitive learning in children. Theories and strategies.* New York: Academic Press, 1976.

London, P. The end of ideology in behavior modification. *American Psychologist*, 1972, *27*, 913–920.

Lovaas, O. I., Freitag, G., Gold, V. J., & Kassorla, I. C. Experimental studies in childhood schizophrenia: Analyses of self-destructive behavior. *Journal of Experimental Child Psychology*, 1965, *2*, 67–84.

Lovaas, O. I., Schaeffer, B., & Simmons, J. A. Experimental studies in childhood schizophrenia: Building social behavior in autistic children by use of electric shock. *Journal of Experimental Research in Personality*, 1966, *1*, 99–109.

Luria, A. R. *Speech and development of mental processes in children.* London: Staples, 1959.

Majorski, L. V., & Clement, P. W. Children's lever-pulling rates under variable interval percentage schedules. *Journal of Experimental Child Psychology*, 1977, *23*, 212–225.

McCandless, B. R. Editorial. *Developmental Psychology*, 1970, *2*, 1–4.

Meichenbaum, D. Cognitive factors in behavior modification: Modifying what clients say to themselves. In C. M. Franks and G. T. Wilson (Eds.), *Annual review of behavior therapy theory and practice* (Vol. 1). New York: Brunner/Mazel, 1973.

Miller, L. B., & Estes, B. W. Monetary reward and motivation in discrimination learning. *Journal of Experimental Psychology*, 1961, *61*, 501–504.

Miller, N. E., & Dollard, J. *Social learning and imitation.* New Haven: Yale University Press, 1941.

Mischel, W. A social learning view of sex differences in behavior. In E. E. Maccoby (Ed.), *The development of sex differences.* Stanford, Calif.: Stanford University Press, 1966.

Mowrer, O. H. *Learning theory and personality dynamics.* New York: Ronald, 1950.

Mowrer, O. H., & Mowrer, W. N. Enuresis: A method for its study and treatment. *American Journal of Orthopsychiatry*, 1938, *8*, 436–459.

Munn, N. Learning in children. In L. Carmichael (Ed.), *Manual of child psychology* (2nd ed.). New York: Wiley, 1954.

Nuttin, J. R. Motivation and reward in human learning: A cognitive approach. In W. K. Estes (Ed.), *Handbook of learning and cognitive processes* (Vol. 3). Hillsdale, N.J.: Erlbaum, 1976.

Oliver, P. R., Acker, L. E., & Oliver, D. O. Effects of nonreinforcement histories of compliance and noncompliance on nonreinforced imitation. *Journal of Experimental Child Psychology*, 1977, *23*, 180–190.

Paris, S. G. The development of inference and transformation as necessary operations. In P. A. Ornstein (Ed.), *Memory development in children.* Hillsdale, N.J.: Erlbaum, 1978.

Pelham, W. E. Selective attention deficits in poor readers. Dichotic listening, speeded classification, and auditory and visual central and incidental learning tasks. *Child Development*, 1979, *50*, 1050–1061.

Perry, D. J., & Garrow, H. The "social deprivation-satiation" effect: An outcome of frequency or perceived contingency? *Developmental Psychology*, 1975, *11*, 681–688.

Peterson, J. Learning in children. In C. Murchison (Ed.), *A handbook of child psychology* (2nd ed.). Worcester, Mass.: Clark University Press, 1933.

Reese, H. W. Verbal mediation as a function of age level. *Psychological Bulletin*, 1962, *59*, 502–509.

Resnick, L. B. Instructional psychology. In M. R. Rosenzweig and L. W. Porter (Eds.), *Annual review of psychology* (Vol. 32). Palo Alto, Calif., 1981.

Samelson, F. J. B. Watson's little Albert, Cyril Burt's twins, and the need for critical science. *American Psychologist*, 1980, *35*, 619–625.

Sameroff, A. J. Learning and adaptation in infancy: A comparison of models. In H. W. Reese (Ed.), *Advances in child development and behavior* (Vol. 7). New York: Academic Press, 1972.

Scott, M. S., & House, B. J. Repetition of cues in children's oddity learning and transfer. *Journal of Experimental Child Psychology*, 1978, *25*, 58–70.

Sears, R. R., Maccoby, E. E., & Levin, H. *Patterns*

of child rearing. Evanston, Ill.: Row-Peterson, 1957.

Sears, R. R., Rau, L., & Alpert, R. *Identification and child rearing*. Stanford: Stanford University Press, 1965.

Skinner, B. F. *The behavior of organisms: An experimental analysis*. New York: Appleton-Century-Crofts, 1938.

Skinner, B. F. *Contingencies of reinforcement*. New York: Appleton-Century-Crofts, 1969.

Skinner, B. F. Selection by consequences. Paper presented at the meeting of the American Psychological Association, Montreal, August 1980.

Smiley, S. S., & Weir, M. W. Role of dimensional dominance in reversal and nonreversal shift behavior. *Journal of Experimental Child Psychology*, 1966, *4*, 296–307.

Sobel, B. A study of the development of insight in preschool children. *Journal of Genetic Psychology*, 1939, *55*, 381–388.

Spelt, D. K. The conditioning of the human fetus in utero. *Journal of Experimental Psychology*. 1948, *38*, 338–346.

Spence, K. W. The differential response in animals to stimuli varying within a single dimension. *Psychological Review*, 1937, *44*, 430–444.

Spiker, C. C., & Cantor, J. H. Introtacts as predictors of discrimination learning performance in kindergarten children. *Journal of Experimental Child Psychology*, 1977, *23*, 520–538.

Stamps, L. E., & Porges, S. W. Heartrate conditioning in newborn infants: Relationships among conditionability, heart rate variability, and sex. *Developmental Psychology*, 1975, *4*, 424–431.

Stevenson, H. W. Children's learning. In P. H. Mussen (Ed.), *Manual of child psychology* (3rd ed.). New York: Wiley, 1970.

Tarver, S. E., Hallahan, D. P., Kauffman, J. M., & Ball, D. W. Verbal rehearsal and selective attention in children with learning disabilities: A developmental lag. *Journal of Experimental Child Psychology*, 1976, *22*, 375–385.

Thom, D. A. *Everyday problems of the everyday child*. New York: Appleton, 1928.

Thorndike, E. L. Animal intelligence: An experimental study of the associative processes in animals. *Psychological Review Monograph Supplements*, 1898, *2*, No. 8.

Thorndike, E. L. *Educational psychology, briefer course*. New York: Teacher's College, Columbia University, 1924.

Thorndike, E. L. *Human learning*. New York: Century, 1931.

Thorndike, E. L. *Selected writings from a connec-

tionist's psychology*. New York: Appleton-Century-Crofts, 1949.

Tighe, L. S., & Tighe, T. J. Discrimination learning: Two views in historical perspective. *Psychological Bulletin*, 1966, *66*, 353–370.

Tighe, L. S., & Tighe, T. J. Transfer from perceptual pretraining as a function of number of stimulus values per dimension. *Psychonomic Science*, 1968, *12*, 135–136.

Vasta, R., & Teitelbaum, M. Reception training effects in the production of modeled language construction. *Journal of Experimental Child Psychology*, 1976, *22*, 67–72.

Vurpillot, E. *The visual world of the child*. London: George Allen and Unwin, 1976.

Vygotsky, L. *Thought and language*. Cambridge, Mass.: MIT Press, 1962.

Vygotsky, L. S. *Mind in society. The development of higher psychological processes*. Cambridge, Mass.: Harvard University Press, 1978.

Watson, J. B. *Psychological care of infant and child*. New York: Norton, 1928.

Watson, J. B. In C. Murchison (Ed.), *A history of psychology in autobiography* (Vol. 3). Worcester, Mass.: Clark University Press, 1936.

Watson, J. B., & Rayner, R. Conditioned emotional reactions. *Journal of Experimental Psychology*, 1920, *3*, 1–4.

White, S. H. Evidence for a hierarchical arrangement of learning processes. In L. P. Lipsitt and C. C. Spiker (Eds.), *Advances in Child Development and Behavior* (Vol. 2). New York: Academic Press, 1965.

Whiting, J. W. M., & Child, I. L. *Child training and personality: A cross-cultural study*. New Haven: Yale University Press, 1953.

Wickens, D., & Wickens, C. A study of conditioning in the neonate. *Journal of Experimental Psychology*, 1940, *26*, 94–102.

Wilkinson, A. Counting strategies and semantic analyses applied to class inclusion. *Cognitive Psychology*, 1976, *8*, 64–85.

Wingfield, R. C. A study in alternation using children in a two-way maze. *Journal of Comparative Psychology*, 1938, *25*, 439–443.

Wooley, H. T. Eating, sleeping, and elimination. In C. Murchison (Ed.), *A handbook of child psychology*. Worcester, Mass.: Clark University Press, 1931.

Zeaman, D., & House, B. J. The role of attention in retardate discrimination learning. In N. R. Ellis (Ed.), *Handbook of mental deficiency*. New York: McGraw-Hill, 1963.

DEVELOPMENTAL SYSTEMS: CONTEXTS AND EVOLUTION* | 6

ARNOLD J. SAMEROFF, *Institute for the Study of Developmental Disabilities and Department of Psychology—University of Illinois at Chicago*

CHAPTER CONTENTS

Since the beginning of attempts to explain the process of development, individual growth has been seen as an organized system. The Greeks saw the transformations in growth as a movement from the imperfect to the ideal; the forms of maturity were implicit in the beginnings of life. Literally interpreted, development has meant an unfolding process; the analogy usually given in dictionaries is to the "development" of exposed photographic film in which some latent image is revealed.

The sequence of changes from an exposed piece of film to a fully defined image is not really transformation at all because the image was there all the time. In behavioral development this position is most explicitly stated by Gesell and his associates

*The author wishes to thank William Kessen, Ronald Seifer, David Lewkowicz, and Martin Stanford for their help in the clarification of the ideas presented in this chapter, and Patricia Lawrence and Helen Brown for translating abstractions and chicken-scratches into a readable typescript.

(Gesell & Amatruda, 1945). The changes seen in behavior are interpreted as an orderly unfolding in a predetermined sequence. Individual differences can be explained by differences in the timing of universally human characteristics. But what of children who do not go through the universal human sequence of behavior and still emerge as competent human adults? What of those individuals with deafness, blindness, or other severe developmental disabilities that should keep them from the possibility of normal outcomes but sometimes do not?

The case of Helen Keller is probably the most telling counterpoint to the maturational view (Keller, 1904). The story of this deaf-blind woman highlights the need for a comprehensive model of development that incorporates the maturational blueprint as only one element in the equation for growth. How a handicapped and retarded child became a brilliant adult might be thought to have clearly demonstrated the powerful influence of environment on human development. The ability of environmental intervention to change the course of development for many children thought to be certain candidates for a life of institutionalization has been well documented (Clarke & Clarke, 1976). Despite this documentation there still is a major reluctance on the part of society to accept environmental intervention as a natural part of the educational system (Sarason & Doris, 1979). Despite the compelling example of Helen Keller as early as the turn of the century, it took 50 years for the next deaf-blind person to graduate from college, and there have been very few others since then (Blatt, 1981).

The reluctance that can be interpreted as social irresponsibility does have a scientific rationale. Although there appears to be strong evidence that environmental manipulation has powerful effects on developmental outcome, there are alternative explanation for the same results based on maturational views (Mendelsohn, 1980). The reduction of the intellectual behavior of individuals (Jensen, 1980), and even the social behavior of groups (Wilson, 1975), to the organization of inherited genes is a major part of the current debates in developmental psychology. The striking point that the same facts can give rise to quite different theoretical interpretations will serve as a prologue to the discussions of development to follow.

Organization has been an implicit characteristic of the developmental process from the first usages of the term, but the nature of that order has been debated explicitly only in recent times. This chapter will be devoted to a presentation of our current understanding of the sources, the course, and the future of human development. What must be examined is the uniqueness of the principles of explanation necessary for such an enterprise. Are the principles of human psychological development similar to the principles of development of life in general? This question must be further broken down between principles that apply to the human individual and those that apply to the development of the human species. Do the ontogenetic processes that move the individual from the fertilized egg to the socialized adult in some way correspond to the phylogenetic processes that moved the species from the macromolecules of the primordial sea to contemporary human civilization?

A number of areas of development must be examined in this effort—evolutionary, biological, psychological, and social. Within each of these arenas there are many structures and functions, species and institutions, that follow their own individual trajectories. Will a multiplication of developmental principles be required to explain the course of each? Conversely, biologists and philosophers have continually been involved in attempts to find the *one* guiding principle, the *one* explanation for all such progressions. Single explanations began with the "divine plans of the gods" and have continued to the current "strategy of the genes." The central focus of this chapter will be to see how adequately such formulations have fit the data of development. What will emerge is a perspective that not only recognizes the uniqueness of the concrete manifestation of each developmental course but also attempts to recognize the generality of a set of properties that characterize the developmental process in any context. This set of properties may be found in the domain of general systems theory.

An initial survey of historical definitions of development will be followed by a survey of the models that have been used to summarize the principles of development. The organismic model will be examined in detail to determine how well its properties fit the data of biological development and evolution. A general systems theory of development will be outlined that adds to the organismic model a principle of dialectical movement and a stronger consideration of environmental organization. Research in social and cognitive development will then be reviewed to determine whether the proposed general systems approach adds anything to current practice. A final summary will emphasize the analysis of context as a necessary part of developmental investigations.

CONCEPTS OF DEVELOPMENT

While behavioral changes are the central concern of the developmental psychologist, the organization of behavioral change is relatively hidden compared to the biological changes during individual human growth from zygote to maturity. The Greeks were already concerned with explaining such changes. Aristotle was able to differentiate between two alternative processes that moved life along on its path to perfection. *Preformationism* is the idea that within the fertilized egg there are parts corresponding with each of the parts of the adult. Growth is a simple process of enlargement from the small seed to the adult form. The homunculus, the little man, that early microscopists claimed to have seen in the sperm cell was thought to be the final evidence for the preformationist position. In modern times, such homunculi are regarded more abstractly as contained in the hereditary material, each gene a preformed aspect of the adult organ. The second idea is called *epigenesis*. In this view the organism initially contains only a few basic elements. All later complex structures are the result of the interaction of these original units with each other. Local interactions have more to do with developmental outcomes than either divine or genetic plans. The epigenetic approach has been consistently the more complex, for its focus has always been on the interaction of parts in the developing system, and especially in its modern manifestation, on the interaction of the parts with their environments. Because both views contain in their original formulations the same idea that there is an ideal outcome that is prefigured in the developmental process, it has always been simpler for a preformist theory which can ignore the historical experience of the system, than it has for an epigenetic theory to explain the actual route to such an ideal outcome. An epigenetic view needs additional formulations that can explain how similar organisms, faced with differing environments, can reach the same end point.

The Rise of Natural Science

Predetermined developmental end points were seriously undermined as explanations for the directed course of growth with the rise of the natural sciences in the seventeenth and eighteenth centuries. Theories attempting to explain the physical world on the basis of a divine plan were rejected in favor of appeals to mechanical hypotheses. The dilemma for scientists trying to understand the nature of living things is summarized by Jacob (1976).

The seventeenth century found itself in a universe whose center of gravity had shifted: a universe in which stars and stones obeyed the laws of mechanics. Henceforth, there were only two alternative ways to assign a place to living beings and to explain their functions. Either living beings were machines . . . or they remained beyond the reach of mechanical laws, in which case the attempts to find unity and coherence in the world had to be abandoned. Faced with this choice neither philosophers, nor physicists, nor even physicians could have a moment's hesitation: all nature was a machine, just as a machine was nature. (p. 33)

A contrasting position was to find a new source of control to explain the complexity of living things that would free them from ties to mechanistic constraints. Claude Bernard summarized the position of vitalism in 1878 as follows:

Even if we assume that vital phenomena are linked to physiochemical manifestations, which is true, this does not solve the question as a whole, since it is not a causal encounter between physiochemical phenomena which creates each being according to a predetermined plan and design . . . . Vital phenomena certainly have strictly defined physicochemical conditions, but at the same time they are subordinated and succeed each other in sequence according to a law laid down in advance . . . . There is a kind of pre-established design for each being and each organ, so that, considered in isolation, each phenomena of the harmonious arrangement depends on the general forces of nature, but taken in relationship with others it reveals a special bond: some invisible guide seems to direct it along the path it follows, leading it to the place which it occupies. (cited in Jacob, 1976, p. 4)

Simpson (1967) summarized the three positions most often taken to explain evolutionary progress: materialist or causalist, vitalist, and finalist. In its simplest form the materialist belief is that there is nothing in the universe but pure mechanism and there is no essential difference between life and nonlife. The vitalist belief is that there are nonmaterial forces that characterize life, that cannot be explained by mechanical principles. For the finalist, development is a progression toward a goal or end. The end state is not the result of the means to get there but rather the cause of those means. The finalist position is usually associated with vitalist views, although this need not be the case. For the finalist, the end, and especially the human end, is seen as the organizer of the processes that produce it.

Modern versions exist for each of these positions. Current materialists do not argue that life and nonlife are the same but rather argue that, whatever their differences, life and nonlife are explainable by a single set of principles. Modern vitalists do not reject causal explanations, but do argue that the explanatory principles are different for nonliving and living processes. The most complexity is found in current finalistic views that require manifold system explanations in order to place the beginning and end state within the same structure. For most biologists, such as Jacob (1976), the conflicts among mechanism, vitalism, and even finalism no longer exist. There is a sense that the "pre-established design" had been identified in the genetic program carried by each individual. Psychologists, on the other hand, still seem to have problems in specifying the locus of the design.

Psychological Development

Whereas biologists have established causal models with principles that operate in addition to those of the physical sciences (Pattee, 1973), psychologists have been less fortunate within their area of concern. The interim solution of the first half of the twentieth century was to deny the complexity of the problem by denying the complexity of development. Instead of viewing the developing human being as reaching new levels of organization in functioning, the more complex behaviors of the adult were seen as accumulations of the simpler behaviors of younger children. Development was a quantitative change rather than a qualitative one. The definition of development was no longer an unfolding, but was rather synonymous with growth—the older you were, the bigger you were, and the more you knew. Sears (1957) typified developmental change as characterized by changes in the precision, efficiency, and speed with which behavioral acts are performed. He also noted changes in the length and complexity of action sequences as, for example, between the infant's simple sucking and the older child's sequence of coming into the house, washing, going to the table, and asking for something to eat. These changes in complexity, however, were seen as changes in quantity on uniform dimensions rather than as changes in quality. There is a place for qualitative changes in this view but these reside in the physical maturation of the child. Biology was acknowledged as a substrate for psychology, but not as a source of developmental principles. The primary allegiance was still to the natural sciences of chemistry and physics. Unfolding of behavior was not an acceptable principle since its causes are unobservable. Instead there was a faith that observation is sufficient to identify all the factors necessary to explain behavioral change. The growth that psychologists were most concerned with was mental growth. Mental growth was seen as a manifestation of learning. Learning could be observed in the changing responses of the individual as a function of environmental contingencies that were thought to control these responses and that also could be observed. The most extreme version of this position was taken by Watson (1930), at least rhetorically:

> Give me a dozen healthy infants, well-formed, and my own specified world to bring them up in and I'll guarantee to take any one at random and train him to become any type of specialist I might select—doctor, lawyer, merchant-chief and, yes, even beggar-man and thief, regardless of his talents, penchants, tendencies, abilities, vocations, and race of his ancestors. (p. 104)

Bijou and Baer (1961) attempted to articulate a rigorous contemporary theory of development based on learning principles. They defined "psychological development" as the progressive changes in the way an organism's behavior interacts with the environment. Whether a particular response is likely to occur depends on environmental stimulation. Rather than looking at where the organism is going in its progress, Bijou and Baer viewed developmental psychology's concern as "the history of the organism's previous interactions" (p. 14). History is observable, the future is not.

Another approach to the definition of development sidestepped the issue of qualitative versus quantitative change by correlating developmental changes with age-changes. Kessen (1960) proposed that "a characteristic is said to be developmental if it can be related to age in an orderly or lawful way" (p. 36). Developmental psychologists were described most generally as studying $R = f(A)$, responses as a function of age. In later writings, Kessen (1962) went on to describe a greater variety of ways that development can be conceptualized, either as a continuous variable, or into metaphoric stages in which young children can be described as engaging in different kinds of activities than older children, or into theoretical stages in which the underlying organization of behavior qualitatively shifts as the child grows older. More recently, Wohlwill (1973) argued at length that change in behavior over time is the basic subject matter of any developmental investigation. He reiterated the idea of a developmental function defined as the relationship between chronological age and changes in response, but he added two emphases: one on the study of these changes in individuals (i.e., the need for a longitudinal approach); the other on the form or mode of the developmental function. For most specified dimensions of behavior, such forms of the function are either steplike, monotonically increasing, or U-shaped.

When behavior is divided into separate functions, it becomes easy to reconcile the qualitative-quantitative debate by asserting that certain types of behavior follow a continuous function in their development while others follow a discontinuous function but the result is a fragmented view of the child's growth. The original unfolding process was separated from the effects of experience by a division between biological and psychological development. Maturation accounted for the former; learning accounted for the latter. Such descriptions redefined development in terms of maturation and learning. Whatever qualitative changes could be identified in development were attributed to maturation (i.e., the unfolding of the individual's biological heritage), while behavioral development was seen as an overlay on biological structure (Hamburger, 1957).

However, the division of development into a biological and a psychological realm with different mechanisms was resisted by a group of psychologists who argued for the unity of process in the two realms. These scientists were primarily comparative psychologists who rejected the modern preformationist solution offered by geneticists for biological development (Jacob, 1976) and more recently for social development (Wilson, 1975); instead, they turned to an approach based on epigenetic concerns. Kuo (1967), for example, defined behavioral epigenesis as a continuous developmental process from fertilization to death, resulting from the continuous dynamic exchange of energy between the developing organism and its endogenous and exogenous environment.

In these epigenetic processes, at every point of energy exchange a new relationship between the organism and the environment is established; the organism is no longer the same organism and the environment is no longer the same environment as they were at the previous moment. Thus, in ontogenesis, both patterns of behavior and patterns of environment affect each other and are therefore in a constant state of flux; that is,

changes in the environmental patterns produce changes in behavior patterns which in turn modify the patterns of environment. The epigenetic view of behavior is bidirectionalistic . . . rather than environmentalistic, as it considers every behavior pattern as a *functional product* of the dynamic relationship between the organism and the environment, rather than as a passive result of environmental stimulation. (pp. 11–12)

Cairns (1979) shortened the definition to "the dynamic organization of behavior over time, from fertilization to death," where dynamic organization is seen as a "fusion" between the effects of experience and the processes of maturation and growth. For Cairns, biological maturation is no more an unfolding process than any psychological development. The experience necessary for behavioral growth is presumed to be necessary for biological growth. Examples of the inseparability of structure and function in development have been provided by Gottlieb (1976) and Oppenheim (1974), who perceive neural activity, sensory stimulation, and feedback from motor movements as acting together in inducing, facilitating, and maintaining neuroembryological behavior.

Organism-in-Environment

Zing-Yang Kuo and T. C. Schneirla are credited by Cairns (1979) with independently defining the principles of the modern approach to behavioral development through their interests in developmental psychobiology. Both had developed their positions during the 1930s by stating the need to see the study of behavior as a synthetic science requiring knowledge of biological, psychological, and social disciplines. Kuo (1967) focused on breaking down the boundaries between these disciplines in order to reject, on the one hand, mechanistic conceptions of development, which treat biology and psychology as obeying separate principles, and, on the other, teleological conceptions, which separate organisms from their environments.

Schneirla (1957) also had a wholistic view of developmental theory and required that any behavioral pattern be analyzed in the light of the biosocial organization of the individual and the group to which it belongs. He saw these as developmental conditions in which organisms display patterns of adaptive activity characteristic of their species. The emphasis on adaptation was important to the conceptualization of developmental direction within psychology.

The specific application of these principles to

developmental psychology had already been fore-shadowed in the writings of Baldwin (1906) and his discussion of assimilation and accommodation in the service of adaptation. But it remained for Piaget (1950) to provide a theory that was explicit enough both in its theoretical structure and in its data base to impress developmental psychology with the possibility of some unity of developmental process between biology and psychology. The unity centered on the adaptive efforts of organisms to construct themselves using as raw materials the results of interchanges with the environment. In the biological sphere, where organisms assimilate nutrients from a biochemical environment in order to develop, the exchanges are material; in the psychological sphere, where the patterning of experience is the nutrient for growth, the exchanges are informational. In both arenas, however, the environment was never seen as shaping the organism because both material and informational nutrients have to be assimilated to an already existing structure. On the other hand, the environment was considered a necessity since neither biological nor psychological progress can occur in the absence of exchanges with the environment.

While radical behaviorists had fully concentrated on the shaping forces in the environment as the primary determinants of psychological growth (Skinner, 1981), and while modern preformationists saw the transformations in psychological functioning with age as the unfolding of a genetic timetable, Piaget offered the third alternative, the progression of organismic development in an inseparable unity with experience. Despite his emphasis on the necessity for an environment to provide the developing child with a milieu for development, Piaget was not concerned with the organization of that environment. He saw the development of logical functioning from a Platonic perspective as a sequence from the imperfect to the ideal. Since the end point was always the same in this view, there was little need to worry how variations in experience might produce different mature modes of psychological functioning.

The recent growth of lifespan developmental psychology (Baltes, 1979), which concentrates on adult behavior, has raised issues about aspects of thought for which no perfect forms exist. Presumed logical universalities have been found to vary with context much more than expected from a Piagetian perspective (Riegel, 1973). This variation has led investigators to argue that adult concepts, especially social ones, are more related to adult environments than to a perfect form (Labouvie-Vief & Chandler, 1978). Human adult identity is seen as being orga-nized around the interaction of a person's concepts of self and social roles within particular cultural relationships. The need to specify such relationships has pushed toward a much more precise approach to the study of environments in a variety of psychological domains (Wapner, Kaplan, & Cohen, 1973). Experience may thus be not only a nutrient for intellectual growth but it may set the constraints determining which of a number of behavioral psychological systems will develop.

Environments as Systems

One of the major themes that will be explored in this chapter is the character of the functional environment that affects development. Although it is no longer a revolutionary idea for developmental psychologists to see the organism as having psychological structure (thanks primarily to Piaget), few current theories credit the environment with the same property. The difference between typical biological and typical psychological thinking about environments reflects this problem. Psychologists see the environment as the source of stimuli that either control or regulate behavior. The range of such stimulus conditions is infinite, and it is mere accident that a child experiences one set of environmental circumstances rather than another. On the other hand, some biologists see the functional environment as so tightly organized and specific to each organism that it is no longer seen as an environment, but rather as part of the organism. Embryology is the biological area where this perspective is most overt.

The embryologist Waddington (1962) has attempted a synthesis in which the preformed parts of the organism defined by the geneticists must now be viewed "epigenetically." Here the genes should be seen not as the determinants of later structure, but as interacters with each other and with the cytoplasm of the egg in a dynamic developmental process. At one level, the environment in which these interactions occur is a constant, since human fetal growth occurs in a highly insulated amniotic environment. At another level, however, many environmental features influence the activity of the genetic system, but these features are primarily other parts of the genetic system. In other words, the development of any part of the embryo is determined by its interaction with its environment, but that environment is also controlled, at the same time, by other parts of the same genetic structure.

One of the aims of this chapter is to determine if such principles, which apply to biological functioning, can be extended to psychological and social functioning. The question of how to define environments is also of significance at the level of social organization, where individual psychological development is shaped by the interaction between a person and other members of a given society. But if society controls the specific environment of each individual, possibly even fitting the environment to that individual, to what degree can it then be said that an individual contributes to his or her own developmental outcome?

The analysis of developmental systems that follows will attempt to find unifying characteristics in both biological and psychological development. A "modern synthesis," one that has been accepted in evolutionary theory, will be generalized to a psychological theory in which all development is seen as the result of an inseparable unity of organism and experience. In pursuing this effort, I will not attempt to reduce the principles of psychological development to the principles of biological development, even though they are far richer than the principles of physics, which have received psychology's traditional allegiance. Rather, I will attempt to enrich the understanding of both disciplines by sharing emphases. The effects of dynamic, changing environments need to be emphasized in what are more generally thought of as highly controlled biological processes, especially in embryogenesis. Conversely, the constraints existing in both the biological and social environment need to be emphasized for the understanding of psychological development, which has been more generally thought of as open ended in its directions and forms.

THE ROLE OF THEORY IN THE STUDY OF DEVELOPMENT

The rationalist tradition that accompanied the rise of natural science diminished the role of speculation and philosophy in science in favor of obtaining a "true" view of the operation of the universe through the careful collection of facts. This view could be supported as long as the facts and their interrelationships are considered to exist independently of the scientific lens through which they are viewed.

More recently, a contrasting position has been developing within the history of science: theory acts to select certain facts as more relevant than others and to impose an organization on observations rather than to be determined by the observations. Even Einstein drew back from a determining view of data: "It may be heuristically useful to keep in mind what one has observed. But on principle, it is quite wrong to try founding a theory on observable magnitudes alone. In reality the very opposite happens. It is the theory which decided what we can observe" (Einstein cited in Heisenberg, 1971, p. 63). It is not implied here that scientists make up theories which have nothing to do with the facts but rather that there is a reciprocal relationship between theory and facts in which both have an inseparable role. This transactional position—in which what the scientist observes is strongly influenced by what theory is held and at the same time what theory is held is strongly influenced by what facts are observed—is analogous to what has come to be called the "constructivist" position in developmental psychology (Piaget, 1970).

Constructivism when applied to understanding psychological development focuses on the active role of children in creating their cognitive and social worlds. In their widely separate domains, developmental biologists (e.g., Waddington, 1962) and historians of science (e.g., T. S. Kuhn, 1962) have arrived at similar positions in which the organism in the former case and the scientist in the latter engage in constructive efforts imposing order on their environments.

T. S. Kuhn (1962) has made a major contribution to understanding the development of theory by documenting what he calls paradigm shifts in the history of any science. He has stayed away from more philosophical debates about alternative world hypotheses and instead has examined the history of theories germane to specific disciplines, especially physics and chemistry. By avoiding speculation and detailing relevant historical examples, he has been especially persuasive in demonstrating that it is not critical experiments that determine the validity of theories but rather their ability to deal better with the totality of data within a discipline. For example, the shift in chemistry from the phlogiston theory to the oxygen theory of combustion was not the result of the discovery of oxygen, since both theories found ways to explain that discovery, but rather that Lavoisier's oxygen combustion explanation opened the way toward an atomic theory of matter which explained many other previous inconsistencies and that Priestly's explanation was only another patch on the already problematic phlogiston theory. Of more recent note, Mitroff's (1974) study of the scientists who received samples of rocks brought back from the moon reveals that the same empirical observations were assimilated into a wide variety of viewpoints. The most open-minded of the scientists were those who tended to stay away from theory. They were also the most junior and did not include any

Nobel laureates. Open-mindedness in this sense becomes a good basis for scientific description but a poor basis for scientific understanding.

The same point is made even more strongly by Brush (1974) in an article with the provocative title, "Should the history of science be rated X?" Brush argues that the standard textbooks in most university introductory courses present the sum of knowledge in a discipline as a continuous discovery of facts, in which each new fact goes a bit beyond the previous ones. If students took these textbooks seriously, they would believe that their professional careers would make contributions to the progress of science by careful experiments to add more facts to the accumulated knowledge of their discipline. In reality, science does not proceed in such a continuous mechanistic manner, each new fact being as valuable as the one that came before. Following T. S. Kuhn's (1962) approach, Brush gives historical examples in which the majority of scientists believed a new theory—even though it went against the existing facts—because the new theory offered a hope for explaining anomalies that were highly problematic for the older views. Furthermore, when new theories are accepted as the new standard for a discipline, many of the older data become obsolete or irrelevant. Within psychology one can find many examples of whole areas of data that seemed important to collect at the time, that now are considered irrelevant. Some good examples are the data collected on nonsense syllables to study memory or even the greater compilations of data on maze learning in rats to study cognition.

Brush suggests that if the truth were written in the university textbooks, it would be that the role of the researcher practicing standard science is to find anomalies that cannot easily be explained by the current normal science. When enough of these anomalies are produced, the accepted theory will become so overextended that most students will be dissatisfied with its explanatory power. With this groundwork of anomalies, the opportunity will exist for someone to present a new theory as a better integration for the field. What would be even more depressing for scientists within the field, and thus should definitely be rated "X," is that these new theories frequently arise outside the field, or they are suggested by someone in another discipline.

The importance of theory may be discouraging to researchers who see scientific progress in the gathering of experimental facts. The *historical* facts are that it is attention to theory that has produced scientific progress, albeit theory focused on empirical data. This chapter will focus on data but only in the service of better understanding the kind of theory that will be necessary to explain the findings of developmental psychology. By starting at a very general level, a context will be described in which specific developmental theories and sets of empirical observations can be embedded. This most general level is that of world hypotheses.

World Hypotheses

In exploring definitions of development earlier, it was noted that there is overlap in developmental concepts used by psychology and biology. At the level of world hypotheses, similarities can be explored beyond the definition of development into many other communalities of principle between psychology and biology, and at the same time these communalities can be explored in many other scientific disciplines in addition to biology and psychology.

What follows will be an effort to understand how such similarities have been conceptualized. These efforts have ranged from those who see each level of human functioning reflected in different disciplines obeying different principles, to those who see the separateness of scientific arenas but also see analogies among their principles, to those who perceive a unity in which all fields of science share the same principles.

One major source of unity between the empirical and theoretical world is to model one after the other. From this perspective, philosophies are fashioned in correspondence to theories of how the material world functions. Scientific understanding becomes a model for philosophical understanding. The debate between philosophical positions then becomes a debate between how well the metaphor fits the functioning of the material world.

> A man desiring to understand the world looks about for a clue to its comprehension. He pitches upon some area of common sense fact and tries if he cannot understand other areas in terms of this one. The basic idea becomes then his basic analogy or root metaphor. He describes as best he can the characteristics of this area, or, if you will, discriminates its structure. A list of its structural characteristics becomes his basic concepts of explanation and description. . . . He undertakes to interpret all facts in terms of these categories. (Pepper, 1942, p. 91)

Pepper attributes the first self-conscious world theory in European thought to Thales, who, dissatisfied with the explanations of mythology, suggested, "All things are water." This root metaphor represented common sense for a Greek islander whose universe was permeated with water. As science has changed, the common sense that can be used to generate these root metaphors has become more complex.

Pepper proposed four "world hypotheses" that he claimed have been the basis for most modern scientific theories: formism, mechanism, contextualism, and organicism. At various times during this century one or another of these hypotheses has been emphasized in the dominant developmental theories, although traces of each can be found at any one time. Formism is based on Plato's philosophy of ideal forms. Concrete manifestations are viewed as the expression of abstract universals. Formism is not a popular metaphor within developmental psychology because it denies development. However, it is popular as an explanation for developmental phenomena among nondevelopmentalists. Theories that explain social organization on the basis of genetic determinants (Wilson, 1975) or language on the basis of universal innate grammars (Chomsky, 1975) derive from the formist metaphor.

Where formism has not been found useful as a metaphor for development because of its simplicity, contextualism has not been seen as useful because of its complexity. Pepper sees the historical event as the metaphor of contextualism with the implication that the universe is a unique network of many causes interacting to produce uniquely determined events. Since each context has a different set of determinants, each development is nonreproducible as well as nonpredictable. Despite its complexity, contextualism has seen a recent popularity in the theories associated with life-span developmental psychology (Baltes, 1979). The need to explain developmental changes in adulthood, where intrinsic biological factors are thought to play a minor role, has moved theorists to a greater consideration of the organization of the environment, that is, the context of development (Lerner & Busch-Rossnagel, 1981).

Mechanism and organicism have been the most popular metaphors for theories of developmental psychology. A number of papers have been explicitly devoted to contrasting the models derived from these two world views (D. Kuhn, 1978; Langer, 1969; Overton & Reese, 1973, Reese & Overton, 1970).

Mechanistic and Organismic Models of Development

Reese and Overton (1970) have discussed organismic and mechanistic models as applied to developmental phenomena in detail because they felt that these radically different models have had a pervasive effect generally on the nature of psychology and specifically on that of developmental psychology. Because each model has served as a lens through which scientists view their subject matter, Reese and Overton described a number of issues on which the two models differ with respect to the categories they impose on developmental research.

The first issue on which the models differ is the root metaphor, the machine versus the organism. When the universe is regarded as a machine, it is seen as being composed of discrete pieces. The pieces and their relationships form the basic reality to which all other complex phenomena can be reduced. Such a reality is capable of quantification, so that functional equations can be constructed that map the relationships between the pieces in operation. The model is derived from the Newtonian version of the cosmos: The same laws that apply to irreducible fundamental elements, and their interactions also apply to all more complex interactions. In the hands of the early learning theorists, equations were proposed that would typify the behavior of all animals independently of their phyletic level (Hull, 1943). For example, the monotonically negatively accelerating relationship between strength of response and hours of food deprivation applies equally well to a sponge, a blow-fly, and a rat; only the exponent differs in the equations. The fact that no central nervous system mediates the response in the sponge, a single nerve mediates it in the blow-fly, and a combination of peripheral and central systems mediates it in the rat are irrelevant, since the same curve can be used for all.

In contrast, when the universe is regarded as a living organized system, the parts gain some of their meaning from the whole in which they are embedded. From this perspective, research is directed toward discovering principles of organization, toward the explanation of the relations of parts and wholes rather than toward the derivation of the whole from some set of elementary processes. For example, "vision," a property of the visual system, is not reducible to the sum of its parts—the cornea, retina, optic nerve, and brain. The interpretation of an observable bit of behavior like the human smile will have different meanings depending on the developmental stage and situational context of the behavior. For the newborn, it is an endogenous concomitant of a particular stage of sleep (Emde, Gaensbauer, & Harmon, 1976); for the older infant, it is the reflection of contingency awareness (J. S. Watson, 1972); for the adult, it may be a sign of manipulation, of anxiety, or (possibly) of genuine happiness.

The second issue on which the models differ is in the source of motivation. Reese and Overton describe the mechanistic position as the "reactive, passive, robot, or empty organism model of man." The organism is inherently at rest, only becoming active under the influence of outside forces. This Newtonian machine must have a source of power external to the central function. Human beings must have extrinsic drives that motivate thought, perception, and activity. In contrast, from the organismic perspective the essence of substance is not its parts but its activity. From this base it follows that the organism is in a continuous transition from one state to another in unceasing succession. No outside source of motivation is necessary since activity is given in the definition of life. Herein is the basis for the active organism model of man.

A third issue on which the models differ is in their epistemological position, the way one comes to know the universe. From the mechanistic perspective, the position is one of naïve realism, "a copy theory of knowledge according to which the knower plays no active role in the known, and inevitably apprehends the world in a predetermined way" (Reese & Overton, 1970, p. 132). John Locke formulated this position in his concept of the *tabula rasa* (i.e., nothing is known to the mind which does not first enter through the senses). The human brain copies reality without adding to it. From the organismic perspective, epistemology is one of constructivism, already mentioned above in regard to the use of scientific models. The knower participates in the construction of known reality on the basis of inherent activity and organization. Knowledge is a product of the interaction between the active knower and external reality. It is on the basis of past organization applied to reality that new organization can arise. As a consequence, mechanistic attempts to reduce or explain new levels of organization by appealing to prior levels is, in principle, impossible.

The several differences between the two models make for differences in the way the two models would study developmental change. The organicist would emphasize the study of processes over products and qualitative change over quantitative change (Reese & Overton, 1970). As applied to research, the method of the organicist would be to describe structures at each identifiable period, to discover the rules of transition from one period to another, and to determine the experiences that would enhance or retard these transitions. The mechanist, on the other hand, would focus on the basic parts and their principles of relationship to which complexities of organization can be reduced. Since there is presumed to be a universal set of principles that would explain the operation of parts at all levels of functioning, the

only differences between the levels for the mechanist would be quantitative ones, so that development becomes analogous to simple growth; just as the body enlarges, knowledge enlarges.

A corollary to the different views of quantitative and qualitative change inherent in these models is that stages of development take on different significances. When an organismic view is taken, the concept of stage becomes a theoretical concept that is applied to different levels of organization at which new system properties emerge and become functional. When a mechanistic view is taken, the concept of stage, if used at all, is merely a description for changes in the complexity of functioning. Stages are conveniences only, because a full description would require, according to the basic definitions of the mechanistic view, a lengthy reduction to the first parts of the system.

These different meanings attached to the concept of stage can be nested within the larger array of meanings described by Kessen (1962). He made a distinction between the use of stage as a description of the state of the organism as opposed to the use of stage as a broader concept that includes not only description of the state but the rules of transition to that state and from that state.

In summary, the mechanistic and organismic world views have different categories for organizing searches for and ascribing meaning to empirical data. These interpretative schemes differ from one another in their units of investigation, sources of motivation, bases of knowing, concepts of developmental change, and possibilities of predicting such changes. They also differ in how they account for changes: Are new structures and functions genuine novelties? Or are they complexifications of prior elements?

In discussing these two models of development, Reese and Overton (1970) have explored an additional emphasis in the incompatibility of the two models. They argue that the mechanistic and organismic perspectives are two different ways of viewing the world that cannot be amalgamated into a single coherent theory. The theories based on these models can be contrasted heuristically in terms of their accuracy, precision, or scope, but they cannot be falsified in direct comparisons in single experiments. The models differ in their criteria of truth and only overlap partially in subject matter. As a consequence, only some form of internal validation is possible.

D. Kuhn (1978) has argued that in the specific case of developmental psychology the mechanistic and organismic paradigms have been too narrowly applied. Social development as conceptualized in social learning theory has been strongly mechanistic, while cognitive development as studied from a Piagetian perspective has been strongly organismic. She adds that neither theory is sufficiently articulated to be able to offer a remedy for the shortcomings of the other. Her conclusion is that both paradigms must ultimately incorporate the viewpoints of the other and in the process construct a new paradigm. Although it makes sense that models applied to social development should include cognition (since social development relies heavily on cognition and vice versa), from the viewpoint of models as models, such incorporations are inappropriate. Pepper (1942) and Reese and Overton (1970) take a strong stand against mixing metaphors. An alternative approach might be to take a closer look at the metaphor of each model to determine if, perhaps, some missed property would resolve the inadequacies of current applications.

Of direct concern here is developmental psychology. How should these facts be viewed and organized into an adequate theory? Kitchener (1982) argues that if the organismic model is to stimulate a plausible research program, a logical analysis of the basic concepts and assumptions of the model is necessary. Organismic theories have been constructed by Heinz Werner and Jean Piaget. Werner's (1957) is the more general and has been applied to a variety of domains of development. Using the concept of "genetic parallelism," Werner argued that the same developmental principles apply to the development of the individual, the species, and culture. Piaget (1950) has generally limited himself to applying the principles of biological development to the data of psychological development or, more narrowly, to cognitive development. For both thinkers, there is a strong analogy between the two disciplines, for biology provides the basic model, or in Pepper's (1942) terminology, the root metaphor.

In order to test the adequacy of such generalizations, it would be useful to examine the characteristics of the metaphor to determine the source of the abstracted properties of the model. In the process, additional properties of the organismic model that can enrich the analogies from biology to other developmental domains may be unearthed. From an intellectual perspective, it would be interesting if a general model that organized the data of several different scientific domains could be found. From a practical perspective it is far more useful and exciting, as well, if the application of the model would reveal previously unnoticed relationships in the domain of interest (i.e., if relationships found in the metaphor would be found in the new area of application). A major question from the perspective of developmental psychology would be the identification of the controls of growth. Are they within the individual, the environment, or some combination of the two? The area of biology that is most concerned with development and is the source of many analogies to developmental psychology is embryology. An examination of the principles of embryonic development may illuminate these analogies.

EMBRYOLOGY AS A DEVELOPMENTAL SYSTEM

Embryology is the study of the development of an individual from conception to birth. This science epitomizes the complexity of biological organization and function while following an individual from the simple beginnings in a single cell to the complex hierarchical functioning of masses of specialized cells that characterize the adult form. The fascination for developmentalists in the study of embryology is that the processes of transformation that are hidden to evolutionists by the slow pace of history and to psychologists by the ephemeral nature of mental concepts, are revealed to view. In Waddington's (1966) words, the developing embryo is seen as:

a simple lump of jelly that, isolated in a drop of water or sitting on a dry surface, begins changing in shape and texture, developing new parts, sticking out processes, folding up some regions and spreading out in others, until it eventually turns into a recognizable small plant or worm or insect or some other type of organism. Nothing else that one can see puts on a performance which is both so apparently simple and spontaneous and yet, when you think about it, so mysterious. (p. v)

This mystery has steadily yielded to the onslaught of biologists who have been particularly interested in the determinants of growth and development. The most exciting recent advances have been in the area of gene activity, but there was a time when genes were considered to be either irrelevant to embryology or at best minor factors (Waddington, 1966). At the beginning of the century, the field was called developmental mechanics or developmental physiology because there was a belief that development resulted only from the mechanical interaction of the growing parts of the embryo. The contributions of T. H. Morgan (1919) moved embryologists to consider genetic influences seriously, but it is only recently that it has become clear that the main thrust of embryological investigation must be to determine how the activities of genes are controlled.

Differentiation and Integration

The basic problem of embryology is to understand how a single fertilized cell with a spherical shape can be transformed into an adult with multitudes of different cells in multitudes of different shapes. Waddington (1966) describes the task of embryology as the analysis of the causes of these changes. The central process he identifies is differentiation, which he subdivides into three major categories of change: differentiation in time, differentiation in space, and differentiation in shape.

The fertilized egg is a eukaryotic cell with an enclosed nucleus containing most of the genetic material in a cytoplasmic environment that has various biochemical and structural components. The genetic material of the nucleus has been contributed by both the mother and father, while the cytoplasm is primarily a maternal contribution. In the first phase of development the original egg cell becomes subdivided into a larger number of small cells through the process of cleavage. At the end of this period, there is formed a blastula consisting of a spherical collection of cells that is hollow in the middle. Immediately, a process of gastrulation occurs in which cell masses are folded and move from one place to another. During this process one side of the sphere of cells from the blastula moves inward like a tennis ball being squeezed at one point.

The result of these movements is an embryonic form with three layers of cells. The layer of cells remaining on the outside becomes the ectoderm, which will later produce the skin and the nervous system. The inside layer that has moved from the outside, becomes the endoderm and will give rise to the intestines and other internal organs. In the space between the ectoderm and the endoderm, a third layer of cells, the mesoderm, which will produce the muscles, is formed. Once all three layers are differentiated, they start to develop into the organs of the adult. From then on, the particular course of development that will lead to the organs will be very different for different animals. For example, will the end result be a sea urchin or a human being? However, the initial stages are generally the same. Why this is so will be left for a later discussion of evolution.

How are the three processes of differentiation reflected in these developments? As it occurs in time, differentiation reflects the transitions as a region of the fertilized egg becomes one of the new cells formed during cleavage. Provided with its own nucleus and cell membrane, each of these early cells will grow into a mass of cells, originally fairly general in characteristics, but after gastrulation taking on the specialized forms necessary to the functioning of the particular organ that is being formed, for example, a muscle, the liver, a bone. These transitions in time, during which chemical changes are the primary mode of differentiation from each region of the egg to the specialized tissues of the adult, are called *histogenesis*.

Differentiation in space reflects the transformation of the egg from its relatively simple organization into the many different parts of the body. These parts begin with a fairly homogeneous organization in the blastula, but soon they begin to form the wide variety of different organs that characterize the adult. One group of cells becomes the substrate for the brain, which then differentiates into the forebrain, midbrain, and hindbrain. The part destined to become the intestines further differentiates into the esophagus, the stomach, and the other organs of the digestive tract. This process by which the different parts of the embryo take on different functions is known as *regionalization*.

As described by Waddington, the third process of differentiation is that of differentiation in shape. The almost spherical form of the initial egg cell is transformed into the later complexities of external form (e.g., the human array of arms, legs, trunk, and head) and into those of internal form (e.g., lungs, heart, nerves, vessels—all the organs that compose the body). The process by which these changes in shape occur is called *morphogenesis*.

Although these three processes can be defined independently, they are going on, as Waddington points out, simultaneously, and they are in intimate connection with each other. The organismic model has as one of its basic properties, the wholistic integration of development, exemplified in the intimacy of differentiation processes as already described in the embryological metaphor. However, as described, none of these processes necessarily exclude a mechanical interpretation of embryology. Genes in a predetermined arrangement within the genotype could interact with the cytoplasmic material, whose structure has been determined by the mother's genes, and then continue to engage in a series of mechanistic chemical interactions to produce the adult form. What need is there to appeal to wholistic processes or new levels of functioning emerging from new levels of organization?

In fact, such an orientation is taken by the field of behavior genetics. ''Behavior genetics has traditionally been concerned with correlating classes of genotypes . . . with classes of behavior . . . relating gene differences to behavior differences'' (Thiessen, 1972, p. 113). The interest here is not in how genes provide the structures that permit behavior but rather how differences in genes produce the variations of structure. The issue of development, which might be thought to be central to the exploration of gene-behavior relationships, is here ignored because in the mechanistic causal equation development is irrelevant.

McCall (1981) makes a similar point in discussing two realms of development akin to Cronbach's (1957) two disciplines of scientific psychology. One realm is the study of longitudinal changes that characterize all individuals in a given species; the other realm is the study of the consistency of differences between members of a given species. McCall's biases seem clear when he states, ''Relying solely on individual differences is like studying the consistency of a difference of a few inches in the heights of giant sequoia trees from seedlings to maturity while ignoring the issue of how all trees grow to be over 300 feet tall'' (p. 3).

The individual differences position was taken in psychology by adherents of radical behaviorism or the black-box approach. In this early Skinnerian view (Skinner, 1950), there was no need to take the organism into account when studying the functional relationships between stimuli and responses. There was no rejection of the notion that the organism was necessary to connect the two, but the organism added nothing to the relationship. If one knew the differences in input and output specifications, one could predict changes in output as a function of changes in input alone. Manipulations of stimulus characteristics (i.e., environmental contingencies) would produce lawful changes in response characteristics.

The black box has also come to the fore in recent theories of evolution. Sociobiologists (Dawkins, 1976; Wilson, 1975) propose that the essential relationships in evolution are between the genes and adult reproductive fitness. From this perspective, ontogeny can be treated as a mechanical causal connection between the two, a connection that adds nothing to the functional relationship.

Wholistic Process in Embryology

If the metaphor of the living organism is to be the basis of an organismic model, it should not be explained by mechanistic principles. For example, there should not be one-to-one relationships between gene activities and phenotypic structures in a theory of embryology derived from an organismic model. Whenever such relationships seem to exist, they must be the consequence of complex organizational activities mediating between the initial state and the final state and not a simple linear chain of causality. Several embryological processes do seem to have these required organismic properties.

Genetic Control Mechanisms

One can begin with the biochemical processes in histogenesis that seem to be the clearest cases of genetic influences on development and therefore the best examples of linear causality. Each cell of an organism contains an identical set of genes, yet each cell follows a different developmental course. In large part, this is due to the chemical heterogeneity of the cytoplasm within the cell. As the cell undergoes cleavage, forming a set of smaller cells, each of the new cells has differing chemical constituents since its cytoplasm came from a different area in the maternal egg, thus providing a differing environment for the same genetic material. At this most primitive of biological levels, the processes of development already include environmental interactions. Most of these processes involve the transformation of simple organic compounds such as amino acids into complex proteins through a series of steps. For example, in the synthesis of arginine the process begins with the conversion of sugar and ammonia into ornithine, then ornithine into citrulline, and finally citrulline into arginine (see Figure 1). Each of these steps is controlled by the catalytic action of an enzyme. The production of these enzymes is in turn controlled by the action of specific genes, seven in the case of arginine synthesis (Beadle & Tatum, 1941).

In these chains of chemical transformation, the quantity of the end product is not necessarily connected to the quantity of initial substance, which is evidence against simple causal chains. In many cases the end product of the sequence acts as an inhibitor of the activity of some enzyme acting at an intermediate step. When sufficient end product is present, the producing system shuts down through what is known as end-product inhibition (Waddington, 1966). If the end product was produced by one of the multitude of other biochemical processes going on in the cell, the chemical chain would not occur at all; while if there were insufficient quantities of the initial compounds necessary in the chain, other processes might be activated to produce the

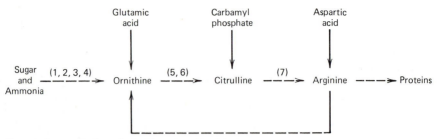

Figure 1. Sequence for the synthesis of the amino acid arginine in the mold *Neurospora*. Genes (1–7) control the formation of enzymes that act at the successive steps. Each of the amino acids in the sequence can be synthesized through other pathways indicated by the descending and ascending arrows.

required chemicals from other sequences of reactions. In the case of the arginine sequence described above, each of the intermediate products, ornithine and citrulline, are produced by at least two different metabolic pathways. This redundancy is important as a safety device in the embryonic system, but it requires at the same time a greater complexity of control than a simple linear system.

The discovery of the mechanisms by which these processes are controlled has produced another exciting view of the developmental process. Genetics had been originally concerned with structural genes that were highly correlated with specific features of the phenotype. However, it became clear that structural genes accounted for only a small percentage of the total number of genes in an organism. Most of an organism's genes are involved in control functions that modify the activity of other genes. An analysis of these functions in prokaryotic cells (i.e., those without nucleuses) led Jacob and Monod (1961) to propose an operon model of gene control. Operator genes act as switches turning on and off the structural genes, while regulator genes produce repressors that turn the operator genes on and off. Depending on the chemical environment in the cell, various regulator genes, operator genes, or structural genes will be activated. But it is the action of the genes that changes the chemical environment of the cell. Analyses of the control of genes in eukaryotic cells (i.e., those with nucleuses, which comprise all multicellular organisms) have not reached the detail of understanding of gene activity in prokaryotic cells. However, what is known indicates that the regulatory functions are far more complex and involve many levels of interactions between genes and gene products (Brown, 1981). Rather than mechanical *interactions* in which a series of genes function in a sequence to produce a series of proteins, there are dynamic *transactions* in which it is the initial state of the environment that changes the genetic

systems by activating certain genes; these genes change the environment by producing new chemicals that, in turn, act back on the gene system by inhibiting the action of the first set of genes and by activating another set of genes.

In such a system there can be no appeal to reductionism in attempting to explain the end product in terms of the initial conditions. The end product can only be explained through the spelling out of the dynamic transactions in which genetic system and cytoplasmic environment reciprocally alter each other's composition and activity. On the other hand, there are clear local causal sequences within these transactions; furthermore, there is a control system that moves these chemical reactions toward a specific state of equilibrium. Here one can see the action of finalistic strategies that have been imputed to living systems. The cell is organized in maintaining a specific chemical composition at any point in time. The manner of achieving this balance is not specifically determined. A specific metabolic end state can be reached through a variety of pathways involving different biochemical intermediates at the same time the same biochemical intermediates can contribute to different metabolic sequences. Similarly, many different genes participate in any one of these transformations, while each individual gene can participate in a number of different sequences. There appears to be an equilibrium that controls many chemical chains. The equilibrium state is a property of the cell as a whole and not of its initial biochemical constituents. The basic premise of modern embryology is that genes control all of the developmental processes, but the control is dynamically organized and sensitive to shifting biochemical characteristics within the cell.

Canalization

A more general model of wholistic processing has been provided by Waddington (1962) in his concept of the canalization of development. While single genes that influence various aspects of developing organs can be identified, the control systems that monitor these activities have not lent themselves to such easy analyses. The fruit fly, *Drosophila pseudoobscura,* has been the subject of many genetic analyses. The wing of the fruit fly is influenced by some genes that act specifically on the length of the wing, others that act on the width of the wing, and still others that act on the thickness of the wing. Rather than each of these genes specifying a dimension of the wing, they operate as an interacting system in which the final product is a balance between competing forces acting to make the wing longer, wider, or thicker. If a major mutation occurs, or is induced to suppress the genes acting on one dimension, the resulting wing will be enlarged in the other two dimensions. However, deviancy only occurs in extreme cases. In general, when there are deviations in the activity of the genes controlling one of the dimensions, the genes controlling the other dimensions will either increase or decrease their activity so that the net result is a normal wing. At some level of the system there is a monitoring function doing the balancing. For Waddington, once a differentiated area begins its course toward becoming a specific organ, it is canalized so that deviations from the course are compensated by a "self-righting tendency."

There are many examples of such compensating systems in embryology. Waddington suggests that canalization is the developmental explanation for the phenomenon of dominance and recessivity in genetics. A homozygous individual will have twice as much of the dominant gene as a heterozygous individual, yet the adult form will be identical for the two. Identical twins are formed when the early embryo splits, yet the two adults are full size even though they began with only half of the usual cytoplasmic material. Experimental embryology has shown that if the egg cell is spun in a centrifuge so that the chemical material is homogenized, the various constituents will return to the appropriate areas in the cytoplasm when the cell is left to itself.

The pathways by which a region of the early egg becomes a specific organ is canalized in the "sense that the developing system has an inbuilt tendency to stick to the path, and is quite difficult to divert from it by any influence, whether an external one like an abnormal temperature or an internal one like the presence of a few abnormal genes" (Waddington, 1966, p. 48). Waddington goes on to point out that reaching the adult state is not guaranteed by this process, only that there is a tendency to do so which resists temporary abnormalities. There is no mysti-

cal explanation necessary for these organizing tendencies in embryology. Waddington presents them as principles that will ultimately yield to causal analysis, but an analysis based on dynamic considerations of a multifaceted developing system integrated around a pathway to a specific developmental end point.

Waddington (1962) labeled the process of regulation "homeorhesis." He termed such a developmental pathway in embryology a "chreod," a Greek word meaning necessary path. The chreod is the trajectory that is followed from the early egg to the finished organ. When a deviation occurs from this trajectory, the self-righting tendencies come into play and the normal final state is reached as if the developmental trajectory had been normal. Tanner (1963) discusses catch-up growth in which mammals achieve a normal adult size at the right time even though deviations had occurred earlier. Preterm human infants are another example of such a catch-up phenomenon, in which their growth rates are accelerated with respect to full-term infants during the first two years after birth. In other words the embryological control system does not have the relatively simple task of maintaining a particular set of parameters, but the far more complex task of maintaining a changing set of parameters over a long period of time.

Regeneration

Although this discussion of embryology is devoted to illuminating the characteristics generally attributed to the organismic model of development, there are some ancillary characteristics of the metaphor that are quite interesting in the possible analogies to psychological development. One of these is the issue of the reversibility of differentiation. The question is whether the system can reverse itself and go back to an earlier embryonic condition once a set of cells enter a chreod. When such a set of cells is isolated from the setting in which it is growing, the evidence is somewhat mixed. When placed in a neutral nutritive medium, the cells appear to return to an embryonic condition but still retain some aspects of their previously differentiated state as well.

However, in the case of those vertebrates that have the ability to regenerate parts of the body, the evidence is much clearer. If the lens of the eye of a frog or newt is removed, a small growth will appear in some part of the eye which will eventually produce a new lens. The growth may form in the cornea or in a completely different group of cells in the retina. These are highly specialized cells that lose their differentiation by simplifying and then developing along a new pathway to become a lens. The property of regeneration, then, is not specific to a particular tissue, but is rather a property of the whole eye. In the case of the newt or frog, it is not the lens tissue alone that is in a chreod, but the whole visual organ.

Embryonic Induction

The wholistic properties of the embryonic system are most excitingly demonstrated in regionalization—differentiation in space. As described earlier, different parts of the early egg become the basis for different organs of the body. Following gastrulation, the process in which the part of the blastula that will be the endoderm folds in under the part that will become the ectoderm, a plate of cells differentiates within the ectoderm which will become the neural tube and later the spinal cord. One of the interesting early questions in embryological research was to discover at what point the cells that form a neural plate are determined in that direction. Spemann (1927) early in the century thought of an ingenious experiment; he removed a piece of the endoderm which lay under the ectoderm that was to become the neural plate and transplanted it so that it lay under a different part of the ectoderm. The result was that the neural plate did not appear in its usual location, but appeared above the transplanted endoderm instead. The process by which one area of the embryo interacts with some neighboring part to make that area develop into an organ is called "embryonic induction." This induction process is very common in embryology. In vertebrates, a sequence of inductions has been demonstrated: First the front area of the neural tube is induced to become the brain; then the front tip of the brain induces the formation of the nose organs. Slightly behind the nose area, two growth areas on each side of the brain, which will later grow into the eyes, induce the neighboring skin to form the lenses. The destiny of a particular set of cells does not appear to be a property of that set of cells but rather of the interaction between sets of cells. Ebert and Sussex (1970) state that during the course of development, few—if any—vertebrate structures develop without an initial interaction between different tissues. Evidence that the determination of cells along a differentiated path has taken place is found only after permanent changes have occurred in the nuclear material. These changes in the genetic material do not happen until after the blastula stage, when the differentiation into the first three tissues has occurred.

The results of the study of the biochemical processes that produce histogenesis and regionalization have demonstrated an early equipotentiality of cells

to become various organs of the body. It is only through being in different environments (i.e., different positions in the early embryo) that places cells in different chemical contexts and sets them on their separate paths toward their respective adult features. Ebert and Sussex (1970) not only have described the inductive paths by which one tissue affects the other but also have reviewed evidence for the bidirectionality of these effects, where the induced tissue acts back on the inducer. Embryological development is characterized by an interaction of systems at all levels. To the extent that the interactions are altered, either through the sequential action of the genes or through interactions with other developing tissues or experimental manipulation, the outcome for any particular tissue is altered.

The final point to be made in this exposition of embryological development involves the process of morphogenesis—changes in shape. The importance of this process is that it brings into play nonchemical forces that move parts of the embryo from one position to another and affect the physical form that different cells, tissues, and organs will take. Without going into detail (e.g., see Carlson, 1981; Ebert & Sussex, 1970; Waddington, 1966), the characteristics of cell surfaces influence the way the cells will attach to one another as in tissue formation, or move past one another, as in gastrulation. Morphogenesis is not a property of single cells but another property of groups of cells or tissues in interaction.

Ebert and Sussex (1970) summarize by stating that "each differentiating tissue cell has had its own inner controls. Yet in its development the cell is part of a larger whole; during its differentiation the cell must respond to control factors extrinsic to it" (p. 241). It is in the balance between individual and collection, part and whole, that the organismic model derives its metaphor. By examining embryological development in detail, it is possible to see how a wholistic emphasis is necessary to understand living systems. The parts, whether genes or cells or tissues, have an activity of their own, but it is only in the discipline of the collectivity that the developmental goal is reached. How that collectivity is controlled is the next topic to which our attention must be turned.

The Organismic Metaphor

In describing embryological development, the aim here is to illuminate the metaphor of the organismic model of development; thus, each of the model's characteristics should be evident in the metaphor. Emphasis on a wholistic, actively functioning entity that constructs itself out of transactions with the environment is derived from the properties of biological development. In their development, the more complex biological organisms pass through stages in which the characteristics of life in the single cell become structurally differentiated; at the same time, new functions appear as properties of the new cell collectivities. For example, each fertilized cell can interact with the environment by ingesting and excreting various biochemical products. In the adult, these same functions are carried out by organs composed of specialized groups of cells; however, although the function can be seen as the same, the range of nutrients that can be ingested is greatly expanded. The differentiation of cells into specialized tissues and the integration of these tissues into specialized organs is coordinated with the integration of the organs into coordinated activity of the whole animal. For example, the ability to get nutrition from a wide range of foods is accompanied by an increase in locomotor ability that permits the animal to cover wide areas in search of these foods.

The use of this metaphor for describing development has been a common practice among developmental psychologists of organismic persuasion. Werner's (1957) *orthogenetic principle* is a generalization to all developmental processes and states that "wherever development occurs it proceeds from a state of relative globality and lack of differentiation to a state of increasing differentiation, articulation, and hierarchic integration" (p. 126). Piaget (1971) defines the most general characteristics of development as "the temporal transformation of structures in the double sense of differentiation of substructures and their integration into totalities" (p. 71). The analogies with the data of psychological development will be dealt with more fully in a later section, but at this point one can already see the shape of the theoretical applications. Both theorists explicitly appeal to a leading contemporary embryologist to justify part of their model, Paul Weiss (1939) for Werner, and C. H. Waddington (1957) for Piaget. But beyond these generalizations, there has been less of a focus on the particulars of the embryological metaphor.

The current debate by researchers in cognitive development on the generality of Piagetian stages largely ignores the organismic metaphor, and even the organismic model, as a source of hypotheses. Two key questions now confronting researchers in cognitive development are whether or not the acquisition of knowledge occurs in a fixed sequence within every task domain and whether or not the level achieved in one domain is structurally related

to levels in other domains (see Gelman & Baillargeon, 1983). Investigators who are empirically oriented restrict their analysis of these questions to investigations of specific cognitive tasks in children of different ages. Investigators who are more theoretically oriented tend to expand their analyses by examining the organismic model on which Piagetian theory is based. These broader examinations require analyses of the universality of stages in the development of the biological metaphor. These analyses thus focus on the questions stated previously: Does cell differentiation into tissues and integration into organs occur in a fixed sequence in every functional domain? Is the level of differentiation and integration reached in one domain structurally related to levels in other domains? Although answers to these embryological questions do not answer the cognitive question, the supposition of the organismic model is that they may illuminate principles of organization that can be applied in building testable answers.

There thus appears to be a major contrast between conceptualizers of a theory and the empiricists who test or use the theory. Theorists, such as Werner or Piaget, integrate broad ranges of developmental data around a model derived from an explicit metaphor. Experimenters engaged in operationalizing the theory for a specific research project rarely appeal to the model or to the metaphor as a source of hypotheses about the relationships expected to emerge. Does this neglect represent a major loss in sources of hypotheses, or is it a realistic view of the limits of analogies (Chapanis, 1961)?

One aim of this chapter is to examine the limits of generalizations from biological development that can be applied to psychological development. Before reaching that step, a further expansion is required in the analysis of biological change. Developmental biology in the specific form of embryology is discussed above; in the next section the principles of evolutionary biology are explored.

EVOLUTION AS A DEVELOPMENTAL SYSTEM

The description of ontogenetic development emphasizes the wholistic processes of the organism in which each developmental step is regulated by a constellation of interacting systems. The organization of each organ through time is seen to be dynamically regulated (e.g., Waddington's [1966] canalization controlled by the organism's self-righting tendencies). There appears to be a tight control over the variability in developmental outcomes. Given the millions of cell divisions that occur during fetal growth, each with the opportunity of introducing more variability into the product, it is amazing that the outcome is so uniform. Except for very rare anomalies, human babies all have the same number of limbs, sensory organs, and internal systems. The control system that produces this uniformity within the species is rooted in the genetic structure of the individual. Even for the developmentalist who has a strong belief in the epigenetic transactions between cells, organs, and their environments, it is the genetic structure that responds to these interchanges and initiates or terminates biochemical processes to insure that the system is on the right track. But how did the genes acquire this capacity? What were the forces that shaped the genetic control system? Answers to these questions lie in the evolutionary history of the organism.

The impact of evolutionary biology on psychological thinking has been primarily in the area of comparative psychology rather than in that of developmental psychology. Although Werner and Piaget liberally acknowledge in their works the principles of ontogenetic development as found in embryology, they place less emphasis on the principles of phylogeny, even though both theorists were influenced by evolutionary thinking. Werner (1948) made strong reference to the analogies to be found between individual development and the development of the species, but only in the form of the very general orthogenetic principle. On the other hand, Piaget (1971) paid little attention to the details of evolution but great detail to the phylogenetic principle of adaptation, which became a cornerstone of his theory of cognitive development. The invisibility of most psychological processes can be a stimulus to search for disciplines in which analogous processes are more observable. Embryology provides a visible analog for the processes of differentiation and hierarchic integration. Evolution provides a historical analog of adaptation.

The field of developmental biology can be conceived of as two separate subfields that differ in methods and in approaches to the problem of cause and effect. These two are *functional biology* and *evolutionary biology*. Mayr (1961) describes the functional biologist as primarily interested in the operation and interaction of structural elements in an attempt to answer the question, ''How?'' By using mainly experimental techniques, the functional biologist tries to determine how things operate. The evolutionary biologist's primary question is, ''Why?'' By seeing every individual and species as the result of a long history dating back several billion years, the evolutionary biologist views all biological phenomena as time-bound and space-bound in contrast with the phenomena of physics, which are usually treated as absolutes. Structures and functions of the organism cannot be understood outside of a historical context. The evolutionary biologist attempts to understand the diversity of biological forms and the pathways by which they have been achieved. In terms of the genetic program, for example, the functional biologist is primarily interested in how gene organization is decoded to produce a phenotype; the evolutionary biologist is interested in how the code came to exist in its present form.

These differing interests within biology have led scientists to search for two different sets of causal factors, ultimate causes and proximate causes (Mayr, 1961). Ultimate causes have a historical impact through thousands of generations of natural selection. Proximate causes are the immediate influences on changes in structure or behavior. As an example, Mayr analyzes why a particular bird begins its migration south on a particular day. The proximate causes are physiological responses in a system sensitive to decreases in the number of hours of daylight and a drop in temperature. The ultimate causes are ecological, because an insect-eating bird would not survive winter in northern regions, and genetic, because the bird has a particular constitution that induces it to respond in a particular way to environmental stimuli.

For Wilson (1975), a sociobiologist, ultimate and proximate causes not only require different scientific approaches, but should probably be ''decoupled,'' since attention to the proximate causes of the developmental biologist, such as the anatomical, physiological, and behavioral machinery of the individual, only confuses the search for the ultimate prime movers of evolution that created the machinery. The desire to separate evolutionary biology from developmental biology expressed by sociobiologists has important consequences and will be treated later in a discussion of social organization.

The Synthetic Theory of Evolution

Evolution at its most general can be described as continuous change on some directed course, best defined as a change in the diversity and adaptation of populations or organisms (Mayr, 1970). These two concepts of diversity and adaptation were the compelling aspects of the Darwinian revolution that reshaped biological thought. The ancient and medieval view of life was that there was a set number of species in natural harmony since the time of creation. The later analysis of the historical record led Lamarck to propose the first consistent theory of evolution (Jacob, 1976; Simpson, 1967). Lamarck described species as having the ability to adapt to circumstances while moving in the direction of perfection. He is most remembered for his hypothesis on how these adaptations were transmitted from one generation to another by the inheritance of acquired characteristics. Although his theory of change was subsequently disproved, his emphasis on adaptation became a cornerstone of modern evolutionary theory.

The sources of diversity were the main theme of Darwin's work. Darwin proposed that there was a great variability within and between species. He agreed with Lamarck that species were evolving, but he did not see them evolving toward perfection. The diversity of modern species is the consequence of differential selection pressures in different environments. Darwin's two-step process was first, the production of variation, and second, selection through survival in the struggle for existence.

A contrasting approach to evolutionary theory rejected the idea of adaptation and selection in favor of the idea of species change by mutation. In this view, new species were to be attributed to random changes in the genetic structure of existing species. The sources for change resided wholly in the individual and not in the relationship between the individual and the environment. These views were supported by the rediscovery of Mendel's work at the turn of the century and the research activity identifying and elaborating the role of genes in the process of heredity. The mutationists believed that no theory of gradual changes through adaptation could explain the discontinuous nature of species. Mayr (1970) suggests that these views were rejected when it was demonstrated that there was less genetic discontinuity between related species and more variability within a species. In addition, naturalistic explanations based on geographical alterations were found for the evolution of existing discontinuities.

The rejection of the theory of inheritance of acquired characteristics by the early geneticists centered on the clear separation between the genotype and the phenotype in the course of hereditary transmission. The genes are fully insulated from normal environmental influences and therefore cannot be altered by experience. The genetic view of evolution during the first third of the century was seen as an alternative rather than a complement to the Darwinian position. Whereas Darwin had focused on the continuity of variation, the early geneticists centered on distinctive characteristics that contrasted sharply with each other (Jacob, 1976).

The complementarity of the research by naturalists and paleontologists on selection and the work of the geneticists as they moved toward population considerations became the basis for what J. Huxley (1942) termed the "modern synthesis" in evolution. Dobzhansky (1937) is generally credited with being the architect of the synthesis (Mayr, 1970), but many others were involved in elaborating the ideas involved. The basic position is that species members are not genetically uniform but contain a great deal of genetic variation held in place by selection. Genetic analyses indicate that no two cells are identical even within a single organism and uniqueness is a characteristic of all individuals, species, and ecosystems. Mutation becomes a secondary mechanism of change in genetic material. The primary mechanism is selection among the wide array of existing variation.

The modern idea of selection differs from Darwin's original position of the struggle for survival. It is not the death of certain individuals that permits others to flourish, but the better adaptiveness of certain individuals to utilize the resources in the environment to reproduce themselves. Population genetics has thus laid the basis for explaining evolution more in terms of differential reproductivity and less in terms of the elimination of weak members of the species (Simpson, 1967). Those individuals that leave more survivors will alter the frequency of certain genes and gene combinations that are more or less adaptive at a particular place and time. The selection process in terms of the characteristics of the environment will determine the direction of evolution.

The modern synthesis is that evolution is neither a random process of genetic mutation nor a directed path toward perfection. Depending on the environmental context, the course of evolutionary change can alter direction repeatedly. Mayr (1970) described selectionist evolution as neither a chance nor a determined process, but a combination of the two that is qualitatively different from either. The processes of organic evolution are consistent with the laws of the physical sciences but cannot be reduced to physical laws. The crucial aspects of evolution are changes in diversity and adaptation. Without a representation of the environment in the form of pressures for adaptation, the particular course that evolution has taken would not have occurred. Each individual consists of a duality, a genotype and a phenotype. The genotype is part of the gene pool of the population and provides a number of potential developmental trajectories toward the individual's phenotype. The phenotype will be shaped by the interaction between the genes and the environment into an individual who will compete with other phenotypes for reproductive success.

The Origin of Life

The need to appeal to a spotty historical record makes the study of evolution difficult. However, the increasing sophistication of dating techniques and the increased understanding of geological movements through history have illuminated much of the past. A theoretical discussion of the selective role of environments acting on genetic variability, as in the modern synthesis, is interesting, but a fine fit between the theory and the data would be more convincing.

Genetic variability was not an issue in evolution until genetic material evolved. But even before that time selection forces acting on systems with differential reproductive capacity were a characteristic of the earliest terrestrial environments. Current estimates put the age of the earth at approximately 4.6 billion years. Surprisingly, life in the form of cells resembling bacteria appeared relatively shortly thereafter, about 3.2 to 3.4 billion years ago. After this step from nonbiological organic matter to life, the step from the original one-celled bacteria to cells with nuclei and multicellular organisms took twice as long, almost 2 billion years (Dickerson, 1978). There is a fairly good fossil record from the first evidence of multicellular organisms about 1.5 billion years ago, through the emergence of man about 1.8 million years ago, to modern times.

The first transition to life involved processes at the core of all developmental phenomena, the necessity for identity and the necessity for transformation. If an organism is continually being transformed into something else, it cannot be said to have an identity. On the other hand, if an organism does not change, it will neither evolve nor reproduce itself. Dickerson (1978) describes the problem in the transformation from nonliving to living molecules. The living cell has two talents, metabolism and reproduction. Metabolism allows the cell to rearrange ingested compounds into molecules necessary for its own maintenance. Reproduction extends this metabolic capacity by permitting the cell to produce offspring that will have similar metabolic capacities. The debate about the origins of life became organized around the question: Which came first, metabolism or reproduction? The answer according to Dickerson is both. Nucleic acids, the material of reproduction, cannot replicate without the presence of enzymes, and enzymes, the catalysts of metabolism, cannot be formed without nucleic acids. In the primordial soup these molecules evolved in parallel and then mated

to form the first reproducing cell. Many steps were necessary for this transition including the formation of the planet and its chemicals, the synthesis of simple biological molecules, and then the combination of these molecules into primitive protein and nucleic acid chains. The achievement at the end was the combination of a protein molecule that could form a membrane around a nucleic acid molecule that could reproduce not only itself but also its protein casing.

The capacity for continued identity is one of the basic distinctions between life and nonlife. Molecules in solution are generally in a state of dynamic equilibrium, constantly forming and reforming as ions move back and forth between different chemical structures. In order to reach a point where a molecule could show greater individual stability, it needed to be localized and the amount of water available reduced. In order for a living organism to survive, it must be set off from the environment by a boundary surface, or else it will be diluted out of existence. Research in this area has demonstrated that the activity of complex molecules (i.e., polymers) in solution will produce droplets with some minor degree of cohesiveness. Dickerson suggests that among these microsystems those that had the ability to carry out simple reactions to increase their mass or strengthen their membrane were the most likely to survive for at least a short period of time. Within a boundary, there can occur changes that may further lengthen the survival of the system. Coordination of encapsulated biochemical functions would ultimately permit the composition of a reproductive process that would allow the organism to continue functioning beyond its own boundaries, that is, within the boundaries of its offspring.

There is no evidence that the solution to the problem of life was a unique one. Many such systems are possible, but those with the least stability or reproductive capacity were displaced by those with better stability and reproductive capacity. In principle, there is no difference between the selection pressures of the earliest chemical environment and those of later, more familiar, biological ones. Experiments attempting to reproduce the earlier conditions of molecular evolution have found that in addition to forming the amino acids, which are the current basis of all living proteins, other amino acids, which are not part of current proteins, were formed (Miller & Orgel, 1974). The choice of the 20 amino acids in the genetic code was not predetermined. These 20 were the results of competition with other amino acids, which may have been part of other possible genetic codes (Doolittle, 1981).

This discussion of research on the formation of

the first cells is important in exploring the interface between biology and chemistry, between life and nonlife. Every step in the sequence is grounded in physical chemistry, yet the explanation for the transition is based on local circumstances that permitted some molecules to develop new capacities in coordination with other molecules. Even at this earliest point in evolution, there was no separation between heredity and environment, between nature and nurture. There is no evidence that there was ever a naked gene. Survival was the achievement of those combinations of molecules that could make the best utilization of energy to maintain their structure and were most competent at accurately reproducing themselves. These were the first organisms to solve the problem of identity and transformation.

The Changing Environment

The next step in the evolution of cells was a change in the chemical process by which energy is produced, a change that dramatically altered the earth and the kind of life that developed thereafter. Some cells changed their ability to use sunlight in metabolism; they evolved a system of using sunlight in the manufacture of glucose, a step that gave them a great advantage in energy production. Proliferating rapidly, they produced oxygen as a by-product of their photosynthesis and thereby slowly changed the chemical composition of the atmosphere. In this new environment, the first organisms to evolve could merely tolerate oxygen, but subsequently there evolved cells that could utilize oxygen as part of their metabolic processes. This capacity permitted them an even greater advantage in getting energy out of available nutrients.

The developmental principle to be derived from this succession again emphasizes the intimate relationship between organism and environment in which both are active contributors. Transactions occur in which the activity of the organism changes the environment; this in turn produces new selective pressures for future changes in the organism. Not until oxygen occurred in the environment could oxygen-utilizing cells evolve, but the source of that oxygen was in the activity of prior cells. Of additional importance is another result: Abundance of oxygen in the environment eliminated many of the cell lines that led to the photosynthetic process because they could no longer survive in the oxygen-rich environment.

Wholistic processes that were seen to characterize embryological development were evident in the earliest stages of evolution. It has become fashionable to point to human beings as the only species

with the capacity to change the whole earth, yet this capacity was already present in those single-cell oxygen-producing organisms that set the stage for human beings to evolve at all. This theme of the inseparability of organism and environment will reoccur in later discussions of roles and society and of concepts and knowledge. In each case, development will be seen to occur only in those cases where there is a transaction between the system of concern and its surround.

In cellular evolution, during the period that the amount of oxygen in the atmosphere was changing, a major change in structure occurred that significantly altered the reproductive rate of cells and increased the potential genetic variability of cellular offspring.

Eukaryotic cells appeared in which the genetic material was collected within a cell nucleus and bounded by a membrane. In contrast with the earlier prokaryotic cells, in which the genetic material was diffused throughout the cell, the localization of the material presented the possibility for organized gene interchanges and laid the basis for sexual reproduction, which even further enlarged the capacity for genetic variability. Evolution of the nucleus was the precursor to all multicellular forms that began to evolve shortly thereafter (Margulis, 1970). While the prokaryotes vary in ability to tolerate or use oxygen in their metabolism, the eukaryotes are all oxygen-dependent and could not have evolved until the atmosphere had changed. The bases for evolution at this time were biochemical and metabolic innovations that increased the efficiency of certain cells to produce energy for self-maintenance. During this period, the influence of life on the environment was at least as important as the influence of the environment on life. The belated ecological concerns of the last few decades are with a process that already was in operation billions of years ago.

From Single Cells to Human Beings

The directedness of evolutionary progress that gave rise to vitalist and finalist theories seems to move toward differentiation and hierarchic interaction. The question for the evolutionary biologist is why? What advantages accrue in moving from a single cell to a multicellular organism? The chief advantage appears to be the redundancy of cellular machinery. This feature allows the organism to live longer, since individual cells can be replaced, and to do specialized functions more efficiently, since groups of cells can be set to each task (Valentine, 1978). As cells become differentiated into nerves or muscles or reproductive units, they can provide the organism with the possibility of a more stable internal physiology as well as the ability to take different shapes to better interact with the environment. Although each of these evolving specialized cells could not survive alone as their single-cell ancestors did, their union as members of a single organism permitted them to take energy from the environment and to reproduce themselves more effectively than their antecedents.

As with most evolutionary steps, there does not appear to be a single thread of change from single cells to multicellular organisms. It is estimated that the more complex organisms evolved at least 17 times from single cells before the transformation was fully successful (Stebbins, 1950). The specializations that different cell groups in the organism assume seem to be related to their location in the organism. Covering cells became supportive of the animal and formed protective coatings or shells. Marginal cells differentiated toward a locomotive function, initially as flagella and then into limbs. Well-nourished cells surrounding the digestive area took on the function of reproduction.

As major steps are completed, there are periods of rapid development in which a new species radiates widely across the environment. As those movements occur, species not only interact with the environment but also with each other. Nutritional sources that had been restricted to simple compounds for the single-cell life forms now became more complex as life became more complex. The evolution of jaws expanded the possibility for food supplies. The colonization of land by plants provided a base for animals to follow. Smaller animals provided a food source for larger animals. Amphibians had been limited to the water for reproduction, but reptiles developed the egg that gave them the capacity to live completely on land. Mammals, who developed placental reproduction and could thus provide a highly stable insulated early environment for their offspring, were even more independent of the environment.

Each step in the evolutionary sequence provided new opportunities for adaptation. Whenever the environment changed, either as new species emerged or, through geological changes as tectonic plates shifted, new adaptations were possible so that new selective advantages could be achieved for one species or another. Organisms form a part of each other's environments as competitors, predators, hosts, or habitats. Changes that were opportunities for some species were foreclosures for others and extinctions are found in every period of evolution. These environmental changes were fortuitous and probabilistic; they depended on local conditions, and, therefore, they were almost unique and unlikely to be repeated. The probability that two tectonic plates containing sets of different species should collide at a specific point in evolutionary history so that their flora and fauna would mix in a specific way is infinitesimal. The course that evolution took was unique for every species. However, can one say that the general functions assumed by more advanced forms relative to less advanced forms were also unique?

Progress in Evolution

As one views the changes that have occurred in life across the billions of years of evolution, one is frequently struck by the seemingly progressive movement along a number of dimensions. Size is the most obvious, but changes in size are well correlated with changes in organizational complexity and functional possibilities. The path through evolution is frequently seen finalistically, a progress toward an ideal that has human beings as its end point, rather than as a way station in life's development. Although humans are acknowledged to be not the biggest, not the fastest, not the strongest animals, they are thought to compensate by being the most adaptable. However, from the perspective of the evolutionary biologist, even adaptability is only a relative construct.

Simpson (1970), a paleontologist who made major contributions to the modern synthesis, feels that several definite directional statements can be made about biological history: the number of kinds of organisms has vastly increased; the distinction between them in structure, function, and ecology have become greater; and average complexity has increased on the whole. Having made that analysis, Simpson went on to note that these trends do not characterize all phases of evolutionary history; nor do they characterize the evolutionary history of all species. In stable environments there is little increase in the kinds of organisms present. Species distinctions have been far from unidirectional, thus, any notion of a central line of evolutionary development is artificial. In regard to complexity, Simpson accepts that the evolution from unicellular to multicellular organisms with differentiated organs represents an increase in complexity, but once the latter stage is reached, further increases in complexity are not always evident. Simpson (1967) analyzed the notion that one direction in evolution is to increase body size. He found changes that are inconsistent in direction; in some cases, a number of reversals have led to descendant species that are smaller than their ancestors. Pressure for change occurs when the ecological niche to which an organism is already adapted is itself in a state of change. The niche is a multidimensional description of the environment that includes the way of life of the organisms occupying that niche. Because organisms help to create their respective niches, ''empty'' niches cannot be defined prior to the arrival of the species that will occupy them. For Lewontin (1978), evolution can still be conceived of as adaptation, but adaption to a dynamically changing environment in which to stand still is to fall behind rather than adaptation to a set of static parameters.

Even with the constant changes in environments, it must also be noted that there has been a remarkable stability in life forms over the history of evolution. Simpson (1967) observes that of the major phyla that have evolved most are still in existence. Despite the wide array of millions of species that have occupied the earth at one time or another, they represent variations on a small number of basic types of organization. Phyla are identified by zoologists as groups of species that represent the broadest of these themes; each group has a specific anatomical organization that permits a particular set of life functions. These basic types of biological organization still survive even though given species within each phylum are constantly emerging and being extinguished.

The conclusion that Simpson draws from the continuity of the phyla is that they each represent an adaptation to some continuing feature of the terrestrial environment—they each have their niche. Simpson cites an analogy credited to T. H. Huxley in which filling the earth with life is like filling a barrel full of apples. The barrel can be overflowing, but there is still plenty of space for quantities of small pebbles between the apples. After the pebbles are added, there is still space for a load of sand to fit, and finally there is still room for quarts of water to be added, before the barrel can hold no more. The phyla are likened to the varied ingredients of the barrel. There are many possible modes of existence on earth and no single species can fill them all. As long as the earth has a particular organization, then the creatures that have adapted to that organization will continue to survive. In other words, no species is any better adapted than another when judged on the basis of its anatomical and functional characteristics. It is only in relation to a specific environmental context that such judgments can be made. Progress, therefore, cannot be directly related to the concept of adaptation since the paramecium and the cockroach may be better adapted to their environments than human beings are to theirs.

Werner (1957), in dealing with psychological processes, was struck by the contrast between the unilinearity of development as idealized in his orthogenetic principle and the multilinearity of actual developmental forms. Multilinearity was seen as opening the way for the study of behavior not only from the perspective of universal sequences but also from that of individual variations leading to specialized branching-out. Adult esthetic experience can be interpreted as a different line of development from the growth of logical thinking; but both are equally valid because there are differing adult contexts for each of these behavioral developments. From Werner's perspective, the qualities of the psychological niche permit the simultaneous existence of different orders of thought and experience.

Viewing development in an evolutionary context can help to unravel the continuities in life from the discontinuities. Tobach (1981) defines a continuous process as one that is present in some form at all phyletic levels. Variations in the mechanisms that perform the process provide for the discontinuities. Using the example of irritability (i.e., the ability of organisms to respond to perturbation by involvement of parts not directly effected by the change), Tobach argues that the process is both continuous (i.e., present in all species) and discontinuous (i.e., its organizational relation to other structures and functions is qualitatively different among most species).

There is another importance for evolutionary change in the continued existence of phyla at different levels of biological complexity. Without the existence of the lower orders, the higher ones would not only not have evolved but they would also not be able to survive. Ecologists (May, 1973) have noted that there are many more smaller species than larger ones in any given setting. One explanation is that there is a much greater variety of small niches than large ones. Another relates to the relationship of species in a ''food web.'' These webs are organized into trophic levels through which energy flows up the system. In general, these webs consist of only four or five levels or orders of what eats what (May, 1973). At the lowest level, plant primary producers convert inorganic compounds into organic ones and are eaten by second level insect herbivores, who are eaten by first carnivores like spiders and frogs. These in turn can be eaten by second carnivores like birds and snakes. The point is that without the continuing existence of the lower orders in these food webs, the higher orders could not evolve or survive.

The relationship between the stages in Piaget's (1950) theory of cognitive development can be seen as analogs of levels in the food web. Piaget's view is that each stage incorporates the structures of the next lower stage, from the here-and-now interactions with material objects to successively removed levels of interaction with abstracted objects of thought. However, the functioning characteristic of each stage is maintained even in the most advanced individual. A human cannot function without sensorimotor interactions with the physical and social environment, nor without the perceptually organized thought of preoperations, even when engaged in concrete or formal operations. Piaget admits that biological maturation plays a role in stage transitions, but the basis of each new stage requires as its primary constituent the achievements of the previous stage. The representation of objects serves as the basis for concepts that serve as the basis for group structures that serve as the basis for logical systems. Piaget (1970) interprets cognitive development as the result of an individual reflecting on his or her own thought. The phylogenetic analogy would require much greater attention to be placed on the structure of the environment and complexity of the adaptive demands placed on the individual by that environment.

Progress can be reconnected to the concept of adaptation but only as an approximation from a specific point of view. Greater organizational complexity is adaptive only in situations where that increased complexity adds to the reproductive fitness of a species. One evolutionary trend is for life to engage in the process of building on itself. As life forms move into new spheres, new opportunities are created for other forms of life. Although the trend for later larger forms to feed on earlier smaller forms can be emphasized, the opposite is also true. The rise of the vertebrates provided new niches for bacteria and protozoa in their intestines and blood streams. The rise of human beings and their societies provided new opportunities for cockroaches and rats to share their dwellings.

Analogously, human sensorimotor and affective experience is enlarged by the development of higher cognitive processes. The conscious manipulation of experience through art and education increases the range of possible emotional, perceptual, and cognitive sensibility.

The final point to be made about evolution is that each new adaptation can only occur on the basis of what already exists. Simpson (1967) emphasizes the dual controls on evolutionary change in the nature of the environment and in the characteristics of the organism. Environments are not limitless. Thus there are constraints on the ways in which organisms can survive. Similarly, there are limits to the new forms that organisms can assume, based on what those organisms have already become. Evolution has many possibilities, but these potential directions are constrained and continuous with what has come before for both organism and environment.

If this view were correct, one would expect that the same environmental opportunity would be exploited differently by different species or different groups. The evolution of flight is a demonstration of how evolution works with the material at hand. Wings developed three times from vertebrate forelimbs: in the reptilian pterodactyl, the birds, and the mammalian bat. Each of these homologous evolutions from a common ancestor reached a different structural solution. The solution was radically different for the analogous development of wings in insects.

Similarly, one would expect that the same species would evolve differently given different environmental opportunities. The diversity of species stimulated Darwin to his theories through his observations of the way birds are more or less related as a function of proximity and climate. What he recognized from these studies is the conditioning of evolution by the selective pressure of the environment.

Phylogeny, Ontogeny, and the Organismic Model

The properties of the organismic model were derived from the properties of living organisms. In describing the data of embryological growth, a number of properties were identified as defining the biological metaphor. The ensuing discussion of evolution was aimed at determining how many of these organismic principles will generalize from ontogeny to phylogeny, from embryology to evolution.

The results of this analysis seem to indicate that there is a good correspondence between the defined properties of the metaphor, and the two fields of biology. In both developmental domains, the characteristics of the parts, the cells in embryology, and the species in evolution cannot be separated from the characteristics of the context. In different contexts, the parts exhibit different contemporary characteristics, and the direction of their development will be altered. The properties exhibited at any point in time cannot be reduced to the interaction of previous properties because they are the result of transactions between those previous properties and the previous environments. Future outcomes are neither determined nor predictable because in each domain further development depends on probabilistic interactions between parts and their environments.

One major difference between the two developmental progressions is that the environment is much more predictable in ontogeny than in phylogeny. The self-righting tendencies that Waddington (1962) attributed to embryological growth are mechanisms designed to stabilize the interactions between organism and environment. In fact, it was the stabilization of these functions that took so much evolutionary time. To produce the genetic code took a billion years. To get the code to the point where ontogeny could occur took 2 billion years, when nucleated cells had evolved to provide the basis for multicellular organisms. Each evolutionary step to a new form was based on a previous stabilization of ontogeny in the ancestral form. The basis for Haeckel's theory that ontogeny recapitulates phylogeny is that the embryological development of individuals in more complex species seems to repeat the evolutionary history of the species. What was soon realized is that the embryological recapitulation is not of a sequence of adult ancestors but of embryological stages of ancestors (Waddington, 1966). For example, human embryos go through a phase in which they have the appearance of embryonic fish, not adult fish. Evolutionary changes, especially among the vertebrates, are based on later stages in embryogenesis when small alterations will not endanger the viability of the individual. When large changes occur early in fetal growth, the embryo is aborted because it is so divergent from the adapted relationships within the placenta. Gould (1977) has made the case that phylogenetic changes are more the result of alterations in the timing of embryological processes than the action of new structural genes. He analyzes the relationship between changes in the rate of somatic growth and reproductive maturation in terms of progenesis and neoteny. These processes are the result of subtle alterations in entire genetic systems rather than major innovations in discrete areas.

Despite the complexities of structure evident in the mammals, the variability of fetal outcomes is relatively small. The reason is that so much of that development occurs in the highly stabilized placental environment discussed earlier. When the individual emerges into the far more variable outside environment, which is not subject to the same tight genetic regulation, other forms of regulation must take over to shape development. For humans, these other forms of regulation are psychological and social. There are aspects of these regulations that reflect the developmental codes inherent in embryological development and aspects that reflect the dialectic of evolution in which a changing organism is further altered by the changes it induces in its environment.

Should these aspects of psychological and social growth of the individual be considered as mere extensions of ontogeny and phylogeny, or is there a need for a more general model for understanding such processes? The organismic model is a suggestion in this direction, but at heart it is only a metaphor. What is required is a more rigorous theory that embodies the principles of the organismic model but places them in a more generalized context. The most articulated effort at such a conception is general systems theory.

GENERAL SYSTEMS THEORY

At the outset we must make a distinction between systems approaches and general systems theory. A *systems approach* is usually treated synonymously with an interactionist position in which one cannot examine the bits and pieces of behavior in isolation. On the other hand, a *general systems approach* incorporates this phenomenological position into a theory that attempts to describe the organization of the systems. Whatever their specific contents or scientific domains, systems are seen as having some general properties, which can be studied in their own right, independently of their concrete manifestations as they occur in biology or psychology. General systems theorists have concerned themselves with a number of these general properties.

General systems theory has come to describe a level of theory midway between highly generalized constructions of pure mathematics and the specific theories of the specialized disciplines. Boulding (1956) saw a need for theoretical constructs about the general relationships of the empirical world, which lie between "the specific that has no meaning and the general that has no content." He saw the lowest level of ambition for such a theory to be the pointing out of similarities in the theoretical constructions of different disciplines. At a higher level of ambition is the development of a spectrum of theories to produce a system of systems that will illuminate gaps in theoretical models and even point the way toward methods for filling the gaps, much like Mendeleyev's periodic table of the elements did for chemistry.

Boulding suggested two approaches to such theorizing. The first is to search for analogous phenomena that occur in a number of different disciplines. The second approach is to arrange the empirical fields into a hierarchy of complexity. Examples that might evolve from the first approach are that almost all disciplines deal with populations of elements to which new ones are added or born and old ones are subtracted or die. These elements interact with some kind of environment and express some form of behavior. Among these behaviors are growth and, of most interest from an organizational framework, transmission of information between the elements. Boulding's hope was that the integration of such universal phenomena across disciplines could potentially lead to a general field theory of the dynamics of action and interaction.

As an example of the second approach, Boulding organized the elements of concern to each science into a hierarchical arrangement encompassing nine levels. The first level is labeled *frameworks,* that is, static descriptions of the relationships of elements in space. Next on the scale of complexity are *clockworks,* simple dynamic systems that have predetermined movements; these are followed by *thermostats,* cybernetic systems that can transmit and interpret information. At the fourth level, biology begins with the *cell,* where life differentiates from nonlife by adding the property of a self-maintaining structure. The fifth level is the *plant,* in which the cells have a division of labor into various tissues as well as the separation between genotype and phenotype. The level of the *animal* is sixth; here there are specialized information receptors, a central structure for information processing in the brain, and the property of self-awareness. The seventh level is the *human;* here there is added a self-reflective quality to the central brain structures as well as the ability to produce, absorb, and interpret symbols. At the eighth level, the *societal* level, the unit is the abstracted role that is tied into a social network by channels of communication which incorporate value systems in addition to semantic and symbolic systems. Boulding added a ninth level of complexity labeled the *transcendental* to contain ultimates, absolutes, and inescapable unknowables that he imagined to have systematic structures and relationships similar to those of the lower-level knowables.

Boulding recognized that such a hierarchy in itself adds little to our understanding of science. But through it one can recognize deficiencies in both empirical and theoretical analyses. Adequate *theoretical* models currently exist only at the level of the cell. For example, the organismic model in developmental psychology is at this level (Reese & Overton, 1970). *Empirical* knowledge is deficient at all levels of the hierarchy.

If one examines the explanatory systems applied by workers in the social sciences, one finds that while the concern is with the eighth level of complexity, most theories are at the second level moving toward the third, that is, mechanistic theories at the level of complexity of clockworks and thermostats are used to explain the phenomena of social systems.

For example, social learning theory based on a set of principles mechanically relating stimuli, reinforcements, and responses is used to explain the behavior of individuals operating in a social collective comprised of roles, norms, and institutions to which these learning principles might not apply. From a general systems perspective, the behavior of individuals is an ingredient in the operation of social systems, but group activity can take on a character not explicable by the behavior of individuals studied apart from the group (Pepitone, 1981). Individuals studied alone would not typically place themselves in life-threatening situations, but individuals as part of certain social groups like armies would. In contrast, Skinner (1966, 1981) argues that selection by consequences acting on individual behavior will explain the evolution of culture and all forms of group behavior. While having hypotheses at any level is better than not having them, eventually a level of theorizing appropriate to the level of complexity will be a necessity.

These hierarchies, while of interest to the general systems theorists, may be less so to developmental psychologists. Of necessity there should be interest in the importance of directing explanatory efforts toward an appropriate level of analysis, but these efforts should be devoted to the processes that may emerge from general systems theory as well as from the structures. An overview of such processes must begin with the work of Ludwig von Bertalanffy.

The idea of a general systems theory is generally attributed to Bertalanffy (1968), who recognized the need to view biology, at least, as an organized system. In the 1930s he promulgated an interdisciplinary doctrine that elaborated principles and models that apply to systems in general, irrespective of the particular kind of elements and forces involved. He saw classical science, represented by the diverse disciplines of chemistry, biology, psychology and the other social sciences, as trying to isolate the elements of the observed universe—simple chemical compounds, enzymes, cells, sensations, habits, or individuals, as the case may be, with the expectation that by putting these elements together again, the whole would be intelligible.

In contrast, Bertalanffy argued that to understand science one needs to understand not only the elements but, more importantly, their interrelations. In addition, he argued that there are correspondences or isomorphisms between systems in totally different fields. The concept of wholeness, which has heretofore been treated as some metaphysical notion, is now to be interpreted by concepts of hierarchic structure, stability, teleology, differentiation, steady state, and goal directedness. As avenues for their study, these properties gave rise to new disciplines such as automata theory, set theory, net theory, and graph theory within mathematics and to the more technology-oriented disciplines of cybernetics, control engineering, and computers. Bertalanffy felt that the study of these interdisciplinary isomorphisms might further the ambitious aim of the unification of science.

He argued against existing mechanistic views that represent the world as ''a Shakespearean tale told by an idiot,'' and argued for an organismic outlook that sees the world as a great organization. He rejected the notions of logical positivism based on physicalism, atomism, and the copy theory of knowledge; and, emphasizing the contributions of the biological sciences, he focused concern on properties of the whole such as interaction, transaction, and teleology. From his work he developed a philosophy that sees man as part of a hierarchy of systems rather than a heap of physical particles. At each level of this hierarchy, truth is not represented in some objective absoluteness but as a *relationship* between the elements and the system. Human knowledge is not seen as an approximation of truth but rather as the expression of a relationship between knower and known.

Bertalanffy (1968) spent his last efforts developing a philosophy that he called perspectivism. Each epoch of history has a view of reality appropriate for that epoch but also unique to that epoch. It was only by appreciating the universal processes of life and their organization that one could hope to approach some general theory of life that would incorporate these various uniquenesses.

System Properties

Because general systems theory is a discipline rather than a theory, it is natural that there are many different views as to what a general systems theory should look like. Boulding (1980), while reflecting on the founding of the Society for General Systems Research in 1954, pointed out that a general system was defined at that time simply as any theoretical system of interest to more than one discipline. From this view, he felt there should be many general systems theories, not one. The reason for this is not so much because one cannot be produced but rather because there is more than one general system in the real world.

As in other disciplines where the mechanistic and organismic metaphors have been used to differentiate theoretical perspectives, a similar division can be used to differentiate systems theories. For example, Ashby, one of the early pioneers in the area, uses a cybernetic general systems model that seems basically to be an updated version of the machines of Descartes. Although such new properties as teleology (i.e., self-correcting, goal-directed behavior) have been admitted to the system, these properties are clearly rooted in such elementary units as the servomechanism. Ashby's (1952) version of systems theory, which he detailed in his pioneering book, *Design for a Brain,* is only at Boulding's third level, that of the thermostat.

Of more interest are those systems theories that use the biological metaphor of the organismic approach, because they cut across many more levels of the hierarchy of life and because they clearly introduce the concept of most concern here, development. In this vein, Bertalanffy's (1968) concept of open and closed systems was a major step forward. The *open system* is defined as a structure that maintains its organization despite exchanges in its parts, (i.e., there is a throughput of material constituents) while the whole maintains its identity. As a simple analogy, a river and a flame are given as examples of structures whose components are constantly changing while the whole, the river or the flame, continue. However, there is no organized differentiation within these wholes. At a level more meaningful to the study of life, the cell is an organization that maintains itself as a whole while the individual molecules of which it is composed are constantly being exchanged through metabolic processes.

The *closed system* fits a mechanistic model in that its structure can be specified and its operation is reducible to a few principles, as in Boulding's level of clockworks. Cybernetics have greatly extended the range of functioning of closed systems through the use of feedback. In contrast with simple machines, cybernetic systems can interact with the environment on the basis of information, but, in contrast with living systems that are open to material exchanges with the environment, they cannot alter their fundamental structure. Bertalanffy may have been limited in his expectations regarding the future of cybernetics, since today it is becoming more conceivable that the self-regulation of computers can be extended to the possibility of altering their hardware and mainframes. However, from the perspective of systems theory, this possibility would not change the definitions of closed and open systems, but only those systems that fall into one or the other category.

For the developmental psychologist, most systems of concern are open in their characteristics. The growth of behavior involves the self-directing interaction of children and their environments and the progressive changing of the organization of behavior as a function of experience. Consequently, the possibilities for each individual's development require an analysis of at least three levels of functioning. Each child is constrained by biological characteristics that structure the ways in which the environment can be experienced and acted on (i.e., the structures for perception and motor activity produced by phylogenetic and ontogenetic processes). Each child is further constrained by the social and technical structures of the culture in which he or she is being raised. Between these levels lie the psychological systems of direct interest.

From the beginnings of general systems theory with its descriptive emphasis on self-organizing properties of structures in hierarchical systems, there has been an increasing formalization of various aspects of the theory. Recently, a major presentation of the theory was attempted by J. G. Miller (1978). He details a general living systems theory exclusively concerned with a subset of all systems, the living ones, that run through seven levels from the cell to supranational systems. In exhaustive detail, he analyzes each of these seven levels of the hierarchy in terms of 19 subsystem processes which use the concepts of thermodynamics, information theory, cybernetics, and systems engineering as well as the more classical concepts of physics. Miller sees his purpose as producing ''a description of living structure and process in terms of input and output, flows through systems, steady states and feedbacks which will clarify and unify the facts of life'' (p. 42). These process variables include such things as ingestors, distributors, transducers, decoders, and deciders, which deal with both matter-energy and information.

A somewhat simpler presentation is that of Ervin Laszlo (1972), who deals with only four levels and four process variables. The four levels are: physical systems; biological systems; cognitive systems; and social systems.

Laszlo defines each system level as a joint function of four independent system properties. These are: first, the property of wholeness and order; second, the property of adaptive self-stabilization; third, the property of adaptive self-organization; and fourth, the property of hierarchical structuring.

Wholeness and Order

The first property of *wholeness and order* is a complex version of the historic organismic notion that the whole is more than the sum of its parts. Put simply, a whole adds the property of relationship to the parts. A part taken alone cannot define a relationship. It is only in the company of other parts that the relationship can exist. The classic gestalt examples of such patterns as melodies are appropriate here. The pitch of the notes that make up a melody can vary over a wide range as long as the relationship between the notes remains the same. At a more complex level, Simon (1973) points out that the same computer program written in FORTRAN, for example, can be executed by different computers using different machine languages. These machine languages interface between the electronic deep structure of the computer and the logical surface structure of the program.

The contrary position has been that of the reductionists, who see no problem in attempting to explain the complexity of functioning found at higher levels by using principles derived from lower levels. In other words, there are no properties of collections of individuals that cannot be explained by the properties of the individuals analyzed apart from the collection. In an attempt to clarify the relationships between fundamental laws and the various fields of knowledge, P. M. Anderson (1972), a physicist, has subdivided reductionism into legitimate and illegitimate reductionism. He argues that the ability to reduce everything to simple fundamental laws does not imply the ability to start from those laws and reconstruct the universe. He sees reductionism as legitimate if it is restricted to the hypothesis that the functioning of higher levels of complexity are based upon and cannot violate the laws of functioning of lower levels of complexity. Biological functioning cannot violate the laws of chemistry and physics that constrain the activity of an organism's constituent atoms and molecules. On the other hand, Anderson regards a ''constructionist'' use of reductionism, which attempts to argue that higher levels of complexity can be explained by the principles of the lower levels, to be illegitimate. The laws of chemistry and physics do not explain biological functioning.

The genetic code is a good example of this point. The structure of DNA cannot violate the constraints placed upon it by its chemical structure; however, the laws of chemistry do not explain the genetic code (Polanyi, 1968). The code by which the four bases of the molecule are translated into the 20 amino acids is a biological law that has only an arbitrary connection to its chemical substrate. There is no chemical reason why any specific combination of bases should translate into any specific amino acid.

In the current debates on reductionism there is a certain irony. The physicists, who have traditionally held the role of fundamentalists by studying the basic units of the universe, have begun to turn more and more to metaphysical speculations (Gal-Or, 1972; Soodak & Iberall, 1978). Physicists are facing an uncomfortable fact: Whenever they seem to discover the ultimate building blocks of nature, someone discovers a more fundamental level, be it electrons, hadrons, or quarks. Even more interesting are the names, such as color and charm, chosen to identify these new units; they reflect abstract process or system properties rather than any concrete characteristic of the particles. Moreover, these particles cannot exist in isolation, but they must always be parts of a system.

The traditional view of the relationship among the sciences has been that they represent a pyramid with physics providing the material base and the social sciences nebulously surmounting the summit. A more recent view is still of a pyramid, but one hanging in space, where the emergence of softer areas of science at the tip is matched by the dissolution of the harder areas at the bottom as each purported ultimate particle gives way to the next newly discovered ultimate particle. But most important, physicists have come to see that what appears as material, in reality, represents an organization in time and space of some underlying dynamic process. Nothing that can be defined as a thing-in-itself has been found to exist. In each case, there are dynamic processes that give rise to the unit's appearance and continued existence.

Trefil (1980) after reviewing the history of the search for simplicity in physics feels that "the dream of explaining the entire physical world in terms of a few basic building blocks does not look realizable" (p. 208). Instead the explanation may involve something very similar-sounding to a general systems theory.

> The road that led us to quarks started with the assumption that nature was simple in the sense that it could be understood in terms of a few simple constituents. We could call this a search for structural simplicity. We can imagine another kind of simplicity, however. We can imagine a world in which we understand processes in terms of a few general principles. The simplicity here would be of an abstract and purely intellectual nature. . . . In practice, the search for intellectual simplicity has been concerned not so much with the structure of particles as with their interactions. Thus, instead of concentrating on the search for quarks, the theorist would concern himself with studying the fundamental interactions between elementary particles. (p. 208)

The emphasis of the new physics is on interactions

rather than objects. The ultimates will not be found in products, but rather in processes.

In short, scientists at *every* level of complexity now have difficulty clearly defining the essential parts of their science. At the atomic level, physicists no longer consider the solar system view of the atom with its electrons spinning around a nucleus core. Instead there is the conception of a series of fields within which are embedded particlelike concentrations of energy and spin. The atom is currently conceived of as functionally interacting nuclear and electronic fields rather than the older notion of mechanically interacting parts (P. M. Anderson, 1972). At the biological level, wholeness and order are found to characterize all systems. Modern definitions of any biological element or structure interpret these as only visible indices of regularities of the underlying dynamics operating in their domains (Weiss, 1969). In other words, static entities are illusions; at heart everything is process.

The task assumed by physicists and chemists is to discover the forces binding energy together so that more complex organizations become possible. The existence of high orders of structure was thought to run against a basic principle of physics, entropy. This second law of thermodynamics states that all systems move toward a state of equal probability. This characteristic of closed systems meant that if unsymmetrical organizations are isolated, they will move toward symmetry. If two gases are placed in a closed container in which one gas is on one side and the second on the other, over a period of time they will intermingle until the distributions of both gases will be equal in every area of the container. Living systems represent major inequalities in the distribution of chemicals that not only maintain these inequalities but increase them with further development. This counter-entropic property of life was the basis for vitalistic theories discussed earlier. More mechanistically oriented theorists introduced hypothetical constructs such as "negative entropy" to explain the improbable organization of living organisms (Brillouin, 1950).

More recently, significant advances within thermodynamics have led to a new understanding of the spontaneous generation of ordered systems. Prigogine (1978) won a Nobel prize for being instrumental in developing a theory of nonlinear systems, which he labeled "dissipative structures," and for rewriting the second law of thermodynamics. The maintenance of these highly ordered structures requires exchanging matter and energy in a constant flux with the environment. Here at the lowest levels of chemical organization, there is a demonstrated inseparability between the structure and the environment. Without dynamic interchanges, no structures would exist. Life, which began as complex molecules that could produce energy, is no longer considered a thermodynamic anomaly requiring special hypotheses. Ordered systems have been given a legitimate status within the laws of physics.

What Prigogine has proposed describes two principles that are of relevance to psychological development. The first is that organized systems emerge from local irregularities in the distribution of matter; the second is that a throughput of energy is required for the maintenance and further development of these systems. In the evolution of life described earlier, there is the requirement that molecules be isolated in some fashion from the universal water environment and that there be a metabolic process by which the system took energy from the environment. Information processing theories of cognition have been based on the important relationship between signal and noise (G. A. Miller, 1963). Signals represent local regularities of information that are contrasted with the homogeneous background of random inputs. The organism must be able to segment what has meaning in the environment from what is meaningless. This process should be able to occur only when the organism is operating on the environment. It is the flow of experience through the cognitive system that not only maintains it but provides the information for further development.

What have become acceptable questions for physicists should also become acceptable for scientists dealing with the more complex levels of living systems in psychology and sociology. For systems that are in dynamic flux, what is the glue that holds the structure together? Psychological concepts and social institutions, once assumed to be things-in-themselves, must be interpreted as structures maintained dynamically through interchanges with the environment. The basis of constructivist theories, such as Piaget's in psychology, is not that children construct a representation of the world but rather that, through their constructive ability, they build themselves. The ability to reach high levels of cognitive development is not a direct consequence of having the biological equipment for thought but rather the result of the operation of this equipment in interpreting input, in organizing that input into meaningful units based on further activity, and eventually in patterning those meaningful units into whole systems based on intellectual experience. Without the throughput of information, there would be no cognitive development.

Adaptive Self-Stabilization

Laszlo's second general property of natural systems is that of *adaptive self-stabilization*. This property refers to a cybernetic stability that self-regulates the system to compensate for changing conditions in the environment by making coordinated changes in the system's internal variables. This buffering capacity of the system reduces the effects of the environment on its constituent parts. By the use of feedback mechanisms, systems with this property become adaptive entities.

The basic unit of adaptive self-stabilization is the cybernetic negative feedback loop. The feedback is called negative because its function is to reduce the effects of deviation. In the prototypical case of the thermostat, deviations in temperature below the set point feed back to activate the heating unit that will raise the temperature until the set-point is reached and the heating unit deactivated. Control theory or cybernetics as an approach to understanding self-regulating systems has become increasingly common in psychological research. Carver and Scheier (1982) describe the utilization of such a model to understand the control of attentional processes in personality theory, self-regulation in cognitive behavior therapy, and biofeedback processes in health psychology. Carver and Scheier emphasized behavioral self-regulation within the individual but acknowledged the importance of social superstrate and biological substrate as hierarchical constraints on the individual. Theoretically more important is the acknowledgment that while the self-regulation of a system to maintain a particular set-point can be defined within the system, the establishment of the set-point must be hierarchically determined. Goals, values, and roles are established by the context of other superordinate system levels and not only by the subsystem of concern.

If there is a larger range of effective interaction between a system and its environment, there will be a larger effect on the system of perturbations introduced from without. A system that only responds to the temperature of the environment will make fewer internal adjustments than a system that is sensitive to temperature plus oxygen content as well as visual and auditory input. The complexity is even greater when there is an interdependence between the internal subsystems, for example, when the functioning of the subsystem for maintaining visual input levels is dependent on the maintenance of an appropriate internal temperature by the thermoregulatory subsystem.

What is of interest here is that as one moves along the scale of complexity, systems become more and more improbable from a thermodynamic perspective; and, as a consequence, they must rely to an increasing extent on precisely controlled environmental relations. Within the psychological realm, subsystems for motivation and attention can be seen as providing the conditions in which more complex cognitive processes can occur (Carver & Schier, 1982). The maintenance of some level of homeostasis or steady state is essential to the continued identity of a system. At the biological level this is very clear in the case of the regulation of temperature, pH levels, and oxygen saturation, among many other variables. Even small changes in these parameters threaten the integrity of the system.

These self-stabilizing properties can operate in terms of a set steady state, but frequently must follow a more dynamic course. An example discussed earlier is Waddington's (1962) developmental variation of self-stabilization, homeorhesis, in contrast to Cannon's homeostasis. In homeorhetic functioning the set point of the system's steady state changes across time. When self-stabilization occurs, it must be to the appropriate developmental set point rather than to an absolute one. When a deviation occurs during embryological development, for example, the self-righting tendencies must be directed at reaching the developmental level where the fetus should be at the current point in time rather than the developmental level at the point in time at which the deviation occurred. One can imagine the complexity of genetic coding that is required to control the interactions of the developing infant with a temporal series of environmental conditions so that the resulting new born is within minimal range of variability. Considering the number of cell divisions and reorganizations that occur during the prenatal period, this feat of control is magnificent.

Adaptive Self-Organization

The third property of natural systems is that of *adaptive self-organization*. While the second property of self-stabilization allows the system to resist perturbations and return to some steady-state parameter, adaptive self-organization is a reorganization that alters the forces and parameters within the system when it is subjected to the action of new constants in the environment. Laszlo (1972) defines adaptive self-organization as changes made when new external forcings act on internal constraints. The direction of change that is implied by the term

adaptation, is one in which the existing system can best continue to function in the face of new circumstances. Piaget's (1950) concepts of assimilation and accommodation are obvious translations of these processes. To the extent that the system cannot assimilate the new environmental conditions with existing regulatory subsystems, accommodation must occur in the form of new subsystems. The new regulatory functions may be fulfilled by new relationships between existing subsystems, or by the establishment of a higher order subsystem with new functions.

In the sensorimotor period, for example, the infant is able to treat objects initially as if their properties were independent. The object is something to suck or look at or touch, depending on which scheme is brought to bear. As these schemes become coordinated, the object becomes something to suck and to look at and to touch. However, once these coordinations are formed they can no longer support the infant's idea that activity controls the object (i.e., that the reason that an object is seeable is because it is looked at or the reason that it is feelable is because it is touched). Although looking away from the object used to make it disappear, now it is being held while the child looks away, so it does not disappear. For Piaget (1952), the child fills in the gap by imagining the missing dimension stimulating representation and achieving object permanence. Object permanence is a coordination of the object's properties that confer on it a presence even in the absence of the child's action on it. A higher-order system is established to coordinate the subsystems that were previously limited to single properties of the object. This new system now has the additional property of action in thought, where previously the action of the child was restricted to real objects.

It is important to note that adaptively reorganized systems are not necessarily more stable systems. They may deal well with forces that elicit the process of self-organization, but they may not be more resistant to all factors in the general environment. To the extent that self-organization results in a greater complexity of structure, the system becomes thermodynamically more "improbable" and potentially unstable. As a consequence, the evolution of systems is "toward increasingly adapted, yet structurally unstable states, balancing their intrinsically unstable complex structure by a wider range of self-stabilizatory functions" (Laszlo, 1972, p. 44). Although these higher-order structures are more independent of specific environmental pressures, the price they pay for such independence is that they need many more internal control systems. When animals evolved from cold blooded to warm blooded, they increased the range of environments in which they could dwell, but the cost was the need for a variety of fine-tuned homeostatic devices to maintain the internal set point in the face of wide fluctuations in external temperature.

Adaptive self-organization is the most complex of the system properties and is central to a concern with the process of evolution. Though adaptive self-stabilization can provide the feedback requirements for maintaining a steady state in homeostasis, or even the more complex homeorhetic functions of following a developmental course from the fertilized egg to the adult, it does not deal with the changes wrought when new environmental circumstances arise for which there are no existing balancing parameters. Laszlo would argue that the genotype provides for both homeostatic and homeorhetic changes, but in the face of certain contingencies alterations are necessary in the genotype itself. These alterations are the kind of reorganizations of fundamental structures that are called evolution.

It is important to recognize the two types of regulations implied by self-stabilization and self-reorganization. The ontogeny of the individual clearly demonstrates structural changes that lead the organism from one level of complexity to another, from the single cell of the fertilized egg to the multicellular blastula through differentiations into tissues, organs, and the systems that support adult biological functions. The perspective based on systems has emphasized the role of environment in all of these biological encounters. Without the environmental inputs at each developmental epoch, there would be no movement to the next development stage.

However, these developmental progressions, even though they incorporate a need for sensitivity to differentiated aspects of the biological environment, do not reveal the process of evolution, by which new adjustments may occur to the same or different environmental pressures. For this understanding, one must examine adaptive self-organization. However, this is easier said than done, since the study of evolution is for the most part a historical study—a reconstruction of past events, past environments, and past reorganizations—rather than an easily observed contemporary process.

The course of evolution is frequently represented as a tree diagram with a trunk of single-cell organisms subdividing to produce many branches that represent the currently existing species on earth. What is too often forgotten is that there is a similar tree diagram of environments in which the trunk of primordial magma cools to branch into water and land masses that further branch into areas of forest and plain containing continuously changing varieties of flora and fauna. This evolution of environments is part and parcel of the evolution of species; each species is in a continuous adaptive relation to the development of the other (Foerster, 1966). Fish could not leave the water until there was land to go to, primates could not climb into the trees until there were trees to live in (Fig. 2).

Systemic Hierarchies

Laszlo's last property deals explicitly with the ordering of levels within a system. Laszlo argues that systems that have the first three properties of wholeness and order, adaptive self-stabilization, and adaptive self-organization will develop in the direction of increasing hierarchic structuration.

Simon (1973) hypothesized that complex systems will more readily evolve from simple systems if there are stable intermediary forms. Systems that are based on hierarchies are much more stable because failure in organization will not destroy the whole system but only decompose it to the next stable subsystem level. As a consequence, instead of starting all over again, the process of complexification can start from the stable subsystem level and reconstitute the loss in a much shorter period of time. Simon uses a parable about two watchmakers as a nonmathematical example of this point.

Two watchmakers assemble fine watches, each watch containing ten thousand parts. Each watchmaker is interrupted frequently to answer the phone. The first has organized his total assembly operation into a sequence of subassemblies; each subassembly is a stable arrangement of 100 elements, and each watch, a stable arrangement of 100 subassemblies. The second watchmaker has developed no such organization. The average interval between phone interruptions is a time long enough to assemble about 150 elements. An interruption causes any set of elements that does not yet form a stable system to fall apart completely. By the time he has answered about eleven phone calls, the first watchmaker will usually have finished assembling a watch. The second watchmaker will almost never succeed in assembling one—he will suffer the fate of Sisyphus: As often as he rolls the rock up the hill, it will roll down again. (p. 7)

Simon's view is that "nature loves hierarchies." Hierarchical systems are the only ones with time to

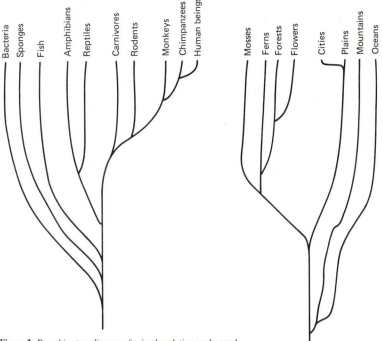

Figure 2. Branching tree diagram of animal evolution can be paralleled by a tree diagram of branching geographical and plant evolution. Trees are environments for each other. Branches within trees are also environments for other branches.

evolve, which explains their prominence among natural systems. It pays for systems to cooperate in evolving more complex functions than to do the job themselves. Systems at about the same level within the same environment will tend to form suprasystems. What is most striking here is that these suprasystems incorporate both the subsystem and the subsystem's environment, which is really just another system. Observable examples can be seen in embryological development. The genetic material of the nucleus in the zygote initially is in interaction with the cytoplasmic material provided by the maternal ovum. Immediately, this small system begins reproducing itself into a small range of similar forms that are coalesced into a new system, the blastula, which includes not only the nuclei but the cytoplasmic environments of the original cell. The blastula, a relatively homogeneous cell mass, begins to differentiate into the gastrula, an organ with specialized tissues as its subsystems. In ontogeny, this process will continue until the biological hierarchy is completed and the child is thrust into the outside world where he or she can begin creating the psychological hierarchy.

The infant's perceptions are modality specific with each observation occurring in the environment of the others. The tactile sensations from the hand are felt in the context of visual, auditory, olfactory, and gustatory properties of the object. As representation develops, the properties of the object that served as perceptual environments for each other are integrated in thought as a superordinate cognitive level—the concept. Further, when children achieve what Piaget calls object permanence, they are able to treat themselves as objects of thought as well. The subject and the object become united in a new cognitive organization that will serve as the basis for further hierarchical developments.

There are no defined upper limits to the systems in which one participates. The sequence of hierarchical levels is only limited by the variety of systems available for inclusion. There are proximal limits placed by the state of evolution of the systems of concern, but there are no ultimate limits in terms of future developments. Each higher level in a hierarchy will have emerged with a greater diversity of functions than any one of its subsystems. On the other hand, there will be a smaller number of actualized higher-level systems than previous subsystems. Molecules are fewer in number than atoms but display a far greater array of functions and properties. Organisms are fewer in number than molecules, and societies are even fewer in number yet incorporate the widest range of functions.

Hierarchic Interactions

An additional aspect of hierarchical organization in natural systems is that systems at each level do not have unidirectional control functions over those of lower levels. There is a dual control (Polanyi, 1968), which is limited by both the nature of the parts and the nature of the whole. The higher levels set boundary conditions for the subsystems, but they do not determine the activity of the subsystems. Polanyi sees these boundary conditions as extraneous to the processes they delimit. Boundary conditions set by higher-order systems harness the properties of the lower systems but cannot violate those properties.

Polanyi analyzes five levels of a hierarchy necessary to produce a spoken literary composition in terms of dual control. Each of the five levels—voice production, word utterance, sentence construction, style organization, and text composition—must conform to the laws that apply to the elements themselves as well as the laws of the entity formed by the elements. Words are based on the rules of sound production, but the rules of sound production do not determine what words will be formed. Sentences are composed of words, but the meanings of words do not determine which sentences will be constructed. A vocabulary cannot be derived from phonetics nor can grammar be derived from a vocabulary. The correct use of grammar does not necessarily produce a good style nor does style produce content, except perhaps in certain rhetorical contexts like politics.

The language hierarchy also illustrates the multiplicative effect of hierarchies on possible functions. Relative to the number of possible sounds and combinations of sounds, there are very few languages in the world. Yet, by combining sets of sounds in an ordered hierarchy, a far greater range of meaning can be expressed by the smaller set of languages than by the greater set of sound combinations.

At a more abstracted level, Simon (1973) discusses how different levels of the hierarchy maintain a degree of independence from each other. For example, when the energies of different physical levels are compared, sharp gradations are found. The energies within atomic nuclei approach 140 million electron volts, while those between atoms in molecules are only of the order of 5 electron volts, while the biological energies within complex molecules are only around one-half of an electron volt. The difference between an atom and a molecule is in the energy levels at which they interact. The smaller the entity the higher the frequency of the interaction. With a three-level hierarchy one could find that the frequency of change at the highest level would be so slow as to be unobservable. At the lowest level the frequencies would be so fast that they could be treated as a constant. It would be at the middle level that the frequencies would be of an observable order and would therefore determine the dynamics of the system under study. Simon refers to a system with these properties as "nearly decomposable," one can ignore the details of the next lower level down and the slow interactions of the next up.

Pattee (1973) adds another interpretation to explain how levels of a hierarchy retain a large degree of independence of the details of each other, yet also have a controlling relationship to each other. Through their constraints, higher levels of a system provide new freedoms. The constraints that the genetic code places on chemistry makes possible the development of life. Only certain amino acids are coded in the genetic system, a limiting factor. On the other hand, there is no need to return to the beginning of evolution to get amino acids. One does not have to start constructing Simon's watch all over again. At the psychological level the constraints of spelling and syntax make possible the free expression of thought. There are only a limited set of letters and words, but each child does not have to reinvent the language system in order to begin expressing the complex ideas of modern knowledge. Again, at the societal level legal constraints provide the basis for individual freedom. By establishing institutional limits to the amount of interference others can have in each person's activity, the possibilities within those limits for personal development are expanded.

When taken out of context, the specific controlling elements exhibit none of the usually observed control functions. Genetic repressors are ordinary molecules that have biological significance only in certain systems. DNA can be seen as the master molecule only in the context of a cell with a variety of other necessary properties that allows DNA to have a control function. Pattee makes an analogy between the controlling functions of DNA and presidents: What each does arises only as a characteristic of the office each holds. Under other constraints, the same molecule or man would appear quite ordinary. Somehow the system itself takes an element and provides it with alternate modes of description. It is these alternate descriptions that define hierarchical control relationships.

The alternative description has significance only in the higher level in which the part is integrated. Simon's example of decomposability is appropriate here, for the details of a complex high-frequency lower system can be ignored and treated "alternatively" as a constant with a specific function relative to the structure in which it is participating. A physiological example can be found in the hierarchical relationships within an organ of the body. The heart is composed of tissues that are composed of cells. A full description of each tissue would require a discussion of the details of the cells that compose it. However, from the perspective of the heart, the description of each tissue is in terms of its function in cardiac activity, for example, contraction to produce a pumping activity. How the tissue uses its cells to perform that function is irrelevant. From the perspective of the circulatory system, the role of the heart is to pump blood. Many cardiac characteristics contribute to this ability, but they are irrelevant to the heart's alternative description with respect to the circulatory system. In fact, the heart can be replaced by someone else's, or even a machine, as long as the pumping function is carried out.

Both Simon and Pattee offer system definitions of the levels of a hierarchy that resist reductionist analyses. The activity of each higher level requires new descriptions and new parameters of activity that only have meaning within the organization of that level. The same element can have alternative descriptions. Within these alternative descriptions, however, are the roots of system transformations. The ability of a part to be interpreted in different ways (i.e., to be incorporated into different systems) provides a source of conflict that can produce changes in the organization of the whole.

Dialectical Movement

The general systems theory described here is based on Laszlo's (1972) set of four principles. However, as mentioned earlier, this is only one of a number of possible general system theories. It matches well with the constructivist, organismic model derived from the study of embryology and evolution described earlier. But it does lack one important general principle that is a clear characteristic of the biological systems described earlier. It is the principle based on the fact that an organism changes its environment through its functioning and thereby creates a new adaptive situation that requires further changes in the organism. This transactional principle has had many names over the years, but its most general formulation has been in theories of the dialectic.

The dialectic was conceived by the Greeks as the process by which truth emerges through the intellectual conflict (*agōn*) of several protagonists. Hegel (1807; Eng. trans., 1910) formulated a modern version of dialectics in which truth emerges through the interaction of subject and object. Prior to Hegel, these two had been separated by Kant, who described the knowing subject as having innate categories of mind and the object as having unknowable

real properties. In contrast, Hegel believed that the categories of mind emerged from the experience with objects, and the properties of objects emerged through the application of mind. Subject and object endow existence on each other. Without objects that differ on a conceptual dimension, the mind does not develop categories. Without a subject to separate the objects on the basis of those categories, the objects do not exist. Development for Hegel is a unified system in which subject and object cannot be separated.

Compare Hegel's philosophical understanding of the developmental relationship between subject and object and the biological relationships between organism and environment discussed earlier. An organism cannot exist separated from its environment, and an environment cannot be defined except from the perspective of an organism. Further, the developmental differentiation and integration of both organism and environment are the result of their exchanges, the organism changing the environment through its activity and the environment changing the organism through its selective opportunities.

In an attempt to apply this approach to developmental psychology, Sameroff and Harris (1979) explored the importance of the concept of dialectical contradiction as the major force motivating cognitive reorganizations. Hegelian dialectics considers development to be motivated by *internal contradictions* inherent in all things. The notion of inherent internal contradiction makes no sense in a psychology based on stable entities. It only makes sense when the focus turns to process. One of the internal contradictions in all systems is that all entities are caught in a two-way stretch; they are, at one and the same time, parts and wholes. They are at once part of someone else's hierarchy while containing their own. Whether the entity be human beings or molecules, the issue is the same. Koestler (1967) has referred to this as the Janus principle. Like Janus, all elements are two-faced, one aimed outward at the wholes of which they are a part and one aimed inward at the parts that make them a whole. There are constraints on our activity placed by the properties of the various social systems in which we participate. At the same time we are constrained by our physical, chemical, and biological constituents.

The contradiction arises out of the possibility for "alternative descriptions" cited above. If each system participated in only one hierarchy, the dialectic would not operate. What we are part of would completely overlap our parts. However, this is rarely the case for complex systems. Coleman (1971) contrasts "whole-person" organizations with institutionalized bureaucracies. In the whole-person society, characteristic of the Middle Ages in Western society, or any social system based on blood lines, each individual is within a group and has no social existence outside the group. Any activity with people outside the group must be carried out through group-relation channels. Bureaucracies, on the other extreme, are composed of abstracted roles in a set of organized relationships that can be filled by anyone who will carry out the required activities. For Coleman, the individual is a *member* of the whole-person group but only a *participant* in the bureaucracy. But the person can participate in a number of bureaucracies, each of which represents an alternative description of that person. These alternative roles could be salesman, student, father, or little-league coach, each requiring different activities and different interpersonal relationships. A child fills alternative descriptions when in the family, the school, or the peer group. The individual in the whole-person group can be diagrammed as nested in a set of concentric circles with similar others. In the institutionalized social system, individuals can increase their range and flexibility of activity and must be diagrammed as the unique intersection of a number of groups or organizations (Fig. 3).

As long as the values of the various roles that the individual fills are similar, there is no source of conflict, nor is there a need for adaptive change. However, when the values in one role are different from those in another, conflict arises. The recent rise of feminism is an example of such a dialectical contra-diction reaching resolution. As long as the roles that men and women filled were nonoverlapping, there was no conflict with the value of equal opportunity. Each sex had the equal opportunity to fill its own roles (i.e., breadwinner vs. homemaker). When women attempted to fill roles traditionally held by men, it became clear that equal opportunity did not exist. The social system had to adapt by either changing the legal code to legitimize unequal treatment or to eliminate sex as a relevant dimension for filling institutional roles. In molecular genetics, repressors produced by regulatory genes can participate in two different systems as a function of the biochemical environment. In one circumstance they can combine with certain genes to prevent their functioning; in another circumstance, in the presence of certain regulatory metabolites, they are coopted into a different structure, and the gene is free to function. At a psychological level, cognitive development presents many comparable instances; for example, as the child grows, older elements are redefined by being included in new systems. The shift from preoperational to operational thinking in the Piagetian system is characterized by a shift from incorporating information into perceptual systems to incorporating it into conceptual systems. Siegler's (1981) studies give examples of how children progress through a series of alternative understandings. The developmental sequences found in children are the result of such shifts: At an early stage, there is only one interpretation placed on information; next, there is a

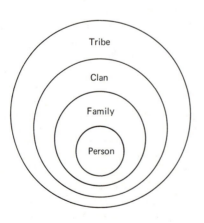

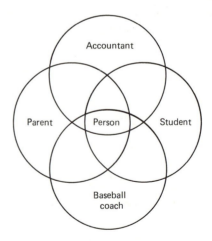

WHOLE–PERSON SOCIETY   BUREAUCRATIC SOCIETY

Figure 3. Whole-person social organization has the individual's role nested completely in a hierarchical structure. In bureaucratic social organizations roles are nested in hierarchies, but individuals participate in a number of these hierarchies depending on the set of roles filled.

period of instability in which the information is coded into two different systems; and, finally, there is a new period of stability in which the information is now coded only into the new system.

Riegel (1976) saw most of the stimulation for development arising from contradictions between four domains that incorporated different aspects of each individual—the biological, the psychological, the social, and the physical setting. Whenever there is change in one area, coordination with other areas is affected, and there is pressure for adaptive change. Adolescence is a sequence of biological events that affects other domains; marriage is an example of a social event that requires adaptive recoordinations.

Mechanism, Organism, and General Systems Theory

Mechanistic and organismic models have been presented as contrasting views of development with different metaphors and properties. In general, the organismic model has been seen as the better approach for understanding developmental psychology, but this is not surprising, for it takes as its metaphor living biological systems (Piaget, 1971; Werner, 1957). However, mechanistic orientations have continued to exert their influence in the form of information processing theories and especially computer models of cognition (Simon, 1979). In an analysis of how biologists who claimed to be reductionists and those who claimed to be wholistic went about their empirical work, Goodfield (1974) was unable to find major differences. This lack of a difference in biological methodology for individuals with such different perspectives may be a consequence of two factors. The first is that biological data are much more amenable to empirical investigation than psychological data and thus "speak for themselves." On the other hand, there is the possibility that organismic and mechanistic models are alternative descriptions of the same phenomena. The universe can be interpreted as being both mechanistic and organismic. Despite the admonitions of Reese and Overton (1970) and Pepper (1942) against mixing metaphors, appeals to unify such perspectives are frequently made (D. Kuhn, 1978; McCall, 1981).

To add to the complexities of interpreting development has been the request of life-span psychologists to replace mechanism and organism with contextualism (Baltes, 1979; Lerner & Busch-Rossnagel, 1981). The contextualists' emphasis on the importance of the structure of the environment is a necessary addition to the emphases of the other two models, especially since the preceding analysis of the biological metaphor revealed such a strong role for context in the determination of embryological and evolutionary direction. However, when taken alone, contextualism is quite arbitrary in the importance given to the multitude of influences impacting on the individual at any time. One of the ways this arbitrariness has been overcome in the past is by recourse to positivism or operationalism (Pepper, 1942) where facts and theories are based on social consensus. Meacham (1981) points out that many theoretical arguments are about boundaries between categories (e.g., heredity and environment, individual and society). He argues that a more fruitful conception would be one of "interpenetration," where as one aspect changes, all others necessarily change simultaneously. Meacham's concept of interpenetration "makes no commitment regarding the existence of boundaries between categories and causes, or whether they might be hierarchically ordered, or what the causal relationships might be" (p. 462). The interpenetration concept makes explicit the enriching aspects of the contextualist position, but also makes clear the impoverishing aspects as well.

Contextual thinking is important as an addition to other models rather than as a substitute for them. Development and evolution may be probabilistic but they are not arbitrary. Every step in development is based on what already exists. The organismic model provides a basis for the continuity of development, just as the contextualist model provides a basis for discontinuity.

General systems theory may provide a framework for the combination of models suggested above. Each system exists in a context of hierarchical relationships and environmental relationships. The analysis of hierarchical interfaces combines both organismic and mechanistic elements. Within such a more general view, interpretations can be made as to why a system appears to function mechanistically from one perspective, organismically from a second perspective, contextually from a third, and, perhaps, dialectically from a fourth. An analogous overview permitted physicists to explain why from one empirical perspective light appeared to have properties of a wave, while from another perspective it appeared to have the properties of a particle.

Although it may be true that any living system is an interconnected network with many components contributing to any observed activity, the relationship between a whole and its parts is one of abstraction. The whole abstracts some aspect of its parts as a criterion for system membership. Bonner (1973) describes the relationships among hierarchical levels in embryology as a series of developmental tests. Levels of the hierarchy act in an all or none fashion to certain chemical regulators, despite the fact that the regulators are always present in some quantity. These biological systems have triggerlike mechanisms that go to a second state if the amount of regulator is above a threshold and remains in the current state if the amount is below the threshold. Such abstracting properties of hierarchies are a common characteristic of perceptual and cognitive systems. Perceptual constancy is the phenomenon when despite an object's changing proximal pattern of stimulation (e.g., perception of a cube being rotated in space), it is still treated as the same cube. Color categories are another such example. In spite of the continuous distribution of light wave frequencies, hues are treated discontinuously.

The Piagetian theory of cognitive development is a sequence of such abstractions in which the content of experience is depreciated relative to some abstracted formal properties as one goes further and further in intellectual development. In order to demonstrate that liquid quantity can be conserved, the child must ignore the different appearances of the liquid in two glasses and infer an underlying logical reality that makes them the same. Yet, at the perceptually based preoperational level, the liquids *are* different.

Hegel based his dialectic on such contradictions. From one perspective, an object has one kind of properties; from another, it has a different kind of properties. In certain contexts the fact that one glass is on the right and the other on the left may make a difference, thus adding the possibility of further conceptual conflict. All reality is organic in that it varies with the constant activity of its components, but in the realm of contemplation, mechanical categorization must intrude. This philosophical point about cognition is equally true for biology, chemistry, and physics. The genetic code is interpreted categorically even though the electrical potentials that characterize the atoms in the DNA molecules are in constant flux.

PSYCHOLOGICAL APPLICATION OF GENERAL SYSTEMS THEORIES

Beginning with an attempt to define the properties of the organismic model of development, I have explored the data of embryology and evolution to determine the common biological characteristics of ontogeny and phylogeny. I then generalized the organismic model into a general systems theory with

applications extending downward into chemistry and physics. This lengthy review of scientific models is a preface to its extension upward into psychology and sociology. It would be possible to examine each domain covered in a handbook of developmental psychology and to impose a systems organization on the data from research in each area. Such an effort would require, however, the writing of a parallel handbook. Instead, two areas will be selected to demonstrate the power of the general systems theory approach; further applications will be left to creative scientists in other areas.

From the literature on general systems theory, five principles have been chosen that should be applicable to each area of developmental psychology. These are (1) wholeness and order, (2) adaptive self-stabilization, (3) adaptive self-organization, (4) systemic hierarchies, and (5) dialectical movement. In the application, the questions to be asked are what a systems approach adds, if anything, to our understanding in each area, how such an approach will identify gaps in our current knowledge, and, lastly, what approaches may be taken to close these gaps.

The first area will be social development and the second will be cognitive development. In each area, both ontogeny and phylogeny will be treated. From the ontogenetic perspective, the course of an individual will be traced and emphasis placed on the environmental regulations that move an individual from neophyte to sophisticate within the existing universe of social and cognitive organization. From the phylogenetic perspective, the emphasis will be on the evolution of the existing social and cognitive organizations.

Social Development

It may be considered a major leap to apply the five theoretical principles, derived from biological functioning as described above, to social behavior, a core topic in developmental psychology. However, such an application is a minor step compared to the proposals of sociobiologists who would replace social psychology with biology.

Social Evolution

In his highly influential book entitled *Sociobiology: The new synthesis,* Wilson (1975) sets as his goal the inclusion of the social sciences into a grander version of the "modern synthesis" than the one that unified evolutionary thinking 40 years earlier. He sees sociology and psychology as well as the humanities as the last branches of biology waiting to be included in the modern synthesis. The current efforts in ethology and comparative psychology are regarded as "ad hoc terminology, crude models, and curve fitting" that will disappear when sociobiology and behavioral ecology are developed at one end and neurophysiology and sensory physiology at the other. Psychology, with its probabilistic descriptions of behavior, will soon lose its rationale for existence when the connections are completed between cellular biochemical activity and social organization. A fundamental theory in sociology must await a full, neuronal explanation of the human brain. Cognition will be translated into neural circuitry; learning and creativity will be defined as the alteration of specific portions of the cognitive machinery regulated by input from the emotive centers. Wilson expresses the hope that psychologists and other social scientists will not be offended by this vision.

Although current principles of sociobiology have been restricted in their application to nonhuman species, and especially to insects, in those arenas they have done very well. The successful analysis of the social organization in ants and termites, which was based on computation of proportions of shared genes, was an exciting breakthrough (Hamilton, 1964). It is hard for sociobiologists to resist extrapolations to social organizations of greater complexity. However, this extrapolation does not seem to make a major contribution when human society is analyzed strictly in terms of kinship systems operating to maximize reproductive success.

Despite this simplification, Wilson (1975) sees something unique about human societies that sets them off from the other three groups of organisms that have achieved social systems (i.e., the colonial invertebrates, the social insects, and the nonhuman mammals). In each of these other groups, social organization evolved a number of times and declined as well. Apparently as the body plan of the individual organisms in the system became more complex through further evolution the efficacy for joining in social efforts was reduced. Individual development reduced cohesiveness, altruism, and cooperation.

In contrast, human society became autocatalytic. Fueled by positive feedback from its own social products, the evolution of the human species began to operate independently of the typical environmental constraints that influence all other evolutionary progressions. In nonhuman cases, species adapt at a much slower pace to changes that they have wrought in their environments or that other species have produced. Cooperative efforts among humans have compounded changes in intellectual capacity, ma-

nipulative skills, and social organization and, finally, in the creation of a symbol system of communication. The rapid pace of human development moved from a linear function to an exponential one with the rise of industrialism in the seventeenth century, at least in terms of technical innovation. As an addendum, Wilson calculates that human society will ultimately reduce this high rate of development to an ecological steady state toward the end of the twenty-first century.

How does one explain this uniqueness of the human species? Wilson sees it as a mystery that will ultimately be solved by using sociobiological principles. The alternative view, which was used to explain human evolution before sociobiology, was that of group selection, in which individuals make altruistic decisions on the basis of a group conscience and awareness. The sociobiologists have argued that such activity can be much better understood, and even predicted, based on the genetic constitution of the individuals in the group. They conclude that the reason humans behave socially is to preserve the genetic material they share with each other (Dawkins, 1976). In contrast, a systems view would argue that other elements human beings share with each other can substitute for the genetic organization, but at a much higher level of organization.

General systems theory offers an alternative explanation to that of the sociobiologists. Systems tend to maintain themselves in the face of variations in environmental perturbations. The direction of evolution has been to produce systems that are more and more capable of minimizing the effects of environmental change through self-stabilizing processes. The evolution of DNA as a repository of genetic information was a major advance in life's self-stabilization. Despite the variation in the development of a given phenotype, the genetic material was protected in a stabilized system. Evolution did not have to reach that point again.

Of more interest to developmental psychology is a further breakthrough in evolution, the establishment of the parental relationship. The newly hatched creature was no longer on its own; it was now part of a social system that endured just as the genetic material had endured at the previous breakthrough in the ability of systems to maintain themselves. If a child dies, evolution does not have to start over. The parents can have another child.

There is yet another evolutionary advance in the cognitive breakthrough that provided the symbol systems of language. Language provided a system that can represent reality and be transmitted independently of that reality. Before language, parents could provide the information they had gleaned from their own experience, but they had no way of transmitting the information of others, which could provide offspring with the ability to live in niches their parents had never considered. Human adaptational capacities had taken a great leap forward.

From the perspective of evolution, all human biological functions arose in the context of better adaptive strategies to ensure better responses to selection pressures. The initial pressures before the rise of human society were from the geological and biological environment. After human organization became autocatalytic, the balance of these pressures arose from within or between human groups.

But beyond these factors, there was a system for encoding and reproducing social systems that constituted the basis for each culture. Flannery (1972) analyzed the evolution of civilization into four types of society, each of which shows progressively more differentiated role structures and institutional organizations. The transitions to the more complex organizations were accompanied by the ability for written encoding of the social system. The "autocatalysis" of human society was really a dialectic in which changes in social complexity required changes in symbolic representation for their encoding. The increasing sophistication of notation and the potential logical operations in grammar offered the possibility for further advances in both social organization and technical achievements. Lévi-Strauss (1966) describes how in his beginning research on primitive human societies he sought primitivity in thought as well. He was struck by his inability to discover such primitivity. Most traditional cultures had already reached high levels of complex thought, which were reflected in their kinship structures and the logic of their mythologies.

Social Systems

The study of individuals functioning within a social structure has taken two major directions; one was an emphasis on the identification of meanings, signs, and communications that help to understand the individual and society. This approach came to be called "symbolic interactionism" (M. F. Kuhn, 1964) because of its focus on the symbolic relationships abstracted from the individuals that participate in them. Symbolic interaction theory has many features of a general system for explaining society. It is rooted in the early work of William James and John Dewey, but had its first explicit statement in the writings of G. H. Mead (1934). The theory sees man's reflection on symbols as the source of a sense of self. Society is seen as preceding the individual, since no individual is ever born into a vacuum. But,

at the same time, society does not exist without individuals. Here is an example of Bertalanffy's open system in which the whole is maintained despite constant changes in the parts, or in society's case, participants.

Another theme in understanding social organization is role theory (Sarbin, 1954). Role theory puts more emphasis on the objective expression of social components. Roles are defined in terms of social norms that have predictability and consistency (Bates, 1956). The quality of role enactment by an individual will vary depending on the clarity of role expectations, the consensus for the role definitions, the congruence between the characteristics of the self and the role, and the energy required to fill the role (Sarbin & Allen, 1968).

The separation of role and individual in the understanding of social organization is one of the prime characteristics of human social organization as opposed to other animal forms. Roles can be filled generally by all members of a species or only by individuals with a certain set of biological characteristics. These latter individuals are defined as belonging to a caste (Wilson, 1975). In insect societies, all roles are filled by castes that differ in morphological features or age group. There is a real sense of biology determining destiny. However, in human societies there has been an evolution away from castes in which individuals born to certain groups are locked into a social stratum throughout their lives. A caste society is another variation of Coleman's (1971) whole-person social organization.

Modern industrial societies, while retaining many inequities in the distribution of actual roles (Jencks, 1972), do operate under the premise that anyone who possesses enough talent is free to fill any role. The social organization is not reduced to the personal characteristics of the individuals composing it. Individuals with different physical characteristics will be able to fill a given role to a better or worse extent, but in general they will not alter the basic characteristics of that role. Most human beings can teach some subject, play baseball, or paint pictures. Some human beings will be much better at one or another of these roles, but the roles will still be those of teacher, baseball player, or artist.

Both symbolic interaction theory and role theory see society as comprised of units defined at some level of abstraction and held together by the organization of a particular society at a particular stage in its development. This orientation is a contrast to the sociobiological assertions that these social networks are reducible to genetic determinants. The uniqueness of symbolic social organizations is that they can assume through their reflective possibilities many of the functions that have fostered evolution at the biological level.

The most important characteristic of the genetic code is that it stabilized the reproduction of individuals by insulating their genetic material from most experiences of individual members of the species and thus equipped species members as a whole to survive across many generations. In a similar fashion, culture stabilizes social organization so that the system will continue to survive by insulating the society against the characteristics of any single individual in that society. In a stable society, individual expression can only occur through roles that exist in a system in which they are related to all the other roles in the system. The rapid pace of technical and institutional change in industrial societies has assured that modern cultures do not stabilize. As a consequence, there are many opportunities for the evolution of new roles or combinations of roles. But these changes will still be coded into an abstracted social system at a level of organization above both biology and psychology.

How much does current psychology recognize this context of human functioning or include it in the analysis of cognition, perception, personality, or even social functioning? Of concern here is what developmental psychology has contributed to the understanding of social development. In its second edition, the Carmichael *Manual* (Carmichael, 1954) contained one chapter on social development that comprised 53 of the 1200 pages of the book. Surprisingly, the authors, Anderson and Anderson (1954) presented a wholistic systems approach to the field that examined how most other domains of developmental research are subsumed in the area of social functioning. They made the point that the history of psychology was conditioned by the discovery of the individual as a behaving unit around the turn of the century. What they did not fully foresee was that this concern with the individual would lead to a lack of concern with the social context. In its third edition, the Carmichael *Manual* (Mussen, 1970) included a full section on socialization in which seven chapters were devoted to topics such as sex-typing, dependency, aggression, morality, and peer interaction; but each was written with little regard to society's contribution to the psychology of individuals. The domain of interest had expanded, however, since the list included chapters on cross-cultural child psychology and on social class and ethnicity.

Socialization

The social order can be described structurally in terms of the organization of roles or symbols. However, this social order rests on each new generation's learning to behave in accord with the imperatives of the society. Orderliness of relationships with others rests in part on each individual having achieved a self that is sensitive to the behavior of others and incorporates the responses of significant others who participate in the same social system (Clausen, 1968). From the sociological perspective, this emphasis in socialization research centers on adolescent and adult socialization in which role learning is primary (Brim, 1966). From the psychological perspective, the concern is less with the learning of roles and more with the relationships between people in the roles. The study of social development involves the establishment, maintenance, and use of social relationships, yet as Lewis (1982) points out, there has been very little effort to study the relationships themselves, especially in their interconnectiveness. Traditionally, socialization has been viewed as the struggle between the self, the family, and society for control of an individual's development. The Freudian model of id, ego, and superego is such a conflictual model. A contrasting model sees the individual, family, and society as coordinated in the support of child development (Inkeles, 1968). The child's need for shelter and emotional support may be completely dependent on the social organization, especially in the case of the human infant. From this perspective the family and the child are *of* society rather than opposed to society.

Most definitions of socialization describe it as the process in which a person acquires the attitudes, values, ways of thinking, need dispositions, and other personal attributes that will allow effective participation in society (Brim, 1966; Inkeles, 1968). Participation in society means participation in a complex social order, yet the traditions of child psychology have been not only to separate the child from family but also to separate as many functions as possible within the child for independent study.

General systems theory has been given importance for the interpretation of developmental data by Dennenberg (1979). He argues that causal relationships purported to be documented by studies using simple experimental manipulations may have other more complex determinants. Of special interest is Dennenberg's point that in cases where no longitudinal correlations are found between two variables, one cannot say that they are unrelated unless the entire developmental system is understood in its interrelationships. Sander, Stechler, and their coworkers (Sander, Stechler, Burns, & Julia, 1970; Sander, Stechler, Burns, & Lee, 1979) have been concerned for a long time with systems aspects of early human development. However, they have made the important point that preoccupation with theoretical discussions of organizational principles can quickly become nebulous and abstract if not related to empirical data (Sander et al., 1979). Their studies focus on a system that includes the individual infant, the infant's caregiver, and the physical environment. The strategy was to identify stable parameters of the total systems, introduce a perturbation or intervention at one of the levels, and then assess developmental effects. The emphasis of their work was to examine behavior in context rather than isolated from context.

Lerner and Spanier (1978) have expressed optimism for a future in which the child, the family, the social system, and their histories will be given equal status in psychological investigations. A necessity is claimed for a multicausal, reciprocal framework for analysis so that the plasticity, multilinearity, and multidirectionality of human development can be explored. Similarly, Wapner et al. (1973) argue for the simultaneous analysis of people in their environments. They criticize earlier emphases on "part processes rather than persons, on instrumentalities *per se* rather than the relationship of the instrumentalities (namely, perceiving, thinking, symbolizing) to the goals and purposes of individuals operating in certain kinds of social-cultural-physical contexts" (p. 261).

An advance over the singular focus on the child's characteristics is the analysis of the child in the family. But even this enlarged view has serious deficiencies. Hartup (1979) notes that a serious oversight in social development research is the lack of information on how the different social worlds of the child interrelate. He feels that childhood socialization should be viewed in terms of reciprocal causalities occurring within various social networks, each a social system in its own right (e.g., peer groups, school groups) in addition to those causalities within the family. Research on the family has typically not taken a systems view but regarded the parents as having a unidirectional socialization impact on the offspring. More recent has been the increasing emphasis on seeing the child as an active contributor to his or her own development, especially on the behavioral organization of the family (Bell & Harper, 1977; Lewis & Rosenblum, 1974).

The move from interpreting the child-parent relationship as bidirectional to explicitly interpreting this relationship in systems terminology has been made in structuralist theories of family therapy (Haley & Hoffman, 1967; Keeney, 1979; Minuchin, 1974). The desire of family therapists to make changes in a system rather than mere observations of it has been a major impetus for using the systems view. When family behavior is only observed, a much wider range of theoretical interpretations is possible than when planned changes have to be made. The experimental manipulation of families necessary to test hypotheses is a possibility more available to therapists engaging families in a helping role than to other researchers. The need of troubled families for interventions has moved therapists to focus on the dynamics of role structures among family members. The interventions in such family therapy are explicitly seen as perturbations in an open system that are directed at producing reorganizations (Watzlawick, Weakland, & Fisch, 1974). However, such applied systems models have been targeted and time-limited rather than generalized to the total developmental process. The increased integration of such applied concerns with academic research would undoubtably enrich both enterprises.

Historical and Cultural Background of Social Development

The extent to which the social world of the child can be expected to change in the future can be extrapolated from how much it has changed in the past. Kessen (1979) has argued that child psychology as a discipline is a recent cultural invention that strongly influences the way we examine and understand children. More significantly, *childhood* itself is a cultural invention. Family, motherhood, and children have not been universal elements historically recognized by society. Ariès (1962), in a major analysis of changes in the concept of the child and family, contended that it was only in the seventeenth century that childhood, and then only middle-class childhood, was recognized as having any unique characteristics, needs, or responsibilities. Previously, infants were not even named until survival was assured. One word, *baby* in English and *enfant* in French, was used to characterize the whole period between birth and adolescence. In paintings of this period, children appear with adult facial features and only their smaller size indicates any difference from adults. The child, the nuclear family, and the home are described by Ariès as evolutionary changes that accompanied the growth of the middle class and the decline of feudalism.

The evolution of Western society has seen the continuous emergence of different stages of childhood in which differentiated behavior can occur and be accepted. Rousseau is frequently credited with initiating the view that children live in a world different from that of adults. Until *Emile* was written in 1762, children were viewed as living in the same psychological life space as adults. Their behavior was evaluated strictly in terms of how well it approximated the behavior of adults within the same life space. The recognition that the life space of the young child could be different from that of the adult was an important prerequisite for the acceptance of different behavior from the child. Over the last few centuries, the stages of infancy, the preschool child, the school-age child, adolescence, and, most recently, youth (Keniston, 1970) have successively emerged as periods in which children are expected to have different behavior. But frequently the basis for this expectation has been placed fully in the child with a corresponding neglect of the different environmental settings in which children of different ages find themselves. While it is fairly easy to justify the different behaviors of children at different ages on a biological basis, it must also be evident that the environments in which these children live are also different and that these differences also evolve.

In Ariès's analysis, it was only when the child was seen as having a soul that requires the moral conditioning of education that childhood became a separate stage. The invention of childhood was inseparably connected with the invention of schools. The possibility of youth becoming a separate stage could only occur in a society in which post adolescents could have a role still separate from the normative adult model. In the case of Western society, this could only occur as a function of a goodly number of individuals in college. In cultures where this stage is not common, individuals enter adulthood immediately following adolescence. This progression is usually accepted for traditional cultures but less so for modern societies. In England, for example, education that emphasizes academic achievement was officially limited to a small portion of the population after age 11, and still only a small percentage of children goes on to higher education. The strong separation of social classes in that country is rooted in clear ecological differences and not necessarily in breeding differences that are the traditional explanations for differences in social status.

The study of social development cannot be isolated from the historical context because, depending on the secular period, the meanings and roles associated with society have changed. Even within a single historical context, social development must still be embedded in a larger institutional structure. Attempts to understand the child isolated from context have not produced an understanding of developmental process or outcome.

Sameroff and Chandler (1975) compared developmental approaches in which a child's outcome was analyzed strictly in terms of the child's characteristics in comparison with approaches in which the

characteristics of the environment were included. A singular focus on the child, whether in the theoretical belief that one could discover the essence of individual differences in behavior or in the empirical hope of finding a simpler unit of analysis for investigation did not produce reliable relationships between initial stage and outcome. What was especially striking was that many biological conditions that should have had enormous impact on later intellectual functioning did not. Whenever a characteristic of the child could be identified that was said to be associated with a specific later outcome (e.g., neonatal anoxia producing mental retardation), other children could be found with the same initial condition who developed quite differently. The socializing environment appears to have some capacity to reduce the effects of biological deviation in producing psychological deviation.

Just as the variability of outcome for human gestation is very narrow considering the multitudes of cell reproductions and the complexity of genetic material, so the outcome for human adults is similarly narrow compared to the many aspects of socialization that a child can experience. Human beings generally grow up to fill a role in their culture. There is a directionality to socialization that is not captured in studies that isolate such behaviors as aggression and dependency from the system of childrearing taken as a whole, or from the characteristics of the culture in which the child is being raised (Whiting, 1963). Erikson's (1950) anthropological explorations of childrearing in several American Indian tribes demonstrated how such behaviors had to be understood in context. He was able to show that what might be defined as deviant in one society would be adaptive in another. Neurotic and psychotic behavior was found to be institutionalized in a number of cultures and was considered a valued part of normal adult behavior.

To understand the differences in outcomes for children, far greater proportions of the variance are explained by appeals to variables in the social environment as against measurements of the young child. These social variables are primarily a function of the possible roles a given child can assume. Different social classes, for example, have developmental agendas preparing their children for different sets of roles with differing cognitive requisites. Kohn (1969) has documented the differing values for children held by parents who varied in social class; the lower-class groups emphasized conformity, the upper-class groups, self-direction. Adult functioning exists in the context of a society with a limited set of possibilities. Developmental outcomes in terms of psychological variables have to be understood in terms of the actual epigenetic path for a given group within a given society.

The control mechanisms of society can be seen as analogues of the control mechanisms in embryology. Waddington's (1962) chreods and self-righting tendencies are found within the institutions of every existing society. There are prescriptions and proscriptions for the various outcomes desired. If a society exists, it must have a developmental agenda for children which brings them to an adequate state of maturity so that they can participate in the adult society. The agenda is part of the culture, but this is not to say that the child does not make a contribution to the developmental process. At each step of the way, cultural interventions are tied to the average expected characteristics of previous children raised by that society. The age when weaning, toilet training, and motor training begin are tied to the presumed physical readiness of children. In other words, there is an intimate timetable relating society's expectations and the child's characteristics (Sameroff, 1982). Presumed readiness is not the same as biological readiness, since many cultures assume quite different schedules for even such highly physically based skills as walking or toilet training (deVries & deVries, 1977).

As the child is socialized, behavior becomes more predictable as the child becomes more and more locked into a developmental chreod toward becoming a member of a given society. To begin to understand differences in children's behavior one must spend time studying their environments.

Psychological Models of Social Organization

Within developmental psychology, the most consistent emphasis on the need to develop ecological models for the understanding of social behavior has been in the work of Bronfenbrenner (1977; see *Bronfenbrenner & Crouter, vol. I, chap. 8*). Bronfenbrenner emphasizes "the progressive accommodation throughout the life span, between the growing human organism and the changing environments in which it actually lives and grows" (1977, p. 513). Bronfenbrenner sees his efforts as an attempt to provide substance to Lewin's (1935, 1936) topographical models.

Lewin (1954) placed great emphasis on the need to interpret behavior within a psychological field. He pointed out that the effect of any given stimulus depends upon the stimulus constellation and upon the state of the particular person at that time. The environment is seen differently by children at different developmental levels—the newborn or the 10-year-old; or in different motivational states—hungry or satiated, energetic or fatigued. Similarly, the environment can produce different states in the person. After encouragement, the child feels different than he does after discouragement; in a democratic group atmosphere, different than he would in an autocratic group atmosphere. Lewin called the totality of factors that influence behavior the "life space" of that individual. He recognized that the specific factors that make up this space have to be studied analytically and specifically distinguished, but he emphasized the mutual interdependence of the coexisting facts.

From the systems perspective, Lewin's contribution can be seen mainly in his attention to differentiations in the social sphere and in his emphasis on the overlapping groups to which the individual belongs. Behavior is an outcome of an overlapping situation, one aspect of which corresponds to the child's own needs and goals and the other to the goals, rules, and values of the group to which the child belongs. Adaptation depends on avoiding too great a conflict between the two sets of forces. The child is seen as participating in many groups including family, friends, church, and school.

Bronfenbrenner (1977) extended the topographical approach by embedding it in a systems hierarchy of a microsystem, a mesosystem, an exosystem, and a macrosystem. The *microsystem* is the immediate setting of a child in an environment with particular features, activities, and roles. The *mesosystem* comprises the relationships between the major settings at a particular point in an individual's development. The *exosystem* is the next higher level in which the mesosystem settings are embedded including, for example, the world of work and neighborhoods. Finally, the *macrosystem* includes the overarching institutional patterns of the culture including the economic, social, and political systems of which the microsystems, mesosystems, and exosystems are concrete expressions. Bronfenbrenner's ecological model has been fruitfully applied in the analysis of a number of social developmental issues. For example, Parke and Colmer (1975) analyzed child abuse in terms of three viewpoints, one focusing on the parent as the cause, another on sociological stress, and a third on the patterns of interaction between parent and child. Belsky (1980) embedded these multiple focuses within the various levels of Bronfenbrenner's systems model. Kurdek (1981) similarly analyzed children's adjustment to divorce in Bronfenbrenner's hierarchical model. Such analyses have moved from approaches that have tried to determine what factors in development account for the most variance in a behavioral outcome to an analysis of the developmental interrelationships between factors. From these systems analyses it is clear that no single factor controls any developmental outcome and that causal analyses must involve many coordinated factors at many levels.

Bronfenbrenner (1977) discusses the major implications of such ecological models for research in child development. He feels that there must be a shift from the heavy emphasis on experimental laboratory paradigms that study "the strange behavior of children in strange situations with strange adults for the briefest possible periods of time" to transformational experiments in which the environment is radically restructured. Such experiments would explore the impact of a manipulation and also provide information on the modifiability of development in larger contexts. Ramey, MacPhee, and Yeates (1982) have been explicit in the use of a general systems theory in attempting to understand and prevent developmental retardation through intervention programs. Such an effort requires the clear specification of subsystems, processes, and targeted assessments at multiple levels. Similarly, Kelly (1979) and his associates have explored coping and adaptation in high school students in a design that allowed the transactions between coping style and school environment to be explored in real social structures.

One of the sources of both social problems and social progress relates to the issue of marginality. Lewin (1954) saw the source of many childhood conflicts in the multiple group membership of the child. Marginality was an important concept in which the individual alternates between the values of the different groups in which he or she is a member. Adolescence is a period of marginality because the child fluctuates between the behavior and feelings of a child and those of an adult.

In many circumstances, the ability of the individual to overcome conflicts related to marginality is strongly influenced by a society's differentiation of its marginal groups. In societies that treat adolescence as a period distinctly separate from childhood, adolescents have far fewer adjustment problems than they do in those societies that acknowledge no boundary between adolescence and childhood (Benedict, 1934; Reuter, 1937).

The marginality issue makes it difficult for certain individuals on the borderline between groups in a culture to make an identification. It also makes it difficult for other individuals in the culture to develop a consistent pattern of interaction with a particular individual. Roskies (1972) has provided a good example in the behavior of parents of physically handicapped children. These children are marginal on a normal-abnormal dimension. Intellectually and emotionally they are quite normal and can be treated as such; however, physically they are abnormal and need to be treated differently. To the extent that parents or society cannot deal with the abnormality, they treat a child as if he or she were normal rather than accepting the physical uniqueness of the child. In the case of some thalidomide babies, the parents would prefer to feed the children themselves for many years, in a manner resembling "normal" eating rather than to have the children feed themselves with their feet. Eating with one's feet may be adaptive for the child, but does not fit normative social behavior. Handicapped children also experience such marginality (Roskies, 1972). Resolution can take the form of fully identifying with one or the other conflicting groups. Deaf individuals will frequently resolve the marginality issue either by hiding their hearing loss and pretending to be nonhandicapped, or by only associating with other deaf individuals and rejecting normal society.

Traditional societies have evolved mechanisms to deal with marginality issues by permitting a wide variety of categories of people, which is based on unique classes, castes, and roles. Our own culture, which emphasizes the equality of all its members and their equipotentiality for development, may be doing a disservice to many of the uniquenesses that fit individuals to more specialized developmental courses.

Parke (1979) reviewed the direction that changes in the study of social and emotional development took in the previous decade. He discerned eight themes that reflect a maturing of such research in its conceptual and methodological foundations: (1) the child plays an active role in his or her own social-emotional development; (2) such development has multiple causes; (3) multiple levels of social influence need to be understood; (4) multiple research strategies are necessary; (5) social-emotional development is context bound and agent bound; (6) it is culture bound; (7) it is affected by secular trends; and, finally, (8) research on social and emotional development influences and is influenced by social policy. These themes represent a good synopsis of the issues that a general systems theory approach would implicate for research in social development.

Systems and Socialization

The principles of general systems theory seem applicable to the study of child socialization. There is a need to emphasize the child as part of a system that cannot be studied in isolation. Each society has self-stabilizing forces for both homeostatic and homeorhetic regulation. Through the reciprocities of social interactions and the resultant learning of appropriate social patterns, each individual is regulated in his or her everyday existence. In each culture the developmental agenda, by emphasizing different behaviors at different points on the path toward adulthood, guides the child's development into the role pattern for that society. Along each path, there are self-righting tendencies that become more institutionalized, and therefore coded, as societies evolve. For slow learners, there are remedial courses; for children who have behavior problems, there are school psychologists; for the handicapped, there are prostheses. In each society categorizations are made as to who will develop along which trajectories. For the Spartans, not all girl babies were allowed to enter the path. For certain cultures, twins are seen as special omens that must be either gotten rid of or valued highly. In our society, abortion functions to eliminate early those children for whom a family is not ready.

Society evolves and reflects the self-organization property of natural systems. The history of society documents the increasing complexity of organization in response to changes in the environmental stresses. As noted above, most of these stresses for human societies are from within rather than from without. Society is hierarchically organized with institutions composed of roles filled by individuals. Since there is no longer a simple nesting of people in roles as in whole-person societies, there is a great complexity of role networks. Multiple individuals filling multiple roles provide a solid basis for contradictions between roles and within individuals. As an example, the contradiction between a social ethic that is based upon equality of opportunity and social roles that place individuals in unequal positions has led to the transformations in race and sex role relations of the last period.

Within this systems approach to social development, psychology has a place despite the contrary views of sociobiologists, but only if it attends to these overarching variables that condition the meaning of every individual's behavior. Society constrains, but so does biology. Each advance of society must be based on the behavioral capacities of its members. In the process of avoiding the fallacy of reductionism, one can fall into the almost equally nonproductive fallacy of disregarding our roots (i.e., our subsystems). The ethologists have been the most persuasive about this issue in their attempts to reconnect psychology to human evolutionary history (Charlesworth, 1976). Indeed, each higher level of

organization, each new stage in evolution or in development, brings with it new principles of organization and functioning because it incorporates so much more than what existed before. But at the same time, the new stage cannot escape its connection to what came before. Human thought processes and experiences are intrinsically connected to the biological substrate that at the same time is transcended by human functioning.

Cognitive Development

The analysis of social development from the perspective of a general systems theory identified a level of organization represented in a symbolic system. There is a general agreement among scientists in biological, psychological, and sociological areas that the ability of human beings to manipulate symbols is a necessary basis for modern societies. The evolutionary relationships between cognitive and social evolution are still a matter of debate (Waterhouse, 1980). Whether the level of cognitive ability necessary to function in a complex organization arose prior to the beginnings of society or whether it was a response to the complexity of social organization is a question that remains to be answered (Crook, 1980). Another problem is to separate the biological substrate of thought from the psychological development of thought and to parcel out to each the contributions of increasing social organization (Jaynes, 1976). Historically speaking, *Homo sapiens* in the form of Neanderthal man appeared about 100,000 years ago and *Homo sapiens sapiens* in the form of modern man about 40,000 years ago (Washburn & McCown, 1978). There is little evidence for biological changes in humans for the last 40,000 years, yet written evidence for complex human thought appears less than 5,000 years ago. It would appear that the conditions for the biological evolution of the human brain were different from those later conditions that gave rise to the psychological expression of advanced cognitive processes.

Systems and Cognition

The application of general systems theory to cognitive development could be considered an afterthought, since Piaget's views incorporate most of the systems principles discussed earlier. Piaget's theories and research are discussed in detail in several chapters in the cognitive development volume of this handbook. In those chapters many important questions are raised about the adequacy of Piaget's formulations and the interpretation of the data from the Geneva laboratory (e.g., Gelman & Baillargeon, 1983). Whatever the validity of these critiques, Piagetian theory is currently a dominant view of cognitive development and will be used here as an illustration of general systems principles. Piaget argues that intellectual development is characterized by a set of functional invariants that operate at every level of cognitive functioning. Each stage of cognitive development will involve different elements and structures, but the functional invariants at each stage remain the same abstractions of process.

These invariants are organization and adaptation. Organization refers to the self-regulated cognitive structures that comprise thought. Adaptation is the process by which these structures change through experience. Piaget's function of organization is akin to the systems property of wholeness and order. The cognitive parts, either sensorimotor schemes, concrete operational groups, or formal operational logics, depending on the stage of cognitive development, are maintained in the whole as aspects of transformational systems with special relationships (e.g., identity or reversibility).

Piaget's function of adaptation includes three systems properties: self-stabilization, self-organization, and dialectical movement. The result of this movement is a hierarchically organized system in which each new stage of cognitive development incorporates the structures of the previous stage as parts in a new whole. The system is open in the sense defined by Bertalanffy (Piaget, 1971) in that it maintains its structure even though the parts are changing as information flows through the system. This information is obtained during the process of adaptation (i.e., *assimilation* and *accommodation*).

One of the most difficult aspects of Piagetian theory to understand is the active nature of knowledge. Just as the cell in biology cannot live without being active, so cognitive structures cannot survive independently of their activity. Knowing only occurs as a part of the active assimilation of experience to existing structures and in the active accommodations of these structures to new experiences (Furth, 1969). This activity is regulated by a general process of equilibration that regulates the balance between the knowing subject and the known object. Equilibration can take the form of *self-stabilization* within the systems so that the cognitive structure is able to make an internal transformation or modification in the service of assimilation. Equilibration can also take the form of *self-organization* within the systems so that a major restructuring that moves cognition into a higher stage of development is necessary.

Piaget has referred to these different aspects of equilibration as *transformation* and *formation* (Piaget, 1970) or *autoregulation* and *auto-organization* (Piaget, 1980).

Dialectical movement is also a major component of the Piagetian system of assimilation and accommodation (Piaget, 1970, 1971). Each assimilation requires some accommodation to occur since no two experiences are ever identical; and each new accommodation means that the next experience will be assimilated somewhat differently since the subject will have been changed. Cognitive activity cannot help but change both the knower and the known in what Piaget sees as neither a linear nor a circular route but rather as a spiral moving into ever higher levels of organization.

Hierarchies of Cognition

A major dimension that characterizes the stages of development in Piaget's spiral is captured in his concept of vertical décalage in which the same content is represented at greater levels of abstraction in each successive loop. The child's understanding of spatial organization is an example of such a progression. Toward the end of the sensorimotor stage, young children can find their way around the house. They can go from one room to another and return to the same place and even use a different route each time. However, if the child is asked to describe the route, either in words or pictures, only vague responses will be made. At this stage they can act, but they cannot represent their actions. During the preoperational stage children become able to translate physical movements in space into represented movements on paper. They can use or draw pictures of the house to reconstruct routes taken. At a later stage spatial representations become even more abstracted from the sensorimotor realm; children are then able to use and construct maps in which points on a piece of paper can substitute for the earlier pictorial representations of space.

Psychological behavior has its beginning when the infant uses a set of biologically organized systems (i.e., schemes) to interpret regularities of patterned stimulation in the environment. These schemes include the modalities of sight, hearing, sucking, touch, and smell. Each of these schemes operates relatively independently, although there is evidence that some specific early coordinations exist (Meltzoff & Moore, 1977; Mendelson & Haith, 1976). Each modality attempts to interpret experience from its own point of view. The sucking scheme interprets all objects experienced in terms of their suckability (i.e., the amount of mouth-opening required, how deeply into the mouth the object can be taken, how much tongue involvement is necessary, etc.). Those objects that are congruent with the existing scheme are better assimilated (i.e., are acted upon more vigorously and for longer periods of time than those objects that are less congruent) (Lipsitt, Kaye, & Bosack, 1966).

Haith (1980) analyzed the newborn's visual behavior in systems terms by studying the "rules that infants look by." In his view, eye movements are regulated by the number of visual contours available for scanning. In the absence of such contours in the visual field, the newborn activates specialized looking patterns to search them out in other parts of the visual display. Haith sees visual behavior in the newborn as a regulated system. He goes on to speculate that the biological correlate of the regulation is to maintain an optimal amount of neuronal firing in the visual cortex. Perturbations in the amount of firing cause the system to make behavioral adaptations to reduce the effect of the altered input.

A discussion of how these independent sensorimotor schemes become intercoordinated from a Piagetian perspective was presented earlier (i.e., the outcome is a new level of stability and the achievement of representation at the end of the sensorimotor period). The achievement of representation or the symbolic function in the preoperational stage permits the manipulation in thought of what can only be manipulated in physical action during the sensorimotor stage. But this symbolic function soon permits thought about structures that do not exist in the physical world (i.e., concepts).

Analyses of classification and categorization in thought have always had, as an implicit characteristic, a hierarchical organization (i.e., higher-order concepts or classes incorporate lower-order ones). Developmental analyses of how these categories are acquired require analyses of the formation of conceptual hierarchies. Concepts arise as contrasts between objects and are not inherent in any single object taken alone. The concept for the color white, for example, is an abstraction. There are objects that have white as a property, but there is no white independent of those objects. A concept is an alternative description of a cognitive subsystem at the next higher level of organization. Each object in the physical world has properties of color, shape, texture, and so on. When these objects are classified (i.e., grouped at a higher level), only a subset of these properties becomes relevant. White objects can be grouped separately from objects with other colors, even though they may share attributes of shape or size more with the other objects than with each other.

The child has the cognitive ability to group and order objects in the environment, but the specific ordering is not a property of the objects themselves. The color categories, or even the number categories, that will be used by a child are strongly influenced by discriminations between categories made by the language and cultural community in which the child is raised. Recent work has shown that the natural frequency of exemplars as well as the correlation of attributes on different dimensions across exemplars will influence the conceptual organizations of the child. Rosch (1978) has identified a level of basic categories that are the first learned by the child for classifying concrete objects (e.g., dogs, chairs, shirts). The members of these categories share significant numbers of attributes, have similar shapes, and are acted upon in similar ways. Rosch sees these basic categories as being at a level with the most adaptive significance for children, since their utilization permits children to divide the environment into units that generalize the most information to the largest number of objects. In addition, these basic categories that children learn first are related to the frequency with which these categories are used by adults in the same culture. The environment of thought becomes a major constraint on the contents of thought.

At a still higher level of cognitive development, the conceptual organization of thought becomes the content for a superordinate organization based on logical analyses. For Piaget formal operations represent the stage in which classes are abstracted in a system of logical relationships. As at lower levels an alternative description is given to a collection of elements that relates them in a higher-order system. Just as different logical systems emphasize different relationships among concepts (i.e., different sets of propositions about the same underlying reality), so, at a lower level, different concepts emphasize different relationships among objects. A major change at the higher level is that thought now takes itself as a content, whereas before the content was the physical world.

The development of children's ability to reflect on their thought processes has become the concern of the relatively new area of metacognition. Metacognition is knowledge about cognition and cognitive phenomena (Flavell, 1979). Such knowledge has to do with people as cognitive beings and with their cognitive tasks, goals, actions, and strategies. Young children have little capacity for thinking about their own thought. When these abilities have developed, they clearly reflect a hierarchical control or monitoring function over thought.

Outside of the mainstream of Piagetian theory, there have been other approaches to the hierarchical analysis of thought. The parallel work of Heinz Werner emphasized many principles similar to those of Piaget and placed strong emphasis on the hierarchical organization of thought embedded in an organismic model (Werner, 1948). Outside of the organismic approach, Harlow (1949) had demonstrated an empirical analog of metacognition in his studies of learning sets (i.e., the learning to learn phenomena). Other analyses concerned themselves with the relationship of thought and communication to social and emotional context. Bateson (1975) was a pioneer in studying the nested behavioral relationships in which the more inclusive setting variables control the interpretation of communications. In Bateson's model the emotional expression accompanying verbal interchanges sets the meaning of the utterance. A reprimand accompanied by a smile might signal a game; if accompanied by a frown, the same reprimand might signal something more serious. Contradictions between the setting signal and the communication have served as the basis for an etiological model of schizophrenia in the "double-bind hypothesis" (Bateson, Jackson, Haley, & Weakland, 1956). In this model, unresolvable conflicts are created for a child when the context of the parent's emotional signals are constantly at variance with embedded verbal ones.

The systems relationships between cognitive and affective factors have been given increasing emphasis in early development. Papousek and Papousek (1979) describe the evolution of their own work from a Pavlovian-based conditioning model to a dialectical system of dynamic interactions uniting the individual parts of the human infant's behavior. They have attempted to combine the informational aspects of learning and its input-output functions with the emotional substrate of an affective orientation-avoidance dimension. In a similar vein, theories relating exploration and attachment as setting conditions for cognitive development have made use of explicit systems descriptions. Sroufe and Waters (1977) have proposed an interactional theory based on Bowlby's (1969) systems conceptualization of attachment cast in terms of set points, goal-correcting behavior, and functional relationships.

Hierarchical models in which higher levels of behavior monitor lower levels have become prominent in the study of mental representations of real-world objects and events. Abelson (1981) suggests that "schemas" such as those hypothesized by Piaget are characteristic of many processes in which higher-order knowledge structures embody expectations guiding lower-order processing of stimulus complexes. He sees one of these schemas, the script concept, as having the potential of unifying central notions in developmental, social, clinical, and cognitive psychology. The importance of such models is that they make a very strong case for embedding any analysis of behavior in a context. The interpretation of that behavior cannot be adequately made without reference to that context.

Context appears to play a role in cognitive development even in later life. If formal operations represent an end point in the development of logic, then adulthood may only be viewed as a period when either a regression of cognitive functioning occurs after the adolescent peak, or as a period in which the fully developed form of logical thought is filled in with specific contents. Labouvie-Vief (1980) takes a contrasting position that adult development brings new and adaptive forms of structural change. These changes involve a higher level of thought that can bring the individual's logical capacities into accord with the possibilities for their utility within the social context. Cognitive development is then removed from a purist isolation and brought into a state of adaptation with a specific social context. The actualized limits of cognitive development may not be qualities of mind but rather determined by societal demands for differing levels of cognitive ability in different domains. Social, subcultural, familial, and individual variables all contribute to the morphology of adult cognition.

Cross-Cultural Aspects of Cognitive Development

The ability to think in symbolic abstractions is a universal characteristic of human beings. The evidence that any particular human actually does think abstractly appears to be intimately connected with the opportunities that each society provides for that person's education and expression. This point is contrary to the view of those that use genetic arguments to explain differences in intelligence test performance (Jensen, 1980). However, it is in accord with those who have analyzed cross-cultural differences in cognition. Lévi-Strauss (1966) has already been mentioned as an anthropologist who expected to find that the thought of humans living in "primitive" cultures would be less complex than those living in relatively underdeveloped modern societies. What he discovered was that although in relatively underdeveloped scientific and technical domains there is little evidence for complex thought, in the understanding and manipulation of kinship relationships and mythological systems there is much evidence that the complexity of logical thinking matches that of individuals in industrialized societies.

Examination of cognitive development in a wide range of traditional cultures using contemporary measures of concept attainment has found both similarities and differences in test performance. However, where such differences in performance are found, it is not clear that these reflect differences in cognitive abilities or differences in the approach to the problems (Cole & Scribner, 1974). In those studies where the concepts to be tested have meaning in the cultural milieu of the child, there are few differences in performance. Although experience with relevant concepts is an important contributor to test performance, cultural differences in attitudes to abstract thinking may be more pervasive influences.

The intricacy of the relationships between thought and cultural values involves a number of systems. Price-Williams (1962) suggests that the use of written symbols is connected with a different orientation than the use of oral symbols. Writing takes a symbol out of its concrete context and is congruent with an impersonal ideology for social relationships. Oral use of symbols is more context bound and congruent with social relationships that emphasize shared functions. Buck-Morss (1975), in a similar vein, has equated Piaget's formal operations with Marx's description of capitalism. In both, the product of labor is alienated from its human origins. For Marx, the value of commodities is no longer tied to the human effort that made them but rather to some abstracted system of value and money. For Piaget, logical thought is freed from the concreteness of real-world appearances and only deals with a symbolic system of transformations. In Buck-Morss's analysis, industrialization produces such cognitive alienation in traditional cultures that have previously maintained a more intimate connection between conceptual and real-world organization.

Studies of the effects of schooling on thought in cross-cultural samples give credibility to these views. Schooling does not produce differences in logical reasoning, although it will affect performance on verbal logical problems. Rogoff (1981) suggests that those individuals who did not go to school are unwilling to accept the premises of an abstract problem like a syllogism. In schools there is an emphasis on verbal instruction out of context from everyday activities. Using logic out of context as an end in itself can be seen as a social invention that has importance only in societies where the scientific and technical supports exist for such modes of thought. Rogoff ends her review of the effects of education by citing a letter written in 1744 by the Indians of Virginia in response to an offer to send some of their sons to attend William and Mary College:

You who are wise must know, that different nations have different conceptions of things; and you will therefore not take it amiss, if our ideas of this kind of education happen not to be the same with yours. We have had some experience of it: several of our young people were formerly brought up at the colleges of the northern provinces; they were instructed in all your sciences; but when they came back to us . . . [they were] ignorant of every means of living in the woods . . . neither fit for hunters, warriors, or counsellors; they were totally good for nothing. We are, however, not the less obliged by your kind offer . . . and to show our grateful sense of it, if the gentlemen of Virginia will send us a dozen of their sons, we will take great care of their education, instruct them in all we know, and make men of them. (Drake, 1834, p. 22)

CONCLUSIONS

A view of development has been examined in this chapter that is based on principles derived from the biological development of the individual and the evolutionary history of the human species. These principles have been abstracted into a model that shares many concepts with general systems theory. Development has been viewed as a dynamic process in which there is a continuous and necessary transaction between the organism of concern and its environment. In each of the areas reviewed, the point is made that behavior cannot be adequately interpreted out of context. Moreover, the limits that have frequently been attributed to an organism's behavior may really be limitations on the possibilities of that organism's development in a given context. Kessen (1979) observed that child psychology in America tends to view the child as a "free-standing isolable being who moves through development as a self-contained and complete individual." This overemphasis on the unit out of context may be changing, but at the cost of an increased complexity of research paradigms. Kessen concludes with a summary of both the bad news and the good, "The image of the child as an epigenetic and continuous creation of social and biological contexts is far more ambiguous and more difficult to paint than the relative simplicities of . . . the self-contained child; it may also illuminate our understanding of children and of our science.''

The biological context of human development has become increasingly accepted through the work of comparative psychology, ethology, and sociobiology. Our biological heritage is thought to have adapted human beings to exist in social units and to have promoted the success of those social units, especially their reproductive success. From a systems perspective, such a one-sided view of context is inadequate. Modern societies are characterized by a wide range of available roles. In earlier social organizations single variables like physical prowess or speed may have served as valid biological metrics for reproductive fitness. However, with increasing institutionalization, social success became multidimensional. Characteristics of intelligence, physical appearance, as well as physical strength, may all have adaptive validity depending on context. An intellectual, a movie star, and an athlete are all permissible roles. Of greater significance is that each of these roles requires a supporting social network of other roles and institutions. Universities require students, motion pictures and athletic events require spectators, and they all require supporting economic institutions. Which of these roles is the most biologically adaptive? Which would provide the most reproductive success? For people living in a modern social order, the question loses most of its meaning. It may be easier to accept oneself as the end product of biological evolution and the conscious organizer of one's constituent parts than to see one's self as a member of some more inclusive social order that can neither be determined nor regulated nor perhaps even understood through individual activity.

If one examines those major turning points in scientific theory that have reshaped our understanding of the universe, one finds they involve a stepping back from limited domains and a placing of the object of inquiry into a broader context. For example, in physics, two of the most notable advances were those of Copernicus and Einstein. Copernicus caused us to step back from seeing our own perspective from earth as the center of the universe to seeing our perspective as only one view of a system that has its center elsewhere. We are only part of an existing system rather than the originators of the system. Similarly, Einstein's theory of relativity forced us to step even further back by demonstrating the necessity of including the observer in the system along with the observed. The only absolute in the system is that the system's properties must be regarded as relative.

Perspectivism is one of the most important lessons that can be taken from a review of general systems theory. Too often the focus has been on the individual unit, be it the child, the parent, the family, or even the culture. Each of these units is in intimate connection with all others, and with their environments in a multitude of relationships; the vast majority of these relationships are in networks that have properties of concern to general systems theory.

Developmental Models

There has been a twofold movement in the elaboration of developmental principles presented here. On the one hand, I have discussed developmental models based on Pepper's (1942) set of world hypotheses. In this discussion the movement has been toward greater complexity as the formist, mechanistic, organismic, and contextualistic models have each been compared with the data of biological development and evolution. In these comparisons each model has been judged to lack some important principle necessary to understand the course of development. The formist and contextualist models are not explicitly developmental, the mechanistic model is reductionistic, and, while the organismic model requires an environment to stimulate developmental changes, neither the organization of that environment nor dialectical exchanges with the environment are given importance.

On the other hand, I have tried to move toward simplicity as captured by a set of general systems principles. Odum (1977), one of the founders of the ''new ecology,'' argued that only by complex multidisciplinary activity could ecosystems be studied and understood in their hierarchical interconnections, but concluded, ''If hierarchical theory is indeed applicable, then the way to deal with large-scale complexity is to search for overriding simplicity'' (p. 195). My excursion into general systems theory was in search of ''overriding simplicity.'' Where classical idealist philosophies dealt with pure forms as static entities, one can conceive of a modern version of formism based on dynamic principles. In the new version these principles are not seen as causing development, but rather as being abstractions derived from a survey of known developing organizations.

Traditionally, social scientists have appealed to the static models of lower-order disciplines for their scientific theories. Currently, however, these disciplines, especially physics, have come to interpret the universe in dynamic terms long familiar to social scientists. Despite these changes, the need for reductionist justification remains strong, even among general systems theorists. In spite of the clear evidence that psychological and societal evolution has been toward greater complexity and organization in opposition to the entropy principle found in the second law of thermodynamics, it is only when a physical scientist, Prigogine, hypothesizes that similar processes occur in distant corners of the universe that social scientists feel comfortable with their own data (Brent, 1978). The cornerstones of physics have become dynamic interactions instead of static entities (Trefil, 1980). So too have we come to see the cornerstones of the social sciences—and of special concern, developmental psychology—as dynamic processes. Dialectical interactions leading to hierarchical organization have been described in biological, psychological, and sociological development. As life has become more complex, the complexity of the interacting systems and the interactions themselves have increased, but the basic processes can still be described in similar terms.

A general systems theory has been described that incorporates principles from mechanistic, organismic, and contextualist models of development. These principles include a structural model based on hierarchical organization in which superordinate levels abstract functions from subordinate levels. These principles also include a dynamic model of self-regulation in which the dialectical relations between systems and their subsystems, and between systems and their environmental context provide the impetus for development and evolution.

Developmental Practice

At this point one must make the jump from theoretical speculation to empirical investigation. The search for research reports that have been explicitly systems oriented in the literature of developmental psychology is relatively unsatisfying, but a trend can be found toward greater frequency. Most such work has been stimulated by attempts at applied research that have forced the investigator into an analysis of contextual variables. If the general systems model is to be taken seriously, it must become part of the forethought of the research design, rather than an afterthought to compensate for unanticipated artifacts.

What is needed for advancement of developmental understanding is a perspective that forces scientists continually to question the context of their observations, an approach that keeps reminding investigators they are not observing absolute phenomena, but rather phenomena existing in a particular setting. Such a perspective will not prevent scientists from investigating variables in limited domains,

for that is where most major empirical advances occur, but it will emphasize that such studies represent a *decision* to ignore the other contexts. What happens all too frequently is that these choices are justified by a belief that the context is irrelevant, for example, that there can be discovered a social science that will have truth outside every particular cultural, political, and historical setting. A truth may be found to generalize across more than one context, but only if those contexts are included in the theory. A universal theory of cognition that focuses only on within-culture tests of thought cannot be found. Such a theory might be found if it includes an analysis of the interaction between a range of cultural contexts and individual cognitions.

What will be the next step in human evolution? From a general systems and dialectical perspective, we need no longer be surprised by either the question or the possibility of an answer. Life moves toward incorporating more and more of its environment into itself and toward reducing the effects of external perturbations. To identify the process of evolution, one needs to analyze existing systems and their environments. At that level, the roots of the next developmental stage will be found. But prediction is only a minor aspect of the greater need alluded to a number of times in this presentation. That greater need is to recognize that all organisms live in an environment and their activities are intimately connected with the characteristics of that environment. Theories of development are conditioned not only by empirical observations but also by the social, economic, and historical conditions of the epoch in which they are proposed. It is only through understanding the relationship between theoretical speculations and the contexts in which they arise that a better understanding of development can be achieved.

REFERENCES

Abelson, R. P. Psychological status of the script concept. *American Psychologist*, 1981, *36*, 715–729.

Anderson, H. H., & Anderson, G. L. Social development. In L. Carmichael (Ed.), *Manual of child psychology* (2nd ed.). New York: Wiley, 1954.

Anderson, P. M. More is different. *Science*, 1972, *177*, 393–396.

Ariès, P. *Centuries of childhood: A social history of the family*. New York: Vintage, 1962.

Ashby, W. R. *Design for a brain*. London: Chapman & Hall, 1952.

Baldwin, J. M. *Mental development in the child and the race* (3rd ed., rev.). New York: Macmillan, 1906.

Baltes, P. B. Life-span developmental psychology: Some converging observations on history and theory. In P. B. Baltes & O. G. Brim, Jr. (Eds.), *Life-span development and behavior* (Vol. 2). New York: Academic Press, 1979. (a)

Baltes, P. B. On the potential and limits of child development: Life-span developmental perspectives. *Newsletter of the Society for Research in Child Development*, 1979 (summer), 1–4. (b)

Bates, F. L. Position, role, and status: A reformulation. *Social Forces*, 1956, *34*, 313–321.

Bateson, G. *Steps to an ecology of mind*. New York: Ballantine, 1975.

Bateson, G., Jackson, D., Haley, J., & Weakland, J. Toward a theory of schizophrenia. *Behavioral Science*, 1956, *1*, 241–264.

Beadle, G. W., & Tatum, E. L. Experimental control of developmental reaction. *American Naturalist*, 1941, *75*, 107–116.

Bell, R. Q., & Harper, L. V. *Child effects on adults*. Hillsdale, N.J.: Lawrence Erlbaum Associates, 1977.

Belsky, J. Child maltreatment: An ecological integration. *American Psychologist*, 1980, *35*, 420–435.

Benedict, R. *Patterns of culture*. Boston: Houghton Mifflin, 1934.

Bertalanffy, L. von. *General system theory*. New York: Braziller, 1968.

Bijou, S. W., & Baer, D. M. *Child development, Vol. 1: A systematic and empirical theory*. New York: Appleton-Century-Crofts, 1961.

Blatt, B. The moral commitment. In F. A. M. Benson, W. Hitzing, & R. Kozlowski (Eds.), *Linking service and training systems in the 1980s*. Columbus, Ohio: Nisonger Center, 1981.

Bonner, J. Hierarchical control programs in biological development. In H. H. Pattee (Ed.), *Hierarchy theory: The challenge of complex systems*. New York: Braziller, 1973.

Boulding, K. General systems theory—The skeleton of science. *Management Science*, 1956, *2*, 197–208.

Boulding, K. E. Universal physiology. *Behavioral Science*, 1980, *25*, 35–39.

Bowlby, J. *Attachment and loss: Vol. 1. Attachment*. New York: Basic Books, 1969.

Brent, S. B. Prigogine's model for self-organization in non-equilibrium systems: Its relevance for developmental psychology. *Human Development*, 1978, *21*, 374–387.

Brillouin, L. Thermodynamics and information theory. *American Scientist*, 1950, *38*, 594–599.

Brim, O. G., Jr. Socialization through the life cycle. In O. G. Brim, Jr. & S. Wheeler (Eds.), *Socialization after childhood*. New York: Wiley, 1966.

Bronfenbrenner, U. Toward an experimental ecology of human development. *American Psychologist*, 1977, *32*, 513–531.

Bronfenbrenner, V., & Crouter, A. C. The evolution of environmental models in developmental research. In W. Kessen (Ed.), *History, theories and methods* (Vol. 1), of P. H. Mussen (Ed.), *Handbook of child development*. New York: Wiley, 1983.

Brown, D. D. Gene expression in eukaryotes. *Science*, 1981, *211*, 667–673.

Brush, S. G. Should the history of science be rated X? *Science*, 1974, *183*, 1164–1172.

Buck-Morss, S. Socio-economic bias in Piaget's theory and its implication for cross-cultural studies. In K. F. Riegel (Ed.), *The development of dialectical operations*. Basel: Karger, 1975.

Cairns, R. B. *Social development: The origins and plasticity of interchanges*. San Francisco: Freeman, 1979.

Carlsen, B. M. *Patten's foundations of embryology*. New York: McGraw-Hill, 1981.

Carmichael, L. (Ed.) *Manual of child psychology* (2nd ed.). New York: Wiley, 1954.

Carver, C. S., & Scheier, M. F. Control theory: A useful conceptual framework for personality-social, clinical, and health psychology. *Psychological Bulletin*, 1982, *92*, 111–135.

Chapanis, A. Men, machines, and models. *American Psychologist*, 1961, *16*, 113–131.

Charlesworth, W. R. Human intelligence as adaptation: An ethological approach. In L. B. Resnick (Ed.), *The nature of intelligence*. Hillsdale, N.J.: Lawrence Erlbaum Associates, 1976.

Chomsky, N. *Reflections on language*. New York: Pantheon, 1975.

Clarke, A. M., & Clarke, A. D. B. *Early experience: Myth and evidence*. London: Open Books, 1976.

Clausen, J. A. A historical and comparative view of socialization theory and research. In J. A. Clausen (Ed.), *Socialization and society*. Boston: Little, Brown, 1968.

Cole, M., & Scribner, S. *Culture and thought: A psychological introduction*. New York: Wiley, 1974.

Coleman, J. S. Social systems. In P. A. Weiss (Ed.), *Hierarchically organized systems in theory and practice*. New York: Harcourt, 1971.

Cronbach, L. J. The two disciplines of scientific psychology. *American Psychologist,* 1957, *12,* 671–684.

Crook, J. H. *The evolution of human consciousness.* Oxford: Clarendon Press, 1980.

Dawkins, R. *The selfish gene.* Oxford: Oxford University Press, 1976.

Denenberg, V. H. Paradigms and paradoxes in the study of behavioral development. In E. B. Thoman (Ed.), *Origins of the infant's social responsiveness* Hillsdale, N.J.: Lawrence Erlbaum Associates, 1979.

deVries, M. W., & deVries, M. R. Cultural relativity of toilet training readiness: A perspective from East Africa. *Pediatrics,* 1977, *60,* 170–177.

Dickerson, R. E. Chemical evolution and the origin of life. *Scientific American,* 1978, *239,* 70–86.

Dobzhansky, T. *Genetics and the origin of species.* New York: Columbia University Press, 1937.

Doolittle, R. F. Similar amino acid sequences: Chance or common ancestry? *Science,* 1981, *214,* 149–159.

Drake, S. G. *Biography and history of the indians of North America.* Boston: Perkins, Hilliard, Gray, 1834. (Cited in Rogoff, 1981.)

Ebert, J. D., & Sussex, I. M. *Interacting systems in development* (2nd ed.). New York: Holt, Rinehart & Winston, 1970.

Emde, R., Gaensbauer, T., & Harmon, R. Emotional expression in infancy: A biobehavioral study. *Psychological Issues Monographs Series, 10.* New York: International Universities Press, 1976. (whole No. 37)

Erikson, E. H. *Childhood and society.* New York: Norton, 1950.

Flannery, K. V. The cultural evolution of civilizations. *Annual Review of Ecology and Systematics,* 1972, *3,* 399–426.

Flavell, J. H. Metacognition and cognitive monitoring: A new area of cognitive-developmental inquiry. *American Psychologist,* 1979, *34,* 906–911.

Foerster, H. von. From stimulus to symbol: The economy of biological computation. In G. Kepes (Ed.), *Sign, image, symbol.* New York: Braziller, 1966.

Foucault, M. *The order of things: An archaeology of the human sciences.* New York: Random House, 1970.

Furth, H. G. *Piaget and knowledge: Theoretical foundations.* Englewood Cliffs, N.J.: Prentice-Hall, 1969.

Gal-Or, B. The crisis about the origin of irreversibility and time anisotropy. *Science,* 1972, *176,* 11–17.

Gelman, R., & Baillargeon, R. A review of Piagetian concepts. In J. H. Flavell & E. M. Markman (Eds.), *Cognitive Development* (Vol. 4), of P. Mussen (Ed.), *Handbook of Child Development.* New York: Wiley, 1983.

Gesell, A. L., & Amatruda, C. S. *The embryology of behavior: The beginnings of the human mind.* New York: Harper, 1945.

Goodfield, J. Changing strategies: A comparison of reductionist attitudes in biological and medical research in the nineteenth and twentieth centuries. In F. J. Ayala & T. Dobzhansky (Eds.), *Studies in the philosophy of biology.* Berkeley: University of California, 1974.

Gottlieb, G. Concepts of prenatal development: Behavioral embryology. *Psychological Review,* 1976, *83,* 215–234.

Gould, S. J. *Ontogeny and phylogeny.* Cambridge, Mass.: Harvard University Press, 1977.

Haith, M. M. *Rules that babies look by: The organization of newborn visual activity.* Hillsdale, N.J.: Lawrence Erlbaum Associates, 1980.

Haley, J., & Hoffman, L. *Techniques of family therapy.* New York: Basic Books, 1967.

Hamburger, V. The concept of ''development'' in biology. In D. B. Harris (Ed.), *The concept of development.* Minneapolis: University of Minnesota, 1957.

Hamilton, W. D. The genetical theory of social behavior. I and II. *Journal of Theoretical Biology,* 1964, *7,* 1–52.

Harlow, H. F. The formation of learning sets. *Psychological Review,* 1949, *56,* 51–65.

Hartup, W. W. The social worlds of childhood. *American Psychologist,* 1979, *34,* 944–950.

Hegel, G. W. F. *The phenomenology of mind* (J. B. Baillie, Ed. and trans.). London: Allen & Unwin, 1931. (Originally published, 1910.)

Heisenberg, W. *Physics and beyond.* New York: Harper & Row, 1971.

Hull, C. L. *Principles of behavior.* New York: Appleton, 1943.

Huxley, J. *Evolution: The modern synthesis.* New York: Harper & Row, 1942.

Inkeles, A. Society, social structure, and child socialization. In J. A. Clausen (Ed.), *Socialization and Society.* Boston: Little, Brown, 1968.

Jacob, F. *The logic of life: A history of heredity.* New York: Vintage, 1976.

Jacob, F., & Monod, J. On the regulation of gene activity. *Cold Spring Harbor Symposia on Quantitative Biology,* 1961, *26,* 193–209.

Jaynes, J. *The origin of consciousness in the break-down of the bicameral mind.* Boston: Houghton Mifflin, 1976.

Jencks, C. *Inequality: A reassessment of the effect of family and schooling in America.* New York: Basic Books, 1972.

Jensen, A. R. *Bias in mental testing.* New York: Free Press, 1980.

Kagan, J. Perspectives on continuity. In O. G. Brim, Jr. & J. Kagan (Eds.), *Constancy and change in human development.* Cambridge, Mass.: Harvard University Press, 1980.

Keeney, B. P. Ecosystemic epistemology: An alternative paradigm for diagnosis. *Family Process,* 1979, *18,* 117–128.

Keller, H. *The story of my life.* Garden City, N.Y.: Doubleday Page, 1904.

Kelly, J. G. *The high school: Students and social contexts in two midwestern communities.* Hillsdale, N.J.: Lawrence Erlbaum Associates, 1979.

Keniston, K. Youth: A ''new'' stage in life. *American Scholar,* 1970.

Kessen, W. Research design in the study of developmental problems. In P. H. Mussen (Ed.), *Handbook of research methods in child development.* New York: Wiley, 1960.

Kessen, W. ''Stage'' and ''structure'' in the study of children. In W. Kessen & C. Kuhlman (Eds.), Thought in the young child. *Monographs of The Society for Research in Child Development,* 1962, *27* (2, Serial No. 83).

Kessen, W. The American child and other cultural inventions. *American Psychologist,* 1979, *34,* 815–820.

Kitchener, R. F. Holism and the organismic model in developmental psychology. *Human Development,* 1982, *25,* 233–249.

Koestler, A. *The ghost in the machine.* New York: Macmillan, 1967.

Kohn, M. *Class and conformity.* Homewood, Ill.: Dorsey, 1969.

Kuhn, D. Mechanisms of cognitive and social development: One psychology or two? *Human Development,* 1978, *21,* 92–118.

Kuhn, M. F. Major trends in symbolic interaction theory in the past twenty-five years. *Sociological Quarterly,* 1964, *5,* 61–84.

Kuhn, T. S. *The structure of scientific revolutions.* Chicago: University of Chicago Press, 1962.

Kuo, Z.-Y. *The Dynamics of behavior development.* New York: Random House, 1967.

Kurdek, L. A. An integrative perspective on children's divorce adjustment. *American Psychologist,* 1981, *36,* 856–866.

Labouvie-Vief, G. Beyond formal operations: Uses and limits of pure logic in life-span development. *Human Development,* 1980, *23,* 141–161.

Labouvie-Vief, G., & Chandler, M. J. Cognitive development and life-span developmental theory: Idealistic versus contextual perspectives. In P. Baltes & O. G. Brim (Eds.), *Life-span development and behavior* (Vol. 2). New York: Academic Press, 1978.

Langer, J. *Theories of development.* New York: Holt, Rinehart & Winston, 1969.

Laszlo, E. *Introduction to systems philosophy: Toward a new paradigm of contemporary thought.* New York: Harper & Row, 1972.

Lerner, R. M., & Busch-Rossnagel, N. A. Individuals as producers of their development: Conceptual and empirical basis. In R. M. Lerner & N. A. Busch-Rossnagel (Eds.), *Individuals as producers of their development: A life-span perspective.* New York: Academic Press, 1981.

Lerner, R. M., & Spanier, G. B. A dynamic interactional view of child and family development. In R. M. Lerner & G. B. Spanier (Eds.), *Child influences on marital and family interaction.* New York: Academic Press, 1978.

Lévi-Strauss, C. *The savage mind.* Chicago: University of Chicago Press, 1966.

Lewin, K. *A dynamic theory of personality.* New York: McGraw-Hill, 1935.

Lewin, K. *Problems of topological psychology.* New York: McGraw-Hill, 1936.

Lewin, K. Behavior and development as a function of the total situation. In L. Carmichael (Ed.), *Manual of child psychology* (2nd ed.). New York: Wiley, 1954.

Lewis, M. The social network systems model: Toward a theory of social development. In T. Field (Ed.), *Review in human development.* New York: Wiley, 1982.

Lewis, M., & Rosenblum, L. A. (Eds.), *Effect of the infant on its caregivers.* New York: Wiley, 1974.

Lewontin, R. C. Adaptation. *Scientific American,* 1978, *239,* 213–230.

Lipsitt, L. P., Kaye, H., & Bosack, T. N. Enhancement of neonatal sucking through reinforcement. *Journal of Experimental Child Psychology,* 1966, *4,* 163–168.

Margulis, L. *Origin of eukaryotic cells.* New Haven, Conn.: Yale University Press, 1970.

May, R. M. *Stability and complexity in model ecosystems.* Princeton, N.J.: Princeton University Press, 1973.

Mayr, E. Cause and effect in biology. *Science,* 1961, *134,* 1501–1507.

Mayr, E. *Populations, species, and evolution*. Cambridge, Mass.: Belknap Press, 1970.

McCall, R. B. Nature-nurture and the two realms of development: A proposed integration with respect to mental development. *Child Development*, 1981, *52*, 1–12.

Meacham, J. A. Political values, conceptual models, and research. In R. M. Lerner & N. A. Busch-Rossnagel (Eds.), *Individuals as producers of their development: A life-span perspective*. New York: Academic Press, 1981.

Mead, G. H. *Mind, self and society*. Chicago: University of Chicago Press, 1934.

Meltzoff, A. N., & Moore, M. K. Imitation of facial and manual gestures by human neonates. *Science*, 1977, *198*, 75–78.

Mendelsohn, E. The continuous and the discrete in the history of science. In O. G. Brim, Jr. & J. Kagan (Eds.), *Constancy and change in human development*. Cambridge, Mass.: Harvard University Press, 1980.

Mendelson, M. J., & Haith, M. M. The relation between audition and vision in the human newborn. *Monographs of the Society for Research in Child Development*, 1976, *41*(Serial No. 167).

Miller, G. A. What is information measurement? *American Psychologist*, 1963, *8*, 3–11.

Miller, J. G. *Living systems*. New York: McGraw-Hill, 1978.

Miller, S. L., & Orgel, L. E. *The origins of life on earth*. Englewood Cliffs, N.J.: Prentice-Hall, 1974.

Minuchin, S. *Families and family therapy*. Cambridge, Mass.: Harvard University Press, 1974.

Mitroff, J. On the norms of science: A report on the Apollo moon scientists. *Communication & Cognition*, 1974, *7*, 125–151.

Morgan, T. H. *The physical basis of heredity*. Philadelphia: Lippincott, 1919.

Mussen, P. H. (Ed.). *Carmichael's manual of child psychology* (3rd ed.). New York: Wiley, 1970.

Odum, E. P. The emergence of ecology as a new integrative discipline. *Science*, 1977, *195*, 1289–1293.

Oppenheim, R. W. The ontogeny of behavior in the chick embryo. In D. S. Lehrman (Ed.), *Advances in the study of behavior* (Vol. 5). New York: Academic Press, 1974.

Overton, W., & Reese, H. Models of development: Methodological implications. In J. Nesselroade & H. Reese (Eds.), *Life-span developmental psychology: Methodological issues*. New York: Academic Press, 1973.

Papousek, H., & Papousek, M. The infant's fundamental adaptive response system in social interaction. In E. B. Thoman (Ed.), *Origins of the infant's social responsiveness*. Hillsdale, N.J.: Lawrence Erlbaum Associates, 1979.

Parke, R. D. Emerging themes for social-emotional development. *American Psychologist*, 1979, *34*, 930–931.

Parke, R. D., & Collmer, C. Child abuse: An interdisciplinary analysis. In E. M. Hetherington (Ed.), *Review of child development research* (Vol. 5). Chicago: University of Chicago Press, 1975.

Pattee, H. H. The physical basis and origin of hierarchical control. In H. H. Pattee (Ed.), *Hierarchy theory: The challenge of complex systems*. New York: Braziller, 1973.

Pepitone, A. Lessons from the history of social psychology. *American Psychologist*, 1981, *36*, 972–985.

Pepper, S. C. *World hypotheses*. Berkeley: University of California, 1942.

Piaget, J. *Psychology of intelligence*. New York: Harcourt, 1950.

Piaget, J. *The origins of intelligence* in children. New York: International Universities Press, 1952.

Piaget, J. *Structuralism*. New York: Harper & Row, 1970.

Piaget, J. *Biology and knowledge*. Chicago: University of Chicago Press, 1971.

Piaget, J. The psychogenesis of knowledge and its epistemological significance. In M. Piatelli-Palmarini (Ed.), *Language and learning: The debate between Jean Piaget and Noam Chomsky*. Cambridge, Mass.: Harvard University Press, 1980.

Polanyi, M. Life's irreducible structure. *Science*, 1968, *160*, 1308–1312.

Price-Williams, D. Abstract and concrete modes in a primitive society. *British Journal of Educational Psychology*, 1962, *32*, 50–61.

Prigogine, I. Time, structure, and fluctuations. *Science*, 1978, *201*, 777–785.

Ramey, C. T., MacPhee, D., & Yeates, K. O. Preventing developmental retardation: A general systems model. In L. Bond & J. Joffe (Eds.), *Facilitating infant and early childhood development*. Hanover, N.H.: University Press of New England, 1982.

Reese, H. W., & Overton, W. F. Models of development and theories of development. In L. R. Goulet & P. B. Baltes (Eds.), *Life-span developmental psychology: Research and theory*. New

York: Academic Press, 1970.

Reuter, E. R. The sociology of adolescence. *American Journal of Sociology*, 1937, *43*, 414–427.

Riegel, K. F. Dialectic operations: The final period of cognitive development. *Human Development*, 1973, *16*, 346–370.

Riegel, K. F. The dialectics of human development. *American Psychologist*, 1976, *31*, 689–700.

Rogoff, B. Schooling and the development of cognitive skills. In H. C. Triandis & A. Heron (Eds.), *Handbook of cross-cultural psychology: Developmental Psychology* (Vol. 4). Boston: Allyn & Bacon, 1981.

Rosch, E. Principles of categorization. In E. Rosch & B. Lloyd (Eds.), *Cognition and categorization*. Hillsdale, N.J.: Lawrence Erlbaum Associates, 1978.

Roskies, E. *Abnormality and normality: The mothering of thalidomide children*. Ithaca, N.Y.: Cornell University Press, 1972.

Sameroff, A. J. Development and the dialectic: The need for a systems approach. In W. A. Collins (Ed.), *Minnesota symposium on child psychology* (Vol. 15). Hillsdale, N. J.: Lawrence Erlbaum Associates, 1982.

Sameroff, A. J., & Chandler, M. J. Reproductive risk and the continuum of caretaking casualty. In F. D. Horowitz, M. Hetherington, S. Scarr-Salapatek, & G. Siegel (Eds.), *Review of child development research* (Vol. 4). Chicago: University of Chicago Press, 1975.

Sameroff, A. J., & Harris, A. Dialectical approaches to early thought and language. In M. H. Bornstein & W. Kessen (Eds.), *Psychological development from infancy*. Hillsdale, N.J.: Lawrence Erlbaum Associates, 1979.

Sander, L. W., Stechler, G., Burns, P., & Julia, H. Early mother-infant interaction and 24-hour patterns of activity and sleep. *Journal of the American Academy of Child Psychiatry*, 1970, *9*, 103–123.

Sander, L. W., Stechler, G., Burns, P., & Lee, A. Change in infant and caregiver variables over the first two months of life: Integration of action in early development. In E. B. Thoman (Ed.), *Origins of the infant's social responsiveness*. Hillsdale, N.J.: Lawrence Erlbaum Associates, 1979.

Sarason, S. B., & Doris, J. *Educational handicap, public policy, and social history: A broadened perspective on mental retardation*. New York: Free Press, 1979.

Sarbin, T. R. Role theory. In G. Lindzey (Ed.), *Handbook of social psychology* (Vol. 1). Cambridge, Mass.: Addison-Wesley, 1954.

Sarbin, T. R., & Allen, V. L. Role theory. In G. Lindzey & E. Aronson (Eds.), *Handbook of social psychology* (Vol. 1, 2nd ed.). Reading, Mass.: Addison-Wesley, 1968.

Schneirla, T. C. The concept of development in comparative psychology. In D. B. Harris (Ed.), *The concept of development*. Minneapolis: University of Minnesota Press, 1957.

Sears, R. R. Identification as a form of behavioral development. In D. B. Harris (Ed.), *The concept of development*. Minneapolis: University of Minnesota, 1957.

Siegler, R. S. Developmental sequences within and between concepts. *Monographs of the Society for Research in Child Development*, 1981, *46*(2, Serial No. 189).

Simon, H. A. The organization of complex systems. In H. H. Pattee (Ed.), *Hierarchy theory: The challenge of complex systems*. New York: Braziller, 1973.

Simon, H. A. Information processing models of cognition. In M. R. Rosenzweig & L. W. Porter (Eds.), *Annual review of psychology* (Vol. 30). Palo Alto, Calif.: Annual Reviews, 1979.

Simpson, G. G. *The meaning of evolution* (Rev. ed.). New Haven, Conn.: Yale University Press, 1967.

Simpson, G. G. Uniformitarianism: An inquiry into principle, theory and method in geohistory and biohistory. In M. K. Hecht & W. C. Steere (Eds.), *Essays in evolution and genetics in honor of Theodosius Dobzhansky*. New York: Appleton, 1970.

Skinner, B. F. Are theories of learning necessary? *Psychological Review*, 1950, *57*, 193–216.

Skinner, B. F. The phylogeny and ontogeny of behavior. *Science*, 1966, *153*, 1205–1213.

Skinner, B. F. Selection by consequences. *Science*, 1981, *213*, 501–504.

Soodak, H., & Iberall, A. Homeokinetics: A physical science for complex systems. *Science*, 1978, *201*, 579–582.

Spemann, H. Organizers in animal development. *Proceedings of the Royal Society of London*, 1927, *102*, 177–187.

Sroufe, L. A., & Waters, E. Attachment as an organizational construct. *Child Development*, 1977, *48*, 1184–1199.

Stebbins, G. L. *Variation and evolution in plants*. New York: Columbia University Press, 1950.

Tanner, J. M. The regulation of human growth. *Child Development*, 1963, *34*, 817–848.

Thiessen, D. D. *Gene organization and behavior*. New York: Random House, 1972.

Tobach, E. Evolutionary aspects of the activity of the organism and its development. In R. M. Lerner & N. A. Busch-Rossnagel (Eds.), *Individuals as producers of their development: A life-span perspective*. New York: Academic Press, 1981.

Trefil, J. S. *From atoms to quarks: An introduction to the strange world of particle physics*. New York: Scribner, 1980.

Valentine, J. W. The evolution of multicellular plants and animals. *Scientific American*, 1978, *239*, 141–158.

Waddington, C. H. *The strategy of the genes*. London: Allen & Unwin, 1957.

Waddington, C. H. *New patterns in genetics and development*. New York: Columbia University Press, 1962.

Waddington, C. H. *Principles of development and differentiation*. New York: Macmillan, 1966.

Wapner, S., Kaplan, B., & Cohen, S. B. An organismic-developmental perspective for understanding transactions of men and environments. *Environment and Behavior*, 1973, *5*, 255–289.

Washburn, S. L., & McCown, E. R. (Eds.), *Human evolution: Biosocial perspectives*. New York: Benjamin/Cummings, 1978.

Waterhouse, M. J. Aspects of the evolution of intelligence. In E. Sunderland & M. T. Smith (Eds.), *The exercise of intelligence: The biosocial conditions for the operation of intelligence*. New York: Garland, 1980.

Watson, J. B. *Behaviorism* (2nd Ed.). New York: Norton, 1930.

Watson, J. S. Smiling, cooing, and "the game." *Merrill-Palmer Quarterly*, 1972, *18*, 323–339.

Watzlawick, P., Weakland, J., & Fisch, R. *Change: Principles of problem formation and problem resolution*. New York: Norton, 1974.

Weiss, P. *Principles of development*. New York: Holt, 1939.

Weiss, P. A. The living system: Determinism stratified. In A. Koestler & J. R. Smythies (Eds.), *Beyond reductionism: New perspectives in the life sciences*. Boston: Beacon Press, 1969.

Werner, H. *Comparative psychology of mental development*. New York: International Universities Press, 1948.

Werner, H. The concept of development from a comparative and organismic point of view. In D. B. Harris (Ed.), *The concept of development*. Minneapolis: University of Minnesota Press, 1957.

Whiting, B. B. *Six cultures: Studies of child rearing*. New York: Wiley, 1963.

Wilson, E. O. *Sociobiology: The new synthesis*. Cambridge, Mass.: Belknap Press, 1975.

Wohlwill, J. *The study of behavioral development*. New York: Academic Press, 1973.

CULTURE AND COGNITIVE DEVELOPMENT* | 7

LABORATORY OF COMPARATIVE HUMAN COGNITION

CHAPTER CONTENTS

*The preparation of this chapter was supported by the Carnegie Corporation and the Ford Foundation. Our thanks to Peggy Bengel and Karen Fiegener for their assistance in making this work possible. The following members of our Laboratory and colleagues from other institutions contributed directly to our efforts: Alonzo Anderson, Denise Borders-Simmons, Michael Cole, Marsha DeForest, Esteban Diaz, Peg Griffin, Jean Lave, Jim Levin, Laura Martin, Jacquelyn Mitchell, Bud Mehan, Luis Moll, Denis Newman, Andrea Petitto, Margaret Riel, Warren Simmons, William Teale, and James Wertsch.

In attempting to understand the relationship between culture and cognition, we have found it useful to examine the historical antecedents of our current assumptions about mind, society, and the means by which we can understand their interrelations. Current debates within developmental and cognitive psychology recapitulate, to a startling degree, debates that occurred within the social sciences a century ago. It is our belief that a reexamination of the nineteenth-century theories of the relationship between mind and society in light of contemporary psychological research yields important suggestions for solutions to *current psychological debates* and provides a useful starting point for our essay.

NINETEENTH-CENTURY ANTHROPOLOGY: FOUR KEY ASSUMPTIONS

Four key assumptions underlie nineteenth-century anthropological assumptions about culture and cognition.

Cognition and Culture Are Aspects of the Same Phenomenon

Nowhere is this idea more clearly stated than by E. B. Tylor (1832–1917). His classic work, *Primitive Culture* (1874), begins with the assertion that "the condition of culture among various societies of mankind, in so far as it is capable of being investigated on general principles, is a subject apt for the study of laws of human thought and action" (p. 1).

Herbert Spencer (1820–1903), another major thinker of the late nineteenth century, shared Tylor's belief in the fusion of mental and cultural phenomena. He also drew an analogy between cultural development on the one hand and mental development on the other.

> During early stages of human progress, the circumstances under which wandering families and small aggregations of families live, furnish experiences comparatively limited in their numbers and kinds; and consequently there can be no con-

siderable exercise of faculties which take cognizance of the *general truths* displayed throughout many special truths. (Spencer, 1886, p. 521)

Spencer invites us to consider the most extreme case; suppose that only one experience was repeated over and over again so that this single event comprised all of a person's experiences. In this case, as Spencer put it, "the power of representation is limited to reproduction of this experience" in the mind. There is nothing else to think *about*. Next, we can imagine that life consists of two experiences, thus allowing at least elementary comparison. Three experiences add to the number of elementary comparisons and the elementary generalizations that we make on the basis of our total experience. We can keep adding experiences to our hypothetical culture until we arrive at the rich variety that characterizes our lives. It follows from this line of reasoning that generalizations (the "general truths" attainable by people) will be more numerous and more powerful the greater one's experience. Society provides experience, and some societies, so it was believed, provide a greater diversity of experience than others, cementing a neat bond between cultural progress and mental progress.

Culture Is Characterized by Levels of Development

This idea, and the associated idea of progress, are also epitomized by Tylor:

> We may fancy ourselves looking on Civilization, as in personal figure she traverses the world; we see her lingering or resting by the way, and often deviating into paths that bring her toiling back to where she had passed by long ago; but, direct or devious, her path lies forward, and if now and then she tries a few backward steps, her walk soon falls into a helpless stumbling. It is not according to her nature, her feet were not made to plant uncertain steps behind her, for both in her forward view and in her onward gain she is of truly human type. (Tylor, 1958, p. 69)

This hyperbolic summary nicely illustrates the intertwining of social and individual aspects of society in Tylor's thinking.

Levels of Culture (or Degrees of Civilization) Are Uniform Within Societies

Tylor's main criteria for judging the stage of a culture were the sophistication of its industrial arts, including the manufacturing techniques for metal tools and agricultural practices, and "the extent of scientific knowledge, the definitions of moral principles, the conditions of religious belief and ceremony, the degree of social and political organization" (1874, p. 27). From this point of view, a stage of culture could be indexed by any of these criteria, since each is characteristic of the society's stage or level.[1]

Change Is the Result of Endogenous Mental/ Social Factors

This assumption is embodied in two central concepts of nineteenth-century evolutionary theory. First, there is the doctrine of psychic unity, the idea that the basic principles of mind are the same in all human groups. Second, there is the principle of independent invention, the idea that cultural change arises from the universal human mind operating on problems universal to a given stage of cultural evolution.

These ideas were attractive because, if true, they would enable anthropologists to fulfill their central task—to establish universal laws of human history by reconstructing the series of steps by which all societies have attained their current rank and the factors that have produced differential movement toward human perfection.

The Boasian Critique

When combined with Darwin's theory of the evolution of species, the grand historical scheme laid out by the fathers of anthropology had a satisfying inevitability to it. As Tylor remarked, it seemed to put the facts in order.

Into this orderly theoretical world stepped Franz Boas (1858–1942), a German scholar whose training brought together several of the major intellectual trends of the nineteenth century. Trained initially in the physical sciences, Boas spent a period in Wundt's laboratory, where research was aimed at constructing a technique to access directly elementary sensations, Wundt's building blocks of mind.

The basic strategy of Wundt's experiments was to get at the very earliest stages of what we would now call information processing. The goal of psychology was to focus on the "raw," "initial" response evoked by very well-specified physical stimuli. It was crucial that the subject not allow any interpretation to intervene between stimulus and response, which was duly recorded in very precise terms—usually reaction time. E. G. Titchener, Wundt's most influential heir in America, went beyond Wundt's plan to insist that the verbal report of sensations, obtained by introspection, had the same precision and reliability as the reaction-time measures.

Significantly, Titchener and other structuralist psychologists believed that if special care was not taken to shear away the subject's elaborated interpretations, raw sensation would be hopelessly mixed with conceptual information (ideas) of an uncontrolled sort, precluding any possibility of discovering the laws by which elementary sensations combine to form ideas. Today, we are familiar with the failure of the structural enterprise in terms of arguments over the irreducibility of thought to elementary sensations, irreconcilable differences arising from conflicting introspective reports, and of American disenchantment with a psychology that precluded the study of practical problems.

Boas questioned the adequacy of such notions on different grounds. It was his belief that the structuralists were mistaken about the purity of the verbal introspective reports they obtained. That is, information other than that narrowly activated by the physical stimulus was affecting the subjects' verbal reports. But because subjects were carefully trained to report as if this were not true, and because procedures were standardized so as to minimize the influence of external information, it *appeared* as if pure sensations were being described. Boas asserted that even "elementary" sensations were conditioned by their contexts of occurrence. His first fieldwork among the Eskimos sought to obtain evidence for this position. Over the course of several decades of research and writing, Boas reconstructed our concept of culture and in the process brought into question the basic assumptions that had guided anthropological research up to this time. (For an outstanding interpretative account, see Stocking, 1968.)

Significantly, Boas was one of the first major figures in anthropology to do fieldwork in societies very different from those of Europe. The theoretical and empirical anthropological work prior to Boas was built largely on the reports of travelers, missionaries, and colonial officers. When he first began his fieldwork, Boas was prepared to find the evolutionary cultural sequence required by the theories of

Spencer and Tylor. However, he was unhappy about the evidence that had been used previously to substantiate such sequences. It was important to evolutionary theorists that "independent inventions" be the dominant form of cultural change to enable historical reconstruction. The diffusion of ideas between groups linked by history and geography was acknowledged, but diffusion was an unwanted source of "noise" in the cultural system, for it obscured the true developmental history. Where two or more groups of people lived in a single locale and shared a common ecology and similar histories, one would expect, of course, to find similar developmental histories at similar rates. But diffusion as a major contributor to culture was downplayed in the ethnological literature.[2]

The assumption of cultural uniformity, which was the basis for ranking cultures in terms of historical development, was equally important to evaluate. Boas's experience among the peoples of the American and Canadian Northwest revealed a pattern of language, custom, and myth that shattered his initial expectations. Instead of uniformity of cultural features, he found diversity that defied either a simple diffusionist or an independent-invention explanation; tribes with the same basic languages were found to adhere to very different myths and beliefs, and tribes with very different languages were found to have almost identical myths and beliefs. Nor was it possible to assign cultural levels to individual features of a culture on the assumption that the course of their development and their current form could be deduced from a common set of rules acting over time. His work on Kwakiutl art emphasized the abstract intellectual work involved in the representation of natural forms. His work on social organization revealed a complexity that badly damaged evolutionary theories of kinship and marriage forms. For example, kinship regulations among the Kwakiutl appeared to result from a mixture of "maternal laws" in a group that was expected to be at a "paternal" stage according to accepted criteria of anthropology at the time. This observation directly contradicted the traditional evolutionary sequence from maternal to paternal forms of kinship regulation.

Moreover, the assumption that different cultural elements will cohere in a uniform manner proved to be incorrect; for, even if a particular cultural product can be said to have been produced by the same historical-cultural process in two cultures, it is unsafe to assume that the same laws apply to other domains within those cultures. Each aspect of culture has to be examined in its own right and its relations to other

aspects within the same society examined to discover the pattern of adaptation that organizes the parts; uniform complexity as a principle of cultural organization does not describe cultural realities. In short, culture features do *not* cohere with respect to any known rules that seem to apply to all cultures in all places. Boas was forced to conclude that each culture represents a combination of locally developed and borrowed features, the configuration of which is an adaptation to the special constraints operating on the people in question.

The contrast between Boas and the evolutionary anthropologist is especially relevant to developmental psychological issues, which were a part of their debate. The notion that "primitives think like children," for example, was much discussed by nineteenth-century anthropologists and psychologists (see Chamberlain, 1901; Gould, 1976). The conclusion is inescapable given the Tylorian premises that mind and society are aspects of the same set of processes, that society is characterized by uniform states of development which allow comparison across societies with respect to level, and that children are less developed forms of adults.

However, if societies are characterized by heterogenous constituent elements, and if all societies can be considered equally valid responses to the historically accumulated problems of survival, there is no basis for comparison across societies *with respect to general levels of development*. Certainly, it is illegitimate to take particular activities out of context as the basis for comparison unless it has been demonstrated that these activities play an equivalent role in the life of the people being compared.

For Boas, not all life's experiences are sewn from the same cloth; they are alternatively simple or complex, depending on the demands made by the total configurations of one's cultural environment. So, too, with mental achievements. If we want to understand thought processes being manifested in any particular context, we need to know the way that this context fits into the current life experiences of the individuals being studied as well as into the past history between and within cultures that have shaped the context in which we make our observations.

Summary

Despite their obvious brevity and the oversimplification that such brevity entails, the foregoing remarks on the modern history of the problem of culture and cognition frame the major issues that have continued to occupy social scientists throughout the twentieth century. We can abstract the following issues from the discussion:

1. It is possible to specify certain adaptive problems faced by all people everywhere because of their common membership in the species, *Homo sapiens*. Their (phylogenetically) common history of problem-solving experiences has resulted in the evolution of a common repertoire of responses to universal aspects of the ecology that are satisfactory in terms of propagation of the species.

2. Many scholars see a single principle of directionality in social history as well as individual biography. The concepts of evolution and development in both anthropology and psychology grow out of a common concern for understanding the origins of humankind as a means to understanding human nature.

3. Despite the overall communality of the life predicaments of *Homo sapiens,* there is variability in the organization of response to these predicaments, depending on the specifics of the "individual" case. The unit that serves as the individual is sometimes the individual person and sometimes the individual culture. There is a very strong tendency among the scholars whose work we have reviewed to draw an analogy between "individuals" at the cultural and personal levels of analysis.[3]

4. It is widely held that the structure and content of early experience shapes the nature of later experience. When Wordsworth asserted that "The child is father to the man," he was speaking for anthropology and psychology as well as for local folk knowledge. Insofar as it is true, this assertion commits the scholar to historical (genetic) analysis in an effort to understand the constraints that shape the current configuration of the system.

5. A major disagreement centers on the problem of uniformity and diversity within whatever unit of analysis the scholar chooses. At the cultural level, the problem of uniformity is central to discussions of cultural evolution. At the individual level, the problem of uniformity is central to discussions of stages of individual development. The issue of uniformity is central to any theory linking individual behavior to cultural experience, and it is central to all theories of change.

In the discussion that follows these issues will appear and reappear in different guises. For example, one prevalent position asserts that there are no important cultural variations in cognition; at most, one can expect to find superficial differences in cog-

nitive content. *Homo sapiens* common phylogenetic history of "problem solving" has produced a common response of the species to its predicaments. We will present Piaget's genetic epistemology as the major example of this position.

Rejection or modification of this universalistic thesis takes several forms. One line of reasoning builds directly from the logic of a universal set of problems by asserting that the specifics of human problem-solving environments are organized by the particulars of their ecology and historically conditioned responses to it. A group's common experience with a local set of unusual constraints will produce between-culture variation, but *within-culture universals*. According to this view, Eskimos and Bushmen share many common problems, but the configurations of adaptation to the specifics of their predicament will produce nontrivial differences in adaptation and, therefore, nontrivial differences in thought. From this perspective, all existing cultures are equally valid responses to unique configurations of historical experience. The "cognitive styles" they produce are said to be correspondingly adaptive. This approach will be reviewed in terms of Berry and Witkin's work.

A second line of reasoning which challenges the tenets of the universalistic thesis and is herein called a context-specific framework, treats culture and cognition as aspects of a single interacting system of coordination between individuals and the socially conditioned contexts of their everyday lives. In effect, the context-specific approach in studies of culture and cognitive development extends Boas's insights concerning the heterogeneity of activity across settings within cultures into psychology. Instead of the universal laws of mind that control development "from above," the context-specific approach seeks to understand how cognitive achievements, which are initially context specific, come to exert more general control over people's behavior as they grow older. The context-specific approach to culture and cognitive development takes "development within domains of activity" as its starting point; it looks for processes operating in the interactions between people within a particular setting as the proximal cause of increasingly general cognitive competence.

For all theories, the rules governing connections between aspects of cultural experience and aspects of mind are a central concern. The solutions proposed by alternative approaches to the question of mind and culture are related insofar as they account adequately for both uniformity and diversity of cultural/mental phenomena.

COGNITIVE UNIVERSALS: PIAGET

Piagetian-inspired cross-cultural research has been the subject of extensive discussion and review (e.g., Dasen, 1972, 1977; Dasen & Heron, 1981; Glick, 1975; Greenfield, 1976; Jahoda, 1980; Laboratory of Comparative Human Cognition, 1979; Price-Williams, 1981). Consequently, our discussion will be highly selective, focusing on central areas of accomplishment and uncertainty.

The cognitive processes that Piaget's theory is intended to explain are the acquisitions of very general schemes that are related to each other in a logical, hierarchically organized sequence.

The basic assumption underlying the bulk of Piaget's work prior to the 1960s was that the basic cognitive achievements observed in Genevan children are universal (for a brief, but comprehensive review, see Piaget, 1970). The basis for this assumption was Piaget's belief that the possible basic forms of interaction between the growing child and his or her environment are defining characteristics of *Homo sapiens*.

However, from very early in his career, Piaget manifested a keen interest in the work of the French sociological school, and particularly the speculation about cultural differences in thought proposed by Lucien Lévy-Bruhl (Piaget, 1955, p. 21). But early remarks about the minds of primitives and children have amounted to no more than speculation on Piaget's part. Almost no appropriate data were at hand to provide concrete tests of such ideas.

Four Factors Contributing to Development

Responding to the growing number of researchers exporting his tasks to non-Western cultures, Piaget (1966, 1974) attempted to clarify the possible contributions of cross-cultural research to his theory. He did so in terms of four theoretically distinct factors that would be expected to contribute to the process of development.

Biological Factor

Piaget draws heavily on biology and particularly biological evolution for his explanation of ontogenetic development (Piaget, 1963). But, as indicated in the passage above, he is careful to distinguish the process of cognitive development from the maturational process of physical development. If the biological factor dominates cognitive development, Piaget would expect little or no effect of the cultural environment on either the developmental sequence

that unfolds or on the rate at which the unfolding occurs.

Equilibration Factor

This factor is at the heart of Piaget's theory of development (Piaget, 1970, 1977). What the child comes to know about the logic of its world is not based solely on relations that are preexisting in the environment nor on the teachings of its caretakers; rather the child must act on and interact with its environment. What the child comes to know is the form of this interaction. Piaget does not deny that children are taught much of what they know or that explicit teaching is not dominated by the equilibration factor. But he does claim that the acquisition of fundamental logical knowledge structures is dominated by this process of equilibration.

The process of equilibration is best considered to be both universal *and* sensitive to the environments created by specific cultures. Cultures may differ in the extent to which their particular practices provide opportunities for experiences or "operational exercises" of the required kind. To the extent that such variations exist, Piaget should predict that different cultures will retard or accelerate the equilibration process but that the sequence of knowledge structures will be universal.

It has proven difficult to interpret Piaget's notion of equilibration in terms of cultural variations in experience. Dasen (1972) and others interpreted equilibration vaguely as "factors, which arise as the young organism interacts with its physical environment" (Laboratory of Comparative Human Cognition, 1978, p. 148). A more thorough examination of Piaget's writing indicates that this interpretation is too narrow, although it describes the vast majority of Piagetian research.

Social Factor of Interpersonal Coordination

Piaget distinguishes between the effect of the teachings of a particular culture (Factor 4) and the effects on development of the features that all societies have in common. In all cultures, there is a socialization process involving social exchanges among children and between children and adults.

Both theoretically and practically, this social factor enters into exceedingly complex relations with Factors 2 and 4. To understand the difficulty of distinguishing social factors from equilibration, we must consider more carefully Piaget's conception of the relationship between the individual and society.

Piaget (1968) describes children engaged in an

activity where they are free to work together or alone:

> Among the younger children, there is no distinct dividing line between individual activity and collaboration. The young children talk, but one does not know whether they listen. Several of them may be at work on the same project, but one does not know if they are really helping one another. Among the older children, there is progress in two directions: individual concentration when the subject is working by himself and effective collaboration in the group. (p. 39)

In contrasting younger and older children in this passage, Piaget shows that he considers "egocentricity" or the lack of it to be a feature of both the children's intellectual structures and the social organization of the work group. The same process of equilibration operates both to coordinate the schemata of the individual and to coordinate collective action. This process operates whether the collective actions include those among peers or between children and cooperative (rather than coercive) adults. If we ask whether the intellectual operations are the cause or effect of cooperation, Piaget answers that it is like the question of "whether the chicken appears before the egg."

> Logic constitutes the system of relationships which permit the coordination of points of view corresponding to different individuals, as well as those which correspond to the successive percepts or intuitions of the same individual. (1968, p. 41)

A new structure of knowledge (logic) cannot arise simply from the internalization of cooperative action, since internal coordination is necessary for cooperation to take place. And it must take place to be available in the child's environment to be internalized.

Then how can "interpersonal coordination" be considered a factor having an independent effect? The distinction can be made, if at all, by shifting our focus from a structural description of the equilibrium of internal and external structures and by considering instead the process by which an individual may achieve that coordination. Piaget (1973) has suggested, and current Genevan research (Doise, Mugny, & Perret-Clermont, 1975) is exploring, the hypothesis of a unique role for the fact that "in any environment individuals ask questions, exchange information, work together, argue, object, etc."

(Piaget, 1974, p. 302). Essentially, the idea is that two children working together may each notice different aspects of the same situation and need to coordinate these perceptions, whereas a child working alone would notice only one aspect which would not need to be coordinated.

While the general structure of interpersonal coordination is independent of content and universal, cultures may vary in the number or nature of opportunities they provide for such interpersonal experiences.

Factor of Educational and Cultural Transmission

The final factor in Piaget's list includes all the specific features that make the social environment of one culture different from that of another. The child learns specific skills and beliefs, both through formal and informal education. This is not to say that learning particular cultural practices does not also include a certain amount of more general experience. In fact, a particular craft—pottery, for example—may provide more operational exercises of some kinds than other practices, such as mapmaking. If some societies provide more overall experience relevant to discovering the nature of the environment, true developmental differences would exist between those cultures in either the rate or final level of development.

It should also be clear from the previous discussion that the final three factors all operate singly and in common to increase the level of a child's thinking through a series of substages and stages. More operational exercise is possible in all three realms; a little more operational exercise leads to a little more development. The problem then is to identify dimensions of cultural difference that are theoretically significant in order to predict the course of cognitive development in different cultures.

Overall Stages

Piaget describes four major stages of development, which form an invariant sequence. Many tests of Piaget's developmental theory are formulated cross-culturally as attempts to confirm the presence of one or more of these four stages. Typically, several age groups are sampled, and the age at which given percentages of the various groups "pass" the test are compared to each other and to the studies conducted in Geneva (or in other cultures of interest). "Passing" may consist not only of giving an answer to the problem that is associated with the stage in question but also of giving an appropriate

302 LABORATORY OF COMPARATIVE HUMAN COGNITION

justification for the answer given. Correct performance on these tasks is used as an index of the presence of the mental operations that are assumed to be necessary for that task.

Obviously, researchers working in the field cannot try out all the tasks that have been used to create modern Piagetian theory. For the most part, the cross-cultural research has focused on the concrete operational stage that, among the Swiss children studied by Piaget and his colleagues, begins at about 7 years. It is supplanted by research on the formal operational stage which begins at around 12 years.

Sensorimotor Intelligence

Piaget has consistently maintained that, in order to understand knowledge, one has to be able to chart its development. In 1936, Piaget published his detailed observations and formulations of the first stage of intellectual development. Sensorimotor intelligence begins at birth and ends with the beginning of symbolic thought during the second year.

Only recently have researchers shown an interest in this early period, and, as yet, there have been very few cross-cultural studies (Dasen, Inhelder, Lavallee, & Reschitzki, 1978; Goldberg, 1972; Kopp, Khokha, & Sigman, 1977). The formulation of a number of ordinal scales of sensorimotor intelligence (Casati & Lezine, 1968; Corman & Escalona, 1969; Uzgiris & Hunt, 1975) has provided cross-cultural researchers with standardized norms that can now be used to investigate the behavior of infants in non-Western cultures. On other measures of infant development, particularly motor skills, African infants have performed at higher levels than Western infants. This precocity makes African infants an interesting population for comparisons of sensorimotor intelligence.

Dasen (1977) reports the results of two recent research studies: one cross-sectional, conducted by Bovet and Othenin-Girard in 1975; and the other longitudinal, conducted by Dasen, Inhelder, Lavallee, and Retschitzki in 1973–1975. In these studies, the performance of Baoulé children from the Ivory Coast was compared to norms established by French children on the Casati-Lezine Scale of Sensori-Motor Intelligence (1968). This scale consists of seven task-series, each composed of hierarchically ordered subtasks. In both studies, no evidence was found for a generalized claim of mental precocity of African infants. Instead, they found that there was a consistent and obvious advancement throughout the age range for African infants on the task-series that involved combinations of objects and the use of objects as instruments. On other task-

series, involving object permanence and object explorations, their behavior more closely paralleled that of the French sample and even showed some slight advances, except in two subtasks, in which there were slight delays.

To understand the reasons for both the advances and the delays, Dasen points to the need to examine the cultural context in which the tasks occur. The few items on which African infants show a delay can be explained in terms of the content of the problem:

> They [the tasks] require the manipulation of some bizarre apparatus, such as rotating a wooden board, or opening a matchbox. It is probably not the lack of familiarity with the test material as such that causes the difficulty; the plastic tube and rake, and toy cars and other objects, used for further tasks, are quite unfamiliar to the infants in the study, and despite this, they manage to use them satisfactorily. Rather, it seems to be the type of manipulation, the rotating around an axle, or sliding the inner part of the box, which is not culturally relevant. Few objects exist in the child's environment that would require such actions. Whereas the European child would usually have plenty of occasions to observe or manipulate toys, furniture, or other objects which involve a rotation or sliding movements. (Dasen, 1977, p. 162)

The differential rates of sensorimotor development are clearly influenced by cultural characteristics, particularly by the predominant mode or quantity of stimulation and by the cultural value placed on particular skills.

Even though there were clear differences in the rate of sensorimotor development between these two groups, Dasen emphasizes the similarity of the overall developmental pattern. The way actions become ordered and integrated into action patterns across cultural groups is highly similar, even when the materials used are unfamiliar to the child. Dasen suggests that the similarities in developmental pattern between very different cultural groups leave open the possibility that there may be generalities in the way infants interact with their environment, constructing knowledge that becomes the basis of later cognitive processes.

Concrete Operations

Attainment of concrete operations is the aspect of Piaget's developmental theory that is most frequently studied cross-culturally. There are perhaps two reasons why this is so. The first involves the nature of the tasks. Concrete operational tasks require the manipulation of physical materials that can be easily transported to exotic cultures or constructed on the spot. A second reason has to do with the activities that constitute the tasks: they can be scored "right" or "wrong." Western psychologists who work in a tradition of quantitative assessment of psychological processes find it easy to standardize the application. Although, in fact, the "clinical" aspect of the concrete operational tasks is fundamental to interpreting responses, the complex interaction required by Piaget tends to drop out of many cross-cultural analyses (cf. Kamara, 1971; Nyiti, 1973).

Population samples from other cultures have been found to achieve concrete operations sooner, at the same time, or later than European and American samples. In some studies, a significant proportion of adults has failed to achieve concrete operations. A variety of explanations, which we will discuss presently, have been offered to account for these results.

Formal Operations

Piaget (1970) characterizes the thinking process of young children as "concrete" operational because it relies on the actual manipulation of objects and events in the immediately present context. Formal operations are not tied to reality in the same way. They enable the adolescent to reason in terms of verbally stated hypotheses.

A second difference between concrete operations and formal operations results from the development of a new organization of cognitive structures. While the concrete operational child reasons from one element to the next, with no overall structure for representing relationships, formal operational adolescents are able to consider systematically the complete set of possibilities.

Genevan adolescents were found to reach the 75% success criterion for each of the substages between 11 and 15 years of age. That is a rare, high level of success.

Although Inhelder and Piaget (1958) used 15 different formal tasks, attempts to assess the presence or absence of formal operations typically use a single task and draw inferences about the whole mental organization of the mind, based on this single task. Neimark's (1975) review of these studies reports a consensus that the level of performance is lower in other cultures than the level reported for comparable ages in Geneva. The older cross-cultural research generally failed to find evidence of formal operational thought among nonschooled, non-Western populations. Recently, there has been some evidence for the existence of formal operational thought

in non-Western, schooled populations. Za'rour and Khuri (1977) found evidence of a shift from concrete performance to formal operational performance on time/distance problems in Jordanian children at about 13 years of age. Saxe (1979) also documented the presence of formal operations in a population of schooled children from Papua, New Guinea. His work represents a break from other studies of formal operations in exotic cultures because he utilized an *indigenous* knowledge system, the birth-order system. Saxe explored the development of the ability to coordinate two reference systems and to generate the possible or hypothetical combinations of birth orders in a family (combinatory logic). He finds evidence of a shift from concrete to formal understandings between the ages of 13 and 19.

Jahoda (1980) presents an especially helpful discussion of the implications of the formal operations cross-cultural research. Citing evidence from the informal reports of explorers and the more formal reports of anthropologists, Jahoda illustrates behaviors that apparently require formal operational thinking among people who have not manifested formal operational thinking in experimental settings. Jahoda's central conclusion is that Piaget's reliance on actions in the physical world is a "bias that may be unjustified, resulting in a misclassification of subjects in traditional societies whose logic gets the main chance to manifest itself in verbal behavior in the social domain" (Jahoda, 1980, p. 119).

Jahoda's suggestion as well as the possibility of domain-specific stage acquisition are two major directions that research on culture and cognitive development have been taking. These themes will recur frequently in the remaining discussion.

Within-Stage Variability

In addition to variability in the age at which children from different cultural groups attain one or another of the global Piagetian stages, there is variability to be accounted for in the manifestation of stage-appropriate behavior *within* stages. Within a Piagetian framework, this kind of variability has traditionally been referred to as *horizontal décalage*. Among Genevan children, for example, there is an ordering of the acquisition of conservation that begins with conservation of quantity, then weight, then volume.

Strictly speaking, studies of horizontal décalage are not motivated by Piaget's theory, since he does not predict within-stage sequences of concept acquisition. They have been of interest to Piagetians partially because they are not properly incorporated into the theory and because obvious lines of accommodation of facts to theory suggest ways in which experience might influence development.

The cross-cultural evidence on the invariance of within-stage concept acquisitions is ambiguous. Early studies found the order of conservation of quantity, weight, and volume to be consistent with Piaget's description among Iranians (Mosheni, 1966), Sicilians (Peluffo, 1967), and Chinese (Goodnow, 1962). Dasen (1970, 1972), Boonsong (1968), and Prince (1968, 1969) found that conservation concepts developed at the same time as each other, while Bovet (1974) and Otaala (1971) found that the sequences of within-stage operational development differed in their samples. Dempsey (1971), using different cultural groups in the United States, found differing décalage among them on time-conservation tasks. Kelly (1977) found effects of schooling on décalage among conservation tasks with New Guinea children.[4]

Piagetian Treatments of Variability

After evaluating the mounting evidence of both the age variability in achieving various "universal" cognitive operations and the within-stage variability in achieving operations connected with the specific materials being manipulated, Piaget (1972) offered three global courses that might explain such performance variabilities.

First, "different speeds would be due to the quality and frequency of intellectual stimulation received from adults or obtained from the possibilities available to children in their environment" (Piaget, 1972, p. 7). Second, Piaget suggests the possibility that formal operations are not the expression of a universal stage, but a form of cognitive specialization (in the manner of an aptitude) that permits certain individuals to penetrate particular domains of experience more deeply than others. The third possibility, the one which Piaget favored, was to assume that all individuals reach a universal stage of formal operations but that formal operations are acquired first (and perhaps only) in fields of adult specialization or in connection with special aptitudes.

None of these possibilities was pursued by Piaget himself, and it is not entirely clear how "aptitude" as a theoretical entity should enter Piagetian theory. However, a number of investigators have been attempting to reconcile Piagetian theory with the evidence that differences in cultural experience underlie developmental delays in performance on Piagetian tasks. In some cases, the reconciliation seeks to explain away the performance differences as the result of experimental artifact; in others, the theory is modified to accommodate the data.

The most traditional approach to this set of problems is to claim that reported cultural differences in cognitive achievement are the result of methodological artifacts. That is, *real* cognitive development is universal; psychologists simply get a mistaken impression of their subjects' competence because of the specific assessment activities that they depend upon.

This conclusion was suggested by Kamara and Easley (1977) and Nyiti (1976). In their investigations these two research teams each used a native speaker as the experimenter who was also a psychologist trained in clinical interviewing. Their developmental curves approximate European norms. Unhappily for the theory, these studies did not manipulate the factors of language and cultural membership of the experimenter. There has been enough variability in previous between-study comparisons to make it unlikely that these factors alone are sufficient to account for many of the cultural differences that have been reported (e.g., in Dasen, 1977).

However, there is no doubt that features of the interactions involved in assessing Piagetian development can materially affect the results. For example, Irvine (1978) sought to reevaluate the difficulties reported for Greenfield's Wolof (Senegalese) subjects who were asked to deal with a conservation-of-liquids problem. As a part of her assessment, Irvine asked subjects to play the role of an informant whose job it was to clarify *for the experimenter* the Wolof terms for resemblance and equivalence. When confronted with the typical Piagetian conflict situation, Irvine's "psychological subjects" gave the "wrong" response: The beaker with water higher on its sides was said to contain more liquid. However, in their role as linguistic informants, these same subjects went on to explain that while the level of the water was "more," the quantity was the same. Greenfield, herself, had noted that conservation was achieved if the children poured the liquids themselves, suggesting that the European-based procedure was eliciting an irrelevant interpretation of the task (Greenfield, 1966). Glick (1975) has offered a useful general discussion of the ways that language may enter into Piagetian assessment.

A closely related interpretation of culturally linked performance differences on Piagetian tasks is to invoke the distinction between cognitive competence and cognitive performance. Dasen (1977) introduced this distinction into the cross-cultural Piagetian literature, drawing upon a formulation offered earlier by Flavell and Wohlwill (1969). Flavell and Wohlwill had suggested that the correct response to a Piagetian task be considered a joint product of the probability that the child has acquired the operational structure and the probability that the relevant task-specific knowledge is applied. To this, Dasen added a third factor identified with cultural factors affecting the probability that the proper knowledge would be brought to bear in "a given cultural milieu."

A major strategy offered by Dasen and his colleagues to address the competence-performance distinction is to conduct training studies, the procedures of which embody a Piagetian theory of the interactions necessary to produce development. For example, Dasen, Lavallee, and Retschitzki (1979) conducted a training study with a large number of Baoulé (Ivory Coast) children, to determine both changes in level of responding to the training task and transfer of training to a variety of other problems requiring the same operations. The central question in this research was to determine if training occurred rapidly and to the hypothetically maximum level. Very rapid and marked effects of training were taken as evidence that the underlying competence existed, but its expression was inhibited. Training in this case was believed to act on the relevant performance factors. Slow learning was interpreted as evidence that the essential competence was initially absent, but instilled by the training. In this study, Dasen and others obtained evidence for learning during the training sessions; the level of performance improved between pre- and posttests. But change was slow enough to best fit the notion that training actually changed the basic competence of the subjects instead of "triggering" an already existing competence. This newly acquired competence transferred to the other appropriate operational tasks. In other studies, change was rapid enough to implicate performance factors, while in some cases training has not been completely successful (see Dasen, Ngini, & Lavallee, 1979).

Dasen (1974, 1980) has sought to provide the most systematic account for performance variability within an overall "ecocultural framework" summarized in Figure 1. Acknowledging the need for methodological rigor in the conduct of studies, Dasen has continued to assume that there are real developmental differences associated with special cultural experience. However, in order to make theory and data fit, he has had to follow that line of Piaget's speculations that relaxed assumptions about the uniformity of developmental levels. (For the most extreme statement of this viewpoint, see Dasen, Berry, & Witkin, 1979.) Working with two groups of Australian Aborigines who differed in the degree of contact they maintained with Euro-Australian culture, Dasen (1974) contrasted performance for two class-es of concrete-operational tasks. He presented three tasks designed to sample spatial thinking on the grounds that traditional Aboriginal culture depends heavily for its survival on the ability to orient in space using cues deemed subtle and obscure to strangers. These spatial tasks were contrasted with standard conservation of number, quantity, volume, length, and seriation, in which, according to the theory, "logicomathematical" concepts predominate. Dasen cites reports that Aboriginal numerical concepts are few and seldom used, to motivate the hypothesis that tasks embodying such concepts will be learned more slowly by Aborigines than spatial tasks, for which the Aborigines have dense practice and cultural aids. On the basis of prior evidence, Dasen predicts the opposite relation among tasks for the European population tested.

The results of this study confirmed the differences in the age of acquisition of general stages and the differences between cognitive domains, all in the direction Dasen predicted. European contact increased performance of the Aboriginal population for the logicomathematical tasks, and the Aborigines found those problems relatively more difficult than the spatial tasks. Linking within-stage performance variations to environmental variations is an important extension of Piagetian research. In recent years, Dasen has systematically explored a variety of strategies for bringing the European-based theory into line with cross-cultural research while maintaining its basic thrust. (For a recent overview, see Dasen, 1980.)

Culture as Independent Variable

How could it be that certain cultures provide more of the theoretically crucial experiences for development? Are these different experiences to be found in the methods of cultural transmission, the informal and formal educational arrangements of the culture? Are they to be found in the interactional patterns or the technology of the culture? Bovet (1974) suggests that the home life of her Algerian subjects is the source of some of their difficulties in responding to her tasks.

A further point to be mentioned is that the eating and cooking utensils (bowls, glasses, plates) of the particular environment studied were of all shapes and sizes, which makes it somewhat difficult to make any comparisons of dimensions. Furthermore, the way of serving food at the table was for each person to help himself from a communal dish, rather than for one person to share it out amongst those present; no comparison of the

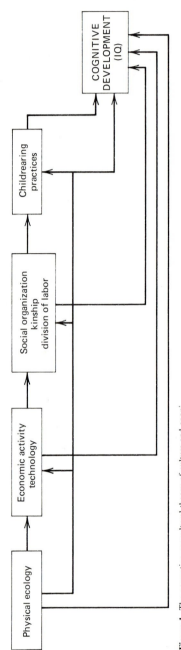

Figure 1. The normative ecocultural theory of culture and cognitive development.

size of the portions takes place. Finally, the attitude of the mother who does not use any measuring instrument, but "knows" how much to use by means of intuitive approximations and estimations, may have some influence on the child's attitude. (p. 331)

Such features of daily life help to explain both why younger children tended not to notice the dimensions of the containers used in the conservation of quantities task and why children in that culture tended to achieve conservation later than in Geneva.

But, of course, the way food is stored and served is but one of a multitude of differences between the two cultures. Bovet's suggestions are plausible, but they do not distinguish between the contributions of social factors and of equilibration; nor do they "unpackage" the sources of experience that might differentially affect development. Other studies have attempted to narrow down the differences by comparing two groups that differ in a single culture in only one "dimension." Among the comparisons that have been made are those between groups that differ in amount of Western contact, urban or rural residence, socialization practices, and amount of schooling. Even when relevant data are collected, the clearly interwoven nature of Factors 2 and 3, if not 4 as well, lead repeatedly to uncertainty (e.g., Dasen, 1974).

Urban and Rural Settings

We have already mentioned Piaget's reference to a study by Mosheni that compared urban and rural children in Iran. A delay of two to three years on concrete operational tasks was found for the rural children while those in Teheran performed roughly as those in Geneva. It might be tempting to attribute these differences to differential exposure to concepts relevant in the Western technological culture in which Piaget's theory was developed. However, Piaget notes that with the exception of biological factors, it is not possible to specify which of his factors should be implicated in the Iranian rural-urban contrast.

Concerning factor 2, Mosheni notices that astounding lack of activity of the young country children who do not go to school and who have no toys, except stones or sticks, and who show a constant passivity and apathy. Thus one finds at the same time a poor development of the coordinations of individual actions (factor 2), of interpersonal actions (factor 3), and educational

transmissions (factor 4), which are reduced since these children are illiterate. This implies a convergence of the three groups of factors. (Piaget 1974, pp. 305–306)

He calls, therefore, for further studies in which these factors (e.g., education) are more clearly controlled.

More recently Opper (1977) compared urban and rural Thai school children. The two samples differed both in their physical environment and in parental occupations (rice farmers vs. government officials or professionals), but in average school performance the samples were similar. Here, again, the rural children lagged behind the children from Bangkok, but the factors responsible for the delay are not entirely clear. The localities differ both in industrialization (and in the resulting "pace of life"), in childrearing practices, and in the quality of the schooling. Although Opper does not link these variables specifically to Piaget's factors, the first two can be seen to resemble Factors 2 and 3, and schooling should be related to Factor 4. Opper notes that although the Bangkok school was superior in equipment and staffing, the lag between the urban and rural samples decreased during the school years. She concludes that "whatever is responsible for the difference between the two groups seems to have occurred already during the pre-school years . . ." (p. 120).

Western Contact

Dasen (1974) compared Australian Aborigines from two different settlements. Both groups were relatively isolated, but differed in the amount of Western contact. The low-contact group was sedentary for part of the year but for about four months "most of the population still leaves on 'walkabout' visiting their ancestral sacred grounds and performing ceremonies, traveling over wide distances in the Western Desert, and living mainly from hunting and gathering" (Dasen, 1974, p. 383). When not on walkabout, children attend school and adults are employed in jobs that do not intersect the European-based economy; or else they live on welfare. The medium-contact group is somewhat more accessible from the nearest European center. These people travel frequently, but they do not go on walkabout. Both groups use their vernacular at home (schools use English), but the medium-contact group has abandoned more of their traditional values. The jobs held by the second group are of the same type as the first, but they have more contact with a cash economy.

Using batteries of conservation tasks that call on logicomathematical and on spatial skills, Dasen established that the rate of development is greater for the medium-contact group than for the low-contact group in the logicomathematical skills but the same for both groups in the spatial skills. It might be expected that the partially nomadic group would develop greater spatial skills by virtue of the practice in hunting and finding their way about the desert. However, Dasen notes that those concepts (conceived as "spatial skills," in other work) which "we are studying are only partly equivalent to those needed for survival by Aborigines (respectively Eskimos), whereas they are the spatial concepts typically relevant to the European culture" (Dasen, 1974, p. 406). Apparently, the skills learned in the desert do not transfer well to Piagetian tasks. (See, however, Kearins, 1980, and Rogoff & Waddell, 1980, which are discussed below.) On the other hand, whatever differences in their lives have been brought about by Western contact do appear to have resulted in some differences in conservation and related abilities.

Schooling

A basic difficulty with interpreting the pattern of cross-cultural data with respect to the influence of schooling on Piagetian concept development is that the theory itself makes no predictions specific to schooling. Clearly, schooling refers to Piaget's Factor 4. But schooling, like any experience, will be expected to promote development of operative understanding only if it provides children with appropriate operative exercises. Different authors have taken different positions on this question.

Greenfield (1966) suggested that schooling increases children's analytic attention to perceptual features of the task and away from the actions involved in the crucial transformations. She also speculates that school may operate indirectly by providing the children with a language (French) that makes distinctions critical to performance and by providing a different set of beliefs that suppress "action magic" interpretations characteristic of her nonschooled subjects. Bovet (1974) disputes these interpretations and attributes Greenfield's results to a kind of "pseudo-conservation." Kiminyo (1977), Armah and Arnold (1977), and Goodnow and Bethon (1966) all argue that schooling should depress the level of operative experience. Goodnow and Bethon and Kiminyo argue that pseudo-conservation occurs among school children because they have been taught procedures specifically applicable to test situations where one does not understand deeply what is going on; nonschooled children have more direct experience with the environment and therefore ought to be more advanced, at least at the concrete-

operational level. Armah and Arnold argue that schooling decreases Ghanaian girls' experience with manipulating objects. All these arguments lead to the prediction of more rapid development among *nonschooled* children. Unfortunately, no differences were found between the schooled and nonschooled populations in overall performance. While the authors seek internal evidence for their hypotheses in the reasons given by individual subjects (e.g., Goodnow and Bethon's), they flounder in their attempts because "performance" and "competence" features of the task demand playoffs against each other: the schooled children are expected to deal more effectively with the "performance" features of the task owing to their greater familiarity with the appropriate discourse forms. These studies did not use the range of techniques suggested by research such as Bovet's, and they remain ambiguous with respect to their theoretical significance.

Strauss, Ankori, Orpaz, and Stavy (1977) found more rapid development of proportional reasoning among unschooled Israeli Arab children up to about 10 years of age. They argue for directly negative effects of specific schooling experience.

One of the most interesting pieces of evidence that culture or task-specific performance factors, not Piagetian competence, underlies differences associated with schooling is provided in a training study by Pinard, Morin, and Lefebvre (1973). Pinard and associates selected a sample of nonconservers on the basis of pretests of schooled and unschooled Rwandian and schooled Canadian 7-year-olds. Control groups did not change their performance over a 2-month period following pretesting. But training that emphasized anticipating the outcome of conservation tests and that provided practice in compensating apparent discrepancies produced a marked improvement in performance; the improvement was equivalent in all the groups. A greater number of unschooled children than schooled children showed an effect of training after only a single session. These results are striking: the fact that so little schooling (the children involved had experienced only 5 months to a year of school) produced an impact on performance and the fact that so little training should remove group differences seem strongly to indicate that these children had a "latent' competence that could easily be "activated" (to use Dasen's, 1977, phrase).

This very brief review of the influence of various experiential/cultural factors on the development of concrete operations illustrates some of the complexities in evaluating the central issue: Does culturally organized experience influence the acquisition of concrete-operational thinking? (For more extensive discussions, see Dasen 1977; Rogoff, 1981.) At present, it is simply not possible to reach a firm answer to this question. The recent advent of training studies and of more sophisticated clinical interviewing techniques holds out the appealing possibility (from the point of view of the theory) that cultural variations can be attributed totally to performance factors, thus preserving the universalist hypothesis with which Piaget began this work. However, such data are few, and there are enough apparently negative cases (summarized in Dasen, 1977) to urge caution with respect to this conclusion.

With respect to formal operations, the situation is quite different. Formal operations seem to show a greater effect of education than do concrete operations. In fact, if formal operational thinking is manifested at all in Piagetian tasks, it occurs mostly for subjects with substantial levels of education (Goodnow, 1962; Goodnow & Bethon, 1966; Laurendeau-Bendavid, 1977). Laurendeau-Bendavid used concrete tasks as well as a formal one that required quantification of probability with schooled, partially schooled, and nonschooled African children up to 17 years of age. Her comments about this work provide a good summary to this overview.

> In sum, school attendance appears to be a facilitating rather than a necessary condition for the attainment of concrete operations and objective causal representations, since some of the children without any schooling do attain these. On the other hand, school attendance is a necessary but not a sufficient condition for the attainment of formal operations, since only subjects with full school experience—and only a few of these—were found to have reached this level. (Laurendeau-Bendavid, 1977, p. 165)

Evaluating the Four Factors

At the time of this writing, 14 years have passed since Piaget first discussed the relevance of cross-cultural research to his theory. Of the four factors he identified, only biological maturation can be firmly ruled out by his criteria. The factors of equilibration, of social coordination, and of specific education all remain as possible, or even plausible, sources of differences in cognitive development.

This remaining uncertainty does not mean that progress has not been made during this period of intense activity. In our view, a decade and a half of hard work has brought more than a proliferation of

data on cultural variations in performance; it has brought increased theoretical and methodological insights into the examination of the theory itself.

With the wisdom provided by added experience and hindsight, it is now apparent that Piaget severely underestimated the difficulties in replicating his basic methods in different cultural settings. Impediments to implementation of the clinical method amount to more than unfamiliarity with the local language. That can be and has been overcome (e.g., Nyiti, 1976). In addition, researchers have had to come to grips with the fact that the modes of discourse that are the medium for the clinical method are themselves so culturally conditioned (Scribner, 1977) that a variety of new techniques has been required to provide the crucial information to assess the cognitive status of children, and that of adults.

Although this work has greatly enriched our knowledge of the within-experiment factors that modify performance, it has simultaneously complicated the already complicated task of disentangling the factors that contribute to development. If no special procedures are employed to distinguish competence and performance, then Piagetians will still be left with the difficult job of "unpackaging" the independent variables. Piaget's comments in his 1966 paper show clearly his sensitivity to this problem which is, after all, a central justification for engaging in cross-cultural work. But each group included in a comparative study may need to be subject to its own, specially tailored, set of procedures to reveal the bedrock level of competence they have acquired. Then, the fullest enterprise will require not only the study of different cultural groups but a "treatment by groups" design in which different amounts of experimentally designed operative practice must be investigated along with different age levels and different cultural groups.

While moving in this direction, researchers within the Piagetian tradition have adopted two differing views of how culturally organized experience ought to be viewed from the standpoint of the theory.

One view is put forth by Heron:

> By this term [cognitive ambience] I mean "values with cognitive relevance that are *implicit* in the total pattern of adult and older sibling behaviour within which (early) development takes place . . . the total pattern of implicit cognitively-relevant cultural values communicated through linguistic and other behaviour by adults and older children." I must re-emphasize what is the vital feature of this "communication of cognitively-relevant cultural values": it is *the unin-*

tentionality, the day-by-day usualness, the taken-for-granted assumptions about what is and what is not important in life. (Heron, 1974, p. 97)

This view matches well the approach assumed by Piaget in his 1966 article and by Piagetian researchers such as Bovet: there are certain concepts essential to all scientific knowledge structures. Development, which proceeds along a unitary path toward mastery of these concepts, may be retarded if a culture fails to provide the requisite experience. If the problems of assessing basic competence can be solved, it is a relatively straightforward matter to determine if a culture has failed to provide the needed experience.

A second approach has been urged by Dasen. He has opted for a modification of Piagetian theory which assumes that different cultures promote development in "certain areas of cognitive development over others." Dasen tells us, "In other words each cultural group is expected to develop specifically those skills and concepts which it most needs" (Dasen, 1977, p. 184). When he found that the nomadic groups acquired spatial concepts earlier than conservation but that the sedentary group acquired conservation earlier than the spatial concepts, he had support for this line of interpretation.

This kind of result has led Dasen and his colleagues to a new formulation of the cross-cultural Piagetian enterprise: "An ecological formulation provides a value-free context for the interpretation of differences as unique adaptations, rather than as differential developments" (Dasen, Berry, & Witkin, 1979, p. 79). Because this apparently multilineal concept of development is still in its formative stages, a good deal of uncertainty necessarily surrounds its interpretation and its relationship to the initial Piagetian enterprise. For example, Dasen, speaking of the differential development of spatial and conservation concepts in nomadic and sedentary groups, says that the cultural differences he observed "do not exclude the universality of the underlying cognitive competence" (Dasen, 1977, p. 184). But asymptotic performance on some of the tasks reached levels no higher than 20% to 30% of the Genevan levels. In some cases, training studies suggest that the differences apply only to performance, but in others, competence is implicated (Dasen, Ngini, & Lavallee, 1979). These results may or may not conflict with the claim for cognitive universals.

Summary

Despite all of the effort represented by the research that we have reviewed under the rubric of Piagetian theory, the basic question of the universality of cognitive competence has not been satisfactorily answered. Responding to massive evidence of culturally conditioned performance variations, more sophisticated experimental techniques have been devised and tested to rescue a universalist conclusion from the evidence of cultural variability. Especially significant, in our view, is Dasen's move toward a domain-specific theory of development. Whether this modification in the theory can be made while retaining a *Piagetian* formulation of cognitive development is an important question to which we will return after we have had the opportunity to review other formulations of the relation between culture and cognitive development.

CULTURAL CONFIGURATIONS

There is a certain irony in the central place that Piagetian theory has occupied in cross-cultural research on cognitive development. Piaget's earlier theorizing suggested that the crucial environmental prerequisites for development would be very widespread in human societies. Relevant cultural variability would be minimal and located in a few, unevenly distributed institutions such as schools. Before the recent appearance of evidence of cultural variability, cross-cultural Piagetian research seemed concerned with proving the null hypothesis: Culture does *not* cause developmental differences in cognitive structures.

In this section, we review two theoretical positions that assume fundamental cultural variation from the outset—the socialization perspective and the psychological differentiation perspective.

The Socialization Perspective

The "socialization perspective" contains the following propositions: (1) the basic economic activities of a people are constrained by physical ecology; (2) cultures elaborate different kinds of social organization to deal with basic life predicaments; (3) cultures transmit their acquired wisdom to their children in ways that fit in with a culturally elaborated system of adjustments representing adult patterns of living. So, for example, simply as a result of direct ecological press, the Kalahari bushman and the Kpelle rice farmer will have to develop different strategies for survival of the individual and the group. Even at a very rudimentary level, these activities will have to be coordinated among members of a culture in order to insure an adequate supply of food, shelter, and care of the young.

When we consider the totality of coordinated responses to life's predicaments as they are experienced by different groups living in different physical ecologies with different histories of culture contact, we arrive at the organized human unit that Franz Boas called a culture. In this view, each culture is a "problem-solving unit." The task of cultural analysis becomes one of describing the "problems" set by the environment and the "solutions" evolved over time to deal with the problems. The task of psychological analysis is to establish how patterns of individual adaptation correspond to cultural adaptation.

During the first half of the twentieth century, this kind of thinking produced two major lines of attack against the idea that psychological development would be controlled by universal, biologically determined features of the species.

Perhaps the most celebrated criticism of psychological universals came when Malinowski presented his analysis of father/son relations among Trobriand Islanders (Malinowski, 1927). Contrary to Freud's claim that Oedipal conflicts would be a universal feature of growing up, Malinowski found no evidence of father/son hostility of the kind predicted.

A number of scholars attempted to rescue the Freudian formulation by modifying it to account systematically for cultural variations. One extremely influential approach was suggested by Kardiner, who characterized psychoanalysis as a psychology that attempts to "follow certain gross maneuvers of the personality over the entire trajectory of the life span" (Kardiner, 1945, p. 11). This analysis assumed certain biological constraints that would set universal problems for human infants.

For example, all infants must obtain food, must be kept free of lethal diseases, must get enough sleep, and so on to survive, or the species will expire. These needs are universal, and so are a very general class of adult behaviors that satisfy them (although not without a great deal of pain and loss). However, the specific conditions under which feeding or sleeping can occur will differ rather markedly depending upon the ecological predicament that a culture faces and the socially elaborated responses

that have been accumulated over time to deal with such predicaments. The attempt to save psychic universals in the face of Malinowski's evidence that Oedipal conflicts are absent among Trobrianders retained the idea of universal *functions*, while arguing cultural differences in the form through which functions were satisfied. The "function" of Oedipal conflicts arising from necessary frustration of infant drives will remain constant across cultures, although the "form" it takes will be different from culture to culture. In some societies, uncles or some other adult figures will be the source of authority and the object of negative feelings instead of fathers.

LeVine's (1974) observations among the Gussii of Kenya provide an excellent example of a socialization theory that characterizes the nature of the ecoculturally mediated constraints on children's experience. Gussii cook their food over an open fire; LeVine noticed that Gussii toddlers around the fire could be subject to burned feet. But this hazard doesn't occur in cultural isolation. Parents, recognizing the danger, arrange matters so that their toddlers spend very little time wandering near fires; they carry their toddlers more than we do. Adults recognize that fires represent a special danger that children have to be protected from once they start to toddle, an insight for which they have an appropriate, summarizing proverb, "Lameness is upright." A wide variety of customs dealing with child care, some of which have less obvious connection to specific dangers, all seem to "solve the problem" of letting toddlers walk on their own (as it were).

Generalizing from many such instances in many cultures, LeVine speculates on three nested goals that are universal to all human societies. He then suggests local conditions as reasons for differential organization, with different consequences for the children.

LeVine's three hypothesized universal goals are:

1. The physical survival and health of the child, including (implicitly) the normal development of his reproductive capacity during puberty.

2. The development of the child's behavioral capacity for economic self-maintenance in maturity.

3. The development of the child's behavioral capacities for maximizing other cultural values—for example, morality, prestige, wealth, religious piety, intellectual achievement, personal satisfaction, self-realization—as formulated and symbolically elaborated in culturally distinctive beliefs, norms, and ideologies.

These goals are nested in the sense that number 1 has to be satisfied before number 2 and number 2 before number 3. They also form a rough developmental sequence; physical health and survival are of deepest concern in the first years of the child's life; self-sufficiency and cultural appropriateness come later.

In short, to understand cultural variability, we must consider different ecologies and the special constraints they might impose. Consider, for example, Liberia and its infant mortality rate, which exceeds 50% in some regions. In such places, the physical well-being of the child should be a paramount concern; hence, customs aimed at ensuring survival of young children should organize a good deal of adult activity. By contrast, consider a society in which the infants' environment is not particularly hazardous, but food is scarce. In that case, parents might urge children to be economically self-sufficient at an early age. These variations in adaptations to local ecological conditions produce a different configuration of experiences.

In each case, the pattern of predicaments that the infant faces will be intricately related to the condition of the physical environment and the conditions of the social environment (i.e., the collective set of coordinated behaviors of the adults in the child's life). Belief in the interlocking, contingent nature of cultural facts and personality development is a central tenet of socialization theorists. As Benedict put it in one of the classic statements of this perspective:

> As a cultural anthropologist . . . I started from the premise that the most isolated bits of behavior have some systematic relation to each other. I took seriously the way hundreds of details fall into overall patterns. A human society must make for itself some design for living. It approves certain ways of meeting situations. . . . People in that society regard these solutions as foundations of the universe. Men who have accepted a system of values by which to live cannot without courting inefficiency and chaos keep for long a fenced-off portion of their lives where they think and behave according to a contrary set of values. They bring about more conformity. They provide themselves with some common rationale and some common motivations. Some degree of consistency is necessary or the whole scheme falls to pieces. (Benedict, 1934, pp. 11–12)

A recent description of the contrasting predicaments of Kipsigi (Kenyan) and American (Cambridge) infants by Super and Harkness (1980) further illustrates the force of these considerations. The Kipsigi are an agricultural people living at a relatively low level of technology. Infants sleep with their mothers for many months following birth and are carried in slings on their mothers' backs. There is no special time set aside for sleeping. The rhythm of the workday operates on a flexible schedule that can be modified to the baby's demands. At night the infant sleeps with the mother who is minimally disturbed if the infant wakes to feed.

Babies born to middle-class parents in Cambridge, Massachusetts, have a different set of demands placed upon them. Especially in cases where both parents work, life is guided by the clock. Unconstrained access to the attention of adults (or of older siblings) is out of the question for a great part of the day; and at night there are severe constraints on feeding posed by the unwillingness of parents to spend part of the night awake. The American norm of sleeping through the night is so strong that our pediatricians use the duration of the longest daily sleep episode as a measure of neurological maturation. Babies in the United States who fail to sleep through the night by the time they are 4 months old are suspected of developmental retardation.

These and similar differences concerning the time-boundness of the constraints on individual activity (both adult and child) led Super and Harkness to offer the following speculation:

> The American infant must learn, in effect, to accept impersonal, externally imposed regularity, while the Kipsigi baby is required to adapt to the needs and behaviors of a small number of particular people. A related contrast holds for adult members of the community and their niches. In Kokwet, the difficult deviant refuses to cooperate with family and neighbors and defies the personal mediation involved in local dispute settlement (Harkness, Edwards, & Super, 1977). In America, the adult who is never on time, misses appointments, or chafes at schedules is the troublesome one. More speculatively, the American baby may be learning about external, invariant, impersonal principles, while the rural Kipsigi infant learns to adapt in particular and personalized contexts. Such a contrast, in one form or another, is frequently drawn in comparing patterns of habitual thought and cognitive performance in rural Africa and urban America (Super, Harkness, & Baldwin, 1977). These parallels, it should be noted, do not necessarily imply an inherent stability of psychological traits; the point is rather that cultures may provide a

continuity of developmental niches supporting particular dispositions. (Super & Harkness, 1980)

Valid or not, these speculations provide an excellent introduction to the large research enterprise that relates cultural adaptation to patterns of individual adaptation (Berry, 1976; Dasen, Berry, & Witkin, 1979; Witkin & Berry, 1975).

Psychological Differentiation Theories

One crucial variable linking cultural and individual adaptation is "cognitive style." *Cognitive styles, in this view, represent the pervasive responses of individuals to pervasive patterns of constraint that arise from ecological and cultural adaptations to which the individual must adapt.* Once the concept of a cognitive style is adopted, it is necessary to find a single framework in which both cultural constraints and individual responses can be represented. One such framework is given by the concept of *differentiation.* The most extensive treatment of this approach to the relation between culture and cognition is provided by Berry (1976).

Berry begins his discussion by considering differentiation at the sociocultural level. He cites Spencer's definition of the evolution of sociocultural systems as a starting point: "Evolution is a change from a state of relatively indefinite, incoherent homogeneity to a state of relatively definite, coherent heterogeneity through continuous differentiations and integrations" (Spencer, 1864, p. 216, quoted in Berry, 1976, p. 21). Berry then reviews attempts to create scales of sociocultural evolution in terms of role differentiation, stratification, and the accumulation of cultural elements.

A good case can be made for temporal sequences of sociocultural changes toward greater social differentiation and complexity. However, sociocultural change is characterized by more than temporal differentiation. Even in Spencer's definition, there is the idea of sociocultural differences in integration (coherence and organization of elements). Here the evidence does not support a linear increase, which leads Berry to reject the idea of a single dimension of sociocultural evolution. Instead, by invoking the distinction between specific and general evolution, he sides with Sahlins and Service (1960), who maintain that "adaptive improvement is relative to the adaptive problem; it is so to be judged and explained. In the specific context each adapted population is adequate, indeed superior, in its own incomparable way" (quoted in Berry, 1976, p. 14).

With this notion of sociocultural differentiation in hand, Berry turns to the ideas of Herman Witkin to characterize individual functioning. Witkin employs the concept of individual differentiation in a way that is attractively similar to the idea of sociocultural differentiation that Berry has formulated in a "neo-Spencerian" manner:

> In broadest terms differentiation refers to the complexity of a system's structure. A less differentiated system is in a relatively homogeneous structural state; a more differentiated system is in a relatively heterogeneous state. The emphasis on "relative" is important for even the most rudimentary system is to some degree differentiated. This is implicit in the very definition of "system."
>
> The description of a system as more differentiated or less differentiated carries definite implications about how it functions. In fact, it is mainly through particular functional manifestations that extent of differentiation of a system may be judged. Before the differentiation concept can be applied to the description of individual behavior or the study of psychological problems its implications for function must be delineated.
>
> Among the major characteristics of the functioning of a highly differentiated system is specialization. The subsystems which are present within the general system are capable of mediating specific functions which, in a relatively undifferentiated state, are not possible or are performed in a more rudimentary way by the system as a whole.
>
> When used to describe an individual's psychological system, specialization means a degree of separation of psychological areas, as feeling from perceiving, thinking from acting. It means as well specificity in manner of functioning within an area. Specific reactions are apt to occur in response to specific stimuli as opposed to diffuse reaction to any of a variety of stimuli. Parts of a perceptual field are experienced as discrete, rather than fused with their background. Impulses are channelized, contrasting with the easy "spilling over" characteristic of the relatively undifferentiated state. More or less discrete feelings and needs are likely to be present. (Witkin, Dyk, Faterson, Goodenough, & Karp, 1962, p. 9)

Just as craft specialization or social stratification may be used as indicators of *sociocultural differ-*

entiation, so various *behavioral* indicators may be used to assess *individual* differentiation. Just as sociocultural indicators of differentiation should cohere, so the individual indicators of psychological differentiation ought to be consistent. As Berry puts it: "[Differentiation] is considered to be a *characteristic of the organism,* and expectations are that tasks which sample differentiation of various kinds of behaviors should yield estimates of roughly similar levels of differentiation" (Berry, 1976, p. 26).

Behavioral Indicators

Key to implementing these ideas is the choice of behaviors that serve as the indicators of differentiation. Differentiation is characterized as a property of "a system's structure," but the referent of the term, "system" is not always clear nor is "structure" clearly specified. In the lengthy passage just cited, "system" sometimes seems to refer to the entire package of individual/environment interactions, sometimes to a subset of interactions that must be investigated in terms of local function, and sometimes to "an individual's psychological system," which can be subdivided into areas labeled by traditional psychological categories (feeling, perceiving, thinking). In order to put these ideas into practice, Witkin's approach was to characterize what he believed to be relevant aspects of organism-in-environment interactions in rather general terms and then to embody these beliefs in psychological tests that appear to have the necessary properties.

Thus, in the area of visual perception, Witkin characterized the relevant characteristics of environment/behavior interactions as follows:

> During development stimulus objects gain function and meaning as a consequence of continuous, varied dealings with them. This acquired functional significance may contribute to the developing discreteness of objects and may serve as the basis for the formation of nongeometrical integrations of the field. We may refer to the increasing discreteness of objects and to the use of more complex principles of field integration as an increase in the articulateness of experience. The person who experiences in articulated fashion has the ability to perceive items as discrete from their backgrounds, or to reorganize a field, when the field is organized; and to impose structure on a field, and so perceive it as organized, when the field has relatively little inherent structure. In this view, the ability to analyze experience and the ability to structure experience are both aspects of increasing articulation. (Witkin et al., 1962, pp. 13–14)

These ideas were embodied in a series of tasks, among which the embedded figures test (EFT) and the rod-and-frame test (RFT) have been most widely exploited. In the EFT, a geometric figure is made a part of a larger design and the subject must locate it. In the RFT, the subject is required to orient a rod "to the vertical." The definition of vertical, however, is ambiguous because the rod is presented within a square frame that can be tilted at various angles with respect to the floor. The key issues are the subject's choice of frame of reference and the physical frame of the tilted square or "true" vertical. Performance of both these tasks is taken as evidence of *perceptual* differentiation. Target items must be perceived as separate from their immediate contexts, and analysis is required to "disembed" the target from the context.

A different set of behavioral indicators are used as indicators of *cognitive* differentiation, which is defined by tasks in which a problem must be analyzed or broken up in order to be solved. Subscales of standard psychometric tests such as matrices, block designs, and picture completion are all said to be measures of cognitive differentiation.

In the *social* domain, differentiation refers to a "sense of separate identity." Witkin suggested three kinds of behavior as indicators of differentiation in the social domain: (1) ability to function with little guidance or support from others; (2) maintenance of direction in the face of contrary social judgments; and (3) stability of self-concept across contexts. The behavioral indicators in this domain have been orientation toward social cues (such as other people's faces), sensitivity to social reinforcers, and preferences for physical distance in social interactions.

The results of correlational studies summarized by Witkin and his associates (e.g., Witkin & Berry, 1975), which suggest consistency of behavior across the indicator tasks, provide the justification for using the concept of "cognitive style" as a link between psychological and cultural adaptation.

Although it would be possible to pursue the study of culture and cognition within a differentiation framework simply by correlating indicators of sociocultural differentiation with indicators of individual differentiation, such evidence would still leave open the question of how cultural experience is transformed into individual behavior. How does the individual come to experience the constraints of the world that mold cognitive style? And, vice versa, how does cognitive style become amalgamated into the totality of coordinated responses to similar experiences?

To answer such questions, Berry and Witkin follow the precedent of the socialization theorists; they look to the early social environment of the child for information about the pattern of constraints that require more and less field-independent, differentiated behavior by the child. In developing indicators of these socialization practices, Witkin has suggested that investigators look at the way that mothers circumscribe their children's activities, whether they regard children as delicate or sturdy, whether they stress conformity and look to the beliefs that they hold about themselves that would affect their behavior toward their children.

Berry (1976) used two different techniques to obtain indicators of the restrictiveness of socialization. First, he used a scale of "compliance-assertion" that had been developed by Barry, Bacon, and Child (1957) to relate child-training techniques to economy and sex differences in socialization (see also Barry, Child, & Bacon, 1959). Barry and associates constructed their scale out of ratings in six categories of interaction involving childrearing. These included obedience training, responsibility training, nurturance, achievement, self-reliance, and general independence training. Using the Human Relations Area files, which contain cross-referenced entries on a wide variety of cultural characteristics, they obtained significant relations between economic activities and socialization practices: compliance increases as food accumulation increases. Second, Berry used a self-appraisal procedure by asking his subjects to rate their own socialization: "When you were growing up, did your mother (father) treat you very strict, fairly strict, or not so strict?" Data generated from these two measures of restrictive socialization practices, which were highly correlated, were combined into a standardized socialization score.

Berry measured ecological factors by using Murdock's classification of subsistence societies in terms of exploitative pattern (animal husbandry, agriculture, etc.), settlement pattern, and size of communities. Acculturation factors were measured by indices that included levels of wage labor and education. Socialization was measured by ranking political and family organization.

Results

With the exception of education and socialization self-ratings, indicators relevant to the ecocultural part of the theory were gathered for 18 subsistence cultural groups ranging from West Africa to Northern Canada to Australia and to three industrialized groups. Data from the Human Area Files were used to code the information about ecological, acculturative, and cultural elements that had been related the-

oretically to sociocultural differentiation. Tests of cognitive style and some control tests were administered to samples within each cultural group. Then the relationships among variables were calculated by using correlation, analysis of variance, and multiple regression techniques. Berry summarizes the results as follows:

> There is systematic covariation between the set of independent variables and the differentiated and acculturative stress behaviors. Cultural groups [and individuals] which are hunting and gathering in subsistence pattern, nomadic in settlement pattern, and loose in sociopolitical stratification emerge as clearly different in cognitive style from those which are agricultural, sedentary, and tight. And within this range of ecological and cultural adaptations, those which occupy intermediate positions ecoculturally also exhibit intermediate behavioral adaptations. . . . Taken at the level of a general overview, it is difficult to avoid the conclusion that the hypothesized relationships have been confirmed. (Berry, 1976, p. 200)

These generalizations have been bolstered by similar studies conducted in many parts of the world on many different populations (see Werner, 1979, for a recent review), making the Berry-Witkin approach to culture and cognitive development one of the most widely tested.

Doubts

Despite these attractive features, there are a number of reasons to question whether the theoretical relationships are either as strong or as broad as they appear to be. One of the major questions raised in recent discussions of the psychological differentiation/cognitive styles research is the issue of domain consistency. The use of the term "style" is motivated by the claim that differentiation manifests itself in all areas of psychological functioning. Thus, key behavioral indicators of field independence and field dependence should cluster within domains (perceptual, cognitive, social, affective) and should correlate highly across domains.

As other writers have noted (e.g., Jahoda, 1980; Werner, 1979), the evidence of domain consistency is not at all strong when one moves from the perceptual and cognitive tasks to the social and affective indicators. Although domain consistency is claimed for intracultural data from the United States, the failure to obtain expected correlations in the cross-cultural arena is considered a problem not only by others but by researchers who take the psychocultural differentiation research perspective (e.g., Dassen, Berry, & Witkin, 1979; Witkin & Berry, 1975, pp. 29–30). There is still the apparent consistency across perceptual and cognitive domains to be considered, however.

Berry, himself, suggests a narrower interpretation of his results because of the difficulty in assigning task to domain.

> In cognition (where perception is also inevitably implicated) differentiation involves the ability to break up or analyze a problem as a step towards its solution, in addition, of course, to many other components (such as background knowledge, general competence, etc.). (Berry, 1976, p. 28)

Goodenough and Karp (1961) are of the opinion that standard psychometric tests such as block designs, picture completion, mazes, and puzzles "appear to involve a capacity to overcome embeddedness." With this justification, supplemented by references to other tasks such as conservation and concept attainment, the separateness of perceptual and cognitive domains is established.

As Jahoda (1980) comments, the lack of process specification creates problems in attempts to evaluate the theory. Nowhere is this truer than in trying to decide if the tasks used to represent cognitive and perceptual domains are sufficiently distinct to warrant the use of the term "cognitive style" when intertask correlations are observed. This issue takes on an added significance in evaluating generalizations from the data because Kohs's blocks and Raven's matrices are widely accepted in American psychological research as indicators of intelligence. (Morrisby's shapes are out of the same mold.) Berry has refused to accept these indicators as valid, but in the absence of a process theory of performance on these tasks, it poses a problem for claiming *differentiation* as the process variable linking individual and cultural adaptation. A "perceptual" task such as the EFT appears to be no less cognitive than any of the cognitive tasks."

Our own view is that evidence of domain consistency is less convincing than current discussions suggest, even for the perceptual and cognitive domains. Serpell (1976) reviewed several such studies and proposed that Witkin and Berry's "cognitive style" is really an increased skill in dealing with pictorial stimuli. For example, Okonji (1969) found the expected correlation between EFT and Raven's matrices, but he failed to find that these two tests correlate with the rod-and-frame test. Okonji also failed to find the expected correlation between EFT, RFT, and socialization factors (see also Siann,

1972). In Berry's study, the rod-and-frame test correlated least with the other measures of field dependence and not at all with measures of socialization or education.

These issues of domain independence and the strength of existing evidence for the theory force themselves on us in two ways. First, they are important to claims that differentiation (disembedding) is the process implicated in the pattern of performance. Berry quite properly included in his battery a test of perceptual discrimination as a process "prior to disembedding (and separate from it . . .)" (Berry, 1976, p. 146). Geometric shapes with gaps in them were presented tachistoscopically and a discrimination score was assigned on the size of a gap necessary to produce recognition. Subjects responded by drawing the figure they saw.

The logic of Berry's analysis leads us to expect that performance on the discrimination task will not correlate highly with performance on the disembedding tasks and will not correlate well with the predicted antecedents of disembedding. Only the first of these expectations is supported by the data; discrimination performance is not as highly correlated with the disembedding tasks as they are with each other, although the correlation is substantial. But discrimination *is* highly predicted by major antecedents. In some cases it is predicted as well as the disembedding task. In light of the truncated range of these scores owing to subjects deleted because they could not draw, the success of the independent variables in predicting discrimination performance is a problem of the sort that motivates a perceptual skills interpretation. According to Berry's statements about the priority of discrimination in the perceptual/analytic process, it would have been interesting to see tests of the effect of ecocultural antecedents with discrimination performance partialed out. No such analysis is offered.

A second concern about the extent to which the implicated *differentiation* is the major process variable controlling performance is the way in which performances generate the classification of subjects in terms of the "cognitive style."

For a task like the rod-and-frame test, the analogy relating performance to process is relatively clear: field independence is indicated when the subject ignores the wooden frame and sets the rod upright with respect to the ground. Field-dependent subjects "depend" on the wooden frame. There are no right or wrong answers, simply different sources of information used to deal with an ambiguous situation.

But for the other tasks used by Berry, there are clear "right" and "wrong" answers. There seems to be no alternative to labeling the performance of someone who cannot identify any of the hidden figures in the EFT as "poor." Certainly when used as psychometric tests, performances like those of many of Berry's groups are so labeled, and so educational researchers focus on remediation through "direct [and] vicarious experiences encouraging conceptual development" (MacArthur, 1973, p. 24).

This close identification between performance on the various indicators of perceptual/cognitive skills is echoed in a recent, comprehensive study of culture and child development: "Studies in both the Western and developing world have shown that children progress from relative field dependence, in which their perception is dominated by the organization of the surrounding field, to relative field independence . . ." (Werner, 1979, p. 187). One might be tempted to conclude from these and similar remarks in the literature that "field dependent" and "less developed" are in some way synonymous, at least within the confines of differentiation theory (Scribner & Cole, 1978). Less differentiated people, like young children, perform poorly on a variety of perceptual/cognitive tasks.

It is this web of factors, vitiating claims of interdomain consistency and mixing tasks interpreted as having "right" and "wrong" answers with tasks having different kinds of answers, that leads us to prefer the idea that Berry and his colleagues have been dealing with a less pervasive set of individual accomplishments than their theory commits them to. By using behavioral indicators that have clear implications of "higher" and "lower" levels of performance, they leave open an interpretation that links field dependence (the "style" that generates low performance) to lower stages of development.

Dasen, Berry, and Witkin (1979) strenuously object to this implication being drawn from their work. They divorce differentiation theory from implications of "higher" and "lower" levels of development by distinguishing between general and specific evolution and by choosing the specific evolution option according to which adaptive improvement is judged by the adaptive problem. This strategy has led cross-cultural differentiation theorists to suggest that the field-dependent and field-independent styles are adaptive to different environments:

Relatively field-independent people are better at cognitive restructuring tasks—that is, tasks which require the person to act on percepts or symbolic representations rather than to adhere to their dominant properties as given. . . .

Relatively field-dependent people are more sensitive . . . to social cues provided by others; they choose to be among others which gives them more experience with people; they have characteristics which are likely to be helpful in relating to other people such as having an interest in others, wanting to help others, and having concern for others. (Dasen, Berry, & Witkin, 1979, pp. 71, 72)

This domain specificity of the adaptiveness of the two styles allows Dasen and others to characterize the theory as "bipolar" and "value free."

Although the claim is not made explicit, it appears that this most recent statement of the theory conceives of societies as either "people oriented" or "object-symbol oriented" in varying degrees that are complementary to each other.

The proposal is that the field-dependent and field-independent cognitive styles, which are process variables, influence the development of patterns of abilities—in this instance, cognitive restructuring skills and interpersonal competencies, combined in an inverse relationship. (Dasen, Berry, & Witkin, 1979, p. 72)

This is an interesting suggestion. However, its empirical basis is very shaky because it rests heavily on claims about domain-specific patterns of reciprocally adaptive behavior that no one else claims in any cross-cultural developmental work. Needed are "bipolar" tasks (such as the RFT) that sample each of the domains in question, and subjects who do well in one domain but poorly in the other *while maintaining the same cognitive style.*

A thought experiment can illustrate how difficult such empirical tests may be. Eskimos are often characterized as field independent. Their talents, therefore, would seem to lie in the cognitive restructuring domain. But do we want to claim of Eskimos that they have less "experience with people," less "interest in others," less "concern for others" than the Temne? Do they have less ability to deal with people than with objects? And if we want to make such claims, how should we establish their validity?

Existing guesses about the real-world analogies for Berry's perceptual tasks also indicate sources of uncertainty in the presumed validity of the perceptual tasks. Berry offers his gap-detecting discrimination task as an experimental analogy to the task facing a hunter: "For discrimination disembedding is not involved; rather the task is to detect an element from a fairly simple gestalt . . ." (Berry, 1976, p. 147). But Wagner (1978), noting the precociousness of 7 to 8-year-old Berber sheep herders on the EFT, surmises: "One might hypothesize that these boys, who are Berbers and who were raised as shepherds before they went to school, had developed certain perceptual skills (such as location of sheep in a variegated terrain) . . ." (Wagner, 1978, p. 150).

Yet another concern is the relationship between psychological differentiation theory (as a theory of individual differences) related to experiences within cultures and the data offered in the cross-cultural literature. Berry (1976) offers analyses at both the individual and cultural levels of analysis. Or so it appears. However, when one considers the nature of the independent variables, it is quickly apparent that, with two exceptions, *the same independent variable codes must apply to all subjects within a cultural group.* The exceptions are years of education and self-rated strictness of childrearing.

Cognizant of this problem, but limited in his ability to carry out within-culture analyses owing to limited variation in the ecocultural index within the cultures, Berry presents within-culture analyses for each group; he relates compliant socialization self-ratings and education to cognitive performance (Berry, 1976, pp. 155–157). Although substantial correlations between cognitive performance and education are obtained, correlations with the socialization index are variable and quite low on the average, in sharp contrast to the general picture given by the between-culture analyses.

The work of Irwin, Engle, Klein, and Yarbrough (1976), who studied the relationship between EFT performance and mother's traditionalism, also suggests that failure to provide within-culture evidence may give a false picture of the factors at work. Similarity of items on their traditionalism scale and Witkin's characterization of the antecedents of field dependence had led them to hypothesize a positive relationship between traditionalism of mothers and field dependence of children. No such relationship was found by Irwin and others. However, ratings of sources of intellectual stimulation did predict EFT performance. Irwin and colleagues argue that Berry's previous research linking field dependence to traditionalism was confounded by variables such as availability of intellectual stimulation.

Summary

Despite the large amount of evidence put forth in support of its basic claims, we remain skeptical about the strength of the psychological differentiation theory as an account of culture's influence on cognition. Our concerns about the claims of this theory are as follows:

1. Evidence of domain consistency may be illusory because the domains in question are either:

a. Not conceptually distinct although they are claimed to be (as, in this case, the perceptual-cognitive contrast), or

b. They do not provide interdomain consistency where distinctiveness of the domain is clearly plausible (as in the lack of EFT/RFT correlation in studies cited).

2. The absence of process specification makes identification of domains ad hoc, or post hoc (e.g., dependent upon response patterns).

3. When process distinctions are made (e.g., the discrimination task), task performance may be predicted as well by control tasks as by the crucial experimental tasks.

4. The bulk of the cross-cultural data relies on between-group data; where within-culture data are available, they fail to confirm the theory.

Our doubts should not lead the reader to conclude that the basic approach linking cultural configurations to configurations of individual cognitive functioning is wrong. Rather, the data in support of specific implications of these ideas are subject to more difficulties than a casual reading of the literature might suggest.

CONTEXT-SPECIFIC APPROACHES

Both the across-culture/universal and within-culture/universal theories emphasize the common processes that can be used to interpret diverse experiences, thus producing coherence in behavior. These theories see as typical cases the following: A child who recognizes that pushing a lump of clay out of shape does not change the amount of clay is a child who knows that pouring water into a different size container does not change the amount of water. Similarly, people who depend upon a tilted frame to define "vertical" are expected to depend on other people for help in defining what is going on and what to do about it in social situations.

This "coherence" assumption was not characteristic of American learning theory in the middle of this century. Influential researchers such as Tolman, Hull, and Skinner evolved very general theories of learning by using very specific tasks as model systems to test the theories. It is a common complaint that each system has its own set of tasks so that no theorist has an easy time accounting for the (tailored) phenomena of a rival.

Some Early Observations

The failure of interdomain coherence as a central organizing principle of behavior is one of the significant characteristics that led to the research program initiated by John Gay and his colleagues in the mid-1960s (Gay, 1973; Gay & Cole, 1967). Gay had begun his work in an effort to pinpoint difficulties that Kpelle (Liberian) children experience when required to master mathematics in American-style schools. In Liberia, like the United States, school difficulties were explained in terms of cognitive skills that seemed to be deficient or lacking. As in America, these deficiencies were related to aspects of the children's home environments. So, for example, it was claimed that Kpelle children have a difficult time discriminating elementary geometric figures such as triangles and squares owing to a lack of perceptual stimulation. This "perceptual deficit" rendered the children virtually helpless when it came to constructing objects or pictures from tinker toys or jigsaw puzzles. There was a great deal of discussion about "African" reliance on rote memory and many other anecdotes about cognitive deficits and their hypothesized origins in Kpelle cultural practices. In each case, a process deficit was linked to *general* features of Kpelle experience.

However, Gay and Cole were forced to conclude that they were dealing with a culture that manifestly produced adults competent in its *own* terms. The juxtaposition of competence and deficiencies allowed Gay and Cole to make a distinction that became characteristic of a good deal of the later work in this tradition. Granted that Kpelle children lack particular kinds of experience that their educated brethren or middle-class American children routinely encounter, Kpelle children are by no means lacking in experience. Gay and Cole decided that it would be necessary to investigate directly Kpelle experience that might represent useful background knowledge for any particular set of skills to be included in the school curriculum. Because mathematics was the area of experience that their project was aimed at, they set out to "know more about the indigenous mathematics so that we can build effective bridges to the new mathematics that we are trying to introduce" (Gay & Cole, 1967, p. 1). The problem, then, became one of discovering through a study of Kpelle activities those that involved one or more elements that would be recognized as relevant to American educators' notion of mathematics, especially those mathematical skills that Liberians wanted to teach more effectively in their schools. Gay and Cole explicitly assumed variability of experience across different life activities with respect to psychological processes.

In exploring the domain of measurement among the Kpelle, Gay and Cole discovered that well-articulated systems of measurement applicable to many problem domains are rare or nonexistent. Each kind of commodity, or each potential "measurable," is dealt with by using a unique system of units. The Kpelle have no well-articulated theory relating, for example, volume or length for a wide variety of materials. They measure length using one of several units, but the appropriate unit is usually associated with a particular kind of material or range of lengths. Cloth is habitually measured in armspans; so are ropes. Another unit, handspans, is used for smaller items like a table top. Footlengths replace handspans for some distances, such as a grave or a floor.

What is striking about these perfectly reasonable-sounding "rules of thumb" is that they are neither standardized nor related to each other in any systematic way. They are different ways to find out how much there is of some quantitative dimension. But there is no single *system* applying to large measurement. When asked to estimate various lengths using each of the possibly applicable metrics (handspans, footlengths, etc.) people were relatively inaccurate and inconsistent when compared with a group of relatively poorly educated Americans. The Americans appeared to mediate their measurements using inches, feet, and yards.

On the basis of these observations, it might be tempting to concede that the Kpelle "have no concept of measurement." However, any such conclusion would have to be tempered by observations that Cole and Gay made concerning measurement of volume, in particular, the volume of rice in various containers.

The Kpelle are rice farmers whose production methods are barely sufficient to get them through the year. In fact, it is not rare for farmers to cut the margin between savings and consumption so close that they experience a "hungry time" just prior to harvesting a new crop. When Gay and Cole investigated measurement in the domain of rice they found a very different picture from that given by their studies of length.

The Kpelle use a system of units applying to rice at the farm, and then a second set of units that applies to rice as a consumable commodity, once it has been threshed. The basic measure in this latter case is the *kopi* (cup) made of a U.S. #1 tin can, which contains almost exactly two English measuring cups. Cups may be aggregated into larger units called tins and tins can be aggregated into bags. Tins contain about 44 cups; these can be aggregated into bags which contain somewhat less than 100 cups. At least at a rough order of exactness, an interlocking scale of units of the sort that we associate with measurement exists among the Kpelle in the case of volume of rice.

An idea of the precision of measurement routinely used for the small amounts of rice used in daily commerce is given by the alternative measuring instruments for a cup. When selling rice to a merchant, the farmer must use a cup provided by the merchant in which the bottom has been pounded down to increase the cup's volume. When buying back rice later, in the frequent and unhappy event that he has not saved enough rice to get to the next harvest, the farmer must use a cup with a flat bottom. The difference in volume is the prescribed margin of profit (which is actually much greater because the farmer sells when prices are low and must buy back when prices are high).

The different cultural experiences with measurement implied by different degrees of precision and differentially developed measuring systems for rice were tested by Gay and Cole in a series of estimation tasks. When Kpelle farmers were contrasted with American subjects of working-class background, the Kpelle were considerably more accurate in estimating the amounts of rice in several bowls of different sizes containing different amounts of rice. Gay and Cole's summary of these results is instructive.

> The most important thing is that measurement is used where it is needed . . . units of measure are, in general not parts of an interrelated system but are specific to the objects measured . . . measurements are approximate unless there is a real need for exactness [and] . . . measures are made quantitative primarily in economic activities. (Gay & Cole, 1967, p. 75)

These conclusions hardly appear startling. But in 1967 they contrasted strongly with the expectations of the times, when coherence in the level of intellectual functioning owing to the application of general cognitive processes was strongly believed in. From that point of view, lack of sophisticated intellectual behavior in one domain led to an expectation of similar lack in others.

A somewhat different, and in a sense more extreme, example of restricted application of an ability was found by Cole, Gay, Glick, and Sharp (1971) in one of their psychological studies of cognitive abilities among the Kpelle. The psychological domain this time was classification, one of the domains about which it is often claimed that tribal African people experience great difficulties. On the basis of pilot work, it was evident that Kpelle people, forest-dwelling rice farmers as they are, have a deep knowledge of the local flora and fauna. Mastery of this knowledge is not a trivial matter. Cole and associates sought to study classification of leaves in a concept-identification task by using two sets of leaves for which Kpelle have well-marked categories. The research was impeded because it was difficult for the American researchers to keep from mixing up the leaves!

The actual experiment involved vine leaves and tree leaves, according to the Kpelle system of classification. In the morning, the research assistant went out to collect 14 leaves; 7 from vines, 7 from trees. These leaves were presented to the subject one by one. The subject was asked to sort the leaves into two classes, according to a criterion the researcher supplied. Feedback was provided and the subject was asked to again sort the objects into the same two classes.

One group was asked to say if the leaves were from trees or from vines. A second group was also expected to make the "tree/vine" classes, but no mention was made of trees and vines. Instead subjects were told that "Some of these leaves belong to Sumo and others belong to Togba." Their job was to name the owner of each leaf as it was presented. In a third group, vine and tree leaves were mixed to form two pseudocategories. Again, subjects were told that half belonged to Sumo and half to Togba. But now there was no real world relation (like tree and vine) to help identify which leaves Sumo and Togba owned.

Overall, the Kpelle subjects mastered this task faster than American college students teaching in Liberia. But the most striking fact was that the Kpelle adults learned very rapidly *only* if the two classes to be formed were called "vine" and "leaf." When asked to name the leaves "belonging to" Sumo and Togba, learning was no faster for the real category than the pseudocategory. The American subjects showed no evidence of categorical learning at all; in fact, they had trouble telling one leaf from another, let alone establishing a response rule (category) for each leaf. In this study the Kpelle subjects clearly manifest knowledge of and use of a cultural category, yet *only when that category is explicitly named.*

Such evidence of very specific localization or context boundness of culture-dependent cognitive skills is by no means restricted to these few examples. Research during the past decade and a half strongly suggests the context-boundness of behavior that is often interpreted in general terms.

In the next section we review a variety of cross-cultural studies of cognition in which the preexperimental expectation (based on common observation, school performance, or test results) has suggested some rather general cognitive differences between cultural population groups. Alternative explanations are then tested in one or a series of studies exploring the relation between the specific activity constituting "the test" and relevant cultural knowledge.

Examples of Context-Specific Research

The general procedure for (if not the logic behind) cross-cultural studies is for a researcher to administer a test or battery of tests to a group of subjects. The test (experimental task, observation) is used as an index of the psychological process believed to control performance. Indices are then compared across cultures. The levels and patterns of performance on the indicator tasks are compared *as if* these performances mean the same thing across populations (e.g., index the same covert activities) and *as if* these performances sample equivalently the designated area of psychological processing with respect to people's everyday experiences.

In the context-specific approach to culture and thought, the "methodological" problems, glossed by *as if*, become the center of theoretical focus. Cultural variation in performance becomes an invitation to discover the relation of tested performance to prior cultural practice. After reviewing several examples of such work, we will turn to the important question of how to reconcile conflicting evidence of culture-general and culture-specific cognitive development within a single analytic framework.

Infancy and Motor Development

All of the measurement problems and questions about the generalized nature of developmental patterns can be seen in the earliest assessments of infants, raised in different cultural settings. A number of different assessment techniques (Bayley Motor and Mental Development Scales, 1965; Neonatal Behavior Assessment Scale as developed by Brazelton & Associates, 1974; Gesell Scales, revised by Gesell & Armatruda, 1947) sample infant behavior and arrive at a general index of both mental and

motor development. Scales typically include such items as: age of walking, crawling, smiling, responding to negative signals, pulling strings to get objects, placing objects in containers. In within-culture studies, one infant is said to be more mature or advanced than another if he or she receives higher scores on these scales. In cross-cultural comparisons, one group of infants is said to be more mature or advanced than another if their mean scores on these scales are higher. Such evaluations have led some researchers to claim an early and general precocity in the mental and motor development of infants from sub-Saharan Africa (Geber, 1974; Geber & Dean, 1957, 1958; for review, see Munroe, Munroe, & Whiting, 1981; Super, 1981; Wober, 1975). While it is claimed that African infants have a head start in development during their first year, it is found that they drop below Western standards in their second or third year.

Super's review of infant development based on such infant development scales entreats the reader to consider carefully the relationship between the specific items used on scales of development and their relationship to the cultural system in which they are embedded. Using spot observations of East African mothers and infants, as well as interviews with the mothers, Super (1976) reported that the Kipsigi (Kenya) make a conscious effort to teach babies to sit and walk; they use standardized procedures for this instruction and employ particular words in their language for characterizing the process. For example, babies are placed in a hole in the ground with blankets, rolled up to provide support. Infants are left in this "sitting" position long before they are able to sit on their own. Super's observations showed that the Kenyan infants are in the sitting position two-thirds more often than infants of comparable age in Cambridge, Massachusetts. As early as the second month of life, walking skills are also exercised; infants' arms are held and they are encouraged to jump. This particular behavioral practice is very similar to the test item found on the Bayley motor scales which is used to indicate readiness to walk, a "developmental milestone."

In summarizing his findings and those of others, Super (1981) concludes that African infants are only more advanced in those behaviors that (1) are specifically taught, (2) are encouraged by providing opportunities for practice, or (3) are both taught and encouraged. The early advancement of particular motor milestones does *not* mean that all motor behaviors are also advanced. For example, the group of Kipsigi infants who were found to sit and walk early, learned to crawl several weeks *later* than the norms established by U.S. infants. It is also the case that these infants spend only a third as much time on the ground as Cambridge infants. The relative importance of a particular behavior and the amount of time that infants are afforded opportunities for practice are reliable predictors of the onset of particular motor milestones.

Another somewhat unusual example of culture-specific learning concerns sleep. It is an instructive example both because sleep is ordinarily considered so close to a biological universal and because of the implied universality of its main characteristic links to everyday life. Super and Harkness (1980) provide an unusual comparison of the sleep/wake cycles in infants in rural Kenya and the urban United States. The length of the infant's longest sleep period (occurring most often during the night hours) has been accepted as a behavioral index of the neurological maturity of the brain. By the third or fourth month, American infants who are developing normally are expected to have maximum sleep periods that last on the average 8 hours. Another assumption about the normal pattern of infant development is that as the infant becomes more mature, less hours of sleep will be necessary. These developments in the infant's sleep/wake cycle have been assumed to be regulated by the infant's needs and not highly influenced by cultural factors. Sleep patterns for Kenyan and American babies are relatively similar during the first months. But after that time, U.S. babies come to sleep more total hours in different patterns than the Kokwet babies in Kenya. By the fourth month, the Kokwet babies are awake on the average of 2 hr. more than the American babies in any 24-hr. period.

Another change is that between the third and fourth months of life babies in the United States begin to concentrate their sleeping into fewer and longer bouts so that the longest single period of sleep lasts on the average 8 hr. and roughly coincides with the sleeping patterns of adults. This is not the case with the Kokwet sample. They continue to have maximum sleep periods of about 4 hr. throughout their first year of life. As mentioned when this work was described in a previous section, these differences in sleep/wake patterns are paralleled by differences in adult structuring of the infant's experience. The caretaking patterns in Kenya arrange for babies to be carried frequently in slings by the mother or some other family member. The productivity of the mother is independent of the sleep/wake cycle of the baby so long as the baby does not become too active, in which case carrying in the sling is impossible. Babies sleep in skin-to-skin contact with their mothers who sleep, except for the infant, alone. The

mother's sleep pattern is only minimally disturbed by a baby who is awake or nursing.

The difference in these two cultural groups controls the contexts that in turn shape the development of behaviors that are assumed to be determined by biological needs within the limits permitted by biology—limits that seem to be much broader than previously believed, in this case.

Super's "context arrangement" interpretation of culture and infant development is supported by a longitudinal research project that demonstrates an empirical correspondence between patterns of specific item precocity in Uganda infants and the culture's child-care practices (Kilbride & Kilbride, 1975). The Kilbrides related the frequency of being in the supine position to early grasping and manipulative behaviors; frequency of being carried at shoulder level was correlated with performance on a task of visual skills; cultural emphasis on early smiling and social behaviors was related to early smiling.

In reviewing the studies of cultural variations in the assessment of infant mental development, Super concludes that, except for conditions of minimal stimulation and/or malnutrition, there is *no* cultural group that shows more rapid *general* cognitive development than another. The literature does, however, provide a number of examples of environmental influences on particular behavior items (Grantham-McGregor & Hawke, 1971; Kilbride & Kilbride, 1975; Leiderman et al., 1973). Because of this relationship, Super challenges the usefulness of standardized psychometric tests in cross-cultural research, a critique that resonates with the ideas expressed in this paper:

> Their future use [of standard psychometric tests] for the purpose of group comparison seems inefficient, at best, because of the enormous amount of detailed empirical work required to explain adequately the pattern of item difference. Only after this Herculean task has been finished can attention be turned to fundamental issues of experiences and development. (1980, p. 106)

In summary, "performance" is used to make general claims about the overall state of infant development; if specific behavioral accomplishments in a culture have been isolated and the infants therein given opportunity and encouragement to practice skills that are components of those specific (and highly prized) behavioral accomplishments, then such infants will be evaluated as "more advanced" or as "having more" of the ability in question than those infants who live in cultures that provide infrequent opportunity and encouragement to practice such component skills or that evaluate the specific accomplishments indifferently.

Perceptual Skills

A number of studies of the behavior of older children relate specific cognitive change to specific experience, the basic assumption of these studies being that supposed differences reflect some underlying general mental ability. Just as early research produced reports of a general motor precocity in African infants, so a sizable body of research now suggests that rural or uneducated African children perform less well than other groups of similar age on pattern reproduction tasks using either pen-and-paper or block designs. Performance on these tasks is often interpreted as indexing the presence or absence of general cognitive abilities: differences in "practical intelligence" (Vernon, 1969); in "cognitive style" (Witkin & Berry, 1975); in "attitudes toward perception" (McFie, 1961); in "sensotypes" (Wober, 1966); in "imagined transformations" (Goodnow, 1969); or in "response organizations" (Serpell, 1969).

These general characterizations of mental ability are then commonly related to general environmental contingencies. Vernon (1969) suggests that retarded practical intelligence is the result of "inadequacies of psychomotor experience . . . and the absence of interest in constructive play or cultural pressures to practical achievements." As we have already mentioned, Witkin and Berry (1975) attribute the field-dependent cognitive style to a complex of environmental relationships but particularly to "the use of strict or even harsh socialization practices to enforce this conformance and by tight social organization." McFie (1961) suggests that "the lack of toys and constructional games which might encourage a more accurate standard of orientation and imitation" are the cause of the perceptual differences he observed.[5]

Suspicious of such inferences, Serpell (1979) designed a study to distinguish between generalized and specific interpretations of representational ability. He selected four perceptual tasks that should all result in lower performance scores for Zambian children than English children, if some general aspect of these children's predicament was responsible for a failure of perceptual abilities to develop. One task required children to copy the positions of the experimenter's hands (mimicry); the second involved copying two-dimensional figures with pen and paper (drawing); the third involved constructing copies of two-dimensional wire objects with strips of wire (molding) and the fourth involved making copies of three-dimensional objects from clay (modeling).

Serpell chose precisely these four tasks because he knew something about the prior experiences of each of the cultural groups on the specific tasks; he based his predictions concerning patterns of cultural differences on function-specific hypotheses linking the role of the model task to known activities in each group. Since skill learning in any culture requires children to attend to and imitate the hand positions of the more competent members, both English and Zambian children should do equally well on the mimicry task. Children in both cultures also had experience modeling with clay, so no differences were expected for that task. Two-dimensional representation with pen and paper is an activity that English children frequently engage in, while Zambian children will have had more practice forming wire into two-dimensional objects, a common activity for them. Therefore, Serpell predicted that the English children would score high on the pen-and-paper task, but not as high on the wire-shaping task. He made the opposite prediction for the Zambian children.

Serpell also wanted to investigate a different kind of general process claim (Wober, 1966) that African subjects process information from different senses in ways that are different from Europeans. For both groups of children, he established a "visual" condition and a blindfolded or "haptic" condition. According to Wober's hypothesis, the Africans should perform better in the "haptic" condition while Europeans should perform better in the visual condition.

The major comparisons were drawn between 8-year-olds in the second grade in Zambian and English primary schools.

The findings support the context-specific hypothesis and present evidence that is difficult to interpret from a general perceptual-deficit approach. The English children did better than the Zambian children in the drawing task and the Zambian children did better in the wire-molding task. There were no significant differences between the groups on the clay-modeling or hand-mimicry tasks. The modality of the task, visual or haptic, did not result in any differences. Contrary to a "sensotype" interpretation between the cultural groups, each group performed better in the visual condition.

Stimulus Equivalence and Familiarity

A great deal of discussion in the claims and counterclaims about culture-cognitive development hypotheses centers on *the* central methodological requirement for valid process inferences in cross-cultural research—subjects must be doing the *same* task if comparisons are to be considered valid (Berry, 1969; several chapters in Triandis & Lambert, 1980). Curiously, this methodological knot shifts status when one takes a context-specific view of learning, as Serpell's study illustrates. From a "central processor" point of view, the fact that one cultural group may have more experience with a particular stimulus configuration than another is a nuisance. It has to be made to go away so that a "clean" comparison can be made. From a context-specific point of view, a stimulus familiarity "control" group is an important source of evidence for the notion that learning is different, depending on precisely how the culture organizes practice with any given stimulus configuration. Exactly those aspects of context for which methodologists keep seeking equivalents represent the description of culturally organized practice. With respect to stimulus equivalence, the folklore of psychological methodologies clearly indicates an area where everyone agrees: culture-specific knowledge controls differences in performance. It is also agreed that these *differences in knowledge can masquerade as differences in process.*

Despite extensive discussions on this topic, there has been no agreed-upon technique for ensuring stimulus equivalence in cross-cultural work or more broadly, comparative cognitive research. In the face of this difficulty, experimental psychologists have usually resorted to intuitive specifications of which tasks are familiar to which groups, and then attempted to produce cross-over effects. That is, they want to demonstrate familiarity effects by showing that people in Culture A perform better on Stimulus A than Stimulus B, while people in Culture B perform better on Stimulus B than Stimulus A. Serpell's study of Zambian and British representation abilities provides an excellent example of a cross-over study. It also demonstrates clearly the tight connection between the "methods" of seeking stimulus equivalence and the theoretical claims of context-specific research. The remaining examples in this section will pursue the implications of differential cultural exposure to relatively specific cognitive demands. Not all such studies are as elegant as Serpell's where a true cross-over was both predicted and obtained. But each provides evidence relevant to the general thrust of context-specific studies of culture and cognitive development.

Classification

A clear example of a cross-over effect can be seen in the research of Irwin, Schafer, and Feiden (1974), who were skeptical of claims that un-

schooled Liberians (Mano) generally lack the ability to classify because they perform poorly when sorting geometric shapes. Examination of Mano cultural practices established that sorting rice is central to Mano economic activity. Rice variations are talked about in everyday discourse. Distinct variations of rice can be used as the logical equivalent of distinct variations in geometric shapes. Two sets of tasks, one using bowls of rice and the other using geometric shapes, were presented to Liberian-unschooled and U.S.-schooled subjects. Subjects had to categorize and, if possible, reclassify each set along three dimensions. These Liberian subjects, as past research indicated, had greater difficulty sorting geometric shapes than Americans, for whom this is typically a trivial task by the time a child is 10 to 12 years of age. But when the material to be sorted was changed to rice, the results were reversed. The African subjects were able to sort the rice, shifting dimensions and accounting for their sorts as skillfully as the U.S. sample had when the task involved geometric shapes. When U.S. subjects were faced with sorting bowls of rice, they demonstrated hesitation and bewilderment like that of the African farmers when faced with geometric shapes.

Fjellman (1971), working with Kamba children in Kenya, studied the relationship between familiarity of materials to be used in a categorization study and the attributes of the stimuli used to form the categories. She was particularly concerned to evaluate generalizations such as the following, based primarily on the application of psychometric tests: "The African way of thinking appears to be a predominantly concrete type, while that of the European white is of a more abstract nature" (Cryns, 1962, pp. 298–299).

Fjellman chose to assess these ideas by using a genre of classification task that had been used widely in the neurological and developmental literature, and for which there was also cross-cultural data. Subjects are presented a set of pictures or objects that can be grouped according to local categories in terms of such dimensions as their color, their shape, their function, or their common membership in some part of a larger conceptual scheme.

Using geometric shapes, several researchers had shown an influence of schooling on category choice (Greenfield, 1966; Serpell, 1969). Children who attend school choose to categorize by form earlier and more readily than those who do not. This finding seemed to mimic developmental increases in form choice and neurological evidence that brain-damaged patients revert to "concrete" attributes like color.

Fjellman was suspicious of these parallels. She noted Price-Williams's (1962) finding that Tiv children (both schooled and unschooled) formed taxonomic categories and did *not* generally rely on color when asked to classify and reclassify *objects common to their everyday experience*. Color as an attribute cropped up when stuffed animals were used as surrogates for the real thing. However, Price-Williams failed to use any of the geometric-form stimuli with which previous schooling effects had been established.

Fjellman remedied this shortcoming by her work with Kamba children who lived in urban or rural settings and who did or did not attend school. Consistent with several other results, Fjellman found that schooling enhanced categorization by form, the more "abstract" attribute. But when 17 pictures of animals known to all the children were used, the judgments of the urban schooled children were markedly more "childish" (according to standard criteria based on the category justifications used) than reasons given by any but the very youngest rural, unschooled children.

In presenting these results, Fjellman makes a very important point about familiarity:

The animals pictured were equally familiar to urban [as to rural] children as measured by ability to identify pictures, but first-hand knowledge which comes from observation of their habits and patterns (particularly for domestic animals) and knowledge of the Kamba system of classification was not. (Fjellman, 1971, p. 104)

Fjellman went on to present other classification tasks involving different objects and different categorizing requirements. Under some conditions there were no differences discernible between groups: cooking and farming implements *whose functions were known to all* elicited a uniformly high level of functional categorizing. When another test was constructed with unknown cooking and farming items, rural boys relied on color rather than functional criteria.

Fjellman's results (only some of which have been summarized here) demonstrate the great care that must be taken to embody problems in materials and procedures whose "fit" with indigenous experience is made a part of the research design. It makes the corollary point, central to this immediate discussion, that because schooling, *by definition*, provides pupils familiarity with new aspects of the world, reliance on experiments whose procedures are examples of *school-based contexts* for problem solving

may err by mistaking differences in stimulus familiarity for deep or general cognitive transformations.

Studies of schooling's putative intellectual consequences have also helped to force closer examination of the different aspects of stimulus familiarity as possible points of contact between schooling and everyday (culturally organized) experience. Each of the studies reviewed thus far suggests strongly that stimulus familiarity cannot be reduced to "frequency encountering stimulus X." Rather, the nature of and variety of interactions with stimuli seem to be important aspects of stimulus familiarity as well.

This point is made forcefully in cases where simple substitution of one set of physical stimuli for another brings about *no* modifications in behavior. Thus, for example, Sharp, Cole, and Lave (1979) conducted a study in which categorization of geometric figures and maize were compared for educated and noneducated children. Consistent with Fjellman's results, classification improved dramatically as a function of years of education. But unlike Fjellman (or Irwin et al., 1974) there was *no* effect of switching to indigenous materials: maize that was red or yellow, large or small, and made up of single or double kernels. Only six out of 32 Mayan adults were able to produce a categorical sorting of the maize; three had sorted the geometric shapes.

This failure to classify in an experimental task cannot be attributed simply to unfamiliarity with the objects or the general inappropriateness of using the classes embodied in the experiment. Varieties, sizes, and configurations of kernels (single and double kernels) were offered by local people in their descriptions of the properties of corn grown in the area. But the task of dividing eight kernels of corn according to three different descriptive criteria for no purpose other than "to see if you can do it" was certainly an unfamiliar task for those who had not been to school. Similar difficulties were encountered by Greenfield (1974), Scribner and Cole (1981), and Gay and Cole (1967).

The role of different kinds of interactions with a "common" stimulus in controlling different aspects of stimulus familiarity is nicely summarized by Childs and Greenfield (1982). Their study concentrated on classification and representation of patterns used in weaving traditional male and female garments in Chiapis, Mexico. Boys (who do not weave) and girls (who do weave) were compared in the way they differentiate patterns. In experimental pattern-representation tasks modeled on weaving, the girls used thin white strips to distinguish patterns as they did when weaving; boys mixed pinks and oranges to get the desired effect as seen from a distance, ignoring the fine-grained structure that produced the effect for the girls who viewed the patterns ''with their fingers.''

Childs and Greenfield summarize the differences in ''stimulus familiarity'' that these very prevalent garments represent to boys and girls.

> The girls' attention to the structural detail of the patterns contrasts with the boys' representation of a difference in superficial appearance, a difference nonetheless important in making the distinction between male and female Zinacanteco clothing. The role requirements of a Zinacanteco woman in relation to clothing are different. Girls need to know and use the detailed aspects of the patterns more than boys and so are more apt to choose those aspects when representing them. (Childs & Greenfield, 1982, p. 13)

From this careful description of precise relations to weaving and its products, we can see that although the patterns used in this ''pattern-representation test'' seem equally familiar to all Zinacantecos, they are not equally familiar in ways crucial to the interpretation of performance. In fact, the very activities that are the source of unequal stimulus familiarity are the source of the differential cognitive consequences.

Memory

The importance of what one is asked to do with familiar materials is posed dramatically in a series of studies by Scribner and Cole (1981, chap. 14). The topic in this case was remembering, in particular, remembering lists of words or pictured objects. The subjects were Vai (Liberian) youngsters and adults who had, or had not, undergone Muslim religious training that requires committing to memory long passages (ideally, all) of the Koran. Scribner and Cole hypothesized that practice in decoding Arabic characters (the Vai do not speak Arabic) and remembering verses should enhance list learning of analogous types. The key problem was to specify a proper analogy. Preliminary study indicated that when given a free recall test where word order in recall is irrelevant, Koranic scholars are no different than the rest of the population. Some indications of superior performance by Koranic scholars appeared when subjects are required to learn words in strict serial order. But a clear superiority appeared only when words or objects are presented in a systematically cumulating fashion that models closely a major teaching technique associated with Koranic recitation. As the familiarity of the *operations* increased, performance increased selectively and accordingly.

In a test of culture-specific remembering tasks that hypothesized nonliterate superiority, Kearins (1980) designed a series of experiments to investigate the relationship of environmental pressures to remembering skills. The Aboriginal inhabitants of the western desert region of Australia, like many other nonindustrial societies, have been shown to perform poorly on a number of standard psychology tests (Dasen, 1972; deLemos, 1969; McElwain & Kearney, 1973). These estimates of intellectual ability contrast with a long history of successful adaptation in a desert region that recent European settlers find to be uninhabitable. Kearins reasoned that requirements of survival in such an environment might result in the development of the ability to attend to small changes in spatial relationships and subsequently to recall the proper locations.

Kearins compared spatial memory skills of Aboriginal Australian children with Anglo-Australian children. The children were shown a number of items arranged in matrices of different sizes for 30 sec. After a few seconds, they were asked to replace the items in the order in which they had been seen. She controlled for object familiarity by using two different types of materials: ''natural'' objects (stone, leaves, stick, etc.) and ''artifactual'' objects (bottle, knife, matchbook). To test for difference in the use of verbal and visual strategies, some displays were made up of objects from the same lexical category (i.e., rocks) varying in size and shape while other displays were made up of objects each from a different lexical category.

The Aboriginal children were consistently better able to reproduce the display regardless of the size of the matrix, the type of materials used, or the degree of similarity among the objects. The Anglo-Australian children's best performance was on the artifactual display in which the objects all came from different lexical categories, but even on this task their score was significantly lower than that of the Aboriginal group.

There were clear behavioral differences in the way each group approached and worked on the problem. Aboriginal children viewed the display in silence and, after stabilizing their position, sat motionless during the 30-sec observation period. When replacing the items, they tended to work at a constant rate, usually holding an item above a location before placing it and rarely moving objects after they had been placed. When asked how they remembered the display, their most frequent response was that they remembered the ''look'' of it. The Anglo-Australian children were more likely to move around the display, pick up, and point to objects and could be heard whispering, muttering, or naming objects.

They moved about restlessly while waiting to re-place the items and then generally replaced four or five immediately, with the rest of the items replaced at a much slower rate. These children were also more likely to move objects around after they had been placed. Their accounts of their remembering suggest the use of verbal strategies: ''I tried to learn around the outside by saying the colors of the bottles'' or ''I remembered what was in it, the shape, the color . . . I described them to myself.''

A memory task performed by Mayan and U.S. 9-year-olds in a study by Rogoff and Waddell (1980) displays related phenomena. When the work of re-membering 20 items was embedded in the recon-struction of a contextually organized three-dimen-sional scene, the memory test performance decrement that had previously been noted for Mayan children disappeared; in fact, the Mayan children's performance appears to have been slightly better than the U.S. children's. Rogoff and Waddell (1980) point to the ''ubiquity of having to remember things in everyday life using the contextual organi-zation of the material as a recall aide.'' They contrast the way their memory task mirrors this everyday situation with the way other memory research puts a premium on memory for isolated bits of information for which external, noncontextual recall aids must be supplied by the subject or by training procedures. The U.S. children appeared to use rehearsal strat-egies while the Mayan children appeared to use spa-tial organization and a more relaxed discussion crite-ria. The important result is not a cross-over effect but the disappearance of an advantage as a more every-day memory task renders impotent the strategies that provide the advantage to U.S. children in other kinds of memory tasks. Both cultures provide for context-specific practice in the Rogoff and Waddell task; a memory deficit of Mayan children does not occur.

Communication

An example in which stimulus familiarity (rather than task familiarity) is usefully reinterpreted in terms of context specificity comes from the work of Lantz (1979). Lantz sought to evaluate the sug-gestion of Bruner, Olver, and Greenfield (1966) that rural unschooled children may lack symbolic repre-sentational skills because their linguistic ability is tied to the immediate context of the referent. Formal education, they said, facilitates the development of language into a fully symbolic tool that can be used for communicating about things in their absence and for mediating other cognitive processes such as clas-sification and memory (Bruner et al., 1966).

Lantz designed a study that would distinguish between the *absence* of symbolic representational skills and the *variable manifestation* of these skills in different contexts. She selected a coding task that would measure communicative accuracy as well as assess classificatory skills and memory. Children were shown an array of objects and asked to describe each item so that it could be distinguished from the others. Sometimes they were told that they were describing stimuli for themselves (Condition 1) or for another child (Condition 2) at a later time. The subjects in this study were rural, unschooled and schooled Indian children, and schooled U.S. chil-dren at three different ages. Two different stimulus arrays were used: a color chip array and a grain-and-seed array.

Lantz reasoned that although the Indian children have a complex color terminology, colors in their culture are frequently substituted for one another with no functional consequence. Grains, on the other hand, are an extremely important part of the village life. Communication about them is important in many contexts. Just the opposite relation between stimulus familiarity and culture was hypothesized for the Americans (on grounds that are not particu-larly well motivated).

As predicted from a context-specific learning hy-pothesis, the rural unschooled children coded and decoded the grain-and-seed array with no difficulty; they performed higher than either the schooled groups, Indian or American, at all ages. The schooled Indian children also scored significantly higher than the schooled U.S. children. This finding clearly shows that children from a nontechnical society without the benefit of formal schooling are able to separate language symbols from the physical refer-ent and to use those symbols for communicating accurately in an artificial situation.

But display of the ability depends upon the stim-uli used. A very different pattern of relative abilities emerges for the results using the color array. The U.S. children scored significantly higher than both Indian groups. The unschooled Indian children did especially poorly on this task. They were unable to decode even their own labels let alone those pro-duced by other children. The schooled Indian chil-dren, when given their own labels to decode, did show higher performance, suggesting that they were able to extract some useful information from the codes they conjured up. But their performance was poor relative to the U.S. sample.

Apparently Lantz's guess that the two classes of stimuli would function symmetrically and op-positely in the two cultural groups was too simple because the specification of ''culture'' as it relates to the arrays used in this study is unclear. The color stimuli may not be embedded in exchanges requiring communications as are dimensions of grain in *either* culture. The subject must then really invent item and category markers in the color task. This facet of intellectual activity, inventing and using thought-structuring ''schemata'' has consistently been found to be a consequence of modern schooling, an institution whose characteristic activities appear very similar in a variety of cultural settings (Jahoda, 1980; Rogoff, 1981; Scribner & Cole, 1973).

The Cognitive Consequences of Literacy

Research on the consequences of literacy based on historical and ethnographic data had suggested very general cognitive consequences of learning to read and write: changes in the nature of deliberate remembering (Havelock, 1978), logical reasoning (Goody & Watt, 1963/1968), and uses of language in a variety of settings (Olson, 1977). (See also, McLuhan, 1962; Vygotsky, 1962.)

Some experimental work aimed at testing these ideas was carried out in the 1960s and early 1970s. But this research all rested on comparisons involving *schooling* (e.g., Greenfield, 1966, 1972). Although reading and writing are clearly central to schooling as we know it, there are many reasons for expecting that practice at learning and reproducing large amounts of novel information organized around modern scientific and social concepts—not the ability to read or write, per se—is the basis for widely reported differences between schooled and unschooled populations on relevant cognitive tasks.

Scribner and Cole (1981) carried out their research among the Vai of Liberia, a culture that provided an unusual opportunity to disentangle literacy from schooling. The Vai are remarkable in that, although their culture is in many respects indistinguishable from the slash-and-burn agricultural groups that live around them, they use not one, but four distinctive systems for writing. Each system is associated with different spheres of activity: literacy in Vai for conducting family and community business; literacy in English for dealing with the government, schools, and modern economic institutions under the control of English speaking Liberians; literacy in Arabic for two purposes—one religious (reading the Koran), the other recordkeeping.

Scribner and Cole conducted several series of studies with these four groups (English, Vai, Arabic, and Koranic literates) to determine the nature and generality of cognitive skills generated by each kind of literate practice. In their initial investigations, they selected a variety of classification, mem-

ory, and logical-reasoning tasks that had produced improved performance for *schooled* literates in previous research (Rogoff, 1981; Sharp, Cole, & Lave, 1979). English schooling produced changes in many, but not all, of the tasks, while the other literacies produced almost none. The most consistent effect of schooling was to improve individuals' abilities to explain the basis of performance on cognitive tasks.

Finding no measurable consequences of Vai literacy, Scribner and Cole then narrowed their focus. They designed a new series of tests to demonstrate *metalinguistic* consequences of becoming literate. Very little evidence for effects of any of the literacies encountered in Vai country were found in this phase of the work. The strongest result to emerge was increased skill on the part of schooled and Vai literates when asked to explain the basis for judgments of grammaticality.

The combined results of these two lines of study discouraged the notion that literacy, per se, produces the general cognitive changes previously associated with schooling. Indeed, while schooling produced changes in performance on many tasks, its effects were by no means uniform.

At this point, Scribner and Cole tested very specific hypotheses about cognitive effects growing directly out of analyses of literate practices. From analyses of a large corpus of letters, they hypothesized that Vai literates ought to be able to communicate more effectively with someone in a remote place. Since writing letters requires practice in formulating descriptions for someone who does not share one's knowledge of the events to be described, Vai literates ought to produce fuller, less egocentric, descriptions. The researchers constructed rebus-like tasks, which required people to code and decode simple graphic symbols that could form propositions. To differentiate among the various literate groups (all of which engage in such activities in order to read or write), Scribner and Cole constructed one task based on syllables (the units of analysis central to Vai script, but only implicit in Arabic or English) and another based on words as the basic units.

The outcome of these studies yielded clearcut evidence of *function-specific* cognitive change, where functions were implemented within different, but overlapping contexts of cultural practice. The two literacies used widely for letter writing, Vai and English, both improved performance on the communication task. All the literacies where understanding the text was important improved performance on the rebus tasks. However, only Vai literacy produced improved performance when the basic graphic units referred to *syllables*.

Context and Practice

Following Scribner and Cole, we wish to interpret these results within a context-specific theory that specifies the within-context structures of activity. In those cases where an outcome does appear to be directly related to reading and writing, the analysis of the social organization and purposes of writing points at literacy-related *practice* as the crucial experience. Thus, the increased ability to explain the basis for one's cognitive performance is attributed to modes of classroom discourse in the case of the schooled students, for whom questions such as "How did you know that?" "What makes you say that?" "Go to the board and show us how you do that" are a routine accompaniment to becoming literate. The improved ability of the Vai literates on the communication task has a straightforward interpretation based on the structure of Vai literacy practices. Their ability to explain the basis of grammatical judgments (but not other cognitive judgments) is again attributed to their custom of discussing the properties of proper Vai speech, occasioned by letters containing unusual constructions. Finally, although the evidence that both English schooling and Koranic-Arabic literacy improve performance on memory tasks is weak and spotty, this evidence is consistent with the fact that these two literacies—but not Vai—require practice in remembering large amounts of novel material, material that is often devoid of specific meaning to the rememberer.

Shortcomings of a Context-Specific Approach

In many cases where generalized cognitive deficits are assumed on the basis of test results modeled on laboratory tasks or psychometric tests (which, we have argued, are historically linked), manipulations of the conditions of the testing, or of the stimulus materials modify performance so that under some restricted set of conditions, a presumably absent ability makes its appearance (as in Cole et al., 1971; Scribner & Cole, 1981). One of the general strategies that has been used by researchers who focus on this situational variability is to take the performance deficit as a point of departure. They seek to explore people's performance on tasks that occur naturally in the culture and that then serve as models for experimental tasks. The goal of such research is to discover

indigenously organized samples of the intellectual behaviors that the experimenter's original task was designed to sample, and then to return to controlled environments in order to "locate" the experimental task with respect to its indigenous variations (Cole, 1975; Scribner, 1975).

Examination of published examples of such work indicates that this approach remains programmatic. Not the least difficulty confronting researchers who have adopted this strategy is that of finding, in everyday life, those enactments of tasks that predominate in experiments (Cole, Hood, & McDermott, 1978).

This work has not been without its successes. In several cases, plausibly analogous indigenous activities have been discovered and used as the basis for further experimentation. But with few exceptions (to be discussed further in a later section) such work has stopped far short of providing a complete map of the domain of inquiry let alone a comprehensive picture of the ways that cultures use to organize the specific contexts where skills are displayed (e.g., see Childs & Greenfield, 1982; Cole et al., 1971; Greenfield, 1974; Lancy, 1977; Scribner, 1977; Super & Harkness, 1980).

In some cases a performance deficit has been manipulated experimentally, without discovering the cause of the specific performance deficit that initiated the research. When this impasse has been reached, the ethnographic literature is searched for plausible reasons for the experimental results. Referring to an example involving a referential communication task, Jahoda nicely captures the limitations of a good deal of context-specific cross-cultural work.

> Cole set out to track down the causes of this poor performance in some detail. (Kpelle farmers had failed to communicate sufficient discriminating attributes of to-be-identified objects.) Some of the empirical work was in fact undertaken, but most of his [*sic*] account consists of listing various possibilities like a seemingly endless trail vanishing at the distant horizon. (Jahoda, 1980, p. 124)

Later, after reviewing suggestions for how to view context-specific effects in a cultural context, Jahoda adds:

> [This approach] appears to require extremely exhaustive, and in practice almost endless explorations of quite specific pieces of behavior, with no

guarantee of a decisive outcome. *This might not be necessary if there were a workable "theory of situations" at our disposal, but as Cole admits, there is none. What is lacking in [the context-specific] approach are global theoretical constructs relating to cognitive processes of the kind Piaget provides, and which save the researcher from becoming submerged in a mass of unmanageable material.* (Jahoda, 1980, p. 126; emphasis added)

The italicized remarks bring us full circle to the issues with which we began. A theory of the relations between culture and mind must include a theory of both phenomena—culture *and* mind—in order to be a theory of their *inter*relationship. And, this theory must be accompanied by a theory of situations in which the interrelationships of mind and culture are enacted. In our opening section, we pointed out that during the nineteenth century culture and mind were viewed as different aspects of the same ordered phenomena. Jahoda counterposes culture ("a theory of situations") and mind ("theoretical constructs relating to cognitive process") as if a theory of culture and cognition could do without one or the other. It cannot, even when the structure of one's language appears to make such a separation inevitable.

The three broad approaches for studying relations between culture and cognitive development reviewed in this chapter should be seen as three guesses about the size of the social unit that will correspond to a given level of "globalness" concerning statements about mind. Piaget's basic guess was that the fundamental environmental predicaments embodied in concrete operational tasks would be universal in all cultures; Witkin and Berry (1975), without denying that possibility, emphasized within-culture universals of environment/child interactions, resulting in global "styles" of adaptation.

In both cases, a failure of behavior to cohere in uniform stages or styles wreaks havoc with the theories. Because generality is the "taken-for-granted-incorrigible-proposition" of these theories, specific variability is the demon they have to cope with, which they do by positing secondary mechanisms to accommodate the inevitable anomalies into the general theory.

The context-specific approach is strongest where the other approaches are weakest. Our specification of cognitive activities in test and experimental situations is as strong as the concurrent theory of behavior in those tasks will allow. The examples in this section demonstrate that there has been some headway

in converting the process of "locating the experiment" from the stage of demonstration to the stage of theory. However, as Jahoda quite correctly points out, there has been no principled way to escape the "endless trail" of particulars.

It strikes us as significant that Jahoda's criticism of the context-specific approach coincides so neatly with Harris' (1968) complaints about Boas' "historical particulars" or White's (1949) concern that Boas had doomed American anthropology to atheoretical detail-mongering. As thoughtful commentators have noted (e.g., Bock, 1980; Stocking, 1968), Boas never rejected the goal of a general theory of mankind built out of the elements of ethnography; but he became badly mired in pursuing evidence of the diffusion of culture elements in the hope that eventually, if not during his lifetime, the material that he and others retrieved would come together to reveal the organization of the grand mosaic.

But Boas's failure to build his critique of nineteenth-century anthropology into a new synthesis did not mean that the critique could be ignored. Twentieth-century anthropology has not yet succeeded where Boas failed; instead, it has mapped with great sophistication the various cul de sacs and promising pathways of the common problems facing all who enter the discussion.

The situation is not far different in contemporary studies of culture and cognition. What we need is a theory that can provide theoretical guidance to allow separation of general laws from the infinite variety of specifics that flood the fieldworker—psychologist and anthropologist alike—who ventures into another culture. But that theory has to be built on as solid a factual and logical foundation as current knowledge will allow.

In the sections that follow, we will reexamine the problem of cultural influences on cognition in the manner suggested by Jahoda's contrast between a "theory of situations" and a "theory of global processes." The central question organizing this discussion will be: How does behavior that is initially context bound and particular become, or appear to become, behavior embodying general characteristics of mind?

FROM THE SPECIFIC TO THE GENERAL

The between-cultural universal, the within-cultural universal, and the context-specific approaches compared and contrasted in the previous sections can be usefully summarized by reference to Figures 2 and 3. Figure 2 represents what we refer to as a *central-processor approach* found in the two univer-

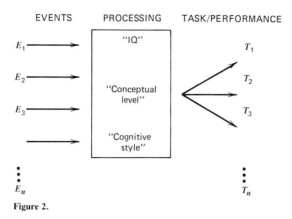

EVENTS · PROCESSING · TASK/PERFORMANCE

Figure 2.

salistic theories. The central-processor approach assumes that experiences operate on the current state of some central cognitive machinery, which in turn guides performance on the range of tasks that individuals encounter. The domain of the processor and its hypothetical structure are different for different theories. For Piaget, the processor corresponds to a universal set of elementary facts about *Homo sapiens* and their shared world. It is endowed with hierarchically organized structural units. For Witkin and Berry, the domains correspond to ecocultural niches, and the processor is structured in terms of hypothetical amounts of differentiation and integration.

Despite differences in terminology, data bases, and the internal structures they posit, both approaches assume that each learning experience (E_1, E_2—E_n) potentially contributes to an increase in power (level, amount) to a central processor that is then deployed to deal with individual performance tasks (T_1, T_2—T_n).

The achievements of these central-processor approaches have been considerable, and they may represent a useful, even correct, approach to the issues. But we think that outstanding sources of disagreement can best be minimized, if not eliminated, by taking a different tack, an extreme version of which is charactered schematically in Figure 3.

Like the central-processor approach, the contrasting ''distributed-processor'' approach sketched in Figure 3 links experiences (E_1) to task performance (T_1) through discrete schemata. However, a ''distributed-processor'' theory places little emphasis on processing that is common to all tasks. Instead, this approach treats cognitive processing as *distributed*. It is distributed in two senses; individual learning is assumed to be context-dependent in the first instance (e.g., distributed by situation), and

processing is *socially* distributed among people within contexts, in the second. This context-specific approach is strong where the central-processor theories are weak; it accounts for variability by specifying the diverging lines between culturally organized practice and task-specific performance. It also offers relatively specific models of culture-specific, task-specific cognitive processing. But the problem with this formulation, as we have noted, is its failure to account for the *generality* in human behavior. Skills and knowledge acquired in one setting often *do* appear in other settings under recognizably appropriate circumstances. In order for a distributed processing approach to work, it must provide some way to represent the fact that the individual events forming the base of the knowledge system are related to each other. The content and distribution of those events, that is, *their* organization, will be an important source of generality that we can ascribe to cognitive processes (e.g., that part of thinking controlled by the internal representations of external events).

In order to explain how generality could be, and is, achieved if learning and development are, in the first instance, context dependent, a theory must an-

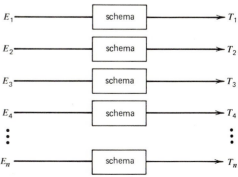

Figure 3.

swer several important questions. First, it must provide a way to describe the basic aspects of the events that constitute the fundamental contexts for activity in many culturally central domains of experience, and the basic unit of analysis in such an approach. Second, we need to understand cultural theories (belief systems) concerning how events are connected by members of any culture. At this point, we do not aspire to a general theory about the cultural constructions of reality. But some systematic ideas concerning what Lave (n.d.) has called "extensional domains descriptive of significant areas of experience" are crucial adjuncts to identifying fundamental events, for the structure of these domains will provide important hypotheses about *event linkages* and, thus, the *generality to be expected* from context-specific learning. Third, we need descriptions of the interactions among people which assemble behavior, indeed, the events that constitute their life experiences. Fourth, we need to consider ways that cultures might control exposure to events so that adult behaviors emerge over time in the behavior of children. The crucial question becomes: What conditions determine whether or not a child will encounter events of the kind necessary to produce change from one stage of generalizations to the next (understanding stage always to mean, "stage-within-context")?

Context Selection

According to the approach we are advocating, the kinds of contexts that children spend their time in are the fundamental units out of which cognitive development is constructed. Therefore, a central role of culture in producing cognitive differences will be context-selection mechanisms that operate on children as they grow up. A recent essay by B. B. Whiting (1980) provides one illustration of how such mechanisms might operate in ways that clearly link to a context-specific cognitive theory.

Previous work by Whiting had treated personality as a variable intervening between culture and individual behavior reflected in expressive and projective behavior. But, in recent years, she has begun to look at personality embodied in the everyday behavior of people and at the way that adults regulate access to important cultural contexts.

> We are interested in the contextual variables defined by culture that are associated with types of social behavior. . . . Our model is designed with the aim of facilitating cross-cultural research which purports to explore the regularities in the contextual components of social behavior. . . .

Our present theory does not deny that there may be some lasting effects of early experiences but dictates that we look as well to other experiences in the life course to explain social behavior. We do not deny the importance of the mother and father in molding the child but our analysis of samples of maternal behavior across cultures convinces us that *the mother and father's greatest effect is in the assignment of the child to settings that have important socializing influences.* (Whiting, 1980, pp. 96–97; emphasis added)

If one considers cognitive skills to be examples of social behavior (an easy allowance in that Whiting and her students have included cognitive tests in their work), it is clear that Whiting is suggesting precisely the kind of selection process that a context-specific theory needs, that is, a way to link contexts in terms of the cultural practices that sustain the group. Summarizing the results of the massive *Six Cultures* studies and more recent work on sex differences, Whiting characterizes the process linking contexts as follows:

> This theory says that patterns of interpersonal behavior are developed in the settings that one frequents and that the most important characteristics of the setting are the cast of characters who occupy the setting. . . . The settings one frequents are in turn related to the activities that occupy males and females of various ages in the normal course of living, activities that are determined by the economic pursuits and social structure and organization variables. (Whiting, 1980, p. 103)

The parameters of human life are described by Whiting in a way that is reminiscent of the ecocultural theory discussed above, and described at length elsewhere (Laboratory of Comparative Human Cognition, in press). But, there is a significant difference between Whiting's proposal and the standard psychological versions of the ecocultural approach. Instead of the ever-present molding of behavior by the accumulated contingencies of history and geography, we have a context-*selection* mechanism for developmental change.

> In the normal course of living, in as much as the settings one frequents change as one grows older and moves from childhood to adolescence to adulthood to old age, a person must be able to learn new behaviors especially if the changes in his/her life style involve interaction with differ-

ent categories of individuals or are in settings focused around new activities, settings with different standing rules of behavior.

Each setting is characterized by an activity in progress, a physically defined space, a characteristic group of people and norms of behavior—the blue print for propriety in the setting. Thus a child moving from the classroom to the playground interacts with adults and peers in different manners. The standing rules for these settings do not prescribe the same type of social interaction. (Whiting, 1980, pp. 103–104)

Many of the age changes that have been reported in the literature on child development may be the result of frequenting new settings as well as gaining new physical and cognitive skills. (Whiting, 1980, p. 111)

A context-selection approach of this sort is needed to begin to handle the problem of the apparent generality of cognitive processes. Whiting's work offers a promising beginning, but a great deal remains uncertain.

Missing almost entirely from Whiting's formulation of context selection and development is a description of the "interpretive procedures" (Cicourel, 1973) that are necessary to account for how people interpret rules in social situations, recognize the social circumstances they confront, and otherwise answer the question: "When is a context?" (Erickson & Schultz, 1977). In order to handle the massive comparative enterprise represented by her theory, Whiting and her colleagues made a series of strategic simplifications. Central was her decision to represent each interaction involving a child by coding what instigated the child's action and the child's response to this instigation. This coding required problematic judgments about people's intentions. All the evidence we have about the assembly of behaviors within the crucial contexts of enculturation indicates that they are complicated interactional events in which stimulus (instigation) and response are very difficult to disentangle (e.g., see Cole, Hood, & McDermott, 1978; Mehan & Griffin, 1980).

A second issue of doubtful status involves the mechanisms of transfer between one setting and the next. Whiting is quite straightforward on this point:

Our theory also hypothesizes that the habits of interpersonal behavior that one learns and practices in the most frequented settings may be overlearned and may generalize (transfer) to other

settings and to other statuses of individuals. These transferred patterns may or may not be appropriate to these new settings and can conceivably lead to maladaptive social behavior . . . . (Whiting, 1980, p. 103)

The mature individual must learn setting-specific patterns of behavior but his dyadic patterns are influenced by previous experience and habits. His/her perceptions of the responses of people in the new setting may be blinded by expectations carried over from the old frequented setting. (Whiting, 1980, p. 104)

What renders the status of these reasonable assertions doubtful is a great deal of evidence indicating that transfer between settings as complex as those considered by Whiting may be minimal or nonexistent (Shweder, 1979a,b, 1980). There is also a sizable literature in psychology indicating that even transfer between problem isomorphs is extremely limited or nonexistent when experimenters pose the problems, even when the problem solvers are college students (Gick & Holyoak, 1980).

Interaction Within Contexts

Contexts are not to be equated with the physical surroundings of settings—classrooms, churches, kitchens. They are constructed by the people present, in varying combinations of participants and audience (Erickson & Schultz, 1977). As McDermott and Roth (1978) have put it, contexts are constituted by what people are doing, as well as when and where they are doing it. That is, people in interaction serve as environments for each other.

We characterize activities such as those from which Whiting obtains her data as *cultural practices,* by which we mean activities for which the culture has normative expectations of the form, manner, and order of conducting repeated or customary actions requiring specified skills and knowledge (see Scribner & Cole, 1981). Cultural practices have to be learned as systems of activity. These settings have "standing rules," what cognitive psychologists term "scripts" (Schank & Ableson, 1977), anthropologists refer to as "contexts" (Frake, 1977), and sociologists call "background expectancies" (Cicourel, 1973; Garfinkel, 1967) that orient people to the behavior that is appropriate for a given situation.

A cultural-practice theory of culture and cognition resists the separation of individuals from the environments in which they live their daily lives.

This means that the relation between culture and cognition represents neither a purely subjective (in the head) nor purely objective (in the world) phenomenon; it is an intersubjective phenomenon, to be found in the interaction between people. Goodenough's notion that "culture consists of whatever one has to know or believe in order to operate in a manner acceptable to its members" (Goodenough, 1964, p. 36) provides a good start toward an interactional conception of culture and cognition. But this knowledge cannot be thought of in static or purely internal terms. Rather, as Geertz (1973, p. 44) suggests, the knowledge is akin to "a set of control mechanisms—plans, recipes, rules, instructions . . . for the governing of behavior." These mechanisms, embodied in cultural practices, are largely accomplished through the *co*operations of individual members of the culture in contexts of practical activity (Leont'ev, 1981).

People must display what they know *to* others and the meaningfulness of behavioral displays is established *by* the interpretation of others. Production and interpretation are mutually informing activities, conducted conjointly in interaction. Furthermore, the interpretation of a behavioral display in the present informs the production of behavior in the future, just as the production of present displays informs subsequent interpretations (G. H. Mead, 1934; Schutz, 1962; Voloshinov, 1973).

"Culture" and "cognition," then, refer jointly to behavior assembled by people in concert with each other. It is for this reason that a cultural practice theory takes cultural contexts, that is, socially assembled situations, not individual persons or abstract cultural dimensions as the unit of analysis for the study of culture/cognition.

Guided Change in Interaction

To our initial proposal that cognitive development is characterized by the mastery of context-specific knowledge about the world, we have now added the ideas that (1) cultures arrange the selection of contexts for children and that (2) one must study seriously the ways in which interactions among participants construct and maintain behavior in those contexts according to standing rules for the conduct of cultural practices. But we have not said much about how within-context interactions result in within-context mastery of essential cultural knowledge. In order to understand how the culture organizes for next steps of within-context development to occur, we turn our attention to the sociohistorical school of

Soviet psychology, which explicitly connects ideas of interaction with the concept of development.

The Relationship Between the Social and the Individual

The sociohistorical approach includes several proposals for how culturally organized social interactional patterns can influence the psychological development of the child. These proposals were made by Vygotsky and his followers in the process of developing a Marxist psychology (El'konin, 1972; Leont'ev, 1978; Luria, 1976; Vygotsky, 1978; Zaporozhets, 1980). A fundamental tenet of this approach is that human cognitive functioning emerges out of social interaction.[6]

The basic idea can be found in Vygotsky's "general law of cultural development."

> Any function in children's cultural development appears twice, or on two planes. First it appears on the social plane and then on the psychological plane. First it appears between people as an interpsychological category and then within the individual child as an intrapsychological category. This is equally true with regard to voluntary attention, logical memory, the formation of concepts and the development of volition. (Vygotsky, 1978, p. 57)

Vygotsky referred to the contexts organizing the social-to-psychological transformation of thinking as "zones of proximal development." Vygotsky defined this zone as the difference between a child's "actual developmental level as determined by independent problem solving" and the level of "potential development as determined through problem solving under adult guidance or in collaboration with more capable peers" (Vygotsky, 1978, p. 86). He demonstrated the usefulness of the notion of the zone of proximal development when dealing with the issues involved in assessing mental ability.

For our present purposes, the most important application of the notion of the zone of proximal development may be seen in Vygotsky's analysis of instruction. In this connection he argued that children can benefit from interaction with more experienced members of their culture only if the level of interaction falls within a certain range specified by the zone of proximal development.

> Instruction is good only when it proceeds ahead of development, when it awakens and rouses to life those functions which are in the process of

maturing or in the zone of proximal development. It is in this way that instruction plays an extremely important role in development. (1956, p. 278)

From the sociohistorical viewpoint, a culture maximizes its impact on a child's development by providing regulative contexts that fall within the zone of proximal development. Of course, there are many ways that more experienced and mature members of a culture can influence the child's environment, but the following four seem particularly important.

First, culture arranges for the *occurrence or nonoccurrence* of specific basic problem-solving environments embodied in cultural practices. Infants are taught to crawl or climb, sleep short or sleep long. Preschoolers learn to model in wire or draw (i.e., model with pen and paper). Students chant the Koran or read the Bible.

Second, the *frequency* of the basic practices is culturally organized. Does one read daily in class or weekly in church? When is it necessary to sort grains? How many times a day does one engage in pottery making and with how many products? Does one sell pottery as well as make it? Culture exerts an overwhelming power in answering such questions.

Third, culture shapes the *patterning* of co-occurrence of events. One may use an interrelated set of units to measure when selling and buying quantities of rice but measure cloth and tables with unrelated quantities. One culture provides for recall of spatial arrays using verbal rehearsal strategies and another without them. Written text is the vehicle for religious activity in some cultures, but not in others.

Fourth, cultures regulate the *level of difficulty* of the task within contexts. This regulation both increases the likelihood that potentially crucial learning events will occur and that costly failure will be averted. Arranging for babies to learn to sit erect by propping them in a hole with a blanket might be a starter task in one culture. Sewing buttons on a shirt may be the starter task toward becoming a master tailor in another. In each case, a series of difficulty levels leading to mastery is elaborated.

In summary, the sociohistorical approach to human cognition offers the following account of the relationship between culture and cognition. First, it proposes that there is indeed a strong connection between the social interactional processes that constitute activity in a culture and the psychological processes of its members. This is so because an individual's psychological functioning is seen to emerge through the process of internalizing various processes involved in social interaction which is itself culturally organized. Second, the zone of proximal development provides the conceptual lynchpin in the process by which members of a culture, children and adults, produce the relationship between social and individual functioning. It is here that the social becomes individual and the individual becomes social.

An Example of Zone-of-Proximal-Development Analysis

An example from research on American children illustrates the way in which adults organize the learning environments of children, thereby creating effective zones of proximal development. Wertsch and his associates (Wertsch, 1978, 1979, in press-a, in press-b; Wertsch, McNamee, Budwig, & McLane, in press) have conducted a series of studies on how mothers help their young children carry out tasks such as assembling a simple puzzle in accordance with a model. The puzzle pieces were cut-out parts of a truck which 5-year-old children were supposed to insert into a frame so that the end product would be identical with the model. Each child was helped by his or her mother through two assemblies of the same puzzle.

The course of the interaction as "the child assembles the puzzle while the mother assists" usually went something like this. During the first try at making the puzzle, the child might insert the pieces in the puzzle, but there is no attempt to make the puzzle in accordance with the model. If the model is used at all, it is because the *mother* negotiates the dyad's activity so she can include the model in the overall strategy. For example, she may make decisions about which pieces are to be used by looking at the model herself, or she may instruct the child to look at the model even though he or she does not understand what role it plays in the task.

During this early stage the child understands only very simple directives by the mother. These directives (which may involve both verbal and nonverbal communicative behaviors) are simple in the sense that they involve minimal understanding of what the mother and experimenter see as the overall task. For example, a regulative utterance such as, "Put the red one here" (with the mother pointing to the correct location) can lead to the appropriate task behavior on the part of the child without his or her understanding the relationship between "the red one," the model, and the puzzle. As the task session progresses, the mother is often able to utilize more complex speech to elicit appropriate task behaviors from the child. For example, she may use a regulative utterance such as, ''Where does the red one go?'' This utterance is more complex in the sense that, unlike the earlier one, it requires the child to identify and execute several substeps of the overall task in order to respond appropriately. Thus in order to identify where the red one goes the child must be capable of regulating her or his own activity to check the model.

Of course, this does not mean that whenever a mother uses a complex regulative utterance the child will respond appropriately. In those cases where an inappropriate response occurs, however, the mother is likely to follow up the child's response by switching to a simple directive that makes explicit the substeps implicit in the complex directive. For example, in the case of the complex directive we mentioned above, the mother might say, ''Look over here [pointing to the model puzzle] and you can see where the red one goes.'' In this way, the child is given a demonstration of how to ''unpack'' complex regulative utterances in the task situation and of how to expand the context of the task and thus to move closer to the overall task definition shared by the mother and experimenter.

The range of semiotic options available to the mother makes it possible for her to provide assistance to the child at various levels. This is a crucial aspect of development since the zone of proximal development can be expected to change as the child's experience with the problem increases. Initially, orientation to the task, selection, comparison, and even motor components of the problem may in large measure be carried out by the mother, who elicits required motor and verbal compliance from the child. The mother is doing more than the child can do, but not so much more that the child cannot participate. As the child comes to take over more of the task, the mother shifts the nature of the work she does (e.g., offering praise or pointing to troubles a few steps ahead).

In a manner reciprocal to adult options, the child can participate in the task at several different levels. These include bare participation where an adult guides the child through the appropriate steps in the task when the child understands little more than that there is a task, or maybe even only that there are a series of small tasks that the child does not yet see as components of an overall task. By participating in interaction understood by the adult (the interpsychological functioning characteristic of the early stages of learning a task), a child can ''accomplish'' the task before the child understands what he or she is doing. Rather than understanding the task

first and then carrying it out, in this sequence of events the child carries out the task (on the interpsychological ''plane'') and then understands it. The child's understanding of the task and of the associated complex regulative speech of the adult is a consequence, rather than a prerequisite, of going through the task. (It is what Cazden, 1981, has aptly called ''performance before competence.'')

The interactive nature of the learning process is highlighted by two facts, so mundane that they invite inattention. First, one never sees the mother sitting next to the child, blithely putting the puzzle together. The child *is always* a participant, and that participation is made possible by the adult. The *nature* of the participation is interactively negotiated by child and adult. Second, the puzzle always gets put together. This puzzle problem is well within the independent problem-solving capacity of one of the participants, so, of course, it gets done. Putting these two facts together, we can see the basis for a claim that development always occurs in a zone of proximal development. Additionally, that zone is dynamically achieved by the *child and others in a social environment*. Initially, it may seem that for any problem the social environment may be doing more than its share of the work, but the achievements of the child/mother in interaction with each other (with the mother carrying a heavy cognitive load) are progressively transformed into achievements of the child, with the mother serving as a distant prop.

The central insight embodied in these ideas about the immediate contexts where development occurs is that crucial events causing change from one level to another heavily involve other people; and in the case of young children, it is generally older people who provide an environment that makes likely the necessary learning. In this sense, important aspects of cognitive development ''come from the outside'' in the form of socially organized information about the goals and constraints regulating behavior. In some cases, the child will quite literally be *told* the necessary information (''You better check the model before you choose a puzzle piece, silly!''); in others, adults only make the important factors salient (''Which piece will fit into the corner?''); and in still others, they may do no more than make it possible for the child to be present while potential learning events are in progress (''Come sit on my lap while I help your sister figure out this puzzle.''). Directly or indirectly, the social environment is likely to be providing important information to sustain and increase the efficiency of thinking. This is not to imply that children have no role in structuring the environments that in turn structure their behavior. As our example from Wertsch's work indicates, the child's behavior provides the adult with crucial information as well as the other way around.

The Zone of Proximal Development in Soviet Cross-cultural Studies

Sociohistorical psychologists never exploited the potential of the zone of proximal development as the locus of development in cross-cultural work. Only one cross-cultural expedition was undertaken at the time these ideas were being developed (described by Luria, 1976), and few have been taken since that time (Tulviste, 1979). Almost all of the scanty Soviet work sought to demonstrate qualitative shifts in the basic activities that underpin cognitive systems for preliterate and industrialized people. No research went into an exploration of how these different kinds of activity systems came into being and how they operate to reproduce themselves across generations.

In view of the fact that the sociocultural theory posits the zone of proximal development as the focus of learning and use of higher psychological functions, it may appear surprising that no work was put into comparative studies of concept acquisition. One can point out the limited attention given to cross-cultural work as an explanation for this neglect. But the failure runs deeper. A commitment to the sociohistorical approach applied cross-culturally is a commitment to looking at how cultures organize learning environments for their members, especially their young. Following his theory, Luria went to Uzbekistan to discover the cognitive consequences of the dramatic shift from traditional pastoralism to literate, technological activities. He conducted interviews and experiments to tap these consequences. But it is in interaction *between Uzbeks* not in interactions between Uzbeks and Russians that the theory predicted the operation and acquisition of Uzbek concepts and problem-solving modes. Nowhere in the world has the sociohistorical research program been carried out. However, a great deal of work has been done that illustrates hypothetical pieces of the overall process.

The Zone of Proximal Development in Anthropological Research

In a wide variety of studies, cultural anthropologists have described the patterns of family interactions called socialization or education "in the broad sense" (M. Mead, 1958; Raum, 1940; for a review, see Mead, 1958). Overwhelmingly, in pretechnological societies, whether of hunter-gatherers (Lee & DeVore, 1976) or agriculturalists or pas-

toralists (Whiting & Whiting, 1975), children are described as participants in a wide variety of social activities that we consider adult. Their role as participants varies as they grow older, but not the fact of their participation. The more detailed ethnographies of the socialization process show that children are routinely assigned tasks commensurate with their current abilities as elements in a larger task guided by their older siblings or adults. Just as developmental psychologists can point to stages of understanding corresponding to logically connected aspects of the environment, anthropologists have pointed out that the sequences of child acquisitions in naturally organized learning environments have a strong element of necessity imposed by environmental constraints. The idea that one must be able to walk before it is possible to run exemplifies this central fact about psychological development's dependence upon the constraints imposed by biological structure and environmental contingencies.

An example of a specialized skill engaged in by adults that is learned in specific contexts regulated by older children and adults is given in the work of Kulah (1973). Kulah studied the use of proverbs in the formal and informal rhetorical discussions of Kpelle (Liberian) elders. He was interested in the way that young Kpelle children come to learn the meaning of the proverbs. His investigation showed that in a very important sense, proverb content and interpretation are not taught; they are "arranged for" through the organization of linked activities. The arranging starts long before any child is expected to know or use proverbs.

All Kpelle children engage in a variety of verbal games including riddling and storytelling. One genre of this game requires teams of children to pose riddles to each other. The riddles consist of two parts roughly akin to a "question" and an "answer." Both questions and answers are part of the traditional lore of the group. They must be learned as pairs. The children line up in two rows and sequentially challenge each other with riddles. The team that answers the most riddles correctly is the winner.

The teams of children are age graded. Children of a wide span of ages (say, from 5 to 15 years) may play; the oldest on each team takes the first turn, then the next oldest, down to the youngest. In this way, even the youngest member of a team is important, and even the youngest is around to learn many new riddles.

This activity is related to adult proverb use in the following way. The question or answer half of the riddles that the children learn are key phrases that will appear in adult proverbs. It is as if the riddle learning serves to teach children the "alphabet" along the way to learning to "read words." For example, a "question" might be something like "rolling stone" and the answer, "no moss."

Kulah's research shows that the potential meaning in combining "rolling stone" and "no moss" is not well understood by young children, even if they know a lot of riddle question/answer pairs. In a task designed to see if the children would group different riddles by the common meaning that the adult interpretation specifies, young children did not respond as if one riddle was related in any way to the other. But as the children grew older, they came more and more to approximate adult groupings of riddles according to their "message." By the time they are old enough to participate in the adult discussions where these proverbs are a rhetorical resource, they show the adult pattern of proverb interpretation. They are ready to learn how to use their now-organized alphabet in a new context, as a component in new, adult, tasks. The adult contexts, in turn, reorganize the "old skill" into a new activity.

While traditional societies such as that described by Kulah provide examples of age-graded activities such as the riddle game, the major educational contexts are unlikely to separate children and adults.

Fortes emphasizes the unity of the social sphere of adults and children among many traditional African peoples.

> As between adults and children . . . the social sphere is differentiated only in terms of relative capacity. All participate in the same culture, the same round of life, but in varying degrees, corresponding to the stage of physical and mental development. (Fortes, 1970, p. 18)

This observation is especially well borne out in recent studies of adults and children engaged in common activities that serve both as contexts for important economic pursuits and for socialization of the young into necessary adult cultural practices.

Lave (n.d.) has recently completed a detailed study of the process of becoming a tailor among Liberian tribal people living in the capital city of Monrovia. A typical tailor shop is peopled by men and boys ranging in age from 6 to 60 years. The range in tailoring expertise is as great as the range in age. Rank beginners and masters work side by side in generally crowded quarters. In this setting, immediate economic necessity and longer term economic security combine to organize the learning activity of apprentices. From their first day in the shop, apprentices have to make themselves useful and masters must begin the task of making them independently productive.

Because the masters cannot sacrifice productivity, a well-worked-out series of steps in the mature practice of tailoring (in this case, making trousers and suits) has evolved, beginning with elementary tasks such as sewing button holes and progressing through a series of tasks (cutting, measuring, sewing zippers) of increasing difficulty. From time to time, Lave observed direct instruction (e.g., when a master ripped out a badly sewn seam to show how it should be done). At other times, masters would arrange special lessons using scraps of cloth or paper to permit practice in cutting or sewing on the machine. However, for the most part instruction was arranged for by including the apprentice in elementary steps *as a part of the adult activity*. In these circumstances, apprentices participate in production of the adult product at the highest level possible because this level is maximally profitable for all concerned.

A crucial feature of such arrangement of this kind of learning environment that fits precisely the idea of a zone of proximal development is that *all* stages of the mature practice are a salient part of the learner's environment, regardless of what "level" in the process he is working at. Thus, the learner is gaining direct practice at one level while observing the skills necessary for later levels. As Lave and many others note, this kind of arrangement ensures progress with relatively few errors while providing constant motivation toward mastery.

Another description of a culture practice organized as a zone of proximal development for novices is provided by the Childs and Greenfield (1982) study of Zinacantieco weaving, referred to earlier. As a part of their research, Childs and Greenfield conducted a careful analysis of the role of social guidance in the mastery of weaving. The guidance was of two kinds. First, there was direct intervention by an adult at points where the learner was making, or was about to make, a mistake. At the beginning of any step in the weaving process (which Childs and Greenfield separate into six major steps), the adult was found to intervene heavily; toward the end of each step, there was little or no guidance. On the child's first garment, the adult spent 93% of the time weaving with the child. If a girl had completed one garment, adult participation was reduced to about 50% of the time. After as many as four successful garments, the adult was still involved directly in weaving about 40% of the time.

This guided instruction is by no means a silent process. Childs and Greenfield show that adult talk is closely tied to the level of skill manifested by the learner and the specific circumstances that the child is facing. Commands dominate early in learning, and these are overwhelmingly of the sort "Do x." In later stages of learning, when the novice weaver's actions are less problematic, the adult talk shifts to statements that point out salient features of the present stage of the work or links between stages.

A second way in which adult Zinacanteco weavers guide practice is to provide children direct exposure to all of the steps of weaving and associated activities *as a part of the process of learning to carry out each of the steps.* We mentioned above that Childs and Greenfield assign six steps to the weaving process. From an early age, long before we might notice that they are learning to weave, girls witness the whole process with all of its six parts. To borrow another phrase from Fortes, "the child is from the beginning oriented towards the same reality as its parents and has the same physical and social material upon which to direct its cognitive and instructional endowment" (1970, p. 19). When it comes time to learn to weave the first garment, the process of applying what one has learned in the past to the circumstances at hand hardly arises.

A number of researchers in anthropology and psychology have focused on the mother/child interaction as the focus of developmentally significant learning experiences. In all cultures, the early life of the child presents child and family alike with a set of problems that are common to all of our species. But depending upon the complexity of environmental factors, the systems of socialization activities that deal with those common problems will be different. They must differ because passing on the culture to children is only a part of what must be done to maintain the species on a day-to-day and moment-to-moment basis. The organization of these other activities must modulate the organization of the child's immediate environment.

Kirk's work relating mother/child interaction to cognitive performance among Ga children illustrates cultural differences in the ways that mothers guide children's problem-solving efforts as a key mediator of improved performance. Kirk (1977) found that certain maternal behaviors correlated with greater skill on conservation tasks, while differences in subcultural groupings (rural, urban, suburban) did not so correlate. Her research shows that mothers who most frequently used specific referents to indicate relationships, and who justified and explained events, had children who performed on higher levels on conservation tasks. This parallels an earlier finding (Kirk & Burton, 1977) from Kenya, where the nonverbal communicative specificity of mothers in teaching interactions was closely associated with the cognitive performance of children. In these studies, as well as those by Rogoff (1978), the terms used to describe the more effective maternal activities are the same terms we would use to describe environments that constitute effective zones of proximal development.

Connections Between Contexts

Thus far we have considered several important issues that have to be resolved in order to build a context-specific approach to culture and cognition into a theory that can encompass the major known phenomena: the ideas that ecocultural constraints operate through context selection, that contexts represent systems of activity, and that cognitive change is often interactionally managed within the significant contexts of socialization.

Still missing is an explicit statement of how a context-specific theory accounts for the ways in which past experience carries over from one context to the next. In both the Piagetian and psychological differentiation approaches, the mechanism invoked to provide for intersituational consistency is called *transfer.* But, as we will see, traditional invocations of this term will not solve the problem.

Current Psychological Evidence

A standard procedure for assessing transfer between different contexts in which the same behavioral principles are believed relevant is to train subjects to solve problems in one form and then to test the influence of this learning in the new, isomorphic problem context. For example, Reed, Ernst, and Banerji (1974) gave college students two isomorphic problems to solve. The first was the classical missionaries and cannibals problem, the second, a logically identical problem involving husbands and wives. The similarity of the task structures was not sufficient to induce transfer between the two problems. *Transfer occurred only when the subjects were explicitly told about the relationship between the two problems.* A similar finding is reported by Wason and Johnson-Laird (1972) concerning a logical problem presented in the form of abstract symbols (vowels and numbers) or in everyday language concerning postmasters, mail, and stamps.

A more recent study by Gick and Holyoak (1980) demonstrates just how difficult it may be to obtain transfer among problems that are extremely similar from the experimenters' point of view, and extremely similar for the subjects too, once they are told about the similarity. What makes the failure of transfer seem odd is that Gick and Holyoak went to a lot of trouble, short of giving verbal hints, to make certain that the relevant analogous information was known to the subjects. But availability of information was not sufficient to induce transfer, because subjects failed "spontaneously" to apply the known, relevant solution. Gick and Holyoak's summary of the obstacles to transfer in their study pinpoints precisely limitations on the amount of "spontaneous" transfer to be expected among the significant contexts of children's lives:

> A potential analogy may often be encoded in a very different context from that in which the [current] problem appears. Indeed, the basic problem in using an analogy between remote domains is to connect two bodies of information from disparate semantic contexts. More generally, successful transfer of learning generally involves overcoming contextual barriers. This may not be easy . . . . (Gick & Holyoak, 1980, p. 349.)

Thus, it appears from the recent psychological literature that transfer (as spontaneous application of analogies among remote contexts) is a weak theoretical reed to use as a central mechanism in any theory of culture and cognitive development.

The perplexity of this work on transfer, when combined with evidence that learning is based on within-context skill mastery, is that all aspects of the emerging theory point to the isolation of cognitive achievements. But our experience of the world does not appear as a mosaic of unconnected fragments. One possible way out of this conundrum is to conclude that the appearance of order is itself an illusion. This position, an extreme version of the "constitutive" perspective described above, is suggested by Shweder's wry comment that:

> The everyday mind accomplishes a very difficult task. It looks out at a behavioral world of complex, context-dependent interaction effects and unsubstantial intercorrelations among events, yet it perceives continuities, neat clusters, and simple regularities. (Shweder, 1980, p. 77)

Although it is certainly true that *Homo sapiens* is engaging in creating order out of disorder, and while it may be true that *Homo sapiens* is more a rationalizing than a rational species, no one, including Shweder, is denying that past experiences operate in the present to influence behavior. The problem is

that detecting an analogy between disparate contexts seems to be a relatively rare *individual* achievement. Valuable as they are, current psychological approaches to the problem of transfer are not likely to provide us the evidence we need to build a theory of culture and cognitive development.

Yet, it seems clear that people *do* use past experience to conduct present behavior; and in this sense, all behavior reflects the transfer of past learning. This is confirmed in the psychological literature on reasoning, particularly that which deals with the reasoning processes that occur in mundane settings. Several contemporary theories of thinking are compatible with the notion that a great deal of knowledge is context specific. According to such views, thinking consists largely of the retrieval of context-specific information that is appropriate for the task at hand. An early theory of this type was proposed by Bartlett (1958) who claimed that in everyday thinking (of the sort that one can sample on afternoon talk shows, dinnertime conversations, and faculty meetings) conclusions are reached (problems are solved) with little consideration of logical alternatives because "in popular thinking the end of the preferred argument sequence itself takes charge of the selection of particular items of evidence" (p. 175).

Furthermore, Bartlett tells us that in everyday life the generalities and conclusions that are put forth and the evidence that is selected are strongly *socially determined*. The generalities and conclusions are usually a part of common wisdom and the selected evidence is more than personal recall; it is "social knowledge, socially distributed" (Schutz, 1962), evidence known as well to others in the group who would be likely to use the same evidence in the same circumstances.

Our problem of relating past context-specific learnings to new or future contexts can be formulated, in the light of Bartlett's work, as a problem of *socially determined retrieval* in the new or future contexts of socially determinded structures and processes. Clearly, there is a possible next step here. One particular process that may be socially determined is the process by which analogies are retrieved. In fact, we suspect that analogy-retrieving processes may well be a form of a culturally elaborated tool for generalizing or transfer (Scribner & Cole, 1973). But, such analogy-retrieving processes arise *in* domains *in* cultures, and an understanding of their use would still require a framework like the culture-practice approach described below.

A Culture-Practice Approach to Transfer

Instead of searching for a central, general mechanism that exists in the head of individual persons as a way to account for transfer, a cultural-practice orientation urges us to look to the organization of the environments in which interactions occur. Emphasizing the importance of social organizations does not dismiss the research on transfer-as-individual-activity. Rather, it emphasizes that in several important ways, *transfer is arranged by the social and cultural environment.* This shift of focus does not so much solve the transfer problem as it dissolves it.

As the work of Lave, of Childs and Greenfield, and of other anthropologists (e.g., Lee & Devore, 1976) strongly suggests, contexts are the "threads" from which are woven the fabric of a society's total adaptation to its circumstances. LeVine (1970) and the Whitings' work (Whiting & Whiting, 1975) contain the same idea cast in a different mold, as does the entire ecocultural movement. If the implications that we are drawing from the research reviewed here are correct, these approaches do not have to depend upon the notion of generalized transfer to accomplish their goals. Overlap in environments and the societal resources for pointing out areas of overlap are major ways in which past experience carries over from one context to another.

Lave emphasizes another point concerning sources of intercontext transfer which applies well to the Childs and Greenfield weaving case and, we believe, to a great deal of our everyday, culturally organized experience. In speaking about the arithmetic problems that tailors encounter, she says:

> Most of the arithmetic problems encountered in everyday life have been seen many times before. They are routine occurrences. This follows from the general routineness of our everyday lives. The tailors come to work six days a week, make trousers, shirts and hats, alongside the same people they have been sewing next to for months or years, for customers many of whom they have known for years. (Lave, 1979, p. 4)

Repetition and redundancy minimize the problem of transfer posed by new and unusual problems such as those that constitute the backbone of psychological research on problem solving.

The single most pervasive resource, and the one that is easily overlooked in a discussion concentrated on learning and problem solving, is language itself. We have already had occasion to note the routine and repeated nature of a great deal of our experience. This routineness and repeatedness is coded in the lexicon, reinforcing whatever analogy-supporting data there may be in the physical characteristics of routine events. Thus, two instances of "weaving a hammock," described with those words, may be

responded to as the same in part because of the conventional and known meanings of the words "weaving" and "hammock," whereas alternative descriptions might not evoke transfer of knowledge. Understanding of this point is a major motivating force behind Whorf's (1956) insistence on the importance of language as a molder of thought; language represents a distilled cultural theory of what goes with what in the world. Children master their culture's theory of the connections between contexts as they master their language. This fact is the basis for Stefflre's (1965) assertion that "an individual will behave toward an object or event in a manner that is similar to the way he behaves toward objects and events that he encodes in the same way" (p. 12).

The importance of language as a code for the sediment of past wisdom concerning the relatedness of elements of experience can be illustrated by reference to the Gick and Holyoak (1980) work on transfer between logically identical problems. Their college students could not transfer problem-solving solutions from one example of a problem to another because they did not apply the appropriate analogy. One problem was embedded in a story of a brain operation; the other involved a military dictator. As separate as these problems sound, audiences hearing a description of this work at a professional conference have no difficulty understanding and instantaneously applying the appropriate analogy. The difference between the lecture and experiment arises because, in describing the two problems, speakers or authors refer to the two problems as "radiation problems" as a part of their description. When language encodes the relevant relation between distinct contexts, the contexts are no longer distinct; *no transfer as an individual invention* is required. We suggest that this phenomenon is extremely widespread and accounts for a great deal of the way that cultures render past problem-solving solutions available for analysis of present problem contexts.

Language, which codes the culture's theory of what goes with what, is a universal resource organizing transfer. In addition, there are culturally elaborated tools for organizing and manipulating information that accomplish generality of cognitive skills. Perhaps the single most important cultural tool for associating contexts among which transfer might occur is literacy. Its history can be seen as a case of the movement from the context specific to the general. If Schmandt-Besserat's (1978) account of the earliest precursors of writing is correct, the earliest writing forms represented no more than tallies for a very circumscribed set of objects in the earliest agricultural settlements. They were devices for recording the number of animals or amount of grain in tiny, protoagricultural settlements. While their contexts of use must be considered quite circumscribed, these tallying devices became standardized for linking information in one immediate context (the amount of grain in a wagon) and the information in another context (the total amount of grain in a shed, or the amount loaned to a neighbor). For something on the order of 6,000 years, these devices remained context specific; only increasing in kind very slightly. But with the advent of bronzeworking technology, improved agicultural techniques, and the rise of trade, a more powerful system of recordkeeping was required. There were many more contexts in which such tallies were needed. As the connections between people became looser because of increased community size, intercommunity trade, and division of labor, people came to inhabit very different contexts from each other, even within the same culture. The tokens proliferated, modes of representing them changed, and eventually an alphabetic system was formed, the system on which contemporary literate practices in American schools are based.

Even from this brief account, it should be clear that writing is not an all-or-none invention. We cannot simply say, "The Greeks invented the alphabet." As the record clearly shows (cf. Gelb, 1963), the alphabet was the end product of many centuries of context-specific adaptations to changing circumstances. Both the way in which literacy is a tool designed and implemented in specific contexts and the linkages it provides between situation have been illustrated in the research by Scribner, Cole, and their colleagues described earlier (Scribner & Cole, 1978, 1981).

Alphabetic literacy is a powerful tool for storing and transferring information across time and distance. It is a transfer-producing tool. But it is not a context-independent tool. Rather, it too is tied very closely to the contexts of activity that constitute adult practice (Cole & Griffin, 1980).

Summary

Throughout this section, we have taken pains to point out that the way in which past experiences carry over from one situation to another is conceived of differently in cultural-universalistic and in context-specific theories. The cultural-practice theory deemphasizes transfer as a central process occurring within the minds of individuals and emphasizes movement of information across contexts as a *social* accomplishment. The tuition of young children by adults, their direct intervention, especially when a mistake is about to be committed, and adults' practice of embedding learning in everyday experiences,

are some of the ways in which environments are arranged for events to reoccur. In fact, the massive redundancy and repetitiveness of learning situations minimizes the occurrence of new situations. In those unusual circumstances when people are confronting new situations, the physical features of those environments, the social distribution of social knowledge, and the presence of a number of cultural resources, notably language and literacy, assist in providing bridges between contexts.

RECAPITULATION AND SYNTHESIS

We began this review of culture and cognitive development with a story of nineteenth-century human sciences in search of the nature of human beings. Our initial contrast was between Tylor, Spencer, and Morgan, who adopted an evolutionary theory of human *Culture* (with a captial "C"), and Boas, who objected to the evidence these three thinkers presented for their evolutionary sequences. He sought the mystery of human nature in the specific, historically accumulated designs for living, and discovered *cultures*, which could not be ranked with respect to uniform scales of development. For the evolutionary theorists, the notion that primitives think like children was a simple lemma, following from their basic assumption. For Boas, the configurations of adult psychological achievements were as variable as the configurations of cultures.

If we turn to developmental and psychological theories applied to a wide variety of cultural settings, we see the same argument recapitulated in a different guise. Evolutionary theory is represented by the most celebrated developmental theorists of the twentieth century, Piaget, whose theory posits a universal series of stages that characterize the organism by qualitatively different psychological structures. And we have Witkin, whose ideas are in several respects similar to Spencer's; they identify differentiation as a core concept of development (see also Werner, 1948). These psychological theories are similar in their belief in the organismwide emphasis on differentiations and integrations as basic elements of development, implications of the psychological states they propose, and in their willingness to order behavior from lower to higher.

The ideas of Boas appear in modern psychological form as context-specific approaches. The research of the Laboratory of Comparative Human Cognition and a good deal of research in contemporary psychology run counter to universalistic theses in several ways (see Bem & Allen, 1974; Cantor & Mischel, 1979; Nisbett & Ross, 1980; Shweder,

1980; Zaporozhets, 1980). Where Piaget and Witkin see uniform stages and levels of information processing, these scholars see context-specific behaviors and attribute less power to central processing mechanisms that control generalization from one setting to the next.

The parallels between competing theories of cultural differences at the end of the nineteenth century and competing approaches to cognitive development in the late twentieth century run deeper than a "specific" versus "general" dichotomy. As we have been at some pains to point out, all theories need to account for both the context specificity and the interconnectedness of human behavior. In the nineteenth century, evolutionary theorists invoked the idea of independent invention to account for similar institutions encountered in different cultures. "Spontaneous invention" is the nineteenth-century anthropologist's equivalent to the twentieth-century psychologist's mysterious process of "spontaneously discovering the analogy." Boas's critique of the idea of spontaneous invention of cultural institutions is repeated in modern psychological discussions of transfer, or generalization, across settings. When we suggested in the previous section that design of contexts and within-context resources, including social resources, account for a good deal of the continuity in the everyday world, we were suggesting that change "diffuses" from outside the unit of analysis. The major difference between our suggestion and Boas's is that we changed the unit of analysis from a "culture" in a geographical locale to "individuals within a culturally organized context."

In reviews such as this, where well-established points of view compete as explanations for a large domain of facts, differences among theories and the facts that are used to substantiate those theories gain easy prominence. But the large areas of agreement among competing approaches are as important as the issues in dispute.

Points of Agreement Among Rival Frameworks

The approaches to culture and cognition discussed in this chapter have existed, in one form or another, for about 100 years. We will not resolve their differences in a single essay. We can, however, review the course of the discussion in search of the areas of general agreement, insights that seem to have broad implications, and crucial points of disagreement. Until rival approaches can agree on what they disagree about, they cannot be of much mutual relevance to each other.

One major point of agreement is captured in the progression from universal to culture-specific to context-specific environments for development. None of the participants in this discussion believe that there is only one proper relationship of cognition to experience and experience to cognition. All approaches recognize the existence of constraints on individual development common to all human groups, of constraints specific to each group, and of constraints that are experienced only by some people some of the time and that vary within and between groups. A second point of agreement concerns the importance of the social and physical worlds as environments for development. All recognize the importance of social interaction for cognitive development. A third point of agreement is that data derived from psychological experimentation are a problematic base on which to construct a theory of culture and cognition. The cultural and social experiences of people, those experiences that comprise the patterns and routines of everyday life, have to be represented in the enterprise. A fourth point of agreement is that development must be understood with respect to the adaptive problems facing the growing child. Insofar as cultures differ in those adaptive demands, the configuration of age-related changes should differ from one culture to another. As Dasen and associates (1979) put it, "We find that an ecological orientation provides a value free context for the interpretation of [cognitive] differences as unique adaptation, rather than as differential developments" (p. 79).

These areas of agreement are substantial. They insure that all participants to the discussion value the same domain of phenomena and that these phenomena are drawn from a wide enough perspective to provide some prospects for a unified theory of culture and cognitive development.

Contrasting Analyses of a Single Activity

At this point, a concrete example may clarify the implications of adopting the various approaches. Consider an activity that has been the focus of several studies reviewed in this chapter—a child learning to make pots from clay. From a Piagetian point of view, pottery making is an opportunity for "operational exercise." It provides an environment in which the child can gain experience with material being transformed in a variety of ways relevant to discovering the basic laws of conservation. As a result of this exercise, the child is more likely to have available a higher-order operation to use when some new material in a new setting is encountered.

From a differentiation perspective, pottery making is an activity that exposes the child to culture-wide constraints that control the kind of mental activity it is most adaptive to engage in. Pottery making is part of a cultural configuration in which very general constraints from the ecology shape the learning environment in which the child learns to pot. Other constraints derive from other parameters: Who gives the instructions? How much innovation is tolerated? Who is permitted to make pots? Whereas for the Piagetian, potting is a token of operational exercise in concrete operations, for the differentiation theorist, it is a token of an environment that promotes more or less reliance on physical objects or persons, and relies more (or less) on individual initiative or social pressure to guide the particulars of the craft.

According to a cultural-practice theory, potting is one of many culturally organized activities that make up the participants' repertoire of knowledge. It involves the exercise of many skills in transforming material. This exercise is embedded in a set of social relations and requires the mastery of culturally transmitted technologies. It is a context that must be mastered as a behavior setting (Barker, 1968). Behavior settings are not disjoint, but the connectedness of the behavior within them cannot be accounted for satisfactorily by listing all the knowledge structures or behavioral constraints common to all, as the Piagetian and differentiation theorists claim. Rather, one has to look to (1) the larger contexts of which they are a part, (2) the actual skills required and mastered in the settings, and (3) the way that potentially shared components of such setting-specific activities are actually linked by the participants. Context-specific retrieval rather than context-general inference and deduction are then given a major role in cognition and development.

For a cultural-practice theory, the craft of pottery making is *simultaneously* an abstract theoretical activity, implicating universal features of the world, an activity that reflects cultural constraints, and an activity that promotes individual skill and personal meaning. Because this activity simultaneously represents these different psychological "elements," we need a systematic method to capture its complexity. The study of the interactional enactment of this craft in its cultural context offers us this possibility. Simultaneously, it provides a unit that characterizes both culture and cognition.

Points of Disagreement and Uncertainty

Despite these broad areas of agreement, parochialism persists, controversy about basic facts

abounds, and leading theorists diverge in their theoretical assertions about the nature of culture-specific cognitive demands as well as the cognitive consequences of dealing with them. The points of disagreement center on the units of analysis on which the competing theories are based and on underlying ideas about the nature of development. The approach we have been arguing for, as crudely contrasted in Figures 2 and 3, suggests that behavior is more situationally constrained and dependent on interaction for its construction and maintenance than central-processor theories would suggest. It characterizes development as more dependent on differences in the knowledge base, and it gives a larger role to contextually sensitive procedures than do the central-processor approaches.

Identifying Constraints

As our previous discussion should have made clear, discerning significant variation in the universal predicaments of human development is a concern of all the theoretical approaches to culture and cognitive development. However, more is involved in resolving differences between rival starting points than finding evidence for general or specific adaptations. All major frameworks assume that the patterns of behavior observed represent the organism's response to constraints. But they do not agree on how these constraints have to be identified by the researcher to provide empirical support for a theory. A crucial source of uncertainty in all these approaches is a well-worked-out theory of what *relevant* constraints are operating at a given time in any of the settings used to test a particular experience/cognition hypothesis. Gravity constrains all human behavior the world over. But gravity is not generally considered a relevant constraint in studies of culture and cognition. Socialization practices are a relevant constraint on young children, but they are not a constraint that is believed to guide children's behavior totally in all the settings they find themselves in.

Rather, all culture and cognition theories include at least implicit assumptions about the settings where crucial constraints are relevant and therefore potentially operative. It is *only* in such settings that the theories are relevant and testable. In this sense, central processor theories also require a theory of situations. So, for example, Witkin asserts that field-dependent people are not expected to rely on social cues *in general*. Rather,

under well-structured conditions field-dependent people do not differ from field-independent people in the use they make of external social referents. When the situation is ambiguous, on the other hand, field-dependent people will seek information from others in their efforts to structure the situation, which they are less able to do without aid. (Jahoda, 1980, p. 100)

Similarly, as Bovet (1974) points out, conservation of quantity does not automatically arise as a potential problem simply because water is being transferred from one container to another. Such transfer must occur under rather well-specified conditions; there must be containers of equal dimensions at one point in the procedure and of different dimensions in another. A "misleading cue" must be present or no test or practice of the conservation principle is possible.

The Interpenetration of the Social and Physical Environments

This issue is fundamental for reconciling different views of culture and cognitive development. Unfortunately, the theoretical assertions that social and physical environments are part of a single system acting on the child has not been matched by techniques that would build such an important assumption into the basic methods on which competing theories rest.

The interpenetration of social and physical experience goes well beyond recognition that there are other people, as well as objects, in the child's environment. As El'konin eloquently pointed out, even most objects cannot be considered asocial; the system "child/thing" is in reality the system "child/social object" because objects are themselves socially defined and shaped.

A major shortcoming of current ecocultural psychological differentiation theory with respect to the relation of social and physical environments is its distinction between "cognitive development" and "the development of social interaction" (Dasen et al., 1979). Combined with the use of presumed culture-free tests of levels of differentiation, this dualism is an impediment to understanding how thoroughly the social and object characteristics of the environment are intertwined. It leads to a narrow focus on only one part of the important process by which the child's contact with a physical and a social world is organized. Ignored by this dualism is the work that takes place in "zones of proximal development," that is, those environments—surrounding, yet external to, the child—which assure that there will be a fit between the needs of the child and the external environment.

It is possible to make a strong case for Piaget's belief in the principled interpenetration of the social and object worlds. But this underlying supposition is really not well represented in the research on which the theory is based. Dasen joins Berry and Witkin in juxtaposing cognitive development to the development of social interactions, even as he calls for reconsidering Piaget's belief that the social and object domains obey the same developmental laws. Although it is true that Piaget uses very similar ideas to account for the structural changes that occur in the social domain and changes in such object-centered domains as conservation, there has been little or no research directed at El'konin's point that objects become social insofar as they interact with people. Nor has there been great success in showing that levels of functioning in one domain correlate well with functioning in the other, as the general stage theory would have us believe.

The root metaphor in Piaget's theory comes from biology, and more specifically, digestion. His model of intellectual development is a metaphoric description of the process of biological growth. In digestion, Piaget tells us, we can see the process by which the organism assimilates food, which undergoes transformations in the process of being accommodated to the existing structure of the organism. Biological growth requires the ingestion of nutrients, the definition or value of which is established by the organism's capacity to process them. These nutrients or "aliments," then become a part of the system, redefining its ability to process future nutrients.

Intellectual growth, for Piaget, operates in a similar fashion. The child, in activity, assimilates new experiences, accommodating mental structures to enable assimilation to be completed. The child can only take in or assimilate those experiences that are defined as relevant by the current state of the processing organization. Once ingested, these experiences form part of the mental organization that will allow for the intake or assimilation of new experiences.

Piaget's work is a relatively faithful embodiment of this biological metaphor in the realm of cognitive development, especially in his discussions of the interactions between an individual and an object. (Cross-cultural research, however, has found it difficult to study the "ingestion process," depending as it does on "digestive products.")

If we extend the digestion analogy a little bit further, we will be able to illustrate the direction we believe Piagetian research needs to take. The biological-nourishment system and the intellectual-experiences system are not determined solely by children's personal and individual efforts. Piaget treats food as if it were a natural object, encountered in nature in its "raw" form. In fact, the range of such natural foods in human history is very small, and the range of humankind's habitat would be very much reduced if *food as a socially structured object* was not the rule rather than the exception. The very fact that fire came under human control and was used to "prepare" food is evidence of the *social* nature of the object, even in Piaget's root metaphor derived from biology.

Parents carefully plan and prepare the food for their young children. But parents are not the only forces operating in the system that assures that the nutritional needs of infants are attended to. Many cultural systems are involved in the preparation and distribution of food for the young as well as for the old. The fact that a great deal of what we eat has been processed, prepared, and is available at the market prior to any preparation that is done in the home also extends Piaget's digestion metaphor further in an interactional direction.

Just as parents carefully prepare the food that children will consume, so, too, parents (and others in the child's environment), prepare and constrain the type of intellectual experiences to which the child will be exposed. Just as children are not left to their own devices, so parents are not forced to operate in isolation when organizing the intellectual environments of their children. And children contribute to this enterprise by displaying both their nutritional and intellectual states to their parents in ways that are both graphic and vocal.

By analogy to the prepared baby food or to the food-processing devices available to parents, the social distribution of social knowledge in any society provides normative guides for the preparation and distribution of "baby experiences" that will lead to the intellectual growth valued by the culture. It is in these ways and by these cultural practices that all reality can be said to be a social reality. Physical reality is both socially constructed and culturally constrained.

From a cultural-practice point of view, the social nature of a great deal of the child's ordinary interactions with the socially organized world is a central focus. The point we have been making about the social nature of the physical world does not mean that interaction with social objects cannot be distinguished and compared to interaction with social beings. Objects and people are distinguishable by the kinds of interactions they allow. Children will come to master interactions with many objects, but

the nature of those interactions will be shaped by the fact that insofar as they are elements in *human* life, they represent socially tailored objects with habitual patterns of interaction built in. In the case of human artifacts, the patterns are built into their very design. Forms of interaction have to be learned, and this learning occurs in culturally organized contexts.

Social Interaction

In order to explore more deeply the problems facing contemporary theories that seek to integrate social and object domains, we need to contrast the way in which each theory treats the interaction of these two domains. Each theoretical approach—whether its origins lie in central processing or in cultural practice—acknowledges that interaction between social and object domains is central to development; but each differs markedly in its treatment of this difficult topic.

Within psychological differentiation theory, interaction is treated as a hypothetical process intervening between parental and child behavior. For purposes of conducting causal analysis, maternal behaviors, for example, are coded as "stimuli" or antecedent variables and child behaviors as consequences. The nature of the child's contribution to this sequence is basically responsive. B. B. Whiting's (1980) coding scheme adopts a similar strategy, reduced to a subcategory of interactions ("mands") for which it is plausible to assume one can code initiator and responder. In Whiting's work, children's behavior, as well as adults', can be seen in the initiator (stimulus) slot, but *interaction* itself is not represented.

For Piaget, interaction is a more central concept. Because Piaget views the child as an active constructor of its world, he places great emphasis on the idea of *co*operations; that is, operations or mental transformations that are formed in concert with others.

The interdependence of social and cognitive development is evident throughout Piaget's theoretical work (Piaget, 1970, 1971), though he claims it is impossible to draw any causal links between the development of "social logic" and "individual logic." They "constitute inseparable aspects of a single reality" (Piaget, 1968, p. 158).

> In the realm of knowledge, it seems obvious that individual operations of intelligence and operations making for exchange in cognitive cooperations are one and the same thing, the "general conditions of actions" to which we have continually referred being an interindividual as well

as intraindividual coordinator because such ''actions can be collective as well as executed by individuals.'' (Piaget, 1971, p. 360)

Because of this unity, Piagetian research has not focused on the development of *co*operations: they are assumed to follow the same developmental path as operational development. But cross-cultural work has forced on Piagetian scholars the realization that the social interactions within which objects are located have to be studied as constitutive of the operations themselves.[7]

The Interpretation of Experimental Data

Although agreement that the interpretation of psychological test data is especially problematic in cross-cultural research is extremely widespread, views about the nature of the uncertainties involved vary greatly between different positions. At one extreme, theorists believe that problems of stimulus equivalence are susceptible to solution with the standard paradigm of intracultural psychological research (e.g., Berry, 1976; Eckensberger, Lonner, & Poortinga, 1979; and many of the other references listed in our bibliography). At another extreme, investigators believe that several features of the psychological tests used in cross-cultural research render the results totally uninterpretable in terms of people's everyday experiences (Lave, 1980; Wolcott, 1972).

Our own view stems directly from our analysis of the origins of psychological experimentation and our field experience. As discussed in the introductory section of this chapter, cognitive psychological experiments began as models of a very special set of human experiences connected closely with theories of specialized mechanical and electrical technology at the end of the nineteenth century. In search of the basic elements of ideas, which he sought in sensations, Wundt constructed a psychology representing interactions between people and physical stimuli (flashing lights, touches, smells, sounds) that could be rigidly controlled and timed in very brief intervals. The way in which sensations became elementary ideas when combined in consciousness was the activity that Wundt set out to model. As previously mentioned, he despaired of modeling more complex interactions (higher psychological functions) relegating that task to folklore and ethnography.

While varying the nature of the antecedent conditions, psychologists down to the present day have retained Wundt's use of an antecedent/consequence framework as a basic means to enable causal analy-

sis. The linearity of the system, from stimulus to response, was essential, for the causal analysis of feedback systems then, as now, was very weak. Gestalt psychologists rebelled against the narrow definitions of stimulus and response, but like other researchers, maintained the framework.

As a consequence of this early strategic decision, the range of interactions that could serve as a basis for the study of human cognition was severely truncated. In effect, psychologists implemented an ''object/person'' model of a human being's interactions with the world. Among its many virtues, this strategy made analogies between psychology and the physical sciences plausible and set the parameters of the kinds of interactions that could be used to *define* basic psychological processes. With the advent of operationalism in the 1940s, psychologists accepted the notion that the meaning of the terms used in their theories were strongly shaped, if not completely determined, by the procedures that were used to evoke and study them. Consequently, short-term memory *means* the behavior exhibited in one or more of the tasks used to study it; forgetting, rehearsal, clustering, inference, compensation, disembedding, and other processes are defined in analogous ways. It is commonplace to point out that tests of psychological abilities are culture bound. But it is less common to point out that these tests arose as cultural practices of a very specific sort.

Binet understood this point very well when he set out to construct a test of school-related abilities. Schools arose in Western Europe specifically to induct children into cultural practices central to the society of the time, among which must be counted reading the Bible as the means to individual salvation, creating forms of social interaction conducive to work in a society that was making the transition to mass production, and recognizing the need for increasingly sophisticated modes of technology. Binet understood the limited nature of his behavior samples and objected to their use as general tests of behavior even for the society in which they arose. He was quite right, of course; schooling was intended as a limited environment for the inculcation of a limited set of the skills required of competent adulthood.

Unfortunately, just as Binet's work was taken out of his hands and put outside the school to provide a model of competent functioning in general, so psychological experiments were taken as models of cognitive processes in general, as if the special set of interactions they were designed to represent exhausted the universe of basic human/environment interactions. When taken outside of the systems of activity that they are designed to model, the fundamental status of behavior in experiments changes. Psychological experiments then cease to be models of that culturally organized activity and become, instead, indeterminate systems of activity, whose correlation with real world models is difficult to specify.

To summarize, psychologists tend to use tests and experiments as measures of the psychological processes that are their basic units of analysis. We are advocating cultural practices as the basic units of analysis. In this view, experiments are models of systems of activity that vary in their goals, the knowledge base they require, and the skills that must be brought to bear in order to achieve the goal. If they are designed as models of recurring systems of activity identified in the culture as routine practices, they are important instruments for the understanding of how culture affects mind.

As models of recurring systems of activity, they are no more or no less "naturally occurring" situations than religious festivals, cockfights, and initiation ceremonies. In both observational and experimental studies, researchers and subjects of research are reflexively related in ways that dissolve simplistic distinctions between "experimental" and "naturally occurring" situations. The cultural practices of twentieth-century industrialized societies, in particular those practices tied closely to technology, are not uniformly distributed in all cultures. Consequently, the model systems that have been developed in these cultural surroundings cannot be assumed to be models of activity in other cultural settings, although they may be. That is a matter for empirical investigation.

It is these kinds of consideration that have led to our earlier emphasis on a theory of situations as an essential aspect of a theory of culture and cognition. Until we can "locate" the experiment with respect to the cultural practices it is intended to model, we cannot make proper headway on interpreting the results that we obtain (Scribner, 1975).

As a consequence of this position, experimentation takes on a very different role in a cultural-practice theory than it does in the central-processor approaches described earlier, where the environment of experiment or test is a universal measure of process. Ideally, cross-cultural experimentation should begin with an analysis of everyday practices and proceed to the construction of model systems to explore the analyst's interpretation of what he or she is observing. This approach uses tasks found in naturally occurring, everyday situations (e.g., situations not designed to study general psychological processes). A model of the structure of the task is then constructed in terms that map the native informant's conceptions. These cultural practices, if described with sufficient formal rigor, become useful domains for comparative analysis (Hutchins, 1980; Lave, n.d.; Quinn, 1976, 1978).

Less than ideally, standard experiments can be used as a starting point of analysis that leads to a search for cultural practices that contain enough constraints in common with the model system to make a claim that the experiment is a model of indigenous practice. The latter approach was used in the work of Cole and others (1971) and is close in spirit to research strategies recommended by Berry and Dasen (1974).

Examples of cultural practices from other cultures suggest just how far the standard psychological experiment is from routine systems of activity. As discussed at length in Bartlett (1958), Cole and others (1978), Lave (1979, 1980), and Vygotsky (1978), there are many differences to be noted between behavior demanded in experiments and problem-solving contexts of everyday life. This reflects the fact that standard experiments are models of schooling, and only part of schooling at that, so we should not be surprised at the discrepancy. It should put us on our guard, however, because the nonrepresentativeness we have been concerned about in cross-cultural work is an issue in our own society. This point is brought home by the work of D'Andrade (1974), Shweder (1977), and Wason and Johnson-Laird (1972), who demonstrate that the everyday thinking of American adults has many of the properties previously attributed as characteristic of nonliterate peoples. It should be noted, too, that efforts in domestic developmental cognitive work to make experiments more closely model young children's experience of the world greatly increase our estimates of the abilities that children possess (Flavell & Ross, 1981; Gelman, 1978; Shweder, Turiel, & Much, 1981).

The Future of Cross-cultural Studies of Culture and Cognition

Our prognostications follow directly from our framework. There is very little in the way of independent invention in the history of human ideas. Change comes about through interaction, where significant discrepancies between our current theory and reality are thrust upon us, where some more inclusive theory is made salient, and where the environment supports higher order generalizations in limited domains. The study of culture and cognition is a true *inter*discipline. Between the domain of the psychologist and anthropologist, it studies that zone of proximal development where the cultural becomes individual and individuals create their culture. This view is a return to the nineteenth-century belief that mind and culture are different aspects of the same phenomenon, a view only slightly modified by the enormous increase in practice and the many local-level insights chronicled in these pages.

NOTES

1. Tylor acknowledged, but did not build on, the fact that "if not only knowledge and art, but at the same time moral and political excellence be taken into consideration, it becomes more difficult to scale societies from lower to higher stages of culture" (1874, p. 29).

2. In an important sense "cultural diffusion" of ideas in anthropological theory is analogous to the "diffusion" of real world knowledge into the controlled, introspective report of a Titchnerian subject; both were attributed to obscure causal sequences in the theories that dominated the period.

3. According to Boas, foreign material adopted by a culture was "adopted and changed in form according to the genius of the people who borrowed it" (quoted in Stocking, 1968, p. 214).

4. Dasen discusses an important difficulty with the studies of décalage: the effects of cultural variables are not discernible in group statistics that present population frequencies of responses at different ages. Individual longitudinal studies would serve to uncover differences in hierarchical development, but such studies are absent from the cross-cultural literature.

5. These studies serve as examples of the way the general ecocultural model discussed in the previous section uses performance on a particular test as an index of *general* cognitive ability—in this case, perception—and then relates this capacity to *general* aspects of the ecological/social network.

6. A complementary view of the relation between mind and society is found in American pragmatism. The most comprehensive elaboration of the pragmatist theory was developed by G. H. Mead (1934). "The behavior of an individual can be understood only in terms of the whole social group of which he is a member, since his individual social acts are involved in larger, social acts which go beyond himself" (Mead, 1934).

7. Recently a group of Genevan scholars (Doise, Mugny, & Perret-Clermont, 1975; Perret-Clermont, 1980) have been pursuing the implications of this line of thinking.

REFERENCES

Armah, K., & Arnold, M. *Acquisition of conservation in Ghanaian children.* Paper presented at the meeting of the Society for Research in Child Development, New Orleans, 1977.

Barker, R. G. *Ecological psychology: Concepts and methods for studying the environment of human behavior.* Stanford: Stanford University Press, 1968.

Barry, H., Bacon, M., & Child, I. A cross-cultural survey of sex differences and socialization. *Journal of Abnormal Social Psychology,* 1957, *3,* 55.

Barry, H., Child, I., & Bacon, M. Relation of child training to subsistence economy. *American Anthropologist,* 1959, *61,* 51–63.

Bartlett, F. C. *Thinking.* New York: Basic Books, 1958.

Bayley, N. Comparisons of mental and motor test scores for ages 1–15 months by sex, birth order, race, geographic location, and education of parents. *Child Development,* 1965, *36,* 379–411.

Bem, D. J., & Allen, A. On predicting some of the people some of the time. *Psychological Review,* 1974, *81,* 506–520.

Benedict, R. *Patterns of culture.* Boston: Houghton Mifflin, 1934.

Berry, J. W. On cross-cultural comparability. *International Journal of Psychology,* 1969, *4,* 119–128.

Berry, J. W. *Human ecology and cognitive style.* New York: Sage-Halsted, 1976.

Berry, J. W., & Dasen, P. R. (Eds.), *Culture and cognition: Readings in cross-cultural psychology.* London: Methuen, 1974.

Blurton-Jones, N. G., & Konner, M. J. Sex differences in the behavior of Bushman and London two- to five-year-olds. In J. Crook & R. Michael (Eds.), *Comparative ecology and behavior of primates.* New York: Academic Press, 1973.

Boas, F. *The mind of primitive man.* New York: The Macmillan Co., 1911.

Bock, P. K. *Continuities in psychological anthropology.* San Francisco: Freeman, 1980.

Boonsong, S. *The development of conservation of mass, weight and volume in Thai children.* Unpublished master's thesis. Bangkok, College of Education, 1968.

Bovet, M. C. Cognitive processes among illiterate children and adults. In J. W. Berry & P. R. Dasen (Eds.), *Culture and cognition: Readings in cross-cultural psychology.* London: Methuen, 1974.

Bovet, M. C., & Othenin-Girard, C. Etude Piagetienne de quelques notions spatio-temporelles dans un milieu africain. *Journal International de Psychologie,* 1975, *10* (1), 1–17.

Brazelton, T. B., Koslosowski, B., & Main, M. The origins of reciprocity: The early mother-infant interactions. In M. Lewis & L. A. Rosenblum, (Eds.), *The effect of the infant on its caregivers.* New York: Wiley, 1974.

Bruner, J., Olver, R., & Greenfield, P. *Studies in cognitive growth.* New York: Wiley, 1966.

Cantor, N. & Mischel, W. Prototypes in person perception. In *Advances in Experimental Social Psychology,* 1979, *12,* 3–52.

Casati, I., & Lezine, I. *Les étapes de l'intelligence sensori-motrice. Manuel.* Paris: Centre de Psychologie Appliquée, 1968.

Cazden, C. B. Performance before competence: Assistance to child discourse in the zone of proximal development. *The Quarterly Newsletter of the Laboratory of Comparative Human Cognition,* 1981, *3,* 5–8.

Chamberlain, A. F. *The child: A study in the evolution of man.* London: Walter Scott, 1901.

Childs, C. P., & Greenfield, P. M. Informal modes of learning and teaching: The case of Zinacanteco weaving. In N. Warren (Ed.), *Advances in cross-cultural psychology* (Vol. 2). London: Academic Press, 1982.

Cicourel, A. V. *Cognitive sociology: Language and meaning in social interaction.* London: Penguin, 1973.

Cole, M. An ethnographic psychology of cognition. In R. W. Brislin, S. Bochner, & W. J. Lonner (Eds.), *Cross-cultural perspectives on learning.* New York: Halsted Press, 1975.

Cole, M., Gay, J., Glick, J. A., & Sharp, D. W. *The cultural context of learning and thinking.* New York: Basic Books, 1971.

Cole, M., & Griffin, P. Cultural amplifiers reconsidered. In D. Olson (Ed.), *Social foundations of language and thought.* New York: Norton, 1980.

Cole, M., Hood, L., & McDermott, R. P. *Ecological niche picking: Ecological invalidity as an axiom of experimental cognitive psychology.* Unpublished manuscript, University of California, San Diego, & The Rockefeller University, 1978.

Corman, H. H., & Escalona, S. K. Stages of sensorimotor development: A replication study. *Merrill-Palmer Quarterly,* 1969, *15,* 351–362.

Cryns, A. G. J. African intelligence: A critical survey of cross-cultural intelligence research in Africa south of the Sahara. *Journal of Social Psychology,* 1962, *57,* 283–301.

D'Andrade, R. G. Memory and assessment of behavior. In H. M. Blalock, Jr. (Ed.), *Measurement in the social sciences.* Chicago: Aldine, 1974.

Dasen, P. R. *Cognitive development in Aborigines of central Australia: Concrete operations and perceptual activities.* Unpublished doctoral dissertation. Canberra: Australian National University, 1970.

Dasen, P. R. Cross-cultural Piagetian research: A summary. *Journal of Cross-Cultural Psychology,* 1972, *3* (1), 29–39.

Dasen, P. R. The influence of ecology, culture and European contact on cognitive development in Australian Aborigines. In J. W. Berry & P. R. Dasen (Eds.), *Culture and cognition.* London: Methuen, 1974.

Dasen, P. R. (Ed.). *Piagetian psychology: Cross-cultural contributions.* New York: Gardner, 1977.

Dasen, P. R. Psychological differentiation and operational development: A cross-cultural link. *The Quarterly Newsletter of the Laboratory of Comparative Human Cognition,* 1980, *2* (4), 81–86.

Dasen, P. R., Berry, J. W., & Witkin, H. A. The use of developmental theories cross-culturally. In L. Eckensberger, W. Lonner, & Y. H. Poortinga (Eds.), *Cross-cultural contributions to psychology.* The Netherlands: Swets Publishing Service, 1979.

Dasen, P. R., & Heron, A. Cross-cultural tests of Piaget's theory. In H. C. Triandis & A. Heron (Eds.), *Handbook of cross-cultural psychology: Developmental psychology* (Vol. 4). Boston: Allyn & Bacon, 1981.

Dasen, P. R., Inhelder, B., Lavallée, M., & Reschitzki, J. *La naissance de l'intelligence chez l'enfant Baoulé de la Côte d'Ivoire.* Berne: Huber, 1978.

Dasen, P. R., Ngini, L., & Lavallée, M. Cross-cultural training studies of concrete operations. In L. H. Eckensberger, W. J. Lonner, & Y. H. Poortinga (Eds.), *Cross-cultural contributions to psychology.* Amsterdam: Swets & Zeitlinger, 1979.

deLemos, M. M. The development of conservation in Aboriginal children. *International Journal of Psychology,* 1969, *4,* 225–269.

Dempsey, A. D. Time conservation across cultures. *International Journal of Psychology,* 1971, *6,* 115–120.

Doise, W., Mugny, G., & Perret-Clermont, A. Social interaction and the development of cognitive operations. *European Journal of Social Psychology,* 1975, *5,* 367–383.

Eckensberger, L., Lonner, W., & Poortinga, Y. H. (Eds.). *Cross-cultural contributions to psychology*. The Netherlands: Swets & Zeitlinger, 1979.

El'konin, D. B. Toward the problem of stages in the mental development of the child. *Soviet Psychology*, 1972, *10*, 225–251.

Erickson, F., & Schultz, J. When is a context? *The Quarterly Newsletter of the Institute for Comparative Human Development*, 1977, *1*, 5–10.

Fjellman, J. A. S. *The myth of primitive mentality: A study of semantic acquisition and modes of categorization in Akamba children of South Central Kenya*. Doctoral dissertation, Stanford University, 1971.

Flavell, J. H., & Ross, L. (Eds.), *Social cognitive development*. Cambridge: Cambridge University Press, 1981.

Flavell, J. H., & Wohlwill, J. F. Formal and functional aspects of cognitive development. In D. Elkind & J. H. Flavell (Eds.), *Studies in cognitive development*. New York: Oxford University Press, 1969.

Fortes, M. Social and psychological aspects of education in Taleland. In J. Middleton (Ed.), *From child to adult: Studies in the anthropology of education*. New York: Natural History Press, 1970.

Frake, C. O. Plying frames can be dangerous: Some reflections on methodology in cognitive anthropology. *The Quarterly Newsletter of the Institute for Comparative Human Development*, 1977, *1*, 1–7.

Garfinkel, H. *Studies in ethnomethodology*. Englewood Cliffs, N.J.: Prentice-Hall, 1967.

Gay, J. *Red dust on green leaves*. East Glastenburg, Conn.: Inter-Culture Associates, 1973.

Gay, J., & Cole, M. *The new mathematics and an old culture*. New York: Holt, Rinehart & Winston, 1967.

Geber, M. La récherche sur le développment psychomoteur et mental à Kampala. *Compte-rendu de la XII réunion des équipes chargées des études sur la croissance et de développment de l'enfant normal*. Paris: Center Internationale de l'Enfance, 1974.

Geber, M., & Dean, R. F. A. Gesell tests on African children. *Pediatrics*, 1957, *20*, 1055–1065.

Geber, M., & Dean, R. F. A. Psychomotor development in African children: The effects of proved tests. *Bulletin of the World Health Organization*, 1958, *18*, 471–476.

Geertz, C. *The interpretation of cultures*. New York: Basic Books, 1973.

Gelb, I. J. *A study of writing* (Rev. ed.). Chicago: University of Chicago Press, 1963.

Gelman, R. Cognitive development. *Annual Review of Psychology*, 1978, *29*, 297–332.

Gesell, A., & Amatruda, C. S. *Developmental diagnosis* (2nd ed.). New York: Hoeber, 1947.

Gick, M. L., & Holyoak, K. J. Analogical problem solving. *Cognitive Psychology*, 1980, *12*, 306–355.

Glick, J. A. Cognitive development in cross-cultural perspective. In T. D. Horowitz et al. (Eds.), *Review of child development research*. Chicago: University of Chicago Press, 1975.

Goldberg, S. Infant care and growth in urban Zambia. *Human Development*, 1972, *15*, 77–89.

Goodenough, D. R., & Karp, S. A. Field dependence and intellectual functioning. *Journal of Abnormal and Social Psychology*, 1961, *63*, 241–246.

Goodenough, W. Cultural anthropology and linguistics. In D. Hymes (Ed.), *Language in culture and society*. New York: Harper & Row, 1964.

Goodnow, J. J. A test of milieu differences with some of Piaget's tasks. *Psychological Monographs*, 1962, *76*, 36.

Goodnow, J. J. Rules and repertoires, rituals and tricks of the trade: Social and informational aspects to cognitive and representational development. In S. Farnham-Diggory (Ed.), *Information processing in children*. New York: Academic Press, 1969.

Goodnow, J. J., & Bethon, G. Piaget tasks: The effects of schooling and intelligence. *Child Development*, 1966, *37*, 573–582.

Goody, J., & Watt, I. The consequences of literacy. In J. Goody (Ed.), *Literacy in traditional societies*. Cambridge: Cambridge University Press, 1968. (Originally published in *Comparative studies in society and history*, 1963, *5*, 27–68.)

Gould, S. J. *Ontogeny and phylogeny*. Cambridge: Harvard University Press, 1976.

Grantham-McGregor, S. M., & Hawke, W. A. Developmental assessment of Jamaican infants. *Developmental Medicine and Child Neurology*, 1971, *13*, 582–589.

Greenfield, P. M. On culture and conservation. In J. S. Bruner, R. P. Olver, & P. M. Greenfield (Eds.), *Studies in cognitive growth*. New York: Wiley, 1966.

Greenfield, P. M. Oral and written language: The consequences for cognitive development in Africa, the United States, and England. *Language and Speech*, 1972, *15*, 169–178.

Greenfield, P. M. Comparing dimensional categorization in natural and artificial contexts: A developmental study among the Zinacantecos of Mexico. *Journal of Social Psychology,* 1974, *93,* 157–171.

Greenfield, P. M. Cross-cultural research and Piagetian theory: Paradox and progress. In K. F. Riegel & J. A. Meacham (Eds.), *The developing individual in a changing world: Historical and cultural issues* (Vol. 1). Chicago: Aldine, 1976.

Harkness, S., Edwards, C. P., & Super, C. M. *Kohlberg in the bush.* Paper presented at the meeting of the Society for Cross-Cultural Research, East Lansing, Mich., 1977.

Harris, M. *The rise of anthropological theory.* New York: Crowell, 1968.

Havelock, E. A. *The Greek concept of justice: From its shadow in Homer to its substance in Plato.* Cambridge, Mass.: Harvard University Press, 1978.

Heron, A. Concrete operations, 'g' and achievement of Zambian children: A non-verbal approach. *Journal of Cross-Cultural Psychology,* 1971, *2,* 325–336.

Heron, A. Cultural determinants of concrete operational behavior. In J. L. M. Dawson & W. J. Lonner (Eds.), *Readings in cross-cultural psychology.* Hong Kong: Hong Kong University Press, 1974.

Hutchins, E. *Culture and inference.* Cambridge, Mass.: Harvard University Press, 1980.

Inhelder, B., & Piaget, J. *The growth of logical thinking from childhood to adolescence.* New York: Basic Books, 1958.

Irvine, J. Wolof "Magical thinking: Culture and conservation revisited." *Journal of Cross-Cultural Psychology,* 1978, *9.*

Irwin, M., Engle, P. L., Klein, R. E., & Yarbrough, C. Traditionalism and field dependence. *Journal of Cross-Cultural Psychology,* 1976, *7* (4), 463–471.

Irwin, M. H., Schafer, G. N., & Feiden, C. P. Emic and unfamiliar category sorting of Mano farmers and U.S. undergraduates. *Journal of Cross-Cultural Psychology,* 1974, *5,* 407–423.

Jahoda, G. Theoretical and systematic approaches in cross-cultural psychology. In H. C. Triandis & W. W. Lambert (Eds.), *Handbook of cross-cultural psychology* (Vol. 1). Boston: Allyn & Bacon, 1980.

Jensen, A. R. *Bias in mental testing.* New York: Free Press, 1980.

Kamara, A. I. *Cognitive development among school-age Themne children of Sierra Leone.* Doctoral dissertation, University of Illinois, 1971.

Kamara, A. I., & Easley, J. A., Jr. Is the rate of cognitive development uniform across cultures?—A methodological critique with new evidence from Themne children. In P. R. Dasen (Ed.), *Piagetian psychology: Cross-cultural contributions.* New York: Gardner, 1977.

Kardiner, A. *The psychological frontiers of society.* New York: Columbia University Press, 1945.

Kearins, J. M. *Visual spatial memory in Australian Aboriginal children of desert regions. Cognitive Psychology,* 1981, *3* (4), 434–460.

Kelly, M. Papua New Guinea and Piaget—An eight-year study. In P. R. Dasen (Ed.), *Piagetian psychology: Cross-cultural contributions.* New York: Gardner, 1977.

Kilbride, J. E., & Kilbride, P. L. Sitting and smiling behavior of Baganda infants: The influence of culturally constituted experiences. *Journal of Cross-cultural Psychology,* 1975, *6,* 88–106.

Kiminyo, D. M. A cross-cultural study of the development of conservation of mass, weight, and volume among Kamba children. In P. R. Dasen (Ed.), *Piagetian psychology: Cross-cultural contributions.* New York: Gardner, 1977.

Kirk, L. Maternal and subcultural correlates of cognitive growth rate: The Ga pattern. In P. R. Dasen (Ed.), *Piagetian psychology: Cross-cultural contributions.* New York: Gardner, 1977.

Kirk, L., & Burton, M. Meaning and context: A study of contextual shifts in meaning of Maasai personality descriptors. *American Ethnologist,* 1977, *4* (4), 734–761.

Kopp, C. B., Khokha, E., & Sigman, M. A comparison of sensory-motor development among infants in India and the United States. *Journal of Cross-Cultural Psychology,* 1977, *8,* 435–452.

Kulah, A. A. *The organization and learning of proverbs among the Kpelle of Liberia.* Unpublished doctoral dissertation, University of California, Irvine, 1973.

Laboratory of Comparative Human Cognition. Cognition as a residual category in anthropology. *Annual Review of Anthropology,* 1978, *7,* 51–69.

Laboratory of Comparative Human Cognition. What's cultural about cross-cultural cognitive psychology? *Annual Review of Psychology,* 1979, *30,* 145–172.

Laboratory of Comparative Human Cognition. Culture and intelligence. In R. Sternberg (Ed.), *Handbook of human intelligence.* New York: Cambridge University Press, in press.

Lancy, D. F. Studies of memory in culture. *Annals of the New York Academy of Science,* 1977, *307,* 285–297.

Lantz, D. A cross-cultural comparison of communication abilities: Some effects of age, schooling and culture. *International Journal of Psychology,* 1979, *14,* 171–183.

Laurendeau-Bendavid, M. Culture, schooling, and cognitive development: A comparative study of children in French Canada and Rwanda. In P. R. Dasen (Ed.), *Piagetian psychology: Cross-cultural contributions.* New York: Gardner, 1977.

Lave, J. *A model of everyday problem solving.* Talk presented to an SSRC Committee on Cognition symposium. La Jolla, Calif., August 1979.

Lave, J. What's special about experiments as contexts for thinking. *The Quarterly Newsletter of the Laboratory of Comparative Human Cognition,* 1980, *2* (4), 86–91.

Lave, J. *Apprenticeship and a cultural theory of learning.* Unpublished manuscript, University of California, Irvine.

Lee, R. B., & DeVore, I. (Eds.). *Kalahari hunter-gatherers.* Cambridge, Mass.: Harvard University Press, 1976.

Leiderman, P. H., Tulkin, S. R., & Rosenfeld, A. (Eds.). *Culture and infancy: Variations in the human experience.* New York: Academic Press, 1977.

Leont'ev, A. N. *Activity, consciousness, and personality.* Englewood Cliffs, N.J.: Prentice-Hall, 1978.

Leont'ev, A. N. The problem of activity in psychology. In J. V. Wertsch (Ed.), *The concept of activity in Soviet psychology.* White Plains, N.Y.: Sharpe, 1981.

LeVine, R. A. Cross-cultural study in child psychology. In P. H. Mussen (Ed.), *Carmichael's Manual of Child Psychology* (3rd ed.) (Vol. 2). New York: Wiley, 1970.

LeVine, R. A. *Culture, behavior, and personality.* Chicago: Aldine, 1973.

LeVine, R. A. Parental goals: A cross-cultural view. In H. J. Leichter (Ed.), *The family as educator.* New York: Teachers College Press, 1974.

Luria, A. R. *Cognitive development.* Cambridge, Mass.: Harvard University Press, 1976.

MacArthur, R. S. Some ability patterns: Central Eskimos and Nsenga Africans. *International Journal of Psychology,* 1973, *8,* 239–247.

Malinowski, B. *The father in primitive psychology.* New York: Norton, 1927.

McDermott, R. P., & Roth, D. R. The social organization of behavior: Interactional approaches. *Annual Review of Anthropology,* 1978, *7,* 321–345.

McElwain, D. W., & Kearney, G. E. Intellectual development. In G. E. Kearney, P. R. deLacey, & G. R. Davidson (Eds.), *The psychology of Aboriginal Australians.* Sydney: Wiley, 1973.

McFie, J. The effect of education on African performance on a group of intellectual tests. *British Journal of Educational Psychology,* 1961, *31,* 232–240.

McLuhan, M. *The Gutenberg galaxy.* Toronto: University of Toronto Press, 1962.

Mead, G. H. *Mind, self, and society.* Chicago: University of Chicago Press, 1934.

Mead, G. H. *The philosophy of the present.* Chicago: Open Court Press, 1954.

Mead, M. *Continuities and discontinuities in cultural evolution.* New Haven: Yale University Press, 1958.

Mehan, H., & Griffin, P. Socialization: A view from classroom interaction. *Sociological Inquiry,* 1980, *50* (3–4), 357–392.

Mosheni, N. *La comparaison des réactions aux épreuves d'intelligence en Iran et en Europe.* Unpublished thesis, University of Paris, 1966.

Munroe, R. H., Munroe, R. L., & Whiting, B. B. (Eds.) *Handbook of cross-cultural human development.* New York: Garland STPM Press, 1981.

Neimark, E. D. Intellectual development during adolescence. In F. D. Horowitz (Ed.), *Review of child development research* (Vol. 4). Chicago: University of Chicago Press, 1975.

Nisbett, R., & Ross, L. *Human inference: Strategies and shortcomings of social judgement.* Englewood Cliffs, N.J.: Prentice-Hall, 1980.

Nyiti, R. M. *A study of conservation among Meru children of Tanzania.* Doctoral dissertation, University of Illinois, 1973.

Nyiti, R. M. The development of conservation in the Meru children of Tanzania. *Child Development,* 1976, *47,* 1122–1129.

Okonji, M. O. The differential effects of rural and urban upbringing on the development of cognitive styles. *International Journal of Psychology,* 1969, *4,* 293–305.

Olson, D. R. From utterance to text: The bias of language in speech and writing. *Harvard Educational Review,* 1977, *47,* 257–281.

Opper, S. Concept development in Thai urban and rural children. In P. R. Dasen (Ed.), *Piagetian psychology: Cross-cultural contributions.* New York: Gardner, 1977.

Otaala, B. *The development of operational thinking in primary school children: An examination of some aspects of Piaget's theory among the Itseo children of Uganda.* Doctoral dissertation, Teacher's College, Columbia University, 1971.

Peluffo, N. Culture and cognitive problems. *International Journal of Psychology*, 1967, *2* (3), 187–198.

Perret-Clermont, A. N. *Social interaction and cognitive development in children* (European Monographs in Social Psychology, H. Tajfel, Ed.). New York: Academic Press, 1980.

Piaget, J. *The language and thought of the child.* New York: World, 1955.

Piaget, J. *The origins of intelligence in children.* New York: Norton, 1963.

Piaget, J. Nécessité et signification des recherches comparatives en psychologie génétique. *Journal International de Psychologie*, 1966, *1*, 3–13.

Piaget, J. *Six psychological studies.* New York: Vintage, 1968.

Piaget, J. Piaget's theory. In P. H. Mussen (Ed.), *Carmichael's manual of child psychology* (3rd ed.). New York: Wiley, 1970.

Piaget, J. *Le structuralisme* (Que sais-je?). Paris: Presses universitaries de France, 1971.

Piaget, J. Intellectual evolution from adolescence to adulthood. *Human Development*, 1972, *15*, 1–12.

Piaget, J. *The psychology of intelligence.* Totowa, N.J.: Littlefield & Adams, 1973.

Piaget, J. Need and significance of cross-cultural studies in genetic psychology. In J. W. Berry & P. R. Dasen (Eds.), *Culture and cognition: Readings in cross-cultural psychology.* London: Methuen, 1974.

Piaget, J. *The development of thought: Equilibration of cognitive structures.* New York: Viking, 1977.

Pinard, A., Morin, C., & Lefebvre, M. Apprentissage de la conservation des quantités liquides chez des enfants Rwandais et Canadiens-Français. *Journal International de Psychologie*, 1973, *8* (1), 15–24.

Price-Williams, D. R. Abstract and concrete modes of classification in a primitive society. *British Journal of Educational Psychology*, 1962, *32*, 50–61.

Price-Williams, D. R. Concrete and formal operations. In R. H. Munroe, R. L. Munroe, & B. B. Whiting (Eds.), *Handbook of cross-cultural human development.* New York: Garland STPM Press, 1981.

Prince, J. R. The effect of Western education on science conceptualization in New Guinea. *British Journal of Educational Psychology*, 1968, *38*, 64–74.

Prince, J. R. *Science concepts in a Pacific culture.* Sydney: Angus & Robertson, 1969.

Quinn, N. A natural system used in infants litigation settlement. *American Ethnologist*, 1976, *3*, 331–361.

Quinn, N. Do Mfantse fish sellers estimate probabilities in their heads? *American Ethnologist*, 1978, *5*, 206–226.

Raum, O. F. *Chaga childhood.* London: Oxford University Press, 1940.

Reed, S. K., Ernst, G. W., & Banerji, R. The role of analogy in transfer between similar states. *Cognitive Psychology*, 1974, *6*, 436–450.

Rogoff, B. Spot observation: An introduction and examination. *The Quarterly Newsletter of the Institute for Comparative Human Development*, 1978, *2* (2), 1–25.

Rogoff, B. Schooling and the development of cognitive skills. In H. C. Triandis & A. Heron (Eds.), *Handbook of cross-cultural psychology* (Vol. 4). Boston: Allyn & Bacon, 1981.

Rogoff, B., & Waddell, K. J. *Memory for an organized scene: A cross-cultural comparison.* Paper presented at the meeting of the Western Psychological Association, Honolulu, 1980.

Sahlins, M. D., & Service, E. R. (Eds.). *Evolution and culture.* Ann Arbor: University of Michigan Press, 1960.

Saxe, G. B. A comparative analysis of the acquisition of numeration: Studies from Papua New Guinea. *The Quarterly Newsletter of the Laboratory of Comparative Human Cognition*, 1979, *1* (3), 37–43.

Schank, R. C., & Abelson, R. P. *Scripts, plans, goals, and understanding: An inquiry into human knowledge structures.* Hillsdale, N.J.: Erlbaum, 1977.

Schmandt-Besserat, D. The earliest precursor of writing. *Scientific American*, 1978, *238* (6), 50–59.

Schutz, A. *Collected papers: The problem of social reality* (Vol. 1). The Hague: Martinus Nijoff, 1962.

Scribner, S. Recall of classical syllogisms: A cross-cultural investigation of error on logical problems. In R. Falmagne (Ed.), *Reasoning: Representation and process.* Hillsdale, N.J.: Erlbaum, 1975.

Scribner, S. *Cultural practice and cognitive skills.* Paper presented at the meeting of the American Anthropological Association, Houston, 1977.

Scribner, S., & Cole, M. Cognitive consequences of formal and informal education. *Science*, 1973, *182*, 553–559.

Scribner, S., & Cole, M. Literacy without schooling: Testing for intellectual effects. *Harvard Ed-*

ucational Review, 1978, *48*, (4), 448–461.

Scribner, S., & Cole, M. *The consequences of literacy*. Cambridge, Mass.: Harvard University Press, 1981.

Serpell, R. The influence of language, education and culture on attentional preference between colour and form. *International Journal of Psychology*, 1969, *4*, 183–194.

Serpell, R. *Culture's influence on behaviour*. London: Methuen, 1976.

Serpell, R. How specific are perceptual skills? A cross-cultural study of pattern reproduction. *British Journal of Psychology*, 1979, *70*, 365–380.

Sharp, D. W., Cole, M., & Lave, C. Education and cognitive development: The evidence from experimental research. *Monographs of the Society for Research in Child Development*, 1979, *44* (Serial No. 178), 1–2.

Shweder, R. A. Likeness and likelihood in everyday thought: Magical thinking in judgments about personality. *Current Anthropology*, 1977, *18*, 637–648. (Reprinted in P. N. Johnson-Laird & P. C. Wason (Eds.), *Thinking: Readings in cognitive science*. London: Cambridge University Press, 1978.)

Shweder, R. A. Rethinking culture and personality theory: A critical examination of two classical postulates (Part 1). *Ethos*, 1979, *7*, 255–278. (a)

Shweder, R. A. Rethinking culture and personality theory: A critical examination of two classical postulates (Part 2). *Ethos*, 1979, *7*, 279–311. (b)

Shweder, R. A. Rethinking culture and personality theory: From genesis and typology to hermeneutics and dynamics (Part 3). *Ethos*, 1980, *8*, 60–94.

Shweder, R. A., Turiel, E., & Much, N. C. The moral intuitions of the child. In J. H. Flavell & L. Ross (Eds.), *Social cognitive development*. Cambridge: Cambridge University Press, 1981.

Siann, G. Measuring field dependence in Zambia. *International Journal of Psychology*, 1972, *7*, 87–96.

Spencer, H. *First principles*. New York: Appleton, 1864.

Spencer, H. *The principles of psychology* (Vol. 5). New York: Appleton, 1886.

Stefflre, V. J. Simulation of people's behavior toward new objects and events. *American Behavioral Scientist*, 1965, *8* (9), 12–15.

Stocking, G. *Race, culture and evolution*. New York: Free Press, 1968.

Strauss, S., Ankori, M., Orpaz, N., & Stavy, R. Schooling effects on the development of propor-

tional reasoning. In Y. H. Poortinga (Ed.), *Basic problems in cross-cultural psychology*. Amsterdam: Swets & Seitlinger, 1977.

Super, C. M. Environmental effects on motor development: The case of African infant precocity. *Developmental Medicine and Child Neurology*, 1976, *18* (5), 561–567.

Super, C. M. Behavioral development in infancy. In R. H. Munroe, R. L. Munroe, & B. B. Whiting (Eds.), *Handbook of cross-cultural human development*. New York: Garland STPM Press, 1981.

Super, C. M., & Harkness, S. The infants' niche in rural Kenya and metropolitan America. In L. L. Adler (Ed.), *Issues in cross-cultural research*. New York: Academic Press, 1980.

Super, C. M., Harkness, S., & Baldwin, L. M. Category behavior in natural ecologies and in cognitive tests. *The Quarterly Newsletter of the Institute for Comparative Human Development*, 1977, *1*, 4–7.

Triandis, H. C., & Lambert, W. W. (Eds.), *Handbook of cross-cultural psychology* (Vol. 1). Boston: Allyn & Bacon, 1980.

Tulviste, P. On the origins of theoretic syllogistic reasoning in culture and the child. *The Quarterly Newsletter of the Laboratory of Comparative Human Cognition*, 1979, *1* (4), 73–80.

Tylor, E. B. *Primitive culture*. London: Murray, 1874.

Tylor, E. B. *The origins of culture*. New York: Harper, 1958.

Uzgiris, I., & Hunt, J. M. Assessment in infancy. *Ordinal scales of psychological development*. Urbana: University of Illinois Press, 1975.

Vernon, P. E. *Intelligence and cultural environment*. London: Methuen, 1969.

Voloshinov, V. N. *Marxism and the philosophy of language*. New York: Academic Press, 1973.

Vygotsky, L. S. *Sobranie Psikhologichescii Issledovanie (Selected psychological investigations)*. Moscow: Akad Ped Nauk RSFSR, 1956.

Vygotsky, L. S. *Thought and language*. Cambridge, Mass.: MIT Press, 1962.

Vygotsky, L. S. *Mind in society: The development of higher psychological processes* (M. Cole, V. John-Steiner, S. Scribner, & E. Souberman, Eds.). Cambridge, Mass.: Harvard University Press, 1978.

Wagner, D. A. The effects of formal schooling on cognitive style. *Journal of Social Psychology*, 1978, *106*, 145–151.

Wason, P. C., & Johnson-Laird, P. N. *Psychology of reasoning: Structure and content*. London:

Batsford, 1972.

Werner, E. E. *Cross-cultural child development.* Monterey, Calif.: Brooks/Cole, 1979.

Werner, H. *Comparative psychology of mental development.* New York: Science Editions, 1948.

Wertsch, J. V. Adult-child interaction and the roots of metacognition. *The Quarterly Newsletter of the Institute for Comparative Human Development,* 1978, *2,* 15–18.

Wertsch, J. V. *A state of the art review of Soviet research in cognitive psychology.* Manuscript, Department of Linguistics, Northwestern University, 1979.

Wertsch, J. V. The significance of dialogue in Vygotsky's account of social, egocentric and inner speech. *Contemporary educational psychology,* 1980, *5,* 150–162.

Wertsch, J. V. *Adult-child interaction as a source of self-regulation in children.* Paper presented at conference entitled "The Growth of Insight during Childhood." University of Wisconsin-Madison, October 1979. (Revised version to appear in S. Yussen (Ed.), *The growth of insight during childhood.* New York: Academic Press, in press.

Wertsch, J., McNamee, G. D., McLane, J. B., & Budwig, N. A., The adult-child dyad as a problem solving system. *Child Development,* 1980, *51,* 1215–1221.

White, L., *The science of culture.* New York: Wiley, 1949.

Whiting, B. B. Culture and social behavior: A model for the development of social behavior, *Ethos,* 1980, *8,* 95–116.

Whiting, B. B., Whiting, J. W. M. *Children of six cultures: A psychocultural analysis.* Cambridge, Mass.: Harvard University Press, 1975.

Whorf, B. L. *Language, thought and reality.* New York: Wiley, 1956.

Witkin, H. A., & Berry, J. W. Psychological differentiation in cross-cultural perspective. *Journal of Cross-Cultural Psychology,* 1975, *6* (1).

Witkin, H. A., Dyk, R. B., Faterson, H. F., Goodenough, D. R., & Karp, S. A. *Psychological differentiation.* New York: Wiley, 1962.

Wober, M. Sensotypes. *Journal of Social Psychology,* 1966, *70,* 181–189.

Wober, M. *Psychology in Africa.* London: International African Institute, 1975.

Wolcott, H. Cognitive development of primitive peoples: A review of Cole et al. *The cultural context of learning and thinking. Phi Beta Kappan,* 1972.

Zaporozhets, A. V. Thought and activity in children. *Soviet Psychology,* 1980, *18* (2), 9–23.

Za'rour, G. I., & Khuri, G. A. The development of the concept of speed by Jordanian school children in Amman. In P. R. Dasen (Ed.), *Piagetian psychology: Cross-cultural contributions.* New York: Gardner, 1977.

THE EVOLUTION OF ENVIRONMENTAL MODELS IN DEVELOPMENTAL RESEARCH* 8

URIE BRONFENBRENNER, *Cornell University***
ANN C. CROUTER, *Pennsylvania State University*

CHAPTER CONTENTS

*In preparing the final version of this chapter, we have profited immeasurably from the thoughtful and thorough review of the penultimate draft by the editor of this volume, Professor William Kessen of Yale University. This final version reflects not only his editorial skill but, to an even greater degree, his scientific insight, wisdom, and comprehensive knowledge of the field. We are also indebted to the following colleagues who reviewed earlier drafts of the manuscript and contributed useful criticisms and suggestions: Jay Belsky, Glen Elder, Jacqueline Goodnow, Melvin Kohn, Phil Schoggen, Robert R. Sears, and Sheldon White. Finally, the authors express their deep appreciation to Gerri Jones who provided invaluable assistance in bibliographical research and in the preparation of innumerable revisions of the manuscript.

**The work of the senior author on this chapter was completed while he was on sabbatic leave, and was supported in part by grants from the W. T. Grant Foundation and the Russell Sage Foundation.

PURPOSE, PROCEDURE, AND PREVIEW

The title of this chapter is at once accurate and misleading. The text is indeed devoted in its entirety to the analysis of research designs in studies of human development. But the reader who expects a methodological treatise on such topics as techniques of data collection, sampling design, or statistical models will have to look elsewhere, for the analysis that we have undertaken focuses wholly on the implications of research design for theory and substance. Specifically, our aim is to trace the evolution, over a period of more than a century, of the scientific paradigms used in systematic research on human development. In particular, we are interested in analyzing the changing conceptions, across time, of the relation between a growing human organism and its environment.

Stated in these terms, the proposed task may appear quite straightforward: carrying out, for the field of developmental psychology, a historical analysis of what Kuhn (1962) has called "paradigm shifts"; that is, new theoretical ideas that lead to the recognition of previously unrecognized domains of investigation requiring new types of research design. Were this alone the scope of inquiry, this chapter would have been much shorter, and less interesting. What made our task challenging, and potentially more rewarding for science, was a broadening of Kuhn's concept of paradigm. His usage of the term is clearly limited to explicit theoretical formulations. We presume to expand the construct to include implicit schemata as well. Our reason for doing so was the expectation—put to the test in the following pages—that many important advances in analyzing the relation between environment and development are made not directly through conceptual redefinition but indirectly by introducing additional distinctions and elaborations into the research design. Such "latent paradigm shifts" become apparent only when one analyzes the operational definitions employed by developmental researchers. Our task, then, is to trace how the construct of environment, and its possible relation to development, has been operationalized over time, and how these successive operationalizations have functioned to delimit or expand the scope of the knowledge acquired.

The reader will note a significant omission in the above statement of purpose. We might also have undertaken to trace the evolution of scientific conceptions of the developing person. This omission was deliberate. Although the analysis would have been fascinating and scientifically worthwhile, the wealth of relevant material would have more than doubled an already overwhelming task. Our choice to focus on changing scientific conceptions of the environment rather than of the person was prompted by the comparative lack of attention given to the former construct by developmental researchers. For an elaboration of this point, see Bronfenbrenner (1979).

It is our hope and belief that an analysis of this kind will have some scientific utility in two respects. First, it may contribute to achieving a more comprehensive view of the evolution and present state of research on development-in-context. Second, by identifying the strengths, gaps, or blind alleys in contemporary research trajectories, the analysis may point to promising pathways (or likely pitfalls) for future investigations. In short, to draw an unorthodox inference from Freud, we trust that, in science as in the psyche, making the latent manifest will lead both to more effective control and to the liberation of previously unrecognized creative potential.

Criteria and Resources

In order to search the literature for relevant material, we had to formulate working definitions of four terms central to our concern: *systematic research, human development, environment,* and *research model* (including its emergence in a new form). All of these formulations had to be sufficiently broad to encompass a wide range of possible operationalizations.

1. *Systematic research* refers to a procedure involving the collection of data that could violate the expectations of the investigator in so salient a fashion as to make it difficult to disregard contradictory evidence. In keeping with this general criterion we stipulate two, more specific requirements:

a. To qualify, the investigation must go beyond the analysis of single cases to seek generalizable findings across individuals or groups.

b. Recognition must be given to the issue of sampling, both in terms of representativeness and as a source of random error.

2. *Human development* involves a change during the life course in enduring patterns of behavior or perception resulting from the interplay between the evolving biological characteristics of the person and features of the environment in which that person lives.

3. *Environment* encompasses any event or condition outside the organism that is presumed to influence, or be influenced by, the person's development.

4. A *research model* refers to the conceptualization of the environment, and its role in development, that is explicit or implicit in the operational definitions employed by the investigator. Any change in the domains encompassed by the environment, or in the relation of these domains to the developing person, or to each other, defines a different research model.

Although the application of these four criteria considerably reduced the range of eligible studies, we were still confronted with a mountain of material to review. To make manageable the task of selection, and to minimize the awesome responsibility for choice, we decided to rely initially on compendia compiled by others—the definitive histories and handbooks in the field. In looking at the former, we discovered a curious and, for us, disappointing fact—the treatment given to our subject matter was minimal at best. Insofar as we have been able to determine, no comprehensive account has been written of the growth of knowledge about human development. There are, of course, histories of theories and theorists of childhood from James Mark Baldwin (Cairns, 1980) to Jean Piaget (Boden, 1980; Ginsburg & Opper, 1979; Rothman, 1977; Vuyk, 1981a, 1981b). There are also comprehensive histories of childhood itself (Ariès, 1962; Bremner, 1974). But, in contrast to other branches of psychology—notably experimental—there has been no systematic historical account of the accumulation of empirically based knowledge in this field.[1]

In the absence of guidance from secondary sources, we were faced with the overwhelming prospect of searching for early studies on our own. Fortunately, we had a solid starting point in Wayne Dennis's collection of historical readings in developmental psychology (1972). The studies reprinted in this volume conveniently extend into the 1930s

and 1940s, when "the great Handbooks," to use Sears's term (1975), take over. These manuals then became our primary source. We examined the two original volumes edited by Murchison (1931, 1933), two by Carmichael (1946, 1954), one by Goslin (1969), and two by Mussen (1960, 1970), the last consisting of two weighty tomes. Luckily we were spared the task of working through the four volumes of the present edition, but there were five others available in the series of *Reviews of Child Development Research* (Caldwell & Ricciuti, 1973; Hetherington, 1975; Hoffman & Hoffman, 1964, 1966; Horowitz, 1975). The first, edited by Hoffman and Hoffman, appeared in 1964; the last one we surveyed was number 5 (Hetherington, 1975), but there are two more already in process. Our heart goes out to our successors.

To find relevant recent studies, we searched through abstracts and circularized a request to colleagues in the field. Finally, for dessert, we turned to lighter fare and sampled successive editions of two widely used textbooks in developmental psychology. The first by Mussen and Conger (later joined by Kagan) ran to six editions between 1956 and 1979. The second covered an even longer time span. Hurlock's *Child Development* first appeared in 1942. The most recent lineal descendent of the same volume was published in 1980 under the title *Developmental Psychology: A Life-Span Approach*. Hurlock has produced a revised text about every 4 years during almost half a century, surely something of a record.

Our procedure was to scan these materials and take note of any study that appeared to meet our criteria. We then consulted the original source and pursued any additional relevant references cited therein. Such a procedure is, of course, subject to a variety of sampling biases of an undetermined and probably undeterminable nature. Nevertheless, we felt we learned something from our labors that merited the attention of workers in the field. The reader alone can make the final judgment.

Overview and Organization

By way of general orientation, it may be useful to summarize our findings in their broadest perspective. Our analysis revealed three successive stages in the evolution of models for research on development-in-context, with each stage building upon the preceding. The earliest period, dating from about 1870 to 1930, was also the longest. It was characterized by the emergence of paradigms, both implicit and explicit, that are essentially descriptive, involving the comparison of developmental outcomes between persons, mainly children, raised in different locations as defined either by geography or social background. The early 1930s brought a sudden and revolutionary change manifested by the application in research designs of explicit theories of developmental processes constructed by such famed paradigm makers as Freud, Piaget, Lewin, Hull, Vygotsky, and others.

An unexpected feature of this middle phase was the long interval between the exposition of a new theoretical paradigm and its actual application in research. We will consider factors that may account for this lengthy "refractory period."

Toward the end of this second stage, the dynamic process models were combined with earlier structural paradigms. The resulting fusion, in turn, gave rise to a new scientific trajectory, beginning in the early 1960s and perhaps best characterized as the evolution of *latent structures*. These were revealed in progressively more complex operational definitions of environmental domains and their relation to the developing person and to each other. Taken together, these latent structures constitute a redefinition of the environment as a context for human development. In place of a series of theoretically and functionally disconnected variables (e.g., class, ethnicity, family structure, socialization processes, etc.), the environment becomes conceived, at least implicitly, as a series of interdependent systems. Some of these systems contain the developing person and directly influence, and are influenced by, that person's perceptions, behavior, and development. Other systems are more remote, but no less powerful in their ultimate effect on developmental processes and outcomes. Historically, we are still in the midst of this most recent phase, which involves the evolution of latent structures that coalesce into implicit research paradigms. Finally, these interdependent systems are treated as changing and evolving over time, so that not only the person, but also the context, undergoes a course of development. The aim of the present analysis is to make the hidden models explicit, but to do so we must first trace their origin in earlier stages.

EARLY PARADIGMS

The first studies we have been able to find that satisfied our four criteria did not appear until the 1870s. Interestingly enough, they encompass two of the major conceptions of developmentally relevant aspects of the environment that still prevail today.

The first study is the report of a survey, conducted by the Pedagogical Society of Berlin (Schwabe & Bartholomai, 1870), on children's knowledge of concepts on entering school. The work originally appeared in the yearbook for the city of Berlin, and was published in an English translation 30 years later in the annual report of the U.S. Commissioner of Education published in 1902. A passage describing the purpose of the inquiry has a curiously modern ring:

> It is an undeniable fact that the average individuality of the child in a metropolis, hence also in Berlin, is a different one, in consequence of the influence of his surroundings, from that of a child living in a rural district or in a small town. It is also a fact that the conditions of the various parts of the city exercise different influences upon the individuality of children, in consequence of which the mental receptivity of children of different wards show a noticeable inequality. (U.S. Commissioner of Education, 1902, p. 710)

Although the survey sample was gratifyingly large, over 1,000 children, the method of administration, the content of the questions, and, especially, the scope of the findings left much to be desired from a contemporary scientific perspective. The children were asked to answer questions orally in groups of ten. The questions themselves dealt primarily with facts of nature and geography and were phrased in rather abstract terms; for example, the children were asked, "How many have an idea [*Begriff*] of a birch, oak, or pine tree standing in the woods?" The concepts inquired about included supposedly familiar locations in the city, numbers, fairy-tale characters, as well as God, Christ, and Biblical stories. At the end of the survey, the children were asked how many had attended a concert, could sing a song, or recite a memorized poem.

Curiously enough, the reported results have nothing to do with the opening statement of the scope of the study. The assertion that "conditions of the various parts of the city exercise different influences upon the knowledge of children" had not been based on empirical findings, but appeared in a circular letter sent to teachers to induce their cooperation in the research. No analyses bearing on this issue are reported in the 13 tables summarizing survey results, perhaps because the members of the Society were overwhelmed by their two major findings. The first had to do with marked sex differences, and the second with even more pronounced variations between children who had entered school directly from home versus those who had had prior experience in a kindergarten or daycare center. To quote the authors of the report:

> From the foregoing table, we see that by far the greater number of ideas . . . were found more frequently in boys than in girls. Greater even than that is the difference between children coming directly from home and those coming from the kindergarten. The latter have a much greater wealth of ideas then the former. The difference is less marked between children coming directly from home than those having been kept in crèches [*Bewahranstalten*]. It is plain, therefore, that the school must assume an attitude with reference to boys different from that assumed toward girls; likewise different attitudes as regards home children, kindergarten children, and children from crèches. (p. 718)[2]

With respect to sex differences, there were a few areas in which the girls surpassed the boys in a pattern that was to become familiar in the decades to follow; females recognized more of the concepts having to do with home and family. According to the authors, this finding reflects

> the more introspective life of the girls . . . in contrast to the life of boys, which is directed, even in early childhood, toward the outside world. . . . That the concepts of thunderstorm and its attendant phenomena should be more lasting in girls than in boys shows that the girls have a greater disposition to fear and apprehension. (p. 720)

The members of the Society were particularly impressed by the greater number of responses produced by children with preschool experience. This contrast prompted a strong policy recommendation, uttered with some conviction in 1870, that speaks provocatively to issues of preschool intervention arising a century later.

> The greater wealth of ideas among children coming from the crèches (*Bewahranstalten*), and the still greater wealth among children coming from the kindergarten as compared with those who have attended neither of these institutions, is so striking that the decision as to whether kindergarten for the prescholastic age is desirable or not cannot remain doubtful for a single moment. (p. 720)

The Social Address Model

Turning from issues of public policy to our basic scientific concern, we may now ask our key question: "What is the model of the environment, and its relation to the development of the child, that is explicit or implied in this pioneering investigation?" The stated purpose of the inquiry, although never fulfilled, provided (one presumes) an answer to this query—the geographic location in which a child lives (country vs. city, neighborhood vs. neighborhood in the city) was thought to produce differing degrees and types of knowledge about the natural environment. In addition, the actual findings of the study prompted the investigators to add other elements to their model. Thus considerable importance was attributed to the exposure of children to supervised preschool settings. And perhaps surprising in an era dominated by the biological determinism of Darwin (albeit less so in Germany), sex differences were explained as a function of the differential treatment of boys and girls within the school setting. It is noteworthy that no reference was made to an analogous possibility in the sphere of parental upbringing. As we will see, it would take half a century before the family came to be seen as the primary environmental influence on children's development. And even within the educational context, the Berlin researchers made no provision for obtaining information about the actual experience of children in preschool or school settings.

We are now in a position to formulate the first and most primitive paradigm employed for investigating development-in-context; it can be described as *the comparison of children living at different social addresses*. As our investigation reveals, this paradigm becomes a pervasive and enduring design in research on human development. Although the social addresses become more sophisticated, this century-old model continues to characterize the majority of investigations being conducted today. For this reason, it is important to take note of three distinctive and delimiting properties of the paradigm. First, the model may be characterized as child centered, in the sense that no one else's behavior is being examined except the child's. Second, the model is unidirectional, since the child is seen as a passive recipient and product of environmental influences. Third, no explicit consideration is given in research operations to intervening structures or processes through which the environment might affect the course of development. One looks only at the *social address*—that is, the environmental label—with no attention to what the environment is like, what people are living there, what they are doing, or how the activities taking place could affect the child. In Lewin's terms (1935), the model is class-theoretical rather than field-theoretical; observed differences in children from one or another setting are "explained" simply as attributes of children in a given context.

Galton's Nature/Nurture Model

The comparison of children living at different social addresses was not the only model for research on development-in-context to emerge in the 1870s. A rather contrasting conception of the environment was implied in Galton's classic study, published during the same period, on "The History of Twins as a Criterion of the Relative Power of Nature and Nurture" (1876). In his report, Galton proposed and applied what he called "a new method" for unraveling the effects of heredity and environment. It involved the comparison of two groups of twins: those who were perceived by family and close acquaintances as having been much alike in childhood versus those who were described as rather dissimilar during the same early period. The relative impact of nature versus nurture could then be assessed, Galton argued, by inquiring as to whether over the years the twins in each of the two groups became more similar or less similar. Although Galton was aware that some twins were born from the same ovum and others from two different ova (p. 392), at the time no reliable technique existed for differentiating monozygotic and dizygotic twins. Hence Galton's strategy represents an ingenious approximation of this distinction made on the basis of the twins' external appearance and behavior.

Galton's examination of data on 55 cases that he studied intensively brought him to a conclusion that "was very distinct, and not at all what I had expected" (1876, p. 401). He found that the degree of reported similarity between twins showed very little variation throughout life despite exposure to very different conditions. The few instances in which marked departures occurred could be ascribed, Galton felt, almost entirely to some form of illness. Galton's conclusion: "The impression that all this evidence leaves on the mind is one of some wonder whether nurture could do anything at all, beyond giving instruction and professional training" (p. 404). It should be noted, however, that in at least one instance Galton qualified his generalization by a critical caveat: "There is no escape from the conclusion that nature prevails enormously over nurture *when the differences of nurture do not exceed what is commonly to be found among persons of the same rank of*

society and in the same country" (p. 404, emphases added).

The above qualification is, of course, critical, for, in effect, it restricts environmental variation substantially by limiting comparisons to persons living in similar social strata of the same society. As a result, Galton's generalization regarding the primacy of nature over nurture risks criticism as a foregone conclusion. Moreover, the criticism does not rest with Galton's ingenious pioneering study, for the conception of the environment implicit in his research design has survived and flourished in the work of later investigators—most notably Burt (1972) and Jensen (1980). Galton's implied conception, and that of his successors, may be described as a definition by exclusion; that is, the environment becomes that portion of the variance that cannot be explained by genetic factors, under conditions in which major potential sources of environmental influence are excluded. Unfortunately, most researchers who employed Galton's model in subsequent decades failed to heed his caveat and its often contradictory implications for the conclusions drawn.

Ironically, although Galton is regarded as the archchampion of hereditarianism, it was also he who identified a number of environmental factors that have proved, ever since, to be among the most powerful mediators of developmental processes and outcomes. Two years prior to the study of twins, he had published his classic monograph entitled *English Men of Science: Their Nature and Nurture* (1874). Therein he documented a statistically significant relation between scientific eminence and primogeniture, since a heavily disproportionate number of his sample outstanding scientists were firstborns. Thus Galton can be credited as the first to introduce family structure as a key environmental context affecting the course of human development.

Galton also went beyond structure to investigate family functioning by calling attention to the importance of parents in the early lives of his subjects. "Nearly a third of the scientific men have expressed themselves indebted to encouragement at home" (p. 205). In Galton's view, however, the influence of parents was qualified in two respects. The first concerns genetic factors; the second relates to the comparative influence of fathers versus that of mothers.

I ascribe many of the cases of encouragement to the existence of an hereditary link; that is to say, the son had inherited scientific tastes, and was encouraged by the parent from whom he had inherited them, and who naturally sympathized with him.

> Attention should be given to the relatively small encouragement received from the mother. . . . In many respects the character of scientific men is strongly anti-feminine. . . . In many respects they have little sympathy with female ways of thought. It is a curious proof of this, that in the very numerous answers which have reference to parental influence, that of the father is quoted three times as often as that of the mother. (pp. 206–207)

Although Galton's conclusions in this domain reflect more than a dash of subjectivity, the fact remains that he appears to be the first researcher to have investigated (but then dismissed as genetic in origin) the possible effect of parents on the development of their offspring through the medium of personal interaction. It would take more than half a century, however, before this interpersonal context would become a primary focus of scientific study. In addition to the impact of parents, Galton also discussed the influence of friends, teachers, and "travel in distant parts." The material was essentially anecdotal, however, and therefore does not meet the criteria we have adopted for defining a systematic scientific study.

Yet another aspect of the environment investigated by Galton was to find somewhat quicker adoption as an essential consideration in developmental research. Galton was concerned not only with the position of the child within the family, but also with the position of the family in the external world. To assess what he called "position in life," he classified the parents of his 96 outstanding scientists into five categories, ranging from "farmers" to "noblemen and private gentlemen" (pp. 21–22). The resulting distribution led him to the following conclusion:

> There can be no doubt but that the upper classes of a nation like our own, which are largely and continually recruited from selection from below, are by far the most productive of natural ability. The lower classes are, in truth, the "residuum." (p. 23)

Here we see the origin of the scales of occupational and socioeconomic status that today constitute the backbone of environmental assessment in studies of human development.[3]

Taking into account the range of Galton's contri-

butions, he emerges as the first of the great paradigm makers in developmental research. What is perhaps most remarkable about his work is that he not only provided operational definitions for some of the most powerful measures we have of both biological and environmental influences on development but also identified important limitations of these measures that have seldom been taken into account in subsequent research. In particular, Galton made clear that the extent to which the environment mediates the expression of genetic potential among individuals or groups is necessarily limited by the degree of environmental variability to which the particular individuals or groups are exposed. If the range is restricted, then observed psychological differences will be due mainly to variations in genetic endowment. Conversely, if the environmental variation is pronounced, it will account for most of the individual or group differences. Galton also identified social class and family structure as major sources of environmental variability. At the same time, he emphasized that the first of these variables, socioeconomic status, could itself be the product of genetic selection. Finally, he considered the possible influence of parental encouragement on the child's development, but, because of his strong hereditarian stance, he missed the opportunity to recognize its power as an environmental agent.

Notwithstanding Galton's impressive contributions, there were many other key environmental dimensions still to be discovered. One of them was introduced in a replication of the Berlin survey in Boston, Massachusetts, by the renowned American psychologist, G. Stanley Hall in 1883. The new parameter is adumbrated in his introductory comments about the original Berlin study, which Hall saw in cross-cultural perspective.

> It is more common in that country than in our own to connect songs, poems, reading exercises, and object lessons, instruction in history, geography, botany, geology, and other elementary branches with the locality. . . . [There] much importance is attached to holiday walks which teachers are expected to conduct for educational purposes. (Hall, 1883, p. 249)

In the light of these considerations, Hall eliminated some of the original German questions that he thought were inappropriate to the American scene and added others he regarded as more suitable. The two major findings of the original Berlin study reappeared in Boston two decades later and 4,000 miles away. As in the German sample, boys surpassed girls except in the area of home and family life (as well as in knowledge of parts of the body). Similarly, a comparison of children entering first grade with and without previous kindergarten experience revealed "in a striking way the advantage of the kindergarten children, without regard to nationality, over all others" (p. 270). Moreover, Hall was not unaware of the possible selective bias: "Many were from charity kindergartens, so that superior intelligence of home surroundings can hardly be assumed." He also made a comparison anticipated, but never carried out, in the original German survey. Of the total sample of over 200 children, there were 36 from rural backgrounds, and these tested higher than their urban counterparts. In explanation, Hall pointed out that the content of primers being used in the schools at that time dealt in substantial measure with country life, and that experiences of nature appeared to have a powerful impact on the young. "Many children locate all that is good and imperfectly known in the country, and nearly a dozen volunteered the statement that good people when they die go to the country—even here from Boston" (p. 256). Consistent with his cross-cultural perspective, Hall then proceeded to examine two additional contrasts. The first was between the Boston and the Berlin children on the 11 questions that were common to the two groups: there were no appreciable differences. The next assessment was in terms of ethnic background; a comparison of responses given by "children of Irish and American parentage" (p. 269). The former achieved significantly lower scores. The differences were especially marked for Irish boys, a finding that prompted Hall to speculate whether "the five and six year old Irish boys are not after all so constituted as to surpass their precocious American playmates later in school or adult life," as slow children "are purported to do."

Although Hall's findings are not without substantive interest, what is significant about them from our perspective is that they extend the concept of social address along a new dimension. To our knowledge, his is the first systematic cross-cultural study. Moreover, it was carried out not only across but also within national boundaries. In the latter instance, the criterion of classification was no longer where the children lived, but the country of origin of their parents and grandparents.

It is clear from the foregoing accounts that by the late 1800s, the characteristics of the environment selected for study had become more complex, primarily through involving aspects of social structure both within the family and in the society at large.

The addresses employed for classifying and comparing the characteristics of the children were becoming increasingly more social and no longer linked solely to a geographic location. Specifically, the social environment was being analyzed at two different levels, each still defined by a social address. In one instance the address described the social location of the child, whereas in the second it was determined by the location of the family within the larger society. Examples of the former include the child's ordinal position, or his exposure to different settings (e.g., home vs. kindergarten). The latter is represented by differences in parental occupation and the family's ethnic background. At each level, there is the presumption that, somehow, the child's experience in these different contexts influences the course of development, but, at the turn of the century, the processes through which environmental factors might influence the child's behavior and development had not yet become an explicit focus of investigation, primarily because no theory of transmission had been proposed capable of being translated into operational terms. The prototypes of such theory, however, can be detected in discussions of the child's immediate environment. Thus the pedagogues of Berlin suggested that the sex differences observed in their pupils might be a function of the different ways in which boys and girls were dealt with in the school. And within the family, Galton saw parental example and encouragement as significant forces impinging on the child's motivation and choice of career.

THE PROLIFERATION AND REFINEMENT OF STRUCTURAL MODELS

The first three decades of the present century saw no significant transformations in research paradigms for studying development-in-context. The existing structural models easily held the field, improved in efficiency, and multiplied in kind almost without limit. The principal scientific developments to occur involved the use of more rigorous methods and designs, and the discovery of new social addresses at which children could be found, and hence compared. For example, a series of investigators conducted studies of twins following Galton's model but improved on his methods by employing standardized tests as measures of intellectual development and by using progressively more accurate techniques for distinguishing between identical and fraternal twins (Lauterbach, 1925; Merriman, 1924; Thorndike, 1905; Wingfield, 1928). In general, the findings were interpreted as supporting Galton's conclusion regarding the primacy of nature over nurture, but with no acknowledgement of the ever-present restrictions on environmental variance. The context in which the twins were growing up remained a void, indexed only indirectly by the greater difference between test scores of fraternal when compared with identical twins, or with those who had been separated rather than brought up together. Not noted was the fact that each pair had been raised within the relatively homogeneous environment either of the same home or in families living in similar strata of society.

The majority of investigations conducted after the turn of the century, however, followed the Berlin model of comparing children living at different social addresses. Some of these were simply new residences along familiar streets; others involved new locations laid out by drawing additional boundaries on the social map that defined further distinctions of status and structure. Let us cite an example of each. Just before the turn of the century, Bohannon (1898), a researcher in Hall's laboratory at Clark, published what appears to have been the first American study[4] of the development of only-children. In that era of large families, the only-child turned out to be an ill-fated and infrequent exception born to parents who had no further offspring, either for reasons of health or of family and personal instability. The slow pace of social and scientific change is reflected in the fact that the first investigation we were able to find of children growing up in single-parent homes was not published until 30 years later, and took the form of an inquiry into the environmental sources of juvenile delinquency (Crosby, 1929). Following Galton's lead, research on persons of intellectual eminence continued to focus on the impact of the family's social background but used more systematic measures of the parents' occupational status (Castle, 1913; Cattell, 1906; Cattell, 1915; Ellis, 1904). A new departure was introduced by Terman (1916) in his analysis of standardization data from the first Stanford-Binet. He asked teachers to estimate the social class to which the child belonged on the basis of the parents' "intellectual level, the culture, and the general level of the home environment." The ratings were made on a 5-point scale. A difference of 14 points in IQ between children from families rated "very inferior" and "very superior" led Terman to conclude "that the children of successful and cultured parents test higher than children from wretched and ignorant homes for the simple reason that their heredity is better" (p. 115). In justification of this conclusion, Terman asserted, on the basis of the evidence available to him at the time, that "prac-

tically all of the investigations which have been made of the influence of nature and nurture on mental performance agree in attributing far more to original endowment than to environment."

Terman's conclusion gained further support from another ingenious application of Galton's nature/nurture model, the comparison of adopted and biological children (Burks, 1928; Leahy, 1935). The fact that the correlations in mental test scores between parent and child were substantially higher for biological than for adopted children seemed clear evidence for the primacy of genetic over environmental influences.

The culmination of methodological and substantive advances made during this period is perhaps best reflected in the first volume of Terman's monumental work *Genetic Studies of Genius* published in 1925. In assessing environmental influences in the development of 1,000 gifted children, Terman and his associates employed a variety of systematic measures of family background including a scale of the father's occupational status, the mother's report of family income, the ethnic background of both parents, the number of years of schooling received by parents and grandparents, family size, data on divorce and separation of parents, teachers' evaluations of the child's home environment, and fieldworkers' ratings of the quality of the neighborhood and the home environment (including such variables as size of home, utilities, neatness, number of books in the home library, the relationship between the parents, and the extent of parental supervision). Although the sample of gifted children showed significant differences on practically all these variables when compared with matched control groups, Terman nevertheless concluded that superior abilities are primarily genetic in origin. His argument is essentially that used by Galton half a century earlier:

To explain by the environmental hypothesis the relatively much greater deviation of our group from unselected children with respect to intellectual and volitional traits appears difficult if not impossible. . . . The fact that in a State which justly prides itself on the equality of educational opportunity provided for its children of every class and station an impartially selected gifted group should draw so heavily from the higher occupational levels and so lightly from the lower throws heavy burden upon the environmental hypothesis. In spite of all our effort to equalize educational opportunity, the ten year old child of a California laborer competes for high IQ rank no more successfully than the laborer's son competed for the genius rank in Europe 100 years ago. This statement is based upon a comparison of the relative number in our group and in the Galton-De Candolle-Ellis Genius-Groups of individuals whose parents belonged to the unskilled or semi-skilled labor classes. Previous studies had only demonstrated the superiority of the higher occupational and social class with respect to the number of finished geniuses produced, and it was only natural that many should prefer to explain this superiority on the ground of educational opportunity. We have demonstrated that the superiority of the same occupational and social classes is no less decisive when the compared offspring are at an age at which educational opportunity is about as nearly equalized as an enlightened Democracy can make it. (p. 635)

We quote the foregoing passage not for its substantive conclusion, but for the evidence it provides of the weak explanatory power of the then existing research model of the environment compared to the strong case for genetic influences made by Galton's paradigm. We do well, therefore, to understand the precise nature of this environmental model and its limitations. By 1930, the operational strategy for assessing environmental influences on child development had become well established. As noted previously, two types of comparisons were being made, but now on a much broader scale. The first focused on the child's location in the microenvironment in terms of such variables as ordinal position, family size, mother's marital status, and amount of experience in preschool or school. The second dimension related to the location of the family in the larger macrosystem as defined by such contrasts as rural versus urban setting, ethnicity, and socioeconomic status and its several components, many of which were treated as linear variables. These categories and continua were well-suited for statistical analysis. In the absence of modern high-speed computers, researchers sat for hours at hand and electric calculators to generate the now-familiar patterns of association between developmental indices and measures of social status and structure both within and outside the family.

Certain defining properties of the paradigm can now be clearly discerned. It is a social structural model consisting of discrete variables. The term "discrete" applies in two respects. First, the variables are dealt with solely as main effects. Although the first edition of Fisher's classic text had been published in 1925, analysis of variance designs per-

Table 1. **Evolution of Environmental Models in Developmental Research**
Stage I: Early Prototypes (1870–1930)

Social Address Models
  Comparison of children (Schwabe & Bartholamai, 1870; Terman, 1916)
  Comparison of adults (Cattell, 1906; Galton, 1874; Terman, 1926)

Nature-Nurture Models
  Comparison of twins (Galton, 1876; Thorndike, 1905)
  Comparison of adopted versus biological children (Burks, 1928; Leahy, 1935)

mitting the assessment of interactions were not adopted in psychological research until the following decade. More significant from our perspective, the social structural variables used in analysis had not been related to each other in any overarching conceptual framework. Most critical, however, was the continuing absence of any theoretical ideas about the processes through which the environment could influence the course of development.

We have now completed our analysis of the first stage in the evolution of models of person/environment interaction in research on human development. For the convenience of the reader, we summarize in Table 1 the two principal paradigms, and their subvariants, that emerged in this period. We also cite the studies in which, to the best of our knowledge, each type of model was first employed.

THE TRANSITION FROM STRUCTURAL TO PROCESS MODELS

As our analysis of studies of development-in-context entered the 1930s, we encountered a striking phenomenon. Having remained essentially unchanged for six decades, the research designs employed by investigators in this domain began to show radical transformations. The first studies were conducted on a small scale, with crude concepts and measures, but these were soon refined and applied on a broader front. The new developments took the form of three successive research trajectories.

The Parent/Child Paradigm

The scientific revolution began with the emergence of research on parent/child relationships and their effect on the child's behavior and development. The initiator and protagonist of this work was David Levy. His first analysis was buried in an article burdened with an awesome and awkward title: "A Method of Integrating Physical and Psychiatric Examination with Special Studies of Body Interest, Over-protection, Response to Growth, and Sex Differences" (1929). Working in collaboration with colleagues at the Smith College School of Social Work, Levy proceeded to gather and analyze systematic clinical data on cases representing contrasting patterns of parent/child relationship along the continuum from what he called "rejection" to "over-protection." The results were published in a series of papers by Levy and his students (Figge, 1931, 1932; Foley, 1932; Hough, 1932; Levy, 1930, 1932, 1933; Lewenberg, 1932; Lewis, 1930). The sphere of inquiry also included the role of the father (Barlow, 1924) and the developmental significance of sibling rivalry (Ross, 1931; Sewell, 1930). Although Levy's statistics were primitive, they revealed consistent relationships between modes of parental care and the corresponding behavior and personality characteristics of children. Levy continued to accumulate and follow up cases so that, by 1943, he was able to publish data on 100 children, 20 of whom had been studied longitudinally for 10 to 15 years (Levy, 1943).[5]

In the interim, Percival Symonds, a psychologist at Columbia, conducted a study based on Levy's work, but he employed a more rigorous design by supplementing clinical interviews with checklists and behavior-rating scales filled out by teachers and other professional personnel who had worked with the children. The results were published in a volume entitled *The Psychology of Parent-Child Relationships* (1939). A new era in developmental research had been born. Levy's and Symond's investigations constitute the prototype for a sequence of more sophisticated studies of childrearing in succeeding decades, notably the work of Baldwin (1946, 1948, 1949; Baldwin, Kalhorn, & Breese, 1945), Sears, Maccoby, and Levin (1957), and Baumrind (1967, 1971, 1980; Baumrind & Black, 1967).

Socialization and Social Structure

A second major wave of investigations followed upon the first. The underlying model can be viewed as a grafting of the new paradigm onto the old—the comparison of persons living at different social addresses is now expanded to include not just children but also parents. The initial contrasts to be investigated were those by socioeconomic status. In a se-

ries of surveys conducted in 1932 for the White House Conference on Child Health and Protection (Anderson, 1936), data were reported on social class differences in parent practices, including onset and duration of breast feeding, scheduled versus self-demand feeding, toilet training, permissiveness, modes of punishment, and training for independence. This was the first in what was to become a series of investigations of socialization and social class over a period spanning a quarter of a century. The accumulated results were analyzed midway by Bronfenbrenner (1958), who identified a secular trend, over a 25-year period, toward greater permissiveness, especially on the part of middle-class parents, who reversed their relative position vis-à-vis the working class in this respect. Curiously, there has been no follow-up study of these trends from the 1950s to the present.

Although ethnographic studies of cultural differences in childrearing had become a major focus of anthropological research by the late 1920s, primarily through the work of Margaret Mead (1928), the first work in this domain meeting our methodological criteria seems to have been Davis and Havighurst's (1948) investigation of "Color Differences in Child Rearing" within American society. Within a decade, however, systematic information about differences in childrearing at social addresses scattered all over the world was made available through the publication of Whiting and Child's volume *Child Training and Personality* (1953).

Variations in parent/child relationships associated with internal family structure were first reported in relation to the sex of the child (Cavan, 1932; Wang, 1932). The findings were soon further qualified by sex of parent (Mott, 1937; Simpson, 1935; Terman, 1938). For example, Mott, in interviews with 500 elementary-age children, found that boys were more often spanked by fathers, girls by mothers. Curiously enough, variations in parental treatment associated with other aspects of family structure were relatively late in attracting the attention of investigators. Thus reports on differences in patterns of childrearing associated with family size and birth order do not begin to appear until the middle 1950s (Bossard and Boll, 1956; Koch, 1954; Lasko, 1954; Sears, Maccoby, & Levin, 1957). More striking is the paucity of research, even up to the present day, on patterns of childrearing in families consisting of only one adult. Despite the now extensive literature on the effects of the father's absence, such studies were not initiated until after

World War II (Bach, 1946; Sears, Pintler, & Sears, 1946). The first investigation to focus direct attention on the childrearing behavior of the single-parent mother was apparently Hetherington's work published in 1978 (Hetherington, Cox, & Cox, 1978).

Models of Group Context

The third major development in research designs involved provision for analyzing children's groups as contexts for human development. Two types of models can be distinguished in the early investigations conducted in this sphere. The first focused primarily on relations between children and adults, the second on relationships among children themselves. In the former category, the earliest studies were conducted in children's institutions. Although the best known of these is the investigation by Spitz (1946a, 1946b), the pioneering study in this domain appears to have been conducted in Austria more than a decade earlier by Durfee and Wolf (1933).[6] These investigators compared developmental quotients of 118 infants in various institutions and correlated the scores with the amount of maternal care that the infants had been given. No differences in performance were discerned before the age of 3 months, but thereafter the developmental levels dropped in inverse relationship to the amount of maternal care received. Children who had been institutionalized for more than 8 months during the first year manifested such severe psychological disturbances that they could not be tested. The study marks the beginning of a series of investigations of institutional deprivation by Spitz, Goldfarb (1943a, 1943b, 1955), Bowlby (1951), Dennis and Najarian (1957), Pringle and Bossio (1958), through the contemporary work of Tizard (Tizard, Cooperman, Joseph, & Tizard, 1972; Tizard & Rees, 1974, 1976; Tizard & Hodges, 1978).

The second and complementary line of research, using a rather different model, also had its origins in the late 1930s in the work of Skeels, Updegraff, Wellman, and Williams (1938). This investigation preceded Skeels's better-known longitudinal study of orphanage children placed for care on a ward of an institution for mentally retarded adults (Skeels, 1942, 1966; Skeels & Dye, 1939). The earlier research also involved an experimental intervention. The sample consisted of 21 pairs of children matched on chronological age, sex, intelligence, nutritional status, and length of residence in the orphanage. The experimental group was randomly assigned to a preschool established on the premises and remained there for 3 years; the control group continued under the established orphanage regime. In contrast to their controls, the experimental children showed impressive gains in IQ, vocabulary, and social adjustment, but were still below the norms for their age. The most dramatic findings of the study were related to the effects of upbringing in the institutional environment. At the outset of the experiment, both groups were described as "lacking in information about the commonest of objects and experiences . . . either lethargic or destructive . . . lacking in flexibility, and tied to nothing in past experience" (p. 184). All of these characteristics were aggravated for the children in the control group, who remained under the institutional regime:

> Certainly no one could have otherwise predicted, much less proved, the steady tendency to deteriorate on the part of children maintained under what had previously been regarded as standard orphanage conditions. With respect to intelligence, vocabulary, general information, social competence, personal adjustment, and motor achievement the whole picture is one of retardation. The effect from one to three years attendance in nursery school . . . was to reverse the tide of regression which, for some, led to feeble-mindedness. (p. 2)

Again, our purpose in citing this study is not to focus on its substantive findings, but to illustrate a new departure in research design. To our knowledge, this investigation by Skeels and his colleagues represents the first example of experimental early intervention as a strategy for studying the impact of the environment on human development. Thus it marks the beginning of a long trajectory reflected in the work of such investigators as Kirk (1958), Gray and Klaus (1965), Weikart (1967), Karnes, Studley, Wright, and Hodgins (1968), Gordon (1971), Levenstein (1970), and Heber, Garber, Harrington, and Hoffman (1972).

Complementing studies of the developmental effects on children of deprived social environments were investigations focusing on the power of the group to shape and sustain the behavior of its members. Perhaps the first work in this regard was Shaw's analysis (1933) of juvenile delinquency as a gang phenomenon. Shortly thereafter, Murphy (1937) documented the role of the group in shaping and sustaining the behavior of nursery school children. This line of investigation entered an experimental phase with the classic study by Lewin, Lippitt, and White on group atmospheres (1939), a work that set the stage for an evolving trajectory of research on group influences and child behavior and development (for a summary, see Hartup, 1970).

THE ORIGIN AND IMPLEMENTATION OF EXPLICIT THEORETICAL PARADIGMS

How can one account for the remarkable innovation and enrichment that suddenly emerged during the 1930s in the conceptions underlying research models for the study of human development in context? Although a number of factors contributed to this rapid evolution, the main sources of significant change were new theoretical ideas that postulated linkages between particular features of the environment and the developing organism.

The Paradigm Makers

Before the 1930s, the only theory employed in empirical work that approximated this requirement was classical conditioning (Holt, 1931; Pavlov, 1928), but it was not equal to the task, despite Watson's grandiose promise[7] (1918). But there were three candidates waiting in the wings, and their formal admission into the scientific establishment of psychological science was signified by their inclusion in the first edition of Murchison's *Handbook* in 1931. The three were Freud, Piaget, and Lewin. Freud's name is of course much more closely associated with theories of intrapsychic structure than with the analysis of external contexts. Nevertheless, it was on Freud's clinically derived theoretical ideas about family dynamics that Levy explicitly relied in designing his research on parent/child relationships and their developmental effects. Similarly, it was Freud's emphasis on the importance of the mother/infant bond that provided the framework for the early investigations of the effects of institutionalization by Durfee, Wolf, Spitz, and their successors.

A rather different view of the organism/environment interface was presented by both Piaget and Lewin. Whereas for Freud the primary context was one of intense emotional relationships, Piaget saw the environment through the eyes of the child as a cognitive structure incorporating physical as well as social dimensions. Moreover, children were no longer passive victims of external forces as conceived in Freud's formulation, but active creators and transformers of the world about them. In support of this view, Piaget adduced experimental evidence showing how the child used objects, shapes, and activities available in the environment to achieve the child's own "construction of reality" (Piaget, 1926, 1954).

While sharing Piaget's phenomelogical orientation, Lewin assigned to the environment an even more explicit and powerful role. He conceptualized it as having "demand characteristics" that attract or repel, and he cited experiments showing how the child's behavior could be changed by altering the psychological situation (Lewin, 1935). Lewin's abstractly defined field theory was to generate his classic experiments on group atmospheres (Lewin et al., 1939) and to culminate ultimately in the conception and execution of what he called "action research" (Lewin, 1948); that is, an investigation deliberately designed to create a new environment that, in turn, can induce changes in behavior and development.

Credit for the next paradigm shift in research on environmental factors in human development belongs to a psychologist whose star seems to have fallen. Whereas references to Freud, Piaget, and Lewin in scientific journals and texts have remained frequent throughout recent decades, Clark Hull appears to have reached his peak of prominence in the middle 1950s. Yet, the long-range impact of his learning theory on investigations of environmental influences has been profound. There is a direct line from his experiments on contingent reinforcement to the strategies of behavior modification so widely used in contemporary studies and applied programs of experimental intervention in clinics, schools, and social institutions. But even more significant from an environmental perspective is the indirect contribution of Hull's work to the explosion of research on *socialization* that occurred in the middle 1950s. Like some other explosions, this one also derived from theoretical work—the systematic integration, in a series of seminars planned and directed by Hull at Yale, of concepts from learning theory, psychoanalysis, sociology, and cultural anthropology. For a firsthand account of the seminar see Sears (1975). The theoretical integration gave rise to a series of empirical studies linking processes at the individual and cultural level (Dollard, 1939; Le Vine, 1970; Miller & Dollard, 1941; Whiting & Child, 1953). Moreover, in contrast to earlier social-address paradigms, the research designs employed by the Yale group posited a more complex causal model. Whereas the former envisioned only a unidirectional process in which culture was the independent variable, Whiting, Child, and their colleagues saw early childrearing practices as the principal mechanisms for producing and sustaining cultural values and customs.

Emerging from a contrasting social and intellectual milieu, a dramatically different paradigm of the role of culture in human development is found in the work of the two Soviet psychologists Vygotsky and Luria. The hallmarks of this orientation are telegraphed in the titles that Michael Cole, their American editor, has given to the two books that present these ideas in English translation: the volume by Vygotsky is called *Mind in Society* (1978); the one by Luria, *Cognitive Development: Its Cultural and Social Foundations* (1976). Both volumes assert the general thesis that the evolution of cognitive processes in the individual is shaped by the definitions of reality provided by the broader cultural context, with particular emphasis on the impact of large-scale social changes, both planned and unplanned. The origins of the theory, and its first application, date back to the late 1920s and early 1930s, when Vygotsky and Luria undertook to test their hypotheses by investigating the effects on cognitive functioning of the transformation of Soviet society that followed the October Revolution. The fieldwork, which involved intensive psychological interviews and tests, was carried out by Luria himself in the remoter regions of Soviet Asia. (Vygotsky was too ill from tuberculosis to be able to leave Moscow.) The investigation focused on a comparison of cognitive functioning in members of communities that had been exposed in varying degrees to the planned social changes being introduced across the entire country.

The results of the study are best conveyed in Luria's own words:

> The facts show convincingly that the structure of cognitive activity does not remain static during the different stages of historical development and that the most important forms of cognitive processes . . . vary as the conditions of life change and the rudiments of knowledge can be mastered. (Luria, 1976, p. 161)

Because Luria's reliance on psychological tests was incompatible with the Communist ideology of the 1930s and succeeding decades, he was not permitted to publish the results of his research until 40 years later, just before his death in 1976. In the middle 1960s, however, Michael Cole, then an exchange graduate student at Moscow University, had the opportunity to work with Luria. He subsequently applied sophisticated elaborations of the Soviet cultural cognitive model in an influential series of studies conducted both in Africa and the United States (Cole, Gay, Glick, & Sharp, 1971; Cole & Scribner, 1974). In the Vygotsky-Luria paradigm, major emphasis is given to the nature of the *activities* conducted within a particular social context. These ac-

tivities are seen as critical elements defining the nature of the environment and constitute the principal mechanisms for affecting developmental change (Wertsch, 1981).

The last two paradigm shifts that can be identified with any confidence both have their roots in biological research, one line being naturalistic, the other experimental. The former is reflected in the impact on developmental psychology of the ethological conceptions of the Austrian Nobel laureate, Konrad Lorenz (1935, 1965), and their subsequent refinement by Tinbergen (1951) and Hinde (1966). The framework has been particularly influential in research on mother/infant relations and the evolution of social behavior in the young (Ainsworth, 1963; Ambrose, 1961; Blurton-Jones, 1974; Schaffer, 1963). A second biological model stems from the experiments of a Canadian psychologist, Donald Hebb, on the effects of environmental restriction and enrichment on development in rats (1937a, 1937b, 1938, 1949). Hebb's work served as a major theoretical and empirical base for Hunt's (1961) influential volume on the effects of infant stimulation, which, in turn, contributed to the rationale for establishing early intervention programs in the middle and late 1960s (Bronfenbrenner, 1974a; Horowitz & Paden, 1973). The principal innovation brought about by these models was a shift in the conception of the child's relation to its environment. Instead of being merely the object of external forces, the child was seen and studied as an active organism seeking stimulation, provoking responses from, altering, and even creating its own surroundings.

Finally, although the evidence is as yet meager and most of it indirect, it appears that another theoretical paradigm of long standing is at last beginning to be implemented in investigations of human development. We refer to the symbolic interaction theory of the "Chicago School" of sociologists, chief among them being Cooley (1902), G. H. Mead (1934), and W. I. and D. S. Thomas (Thomas, 1927; Thomas & Thomas, 1928; Thomas & Znaniecki, 1927). Their theory of socialization focused on the evolution of a concept of self through the person's interaction, throughout the lifespan, with "significant others," both within and outside the family. It is a reflection of the long history of isolation between disciplines that only in recent years has this conception begun to influence research in child development, an area of inquiry heavily dominated by psychologists. The scholar who finally broke the disciplinary barrier was a sociologist, Glen Elder. Using longitudinal data gathered by psychologists, Elder assessed the impact of the Great Depression

(Elder, 1979) on the development of children at successive stages of transition in their lives. Elder explicitly credits the Chicago School, particularly Thomas and Znaniecki's study of *The Polish Peasant in Europe and America* (1927), as the source for the research model on which his investigation was based. His work, in turn, has stimulated other researchers (e.g., Furstenberg, 1976) to use similar designs in pursuing what Elder has called "the life course" approach in studies of human development. The approach focuses attention on stability and shift in developmental trajectories as a function of the role statuses and transitions experienced by a particular age cohort during a given period in history.

Although our analysis yielded few surprises in identifying the originators of paradigm shifts in conceptions of the role of the environment in human development, it illuminated aspects of the evolution of operational concepts that we had not previously recognized. First, we had not appreciated the extent to which the most influential theoretical ideas have been produced by scholars from other countries and other disciplines. Second, we had not realized how long the typical "refractory period" is between the publication of a theory and its application in scientific work. Indeed, it is this "sleeper effect" that makes it difficult, as we approach our own times, to identify which contemporary theoretical ideas, if any, will eventually lead to new and fruitful directions in scientific work.

Theory Translators

Confronted with this phenomenon, we pondered on the forces that might account for its existence. Fortunately, our labors yielded some relevant evidence. In the course of our analysis, we found ourselves identifying not only persons whom we called "creative theorists," but also "theory translators"—those who were able to transform new, highly general and often strange theoretical ideas into delimited, researchable problems and corresponding operational definitions. Inventive translators were not always at hand at the time the theory was conceived. It often took a decade or two before the translation was finally accomplished. Thus, as we have seen, the first implementation of Freud's theories in systematic research on parent/child relationships did not take place until the early 1930s; moreover, the innovation occurred from outside developmental psychology in the person of David Levy, who was a psychoanalytically oriented psychiatrist. It was only then that a psychologist (Symonds) entered the picture, primarily to provide a more rigorous research design and more objective methods of data gathering and analysis.

Another productive Freudian research trajectory was also set in motion by a psychiatrist and a psychologist, with the latter again contributing a more objective methodology. Bowlby (1951, 1958, 1969) gave sufficient theoretical concreteness to Freud's concept of maternal attachment so that Ainsworth and her colleagues (1969) were able to develop the widely used "strange situation" experiment as a method for assessing the quality and consequence of stability versus disruption in the mother/infant bond.

The implementation of Freud's theory of identification ran a more convoluted course via a detour through learning theory. It finally emerged in somewhat altered but more easily operationalized form in the concept of modeling as developed and applied by Bandura and his colleagues (Bandura, 1969; Bandura & Huston, 1961).

Analogous roles in relation to Piaget's theories of social influences in development were played by Berenda (1950) and Kohlberg (1963, 1964). Similarly, it was Lewin's students—and later colleagues—Lippitt and White who applied his field theory to the study of children's groups. Some years later, Barker translated Lewin's elusive concept of "life space" into concrete naturalistic "behavior settings," thereby establishing a new research domain of ecological psychology (Barker, 1965, 1968; Barker & Wright, 1951, 1955).[8] Vygotsky and Luria's model of cultural cognition hibernated for four decades before it could be exported into a warmer scientific climate by Cole and his colleagues.

We have already commented on the critical contribution of Hull's interdisciplinary seminar in integrating his learning theories with psychoanalytic and anthropological approaches, thus setting the stage for field studies of socialization processes and outcomes. The fact that the gap between conception and application was far longer in the case of role theory at the University of Chicago indicates that borders between disciplines can be as powerful barriers as those of language and geographic distance.

Our purpose in documenting the distant origin and delayed and devious course characterizing the early life history of new research paradigms is to alert workers in the field to the typically unorthodox sources of scientific advance, and to the critical role played in the process by other persons besides the creative theorists. The lessons to be learned are those of openness to ideas from other scientific traditions and of the importance of early efforts to operationalize a new paradigm before making a final judgment about its scientific merit.

It is instructive to ask whether an examination of empirical work reveals any other sources of new operational definitions of the environment besides those generated by overarching theoretical systems. One such creative influence may be described by the term "domain theory"—that is, a conception that identifies a hitherto unexplored area of investigation and offers descriptive concepts and methods appropriate for exploring the uncharted terrain. A classic example is Moreno's invention of sociometry (1934) as a technique for analyzing the social structure of a group and the individual's position within it. Moreno's constructs and procedures provided the impetus for a large number of studies of social development, in which the child's sociometric status was used either as the independent or the dependent variable. A related example of domain theory is found in Bott's (1957) analysis of family social networks and their recent reinterpretation by Cochran and Brassard (1979) as support systems for family functioning and child development.

A significant and sophisticated contribution in domain theory is represented by Baltes and Schaie's development of a methodological framework for the systematic study of what they have called "life span developmental psychology" (Baltes, 1968; Baltes & Schaie, 1973). Their formulations have two important implications. First, their work focuses attention on the developmental impact of the contexts that human beings enter in the years following adolescence. Second, and more important, it introduces a major reconceptualization in research design. Until the late 1960s, the results of longitudinal studies in human development had been interpreted as revealing psychological growth as a function of age. Then, the sophisticated analyses of Baltes, Schaie, and their colleagues (Baltes, 1968; Nesselroade & Baltes, 1979; Schaie, 1970) demonstrated the confounding effects of age and cohort. Not only did persons in the same age group share a life history of common experience, but those of a given age in different generations could have quite diverse experiences depending on the period in which they lived. Baltes and his associates sought to clarify these complexities through the use of ingenious statistical models designed to separate out the influences of age and cohort. It remained for a group of sociologists (Elder, 1974; Furstenberg, 1976; Riley, 1973) to turn a methodological problem into a substantive solution by transforming the individually-oriented study of life span development into a context-oriented analysis of the progression of particular groups along contrasting social trajectories throughout the life course.[9]

We are now in a position to summarize, in Table 2, the major advances occurring in the second stage in the evolution of research models, a phase stimulated by the sudden proliferation of theories about developmental processes. The theorists, and a capsuled description of their theories, appear in the first column of the table. In the second column, we list the principal investigators who first succeeded in translating each theory into operational form, along with a reference to specific studies in which this implementation was accomplished. Similarly, the third column lists domain theorists and relevant researches.

HISTORICAL CHANGE AS A SOURCE OF SCIENTIFIC INNOVATION

History exerted its influence on research designs long before developmental researchers gave it explicit recognition. We refer to the impact of historical and cultural changes in focusing the attention of investigators on new features of the environment that could affect developmental processes. For example, the scientific revolution of the nineteenth century clearly set the stage for Galton's studies of the genesis of scientific genius. Freud's neurotics were the products of a special brand of Viennese Victorianism. As clearly revealed in his first published paper (Lewin, 1917), Lewin's theoretical ideas were stimulated by his experience as an infantryman in World War I. In this analysis of a *Kriegslandschaft* (war landscape), he describes how the perceived reality of the landscape changes, as the soldier nears the front line, from one of pastoral peace to threatening terrain.

History can also speak to the researcher without the intervening translation of a theorist. For instance, the first studies of the impact of the father on the family as a childrearing system were prompted by massive unemployment during the Great Depression (Angell, 1936; Caven & Ranck, 1938; Komarovsky, 1940; Morgan, 1939). A second flurry of investigation in this sphere occurred some years later when World War II gave rise to a spate of studies on the effects of father absence on children's development (Bach, 1946; Sears et al., 1946; Stolz, 1954). Research on the impact of maternal employment first appeared in the 1930s as women began to enter the labor force in larger numbers to supplement family income in the aftermath of the Great Depression (Glueck & Glueck, 1934a, 1934b; Hodgkiss, 1933; Mathews, 1934). Interestingly enough, this line of work was initiated with exactly the opposite hypothesis to that serving as the point of departure in re-

Table 2. Evolution of Environmental Models in Developmental Research
Stage II: The Emergence of Paradigm Makers and Implementers (1930–)

Process Theorists		Translating Theorists	Domain Theorists	
FREUD:	Environment as interpersonal relations	Bandura & Huston, 1961; Bowlby, 1951; Bühler, 1937; Durfee & Wolf, 1933; Levy, 1929; Skeels, 1936; Spitz, 1946; Symonds, 1939	SOCIOMETRY:	Moreno, 1934
LEWIN:	Environment as psychological field (life space, group climate)	Lewin, Lippitt, & White, 1939	SOCIAL NETWORKS:	Bott, 1957; Cochran & Brassard, 1979
PIAGET:	Environment as child's construction of reality	Berenda, 1950; Kohlberg, 1963	LIFESPAN DEVELOPMENT:	Baltes, 1968
HULL SEMINAR:	Environment as socialization in cultural context	Dollard, 1939; Miller & Dollard, 1941; Whiting & Child, 1953; Sears, Maccoby, & Levin, 1957		
VYGOTSKY-LURIA:	Changing society as cognitive context	Cole, 1971, 1974		
LORENZ:	Environment as biological ecology	Ambrose, 1961; Ainsworth, 1963		
HEBB:	Environment as stimulation	Hunt, 1961		
CHICAGO SCHOOL:	Environment as historical life course	Elder, 1974; Furstenberg, 1976		

search on fathers. In the latter case, the *unemployment* of the parent was seen as potentially detrimental to the child's development, whereas in the case of the mother it was *employment* that was presumed to have undesirable effects. As more and more women entered the labor force in the 1960s and 1970s, studies on effects of maternal employment rose to a new plateau and have remained there ever since (Bronfenbrenner & Crouter, 1981). A resurgence of interest in the developmental impact of fathers' employment still lies ahead.

In a different domain, the experiment with orphanage children conducted by Skeels and his colleagues in the 1930s was stimulated not by a theoretical concern with the effects of maternal deprivation but by a change in school practice. The investigation was designed to assess the educational effect of kindergartens, which were then becoming more common on the American scene. Despite the promising result of this and other studies (reviewed in Bronfenbrenner, 1974a), research on the effects of preschool intervention exhibited a low profile through the 1940s and 1950s, but it became a major social science industry in response to President Johnson's call to arms for a "War against Poverty" and a "Head Start" for poor children and their fami-

lies. With the growing divorce rate and entry of mothers into the labor force, single parenthood and daycare became primary research concerns of the 1970s. As we look ahead to the 1980s, should we anticipate new scientific knowledge, and possibly new theory as well, about the effects on children and families of inflation, energy shortages, unemployment, and the drastic reduction in health and social services? Time will tell. In the interim, we had better begin to heed the methodological requirements of what may be called the "new demography." The well-designed study of the future must not only control for the familiar confounding variables of class and race; to these we must add new forms of family structure, both mothers' and fathers' employment status, the type and extent of substitute care, and—perhaps soon—the number of hours spent by fathers in housework and childrearing. Such are the forces determining the future of our science.

THE EVOLUTION OF LATENT STRUCTURES IN SOCIAL ADDRESS MODELS

The role of historical and social changes in prompting social scientists to introduce new elements into their research designs represents an instance of what we have termed the evolution of *implicit* research models. For example, the investigators cited above who saw the opportunity during World War II of assessing the impact of father absence on the mother's treatment of the child did not describe themselves as introducing a new research paradigm; but, in fact, they were breaking new ground. An established dyadic model of the parent/child relationship was being transformed into a three-person structure exhibiting the properties of a system in which each participant could influence, and be influenced by, the interaction between the other two.

The foregoing example illustrates several distinctive features of the development of implicit paradigms. The evolution entails not only the addition of new environmental domains but also the formation of more complex structures that become more differentiated both in form and in function. To anticipate the results of analyses to follow, the initial impetus for this progression came from the confrontation and resulting fusion between the earlier social address models and the later process paradigms. To pursue our original analogy, the process provides a key for opening the doors at diverse social addresses, thereby disclosing dwellings in which human beings relate to one another and engage, separately and jointly, in a variety of activities characteristic for a particular address. These contrasting patterns of activities, as they persist over time, generate differences in the development of persons living at each address. Moreover, the various locales are no longer isolated from each other. They are linked together in complex ways that, in turn, influence the operation and outcome of processes taking place within each setting. Finally, we encounter what is perhaps the most intriguing aspect of this scientific evolution; for the most part, it did not appear to have been the result of any conscious, coordinated effort. Rather, it emerged as an unplanned achievement, the product of seemingly ad hoc innovations by different investigators working independently, but nevertheless proceeding in complementary and convergent directions. The resultant structures have not been made explicit, but they can be inferred from the operational designs employed by investigators in the field. The implicit evolution has proceeded by stages. The evolving models, however, do not spring de novo from contemporary research; they have their roots in the earlier paradigms, both explicit and implicit, that we described in the preceding pages.

An analysis of this evolutionary process is potentially rewarding in two directions. On the one hand, by making latent paradigms explicit, it can illuminate the path of progress in the past. On the other hand, this same analytic process can adumbrate a trajectory of possible scientific advance for the future.

The earliest latent structures in research designs for studying development-in-context were, as we have seen, comparatively simple. Indeed, the first was scarcely worthy of the name, since it verged on the obvious and inescapable. But because it served as a building block for more complex structures to come, it deserves brief mention. The initial step involved merely a grafting of the newer process models on the previously existing taxonomy of social addresses. Up to that time, this taxonomy had been applied solely to compare characteristics of children or adults growing up in contrasting environments. But once Levy and his colleagues had documented the developmental importance and technical feasibility of measuring patterns of childrearing, it was a natural and easy shift to expand the traditional social address model beyond the child to the parent. The result was a proliferation of studies documenting differences in parent/child relationships across a variety of contexts. The data generated by these research trajectories provided a basis for explaining differences in the characteristics of children growing up in diverse environments. The interpretation followed a simple syllogism: parental treatment was known to affect the development of the child; since parents in different environments had now been shown to treat their children differently, this fact could account for the observed contrasts between children brought up in the diverse settings. The interpretation rested, however, on the assumption that the processes linking the behaviors of parents and children were universal; that is, they remained the same irrespective of the characteristics of the participants or the contexts in which the processes were occurring.

A Person-Process-Context Model

Insofar as we have been able to determine, this assumption remained unchallenged in empirical work until the 1960s. At that time, studies began to appear reporting differences by social address not only in the characteristics of parents and children, but in the relation between the two. Thus, Bronfenbrenner (1961), using a factorial covariance design, analyzed the relations between parental and child behavior separately by sex of parent and sex of child. The results revealed that the "same" parental treatment had different effects depending on the combination of roles involved. A higher level of responsibility in the son was associated with greater nurturance and affection, especially from the mother, and—even more markedly—with increased discipline and authority from the father. By contrast, among girls the same kinds of parental variables were negatively related to level of responsibility; again, it was the father whose behavior seemed to be especially crucial. Bronfenbrenner interpreted these results as suggesting differential susceptibility to similar socialization practices directed at boys and girls, but he pointed to the difficulty of resolving issues of causality from correlations among measures obtained at the same point in time.

The limitations of a cross-sectional design were overcome in two subsequent longitudinal studies: parental treatment in early childhood predicted subsequent behavior in adolescents much better for boys than for girls (Kagan & Moss, 1962; Schaefer & Bayley, 1963). At a cross-cultural level, Caudill and Weinstein (1969) found that similar behavior toward infants by mothers in Japan and in the United States led to different consequences in the two societies. To investigate the possibility that these differences might have a genetic base, Caudill and Frost (1975) replicated the study with a sample of Japanese mothers living in the United States. The differences were still present, but much reduced. The authors interpret their results as ruling out genetic factors in favor of the influence both of cultural change and cultural persistence, with the former being much the stronger.

Even earlier in life, the same prenatal and perinatal traumas (e.g., birth injuries) correlated with later IQ for children from lower-class families but not for those from middle-class homes (Drillien, 1964; Werner, Simonian, Bierman, & French, 1967; Willerman, 1972; Willerman, Naylor, & Myrianthopoulos, 1970). Conversely, the association between adolescents' reports of parent/child·relationships and ratings of their behavior at school by teachers and peers was stronger for middle-class than for lower-class groups (Bronfenbrenner, 1961). It appears that both biological and interpersonal influences can have different effects depending on the context in which they operate. To put it more colloquially, good things get better for those who are well-off to start with, and bad things get worse for those who are not.

The dynamics of the processes involved in such contextual contrasts were illuminated in a series of studies by Tulkin and his colleagues (Tulkin, 1973a, 1973b; Tulkin & Cohler, 1973; Tulkin & Covitz, 1975; Tulkin & Kagan, 1972). These investigators focused on differences in development during infancy and early childhood as a function of the family's socioeconomic status. To control for the child's sex and ordinal position, the sample was limited to firstborn girls, first studied when they were 10 months old. The initial publication (Tulkin & Kagan, 1972), based on home observations, reported that middleclass mothers engaged in more reciprocal interactions with their infants, especially in verbal behavior, and provided them with a greater variety of stimulation. The second study (Tulkin & Cohler, 1973) documented parallel differences in maternal attitudes; middle-class mothers were more likely to subscribe to statements stressing importance of perceiving and meeting the infant's needs, the value of mother/child interaction, and the moderate control of aggressive impulses. Furthermore, the correlations between maternal behavior and attitudes were substantially greater in middle-class than in lowerclass families. Next, in two experiments Tulkin (1973a, 1973b) found that middle-class infants cried more when separated from their mothers, but were better able to discriminate the mother's voice from that of an unfamiliar female from the same social class. Finally, several years later, Tulkin and Covitz (1975) reassessed the same youngsters after they had entered school. The children's performance on tests of mental ability and language skill showed significant relationships to the prior measures of reciprocal mother/infant interaction and strength of maternal attachment and voice recognition when the children had been 10 months old. Once again, the observed correlations were higher for middle-class families. Even more important from a developmental perspective, the relationships of maternal behavior at 10 months to the child's behavior at age 6 were considerably greater than the contemporaneous relationships between both types of variables in the first year of life. The investigators, however, were quick to reject the hypothesis of a delayed "sleeper effect." Rather, they argued that mothers who engage in adaptive reciprocal activity with their infants at early ages are likely to continue to do so as the child gets older, thus producing a cumulative trend.

If one considers the foregoing series of studies as a body and analyzes the elements of the research designs employed, one can discern the latent structure of a newly emergent model for investigating development-in-context. The model has the following features:

1. It envisages the possibility of differences by social class not only in childrearing practices and

outcomes, but also in the processes that interconnect them.

2. Developmental processes are assumed to vary as a joint function of biological and environmental factors.

3. Childrearing attitudes and belief systems are treated as important mediators of childrearing behavior.

4. Recognition is given to the possibility of reciprocal influences; not only does the environment influence the child but the child also influences the environment.

5. Developmental effects can be cumulative over time.

In the light of these defining properties, we refer to this evolutionary paradigm as a *person-process-context model,* since it takes into account the characteristics of each of these elements and the interaction among them.

Galton's Nature/Nurture Paradigm in a Process Perspective

It is instructive to apply the person-process-context model to the findings and conclusions of studies based on Galton's classical paradigm and its later derivatives. One of the most important of these derivatives involves the comparison of children raised by adoptive versus biological parents (Burks, 1928; Horn, Loehlin, & Willerman, 1979; Leahy, 1935; Scarr & Weinberg, 1976). Here the typical finding is that the correlation between IQs of biological parents and children raised from an early age in adoptive homes is considerably greater than the corresponding correlation between IQs of adoptive parents and of their adopted children. Whereas the coefficients for the first group range between .40 and .60, those for the second fall between .09 and .20 and are nonsignificant. Implicit in this comparison are two assumptions. The first, which appears entirely warranted, is that the substantial correlations obtained between the IQs of biological parents and children separated from them early in life must reflect primarily the influence of heredity. The second assumption can be called into question since it presumes that the IQ of the adoptive parent measures, or is highly correlated with, aspects of the environment that are most relevant for a child's intellectual development. To the extent that this measure misses the mark, the resulting correlations would necessarily be reduced. In the light of numerous findings from socialization research, some of them mentioned in this review, a more valid index would be provided by measures of parent/child atti-

tudes and interactions of the type used by Tulkin and Kagan in the study described above. Correspondingly, a more appropriate analytic model for assessing the joint contributions of environment and heredity in adoptive versus biological families would involve a multiple regression design in which both parental IQs and measures of childrearing processes would be entered in the same equation. The relative size of path coefficients would then offer an indication of the relative contribution of genetic and environmental factors to intellectual development of the children. Then, in the case of the adopted children, if the IQ of the biological parent washed out any effects of socialization by the adoptive parent, the hypothesis of genetic primacy would be strongly supported. Such a finding seems unlikely given the many studies documenting the significant impact of socialization processes on psychological development.

A more probable state of affairs requires for its detection a person-process-context design that takes into account the possibility of interaction effects between genetic and environmental processes. Such designs have come to be applied only recently. For example, in a series of adoption studies conducted in Denmark, the investigators (Goodwin, 1976; Goodwin, Schulsinger, Hermansen, Guze, & Winokur, 1973; Goodwin, Schulsinger, Møller, Hermansen, & Winokur, 1974; Schuckit, Goodwin, & Winokur, 1972) identified samples of men who had been adopted before the first 6 weeks of life, but one of whose biological parents had been hospitalized for alcoholism. Compared to a matched control group of adoptees born of nonalcoholic parents, the biological sons of alcoholics had a higher rate of alcoholism. When the same design was replicated with samples of adopted women (Goodwin, Schulsinger, Knop, Mednick, & Guze, 1977a, 1977b), however, there were no differences. The investigators suggest that the daughters of alcoholics may be "as genetically susceptible to alcoholism as are their sons, but that because of cultural and possibly counteractive biological factors, women are 'protected' from becoming alcoholic'' (Goodwin et al., 1977b, p. 1008).

The interaction of genetic and social factors emerges as even more salient in recent studies of forces affecting the development of criminality and antisocial behavior (Hutchings & Mednick, 1973; Robins, 1973; Schulsinger, 1972). The investigators evaluated the incidence of criminal offenses among adoptees as a function of whether the adoptive versus the biological father had a police record. The results were compared to those for a control group of nonadopted children matched on family background characteristics. Minor infractions were distinguished from serious crimes. On both counts, the findings revealed that criminality in either the biological or the adoptive father had a significant effect, but the influence of rearing by a father with a criminal record was greater when a genetic predisposition was also present—a nice instance of organism/environment interaction detected by applying a person-process-context model.

The existence of such interaction beyond the family context is revealed in a similar study conducted in the United States (Crowe, 1972, 1974, 1975), this time with adopted children born to female offenders 90% of whom were felons. The control group consisted of adoptees selected by choosing the next entry from the state adoption registry matched by age, sex, race, and approximate age at adoption. Psychiatric diagnoses were made by judges blind to the family background of the adoptee. At the time of examination, the children averaged 26 years of age, with a range from 15 to 45. The only significant difference between the two groups was in the frequency of a diagnosis of antisocial personality. Other types of personality disorders were distributed equally between adoptees born of mothers with and without a criminal record. In a secondary analysis, however, two related environmental factors were reliably associated with an antisocial outcome: earlier age at adoptive placement and longer time spent in orphanages and temporary foster homes. These environmental effects were more pronounced among adoptees whose biological mothers had been offenders. The author interprets his findings as indicating "that the interaction of genetic and environmental factors was more important in leading to an antisocial outcome than either alone" (Crowe, 1974, p. 789).

Our final example applies a person-process-context model on an even broader scale. As reported in another volume of this *Handbook*, Scarr and her associates (Scarr & Barker, 1981; Scarr, Pakstis, Katz, & Barker, 1977; Scarr, Weber, Weinberg, & Wittig, 1981) compared black and white samples to test the general hypothesis that individual differences in mental test scores will be more influenced by environmental factors for black children than for white because the former live in a "more repressive environment." In accord with theoretical predictions, black youngsters exhibited less genetic variability in their scores, showed higher twin correlations, lower differences between twin coefficients for monozygous and dizygous pairs, and scored relatively worse on tests that were more cul-

turally loaded for white middle-class groups. The investigators interpret the findings as supporting the thesis that "black children are being reared in circumstances that give them only marginal acquaintance with the skills and knowledge being sampled by the tests" (Scarr & Barker, 1981). Implicit in the research of Scarr and her colleagues is a more general theoretical model that posits variation in the expression of genetic potential as a function of environmental conditions.

As the foregoing examples demonstrate, the application of a person-process-context model to correlations yielded by twin or adoption studies leads to interpretations that are rather different from those obtained by applying the classical Galton paradigm. In addition, the person-process-context model can generate provocative research questions not previously raised. For example, one might hypothesize that socialization practices employed by adoptive parents would be more effective with children whose biological parents were of higher intelligence. Still another possibility rests on the assumption that some degree of genetic similarity facilitates socialization processes. If so, one would predict that the correlation between measures of socialization process and outcome would be higher for children being brought up by their biological parents than for those raised by adoptive parents. To date we have been able to find no studies investigating relationships of this kind—a situation that we hope will change as the person-process-context model receives recognition and acceptance as a powerful paradigm for investigating development-in-context.

Limitations of the Person-Process-Context Model

Despite its scientific advantages, this model is not without some shortcomings. There are four that merit our attention.

1. The processes incorporated within the paradigm have thus far been confined to the sphere of interpersonal relations.

2. Even within the interpersonal sphere, the structure serving as the instrument of transmission between the environment and the child is limited to a dyadic model. Such a model takes into account only direct single-step causal relationships between the environment and the developing person and does not provide for possible mediating influences of other external factors.

3. All the causal elements in the model are confined within the boundaries of the immediate setting containing the child—mainly, the family. Although

the studies offer considerable evidence that the operation of intrafamilial processes is affected by the external contexts of class and culture in which the family resides, the research designs do not provide for any analysis of the processes through which these external contexts impinge on the family.

4. Although the longitudinal designs employed in these studies add to the child's environment a new dimension of time, they leave a large temporal terrain unexplored. While the investigations permit an evaluation of the impact of the child's early environment on later development, they do not provide for the assessment of environmental changes in the intervening period. Like the early studies of place, in which the houses were left empty, these pioneering investigations of environment over time involve long intervals in which "nothing happened."

Fortunately, this was not the state of affairs with respect to research activity during this period. Concomitantly with the evolution of person-process-context models, other developments were occurring that were to remedy the deficiencies we have just described. These developments were first manifested in research designs that reflected a more complex and differentiated conception of the immediate settings in which children lived. Initially, these designs were stimulated by explicit theoretical paradigms, but soon they took on an implicit momentum of their own.

THE EVOLUTION OF SETTINGS AS MICROSYSTEMS

The first alternative to the psychonanalytically derived parent/child model of the immediate environment also had European theoretical roots, in this instance stemming from the formulations of Kurt Lewin (1936). Lewin had emphasized the power of the immediate environment in steering the child's behavior, and the importance of the activities taking place in that environment as a context for evoking behavior. As previously noted, these theoretical conceptions were ultimately translated into research operations by Barker, Wright, and their colleagues (Barker, 1965, 1968; Barker & Gump, 1964; Barker & Schoggen, 1973; Barker & Wright, 1951, 1955). These investigators have provided impressive evidence in support of their thesis that most of the variance in the behavior of children, and indeed of human beings generally, is accounted for by the settings in which they are located. Furthermore, the capacity of these settings to function effectively depends upon the availability of human beings possessing the skills required for the activities expected in these settings. On the basis of their observations, Barker and his colleagues have developed a "theory of undermanning" which they apply to explain the growth and decline of behavior settings in various social contexts such as schools, neighborhoods, communities, and cultures. Implicit in the research model is the implication that the child's experience in a particular setting has an effect on his subsequent development. The validity of this assumption will be discussed below, after we have examined other operational models of the immediate context of child development that emerged during this same period.

Another major step in the delineation of developmentally relevant features of the immediate setting occurred with the differentiation between social and physical aspects of the environment. The first to operationalize this distinction was Spitz. In his original study (1945), he had called attention to the fact that the progressive deterioration exhibited by the institutionalized infants could be due not only to the severing of the mother/infant relationship but also "to other factors . . . such as the perceptual and motor deprivations from which they suffer" (1945, p. 66). Although it is not generally acknowledged, he then undertook a second investigation designed to make a critical test between his two hypotheses (Spitz, 1946b). Thus he showed that within the institutionalized environment only those children who had been separated from the mother within a limited age range exhibited severe symptoms of deterioration. Also, he successfully reversed the deterioration by introducing mother substitutes for several of the most seriously deprived children. At the same time, Spitz emphasized that the provision of the mother substitute was not a sufficient condition, since with young children, opportunity for locomotion was also a necessary prerequisite for social contact.

The Setting as a Physical Environment

The first systematic investigations of the role of the physical environment in children's behavior and development, however, occurred in quite a different sphere; namely, the impact of television viewing on children. These studies were of two kinds. The great majority examined the direct impact of television on children's behavior, both social and cognitive (Bandura, Ross, & Ross, 1963; Liebert, Neale, & Davidson, 1973; Stein & Friedrich, 1975). A second group of researches focused on the effects of television not directly on the child, but on patterns of activity and interaction in the family as a whole— what Parke has called the role of "TV as a family member'' (1978). The first study of this type was conducted by Maccoby in 1951. In a field survey, she found that over three-quarters of the respondents indicated no conversation had occurred during television viewing except at specified times such as commercials. Other studies have evaluated the effects of TV watching, and TV breakdown, on family tension, and the use of television as a babysitter (Rosenblatt & Cunningham, 1976; Steiner, 1963).

More recent investigations have illuminated yet another aspect of the immediate physical environment significant for the child's psychological growth—toys and their effects on the child's behavior and development. In a pioneering study, McCall (1974) demonstrated that the extent to which an infant played with a toy depended on its ''contingent responsiveness''—the extent to which the object could be manipulated or made to react, as opposed to remaining unchanged in response to the infant's efforts. In a subsequent study, Yarrow, Rubenstein, and Pederson (1975) found that experience with responsive toys predicted the child's subsequent development of motor coordination and such goal-directed actions as reaching, grasping, and exploring novel objects. An even broader range of motor and mental activities was related to the variety of play materials and household objects available in the infant's environment.

The Setting as a Structured Environment

A transition to another level of analysis can be discerned in a study by Wachs (1976). In this research, the physical features of the home environment were analyzed as a reflection of parental strategies in dealing with the child. For example, Wachs found that the absence of physical or visual restraints in early infancy was related to later cognitive development as measured by a standardized test administered at 2 years of age. On a broader front, Caldwell and her associates, in a series of reports from a longitudinal study (Bradley & Caldwell, 1976a, 1976b; Elardo, Bradley, & Caldwell, 1975, 1977), cite evidence that observational measures of home arrangements for 6-month-old infants were significantly related to IQ scores for the same children at 4½ years of age. Specifically, coefficients ranging between .30 and .44 were obtained for the following environmental variables: *provision of appropriate play materials, organization of physical and temporal environment,* and *opportunities for variety and daily stimulation.* Correlations with measures of mother/infant interaction were also positive, but of marginal statistical significance. When the observa-

tions were repeated part way through the study (at age 2), all of the coefficients rose in magnitude, in particular those pertaining to maternal involvement with the child and to the emotional and verbal responsiveness of the mother (Bradley & Caldwell, 1976b). In the authors' view, these results point to the importance, for the child's future cognitive development, of the parents' organizing the infant's physical environment beginning in the first year of life. Thereafter, Bradley and Caldwell suggest, children may be able to provide many needed kinds of experiences for themselves. The importance of the mother's emotional and verbal responsiveness, however, increases in the second year of life as the infant begins to use verbal communication as a means of expressing and satisfying its needs.

The developmental significance of the child's early physical environment is also demonstrated by the results of a previous study by these same investigators reporting developmental outcomes at the age of 3 (Elardo, Bradley, & Caldwell, 1975). At that time, correlations between IQ and observational measures of the home at 6 months were appreciably higher than predictions based on the Bayley Test of Mental Development administered at the age of 6 months and again at 1 year. In short, the child's later development was better predicted by characteristics of the infant's environment at the age of 6 months than by direct measures of the infant's developmental status at the same early age.

From our perspective, what is especially significant about these studies is not the findings they have yielded—valuable as they are—but the new conception, implied in the research designs, of the process through which parents, teachers, or other adults can affect the development of the young. In all the classical paradigms we have examined previously, the process was presumed to take place through direct social interaction; that is, the parent or other socializing agent had to be present and doing something with the child. In the studies by Caldwell and her colleagues, the mother can influence the child in her absence through the prior structuring of the environment so as to evoke certain kinds of activities and discourage others. Such structuring is accomplished by providing materials, arranging the physical environment, and—at later ages—giving instructions and setting time schedules and deadlines. By adapting such structure to the child's changing capacities, the parent or teacher is able to encourage and shape the child's psychological growth. We see here an elegant example of Lewin's (1936) conception of ''environment steering behavior and development.''

At a more concrete level, studies of the setting as a structured environment illuminate two additional features of the microsystem. First, the immediate setting containing the child is viewed as including physical stimuli and objects that can directly affect the child's behavior and development. Second, the influence of these physical stimuli can operate in a more complex fashion involving indirect as well as direct effects. For example, as in the case of television, a physical stimulus can reduce the frequency of parent/child interaction with possible consequences for the child's behavior and development. Conversely, the impact of physical stimuli on the child can be mediated through the parents' structuring of the child's environment.

Triadic Models and Second-Order Effects

Such processes of indirect influence can involve not only physical objects, but also people. As previously noted, this possibility was first suggested by researchers investigating the effects of father absence during World War II (e.g., Bach, 1946; Sears et al., 1946). In keeping with the then-prevailing research model, these workers collected systematic data only on the perceptions and behavior of the child. But in interpreting their findings, the investigators proposed that the child may have been affected not only directly by the absence of the role model, but also indirectly through the impact of the husband's absence on the parental behavior of the mother. It took a decade before this possibility was investigated systematically; it was confirmed in Tiller's study of children in Norwegian sailor families (Gronseth & Tiller, 1957; Tiller, 1958, 1961). The operational model of the parent/child relationship was thereby expanded from a dyad to a three-person system. It was not until the 1970s, however, that the model was formally explicated (Bronfenbrenner, 1974b, 1979; Lewis & Feiring, 1979) and applied in a still growing number of investigations. The basic mechanism revealed in such studies has been referred to by Bronfenbrenner (1974b) as a "second-order effect"—the mediation of a dyadic process through the influence of a third party. Explicit second-order effects were first demonstrated in studies documenting the impact of the father on the mother's treatment of the child (Parke, 1978; Pedersen, 1976). More recently, in a symposium on second-order effects, Pederson and his colleagues (1981) reported that 5-month-olds timed their bids for parental attention to periodic lapses during conversations between husband and wife. The authors comment: "In spite of the complexity of selective engagement and disengagement of the different dyadic units, the five-month-old infant appears suf-

ficiently sensitive and adaptive to maintain synchrony with these changes" (p. 3). In the same symposium, Rubenstein, Howes, and Pedersen (1982) described an experiment in the home in which the dyadic model was successively expanded to encompass a four-person system involving both children and adults. Mothers and their 19-month-old infants were observed on four different days under four counterbalanced conditions: only mother and infant present; mother, infant, and an infant friend; mother, infant, and an adult friend of the mother; mother, infant, peer, and peer's mother. The results revealed a complex but consistent pattern. For example, the presence of peers seemed to reduce the intensity of maternal behavior. In contrast, the presence of a second familiar adult increased affiliative behaviors on the part of the infant. The relative inaccessibility of the mother when involved with her own adult friend evoked signs of stress in her child only when there was no peer present.

Properties of the Microsystem

The complexity of structure, process, and outcome revealed by the research designs of the types employed in the foregoing studies stands in sharp contrast to the simplistic schemata of half a century earlier, when settings were differentiated solely by their geographic or social address. Implicit in the more recent designs is a conception of the setting as an organized complex of a number of critical elements. Taken together, these elements constitute what Bronfenbrenner, following Brim (1975), has referred to as a *microsystem*, defined as "a pattern of activities, roles, and interpersonal relations experienced over time by the developing person in a given setting with particular physical and material characteristics" (1979, p. 22). A *setting* is a place where people can readily engage in face-to-face interaction, such as a home, daycare center, play group, classroom, work place, and so on. The factors of activity, role, interpersonal relations, time, and material characteristics constitute the elements, or building blocks, of the system. The system also has its dynamics, since the emergent structure provides the context for influence processes, operating both directly and indirectly, to evoke and sustain patterns of reciprocal interaction between an always active organism and its immediate physical and social environment. These patterns of interaction, as they persist and evolve through time, constitute the vehicles of behavioral change and individual development.

Implicit in this microsystem model is the emergence of a more dynamic and differentiated concept of the child's immediate environment.

Through its physical and temporal organization, the near environment can steer behavior and development, a circumstance that enables parents, teachers, and other socializing agents to influence the child's activities—and through them the child's development—over extended periods of time. The differentiation in structure and function is further manifested in the expansion of focus from dyads to triads and higher order structures as the proximal contexts of the socialization process. Bronfenbrenner has referred to such higher order structures as N + 2 systems. As indicated in the example cited, these more complex systems can become units of analysis in their own right. Whereas, previously, the primary object and agent of environmental influence was seen to be the individual child, now dyads and triads are treated as dynamic structures that can affect and be affected by external forces.

Finally, these complex conceptualizations are not merely theoretical abstractions; they can now be operationalized and even counted. Thirty years ago, in his presidential address to the American Psychological Association, Robert Sears (1951), a student of Hull who had made major contributions to the synthesis of psychoanalytic and learning theory, called upon psychological science to move from monadic to dyadic units of analysis. It took three decades before developmental researchers implemented Sears's prescient paradigm, and, in the process, they have done him one better—and more; triads and still higher-order structures are now matching the dyads as primary contexts for the analysis of human behavior and development.

Ecological Transitions

At the same time, the newly emergent models are not without significant limitations. Although the research designs employed permit the assessment of complex structures and processes, they leave two critical questions unresolved. First, since all of the investigations cited are cross-sectional, the direction of influence remains ambiguous. Second, even if the causal link were established, the possibility remains that the second-order effects are purely situational and have no significant developmental impact on patterns of perception or behavior. A much underused strategy for dealing with both of these problems involves exploiting a recurring human experience to which Bronfenbrenner (1979) has applied the term *ecological transition. An ecological transition takes place whenever, during the life course, a person undergoes a change in role either within the same or in a different setting.* Such transitions occur at all ages and often serve as the impetus for developmental change. In infancy and early childhood, they are

typically occasioned by the action of someone else, but—especially from adolescence onward—they can be self-initiated as well. To cite some examples—a new sibling is born, a child enters daycare or school, the mother goes to work, the family moves to another community, the parents divorce, remarry again, a parent changes careers—or, to turn to even more universal themes—family members become sick, get well again, go on vacation, return to work, retire, or undergo the final transition to which there are no exceptions: dying.

Yet, few scientific investigators have exploited naturally occurring events of this kind. Early on, Baldwin (1947) observed the mother's behavior toward the first child before, during, and after the mother's pregnancy with a second child. More recently, Hetherington (1978) has traced the progressive influence of divorce on the mother/child relationship and the child's behavior in school. The disruptive effects of separation reached their peak one year afterwards and declined through the second year, although the divorced mothers never gained as much influence with the child as their married counterparts experienced. Evidence for a second-order effect appeared in the finding that the mother's effectiveness in dealing with the child was directly related to the amount of support she received from her ex-husband. Unfortunately, studies of this kind are rare. With a few exceptions to be noted below, the common transitions of life, especially during adolescence, youth, and adulthood, have yet to be investigated.

From the point of view of scientific method, every ecological transition has the virtue that it constitutes a readymade experiment of nature with a built-in, before/after design in which each subject can serve as his own control. In addition, the ecological transition offers another strategic advantage of particular significance for the concerns of this chapter; it is especially well suited for investigating development as a product of environmental change.

Developmental Validity

This brings us to a critical question in research on development-in-context; namely, what constitutes an operational definition of development? Or to put the issue in another way, what kind of research design is necessary to demonstrate that development has in fact occurred as a function of environmental conditions? For example, most of the investigations we have just reviewed, from Barker's field studies of psychological ecology to the demonstration of second-order effects within the family, provide dramatic evidence for the impact of the immediate environment on the behavior of the child. But *behavioral change cannot be equated with developmental change.* The former could simply represent a temporary adaptation to an immediate situation and hence involve no lasting effect. By contrast, the latter implies a process of growth in which patterns of behavior are internalized and maintain some degree of consistency and independence across environmental settings. As has been documented elsewhere (Bronfenbrenner, 1979), most research on human development takes such generalization for granted without actually providing for its demonstration in the research design. This comment applies both to past and more recent work. For example, in research on ecological psychology, it remains to be shown that the exposure of children to particular behavior settings in the community has any enduring impact on their subsequent behavior in other contexts. Similarly, it is still an open question whether second-order effects have any lasting effect outside the specific situation in which they are generated. Resolution of this issue requires data on the child's behavior in at least one other microsystem that is removed both in structure and time from the original setting in which the behavior was produced. In other words, if patterns of action or attitude evoked in one setting carry over to another time and place, this constitutes evidence for the occurrence of developmental change. We refer to this design criterion as *developmental validity.*

The foregoing criterion was in fact met in a number of the research designs we have presented in the course of this chapter, but its application was not explicitly recognized or given formal statement by the investigator. Here we have yet another instance of the emergence of what we have called "latent structures" in the evolution of scientific models for studying development-in-context. The most common de facto demonstration of developmental validity is provided by evidence that behavior changes induced within the family are carried over into other settings, most notably preschool, school, and perhaps most frequent of all, the psychological laboratory. Indeed, the use of the laboratory experiment as a method for demonstrating that development has in fact occurred represents one of the most important and ecologically valid applications of the laboratory as a basic tool in developmental research.

The perceptive reader will observe that, in our examination of the more differentiated structure of the environment implicit in contemporary research models, we have already passed beyond the boundaries of a single immediate setting containing the developing person. Thus our examples of ecological transition have included shifts in role outside as well as within the family. And in our explication of the criteria for developmental validity, we have stipulated the necessity of including at least two contrasting microsystems in the research design. This expansion of focus beyond one setting is also manifested in the designs employed by investigators of development-in-context during the past two decades. We turn next to an examination of this further evolution of latent structure in developmental research.

RESEARCH MODELS OF RELATIONS BETWEEN DEVELOPMENTAL SETTINGS: THE MESOSYSTEM

Beginning with the earliest studies of socialization, there has been a recurring, but apparently unremarked, discrepancy in the types of experimental designs being employed. In investigations of the effects of parental childrearing practices, some workers measured the developmental outcomes in the home, others in some external settings like nursery, preschool, school classroom, or, as we have just noted, in the laboratory. This difference in research design has a theoretical implication. In addition to permitting the assessment of developmental validity, the second model assumes a more complex definition of the environment as involving at least two settings. The notion that two or more settings can simultaneously affect the behavior and development of the child has evolved only gradually. Once again, the process has been one of progressive elaboration in the latent structure of research designs. A research design that implicitly treats behavior or development as a function of processes occurring in two or more settings, or of the relations between these settings, is referred to as a *mesosystem model.*

Insofar as we have been able to discover, the possibility of multisetting influences on development first received recognition in Hartshorne and May's classical experiments on deceit (1928), in which the authors reported on the relative impact of parents' versus peers' values on the child's attitudes about right and wrong. This study is a forerunner of a research trajectory that reemerged in the 1950s—Neiman (1954); Harris and Tseng (1957); Hess and Goldblatt (1957); Stukat (1958); and Bowerman and Kinch (1959)—and that reached its climax in the 1960s and 1970s. In a large-scale survey, Coleman (1961) documented the relative impact of parents versus peers on high school achievement. A few years later, cross-cultural comparisons of peer group influences were reported in the work of Bronfenbrenner and Devereux (Bronfenbrenner, 1967, 1970; Bronfenbrenner, Devereux, Suci, & Rodgers,

1965; Devereux, 1965, 1966; Devereux, Bronfenbrenner, & Rodgers, 1969; Rodgers, 1971) and of Kandel and Lesser (1972). While studies of this kind offered powerful evidence of complementary and differential effects of exposure to diverse settings, the research designs employed did not provide for a comparative analysis of the environmental structures and processes that produced the obtained effects.

The Comparative Analysis of Microsystems

The first investigators to carry out such systematic comparisons were the psychological ecologists. Barker and Gump (1964) compared the experience of pupils in big schools versus those in small schools and demonstrated that, in accord with Barker's theory of undermanning, children in the latter setting participated in a far greater variety of roles in contrast to the large high school in which many students must compete for a restricted number of opportunities and hence become marginal participants in school society. It is only recently, however, that comparative studies of this kind have been extended to other types of childrearing settings. For example, our examination of the scores of studies conducted during the past decade on children in daycare (for a summary, see Belsky, Steinberg, & Walker, 1982), revealed that the overwhelming majority employed what we have called a social address model; that is, a comparison of children reared at home versus those reared in daycare settings. A far smaller number of investigations examined the significance of daycare for the mother, or for the family as a whole. Rarest of all were studies comparing the actual experiences of children in home and daycare settings. The most systematic research in this area is a series of studies, within a longitudinal design, conducted in Sweden by Cochran and Gunnarsson (Cochran, 1975, 1977; Cochran & Robinson, 1982; Gunnarsson, 1978). Early analysis revealed that, although youngsters in the two settings had many common experiences, interactions between adults and children, particularly in the cognitive-verbal sphere, were more frequent in homes than in daycare centers, thus providing greater opportunity for socialization by adults. An important factor in this regard was the reduced need for explanation and restriction in the more homogeneous, predominantly child-oriented center environment as compared to the home; the latter also contained adult possessions and areas of adult activity. The lower level of adult/child interaction in the daycare setting was especially marked for boys, who were more likely to concentrate their activities in the peer group. This effect tended to increase with the age of the child. Gunnarsson (1978) hypothesized that the observed difference may be related to the absence of male caregivers in center settings. Unfortunately, the question of whether the experience in the two contrasting settings had any effect on the children's development is clouded by an unresolved issue of developmental validity. Each child was observed only in a single setting, a circumstance Gunnarsson identifies as one of the major limitations of the study.

This shortcoming was remedied in an investigation of communication in home and school settings conducted by Philips (1972). The subjects were children living on an Indian reservation. The results indicated that much of the Indian children's confusion and "inappropriate behavior" as perceived by school personnel appeared to be the result of the cultural incongruity between the worlds of home and school. A nicely complementary investigation shifts the focus from the children to the teacher. Erickson and Mohatt (1982) studied two elementary school classrooms on an Indian reservation. One of the classes was taught by an Indian teacher, the other by a non-Indian. The stated purpose of the investigation was to examine "the similarities in . . . two classrooms of culturally similar children who were taught by teachers whose cultural backgrounds differed" (p. 2). The research revealed consistent disparities in the way the two teachers organized the lesson format, paced the discussion, and seated the children. For example, the Indian teacher tended to create participation structures in the classroom that were more congruent with tribal etiquette than those introduced by the non-Indian instructor. The fact that there was only one teacher of each race limits the generalizability of the findings but not the scope of the environmental model underlying the research design.

The foregoing studies have in common the feature that they involve a comparative analysis of different microsystems. Although there can be no question of the scientific utility of this comparative paradigm, it exhibits a now familiar missing element, the absence of information on any developmental effects as manifested by the behavior of the children themselves in other settings at other times.

Setting Transitions

One research strategy that contributes to the solution of this problem involves tracing changes in the behavior of the same children as they move from one type of setting to another; that is, they undergo what we have called an ecological transition, now not

merely within settings, but across them. An ingenious application of this strategy is provided by
Hayes and Grether's (1969) unorthodox analysis of
achievement test scores for several thousand students enrolled in grades two through six of the New
York City school system. Instead of examining academic gains only in the usual fashion by analyzing
changes from fall to spring, Hayes and Grether also
looked at the remaining interval from spring to fall—
at what happened during the summer.

During the vacation, white pupils from advantaged families continued to gain about the same rate,
whereas those from disadvantaged and black families not only progressed more slowly but actually
reversed direction and lost ground so that by the time
they returned to school they were considerably farther behind their classmates from more favored circumstances. The authors conclude that the substantial difference in academic achievement across
social class and race found by the end of the sixth
grade is not "attributable to what goes on *in* a
school, most of it comes from what goes on *out* of
school" (p. 6). Hayes and Grether's findings, and
conclusion, have been replicated in a subsequent
investigation by Heyns (1978).

An analogous research design was employed in a
longitudinal study of transition from elementary to
junior high school (Blyth, Simmons, & Bush, 1978;
Simmons, Blyth, Van Cleave, & Bush, 1979). In
addition to the shift in setting, the investigators took
into account a biological transition, the onset of
puberty. The dependent variable in this study was an
overall measure of self-esteem. The results indicated
that entrance into high school had the effect of
lowering the young person's evaluation of the self,
particularly among girls who were experiencing the
onset of puberty at the time of transition.

While these investigations document the psychological impact of moving from one life setting into
another, the research designs do not provide for any
analysis of the structures and processes in the setting
that mediate the observed changes. The scientific
gains to be attained through an analysis of processes
accompanying the change are illustrated in two sets
of studies that document ecological transitions at
opposite ends of the lifespan. In their longitudinal
investigation of the effects of divorce, Hetherington
and her colleagues (1979) observed the changes in
the behavior of children both at home and at school.
The findings revealed that boys and girls in recently
divorced households exhibited behavior patterns at
school that were less socially and cognitively mature
than those of children in nondivorced families, with
the former group showing higher rates of dependent
help-seeking behavior, acting out, and non-

compliance. These effects were more marked for
boys than for girls. Moreover, even when the behavior of the boys in divorced families improved, they
were still "viewed and responded to more negatively by peers and teachers than were children from
non-divorced homes or girls from divorced homes"
(pp. 26–27). These results clearly demonstrate the
spillover aftereffects of experience from one setting
into another.

Hetherington and her colleagues also examined
the stability of behavior across three settings—
home, school, and laboratory. In what may appear
as a counterintuitive result, they found that children
from divorced homes exhibited greater continuity
across settings than their counterparts in the control
group, particularly in the first year following the
family breakup. The authors explain this finding
with the speculation that "In the first year following
divorce, the distress, anxiety, and problems in coping with their new family situation are most intense. . . . Under such disturbed conditions, the internal state of the child, rather than external
variations may control the behavior of the child" (p.
44). In other words, the divorced children were not
as responsive to the differential demands of setting
as those whose family life was more stable.

An investigation published in the same year sheds
additional light on the dynamic governing the cross-
setting effect of parental divorce on the child's behavior in school. Hess and Camara (1979) showed
that the degree of disturbance, aggressive behavior,
and impaired performance at school was a function
of the quality of the emotional relationship maintained after the divorce between the child and both
parents.

In the foregoing examples, ecological transitions
are employed to maximal scientific advantage by
analyzing the specific properties of the microsystem
in one setting that induce particular kinds of effects
in the other. This strategy is profitably applied to
experimental as well as naturalistic studies. An instructive example is provided by the Abcedarian
Project (Ramey & Haskins, 1981, 1982). From 1972
to 1977, four cohorts of children at high risk for
school failure and psychosocial retardation were
randomly assigned to an experimental and a control
group. The former were exposed to an intensive
daycare program from the age of 3 months to the
time of entry into public kindergarten. The program
offered a cognitive and socially oriented curriculum
emphasizing language. In addition, social work,
medical, and nutrition services were provided. The
control group children were not enrolled in daycare,
but their families received the other three types of
service. An analysis of followup data obtained upon

the children's entry into school led the investigators to the following conclusion:

> This experiment, and particularly the experience of children once they enter the public schools, has caused us to reexamine what might be called the psychological approach to understanding development. . . . We have tended to see the problem as residing within individual children or their families. Similarly, we have tended to view the objective intervention programs as changing individual children or their families. Yet the results we are beginning to report concerning children's homes, neighborhoods, and schools have forced us to consider the social environment within which children develop. (Ramey & Haskins, 1982, pp. 32–33)

Setting transitions continue to have developmental impact throughout the lifespan. An experimental program designed by Blenkner, Bloom, and Nielson (1971) to improve protective services for the elderly was successfully implemented, but produced an unhappy boomerang effect. The sample consisted of noninstitutionalized persons over 60 years of age who were deemed incapable of adequately caring for themselves and were being carried on social agency rolls. Cases were randomly allocated to experimental and control groups. The former were given "considerably greater service of a more varied nature than was ordinarily available in the community" (p. 489). Four highly qualified caseworkers were hired to implement the special program. The control group received the "standard treatment" provided by local social agencies. Although the experimental group clearly experienced a higher level of protective services, findings on measures of functional competence administered after 1 year failed to show a reliable advantage for the special program. In fact, such differences as there were favored the control group, and mortality rates—referred to by the authors as "the ultimate deterioration in competence"—showed a similar trend. Concerned by these findings, the investigators continued to gather followup data on mortality rates in the two groups. At the end of 4 years, the survival rate in the experimental group was significantly lower than that for the controls. Upon further investigation, the researchers discovered the source of the paradox. The more intensive casework conducted in the special program had led to earlier and higher rates of institutionalization; placement in the institution, in turn, was associated with a higher mortality rate.

A study by Aldrich and Mendkoff (1963) sheds light on the dynamics through which the environment accelerates departure from life. The investigators exploited an experiment of nature provided by the impending closing of a home for disabled elderly persons and the transfer of residents to other similar facilities. The principal outcome measures were deviations from expected mortality rates for age during three successive periods: before patients learned of the projected relocation, while patients were still in the home and awaiting transfer, and after relocation had taken place. Rates rose markedly during the first 3 months following relocation and declined gradually thereafter.

Linkages Between Settings

The foregoing studies at both ends of life's continuum share in common a research design that by implication defines the context of development as consisting of more than one setting; thus it meets the criterion for a mesosystem model. In its fullest form, however, such a model contains one additional feature not represented in the investigations discussed thus far. In none of these studies was any explicit consideration given to the nature of possible connections between different settings and to the role of such connections in mediating the impact of each setting on the developing person. The first investigation we have been able to find that takes such linkages into account was conducted in the early 1950s by Prugh, Staub, Sands, Kirschbaum, and Lenihan (1953). These investigatiors took advantage of a planned change in hospital practice to conduct a comparative study of the reaction of children and their parents to two contrasting modes of ward operation. The groups were matched in age, sex, diagnosis, and past and current periods of hospitalization. The control group consisted of children admitted and discharged over a 4-month period prior to the introduction of the contemplated change. The young patients hospitalized during this period experienced "traditional practices of ward management" (p. 75) in which parents were restricted to weekly visiting periods of 2 hr. each. The experimental group, admitted during the next period, could receive visits from parents. In addition, the parents accompanied the child on admission to the ward, were introduced to staff, and were encouraged to participate in ward care. Greater emotional distress was observed among the children in the control group, not only while they were in the hospital but also during followup visits to the home conducted periodically throughout the year following hospitalization. The distinctive feature of this experiment is the introduction of familiar figures from one environment into the other in order to ease the process of transition for the child.

The above strategy illustrates the use of a meso-system model for intervention research that involves strengthening of *interpersonal linkages between settings*. A decade later, this same strategy was employed as the principal element of a preschool intervention program emphasizing parental involvement in the preschool as well as the school (Gray & Klaus, 1965; Karnes, 1969; Weikart, 1967), but this meso-system paradigm has seldom been applied at older ages. A notable exception is Smith's "School and Home" experiment (1968). Smith saw the growing alienation between parents and schools prevailing many segments of our society as a basic problem of American public education. With this issue as the focus, she designed a program to improve school performance of low-income minority pupils in the elementary grades. The project involved approximately 1,000 children from low-income families, most of them black, attending public elementary schools. The principal strategy employed for enhancing children's school performance was that of involving parents and teachers "as partners, not competitors, in the child's learning process." A core group of low-income parents mobilized others to become involved in the program. Parents were urged to provide supports for their children. Youngsters were given tags to wear at home that said, "Please read to me." Older children were given tags imprinted: "May I read to you?" Business students from the high school typed and duplicated teaching materials thus freeing teachers to work directly with the children. Teachers' in-service sessions focused on the influence of environmental factors in the children's classroom behavior and performance. In short, reciprocal support systems were established for all participants in the program. Regrettably, the innovativeness of Smith's intervention strategy was not matched by equal originality in the selection of outcome measures. Measured effects were limited to significant gains on tests of reading achievement, and overwhelmingly favorable attitudes expressed toward the program in a questionnaire that brought a gratifying response rate of 90%, unusually high in research with low-income families.

Since Smith's work was published, there has been only one substantial foray into the borderland between family and school, an ethnographic study by Lightfoot (1978), appropriately entitled "Worlds Apart."

The conception of the environment implicit in the Smith study and other mesosystem designs that we have just examined is obviously more complex than that implied in models considered previously. Nevertheless, as these same investigations demonstrate, this complex conception *is* translatable into research operations, which in turn can yield new scientific knowledge regarding the role of environmental factors in human development.

Galton's Nature/Nurture Model Reanalyzed as a Mesosystem

A mesosystem model can also place old knowledge in new perspective. This point is illustrated in Bronfenbrenner's (1975a) reanalysis of published data from studies of identical twins reared together and reared apart (Juel-Nielsen, 1964; Newman, Freeman, & Holzinger, 1937; Shields, 1962). Studies of this kind typically report correlations between IQ scores of twins reared apart that are only slightly lower than those for twins reared in the same home; specifically, Erlenmeyer-Kimling and Jarvik (1963) report a mediant correlation of .75 for the former group versus .87 for the latter. This finding is ordinarily interpreted as testifying to the primacy of genetic influences in the determination of intelligence (e.g., Burt, 1966; Jensen, 1969, 1980; Loehlin, Lindzey, & Spuhler, 1975; Willerman, 1979). Underlying this interpretation is the assumption that twins reared in the same family share a common environment, whereas those reared apart are experiencing widely different environments. A mesosystem model calls this assumption into question on the grounds that, even though they are not living in the same home, the twins may be sharing common environments in other settings. To test this hypothesis, Bronfenbrenner recalculated correlations based on subgroups of twins sharing common environments as follows:

1. Among 35 pairs of separated twins for whom information was available about the community in which they lived, the correlation in Binet IQ for those raised in the same town was .83, for those brought up in different towns, .67.

2. In another sample of 38 separated twins, the correlation for those attending the same school in the same town was .87; for those attending schools in different towns .66.

3. When the communities in the preceding samples were classified as similar versus dissimilar on the basis of size and economic base (e.g., mining vs. agricultural), the correlation for separated twins living in similar communities was .86; for those residing in dissimilar localities .26.

Mesosystems Summarized

The lowest common denominator in all the studies we have examined is a conception of the environment that takes into account the experience of the developing person in more than one setting. Within this general paradigm, three types of research designs have been employed.

1. *Cross-sectional Mesosystem Models*. In this design the behavior and development of the child are analyzed as a joint function of influences deriving from the child's participation in two or more settings simultaneously.
2. *Transitional Mesosystem Models*. Here developmental changes in the child's behavior, and in the behavior of others with whom the child commonly interacts, are related to the child's transition from one setting into another.
3. *Linkage Mesosystem Models*. The designs incorporate not only environmental influences arising within settings; they also examine the developmental impact, within settings, of the degree and nature of the interconnections existing between these settings.

Ideally, a comprehensive mesosystem model would involve a synthesis of elements from all three of the above research designs. Such synthesis is present only to a partial extent in investigations conducted to date.

A mesosystem model might appear to be sufficiently complex to be applicable to almost any environmental situation that the developmental researcher could encounter. Yet, there is one other significant environmental terrain that they do not encompass. All of the research models we have examined thus far have been limited to settings containing the developing person. Thus they do not take into account the possibility of forces emanating from external contexts that affect processes within immediate settings. We turn next, and last, to the evolution of research paradigms incorporating this domain.

EXTERNAL CONTEXTS INFLUENCING DEVELOPMENTAL PROCESSES: EXOSYSTEM MODELS

The first systematic effort to assess the impact of an external setting on socialization processes and outcomes appears in research on the effects of maternal employment. The earliest studies of this kind were published in the 1930s (Glueck & Glueck,

1934a, 1934b; Hodgkiss, 1933; Mathews, 1934). The basic paradigm then, as it still is today, was the comparison of children at different social addresses, in this instance defined by the mother's work status. In addition, most of the early studies were flawed by serious errors in research design, in particular the failure to control for social class and family structure. There were a few notable exceptions. The first of these was also far ahead of its time in the conception of the environment implicit in the research design that was employed. In 1934, Mathews published an investigation of differences in parental behavior and conditions in the home, based on questionnaires from 200 children in grades five through nine. Half of the children had mothers with full-time jobs outside the home; the other half had mothers who were not employed. The children were pair matched on sex, grade, school, community, and father's occupation. The statistically significant differences that emerged fell into a pattern: a higher percentage of working mothers' children wore soiled clothes to school, had a sense of hurry around the home, were scolded by a tired mother, and sometimes had to make their own breakfasts. Contrary to expectations, their fathers were less active in the home, and fewer of them took responsibility for the care of the children or played games with them. Many years later, a reviewer pointed out that the study by Mathews had been conducted at a time "when full-time working hours could be as much as 10 or 11 hours a day, when automatic machines were rare in housekeeping, and when fathers lost status (in their own eyes at least) when they participated in family chores" (Stolz, 1960, p. 767). Although Mathews could not have forseen the social changes that were to occur, she did anticipate future developments in research models. Not only was her investigation the first to broaden the focus of studies of maternal employment to include the mother as well as the child, but she also investigated the indirect effects of mother's work on the parental behavior of the father. Such a triadic model was not to reappear in studies of maternal employment for a quarter of a century.

The Evolution of Research Models in Studies of Maternal Employment

In the interim, scientific development in this sphere followed a more gradual and now familiar course, in which three successive stages can be usefully distinguished. (For a more detailed analysis, see Bronfenbrenner & Crouter, 1981). As already noted, the earliest and most enduring line of investigation focused on the identification of differences in the characteristics of children as a function of the mothers' work status. The principal developments in this initial phase occurred mainly in the area of research design. By the late 1950s, imposing controls for such confounding factors as family structure and socioeconomic status brought about a reversal in the research findings. Whereas, previously, study after study had reported deleterious effects of maternal employment on children, the use of more rigorous methods resulted in the complete disappearance of this main effect, but the occasional emergence of interactions, particularly by sex of child, that challenged ready interpretation.

These interactions became more frequent and more pronounced in a second major wave of inquiry that emerged in the 1960s and was stimulated by and exemplified in the work of Hoffman (1963). This line of investigation focused on the mediating role of maternal attitudes in influencing the impact of the mother's employment status on the child. Mothers who liked their work reported stronger feelings of attachment to the children and imposed less severe discipline than those not working outside the home. Their children, in turn, expressed more positive attitudes toward the mother and exhibited greater impulse control in school. In contrast, mothers who did not like their work described less power assertion over their children, but significantly more assertiveness of the child toward the mother. The children of these mothers reported more regular participation in household tasks, used physical force more often, and responded to frustration in a less adaptive way. The findings of these studies also suggested that the consequences of maternal employment might differ for the two sexes, being more beneficial to girls than to boys.

These themes became the major preoccupation of research on maternal employment in the third and final phase extending from the early 1970s to the present day. The hallmark of these studies is a pattern of findings characterized by complex but consistent interactions by sex and social class. By 1980, there accumulated an appreciable body of evidence indicating that the mother's working outside the home tends to have a salutary effect on girls, but is associated with some negative outcomes for boys. The findings for girls are not only firmer, but also point to the nature of the underlying process involved. The relevant studies have been carefully and comprehensively reviewed by Hoffman (1980). The results indicate that daughters from families in which the mother works tend to admire their mothers more, have a more positive conception of the female

role, and are more likely to be independent. None of these trends is apparent for boys. Instead, the pattern of results, especially in recent investigations, indicates that the mother's working outside the home is correlated with reduced academic achievement for sons in middle-class but not in low-income families (Banducci, 1967; Brown, 1970; Gold & Andres, 1978a, 1978b; Gold, Andres, & Glorieux, 1979). Although, in several of these same studies, daughters of working mothers obtained slightly higher scores than daughters of mothers who remained at home, none of these differences is significant, nor are the results qualified by social class.

The processes underlying these findings are illuminated by the results of a study currently being conducted by the senior author and his colleagues on a sample of 152 two-parent families, each with a 3-year-old child (Bronfenbrenner, Alvarez, & Henderson, 1982). The basic data consisted of parents' free descriptions of the 3-year-old child given in an open-ended interview. A systematic content analysis revealed that the most flattering portrait of a daughter was painted by mothers who were working full-time, but this was also the group that portrayed a son in the least favorable terms. A further breakdown by mother's education status indicated that the enthusiastic view of a daughter in the full-time group occurred primarily among those mothers who had some education beyond high school. For those with limited schooling, the trend was actually reversed, with daughters of mothers working full-time being described least favorably. In the light of both quantitative and qualitative findings, the authors make the following interpretative comment: ''The pattern brings to mind the picture of an aspiring professional woman who already sees her three-year-old daughter as an interesting and competent person potentially capable of following in her mother's footsteps'' (p. 12). The most salient feature of the findings for sons was the exceptionally positive description given by mothers working part-time in contrast to the much lower evaluation offered by those fully employed. The advantages of part-time employment, so far as maternal perceptions are concerned, were appreciably greater for a son than for a daughter. Regarding the basis for this sex difference, the authors speculate as follows: ''One possible explanation draws on the recurrent and generally accepted finding in research on early sex differences (Maccoby & Jacklin, 1974) that male infants tend to be more physically active from birth and hence require more control and supervision. Full-time work may limit opportunities for such necessary monitoring. Viewed from this perspective, the findings suggest that the reported sex differences in effects of maternal employment derive from the cumulative interaction of perceptual and organismic factors evolving in a larger socioeconomic context'' (pp. 12–13).

In a separate interview, the results of fathers' interviews revealed the same highly differentiated demographic profile, but in somewhat lower relief. No such pattern appeared, however, in descriptions given by parents of themselves or of their respective spouses. It would seem, therefore, that maternal work status may have a distinctive impact on the parents' perceptions of their preschool children and that the number of hours the mother works is an especially critical factor. It remains to be seen, however, whether these early descriptions have any lasting consequence. A follow-up assessment is currently under way of the children's behavior and performance in the first grade.

Further elaborations of the underlying research model are reflected in two other sets of findings during this period. A longitudinal study by Moore (1963) reported some long-range effects of maternal employment. Children whose mothers worked when the child was under 2 years of age exhibited greater dependence and insecurity after entering school. Similar trends are apparent in a retrospective study by Burchinal (1963); consistent with the results of cross-sectional designs, the finding of impaired functioning was specific to intellectual performance in boys. In a different domain, a number of investigators reported that husbands of working mothers engaged in more household tasks (e.g., Blood, 1963, 1967; Blood & Hamblin, 1958; Sanfilios-Rothschild, 1970), but this conclusion was subsequently called into question by Pleck (1981).

Once again, we summarize these investigations not for their substantive findings, but for the insight they provide regarding the evolution of research models in field studies of human development. From this perspective, what we observe in studies of influences from external settings, in this instance from the workplace, is a recapitulation of the sequence we previously detected in the development of latent structures in other spheres of inquiry. Thus the earliest paradigms were simple comparisons of children at different social addresses; in this instance, the addresses were outside the home at the mother's workplace. With the advent of process theories focused around the parent/child relationship, the parent was added as an addressee. With the introduction in research designs of multiple demographic variables, the effort to control for each introduced investigators to a new phenomenon: the possibility

that processes operate differently in different social contexts, with parental attitudes functioning as a powerful intervening variable. The scientific paradigm then shifted to what we have called a person-process-context model. Application of this model confirmed that the external context, the mother's participation in work, evokes differing socialization processes and outcomes in diverse social contexts. There are indications that these processes can be mediated by second-order effects and can have long-range consequences in the life of the developing person.

At the same time, the exosystem model that has evolved for the study of the effects of maternal employment lacks certain features of paradigms we have examined in other areas. Specifically, the work setting remains essentially a social address devoid of any dynamic structure of its own or of the system of interconnections with the microsystem containing the developing persons. These missing features become, as we will see in the following section, quite prominent in research designs employed for studying the influence of the father's employment on family functioning and the development of the child.

Research Paradigms for Investigating the Effects of Father's Occupation

Until very recently, researches on the impact of work on family life have treated the job situations of mothers and fathers as separate worlds, having no relation to each other and leading to rather different results. To be sure, when both lines of investigation first began in the 1930s, they focused on the same problem area—a concern with the effects of whether the parent had a job. But the initial assumptions were already addressed to opposite poles. For mothers, it was the fact of being employed that was presumed to be damaging to the child, whereas for fathers it was being unemployed that was seen as the destructive force. Moreover, in contrast to an initial preoccupation with the direct effects of maternal employment on the child, studies of paternal occupation centered, from the very outset, upon effects on the father himself, and on the functioning of the family as a whole. Child outcomes were slow to emerge as foci of scientific attention, and, even then, were viewed mainly as indirect effects of the impact of the father's work situation on parental patterns of childrearing.

Once again, several stages can be distinguished in the development of research in this area. The first studies appeared in the late 1930s and dealt with the impact on the family of the father's loss of a job during the Great Depression (Angell, 1936; Cavan

& Ranck, 1938; Komarovsky, 1940; Morgan, 1939). The husband's unemployment resulted in a loss of status within the family, a marked increase in family tensions and disagreements, and a decrease in social life outside the home. At the same time, the father became increasingly unstable, moody, and depressed.

Once the Depression was over, the interest in fathers declined. Indeed, during the next 20 years, the father was remembered by researchers only for his absence in World War II. It was not until the late 1950s that Miller and Swanson (1958) published a study focusing on characteristics of the father's work situation affecting parents' childrearing values and practices. The investigators distinguished two main types of work organization: *bureaucratic* and *entrepreneurial*. The first, represented by large-scale businesses, was characterized by relatively more secure conditions of work, which were manifested by such features as regular hours, stabilized wages, unemployment insurance, and retirement funds. The second, exemplified by small-scale family-owned businesses, involved greater initiative, competitiveness, risk taking, and insecurity regarding the future. Miller and Swanson reported that wives of men from bureaucratic backgrounds described styles of upbring that were more permissive and laid greater stress on the development of interpersonal skills; by contrast, wives of husbands working in entrepreneurial settings were found to be more concerned with individual achievement and striving. Unfortunately, the investigators based their findings on the analysis of each group separately, without ever making a direct comparison between the two. Although similar findings based on Miller and Swanson's occupational dichotomy were obtained by Caudill and Weinstein in Japan (1969), a later effort to replicate their original results in the United States did not prove successful (Maccoby, 1981), perhaps because of the progressive bureaucratization of entreprenurial settings in recent decades.

A more refined and methodologically rigorous analysis of the father's work situation was published by Kohn in 1969. He proposed that the structure and content of activities in the father's job shaped his value orientations to other aspects of his life, including the ends and means of childrearing. Kohn proceeded to test this hypothesis in a series of studies of middle-class and working-class men and their childrearing values. As predicted, working-class men whose jobs typically require compliance with authority tended to hold values that stressed obedience in their children; by contrast, middle-class fathers expected self-direction and independence, the qualities required by the demands of their occupation. The values were also reflected in childrearing practices. Subsequently, Kohn and Schooler (1973, 1978) examined the nature of work in a more fine-grained analysis, focusing on the dimension of "occupational self-direction"—the extent to which a job requires complex skills, autonomy and lack of routinization—and its relation to workers' "intellectual flexibility" as measured in a series of standardized tests. Using causal modeling techniques with longitudinal data, the investigators demonstrated that the occupational self-direction of a job could affect one's intellectual flexibility 10 years later. This finding has recently been replicated in a comparative study including samples both from the United States and Poland (Slomczynski, Miller, & Kohn, 1981). Unfortunately, no evidence is yet available on how the opportunity for self-direction at work, and the intellectual flexibility that it generates, relate to parental patterns of childrearing, and how these, in turn, affect the behavior and development of the child.

The full causal sequence is documented for a different psychological domain, however, in a study by Mortimer (1974, 1976) based on Kohn's theoretical model. In a reanalysis of longitudinal data from a panel study, she found a strong tendency for sons to choose an occupation similar to their father's as analyzed along the dimensions of work autonomy and the function of work activities. The special strength of Mortimer's study lies in the inclusion of parent/child relationships as an intervening link in her model. She found that the most effective transmission of vocational value and choice occurred under a combination of a prestigious parental role model and a close father/son relationship.

Research Models of the Work/Family Interface

A third line of investigation, emerging in the middle 1960s, reflects a significant elaboration in the latent structure of research designs in this sphere. The earliest studies in this domain focused on the effects of conflicting time schedules. For example, Mott, Mann, McLoughlin, and Warwick (1965) found that workers on the late afternoon shift rarely saw their school-age children during the work week. The job of discipline fell to the mother, and the shortage of time shared by both parents produced family conflicts over what to do with that time. A subsequent study (Landy, Rosenberg, & Sutton-Smith, 1969) examined the impact on daughters of the father's working on a night shift. The daughters of men so employed showed significantly lower scores in tests of academic achievement.

In 1977, Kanter introduced the concept of "work

absorption'' to describe the extent to which work made demands on one's physical and mental energy. In the same year, Heath (1977) studied the effects of this phenomenon and reported that it had a ''narrowing effect'' on men who had little time for nonwork activities, including spending time with their children. Work absorption tended to generate guilt and increased irritability and impatience in dealing with the child.

More recently, Bohen and Viveros-Long (1981) exploited an experiment of nature to investigate the impact of flexible work hours (flexitime) on family life. They compared two federal agencies engaged in similar work and staffed by similar personnel, but differing in arrangement of working hours. In one agency the employees worked a conventional schedule from 9 A.M. to 5 P.M.; in the other, they could choose to arrive within a 2-hr. range in the morning and adjust their leaving time accordingly. The results of the experiment were somewhat ironic. Measures of family strain and participation in home activities showed a significant difference favoring flexitime for only one group of families—those without children. Two explanations are proposed for the absence of effects on families with children. One argues that flexitime arrangements do not go far enough to meet the complex scheduling problems experienced by today's parents. A second interpretation suggests that the flexible time may have been used for activities outside the home unrelated to childrearing, such as recreation, socializing, or even moonlighting. Unfortunately, no data were available to verify either hypothesis.

The study by Bohen and Viveros-Long included data on mothers as well as fathers. In this respect, it reflects a recent and long-delayed convergence for the two hitherto separate lines of research on maternal and paternal employment and their effects on family life. The first manifestation of this convergence appeared in a field study conducted by Rapoport and Rapoport (1971) of the everyday problems, tensions, and experiences of dual-career families in England. This same theme has been followed up in the United States by a number of investigators (Golden, 1975; Hood, 1980; Hood & Golden, 1979; Piotrkowski, 1979; Pleck, 1983; Pleck, Staines, & Lang, 1980). The studies document the spillover of tensions in the work situation into the family, and vice versa.

Exosystems Through Time and Space

The research designs of the foregoing studies reflect the development of a complex, reciprocal model of exosystem structures, processes, and effects. At the same time, they exhibit two now-familiar limitations. First, the primary research focus is on family functioning rather than the resultant behavior and development of the child. Second, since all the designs are cross-sectional, they do not permit an assessment of the evolution of process-in-context over time or of long-range developmental effects on the child.

These limitations are transcended in Elder's reanalysis of archival data from two longitudinal studies conducted in California with samples of children born in the early versus late 1920s (Elder, 1974, 1979, 1981; Elder & Rockwell, 1979; Rockwell & Elder, 1982). Like his predecessors in earlier decades, Elder saw an opportunity to investigate the impact of the Great Depression on family life, but to do so in the context of a much more powerful research design. The samples for both studies had been selected before the Depression had occurred. As happens in a mighty storm, some families were directly hit by the subsequent disaster, and others spared. Insofar as individual households were concerned, these strokes of fortune fell in a virtually random pattern as this factory closed and that one remained in operation, one stock collapsed and another survived on the Big Board. Elder took advantage of this natural experiment to divide his sample into two otherwise comparable groups differentiated on the basis of whether the loss of income as a result of the Depression exceeded or fell short of 35%. Both of these groups were also stratified on the basis of the family's socioeconomic status prior to 1929. The availability of longitudinal data on the children made it possible to assess long-range developmental outcomes through late childhood, adolescence, and adulthood. Finally, the fact that the children in one sample were born 8 years earlier than those in the other permitted a comparison of the effects of the Depression on youngsters who were adolescents when their families became economically deprived versus those who were still young children at that time.

The results for the two groups presented a dramatic contrast. Paradoxically, for youngsters who were teenagers during the Depression years, the family's economic deprivation appeared to have a salutary effect on their subsequent development, especially in the middle class. As compared with the nondeprived who were matched on pre-Depression socioeconomic status, deprived boys displayed greater desire to achieve and a firmer sense of career goals. Boys and girls from deprived homes attained greater satisfaction in life, both by their own and by societal standards. Though more pronounced for adolescents from middle-class backgrounds, these favorable outcomes were evident among their lower-class counterparts as well. Analysis of interview and observation protocols enabled Elder to identify what he regarded as the critical factor in instigating this favorable developmental trajectory: the loss of economic security forced the family to mobilize its own human resources, including its teenagers, who had to take on new roles and responsibilities both within and outside the home and to work together toward the common goal of getting and keeping the family on its feet. This experience provided effective training in initiative, responsibility, and cooperation. In the words of the Banished Duke, "Sweet are the uses of adversity."

Alas, adversity was not so sweet for male children who were still preschoolers when their families suffered economic loss. The results were almost the opposite of those for boys in the earlier investigation. Compared with controls from nondeprived families, these youngsters subsequently did less well in school, showed less stable and successful work histories, and exhibited more emotional and social difficulties, some still apparent in middle adulthood. These negative outcomes were much more marked in boys than in girls and were accentuated in families from lower-class backgrounds.

Elder's research design completes the exosystem model by adding the revealing dimension of time as a context for assessing the processes, both environmental and intrapsychic, set in motion by a major change in the exosystem of the developing person. The time dimension has been explored by other investigators as well. For example, Furstenberg (1976) has shown that, in contemporary America, when a teenager becomes pregnant before marriage, much of the rest of her life is foreordained and, indeed, foreclosed in terms of future education, work opportunities, income, marriage, and family life. In other domains, Entwistle and Doering (1981) have traced the effect of changing patterns of prenatal education over the years on a mother's birth experience and on her subsequent treatment of the infant; and Hogan (1981) analyzed how the transition from adolescence to adulthood has changed in successive cohorts since 1900.

The Parents' Social World as an Exosystem

Another external context affecting developmental processes that has not yet received the attention it deserves is represented by the parents' social life, in particular their interactions with relatives, friends, and neighbors in the community. Research models in this sphere have evolved only in the last few years

and have not been developed as fully. The earliest example we have been able to find is a study of child neglect among low-income families conducted by Giovannoni and Billingsley (1970). The investigators sought to identify the environmental conditions associated with the parents' treatment of the child. Among other environmental factors identified as having a preventive effect was the existence of a functional kinship network and church attendance. The authors conclude that "among low-income people, neglect would seem to be a social problem that is as much a manifestation of social and community conditions as it is of any individual parent's pathology" (p. 204).

Corroborative data come from a large-scale correlational analysis of child abuse reports and socioeconomic and demographic information for the 58 counties in New York State (Garbarino, 1976). In the investigator's words, "A substantial proportion of the variance in rates of child abuse/maltreatment among New York State counties . . . was found to be associated with the degree to which mothers do not possess adequate support systems for parenting and are subjected to economic stress" (p. 185).

The importance of this phenomenon on a broader perspective is indicated in a recent study by Kamerman entitled *Parenting in an Unresponsive Society* (1980). Content analysis of the mothers' responses revealed a high degree of stress experienced by both single-parent and two-worker families around the issues of coordinating the burdens of work, household tasks, childrearing, and child-care arrangements. A key role in alleviating strain was played by informal support systems consisting of neighbors, friends, and, especially, immediate family members and relatives. "Whether for child care purposes, emergencies, advice, or just encouragement and sympathy, most of these women view 'family' as an essential support system" (p. 108). Unfortunately, none of these investigations obtained evidence on the critical last two links in the causal chain: the direct impact of family support systems on family functioning, and the second-order effect on the behavior and development of the child.

As with systems at more proximal levels, influences from the exosystem can be physical as well as social. A classical and early example is the finding that children's disturbed reactions to heavy bombing during the London blitz were a function of the degree of anxiety communicated by their parents (John, 1941). An exosystem effect capable of interpretation at two different levels is documented by Cohen, Glass, and Singer (1973) in a study of the influence of traffic noise on children's auditory and verbal skills. Children living on the lower floors of a 32-story building showed greater impairment of auditory discrimination and of reading achievement than those living in apartments on higher floors. The degree of impairment was also related to length of residence in the building. The relationship was independent of social class. The investigators viewed their research as a real-life counterpart to laboratory experiments demonstrating degradation of task performance as a direct aftereffect of exposure to noise. The two situations are not precisely analogous, however, since the real-life setting included other persons besides the children—namely, their parents and other family members who were also exposed to traffic noise and in all likelihood affected by it. Thus the possibility remains that the impairment of the child's auditory discrimination and verbal skills came about not only as a function of personal difficulties in hearing and sustaining attention in a noisy environment but also because others in the home were similarly affected and engaged less frequently in conversations, reading aloud, or correction of the child's verbal utterances. No data were available to evaluate the existence of such second-order effects.

It should now be apparent that the evolution of exosystem models in field studies of human development parallels the course exhibited by analogous models at the more proximal levels of the meso- and microsystem. The progression has been one from the use of simplistic class-theoretical categories to the elaboration of complex latent structures permitting the assessment of direct and indirect effects both within and between different levels of the environment. By way of summary, the evolution of these latent structures is outlined in Table 3, together with references to early and representative investigations at successive levels of development.

We have now completed our task of making the latent content manifest and are in a position to test the validity of our hope that explication of the implicit will provide a guide for promising pathways to future investigation.

RETROSPECT AND PROSPECT

In our analysis, we identified three major sets of forces contributing to the evolution of research models in field studies of human development. The first,

Table 3. **Evolution of Environmental Models in Developmental Research**
Stage III: The Emergence of Latent Structures (1950–   )

Social Address Models	Microsystem Models	Mesosystem Models	Exosystem Models
Comparison of Socializing Agents	*Setting as Physical Environment*	*Unidirectional and Joint Effects of Multiple Settings*	*Impact of External Settings*
(Cavan, 1932; Wang, 1932; Anderson, 1936; Mott, 1937; Davis & Havighurst, 1948)	(Spitz, 1945; Maccoby, 1951; Steiner, 1963; McCall, 1974; Yarrow et al., 1975)	(Hartshorne & May, 1929; Neyman, 1954; Bowerman & Kinch, 1959)	(Hodgkiss, 1933; Mathews, 1934; Angell, 1936; Cavan & Ranck, 1938; Miller & Swanson, 1958; Kohn, 1969; Giovanni & Billingsley, 1970; Garbarino, 1976)
Person-Process-Context Models	*Setting as Prestructured Environment*	*Reciprocal Linkages between Settings*	
(Bronfenbrenner, 1961; Kagan & Moss, 1962; Schaefer & Bayley, 1963; Drillien, 1964; Werner et al., 1967; Tulkin, 1972; Willerman, 1972)	(Bradley & Caldwell, 1975; Wachs, 1976)	(Prugh et al., 1953; Gray & Klaus, 1965; Smith, 1968)	*Exosystem Linkages, Transitions and Feedback*
	Triadic Models and Second-Order Effects		(Mott et al., 1965; Kanter, 1970; Bohen & Viveros-Long, 1981)
	(Bach, 1946; Sears et al., 1946; Tiller, 1958; Bronfenbrenner, 1974)	*Ecological Transition and Feedback Between Settings*	*Exosystem Trajectories*
		(Hayes & Grether, 1969; Simmons et al., 1979; Hetherington et al., 1979)	(Elder, 1974; Entwistle & Doering, 1981; Furstenburg, 1976)
	Ecological Transitions Within Settings		
	(Baldwin, 1947; Hetherington, 1978)		

and the most explicit, were new theoretical paradigms developed by scientists themselves. We observed that the creators of these paradigms are frequently theorists from other disciplines and other cultural backgrounds, and we suggested that this fact may account for the frequently long refractory period between the exposition of a theory and its ultimate application in empirical research. We noted that a critical role in this regard is played by researchers whom we referred to as "translating theorists," those who are able to operationalize unorthodox concepts in more orthodox ways. Finally, we recognized the constructive contribution of those whom we called "domain theorists," investigators who call attention to previously uncharted domains and provide tools for their systematic mapping.

Having established that theorists have made creative contributions to scientific progress, what use can we make of this hardly surprising discovery in order to advance scientific work in the future? Our puerile progress in understanding the conditions conducive to human development relegates to science fiction any possibility of raising the quantity and quality of creative scientists themselves in years to come. But if we cannot create paradigm makers for the future, we can still learn from paradigm makers in the past. As we will indicate, we have yet to reap the full harvest of their revolutionary conceptions.

The second stimulus to scientific progress identified in our analysis emanates from a source outside the pale of science itself. It would appear that, over the decades, developmental researchers have been carrying on a clandestine affair with Clio—the Muse of history. To put the issue more discreetly, the course of social change has itself provoked investigators to a broader and more complex conception of the environment as it affects processes of human development. Initially, this broader conception involved recognition of newly emerging social structures in the society, but more recently history has provided the framework for tracing what Elder has called "the life course" of human beings living in the same cultural epoch and, thereby progressing together through a distinctive succession of common experiences, critical events, and ecological transitions. To be sure, social scientists cannot shape the course of history; but they can learn to pay attention to its vicissitudes. We suggest that, after so many years, the developmental researcher's illicit liaison with Clio is no longer a tenable arrangement; it is time we embraced her as a legitimate partner in our creative scientific efforts.

Finally, we have discovered that, over the last three decades, the most significant change that has occurred in the evolution of scientific models in the study of human development has been a closet phenomenon—the gradual elaboration of latent structures underlying the research designs employed by investigators in the field. We propose that herein lies the greatest promise for moving forward in our scientific endeavors. The evolution of these latent structures has proceeded at an uneven pace, with greater advances in some sectors than in others; as a result, some regions have been bypassed, leaving gaps in the terrain. These gaps not only reveal the scope of our ignorance; they also delineate the ground for useful exploration. More importantly, the latent structures are not static forms, but dynamic trajectories with a momentum of their own. In Lewin's terminology, they represent uncompleted tasks that call for scientific closure. Our opportunity lies in recognizing and responding to that challenge by selecting those trajectories that have penetrated farthest into new scientific terrain and accelerating their momentum.

Toward this end, we conclude by reviewing the successive stages we have discerned in the evolution of research models in order to identify those paradigms that may have outlived their usefulness, others that are still viable, and others still that offer the richest promise for scientific advance.

The Comparison of Children at Different Social Addresses

Since its first introduction over a century ago, this early prototype has been applied to an increasing variety of environmental contexts. From the crude geographic and national contrasts of the late nineteenth century, the comparison shifted to indices of family structure, socioeconomic status, and, in recent decades, to the analysis of concrete naturalistic settings (e.g., home, school, peer group, daycare, workplace) and to the assessment of experimental programs of environmental intervention. Each new environmental contrast involved an assessment of the behavior and characteristics of children exposed to the contexts in question.

Although this traditional trajectory has shed little light on the processes through which the environment influences behavior and development, it still has important scientific utility in at least two respects. First, it remains a strategy of choice for exploring the developmental potential of newly emerging domains. For example, increasing numbers of children are growing up in so-called "merged families," in which children of different biological parents are living in the same household. The effects of remarriage on children is as yet an uncharted terrain for which the social address model is well suited as a tool for scientific discovery. A second area, defined more by practical than scientific needs, is that of program evaluation where child outcomes define the major goals to be achieved. The exclusive use of a social address model for either of the above purposes does not imply that more scientific knowledge would not be gained through application of the more sophisticated paradigms described below. But with limited resources, this model represents the minimal strategy adequate to the problem at hand.

Implementation of Theoretical Paradigms

In our view, the implementation still has some distance to go. For example, the constructs of Piaget, Lewin, and Vygotsky have yet to be applied in Freud's dyadic paradigm. The three cognitively oriented theorists share in common an emphasis on the importance of goal-oriented activities both as the producers and the products of developmental advance. In consequence, the research that these perspectives have generated has involved extensive observation of the ways in which children act upon, transform, and even create their environment. But the fact that all three theories are essentially child centered has inhibited recognition of their implications for adult/child interaction. Specifically, neither the originators of these cognitive paradigms, nor their scientific descendents, have spent much time observing the cognitive activities of parents, or other social agents, jointly with or in the presence of children. Yet, given the assumption of organism/environment reciprocity common to all three theories, it is not unreasonable to expect that the content and complexity of parent/child activities, analyzed in terms of the concepts of Piaget, Vygotsky, or Lewin, would bear some systematic relation to the content and complexity of the activities subsequently initiated by children when alone, with other children, or with adults.

There is also the unexplored question of how socialization activities, viewed in cognitive terms, are differentially distributed across even the well-established socioenvironmental contexts of social class, ethnicity, and family structure. The same issue can be raised with respect to the much researched socialization mechanisms of reinforcement and modeling. Are these equally prevalent in families of varying structure and cultural background? Finally, there is the question of the socialization correlates of the ''new demography.'' As we have seen, since

1960 a steadily increasing number of investigations has assessed differences in the behavior and characteristics of children of working versus two-parent households, or youngsters reared entirely at home versus those exposed to daycare settings. But few researches have focused on the socialization practices of the parents of these children. Do parents begin to treat their child differently when the mother takes a job, when the child enters daycare, or goes to school? Such unanswered questions highlight our ignorance about the distribution across diverse contexts of the basic cognitive and social processes discovered by the paradigm makers.

Applications of the Person-Process-Context Model

The foregoing examples illustrate some of the missing cells that become apparent in a matrix generated by the intersection of socialization practices with social structures. The number of lacunae becomes even greater when one asks whether the practice affects the behavior of the child. Indeed, except for a few isolated plots, the entire matrix constitutes a terra incognita for developmental research, since we know very little about whether or how socialization processes differ in their effectiveness from one social context to another. Does social reinforcement operate more successfully in certain types of family structure? Does modeling produce behavior change more quickly in conforming societies? Do socialization processes become less effective for families under severe economic stress, or those undergoing ecological transition? At a more general level, what are the external conditions that affect the capacity of a family, school classroom, or other socialization contexts to function efficiently? Moreover, as indicated in our review, an analogous question can be posed with respect to the operation of biological factors in human development; namely, under what environmental circumstances are genetic potentials most fully realized, or biological limitations most readily transcended? The application of a person-process-context model not only poses such questions but provides a revealing research design for their investigation.

In applying such a model, future investigators can profit by three lessons from the work of their predecessors. First, whatever the context, one can be almost certain that the process will differ by sex of child. Second, the most powerful environmental factors influencing both the effectiveness of socialization processes and the impact of biological factors are likely to be those associated with the family's socioeconomic status. Third, the scientific power of the person-process-context paradigm can be enhanced by incorporating the more differentiated conception of the environment implicit in what we have called microsystem, mesosystem, and exosystem models.

Microsystem Designs

In relation to the immediate environment of the child, this more differentiated conception involves such diverse elements as physical objects and toys, the manner in which the environment is organized by adults, physically and temporally, and the interpersonal structures in which the child becomes engaged with other persons in the setting. Critical features of these structures include their complexity (dyad, triad, N + 2 system), and the roles of the participants (e.g., mother, father, siblings, other adults). All of these factors have been shown to influence the child by activating and shaping distinctive patterns of behavior and response that then acquire a momentum of their own. The principal scientific promise of this microsystem model lies in expanding it beyond the somewhat restricted boundaries within which it has thus far been applied. The first of these limitations has been the age of the child. The most sophisticated microsystem designs have been employed almost exclusively with infants or youngsters of preschool age. Would analogous findings be obtained for school-age children or adolescents? For instance, does the extent of the father's support of the mother (or vice versa) increase each parent's effectiveness in dealing with a teenage daughter or son?

The foregoing examples reflect the restricted range of third parties in the studies thus far conducted. In these investigations, the triadic model has been applied only to the members of the nuclear family; yet it has much wider implications. For instance, the third-party role can be played, with as yet unknown effects, by grandparents (including the much maligned but as yet unresearched role of the mother-in-law), aunts and uncles, other members of the extended family, friends and neighbors, as well as teachers, counselors, and others providing services to children and families. Of particular interest in the latter group is the person who, after the parents, is probably the most pervasive but forgotten figure in the lives of American children and in the research designs of the investigator—the babysitter.

A third boundary to be transcended in microsystem studies relates to the broader social context. Few researchers to date have compared microsystems in different social groups. We have hardly begun to learn how such microsystem factors as pa-rental structuring of the home environment, the organization of time, or the pattern of triadic situations and second-order effects differ in families of varying socioeconomic levels, ethnicity, family structure, or maternal (and paternal) work status.

But the largest lacuna in microsystem research is the paucity of studies establishing the developmental validity of microsystem processes; that is, the demonstration that children exposed to particular physical and interpersonal structures in the home behave in a distinctive fashion in other settings such as daycare, school, peer group, neighborhood, and vice versa. In short, do microsystem variations make any difference for development?

Mesosystem Designs

As we have previously noted, establishing developmental validity by demonstrating carry-over of behavior from one setting to another meets the minimal condition for a mesosystem model—one that takes into account the child's experience in at least two different settings. In the light of our analysis, such a model offers a number of unexploited opportunities for research on development-in-context.

Setting Transition and Feedback

The entry of a child into a new setting permits observing the effects of that transition in the other major settings in which the child is a participant. We refer to this phenomenon as *transition feedback*. Its effects are manifested not only in the behavior of the child but also in the behavior of others. For example, how does the child's enrollment in daycare alter the pattern of activities and interactions occurring within the family? How are these patterns further modified when the child enters school? And what happens in both home and school settings as a function of the youngster's involvement in supervised or unsupervised peer groups in the community?

Empirical answers to these questions not only provide a basis for assessing the impact of each ecological transition on the child's development; they also document the microsystem transformation that invariably occurs and then becomes the context for the next stage of development. Placing a child in daycare may be as important for its effect on the parents as on the child. By providing a support system to the family, daycare may enable parents to function more effectively in their childrearing role. From a somewhat different perspective, once the child enters daycare or school, parents may change the structure of the home environment, the activities they engage in with the child, their disciplinary practices, and even the character of the affectional relationship between parent and child. The nature of these changes will also be affected, however, by alterations in the child's own behavior induced by participation in the new situation in school.

These two-way processes, and their implications for development, are yet to be researched systematically. Moreover, the opportunity for investigations of this kind are manifold. Setting transitions, and their accompanying feedback effects, are not limited, of course, to childhood; they recur through life in such experiences as entering high school or dropping out, graduating or going to work, doing military service, becoming engaged, marrying, changing jobs, having a child, being promoted, becoming seriously ill, moving, losing a job, becoming divorced, remarrying, or retiring. Each of these events offers an occasion for observing the condition, course, and consequence of developmental changes not only for the child but also for the other participants in the child's world. The resulting observations then provide a basis for inducing general parameters and principles regarding the interplay between environmental and individual factors in human development.

Mesosystem Dissonance and Complementarity

One general parameter emerging from those studies that have employed an implicit mesosystem model is the extent to which the settings containing the developing person, and their constituent microsystems, conflict with or complement each other in terms of the demands they place on that person. For example, to what extent are the patterns of behavior exhibited by or expected of the child at home compatible with those he or she experiences at school or in the peer group?

The analogous question may be raised for successive ecological transitions throughout the life course. The more critical issue, however, pertains to the role such compatibility plays in the process of development. Clearly, complete continuity would only perpetuate the status quo, but, at the opposite extreme, sharply conflicting demands could lead to developmental arrest or retrogression. A middle ground seems to be indicated on a priori grounds, but the relevant empirical evidence awaits the application of appropriate mesosystem models.

Linkages Between Settings

Mesosystem designs also focus attention on structural features of the environment that are especially likely to affect the ease of transition from one setting to the next and the degree of compatibility between settings. These structural features are the interconnections between settings—linkages that already exist or can be constructed to facilitate movement, communication, and reciprocal adaptation between microsystems. Examples of such linkages include: prior visits to the daycare center, preschool, or school by the child in the company of a parent; having an older sibling in school; providing parents with information about school procedures; inviting the child's friends into the home; involving parents as leaders of activities in groups in which their children are participants; encouraging parents to observe in children's classrooms. All of these are familiar practices employed to greater or lesser degree within modern society. What is unknown relates to the issue of primary interest to the developmental researcher—the effect of these practices on the behavior and development of the child. Does establishing links between home and school prior to entering kindergarten or first grade facilitate a child's subsequent adjustment to school? Do the relations between parent and teacher in successive grades have reciprocal effects on the child's experiences at school and at home, as reflected in the teacher's behavior, the child's academic achievement, patterns of parent-child interaction, or the child's susceptibility to peer group influence? Do children whose parents are active as leaders of children's groups exhibit a different developmental course from those whose parents remain uninvolved? These are questions that mesosystem designs invite us to explore.

Mesosystem Models in Program Evaluation

If a mesosystem is to encompass relations between the principal settings in which the growing child is a participant, then for many American children it must include the services and social programs in which the child, or the family as a whole, are enrolled as participants. Over the past decade, the evaluation of such programs, both in the public and private sector, has become a major social science industry. Although much of this effort is concerned with issues of program delivery, administration, and cost effectiveness, major attention has also been accorded to the analysis of program effects. In the case of programs serving children, this has usually meant an assessment of the child's physical, intellectual, and socioemotional development on outcome measures administered within the program setting. A mesosystem perspective argues for expanding the focus of evaluation beyond a single setting, and beyond the child per se, to include the analysis of the other microsystems in which the child is a participant. For example, does the program bring about a change in parental attitudes and behavior toward the child? Do the parents begin to structure the home environment in a different way? Will there be greater involvement in childrearing by the father, or greater support offered by other family members to the persons primarily engaged in the care of the child? Does the program result in increased linkages or improved relations between the home and other settings in which the child spends his or her time? Does it increase the child's involvement in the activities of adults outside the immediate family such as relatives, friends, and neighbors? And if so, there is always the ultimate question that determines the relevance, or irrelevance, of all the others: What difference do these involvements make for the child's development?

Diversity in Roles and Role Models

The child's increasing participation in multiple settings with increasing age entails two consequences of possible developmental import. First, a shift in setting implies also a shift in role from a son or daughter at home, to a pupil in school, a group member in a club or street gang. Second, the child is correspondingly exposed, and expected to be responsive, to an ever greater variety of roles occupied by others—teachers, principals, recreation workers, counselors, policemen, shop clerks, and community residents. The existence of these concurrent phenomena raises the question whether and how exposure to a variety of roles can affect the course of development. There appears to be no empirical evidence bearing on this issue. The basic theses of role theory as developed by G. H. Mead (1934), the Thomases (1927, 1928), Sullivan (1947), and Cottrell (1942) would seem to imply that such exposure should facilitate the process of psychological growth. All these theorists view personality development as the outcome of a process of progressive role-differentiation involving two complementary phases. In the first instance, the child's psychological growth is facilitated by exposure to persons occupying a diversity of roles—first within the home, and then beyond. At the same time, as a function of interaction with persons in different social positions, the child is placed in new roles and thereby develops a more complex identity as he or she learns to function as a daughter, son, sister, brother, grandchild, cousin, friend, pupil, teammate, and so on.

These hypotheses could be explored in mesosystem models in which the characteristics of the developing person's role performance in one setting (e.g., as a high school student) are examined as a function of exposure to roles in other settings. One measure of the latter might be the variety of occupations and ethnic backgrounds of adults with whom the young person has had close association, although this index might exhibit a restricted range in contemporary American society.

The Mesosystem in Social-Structural Perspective

The foregoing comment alerts us to a sixth and last domain of inquiry that invites exploration with mesosystem models—an examination of how mesosystem relations vary as a function of social context. Thus we do well to understand how cross-setting transitions, dissonances, linkages, and variations in role differ for children from varying social backgrounds as defined by social class, ethnicity, family structure, mother's work status, and other structural contrasts. The documentation of such diversity then sets the stage for the more critical question of its consequences for developmental processes and outcomes.

Exosystem Designs

The above research perspectives derived from mesosystem models have their counterparts at the level of exosystems. But rather than analyzing these analogues as formal structures, we shall indicate their research potential by focusing on substance; that is, by examining those exosystems that appear to offer the most promise for scientific investigation as external contexts for human development. Our review has highlighted the importance of three domains in this regard: (1) the world of work; (2) the family's social world; and (3) social changes in the larger society.

The World of Work as an Exosystem in Children's Development

The studies we have reviewed in this domain reveal significant and complex effects of parental employment in the behavior and development of children. The impact of such effects is likely to become more salient if present demographic trends continue, especially among families with children under three; in such families the rates of maternal labor force participation are increasing most rapidly (Bronfenbrenner, 1975b, 1982). From a research perspective, a promising trajectory in this sphere lies in the full convergence of two lines of investigation long pursued separately in studies of the mother's and father's employment. We suggest that the time has passed when researchers can examine one of these domains without giving simultaneous consideration to the other. One important aspect of this convergence involves applying to each parent's work situation the research designs and underlying conceptual frameworks that heretofore have been employed almost exclusively to the working world of the other parent. For example, investigators have yet to assess the impact on family and child of the number of hours the father works, or his attitudes toward his job and its relation to the family life—factors that have been repeatedly examined in studies of maternal employment. Conversely, there has been no research on the effects of the mother's loss of a job on her family and children, despite the fact that more than a fifth of the nation's children live in female-headed families and that the unemployment rates for this group are especially high (Bureau of Labor Statistics, 1980). Nor have students of human development analyzed how the content of the mother's job, or the organizational structure at work, affects maternal childrearing values and practices, and, thereby, the behavior and development of children. The application of research designs from one parent's work domain to the job situation of the other parent must also take into account the almost certain probability that developmental processes and outcomes associated with parental occupations will exhibit systematic differences as a function of sex of parent, sex of child, the age of the child, the duration of employment, and the family's socioeconomic status.

Moreover, given the likelihood of mesosystem influences, it becomes important, in future research in this area, to obtain systematic information about the settings in which children are placed when parents are at work, since the nature of this experience is likely to be even more consequential for the child's development than the circumstances of parental employment. A key factor in this regard is the exposure of the child to peer group influences in the absence of adult supervision.

Finally, a critical aspect of the exosystem associated with the parental work situation is the degree of conflict between the demands of work and family life experienced by each parent, and the availability of support systems both within and outside the work situation for minimizing the conflict and maximizing the rewards of participation in both settings. Particularly significant are fringe benefits being offered by many employers through extended maternity and paternity leaves, flexitime, job sharing, on-site daycare, sick leave when the child is ill, and so on. Although the consequences of such policies are presumed to be beneficial both to parents and children, no research appears to have been conducted as yet on their actual effect on childrearing processes and outcomes. Moreover, the assessment is complicated by the confounding of the availability of such policies with social structural factors. For example, Kamerman and Kingston (1981) point out that large firms are more likely to have benefit packages for their employees than small firms, an observation reminiscent of Miller and Swanson's (1958) distinction between entrepreneurial and bureaucratic work environments. It will be recalled that, in that study, bureaucratic structures were associated with childrearing practices less conducive to the development of the child's initiative, responsibility, and achievement. As previously noted, Miller and Swanson's findings are still to be replicated in the American context in a design that meets criteria of developmental validity. There is clearly both need and opportunity for well-designed investigations on large versus small work settings, their policies with regard to families, and the consequences of these policies for parents and children.

The Family's Social World as an Exosystem

The unanswered questions raised by consideration of parental work as an exosystem for the developing child have their analogues in relation to the extent and nature of the parents' social relationships outside the immediate family. There appear to be at least three ways in which such relationships can influence childrearing, only one of which has received research attention to date; and even there the investigations have yet to trace the critical last link in the causal chain. Cochran and Brassard (1979) have argued persuasively that the family's social networks—made up of relatives, friends, neighbors, and coworkers—can play an important role by serving as sources of information, by exchanging goods and services, and by offering emotional support. It still remains to be shown, however, that such networks do in fact influence the effectiveness of the family as a childrearing system. The same need for establishing developmental validity applies to Bronfenbrenner's thesis (1979) that social networks facilitate family functioning to the extent that they provide access to sources of power within the community. Bronfenbrenner suggests that one of the debilitating factors in the lives of lower-class families is that their social networks typically do not extend into the circles of power that control the allocation of resources and determine the capacity of parents to manipulate the social environment so that it becomes more responsive to their own and their children's needs. Finally, the parents' social networks may disrupt as readily as they facilitate childrearing processes. Just as in the work domain the decisive factor becomes the degree of dissonance versus complementarity between systems. The decisive factor becomes the extent to which the demands in each domain can or cannot be accommodated to each other. For example, can the responsibilities of home and children become so pressing as to isolate the family from its social milieu, thus cutting off needed external supports and developmental opportunities both for parents and children? Does the parents' social life, or civic obligations, reinforce or remove them from family activities? How are children's experiences and life courses affected as a result? These are issues of our time that have scarcely been explored in research on development-in-context.

Social Policies and Programs as Exosystems

The middle 1970s witnessed a sudden and rapid growth of interest by social scientists in the area of child and family policy (Keniston, 1977; *Toward a National Policy*, 1976; Zigler, Kagan, & Klugman, in press). Several major universities have established centers for the conduct of research in this sphere, and the National Academy of Sciences has established a high-level standing committee to encourage further scientific work in this domain (Handler & Zatz, 1982; Hayes, 1982; Heller, Holtzman, & Messick, 1982; Kamerman & Hayes, 1982; Travers & Light, 1982; *Services for Children*, 1981). From the perspective of the present analysis, such developments represent steps in a welcome direction.

But the same perspective also implies a caveat. The analysis of exosystems cannot be confined to the study of policies and programs alone; it must also trace the effects of these policies and programs on the more proximal meso- and microstructures in which developmental processes actually occur. As one of the present authors has pointed out elsewhere (Bronfenbrenner & Weiss, 1983), studies of child and family policy have gained such strong momentum that, in many instances, they have run out of range and broken the connection from the center around which they presumably focus. In other words, policies and programs are being analyzed as ends in themselves, without examining their effects on the presumed beneficiaries—children and those responsible for their care. In the developmental research of the future, research that does not investigate these intervening links ceases to be developmental.

Social Change as an Exosystem

It may be a reflection of the historical naïveté of behavioral scientists that, in the course of our analysis, we were surprised by the role that history played in the evolution of research models for field studies in human development. We first observed the workings of our sister science in confronting developmental researchers with newly evolving social addresses at which the development of children—and adults—could be compared: the emergence of new types of educational settings; new family forms; new patterns of parental role differentiation in work and family life; new modes of child care outside the family; and new types of services, programs, and benefits provided to families and other childrearing institutions. In a broader perspective, history has altered the course of human development through the impact of major historical events—wars, migrations, periods of economic depression or affluence. Taking Thomas and Znaniecki's classical study of Polish peasants in America (1927) as a model, Elder and other protagonists of the life-course approach (for a recent review, see Featherman, 1982) have traced the subsequent experiences of individuals in the family caught in the wake of these large-scale social and cultural changes. In the ideal case, such investigations require rich archival data from longitudinal studies conducted over extended periods of time. Such archival sources are rare, but their potential yield justifies their fullest exploitation, as well as the search for as yet undiscovered sources buried in libraries or institutional records. From a developmental perspective, the principal shortcoming of such records is likely to be the paucity of data on developmental outcomes. One may readily discover which person or family was exposed to one set of historical circumstances, and which to another, but information on subsequent life course is likely to be limited to educational or occupational careers or, in extremis, to age of death.

For this reason, the richest prospect for assessing the impact of historical events on human development lies in retrospective studies of persons still living whose life courses followed contrasting historical trajectories. The trajectories need not go very far back. For example, one cohort of special interest are those who were adolescents during the turbulent 1960s. Some experienced a fairly traditional family life and education; others dropped out of school, left home, and adopted new lifestyles. Both groups were subsequently confronted by a tight job market in the 1970s. Many now have families and children of their own. A systematic investigation of the life careers of contrasting subgroups, including an examination of their present characteristics as parents, workers, and citizens, offers a rich return for developmental research.

A historical perspective also alerts us to another

reality that needs to be taken into account in research designs for field studies. Especially in cross-cultural investigation, the dimension of time is often left completely out of consideration. The social structural characteristics of the family are recorded at the time of investigation, and treated as bases for comparison or control, without regard to how long the child or the family may have been living under the circumstances in question. Thus families are classified in terms of household structure, maternal employment status, father's occupation, use of daycare services, and the rest, at a particular point in time without taking into account how long and during what ages the child was exposed to the given context. Especially in a period of rapid social change, this practice results in the confounding and serious underestimation of short-term and long-term effects. Such distortion is likely to occur because both age and length of exposure function as critical factors in determining developmental impact. In addition, the failure to take cognizance of changes in status over time overlooks the possibility that stability versus instability in the child's environment may be as consequential for development as the nature of the particular contexts to which the child is exposed. For these reasons, we do well to introduce, as a standard requirement in the design of studies of human development, taking an "environmental history" of the socialization contexts in which the child has lived as defined by age-associated changes in family structure, parents' occupational status, income, and forms of substitute care. Viewed as a whole, the life-course perspective focuses attention on the nature and sequence of the environments and events a person experiences from early childhood onward, and the effect of these experiences on subsequent development. Once set in motion, such developmental trajectories (Bronfenbrenner, 1979) have a momentum of their own. To employ an outmoded metaphor, development takes place on a moving train. One can walk forward or backward through the cars, but what really matters is where the train is going, for in most countries there are few places where one can change tracks. America probably presents more possibilities in this regard than many other societies, but even here, many transfers are forced rather than free, especially those leading to unwelcome destinations. Within a particular culture, opportunities to change trains vary with one's age, social position, and the period of history in which one lives. The life-course approach involves the systematic study of such variations and its effects on development. By transforming elapsed time into historical time, the workers in this domain have added a new third dimension to developmental research that endows substantive content to what had previously been mere temporal duration.

But the principal lesson of history for developmental researchers relates not to the study of the past, but to the study of the future. History alerts us to the importance of recognizing and analyzing major social changes as they affect the capacity of families and other childrearing institutions to function effectively as contexts of human development. As these words are being written, American society is undergoing profound changes in the conditions of life for many of its families and children. Social researchers are subject to an ethical code that prohibits them from exposing children to situations that are injurious to their welfare. Unfortunately, there is no such restriction on the nation as a whole, and its duly empowered leaders and policy makers. The latter are free to run their economic and social experiments without such niceties as prior parental consent or review by qualified professionals. It remains the responsibility of researchers, however, to monitor these experiments and give early warning of any unintended effects. In doing so, we must use the best scientific methods at our command. There may be some difficulties in finding matched control groups, but there should be no problem with sample size. It is the irony and limitation of our science that the greater the harm done to children, the more we stand to learn about the environmental conditions that are essential for making—and keeping—human beings human. As we enter the 1980s, there are indications that these essential conditions are being seriously undermined in broad segments of American society. It therefore becomes our professional obligation to employ the most advanced research designs at our disposal in order to forestall the tragic opportunity of significantly expanding our knowledge about the limits of the human condition for developing human beings.

NOTES

1. The closest approximations we have been able to find are three essays. Two are compact histories of child development as a total field (Hartup, 1978; Sears, 1975); the third is a historical and comparative survey of socialization theory and research by Clausen (1968). We are grateful to these colleagues both for information and insight.

2. The present authors take issue with the English translation of the last sentence. The original German text reads: *Man sieht also, dass die Schule zu den Knaben eine andere Stellung einnimmt als zu*

den Maedchen, zu den Kindern, die nur in der Familie erzogen worden sind, eine andere als zu denen, die in einem Kindergarten oder in einer Bewahranstalt vorbereitet wurden (1870, p. 69). The verb *einnimmt* carries no connotation of compulsion. In our view, the translation should read: "One sees that the school takes a different attitude toward boys and toward girls, and toward children with and without prior experience in crèche or kindergarten."

3. Strictly speaking, Galton was actually not the first to examine systematically the social background of eminent scientists. A year earlier, Candolle (1873) had published a study of French *savants* in which he divided his sample into three social classes.

4. A German study by Kolrausche (1891) had been published 7 years earlier. Through direct observation, the investigator found that only-sons were less active in school play than later-borns.

5. Basically the same parent-child paradigm was developed independently some years later in Vienna by Charlotte Bühler (1937), but, unfortunately, the model does not appear to have been followed up either in Europe or in the United States.

6. The Kaethe Wolf who was the coauthor of this pioneering study was subsequently acknowledged in a footnote as having served as a collaborator in Spitz's work (1946a, p. 56).

7. "Give me a dozen healthy infants, well-formed, and my own specified world to bring them up in, and I'll guarantee you to take any one at random and train him to become any type of specialist I might select—doctor, lawyer, artist, merchant-chief, and, yes, even beggarman and thief, regardless of his talents, tensions, tendencies, abilities, vocations, and race of his ancestors" (Watson, 1930, p. 82).

8. Although Barker equates his conception of the psychological environment with "the life space in Kurt Lewin's terms" (1968, p. 1), he also credits another psychological theorist of European origin, Brunswik (1956), as influencing the definition of environment as employed in ecological psychology (Barker, 1965, p. 1).

9. In more recent work, Baltes and his colleagues (Baltes, 1979, Baltes, Reese, & Lipsitt, 1980) have proposed a substantive distinction among three types of events linked with age. First, there are "normative age-graded" processes associated with biological maturation and stages of socialization common to all members of the culture. Second, there are "normative historical" events specific to a particular period but again affecting most members of the society (such as wars, revolutions, or economic depressions). Finally, there are "nonnormative" life events experienced by particular individuals at different times, such as changes in marital status, illnesses, career shifts, or accidents. Each of these three types of age-associated phenomena is presumed to influence development in different ways. Baltes' progression from a methodological to a substantive focus, as it is implemented in empirical work, will mark a significant convergence between lines of research originating in the psychological tradition of psychometrics, emphasizing cohort effects, and the paradigms introduced by the Chicago School of Sociology highlighting the impact of changes in life course on human development.

REFERENCES

Ainsworth, M. D. S. The development of infant-mother interaction among the Ganda. In B. M. Foss (Ed.), *Determinants of infant behavior* (Vol. 2). London: Methuen, 1963.

Ainsworth, M. D. S., & Wittig, B. A. Attachment and exploratory behavior of one-year-olds in a strange situation. In B. M. Foss (Ed.), *Determinants of infant behavior* (Vol. 4). London: Methuen, 1969.

Aldrich, C. K., & Mendkoff, E. Relocation of the aged and disabled: A mortality study. *Journal of the American Geriatrics Society*, 1963, *11*, 185–194.

Ambrose, J. A. The development of the smiling response in early infancy. In B. M. Foss (Ed.), *Determinants of infants' behavior* (Vol. 1). New York: Wiley, 1961.

Anderson, H. E. *The young child in the home*. New York: Appleton-Century, 1936.

Angell, R. C. *The family encounters the Depression*. New York: Scribner, 1936.

Ariès, P. *Centuries of childhood*. (Robert Baldick, Trans.) New York: Knopf, 1962.

Bach, G. R. Father-fantasies and father-typing in father-separated children. *Child Development*, 1946, *17*, 63–80.

Baldwin, A. L. Differences in parent behavior toward three- and nine-year-old children. *Journal of Personality*, 1946, *15*, 143–165.

Baldwin, A. L. Changes in parent behavior during pregnancy. *Child Development*, 1947, *18*, 29–39.

Baldwin, A. L. Socialization and the parent-child relationship. *Child Development*, 1948, *19*, 127–136.

Baldwin, A. L. The effect of home environment on nursery school behavior. *Child Development,* 1949, *20,* 49–62.

Baldwin, A. L., Kalhorn, J., & Breese, F. H. Patterns of parent behavior. *Psychology Monographs,* 1945, *58,* No. 5.

Baltes, P. B. Longitudinal and cross-sectional sequences in the study of age and generation effects. *Human Development,* 1968, *11,* 145–171.

Baltes, P. B. Life-span developmental psychology: Some convening observations on history and theory. In P. B. Baltes & D. G. Brim (Eds.), *Life-span development and behavior* (Vol. 2). New York: Academic Press, 1979.

Baltes, P. B., Reese, H. W., and Lipsitt, L. P. Life-span developmental psychology. *Annual Review of Psychology,* 1980, *31,* 65–110.

Baltes, P. B., & Schaie, K. W. *Life-span developmental psychology: Personality and socialization.* New York: Academic Press, 1973.

Banducci, R. The effect of mother's employment on the achievement, aspirations, and expectations of the child. *Personnel and Guidance Journal,* 1967, *46,* 263–267.

Bandura, A. *Principles of behavior modification.* New York: Holt, Rinehart & Winston, 1969.

Bandura, A., & Huston, A. C. Identification as a process of incidental learning. *Journal of Abnormal and Social Psychology,* 1961, *43,* 311–318.

Bandura, A., Ross, D., & Ross, S. A. Imitation of film-mediated models. *Journal of Abnormal and Social Psychology,* 1963, *66,* 3–11.

Barker, R. G. Explorations in ecological psychology. *American Psychologist,* 1965, *20,* 1–14.

Barker, R. G. *Ecological psychology.* Stanford, Calif.: Stanford University Press, 1968.

Barker, R. G., & Gump, P. V. *Big school, small school.* Stanford, Calif.: Stanford University Press, 1964.

Barker, R. G., & Schoggen, P. *Qualities of community life: Methods of measuring environment and behavior applied to an American and an English town.* San Francisco: Jossey-Bass, 1973.

Barker, R. G., & Wright, H. F. *One boy's day.* New York: Harper, 1951.

Barker, R. G., & Wright, H. F. *Midwest and its children: The psychological ecology of an American town.* New York: Row, Peterson, 1955.

Barlow, D. *The passive father as a factor in the adjustment of the child.* Northampton, Mass.: Smith College Studies in Social Work, 1924.

Baumrind, D. Child care practices anteceding three patterns of preschool behavior. *Genetic Psychology Monographs,* 1967, *75,* 43–88.

Baumrind, D. Current patterns of parental authority. *Developmental Psychology Monographs,* 1971, *4* (1), 1–102.

Baumrind, D. New directions in socialization research. *American Psychologist,* 1980, *35,* 63–661.

Baumrind, D., & Black, A. Socialization practices associated with dimensions of competence in preschool boys and girls. *Child Development,* 1967, *38,* 291–329.

Belsky, J., & Steinberg, L. D. The effects of day care: A critical review. *Child Development,* 1978, *49,* 929–949.

Belsky, J., Steinberg, L., & Walker, A. The ecology of day care. In M. E. Lamb (Ed.), *Non-traditional families: Parenting and child development.* Hillsdale, N.J.: Erlbaum, 1982.

Berenda, R. W. *The influence of the group on the judgments of children.* New York: King's Crown Press, 1950.

Blenkner, M., Bloom, M., & Nielsen, M. A research and demonstration project of protective services. *Social Casework,* 1971, *52,* 483–499.

Blood, R. O., Jr. The husband-wife relationship. In F. I. Nye & L. W. Hoffman (Eds.), *The employed mother in America.* Chicago: Rand McNally, 1963.

Blood, R. O., Jr. *Love match and arranged marriage.* New York: Free Press, 1967.

Blood, R. O., Jr., & Hamblin, R. L. The effect of wife's employment on the family power structure. *Social Forces,* 1958, *36,* 347–352.

Blurton-Jones, N. G. *Biological perspectives on parenthood. The family in society: Dimensions of parenthood.* London: Her Majesty's Stationery Office, 1974.

Blyth, D. A., Simmons, R. G., & Bush, D. M. The transition into early adolescence: A longitudinal comparison of youth in two educational contexts. *Sociology of Education,* 1978, *51,* 149–162.

Boden, M. A. *Jean Piaget.* New York: Penguin Books, 1980.

Bohannon, E. W. The only child in a family. *Pedagogical Seminary,* 1898, *5,* 475–496.

Bohen, H., & Viveros-Long, A. *Balancing jobs and family life: Do flexible working schedules help?* Philadelphia: Temple University Press, 1981.

Bossard, J. H. S., & Boll, E. S. *The large family system.* Philadelphia: University of Pennsylvania Press, 1956.

Bott, E. *Family and social network.* London: Tavistock, 1957.

Bowerman, C. E., & Kinch, J. W. Changes in family and peer orientation of children between the fourth and tenth grades. *Social Forces*, 1959, *37*, 206–211.

Bowlby, J. *Maternal care and mental health*. Geneva: World Health Organization, 1951.

Bowlby, J. The nature of the child's tie to his mother. *International Journal of Psychoanalysis*, 1958, *39*, 350–373.

Bowlby, J. *Attachment and loss* (Vol 1: *Attachment*). London: Hogarth, 1969.

Bradley, R. H., & Caldwell, B. M. Early home environments and changes in mental test performance in children from 6 to 36 months. *Developmental Psychology*, March 1976, *12* (2), 93–97. (a)

Bradley, R. H., & Caldwell, B. M. The relation of infants' home environments to mental test performance at fifty-four months: A follow-up study. *Child Development*, December 1976, *47* (4), 1172–1174. (b)

Bremner, R. H. (Ed.). *Children and youth in America*. Cambridge, Mass.: Harvard University Press, 1974.

Brim, O. G. Macro-structural influences in child development and the need for childhood social indicators. *American Journal of Orthopsychiatry*, 1975, *45*, 516–524.

Bronfenbrenner, U. Socialization and social class through time and space. In E. E. Maccoby, T. M. Newcomb, & E. L. Hartley (Eds.), *Readings in social psychology*. New York: Holt, Rinehart and Winston, 1958.

Bronfenbrenner, U. Some familial antecedents of responsibility and leadership in adolescents. In L. Petrullo & B. L. Bass (Eds.), *Leadership and interpersonal behavior*. New York: Holt, Rinehart and Winston, 1961.

Bronfenbrenner, U. Response to pressure from peers versus adults among Soviet and American school children. *International Journal of Psychology*, 1967, *2*, 199–208.

Bronfenbrenner, U. *Two worlds of childhood: U.S. and U.S.S.R.* New York: Russell Sage Foundation, 1970.

Bronfenbrenner, U. *Is early intervention effective? A Report on Longitudinal Evaluations of Preschool Programs* (Vol. II). Washington, D.C.: Department of Health, Education and Welfare, Office of Human Development, 1974. (a)

Bronfenbrenner, U. Developmental research, public policy, and the ecology of childhood. *Child Development*, 1974, *45*, 1–5. (b)

Bronfenbrenner, U. Is 80% of intelligence genetically determined? In U. Bronfenbrenner & M. Mahoney (Eds.), *Influences on human development* (2nd ed.). Hinsdale, Ill.: Dorsey Press, 1975. (a)

Bronfenbrenner, U. Reality and research in the ecology of human development. *Proceedings of the American Philosophical Society*, 1975, *119*, 439–469. (b)

Bronfenbrenner, U. *The ecology of human development: Experiments by nature and design*. Cambridge, Mass.: Harvard University Press, 1979.

Bronfenbrenner, U. New images of children, families, and America. *Television and Children*, 1982, *4*, 3–16.

Bronfenbrenner, U., Alvarez, W., & Henderson, C. R., Jr. Working and watching: Maternal employment status and parents' perceptions of their three-year-old children. Ithaca, N.Y.: Department of Human Development and Family Studies, Cornell University, 1982.

Bronfenbrenner, U., & Crouter, A. C. *Work and family through time and space*. In S. Kamerman & C. D. Hayes (Eds.), *Families that work*. Washington, D.C.: National Academy Press, 1982.

Bronfenbrenner, U., Devereux, E. C., Jr., Suci, G. J., & Rodgers, R. R. *Adults and peers as sources of conformity and autonomy*. Paper presented at the Conference on Socialization for Competence, sponsored by the Social Science Research Council, Puerto Rico, April 1965.

Bronfenbrenner, U., & Weiss, H. Beyond policies without people: An ecological perspective on child and family policy. In E. Zigler, S. L. Kagan, & E. Klugman (Eds.), *Children, families, and government: Perspectives on American social policy*. Cambridge, Eng.: Cambridge University Press, 1983.

Brown, S. W. *A comparative study of maternal employment and nonemployment*. Unpublished doctoral dissertation. University Microfilms 70–8610, Mississippi State University, 1970.

Brunswik, E. *Perceptions and the representative design of psychological experiments*. Berkeley: University of California Press, 1956.

Bühler, C. *Kind und Familie*. Vienna: Fischer, 1937.

Burchinal, L. G. Personality characteristics of children. In F. I. Nye & L. W. Hoffman (Eds.), *The employed mother in America*. Chicago: Rand McNally, 1963.

Burks, B. S. The relative influence of nature and nurture upon mental development: A comparative study of foster parent-foster child resemblance and true parent-true child resemblance. *Yearbook of the National Society for the Study of Education,* 1928, *27* (I), 219–316.

Burt, C. The genetic determination of differences in intelligence: A study of monozygotic twins reared apart and together. *British Journal of Psychology,* 1966, *57,* 137–153.

Burt, C. Inheritance of general intelligence. *American Psychologist,* March 1972, *27* (3), 175–190.

Cairns, R. B. Developmental theory before Piaget: The remarkable contributions of James Mark Baldwin. *Contemporary Psychology,* 1980, *25,* 438–440.

Caldwell, B. E. & Ricciuti, H. N. (Eds.) *Review of child development research* (Vol. 3). Chicago: University of Chicago Press, 1973.

Candolle, A. L. P. *Historie des sciences et des savants depuis deux siècles, suivie d'autres études sur des sujets scientifiques, en particulier sur la sélection dans l'espèce humaine.* Geneva: H. Georg, 1873.

Carmichael, L. (Ed.). *Manual of child psychology* (1st ed.). New York: Wiley, 1946.

Carmichael, L. (Ed.). *Manual of child psychology* (2nd ed.). New York: Wiley, 1954.

Castle, C. S. A statistical study of eminent women. *Archives of Psychology,* 1913, *4* (27), vii + 90.

Cattell, J. M. A statistical study of American men of science, the selection of a group of one thousand scientific men. *Science,* N.S., 1906, *24,* 658–665, 699–707, 732–742.

Cattell, J. M. Families of American men of science. *Popular Science Monthly,* 1915, *86,* 504–515.

Caudill, W., & Frost, L. A comparison of maternal care and infant behavior in Japanese-American, American, and Japanese families. In U. Bronfenbrenner & M. Mahoney (Eds.), *Influences on human development* (2nd ed.). Hinsdale, Ill.: Dryden Press, 1975.

Caudill, W., & Weinstein, H. Maternal care and infant behavior in Japan and America. *Psychiatry,* 1969, *32,* 12–43.

Cavan, R. S. The wish never to have been born. *American Journal of Sociology,* 1932, *37,* 547–559.

Cavan, R. S., & Ranck, K. H. *The family and the Depression: A study of 100 Chicago families.* Chicago: University of Chicago Press, 1938.

Clausen, J. A. *Socialization and society.* Boston: Little, Brown, 1968.

Cochran, M. M. *The Swedish childrearing study: An example of the ecological approach to the study of human development.* Paper presented at the Second Biennial Conference of the International Society for the Study of Behavioral Develop-

ment, University of Surrey, 1975.

Cochran, M. M. A comparison of group day and family childrearing patterns in Sweden. *Child Development,* 1977, *48,* 702–707.

Cochran, M. M., & Brassard, J. Child development and personal social networks. *Child Development,* 1979, *50,* 601–616.

Cochran, M. M., & Robinson, J. Day care and sex differences. In S. Kilmer (Ed.), *Advances in early education and day care* (Vol. 3). Greenwich, Conn.: J.A.I. Press, 1982.

Cohen, L. B. Our developing knowledge of infant perception and cognition. *American Psychologist,* 1979, *34,* 894–889.

Cohen, S., Glass, D. C., & Singer, J. E. Apartment noise, auditory discrimination and reading ability in children. *Journal of Experimental Social Psychology,* 1973, *9,* 407–422.

Cole, M., Gay, J., Glick, J. A., & Sharp, D. W. *The cultural context of learning and thinking.* New York: Basic Books, 1971.

Cole, M., & Scribner, S. *Culture and thought: A psychological interpretation.* New York: Wiley, 1974.

Coleman, J. *The adolescent society.* New York: Free Press, 1961.

Cooley, C. H. *Human nature and the social order.* New York: Scribner, 1902.

Cottrell, L. S. The analysis of situational fields in social psychology. *American Sociological Review,* 1942, *7,* 370–382.

Crosby, B. A. A study of Alameida County delinquent boys with special emphasis upon the group coming from broken homes. *Journal of Juvenile Research,* 1929, *13,* 220–230.

Crowe, R. R. The adopted offspring of women criminal offenders. *Archives of General Psychiatry,* November 1972, *27,* 600–603.

Crowe, R. R. An adoption study of antisocial personality. *Archives of General Psychiatry,* December 1974, *31,* 785–791.

Crowe, R. R. An adoptive study of psychopathy: Preliminary results from arrest records and psychiatric hospital records. In R. R. Fieve, D. Rosenthal, & H. Brill (Eds.), *Genetic research in psychiatry.* Baltimore: Johns Hopkins University Press, 1975.

Davis, A , & Havighurst, R. J. Social class and color differences in child rearing. *American Sociological Review,* 1942, *7,* 370–382.

Davis, A., & Havighurst, R. J. Color differences in child rearing. *American Sociological Review,* 1948, *11,* 698–710.

Dennis, W. *Historical readings in developmental*

psychology. New York: Appleton-Century-Crofts, 1972.

Dennis, W., & Najarian, P. Infant development under environmental handicaps. *Psychological Monographs*, 1957, *71* (7).

Devereux, E. C., Jr. *Socialization in cross-cultural perspective: A comparative study of England, Germany, and the United States*. Paper read at the Ninth International Seminar on Family Research, Puerto Rico, 1965.

Devereux, E. C., Jr. *Authority, guilt and conformity to adult standards among German school children: A pilot experimental study*. Paper presented to the Upstate New York Sociological Association, Rochester, N.Y., May 1966.

Devereux, E. C., Bronfenbrenner, U., & Rodgers, R. R. Child rearing in England and the United States: A cross-national comparison. *Journal of Marriage and the Family*, 1969, *31*, 257–270.

Dollard, J. Culture, society, impulse, and socialization. *American Journal of Sociology*, 1939, *45*, 50–63.

Drillien, C. *The growth and development of the prematurely born infant*. Baltimore: Williams & Wilkins, 1964.

Durfee, H., & Wolf, K. Anstaltspflege und Entwicklung im ersten Lebensjahr. *Zeitschrift fur Kinderforschung*, 1933, *42*, 273–320.

Elardo, R., Bradley, R., & Caldwell, B. M. The relation of infants' home environments to mental test performance from six to thirty-six months: A longitudinal analysis. *Child Development*, March 1975, *46* (1), 71–76.

Elardo, R., Bradley, R., & Caldwell, B. M. A longitudinal study of the relation of home environments to language development at age three. *Child Development*, 1977, *48*, 595–603.

Elder, G. H., Jr. *Children of the Great Depression*. Chicago: University of Chicago Press, 1974.

Elder, G. H., Jr. Historical change in life patterns and personality. In P. Baltes & O. Brim (Eds.), *Life-span development and behavior* (Vol. 2). New York: Academic Press, 1979.

Elder, G. H., Jr. Scarcity and prosperity in postwar childbearing: Explorations from a life course perspective. *Journal of Family History*, Winter 1981, *5*, 410–431.

Elder, G. H., Jr., & Rockwell, R. C. The life-course approach and human development: An ecological perspective. *International Journal of Behavioral Development*, 1979, *2*, 1–21.

Ellis, H. *A study of British genius*. London: Hurst and Balckett, 1904.

Entwistle, D. R., & Doering, S. G. *The first birth: A family turning point*. Baltimore: Johns Hopkins University Press, 1981.

Erickson, F., & Mohatt, G. Cultural organization of participation structures in two classrooms of Indian students. In G. Spindler (Ed.), *Doing the ethnography of schooling: Educational anthropology in action*. New York: Holt, Rinehart & Winston, 1982.

Erlenmeyer-Kimling, L., & Jarvit, T. F. Genetics and intelligence: A review. *Science*, 1963, *142*, 1478–1479.

Featherman, D. L. The life span perspective in social science research. In *The 5-year outlook on science and technology* (Vol. 2). Washington, D.C.: National Science Foundation, 1982.

Feinman, S., & Feiring, C. *Social referencing and second-order effects in ten-month-olds*. Paper presented at the Biennial Meetings of the Society for Research on Child Development, Boston, 1981.

Figge, M. The etiology of maternal rejection: A study of certain aspects of the mother's life. Abstracted in *Smith College Studies in Social Work*, June 1931, *1*, 407.

Figge, M. Studies in maternal overprotection and rejection: V. Some factors in the etiology of maternal rejection. *Smith College Studies in Social Work*, March 1932, *2*, 209–223.

Fisher, R. A. *Statistical methods for research workers*. Edinburgh: Oliver & Boyd, 1925.

Foley, P. Studies in maternal overprotection and rejection: III. Early responsibility and affect-hunger as selective criteria in maternal over-protection. *Smith College Studies in Social Work*, March 1932, *2*, 209–223.

Furstenberg, F. *Unplanned parenthood: The social consequences of teenage child bearing*. New York: Free Press, 1976.

Galton, F. *English men of science: Their nature and nurture*. London: Macmillan, 1874.

Galton, F. The history of twins as a criterion of the relative power of nature. *Anthropological Institute Journal*, 1876, *5*, 391–406.

Garbarino, J. A preliminary study of some ecological correlates of child abuse: The impact of socioeconomic stress on mothers. *Child Development*, 1976, *47*, 178–185.

Ginsburg, H., & Opper, S. *Piaget's theory of intellectual development* (2nd ed.). Englewood Cliffs, N.J.: Prentice-Hall, 1979.

Giovannoni, J., & Billingsley, A. Child neglect among the poor: A study of parental adequacy in families of their ethnic groups. *Child Welfare*, 1970, *49*, 196–204.

Glueck, S., & Glueck, E. *One thousand juvenile delinquents*. Cambridge, Mass.: Harvard University Press, 1934. (a)

Glueck, S., & Glueck, E. *Five hundred delinquent women*. New York: Knopf, 1934. (b)

Gold, D., & Andres, D. Developmental comparisons between adolescent children with employed and nonemployed mothers. *Merrill-Palmer Quarterly*, 1978, *24*, 243–254. (a)

Gold, D., & Andres, D. Developmental comparisons between 10-year-old children with employed and nonemployed mothers. *Child Development*, 1978, *49*, 75–84. (b)

Gold, D., Andres, D., & Glorieux, J. The development of Francophone nursery-school children with employed and nonemployed mothers. *Journal of Behavioural Science*, 1979, *11*, 169–173.

Golden, S. Pre-school families and work. Doctoral dissertation, University of Michigan. *Dissertation Abstracts International* 13969, 1975 (University Microfilms No. 15347).

Goldfarb, W. The effects of early institutional care on adolescent personality. *Journal of Experimental Education*, 1943, *12*, 106–129. (a)

Goldfarb, W. Infant rearing and problem behavior. *American Journal of Orthopsychiatry*, 1943, *13*, 249–265. (b)

Goldfarb, W. Emotion and intellectual consequences of psychological deprivation in infancy: A re-evaluation. In P. H. Hoch & J. Zubin (Eds.), *Psychopathology of childhood*. New York: Grune and Stratton, 1955.

Goodwin, D. W. *Is alcoholism hereditary?* New York: Oxford University Press, 1976.

Goodwin, D. W., Schulsinger, F., Hermansen, L., Guze, S. B., & Winokur, G. Alcohol problems in adoptees raised apart from alcoholic biological parents. *Archives of General Psychiatry*, February 1973, *28*, 238–243.

Goodwin, D. W., Schulsinger, F., Knop, J., Mednick, S., & Guze, S. B. Alcoholism and depression in adopted-out daughters of alcoholics. *Archives of General Psychiatry*, July 1977, *34*, 751–755. (a)

Goodwin, D. W., Schulsinger, F., Knop, J., Mednick, S., & Guze, S. B. Psychopathology in adopted and nonadopted daughters of alcoholics. *Archives of General Psychiatry*, September 1977, *34*, 1005–1009. (b)

Goodwin, D. W., Schulsinger, F., Møller, N., Hermansen, L., Winokur, G., & Guze, S. B. Drinking problems in adopted and nonadopted sons of alcoholics. *Archives of General Psychiatry*, August 1974, *31*, 164–169.

Gordon, I. J. *A home center learning approach to early stimulation*. Gainesville, Fla.: Institute for Development of Human Resources, 1971.

Goslin, D. A. *Handbook of socialization theory and research*. Chicago: Rand McNally, 1969.

Gray, S. W., & Klaus, R. A. Experimental preschool program for culturally deprived children. *Child Development*, 1965, *36*, 887–898.

Grønseth, E., & Tiller, P. O. Father absence in sailor families. In *Studies of the family* (Vol. II). UNESCO Seminar in Family Research. Gøttingen: Vandenhoek et Ruprecht, 1957.

Gunnarsson, L. *Children in day care and family care in Sweden: A follow-up*. Gothenburg, Sweden: University of Gothenburg, 1978.

Hall, G. S. The contents of children's minds. *Princeton Review*, January–June 1883, 249–272.

Handler, J. F., & Zatz, J. *Neither angels nor thieves*. Washington, D.C.: National Academy Press, 1982.

Harris, D., & Tseng, S. Children's attitudes toward peers and parents as revealed by sentence completions. *Child Development*, 1957, *28*, 401–411.

Hartshorne, H., & May, M. *Studies in deceit*. New York: Macmillan, 1928.

Hartup, W. W. Peer interaction and social organization. In P. H. Mussen (Ed.), *Manual of child psychology* (Vol. 2). New York: Wiley, 1970.

Hartup, W. W. Perspectives on child and family interaction: Past, present, and future. In R. M. Lerner & G. B. Spanier (Eds.), *Child influences on marital and family interaction*. New York: Academic Press, 1978.

Hayes, C. D. (Ed.). *Making policies for children*. Washington, D.C.: National Academy Press, 1982.

Hayes, D., & Grether, J. *The school year and vacation: When do students learn?* Paper presented at the Eastern Sociological Convention, New York, 1969.

Heath, D. B. Some possible effects of occupation on the maturing of professional men. *Journal of Vocational Behavior*, 1977, *11*, 263–281.

Hebb, D. O. The innate organization of visual activity: I. Perception of figures by rats reared in total darkness. *Journal of Genetic Psychology*, 1937, *51*, 101–126. (a)

Hebb, D. O. The innate organization of visual activity: II. Transfer of a response in the discrimination of brightness and size by rats reared in total darkness. *Journal of Comparative Psychology*, 1937, *24*, 277–299. (b)

Hebb, D. O. Studies of the organization of behavior: I. Behavior of the rat in field orientation. *Journal of Comparative Psychology*, 1938, *25*, 333–352.

Hebb, D. O. *The organization of behavior*. New York: Wiley, 1949.

Heber, R., Garber, H., Harrington, S., & Hoffman, C. *Rehabilitation of families at risk for mental retardation*. Madison, Wis.: Rehabilitation Research and Training Center in Mental Retardation, University of Wisconsin, 1972.

Heller, K. A., Holtzman, W. H., & Messick, S. (Eds.). *Placing children in special education*. Washington, D.C.: National Academy Press, 1982.

Hess, R. D., & Camara, K. A. Post-divorce family relationships as mediating factors in the consequences of divorce for children. *Journal of Social Issues*, 1979, *35* (4), 79–96.

Hess, R. D., & Goldblatt, J. The status of adolescents in American society: A problem in social identity. *Child Development*, 1957, *28*, 459–468.

Hetherington, M. (Ed.). *Review of child development research* (Vol. 5). Chicago: University of Chicago Press, 1975.

Hetherington, E. M., Cox, M., & Cox, R. The aftermath of divorce. In J. H. Stevens, Jr. & M. Mathews (Eds.), *Mother-child, father-child relations*. Washington, D.C.: National Association for the Education of Young Children, 1978.

Heyns, B. *Summer learning and effects of schooling*. New York: Academic Press, 1978.

Hinde, R. A. *Animal behavior: A synthesis of ethology and comparative psychology*. New York: McGraw-Hill, 1966.

Hodgkiss, M. The delinquent girl in Chicago: II. The influence of broken homes and working mothers. *Smith College Studies of Social Work*, 1933, *3*, 259–274.

Hoffman, L. W. Mother's enjoyment of work and effects on the child. In F. I. Nye & L. W. Hoffman (Eds.), *The employed mother in America*. Chicago: Rand McNally, 1963.

Hoffman, L. W. The effects of maternal employment on the academic attitudes and performance of school-aged children. *School Psychology Review*, 1980, *9*, 319–335.

Hoffman, M. L., & Hoffman, L. W. (Eds.) *Review of child development research* (Vol. 1). New York: Russell Sage Foundation, 1964.

Hoffman, M. L., & Hoffman, L. W. (Eds.) *Review of child development research* (Vol. 2). New York: Russell Sage Foundation, 1966.

Hogan, D. *Transition in social change: The early lives of American men*. New York: Academic Press, 1981.

Holt, E. B. *Animal drive and the learning process* (Vol. 1). New York: Holt, 1931.

Hood, J. *Becoming a two-job family*. Unpublished doctoral dissertation, University of Michigan, 1980.

Hood, J., & Golden S. Beating time/making time: The impact of work scheduling on men's family roles. *The Family Coordinator*, 1979, *29*, 575–582.

Horn, J. M., Loehlin, J. C., & Willerman, L. Intellectual resemblance among adoptive and biological relatives: The Texas Adoption Project. *Behavior Genetics*, 1979, *9*, 177–207.

Horowitz, F. D. (Ed.) *Review of child development research* (Vol. 4). Chicago: University of Chicago Press, 1975.

Horowitz, F. D., & Paden, L. Y. The effectiveness of environmental intervention programs. In B. M. Caldwell & H. N. Ricciuti (Eds.), *Review of child development research* (Vol. 3). Chicago: University of Chicago Press, 1973.

Hough, E. Studies in maternal overprotection and rejection: II. Some factors in the etiology of maternal overprotection. *Smith College Studies in Social Work*, March 1932, *2*, 188–208.

Hunt, J. McV. *Intelligence and experience*. New York: Ronald Press, 1961.

Hurlock, E. B. *Child development* (Vol. 1). New York: McGraw-Hill, 1942.

Hurlock, E. B. *Child development* (Vol. 2). New York: McGraw-Hill, 1959.

Hurlock, E. B. *Child development* (Vol. 3). New York: McGraw-Hill, 1968.

Hurlock, E. B. *Child development* (Vol. 4). New York: McGraw-Hill, 1975.

Hurlock, E. B. *Developmental psychology: A life-span approach*. New York: McGraw-Hill, 1980.

Hutchings, B., & Mednick, S. A. Registered criminality in the adoptive and biological parents of registered male criminal adoptees. In R. R. Fieve, D. Rosenthal, & H. Brill (Eds.), *Genetic research in psychiatry*. Baltimore: Johns Hopkins University Press, 1973.

Jensen, A. R. How much can we boost I.Q. and scholastic achievement? *Harvard Educational Review*, Winter 1969, 1–123.

Jensen, A. R. *Bias in mental testing*. New York: Free Press, 1980.

John, E. A study on the effects of evacuation and air raids on children of preschool age. *British Journal of Educational Psychology*, 1941, *11*,

173–182.

Juel-Nielson, N. *Individual and environment*. Copenhagen: Munksgaard, 1964.

Kagan, J., & Moss, H. A. *Birth to maturity*. New York: Wiley, 1962.

Kamerman, S. B. *Parenting in an unresponsive society*. New York: Free Press, 1980.

Kamerman, S. B., & Hayes, C. D. (Eds.), *Families that work*. Washington, D.C.: National Academy Press, 1982.

Kamerman, S. B., & Kingston, P. Employers' responses to family responsibilities. In S. B. Kamerman & C. D. Hayes (Eds.), *Families that work*. Washington, D.C.: National Academy Press, 1982.

Kandel, D. B., & Lesser, G. S. *Youth in two worlds*. San Francisco: Jossey-Bass, 1972.

Kanter, R. M. *Work and family in the United States: A critical review and agenda for research and policy*. New York: Russell Sage, 1977.

Karnes, M. B. *Research and development program on preschool disadvantaged children: Final report*. Washington, D.C.: U.S. Office of Education, 1969.

Karnes, M. B., Studley, W. M., Wright, W. R., & Hodgins, A. S. An approach to working with mothers of disadvantaged preschool children. *Merrill-Palmer Quarterly*, 1968, *14*, 174–184.

Keniston, K., & The Carnegie Council on Children. *All our children: The American family under pressure*. New York: Harcourt Brace Jovanovich, 1977.

Kirk, S. A. *Early education of the mentally retarded*. Urbana, Ill.: University of Illinois Press, 1958.

Koch, H. L. The relation of "primary mental abilities" in five- and six-year-olds to sex of child and characteristics of his sibling. *Child Development*, 1954, *25*, 209–223.

Kohlberg, L. Moral development and identification. In H. W. Stevenson (Ed.), *Child psychology*. Chicago: National Society for the Study of Education, 1963.

Kohlberg, L. The development of moral character. In M. L. Hoffman & L. W. Hoffman (Eds.), *Review of child development research* (Vol. 1). New York: Russell Sage, 1964.

Kohn, M. L. *Class and conformity: A study in values*. Homewood, Ill.: Dorsey, 1969.

Kohn, M. L., & Schooler, C. Occupational experience and psychological functioning: An assessment of reciprocal effects. *American Sociological Review*, 1973, *38*, 97–118.

Kohn, M. L., & Schooler, C. The reciprocal effects of the substantive complexity of work and intellectual flexibility: A longitudinal assessment. *American Journal of Sociology*, 1978, *84*, 24–52.

Kolrausche, E. Jugendspiele und Einzelsöhne. *Zeitschrift für Schulegesundheitspflege*, 1891, *4*, 178.

Komarovsky, M. *The unemployed man and his family*. New York: Dryden Press, 1940.

Kuhn, T. S. *The structure of scientific revolutions*. Chicago: University of Chicago Press, 1962.

Landy, F., Rosenberg, B. G., & Sutton-Smith, B. The effect of limited father absence on cognitive development. *Child Development*, 1969, *40*, 941–944.

Lasko, J. K. Parent behavior toward first and second children. *Genetics Psychological Monographs*, 1954, *49–50*, 97–138.

Lauterback, C. E. Studies in twin resemblance. *Genetics*, 1925, *10*, 525–568.

Leahy, A. M. Nature, nurture, and intelligence. *Genetic Psychology Monographs*, 1935, *17*, 236–308.

Levenstein, P. Cognitive growth in preschoolers through verbal interaction with mothers. *American Journal of Orthopsychiatry*, 1970, *40*, 426–432.

Le Vine, R. A. Cross-cultural study in child psychology. In P. H. Mussen (Ed.), *Carmichael's manual of child psychology* (3rd ed.). New York: Wiley, 1970.

Levy, D. A method of integrating physical and psychiatric examination with special studies of body interest, overprotection, response to growth, and sex differences. *American Journal of Psychiatry*, 1929, *9*, 121–198.

Levy, D. Paper on maternal overprotection. *American Journal of Psychiatry*, 1930, *9*, 904.

Levy, D. On the problem of delinquency. *American Journal of Orthopsychiatry*, 1932, *2*, 197–211.

Levy, D. Relation of maternal overprotection to school grades and intelligence tests. *American Journal of Orthopsychiatry*, 1933, *3*, 26–34.

Levy, D. *Maternal overprotection*. New York: Columbia University Press, 1943.

Lewenberg, M. Marital disharmony as a factor in the etiology of maternal over-protection. *Smith College Studies in Social Work*, 1932, *2*, 224–236.

Lewin, K. Kriegslandschaft. *Zeitschrift für Angewandte Psychologie*, 1917, *12*, 440–447.

Lewin, K. *A dynamic theory of personality*. New York: McGraw-Hill, 1935.

Lewin, K. *Principles of topological psychology*. New York: McGraw-Hill, 1936.

Lewin, K. *Resolving social conflicts, selected papers on group dynamics.* New York: Harper, 1948.

Lewin, K., Lippitt, R., & White, R. K. Patterns of aggressive behavior in experimentally created "social climates." *Journal of Social Psychology,* 1939, *10,* 271–299.

Lewis, M. How parental attitudes affect the problem of lying in children. *Smith College Studies in Social Work,* 1930, *1,* 403.

Lewis, M., & Feiring, C. The child's social network: Social objects, social functions, and their relationship. In M. Lewis & L. A. Rosenblum, *The child and its family.* New York: Plenum, 1979.

Liebert, R. M., Neale, J. M., & Davidson, E. S. *The early window: Effects of television on children and youth.* New York: Pergamon Press, 1973.

Lightfoot, S. L. *Worlds apart.* New York: Basic Books, 1978.

Loehlin, J. C., Lindzey, G., & Spuhler, J. N. *Race differences in intelligence.* San Francisco: Freeman, 1975.

Lorenz, K. Z. Der Kumpan in der Umwelt des Vogels. *Journal für Ornithologie,* April 1935, *2,* 137–413.

Lorenz, K. Z. *Evolution and modification of behavior.* Chicago: University of Chicago Press, 1965.

Luria, A. R. *Cognitive development: Its cultural and social foundations.* Cambridge, Mass.: Harvard University Press, 1976.

Maccoby, E. E. Television: Its impact on school children. *Public Opinion Quarterly,* 1951, *15,* 421–444.

Maccoby, E. E. Personal communication, 1981.

Maccoby, E. E., & Jacklin, C. N. *The psychology of sex differences.* Stanford, Calif.: Stanford University Press, 1974.

Mathews, S. M. The effects of mothers' out-of-home employment upon children's ideas and attitudes. *Journal of Applied Psychology,* 1934, *18,* 116–136.

McCall, R. B. Exploratory manipulation and play in the human infant. *Monographs of the Society for Research in Child Development,* 1974, *39* (No. 155).

Mead, G. H. *Mind, self, and society.* Chicago: University of Chicago Press, 1934.

Mead, M. *Coming of age in Samoa.* New York: Morrow, 1928.

Merriman, C. The intellectual resemblance of twins. *Psychology Monographs,* 1924, *33,* 58.

Miller, D. R., & Dollard, J. *Social learning and imitation.* New Haven, Conn.: Yale University Press, 1941.

Miller, D. R., & Swanson, G. E. *The changing American parent: A study in the Detroit area.* New York: Wiley, 1958.

Moore, T. W. Children of working mothers. In S. Yudkin & H. Holme (Eds.), *Working mothers and their children.* London: Michael Joseph, 1963.

Moreno, J. L. *Who shall survive? A new approach to the problem of human inter-relations.* Washington, D. C.: Nervous and Mental Disease Publishing Co., 1934.

Morgan, W. L. *The family meets the Depression.* Minneapolis: University of Minnesota Press, 1939.

Mortimer, J. T. Patterns of intergenerational occupational movements: A smallest-space analysis. *American Journal of Sociology,* 1974, *79,* 1278–1299.

Mortimer, J. T. Social class, work, and the family: Some implications of the father's career for familial relationships and son's career decisions. *Journal of Marriage and the Family,* May 1976, 241–256.

Mott, P. E., Mann, F. C., McLoughlin, Q., & Warwick, D. P. *Shift work: The social, psychological, and physical consequences.* Ann Arbor: University of Michigan Press, 1965.

Mott, S. M. Mother-father preference. *Character and Personality,* 1937, *5,* 302–304.

Murchison, C. (Ed.) *A handbook of child psychology.* Worcester, Mass.: Clark University Press, 1931.

Murchison, C. (Ed.) *A handbook of child psychology.* Worcester, Mass.: Clark University Press, 1933.

Murphy, L. B. *Social behavior and child personality.* New York: Columbia University Press, 1937.

Mussen, P. H. (Ed.) *Handbook of research methods and child development.* New York: Wiley, 1960.

Mussen, P. H. (Ed.) *Carmichael's manual of child psychology.* New York: Wiley, 1970.

Mussen, P. H., & Conger, J. J. *Child development and personality* (1st ed.). New York: Harper, 1956.

Mussen, P. H., Conger, J. J., & Kagan, J. *Child development and personality* (2nd ed.). New York: Harper, 1963.

Mussen, P. H., Conger, J. J., & Kagan, J. *Child development and personality* (3rd ed.). New York: Harper, 1969.

Mussen, P. H., Conger, J. J., & Kagan, J. *Child development and personality* (4th ed.). New

York: Harper, 1974.

Mussen, P. H., Conger, J. J., & Kagan, J. *Child development and personality* (5th ed.). New York: Harper, 1976.

Mussen, P. H., Conger, J. J., & Kagan, J. *Child development and personality* (6th ed.). New York: Harper, 1979.

Neiman, L. J. The influence of peer groups upon attitudes toward the feminine role. *Social Problems*, 1954, *2*, 104–111.

Nesselroade, J. R., & Baltes, P. B. *Longitudinal research in the study of behavior and development*. New York: Academic Press, 1979.

Newman, H. H., Freeman, F. N., & Holzinger, K. J. *Twins: A study of heredity and environment*. Chicago: University of Chicago Press, 1937.

Parke, R. D. Children's home environments: Social and cognitive effects. In I. Altman & J. F. Wohlwill (Eds.), *Children and the environment*. New York: Plenum Press, 1978.

Pavlov, I. P. *Lectures on conditioned reflexes*. (G. V. Anrep, Trans.) London: Oxford University Press, 1928.

Pederson, F. A. *Mother, father, and infant as an interaction system*. Paper presented at the annual meeting of the American Psychological Association, Washington, D.C., 1976.

Pederson, F., Cain, R., & Anderson, B. *Second-order effects involving interactions among mother, father, and infant*. Paper presented at the Biennial Meeting of the Society for Research on Child Development, Boston, 1981.

Philips, S. Participant structures and communicative competence: Warm Springs children in community and classroom. In C. Cazden, D. Hymes, & V. John (Eds.), *Functions of language in the classroom*. New York: Teachers College Press, 1972.

Piaget, J. *The language and thought of the child*. New York: Harcourt, Brace, 1926.

Piaget, J. Piaget's theory. In P. H. Mussen (Ed.), *Carmichael's manual of child psychology* (Vol. 1). New York: Wiley, 1946.

Piaget, J. *The construction of reality in the child*. (M. Cook, Trans.) New York: Basic Books, 1954.

Piotrkowski, C. S. *Work and the family system: A naturalistic study of working-class and lower-middle-class families*. New York: Free Press, 1979.

Pleck, J. H. *Wives' employment, role demands and adjustment: Final report*. Unpublished manuscript, Wellesley College Center for Research on Women, 1981.

Pleck, J. H. Work schedules and work—family conflict in two-earner couples. In J. Aldous (Ed.), *Dual-earner families*. Beverly Hills, Calif.: 1983.

Pleck, J. H., Staines, G., & Lang, L. The conflict between work and family life. *Monthly Labor Review*, March 1980, 29–32.

Pringle, M. L., & Bossio, B. A study of deprived children. *Vita Humana*, 1958, *1*, 65–92, 142–170.

Prugh, D. G., Staub, E. M., Sands, H. H., Kirschbaum, R. M., & Lenihan, E. A. A study of the emotional reactions of children in families to hospitalization and illness. *American Journal of Orthopsychiatry*, 1953, *23*, 70–106.

Ramey, C., & Haskins, R. The causes and treatment of school failure. Insights from the Carolina Abecedarian Project. In M. Begab (Ed.), *Psychosocial influences and retarded performance: Strategies for improving social competence* (Vol. 2). Baltimore: University Park Press, 1981.

Ramey, C., & Haskins, R. The modification of intelligence through early experience. *Intelligence*, 1981, *5*, 5–19.

Rapoport, R., & Rapoport, R. *Dual-career families*. Baltimore: Penguin, 1971.

Riley, M. W. Aging and cohort succession: Interpretations and misinterpretations. *Public Opinion Quarterly*, 1973, *37*, 35–49.

Robins, L. N. Discussion of genetic studies and criminality and psychopathy. In R. R. Fieve, D. Rosenthal, & H. Brill (Eds.), *Genetic research in psychiatry*. Baltimore: Johns Hopkins University Press, 1973.

Rockwell, R. C., & Elder, G. H., Jr. Economic deprivation and problem behavior: Childhood and adolescence in the Great Depression. *Human Development*, 1982, *25*, 38–88.

Rodgers, R. R. Changes in parental behavior reported by children in West Germany and the United States. *Human Development*, 1971, *14*, 208–224.

Rosenblatt, P. C., & Cunningham, M. R. Television watching and family tensions. *Journal of Marriage and the Family*, February 1976, *38* (1), 105–111.

Ross, B. M. Some traits associated with sibling jealousy in problem children. *Smith College Studies in Social Work*, 1931, *1*, 364–376.

Rothman, B. *Jean Piaget: Psychologist of the real*. Ithaca, N.Y.: Cornell University Press, 1977.

Rubenstein, J. L., Howes, C., & Pedersen, F. A. *Infant Behavior and Development*, 1982, *5*,

185–194. *Second-order effects of peers on mother-toddler interaction.*

Sanfilios-Rothschild, C. The study of family power structure: A review, 1960–1969. *Journal of Marriage and the Family,* 1970, *32,* 539–552.

Scarr, S., & Barker, W. The effects of family background: A study of cognitive differences among black and white twins. In S. Scarr (Ed.), *IQ: Social class and individual differences.* Hillsdale, N.J.: Erlbaum, 1981.

Scarr, S., & Kidd, K. K. Developmental behavior genetics. In M. Haith & J. Campos (Eds.), *Mussen handbook of child psychology* (Vol. 4). New York: Wiley, 1983.

Scarr, S., Pakstis, A. J., Katz, S. H., & Barker, W. B. The absence of a relationship between degrees of white ancestry and intellectual skills within a black population. *Human Genetics,* 1977, *39,* 69–86.

Scarr, S., Webber, P. L., Weinberg, R. A., & Wittig, M. A. Personality resemblance among adolescents and their parents in biologically-related and adoptive families. *Journal of Personality and Social Psychology,* 1981, *40,* 885–898.

Scarr, S., & Weinberg, R. A. IQ test performance of black children adopted by white families. *American Psychologist,* 1976, *31,* 726–739.

Scarr, S., & Yee, D. Heritability and educational policy: Genetic and environmental effects on IQ, aptitude, and achievement. *Educational Psychologist,* 1980, *15,* 1–22.

Schaefer, E. S., & Bayley, N. Maternal behavior, child behavior, and their correlations from infancy through adolescence. *Monographs of the Society for Research on Child Development,* 1963, *28* (3, Serial No. 87).

Schaffer, H. R. Some issues for research in the study of attachment. In B. M. Foss (Ed.), *Determinants of infant behavior.* New York: Wiley, 1963.

Schaie, K. W. A reinterpretation of age-related changes in cognitive structure and functioning. In L. R. Goulet & P. H. Baltes (Eds.), *Life span developmental psychology: Research and theory.* New York: Academic Press, 1970.

Schuckit, M. A., Goodwin, D. A., & Winokur, G. A study of alcoholism in half siblings. *American Journal of Psychiatry,* March 1972, *128* (9), 1132–1136.

Schulsinger, F. Psychopathy: Heredity and environment. *International Journal of Mental Health,* 1972, *1,* 190–206.

Schwabe, H., & Bartholomai, F. Der Vorstellungskreis der Berliner Kinder beim Eintritt in die Schule. In *Berlin und seine Entwickelung: Städtisches Jahrbuch für Volkswirthschaft und Statistik Vierter Jahrgang.* Berlin: Guttentag, 1870.

Sears, R. R. Personality development in contemporary culture. *Proceedings of the American Philosophical Society,* 1949, *92,* 363–370.

Sears, R. R. A theoretical framework for personality and social behavior. *American Psychologist,* 1951, *6,* 476–483.

Sears, R. R. Your ancients revisited: A history of child development. In E. M. Hetherington (Ed.), *Review of child development research* (Vol. 5). Chicago: University of Chicago Press, 1975.

Sears, R. R., Maccoby, E. E., & Levin, H. *Patterns of child rearing.* Evanston, Ill.: Row, Peterson, 1957.

Sears, R. R., Pintler, M. H., & Sears, P. S. Effect of father separation on preschool children's doll play aggression. *Child Development,* 1946, *17,* 219–243.

Services for children. Washington, D.C.: National Academy Press, 1981.

Sewell, M. Some causes of jealousy in young children. *Smith College Studies in Social Work,* 1930, *1,* 6–22.

Shaw, C. R. *Juvenile delinquency—a group tradition* (Child Welfare Pamphlets, No. 23). Bulletin of the State University of Iowa, News Service, No. 700, 1933.

Shields, J. *Monozygotic twins brought up apart and brought up together.* London: Oxford University Press, 1962.

Simmons, R. G., Blyth, D. A., Van Cleave, E. F., & Bush, D. M. Entry into early adolescence: The impact of school structure, puberty, and early dating on self-esteem. *American Sociological Review,* 1979, *44,* 948–967.

Simpson, M. Parent preferences of young children. *Teachers College Contributions to Education,* No. 652, 1935.

Skeels, H. M. A study of the effects of differential stimulation on mentally retarded children: A follow-up report. *American Journal of Mental Deficiency,* 1942, *46,* 340–350.

Skeels, H. M. Adult status of children with contrasting early life experience. *Monographs of the Society for Research in Child Development,* 1966, *31*(3, Serial No. 105).

Skeels, H. M., & Dye, H. B. The study of the effects of differential stimulation on mentally retarded children. *Proceedings and Addresses of the American Association of Mental Deficiency,* 1939, *44,* 114–136.

Skeels, H. M., Updegraff, R., Wellman, B. L., &

Williams, H. M. A study of environmental stimulation: An orphanage preschool project. *Iowa State Studies in Child Welfare*, 1938, *15* (4).

Slomczynski, K. M., Miller, J., & Kohn, M. Stratification, work, and values: A Polish-United States comparison. *American Sociological Review*, 1981, *46*, 720–744.

Smith, M. B. School and home: Focus on achievement. In A. H. Passow (Ed.), *Developing programs for the educationally disadvantaged.* New York: Teachers College Press, 1968.

Spitz, R. A. Hospitalism: An inquiry into the genesis of psychiatric conditions in early childhood. *Psychoanalytic Study of the Child*, 1945, *1*, 153–172.

Spitz, R. A. Hospitalism: A follow-up report on investigation described in volume 1, 1945. *Psychoanalytic Study of the Child*, 1946, *2*, 113–117. (a)

Spitz, R. A. Anaclitic depression: II. An inquiry into the genesis of psychiatric conditions in early childhood. *Psychoanalytic Study of the Child*, 1946, *2*, 313–342. (b)

Stein, A. H., & Friedrich, L. K. Impact of television on children and youth. In E. M. Hetherington (Ed.), *Review of child development research* (Vol. 5). Chicago: University of Chicago Press, 1975.

Steiner, G. A. *The people look at television.* New York: Knopf, 1963.

Stolz, L. M. *Father relations of war-born children.* Stanford, Calif.: Stanford University Press, 1954.

Stolz, L. M. Effects of maternal employment on children: Evidence from research. *Child Development*, 1960, 31, 749–782.

Stukat, K. G. *Suggestibility: A factorial and experimental analysis.* Stockholm: Almquist and Wiksellt, 1958.

Sullivan, H. S. *Conceptions of modern psychiatry.* Washington, D.C.: William Alanson White Psychiatric Foundation, 1947.

Symonds, P. M. *The psychology of parent-child relationships.* New York: Appleton-Century, 1939.

Terman, L. M. *The measurement of intelligence.* New York: Houghton Mifflin, 1916.

Terman, L. M. *Genetic studies of genius.* Stanford, Calif.: Stanford University Press, 1925.

Terman, L. M. *Psychological factors in marital happiness.* New York: McGraw-Hill, 1938.

Thomas, W. I. *The unadjusted girl.* Boston: Little, Brown, 1927.

Thomas, W. I., & Thomas, D. S. *The child in America.* New York: Knopf, 1928.

Thomas, W. I., & Znaniecki, F. *The Polish peasant in Europe and America.* Chicago: University of Chicago Press, 1927.

Thorndike, E. L. *Measurement of twins.* New York: Science Press, 1905.

Tiller, P. O. Father absence and personality development of children in sailor families. Copenhagen, Denmark: *Munksgaard Nordisk Psykologi's Monograph Series*, 1958, *9*.

Tiller, P. O. *Father separation and adolescence.* Oslo: Institute for Social Research, 1961.

Tinbergen, N. *In the study of instinct.* London: Oxford University Press, 1951.

Tinbergen, N. On aims and methods of ethology. *Zeitschrift für Tierpsychologie*, 1963, *20*, 410–433.

Tizard, B., Cooperman, O., Joseph, A., & Tizard, J. Environmental effects on language development: A study of young children in long-stay residential nurseries. *Child Development*, 1972, *43*, 337–358.

Tizard, B., & Hodges, J. The effect of early institutional rearing on the development of eight year old children. *Journal of Child Psychology and Psychiatry*, 1978, *19*, 99–118.

Tizard, B., & Rees, J. A comparison of the effects of adoption, restoration to the natural mother, and continued institutionalization on the cognitive development of four-year-old children. *Child Development*, 1974, *45*, 92–99.

Tizard, B., & Rees, J. A comparison of the effects of adoption, restoration to the natural mother, and continued institutionalization on the cognitive development of four-year-old children: Further note (December 1975). In A. M. Clarke and A. D. B. Clarke (Eds.), *Early experience: Myth and evidence.* London: Open Books, 1976.

Toward a national policy for children and families. Washington, D.C.: National Academy of Sciences, 1976.

Travers, J. R., & Light, R. J. (Eds.). *Learning from experience.* Washington, D.C.: National Academy Press, 1982.

Tulkin, S. R. *Mother-infant interaction in the first year of life: An inquiry into the influences of social class.* Unpublished doctoral dissertation, Harvard University, 1970.

Tulkin, S. R. Social class differences in infant's reactions to mother's and stranger's voices. *Developmental Psychology*, Jan. 1973, *8* (1), 137. (a)

Tulkin, S. R. Social class differences in attachment behaviors of ten-month-old infants. *Child Devel-*

opment, March 1973, *44* (1), 171–174. (b)

Tulkin, S. R., & Cohler, B. J. Child-rearing attitudes and mother-child interaction in the first year of life. *Merrill-Palmer Quarterly, 1973, 19,* 95–106.

Tulkin, S. R., & Covitz, F. E. *Mother-infant interaction and intellectual functioning at age six.* Paper presented at the meeting of the Society for Research in Child Development, Denver, April 1975.

Tulkin, S. R., & Kagan, J. Mother-child interaction in the first year of life. *Child Development, 1972, 43,* 31–41.

U.S. Bureau of the Census, Current Population Reports, Series P-60, No. 127. *Money income and poverty status of families and persons in the United States: 1980.* Washington, D.C.: U.S. Government Printing Office, 1981.

U.S. Commissioner of Education, *Annual Report for 1900/1901* (Vol. 1). Washington, D.C., 1902.

Vuyk, R. *Overview and critique of Piaget's genetic epistemology 1965–1980* (Vol. 1). New York: Academic Press, 1981. (a)

Vuyk, R. *Overview and critique of Piaget's genetic epistemology 1965–1980* (Vol. 2). New York: Academic Press, 1981. (b)

Vygotsky, L. S. *Mind in society: The development of higher psychological processes.* Cambridge, Mass.: Harvard University Press, 1978.

Wachs, T. D. Utilization of a Piagetian approach in the investigation of early experience effects: A research strategy and some illustrative data. *Merrill-Palmer Quarterly,* January 1976, *22* (1), 11–30.

Wang, C. K. A. The significance of early personal history for certain personality traits. *American Journal of Psychology, 1932, 44,* 768–774.

Watson, J. B. *Psychology from the standpoint of a behaviorist.* Philadelphia: Lippincott, 1918.

Watson, J. B. *Behaviorism* (2nd ed.). New York: Norton, 1930.

Weikart, D. P. *Preschool intervention: A preliminary report of the Perry Preschool Project.* Ann Arbor, Mich.: Campus Publishers, 1967.

Werner, E., Simonian, K., Bierman, J. M., & French, F. E. Cumulative effect of perinatal complications and deprived environment on physical, intellectual, and social development of preschool children. *Pediatrics, 1967, 39,* 480–505.

Wertsch, J. *The concept of activity in Soviet psychology.* Armonk, Sharpe, 1981.

Whiting, J. W. M., & Child, I. L. *Child training and personality: A cross-cultural study.* New Haven, Conn.: Yale University Press, 1953.

Willerman, L. Biosocial influences on human development. *American Journal of Orthopsychiatry, 1972, 42,* 452–462.

Willerman, L. *The psychology of individual and group differences.* San Francisco: Freeman, 1979.

Willerman, L., Naylor, A., & Myrianthopoulos, N. Intellectual development of children from interracial matings. *Science, 1970, 170,* 1329–1331.

Wingfield, A. H. *Twins and orphans: The inheritance of intelligence.* London: Dent, 1928.

Yarrow, L., Rubenstein, J. L., & Pederson, F. A. *Infant and environment: Early cognitive and motivational development.* Washington, D.C.: Hemisphere, 1975.

Zigler, E., Kagan, S. L., & Klugman, E. (Eds.), *Children, families, and government: Perspectives on American social policy.* Cambridge: Cambridge University Press, in press.

DESIGN AND ANALYSIS IN DEVELOPMENTAL PSYCHOLOGY* | 9

MARK I. APPELBAUM, *University of North Carolina at Chapel Hill*
ROBERT B. McCALL, *Boys Town Center, Boys Town, Nebraska*

CHAPTER CONTENTS

PROLOGUE

Developmental psychology is the study of behavioral change within organisms over age. And, like other areas of psychology, it aims to describe, understand, predict, and control behavior by studying factors that are necessary, that are sufficient, or that influence both behavior in general and behavioral differences between individual organisms. But in contrast to other specialties, the study of development is the study of *change*—change within organisms over age. Wohlwill (1973) has argued that the methodology appropriate for the study of static behavioral phenomena must be modified in crucial ways when applied to the study of change. But developmental psychology has not often been truly developmental, and therefore it has not seriously faced the methodological issues unique to its definitional purpose (McCall, 1977; Wohlwill, 1973; but see also Overton & Reese, 1981).

These criticisms represent challenges to the broad purpose of developmental psychology, the nature of the questions it asks, and the ways in which it researches them and interprets the results achieved. In addition, developmental methodology also in-

*We thank Craig Edelbrock and Kenneth Spenner for making several valuable suggestions in the development of this chapter, Patricia Mordeson and Betsy Schopler for assembling material, Mary Pat Roy for typing a difficult manuscript, and Suzanne Appelbaum for proofreading. Portions of this work were supported by a Fulbright Fellowship to Mark I. Appelbaum.

cludes specific techniques of design and statistical analysis that must be appropriate to the general strategy of the research. The field of applied statistics has made great strides in recent years, but as is often the case, innovations in statistical methods are slow to trickle down to the researchers who need them. This gap between statistical knowledge and research practice limits a discipline, and one could argue that a major shift in developmental psychology toward the study of change over age is not likely to occur unless the research community is acquainted with statistical methods that can answer such questions.

The broad purpose of this chapter is to attempt to narrow the knowledge gap between statisticians and researchers. We will consider issues and techniques that are basic to all specialties of psychology as well as those that are especially applicable to the study of development.

As stated above, methodology and statistics serve a higher master—the broad strategic goals of the discipline. Therefore, we begin with a brief history of developmental strategy to establish a structure for considering the specific methods to be presented in the body of this chapter.

Our Methodological Roots

About 1930, developmental psychology commenced a new era when many of the major longitudinal projects were initiated at Fels, Berkeley, and elsewhere. These studies were observational in nature and emphasized mental tests and sometimes naturalistic observations in nursery school and at home. The resulting data, analyzed primarily in terms of correlations within and across age, reflected the researchers' attempts to find correlates of important behaviors and stabilities in individual differences across age. Although these longitudinal studies did not constitute the totality of developmental psychology at the time, they and their basic strategies did represent a major thrust.

In the late 1950s and early 1960s, developmental psychology was joined by experimentalists, many of whom had formerly studied basic issues of sensation, perception, and learning in animals. They continued to research essentially the same topics, but now they did so in the human infant rather than in the pigeon and white rat. This shift in organisms-for-study was sufficient for these experimentalists to be called "developmental psychologists." Partly as a result, infancy blossomed as a focal area, and because of their experimental research orientation and expertise, the newcomers improved the scientific image of developmental psychology.

The two groups, the traditional correlationalists and the experimental-child types, have rarely coordinated their efforts or cooperated with each other just as they have failed to do in other areas of psychology. For example, in 1957, Cronbach called attention to the two disciplines of psychology. One emphasizes observational methods, sometimes made in naturalistic contexts, and correlational analyses. The other pursues the experimental manipulation of variables in the laboratory, looking for differences between means with the analysis of variance. Such a schism is not necessary, but it seems to continue in psychology in general as well as in developmental psychology in particular (McCall, 1977). Therefore, it is crucial to examine this methodological distinction and evaluate whether it serves us well.

The Two Realms of Development

Basically, these two research attitudes represent allegiances to methodological strategies grounded in different values. Experimentalists contend that their approach can determine the causality between independent and dependent variables. Therefore, they tend to study experimentally induced main effects on groups of subjects. In contrast, correlationalists stress that they study development as it naturally occurs in ecologically valid contexts that are usually less amenable to experimental manipulation. As a result, they tended to observe factors that relate to differences between individuals in single representative groups. Both sides need to understand that these two methodological approaches are not contradictory and that each is necessary for progress in the discipline. Moreover, each camp needs to be developmental. Let us look more closely at this schism, especially from the standpoint of studying developmental change over age.

The Developmental Function. One aspect of developmental inquiry concerns the *developmental function* (Wohlwill, 1973). Essentially, this is the average value of a dependent variable plotted over age. A prototypical example is a growth chart for height or weight in which a sample of individuals is measured successively and the average for the group is plotted as a function of age. If the sample is representative of the species, then the resulting plot is a *species-general developmental function*. Developmental functions also may be plotted for a subgroup of the species and even for an individual. When experimentalists are developmental, they tend to study group differences in developmental functions as a consequence of an experimental manipulation.

Developmental functions are *continuous* or *dis-*

continuous. A developmental function is continuous when there are only quantitative, not qualitative, changes in the characteristic over age. Height is a continuous developmental function because the fundamental nature of height does not change over age, although the average value in the sample may, and usually does, change. Piaget's sensorimotor intelligence is a discontinuous developmental function because the fundamental character of sensorimotor intelligence changes from one stage to the next.

It should be noted that the distinction between continuous and discontinuous developmental functions is a theoretical one. Intelligence, for example, can be measured with a single relative score (e.g., IQ) across age, but the qualitative nature of the concept nevertheless might change from age to age. Therefore, intelligence may be conceptually discontinuous even though its measurement may be continuous. The choice of appropriate statistical methods may depend on the continuous/discontinuous distinction.

Individual Differences.   The other realm of developmental inquiry concerns individual differences. The phrase *individual differences* refers to the variability of performance between individuals about their group mean. Developmentally speaking, individual differences are either *stable* or *not stable*. They are stable if individuals maintain approximately the same relative ordering within their group at one age as they do at another age. The correlation coefficient is the classic measure of cross-age stability.

Independence.   Conceptually, the continuity, discontinuity, and form of the developmental function are independent of the stability or lack of stability in individual differences from one age to the next. For example, height shows a progressive increase during the first years of life. In contrast, individual differences are not very stable during the first months following birth but become more stable by the end of the first year. Early intelligence can be conceived to follow a discontinuous developmental function, with individual differences not stable early but more stable later as the developmental function becomes more continuous. It is also possible to view early mental development as a sequence of stages in which individual differences are relatively more stable within stage but less stable across stage boundaries (McCall, 1979). The important point is that the relationship between the nature of the developmental function and the stability of individual differences is an empirical question; conceptually, it is possible for any combination of characteristics to exist.

Examples of Confusing the Two Realms.   As we have seen, researchers have tended to emphasize either issues pertaining to the developmental function or those pertaining to individual differences. Although these two groups emerged from independent historical traditions, they have not always borne in mind the potential independence of these two conceptual realms when drawing inferences.

Consider, for example, the development of intelligence. Bloom (1964) suggested that approximately one-half of a person's intelligence is determined by the age of 4. This often-quoted statement reflects the empirical finding that the correlation between IQ test performance at 4 and at 18 years of age is approximately 0.71, the square of which is 0.50. While it is accurate to say that approximately 50% of the differences between individuals at age 18 is associated with differences one can observe in those same individuals at age 4, it is not correct to conclude that one-half of a person's intelligence is determined by age 4. This erroneous inference is a case of extrapolating from data on individual differences to the developmental function. The statement ignores the fact that a person's absolute amount of information and intellectual skills (i.e., the developmental function) may increase several fold between 4 and 18 years of age.

Unfortunately, we make this error frequently. For another example, consider the nature/nurture issue with respect to intelligence. The heritability of a characteristic is the proportion of individual differences in that trait which is associated with individual differences in genetic background. All procedures in population genetics rely on individual differences. Therefore, if a characteristic, such as intelligence, has a heritability of .50, this suggests that 50% of the variability between individuals within a group is associated with their genetic background, but it says nothing about the species-general developmental function or group differences in it. That is, it is possible for all members of the species to pass through a series of qualitative steps laid down in the maturational plan of the species which transform a nonverbal, nonthinking organism to one capable of abstract reasoning and syllogistic logic without the fact ever being considered in the calculation of the heritability of intelligence. From this perspective, the task of population genetics is analogous to measuring differences in the heights of the seedlings of giant sequoia trees and trying to predict the relative difference in heights of those trees at maturity, while ignoring the fact that the trees may grow to be over 250 feet tall.

Another cost of failing to see individual differences and developmental function as two separate aspects of the same problem concerns the distinct possibility that individual differences are governed by one set of factors and the developmental function by another set of factors. For example, the famous Skodak and Skeels study (1949; Honzik, 1957) showed that the IQs of adopted children correlated .38 with those of their biological parents but essentially .00 with an estimated index of intelligence for their rearing parents. However, the average IQ of the children was 21 points higher than the average of their biological parents and nearly identical to the estimated average of their rearing parents. This study suggests that individual differences in IQ may be more associated with genetic circumstances while the average IQ of the group is more influenced by environmental factors.

Of course, this dichotomy oversimplifies the development of intelligence, but it does illustrate how, in a single sample, different factors can influence the developmental function and individual differences. Jensen (1973) has demonstrated that these two pieces of information are not contradictory for this case. While the remainder of this chapter will maintain the distinction between these two potentially independent realms, they are not likely to be independent in nature, and both must be seen as two pieces of the same puzzle if we are to emerge with a comprehensive understanding of the nature of development (McCall, 1981).

Being Developmental. The word development means change, change over time within organisms. Regardless of which of the two realms of developmental study one considers, we have rarely been truly developmental.

For example, very few of our studies in any tradition are conducted over age. Rather, they are primarily studies of immature organisms at a single age. And, even when age is a variable, we must ask whether we are studying age differences or age changes (Wohlwill, 1973). If our goal is to describe the difference between a "typical" 6- and a "typical" 12-month infant, then cross-sectional research will suffice. But if we wish to study age changes within organisms, then longitudinal methodology is required. Unfortunately, the number of longitudinal studies conducted is woefully small.

Moreover, during the last two decades the longitudinal method has come under attack for confounding age changes with secular change and repeated testing experience (Baltes & Schaie, 1973; Nesselroade & Baltes, 1974; Schaie, 1965). Although research designs have been offered that are supposed to deal with these confounds (see below),

it is not clear that they in fact handle the problems or are always necessary (for a discussion, see McCall, 1977). Nevertheless, the effect of these criticisms has been to define "proper" longitudinal methodology out of the time and financial means of the discipline and to excessively tarnish the image of the longitudinal method, which, as difficult as it may be, is the lifeblood of a developmental science. While developmental psychology should be indebted to these scientists for calling our attention to these confounds and for creating new approaches, the "movement" may have fed upon itself, temporarily gone too far, and hampered progress in our discipline (McCall, 1977).

The observationalists have been more likely than the experimentalists to conduct longitudinal studies, but they have fared no better in describing developmental change. Typically, they analyze their pregnant longitudinal data in ways that ignore completely any change in the developmental function and reveal stability, not change, in individual differences.

For example, our customary approach to analyzing longitudinal data is to calculate correlations between similar measures assessed at two different ages. If the correlation is significant, we proclaim stability in the characteristic, which is to say that a lack of change in the relative position of individuals within the group has been observed. Notice that we sometimes draw this conclusion even if more instability than stability is observed (i.e., r is less than .71). On the other hand, if a significant correlation is not found, we cannot infer that change has occurred because that would be accepting the null hypothesis.

Not only do we not look for change, but the failure to find stability is often interpreted as a black mark on a variable's reputation and utility. When a longitudinal correlation is not found, we sometimes question the meaningfulness of the measure. True, if a variable lacks meaningful correlates, it may reflect random or uninteresting variation. But some have proposed that infant tests be discarded, for example, because they do not predict later IQ. Instead, the infant tests may be adequate assessments of contemporary performance, and the lack of developmental stability may be associated with the possibility that mental ability changes its fundamental nature over age.

Regardless of tradition, these are curious strategies for those who should be studying change. We need to have attitudes and methods oriented toward revealing change as well as continuity and stability.

Relevant Developmental Psychology

As argued elsewhere in this volume, developmental psychology has spent the last two decades in methodological narcissism. Stated extremely, we have been much more concerned with studying something in a methodologically precise manner than with learning something important about development. It is—or was—a natural stage in the development of a new discipline. But one might argue that we have now emerged from this phase with the confidence that we do know something about how to study development and that we should be about the business of asking bigger questions, some of which should have direct social relevance and application. But, to be truly relevant to social concerns, developmental psychology will need to do more than simply turn toward studying topics of greater public interest. New thinking and new methods are required.

Can *Versus* Does *Questions*. The great advantage of experimental methods is that they address cause-and-effect questions: Can the presence of X cause a change in the dependent variable Y? To test this proposition, we typically construct a laboratory experiment, manipulate the presence or level of X, and observe dependent changes in Y. But often the laboratory circumstances are not the same as the circumstances characteristic of the natural environment of individuals. Therefore, from a practical standpoint, the results of the experimental research tend to answer the question of whether X *can* cause Y, but do not directly answer the question of whether X *does* cause Y in society. Adults *can* learn nonsense syllables, for example, but they rarely *do;* children can be classically conditioned, but this may or may not be the process by which they learn most or even many behaviors; and children can be made to display more aggressive actions by viewing violent television programs, but television may or may not play a major role in producing violent crime in society or even aggressive behavior in nursery schools. Of course, if the experimental manipulation could be performed with random assignment and in a naturalistic context (e.g., typical television fare introduced into a community that previously had no television at all; Murray & Kippax, 1977), one would be on better inferential ground. But even then it will be difficult to firmly conclude that television violence indeed does cause the criminal violence we read about in the newspapers.

Interpreting the Effects of Manipulations on Development. A second problem in studying naturalistic development points up the necessity for interpreting experimental results differently when the manipulation impinges on a developmental rather than on a static phenomenon (Wohlwill, 1973). Suppose it were ethically possible to deprive children of certain nutritional needs at a specified point in development. It is likely that growth rates would slow relative to controls during the period of deprivation. But after proper nutrition is reinstated, the growth rate might actually exceed the normal for a short period of time (Tanner, 1963). Typically, we infer that the treatment effect causes the change we observe in the dependent variable. But should we say that the deprivation experience caused an accelerated or catchup growth rate? Or was it the termination of the deprivation condition or the reinstatement of normal nutrition that produced it? To adequately explain catchup growth, one must consider not only the experimental treatment but its interaction with normal developmental processes not under experimental control. It is clear that discovering the sufficient causes of development will be difficult.

Unraveling the necessary causes of naturalistic development is every bit as arduous and complex an undertaking. Necessary causes are usually determined by depriving the organism of the hypothesized factor. However, when children are the subject of study, ethical considerations obviate many experimental deprivations. Therefore, we are no more likely to uncover many of the necessary causes of development as we are the sufficient ones.

The Need for Both. The purpose of this chapter is not to denigrate one approach or another or to prophesy developmental nihilism. Rather, explaining developmental change in naturalistic contexts is a formidable task that requires modifications in our thinking and our methods. We are going to be more limited in what we will be able to conclude than we might have hoped. For example, we must accept the possibility that we will probably never be able to demonstrate unequivocally that certain cognitive experiences in the first 18 months of life are *necessary* for the development of language or intelligence in the second and third years.

We should not give up these quests, however, but we should change our methods and alter our expectations. Other sciences face these same realities. Paleontology, geology, and astronomy seem to be alive and well without manipulating fossils, continents, or heavenly bodies. Maybe it would be more fruitful and less frustrating if we strove to be like epidemiology rather than like physics. Epidemiologists are apparently less intimidated by such logical limitations, perhaps because they do not have a history of deifying the manipulative experimental method above all others. Rather, they approach their problems by marshaling evidence from as many strategies as possible and realize that each strategy, in itself, is deficient. For example, if a laboratory study demonstrates that under certain conditions X can lead to Y, if there is a relationship between X and Y in naturalistic settings, if X can be imposed in a naturalistic or quasi-naturalistic environment and it leads to Y, and if X exists in sufficient magnitude in society, then these several observations coalesce on the tentative proposition that X does cause Y in naturalistic circumstances. Each approach is inadequate by itself, but each makes a vital contribution to the conclusion.

What developmental psychologists need is the self-confidence that we possess skills and methods that are either adequate to the task or can be modified to be adequate. Stated extremely, we must shift our value for discovering certainty about trivia to discovering somewhat less certain knowledge about more relevant and useful questions. And we must seek to describe *change* as vigorously as we have sought to describe consistency in developmental function and in individual differences.

The Role of Research Methods and Analysis

The historical themes and allegiances described above shape the questions we ask and the answers we obtain, and they form a structure with which to organize specific techniques. Our purpose in this chapter is to broaden the developmentalist's perspective and to improve the quality of design and analysis in the pursuit of our goals. But we do not provide a complete survey of design and analysis in developmental psychology, or even in-depth coverage of specific topics. Many such treatises already exist, principally Wohlwill (1973), Achenbach (1978), Nesselroade and Baltes (1979), Nesselroade and Reese (1973), Osofsky (1979), and Sackett (1979), to name only a few. Rather, we have preferred to deal with several design and statistical situations that are common in developmental psychology but that are often handled in less appropriate or less sophisticated ways than are possible. Occasionally much more advantageous methodologies exist than we are currently employing, while in other contexts we have forgotten the "common wisdom" of an earlier age.

While we have tried to bring developmentalists more up-to-date statistically, we do not claim to present new techniques in all their detail and potential. Rather, we have tried to introduce some approaches, but not cover them comprehensively. We have been more interested in communicating what should be done and why than in the basic procedures of how actually to do it. In addition, we acknowledge that many procedures have been omitted and that other authors might choose to emphasize different topics. We can only hope we have been of some help to some researchers.

We further note that while much of the chapter is statistical, no amount of statistical expertise can replace careful phrasing of research questions, appropriate sampling, precise measurement, incisive design, and proper inferences. Throughout our review we have tried to keep our eye on the importance of studying both the developmental function and individual differences for the purpose of describing and understanding change over age within organisms.

DEVELOPMENTAL FUNCTIONS: FACTORIAL DESIGNS

Developmental functions imply a pattern across age either of means or of another measure of group performance. The statistical tools used to describe such functions include the most common methods of analysis, for example, the analysis of variance. There is no need to provide a short course on the analysis of variance here (see, for example, Winer, 1971). Rather, we have concentrated on new techniques and situations in which statistical advances have eclipsed more traditional methods.

We begin with a discussion of the nature of the data; move next to reliability, to cross-sectional designs involving qualitative—followed by those involving quantitative—data, and then to multivariate analysis; and end with longitudinal or repeated measures analyses.

The Nature of the Data

Selecting appropriate analyses requires knowing something about the nature of data, specifically the observational unit, the type of measurement, and the reliability of the measurement.

Observational Unit

The fundamental logic of the randomized design—the traditional independent-groups analysis of variance—and many other statistical techniques rest on the assumption that observational units, typically subjects, are randomly and independently sampled and randomly assigned to treatment conditions. Such random and independent sampling and assignment are crucial assumptions of the statistical analysis and the logical basis of our ability to draw the inference of causality.

But sometimes actual circumstances become a

little complicated. Suppose 20 children are enrolled in a single preschool enrichment program with one teacher, and they are to be compared with 20 children selected from the community who had no preschool experience. If each pupil is given a test of basic skills, the researcher will have two groups of 20 scores.

What is the observational unit in this situation? Notice that the home-reared children are independent from one another, but the children in the single preschool classroom are not mutually independent because they share a common relevant experience—their teacher and all the elements of their particular preschool classroom experience.

Nonindependence between observational units may result in decreased within-group error variance, artificially inflated t (or F) values, and too many rejections of the null hypothesis. Because the independent observational units are a single classroom composing one "group" and 20 individual children composing the other group, these data cannot be analyzed by conventional analysis of variance methods.

Suppose the researcher implemented the enrichment program in five classrooms with five different teachers and compared the performance of these children with those from five other classrooms taught by five other people who used a traditional curriculum. What is the observational unit? We are prone to simply ignore classroom and compare the scores of the students receiving the special program with those receiving the traditional program. But students within a classroom are not independent of one another while classrooms are. Therefore, classroom is technically the observational unit. In this case, the practical problems of analysis can be handled by using a nested or hierarchical design in which classroom is nested within the curriculum factor (Winer, 1971).

All "groups" of subjects do not necessarily constitute an observational unit. For example, college students might be given a paper-and-pencil test in groups, but the observational unit might still be the individual student if it can be assumed that the individuals would have performed the same if they had been administered the test individually. A general rule of thumb in this regard is to ask if the results would be the same if each subject were assessed individually. The answer is probably "yes" in the paper-and-pencil study described immediately above, but it would be "no" in the preschool enrichment study described initially.

Another problematic circumstance occurs when dyads or other small groups are studied, as in mother/infant interaction or family groups. Obviously,

the members of such groups are not independent, and the dyad or family is the observational unit. Usually this will mean that the dependent variable is a single number that reflects something about the family unit. For example, it might be the number of minutes the dyad spends in positive social interaction. But we often make observations on each member of the dyad, such as, the number of smiles or touches by the mother, the number of coos by the baby, and so on. In such cases, it may be useful to keep the dyad as the observational unit, but to conceive of that unit as having more than one dependent variable (e.g., mother smiles, baby coos, etc.). Then dyads might be analyzed with multivariate procedures that are designed to handle more than one dependent variable simultaneously (see below).

Scales of Measurement

Another aspect of the data that determines what statistical technique can be used is whether differences between scores on the dependent variable are qualitative or quantitative in nature.

Qualitative Variables. Qualitative dependent variables are ones whose underlying scale is either nominal or ordinal (Stevens, 1951). For example, the dependent variable may simply be the presence or absence of a specific attribute: a child may imitate or not imitate a model; an infant may smile or not smile during a stimulus presentation; or a baby may not vocalize at all, vocalize some, or vocalize a good deal. Observations of this kind are sometimes referred to as *count data*, because the dependent variable is essentially a count of the number of individuals in each of several mutually exclusive (such as religious preference), or ordinal (the amount of vocalization) categories.

Usually, a subject produces only a single count or tally in a single category. That is, either the subject imitates or the subject does not imitate; the subject does not do both. These are called *single-response data* if each subject is assigned to one of several mutually exclusive categories (Bock, 1975). On the other hand, it is sometimes the case that an individual could contribute a tally to more than one category. If each subject in the sample makes a number of responses, and each response is assigned to one of several categorical schemes, the resulting frequencies represent *multiple-response data* (Bock, 1975).

Quantitative Variables. In contrast to qualitative measurements, a dependent variable is *quantitative* if a numeric value reflects the *amount* of the attribute present in the observational unit along an interval or ratio scale. For example, two possibilities are height in inches or ratings of the aggressiveness of nursery school children on a 10-point scale (assuming the scale does possess equal intervals).

The distinction between qualitative and quantitative dependent variables is often related to the distinction between discrete (discontinuous) and continuous random variables (qualitative data tend to be discrete; quantitative data tend to be continuous). Notice also that the qualitative/quantitative or discrete/continuous distinction applies to the *conceptual* dependent variable, not to its operational measurement. For example, aggressiveness in nursery school children could be conceived to be a continuous dependent variable, but it might be measured by counting the number of discrete aggressive acts. Each item on a test may constitute a discrete measurement, but the total of such items may reflect a value for a continuous (i.e., quantitative) dependent variable called achievement.

Often only one dependent variable or attribute is considered at a time, and each subject contributes one score to the data set. This is called *univariate* data. However, a subject might be measured on several different attributes, in which one has *multivariate* data. Multivariate data must be distinguished from *repeated measurements*. Multivariate data involve the assessment of several different attributes of the same unit (i.e., subject), while repeated measurements involve the assessment of a single attribute of each unit on two or more occasions. The univariate versus multivariate distinction is the quantitative analog to the single-response versus multiple-response distinction for qualitative data. The appropriate statistical technique partly depends on these distinctions.

Reliability

When a psychometric test is developed, one of the first questions we ask is, "What is its reliability and its validity?" Procedures for determining an index of reliability for paper-and-pencil tests are well-known. But researchers tend to be less sophisticated about determining reliability in other research contexts, especially in experimental factorial designs.

Classical Reliability for Quantitative Data. Classical methods of assessing reliability for quantitatively measured attributes are well understood and documented. Numerous texts that describe both the theory and practice of classical reliability (e.g., Nunnally, 1967; Cronbach, 1970) are available. An excellent chapter by Stanley (1971) is especially recommended to researchers.

Classical reliability theory and methods were developed in the context of measuring mental performance and test construction. As a result, they tend to

assume that quantitative data are available and that the dependent variable is continuous and unidimensional (e.g., all items on the test measure the same basic attribute). Moreover, a score X_i for individual i is assumed to be composed of a true score, T_i, for that individual and an error component, e_i, which is conceived to be a combination of all factors and influences that prevent the observed score from being "exact." The e_i are usually presumed to be normally distributed, mutually independent, and independent of the true scores. In theory, the *index* is simply the correlation of the true score with the observed score, and the *reliability* of the test is the proportion of the total variance of the observed score attributable to the variability of the true scores.

This concept of reliability is simple enough in theory. In practice, however, we never have a measure of the true scores to correlate with the observed scores. To deal with this practical problem, one assumes that the true score component is identical for two observed scores and the error is randomly distributed and uncorrelated with the true score component. Then an assessment of reliability can be determined by correlating the two observed scores. The correlation will be high to the extent that the error variability is small relative to the common true score variability in the two observed scores.

To obtain the two observed scores, one of two concepts are needed. The first is *domain sampling*, which assumes that a unidimensional test is made up of a sampling (perhaps random) of items from the domain of interest and that subsamples of items within that domain are theoretically comparable observed scores. Reliability is then assessed by the split-half method, Kuder-Richardson Formula 20, or other indices based upon the idea of the average intercorrelation among items. Notice that these approaches require that the test be unidimensional and that the error variability for the two scores be uncorrelated in order for the split-half reliability coefficient to accurately reflect the proportion of observed-score variability attributable to true score variability. But the assumption of uncorrelated error may not be met in this context. For example, if one subject is tired and another is not, this difference will exist for both halves of the assessment. Therefore, assuming that fatigue is error, the split-half reliability could incorrectly estimate the reliability of the measurement.

Instead of domain sampling, another assumption could be made. If *parallel forms* of the assessment existed (i.e., two comparable measuring instruments), they could be administered at two different times sufficiently spaced to decrease the likelihood that temporary error variability on the two occasions will be correlated. One version of this assumption leads to test/retest reliability procedures, which may yield lower reliabilities than split-half procedures to the extent that they correct for correlated error.

Not only is there a problem applying reliability theory to psychometric data, but new problems arise when the data are developmental. For example, consider the task of determining the reliability of the Brazelton Neonatal Assessment Scale. Split-half reliabilities cannot be performed over the entire instrument because the items do not all assess the same characteristic or dimension. Moreover, since the behavior of the newborn is so dependent on state, which is typically unstable, it might be very difficult to assess the same behavior twice under identical state conditions even if the items were unidimensional.

Consequently, test/retest reliability appears to be the method of choice, but in this case it brings its own problem. A newborn is developing so rapidly that a test/retest interval of one day may be too long. As a result, test/retest correlations may be low, not because the measurement instrument is unreliable, but because the baby has changed from one day to the next. This confusion between the reliability of the measurement and the stability of the trait represents one of those special problems with which developmentalists must cope when they try to deal with change by using analytical methods determined for the static case (Jensen, 1980). Some of these problems can be sorted out and assessed if the researcher has a model that specifies what aspects of the data are error, stable or nonstable individual differences, and so on (Wheaton, Muthén, Alwin, & Summers, 1977).

Reliability for Qualitative Data.   Often the data consist of categorical responses (e.g., the child imitated perfectly, imitated approximately, did not imitate). Usually classical methods of reliability are not appropriate for qualitative data because the variable in question is not continuously distributed for either true score or error.

In the qualitative situation we often want to know the reliability of two observers who are making categorical judgments about the behavior of a subject. Our usual procedure is to report the proportion of total judgments on which the two raters agree. This approach has several serious problems, principally that the result depends on the rates of occurrence of the dependent variable and that this method fails to consider the chance and maximum percent agreements. We illustrate with some hypothetical interobserver reliability data that are presented in Part *i* of

Table 1 for the occurrence of smiling in infants while they are being shown pictures of social stimuli. Invoking the strategy of determining the percent of the total on which the two judges agree (i.e., smile/smile and no-smile/no-smile judgments), we find an apparently respectable reliability of 92%.

This high reliability is a little deceiving. Consider the table from another perspective. Given that one judge decides no smiling has occurred, the probability is $88/92 = .96$ that the other judge also decides no smiling has occurred. In contrast, given that one judge decides a smile has occurred, the probability is only $4/8 = .50$ that the other judge also decides that a smile has occurred. The example points out that overall percent agreement is very dependent on the relative frequencies of the events being judged. General percent agreement reliabilities will tend to be high when the trait being assessed has a very low or very high frequency.

Another way to view this set of data is to assume the low frequency of the behavior and to determine the chance level of agreement given that frequency. The chance data for this hypothetical base rate are given in Part *ii* of Table 1. The values in the cells are determined in the same way that expected frequencies are determined in chi-square tables (i.e., multiply the row and column totals for a particular cell and divide by the grand total: $(8)(8)/100 = .64$). Given that each judge guessed at the same base rate of 8% smiling, the percent agreement by chance alone is approximately 85%. The observed reliability of 92% is not much greater than the chance value of 85%.

Notice, however, that the two judges estimated the identical base rate of smiling (i.e., 8%). In such cases, the maximum possible percent agreement is 100%. But, the judges are actually likely to differ in their estimate of base rate, and when this occurs the maximum possible percent agreement is less than 100%. In this case, observed percent agreement must be evaluated against chance agreement on the one hand and maximum possible agreement given the marginal distributions on the other. In Part *iii* of Table 1, one judge records 20% and the other 40% smiling. The raw data are symbolized by *d*, the maximum agreement given the marginals is represented by *mx/m,* and the chance agreement given the marginals is symbolized by *c/m.* The percent agreement for the raw data is 70%, which is a little more than half way between the chance level of 56% and the maximum possible of 80%.

Finally, one could argue that the disagreement between judges in the estimated base rate of smiling is itself unreliability, and that the chance rate and maximum possible agreement should be based on

Table 1. Interobserver Reliability
for the Dichotomous Variable of Smiling

i. *Hypothetical data*

Judge B

		Smile	No Smile	
Judge A	Smile	4	4	8
	No Smile	4	88	92
		8	92	100

ii. *Chance data given the base rate of smiling*

Judge B

		Smile	No Smile	
Judge A	Smile	.64	7.36	8
	No Smile	7.36	84.64	92
		8	92	100

iii. *Hypothetical data when the marginal distributions are not equal*

Judge B

		Smile	No Smile	
Judge A	Smile	d:15 mx/m:20 c/m: 8	d: 5 mx/m: 0 c/m:12	20
	No Smile	d:25 mx/m:20 c/m:32	d:55 mx/m:60 c/m:48	80
		40	60	100

d: Data: Percent agreement for raw data = $(15 + 55)/100 = 70\%$

mx/m: Maximum agreement given the marginals = $(20 + 60)/100 = 80\%$

c/m: Chance agreement given the marginals = $(8 + 48)/100 = 56\%$

iv. *Hypothetical chance data that produces a significant chi square*

Judge B

		c_1	c_2	c_3	
Judge A	c_1	30	20	0	50
	c_2	13	9	8	30
	c_3	17	1	2	20
		60	30	10	100

chi square = 25.17, $p < .001$
Percent agreement = 41%

v. *Definition and computation of* kappa *for data in Part iii*

Judge B

		Smile	No Smile	
Judge A	Smile	a 15	b 5	e 20
	No Smile	c 40	d 55	f 80
		g 40	h 60	j 100

$$\text{kappa} = \frac{P_o - P_c}{1 - P_c} = \frac{.70 - .56}{1 - .56} = \frac{.14}{.44} = .32$$

in which

P_o = observed proportion of agreement = $\frac{a + d}{j}$

$= \frac{15 + 55}{100} = .70$

P_c = proportion of agreement expected by chance

$= \frac{eg + fh}{j^2} = \frac{20(40) + 80(60)}{(100)^2}$

$= \frac{800 + 4800}{10000} = .56$

the average of the two judges' base rate $((.20 + .40)/2 = .30)$ which yields a 58% chance level and a 100% maximum (i.e., for equal marginals). In this case, 70% agreement next to a theoretical chance level of 58% and a theoretical maximum of 100% is not too impressive.

Would not chi square and a test of significance on this contingency table solve this problem? No. Consider the data in Part *iv* of Table 1. In this case of a three-category judgment, the chi square is 25.17, which is highly significant. On the other hand, the percent agreement is only 41%, which is precisely the value one could expect by chance given the marginal distributions. Therefore, chi square does not take into consideration the chance level, and "chance" agreement can nevertheless produce a "significant" chi square.

These and other problems with measures of agreement have been reviewed by Fleiss (1975). To solve these problems, Cohen (1960) has introduced a statistic, *kappa*, which is an index of agreement that is corrected for chance. The definition of kappa and a numerical example is given in Part *v* of Table 1 for the data presented in Part *iii*. The value of kappa will be 0 when the percent agreement is at chance level and kappa will equal 1.0 in the case of perfect agreement when the marginal distributions for the two judges are equal. If it is assumed that deviations in the marginals are also a source of unreliability, then 1.00 is always the appropriate maximum; otherwise, kappa could be calculated for the maximum percent agreement given the marginals (Cohen, 1960, pp. 42–43).

Methods exist (Everitt, 1968; Fleiss & Cicchetti, 1978; Fleiss, Cohen, & Everitt, 1969) for testing the significance of kappa (i.e., is there significant agreement between judges?) and for the difference between two independent kappas. Significance tests are not usually helpful in assessments of reliability when agreement is assumed to be quite high, but they may be useful for tests of agreement between categorical judgments in other contexts. Note, however, that large samples are necessary for good approximations to probabilities for certain comparisons (see Fleiss & Cicchetti, 1978).

Reliability in Experimental Research. Assessments of reliability are common in psychometrics and in one-sample observational research, but the need for reliability information is often equally essential in experimental research in which different treatments are experimentally imposed or in which there are naturally defined subgroups in the design (e.g., sex).

In experimental research, we typically assess reliability by having two observers make comparable judgments at the same observational session. Notice that this is different from the reliability we have just discussed. In experimental research we rarely ask about the stability of the trait over time or the ability of our measurement procedures to record the same response on two separate occasions or even on alternate minutes of the same assessment. There are several questions that could be asked in this situation: (1) Is the measuring instrument reliable (interobserver reliability)? (2) Are individual differences reliable over short periods of time (test/retest) or over comparable assessments (parallel measurements)? (3) Is the characteristic stable over a longer period of developmental time (developmental stability)? These questions apply to individual differences; one could also ask about the reliability and stability of group differences.

For example, suppose one were assessing attention in 4-month-old infants and divided the sample into boys and girls. To answer the above questions, one might have (1) observations of the dependent variable (e.g., fixation time) recorded simultaneously by two observers to determine the interobserver reliability of the measuring instrument, (2) two assessments of attention closely spaced in time to determine the reliability within subjects of individual differences in fixation time, (3) another followup session some time later to determine the developmental stability of fixation time as a trait, and (4) two equivalent groups of boys and girls at each assessment to determine the reliability of group differences between boys and girls. This happens to be a typical area in which sex differences sometimes occur and sometimes do not; and when they occur, they do not always favor the same sex (Cohen & Gelber, 1975; McCall, 1971; McCall & McGhee, 1977). Some data suggest that the sex differences may be based partly on age, the developmental pattern of girls preceding that of boys by a few weeks (McCall, 1973). Perhaps a great deal of confusion in the literature could have been avoided if the suggested study had been carried out.

Another issue in determining reliability in experimental research is that the reliability must be calculated on the same data that are to be analyzed. If fixation time is recorded on six presentation trials of a stimulus but only total looking time is analyzed for group differences, then reliability should be assessed on total looking time, not on the length of a look during a single trial. Similarly, some studies of infant attention calculate reliability on actual fixation time in seconds, but the data are analyzed in terms of the percent fixation to the novel of two stimuli. The reliability of the former does not guarantee the reliability of the latter variable.

A special, but common, case of determining the reliability of the wrong variable involves the reliability of difference scores. For example, suppose a familiar stimulus is presented several times until a criterion of habituation is reached, and then a novel stimulus is introduced. Because the habituation criterion can be a relative one (two adjacent trials on which the fixation time is 50% of the first two trials), not all subjects will be fixating a comparable length of time before the introduction of the new stimulus. To determine the relative response to the new stimulus, the researcher may take the difference between fixation time to the first presentation of the novel stimulus minus the fixation time to the last presentation of the familiar stimulus. But the reliability may be reported for fixation time on a single trial, not for the difference score. This is not appropriate, because the reliability of a difference score is inversely proportional to the correlation between the two scores used to calculate the difference. That is, the higher the correlation, the lower the reliability. This makes sense because when the correlation is high, a great deal of common true-score variance is subtracted out, leaving a difference score that is mostly error.

Specifically, assuming the variances are equal for the two distributions, the reliability of a difference score is given by the formula

$$r_{dd} = \frac{r_{11} + r_{22} - 2r_{12}}{2(1 - r_{12})}$$

If the reliability for each trial is $r_{11} = r_{22} = .90$ and the correlation between trials is $r_{12} = .80$, then the reliability of the difference score is only .50. Difference scores have a variety of problems, and researchers who feel a need to use a difference score should consult Cronbach and Furby (1970), Harris (1967), and a later section of this chapter for the merits and limitations of several approaches.

Not only should the reliability be reported for the same data to be analyzed, it should also be reported on the same sample. For instance, some educational test manufacturers report reliability for a single sample of children in grades one through six, but the suggested use of the test is to pick out reading-disabled students in a particular grade. The reliability for the total sample may be extraordinarily high because of the great range of ability, but it could be quite low if the sample were restricted to the third grade.

The problem becomes messier in factorial designs. For a single-factor design with few subjects, one might prefer to assess reliability using the analysis of variance rather than with correlations (see Winer, 1971). However, suppose a factorial design with sex and grade as independent variables is conducted on reading achievement. In this case, the reliability of the dependent variable is often assessed on a single subsample of children taken from both sexes and all grades. But reliability calculated by ignoring group membership may be quite different than reliability within groups. For example, average group differences—treatment effects—can affect reliability enormously. A much different reliability might be obtained if the cell mean were subtracted from each subject's score and then the reliability calculated ignoring group membership, a statistic called the *pooled within-cell correlation.*

Which approach is appropriate? Some might argue that for the overall analysis of variance, the traditional method of ignoring group affiliation may be appropriate. But when specific comparisons are made, or when individual differences in reading achievement are correlated with other variables separately within groups—boys and girls or grades, for example—then the overall reliability is not appropriate and some within-cell correlation, either specific to certain groups or pooled over the entire design, is more appropriate. Others would contend that the within-cell correlations are the only appropriate assessment of reliability because they are not influenced by treatment effects.

Univariate Independent Groups—Cross-Sectional Designs

Most studies in developmental psychology involve comparisons of means or other measures of group performance for independent groups of subjects. We first consider some advances in analyzing such designs when the data are qualitative in nature.

Qualitative Data

Most often our measurements are continuous or close to being continuous, such as IQ scores, rating scales of five or more points, etc. In such cases, the traditional analysis of variance (see below) may be appropriate. But when the data are definitely qualitative—pass-fail, normal-questionable-abnormal—analysis of variance procedures are usually not appropriate because of the extreme nonnormality of the data and certain problems of independence.

In such cases, we have usually employed chi-square tests for contingency tables or ignored the violations of assumptions and used the analysis of variance anyway. Recently, extensive work has been conducted by biostatisticians on analyses of binary and categorical (i.e., discrete) data that follow more closely the logic of the analysis of variance. Some of the major references in this field include Bishop (1969); Bishop, Fienberg, and Holland (1975); *Fienberg (1977); *Finney (1971); *Fleiss (1981); Goodman (1970); Grizzle, Starmer, and Koch (1969); Koch, Imrey, and Reinfurt (1972); Ku, Varner, and Kullbach (1971); *Landis and Koch (1979). (More applied references have been asterisked.) We outline two types of analysis.

Probit/Logit Analysis. One of the more common questions in developmental psychology is, ''At what age do children accomplish a certain behavior or skill, such as, sitting alone without support, walking, or talking?'' Assuming the intent is to describe age differences rather than age changes in this pass/fail task, a cross-sectional sample of subjects at various ages might be obtained to determine the percentages of the children who display the behavior at each age. But one would like to estimate accurately the age at which half the sample (or any other specific percentage) complete the task. Moreover, it would be of interest to be able to compare such functions for two or more abilities to know, for example, whether walking precedes talking.

The analysis for this question comes from biology. A biologist wants to know the dose of a given drug that will produce one or another response. Such a relationship is called a *dose-response curve* or *tolerance curve* in which a binary response (either a natural occurring binary or an artificially dichotomized response) is the dependent measure and dosage level is the independent variable. The dose-response or tolerance curve is a *theoretical* function that is integrated from zero to a specific dosage level to obtain the percentage of subjects who respond.

The critical problem in the analysis is to determine the form and parameters of the function. If the form of this curve is normal using the log of the dose, the analysis is called a *probit analysis;* if the curve is logistic, the analysis is called a *logit analysis.* Because the dosage scale can be transformed in several ways, a whole variety of functions can be tested to determine the best fit. Then the age corresponding to any specific percentage of subjects passing the item may be estimated. Typically, one looks for the dosage level at which 50% of the subjects respond, a point called LD50 (from the ''lethal dosage for 50%'' of the subjects), but virtually any other percentage can be obtained and confidence limits calculated.

Suppose one wanted to determine the age at which 50% of infants are able to sit unsupported. A sample of subjects might be selected at each of several preselected ages from one at which no infant sits to one at which all subjects do so. The number of subjects per age need not be equal, and ages need not be equally spaced. In fact, it is often wise to concentrate more assessments near the point where subjects are most likely to accomplish the task. Notice that the sampling is cross sectional and the design looks appropriate for a one-factor, independent-groups, analysis of variance with a dichotomous dependent variable. No statistical investigations have studied the effects of repeated measures on the probit solution.

The analysis is described fully by Finney (1971) and may be calculated by hand or by computer (e.g., SAS, 1982). To illustrate, Table 2 presents some data from Gesell and Thompson (1934) on the number of infants sitting unsupported for at least one minute at different ages (lunar weeks). These data are the input to a probit program that produces an iterative maximum likelihood solution to a regressionlike problem of fitting an equation in $\log_{10}$ (age) to a function of the observed proportions of children at each age who exhibit the behavior. This dose-response curve will be log normal under the logistic, and a chi-square test of goodness of fit will be reported in the output. A significant chi square suggests a *departure from a good fit,* implying that a function other than log normal should be tried.

The output also includes the parameters of the regression line, estimates of LD50 and other percentiles, and upper and lower limits, called *fiducial limits,* which are functionally similar to confidence limits but with different theory and logic. If the function is indeed normal, then half the children in the population would exhibit the target behavior at 30.505 lunar weeks. Moreover, the fiducial limits for LD50 are 29.44 and 31.55 weeks with probability .95. It should be noted that the fiducial limits are not usually symmetric about the LDx value in the original metric of the independent variable.

For the present data, the log normal function is not appropriate because the chi-square test of goodness of fit is 27.7759 with df = (number of ages) − 2 = 13 and $p \leq$ .0097. Remember, a significant result implies a departure from a good fit. Thus, a logit transformation, or no transformation at all, might be tried next as a better approximation to the data.

The above example is the simplest form of probit analysis. The technique can be extended to studying two characteristics, for example, the ages of talking and walking. Thus, one could ask whether one skill lags behind the other by a constant amount (e.g., are the probit regression lines parallel?).

One might also wonder if boys and girls differ in their probit function for a single behavior. This analysis is logically similar to a two-factor analysis of

Table 2. **Probit Analysis of Age of Sitting Unsupported**
(Data from Gesell & Thompson, 1934)

i. Data (cross-sectional)

Age (lunar weeks)	n (independent groups)	Number Sitting
4	100	0
6	100	0
8	100	0
12	100	0
16	100	0
20	100	3
24	100	6
28	100	24
32	100	61
36	100	80
40	100	100
44	100	100
48	100	100
52	100	100
56	100	100

ii. Analysis

Probability	Dose (i.e., Age)	95% Fiducial Limits	
		Lower	Upper
.01	21.12	19.13	22.65
.05	23.52	21.80	24.85
.10	24.91	23.35	26.13
.50	30.51	29.44	31.55
.95	39.56	37.67	42.30
.99	44.06	41.36	48.16

Test of Goodness of Fit:
chi square = 27.78, $df = k - 2 = 13$, $p < .0097$

Therefore, the model does *not* fit; try another.

variance (sex, age) design with a dichotomous dependent variable. One might be specifically interested in whether 50% of the children pass each task at the same age (e.g., does LD50 for walking = LD50 for talking?). Finally a more complicated probit analysis can be used to study the interactive effect of two independent variables on a dichotomous dependent variable, for example, the effect of infant risk status and socioeconomic level on the passage of early milestones. This approach might be applied in the study of Sameroff and Chandler's (1975) transactional model of development. Details of the analysis of these designs can be found in Chapters 6 and 11 of Finney (1971).

Contingency Table Analysis. The newer methods of analyzing categorical (i.e., discrete) and count data have been called by different names—contingency table analysis, log-linear models, analysis of categorical data. Fundamentally, however, these techniques are outgrowths of the well-known chi-square contingency table procedures, and they are now developed to handle several independent and dependent variables.

We illustrate these methods with an example that involves two independent and two dependent variables. Suppose 100 children from urban environments and 100 from rural environments are randomly selected and assigned in equal numbers to an intervention program designed to improve their social and intellectual skills and to a control program. At the end of the treatment phase, the children are assessed by a variety of clinical means and judged to be either adequate or not adequate with respect to social adjustment and with respect to intellectual progress. The data might be laid out as in Table 3. The n_{ij} indicate the number of children in each of the four intervention-control/urban-rural groups who were judged to be adequate or inadequate on social and intellectual criteria, with the first subscript denoting the row and the second subscript the column of the table. (The dot subscript signifies that the corresponding dimension has been collapsed.)

The rows of the data table constitute the separate and independent samples of the design. Owing to the design of the experiment, a subject is in one and only one of these four groups. The columns represent the different response combinations or categories into which subjects might be classified. Notice that although this design looks something like a multivariate analysis (e.g., each subject has both a social and an intellectual score), subjects are actually in one and only one of the four combinations of adequacy/inadequacy on these two dimensions. Analyses of this kind deal with the distribution of cases across the columns of the array, both within and between groups.

In general, analyses of this type are based on some function of the multinominal distribution. That is, the true probability that an individual should be classified in the ith row and the jth column is estimated by $n_{ij}/n_{i.}$, and the expected frequencies (or proportions) are calculated according to the multinominal distribution under various null models. Analyses provide information on the two between-subjects factors (i.e., intervention versus control and urban versus rural), the within-subjects dimensions (i.e., social and intellectual assessments), and all interactions, much like an analysis of variance but with chi-square, rather than an *F*, test statistics.

Table 3.   Example of Contingency Table Analysis Design

		Socially Adequate		Socially Inadequate		
		Intellectually Adequate	Intellectually Inadequate	Intellectually Adequate	Intellectually Inadequate	
Intervention	Urban	n_{11}	n_{12}	n_{13}	n_{14}	$n_{1.}$
	Rural	n_{21}	n_{22}	n_{23}	n_{24}	$n_{2.}$
Control	Urban	n_{31}	n_{32}	n_{33}	n_{34}	$n_{3.}$
	Rural	n_{41}	n_{42}	n_{43}	n_{44}	$n_{4.}$
		$n_{.1}$	$n_{.2}$	$n_{.3}$	$n_{.4}$	$n_{..}$

The actual statistical calculations and tests may follow one of three slightly different procedures. The Grizzle-Starmer-Koch (GSK) strategy is a weighted least-squares approach (Grizzle et al., 1969); Bishop (1969) and others have offered a maximum likelihood strategy; and Ku and colleagues (1971) have presented a technique based upon a "minimum discrimination information" strategy. Fortunately, for large samples, these three approaches provide nearly identical solutions, and the selection of an approach will generally be dictated by personal preference or by the availability of computer facilities. Kleinbaum and Kupper (1978) provide a very readable presentation of the analysis of categorical data, particularly by the GSK method. Interested readers may also consider the procedures, developed by Leo Goodman and explained less technically by Davis (1974), which permit the analysis of hypothesized models in the context of multivariate contingency tables.

A number of computer programs are available, including GENCAT (Landis, Stanish, Freeman, & Koch, 1976; obtainable from the Program Librarian, Department of Biostatistics, School of Public Health, University of North Carolina, Chapel Hill, NC 27514), PROC FUNCAT in *SAS User's Guide: Statistics* (1982), and BMDP-P3F, Multiway Frequency Tables-Log-Linear Models (Dixon, 1981).

From a practical standpoint, two cautions are in order. First, count and categorical analyses require large numbers of subjects. Just as a minimum expected frequency of 5 is usually required for chi-square contingency tables, all observed frequencies in contingency table analysis should be 10 or more. Since the number of response categories is the product of the number of "levels" of each dimension assessed, the number of different possible "responses" rapidly becomes quite large, requiring a large sample to avoid cells with frequencies below 10. This becomes an even greater issue when repeated-measures versions of these procedures are used (Landis & Koch, 1979; see below). Researchers should note that while it is common practice to combine categories to increase cell frequencies, technically this should be done a priori and not after examination of the data, since judicious combinations of categories can enhance or minimize effects.

A second caution is that most computer programs for contingency table analyses are very complex to use because they permit a wide variety of options, many of which are likely to be irrelevant to the researcher's specific purpose. First-time users are advised to seek the guidance of an experienced colleague and to test their use of the program by replicating a textbook example (e.g., from Kleinbaum & Kupper, 1978) before analyzing their own data. This suggestion, in fact, is useful to follow any time a program is first used.

Quantitative Data

Most often, the researcher has quantitative data (e.g., continuous) on an interval or ratio scale; fortunately, procedures for analyzing such designs are well-known to most researchers. Winer (1971), among other textbooks, covers randomized factorial designs and the analysis of variance for independent groups, including tests on trends. Such procedures need not be discussed here. Rather, we take up a few specific issues in which current practice in developmental psychology is sometimes not consistent with the best statistical procedures.

A Posteriori Comparisons.   Developmental researchers often perform a host of after-the-fact multiple comparisons, usually after finding a significant interaction in factorial experiments. Two issues arise. First, are such paired comparisons necessary? A significant two-factor interaction means that the performance across levels of one factor is significantly different from the performance across levels of the other factor. If there is a sex-by-age interaction, for example, it means the developmental function for the two sexes is significantly different. This result is interpretable without additional tests: Males and females have different developmental functions within the research context, and one may describe the difference as long as the description applies to the *entire* observed function (e.g., one rises more rapidly than the other). Additional comparisons are not necessary for such conclusions.

More specific comparisons are required, however, if more specific interpretations are desired. For example, one may want to specify the age at which the sexes first become significantly different. The statistical problem is to control the significance level of a set of tests so that the probability of one or more statements being false in a set of statements about mean differences is less than a specified level—*alpha*. Procedures to accomplish this goal are presented in Winer (1971). We provide a simplified guide below.

If one or two comparisons are to be made only to explicate the specific form of a particular significant main effect or interaction, they are called tests of *simple effects*. The significant omnibus effect (i.e., main effect, interaction) is sufficient protection for α.

If several comparisons are pre-planned (i.e., not conducted as a consequence of observing the values of the means), the simplest and most powerful strategy that controls the alpha level at a prespecified value is the Dunn or Bonferroni procedure which requires that the usual test of a contrast be evaluated at the α/C level of significance, where C is the number of comparisons being tested. If this procedure is followed, the resulting set of tests has an overall Type I error of α.

If the comparisons are not pre-planned but performed as a consequence of observing the obtained means, then Tukey's HSD (Honestly Significant Difference) method is the appropriate post-hoc technique, provided the comparisons are to be conducted pairwise (i.e., two groups at a time). If the post-hoc comparisons involve more than two groups at a time, Scheffe's S method is the appropriate technique.

Both these latter strategies allow for all possible comparisons of the specified type (pairwise or general). As a result, rather large differences are required to obtain significance. An alternative approach that is more powerful in many circumstances requires the researcher to specify before the experiment is con-

ducted a set of comparisons which represent the set of contrasts that will be tested *if* the appropriate omnibus test of the analysis of variance is significant. These pre–planned contrasts are then tested using the Dunn/Bonferroni procedure. Although the *p*-value required for significance (i.e., $p = \alpha/C$) may be quite small, it will usually be less stringent than that required by the HSD method and almost certainly larger than that required by the Scheffe procedure while still maintaining the proper control of alpha. Of course, the fewer the tests planned, the smaller C, and the larger is the required p.

It should be noted that we have *not* recommended the commonly used Neuman-Keuls or Duncan Multiple Range procedures.

Nonorthogonal (unequal n*s*) Designs. Most introductory discussions of factorial designs consider only the case of equal cell frequencies. But unequal cell size is the rule in "real" research. Typically, researchers faced with unequal *n*s invoke a computational method developed before the prevalence of high-speed computers (e.g., unweighted means) or other methods that provide approximate solutions. Today, such methods no longer seem defensible, but straightforward descriptions of precise methods are not widely available to most researchers.

In the discussion below, which follows Appelbaum and Cramer (1974), we assume that the design is nonorthogonal for one of two reasons. First, the inequality may reflect a state of nature. For example, in a random sample of American school children, there will be fewer blacks than whites because the races are not equally represented in the population. Second, subjects may be missing at random. In either case, the inequality is *not* related to the independent or dependent variables under investigation. In contrast, suppose subjects are missing because more infants became bored and cried while viewing geometric forms and could not be used in the analysis than infants who watched pictures of human faces. This systematic cause *is* related to the experimental conditions, and little can be done to "correct" this confound.

Technically, the unequal *n* condition is called *nonorthogonality* because the estimates of effects are not independent of one another. An extreme example will illustrate this lack of independence. In Part *i* of Table 4, a simple two-factor design is displayed in which subjects were sampled only in cells a_1b_1 and a_2b_2, with means equal to 10 and 20, respectively. The question is, "What effects do we have here?" One could argue that there might be an effect for Factor *A*, there might be an effect for Factor B, and there might be an interaction. But we cannot tell because these possibilities are confounded.

Another way of understanding the confounds is to note that if we ignore the possible effect for B and the AB interaction, then there appears to be an effect for A. Similarly, if we ignore the effect for A and AB, then there appears to be an effect for B. Finally, if we ignore the effects for A and B, then there is an AB interaction. However, if we eliminate, rather than ignore, the effect for B (by subtracting the column means from the cell means), then there is no effect for A or for AB. Similarly, if we eliminate the effect for A, there is no B or AB effects, and if the effect for AB is eliminated, there are no main effects. The distinction between *ignoring* other effects and *eliminating* other effects is crucial to the following discussion.

The same problem of confounding observed above can exist in designs that do not have empty cells but have unequal numbers of subjects per cell. An illustration is presented in Part *ii* of Table 4. This is a somewhat extreme sample of this circumstance, but the reader should note that even small inequalities can sometimes produce dramatic confounds.

The table gives the mean, the number of subjects, and the confidence interval (CI) for each cell. Notice first how differences in the stability of estimates for the population means, as expressed by the confidence intervals, can influence the possible true state of the population means. In Part *iii* of Table 4, cells a_1b_1 and a_2b_2 have large numbers of subjects and relatively small confidence intervals. Therefore, their potential population means remain at 10 and 20, respectively. But because of the small numbers of subjects in the other two cells and the large confidence intervals accompanying them, the true population means for these cells could range between 10 and 30, thereby producing or eliminating main effects for A, B, and the AB interaction as illustrated. Consequently, a certain amount of indeterminacy in the results is associated with the fact that confidence intervals about sample means vary as a function of cell size.

The same comparison between ignoring and eliminating an effect that was made above for the missing cell design can be conducted for the unequal n case, which is done in Part *iv* of Table 4. At the left, any effect for A is ignored by collapsing subjects over the two levels of A and then calculating the means for the levels of B over the 27 subjects in each column. This yields means of 10.7 and 19.3, an apparent effect for B if A is ignored.

At the right of Part *iv*, the A effect is eliminated rather than ignored. This is accomplished by subtracting the row mean from the cell mean for each level of A. The residual represents what is left in B after the effects of A have been eliminated. In this case, all the residuals are 0. Consequently, no B effect remains once the effect for A is eliminated.

This example illustrates the vast difference between a test of B ignoring A versus a test of B eliminating A. No effect for B exists after eliminating A, and no effect for A exists after eliminating B. Yet in each case there is an effect for B ignoring A and for A ignoring B. Once again, the effects are confounded—something is happening, but because of the confound between A and B, we cannot tell whether the effect resides in A or B or both. When the number of subjects per cell is equal across all cells, the effect for B ignoring A is identical to the effect for B eliminating A. But this is not the case when cell size is unequal.

How, then, do you analyze such data? The recommended statistical procedure consists of testing one model versus another for the data (Appelbaum & Cramer, 1974). For example, the possible models for a two-factor analysis of variance are given in Part *v* of Table 4. Model 1 is the model typically used when all cell sizes are equal. In this case, the estimates of the parameters for the grand mean (μ), Factor A (α), Factor B (β), the AB interaction ($\alpha\beta$), and error (ϵ) are all independent of one another. But this is not the case when cell sizes are unequal. Therefore, we need the additional models presented in Part *v* in which the several parameters are progressively eliminated. The steps in the procedure are as follows.

1. Test for a significant interaction by comparing Model 1 with Model 2. If the result is significant, no tests on main effects are appropriate (in the orthogonal or nonorthogonal cases), although one may want to test certain contrasts (simple effects tests) to aid in the interpretation of results. If the test for interaction is not significant, proceed to the next step.

2. Test A eliminating B by comparing Model 2 versus Model 3, and test B eliminating A by comparing Model 2 versus Model 4. If either one or both of these tests are significant, interpret these results and stop. If neither of these tests is significant, proceed to the next step.

3. Test A ignoring B by comparing Model 4 with Model 5, and B ignoring A by comparing Model 3 with Model 5. If both of these tests are significant (as they are in this example), you may conclude that

Table 4. Testing Effects in the Nonorthogonal (Unequal Cell Size) Design
(Adapted from Appelbaum & Cramer, 1974)

i. *Missing cells design*

$$B$$

	b_1	b_2	
a_1	10		10
a_2		20	20
	10	20	

A

ii. *Unequal* n*s design*

$$B$$

	b_1	b_2	
a_1	$\overline{X}_{11} = 10$ $n_{11} = 25$ CI = 3.97 to 16.03	$\overline{X}_{12} = 10$ $n_{12} = 2$ CI = −11.32 to 31.32	10
a_2	$\overline{X}_{21} = 20$ $n_{21} = 2$ CI = −1.32 to 41.32	$\overline{X}_{22} = 20$ $n_{22} = 25$ CI = 13.97 to 26.03	20
	10.7	19.3	

A

iii. *Some possible population means*

	B					B					B		
	b_1	b_2				b_1	b_2				b_1	b_2	
A a_1	10	10	10		A a_1	10	20	15		A a_1	10	20	15
a_2	20	20	20		a_2	10	20	15		a_2	30	20	25
	15	15				10	20				20	20	

something has happened but that you are unable to decide whether it is an *A* or a *B* effect. If either one of these tests is significant, you may conclude that there is possibly an effect for that factor but that as in the present study it is seriously confounded with the other factor.

Most linear model statistical analysis computer programs (e.g., MANOVA, MULTIVARIANCE, SAS) permit the user to specify the models and the tests in the way outlined in Table 4. Further, the procedure can be generalized to any number of factors (see Appelbaum, 1975), but the first test is al-

ways made on the highest order interaction, followed by all of the elimination tests for the next highest order of interaction, and so on until the last tests are performed on the main effects. It should be noted that the recommended procedure described here may not yield the same results as the unweighted means analysis or the unweighted least-squares procedures commonly used and outlined in Winer (1971).

Analysis of Covariance. In the independent-groups factorial design, the error mean square is composed of the variability of subjects about their respective cell means pooled over all cells in the

Table 4—Continued

iv. *Comparison of "B ignoring A" and "B eliminating A"*

		B ignoring A		
		b_1	b_2	
A	a_1	$\overline{X}_{11} = 10$ $n_{11} = 25$	$\overline{X}_{12} = 10$ $n_{12} = 2$	10
	a_2	$\overline{X}_{21} = 20$ $n_{21} = 2$	$\overline{X}_{22} = 20$ $n_{22} = 25$	20
		$\overline{X}_{.1} = 10.7$ $n_{.1} = 27$	$\overline{X}_{.2} = 19.3$ $n_{.2} = 27$	

	B eliminating A		
	b_1	b_2	
a_2	$\overline{X}_{11} - \overline{X}_{1.} = 10 - 10$ $= 0$	$\overline{X}_{12} - \overline{X}_{1.} = 10 - 10$ $= 0$	10
a_2	$\overline{X}_{21} - \overline{X}_{2.} = 20 - 20$ $= 0$	$\overline{X}_{22} - \overline{X}_{2.} = 20 - 20$ $= 0$	20
	0	0	

v. *Models in a two-factor analysis of variance*

1. $X_{ij} = \mu + \alpha_i + \beta_j + \alpha\beta_{ij} + \varepsilon$
2. $X_{ij} = \mu + \alpha_i + \beta_j \qquad + \varepsilon$
3. $X_{ij} = \mu \qquad + \beta_j \qquad + \varepsilon$
4. $X_{ij} = \mu + \alpha_i \qquad\qquad + \varepsilon$
5. $X_{ij} = \mu \qquad\qquad\qquad + \varepsilon$

vi. *The complete nonorthogonal analysis of variance*

Source	Models	df	MS	F	p
AB	1 vs. 2	1	.00	.00	1.00
A eliminating *B*	2 vs. 3	1	370.37	1.65	.21
B eliminating *A*	2 vs. 4	1	.00	.00	1.00
A ignoring *B*	4 vs. 5	1	1349.99	6.00	.02
B ignoring *A*	3 vs. 5	1	979.63	4.35	.04
Within cells		50	225.00		

design. The larger this within-cell variability, the more difficult it is to obtain a significant effect for a specific difference in means. Therefore, it is desirable to have the within-cell variability as small as possible.

One way to reduce within-cell variability is to specify some other variable that is associated with individual differences in the dependent variable. For example, if one is assessing the relative merits of different types of enrichment programs on the acquisition of basic reading skills, one might suppose that all subjects in the design, regardless of the particular educational program they receive, will vary in reading skills as a function of social class or intelligence. If the data are sparse and one has only high, medium, and low socioeconomic class designations for the parents of each child, then subjects can be "blocked" on this variable. That is, social class becomes an additional independent variable. Because a good part of the variability within a cell is associated with parental social class, that variability will now be attributed to the independent variable of social class, and thus it is removed from the general error term. This permits tests on the dependent variables to be made with increased precision.

But suppose an intelligence test had been given to

each pupil before the educational program was instituted. The intelligence test score could be used as a covariate. That is, the regression between intelligence and reading score could be calculated and the variability in reading score that is associated with intelligence partialed out, leaving a residual within-cell variability that is smaller than the original. Basically, the analysis of covariance performs these operations.

It is important, however, to be aware of the assumptions involved in an analysis of covariance, because violation of these assumptions can have a substantial effect, sometimes distorting the results considerably. In simple analysis of covariance it is assumed:

1. The relationship between the covariate (e.g., intelligence) and the dependent variable (e.g., reading skill) is nontrivial (e.g., the pooled within-cell regression is significant at $p < .10$ or smaller).

2. This relationship is linear.

3. The slope of the regression line is identical in all cells of the design.

Since the analysis of covariance is not robust with respect to violations of these assumptions, especially the assumption of homogeneity of the slope of the regression line across all cells, it is desirable to conduct preliminary tests on these assumptions before using the analysis of covariance.

It is also important to note that the purpose of the analysis of covariance is to reduce the within-cell error variability, *not to erase group differences on the covariate*. If, after assigning children to educational programs, significant differences in intelligence exist between the groups, the analysis of covariance is *not* designed to equate the groups on intelligence. While the analysis does alter the group means on the dependent variable as well as reduce the within-cell variability as a function of mean differences between groups on the covariate, it is likely under such circumstances that the assumptions of the analysis of covariance will be violated, thereby compromising the validity of the results.

As a general rule, the analysis of covariance simply is not designed to make up for sampling biases and initial differences on the covariate, despite the fact that many people believe such situations are precisely the ones calling for covariance adjustment. However, analysis of covariance can be used to adjust for initial group differences under certain very restrictive conditions (Overall & Woodward, 1977), but researchers who use the technique for this purpose have the responsibility of demonstrating that

their particular circumstances meet these required conditions. There is no adequate substitute for random or probability sampling (see later section on field research).

Multivariate Analysis of Independent Groups— Factorial Designs

Sometimes it becomes useful to consider the effect of different treatments on a set of dependent variables rather than on just one. Typically, this will occur when the conceptual dependent variable is multidimensional or when several measurements reflect different facets of a single concept. The generalization of univariate analysis of variance to consider simultaneously more than one dependent variable (two or more different variables, to be distinguished from "repeated measurements" of the same variable) is called multivariate analysis of variance (abbreviated MANOVA, which is to be distinguished from a computer program of the same name).

There are two basic advantages to using MANOVA as opposed to analyzing several dependent variables one at a time. First, multivariate analysis utilizes information about the relationships (i.e., correlations or covariances) among dependent variables in drawing conclusions about treatment effects. This information is ignored completely when a series of univariate tests is conducted. Statistically, it is quite possible, and not unusual, to find a significant multivariate effect when no univariate differences are significant. This can occur because the relationships among dependent variables are considered in multivariate tests. Psychologically, behavioral effects are rarely expressed in a single variable or as independent differences in several measures. Rather they occur as a set of interconnected effects expressed in many variables, and we should describe these effects with procedures that are sensitive to this complexity.

The second advantage of multivariate procedures is that they maintain proper control over alpha, the Type I error rate. In a two-group design in which the groups are actually identical in the population, the probability that we will nevertheless find a significant difference at the .05 level is .05. But if we separately analyze k-dependent variables, the probability of finding at least one significant difference at .05 is approximately k *times* .05. Multivariate tests keep the probability of a Type I error at alpha for the set of variables being considered. This function is similar to the reasoning that calls for an overall analysis of variance rather than several t-tests in a one-factor univariate analysis.

Manova

There is more to performing a multivariate (M) analysis (AN) of variance (OVA) than sending the data off to the computer to be analyzed by one of the several appropriate statistical programs. A nontechnical introduction to MANOVA and some other multivariate procedures is given by McCall (1970). We discuss only a few points here.

Selecting the Variables. Picking the set of dependent variables to be analyzed is as crucial a part of multivariate research as selecting a single measure for a univariate design. For one thing, you do not throw every available variable into a MANOVA to see what comes out. Dependent measures need to be picked deliberately. They must form a logical set that can be interpreted *as a set*. For example, in a habituation paradigm in which a single stimulus is repeatedly shown to an infant, the length of fixation on the first trial, the trial of the longest fixation, number of trials from the trial of longest fixation to criterion, and the average fixation per trial all form a cohesive set of measures of the habituation process. It would not be particularly useful to include in the dependent variable set socioeconomic status, baby's age, or differential heart-rate response to an auditory discrepancy obtained from another assessment. These do not fit the set of variables that define the infant's visual response to repeated visual stimuli. They might be used in other analyses, as correlates, as covariates, or as blocking factors. Moreover, adding the variable "trials to criterion" would not be appropriate because it is redundant with the sum of "the trial of the longest fixation" and "number of trials from the trial of longest fixation to criterion." Therefore, dependent variables must form a conceptually cohesive and meaningful set and must not be linearly, logically, or procedurally dependent on one another, although they may be correlated with one another.

It is also helpful to keep the number of dependent variables small, at least relative to the number of subjects. A very general rule of thumb is that there must be at least three times the number of subjects *per cell* as dependent variables. This is a minimum. Too many variables can have undesirable consequences. For example, they increase the critical value, thus making it more difficult to reject the null hypothesis. This is a special problem when many of the variables are highly correlated. The sampling distribution for the multivariate test of significance detects a large amount of discrimination among the levels of a factor *per dependent variable*. So, when variables that are highly correlated with other variables in a dependent set are added to that set, their

discriminating power may be redundant. Therefore, adding redundant variables raises the critical value but not the discriminating power of the set, and this can so dilute the effects of "good" variables that no significant multivariate difference is obtained when it would have been if the variables had been selected more thoughtfully.

In many cases, the researcher has more variables than are reasonable to analyze for the subjects available. Some selection of variables must be made. How does one go about this? The best way is to mentally group variables into small sets that conceptually hang together as described above. This should be done before any analyses are conducted. Some investigators would like to select variables on the basis of certain preliminary data analyses. Most such maneuvers bias the probabilities of the multivariate test. For example, one might be tempted to pick variables that are relatively uncorrelated with one another. As indicated, the elimination of redundancy increases the likelihood of a significant multivariate result, so one is biasing the set in the direction of significance. That may be only a misdemeanor, but a real felony is to pick out those variables that have univariate significance. Other researchers want to factor the dependent variable set and submit the factor scores to MANOVA. Depending on the factoring, this may be doing the same thing as selecting modestly or uncorrelated variables. In addition, factor scores are problematic, and you will have to interpret abstract rather than concrete measurements. It is best to select variables conceptually and a priori.

Nature of the Output. A MANOVA and a discriminant analysis (mathematically equivalent in result to a one-factor multivariate analysis of variance but with a somewhat different rationale) provide the following information for each effect tested:

1. *A multivariate test of significance.* This indicates whether a significant discrimination is possible between the levels of this factor on the basis of a composite score (i.e., discriminant function) composed of the sum of each variable weighted by its corresponding coefficient (i.e., standardized discriminant function coefficients, see below). There may be more than one multivariate significance test for a single effect (but not more than either the number of dependent variables or one less than the number of groups). If the first multivariate test is significant, the discriminant function is regressed from the set of dependent variables. Then a new set of coefficients is computed for the residuals and tested to determine if this second function discriminates between the levels of this factor. Thus, two or more

sets of standardized discriminant coefficients and multivariate tests would be reported. When two or more discriminant functions are significant, it means that the levels of this factor are significantly different from one another along two or more orthogonal dimensions (see Item 6 below).

2. *The standardized discriminant coefficients* for each dependent variable. The program has determined that these weights will produce a composite variable (i.e., the discriminant function) that maximally discriminates between the levels of this factor. These weights are analogous to beta weights in multiple regression and often may be interpreted in similar ways with similar cautions (see below). Be sure that these coefficients are standardized, otherwise they cannot be compared across variables.

3. *The cell means and variances* for each of the original variables.

4. *Univariate significance tests* for each dependent variable (i.e., a complete univariate analysis of variance is performed separately for each dependent measure).

5. *A table of within-cell correlations*. These are produced by subtracting the cell mean from each subject's score for each dependent variable and then correlating all dependent variables by ignoring group membership. In this manner, mean differences between the groups are removed, and subjects may be pooled across groups to produce a single matrix of intercorrelations. Such correlations are vastly preferred for almost all correlational work within the context of factorial designs, because otherwise mean differences between the groups can produce spurious relationships between variables. However, while within-cell correlations remove group differences in means, they do not eliminate group differences in variance or in the direction and magnitude of correlations. The groups are assumed to be homogeneous with respect to their variance/covariance matrices.

6. *The group means on the discriminant function scores for each significant discriminant function and the correlations between the discriminant function and the original measures*. When two or more discriminant functions are significant, it is sometimes helpful to plot the means for each group along axes defined by each discriminant function. That is, draw axes corresponding, for example, to Function 1 and Function 2, locate a point for each group corresponding to that group's mean on Function 1 and Function 2, and project each point onto each axis (i.e., draw a perpendicular from the point to each axis). Now you will be able to see which groups are maximally separated by Function 1 and which are separated by Function 2 (and so forth).

Interpretation. Unfortunately, no set of five easy rules exists for interpreting a multivariate analysis of variance. There is no substitute for understanding something about what the analysis attempts to do, how the analysis accomplishes these goals, and how to interpret the results obtained. At the risk of oversimplification, however, here are some very rough guidelines.

1. MANOVA is simply an extension to the multivariate case of univariate analysis of variance, and it should be interpreted in the same way except that multivariate results apply to the *set* of dependent variables. Problems occur when researchers attempt to interpret results in terms of the relative "importance" of one or another of the original variables. These problems are similar to those encountered when one tries to determine the relative importance of variables in a multiple regression system (see below).

2. If one must "pull apart" a multivariate result, then the following steps may be of some help.

a. Plot the group means for the original variables as one would do for a univariate ANOVA. This will help you to visualize the relative positions of the groups on each of the original variables.

b. Plot the group means on the significant discriminant functions to visualize the relative positions of the groups on the composite variables.

c. Examine the univariate test results and the standardized (not unstandardized) discriminant function coefficients (i.e., weights). In general, if an original variable has both a significant univariate F and a coefficient that is large in absolute value, the variable should probably be considered "important."

d. If the univariate F is not significant and the coefficient is less than $\pm.20$, then the variable is probably "not important."

e. If the univariate F is significant but the coefficient is small, the variable is probably redundant (i.e., correlated) with one or more other variables in the set. Such a variable is probably "not important" in the sense that it adds relatively little to the other variables in the set.

f. If the univariate F is nonsignificant but the coefficient is large, the variable probably is "not important" by itself but complements other variables in the set in assessing the multivariate effect (see McCall, 1970, for additional suggestions).

3. MANOVA creates a discriminant function by weighting the original variables in a way that produces the maximum discrimination between the groups (i.e., treatment effect). As such, researchers sometimes want to interpret the nature of the discriminant function. However, as in multiple regression, it is very difficult, if not impossible, to do this on the basis of the coefficients alone (Mosteller & Tukey, 1977). There are two major reasons for this:

a. The coefficients depend on the other variables in the set (i.e., in a sense they are like partial regression coefficients; see below). As indicated above, a variable may be substantially redundant with another variable and not be important if that other variable is included but be very important if the other variable is not in the set. Adding or deleting variables may drastically change all of the coefficients.

b. The coefficients are extremely unstable, particularly if the variables are highly correlated. Replication of the coefficients is usually needed before stability can be assumed.

4. If, despite these warnings, researchers still want to interpret the discriminant function, they will need to use in concert all of the information contained in the discriminant function coefficients, group means for the original variables and for the discriminant function, and the within-cell correlations of the original variables. Particular care must be taken when the signs of the coefficients differ, because then it is possible for two groups with quite different characteristics (i.e., means on original variables) to have similar means for the discriminant function.

5. Another approach to interpreting the nature of the discriminant function is to ignore the coefficients but to examine the correlations between the original variables and the discriminant function. These correlations (called structural coefficients) may be interpreted directly and are much less troublesome than discriminant coefficients. Unfortunately, many computer programs for MANOVA do not automatically provide these coefficients.

6. It is possible to obtain a significant multivariate effect with no significant univariate results. In this case, one must inspect carefully all the available information to make an interpretation in terms of the original variables.

7. Once you have narrowed the set of dependent variables to those you believe "important" and those "unimportant" to making the significant discrimination, you can check your interpretation (for an illustration, see McCall, Appelbaum, & Hogarty, 1973).

a. Will the set chosen as important discriminate without the other variables? Reanalyze this effect using only the "important" variables as the dependent measures.

b. Do the "unimportant" variables share any variance pertinent to the discrimination with the "important" variables? To assess this, covary the "unimportant" from the "important" variables.

c. Can the "unimportant" variables discriminate? Repeat the analysis using only those variables thought to be "unimportant."

d. If the "unimportant" variables do discriminate, will they do so if the "important" variables are covaried? So, covary the "important" from the "unimportant" variables.

8. It is possible for the multivariate test not to be significant, but to have one or more significant univariate results. The proper interpretation is that you have nothing to report. The multivariate test was not significant, and you are not permitted to look at individual variables anymore than you are permitted to do post-hoc comparisons without an overall effect in a univariate analysis of variance. It may be a bitter pill, but to do otherwise violates the control of alpha (i.e., Type I error). Therefore, judiciously select dependent variables for analysis.

Repeated Measures

Designs in which the same sample or samples of subjects are assessed more than once on the same dependent variable (or variables) pose special statistical problems.

Qualitative Data. The strategy underlying the statistical tests described above for categorical data have recently been extended to apply to longitudinal studies (Landis & Koch, 1979). However, the procedure rests on the strategy of creating as many response categories as there are possible response *combinations*. That is, a three-category response scale (e.g., high, medium, low) assessed on four different occasions has $3 \times 4 = 12$ possible response patterns, and any single subject can display only one of these patterns. However, with the requirement of at least 10 tallies in each cell, from 150 to 200 subjects would be required for a single group design and nearly 500 for a three-group design. Therefore, the minimum number of subjects required to analyze such a design may preclude its use, although one can find published studies employing far fewer subjects.

Quantitative Data, Univariate Factorial Design. A univariate factorial design with one repeated factor having more than two levels raises special problems. The traditional analysis of variance for such designs (e.g., Winer, 1971) makes some additional assumptions. Specifically, these procedures require that the correlations (or covariances) between all pairs of repeated assessments are equal. If more than one group of subjects is involved, these correlation matrices must be identical from group to group. This assumption is called *homogeneity of covariance* or *compound symmetry*.

In much developmental research, this assumption cannot be met. For example, year-to-year correlations of IQ are highest for the shortest test/retest interval, and they progressively decline as the interval between assessments increases. This clearly violates the assumption of compound symmetry. In contrast, time spent playing with five different toys might produce relatively homogeneous correlations between the five stimuli. Also, if the experiment has only one group and only two levels of the repeated factor, there is only one correlation and this assumption is met. But when such a design has *several* groups of subjects, this *r* must be the same for each group in the design. While the analysis of variance is rather robust with respect to violations of the assumption of homogeneity of variance, it is not robust with respect to violations of the assumption of compound symmetry. Such violations lead to too many rejections of the null hypothesis.

McCall and Appelbaum (1973) have considered this problem and evaluated several approaches to solving it. Both Box (1954) and Greenhouse and Geisser (1959) have suggested corrections to the degrees of freedom of the traditional *F* test. These procedures are relatively simple to use, but they have been shown to be overly conservative (i.e., some results are not found to be significant which should have been). We believe these and other approximate adjustments have little to recommend them, except for simplicity, because an exact solution that makes no assumptions about compound symmetry is available.

McCall and Appelbaum (1973) have described and numerically illustrated in nontechnical fashion how to use multivariate analysis of variance to analyze data from a univariate repeated-measures design. The general strategy requires that the repeated dimension be transformed from an independent variable to a dependent variable. To do this, a set of orthogonal contrasts, typically the orthogonal polynominal contrasts, is determined for the repeated dimension (e.g., the linear, quadratic, cubic, etc. contrasts scores are produced for each subject by multiplying the appropriate coefficients times the subject's scores). These contrasts then constitute a set of dependent variables representing the repeated dimension, and a strictly between-subjects multivariate analysis of variance is performed on this set of contrasts. Multivariate results for the between-subjects factors constitute tests of those factors in interaction with the repeated dimension. A between-subjects analysis of variance conducted on the mean (or total) score over all repeated levels is equivalent to the between-subject effects in a univariate analysis of variance. Finally, a multivariate test of the grand mean of the set of dependent contrasts constitutes a test of the main effect for the repeated dimension.

Multivariate Repeated Measures. Suppose one has several dependent measures each assessed on several occasions. The analytic strategy is the same as described immediately above, except that a set of contrasts must be determined for each dependent variable (e.g., the linear, quadratic, and cubic contrast for Variable 1; the linear, quadratic, and cubic contrast for Variable 2; etc.). All of these contrasts then constitute the set of dependent variables, and one follows the procedure outlined immediately above. Note that the number of dependent variables increases rather quickly, perhaps requiring a large number of subjects.

Unequal Spacing in Trend Analysis. It should be noted that tables of orthogonal polynominal coefficients almost invariably are for the case in which the levels of the factor are equally spaced. But when the factor is age, the intervals may be unequally spaced. For example, we may make an assessment at 1, 2, 4, and 8 years of age. The common coefficients are not appropriate for this case. Robson (1959) has described a method for constructing coefficients for unequally spaced intervals, or researchers can use the MANOVA program (Cramer, 1976) or the ORPOL function of PROC MATRIX in the SAS system (SAS, 1982) to generate these coefficients.

Measuring Change

If developmental psychology's focus is to describe and explain behavioral change within organisms over time or age, then investigators are likely to want to use measures that represent a difference or change from one occasion to the next. For example, one might want to calculate the simple gain, posttest minus pretest score, to measure the change in performance produced by an enrichment program and to correlate this index with other variables of interest.

But for many years, statisticians have warned researchers against the uncautious use of change scores. For example, in a review of such methods, Cronbach and Furby (1970) concluded that "gain scores are rarely useful, no matter how they may be adjusted or refined. . . . 'Raw change' or 'raw gain' scores formed by subtracting pre-test scores from post-test scores lead to fallacious conclusions, primarily because such scores are systematically related to any random error of measurement. Although the unsuitability of such scores has long been discussed, they are still employed, even by some otherwise sophisticated investigators'' (p. 68).

Investigators who feel they must use some form of change or difference score should become thoroughly familiar with Harris (1967) and Cronbach and Furby (1970). Although they recommend against change scores, Cronbach and Furby point out that if they must be used, raw gain is not as good a measure of change as difference scores that are refined by using certain regression procedures. Moreover, special methods are required when the two scores entering the calculation of change are "linked," either because they are both obtained from a single test or test battery administered at one sitting or because observations on two different occasions are made by the same observer.

Cronbach and Furby recommend alternative procedures of analysis in several situations in which investigators have commonly used change scores. We summarize their suggestions briefly, but advise researchers to consider their article in detail.

Pre-Post Randomized Experiments. In a single-group, pre-post experiment, there is no need to calculate a gain or a change score. A correlated *t*-test will suffice to test the difference between pretest and posttest assessments.

In a randomized factorial experiment involving a pretest and posttest, it is assumed that subjects are randomly assigned to treatment groups and that such assignment produces comparable groups on the pretest score. If so, one option is simply to test the difference between treatment groups on the posttest measure alone, completely ignoring the pretest score except to verify that the random assignment of subjects indeed produced equal pretest group means.

An alternative is to use the analysis of covariance (see above). In this case, the pretest would constitute the covariate and the posttest the dependent variable. If other measures assessed prior to treatment are also available and correlate with posttest scores, then pretest score plus these other variables may constitute multiple covariates to be simultaneously regressed from posttest scores to increase precision. Remember, however, from the discussion of covariance above, groups must not differ significantly on the covariate(s), the regression of covariate on dependent variable must be substantial (e.g.,

if the correlation is less than .40, consider blocking subjects rather than using covariates), and the regression lines must be linear and homogeneous from group to group (e.g., $p \geq .25$). Even then, substantial error may be introduced from nonsignificant differences in slope. If within-group regressions are significantly different in slope, the main effect for groups (e.g., treatments) is not interpretable because it depends on group differences in pretest means.

Comparison of Groups Not Formed at Random. When treatment groups are formed by procedures other than randomization or a randomization procedure is unsuccessful in producing comparable groups on the pretest, the assessment of group differences in response to differential treatments is usually not possible (but see Overall & Woodward, 1977). "There simply is no logical or statistical procedure that can be counted on to make proper allowances for uncontrolled preexisting differences between groups" (Lord, 1967, p. 305). We consider such cases further in the section on field studies.

Correlational Studies. Sometimes investigators want to correlate a person's developmental change (e.g., increase in height, improvement in test scores) with other variables. We often do this by calculating a simple change score between two assessments and correlating it with other variables. It would be better to compare regressions of the pretest on the posttest with or without the other variables of interest, or to regress pretest from posttest before correlating the residual with other variables. The latter index is called the "part" correlation, which should be distinguished from the "partial" correlation in which the covariate is regressed from both measures (see below).

Selecting High or Low Gainers. Sometimes a researcher is interested in selecting for further study individuals who gained substantial amounts or those who did not gain substantial amounts from a given treatment. Although many researchers calculate raw gain or difference scores, this procedure cannot be recommended because such scores tend to show a spurious advantage for persons who begin with low scores on the initial assessment.

A more reasonable approach is to predict with regression procedures scores on the posttest criterion using all of the information available. Then select those who actually score substantially above this prediction and those who score substantially below it. However, Cronbach and Furby (1970) have determined special regression procedures for this situation which are recommended over traditional techniques. Other problems associated with defining unusually high or low scoring individuals on the basis of their deviations from scores predicted by regression procedures are discussed extensively by Appelbaum and Cramer (1983).

Defining a Construct as a Gain. Sometimes we operationally define a concept in terms of a difference. For example, self-satisfaction may be defined as the difference between the ratings of actual self and ideal self on a scale of self-esteem.

In this case, researchers often calculate the difference between the two variables as an index of the concept (i.e., self-satisfaction). This assumes that the slope of the regression between the two variables is linear and equals 1.0. But this assumption can be assessed empirically. Even if the regression is linear, the slope may not be 1.0. It may be better to define the construct as $Y - mX$, in which Y is actual self, X is ideal self, and m is the slope of the regression of X on Y determined empirically.

In the past few years, there has been renewed interest in the concept of change and its assessment in developmental psychology. Interested readers might consult Baltes, Nesselroade, and Cornelius (1978), Bentler (1973), Labouvie (1980), and McCall (1977).

The Analysis of Spread or Variability

Most researchers interested in group comparisons are oriented only toward finding differences in the mean performance of treatment groups. But certain treatments could have a profound effect on individuals that would not be reflected in the means. For example, suppose one group of children were given a test assessing their ability on a certain task. Another group was administered the same test, but it was advertised to be extremely difficult and challenging. Some children in this group may take up the challenge and work extra hard, scoring extremely well. Conversely, other children may be intimidated by the instructions and give up, thereby scoring poorly. The two group means may be equal, but the variability of scores in the challenged group may be much greater. How does one assess differences in spread or variability?

Parametric Tests. There are several well-known tests of variances, including the F test (Hays, 1981) of the difference between two independent variances and the F-*max* and Bartlett's tests (both discussed in Winer, 1971) designed to compare the variances of several independent groups. However, these procedures are extremely sensitive to departures from normality, and they must be used only with great care, if at all, when distributions are nonnormal.

Other parametric tests of the equality of variances, procedures collectively called the analysis of "spread," are discussed by O'Brien (1978). O'Brien's work is based on a variety of statistical procedures that may not be familiar to applied researchers, and statistical consultation may be needed to implement them.

Nonparametric Tests. A limited number of nonparametric alternatives exist to test the equality of two independent variances. In this context, the issue is called the "two sample scale problem." The two most popular approaches are the Ansari-Bradley (Ansari & Bradley, 1960) and the Siegel-Tukey (Siegel & Tukey, 1960, 1961). Both procedures operate in similar fashion, and neither is preferred over the other.

Confounding in Developmental Designs

In 1965, Schaie pointed out that the typical cross-sectional or longitudinal study confounded age with the time of birth of the subjects (i.e., cohort) and the time at which the measurements were made.

For example, a cross-sectional study of three ages conducted in a given year confounds age with year of birth, because if the study were conducted in 1980 the 5-year-olds would be born in 1975, the 10-year-olds in 1970, and so on. Are the observed age effects in such a study really associated with age or with the fact that children born in 1975 are somehow different from those born in 1970, and so forth?

Similarly, in a longitudinal study of a single group of children born in 1970, age effects would be confounded with the year of measurement. That is, the 5-year assessment would be made in 1975, the 10-year assessment in 1980, and so on. In this case, one cannot tell whether age effects are associated with age changes or with secular changes (e.g., shifts over the calendar years of attitudes toward children, working mothers, social permissiveness, etc.).

Schaie was also concerned that the experience of being tested at periodic intervals was also a confound in longitudinal research. Increasing levels of performance over age might be associated with increasing familiarity with the test or improvement in test-taking skills, and not with increasing ability with age.

These criticisms received enthusiastic endorsement by a large segment of the discipline. In principle, these were justifiable concerns, and the awakening of developmental researchers to these potential confounds was a major contribution. But, in the opinion of some (e.g., McCall, 1977), the movement got out of hand. Longitudinal research, both past and future, was almost dismissed outright if no controls for cohort or secular change were included. The new methods required legions of control groups for each age to be considered (see below). The result was that "proper" developmental studies were beyond the financial and professional means of the discipline. In addition, as often happens in such rapid, major turnarounds of thought, certain methods for controlling these extraneous variables became favored, sometimes without regard to the specific question addressed by the research, the nature of the behavior being studied, or the particular ages of the subjects.

In our view, the longitudinal method is the life-blood of developmental science. It is the only way researchers can study change within organisms over age. Moreover, age is inextricably confounded with time of birth and time of assessment, and there is no logical way to separate these three factors perfectly any more than there is to separate mental age, chronological age, and IQ. Therefore, some assumptions must be made regarding at least one of the three factors, and these assumptions should be based upon the best available theory and data pertinent to the specific problem, variables, ages, and times involved.

For example, it may be reasonable to assume that neither time of birth nor time of assessment affects the quality and timing of Piagetian sensorimotor stages. In contrast, these two factors may be crucial in the study of adolescent attitudes toward sexual behavior. But even in this latter case, their influence may depend on the particular age range, years of birth, and time of measurement being studied. In addition, assumptions about these factors might be different for studies of developmental function than for studies of individual differences. McCall (1977) pointed out that in a large study of mental abilities and personality among adolescents (Nesselroade & Baltes, 1974), birth year had an effect throughout the age range considered, repeated testing influenced the second but not the third assessment, and neither of these variables was systematically related to the pattern of cross-age correlations.

Wohlwill (1973) has discussed the relative merits and limitations of the several designs offered by Schaie, Baltes, and others in this context, and his presentation has been summarized in Table 5. The issues can be seen in the diagram at the top of this table. The rows of this scheme represent years of birth and the columns are years of measurement. These two variables completely define age, which is

given in the cells of the diagram. Therefore, time of birth, time of measurement, and age are inextricably confounded.

The first step for the researcher is to decide which of the variables is of primary interest. Typically this will be age. The second step is to decide on the basis of theory and research which of the other factors are also likely to affect the behavior to be studied. The third step is to select control groups to assess the influence of these other variables.

Three general approaches have been proposed, depending upon the assumptions the researcher is willing to make. These designs are described briefly in the remainder of Table 5. For example, the *cohort-sequential design* (i.e., the dashed-line parallelogram) is the classic longitudinal design, but replicated over several cohorts born in different years. In its most basic form, one has an Age × Cohort design, and presumably age effects should emerge with cohorts without a serious qualifying interaction. However, assumptions must be made about the role of time of measurement, because it is confounded with both factors.

The *time-sequential design* (i.e., the solid-line parallelogram) is the classic cross-sectional design, but it is replicated at different times of measurement. Presumably, age effects should run roughly parallel within each assessment year. But time of birth, and therefore cumulative history, is confounded with these factors, and interpretation may rest upon certain assumptions in this regard.

If one's major interest is in time of birth and measurement effects, not in age, then the *cross-sequential design* may be appropriate. However, since this approach relegates age to the role of a confound, it will probably not be used often by developmentalists.

Ideally, one should assess all the groups in Table 5 and conduct all three designs, hoping that the results converge on a few main themes without serious qualifications associated with various confounded interactions. Notice, however, that for a study spanning five ages assessed yearly, 21 different assessments are required covering 7 years plus controls for repeated testing in longitudinal studies (e.g., groups tested for the first time at various points during the assessment schedule). The financial and time commitments are enormous. While certain "shortcuts" have been proposed, most trade convenience for certain assumptions in addition to those required for these designs (Wohlwill, 1973).

What does one do? The best one can. Which design and approach is most appropriate can only be

Table 5.   Summary of Developmental Designs (adapted from Wohlwill, 1973)

Cohort (Year of Birth)	1975	1976	1977	1978	1979	1980	1981
1970			7				
1971			6	7			
1972	3	4	5	6	7		
1973		3	4	5	6	7	
1974			3	4	5	6	7
1975				3	4		
1976				3			

(Year of Measurement across columns)

Design	Independent Variables	Features
Cohort-Sequential (dashed-line parallelogram)	**Age, Cohort**	1. Classic longitudinal design, replicated over cohorts 2. Provides information on age differences (if independent groups) or age changes (if longitudinal) and on isolated and cumulative cohort and historical factors 3. Confounds Age × Cohort interaction with Time of Measurement (i.e., assumes no Time of Measurement effects) 4. Requires longer research investment
Time-Sequential (solid-line parallelogram)	**Age, Time of Measurement**	1. Classic cross-sectional design, replicated over time 2. Provides information on age differences (if independent groups) or age changes (if longitudinal) and some information on time of measurement 3. Confounds Age × Time of Measurement with Cohort (i.e., assumes no cohort effects and no cumulative historical effects) 4. Requires shorter research investment
Cross-Sequential (dotted-line rectangle)	**Cohort, Time of Measurement**	1. Provides information on historical and cohort differences 2. Confounds Cohort × Time of Measurement with Age (i.e., assumes no Age effects)

decided individually for each set of particulars. While conducting all groups would be optimum in many cases, it may not be possible or even worthwhile. Make your assumptions on the best theory and data available for each specific case, and remember those assumptions when interpreting the results. But to ignore questions of intraindividual change altogether because of methodological complexity or to denigrate virtually any study that does

not assess all possible confounds cheats the discipline of a significant part of its *raison d'être*.

INDIVIDUAL DIFFERENCES

In addition to developmental functions, a second major task of developmental psychologists is to specify the stability or lack of stability of individual differences in behavioral characteristics over developmental time and the interrelationships of attributes within or across time. Typically, such questions are addressed with correlational analyses, from the simple Pearson correlation coefficient to complex factoring procedures. We consider some of these techniques in this part.

The Classical Bivariate Indices of Relationship

Most methods assessing the relationship between attributes are based on the correlation coefficient. This index has been extensively studied, but problems in applying it to various research contexts are legion. In this section we present some fundamental information about correlations. We consider the basic tests of hypotheses regarding correlation coefficients, factors that affect the size and interpretation of correlation coefficients, some robust measures of correlation, and some noncorrelational indices of relationship.

Correlations and Tests Based on Multivariate Normal Models

Given the assumption of normal distributions, we begin with the simplest circumstance, the one-sample study.

One Sample, One Correlation. Most elementary statistics texts for psychologists include a *t*-test for the hypothesis that in the population a single correlation on a single sample is within sampling error of a population correlation of .00. Sometimes, however, we wish to test an observed correlation against some theoretical or population correlation that is not .00. An observed correlation can be tested against this theoretical value by using the common *r*-to-*z* transformation and the formula

$$Z = (z_r - z_\rho)/\sqrt{n - 3}$$

in which z_r is the *r*-to-*z* transformation of the observed correlation, z_ρ is the *r*-to-*z* transformation of the theoretical or population correlation, and *n* is the sample size. Under the null hypothesis Z is distributed according to the standard normal distribution.

One Sample, a Matrix of Correlations. Other issues arise in the more typical case in which several dependent variables are assessed on a single sample and the entire matrix of correlations is calculated. With *k* variables, there are $k(k - 1)/2$ bivariate correlations possible. What researchers typically do in this case is test the significance of each correlation in the matrix and discuss all the significant results. This is an inappropriate strategy. For one thing, a

certain number of correlations in a large matrix will be significant by chance alone, although the precise error rate is difficult to determine. It is *not* accurate to say, as is commonly declared, that 5% are expected to be significant at the .05 level, because the correlations are not independent of one another. A strategy invoked in other contexts to overcome this type of problem is to proceed to individual tests only after an overall test is significant. The same approach can be used in this context.

Testing several correlations from a single sample can occur in two general contexts. The first is when the *k* variables and their relationships to one another constitute a conceptually integrated and meaningful set (the same circumstance discussed above under MANOVA). Then a test on the set *as a set* is appropriate, and such tests are called ''simultaneous tests.''

To conduct one type of simultaneous test, assume *k* variables form some meaningful set and have a multivariate normal distribution. Then the first question in a one-sample study should be whether the *matrix* of $k(k - 1)/2$ correlations is within sampling error of a population *matrix* of zero values with 1s along the diagonal (i.e., the identity matrix). Following the procedure proposed by Bartlett (1954) and reported in many standard multivariate texts (e.g., Morrison, 1976), the test statistic is a likelihood ratio statistic following an asymptotic chi-square distribution. Specifically, it is

$$x^2_{\text{obs}} = - \left| (n - 1) - \frac{2k + 5}{6} \right| \ln | \mathbf{R} |$$

where *n* is the sample size, *k* is the number of variables, and $\ln | \mathbf{R} |$ is the natural logarithm of the determinant of the sample correlation matrix (computer subroutines to calculate the determinant of a matrix are widely available). Under the null hypothesis that the population correlation matrix is the identity matrix (1s along the diagonal and 0s elsewhere), this test statistic follows the chi-square distribution with $k(k - 1)/2$ degrees of freedom.

Significant (i.e., large) values of chi square suggest rejection of the null hypothesis that all off-diagonal correlations are .00. If this null hypothesis is rejected, then the researcher is permitted to discuss bivariate relationships within the matrix that have apparently contributed to this significant general result. Other procedures for this case and techniques for conducting a posteriori tests within a significant matrix are reviewed by Larzelere and Mulaik (1977).

In contrast to the simultaneous test described

above for a conceptually integrated set of variables, other procedures are appropriate when the several variables do not form a cohesive set. Typically, in this case, several a priori tests are to be conducted on correlations from a single sample, and some method is required to control for the Type I error rate over the family of such tests. Then "multiple test procedures" are required.

Larzelere and Mulaik (1977) recommend a computationally simple approach they call a "multistage Bonferroni procedure." In the first stage, conduct each individual significance test using a significance level equal to alpha (usually .05) divided by m, the number of a priori tests to be made. If no correlation is significant in this family of tests, stop the analysis and conclude that no evidence exists to reject the null hypothesis that no correlation in the tested group reflects a population value other than zero.

So far, the procedure has followed the standard Bonferroni approach, but Larzelere and Mulaik (1977) feel this is too conservative. If at least one correlation is found to be significant in the first stage of tests described above, they recommend proceeding to a second stage. Specifically, if k of the m tests were significant in the first stage, retest the $(m - k)$ previously nonsignificant correlations using a significance level equal to alpha divided by $(m - k)$. Repeat this second-stage procedure, calculating a new significance level each time, until no remaining correlation is found significant in an analysis stage. With this approach, the probability of making at least one Type I error in the family of tests is less than or equal to the nominal level (e.g., .05).

It is also possible to test whether an observed matrix of correlations is significantly different from some known or hypothesized population matrix other than the identity matrix. One solution to this problem was offered by Jennrich (1970), and other approaches relying on the analysis of covariance structures have been briefly reviewed by Larzelere and Mulaik (1977). Researchers should note that these procedures can be used to test specific hypotheses about a sample correlation matrix. If the scientist can specify the values of all, or even just some, of the correlations before the observations are made, such hypotheses can constitute the "known" matrix against which the observed matrix is tested (see later section on analyzing covariance structures).

Within a matrix of correlations derived on a single sample, it is sometimes necessary to test a priori the significance of the difference between two correlations based on the same subjects. For example, one might be interested in whether the IQs of mothers or of fathers correlates more highly with the ver-

bal performance of their children. Not only are these two correlations based on the same sample of subjects, but they involve a common variable—verbal performance of the child. A number of techniques for dealing with nonindependent correlations have been suggested, but Appelbaum and Cramer (1976) have shown that the one proposed by Olkin (1967) is preferred over a wide range of conditions, particularly when the sample size is greater than 24.

To test the hypothesis that $\rho_{jk} = \rho_{jl}$ against either unidirectional or bidirectional alternatives, form the statistic

$$Z = (r_{jk} - r_{jl})/s_{d'}$$

where

$$s_{d'} = [1/(n - 1)][(1 - r_{jk}^2)^2 + (1 - r_{jl}^2)^2 - 2r_{kl}^3 - (2r_{kl} - r_{jl}r_{jk})(1 - r_{jk}^2 - r_{jl}^2 - r_{kl}^2)].$$

Under the null hypothesis, Z is distributed as the standard normal with mean 0 and standard deviation 1.

Suppose the two correlations do not involve a common variable as above, but they are computed on the same sample of subjects. Steiger (1980) presents a modification of a procedure developed by Dunn and Clark (1969) for handling this situation, and we present the computational formulas in Table 6.

More Than One Sample, Two Variables. Suppose we want to compare two independent groups

---

Table 6. **Testing the Difference Between Two Correlations Involving Different Variables That Are Calculated on One Sample of Subjects (from Steiger, 1980)**

To test the hypothesis that rho$_{jk}$ = rho$_{lm}$

Calculate

$$\hat{Y}_{jk,lm} = 1/2 \{[(r_{jl} - r_{jk}r_{kl}) \times (r_{km} - r_{kl}r_{lm})]$$
$$+ [(r_{jm} - r_{jl}r_{lm}) \times (r_{kl} - r_{kj}r_{jl})]$$
$$+ [(r_{jl} - r_{jm}r_{ml}) \times (r_{km} - r_{kj}r_{jm})]$$
$$+ [(r_{jm} - r_{jk}r_{km}) \times (r_{kl} - r_{km}r_{ml})]\}$$

$$\bar{r} = 1/2 (r_{jk} + r_{lm})$$

$$\bar{s} = \hat{Y}_{jk,lm}/(1 - \bar{r})^2$$

Under the null hypothesis, the statistic

$$Z = (n - 3)^{1/2}(z_{jk} - z_{lm})(2 - 2\bar{s})^{-1/2}$$

is distributed as the standard normal, where z_{jh} and z_{lm} are the r-to-z transformed values of r_{jh} and r_{lm}. The test may be performed either as a directional or nondirectional test.

---

with respect to the correlation between two variables. Elementary statistics texts offer the familiar r-to-z transformation and a test of the difference between two independent correlation coefficients using the standard normal distribution.

Sometimes researchers attempt to interpret two separate tests of the significance of a correlation (H_0: $\rho = .00$) as if they constituted a test of the difference between the two correlations. For example, if a correlation between two variables is significant for boys but not for girls, the researcher may subtly or overtly conclude that the relationship is greater for boys than for girls. Such a conclusion requires a test of the difference between those two independent correlations. It is quite possible for the relationship to be significant for boys but not significant for girls, yet the difference between the two correlations be non-significant (which would be the case if the correlations were .45 and .40 for ns of 20).

Suppose now that we are interested in the difference between more than two independent groups with respect to the correlation among two variables. For example, consider the relationship between some aspect of maternal language and child IQ for black and white, male and female, children. Specifically, the null hypothesis is that in these four populations the correlations are all equal to a single value.

Notationally, we have $k = 4$ groups of sizes n_1, n_2, . . . , n_k, respectively, with observed sample correlations $r_1, r_2, . . . , r_k$. The calculation begins by determining Fisher's r-to-z transformation for each of the sample correlations and then defining the quantity W to be

$$W = \sum_{i=1}^{k} (n_i - 3)(z_i - \bar{z})^2$$

where

$$\bar{z} = \sum_{i=1}^{k} (n_i - 3)z_i \bigg/ \sum_{i=1}^{k} (n_i - 3)$$

Under the null hypothesis for reasonably large ns ($n > 25$), W is distributed asymptotically as chi square with $k - 1$ degrees of freedom. Large observed values of W suggest rejection of the null hypothesis of homogeneity of the k-independent correlations.

This method might find use in factorial research designs originally intended to test mean differences between the groups. Rather than limiting data analysis to tests on means, the correlations between pairs of variables within groups also might be examined. The above approach constitutes an overall test of whether differences in a relationship exist for this *set of groups*. If the test statistic is significant, correla-tions for individual groups may be examined to explain this overall finding.

It should be noted that under the assumptions of these statistical tests, mean differences are conceptually independent of the pattern of correlations (i.e., all combinations of results for means and for correlations are theoretically possible). Therefore, analyses on both means and correlations can provide distinct and complementary information and are likely to lead to greater understanding of the behaviors under investigation.

More Than One Sample, Matrices of Correlations. We often have a set of dependent variables, not just one pair, on two or more groups. For example, suppose we are interested in several characteristics of children whose parents have recently divorced. We may obtain four samples: firstborn sons or daughters in the custody of their mothers or fathers. Initially, we are likely to perform an analysis of variance to determine if mean differences exist on the set of variables in this 2×2 factorial design. Then we may be interested in whether the entire matrices of correlations between the dependent variables differ across the set of four groups. As an initial step, a general test of the homogeneity of these four correlation matrices is vastly preferred to testing the significance of all pairs of correlations across all four groups.

Testing the equality of entire correlation matrices obtained from several independent samples is far more complicated theoretically and computationally than the procedures outlined above. The most widely accepted tests of this kind are due to Jennrich (1970). In Table 7 we present the computational formulas for two cases, the first involving just two independent groups and the second involving k-independent groups.

It should be noted that for the estimated probabilities to be accurate both tests require rather large samples—three times the number of subjects as variables or $n = 25$ per group, whichever is larger. In addition, both tests are sensitive to departures from the null hypothesis, and the null hypothesis will be rejected even if all but a few of the correlations are nearly equal. Further, a glance at Table 7 will indicate that the computations are complex. While programs to perform these tests directly are not widely available, such a program can be constructed using matrix manipulation subroutines contained in standard statistical computer packages. Further, Sörbom and Jöreskog's COFAMM program (1976) can be used to test most of these maximum likelihood hypotheses with some "fidgeting."

Correlations Within Pairs of Subjects—The In-

Table 7. **Testing the Difference between Matrices of Correlations for Two or for *k* Independent Samples**

i. *Two independent samples; A and B; H_o: $P_a = P_b$*	**ii.** *k independent samples; H_o: $P_a = P_b = \ldots = P_k$*

i. *Two independent samples; A and B; H_o: $P_a = P_b$*

R_a is the correlation matrix of p variables for sample A containing N_a observations with typical bivariate correlation $_a r_{ij}$

R_b is the correlation matrix of p variables for sample B containing N_b observations with typical bivariate correlation $_b r_{ij}$

$\overline{R}$ is the matrix of mean correlations weighted for sample size in which a typical element is

$$\bar{r}_{ij} = \frac{(n_a)(_a r_{ij}) + (n_b)(_b r_{ij})}{n_a + n_b}$$

$\overline{R}^{-1}$ is the inverse of $\overline{R}$ with typical element $\bar{r}^{ij}$

S is a matrix with typical element
$s_{ij} = v_{ij} + (\bar{r}_{ij})(\bar{r}^{ij})$
where $v_{ij} = 1$ if $i = j$; 0 otherwise

$c = n_a n_b / (n_a + n_b)$

$Z = c^{1/2} \overline{R}^{-1}(R_a - R_b)$

Under H_o: $P_a = P_b$
Chi square$_{obs}$ = 1/2 tr(Z^2)
$\qquad$ − diag'(Z)S^{-1}diag(Z)
$\qquad$ with $df = p(p - 1)/2$
$\qquad\qquad$ where p equals the number of variables
Large values of the observed chi square suggest rejection of the null hypothesis.

ii. *k independent samples; H_o: $P_a = P_b = \ldots = P_k$*

R_a, R_b, $\ldots$ R_k are as above

$\overline{R}$ is the matrix of mean correlations weighted for sample size in which a typical element is

$$\bar{r}_{ij} = \frac{(n_a)(_a r_{ij}) + (n_b)(_b r_{ij}) + \ldots + (n_k)(_k r_{ij})}{n_a + n_b + \ldots + n_k}$$

$\overline{R}^{-1}$ is the inverse of $\overline{R}$ with typical element $\bar{r}^{ij}$

S is a matrix with typical element
$s_{ij} = v_{ij} + (\bar{r}_{ij})(\bar{r}^{ij})$
where $v_{ij} = 1$ if $i = j$; 0 otherwise

For each group A, B, $\ldots K$ form
$Z_i = (n_i)^{1/2}\overline{R}^{-1}(R_i - \overline{R})$
where $i = a, b, \ldots k$

Under H_o: $P_a = P_b = \ldots P_k$
Chi square$_{obs}$ = $\sum\limits_{i=1}^{k}$ [1/2 tr(Z_i^2)
$\qquad\qquad$ − diag'(Z_i)S^{-1} diag(Z_i)]
$\qquad df = (k - 1)p(p - 1)/k$
$\qquad\qquad$ where p equals the number of variables and k equals the number of samples
Large values of the observed chi square suggest rejection of the null hypothesis.

---

traclass Correlation. A special case occurs when the scores entering the correlation are observed on the members of pairs of subjects. A classic example occurs when the intelligence of siblings or twins is correlated. The problem in applying the traditional Pearson r to such data is determining which sibling shall be "the first" (i.e., the X variable) and which shall be the "second" (i.e., the Y).

The intraclass correlation was proposed as a solution to this problem. One simply enters each pair of siblings twice into the calculation of an ordinary Pearson correlation, once with one sibling taking the role of the "first" element and once with the other sibling taking the role of the "first" element. Moreover, if there are three siblings, all six pairwise permutations of the scores would be entered. If there are only two members in each family, the significance of the intraclass correlation, r_i, may be tested by first transforming the observed intraclass correlation to a z score by the familiar r-to-z transformation. Then compare the observed correlation against a standard normal distribution with a population mean equal to the z transform of the hypothesized intraclass correlation and a population standard deviation equal to $1/(n - 3/2)$, where n is the number of *pairs of subjects*, not pairs of scores.

Intraclass correlations also have been developed in terms of the analysis of variance. For example, the sibling data described above could be conceived as a randomized blocks analysis of variance with families serving as blocks and siblings as "treatments." (One sibling is arbitrarily selected to be "the first.") In this case, the intraclass correlation may be determined in one of two ways, either as

$$r_i = (SS_B - SS_W)/(SS_B + SS_W)$$

or as

$$r_i^* = (MS_B - MS_W)/(MS_B + MS_W).$$

These two estimates do not give the same values,

and the one based on mean squares is generally considered to be slightly less biased on the average.

Care must be taken in the interpretation of the intraclass correlation, and a substantial number of researchers are uncomfortable with its use. For example, the three estimates may yield quite different values when the means or standard deviations of the two distributions are not equal. Although this may not be a concern in some situations, it can be a problem if one sibling was reared at home in disadvantaged circumstances and the other was adopted into an advantaged family. A small illustration of the problem is given in Table 8. Here the Pearson r is 1.00, the intraclass correlation based on the sums of squares is .723, and the intraclass correlation based on the mean squares is .772. Further, if the scores are standardized separately within each group, then the intraclass correlation based on the sums of squares would be identical with the Pearson estimate. Therefore, while the Pearson r is not influenced by linear transformation of the variables, the intraclass correlations based on the sums of squares and mean squares are changed with a change in mean and variance.

This example represents but one of many issues surrounding the several versions of intraclass correlations and their application to different situations. Researchers might begin studying these problems by consulting Bartko (1976, 1978) and Shrout and Fleiss (1979).

Factors That Affect the Size of Correlations. Most correlational statistics are appropriate for quantifying a relationship between two variables in a sample drawn randomly and independently from a single population. Then, and only then, can the resulting correlation be generalized to that population. But correlational indices may be calculated on samples that are not random and therefore not representative of the population to which the researcher wishes to generalize. Although explanations of factors that affect the size of the correlation coefficient can be found in elementary text books (e.g., McCall, 1980), errors persist in the developmental literature, especially when several groups of subjects are involved. Therefore, these issues will be mentioned briefly here to refresh memories.

Restricting or truncating the range of a random variable can influence the size of the correlation. If extreme scores are eliminated in the sampling process, correlations may be reduced in absolute value; if scores in the middle range are omitted, as in the selection of extreme groups, correlations may be spuriously inflated. The classical example is the difficulty in validating the Scholastic Aptitude Test as a

Table 8. **Comparison of Three Methods for Estimating the Intraclass Correlation When the Mean and Standard Deviation Are Not Equal**

Family	Younger Sib	Older Sib
a	114	124
b	94	104
c	103	113
d	121	131
e	87	97

$$r(\text{Pearson}) = 1.000$$
$$r_i(\text{SS}) = .723$$
$$r_i^*(\text{MS}) = .772$$

predictor of college grades, because only students in the upper end of the range of scores on the SAT tend to be admitted to college. In contrast, when researchers deliberately select extreme groups (e.g., high and low readers, high-risk and normal infants), correlations across groups cannot be generalized to the broader population (although rs calculated within a group may generalize to the population from which that group was sampled). Notice also that sampling extreme groups can influence the size of correlations involving other variables if those variables are correlated with the sampling criteria.

Ordinarily, separate groups cannot be lumped together in a single sample for correlational purposes unless the means and variances of the subgroups are comparable or the combined sample is representative of a population of interest. This problem may occur when correlating variables across groups in factorial designs when the analysis of variance show that the groups have significantly different means. The overall correlation may be higher, lower, or even opposite in sign to the correlations found within each group. If sample size is sufficient, separate correlations for each group are best, but a pooled within-cell estimate of correlation (i.e., subtract the cell mean from each score and correlate for all subjects ignoring group membership) may be used if there is evidence that the correlation is homogeneous from group to group or when hemogeneity of the correlation matrices is assumed (as in MANOVA). Notice that within-cell correlations deal with the problem of mean differences between groups, but they do not deal with differences in variance or the possibility that the size and direction of correlations may be different from group to group.

Developmental psychology is especially prone to problems of floor and ceiling effects in which scores pile up at the bottom or top of a bounded scale. This is a common problem in longitudinal studies and in developmental testing in which young children are unable to pass any items while older children pass them all. There is no neat solution to this problem. If one changes the test to make it maximally appropriate for each age, then one has confounded test form with age. Transformations may help "normalize" the data, but they do nothing for the conceptual problems.

Correlational Indices of Relationship Between Attributes Measured with Qualitative Scales

The techniques described above assume multivariate normal distributions. Suppose this assumption does not hold because the measurement scales are noncontinuous, qualitative, categorical, or binary. Numerous approaches to the measurement of correlation for noncontinuous data have been proposed. Carroll (1961) discusses the nature of these procedures, and Glass and Stanley (1970) present a good elementary treatment of them. We shall mention only a few of the problems in the assessment of interrelationship for noncontinuous data.

Selecting a Technique. The technique of choice depends largely on the theoretical scale underlying the dependent variable. There are three basic ways noncontinuous data can arise.

First, the measures may be logically noncontinuous, as when a symptom is either present or absent or a particular response either occurs or it does not occur. In addition, a number of demographically defined variables are categorical by nature, for example, sex, race, and religious affiliation. Note, however, that variables involving more than two categories are useful in a correlational sense only if they fall along a scale having at least ordinal properties. If the categories are truly nominal (e.g., religious group), correlational methods are generally not appropriate, and one needs to employ cross-classification indices of association in these situations (see below).

The second type of noncontinuous data arises when attributes possess a truly continuous underlying distribution but we artificially dichotomize or polychotomize the measurement. For example, body temperature has an underlying theoretical scale that is continuous, but we may artificially divide individual scores into two categories—febrile or nonfebrile. We may believe in a continuous scale of risk for newborn infants, but nevertheless classify babies into abnormal, questionable, and normal.

The third situation leading to noncontinuous data occurs when we retain only the rank-order properties of the measurements, either because that is the form of the original measurements (e.g., teachers rank order students on a specific trait) or because we do not have confidence in the equal-interval properties of the measurements that we then convert to ranks (e.g., length of infant vocalization may be timed, but subjects are then rank ordered).

The Measurement Is Logically Noncontinuous. When the measurement is logically noncontinuous, cross-classification (i.e., noncorrelational) indices of association are generally the most appropriate methods (see below). But within the correlational tradition, the most common index is the phi coefficient. If we have two variables, X and Y, both of which are naturally dichotomous (e.g., scored 0 or 1), we may form the 2×2 table in Table 9 and calculate phi as indicated.

When interpreting the phi coefficient, one must remember that it is highly dependent on the marginal distributions, which may restrict its range and lower its maximum value well below 1.00. Attempts to rescale phi by using the ratio of the observed phi to the maximum possible phi given the marginals are generally unsuccessful (Carroll, 1961). It is often preferred to reformulate the problem to be a question of group comparisons instead of correlations.

It is sometimes of interest to have a measure of the degree of association between a dichotomous classification of subjects (independent variable) and a continuous dependent variable. The *point biserial* correlation is the ordinary Pearson correlation coefficient with the dichotomous classification variable scored 0 or 1. No special computational method is needed. The point biserial simply provides an in-

Table 9. **Calculation of the Phi Coefficient for Two Logically Dichotomous Variables**

		Variable Y		
		0	1	
Variable X 0		a	b	$a + b$
1		c	d	$c + d$
		$a + c$	$b + d$	n

$$\text{phi} = \frac{bc - ad}{\sqrt{(a + c)(b + d)(a + d)(c + d)}}$$

dex of the degree of association between independent and dependent variables which may supplement tests of significance on the group means.

We are not aware of adequate indices for the correlation of a truly dichotomous variable with either an artificially dichotomized or a rank-order variable.

Artificially Dichotomized Variables with Underlying Theoretical Normal Distributions. The tetrachoric correlation is the most appropriate index for this situation, yielding an estimate of the population Pearson correlation that would be obtained if the variables had been measured on a continuous scale.

To calculate the tetrachoric, cast the data in the form of Table 9. If $(a + b)/n$ and $(b + d)/n$ are between .30 and .70, then the tetrachoric correlation can be estimated by the formula

$$r_{\text{tet}} = \cos \frac{180}{1 + \sqrt{bc/ad}}$$

If these proportions are not between .30 and .70, the exact computation requires a computer (e.g., Routine BECTR, IMSL, 1979).

Rank-Order Data. Techniques for correlating ranked data (e.g., Spearman rank-order correlation, τ) are described in most nonparametric statistical references.

A Word of Caution. Some correlational techniques for noncontinuous data are essentially Pearson correlation coefficients applied to this particular data form (e.g., biserial, point biserial) while other indices are not Pearsonian (e.g., tetrachoric). In many instances these latter indices do *not* have the same properties as the Pearson r. This fact is particularly important when trying to use such correlations in more complicated techniques, such as, factor analysis, path analysis, and most multivariate hypothesis testing methods. In general, one should never mix different correlational indices in a single matrix (e.g., the input matrix for a factor analysis), because important properties of the matrix (e.g., positive definiteness) may be destroyed and the results of the subsequent analyses may be incorrect or misleading. Not only is mixing types of correlations inadvisable, but a factor analysis of all binary items may produce special problems, especially if the items are age scaled (see below).

Noncorrelational Indices of Relationships

Correlational methods are often not appropriate when dealing with noncontinuous data, particularly polychotomies in which the categories do not possess ordinal properties. In these circumstances it may be better to use measures of association based on cross-classifications.

Chi-Square Contingency Tables. The most traditional index of this type is the chi-square contingency test of independence. This procedure is well-known and described in most basic statistical textbooks, but it is often misused, either because of a failure to meet the assumptions or because it is not designed to provide the information the researcher desires.

The major assumptions of the chi-square test are that subjects are independently and randomly sampled and contribute a tally to one and only one cell of the contingency table. Therefore, it is usually *not* appropriate to use chi-square contingency tests to determine mother/infant contingencies within a single dyad, for example, because the same two subjects provide all the tallies in the table.

For most applications, another requirement for the chi-square procedure to yield appropriate results is that the *expected* frequency of *each cell* must be at least 10 for a 2 × 2 contingency table and at least 5 in larger tables. When expected cell frequency is below these minimums, chi square is inappropriate, although the Fisher Exact Test may be used for small samples in the case of a 2 × 2 table. When the number of observations per cell is in the range of 5 to 10, it is often desirable to use the correction for continuity given in most textbooks.

Much attention has been paid to the special case of 2 × 2 tables (see Goodman & Kruskal, 1954). A number of measures of association have been proposed, including two indices (Q and Y) developed by Yule; the mean square contingency denoted as "phi squared"; Pearson's variation of phi squared, called C; and T, an average chi square. Some of these produce indices that vary between 0 and 1, in which 0 indicates a complete lack of association and 1 indicates perfect association.

Classical chi-square contingency tables and related indices have some definite limitations and liabilities. For one thing, users should be aware that these statistics are highly dependent on the marginals that are treated as if they were population values. In many cases, the marginals are highly dependent on the sampling plan and conclusions must be restricted to that plan. If the marginals are not an accurate reflection of the population, the results of these statistics will not accurately generalize to that population. Moreover, departures from expectancy may be concentrated in a few cells that alone can produce a significant result. (Note that a few extreme cases can also produce a large Pearson correlation.) Finally, the range of possible values may not convey directly the degree of association, or a correlationlike index may not range between 0 and +1. Because of these limitations, some statisticians have claimed to be "unable to find any convincing published defense of chi square-like statistics as measures of association" (Goodman & Kruskal, 1954). Many of these problems have been solved by more recent innovations in discrete multivariate analysis and more sophisticated readers are encouraged to consult Bishop, Feinberg, and Holland (1975) and Davis's (1974) presentation of Goodman's approach.

Correlation-Type Indices: Lambda Statistics. Instead of testing hypotheses about the structure of categorical responses as in the above techniques, Goodman and Kruskal (1954) and others have proposed a number of alternative indices for the measurement of the degree of association in cross-classification tables. The logic of these statistics is quite different from that of the chi-square analysis of contingency tables. For example, in the case of the lambda statistics to be discussed below, the logic is much closer to that of the Pearson correlation than to the logic of contingency tables. Specifically, the Pearson correlation coefficient represents, among other things, the percent of the total variance in a variable that is saved by predicting it from knowledge of the other variable relative to predicting it without knowledge of that variable. Similarly, the lambda statistics are based on providing an index for categorical data which represents the reduction in

Table 10. Calculation of Asymmetric and Symmetric Lambda Statistics of Relationship for Unordered Categories

i. Raw data

	Factor B				
	b_1	b_2	b_3	b_4	
a_1	6	17	16	8	47
Factor A a_2	17	33	91	42	183
a_3	20	30	70	150	270
	43	80	177	200	500

ii. Unidirectional prediction: Asymmetric lambda

(Errors in B/No A)   = The number of *errors* when predicting B with *no A* information.
                       = Predict all cases to be the most frequent B category, which is b_4. We would be correct in 200 of 500 cases, so we would be in *error* in 300 of 500 cases.

(Errors in B/No A)   = 300

(Errors in B/With A) = The number of *errors* when predicting B *with A* information.
                       = Predict for each category of A the most frequent category of B:

Category of A	Predict B	Ss Correct	Ss Incorrect
a_1	b_2	17 of 47	30
a_2	b_3	91 of 183	92
a_3	b_4	150 of 270	120
			242

(Errors in B/With A) = 242

$$\text{Asymmetric lambda} = \frac{\text{(Errors in B/No A)} - \text{(Errors in B/With A)}}{\text{(Errors in B/No A)}} = \frac{300 - 242}{300} = \frac{58}{300}$$

Asymmetric lambda = .193

total errors when predicting the category of one variable on the basis of knowing the category of the other variable relative to not knowing any information about that variable.

We now describe *asymmetrical lambda* for unidirectional prediction in situations in which we have two polychotomies, Factor A and Factor B. Assume no relevant underlying continuous scale and no mutual ordering among the categories of either factor. But an asymmetrical relationship must hold between the two factors—that is, the A classification logically precedes the B classification, either chronologically, causally, or in some other way.

Suppose we are interested in predicting the B category membership for a single subject. Given no additional information, a rational strategy is simply

to predict that any subject belongs in that category of B which has the greatest frequency over the entire sample (i.e., the most highly probable B category). On the other hand, if we know the category of A to which our subject belongs, then the optimal strategy would be to place the subject in that B category which has the greatest frequency *for subjects within that particular* A *category*. If we were to do this for all categories of A and if there were some association between A and B, then fewer prediction errors should occur when using the A information to predict B category membership than when not using the A information. The percent of error reduction is essentially the lambda statistic.

Sample data for the asymmetric lambda are given in Table 10. Perhaps Factor A consists of infants

---

Table 10.—Continued

---

iii. *Bidirectional prediction: Symmetric lambda*

(Errors in B/No A)   = 300 (see *ii* above)

(Errors in B/With A) = 242 (see *ii* above)

(Errors in A/No B)   = 500 − 270 = 230

(Errors in A/With B) = (43 − 20) + (80 − 33) + (177 − 91) + (200 − 150) = 206

$$\text{Symmetric lambda} = \frac{\begin{array}{c}(\text{Errors in } B/\text{No } A) + (\text{Errors in } A/\text{No } B) - \\ (\text{Errors in } B/\text{With } A) - (\text{Errors in } A/\text{With } B)\end{array}}{(\text{Errors in } B/\text{No } A) + (\text{Errors in } A/\text{No } B)} = \frac{300 + 230 - 242 - 206}{300 + 230} = \frac{82}{530}$$

Symmetric lambda = .155

---

iv. *Comparison between chi square and lambda*

		Factor B				
		b_1	b_2	b_3	b_4	
	a_1	16	8	6	17	47
Factor A	a_2	33	42	17	91	183
	a_3	14	29	27	200	270
		63	79	50	308	500

Chi square = 60.1*** (Chi square, df = 6, .001 = 22.5)
Asymmetric lambda = 0
Symmetric lambda = .076

classified at birth as being high risk, suspect, or normal. Factor B may reflect a categorical outcome scheme, such as, no school problems, underachievement, learning disability, hyperactivity, and so on. Alternatively, infants might be classified as avoidant, secure, or resistant at 12.5 months, and the same infants might be classified by the same scheme again at 19.5 months to determine the stability of individual differences in attachment behaviors (e.g., Thompson, Lamb, & Estes, 1982). Notice in both examples, a subject is tallied in one and only one category, and the categories have no underlying ordinal basis. (If they do, this analysis ignores it.) Further, prediction is in only one direction: We are interested in predicting *from* early-risk status *to* later school problems, or from 12.5 to 19.5 months. The degree of accuracy in predicting in the reverse direction may be different.

The calculation of the asymmetric lambda is given in Part *ii* of Table 10. First determine the number of errors when predicting the B category with no A information. If we had no information about the risk category to which an infant belongs (i.e., category of Factor A), we would predict the most probable B category, which is b_4. We would be correct in 200 of the 500 cases, so we would be in error on 300 cases. On the other hand, if we knew the category of A to which a subject belongs, then we would predict which B category is the most likely (i.e., has the most cases) within that category of A. For example, within a_1 the most frequent B category is b_2. In predicting b_2 within a_1, we would be correct 17 out of 47 times and incorrect 30 times. When this process is repeated for each A category and the errors summed over A categories, we have the number of errors when predicting B with A information—242 in this case. Asymmetric lambda is simply the errors in predicting B with no information about A minus the errors in predicting B with information about A, all divided by the errors in predicting B with no information about A. In the present case, asymmetric lambda is .193.

The lambda statistic is free to range between 0 and 1. Lambda will have a value of 0 if and only if knowledge of the A classification is of no use at all in predicting B category membership; it will have a value of 1.00 if and only if knowledge of A classification membership predicts B category membership without error.

The above statistic assumes unidirectional prediction, that is, that Factor B is being predicted from Factor A, not the reverse. However, in many cases we are simply interested in the degree of association between two variables and the direction of prediction is irrelevant. In such cases, the degree of association should reflect predicting B from A as well as A from B. The *symmetric lambda* statistic follows this logic. The calculation of symmetric lambda is given in Part *iii* of Table 10. For the data presented in Part *i*, the symmetric lambda is .155.

It is important to notice the difference between measures of contingency based on expected frequencies determined from marginal distributions and measures of association based on accuracy of prediction. In Part *iv* of Table 10, a set of data is presented and chi square is calculated to be 60.1, which is highly significant. However, for the same set of data, asymmetric lambda is 0, indicating no advantage at all in predicting B from knowledge of A, and symmetric lambda equals .076, indicating very little relationship in either direction. Researchers must decide which of these methods fits their purpose in each specific case.

Confidence limits and tests of significance for the lambda statistic, and issues pertaining to these items, are discussed in Goodman and Kruskal (1972).

Multivariate Relationships

Most phenomena occur in a context. They may be imbedded in a network of relationships with other variables, part of a developmental progression, and so forth. Therefore, most relationships will be multivariate, either contemporaneously, longitudinally, or both. In this section we consider first some deceptively simple techniques involving more than one pair of variables or repeated assessments of the same variables over age which sometimes turn out to be very difficult to interpret. We then consider multiple regression and, finally, a few factoring techniques. Although many of these procedures are statistically related, we present them separately here.

Developmental Application of Regression

In the last decade, developmentalists have become infatuated with partial correlations, path analysis, and cross-lagged panel analysis as methods to discover causality from essentially nonexperimental, observational, individual-difference data. The acceptance of some of these methods has been wholesale in some quarters. In our experience, data analyzed with these techniques often do not meet the required assumptions, or, if that hurdle is cleared, the results may be improperly interpreted. While these techniques have some utility for developmentalists, especially in conceptualizing developmental issues, they are nowhere near the panaceas that some people believe. The most readable presentation of these and other procedures by a proponent of them can be found in Kenny (1979), and readers are strongly urged to read Chapter 13 of Mosteller and Tukey (1977).

Part and Partial Correlations. The *partial* correlation between X and Y with W partialed out consists of the Pearson bivariate correlation between the residuals of X and Y after W has been regressed *from both X and Y.* The formula for such a correlation is

$$r_{xy \cdot w} = \frac{r_{xy} - r_{xw} r_{yw}}{\sqrt{1 - r_{xw}^2} \sqrt{1 - r_{yw}^2}}$$

A *part* correlation is the correlation between X and the residual of Y after W has been regressed out of Y (but not out of X). The formula for a part correlation is

$$r_{x(y \cdot w)} = \frac{r_{xy} - r_{xw} r_{yw}}{\sqrt{1 - r_{yw}^2}}$$

Partial and part correlations usually provide different pieces of information. For example, one might be interested in the relationship between maternal encouragement and childhood IQ "over and above" the influence of maternal IQ on both variables. A partial correlation removing maternal IQ from maternal encouragement and from child IQ presumably would reflect the extent to which that aspect of encouragement not linearly associated with maternal IQ is correlated with that aspect of child IQ not linearly associated with mother's intelligence. But it might be of interest to calculate the part correlations. That is, to what extent does that part of maternal encouragement unrelated to maternal IQ relate to child IQ, and to what extent does maternal encouragement relate to that part of child IQ that is not linearly associated with mother's intelligence?

Part correlations are often more reasonable than partial correlations in situations in which the two variables are separated by developmental time. That is, if maternal encouragement and maternal IQ are measured at 12 months but child IQ is measured at 4 years, it may be more reasonable to calculate the part correlation regressing out maternal IQ only from maternal encouragement. In any event, researchers should consider the difference between these indices and select the one most appropriate to the information they want.

Of greater concern is how part or partial correlations are interpreted. Consider the diagram in Table 11. Suppose we have an assessment of socioeconomic status (SES), IQ, and school achieve-

ment for a group of children. Suppose further that SES and IQ each correlates .50 with achievement (hypothetical data). Now let us calculate some partial correlations. For example, suppose we partial out SES and observe that the correlation between IQ and achievement goes from .50 to .03. The conclusion is that IQ makes no particular contribution to achievement after removing the influence of SES. That is correct, but this statement sometimes leads to the assertion that achievement is really a function of SES and not of IQ. The latter interpretation is not necessarily true. What if IQ were regressed out and the partial correlation of .50 between SES and achievement were reduced to .06. By the same logic, one would now conclude that SES had no influence on achievement over and above IQ. Given this set of outcomes, very little can be said about the relative contributions of SES and IQ because they are so highly correlated with one another. It is possible for SES and IQ to both make a contribution to achievement or for one and not the other to do so.

A similar problem of interpretation occurs when an index variable, such as SES, and a potentially more functional variable, such as maternal encouragement, are used to predict some achievement measure of infants or young children. What often happens is that once SES is removed, either by partial or part correlations, maternal encouragement no longer has predictive significance. We then tend to dismiss maternal encouragement as not being important. In reality, maternal encouragement might functionally cause the achievement, but because the index variable (SES) correlates with maternal encouragement and other predictors of achievement, it has a higher part or partial correlation with achievement than does encouragement.

These examples illustrate a major point. Part or

Table 11. **Hypothetical Relationships Between SES, IQ, and Achievement**

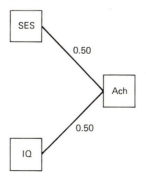

partial correlational procedures (which are also involved in path analysis and stepwise regression, see below) are often more useful for sheer prediction purposes than for understanding the functional or causal relationships among the variables. If you want to predict some outcome criterion, these procedures can help you select an efficient set of predictors, but those predictors may not actually be the functional causal agents.

Path Analysis. Path analysis has had a certain appeal to developmentalists, not only because they have assumed that it can reveal patterns of causality, but because developmental data readily lend themselves to path analysis. While path analysis can provide useful information, it is often used and interpreted naively and sometimes without regard to violations of its assumptions. A good, nontechnical introduction to path analysis has been provided by Kerlinger and Pedhazur (1973), which we follow here. A somewhat more complete and more favorable account is available in Kenny (1979).

Path analysis is essentially a model-testing procedure relying on correlations and partial correlations among a set of variables in which certain hypotheses can be made regarding the existence and direction of presumed influences between the variables. Because one can more readily make assumptions about the direction of causality when variables are measured at two points in time, developmental data lend themselves nicely to path analysis.

The assumptions for path analysis are that (a) the relations among variables are linear, additive, and presumably causal; (b) all relevant variables are included in the analysis (which assumption requires that the researcher either knows a good deal about the behavior being studied or is willing to restrict generalizations to the situation defined by the variables assessed, no more and no fewer); (c) there is a one-way causal flow in the system; and (d) variables are measured at least on an interval scale.

The analysis begins by specifying the variables and by hypothesizing the existence and direction of influences between variables. Path analysis is mostly a hypothesis-testing or model-fitting procedure, so the researcher must specify a model to be tested. This can become complex very quickly. For example, consider Table 12, which presents certain models for the simplest practical case of three variables (all of which are standardized). Part *i* represents one model, although *12 different models are possible even for the simple case of three variables!* Specifically, it is suggested that *X* and *Y* precede or have an influence on *W*, but *W* does not influence *X* or *Y*. If *X* and *Y* are measured at time 1 and *W* at time

Table 12. **Some Examples of Path Analysis**

---

i. *One simple model*

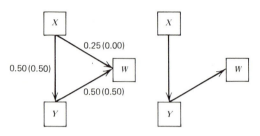

ii. *A second model that fits the data equally well*

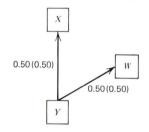

2, this assumption at first seems plausible. However, to the extent that *W* also exists at time 1 but was not measured then and that *W* has some longitudinal stability, we have already violated one of the assumptions that all variables are included in the model.

Proceeding anyway, the arrows in Part *i* suggest a specific model: *X* influences *W* directly and indirectly through its influence on *Y*, and *Y* influences *W* directly. The observed simple correlations are given next to each arrow. Path coefficients are given in parentheses. In the case in which a standardized variable is influenced by one and only one standardized variable, that is, *Y* is influenced only by *X*, its path coefficient is equal to the simple correlation between *X* and *Y*. However, *W* is influenced by both *X* and *Y*, so the path coefficients for the arrows leading to it are partial correlations. Therefore, the partial correlation between *Y* and *W* with *X* removed is .50, while the partial correlation between *X* and *W* with *Y* removed is .00. This result suggests that the model can be simplified by deleting the *X*-to-*W* arrow entirely. The question then is whether this simplified model can reproduce the observed correlations, and procedures for doing this reveal that it can. Presumably, then, the data are consistent with the causal flow diagrammed at the right in Part *i*. The conclusion is likely to be that *X* has no influence on *W* directly, but it does influence *W* indirectly through its influence on *Y*.

Two cautions are urged. First, recall our discussion of partial correlation. If X were maternal encouragement and Y were SES, we would conclude that maternal encouragement has no direct effect on child achievement (W), only an indirect one through socioeconomic class. Conceptually, the opposite seems more reasonable. The second caution is that just because the observed correlations can be reproduced by the model at the right of Part i does not mean that this particular model is the only one that can reproduce the pattern of correlations. Indeed, one would have to test all 12 possible models before one could argue that one model is better than the others at reproducing the observed correlations. And if more than one model can reproduce the observed correlations, what criteria shall we use to compare models?

For example, consider now Part ii of Table 12. Here is an alternative model for this case. It suggests that Y produces both X (contemporaneously) and W (predictively). For example, SES might be related to maternal encouragement contemporaneously and also predict later child achievement, with earlier maternal encouragement not influencing later achievement at all. In fact, this model is equal to the first in reproducing the observed pattern of correlations despite the fact that the direction of causality was reversed in one of the two causal specifications. Therefore, it is sometimes possible to have directly opposite causal hypotheses in two models, both of which fit the data equally well.

The testing of hypotheses in path analysis is most directly performed with statistical technology developed for the analysis of covariance structures (see below). These techniques include methods for testing the adequacy of a simple model, the comparison of competing models, and the assessment of incremental fit. A relatively nontechnical discussion of these models and their applications has been presented by Bentler and Bonett (1980).

The advantage of path analysis is to eliminate possible models. But the number of possible models meriting assessment can be enormous, and selection of one model may not always be possible, as we have seen. Moreover, one must keep a careful eye on the assumptions and the cautions voiced above with respect to interpreting partial correlations. Therefore, while path analysis may be a useful technique, especially for achieving parsimonious models with high predictive efficiency, its ability to determine causality from observational data is probably more limited than many suppose.

Cross-lagged Panel Analysis. What could be better for developmentalists concerned with indi-

vidual differences than a procedure that could determine developmental causality from strictly observational longitudinal data and that requires nothing more complicated than the computation of a few simple correlation coefficients? No wonder cross-lagged panel analysis has been greeted so enthusiastically by some developmentalists. But the promise and simplicity of cross-lagged analysis must be purchased at the dear cost of a highly restrictive set of assumptions that are not often met by developmental data. And even when they are met, some specialists feel that conclusions derived from cross-lagged analysis may be inaccurate or misleading.

The logic and procedure of cross-lagged panel analysis is illustrated in Table 13. Suppose a mental test was administered during infancy and again during childhood to a sample of children, and their mothers were assessed for some aspect of intellectual stimulation or encouragement at these same points in time.

There are three types of correlations in such a "panel." First, child IQ can be correlated with mother's stimulation during infancy and again during childhood. Because these correlations are calculated on variables assessed at the same time, they are called *synchronous correlations*. Second, IQ can be correlated with itself across age and maternal stimulation can be correlated with itself across age. These longitudinal relationships between the same variables are called *stability correlations*. Third, the diagonals of the panel represent correlations across variables and across developmental time. They are the *cross-lagged correlations*.

Presumably, if the cross-lagged correlations are significantly different from one another, one has evidence suggesting causality. In the example, we would look for the correlation between maternal in-

Table 13.   **General Scheme for Cross-Lagged Panel Analysis**

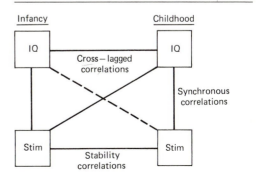

fant stimulation and childhood IQ to be statistically higher than the correlation between infant IQ and maternal childhood stimulation. Presumably, such a result would suggest that early stimulation by the mother produces a brighter child.

We offer several cautions. First, the statistical test comparing the two cross-lagged correlations must take into account the fact that the two rs are not independent. Researchers rarely consider this point. We have presented an appropriate test in Table 6 for the case of comparing two correlations involving four variables assessed on a single sample.

The next problem with cross-lagged panel analysis is that the desired interpretation depends on several assumptions that are unlikely to be met by the data and even more frequently disregarded completely by researchers. These assumptions include the following:

1. *The causal relationships for* X *and* Y *do not change over time.* A necessary, but not sufficient, sign that this assumption is met is that the synchronous correlations are equal. In our example, the correlation between maternal stimulation and child IQ must be the same during infancy as during childhood. But even if this assumption is supported by the data, Rogosa (1980) has shown that unequal cross-lagged correlations may nevertheless reflect a noncausal association.

2. *The stability correlations must be equal.* This implies two requirements. First, the two measures associated with Time 1 must be assessed at the same time, and the measures associated with Time 2 must also be measured at the same time. Second, the stability correlations must be equal. In our example, the stability for child IQ must be identical to the stability for maternal stimulation. In parent/child work, it might be expected that the stability of the parent variable will be greater than the stability of the child variable, thus violating this assumption.

3. We believe, in addition to these assumptions, interpretation is very difficult unless *all important variables have been measured and are included in the panel.* In the example in Table 13, many results consistent with these assumptions and a causal interpretation could be explained noncausally if IQ were genetic or if maternal stimulation was a correlate of maternal intelligence (and therefore of child intelligence).

Not only are these assumptions restrictive, but as Rogosa (1980) has pointed out, the interpretation of a cross-lagged panel analysis is not straightforward, *even when the assumptions are met.* The reason, in part, is that the relative sizes of the correlations (not just their significance or nonsignificance) are important. For example, moderate correlations between maternal stimulation and later child IQ on the one hand and maternal infant stimulation and maternal childhood stimulation on the other might mean that the mothers who stimulate early are not necessarily the same mothers who stimulate later. In addition to the size of the correlations, it seems necessary to have all of the relevant variables involved in the system, and multiple variates and several assessment occasions might be more informative.

Several statisticians and methodologists have recently suggested that cross-lagged analysis simply does not fulfill its promise as a method of discovering causality (Rogosa, 1980; Wohlwill, 1973). Rogosa (1980) is particularly blunt: "No justification was found for the use of CLC" (cross-lagged correlations) and "CLC should be set aside as a dead end" (p. 257). Other statisticians would suggest using general simultaneous equation models and the analysis of covariance structures instead of cross-lagged procedures.

A more moderate view suggests that these methods may help in eliminating some alternatives, just as in the case of path analysis, especially if part and partial correlations are calculated within the panel (i.e., the panel is treated somewhat like a path analysis). Even then, considerable interpretive caution is required, and one must always be on the lookout for variables that are not assessed but that may underlie the observed relationships.

Multiple Regression

Although multiple regression is commonly known to developmental researchers, it is but one technique in an extensive collection of regression methods that are less familiar, some of which have been discussed above. Indeed, some statisticians would argue that regression techniques underlie almost all statistical methods and that applied statistics will someday be taught from this perspective.

We present here only a general introduction to multiple regression. Readers are referred to several comprehensive textbooks and articles on the subject. Draper and Smith (1981) is a more-or-less classical text stressing the fundamentals of regression analysis; Green (1978) and Kleinbaum and Kupper (1978) are somewhat more advanced yet applied books that consider regression as part of general multivariate methods; and Mosteller and Tukey (1977) present regression analysis in the context of data analytic and robust methods. Darlington (1968) offers a brief and readable overview of multiple regression.

In its simplest and most commonly applied form, multiple regression is a technique for determining the relationship between a set of predictors and a single criterion in a single population of subjects. One begins by positing a model that states the linear relationship between a single criterion, Y, and a set of k predictors, $X_1, X_2, \ldots, X_k$, called the *stock:*

$$Y_i = \beta_0 + \beta_1 X_{1i} + \beta_2 X_{2i} + \cdots + \beta_k X_k + e_i.$$

Typically, the goals of regression analysis are (1) to determine if the stock of X variables improves the prediction of Y over what could be achieved by predicting the mean of Y for each individual (i.e., significance testing), (2) to determine if some simpler model with fewer predictors can do the job of predicting as efficiently (i.e., model simplification), and (3) to estimate and interpret the parameters (i.e., the beta coefficients) in the minimally adequate model obtained above (i.e., estimation and interpretation).

Significance Testing. The classical approach to significance testing begins with a set of assumptions about the nature of the terms in the model and then employs a criterion to assess the adequacy of the fit.

In addition to assuming the basic form of the model and the variables composing the stock, one also assumes that (1) the ith observation (Y_i) is the sum of two parts, a fixed part that is $\Sigma \beta_j X_i$ plus a random part, the e_i ; and (2) the errors, e_i, are independent from subject to subject and normally distributed with a mean of 0 and variance σ^2. The criterion employed, the least-squares criterion, specifies that the parameters of the model (i.e., the β_j) are such that the sum of the squared errors of prediction is a minimum.

Although it is almost universally employed, the least-squares criterion is more useful for some applications than for others. For example, the least-squares criterion usually allows a relatively small error for each individual rather than predicting perfectly for most subjects but making very large errors on those few cases. Thus, the least-squares criterion may not be a desirable criterion for military gunnery or certain types of medical diagnoses in which it is better to be perfectly accurate for as many cases as possible rather than to miss every one by "just a little bit."

The overall regression may be tested by comparing two models for adequacy of fit:

$$H_0: Y = \beta_0 + \beta_1 X_1 + \cdots + \beta_k X_k + e$$
$$H_1: Y + \beta_0 + e$$

Should the test determine that the second model with

k fewer parameters is not substantially worse in predicting the Y_i than the more elaborate model, we will conclude that, relative to the number of parameters that must be estimated, we will not do better than simply predicting the mean of the Y for each individual. This model comparison may be accomplished by comparing the mean square for regression with the mean square for error or by testing that the squared multiple correlation is zero in the population. These two approaches yield the same p values. It should be noted, however, that the sample squared multiple correlation is a somewhat biased estimate of the population value. This bias can be reduced, but not eliminated, by calculating

$$R^2_{\text{adjusted}} = 1 - (1 - R^2)(n - 1)/(k - n - 1).$$

When the ratio of the number of predictors to the sample size is relatively large, the adjusted value is the superior descriptive index, but the test of significance is based upon the *un*adjusted R^2.

Model Simplification. Following a significant overall test of regression, one often seeks to determine which of the predictors in the stock are useful and to simplify the model by eliminating unimportant variables. The first temptation is to look at the standardized partial regression coefficients (i.e., the betas), and assume that the variables receiving the highest weights are most important and those receiving the smallest weights are of little consequence. This approach is almost certainly wrong and can lead to very poor conclusions. Mosteller and Tukey (1977) discuss many of the problems in the testing of individual weights. Cramer and Appelbaum (1976) provide cases in which variables with large standardized weights are less important than variables with much smaller weights and cases in which variables with relatively modest weights may be crucial to the level of prediction.

One reason for this is that the estimates of these weights are rather unstable, particularly when the variables are highly intercorrelated. Replication is required if any conclusion rests on the actual magnitudes of the regression weights. Another reason is that the beta weights are *partial* weights. That is, a beta weight indexes the contribution of the variable *given* that all of the other variables are already in the regression. Thus, if variables A and B are equivalent predictors of the criterion, A will contribute nothing to the prediction in the presence of B, and B will contribute nothing in the presence of A. It is quite critical that researchers understand that the tests of individual beta weights in a regression system are tests *both* of the particular regression coefficients and the other variables in the stock. A change in the stock can, and usually will, change both the estimate of an individual beta and its "significance."

The results of the overall test of regression and the tests for individual coefficients can fit any one of the following possibilities:

1. R^2 (overall regression) and all betas are significant.
2. R^2 and some, but not all, betas are significant.
3. R^2 is significant but none of the betas are significant.
4. R^2 is not significant, but all betas are significant.
5. R^2 is not significant, but some, although not all, betas are significant.
6. R^2 and all betas are not significant.

The interpretation of these several possibilities follows that given by Cramer (1972). If patterns 4, 5, or 6 are obtained, proceed no further and conclude that the regression stock is not useful in predicting the criterion. This situation, especially patterns 4 and 5, are not unlike other cases in which an overall test is not significant but individual variables or comparisons are. If the overall test is not significant, that is that.

Of course, in the event of either pattern 4 or 5, two possibilities are present. One is that the observed relationship for a particular variable is chance. Second, it may be that one or more of the variables is really a useful predictor, but the researcher unwisely chose to combine in the stock such variables with other quite useless variables or used very highly intercorrelated variables, thereby diluting the effect of "good" predictors.

This possibility highlights the importance of picking the stock carefully. Multiple regression is a method for determining whether *a set* of variables predicts better than chance (i.e., than the mean of the Y), and a test of that proposition was nonsignificant in this case. If there was a good a priori reason for testing the predictability of individual variables, this should have been the course of action rather than the multiple regression. Of course, there is no way to discriminate between these two possibilities except through a replication sample. This is one reason why it is often recommended to have a sample sufficiently large to divide into a primary sample of two-thirds the cases and a replication sample of one-third.

Should patterns 1, 2, or 3 occur, one concludes that the stock is "useful" in predicting the criterion. If pattern 1 is the case, no simplification in the model is possible because the partial F-tests show that every variable is useful, given the other variables in the system. If pattern 2 is the case, a series of model comparisons may serve to simplify the regression equation. Note, however, as stated above, one must not simply delete variables with nonsignificant betas. Finally, if pattern 3 occurs, one or more of the variables contributes to the regression, but no single variable is itself so "major" that it is needed *if* the other variables are in the system.

Researchers often automatically select a stepwise regression procedure as a method of reducing the model. There are many variations on the criteria used in stepwise procedures, and researchers should be aware of the particular one invoked by the computer programs they employ. In some cases, the method selects the best single-variable predictor in step 1, the best two-variable prediction stock in step 2, the best three-variable prediction stock in step 3, and so on. In this option, a variable may be included in an earlier step but not in a later one. Another criterion is that the variable with the highest simple correlation with the criterion is entered first; step 2 consists of regressing out that variable from the others in the stock and asking which remaining variable has the best residual correlation with the criterion (e.g., the best partial correlation with the first variable regressed out); and so on.

Often in this context researchers simply accept a model composed of variables that contribute a significant increment in predictive accuracy and discard the others. It is easy to conclude that the other variables play no significant role in predicting the criterion. As explained under partial correlation, this may not be an accurate interpretation at all. A global variable, such as SES, may predict the criterion (e.g., IQ) best. Other variables (e.g., maternal encouragement, extent of father's involvement with the child) may not contribute beyond that level of prediction, but they may be important causes of the criterion behavior. Stepwise regression is a good procedure for determining predictive efficiency (e.g., maximum predictive accuracy with the fewest number of variables), but this may or may not be what is needed for the proper interpretation and understanding of the behavior in question.

If stepwise procedures are desired, we recommend backward selection with provisions for reentry of variables at later stages. This procedure reduces capitalization on chance, and it is most consistent with the model comparison strategy that we favor. Basically this approach starts with a full model that is compared with one in which the "weakest" variable has been eliminated. If there is no significant decrease in the R^2, then perhaps that "weak" predictor could be eliminated, and the process repeated for the next "weakest" variable. However, once a variable is eliminated in this way, provisions are made to reenter it on subsequent model comparisons.

Interpretation. Once all the statistics are calculated, problems of interpretation may persist. For example, one practical application of multiple regression is in predicting who will succeed and who will not. Suppose the overall regression is highly significant, and we have a predicted criterion score for each individual plus their actual observed score. Therefore, it is possible to determine who has actually scored higher and who has actually scored lower than was predicted. If the criterion were achievement, these differences between actual and predicted scores might define overachievers and underachievers.

Appelbaum and Cramer (1983) have shown that the nature of the least-squares regression system produces some problems in this application. Specifically, there will be a natural tendency to underpredict high scorers and to overpredict low scorers, which means that the statistical system will cause a disproportionate number of high scores to be regarded as overachievers (having predicted somewhat lower levels of performance for them) and a disproportionate number of low scores to be underachievers (having predicted somewhat higher scores for these individuals).

Another problem in interpreting the implications of a multiple regression equation rests on the apparent possibility that very low scores on one variable could, in theory, be totally compensated by extremely high scores on another variable (i.e., could large amounts of maternal stimulation compensate for severe risk status at birth?). This problem of "infinite substitutability" is of greatest concern when one attempts to apply the regression equation in situations in which one or another of the predictor variables contains a value beyond the range of those included in the formation of the original regression equation. Therefore, as in simple regression, it is wise not to use the equation for predictor variables having values exceeding the original range used to determine the prediction equation.

An error of interpretation is sometimes made by assuming that increasing the value on one predictor variable will increase the criterion behavior of a subject, the "intervention fallacy." For example, suppose family income was one of several potent variables in the prediction of school success. It might be assumed that increasing income through an income

maintenance or other transfer program would increase school success. But recall that family income is one of several predictors in the stock and its influence cannot be separated from them, so increasing family income is likely to influence the other variables as well. Moreover, this is strictly observational research, and there is no guarantee that family income causes the criterion.

Factor Analysis

A goal of science is to explain a variety of observed phenomena with a few general underlying principles. One mathematical technique that directly attempts to accomplish this goal is factor analysis. Suppose we measure a variety of characteristics on a single sample of subjects and wonder whether there are a small number of fundamental dimensions underlying the behavior which will account for most of the interrelationships found among the observed variables and thereby reflect the total behavioral domain in fewer dimensions than originally measured. This is the aim of factor analysis.

Factor analysis is a vast special topic requiring considerable background before a researcher actually conducts such an analysis. The prevalence of computers and statistical program packages make it much easier to compute a factor analysis than to understand or interpret it. There are a variety of decisions that must be made before conducting any factor analysis, and the appropriateness of one versus another alternative and the interpretation of the results requires a good deal of study. Therefore, we strongly urge researchers to read at least one basic reference before preceding. For example, Harman (1967), Mulaik (1972), and Thurstone (1947) are standard texts.

Basic Strategy. The starting point of factor analysis is the *fundamental equation* for an observed variable (sometimes called "manifest" variable) that is in standardized form (i.e., mean of 0 and standard deviation of 1). The equation reads

$$Z_i = f_{i1}F_{i1} + f_{i2}F_2 + \ldots + f_{ik}F_k + u_iU_i.$$

Thus, any given variable in the set of p variables is conceived as being made up of several components, the F_k, the underlying or *latent factors* that are common to all the variables in the set being analyzed. In addition, there is a set of coefficients for each variable, the f_{ik}, which express the direction and extent to which that variable contains each latent factor. These regressionlike weights are called *factor loadings,* and they indicate the relative weighting of each of the k factors in making up the observed variable Z_i. In addition to the k factors, there is one additional factor specified by U_i which is called the *unique factor.*

The goal of factor analysis is to determine the k underlying factors that will, under an optimal situation, account for the interrelationship among the p observed variables. This amounts to determining the factor loadings for all observed variables on each of the hypothesized factors.

There are several assumptions and choices that must be made in order to accomplish this factoring. In practice, these choices are sometimes made not on the basis of what is appropriate to the problem at hand but on ''what is most often done'' or ''what is convenient.'' These are not sound bases for such decisions. We consider a few of these issues below.

Principal Components and Common Factor Analysis. The first question is what aspects of the interrelationship of variables should be reproduced? In the *principal components* analysis one attempts to reproduce exactly the intercorrelations (or some other measure of association) among the battery of observed variables and, at the same time, to account for all of the variance in each and every observed variable.

On the other hand, in *factor analysis* one first conceives of the variance of a variable as being broken down into two fundamental components. One variance component is shared with some or all of the other variables in the battery; it is the *common variance* of the item or variable. The other component is the *unique variance* of the item. It is a component unique to that particular measure and is not shared with any other variable in the battery. The unique variance also includes the error variance of the item.

It is important to note that the term ''factor analysis'' technically refers to a common factor analysis, that is, a factor analysis of the common space variability in the test battery. Although the mathematics of factor analysis and principal components analysis are similar, they are based on different models and on different conceptions of what appropriate interrelationships should be reproduced. If one wants to simply duplicate the battery of variables in a set of orthogonal summary variables in which each explains a smaller percentage of the variance than the last, then one is describing a principal components analysis. Basically, it is a summary or descriptive procedure. On the other hand, if one wants to define common underlying dimensions that may explain a set of interrelationships, one wants a factor analysis.

Since a principal components analysis attempts to reproduce the correlations among the observed variables and account for the total variance, the diagonals of the correlation matrix to be factored contain the value 1.00. On the other hand, in a factor analysis, only the common variance is of interest, and therefore the diagonal elements of the correlation matrix are reduced to the degree to which variance of that variable is common variance. Just how to estimate the common variance of each variable is known as the *communality estimation problem.* Unfortunately, no simple solution exists to this problem because the estimate of communality depends partly on the number of factors one believes to be included in the system. Therefore, estimating communalities and determining the number of factors are inherently confounded in factor analysis. A number of methods are available to estimate communalities, the most common of which is to use the squared multiple correlation of the variable in question with the other variables in the battery. This squared multiple correlation (SMC) may either serve as an estimate of the communality or be a starting point for communality estimation in iterative factor analytic procedures in which the estimation of the communalities and the number of factors are changed until the results converge on a stable solution.

Related to the issue of communalities is the task of determining the number of factors in the final model. Of the several methods available, the easiest is Kaiser's *Little Jiffy* method, which calls for the retention of all factors with eigenvalues greater than 1. Experience has shown that for many situations the Little Jiffy criterion seems to provide an adequate solution to the number-of-factors problem. Another method is the *Scree* criterion. To use this approach, plot the factors along the X axis in order of extraction and the eigenvalues associated with each factor (before rotation) along the Y axis. Then connect the points. One searches this ''root plot'' for a break (i.e., an especially large gap between factors in relative root size) and then selects the number of factors immediately preceding the break. A third criterion, called *interpretability*, simply suggests the researcher retain as many factors as can be easily interpreted. Of course, this approach may rest with the interpretive skill or imagination of the investigator, not with the quantitative structure of the data. Finally, if one uses an *iterative* technique (see above), then the number of factors is fundamentally left to the mathematical fit of the model to the data, and usually the investigator does not make an active decision regarding the number of factors to retain.

The Nature of the Latent Variables. Another question to be faced is how the latent variables or factors should be represented. It is common practice to conceive of the factors as orthogonal or uncorrelated with one another, but this is not a necessary restriction. Indeed, the goal of reproducing the original correlation matrix is possible with a variety of different representations of factors. The selection of a particular factor structure rests more on personal preference and philosophy of science than on a mathematical criterion. For example, if one views factors as simply the result of human thought aimed at a parsimonious description of nature, then one may chose to represent the underlying dimensions as orthogonal or uncorrelated with one another. This alternative certainly simplifies one's view of nature.

On the other hand, one may feel that the orthogonality or nonorthogonality of the factors should be an empirical question and not imposed on nature by psychologists. Therefore, the factors should be allowed to be nonorthogonal if appropriate, although other assumptions about nature are usually made in this process. Therefore, the choice depends on which assumptions one wishes to impose on the data. For example, most factor analytic programs, such as principal axis programs (see below), produce a set of factors that are initially uncorrelated with one another. After this intermediate solution is obtained, rotational programs may rotate the axes to meet some other requirement or criterion to produce nonorthogonal factors or orthogonal factors with certain desirable properties.

How Should the Factors be Extracted?   The most frequently used method of factor extraction for the common factor model is principal axis factor analysis. There are several principal axis programs, either with or without iterations, and the user should select one of these methods plus a communality estimation procedure. In general, iterative procedures are usually preferred, although other techniques of factor analysis are available including image analysis, canonical factor analysis, and alpha-factor analysis. These methods differ mainly in the way they approach some rather technical problems in factor analysis, and each technique produces slightly different results, which may be preferred in one situation or in another (see Mulaik, 1972, chap. 8).

Rotational Criteria.   Another choice required by users of factor analysis is to select a criterion for rotation of the factors. The most commonly used criterion is varimax. Simply put, this procedure rotates the factors to a simple structure in which each variable is weighted maximally on a few factors and minimally on all the others. This helps interpretation of the factors because they tend to be defined by a few of the observed variables that will have high loadings while the other variables will have small loadings.

Interpretation of Factors.   The first issue regarding the interpretation of factors concerns whether one believes they are "real" or not. On one hand, one may argue that the obtained factors are simply a convenient method of thinking about nature. On the other hand, some researchers believe that the obtained factors estimate real dispositions or entities of nature. Whether factors are the researcher's abstraction or real entities is a matter of philosophy and judgment.

Another issue of interpretation concerns loadings. For one thing, how large does a loading have to be before one interprets it? Common wisdom suggests that factor loadings of .40 or above should be interpreted, but there is no objective criterion to answer this question.

In addition, how shall negative loadings be interpreted? Here one is faced with a problem similar to interpreting beta weights in regression (see above). The sign of a weight depends on the direction of scoring of the variables and the direction of the intercorrelations. It is sometimes desirable to "reflect" (i.e., multiply by -1) all of the loadings on a factor to improve interpretability, but then one must remember that such reflection will change the sign of the correlations between that factor and other factors (if factors are nonorthogonal) and variables.

Finally, factor loadings and especially factor scores should be interpreted with caution. Like beta weights, they are not very stable and can change dramatically with the addition or subtraction of a variable or in a replication sample. Factor scores, the coefficients assigned to individual subjects reflecting the direction and extent to which each factor represents a subject's particular performance, are very problematic, and some specialists caution that one should generally not use factor scores. If one does use factor scores obtained by the common regression method, the researcher should be aware that the factor scores may not be uncorrelated even if the factors themselves are orthogonal. Further, they may not have a mean of 0 and a variance of 1, even though the common factors are so constructed.

Developmental Applications of Factor Analysis

In the following sections we mention a few factoring techniques that may be of special interest to the developmental researcher. In doing so, we will assume that the reader is reasonably well acquainted with basic factor analysis.

Individual Differences in Developmental Function.   Recall at the beginning of this chapter that a developmental function is a plot of the amount of a characteristic in a sample over age. Of course, there will also be individual differences in the form of this growth curve. Years ago, psychologists debated whether the prototypical group ogive learning curve was typical of any particular subject within the sample. Similarly, one also can inquire about individual differences in developmental functions.

Tucker (1960, 1966a) developed a factor analytic approach to determine the major individual differences in learning curves for a sample of subjects who were repeatedly assessed on a single dependent variable. McCall et al. (1973), who applied the analysis to longitudinal IQ data, described five major patterns of IQ change over 17 ages for a middle-class sample. McCall (1979) also used the same procedure to characterize individual differences in habituation pattern for infants responding to repeatedly presented visual or auditory stimuli.

In the case of the IQ data, Tucker's procedure decomposes the Subjects × Occasions IQ score matrix by the Eckart-Young procedure, which yields a set of components constituting generalized patterns of IQ change over age plus, for each subject, a matrix of component scores that represent the direction and extent to which that subject's actual pattern of IQ change is approximated by the generalized components. The first component is often related to the grand mean of the variable over age for the entire sample, and a subject's component score reflects not only the extent to which the subject's developmental IQ profile follows the average group trend but also how much that subject's general level is above or below the mean level. Component scores for the subsequent, mutually orthogonal, components reflect the extent to which that subject's actual IQ pattern deviates from the main trend in the manner described by each component. Because the psychological meaning of the components themselves is controversial (see below), subjects were then clustered by a direct cluster rotation (Overall & Klett, 1972) on the basis of their component scores for the first four components. The clustering analysis produced five subgroups of subjects whose average raw IQ at each age was then plotted to reveal five major "patterns" of IQ change over age for this sample.

Presumably, Tucker's procedure could be applied to any case in which a single dependent variable is repeatedly assessed on a sample consisting of at least 3 to 4 times as many subjects as assessment occasions. Thus far, the procedure has only been applied in observational research, but it could be used in experimental contexts in which subjects are assessed repeatedly from the beginning of one or more treatments through a followup period. All subjects could be analyzed simultaneously, and then it could be determined if subjects receiving one treatment versus another were disproportionately represented in one developmental pattern or another.

For example, an enrichment program might produce an early advantage that diminishes over time for some pupils while it might have no early effect but later advantage for other students. An intervention group composed of these two subtypes might not differ in average performance from a control group; nevertheless, these different responses to the treatment might demonstrate that the program had an effect, but it influenced subjects differently.

If we are ever to escape the "one-size-fits-all" mentality in education and other fields, we will need to explore such individual differences in longitudinal response to treatments. But a caution is in order. In any sample of subjects, individual differences in developmental profile are likely to occur regardless of treatment. Therefore, it will almost always be possible to find some subjects who apparently benefited from an intervention program.

In order to distinguish random from real individual differences in profile, several precautions must be taken. First, the groups of subjects that the analysis says have different profiles should be tested to determine whether those profiles are indeed statistically different from one another. Second, it helps if other information on the subjects can be used to discriminate between profile groups and aid the interpretation of the developmental patterns determined by the analysis. Third, when some profiles are consistent with prediction or theory and others are not, categorical statistics or binomial probabilities sometimes can be used to determine whether a significantly disproportionate number of subjects showed the predicted pattern. Finally, replication is very compelling, but remember that the same variables (in this case, the same number of repeated assessments) are recommended for the replication study as in the original investigation.

It should also be noted that the developmental profiles produced by this method are not "prototypical" but are simply one of many possible descriptions of the individual differences in the data set. Several design and statistical decisions that can influence the result are made, and therefore the utility of this approach rests mostly in demonstrating that the observed profiles are descriptively useful in some way and are interpretable in terms of correlates of one pattern versus another.

Factoring Developmental Data. The above procedure involves factoring the Subjects × Occasions correlation matrix. Such a matrix often has high correlations along the diagonal and progressively smaller correlations as one moves off the diagonal. When this is perfectly true, the matrix is called a "simplex," and approximations to simplex matrices are common in longitudinal research. When simplex matrices are factored, the plot of factor loadings for occasions is predictable. The first factor tends to be linear across occasions, the second quadratic, the third cubic, and so on. This fact was pointed out by Cronbach (1967), who criticized the factoring of year-to-year mental test scores because it produced spurious or uninterpretable factors. Although most actual data matrices are not perfectly simplex in nature, factors can nevertheless approximate the prototypical expected factors and thus be uninterpretable in themselves. However, as suggested above, Tucker's factoring approach can be used as an intermediate step to reduce the data base to a few dimensions prior to clustering. Other procedures, for example, clustering orthogonal polynomial contrast scores, could be employed, but the latter reduce the original data along dimensions defined a priori.

Factoring Mental Test Items. It is common for developmentalists to factor the items of omnibus tests (e.g., infant tests, IQ tests, etc.) to observe the conceptual dimensions underlying such behavior at various ages. Often, the items are scored pass or fail and are age graded. This means that items are ranked according to difficulty, and that at any single age some items are passed by no one, others are passed by everyone, and some produce reasonable variability of response. When such item responses are factored at a single age, it is possible to obtain factors composed of items that reflect common age placements rather than common psychological processes.

Some options are open to the researcher in this situation. For one thing, the analysis can be restricted to items that have substantial variance (e.g., at least 10% but not more than 90% of the subjects pass the item). Then, after the analysis, assessments can be made to determine if the factors are simply reflections of common item difficulty. For example, if general maturation were the only determinant of factor composition, then the scatter plot of principal component scores on the first component against those on the second component should be parabolic in form, although the orientation of the parabola will vary arbitrarily with the signs attached to the item loadings (McDonald, 1967). Notice that these plots are in terms of component, not factor, scores (i.e., the results of a principal components analysis before any rotations are conducted). Finally, if the factor analyses are conducted at several ages and common

age placement determines factor composition, then component scores on the first principal component should be highly correlated with component scores on the first principal component at adjacent ages, the second principal component should be correlated with the second at adjacent ages, and so forth. If these checks are passed (i.e., the plot is not parabolic and the correlations across corresponding components are not uniformly high), then it is likely that the factor composition does not simply reflect the age placement or difficulty of the items.

Longitudinal Multivariate Factor Analysis. Suppose not one but several dependent measures are assessed at more than one age on a sample of subjects. Such a design produces a Subjects × Variables × Occasions data matrix. Factor analytic procedures described above are designed to factor a two-dimensional matrix, but what about this three-dimensional case in which the Subjects × Variables matrix exists for several occasions? For example, is the factor structure at one age similar to the factor structure at the next age? Are there factors common across all ages? Are there "interaction" factors representing qualitative changes in the pattern of interrelationships across occasions? In some sense, these are fundamental questions for developmental psychology, and while some procedures exist for answering them, rarely have they been used.

When only two occasions or ages are involved, certain factoring procedures are available that determine a single set of factors that is most representative of the common factor structure at the two ages. Other procedures use other criteria, and the interested reader is referred to Nesselroade (1970) for a discussion of such procedures.

If there are more than two occasions, other procedures must be used. One technique is three-mode factor analysis (Tucker, 1966b). To our knowledge this technique has never been reported using developmental data. It yields one set of factors for individuals, one set for variables, and one set for occasions. In addition, a "core" set of factors describes the relationships among these three sets of factors. This core set of factors permits one to trace changes in the factorial structure of the variables over time and thus provides one glimpse of the changing relationships of behaviors with development.

Three-mode factor analysis is essentially a descriptive technique that makes a minimum set of constraints on the data. A similar approach called PARAFAC has been described by Harshman and Berenbaum (1980). Another procedure, developed by Jöreskog (1969, 1973, 1979), requires the user to specify certain parameters of the model, and therefore it can be used to test certain hypotheses about the variables and their interrelationships (see also covariance structures below). Jöreskog's procedure provides for three kinds of factors—general, occasion specific, and test specific. However, it is somewhat less suitable than Tucker's procedure for determining the nature of the interaction or change in relationships across occasions or age (Wohlwill, 1973).

Although we encourage developmental researchers to consider these analyses, computation and interpretation are very complex, and the limits and utility of these approaches in developmental psychology have not been explored. Researchers are advised to attempt such analyses only with the cooperation of a statistician who specializes in such procedures.

Analysis of Covariance Structures. Factoring and other multivariate procedures are often criticized for being purely descriptive, capitalizing on chance and interpreting naturalistic phenomena in an entirely post hoc (''clinical'') manner. What should be done, these critics argue, is to specify in advance the relationships to be observed and then perform ''confirmatory'' analyses to test the soundness of these hypotheses.

The most general approach to testing a set of a priori hypotheses involving the structure of a correlation (or covariance) matrix or the equality of the structures of several such matrices is called the *analysis of covariance structures*. The fundamental ideas of this approach were first introduced by Bock and Bargmann (1966), but they have been developed most vigorously since then by Jöreskog (e.g., for an introduction see Jöreskog, 1979) who has also produced several computer programs to perform the highly intricate computations (e.g., ACOVSM by Jöreskog, van Thillo, & Gruvaeus, 1970; LISREL by Jöreskog & Sörbom, 1978; COFAMM by Sörbom & Jöreskog, 1976). The application of this class of technique to longitudinal data is well illustrated in Jöreskog (1975). These techniques are very broad and extremely complicated. We present here only a very elementary description and application of these procedures.

The basic purpose of the analysis of covariance structures is the decomposition of correlation (or covariance) matrices into a set of basic structural matrices that conform to a priori sets of hypotheses concerning the nature of the interrelations of continuously measured variables. At the risk of misrepresenting or oversimplifying the approach, it is somewhat akin to testing the fit of a priori defined or partially defined factors in factor analysis. Thus,

instead of simply describing a covariance matrix in terms of factors generated by the data, these procedures require the researcher to specify some or all of the loadings on some or all of the factors on the basis of previous research or theory and then to test the goodness of fit of those specifications with the data. Actually, the user specifies parameters, not factor loadings, in one of three ways. First, parameters may be assigned a particular value on the basis of theory or prior research (e.g., as simple as 0 for no involvement, 1 for strong involvement). Alternatively, some parameters may be constrained in that their values are unknown but they are set equal to or less than other parameters in the system. Finally, some parameters may be free. Their values are unknown and unconstrained, and will be estimated from the data.

Bronson and Pankey (1977) reported one of the few developmental applications of this method to their study of the wariness of toddlers in small-group nursery-school play sessions during the second year of life. The youngsters were observed ten times during the year. After discarding the first session, the remaining nine were divided into three ''occasions''—the first, second, and third trimesters. The basic data then consisted of 40 children (Subjects) each having three ''freedom-in-playspace'' scores (i.e., ''nonwariness'' variables) during each of three trimesters (i.e., occasions).

Bronson and Pankey (1977) tested three models of the development of this behavior. Model *A* asserted that individual differences across the entire set of occasions reflected differences in wariness inherent in individual children. This hypothesis was represented by a single factor at each trimester. These three general factors should account for the vast bulk of the correlations among the three assessments within and across trimesters.

Model *B* predicted that wariness was based upon accumulated experience with peers. This hypothesis was reflected in three ''occasion-specific'' factors with the constraint that each developmentally successive factor include a portion that reflected the child's previous experience (i.e., the partial regression of the previous trimester[s] data) plus a new component.

Model *C* hypothesized that both Models *A* and *B* operate, but with the additional constraint that the general wariness factor (from Model *A*) should decline in importance over trimesters (i.e., have progressively smaller loadings over trimesters).

After loadings (i.e., parameters) are specified in accord with a model, the analysis estimates the unspecified parameters and attempts to reproduce the observed intercorrelation matrices given the hypothesized specifications. A residual matrix reflecting the differences between the observed and the reproduced correlations is created, and chi-square test of goodness of fit evaluates the size of this residual as a function of the number of unconstrained parameters that must be estimated. In this study, the results indicated that Model *A* was not adequate, Model *B* was much better, and Model *C* represented a very good fit.

However, like other techniques, the analysis of covariance structures has limitations. For one thing, the statistical theory and mechanics are extraordinarily complicated. Most of us are not able to rip off one of these analyses without substantial preparation and help.

Second, the very purpose of the approach is confirmatory, which requires the researcher to know or hypothesize a priori the nature of the relationships among the variables and specify parameters of a model. Therefore, if you have a highly specific theory or are working in a well-researched area and are able to specify one or more models to be tested, this approach has definite value. If not, the analysis of covariance structures is probably best left for another day.

Third, as with three-mode factor analysis and some other new procedures, the technique is still being developed and investigated, so there may be little in the published literature to guide us in the application of the procedure. Test statistics may require larger samples than are common, and multivariate results over several occasions can strain the interpretative capabilities of some experienced researchers.

Finally, as with almost all model-fitting procedures, just because one model can be shown to fit the data does not preclude the possibility that other models based on quite different hypotheses will also fit the data. Since the number of possible models rapidly approaches the uncountable as variables and occasions multiply, the technique is best suited for deciding between two or more theoretically prominent competing models, not for finding the "best model of all."

Despite these and other limitations, this approach has considerable merit when applied in appropriate circumstances, and it should be used more often in developmental research.

SPECIAL TOPICS

In this section we treat two special topics, the design and analysis of social interaction studies and

a few designs developmentalists might use in the analysis of quasi-experimental and field studies.

The Analysis of Social Interaction Data

Bronfenbrenner (1974, 1979) has chastised developmentalists for studying children isolated from their natural contexts, both their natural physical environments (e.g., homes, neighborhoods) and their social milieus (e.g., families, classrooms). In addition, Sameroff and Chandler (1975) urged their colleagues to think about development as a series of transactions between child and parent, for example, in which each person reciprocally influences the other during a continuing stream of interaction.

Few would argue that major segments of development are indeed transactional, and some have attempted to study such reciprocal social influencing. But such research, even in its simplest form, may be the most complicated and difficult methodologically and statistically of any major endeavor in the discipline. Below, we consider two general types of social interaction questions. Unfortunately, we offer more cautions than solutions. In recent years, a number of advances have been made in the analysis of social interaction and in sequential analysis, but in our judgment all are initial ventures. The proposed solutions are either approximate, specific to a very narrow set of circumstances, or require strong sets of assumptions (e.g., see Bakeman & Dabbs, 1976; Cairns, 1979; Kraemer, 1975; Kraemer & Jacklin, 1979; Sackett, 1978, 1979).

The two classes of problems discussed below are both addressed to making statements about *individuals* within dyads or larger groups, either as a function of the type of group or the behavior of other group members. If, however, the researcher wants to draw conclusions only about the dyad or group, not members within it, then the measure is for the group as a whole; the "group" is the unit of analysis rather than "subject," and the conventional methods of analysis may suffice. For example, one might study pairs of 2-, 3-, and 4-year-old peers in free play and simply be interested in the number of cooperative and aggressive acts per dyad as a function of age. In this case, dyad is the unit of analysis and traditional statistical techniques can be used.

Problems arise, however, when the focus is not on the group but on the behavior of *individuals within groups,* because those individuals are not independent of one another. Indeed, a focal assumption of such research is that individuals are influenced by other group members.

To deal with this problem, researchers have

sometimes analyzed data from only one individual per group. Others have used a confederate who is treated as a constant for all subjects, a debatable assumption in some cases. At other times the dependent variable has been defined as a joint action of both pair members (e.g., the number of times a mother touch is followed by a baby smile). Sometimes these approaches are satisfactory, but Kraemer and Jacklin (1979) point out that they also may fail to reflect the dependency between pair members that is the object of the study. For example, they may not permit one to obtain information about partner effects or the sequential interaction of subject and partner. In this case, other methods are required, depending on the nature of the research question.

Analysis of Summary Scores for Members of Dyads

Suppose a researcher is interested in the general social behavior of types of individuals or types of dyads. Each member of a dyad contributes a single score based upon an observation of the dyad, and dyads are of two or more general types. The analysis depends on the nature of the scores and of the questions to be answered about the role of pair members.

Single Dependent Variable, Unbalanced Pairs. Suppose one observed boy/boy, boy/girl, and girl/girl pairs of 2-year-olds in a play session and counted the number of social initiations each child made. One might want to know whether girls made more or fewer overtures than boys and whether each sex differed as a function of the sex of their partner. Notice the unit of analysis is subject type (i.e., sex) and conclusions will be drawn about boys versus girls as a function of sex of partner. Importantly, no direct observations of sequential dependencies between pair members within the stream of interaction will be evaluated—only a summary score per subject.

Kraemer and Jacklin (1979) have presented a method for analyzing this type of data. It is based upon a two-factor univariate analysis of variance in which the factors are sex of subject and sex of partner. Notice, however, that sex of subject or partner is not balanced across pairs (i.e., no boys are in girl/girl pairs). Also, the pairwise correlations are non-zero (i.e., subjects are not independent within dyads), and the cell variances may not be equal. Therefore, the usual analysis of variance procedures are not appropriate.

Kraemer and Jacklin (1979) present relatively simple formulas for determining effects for these two factors and their interaction, as well as an extension of their method to triads and beyond. In addi-

tion, they suggest calculating intraclass correlation coefficients (see above) separately between paired individuals in the same-sexed pairs and the product moment correlation for the cross-sexed pairs if the variances for the two sexes are different. These correlations can be tested for significance and homogeneity, and if they are similar, the pooled correlation can be tested (Kraemer, 1975; Kraemer & Jacklin, 1979).

One or More Dependent Variables, Balanced Pairs. In the above case, sex of subject and sex of partner are not completely balanced across the three groups of dyads (e.g., there are no boys in the girl/girl pairs). This is likely to be the case when one is interested in the response of different categories of subjects as a function of some category of partner. Suppose, however, one were studying mother/daughter pairs from two-parent, single-parent, and reconstituted families. Now the membership of the dyads is balanced across category of dyad (i.e., a mother and a daughter are in each pair), and the research question focuses on differences between types of dyads, not differences between types of subjects within dyads.

This design may be analyzed as a single factor (type of family) multivariate analysis of variance with two dependent variables (one for the mother and one for the daughter). Within-cell correlations can also be obtained.

Notice that this approach is quite general. For example, the measure made on the mother does not have to be the same qualitative dependent variable as that made on the daughter. One could measure, for instance, the number of commands made by the mother and the number of disobedient acts displayed by the daughter. Further, more than one measure per subject could be analyzed simultaneously, and there could be three measures on mothers and two, for example, on the daughters. Of course, more than one independent variable also could be involved. The use and interpretation of multivariate analysis of variance is discussed above.

Sequential Dependencies

A single score derived from a dyadic interaction episode may obscure the researcher's main interest. It is not simply how many commands and how many disobedient acts are displayed by a parent–child pair of one type or another, but how many times a command directly produces a consequence of disobedience. At first thought, the analysis of contingencies seems straightforward. One counts up the number of commands and the number of times each command was followed by disobedience versus the number of times it was obeyed. These two proportions constitute the assessment of relative contingency for a single pair.

Looks are deceiving. In fact, the design and analysis of sequential dependencies is perhaps the most difficult and problematic of any focus of developmental study. Here are a few reasons why.

Defining the Variables. The first problem may be deciding how to define and sample the behaviors of interest. Suppose we want to study maternal behavior and infant smiling. Besides the problems of distinguishing a smile from a nonsmile, one must decide how long after the mother's stimulus behavior one can wait for the smile to occur. Is it a smile if it occurs within 5, 10, 15 seconds of the stimulus, or simply if it is the next behavior? Suppose the baby does something else before smiling—perhaps vocalizes and then smiles. Is this a two-part response unit and the smile should be counted as a response, or is the vocalization the response and the smile a spontaneously emitted behavior? Another problem is that a smile could be both a response and a stimulus. The mother might smile, baby smiles, and mother smiles again. Here the baby's single smile is both a cause and an effect, and the mother's two smiles, while behaviorally identical, are stimulus and response, respectively. It is often very difficult to define the behaviors of interest and to determine which are stimuli, which are responses, and which are both.

Another problem of definition is specifying a set of categories of behaviors for each member of the dyad that satisfies the requirements of the research question and of the statistical analysis. For example, most researchers strive for a set of mutually exclusive and exhaustive behavioral categories—every act of both individuals is scored in one and only one category. But, as we have seen, the problems of interpreting a given response promote establishing more and more, finer and finer, categories. Not only does one encounter the problem of the upper limit of observers to code so many behaviors for two individuals reliably but also the size of the transition matrix; for example, the matrix of tallies of each infant behavior that follows each maternal behavior increases geometrically with the number behavioral categories. The result is often unwieldly matrices with many cells containing small or zero frequencies, which create serious problems for most statistical analyses.

Categorial Data. Although it is possible to study sequential events with continuous variables (i.e., time series analysis), most often the variables have been categorical. In theory this is not a problem, because the statistical treatment of categorical data is well-developed for many circumstances. But researchers are not always familiar with these developments.

As we have seen in previous sections on the analysis of categorical data, the outcome is often very dependent on the marginal distributions. For one thing, the results may not generalize to situations having different marginal distributions. In addition, the results often are not readily interpretable unless some attempt has been made to correct for, or to compare the findings with, chance levels.

For example, suppose one wanted to know if maternal commands were more likely to lead to aversive language or ignoring by teenagers. The conditional probabilities might be .75 that a command is followed by aversive language versus .30 that it is followed by ignoring. We are tempted to conclude that commands lead to aversive language. But this may not be true, depending on the marginals. It is possible that aversive language is such a common teenage behavior (i.e., its marginal frequency is very high) relative to ignoring (i.e., its marginal is low) that aversive language is no more contingent on commands than ignoring. In fact, neither behavior may be more contingent than chance. Therefore, some attempt must be made, statistically or in the design, to control for the marginals and chance associations. Carroll (1961) has discussed these statistical problems, and we have described above some of the corrections for chance in measures of association for categorical data. But these corrections do not usually solve all the problems of interpretation in sequential dependency studies.

Independence. The very reason for studying sequential dependencies—the cause-effect contingencies—creates major statistical and interpretive problems. That is, the observations are not independent.

Unfortunately, many statistical techniques designed for categorical data assume independence of behavioral events within each of the categorical schemes. Presumably, then, each behavior the mother displays must be independent of every other maternal behavior, and the same must be true for the teenager. This assumption is met when each subject provides one and only one tally to the matrix, but this is not the case in sequential dependency studies. If chi-square contingency analysis is applied to such a mother/teenager transition matrix as has been suggested (Castellan, 1979), the null hypothesis will be rejected too frequently.

The reason is that the chi-square test cannot distinguish between dependencies within a categorical scheme (e.g., in mother's behavioral sequence) and dependencies between two categorical schemes (e.g., between mother and teenager). Usually, this problem is solved by assuming each observation within a scheme is independent. When this is so, rejection of the null hypothesis implies that the two categorical schemes are not independent. But when dependencies exist within a scheme—that is, when mothers do not behave randomly from moment to moment and teenagers do not behave randomly from moment to moment—chi square can be significant even though mother and teenager are not paying any attention to one another and are behaving independently of one another (Appelbaum, in press).

Such dependencies within a categorical scheme can become still messier. In certain dyads we are interested in the behavior of one particular individual, for example, the mother, on another identified person, the teenager. This conceptual interest dictates whose behavior is the stimulus and whose behavior is the response. But if we are to accept the tenet of transactional theory (Sameroff & Chandler, 1975) that both members of the dyad influence each other, then the same data also should be examined from the standpoint of the teenager as stimulator and the parent as responder. Ideally, this reciprocal interaction should be assessed in the same analysis, but, for the most part, techniques to investigate the reciprocal interaction do not exist. At least, both separate analyses should be conducted in such cases. Notice, however, that when the two members of a dyad are not conceptually distinct (e.g., same-age, same-sex peers), who is the stimulator and who is the respondent may not be of interest. Nevertheless, separate analyses should be conducted to avoid the possibility that the same event is recorded in both categorical schemes in the same analysis (i.e., is regarded once as a stimulus and once as a response).

Finally, some researchers produce transitional matrices that are simply the sums of raw response frequencies over all dyads. Here again we have independence problems. For one thing, some of the tallies are based on the same subjects while others are between subjects—a very messy circumstance for most statistical techniques. Further, some dyads will contribute more to the group total than others because they display more of the behaviors of interest. Calculating transitional probabilities for each dyad before combining across dyads may be better in some situations.

Conclusion. Given the above litany of cautions, the reader may decide to avoid the study of social interaction at all costs. That would be unfortunate. While some consideration must be given to the availability of techniques, the substantive value of the problem should be the primary determinant of what we choose to study. Our point in this section is to mention some of the problems in this area and to warn researchers that their choices in these matters make a difference. We urge them to consult more detailed references (Bakeman & Dabbs, 1976; Cairns, 1979; Cook & Campbell, 1979; Kraemer, 1975; Kraemer & Jacklin, 1979; Sackett, 1978, 1979).

Quasi-Experimentation and Field Research

At the beginning of this chapter, we argued that while much experimental research addressed questions of the form, "*can X* cause *Y*," it was also useful to consider whether "*X does* cause *Y*" in naturalistic, ecologically valid contexts. It was acknowledged that the science of relevant or applied child development will be less tidy methodologically than laboratory experimentation, and that conclusions will be more ambiguous and tentative. But the pursuit is required if developmental psychology is to achieve its potential contribution to human welfare.

Psychology in general has moved more in this direction during the last decade, and a variety of techniques have been developed to deal with less-than-ideal research circumstances, ones typical of naturalistic, applied, and field settings. While some of these research efforts are devoted to detailed description, diagnosis, assessment, and descriptive evaluation, the greatest methodological interest has focused on attempts to draw causal inferences concerning the consequences of an event or treatment when subjects are not randomly assigned to groups, when a priori differences exist between the experimental and control groups, when no control group is available, when the dependent variable assessed on the treatment group is qualitatively different than that assessed on the control group, and so forth. These topics fall under the label "quasi-experimentation."

By definition, no perfect solutions exist for impossible problems, but under certain circumstances useful conclusions can be drawn from quasi-experimentation. Indeed, if we are to make progress in evaluation research, that is, to understand naturalistic development and to apply our knowledge and skills to real human concerns, we must become more sophisticated in these methods.

While the call for relevant and ecologically valid research in developmental psychology is now common (see Bronfenbrenner, *vol. I, chap.* 8), a main source of resistance to this movement is the untidy character of the design and analysis of such studies. With each departure from the prototypical laboratory experimental ideal, the researcher must contend with more threats to the validity of research results. Cook and Campbell (1979) have described in very readable form these threats as well as a variety of designs and statistical analyses common in field research. Anderson et al. (1980) provide a particular nice review of quantitative methods available for these types of designs. Below we mention only a few designs which might be employed by developmentalists.

Nonequivalent, Untreated Control Group with a Common Pretest and Posttest

In this design, an experimental group is administered a pretest, then the treatment, and finally a posttest, while a control group, not composed of subjects from the same population as the treatment group and therefore "nonequivalent," is given the same pretest and posttest but no treatment. All the pretests and posttests consist of the assessment of the same dependent variable.

For example, suppose a special television program designed to improve the mathematical knowledge of preschool children is introduced nationwide. A sample of children are selected and given a mathematics pretest. Then some of the children choose to watch the program while others do not, forming a treatment and a control group. Because the children were not randomly assigned to groups, these are nonequivalent groups. After the series of programs was broadcast, the same mathematics test was administered to all of the original children.

From a practical standpoint, this may be one of the most ideal research circumstances that can be expected in a naturalistic situation. Random assignment to special treatments or programs versus control conditions is rarely possible because a special government program may be aimed only at a group of people with particular characteristics (e.g., low income), people who seek services may be different from those who do not seek those services, and law and ethics prohibit denying services to eligible citizens.

Threats to Validity. The nonequivalence of the experimental and control group opens the door to a variety of threats to the validity of causal inferences. These problems are even more severe and complicated if the pretest and posttest are not the same dependent measures, if the pretests and posttests are made on separate samples, or if the treatment and control groups are assessed with different dependent

measures (cases discussed by Cook & Campbell, 1979).

While most veteran laboratory researchers would immediately conclude that no causal inferences can be drawn from such designs, some level of inference can be made if these threats to validity can be eliminated or minimized by methods other than randomization.

One general strategy is to alter the design so that a validity threat can be examined empirically. For example, one threat to the validity of the illustrative case is differential maturation—those children who watch the treatment TV series are developing at a faster rate than those who do not watch. Differences between posttests and pretests result from their faster inherent growth rate, not from any benefit of the TV programs. To assess this threat, an extra pretest might be added to the design so that a Pretest 1, Pretest 2, Treatment (experimental group only), and Posttest would be conducted with assessments equally spaced in time. Then one can look at change between Pretests 1 and 2 to determine if growth rates are different for the two nonequivalent groups.

A second approach to dealing with threats to validity in this context is less laborious but more chancy. Some patterns of results from this design are more interpretable than others because they obviate certain interpretations. For example, suppose the mean of the control group was the same on the pretest and the posttest, but the mean of the treatment group was below the control group on the pretest and above the control group on the posttest. Assuming pairwise statistical significance, this crossover pattern minimizes the threat of alternative explanations based on regression toward the mean, simple maturation (but not some complex forms), and certain problems associated with the scale of measurement.

Analysis. The analysis of such designs has been discussed extensively by Reichardt (1979) and Anderson et al. (1980). Statistically, the easiest and least problematic, but the least sensitive, approach is to use the analysis of variance to test for an interaction between experimental/control groups and pretest/posttest followed by paired comparisons. Since the experimental and control groups are nonequivalent, they may differ on the pretest. Consequently, one is looking for a contrast in pretest/posttest scores for the two groups, namely, an interaction. However, the pretest scores may not be terribly different, and the control group may not change much between assessments. In this case, one is asking the analysis of variance to be sufficiently sensitive to reveal an interaction in which only one of four points deviates from the others.

Some researchers deal with this problem by testing the difference between the two groups on pretest, and finding no difference, they proceed to analyze the posttest data alone. There are two problems with this approach. First, it involves accepting the null hypothesis with respect to the pretest data and then assuming the points are identical (not just similar enough to fail to reject the null hypothesis). If the pretest scores are different at $p < .10$ but the posttest scores are at $p < .03$, are the pretest differences significantly different from the posttest differences? This is the real question under investigation, and it is addressed by the interaction term of the analysis of variance. A second problem to ignoring the pretest data is that this strategy assumes that *all of the non-equivalence* between experimental and control groups is reflected in the pretest measure, which is unlikely in the social sciences.

Another common approach to analyzing this design is to use the pretest score as a covariate in an analysis of covariance on the posttest scores. This is a recommended approach in randomized designs (Cronbach & Furby, 1970), but serious problems can occur when applying this method to nonequivalent groups (Reichardt, 1979), especially if the groups differ on the pretest. As indicated above, covariance will mathematically adjust the dependent variable for group differences on the pretest, but the adjustment may not be appropriate. For example, if the covariate is an errorful measure, as it usually is, group differences can be produced where none actually exist and obliterated when they actually do exist (for an excellent explanation, see Reichardt, 1979). Therefore, in most situations, the analysis of covariance, while appropriate for randomized designs, will probably not be useful for nonequivalent group designs (Cronbach, Rogosa, Floden, & Price, 1977).

A blocking approach is also tried in such situations. Subjects in both experimental and control groups are assigned to comparable blocks on the basis of the pretest. But this approach has all of the statistical problems of the analysis of covariance. Moreover, blocking and other methods that restrict the samples to subjects in both experimental and control groups to those scoring in a common range on the pretest impose an additional selection bias and raise serious questions about external validity. For example, to what population shall the results be generalized when the samples in both treatment and control groups are not representative of people in society who are actually eligible for the treatment or not eligible for it?

Finally, gain scores are sometimes used in this design. But, as discussed above, the use of gain scores is not usually appropriate.

There is no perfect analysis for the nonequivalent design or a one-size-fits-all strategy for dealing with this case. The statistical approach will depend in part on the nature of the nonequivalence, the nature of the treatment and the results, and other factors (see Anderson et al., 1980; Reichardt, 1979).

Regression/Discontinuity Design with Pretests and Posttests

A special case of the previous design may occur when a government program, for example, is implemented for a specific group of people in society and when eligibility requirements for admission to it mean that the treatment and control groups are not only nonequivalent but essentially nonoverlapping on the pretest. For example, certain welfare and educational programs are available only for families below certain financial or performance levels. If pretest data are available for all subjects, then one may combine treatment and nontreatment groups into a single plot of posttest scores as a function of pretest score. If the treatment had an effect, there should be a discontinuity of regression with an inflection point of some sort at the cutoff or minimum eligibility level of the pretest.

In this case, the analysis of covariance could be used with the pretest as covariate, even if the pretest is not error free. Such an analysis essentially compares the intercept of the pretest/posttest regression at the cutting score point on the pretest. Such an analysis assumes the regression lines within the treatment and nontreatment subgroups are linear and have comparable slope. Of course, a sufficient range of scores within each group must be available to determine the slope and linearity of the regression line within that subgroup. If the slopes are different or nonlinear, other procedures must be used (see Reichardt, 1979).

Interrupted Time-Series Design

This design consists of frequent and periodic assessments on an experimental sample with a treatment interposed approximately in the middle of the assessment series. A nonequivalent, no-treatment control group can be added, the treatment may be repeated at several points during the assessment schedule, or the treatment may be interposed at one point and the antithesis of the treatment (if feasible) interposed at another point.

Behavior modification researchers often use variations of this strategy, for example, when they make baseline observations, begin reinforcement, withdraw reinforcement, reintroduce reinforcement, withdraw it, introduce negative reinforcement, withdraw it, and reinstitute reinforcement.

Another example of the interrupted time-series design is the plot of height before, during, and after a serious illness that shows a decline in growth rate during the illness and "catch up" growth for a short time after illness (Tanner, 1963). Such designs and their analysis have been discussed extensively in the context of field experiments by Cook and Campbell (1979) and McCain and McCleary (1979).

Assuming the simplest interrupted time-series design with one experimental group and one treatment, a plot of the dependent variable as a function of assessment occasion might reveal several kinds of effects after the treatment. First, there may be a change in level in which the general trend over repeated assessments remains the same but a sharp discontinuous elevation of the trend line occurs immediately following the treatment. Second, the slope of the trend over occasions may steepen or flatten after the treatment. Third, the variances around the means may increase or decrease; and fourth, a pattern evident over the pretreatment assessments may be altered, shifted out of phase, or modified in some other way following treatment. Whatever the effects, they may persist for a short time or a long time, and they may be manifest immediately following the treatment or only after a period of time.

Threats to Validity. One of the problems with interrupted time series, especially for developmentalists, is the presence of growth spurts or developmental change. If the treatment is introduced at the beginning of the adolescent growth spurt, for example, a nontreatment control group would be necessary to separate maturation from treatment effects. Such a control would also help to minimize the threat of seasonal or secular change and a variety of other validity threats (see Cook & Campbell, 1979).

Analysis. Statistically, the most sophisticated methods for analyzing such data have been proposed by Box and Jenkins (1976), which have been presented in an introductory and applied manner by McCain and McCleary (1979) and in textbook format by Glass, Willson, and Gottman (1975) and by Hibbs (1977). However, the Box and Jenkins approach, called the *autoregressive integrated moving average* (ARIMA) or the transfer function approach, typically requires 50 to 100 assessment occasions, far more than developmentalists are likely to measure. Therefore, a repeated measures analysis of variance that is performed with the multivariate analysis of variance strategy advocated above and that includes planned comparisons may be the most appropriate method of analysis (McCain & McCleary, 1979). Depending on how many assessments are made and the pattern of means prior to the introduction of a treatment, one might use regression procedures to extrapolate the pretreatment trend as a means of determining whether the treatment is associated with an altered pattern of response.

EPILOGUE

Often growth in one discipline outpaces growth in another, and sometimes lessons learned long ago are forgotten in the rush of advances in one area or another. In some cases, applied statistics has advanced substantially beyond the developmentalist's knowledge of that field. We have tried to bring researchers more up to date in this regard, acknowledging the limits of this presentation.

At other times, however, developmental psychology has pushed beyond the ability of applied statistics to provide unequivocal solutions. While some scientists may despair and avoid such topics, we urge them to proceed carefully, but to proceed nonetheless. Inadequate techniques sometimes necessitate crude or approximate research and produce some ambiguity in our results. But while crude research is sometimes necessary, sloppy design and analysis are never justified. We hope this chapter contributes in some small way in helping all of us to recognize the difference.

REFERENCES

Achenbach, T. M. *Research in developmental psychology: Concepts, strategies, methods.* New York: Free Press, 1978.

Anderson, S., Auquier, A., Hauck, W., Oakes, D., Vandaele, W., & Weisberg, H. *Statistical methods for comparative studies.* New York: Wiley, 1980.

Ansari, A. R., & Bradley, R. A. Rank-subtest for dispersion. *Annals of Mathematical Statistics,* 1960, *31,* 1174–1189.

Appelbaum, M. *The MANOVA program: II. Complete factorial designs.* Chapel Hill, N.C.: L. L. Thurstone Psychometric Lab, Research Memo No. 44, January 1975.

Appelbaum, M. Sequential dependencies and association—Can they be separated? *Psychometric Lab Report,* in press.

Appelbaum, M. I., & Cramer, E. M. Some problems in the nonorthogonal analysis of variance. *Psychological Bulletin,* 1974, *81,* 335–343.

Appelbaum, M. I., & Cramer, E. M. *A comparison of several methods for dependent correlations.* Southern Society for Multivariate Experimental Psychologists, New Orleans, March 1976.

Appelbaum, M., & Cramer, E. M. $E(\hat{Y}/Y)$—or direction and selection count. Chapel Hill, N.C.: Psychometric Laboratory Report, University of North Carolina, 1983.

Bakeman, R., & Dabbs, J. M. Social interaction observed: Some approaches to the analysis of behavior streams. *Personality and Social Psychology Bulletin*, 1976, *2*, 335–345.

Baltes, P. B., Nesselroade, J. R., & Cornelius, S. W. Multivariate antecedents of structured change in development: A simulation of cumulative environmental patterns. *Multivariate Behavioral Research*, 1978, *13*, 127–152.

Baltes, P. B., & Schaie, K. W. On life-span developmental research paradigms: Retrospects and prospects. In P. B. Baltes & K. W. Schaie (Eds.), *Life-span developmental psychology: Personality and socialization*. New York: Academic Press, 1973.

Bartko, J. J. On various intraclass correlation reliability coefficients. *Psychological Bulletin*, 1976, *83*, 762–765.

Bartko, J. J. Reply to Agina. *Psychological Bulletin*, 1978, *85*, 139–140.

Bartlett, M. S. A note on multiplying factors for various chi-squared approximations. *Journal of the Royal Statistical Society* (Series B), 1954, *16*, 296–298.

Bentler, P. M. Assessment of developmental factor change at the individual and group level. In J. R. Nesselroade & H. W. Reese (Eds.), *Life-span developmental psychology: Methodological issues*. New York: Academic Press, 1973.

Bentler, P. M., & Bonett, D. G. Significance tests and goodness of fit in the analyses of covariance structure. *Psychological Bulletin*, 1980, *88*, 588–606.

Bishop, Y. M. Full contingency tables, logits, and split contingency tables. *Biometrika*, 1969, *25*, 383–399.

Bishop, Y. M., Fienberg, S. E., & Holland, P. W. *Discrete multivariate analysis: Theory and practice*. Cambridge, Mass. MIT Press, 1975.

Bloom, B. S. *Stability and change in human characteristics*. New York: Wiley, 1964.

Bock, R. D. *Multivariate statistical methods in behavioral research*. New York: McGraw-Hill, 1975.

Bock, R. D., & Bargmann, R. E. Analysis of covariance structure. *Psychometrika*, 1966, *31*, 507–534.

Box, G. E. P. Some theorems on quadratic forms applied in the study of analysis of variance problems. II. Effects of inequality of variance and of correlation between errors in the two-way classifications. *The Annals of Mathematical Statistics*, 1954, *25*, 484–498.

Box, G. E. P., & Jenkins, G. M. *Time-series analysis: Forecasting and control*. San Francisco: Holden-Day, 1976.

Bronfenbrenner, U. Developmental research, public policy, and the ecology of childhood. *Child Development*, 1974, *45*, 1–5.

Bronfenbrenner, U. *Ecology of human development: Experiments by nature and design*. Cambridge: Harvard University Press, 1979.

Bronson, G. W., & Pankey, W. B. On the distinctions between fear and wariness. *Child Development*, 1977, *48*, 1167–1183.

Cairns, R. B. (Ed.). *The analysis of social interaction*. Hillsdale, N.J.: Erlbaum, 1979.

Campbell, D. T. Factors relevant to the validity of experiments in social settings. *Psychological Bulletin*, 1957, *54*, 297–312.

Campbell, D. T., & Stanley, J. C. Experimental and quasi-experimental designs for research on teaching. In N. L. Gage (Ed.), *Handbook of research on teaching*. Chicago: Rand McNally, 1963.

Carroll, J. B. The nature of the data, or how to choose a correlation coefficient. *Psychometrika*, 1961, *26*, 347–372.

Castellan, J. The analysis of behavior sequences. In R. B. Cairns (Ed.), *The analysis of social interaction*. Hillsdale, N.J.: Erlbaum, 1979.

Cohen, J. A coefficient of agreement for nominal scales. *Educational and Psychological Measurement*, 1960, *20*, 37–46.

Cohen, L. B., & Gelber, E. R. Infant visual memory. In L. B. Cohen & P. Salapatek (Eds.), *Infant perception: From sensation to cognition* (Vol. 1). New York: Academic Press, 1975.

Cook, T. D., & Campbell, D. T. *Quasi-experimentations: Designs and analysis issues for field settings*. Chicago: Rand McNally, 1979.

Cramer, E. M. Significance tests and tests of models in multiple regression. *The American Statistician*, 1972, *26*, 26–29.

Cramer, E. M. *MANOVA II*. Chapel Hill, N.C.: L. L. Thurstone Psychometric Laboratory (mimeo), 1976.

Cramer, E. M., & Appelbaum, M. I. Interpreting standardized regression coefficients. Southern Society of Multivariate Experimental Psychologists, New Orleans, March 1976.

Cronbach, L. J. Year-to-year correlations of mental tests: A review of the Hofstaetter analysis. *Child Development*, 1967, *38*, 283–290.

Cronbach, L. J. *Essentials of psychological testing* (3rd ed.). New York: Harper & Row, 1970.

Cronbach, L. J., & Furby, L. How should we measure ''change''—or should we? *Psychological Bulletin*, 1970, *74*, 68–80.

Cronbach, L. J., Rogosa, D. R., Floden, R. E., & Price, G. G. *Analysis of covariance in nonrandomized experiments: Parameters affecting bias.* (Occasional paper.) Berkeley, Calif.: Stanford University, Stanford Evaluation Consortium, 1977.

Darlington, R. B. Multiple regression in psychological research and practice. *Psychological Bulletin*, 1968, *69*, 161–182.

Davis, J. A. Hierarchical models for significance tests in multivariate contingency tables: An exegesis of Goodman's recent papers. In H. L. Costner (Ed.), *Sociological Methodology, 1973–1974.* San Francisco: Jossey-Bass, 1974.

Dixon, W. J. (Ed.). *BMDP Statistical Software.* Berkeley, Calif.: University of California Press, 1981.

Draper, N. R., & Smith H. *Applied regression analyses* (2nd ed.). New York: Wiley, 1981.

Dunn, O. J., & Clark, V. A. Correlation coefficients measured on the same individual. *Journal of the American Statistical Association*, 1969, *64*, 366–377.

Everitt, B. S. Moments of the statistic kappa and weighted kappa. *British Journal of Mathematical and Statistical Psychology*, 1968, *21*, 97–103.

Fienberg, S. E. *The analysis of cross-classified categorical data.* Cambridge, Mass.: MIT Press, 1977.

Finney, D. J. *Probit analysis.* Cambridge: Cambridge University Press, 1971.

Fleiss, J. L. Measuring agreement between two judges on the presence or absence of a trait. *Biometrics*, 1975, *31*, 651–659.

Fleiss, J. L. *Statistical methods for rates and proportions* (2nd ed.). New York: Wiley, 1981.

Fleiss, J. L., & Cicchetti, D. V. Inference about weighted kappa in the non-null case. *Applied Psychological Measurement*, 1978, *2*, 113–117.

Fleiss, J., Cohen, J., & Everitt, B. S. Large sample standard errors of kappa and weighted kappa. *Psychological Bulletin*, 1969, *72*, 323–327.

Gesell, A., & Thompson, H. *Infant behavior.* New York: Greenwood Press, 1934.

Glass, G. V., & Stanley, J. C. *Statistical methods in education and psychology.* Englewood Cliffs: Prentice-Hall, 1970.

Glass, G. V., Willson, V. L., & Gottman, J. M. *Design and analysis of time-series experiments.* Boulder, Colo.: Colorado Associated University Press, 1975.

Goodman, L. A. The multivariate analysis of qualitative data: Interaction among multiple classifications. *Journal of the American Statistical Association*, 1970, *65*, 226–256.

Goodman, L. A., & Kruskal, W. H. Measures of association for cross classifications. *Journal of the American Statistical Association*, 1954, *49*, 732–764.

Goodman, L. A., & Kruskal, W. H. Measures of association for cross classification. IV: Simplification of asymptotic variances. *Journal of the American Statistical Association*, 1972, *67*, 415–421.

Green, P. E. *Analyzing multivariate data.* Hinsdale, Ill.: Dryden Press, 1978.

Greenhouse, S. W., & Geisser, S. On methods in the analysis of profile data. *Psychometrika*, 1959, *24*, 95–112.

Grizzle, J. E., Starmer, C. F., & Koch, G. G. Analysis of categorical data by linear models. *Biometrika*, 1969, *25*, 498–504.

Harman, H. H. *Modern factor analysis* (2nd ed.). Chicago: University of Chicago Press, 1967.

Harris, C. W. *Problems in measuring change.* Madison, Wis.: University of Wisconsin Press, 1967.

Harshman, R. A., & Berenbaum, S. A. Basic concepts underlying the PARAFAC-CANDECOMP three-way factor analysis model and its application to longitudinal data. In D. H. Eichorn, P. H. Mussen, J. A. Clausen, N. Haan, & M. P. Honzik (Eds.), *Present and past in middle life.* New York: Academic Press, 1980.

Hays, W. L. *Statistics* (3rd ed.). New York: Holt, Rinehart & Winston, 1981.

Hibbs, D. A., Jr. On analyzing the effects of policy interventions: Box-Jenkins vs. structural equation models. In D. R. Heise (Ed.), *Sociological Methodology, 1977.* San Francisco: Jossey-Bass, 1977.

Honzik, M. P. Developmental studies of parent-child resemblance in intelligence. *Child Development*, 1957, *28*, 215–228.

Jennrich, R. J. An asymptotic χ^2 test for the equality of two correlation matrices. *Journal of the American Statistical Association*, 1970, *65*(330), 904–912.

Jensen, A. R. Let's understand Skodak and Skeels, finally. *Educational Psychologist*, 1973, *10*, 30–35.

Jensen, A. R. *Bias in mental testing.* New York:

Free Press, 1980.

Jöreskog, K. G. Factoring the multitest-multi-occasion correlation matrix. Princeton, N.J.: Educational Testing Service. Research Bulletin, 1969, No. 69–62.

Jöreskog, K. G. Analysis of covariance structures. In P. R. Krishnaiah (Ed.), *Multivariate analysis-III*. New York: Academic Press, 1973.

Jöreskog, K. G. Statistical models and methods for analysis of longitudinal data. *British Journal of Mathematics and Statistical Psychology*, 1975, 28, 138–151.

Jöreskog, K. G. Statistical estimation of structural models in longitudinal-developmental investigations. In J. R. Nesselroade & P. B. Baltes (Eds.), *Longitudinal research in the study of behavior and development*. New York: Academic Press, 1979.

Jöreskog, K. G., & Sörbom, D. *LISREL IV—A general computer program for estimation of linear structural equation systems by maximum likelihood methods*. Chicago: International Educational Services, 1978.

Jöreskog, K. G., van Thillo, M., & Gruvaeus, G. ACOVSM. A general computer program for analysis of covariance structures including generalized MANOVA (*Research Bulletin, 70–01*), Princeton, N.J.: Educational Testing Service, 1970.

Kenny, D. A. *Correlation and causality*. New York: Wiley-Interscience, 1979.

Kerlinger, F. N., & Pedhazur, E. J. *Multiple regression in behavioral research*. New York: Holt, Rinehart & Winston, 1973.

Kleinbaum, D. G., & Kupper, L. L. *Applied regression analysis and other multivariable methods*. North Scituate, Mass.: Duxbury, 1978.

Koch, G. G., Imrey, P. B., & Reinfurt, D. W. Linear model analysis of categorical data with incomplete response vectors. *Biometrika*, 1972, 28, 663–692.

Kraemer, H. C. On estimation and hypothesis testing problems for correlation coefficients. *Psychometrika*, 1975, 40, 473–485.

Kraemer, H. C., & Jacklin, C. N. Statistical analysis of dyadic social behavior. *Psychological Bulletin*, 1979, 86, 217–224.

Ku, H. H., Varner, R., & Kullback, S. Analyses of multidimensional contingency tables. *Journal of the American Statistical Association*, 1971, 66, 55–64.

Labouvie, E. W. Measurement of individual differences in intraindividual changes. *Psychological Bulletin*, 1980, 88, 54–59.

Landis, J. R., & Koch, G. G. The analysis of categorical data in longitudinal studies of development. In J. R. Nesselroade & P. B. Baltes (Eds.), *Longitudinal research in the study of behavior and development*. New York: Academic Press, 1979.

Landis, J. R., Stanish, W. M., Freeman, J. L., & Koch, G. G. A computer program for the generalized chi-square analysis of categorical data using weighted least square (GENCAT). *Computer Program in Biomedicine*, 1976, 6(4), 196–231.

Larzelere, R. E., & Mulaik, S. A. Single-sample tests for many correlations. *Psychological Bulletin*, 1977, 84, 557–569.

Lord, F. M. A paradox in the interpretation of group comparisons. *Psychological Bulletin*, 1967, 68, 304–305.

McCain, L. J., & McCleary, R. The statistical analysis of the simple interrupted time-series quasi-experiment. In T. D. Cook & D. T. Campbell (Eds.), *Quasi-experimentation: Design & analysis issues for field settings*. Chicago: Rand McNally, 1979.

McCall, R. B. IQ pattern over age: Comparisons among siblings and parent-child pairs. *Science*, 1970, 170, 644–648.

McCall, R. B. Attention in the infant: Avenue to the study of cognitive development. In D. Walcher & D. Peters (Eds.), *Early childhood: The development of self-regulatory mechanisms*. New York: Academic Press, 1971, 107–140.

McCall, R. B. Encoding and retrieval of perceptual memories after long-term familiarization and the infant's response to discrepancy. *Developmental Psychology*, 1973, 9, 310–318.

McCall, R. B. Challenges to a science of developmental psychology. *Child Development*, 1977, 48, 333–334.

McCall, R. B. The development of intellectual functioning in infancy and the prediction of later IQ. In J. D. Osofsky (Ed.), *Handbook of infant development*. New York: Wiley, 1979.

McCall, R. B. *Fundamental statistics for psychology* (3rd ed.). New York: Harcourt Brace Jovanovich, 1980.

McCall, R. B. Nature-nurture and the two realms of development: A proposed integration with respect to mental development. *Child Development*, 1981, 52, 1–12.

McCall, R. B., & Appelbaum, M. I. Bias in the analysis of repeated measures designs: Some alternative approaches. *Child Development*, 1973, 44, 401–415.

McCall, R. B., Appelbaum, M. I., & Hogarty, P. S. Developmental changes in mental performance. *Monographs of the Society for Research in Child Development,* 1973, *38*(Serial No. 150).

McCall, R. B., & McGhee, P. E. The discrepancy hypothesis of attention and affect in human infants. In I. C. Uzgiris & F. Weizmann (Eds.), *The structuring of experience.* New York: Plenum, 1977.

McDonald, R. P. Numerical methods for polynomial models in nonlinear factor analysis. *Psychometrika Monographs,* 1967, *32,* 77–112.

Morrison, D. F. *Multivariate statistical methods.* New York: McGraw-Hill, 1976.

Mosteller, F., & Tukey, J. W. *Data analysis and regression.* Reading, Mass.: Addison-Wesley, 1977.

Mulaik, S. *The foundations of factor analysis.* New York: McGraw-Hill, 1972.

Murray, J. P., & Kippax, S. Television diffusion and social behaviour in three communities: A field experiment. *Australian Journal of Psychology,* 1977, *29,* 31–43.

Nesselroade, J. R. Application of multivariate strategies to problems of measuring and structuring long-term change. In L. R. Goulet & P. B. Baltes (Eds.), *Life-span developmental psychology: Research and theory.* New York: Academic Press, 1970.

Nesselroade, J. R., & Baltes, P. B. Adolescent personality development and historical change: 1970–1972. *Monographs of the Society for Research in Child Development,* 1974, *39*(Serial No. 154).

Nesselroade, J. R., & Baltes, P. B. (Eds.). *Longitudinal research in the study of behavior and development.* New York: Academic Press, 1979.

Nesselroade, J. R., & Reese, H. W. *Life-span developmental psychology: Methodological issues.* New York: Academic Press, 1973.

Nunnally, J. C. *Psychometric theory.* New York: McGraw-Hill, 1967.

O'Brien, R. G. Robust techniques for testing heterogeneity of variance effects in factorial designs. *Psychometrika,* 1978, *43,* 327–342.

Olkin, I. Correlations revisited. In J. Stanley (Ed.), *Improving experimental design and statistical analysis.* Chicago: Rand McNally, 1967.

Osofsky, J. D. (Ed.). *Handbook of infant development.* New York: Wiley, 1979.

Overall, J. E., & Klett, C. J. *Applied multivariate analysis.* New York: McGraw-Hill, 1972.

Overall, J. E., & Woodward, J. A. Nonrandom assignment and the analysis of covariance. *Psycho-logical Bulletin,* 1977, *84,* 588–594.

Overton, W. F., & Reese, H. W. Conceptual prerequisite for an understanding of stability-change and continuity-discontinuity. *International Journal of Behavioral Development,* 1981, *4,* 99–123.

Reichardt, C. S. The statistical analysis of data from nonequivalent group designs. In T. D. Cook & D. T. Campbell (Eds.), *Quasi-experimentation: Design & analysis issues for field settings.* Chicago: Rand McNally, 1979.

Robson, D. S. A simple method for construction of orthogonal polynomials when the independent variable is unequally spaced. *Biometrics,* 1959, *15,* 187–191.

Rogosa, D. A critique of cross-lagged correlation. *Psychological Bulletin,* 1980, *88,* 245–258.

Sackett, G. P. (Ed.). *Observing behavior: Data collection and analysis methods.* Baltimore: University Park Press, 1978.

Sackett, G. P. The lag sequential analysis of contingency and cyclicity in behavioral interaction research. In J. D. Osofsky (Ed.), *Handbook of infant development.* New York: Wiley, 1979.

Sameroff, A. J., & Chandler, M. J. Reproductive risk and the continuum of caretaking casualty. In F. D. Horowitz (Ed.), *Review of child development research* (Vol. 4). Chicago: University of Chicago Press, 1975.

SAS User's Guide: Statistics. Cary, N.C.: SAS Institute, 1982.

Schaie, K. W. A general model for the study of developmental problems. *Psychological Bulletin,* 1965, *64,* 92–107.

Shrout, P. E., & Fleiss, J. L. Intraclass correlations: Uses in assessing rater reliability. *Psychological Bulletin,* 1979, *86,* 420–428.

Siegel, S., & Tukey, J. W. A non-parametric sum of rank procedure for relative spread in unpaired samples. *Journal of the American Statistical Association,* 1960, *55,* 429–455.

Siegel, S., & Tukey, J. W. Correction. *Journal of the American Statistical Association,* 1961, *56,* 1005.

Skodak, M., & Skeels, H. M. A final follow-up study of 100 adopted children. *Journal of Genetic Psychology,* 1949, *75,* 85–125.

Sörbom, D., & Jöreskog, K. G. *Confirmatory factor analysis with model modification.* Chicago: International Educational Services, 1976.

Stanley, J. C. Reliability. In R. L. Thorndike (Ed.), *Educational measurement.* Washington, D.C.: American Education, 1971.

Steiger, J. H. Tests for comparing elements of a

correlation matrix. *Psychological Bulletin,* 1980, *87,* 245–251.

Stevens, S. S. (Ed.). *Handbook of experimental psychology.* New York: Wiley, 1951.

Tanner, J. M. The regulation of human growth. *Child Development, 1963, 34,* 817–848.

Thompson, R. A., Lamb, M. A., & Estes, D. Stability of infant-mother attachment and its relationship to changing life circumstances in an unselected middle-class sample. *Child Development, 1982, 53,* 144–148.

Thurstone, L. L. *Multiple factor analysis.* Chicago: University of Chicago Press, 1947.

Tucker, L. R *Determination of generalized learning curves by factor analysis.* Educational Testing Service Technical Report, 1960.

Tucker, L. R Learning theory and multivariate ex-

periment: Illustration by determination of generalized learning curves. In R. B. Cattell (Ed.), *Handbook of multivariate experimental psychology.* Chicago: Rand McNally, 1966. (a)

Tucker, L. R Some mathematical notes on three-mode factor analysis. *Psychometrika, 1966, 31,* 279–311. (b)

Wheaton, B., Muthén, B., Alwin, D. F., & Summers, G. G. Assessing reliability and stability in panel models. In D. R. Heise (Ed.), *Sociological Methodology 1977.* San Francisco: Jossey-Bass, 1977.

Winer, B. J. *Statistical principles in experimental design.* New York: McGraw-Hill, 1971.

Wohlwill, J. F. *The study of behavioral development.* New York: Academic Press, 1973.

ASSESSMENT OF CHILDREN | 10

SAMUEL MESSICK, *Educational Testing Service*

CHAPTER CONTENTS

This chapter addresses both the psychometrics of child assessment and the psychometrics of child development—that is, both the assessment of human characteristics at a given point in time and the assessment of differences over time in variables and structures. Basic concepts of standard psychometric theory are reviewed in depth: such theory essentially comprises a psychometrics of stasis or steady state. Moreover, because several standards of psychometric adequacy tend to break down in the face of rapid development of the processes being assessed, the clear need for a formal psychometrics of change is underscored.

The major facets and media of assessment are examined, and the role of context is analyzed as both a contaminant and facilitator of measurement interpretation. Throughout, it is assumed that psychological measurement must be justified on a value basis in terms of the social consequences of its use, as well as on a scientific basis in terms of psychometric evidence. Indeed, in our view, as explicated elsewhere, social values must be explicitly incorporated within the central unifying concept of validity (Messick, 1980, 1981b). And because we hold validity to be an overall judgment, along with supporting data and rationales, of the adequacy *and appro-*

priateness of inferences and actions based on test scores, we maintain that the ethics of assessment is an integral part of the assessment process.

In the assessment of children's characteristics, the emphasis is on the dependability of test scores, which is the issue of reliability, and on the trustworthiness of inferences derived from them, which is the issue of construct validity. The concern is not to explain any single behavior or item response, which almost certainly reflects a confounding of multiple determinants, but rather to account for *consistency* in behaviors or item responses, which frequently reflects a small number of distinguishable determinants. As opposed to treating the item responses or behaviors in question separately as a conglomeration of specifics, these behavioral and response consistencies are typically summarized in the form of total scores or subscores, which then serve as measures or indicants of the underlying determinants. We thus move from the level of discrete behavior to the level of measurement, the key point being that in educational and psychological measurement inferences are drawn from *scores*, a term used here in the most general sense of any coding or summarization of behavioral consistency on a test, observation procedure, or other assessment device.

The emphasis in psychometrics is on scores or measurements as opposed to tests or instruments because the psychometric properties that signify adequate assessment are properties of scores, not tests—tests do not have reliabilities and validities, only test responses do. This is an important point because test responses are a function not only of the stimulus conditions, items, or tasks but of the *persons* responding and the *context* of assessment. Thus, as we shall see, the generalizability of psychometric properties across population groups and situational contexts becomes a pervasive and perennial empirical question.

In the assessment of development or change, the emphasis is on three distinct kinds of differences over time: on differences in performance levels and variability, which raise the issue of growth versus decline; on differences in the relative ordering of individuals, which point to the issue of stability versus instability; and, on differences in the structure of interrelationships among measures, which give focus to the issue of continuity versus discontinuity. Central to each of these distinct but interconnected issues is the notion of construct validity and the extent to which it is generalizable over time. This is so because construct validity undergirds the interpretive meaning of measures and constructs, and the resolution of these three basic issues entails a disentangling of developmental changes in the meaning of measures from developmental changes in the meaning of the constructs assessed.

Although this chapter does not cover the evaluation of childhood intervention programs, it should be noted that these same issues of reliability and construct validity arise in program evaluation with respect to the measurement of outcomes and the assessment of change. Program evaluation is even more complicated, however, because of the additional question of whether any observed changes may be causally attributed to a particular program or treatment rather than to the operation of other factors such as normal growth during that period. A further complication is that program evaluation is typically embedded in an ideological context of social values in which concern is not only with program effectiveness or treatment impact but also with such politically salient issues as efficiency of implementation and equity of access. But all inferences and actions based on test scores, whether in the laboratory or applied settings, occur in ideological contexts, which means that the issues of validity and values are inherently intertwined and that the ethics of assessment is a fundamental and continuing concern in all test interpretation and use.

VICISSITUDES OF MEASUREMENT WITH CHILDREN

The key issues in the assessment of children and of early developmental change, as well as in the evaluation of childhood intervention programs, are essentially the same as those arising in assessment and evaluation generally at any age or developmental level (Messick & Barrows, 1972). The major recurring questions are these: What characteristics or variables should be assessed? How adequate is their measurement—in particular, how good are the scores as dependable measures of the constructs they are interpreted to assess? How should observed changes be interpreted—in particular, do scores retain the same meaning over time, or do they reflect qualitatively different relational structures? Can changes associated with intervention programs be causally interpreted—in particular, can they be defensibly attributed to specific childcare or educational treatments? And, finally, can the assessment and evaluation findings be generalized to other populations and other settings? These are difficult questions at best, but they are exacerbated even further during childhood by the vagaries of measurement with young children and by the occurrence of rapid development in the early years.

Vagaries in Test Performance

In the assessment of young children, many problems that are ordinarily handled by the standardization of instructions and procedures and by reliance on the past testing experience and expectations of the respondents become highly magnified by virtue of the limited experience and understanding of many youngsters in coping with novel task demands. These include problems of establishing rapport and motivation; of ensuring that instructions are well understood; of maintaining attention; and, of coping with boredom, distraction, and fatigue. For example, to what extent do the instructions effectively orient the child, and are there procedures for reorientation if the child displays deviant or irrelevant behavior? There are also special problems of orientation associated with the use of fixed time limits because of the mixed messages that timed tasks convey about the relative importance of speed and accuracy.

Features of the assessment setting may also influence behavior in either facilitating or debilitating ways, especially with young children. Assessment occurs in a context of relationships between the child and the physical surround—task materials, furnishings, lighting, ventilation, temperature, and so forth—but, more importantly, between the child and the social surround—including the examiner, other children, and social expectancies such as a sense of freedom, a sense of task orientation, a sense of being evaluated or, indeed, an apprehension over being evaluated. Is there one examiner with one child, or is there group as opposed to individual administration? Apart from instructions that ingenuously call for "playing a game," are there indications of a relaxed, gamelike atmosphere? Or is there a testlike or schoollike atmosphere in which the asking of questions implies the existence of correct or desirable answers?

Given these and many other pertinent questions, it is apparent that the social psychology of the assessment context requires careful attention. Nor should such attention be limited to the assessment setting per se but should also be directed to relevant aspects of the child's background and history. For example, is the task meaningful to the child in terms of prior life experience, or does it assume a special or different meaning in the assessment context? As an instance, a child may exhibit apparent lack of understanding of the preposition "on" when asked in the assessment context to "put the circle *on* the square," while in the classroom setting the same child readily complies with the request to "put the truck on the shelf" (Sigel, 1974).

We are thus faced with the fundamental question of whether the meaning of a psychological measure is context specific or whether it generalizes across contexts. On the one hand, especially in the assessment of young children, we are compelled by a principle of contextualization, which holds that the context in which a task is presented alters its very nature by virtue of constraining or facilitating factors inherent in the specific situation (Sigel, 1974). On the other hand, we note that standardization of testing conditions and the use of relatively novel items or tasks contributes to objectivity and comparability of scores across respondents and settings. Rather than opt for one position or the other, in this chapter we urge that the role of context in test interpretation be repeatedly investigated and continuously monitored as a recurrent empirical question in each new measurement effort. Although later sections of the chapter stress the importance of assessing the context as well as the child and of assessing child characteristics in a context similar to the one for which inferences are to be drawn or predictions made, this is intended not as a deliberate move toward context-specific measurement, though that may indeed be required empirically in particular instances, but rather as a means of facilitating the systematic examination of generalizability across contexts.

One of the major goals of assessment is to maximize the validity of test interpretation and to minimize construct-irrelevant task difficulty, much of which derives from context. But this is typically in the service of predictability to other behaviors, times, and settings. To the degree that standardization or experimental control cannot eliminate construct-irrelevant variance or that contexts differentially influence the response processes and hence bias the meaning of the scores, then interpretation and predictability will need to be moderated by context. But one thing is certain—generality cannot be taken for granted nor can context be ignored.

Rapidity of Early Development

The assessment of children is also rendered problematic by the occurrence of rapid changes, especially during the early years. It is difficult to assess a child's characteristics adequately at a given point in time—to take a psychometric snapshot, as it were—if those characteristics are in effect moving targets. In standard psychometric terms, adequate measurement entails some degree of internal consistency or homogeneity of response across items or tasks and some degree of at least short-term stability. For many characteristics, these properties can be demonstrated and, if continuity of correlational patterns or factor structures can also be established, then growth may be assessed in terms of score increments on variables having relatively constant construct meaning. In other instances, however, internal structure may appear fragmented, or there may be instability of scores even over the short run. Such fragmentation and instability are usually taken as evidence of inadequate measurement, but they may instead indicate that change is taking place. This is one of the main reasons for seeking a psychometrics of change as well as a psychometrics of steady state.

DOMAINS OF MEASUREMENT

This section deals first with some recurrent distinctions concerning the objects and objectives of psychological measurement; then, with the major classes of experimental procedures or media of assessment; and, finally, with the primary systems of variables to be assessed, including variables relevant to the child, to both the measurement and experiential contexts, and to interactions among them. Thus, before proceeding to the assessment of psychological structure in the following section on Psychometrics of Steady State, we place equal emphasis on the nature and choice of variables to be structured and the experimental methods for obtaining basic measurements, on the grounds that these are just as important for the ultimate quality of score interpretations as are the logical and mathematical means of educing generalizations.

Facets of Measurement

A number of distinctions are made in the measurement arena with sufficient persistence that the points ought to be recognized and examined, although not necessarily taken at face value. These distinctions are stated as dichotomous contrasts, but in most instances the contrasts are not sharply etched in actuality—rather, the contrasted concepts frequently overlap or are intertwined or represent two faces of the same coin. They include the following.

Trait versus Response Class

A trait is a relatively enduring characteristic of a person—an attribute, process, or disposition—which is consistently manifested to an appropriate degree when relevant, despite considerable variation in the range of settings and circumstances. A response class is a class of behaviors all of which change in the same or related ways as a function of stimulus contingencies—that is, they all reflect essentially the same change in the person's relation to the environment. Some psychologists interpret behavioral consistencies—whether on tests or in nontest situations—to be manifestations of traits, which serve to organize the behavior or otherwise produce response consistencies (e.g., Allport, 1937, 1961; Cattell, 1957). In this view, traits are "broad patterns of determining tendencies that confer upon personality such consistency as it displays" (Allport & Odbert, 1936, p. 13).

Other psychologists such as Skinner (1971) maintain that behaviors, including test behaviors, are consistently related because they are elicited and maintained by the same or related environmental conditions, especially reinforcement conditions (cf. Anastasi, 1948; Tryon, 1979). In this view, related behaviors form a response class because they enter the same functional relationships with antecedent, concurrent, or consequent stimulus conditions; it is these environmental contingencies, rather than traits, that control their operation. At issue is whether dispositional traits are real attributes of persons or whether the behavioral consistencies they refer to are instead elicited and maintained by environmental or situational factors, which in turn are the real entities (Messick, 1981a). Some psychologists, of course, adopt intermediate views; they attribute some behavioral consistencies to traits, some to situational factors, and some to interactions between them, in various and arguable proportions (Bowers, 1973; Ekehammar, 1974).

Trait versus State

In contrast to connotations of relative stability and enduringness associated with traits, states are conceptualized as temporary conditions of mentality or mood, transitory levels of arousal or drive, and currently evoked activity. States are typically readily reversible, being subject to relatively rapid changes in level. However, the distinction between traits and states appears to be both arbitrary and vague (Allen & Potkay, 1981). For example, when individual susceptibility to a particular state, such as anxiety, becomes chronic, it would appear to qualify as a trait. Furthermore, typical lists of traits and states not only share many labels in common, but the so-called state lists include terms ordinarily classified as traits and vice versa (Allen & Potkay, 1981). Thus, the same label can and often does refer to both a state and a trait.

Moreover, whether a self-report instrument measures a state or a trait apparently depends on the instructions accompanying it, such as "describe yourself today" as opposed to "describe yourself in general." State is thereby often taken as short-term feeling or functioning and trait as a long-term summary or average, with trait scores actually being derived on occasion by summing over units or blocks of state data (Zuckerman, 1979). Patterson and Bechtel (1977), as an instance, explicitly define trait as an average state level measured over many different situations. It would not be surprising, then, if a given trait measure were influenced by the day's states or a state measure were influenced by the individual's trait level—an individual who typically has high anxiety is not very likely to exhibit many low anxious states nor is an individual who typically has low anxiety likely to exhibit many high anxious states in the absence of extraordinary stimulation.

In principle, traits and states may be more effectively disentangled by means of repeated multivariate measurement over relatively short time spans. Under these circumstances, factor structures that have patterns of loadings which are invariant over time and show relatively stable factor scores may be distinguished from similarly invariant structures which show relatively fluctuant factor scores. The latter combination of invariant factor loadings and fluctuant factor scores provides a structural representation of states. The former combination of stable factor scores and invariant factor loadings, along with stable factor scores combined with variant factor loadings, would represent traits—with the invariant loadings signaling relative continuity of process or meaning and the variant loadings signaling relative discontinuity. Indeed, such a multivariate longitudinal perspective might free us from the state/trait distinction altogether by making it clear that stability would be more fruitfully regarded not as a loose dichotomy of state versus trait but as a continuum of values (Buss, 1974; Nesselroade & Bartsch, 1977).

Signs versus Samples

Test behaviors may be taken as signs of other behaviors which they do not ordinarily resemble and as indicants of underlying traits. They may also be viewed as samples of behaviors essentially similar to those for which predictions are to be made (Goodenough, 1949; Loevinger, 1957). For trait theorists, test behaviors are largely signs of psychological structures, whereas for behaviorists and social behaviorists, they are largely samples of response classes (Wiggins, 1973). Many psychologists use tests as both signs and samples, being concerned both with predispositions to respond stably over time across various environmental conditions (traits) and with current patterns of reaction under specific environment conditions (states). This is not to say that signs and samples are coordinate with traits and states, for trait behaviors may be directly sampled and states may be indicated by symptoms or signs.

Structure versus Process

As employed in psychology, the term "structure" is usually contrasted with "process" or "function" in one usage or with "change" in another. Structure is contrasted with process or function even though most examples of mental structure such as ability, attitude, or temperament are inferred directly from process or function, and most mental processes or functions themselves exhibit structure. As a consequence, it is the contrast of structure with change, especially rapid or paroxysmal change, which reveals its essential distinguishing feature. In this light, "structures are stable, relatively enduring components of [psychological] organization that are invoked to account for recurrent similarities and consistencies in behavior over time and over situations" (Messick, 1961, p. 94). A key operative word in this formulation is "relatively," for we are speaking of stability, not fixity.

Psychological structures are usually inferred in one way or another from consistent individual differences in behavior. In factor analytic terms, such intercorrelated behaviors yield factors and organized structures of factorial relationships. Indeed, as Rapaport (1959) and many other theorists have pointed out, structural determiners of behavior were introduced as intervening variables in the first place because of the problem of consistent individual differences—that is, neither external stimuli nor internal motivations accounted for individual behavior uniformly in a one-to-one fashion. Yet, a structure versus process distinction is a fuzzy one at best: processes are often highly *structured* into hierarchies, organized sequences, or stages that are identifiable mainly through consistent individual differences while structures, including factor structures, often reflect commonalities in psychological *processes*. Thus, structure and process appear to go hand in hand. Having noted that this kind of parallelism between structure and process cuts across methodologies, Carroll (1978) opined that "perhaps this is the way things are—the way the world is. That is, perhaps processes are clearly identifiable *only* through their association with individual differences, and perhaps it is inevitable that there should be individual differences associated with any given psychological process" (p. 110).

Normative versus Ipsative Structures

Most test scores in psychology and education serve to order individuals with respect to some attribute or variable. Such scores are called *normative* because they form the distribution of subjects' attribute values in any reference group and allow comparisons *between* individuals in levels of performance or trait. So-called *ipsative* scores, in contrast, serve to order a set of variables or traits for each individual (Cattell, 1944). They allow comparisons *within* individuals in the relative level of each trait vis-à-vis the other traits assessed.

In an ipsative test for a set of variables or traits, the sum of subtest scores for the traits is a constant for each individual. This is because the individual's mean performance level across those subtests is either removed statistically or never assessed in the first place by virtue of employing such systematically restricted response formats as paired comparisons among the traits, rank orderings of the traits, or Q-sorts of the traits by or for each individual (Block 1961; Edwards, 1954; Stephenson, 1953). For a statistically ipsatized measure, the individual's mean score across subtests for the variables or traits is subtracted from each of that individual's trait scores—in contrast to a normative deviation score, in which the mean trait score across the total group of respondents is subtracted from each individual's trait score. That is, for statistically ipsatized scores, the person's mean across the trait subtests is subtracted from that person's subtest scores for each of the traits; whereas for normative deviation scores, the trait subtest mean across persons is subtracted from each person's score on that particular subtest. Similarly, to obtain ipsative *standard* scores, the ipsative score deviation around the person's mean is divided by the person's standard deviation, in contrast with normative standard scores in which the normative score deviation around the test mean is divided by the test standard deviation.

Since trait scores on an ipsative measure are relative to each person's mean level across the traits assessed, the intercorrelations among ipsative trait scores are statistically constrained in important ways because an individual scoring relatively high on some of the traits must score relatively low on other traits. These constraints operate in such a way that the sum of each column in an ipsative intertrait *covariance* matrix must always equal zero (Radcliffe, 1963). Furthermore, if the ipsative trait variances are equal, the sum of each column in an ipsative intertrait *correlation* matrix is also zero, and the average off-diagonal correlation takes on its limiting lower-bound value of $\frac{-1}{n-1}$). Thus, the average correlations of $-.071$ and $-.181$, respectively, reported in the test manuals among the 15 scores on the Edwards (1954) *Personal Preference Schedule* and among the six scores on the Allport, Vernon, and Lindzey (1960) *Study of Values* are statistical

requirements of ipsative measures and do not provide evidence that the variables assessed are relatively independent. Worse still, the covariances of a set of ipsative scores with any normative variable, including various applied criteria of interest, also sum to zero, as do the correlations if the ipsative variables have equal variances (Radcliffe, 1963). Thus, when used normatively—that is, to describe or interrelate orderings of individuals on the particular variables or traits—the score interpretations and resulting intertrait correlations of ipsative measures, as well as their external validity in predicting normative criteria, are constrained in complicated ways.

On the other hand, when used ipsatively—that is, to describe or interrelate orderings of variables or traits for particular individuals—the score interpretations and resulting interperson correlations have straightforward meaning. With respect to score interpretations, ipsative measures portray *intraindividual patterns* of variables or traits. For example, they might describe the relative prominence of an individual's needs or values or other personality characteristics, the relative intensity of a person's interests, or the comparative strengths and weaknesses of a person's abilities or achievements. With respect to interrelationships, interperson correlations reveal between-person similarities in patterns of variables or traits, and factor analysis of interperson correlations—the so-called Q-technique (Cattell, 1978; Ross, 1963; Stephenson, 1953)—reveals clusters or types of individuals who share patterns of traits.

The concept of *ipsative structure*—or the intraindividual organization of attributes or traits—is a potentially important one for developmental measurement and research because key properties of an individual's psychological structure may differ systematically over time (Emmerich, 1968). For example, developmental differences may appear in the number of differentiated attributes or traits in the individual's repertoire and in the manner of their organization; if the organization is hierarchical, there may be developmental changes in the number of levels in the hierarchy or in the location of particular attributes. Moreover, speaking normatively, individuals may also differ one from another in these same structural properties, as well as in the relative complexity versus simplicity of their structures and in the developmental course of structural change. Although not yet widely studied because of methodological difficulties, such ipsative structures and their developmental changes may be at least tentatively addressed by using a variety of factor analytic and scaling techniques, including Q-technique applied to interperson correlations over time (Block, 1971; Cattell, 1978; Wohlwill, 1973).

Nomothetic versus Idiographic Methods

A perennial though controversial and somewhat anachronistic distinction is frequently drawn in psychological assessment between those methods and procedures designed to discover general laws, which are called nomothetic, and those methods attempting to characterize a particular event or individual, which are called idiographic (Allport, 1937, 1961, 1962, 1966; Beck, 1953; Eysenck, 1954; Falk, 1956; Holt, 1962; Meehl, 1954). Although a number of psychologists have attempted to resolve or dismiss this distinction in its "generalizing" versus "individualizing" form, it still persists in a slightly different guise. Eysenck (1954), for example, holds that "*the science of personality must by its very nature be nomothetic*" (p. 341). Holt (1962) maintains that "the idiographic point of view is an artistic one that strives for a nonscientific goal; the nomothetic, a caricature of science that bears little resemblance to anything that exists today. Since no useful purpose is served by retaining these mischievous and difficult terms, they had best disappear from our scientific vocabularies" (p. 402). Yet Allport (1962) insists on preserving a nomothetic versus idiographic distinction, though it is now couched in subtly different phrasing that shifts the emphasis in important ways—he no longer stresses generalizing versus individualizing but rather "seeking general laws" versus "dealing with structured pattern" (p. 408).

Allport's (1962, 1966) view of structured pattern embraces two distinguishable features. One is the point that individuals differ in the ways in which traits are interrelated and organized intraindividually, which is the issue of ipsative structure. The other is that individuals also differ in terms of *which* traits are personally important, relevant, or salient. Since Allport (1966) at one point called methods that attempt to identify and characterize a person's central or salient traits "idiomorphic," that term will be used here to highlight the potential importance of assessing traits in terms of their relevance or personal value. Accordingly, intraindividual patterns of personally important or central traits will here be termed *idiomorphic structures*. In contrast with ipsative structures—which are intraindividual organizations of dimensions or traits applied generically to each individual in terms of level, intensity, or strength—idiomorphic structures are intraindividual organizations of dimensions or traits applicable to the particular individual in terms of relevance, importance, or salience. Idiomorphic structures are predicated on the notion that not all psychological dimensions or traits apply to each person and that a critical source of individual differences derives from precisely which traits are central, important, or valued by the person. As a further complication, the relevance or importance of a trait for an individual's behavior may vary from one situation to another.

A number of idiomorphic methods have been proposed to assess the individual's personally relevant and most consistent traits (Bem & Allen, 1974; Kelly, 1955; Kenrick & Stringfield, 1980; Lamiell, 1981), but since different traits are applicable to different individuals, this approach has profound ramifications for psychological measurement. It is not just that "one simply cannot, in principle, ever do any better than predicting some of the people some of the time" (Bem & Allen, 1974, pp. 511–512), but that in any instance one may assess idiomorphically only some of the people in comparable ways. But it may be possible to assess somewhat more of the people in terms of comparable constructs, albeit the construct measures for various individuals may be topographically dissimilar.

Norm-referenced versus Criterion-referenced Interpretations

In addition to interpreting a person's performance level or trait position normatively in terms of how other individuals score on that dimension or trait, ipsatively in terms of that person's relative scores on other dimensions or traits, or idiomorphically in terms of the relative importance or salience of that dimension or trait in the individual's repertoire, scores may also be interpreted criterially in terms of performance standards or behavioral referents. Scores interpreted within this latter framework are called *criterion-referenced*, typically in contradistinction to *norm-referenced* scores.

A norm-referenced test is one that is constructed to yield scores that optimally discriminate among individuals on the trait measured by the test and that are interpreted in terms of the relative performance of other individuals and groups on the same test. "A criterion-referenced test is one that is deliberately constructed to yield measurements that are directly interpretable in terms of specified performance standards" (Glaser & Nitko, 1971, p. 653). If the items are geared to particular educational or developmental objectives, the test is usually termed an "objectives-referenced'' measure. If the items systematically represent a well-defined content area or if they sample a well-specified domain of tasks, the test is sometimes termed a ''content-referenced'' measure or a ''domain-referenced'' measure. Usually, a criterion-referenced interpretation either describes the individual's level of performance on content similar to the test—for example, ''this vocabulary score implies ability to interpret 80% of words at the difficulty level illustrated by *obvious, overwhelm, persuasive,* and *sentiment*''—or else predicts the individual's behavior in a situation dissimilar to the test—for example, ''a student with this vocabulary score who enters training for accountant has a 4-to-1 chance of completing the course'' (Cronbach, 1970, p. 85).

Since meaningful criterion-referenced interpretations can be made for a single individual in isolation, score distributions are not requisite for criterion-referenced tests as they are for norm-referenced tests. Indeed, score distributions are often quite constrained or truncated in such typical applications of criterion-referenced tests as certification of mastery or minimum competence. However, normative comparisons can of course be made with criterion-referenced tests, either with formal norms or without, at least to the degree that the obtained score variation provides useful discrimination among respondents. Thus, a criterion-referenced test may be used for norm-referenced measurement, but it has the disadvantage that it was not constructed to maximize score variability; on the contrary, criterion-referenced tests frequently yield relatively homogeneous score distributions and thus typically provide less than optimal discrimination among individuals (Hambleton & Novick, 1973). Similarly, a norm-referenced test may be used for criterion-referenced interpretations, but it is unlikely to provide adequate coverage for assessing performance changes because many relevant items that were either too easy or too hard at a particular level of development or training will have been left out since they did not discriminate among individuals.

In addition to this fuzzy overlap in application, there is also a fuzzy overlap in conception. In the present state of the art, all procedures for establishing performance standards for criterion-referenced interpretation require judgment at some point, and these judgments often involve normative comparisons either explicitly or tacitly. But at the level of interpretation, the distinction seems clear: A norm-referenced interpretation compares an individual's test performance with the performance of others, whereas a criterion-referenced interpretation compares it with a performance standard (Messick, 1975).

Competence versus Performance

An important distinction is made in psycholinguistics between competence and performance (Chomsky, 1957, 1965) that seems just as compelling for psychological functioning generally. Applicable as a general principle, this distinction has profound implications for test interpretation. Linguistic competence refers to the system of rules that characterizes a person's abstract knowledge of language structure; it constitutes a formal grammar of that person's language. Linguistic performance refers to the processes involved in actual language behavior in task situations. More generally, competence is the formal structure of what a person knows and can do under ideal circumstances, whereas performance is what is actually done under existing circumstances. Competence embraces the structure of knowledge and abilities, whereas performance subsumes as well the processes of accessing and utilizing those structures and a host of affective, motivational, attentional, and stylistic factors that influence the ultimate responses.

Since these two types of mediating variables—cognitive structures and response factors—may be differentially learned or developed at a given point in time, a child's competence might not be validly revealed in a particular test performance because response factors were inadequately mastered or controlled (Flavell & Wohlwill, 1969; Overton & Newman, 1982). Although competence may be defensibly inferred from *correct* task performance, especially if consistently demonstrated across related tasks, as a general rule it is dangerous to make inferences about competence or incompetence from *incorrect* performance. To do that requires the discounting of a variety of plausible rival sources of poor performance, such as inattention, memory limitations, anxiety, low motivation, or fatigue.

Maximal Performance versus Typical Performance

Measures of maximal performance attempt to assess how well individuals *can* perform at their best; they include tests of ability, knowledge, and competence. Measures of typical performance attempt to assess what individuals are *likely* to do in a given situation or in a broad class of situations; they include tests of interests, attitudes, habits, and personality (Cronbach, 1970). Many tests cut across these categories in a variety of ways. Some measures of cognitive style, for example, attempt to assess what individuals typically do or prefer to do on cognitive tasks when they are striving to do their best (Kogan, 1971; Messick, 1976).

Correctness versus Goodness of Response

In the literature on creativity in contradistinction to intelligence, a distinction is proffered between correctness and goodness as one means of differentiating intellective from creative responses (Jackson & Messick, 1965). Intellective responses are judged in terms of correctness or accuracy, by the degree to which certain objective and logical criteria have been satisfied. The criteria of correctness tend to be categorical—they usally admit only one answer or a relatively restricted set, with all other responses regarded as incorrect or in error. In contrast, creative responses are judged in terms of goodness or worth, by the degree to which certain subjective and psychological criteria have been satisfied. The criteria of goodness tend to be continuous—they admit a wide range of responses that vary in the degree of their acceptability and appropriateness. As Guilford (1957) phrased it, "There are different bases or criteria by which a product is judged. One is its logical consistency with known facts. Another is its less-than-logical consistency with other experiences" (p. 116).

The distinction between correctness and goodness has a number of implications for measurement. One is that although the ubiquitous cumulative scoring model may be eminently acceptable for toting up *correct* answers into total scores, other models that accommodate both frequency and quality in noncompensatory ways may be needed for scoring overall goodness. For example, consider that two individuals have each produced 10 creative responses, with each response being rated on a 10-point scale of goodness. Suppose further that one individual received 10 ratings of unity and that the other received nine ratings of zero and a single rating of 10. Should the same overall score be given to both individuals, as would happen using traditional weighted summations? Another implication is that although correct responses can be scored objectively using answer templates or machines, humanness may be required to judge goodness. As Santayana (1896) put it, "for the existence of good in any form it is not merely consciousness but emotional consciousness that is needed. Observation will not do, appreciation is required" (p. 16).

Content versus Style

All human activity has both a substantive and a stylistic character. However, since each act is intrinsically integral, it is only through a somewhat arbitrary analysis that these two primary aspects may be separately assessed. Nonetheless, the distinction is fundamental in psychological measurement because an individual's style of functioning creates a force field affecting both the interpretation of substantive content and the appraisal of performance levels. Furthermore, since style reflects "the oblique mirroring of personal traits" (Allport, 1961, p. 462), sometimes these personality attributes extend and enhance the substantive or content aspects of performance and sometimes they distort and interfere with substantive functioning, depending upon the nature and intensity of the personality characteristics manifested stylistically. Thus explicit measures of style may not only tap deeper personality structures of interest in their own right, but can contribute directly to a disentangling of substantive and stylistic effects, whether they be mutually supportive or distortive. In short, we wish both to control styles as contaminating influences in content measurement and to measure styles as personality variables of potential importance (Jackson & Messick, 1958).

In regard to measurement, the basic distinction between substance and style contrasts the *content* and *level* of performance—the questions of what? and how much?—with the *manner* or *form* of performance—the question of how? Emphasis on consistent individual differences in level of performance in particular content areas has led to the delineation of psychological dimensions or traits largely in content terms, such as numerical ability, scientific interest, religious attitude, economic value, need for achievement, introversion, and hypochondriasis. Emphasis on consistent individual differences in the manner or mode of performance has led to the delineation of psychological dimensions or traits largely in stylistic terms, such as fluency, preference for complexity, dogmatism, need for variety, impulsivity, and paranoia. In addition to such psychological dimensions characterized primarily in terms of their salient stylistic features, a number of dimensions have been conceptualized intrinsically as *being* styles in a more fundamental sense. These latter styles are especially important from a measurement standpoint because they illuminate the manner and process of performance as opposed to the content and outcome of performance. Furthermore, since these individual styles refer to consistencies in the *way* psychological substance is processed rather than to consistencies in the substance itself, they may entail mechanisms for the organization and control of processes that cut across substantive areas.

Among these basic styles are *response styles* operating in self-description and self-report, such as the tendencies to be acquiescent, critical, socially desirable, or extreme in self-presentation (Berg, 1967; Messick, 1968; Wiggins, 1973); *cognitive styles* operating in perception, remembering, thinking, and problem solving, such as field independence versus field dependence, scanning versus focusing, and broad versus narrow categorizing (Kogan, 1971, 1976; Messick, 1976, 1982); and *expressive styles* operating in facial, motoric, vocal, and graphic expression, such as speed, tempo, and constriction versus expansiveness (Allport, 1961; Ekman, Friesen, & Ellsworth, 1972; Ekman & Oster, 1979). Also of special interest in the assessment of children are behavioral styles of responsiveness to task demands, such as the tendency to make work responses, spontaneous verbalizations, or spontaneous extensions in coping with task requirements (Hertzig, Birch, Thomas, & Mendez, 1968). Because response styles assume their prime significance in connection with self-report, cognitive styles in connection with information-processing tasks, and expressive styles in connection with naturalistic behavior, these three types of styles contribute differentially to score interpretation in the three major media of assessment, respectively—namely, questionnaires, objective performance tests, and real-life observations.

Media of Assessment

There are three basic ways of obtaining data for purposes of psychological assessment. We can ask individuals questions about themselves; we can give them tasks to perform or confront them with situations to cope with; or we can observe their behavior in naturalistic settings. More formally, there are three basic media of assessment. In one, we make inferences from a person's self-descriptions and self-reports, which constitute what Cattell (1946; 1957) calls questionnaire or Q-data; in the second, we make inferences from a person's performance on stimulus tasks and in contrived field situations, which constitute what Cattell calls objective test or T-data; and in the third, we make inferences from a person's behaviors in everyday life settings, which constitute what Cattell calls life-record or L-data.

Each of these three media of assessment is subject to characteristic perturbations or sources of distortion, which collectively are sometimes referred to as "method variance" (Campbell & Fiske, 1959). Method variance includes all systematic effects associated with a particular measurement procedure that are extraneous to the focal variable or trait being measured. Because of their pervasiveness and considerable impact, two types of measurement distortion assume special significance in psychological assessment—namely, instrument effects and observer effects (Cattell, 1968, 1977; Cattell & Digman, 1964).

Instrument effects are response consistencies deriving from interactions of personal characteristics of the individual with the form or format of the assessment device and the conditions of administration or observation. Although irrelevant to the focal variables being assessed, these implicated personal characteristics—by virtue of their responsiveness to the form and conditions of assessment—serve to distort, contaminate, or otherwise interfere with the measurement of the focal variables. Instrument effects may operate in all three assessment media, but they are of primary concern on questionnaires and objective tests, where they are more likely to influence the subject's responses directly. *Observer effects*, on the other hand, operate primarily in life-record and questionnaire data, where information is essentially filtered through a human transducer—either an external observer or the self as observer. In observer effects, the view of any focal trait of the individual may be distorted not only as a function of his or her other characteristics in interaction with the form and conditions of observation, but also as a function of the observer's characteristics in interaction both with the subject's traits and with the form and conditions of observation.

In a sense, both instrument effects and observer effects, deriving as they do from interactions between personal characteristics of respondents or observers with the form and conditions of assessment, are special instances of a more general class of context effects. As we shall see, a differentiated view of context effects that distinguishes the measurement context from both the intrapersonal context of the individual's personal characteristics and the environmental context of the individual's social, cultural, and educational experience provides a powerful complementary framework for taking instrument and observer effects into account in relation to the focal variables measured.

Questionnaires and Their Perturbations

The term "questionnaire" as used here refers to any assessment device that elicits self-descriptions or self-reports. Although such responses ostensibly require introspection or recall, they may be viewed for measurement purposes not only as assertions about the self but as samples of verbal behavior. As assertions about the self, questionnaire responses may be more or less accurate self-estimates or self-revelations, depending upon the individual's degree of relevant self-knowledge. It is more likely, however, that self-descriptions will be variously distorted by the intrusion of nonfocal personal characteristics via mechanisms of self-deception, self-defense, and impression management, yielding instances of the self-observer effects discussed previously. Thus, in one way or another, the interpretation of self-descriptions and self-evaluations must take into account individual differences in accuracy of self-observation, degree of relevant self-knowledge, and attitudes toward the self—which together contribute to biases in self-perception and self-regard—as well as individual differences in attitudes toward the examiner and toward the uses to which the assessment information will be put—which contribute to biases in impression management and self-report (Damarin & Messick, 1965).

As behavior samples, questionnaire responses may be scored for numerous behavioral consistencies that take on all the earmarks of objective test or T-data. In addition to such clear exemplars of questionnaire T-data as latency of item response, number of items omitted, and speed in completing the questionnaire, we must also include as questionnaire T-data—that is, as objective performance measures obtained from a questionnaire—scores for the tendency to respond "true," as an instance, or for the tendency to endorse items judged socially desirable, because it is consistency in item response that is at issue in such scores rather than consistency in self-description (Berg, 1967; Messick, 1968; Wiggins, 1973). Although such stylistic tendencies may be studied as personality variables in their own right, they represent interactions between the respondent's personal characteristics and the form or format of measurement—as does, for example, the tendency to give extreme responses on Likert scales or other multicategory rating options (Hamilton, 1968)—and thus they constitute intrusive instrument effects when content traits are the focus of assessment. Questionnaires, therefore, involving as they do both self-observations and behavioral responses, are particularly susceptible to distortion from both observer effects and instrument effects.

Moreover, just as questionnaires may yield nonQ-data, so may other assessment devices such as interviews yield Q-data. Indeed, the interview may be a truly multimedia device because it not only provides the same kinds of Q- and T-data as questionnaires, but real-life interviews also afford the possibility of recording L-data. Research on questionnaire assessment has been extensive and the fol-lowing sources are suggested for historical and systematic treatments of the field: Cattell (1957, 1977); Edwards (1970); Eysenck and Eysenck (1969); Goodwin and Driscoll (1980); Guilford (1959); Jackson and Paunonen (1980); Selltiz, Wrightsman, and Cook (1976): Wiggins (1973); and, Wilde (1977).

Objective Performance Tests and Their Perturbations

An objective test, according to Campbell (1957), is one in which "the subject is told, either explicitly or implicitly, that there is a correct answer external to himself, for which he should search in selecting his answer" (p. 207). This is in contrast to voluntary self-description, where the subject is usually told that there are no right or wrong answers. Campbell's definition clearly embraces ability and achievement tests, as it must, but in order to make explicit the inclusion of creativity tests, his conception should be modified in the following manner to incorporate standards of goodness as well as correctness: An objective test is one in which the respondents believe that they should emphasize accuracy, correctness, or goodness of response because external standards exist for evaluating their answers. Cattell (1957, 1958) stresses that in an objective test subjects are told what they should try to do, but not what this will be interpreted to mean about the self. For Cattell (1957), an objective test is a "portable, exactly reproducible, stimulus situation, with an exactly prescribed mode of scoring the response, *of which the subject is not informed*" (p. 225). From this perspective, the key feature of objective test or T-data is that test behavior is assessed without the subject being aware of the manner in which that behavior affects the scoring and interpretation.

The objectivity of an objective test derives from the fact that the responses are behavioral as opposed to self-descriptive or self-evaluative and that what is scored is consistency in performance, not self-appraisal. This is true even though that scoring may be judgmental or subjective—within prescribed and replicable procedures, of course—as is typically the case with creativity tests or other open-ended tasks requiring invented or constructed responses. Objectivity of scoring is a different matter entirely—completely specified scoring procedures and keys may be used in all three assessment media, not just objective tests, and are routinely used with questionnaires.

Objective tests, like all assessment media, are susceptible to distortion from a variety of instrument effects. These stem primarily from interactions of the respondents' personal characteristics with the form of the test, with the conditions of administration, and with the situation and life circumstances surrounding the testing (Cattell, 1977). Examples of test-form effects include cognitive styles responsive to particular task requirements, such as reflection versus impulsivity revealed in differential emphasis on carefulness versus speed in performing timed tasks; response styles elicited by particular response formats, such as acquiescence in reporting the presence of stimuli when asked to respond "yes" or "no"; and differential familiarity with particular item formats, such as analogies or sentence completion. Examples of administrative-condition effects are score patterns associated with variations in lighting for tasks requiring visual discrimination or with differential acceptance of an allegedly gamelike atmosphere. Finally, examples of situational effects are response consistencies concomitant with testing some children on weekends and others during school hours or testing some children in a psychological clinic or laboratory and others in classrooms or at home.

Although most widely employed to assess abilities and achievements, objective performance measures are also prevalent in the assessment of perception, memory, thinking, problem solving, and other cognitive processes as well as in the assessment of creativity and motivation. So-called projective tests are also classifiable as objective performance tests within this three-media framework since they are usually conceived as measures of idiosyncratic or distorted perception or cognition, in which the idiosyncracies are attributable to motivational and affective forces (Cattell, 1957). Extensive discussions of objective performance tests appear in Cattell (1957), Cronbach (1970), Eysenck (1970), Guilford (1959), Hundleby, Pawlik, and Cattell (1965), Ishikawa (1977), and Thorndike (1971).

Behavioral Observations and Their Perturbations

Observations of behavior in situ, or L-data, entail the recording and encoding of everyday life behaviors in naturalistic situations and cultural settings. L-data contrasts with questionnaire or Q-data in that it is recorded independently of the subject's self-perception or self-appraisal. Although it shares with objective test or T-data the property of being behavioral, it differs in being perceived by subjects as ordinary experience rather than as a test of their performance. Furthermore, naturalistic settings are neither as portable nor as readily standardized as a test, and hence L-data is more directly situation- and cul-

ture-bound than much of T-data (Cattell, 1957). Thus behavioral observations yield neither subjective self-descriptions nor objective performance measures. Instead, they record behaviors that are spontaneous and natural rather than constrained and reactive to evocative questions or controlled tasks. Observational techniques are also widely used to assess behavioral responses to *contrived* situations in naturalistic field settings (Weick, 1968), but if the contrived situation is standarized and reproducible and the scoring procedures for appraising selected target responses are precisely specified, then the resultant behavior scores technically constitute T-data.

The key feature distinguishing L-data from both Q- and T-data is that—to the degree that the observer and the process of observation are unobtrusive—the subject does not adopt assessment-triggered motivational sets to respond or perform in particular ways. Thus, *unobtrusive* behavioral observations yield *nonreactive* measures in the sense that the measurement procedures do not influence and thereby change the subject's behavior or the event being observed (Webb, Campbell, Schwartz, & Sechrest, 1966); nevertheless, the obtained measures may yet be substantially distorted by a variety of observer and instrument effects in the encoding and recording of the behavior. These distortions derive from interactions of the observer with characteristics of the subject, the setting, and the recording instrument and become increasingly more serious as the degree of inference required of the observer increases from behavior recording and categorization to trait attribution and trait rating. Worse still, situations that are effectively reactive from the subjects' standpoint because of observer obtrusiveness are susceptible to even more fundamental distortions; for, the subjects' spontaneous behaviors may be altered as a consequence of their awareness of being observed and of their attendant interactions with characteristics of the observer and the mode of observation.

Because of the seriousness of these obtrusive observer effects or observer-interference effects (Weick, 1968), it matters whether or not the observer is known to be an observer—that is, whether or not the observer as well as the mode of observation is concealed or disguised—and it matters whether or not the observer is a participant in the events or processes being observed. A known participant observer, by virtue of taking part in the events transpiring, likely affords the most obtrusive or subject-reactive circumstance, while an unknown or concealed nonparticipant observer affords the least subject reactivity. Between these extremes, a known nonparticipant observer is likely more obtrusive than an unknown participant observer. However, the reduced subject reactivity purchased with concealment comes at a high cost. In regard to participant observation, while concealment may control one type of interference—namely, awareness of being observed—it may create another type of interference—namely, inadvertent diversion of a natural event by the bogus participant (Weick, 1968). In regard to both participant and nonparticipant procedures, concealed observation raises basic ethical issues concerning invasion of privacy and informed consent (Amrine & Sanford, 1956; Burchard, 1957). In this connection, some investigators have argued that concealment is justified if the behavior is public (Barker & Wright, 1955) or if the participation is not misrepresented, even though the observer may have additional interests (Riesman & Watson, 1964).

One alternative to concealment is partial concealment; that is, the investigator makes known the fact that observations are being made but conceals who or what is being observed, as in mother/child interactions in which the investigator implies that only the child's behavior is under scrutiny. Another alternative is nonconcealment; that is, we may have to accept the fact that even nonparticipant observers are sometimes conspicuous because they play the unusual role of a nonmember who is always present but never participates (Goode & Hatt, 1952). Under the best of circumstances, such observers may come to be accepted as interested bystanders and be essentially ignored. Fortunately, problems of obtrusiveness and interference tend to be less troublesome in observations of children, especially if they are sufficiently absorbed in their own activities, and "the younger the child, the more natural his behavior in the presence of an observer" (Wright, 1960, p. 76). Moreover, since adults as well as children can become engrossed in events, the observation of behavior in absorbing situations has been proposed as a general strategy for offsetting observer obtrusiveness on the grounds that the participants will forget, at least temporarily, the presence of the observer (Straus, 1964).

Thus, the mere presence of a known observer or a known observation process, even if well blended into the natural setting, may suffice to evoke self-conscious behavior on the part of the subject, which has been called the "guinea pig effect" (Selltiz, Jahoda, Deutsch, & Cook, 1959). Subject awareness of observation may also evoke mechanisms of self-defense or dissembling. In addition, it may lead the subject to choose restrictively from among the many legitimate roles in his or her repertoire the one deemed most appropriate for self-presentation given the presumed purposes of the observation, which has been called the "role selection effect" (Webb et al., 1966). The cues available to subjects as they attempt to decide which roles or behaviors are appropriate under the conditions of observation have been called "demand characteristics" (Aronson & Carlsmith, 1968; Orne, 1962). Although demand characteristics are usually invoked by psychologists in connection with social and psychological experiments, they apply with equal cogency to nonexperimental behavioral observations.

Similarly, observations generally are also prone to the other major source of experimental bias deriving from the unintentional influence of the experimenter—or, in our case, the observer—on the results obtained. The nature and intensity of the subject's reactivity to the observer may be a function, for example, of such demographic characteristics as the observer's sex, age, race, religion, and status and of such personality characteristics as likability, warmth, and anxiety, as these interact with the subject's demographic and personal characteristics. Perhaps the most disquieting of the unintentional observer influences are observer expectancy effects (Rosenthal, 1966), in which the observer's expectations—about the sequence of behavior, trait relationships, likely outcomes, or whatever—subtly influence the results obtained. These influences are manifested not just in terms of subject reactivity but in terms of observer biases in perception, judgment, and overall information processing.

A number of types of specific observer biases have been delineated. These biases differ depending on whether the objective is a *duplicatory* recording of behavioral information with no intended change in form, as in narrative descriptions and specimen records, or whether it is a *reductive* recording in which complex behavior is translated into a simple language, as in sign analysis and category systems (Campbell, 1958; Weick, 1968). Still different biases emerge if the objective is an *inferential* recording involving imputed meaning or trait attribution, as in trait ratings. Examples of such biases are abbreviation, or the dropping of details, and reconstruction, or the generation of details in line with what is familiar or expected—in the extreme, "suppressing remembered detail that does not now seem to fit and . . . confabulating detail where gaps are conspicuous" (Campbell, 1958, p. 342). Other examples include closure or directional distortion and symmetry or balanced distortion, enhancement of contrast, assimilation to stereotypes, assimilation to prior subject behavior, assimilation to expected behavior or to the observer's own attitudes, and assimilation to the observer's evaluative preferences (Campbell, 1958; Weick, 1968).

Examples of instrument effects in behavior rating include *halo error,* or the tendency to rate traits in line with the observer's general impression of the subject; *logical error,* or the tendency to assign similar ratings to traits that seem logically related even though behaviorally independent; *leniency error,* or the tendency to rate liked subjects higher on positive traits; *central tendency error,* or the tendency to use intermediate categories and avoid extremes; and *contrast error,* or the tendency to rate subjects as different from the rater's own perceived position (Guilford, 1954).

This panoply of subject reactivity, observer bias, and instrument effects attendant upon behavioral observations may seem a dismal litany, but it is recited here for two main reasons: First, observational methods are widely used in child assessment and for good reasons; so, we should be alert to their many pitfalls. Second, the pervasiveness of these biases reaffirms the necessity not only for systematic experimental controls but for convergent and discriminant methods of analysis to assure that observational measures of focal variables or traits are not specific to particular observers, observation conditions, and settings but rather generalize across such context effects.

In regard to the first point about the prevalence of use with children, observational methods are important in the assessment of young children for a number of reasons (Goodwin & Driscoll, 1980). Behavioral observations afford a means of measuring many child characteristics that might otherwise be unmeasurable because of the young child's limited verbal response repertoire and limited test-taking skills. In addition, because much observational measurement emphasizes the recording of behavior as it occurs naturally, there is no requirement for the child to stay on task or to attend to the measurement procedure when distracted or fatigued. More positively, young children appear to be relatively open and unperturbed by being observed. As Wright (1960) contends, the observer's presence probably "attenuates especially the bad extremes of behavior from cuss words on down," yet this still "leaves much that experimenters are never going to see in laboratories at their inestimable best" (p. 118). Moreover, observation is particularly well suited for appraising children's affective and socioemotional characteristics (Walker, 1973) and for assessing interaction processes in family, classroom, and play settings. As a further example, observational methods may be used to link children's behavior with naturalistic conditions that vary over time or from one part of the real world to another, thereby contributing descriptively to the ecological study of human development (Bronfenbrenner, 1977; Wright, 1960).

Extensive discussions of observational methodology for the collection and analysis of L-data, including recommended control and training procedures for attenuating the effects of observer bias, appear in Boehm and Weinberg (1977), Brandt (1972), Cartwright and Cartwright (1974), Cattell (1957, 1968), Goodwin and Driscoll (1980), Hammond (1977), Heyns and Lippitt (1954), Lambert (1960), Medinnus (1976), Medley and Mitzel (1963), Selltiz et al. (1976), Stallings (1977), Webb et al. (1966), Weick (1968), Wiggins (1973), and Wright (1960, 1967).

In regard to the second point about the need to appraise the generalizability of observational measures, this of course is truly general and holds with equal force for objective test and questionnaire measures as well. We are concerned about the generalizability of our measures of focal variables or traits not only across observer-bias and observer/instrument effects in observational measurement, but also across subject/instrument effects in objective test and questionnaire measurement and across self-observer effects in the latter. Generalizability theory and methodology will be discussed in a subsequent section, but the basic strategy is simply to appraise the consistency of measurement properties across different observers, conditions, or instruments.

In assessing the degree to which a measure primarily reflects the variable or construct of interest as opposed to contaminating variables, much of the power derives from the requirement of multiple measures and preferably multiple methods of measurement for each construct or trait. Multiple measures might entail different instruments in the same medium or different observers in the same setting, while multiple methods might entail different media such as questionnaires versus behavior ratings or different observational conditions or settings. Consistent relationships among different measures of the same construct or trait, along with empirical distinctiveness for measures of different constructs or traits obtained by the same method, constitute convergent and discriminant evidence, respectively, that the measures transcend instrument effects. Furthermore, if the multiple methods included observational techniques, observer effects as well are transcended (Cattell, 1977; Cattell, Pierson, Brim, & Finkbeiner, 1976). Convergent and discriminant evidence from such multitrait/multimethod designs contribute to an important aspect of construct validity called trait validity (Campbell, 1960; Campbell & Fiske, 1959). Convergent and discriminant evidence are also critical to still broader issues of generalizability in which we are concerned with the generality of a measure's meaning and utility across different population groups and different ecological settings—usually referred to, respectively, as population and ecological validity (Bracht & Glass, 1968; Shulman, 1970) or, more straightforwardly, as population and ecological generalizability (Messick, 1980).

Typologies and Trade-offs in Measurement

Cutting across the three assessment media are a number of conceptual dichotomies, such as structured versus unstructured response formats and direct versus indirect question formats, which generate, on the one hand, a typology of assessment devices but pose, on the other hand, a series of dilemmas or trade-offs in measurement. These dichotomies represent trade-offs because, if the desirable features of one side of the dichotomy are emphasized or refined, then those of the other side are degraded or forgone (Loevinger, 1957).

Campbell (1957), for example, has proposed a typology of nonobservational assessment devices based on the three dichotomies of structured versus free response, direct versus indirect (or disguised) response, and objective versus voluntary response. The trade-off with respect to degree of response structure is between the meaning of the response vis-à-vis the individual and its meaning vis-à-vis the group. "The greater the degree of structure, the more exact can be comparison between every individual and the group, but the less exact is the relation of the test response to the personality trait of the individual" (Loevinger, 1955, p. 3). The trade-off with respect to degree of indirection is between the amount of disguise in the question and the amount of disguise in the answer—that is, direct questions are likely to arouse defensive or disguised reactions. Such distortions contribute nonrandom error variance to the items, which is likely to cumulate in the total score in the same way that trait variance cumulates while at the same time reducing the validity of interpretation. On the other hand, if disguised questions are tangential to each other as well as to the trait in question, they will likely be low in internal consistency or homogeneity, though possibly more valid in the aggregate than the cumulated direct questions. This raises the specter of a trade-off between homogeneity and validity (Loevinger, 1957).

Campbell's (1957) dichotomy of objective versus voluntary tests is similar but not identical to Cattell's (1957) distinction between objective test and questionnaire media. "In the *voluntary* test the respondent is given to understand that any answer is acceptable, and that there is no external criterion of correctness against which his answer will be evaluated. He is encouraged in idiosyncracy and self description" (Campbell, 1957, p. 207). Voluntary devices include questionnaires, to be sure, but also such instruments as the Thematic Apperception Test, which for Cattell qualifies instead as an objective test since the TAT is portable and standardized with detailed scoring procedures and since the respondent is unaware of the way in which his or her verbal behavior affects the scoring and interpretation. The trade-off in this dichotomy is between external criteria and internal criteria, between the subject's orientation toward standards of correctness or goodness and standards of personal relevance or importance.

Some other prominent dichotomies might also be added to embellish this typology of assessment formats, such as bandwidth versus fidelity to accommodate multiple scoring or reactive versus unobtrusive techniques to accommodate observational measures. With respect to bandwidth versus fidelity, the trade-off is between the number of characteristics assessed and the quality of their measurement—the more variables or traits a device embraces in a given time, the less dependable and reliable the multiple scores. With respect to reactive versus unobtrusive procedures, the trade-off pits loss of spontaneity and naturalness against invasion of privacy, thereby raising controversial issues of science versus ethics.

Systems of Variables

It should be apparent by now that the assessment of children and the assessment of developmental change, as well as the evaluation of childhood intervention programs, are influenced by a host of interacting factors that somehow must be taken into account if generalizable interpretations are to be sustained. This recognition of the interactive impact of personal and environmental influences on the subject's responses is in effect tantamount to the adoption of a systems perspective in assessment. That is, we explicitly acknowledge that child assessment entails an extremely complicated *system* involving, at the very least, complex multifaceted organisms changing over time in interaction with diverse environmental forces. Furthermore, this system is composed of differentiated but overlapping subsystems that embrace the child, family, peers, community, communication media, and the cultural setting as well as the school, teachers, and educational programs. Since the concept of system implies a complex entity that functions as a whole by virtue of the interdependence of its parts, it follows that a change or intrusion in one part of the system may interact with and produce unanticipated consequences in other parts of the system.

In attempting to measure any element or characteristic of such a system, we must assess the general context of interdependencies in order to take account of possible interactions of the characteristics measured with other aspects of the system—especially interactions among implicated characteristics of the child as well as interactions of these child characteristics with the measurement process and with situational and sociocultural factors. Otherwise we are at a loss to know how to generalize a given measure and its meaning—or to limit its generalization—across various individuals and groups and across types of situations. This possible relativity of measurement inferences to context has three main implications: first, the need to explicitly consider the child *as* context when particular child variables are assessed; second, the need for direct assessment *of* context, especially of the measurement context and the environmental context of social and educational experience; and finally, the need for focused assessment *in* context to appraise functional child characteristics under realistic conditions of functioning. Before proceeding to elaborate these three points on the importance of context, however, we should first briefly address a critical problem in this connection—namely, we have no systematic way as yet of specifying just what constitutes "context" (Messick, 1982b).

Context is not any and all attributes of the environment but, as in discourse, those aspects of the surround that illuminate or add to the meaning of the focal variables and their functioning. The descriptive measurement of a variety of supplementary dimensions, however salient or pervasive, is not enough for a true assessment of context. Such descriptive measurement may characterize the setting or background, to be sure, but not the operative *context* with its implication of differential or moderating influence on individual behavior.

Current approaches to the delineation of context

effects are typically after the fact of measurement and are generally limited to statistical analyses of possible interactive and moderated or curvilinear relationships among those variables that happened to be assessed for other reasons. What is needed is some form of prior context analysis to guide the measurement process. This might be a type of behavioral analysis to establish empirical relations between stimulus conditions and response classes (S-R analysis), preferably elaborated to take organismic mediators into account (S-O-R analysis). Or it might be a type of functional analysis to conceptualize stimulus conditions and environmental circumstances in terms of the organismic needs and values they serve or satisfy (O-S-R analysis). The former approach, of course, is directly in line with behaviorist tradition (Bijou & Peterson, 1971; Kanfer & Saslow, 1969; Skinner, 1938, 1953), while the latter is more congenial with Murray's (1938) need-press formulation and with Thurstone's (1923, 1924) self-expression reformulation of the stimulus-response "fallacy." Failing some type of prior context analysis, what is usually offered, if anything, is simply a specification of potential sources of context effects (Messick & Barrows, 1972). Such lists may serve a useful heuristic purpose, however, in drawing attention to often overlooked sources of interactive influence that should be anticipated in the assessment design.

Child *as* Context, or a Child's Garden of Variables

Inferences about a particular characteristic or competency of a child should be relative to the intrapersonal context of that child's intellectual and personality makeup, or at least to the salient features of that makeup. Since the child is a very complicated system of interdependencies, one must anticipate that certain traits and characteristics will influence or interfere with the assessment of other traits and characteristics—as when defense mechanisms distort self-description, poor reading comprehension degrades the assessment of subject-matter knowledge, or high verbal skill facilitates the channeling of aggression into satire.

The decision as to which variables to examine in any research or evaluation study must perforce depend to a large degree on the particular research hypotheses being investigated or the particular treatments being evaluated. In each case, the specific research or evaluation questions at issue will serve to focus attention upon certain measures of intended influence (the so-called independent variables that are to be experimentally manipulated or so selected as to provide naturally occurring contrasts) and upon certain measures of expected outcome (the so-called dependent variables that are used as criteria for appraising the significance of findings). The choice of such specific focal variables will not be considered in detail here because they are so closely hypothesis- or objective-bound, but the general strategy of variable selection will be briefly addressed. In particular, it is argued that focusing attention on the presumed causal influences and the anticipated outcomes is not enough—that consideration must also be given to other dimensions of personal and environmental impact, to possible interacting or moderating influences in the subject's makeup or background and in the situational context, and to the possibility of unanticipated outcomes or side effects (Messick, 1970a; 1970b; Messick & Barrows, 1972; Scriven, 1966).

In any particular study, to be sure, it is impossible to measure all of the potentially important variables because practical considerations force us to be selective. In each instance a choice is made determined by value judgments and priorities in the face of practical constraints. The major point here, however, is that this choice should be an explicitly considered one from an array of possibilities that includes the major areas of influence, context, and outcome. The value judgments implicit in the choice of some variables rather than others should be justifiable on rational and ethical grounds and should take into account their relation not only to specific research hypotheses or program objectives but also to broader developmental and educational goals as well as social values (Messick, 1980; Scriven, 1967). A sample array of child variables is presented next, followed in the subsequent section by an array of possible context variables. No claim is made for comprehensiveness, but rather the intention is simply to outline the major measurement areas that should be considered in selecting assessment variables for research and evaluation studies with children, where the possibilities for interaction and differential impact are legion.

The major child variables for typical assessment purposes may be classified into the three broad groups of cognition, personal and social functioning, and health and physical status:

Within cognition, we might list subareas for perception; attention; memory; concept learning; analytical functioning; Piagetian developmental stages; creativity; verbal behavior; general intelligence; assorted specific abilities; and, a variety of academic and artistic achievements.

Within personal/social functioning, we might subsume personal and social motives; adaptive role behavior; controlling mechanisms (including cognitive styles, defenses, and coping styles); attitudes; affects; interests; values; and, dimensions of temperament and personality.

Within health and physical status, we might include gross physical characteristics; auditory and visual acuity; present health status; present mental health and adjustment; the nature and extent of any handicapping conditions; and, personal and family health history.

Since some variables may be conceptualized within each of these categories as traits, states, or response classes, this type of systematic consideration of options should prove generally useful whether the focus is on trait structure, state dynamics, or behavior repertoire. As a further illustration, a more refined survey of child characteristics related to social competency goals of childhood intervention programs appears in Anderson and Messick (1974). Again, in reviewing such an array of possible variables, the intention is not to press for complete coverage but to stimulate the investigator to make rational choices among potentially important alternatives.

Assessment *of* Context, or Consider the Circumstances

Because it is often overlooked in considerations of context, a distinction is drawn here between the measurement or research context on the one hand and the broader environmental context of social and educational influences on the other. Special reference is made to variables associated with the assessment or research per se to serve as a reminder that serious threats to interpretability and generalizability arise whenever examiners or researchers intrude upon the scene, as in the phenomenon of the self-fulfilling prophecy or the celebrated Hawthorne effect. Characteristics of examiners and experimenters should therefore be systematically noted as a possible basis for clarifying any consistent differences in measurement or research results they might obtain. Moreover, inferences about measured characteristics of the child should be relative not only to such examiner effects but to the broader context of the measurement process as a whole. By that we mean not just taking into account critical objective features such as whether the task was timed or untimed, but also tempering interpretations of subject responses in light of the child's general style of reaction to the task, the examiner, and the assessment and research situation.

With respect to the child's reaction to the assessment situation, a number of personal characteristics that the child brings into the situation are especially pertinent, such as familiarity or prior practice with the particular test or type of test, achievement motivation, self-esteem, proneness to evaluative anxiety, and various motivational anomalies such as being culturally unattuned to standardized testing and its ostensible educational and social relevance or evincing countercultural motives to avoid conspicuously good behavior. Other variables in the measurement or research context having potential influence on subject behavior include personality characteristics of the examiner or researcher and demand characteristics of the measurement procedure or research treatment, especially as these might elicit apprehension or defensiveness or otherwise influence the child's spontaneous style of responsiveness.

In this regard, noteworthy characteristics of examiners or researchers—in addition to the pervasive influence of individual differences in their training, experience, and competence—include

sex, race, ethnicity, and language or dialect; their hypotheses and expectations; and, a variety of personality attributes.

Features of the measurement procedure or research treatment that have potentially differential effects on subject behavior include

instrument and observer effects; novelty and disruption effects; atmosphere effects, such as those deriving from evaluative, relaxed, or stressful conditions; degree of obtrusiveness or reactivity; intensity of task orientation as exemplified by time pressure or the use of feedback or probes; and, the presumed purpose of the assessment, such as research, program evaluation, diagnosis, placement, or selection.

Because characteristics of the examiner or researcher and of the measurement or research procedure interact with personal and demographic characteristics of the subject, the social psychology of the testing or research experience has become an issue warranting detailed study in its own right (Allen, Dubanoski, & Stevenson, 1966; Banks, McQuater, & Hubbard, 1978; Katz, Atchison, Epps, & Roberts, 1972; Katz, Henchy, & Allen, 1960; Rosenthal, 1966; Sattler, 1970, 1982). From an assessment standpoint, however, the important issue is not merely the occurrence of differential impact on

the subject's behavior but rather on the subject's scores. For example, the race of the examiner may influence the subject's attitudes or interpersonal behavior in the assessment situation but apparently has little demonstrated effect on intelligence test scores or other measures of cognitive abilities (Sattler, 1982).

In regard to the environmental context of social and educational influence, the general point is that inferences about child characteristics, particularly about competencies, should be relative to the experiential context of learning opportunities in school, home, community, and culture to which the child has been exposed. When inferences about competency are drawn from task performance, it should make a difference whether or not the child has had an opportunity to learn the skills required by the task. Similarly, it should also make a difference whether the child—or the child's teachers, parents, or peers—thought those skills, or any other personal characteristics under scrutiny, were important or relevant.

The major variables of social and educational experience may be clustered for convenience in terms of influences related to the family, peers, classroom, teachers, school, and the larger community and culture in which they are embedded:

The family cluster includes both *status* variables—such as parents' educational levels and occupations; number of adults and children; target child's sex and ordinal position; sibling sex and age; family structure; older siblings' behavior patterns; and, the target child's possessions, learning resources, and areas of stress—and *process* variables—such as control techniques; language processes; parental teaching styles and belief systems; aspirations and expectations; feelings of control over the environment; feelings of alienation; differentiation of the environment; and, the target child's mobility or variety of stimulation.

Peer variables include the target child's popularity; the number and closeness of relationships with same-sex and opposite-sex individuals; the nature and degree of involvement in school-related peer groups, church-related groups, and neighborhood groups; peer groups' attitudes and values; and, the nature and degree of peer pressure.

Classroom variables include salient aspects of child classroom behavior; adult behavior; child/child interactions; child/adult interactions; group structure; and, program activities and materials.

Teacher variables include sex and ethnicity; personality characteristics; training and experience; cognitive skills; general knowledge and specific competence; values, attitudes, and expectations; and, dominant role characteristics such as supportive, authoritarian, or flexible.

The school cluster includes key features of the physical facilities and equipment; teachers and staff; student body; pupil services; extracurricular activities; expenditures; community relations; and, teachers' and administrators' perceptions of the teachers, administrators, students, and their own problems.

Characteristics of the community and larger culture include physical features and facilities; size and nature of the neighborhood; social and political characteristics of the area population and the history of such characteristics; patterns of ethnicity and language use; degree of social organization; degree of urban acculturation; demographic descriptors; and, family perceptions of and attitudes toward these community and cultural characteristics.

The major point is that child assessment results should never be interpreted in isolation. To the extent possible, they should be interpreted in light of the child's cooperation, motivation, and adaptive behavior in the assessment setting—as well as nontest adaptive behavior in other settings—and in light of the child's family and cultural background, learning opportunities, primary language, and handicapping conditions. An example of a comprehensive assessment procedure that systematically utilizes physical, personal/social, and cultural information in the assessment of child characteristics is Mercer's (1979; Mercer & Lewis, 1977, 1978) System of Multicultural Pluralistic Assessment (SOMPA). Unfortunately, from one perspective SOMPA does not go far enough in including relevant contextual variables while from another perspective it goes much too far, especially in light of available research evidence, in modifying standard assessments to reflect a particular cultural context. It is one thing to interpret standardized scores in relation to one or more relevant contexts and quite another thing altogether to bias the scores themselves in the direction of a specific context.

The most critical and controversial feature of SOMPA is the use of multiple regression equations to adjust standard IQs obtained from the Wechsler Intelligence Scale for Children-Revised (1974), or WISC-R, for differential effects of the sociocultural setting in which the child is being reared. These effects are estimated by means of four sociocultural

scales assessing family size, family structure, socioeconomic status, and urban acculturation. When scores on these four scales were used to predict WISC-R IQs separately for blacks, whites, and Hispanics, significant group differences in slopes and intercepts were obtained as were statistically significant, though modest, proportions of explained variance in Verbal (10% to 22%), Performance (4% to 12%), and Full Scale IQ (14% to 18%). These results provide the empirical justification for deriving adjusted IQ scores in SOMPA, which are calculated by adding to 100 the algebraic difference between the child's obtained IQ and predicted IQ and scaled to yield a score distribution with a standard deviation of 15 as in the original WISC-R score distribution (Mercer, 1979).

This procedure, which essentially equates the child's predicted IQ based on sociocultural background measures to a norm of 100 for each racial or ethnic group separately, is carried out only for predicted scores less than 100; children with predicted IQs of 100 or higher are assumed to come from backgrounds for which the standard WISC-R norms are appropriate, so no regression adjustments are made for them. Basing adjustments on statistically distinct regression equations for each racial or ethnic group separately not only effectively eliminates between-group mean differences in adjusted IQ scores, as would the use of separate WISC-R norms for each group, but also takes into account significant IQ-related sociocultural variation within group. The resultant adjusted IQ score, since it is deemed to reflect the child's "intelligence" relative to expectations derived from his or her sociocultural experiences, is interpreted by Mercer (1979) as the child's Estimated Learning Potential (ELP). This is in contrast with the unadjusted IQ, which Mercer interprets as the child's current School Functioning Level (SFL).

Although SOMPA incorporates a number of desirable features, it also entails some serious problems of measurement and interpretation. On the positive side is the use of multivariate measures of physical dexterity, sensory acuity, perceptual/motor development, and health history to screen for physical or biological anomalies that might invalidate WISC-R scores. Also on the positive side is the use of standardized adaptive behavior scales not only to identify emotional and behavioral deviance possibly disruptive of both test and classroom performance, but to appraise a variety of nonintellective, adaptive strengths that might temper diagnoses of mental retardation. On the problematic side is the unsupported utilization of statistically adjusted WISC-R scores to estimate "learning potential," a construct reminiscent of the notion of ''capacity''—which is an inference two steps removed from behavior in the sense that capacity predicts developed ability levels whereas ability merely predicts performance (Diamond & Royce, 1980). The measurement of such a second-order *person* construct as a residual score controlled for *sociocultural* variance raises important conceptual issues as well as methodological ones.

In this regard, it is not just that the published regression equations, being based on restricted samples of California school children, require extensive local or national renorming for widespread application, but that any regression equations based on sociocultural variables exogenous to the child should be used at all for the purpose of measuring child characteristics as opposed to assessing change or treatment effects. While the rationale for regression-based residual scores is usually to eliminate contaminating variance from a particular measure of a construct, the procedure simultaneously partials out any genuine construct variance that is correlated with the contaminants being controlled, thereby yielding in such cases a systematically distorted measure of the construct in terms of its external relationships, not just a decontaminated or purified measure. This could mistakenly lead to a change, subtle or otherwise, in the construct's network of empirical correlations based on the adjusted as opposed to the unadjusted measure and ultimately to a change in the interpreted meaning of the construct itself. In any event, such residual scores are often interpreted not as purified measures of the original construct, but as measures of distinct constructs, as we observe in the shift from IQ to School Functioning Level to Estimated Learning Potential in SOMPA. But such emergent constructs require their own theoretical and empirical justification and cannot trade on construct validity evidence for the original score.

On this point, matters are worse still because the particular child characteristic assessed via regression adjustments in SOMPA—construed as ''learning potential''—is a second-order interpretation that depends profoundly on critical unverified assumptions which, at least with the crude sociocultural control scales used at present, are unlikely to be verified in any serious fashion. As Mercer (1979) herself declaims, ''The user assumes (a) that the four Sociocultural Scales are adequate measures of whatever sociocultural factors separate the culture of the school from the culture of the home and (b) that equating children on the four Sociocultural Scales controls for differences in their opportunity to ac-

quire the skills and knowledge needed to succeed in school, their motivation to acquire the skills and knowledge needed, and their response to test-taking situations'' (p. 145).

Ironically, given the stated purposes of SOMPA to expand educational opportunities and to reduce stigmatization, this unvalidated learning-potential interpretation may be especially insidious for low IQ children, whether or not their scores are increased appreciably by the statistical transformations. Those children whose scores are raised by the regression adjustments may find themselves excluded from special education programs and services that might be beneficial (Clarizio, 1979); whereas for those children whose adjusted scores remain relatively low, the implication that they are ''biologically impaired with poor potential both stigmatizes them and discourages remedial efforts'' (Goodman, 1979, p. 220).

In sum, SOMPA was discussed at length here because it provides an excellent example—with its systematic coverage of medicophysical, sociocultural, and personally adaptive variables—of the comprehensive assessment *of* context, both intrapersonal and environmental. This multifarious contextual information provides a rich foundation for qualifying score interpretations—in this case, IQ score interpretations—in light of individual circumstances. Rather than just modifying score interpretations as a function of context, however, SOMPA also interprets scores modified as a function of context. By so interpreting statistically adjusted scores essentially by fiat, without benefit of supportive psychological theory or research, SOMPA's validated measurement base unfortunately becomes seriously overextended. That is, the statistical modification of IQ scores to generate the derivative construct of ''learning potential'' is both inadequately conceptualized in relation to the procedural steps involved in ''measuring'' this construct and, at least at this time, sorely lacking in either empirical or construct validity (Sattler, 1982).

Assessment *in* Context, or Appraising Traits in Action

The likelihood of interactions between measured attributes of the person and situational factors influencing behavior compels us to view the child's intellect and personality as more than a collection of static traits susceptible to passive attempts at assessment. When confronted with the prospect of interactions, it is not enough to ascertain the strength of a particular attribute or trait under standard or optimal conditions—in addition, one should determine the extent to which the trait operates under a variety of relevant conditions. In particular, especially for purposes of predicting performance in structured settings such as classrooms, a trait should be assessed under conditions that reveal its dynamic interactions with situational demands. This suggests that we should attempt to assess interactive processes and interactive effects directly—that we should measure functional characteristics of the child not merely as general traits but as expressed in the situation and under the conditions to which inferences are to be drawn and predictions made.

From this standpoint, the major assessment task becomes one of identifying pertinent situations for revealing and appraising the behavior in question or else one of eliciting the relevant behavior by appropriate situational manipulations. As a consequence, most approaches to assessment *in* context are embedded in naturally occurring situations of interest or else in contrived situations carefully designed to simulate a real-life counterpart. Prominent examples of assessment in context with adults include the use of stress interviews to assess tolerance for cognitive and emotional strain (Murray, 1948), leaderless group discussions to assess leadership potential (Bass, 1960), and job tryouts or probationary periods and work samples to assess job performance skills (Dunnette, 1976; Guion, 1978).

Examples of assessment in context with children—in addition to behavioral observations in naturally occurring structured settings such as classrooms (e.g., Stallings, 1977) and unstructured settings such as free play (e.g., Emmerich, 1977)—include what has been termed "psychosituational assessment" and "behavioral assessment," which are highly similar approaches. In *psychosituational assessment,* behavior is directly and continuously measured as a function of the immediate antecedent and consequent conditions that evoke, reinforce, and perpetuate the behavior in the situations where it naturally occurs (Bersoff, 1973; Ellett & Bersoff, 1976). Emphasis is on continuous feedback about the child's current performance level—especially about undesirable or maladaptive behavior such as academic failure—in relation to environmental conditions that may be eliciting and maintaining the behavior. Such performance feedback as a guide for adaptively adjusting instructional or other intervention strategies, long a common practice in individually prescribed and computer-assisted instruction (Glaser, 1968; Groen & Atkinson, 1966), is akin to what we have advocated elsewhere in the

form of "continuous evaluation as a basis for adaptive action" (Messick & Barrows, 1972, p. 280).

In *behavioral assessment,* samples of child behavior directly pertinent to treatment decisions are taken in a variety of settings in which the behavior normally occurs, ideally using multiple methods to tap verbal, perceptual, motor, and psychophysiological responses (Ciminero & Drabman, 1977). As in psychosituational assessment, emphasis is on identifying antecedent and consequent conditions in the child's environment that are associated with the child's current response capabilities and problem behaviors as a basis for designing, evaluating, or revising intervention procedures (Bergan, 1977). Thus, behavioral assessment aims at the appraisal of specific functional relationships and interactions between behavior and environment. Discussions and examples of behavioral assessment procedures may be found in Bijou and Peterson (1971), Goldfried and D'Zurilla (1969), Kanfer and Saslow (1969), Mischel (1968), and Wiggins (1973).

Stability and Variability in Measurements

The focus in most psychological and educational measurement is on factors contributing to stability in behavior and task performance. But, as we have seen, there are also numerous factors contributing to systematic variability in behavior and performance. Indeed, much of our concern about context effects pertains to variability in individual performance across situations, times, and tasks and to the possibility that individuals from different family or cultural backgrounds might perform differently if the task conditions were altered. This latter point mirrors Cole's dictum that "cultural differences reside more in differences in the situations to which different cultural groups apply their skills than in differences in the skills possessed by the groups in question" (Cole & Bruner, 1971, p. 874; Cole, Gay, Glick, & Sharp, 1971). In addition to variability in individual performance across *situational contexts,* however, another source of systematic differences in performance is behavioral variability across individuals as a function of personality, motivation, and cognitive styles—which has led to a parallel emphasis on the *intrapersonal context* of the child as a functioning system.

Elaborate statistical machinery has been developed over the years in the form of psychometric theories of mental test scores to address these issues of response stability and variability. In these mathematical formulations, nonsystematic response *vari-*

ability is associated with the concept of measurement error, which is the keystone of test-score theories. Although primary emphasis historically has been on random error generally from whatever source, modern developments delineate a variety of specific sources of error stemming from differences not only in persons but in items, instruments, settings, occasions, observers, and other facets of the measurement context and procedure. Response *stability* in these psychometric models is associated with the concept of true score—or one of its generic variants such as universe score—which is the average or expected value of the obtained score over replications. Systematic response variability is associated with true-score variance or with components of true-score variance reflective of consistent individual differences, as identified by factor analysis or other multivariate statistical techniques. If error is the keystone of test-score theories, then true score, in one guise or another, is the touchstone.

These models typically take it for granted, however, that the person or any other object of measurement is essentially in a steady state such that the errors fluctuate irregularly around zero. The models are reasonably "satisfactory as long as there is no regular trend in performance, . . . [but they] will not deal adequately with the stability of scores that are subject to trends, or to order effects arising from the measurement process" (Cronbach, Gleser, Nanda, & Rajaratnam, 1972, pp. 363–364). This is a problem mainly for undetected trends because, once a trend is detected, it may be handled by applying the score model at two or more selected points in the trend interval and then treating the trend as a functional relationship (Kane, 1982). Models and methods for assessing trends—or more generally, systematic changes in scores and structures as a function of time and intervening events—in most instances involve the comparison of scores or structures obtained in two or more steady states. For this reason, the assessment of change—whether viewed as a difference in level and variability, a difference in relative ordering, or a difference in pattern or dimensional structure—benefits from a careful examination of the extensively developed psychometrics of steady state.

THE PSYCHOMETRICS OF STEADY STATE

Theories of measurement broadly conceived may be viewed as loosely integrated conceptual frameworks within which are embedded rigorously formulated statistical models of estimation and inference about the properties of measurements or scores.

Measurement theories typically treat a rich complex of fundamental issues concerning the interpretation and use of scores, which will be simplified here for purposes of discussion in terms of four main rubrics: first, the issue of consistency and precision of measurements as addressed by concepts of reliability, generalizability, error of measurement, and information; second, the issue of the substantive meaning of measurements—or of the adequacy of theoretical interpretations—as embodied in the concept of construct validity; third, the issue of utility of measurements as complicated by problems of bias and fairness in application; and finally, the issue of the generality of a measure's meaning and utility across different population groups and ecological settings.

Reliability and the Dependability of Measurements

Almost all psychometric theories of test scores are probabilistic in character because of the compelling nature of the concept of measurement error—that is, there is a general expectation that any measurement procedure is subject to disturbance or error from a variety of sources. The respondent might be fatigued or unmotivated, for example, the items too difficult or diverse, the observer inattentive, the response form confusing, the setting distracting, and the time of day or year atypical. These and other sources of influence might affect some respondents or observers more than others at any one moment and might affect individual respondents or observers more at one moment than another. Such "momentary variations in the circumstances of measurement which are unrelated to the measurement procedure itself . . . are assumed to be random" or unsystematic and thereby amenable to definition in statistical or probabilistic terms (Wiggins, 1973, p. 280). Thus, in essence, measurement error is considered to be a random variable representing "a disturbance that is due to a composite of a multitude of factors not controlled in the measurement procedure" (Lord & Novick, 1968, p. 38). Since an individual's observed score (X_{ji}) on a particular test or assessment device, denoted j, undoubtedly contains measurement error (E_{ji}), then clearly that portion without the error ($X_{ji} - E_{ji}$) constitutes the true measurement, usually called the true score (T_{ji}). All theories of reliability conceive of observed measurements in these terms—that is, as comprising two components, one due to error and the other not:

$$X_{ji} = T_{ji} + E_{ji} \qquad (1)$$

Reliability theories differ, however, in the way in

which the nonerror component or true score is conceptualized.

Classical Test Theory

The basic equations of classical test theory can be derived from either a definition of true score or a definition of error score, combined in each case with a definition of parallel tests (Gulliksen, 1950). Once true score is defined, the properties of error can be derived, and vice versa. For example, by assuming that the number of successive independent measurements of the same attribute or trait may be increased indefinitely, true score has been defined as the limit of the average of these measurements; or, what amounts to the same thing, as a person's observed score on an infinitely long test (Gulliksen, 1950; Lord & Novick, 1968). Such conceptions of true score assume that successive measurements are unaffected by the previous measurements and that neither the attribute being measured nor the person's attribute value changes systematically. Alternatively, since random errors are irregular and unsystematic and cancel each other out on the average over a sufficiently large number of observations, error score has been defined as being uncorrelated with both true scores and other error scores and as having a mean of zero (Gulliksen, 1950). Because the concept of measurement error is intuitively compelling while that of true score is philosophically controversial (Loevinger, 1957; Thorndike, 1964) and because the associated mathematics is more simple (though less powerful), we will develop the basic relationships of test theory from the definition of error. These relationships turn out to be essentially the same, however, whether a definition of error or of true score is used as the starting point.

Implications of Measurement Error

Since the mean error score is zero ($M_E = 0$) by definition, it follows from the basic conception of observed score given in Equation 1 that the mean observed score equals the mean true score ($M_X = M_T$). It should be noted that Equation 1 also holds in deviation score form—that is, $x = t + e$, where $x = (X - M_X)$, $t = (T - M_T)$, and $e = (E - M_E = E)$. Furthermore, since true and error scores are uncorrelated ($r_{TE} = 0$), the observed score variance $\left(\sigma_X^2 = \dfrac{\Sigma x^2}{N} \right)$ may also be expressed as the sum of true and error components—namely, the true variance (σ_T^2) plus the er-

ror variance (σ_E^2):

$$\sigma_X^2 = \sigma_T^2 + \sigma_E^2 \qquad (2)$$

Given uncorrelated true and error scores and the statistical formulas for correlation $\left(r_{XY} = \dfrac{\Sigma xy}{N\sigma_X\sigma_Y} \right)$ or covariance $\left(\sigma_{XY} = \dfrac{\Sigma xy}{N} = r_{XY}\sigma_X\sigma_Y \right)$, Equation 1 also yields a representation for the correlation between observed scores and true scores as the ratio of true to observed standard deviations $\left(r_{XT} = \dfrac{\sigma_T}{\sigma_X} \right)$. Consequently, the square of the correlation between observed scores and true scores equals the ratio of true variance to observed variance:

$$r_{XT}^2 = \frac{\sigma_T^2}{\sigma_X^2} \qquad (3)$$

Similarly, the square of the correlation between observed scores and error scores equals the ratio of error variance to observed variance $\left(r_{XE}^2 = \dfrac{\sigma_E^2}{\sigma_X^2} \right)$, and from Equations 2 and 3

$$r_{XT}^2 = 1 - \frac{\sigma_E^2}{\sigma_X^2} = 1 - r_{XE}^2 \qquad (4)$$

Solving Equation 4 for σ_E yields

$$\sigma_E = \sigma_X \sqrt{1 - r_{XT}^2} \qquad (5)$$

which is the familiar formula from statistics for the *standard error of estimate* in the regression of observed score on true score. The statistical formula for the standard error in estimating scores on one variable Y from another variable Z is $\sigma_{Y|Z} = \sigma_Y \sqrt{1 - r_{YZ}^2}$. Thus, σ_E is interpretable as the standard deviation of observed scores for a given true score ($\sigma_{X|T}$).

The relationships developed up to this point follow directly from Equation 1 and the definition of error. The development of formulas for reliability, however, requires some additional definitional assumptions. Specifically, since the intuitive concept of reliability refers to the degree to which repeated measurements with the same or interchangeable instruments are consistent, we need a definition of interchangeable instruments—that is, where it makes no difference which test is used. In classical test theory, interchangeable instruments are called *parallel tests*, denoted j and j', which are defined as yielding measurements having identical true scores ($T_{ji} = T_{j'i}$) and identical error variances ($\sigma_{E_j}^2 = \sigma_{E_{j'}}^2$). Because errors are uncorrelated by definition, we cannot assume that error scores on one test are equal to error scores on a parallel test, but we can postulate equal variability of errors. Thus, parallel tests measure exactly the same thing in the same scale equally well. From this definition and Equation 1, it can be demonstrated that parallel tests have equal observed means ($M_{X_j} = M_{X_{j'}}$), equal observed variances ($\sigma^2_{\bar{X}_j} = \sigma^2_{\bar{X}_{j'}}$), equal intercorrelations ($r_{X_jX_{j'}} = r_{X_jX_{j''}} = r_{X_{j'}X_{j''}}$), and equal correlations with any other test k ($r_{X_jX_k} = r_{X_jX_k} = r_{X_{j'}X_k}$).

We are now in a position to express the correlation between two parallel measurements, which for convenience will be denoted here as $r_{XX'}$ rather than $r_{X_jX_{j'}}$, as a function of their true and error components, where $X = T + E$ and $X' = T + E'$. It follows from Equation 1 in deviation score form, from the properties of parallel tests, and from the definition of uncorrelated errors that

$$r_{XX'} = \frac{\Sigma xx'}{N\sigma_X\sigma_{X'}} = \frac{\Sigma(t + e)(t + e')}{N\sigma^2_{\bar{X}}} = \frac{\sigma^2_T}{\sigma^2_{\bar{X}}} \quad (6)$$

Thus, the correlation between parallel measurements equals the ratio of true-score variance to observed-score variance, which has already been shown in Equation 3 to equal the square of the correlation between observed scores and true scores. Hence, we may write

$$r^2_{XT} = \frac{\sigma^2_T}{\sigma^2_{\bar{X}}} = r_{XX'} \quad (7)$$

Although it is traditional to define reliability as the correlation between parallel tests (Gulliksen, 1950), Lord and Novick (1968) prefer to define it as the squared correlation between observed score and true score (r^2_{XT}) "to emphasize the fact that reliability may be *defined* without using the concept of parallel measurements and because this quantity proves useful in models of wider application" (p. 61). In any event, as seen in Equation 7, the *reliability* of test scores is a measure of the degree of true-score variation relative to observed-score variation. As a variance ratio, reliability cannot be negative and must be a quantity in the interval from 0 to 1.

It follows directly from Equation 6 that the true-score variance, an unobservable quantity, equals the covariance between parallel measurements, a potentially observable quantity:

$$\sigma^2_T = \sigma^2_X r_{XX'} = \sigma_{XX'} \quad (8)$$

It also follows from Equation 6 and Equation 2 that

$$\sigma_E = \sigma_X\sqrt{1 - r_{XX'}} \quad (9)$$

which is known as the *standard error of measurement*. A comparison of Equation 9 with Equation 5

makes it clear that the standard error of measurement is the standard error of estimate for the prediction of observed scores from true scores expressed in terms of potentially observable values. It is also clear from Equations 4 and 7 that the correlation between observed and error scores may similarly be expressed in terms of potentially observable values ($r_{XE} = \sqrt{1 - r_{XX'}}$). These quantities are potentially observable to the extent that the repeated measurements are sufficiently parallel, which may be attested to in large part by verifying empirically the properties of parallel tests—that is, equal observed means, variances, intercorrelations, and correlations with other tests (Lord & Novick, 1968).

The kinds of inferences that can be made when the parallelism of repeated measurements is questionable are addressed by statistical models that relax the requirements of parallelism in various ways. Some of these models will be examined briefly in the next section, but for present purposes a few examples should make the intention of such models clear. For instance, test forms may be considered to be only imperfectly or nominally parallel, but true score is defined as the expected value over a population of such forms. Or, repeated measurements might have identical true scores but different error variances, a condition which is termed "tau-equivalent" or true-score equivalent. Or, they might have true scores that differ solely by an additive constant as well as having different error variances, which is termed "essentially tau-equivalent" (Lord & Novick, 1968). As a final instance, repeated measurements might have true scores that correlate perfectly with each other yet display not only unequal error variances and true-score means as in essentially tau-equivalent tests, but unequal true-score variances as well—a condition known as "congeneric" (Jöreskog & Sörbom, 1979). Although each of these kinds of tests, like parallel tests, may still be said to measure the same thing, they no longer necessarily measure it equally well or in the same scale.

Regression Estimates and Confidence Intervals

Returning now to classical test theory with parallel measurements, we have seen that the standard error of measurement (Equation 9), being the standard error of estimate for the prediction of observed scores from true scores (Equation 5), is the standard deviation of observed scores for a given true score ($\sigma_{X|T}$). Since the regression function of observed score on true score is linear with a slope of unity

(Lord & Novick, 1968), the least squares regression estimate of a person's observed score ($\hat{X}_i$) is, not surprisingly, that person's true score. This is immediately apparent from the least squares linear regression function, which takes the following general form for the prediction of scores on one variable Y from scores on another variable Z:

$$\hat{Y}_i = M_Y - \beta_{YZ}M_Z + \beta_{YZ}Z_i$$
$$= M_Y + \beta_{YZ}(Z_i - M_Z)$$

where the slope or regression coefficient

$\beta_{YZ} = r_{YZ}\dfrac{\sigma_Y}{\sigma_Z}$. The slope of the regression function

of X on T is $\beta_{XT} = r_{XT}\dfrac{\sigma_X}{\sigma_T} = 1$. This follows directly from Equation 3. The estimated observed score is: $\hat{X}_i = M_X - M_T + T_i = T_i$, since $M_X = M_T$.

Although the standard error of measurement (σ_E) is usually employed to establish "reasonable" confidence limits for the inclusion of a person's true score in a band around his or her observed score (Gulliksen, 1950), this is likely to be misleading, possibly grossly misleading (Lord & Novick, 1968; Cronbach et al., 1972). This is partly because σ_E is the standard error of estimate for a given true score, not a given observed score, but mainly because confidence bands should be applied, if at all, around the estimated true score, which is regressed toward the group mean, not around the observed score. Although σ_E may be viewed as the error made in substituting the observed score for the true score (Gulliksen, 1950), this error is symmetric not around the observed score but around the true score. Confidence bands based on σ_E may be established centered around the estimated true score and then legitimately applied with reference to the observed score (Nunnally, 1967). For example, on a test with a mean of 100, a standard deviation of 10, a reliability of .91, and a standard error of measurement of 3, an individual obtaining an observed score of 120 would have an estimated true score regressed toward the mean ($\hat{T}_i = 118$); a confidence band of ± 2 standard errors around the estimated true score (112–124) can be used with the observed score of 120 to indicate the range in which that person's true score is likely to fall with about .95 probability. The resulting confidence zone, which is asymmetric around the observed score ($120 + 4$ to $120 - 8$), reflects the error made in substituting an individual's observed score for his or her true score.

Of much more practical concern, then, is the regression function of true score on observed score. In the least squares linear regression model, the slope of this function, given Equations 3 and 6, is

$\beta_{TX} = r_{XT}\dfrac{\sigma_T}{\sigma_X} = \dfrac{\sigma_T^2}{\sigma_{\hat{X}}^2} = r_{XX'}$. The estimated true score is

$$\hat{T}_i = M_T - r_{XX'}M_X + r_{XX'}X_i$$
$$= r_{XX'}X_i + (1 - r_{XX'})M_X \qquad (10)$$

Thus, the regression coefficient β_{TX} of true score on observed score is equal to the reliability of the test scores, and estimated true scores are equal to observed scores only for perfectly reliable tests. Otherwise, the less reliable the test scores, the more weight is placed on the group mean in the least squares regression estimate of an individual true score. The standard error of estimate for the regression of true on observed score ($\sigma_{T|X}$), given Equations 7 and 8, is

$$\sigma_{T|X} = \sigma_T\sqrt{1 - r_{XT}^2} = \sigma_X\sqrt{r_{XX'}}\sqrt{1 - r_{XX'}}$$

The use of linear regression estimates of true scores has been cautiously recommended by Cronbach and his colleagues (1972), in which case $\sigma_{T|X}$ would be an appropriate standard error for establishing confidence intervals around the estimated true score (Dudek, 1979). Confidence bands based on $\sigma_{T|X}$ reflect the error made in substituting an individual's estimated true score for his or her actual true score. However, because the regression of T on X is generally not linear (Lord & Novick, 1968), the wisdom of using true-score regression estimates in practice has been seriously questioned (Lumsden, 1976).

Correlation Between True Scores

The next relationship to be developed from classical test theory is an extremely important one from the standpoint of both the substantive interpretation and the practical utility of test scores—namely, the correlation between true scores on any two tests j and k. Indeed, in Spearman's articles on "The Proof and Measurement of Association between Two Things" (1904) and on "Correlation Calculated from Faulty Data" (1910), this problem effectively launched the development of test theory as a distinct discipline. The problem is central because psychologists are interested in drawing inferences not about relationships between two test scores or between test scores and criterion scores, all of which contain error, but about relationships between the constructs or traits reliably assessed by these fallible scores. Although we recognize that interpreting true scores on these tests as adequate representations of particular constructs or traits is a separate issue—namely, that of construct validity—nevertheless, the correlations to be appraised in practical as well as scientific applications are those between true scores unaffected by measurement errors, not those between observed scores.

From Equation 1, the covariance of observed scores between any two tests j and k may be written as

$$\sigma_{X_j X_k} = \frac{1}{N} \Sigma x_j x_k = \frac{1}{N} \Sigma (t_j + e_j)(t_k + e_k) \quad (11)$$

Because error scores by definition are unrelated to both true scores and other error scores, this reduces to

$$\sigma_{X_j X_k} = \frac{1}{N} \Sigma t_j t_k = \sigma_{T_j T_k} \quad (12)$$

Thus, the covariance between observed scores is equal to the covariance between true scores. Rewriting this relationship in correlational notation yields

$$\sigma_{X_j X_k} = r_{X_j X_k} \sigma_{X_j} \sigma_{X_k} = r_{T_j T_k} \sigma_{T_j} \sigma_{T_k} = \sigma_{T_j T_k} \quad (13)$$

Since the *predictive validity* of test j in predicting any other test or criterion k is classically defined as the absolute value of the correlation between them, it follows from Equation 13 that the predictive validity of j in relation to k may be written as

$$r_{X_j X_k} = \frac{\sigma_{T_j T_k}}{\sigma_{X_j} \sigma_{X_k}}$$

This leads to the illuminating observation that if j and k were parallel measures, then $\sigma_{X_j} = \sigma_{X_k} = \sigma_X$ and $\sigma_{T_j T_k} = \sigma_T^2$, so that from Equation 6

$$r_{X_j X_k} = \frac{\sigma_T^2}{\sigma_X^2} = r_{XX'}$$

That is, the reliability of a test is its predictive validity with respect to a parallel test.

More importantly, for *nonparallel* measurements j and k, it also follows from Equation 13, given the value of the true-score standard deviation from Equation 8 ($\sigma_T = \sigma_X \sqrt{r_{XX'}}$) and the availability of parallel forms j, j' and k, k' for each test separately, that

$$r_{T_j T_k} = \frac{\sigma_{X_j X_k}}{\sigma_{T_j} \sigma_{T_k}} = \frac{r_{X_j X_k}}{\sqrt{r_{X_j X_{j'}}} \sqrt{r_{X_k X_{k'}}}} \quad (14)$$

This result is a widely used formula called the *correction for attenuation*. The name derives from the fact that the correlation between observed scores, being attenuated by the unreliability of the measurements, is less than the correlation between corre-

sponding true scores. If the reliabilities of the measurements are known or can be estimated, then Equation 14 can be used to correct for the attenuation due to measurement errors, thereby estimating the correlation between true scores. Since the reliability coefficients appearing in the denominator of Equation 14 are numbers less than unity, except for the ideal of perfectly reliable scores, the disattenuated estimate of the true-score correlation will as a rule be greater than the observed-score correlation.

Since it is sometimes desired in predictive validity studies to estimate the correlation between a test and a perfectly reliable criterion, another useful attenuation formula may be derived by a similar line of development—namely, a formula for the correlation between observed scores on one test j and true scores on another test or criterion k:

$$r_{X_j T_k} = \frac{r_{X_j X_k}}{\sqrt{r_{X_k X_{k'}}}} \quad (15)$$

Substituting Equation 15 into Equation 14, we obtain

$$r_{T_j T_k} \sqrt{r_{X_j X_{j'}}} = r_{X_j T_k} \leq \sqrt{r_{X_j X_{j'}}} \quad (16)$$

since $r_{T_j T_k}$ must be unity or less. Thus, the predictive validity of a test j with respect to any criterion k, even a perfectly reliable criterion, cannot exceed the square root of the reliability of the test, which is called the *index of reliability*. In other words, given Equation 7 ($\sqrt{r_{X_j X_{j'}}} = r_{X_j T_j}$), the predictive validity of observed scores with respect to any criterion cannot exceed the correlation with their own true scores. As a consequence of Equation 16, high test-score reliability is a necessary, though not a sufficient, condition for high predictive validity.

Estimating Stability and Equivalence

For these test theory developments to have any practical import, however, some empirical means must be available for estimating the reliability of test scores. In classical theory, what is desired is the correlation between truly parallel measurements taken in such a way that the person's true score does not change in the interim—that is, where no practice, fatigue, memory, mood, growth, or other factors influence the repeated measurements. This ideal correlation, which is called the *coefficient of precision*, represents the extent to which test unreliability is due solely to imprecision of measurement—that is, to inadequacies of the test form and testing procedure—rather than to changes in people over time or to a lack of equivalence of purportedly parallel forms (Lord & Novick, 1968). However, since these other contributions to error variance inevitably operate to some extent in practice, they are compounded with the errors of imprecision to various degrees in the different experimental methods of estimating reliability.

There are three generic methods for estimating reliability with ostensibly parallel measurements— one based on the correlation between repetitions of the same test (the test/retest method), another based on the correlation between alternate test forms (the parallel forms method), and the third based on analysis of consistencies among items or subparts of a single test (the internal analysis method). In the test/ retest method, the correlation between scores from successive administrations of the same test is likely to be inflated by memory and practice effects if the interval between testing is short, thereby yielding an overestimate of the coefficient of precision. However, as the time interval between testings increases, the test/retest correlation typically decreases because changes in the person are likely to become more important than memory effects or even measurement imprecision. For this reason, the test/retest correlation is called a *coefficient of stability*. There are as many coefficients of stability as there are time intervals and testing conditions investigated.

In the parallel forms method, two versions of a test are administered, each containing items different from the other but yielding ostensibly parallel measurements. The correlation between such alternate forms is called a *coefficient of equivalence; it* treats as error not only the imprecision of measurement but also any true-score variance resulting from the lack of strict parallelism in the assumedly parallel scores. However, since alternate forms are administered successively in practice, the correlation between them also includes errors due to variations in the persons and the testing conditions. This may be important whether the forms are administered in immediate succession (e.g., because of practice or fatigue effects) or administered hours or days apart (e.g., because of mood fluctuations or true trait changes). For this reason, the correlation between parallel forms is often termed a *coefficient of equivalence and stability*. In practical applications, when the time interval between administrations is short and the conditions of testing are equivalent, the parallel forms method usually yields a correlation coefficient that approximates, though it tends to underestimate, the coefficient of precision (i.e., its major source of error is the imprecision of the measurements). This is especially so if the order of administration of the alternate forms is counterbalanced to appraise and control for practice and other sequence effects. On the other hand, if major systematic

changes are anticipated as a consequence of practice, measurement error might be better estimated using specialized test theory models that take into account practice effects (Whitely, 1979).

Estimating Internal Consistency

In the internal analysis method, correlations are computed not between repetitions of the same or parallel tests, but between subparts of a single test. Usually, either the test is divided into two subparts, traditionally called "split halves," which are then correlated with one another, or else each item is considered to be a subpart and the item variances and covariances are subjected to analysis. A popular technique for constructing split halves is to place alternate odd-numbered and even-numbered items in the two parts (the odd/even method), but it is better to assign items randomly to the two halves. It is better still to match item pairs on means and standard deviations and then assign one member of each pair randomly to a half-test. Since the correlation between scores on the half-tests estimates the reliability of a test of half-length, we need some means of estimating the reliability of the full-length test which is the composite of the two parts. If the two component half-tests are approximately parallel, this stepped-up reliability of the full-length test may be obtained from the formula for the reliability of a composite of parallel subparts, which is known as the *Spearman-Brown formula* (Gulliksen, 1950; Lord & Novick, 1968). According to this formula, the reliability of a composite X of two parallel components Y and Y' is

$$r_{XX'} = \frac{2r_{YY'}}{1 + r_{YY'}} \qquad (17)$$

The generalized form of the Spearman-Brown formula for the reliability of a composite test composed of K parallel components is

$$r_{XX'} = \frac{Kr_{YY'}}{1 + (K - 1)r_{YY'}} \qquad (18)$$

Thus, the reliability of a composite test increases as its length is increased by adding parallel components. It should be noted that as long as the correlation between component parts is positive, no matter how small, test reliability may be systematically increased in this manner. Indeed, if the numerator and denominator of Equation 18 are divided by K, it is clear that as K increases indefinitely the reliability of the composite test approaches unity. It should also be noted that if the components are in fact not parallel, the Spearman-Brown formula yields too small an estimate of reliability for the full-length test (Lord & Novick, 1968).

This line of argument may be extended to the treatment of each of the K items (Y_g) on a test as a component part—that is, by viewing a test score as a composite of item scores. Although the general Spearman-Brown rationale applies in the case of parallel items, a less restrictive formulation is more widely applicable. This takes the form of a lower-bound estimate of test reliability, called *coefficient* α by Cronbach (1951), which can be computed from the test variance and item variances obtained in a single test administration:

$$\alpha = \frac{K}{K-1}\left(1 - \frac{\Sigma\sigma_{Y_g}^2}{\sigma_X^2}\right) \qquad (19)$$

This formula also holds if Y_g is viewed as a subtest rather than an item. Furthermore, coefficient α *equals* the stepped-up test reliability ($r_{\hat{X}T}^2$), not just the lower bound of reliability, when the subparts or items are essentially tau-equivalent—that is, when their true scores differ solely by an additive constant (Lord & Novick, 1968). Like parallel measurements, this implies unit true-score correlations and equal true-score variances and covariances but, unlike parallel measurements, does not require equal error variances or even equal true-score means.

If the subparts or items are in fact parallel, then coefficient α is equivalent to the general Spearman-Brown formula for the reliability of a composite test composed of K parallel components (Lord & Novick, 1968). Thus, coefficient α is the stepped-up mean item intercorrelation (Stanley, 1957). As in the Spearman-Brown formula, coefficient α increases as the length of the test is increased by adding appropriate items or components. Moreover, with respect to split-halves, coefficient α has the compelling interpretive property that it is the average of the αs for all possible assignments of the items to split-halves. If the K items are assigned to two half-tests randomly, coefficient α for the K items is the expected value of the α for the two random halves (Cronbach, 1951). Because of these and other properties, some measurement specialists feel that coefficient α is one of the most fundamental formulas in all test theory: "It is so pregnant with meaning that it should routinely be applied to all new tests" (Nunnally, 1967, p. 196).

Some widely used special cases of coefficient α were originally derived by Kuder and Richardson (1937) for binary items—that is, items dichotomously scored either zero or unity—and for the further restriction of equal item difficulties. These two special formulas are known as KR20 and KR21, respectively. Since for binary items the variance of item g equals $p_g(1 - p_g)$, where p_g is the proportion of individuals getting the item correct, coefficient α reduces to

$$\text{KR20} = \frac{K}{K-1}\left(1 - \frac{\Sigma p_g(1 - p_g)}{\sigma_X^2}\right) \qquad (20)$$

Further, since for binary items of equal difficulty the mean test score equals K times the average or constant value $\bar{p}$, or $M_X = \Sigma p_g = K\bar{p}$, coefficient α under these circumstances becomes a simple function of the test mean and variance:

$$\text{KR21} = \frac{K}{K-1}\left(1 - \frac{M_X - \frac{1}{K}M_X^2}{\sigma_X^2}\right) \qquad (21)$$

In spite of its computational simplicity, KR21 should rarely be used in practice for other than quick or informal analyses because it is attenuated by variability in item difficulties and hence is typically lower than KR20.

Test reliability based on the internal analysis method—that is, determined from the analysis of item variance or from the correlation between split halves—is called a *coefficient of internal consistency* or, at times, of *homogeneity*. Although the concept of a homogeneous test is variously and imprecisely defined in psychometric literature, it generally conveys the notion of a test whose components all measure the same thing. Lord and Novick (1968) add an important qualification to this general notion based on the excellent rationale that since coefficient α is equal (as opposed to being a lower bound) to the reliability of a composite test if and only if all test components are essentially tau-equivalent, it seems natural to define homogeneity in terms of this property. "Thus a homogenous test is one whose components all 'measure the same thing' in their true-score components" (Lord & Novick, 1968, p. 95). Since essential tau-equivalence, as we have seen, permits unequal error variances and true-score means but requires equal true-score variances and covariances, and since true-score covariance is equal to observed-score covariance by Equation 13, a homogeneous test has equal observed-score covariances among all its components. Since homogeneity is required for coefficient α to be equal to the reliability rather than a lower bound, while the stronger requirement of parallelism is needed for the Spearman-Brown formula, departures from homogeneity contribute to error variance in reliability coefficients based on the internal analysis method.

Multiple Sources of Error

Another source of error for such coefficients is the degree of speededness of the test. This is seen most readily from a consideration of the odd/even method. Since any examinee failing to complete a block of items at the end of a test will receive a score of zero on each of these items, the odd and even scores for that set of items will correlate perfectly and thereby distort the reliability estimate. With speeded or partially speeded tests, reliability should be estimated from the correlation between separately timed alternate forms or repetitions of the same test, or from the α across separately timed component subtests. As a rule, if a test is unspeeded for all practical purposes and either quite homogenous or of substantial length, coefficient α should give a good approximation to the coefficient of precision. Furthermore, "with tests of moderate length that have been specifically designed to measure a single underlying trait, coefficient α should provide a useful approximation to the reliability coefficient for most procedures that do not involve corrections for attenuation" (Lord & Novick, 1968, p. 136).

The latter caveat is a reminder that all experimental methods for approximating reliability, with the possible exception of short-term test/retest coefficients, to some degree yield underestimates. Since these reliability estimates appear in the denominator of the attenuation formula (Equation 14), it follows that the resulting corrections typically produce overestimates, sometimes even yielding disattenuated correlations greater than unity. For example, if the correlation to be corrected (r_{XY}) is between test scores based on single administrations of X and Y close together in time, the measurement error present in the estimate of r_{XY} is primarily due to the imprecision of the two measurements. Yet, in each estimate of $r_{XX'}$ and $r_{YY'}$ at least one additional source of error variance may be introduced that is not present in r_{XY}—for example, item or subtest heterogeneity in internal-analysis estimates, variation between forms in parallel-forms estimates, and changes in persons and conditions in test/retest estimates. Although this state of affairs has led some experts to bemoan that "the correction should never be used" (Lumsden, 1976, p. 256), it seems more appropriate to strive for experimental designs that estimate $r_{XX'}$ and $r_{YY'}$ based on the same sources of error variation as are involved in the estimate of r_{XY} (Winne & Belfry, 1982). More generally, it should be clear by now that many factors contribute to variations among measurements, and the choice as to which factors should or should not be viewed as sources of "error" depends on the intended use of the coefficient and the kind of generalization that is sought.

Effects of Group Heterogeneity

The interpretation of a reliability coefficient depends, however, not only on the specification of its sources of error but on the specification of the population or group on which it is based. Since error variance tends to be characteristic of a measurement procedure if administered under standardized conditions, differences in observed-score variance for different groups usually reflect differences in their true-score variance. Since reliability is the ratio of true variance to observed variance—or to the sum of true variance plus error variance—and since error variance remains relatively constant across groups assessed under the same conditions of measurement, test reliability increases as *group heterogeneity* increases, as does the predictive validity of the scores. For this reason, a reliability coefficient alone is not very informative about a test as a measuring instrument.

Because the size of the reliability coefficient depends on the variability of the group on which it is calculated, to interpret its psychometric import we need to know the observed-score variance as well, or at least some function of the observed-score variance such as the standard error of measurement. Since the standard error of measurement varies directly with observed-score variance and inversely with reliability (Equation 9), it is less sensitive to changes in group heterogeneity than is reliability alone. Indeed, if a relatively low reliability coefficient is obtained on a group having a known restricted variance, its value for a more heterogeneous group having any specified variance may be estimated by a formula simply derived by assuming that the error variances or standard errors of measurement are the same in both groups:

$$ r_{XX'} = 1 - \frac{\sigma_x^2}{\sigma_X^2} \ (1 - r_{xx'}) $$

where X refers to test scores obtained in the more heterogeneous group and x to scores on the same test in the more restricted or curtailed group. This formula, which is called a *correction for restriction of range*, is one of several formulas relating to the effects of group heterogeneity and selection on reliability and predictive validity presented in Gulliksen (1950) and Lord and Novick (1968).

In regard to the effects of group heterogeneity on predictive validity, if the range of scores is curtailed as a consequence of explicit selection on some predictor variable X, then the validity coefficient r_{XY} in the unrestricted group may be estimated by a formula derived by assuming equal linear regression slopes and standard errors of estimate in the selected and unselected sample—that is, by assuming that $r_{xy} \dfrac{\sigma_y}{\sigma_x} = r_{XY} \dfrac{\sigma_Y}{\sigma_X}$ and $\sigma_y \sqrt{1 - r_{xy}^2} = \sigma_Y \sqrt{1 - r_{XY}^2}$: For the simple two-variable case,

$$R_{XY}^2 = \frac{\dfrac{\sigma_X^2}{\sigma_x^2}\, r_{xy}^2}{1 + \left(\dfrac{\sigma_X^2}{\sigma_x^2} - 1 \right) r_{xy}^2} \tag{23}$$

A comparison of Equation 23 with Equation 18 indicates that the square of the validity coefficient in the unselected sample is stepped up in relation to the squared validity in the selected group in the manner of the Spearman-Brown formula, where the multiplying factor $K = \dfrac{\sigma_X^2}{\sigma_x^2}$ is the ratio of predictor variance in the unselected group to that in the selected group (Gulliksen, 1950; Cronbach, 1971).

Another useful index is the *signal-to-noise ratio* (S/N) which, unlike the reliability coefficient, is directly proportional to true-score variance across groups as well as to observed-score variance, assuming group comparability of error variance. As might be expected, the signal-to-noise ratio is the ratio of true-score variance to error variance or of reliability to unreliability:

$$\frac{S}{N} = \frac{\sigma_T^2}{\sigma_E^2} = \frac{r_{XX'}}{1 - r_{XX'}} \tag{24}$$

An important property of this index is that it is directly proportional to test length, in contrast with the stepped-up Spearman-Brown estimate of reliability which is a hyperbolic function of test length. Moreover, the reciprocal of the signal-to-noise ratio multiplied by the length of the test is invariant with respect to test length (Cronbach & Gleser, 1964; Gulliksen, 1950). Thus, as test length increases, the test's unreliability relative to its reliability decreases proportionately in order to maintain a constant product.

True Scores as Expected Values

This exposition of classical test theory shares a common weakness with most traditional presentations—namely, the variables and relationships are represented as sample-based values rather than as estimates of population parameters. However, this is a consequence of opting for simpler mathematics and for the definition of error as the starting point, and it is not an intrinsic limitation of classical test theory per se. For example, Lord and Novick (1968) demonstrated that under very general conditions true and error scores may be defined or constructed so that they satisfy the assumptions of classical test theory—that is, the assumptions of classical test theory are not postulated but are derived from much simpler assumptions.

By hypothesizing the distribution that might be obtained over a sequence of statistically independent repeated measurements or replications for each individual, observed score is conceived as a random variable, and true score is defined as the expected value of the observed score. The error-score random variable is defined as the difference between the observed-score random variable and the person's true score. By repeated random selection of persons from some well-defined population, an observed-score random variable is also defined for the distribution of measurements over people, thereby permitting a link between error variance within persons over replications and group error variance, which is the expected value or average over persons of the within-persons error variances. Similarly, an observed-score random variable may be defined over repeated sampling of test forms for a specific person as well as over repeated sampling of the combination of test forms and persons. Then, by defining the properties of test forms, such as parallelism and tau-equivalence, Lord and Novick (1968) derive the results of classical test theory in terms of expected values of random variables. More importantly, classical test theory proves to be a special case of this more basic formulation, which also provides the mathematical foundation for a number of more general models such as the generic true-score models mentioned briefly in the next section.

Classical test theory has been discussed here at such length because its basic concepts endure in some form or other in modern formulations and because most of the derived relationships still hold in elaborated or generalized form in these more powerful statistical treatments. This extensive review also illustrates the rich panoply of useful results that are derivable from a small number of intuitively plausible assumptions. Moreover, these results still undergird most of current measurement practice. Nonetheless, there are a variety of critical recurrent problems in scientific as well as applied measurement that classical test theory glosses over or downright mishandles but that modern developments promise to resolve. For this reason, we will briefly examine next some of the contributions and implications of generalizability theory and subsequently of item-response theory.

Generalizability Theory

In the classical theory of reliability, observed-score variance is considered to reflect true subject differences—whether among persons or other objects of measurement—combined with random variation among multiple observations, which is attributed to error. However, since multiple observations may arise from a number of sources, such as different test forms or different occasions or different raters, this means that there are a variety of distinct sources of random variation that may contribute differentially to overall measurement error in any given instance. In other words, the conditions of observation may vary along a number of dimensions or facets. But classical test theory presumes that variation along any of these facets yields parallel measurements having equal means and variances as well as zero interactions of subjects with test forms or occasions or raters. This may be quite reasonable for carefully equated parallel tests, but seems less so for other types of measures such as ratings or behavioral observations. Raters are likely to differ, for example, in the average level and spread of their ratings as well as in the particular qualities they attend to, this latter producing a subject-by-rater interaction (Cronbach et al., 1972).

The literature of classical test theory recognizes assorted types of error and in particular differentiates between occasions and stimulus items or test forms as logically separate facets of observation (Thorndike, 1951; Stanley, 1971). Indeed, the distinctions among coefficients of stability, equivalence, and internal consistency were an attempt to cope with this issue. But these distinctions break down in the face of multiple sources of variation because they do not do justice to the many types of operative error that might influence the variability—and hence the interpretation—of particular measurements. As a rule, investigators are not really interested in the particularities of measurement—in the responses given to particular tasks or items, in the context of a particular tester or observer, in a particular setting on a particular occasion. Both scientific and applied researchers usually wish to draw inferences that go beyond the particular circumstances—that is, they assume that at least some of the conditions of measurement could be altered without seriously affecting the import of the scores.

Universe Scores and Generic True Scores

In the terminology of generalizability theory, investigators act as if there were a universe of observations, any of which would provide a usable basis for score interpretation and decision making. The ideal basis would be something akin to the person's mean score over all acceptable observations, which would represent a *universe score*. "The investigator uses the observed score or some function of it as if it were the universe score. That is, he generalizes from sample to universe. *The question of 'reliability' thus resolves into a question of accuracy of generalization, or generalizability*" (Cronbach et al., 1972, p. 15).

From this perspective, a concern about score reliability is a concern about the extent to which one may defensibly generalize from the particular observations to a broader class of observations. In the test/retest method, we primarily inquire about generalizability across time or occasions; in the parallel-forms method, about generalizability to other measures of the same trait that might equally well have been constructed by the same procedure; in the internal consistency method, about generalizability to other items like these that might just as well have been sampled as representatives of the domain; and, in rater reliability or scorer reliability, we inquire about generalizability across different raters or different scorers. Thus, since the same measure may be generalized to several different universes, the investigator must specify the primary universe or universes of generalization before reliability can be appropriately examined. This is so because the type of generalizability at issue should dictate the type of experimental design needed for collecting reliability data.

In the classical approach, the usual designs either permit variation along one facet while presuming control or randomness of the other facets or else confound the facets in a conglomerate treatment of error. In any event, the resulting classical reliability estimates assume that the multiple measurements associated with varying conditions of observation are parallel. But since different sources of error are likely to operate conjointly in practice, the persistent practical problem is to estimate the magnitude of each type of error variation separately and preferably without the unrealistic requirement that all conditions of observation be strictly parallel.

This problem has been attacked in piecemeal fashion over the years until it received systematic treatment in generic true-score theory (Lord & Novick, 1968) and generalizability theory (Cronbach et al., 1972). For instance, an early contribution relaxed the requirement of parallelism by formally allowing inequality of condition means, thereby extending reliability theory realistically to facets of observation other than equated tests, such as ratings (Ebel, 1951). The term "condition" is used here in the very general sense of Cronbach and his colleagues (1972) to refer to either items, test forms, stimuli or tasks, testers, observers, occasions, settings, or other situations of observation; each type of condition is called a "facet" of observation.

In another development, conditions of observations, primarily test items, were conceived to be sampled from some universe or domain, either randomly or in accordance with a stratified design (Lord, 1955a, 1955b; Tryon, 1957). In this domain-sampling approach, tests are not required to be strictly parallel but only randomly parallel, in the sense that their means, variances, and correlations with true scores differ only by chance. A true score or domain score in this context is the score a person would obtain over all the items in the domain. This model yields equations that are straightforward generalizations of those in classical test theory. For example, the square of the correlation between observed score and true or domain score—that is, the reliability—is equal not to the constant correlation between strictly parallel tests, as in Equation 7, but to the average correlation among randomly parallel tests, which is a natural extension if only chance differences in test properties are assumed (Nunnally, 1967; Tryon 1957).

As one might expect, the simultaneous analysis of two or more facets of observation was accomplished through the application of analysis of variance to reliability problems (Burt, 1955; Lindquist, 1953) and subsequently through the analysis of variance components (Finlayson, 1951; Gleser, Cronbach, & Rajaratnam, 1965; Medley & Mitzel, 1963; Stanley, 1961). Test scores had already been treated, ever since the late 1930s, in terms of a persons-by-items analysis of variance—that is, in terms of an experimental design having a single facet for items—and test reliability had been shown to be a function of mean-square terms (Hoyt, 1941; Jackson, 1939). Hence, extension to multifacet designs, though complicated, was a very good bet. By allowing for alternative definitions of error, such multifacet analysis of scores made it clear that several distinct reliability coefficients can be obtained for a given measurement procedure. It also became clear that increasing the number of observations has di-

verse effects on these coefficients, depending on which facet the observations are added to (Lindquist, 1953).

These several distinct reliability coefficients are usually cast in the form of intraclass correlations, which are also readily estimated from mean-square terms in analysis of variance as well as from variance components (Gleser et al., 1965; Pilliner, 1952). Since an intraclass correlation is the correlation between two variables having arbitrarily interchangeable scores—such as between IQs for a set of twins or between split halves of a test—averaged over all possible arbitrary splits (Guilford, 1954), this seems a natural form for reliability coefficients to take. Indeed, many classical reliability formulas, including coefficient α and KR20, have long been recognized to be intraclass correlations (Stanley, 1971).

Variance Components Models

A systematic approach applicable to multiple facets of observation has been formalized by Lord and Novick (1968) for the problem of estimating test parameters when parallel measurements cannot be presumed. The general model they proposed as a foundation for classical test theory—by virtue of defining multiple observed-score random variables not only in terms of repeated measurements of a given person with a given test but also in terms of random sampling of a population of persons for a given test, of test forms for a given person, and of the various test-person combinations—was seen to be a special case of the random-effects model used in variance components analysis. "The true scores of the classical test theory model play the part of main effects and the error scores, the part of within-group variation" (Lord & Novick, 1968, p. 39).

In this more general formulation, an important distinction is drawn between a *specific true score,* which depends on the conditions under which the measurements are taken, and a *generic true score,* which cuts across a specified set or universe of conditions. For example, experimentally independent repeated measurements for a particular observational setting such as a classroom or for a particular observer such as a teacher will yield a specific true score for that condition, defined as the expected value of this specific observed-score random variable. Similarly, experimentally independent repeated measurements for a different observational setting such as a laboratory or for a different observer such as a researcher or school psychologist will yield a specific true score for each of these conditions, as would experimentally independent repeated measurements for the psychologist observer in the classroom or for the teacher observer in the laboratory. If we now consider repeated measurements obtained by a random sampling of these conditions, the true score so defined is the generic true score that generalizes across conditions. A person's specific true scores are likely to differ from one condition to another, but his or her generic true score is the same across conditions. It is also unlikely that measurements will be strictly parallel across conditions but rather only imperfectly parallel at best or nominally parallel or randomly parallel. A test form might be more difficult, for example, in the unfamiliar setting of the laboratory or with an unfamiliar examiner such as a school psychologist than in the familiar classroom setting with a familiar teacher examiner.

A person's generic true score (μ_i) is the expected value over the conditions of measurement or test forms of his or her specific true scores ($\mu_i = \mathscr{E}_j T_{ji} = \mathscr{E}_j \mathscr{E}_r X_{jir}$), where $\mathscr{E}_j$ is the expectation operator indicating the mean over all conditions or test forms in the specified universe of conditions and $\mathscr{E}_r$ is the mean over replications. The generic true score is a random variable over the population of examinees, and its expected value is the average level or general population mean (μ) of the traits measured by all the test forms or conditions ($\mu = \mathscr{E}_i\mu_i$). The difference between a person's generic true score and the general mean is called the *person effect* ($\mu_i - \mu$), and its variance will be denoted $\sigma^2(i) = \mathscr{E}_i(\mu_i - \mu)^2$. Similarly, the expected value over persons of the specific true scores for a particular condition or test form is a condition parameter (μ_j), usually referred to in the case of test forms as test difficulty ($\mu_j = \mathscr{E}_i T_{ji} = \mathscr{E}_r X_{ji}$). This difficulty parameter μ_j reflects the average level of examinee performance on the jth condition or test form. The difference between this parameter and the general mean ($\mu = \mathscr{E}_i\mu_i = \mathscr{E}_j\mu_j = \mathscr{E}_i\mathscr{E}_j T_{ji}$) is called the *condition effect* or the test effect ($\mu_j - \mu$), and its variance is denoted $\sigma^2(j)$.

The *interaction effect* for person i and condition j is the extent to which the corresponding specific true score's deviation from the general mean differs from that expected from knowledge of the person effect and condition effect: $(T_{ji} - \mu) - (\mu_i - \mu) - (\mu_j - \mu) = T_{ji} - \mu_i - \mu_j + \mu$; its variance is denoted $\sigma^2(ij)$. With repeated measurements of persons in conditions, a *replication effect* may also be defined as the difference between the observed score and the sum of all of these effects plus the general mean—that is, the replication effect includes any source of variation in the observed scores that is not

attributable to person or condition or interaction effects. Its variance is an estimate of $\sigma^2(e)$, which is the average over all conditions or tests of the group specific error variance $\sigma^2(e_j)$, which in turn is the average over persons of the specific error variance $\sigma^2(e_{ji})$. If all measurements were strictly parallel, then $T_{ji} = \mu_i$ and $\mu_j = \mu$ so that the interaction term becomes zero. Thus, the occurrence of substantial interaction effects is an indication that measurements are not parallel. For nonreplicated measurements, the interaction and replication effects collapse into a *residual effect* with variance $\sigma^2(ij,e)$.

These effects represent a partitioning of variance by the general linear analysis-of-variance model in a way that is consistent with the test theory model. The general linear model holds that a person's observed score on the rth replication of the jth test or condition is $X_{jir} = \mu + (\mu_i - \mu) + (\mu_j - \mu) + (T_{ji} - \mu_i - \mu_j + \mu) + E_{jir}$ which is equivalent to $X_{jir} = T_{ji} + E_{jir}$. Furthermore, for the random-effects model, the variances of all these effects summate to equal the total observed-score variance, which is why they are called *variance components:* $\sigma^2_X = \sigma^2(i) + \sigma^2(j) + \sigma^2(ij) + \sigma^2(e)$. This model may be readily extended to encompass additional facets. For example, for a second distinct condition facet k, one would add a main-effect variance component $\sigma^2(k)$ for the new facet along with three new interaction components $\sigma^2(ik)$, $\sigma^2(jk)$, and $\sigma^2(ijk)$. By this mode of variance decomposition, random variables for generic true score, condition difficulty, and interactions are constructed that are uncorrelated, over all test forms pooled, both with each other and with residual error (Lord & Novick, 1968).

For n_i persons drawn at random from an infinitely large population and n_j items or tests or conditions drawn at random from a universe of N_j possibilities, these variance components may be estimated from the expected mean squares in the random-effects model of analysis of variance (Cornfield & Tukey, 1956; Winer, 1962). For a one-facet crossed design of persons by conditions or test forms, the expected among-persons mean square is

$$\mathscr{E}(MS_j) = \sigma^2(e) + \left(1 - \frac{n_j}{N_j}\right)\sigma^2(ij) + n_j\sigma^2(i)$$
$$(25)$$

The expected among-conditions mean square is

$$\mathscr{E}(MS_j) = \sigma^2(e) + \sigma^2(ij) + n_i\sigma^2(j) \quad (26)$$

The expected interaction or residual mean square is

$$\mathscr{E}(MS_{ij}) = \sigma^2(e) + \sigma^2(ij) = \sigma^2(ij,e) \quad (27)$$

The variance component for persons, which is the generic true-score variance, is estimated by

$$\frac{\mathscr{E}(MS_i) - \mathscr{E}(MS_{ij})}{n_j} = \sigma^2(i) - \frac{\sigma^2(ij)}{N_j} \quad (28)$$

If the universe of conditions or test forms is infinite, Equation 28 reduces to $\sigma^2(i)$. But in any event, as long as the universe N_j is fairly large, any bias in this estimate of generic true-score variance will be relatively small.

For a nonreplicated crossed design with two condition facets, such as occasions as well as test forms or observers, and assuming random sampling from an infinite population of persons and very large condition universes, the expected mean squares are:

$$\mathscr{E}(MS_i) = \sigma^2(ijk,e) + n_k\sigma^2(ij) + n_j\sigma^2(ik) + n_jn_k\sigma^2(i)$$
$$\mathscr{E}(MS_j) = \sigma^2(ijk,e) + n_i\sigma^2(jk) + n_k\sigma^2(ij) + n_in_k\sigma^2(j)$$
$$\mathscr{E}(MS_k) = \sigma^2(ijk,e) + n_i\sigma^2(jk) + n_j\sigma^2(ik) + n_in_j\sigma^2(k)$$
$$\mathscr{E}(MS_{ij}) = \sigma^2(ijk,e) + n_k\sigma^2(ij)$$
$$\mathscr{E}(MS_{ik}) = \sigma^2(ijk,e) + n_j\sigma^2(ik)$$
$$\mathscr{E}(MS_{jk}) = \sigma^2(ijk,e) + n_i\sigma^2(jk)$$
$$\mathscr{E}(MS_r) = \sigma^2(ijk,e)$$

The unknown variance components are estimated by inserting the actual mean squares from the analysis of variance into these equations in place of their expected values and then solving for the components, starting from the bottom with the residual mean square.

Using variance components analysis with a variety of experimental designs, Lord and Novick (1968) developed formulas for estimating both specific and generic true-score variances, error variances, and reliability coefficients without requiring the assumption of parallel measurements. A rigorous statistical foundation was thereby provided for the application of test theory not only to "situations where it is impossible for practical reasons to obtain parallel measurements, but also [to] situations where it is undesirable for logical reasons to define true score in terms of any single test form" (Lord & Novick, 1968, p. 173). This variance components approach was both anticipated and greatly elaborated by Cronbach and his colleagues (Cronbach, Rajaratnam, & Gleser, 1963; Cronbach et al., 1972; Gleser et al., 1965), who prefer to speak of universe scores rather than generic true scores and of generalizability rather than reliability. Indeed, Cronbach and his colleagues (1972) have gone beyond Lord and Novick in a number of important ways—for

example, in their explicit consideration of multiple additional facets, their detailed treatment of a variety of crossed and nested designs, and their multivariate extensions to multiscore instruments and profiles. For summaries of generalizability theory and of recent developments in that field, see Brennan and Kane (1979) and Shavelson and Webb (1981).

Generalizability Studies and Decision Studies

Among these many high-powered contributions to reliability theory is a deceptively simple but enormously useful distinction that Cronbach and his colleages (1972) draw between generalizability or G studies and decision or D studies. A G study is designed to investigate a measurement procedure in terms of the relationship between observed scores and the universe scores to which they are to be generalized, while a D study applies the measurement procedure for purposes of decision making. Since the same set of data may be employed both for an analysis of generalizability and for decision making, the G and D studies may be one and the same. It is assumed, of course, that the persons assessed in the D study are drawn from the same population as those in the G study and that the conditions sampled in the D study represent the same universe or universes as in the G study. The number of conditions sampled for a particular facet of observation in the G study is denoted n_j while the number of conditions used in a D study is denoted n'_j.

The coefficient of generalizability ($\mathscr{E}\rho^2$), being a counterpart of the coefficient of reliability given in Equation 3, is defined as "the ratio of universe-score variance to expected observed-score variance; this is approximately the expected value of the squared correlation of observed score and universe score" (Cronbach et al., 1972, p. 82). Note the reference to "expected observed-score variance," which did not occur as a concept in classical test theory because the variance of observed scores was directly calculated in reliability studies. In generalizability theory, however, the G study is a basis for thinking about data to be collected in foreseeable or future D studies, so the relevant observed-score variance is not that arising from any single application of the D study design (σ_X^2) but rather the expected value ($\mathscr{E}\sigma_X^2$) over all applications of the design. Depending upon the particular experimental design, the expected observed-score variance is estimated by combining the variance components that contribute to person variance, thereby excluding condition components that are constant for persons such as $\sigma^2(j)$

and $\sigma^2(jk)$ in crossed designs (Cronbach et al., 1972).

In a G study, for example, with a one-facet crossed design—as when a single observer rates n_i individuals on n_j occasions or n_j test forms are administered to n_i examinees on a single occasion—the universe-score variance $\sigma^2(i)$ is estimated from Equation 28, assuming a very large universe N_j of admissible observations, while the expected observed-score variance is estimated from $\sigma^2(i)$ and $\sigma^2(ij,e)$. The coefficient of generalizability for a specified universe of generalizations and a particular D-study design is the ratio of the universe-score variance to the expected observed-score variance for that design, which is an intraclass correlation (Cronbach, et al., 1972). This follows directly from the definition of an intraclass correlation, which has been formulated in variance-components terms as the ratio of the relevant component to the variance associated with that component plus error variance (Snedecor, 1956). Thus for a D study in which a single observer rates subjects on only one occasion but where we are concerned about the generalizability of the ratings across occasions or a D study in which only a single test form is administered but where we are concerned about the generalizability of the scores across forms—that is, D studies in which $n_j' = 1$—the coefficient of generalizability is estimated from Equations 27 and 28 as

$$\rho^2(1) = \frac{\sigma^2(i)}{\sigma^2(i) + \sigma^2(ij,e)}$$

$$= \frac{\frac{1}{n_j}(MS_i - MS_{ij})}{\frac{1}{n_j}(MS_i - MS_{ij}) + MS_{ij}} \qquad (29)$$

$$= \frac{MS_i - MS_{ij}}{MS_i + (n_j - 1)MS_{ij}}$$

This intraclass correlation indicates the extent to which we may generalize from a single condition of observation to other conditions of the facet—hence the designation $\rho^2(1)$.

If the D study contains not one condition of observation but n_j' conditions, in effect we are concerned about generalizing from the composite of these n_j' separate components—that is, from the individual's average rating over n_j' occasions or from the sum or average of n_j' test scores. Accordingly, we need to step-up the generalizability coefficient for a single condition to one for a length of n_j' conditions, just as we stepped-up the reliability of a unit-length test or half-test by the Spearman-Brown formula (Equation 18). The coefficient of generalizability for

a composite of n_j' conditions is

$$\rho^2(n_j') = \frac{n_j'\rho^2(1)}{1 + (n_j' - 1)\rho^2(1)}$$

$$= \frac{n_j'(MS_i - MS_{ij})}{n_j'MS_i + (n_j - n_j')MS_{ij}}$$

$$= \frac{MS_i - MS_{ij}}{MS_i + \left(\frac{n_j}{n_j'} - 1\right)MS_{ij}} \qquad (30)$$

Equation 30 gives the general form of the intraclass correlation when the number of conditions in the G study (n_j) is different from the number in the D study (n_j'). Ordinarily, the G study embraces more conditions of observation than a D study because otherwise the D study would be a better basis for estimating generalizability. If the D study contains only one condition of observation $(n_j' = 1)$, Equation 30 reduces to Equation 29 as a special case.

When the D study contains just as many conditions of observation as the G study $(n_j' = n_j)$, Equation 30 reduces to

$$\rho^2(n_j) = \frac{MS_i - MS_{ij}}{MS_i} = 1 - \frac{MS_{ij}}{MS_i} \qquad (31)$$

which is identical to coefficient α, KR20, Hoyt's (1941) analysis-of-variance procedure, and several other variant formulas. This is readily seen by thinking of the n_j conditions of observation as components of a composite score, such as items comprising a test. The total variance of a composite X of n_j item scores Y_g is equal to the sum of the n_j item variances (σ_g^2) plus the sum of the $n_j(n_j - 1)$ item covariances $(r_{gh}\sigma_g\sigma_h)$. The total variance may consequently be expressed in terms of mean item variances $(\overline{\sigma_g^2})$ and covariances $(\overline{r_{gh}\sigma_g\sigma_h})$ as follows:

$$\sigma_X^2 = n_j\overline{\sigma_g^2} + n_j(n_j - 1)\overline{r_{gh}\sigma_g\sigma_h} \qquad (32)$$

It has also been shown that the interaction mean square MS_{ij} is equal to the mean of the item variances minus the mean of the item covariances ($MS_{ij} = \overline{\sigma_g^2} - \overline{r_{gh}\sigma_g\sigma_h}$) and that the person mean square $MS_i = \overline{\sigma_g^2} + (n_j - 1)\overline{r_{gh}\sigma_g\sigma_h}$ (Gulliksen, 1950; Stanley, 1957). Inserting these values in Equation 31 yields

$$\rho^2(n_j) = \frac{n_j\overline{r_{gh}\sigma_g\sigma_h}}{\overline{\sigma_g^2} + (n_j - 1)\overline{r_{gh}\sigma_g\sigma_h}}$$

$$= \frac{n_j\left(\dfrac{\overline{r_{gh}\sigma_g\sigma_h}}{\overline{\sigma_g^2}}\right)}{1 + (n_j - 1)\left(\dfrac{\overline{r_{gh}\sigma_g\sigma_h}}{\overline{\sigma_g^2}}\right)} \qquad (33)$$

Thus, $\rho^2(n_j)$ is seen to be the ratio of the average item covariance to the average item variance stepped-up to n_j times as long by the Spearman-Brown formula (Equation 18). Furthermore, if the item variances are equal, $\rho^2(n_j)$ reduces to the stepped-up mean item intercorrelation, which has been previously noted as an interpretation of coefficient α. Moreover, since the numerator of Equations 31 and 33 ($MS_i - MS_{ij} = n_j \overline{r_{gh}\sigma_g\sigma_h}$) equals $n_j\sigma^2(i)$ by Equation 28 (assuming a fairly large universe N_j), it follows that $\sigma^2(i) = \overline{r_{gh}\sigma_g\sigma_h}$. Thus the estimated variance component for persons in the random-effects persons-by-items crossed model is the mean of the covariances among the items sampled (Stanley, 1971). If we next multiply the numerator and denominator of the first version of Equation 33 by n_j and insert corresponding values from Equation 32, we obtain

$$\rho^2(n_j) = \frac{n_j\left(\dfrac{\sigma_{\bar{X}}^2 - n_j\overline{\sigma_g^2}}{n_j - 1}\right)}{n_j\overline{\sigma_g^2} + n_j(n_j - 1)\overline{r_{gh}\sigma_g\sigma_h}}$$

$$= \frac{n_j}{n_j - 1}\left(\frac{\sigma_{\bar{X}}^2 - n_j\overline{\sigma_g^2}}{\sigma_{\bar{X}}^2}\right)$$

which is equal to coefficient α (Equation 19):

$$\rho^2(n_j) = \frac{n_j}{n_j - 1}\left(1 - \frac{\Sigma\sigma_g^2}{\sigma_{\bar{X}}^2}\right) = \alpha \qquad (34)$$

Since the generalizability design that yielded this result was a one-facet model, it is not surprising that the resultant formulas should be essentially the same as those in classical test theory with its single facet of items or test forms. Yet, the power of generalizability theory derives from its simultaneous treatment of multiple facets of observation, which yields more complicated procedures that are relatively straightforward extensions of the variance-components approach to multiway designs and multivariate measurements (Cronbach et al., 1972). Consider, for example, the generalizability of ratings of sociability or aggressiveness obtained during a free-play period in school. Some investigators may wish to generalize across observers while others wish to generalize across occasions in the same free-play setting. Alternatively, these investigators may ask how many observers or occasions are needed to produce a coefficient of generalizability at some minimally acceptable level. One theorist may expect to generalize only to school settings while another wishes to generalize to both school and home environments and a third to all interpersonal situations. Although a G study may be designed to assess the degree of generalizability across these several universes—and the broader the G study, the more useful it will be to a variety of investigators—it should be clear that investigators must specify their own universe of generalization before they can either design a G study appropriately or properly utilize the results of an existing G study (Wiggins, 1973).

Limits of Generalizability Theory

We might also note at this point the fuzzy limits of generalizability theory. Since the theory may be applied to the generalizability of multifaceted measures from one point in time—say, performance ratings by teachers in high school—to multifaceted measures at a later point in time—say, performance ratings by professors in college or by supervisors in a work setting—generalizability theory deliberately blurs the traditional distinction between reliability and predictive validity. It should also be clear that the broader the universe of generalization, the more sources of error that must be contended with. Indeed, one way to reduce error variance is to narrow the universe of generalization. But in any event, regardless of how narrow or broad the universe of generalization is specified to be, the degree of interpreted generalizability should be supported by empirical evidence from generalizability studies combined with plausible rationales for extrapolation. Another way of reducing error variance—in addition, of course, to enlarging the sample of observations—is to standardize some aspects of the measurement procedure. This is tantamount to fixing or restricting the conditions on specified facets of observation.

In any generalizability study, only some of the many possible facets of observation are explicitly varied systematically; all of the others, being assumed to vary randomly and independently from observation to observation, are subsumed under the residual component of variance. If one or more of these implicit or hidden facets are confounded with any of the explicit facets or with persons, then the degree of generalizability is jeopardized—although known confoundings may be addressed by qualified interpretations, as when differences among teacher-raters in classrooms and parent-raters in homes are attributed not to rater differences but to combined rater/situation differences. One way to control for tacit interactions is to employ a particular fixed condition or set of conditions on specified facets, so that this same condition enters all observations. Such standardization also limits generalizability but in known ways, so that interpretations can and should be qualified by the conditions that have been held constant (Kane 1982; Shavelson & Webb, 1981).

Cronbach and his colleagues (1972) recommend not only the calculation of generalizability coefficients as empirical support for generalizations, but also their use in regression estimates of universe scores and in determining disattenuated relationships among variables. Although these proposed uses have powerful implications for both scientific and applied work, neither they nor generalizability theory itself are without their detractors. Lumsden (1976), for example, complains that "Cronbach et al. advocate repeated measures without emphasizing the obvious dangers that main effects and interactions with persons are inextricably confounded with sequence effects and their interactions" (p. 258). He also underscores the nonlinearity of the regression of universe scores on observed scores by pointing out that if the reliability or generalizability coefficient is high, the linear regression estimate of universe scores is not worth making and that if reliability is low, such linear estimates may be misleading. The general thrust of Lumsden's apt though cranky critique is that we should be *measuring attributes* rather than estimating true or universe scores. We turn now to theories that take precisely this approach and, in the process, also take explicit account of nonlinearity of regression.

Item Response Theory of Latent Trait Measurement

A major weakness common to both classical test theory and generalizability theory is the sample-dependent nature of the estimation procedures. Regression estimates of true or universe scores as well as estimates of reliability or generalizability coefficients are a function of the particular item set and subject sample from which the data were derived. Thus, a given individual might obtain different estimates of true or universe scores as well as different errors of measurement depending upon the average ability or trait level and the degree of heterogeneity in the particular group he or she was tested with.

The Promise of Parameter Invariance

Item statistics widely used in test construction, such as item difficulty and item discriminating power, are similarly sample-dependent. For example, item difficulty (or the proportion of individuals getting the item correct or responding in the keyed direction) is a function of the ability or trait level of the particular reference group tested. Item discriminating power (or the item-test correlation) is similarly dependent on the particular set of items and sample of respondents involved. This is clearly the case

for dichotomous items if discriminating power is indexed by the product-moment or *point-biserial* correlation, which is a manifest function of item difficulty (Lord & Novick, 1968). In contrast, if the necessary assumptions of normality and linearity of regression hold, the *biserial* correlation between a dichotomous item and the continuous total score is generally invariant over groups of examinees that differ in level of ability or trait but not in heterogeneity or other respects. Either type of item-test correlation coefficient is dependent upon the heterogeneity of the subject sample and upon the characteristics of the particular other items determining the total test score. Thus, the proportion of correct answers to an item is not really a pure or unalloyed measure of item difficulty nor is the item-test correlation an unalloyed measure of item discriminating power. Rather, these ostensible indexes of item properties reflect important characteristics of the group tested as well.

One of the critical properties of the item response theories to be considered next is that item parameters are invariant across groups of examinees while at the same time estimates of examinee ability or trait level are invariant across sets of items measuring the same ability or trait. This invariance is achieved by relating item responses not to total observed score or even to true score but rather to the ability or latent trait being measured, which is commonly designated θ. The true score T and the latent trait θ essentially refer to the same thing except for the scale of measurement used to express them. The critical difference is that the measurement scale for true score depends on the particular items in the test, while the measurement scale for θ is independent of the items in the test (Lord, 1980; Lord & Novick, 1968). This will become clear once the item response model and its properties are described. For a general introduction to item response theory and reviews of its difficulties and applications, see Hambleton (1979), Hambleton and Cook (1977), and Hambleton, Swaminathan, Cook, Eignor, and Gifford (1978).

Modeling the Probability of Success

Item-response theory (IRT) defines the probability of answering an item correctly or of responding in the keyed direction as a mathematical function of level on the ability or latent trait being measured. The mathematical function most widely used for this purpose is the logistic cumulative distribution function, which is highly similar to its major competitor, the cumulative normal function. However, compared with the normal function, the logistic is much more tractable mathematically. The logistic function has one parameter for each individual—namely, ability or trait level (θ)—and from one to three parameters characterizing each item (Lord, 1980; Lord & Novick, 1968). The item parameters reflect difficulty level (b_g), discriminating power (a_g), and likelihood of guessing (c_g).

Let us first consider the simpler case of items that cannot be answered correctly by guessing. In this two-parameter case, the logistic item response function for a dichotomous item g represents the probability $P_g(\theta)$ of a correct or keyed response to the item as follows:

$$P_g(\theta) = \frac{e^x}{1 + e^x} \qquad (35)$$

where $x = Da_g(\theta - b_g)$. In this equation, e is the mathematical constant 2.71828... and D is a scale factor. The scale factor D is usually taken to be 1.7 because at this value the logistic and normal cumulative distribution functions differ by less than .01 for all values of x. The inverse function of Equation 35 is

$$x = Da_g(\theta - b_g) = \log\frac{P_g(\theta)}{1 - P_g(\theta)} \qquad (36)$$

The expression $\dfrac{P}{1 - P}$ is a likelihood ratio that is essentially the same as the familiar concept of "betting odds" and its log is a quantity known as a logit, which is widely used in biological assay work (Berkson, 1953).

Some two-parameter logistic item response functions or item characteristic curves are illustrated in Figure 1. The difficulty parameter b_g is an item-location parameter defined on the same unbounded scale as the ability or trait θ. In the absence of guessing, b_g is the trait level at which the probability of a

correct answer is .5. The more difficult the item, the further to the right the curve appears on the trait scale. Thus, item 2 in Figure 1 is more difficult than item 1. The parameter a_g is proportional to the slope of the curve at the inflexion point, which occurs for logistic functions at $\theta = b_g$. This is the point at which the slope of the item characteristic curve is a maximum. The parameter a_g represents the discriminating power of the item—that is, the degree to which item response varies with changes in ability level. In Figure 1, for example, item 2 discriminates much more sharply between trait levels than does item 1.

A one-parameter logistic model developed by Rasch (1960, 1966) represents the probability of a correct response as a function solely of the difference between ability level and item difficulty, each expressed in comparable units on the same trait scale. The Rasch model may be viewed as a special case of the two-parameter model of Equation 35 in which all items are assumed to have equal discriminating power $\bar{a}$ and hence vary only in difficulty level. That is, $x = D\bar{a}(\theta - b_g)$ and if $D\bar{a}$ is incorporated into the metric of the θ scale (to yield a new metric θ'), the one-parameter logistic model may be written simply as

$$P_g(\theta') = \frac{e^{(\theta' - b'_g)}}{1 + e^{(\theta' - b'_g)}} \qquad (37)$$

Examples of items fitting this one-parameter model appear in Figure 2.

The assumption that all items have equal discriminating power is unduly restrictive—there is substantial evidence that this assumption will be routinely violated except for tests composed of items specifically chosen to have this property (Hambleton

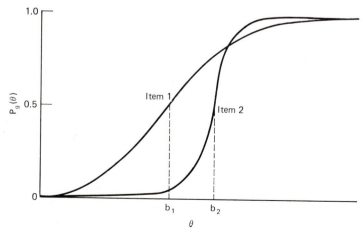

Figure 1. Two-parameter logistic item response functions.

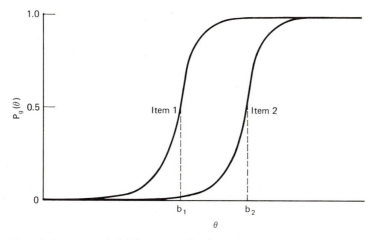

Figure 2. One-parameter logistic item response functions.

& Traub, 1973; Lord, 1980; Lord & Novick, 1968). This is lamentable because simple models often have convenient and attractive features. The one-parameter Rasch model, for example, is the only latent trait model for dichotomous items that is consistent with "number right" scoring. In this one-parameter case, the unweighted sum of correct responses given by a respondent is a sufficient statistic, in the sense that it contains all the information needed, for estimating that person's ability or trait level θ (Lord, 1980; Wright, 1977). In the two-parameter logistic model, in contrast, the estimation of examinee ability or trait level is more complicated because the corresponding sufficient statistic is a weighted score in which each item response is multiplied by the item's discriminating power a_g (Lord, 1980).

For dichotomous items that can be answered correctly by guessing, which includes all multiple-choice items, a three-parameter model is needed to cope with the realities of item response variation. The three-parameter logistic item response function may be written as follows (Lord, 1980):

$$P_g(\theta) = c_g + (1 - c_g)\frac{e^x}{1 + e^x} = \frac{c_g + e^x}{1 + e^x} \quad (38)$$

where $x = Da_g(\theta - b_g)$. The parameter c_g is the lower asymptote of the item characteristic curve and represents the probability that a person completely lacking in the ability or trait will answer the item correctly or in the keyed direction. It is sometimes referred to as a "guessing" or "pseudo-chance" parameter. Examples of three-parameter item characteristic curves are presented in Figure 3. It should be noted that in the presence of guessing, the difficulty parameter b_g is no longer the ability level at which the probability of a correct answer is .5, but

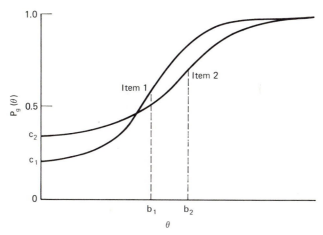

Figure 3. Three-parameter logistic item response functions.

rather the ability level at which the probability of a correct answer is halfway between c_g and unity.

Unidimensionality and Common Scale Meaning

These latent trait models all postulate that the probability of success depends on the difference between the respondent's ability or trait level θ and the item difficulty levels b_g—as weighted by item discriminating power and adjusted for guessing—and on nothing else. If this is true, the items must all measure the same ability or latent trait, and a person's ability or trait level θ is all the information that is needed to determine his or her probability of success on a specified calibrated item. If performance on the items consistently depends on some other trait in addition to θ, then the probability of a correct response would clearly not be a function of only one person parameter θ and the model would fail to hold. Thus, these latent trait models apply only to *unidimensional* sets of items that all measure a single underlying trait, in the sense that only one dimension of response consistency contributes to systematic variations in item difficulty.

Another way of saying this is that the items are interrelated only by virtue of their mutual relationship to the single underlying trait θ. Thus, for fixed values of θ—that is, for individuals having the same ability or trait level—the correlation between any two items should be zero. More rigorously, for individuals having the same value of θ, the distribution of item scores are all statistically independent of each other. This is the property of *local independence*, which follows automatically from unidimensionality and does not constitute an additional requirement (Lazarsfeld, 1959, 1960; Lord & Novick, 1968). Although the requirement of unidimensionality is unlikely to be strictly met in practice, it is tolerably well approximated in many instances (Lord, 1980). In any event, the appropriateness of the assumption may be roughly evaluated for any set of itemized psychological test data by factor analyzing the test items (Hambleton & Traub, 1973). Indeed, even if the item set proves to be multidimensional, it is often possible to cluster items into sufficiently homogeneous groups on the basis of such factor analyses to warrant latent trait scaling of each cluster separately. Thus, within certain restrictions, we can think of θ as the common factor of the items (Lord, 1980).

The item response function can be viewed as the regression of item score on the latent trait θ—a regression that, in the cumulative normal and logistic item response theories, is explicitly nonlinear. As in many statistical contexts, this regression remains the same when the frequency distribution of the predictor variable is changed. This should be especially clear in the case of these item response models because the probability of a correct response to any item g for individuals at a given trait level θ_i depends only on θ_i and not on the number of people at θ_i or on the number of people at any other trait level (Lord, 1980). Since the regression is invariant, the item parameters a_g, b_g, and c_g remain the same regardless of the distribution of the trait in the group tested. This invariance of item parameters across groups affords distinct advantages in test development work over group-dependent classical item statistics such as the proportion of individuals getting the item correct and item-test correlation coefficients.

Another important property of latent trait models is that once a set of items has been calibrated—that is, the item parameters have been determined—a person's ability or trait score may be estimated from any subset of items that have been fit to the model. Thus, estimates of examinee ability or trait level are invariant across sets of calibrated items measuring the same ability or trait. This means that individuals may be compared on a common trait scale even though they may have taken different subsets of items and that items may be added or dropped from the test without affecting the comparability of the scores. Furthermore, separately calibrated tests measuring the same trait can be put on the same scale by means of shared items common to both tests. Tests geared to different age levels, for example, can be so linked provided that they share some overlapping common items. Similarly, tests of the same trait administered at different points in time may be put on the same scale provided there are items common to both administrations (Lord, 1980; Stocking & Lord, in press). Thus, latent trait scores—by virtue of their comparability of meaning across groups, age levels, and times—are especially felicitous for the study of change and trends over time.

Furthermore, because these latent trait scales are unbounded, they are not warped by floor and ceiling effects in the way that percentage correct and total scores are, so they are more likely to be linearly related to other quantitative variables. Indeed, "there is abundant evidence in the biological and psychological literature that the relationships of quantitative variables to percentages are typically linear on the log-odds (logit) scale and not on the percentage scale" (Bock, Mislevy, & Woodson, 1982, p. 6).

Moreover, since both persons and items are placed on the same scale—the former in terms of their estimated trait levels θ_i and the latter in terms of their estimated difficulty levels b_g—the meaning of a scale score may be interpreted by reference to the content of items at various points on the scale. This provides a *criterion-referenced* interpretation of the meaning of each numerical level of ability or trait: the trait score is interpreted in terms of expected performance on typical benchmark items without reference to score distributions of persons being measured. At the same time, however, IRT models yield estimates of the proportion of correct answers expected for typical individuals at each score point in each group assessed. Thus, *norm-referenced* interpretations are also provided by reference to these group distributions.

Information on Local Precision

Another important feature of these item response models of latent trait measurement is the refined approach they afford to the issue of reliability. Since standard errors of measurement are readily computable for each scale score, they may be expressed as a function of θ rather than taken to be constant as in classical test theory. (The squared standard error of measurement of classical test theory is simply the standard error variance for each scale score averaged over all examinees.) This means that measurement precision need not be summarized by a single reliability coefficient for each test but can be more appropriately represented as it varies with values of θ. In item response theory, such a variable index of measurement precision or precision of trait estimation is provided by a measure of the *information* a test conveys at each fixed value of θ (Lord & Novick, 1968).

The information function $I(\theta,x)$ is defined as a quantity inversely proportional to the squared length of the confidence interval for estimating an examinee's trait level θ from test score x (Lord, 1980). Thus, information is high when there are narrow confidence bands around the estimate of θ and low when the confidence bands are wide. It can be shown that this measure of information is equal to the squared slope of the regression of x on θ for a given value of θ, denoted here as $\beta^2_{x|\theta}$, divided by the variance of x for the fixed θ, denoted $\sigma^2_{x|\theta}$ (Lord, 1980):

$$I(\theta,x) = \frac{\beta^2_{x|\theta}}{\sigma^2_{x|\theta}} \qquad (39)$$

In other words, the information function for a test score x is the square of the ratio of the slope of the regression of x on θ for a given θ to the standard error of measurement of x for the fixed θ. Thus, the variation in the information provided by a test score x in estimating θ derives from two distinct sources: First,

the steeper the slope of the regression of x on θ for a given θ—that is, the more sharply x varies with θ in that region—the more information the test provides about θ. Second, the smaller the standard error of measurement for the given θ, the more information the test provides about θ.

The information function of the maximum likelihood estimator of θ is called the *test information function* $I(\theta)$:

$$I(\theta) = \sum_g \frac{P'^2_g}{P_g(1 - P_g)} \qquad (40)$$

where P'_g is the slope of the item characteristic curve for item g at trait level θ. The test information function can be shown to be an upper bound to the information that can be obtained by any estimator or method of scoring the test (Lord, 1980).

The quantity $\dfrac{P'^2_g}{P_g(1 - P_g)}$ in Equation 40, which is the contribution of item g to the test information function, is called the *item information function* $I(\theta,y_g)$. Hence, the information function for the test is simply the sum of the information functions for each item:

$$I(\theta) = \sum_g I(\theta,y_g) \qquad (41)$$

Thus, in item response theory the contribution of each item to the measurement effectiveness of the test does not depend on the particular other items included in the test, as it does in classical test theory. Furthermore, two different tests of the same trait or two different ways of scoring the same test can be revealingly compared by calculating the ratio of their respective information functions, which yields the *relative efficiency* of one score compared to another at each level of θ. Relative efficiency is invariant under any monotonic transformation of the trait scale θ.

Duality and Integration of Measurement Models

Two other aspects of these item-response models are worth noting. First, by virtue of the duality between stimulus scaling and test theory (Mosier, 1940, 1941), IRT models prove to be formally equivalent to special cases of Thurstone's scaling models for comparative and categorical judgment (Torgerson, 1958). This formal equivalence has important ramifications for the development of integrated measurement theory (Brogden, 1977; Lumsden, 1980). To illustrate, in Thurstonian categorical scaling, the probability that a stimulus is judged to fall below a particular category boundary is a function of the difference between the category boundary (t_k) and the stimulus scale value (s_g) on the attribute scale; whereas in item response theory, the probability that a person passes a particular item is a function of the difference between the person's trait level (θ_i) and the item's difficulty level (b_g) on the latent trait scale.

In Thurstonian models, the probability is a cumulative normal function of the difference $(t_k - s_g)$ while in IRT models the probability is typically a logistic function of the difference $(\theta_i - b_g)$. However, this discrepancy is not a critical issue both because the normal and logistic functions are virtually indistinguishable from each other empirically and because either function could be used just as well in either model. For example, paired comparison scaling models using the logistic function have been developed by Bradley and Terry (1952) and by Luce (1959), and IRT models using the normal ogive have been explicated by Lord (1953, 1980) and by Tucker (1952). What is critical is not so much the particular mathematical form of the distribution function employed, as long as it is strictly monotonically increasing, but rather that all of the stimulus (or item) distributions be represented in the *same* mathematical form on a common scale or base line (Adams & Messick, 1958).

As a parallel to Thurstone's (1927) law of comparative judgment, the general model for Thurstonian categorical scaling may be expressed as follows (Torgerson, 1958):

$$t_k - s_g = z_{gk}\sqrt{\sigma_g^2 + \sigma_k^2 - 2r_{gk}\sigma_g\sigma_k} \quad (42)$$

where z_{gk} is the unit normal deviate corresponding to the probability that stimulus g is judged to fall below category boundary k. In various special cases, the covariance term is assumed to be constant or zero and either the boundary dispersions (σ_k) or the stimulus dispersions (σ_g) are taken to be constant, or both. These dispersions arise because of momentary organismic fluctuations in the perception of stimuli and category boundaries.

The special case of constant boundary dispersions $(\sigma_k = k)$ yields $z_{gk} = \frac{1}{\sigma_g'}(t_k - s_g)$, where $\sigma_g' = \sqrt{\sigma_g^2 + k^2}$. This is the Thurstonian counterpart of the two-parameter IRT model of Equation 35 or 36, with θ corresponding to t_k, b_g to s_g, and a_g to $\frac{1}{\sigma_g'}$. The special case of constant stimulus dispersions as well as constant boundary dispersions yields $z_{gk} = \frac{1}{\bar{\sigma}'}(t_k - s_g)$, which is the Thurstonian counterpart of the one-parameter Rasch model

of Equation 37, with $\bar{a}$ corresponding to $\frac{1}{\bar{\sigma}'}$ (Lumsden, 1980). Thus, the reciprocal of the stimulus dispersion in the Thurstone model, being the counterpart of the item discriminating power in the IRT model, is proportional to the slope of the item characteristic curve at its inflexion point.

The existence of boundary dispersions σ_k in the Thurstone model implies that tacit within each IRT model are person characteristic curves with slopes inversely proportional to σ_k. Whereas an item characteristic curve expresses the probability of a correct or keyed response to a particular item as a function of the ability or trait level of persons, a person characteristic curve expresses the probability of a correct or keyed response by a particular person as a function of the difficulty level of items. Person characteristic curves are akin to ROC (receiver operating characteristic) curves in signal detection theory (Green & Swets, 1966).

The two special cases just examined—corresponding to the two-parameter IRT model and the one-parameter Rasch model, respectively—both entail person characteristic curves having equal slopes. A third special case in which the stimulus dispersions are taken to be equal but the boundary dispersions are allowed to vary yields a kind of pseudo-Rasch model having equal slopes for the item characteristic curves but different slopes for the person characteristic curves (Lumsden, 1980). If both stimulus dispersions and boundary dispersions are considered to vary, a two-parameter IRT model results having unequal slopes for both item characteristic and person characteristic curves.

By estimating person characteristic curves as well as item characteristic curves, the adequacy of the IRT model can be appraised not only in terms of item fit but in terms of person fit as well. Thus, the degree of person fit provides a measure of the appropriateness of the IRT model for describing the response patterns of different persons or types of persons (Levine & Rubin, 1980). Furthermore, slope differences in person characteristic curves may be interpreted as differences in person reliability (Lumsden, 1977, 1978). Although person characteristic curves are typically treated as interesting but incidental features of IRT models of cognitive test performance, they occasionally form the central focus of models of personality test performance (Voyce & Jackson, 1977).

The second noteworthy aspect of item response models is the preferred use of the logistic distribution function. This has been justified on the grounds that it is highly similar to, but more tractable mathematically than, the ubiquitous normal function. Since the logistic function approaches its asymptotes somewhat less rapidly than the normal ogive, it is also more robust than the normal ogive in accommodating the inevitable careless errors made by persons high on the ability or trait scale (Lord, 1980). But there is a more basic reason for preferring the logistic function—namely, its uniqueness in relating scaling models based on differences in scale values, such as Thurstone's (1927), to scaling models based on ratios of scale values, such as the Bradley-Terry (1952) and Luce (1959) models and the magnitude estimation models of psychophysics (Stevens & Galanter, 1957; Galanter & Messick, 1961).

The Thurstone models, as we have seen, express the probability P_{gk} that stimulus (or category boundary) k is judged to exceed stimulus g as a function of the difference in their scale values on the attribute scale:

$$P_{gk} = f(s_k - s_g) \qquad (43)$$

Ratio scaling models express this probability as a function of a ratio of scale values. For example,

$$P_{gk} = f'\left(\frac{v_k}{v_g + v_k}\right) \qquad (44)$$

Since the probability that k exceeds g is the same datum in both models, the two formulations may be related as follows:

$$\frac{v_k}{v_g + v_k} = F(s_k - s_g) \qquad (45)$$

where $s_k = \phi(v_k)$. The problem is to determine the possible forms of F whereby Equation 45 holds, as well as the attendant form of ϕ relating s_k and v_k.

Bradley (1953) has shown that if the logistic function is substituted for the normal ogive in the Thurstone model, then $s_k = \log v_k$. Luce (1959) has proven that if s_k is set equal to $\log v_k$, then the distribution function for P_{gk} is logistic. Finally, Adams and Messick (1957) have shown that the *only* monotonic increasing function satisfying Equation 45 is the logistic and that the attendant relationship of s_k to v_k is logarithmic (Luce, 1959).

Much of the power of IRT scales derives from their invariant properties—invariance both of item parameters across respondent groups and of respondent trait levels across subsets of items fit to the model. This means that the trait levels of individuals may be estimated on a common scale, even though they may have taken different subsets of items, and that separately calibrated tests of the same trait can be put on a common scale by means of shared items. As a consequence, if the IRT model fits the response data, individuals can be legitimately compared on scales having a common meaning not only across population groups but across age levels and across different points in time. This makes IRT scaling of unidimensional traits—or of traits that are unidimensional over certain age spans—especially attractive for research in human development (e.g., see Whitely, 1980).

REFERENCES

Adams, E., & Messick, S. An axiomatization of Thurstone's successive intervals and paired comparisons scaling models. Applied Mathematics and Statistics Laboratory, *Technical Report 12,* Stanford University, 1957.

Allen, B. P., & Potkay, C. R. On the arbitrary distinction between states and traits. *Journal of Personality and Social Psychology,* 1981, *41,* 916–928.

Allen, S., Dubanoski, R., & Stevenson, H. Children's performance as a function of race of experimenter, race of subject, and type of verbal reinforcement. *Journal of Experimental Child Psychology,* 1966, *4,* 248–256.

Allport, G. W. *Personality: A psychological interpretation.* New York: Holt, 1937.

Allport, G. W. *Pattern and growth in personality.* New York: Holt, Rinehart and Winston, 1961.

Allport, G. W. The general and the unique in psychological science. *Journal of Personality,* 1962, *30,* 405–421.

Allport, G. W. Traits revisited. *American Psychologist,* 1966, *21,* 1–10.

Allport, G. W., & Odbert, H. S. Trait names: A psychological study. *Psychological Monographs,* 1936, *47* (whole No. 211), 1–171.

Allport, G. W., Vernon, P. E., & Lindzey G. *Manual: Study of values.* Boston: Houghton Mifflin, 1960.

Amrine, M., & Sanford, F. In the matter of juries, democracy, science, truth, senators, and bugs. *American Psychologist,* 1956, *11,* 54–60.

Anderson, S., & Messick, S. Social competency in young children. *Developmental Psychology,* 1974, *10,* 282–293.

Anastasi, A. The nature of psychological 'traits.' *Psychological Review,* 1948, *55,* 127–138.

Aronson, E., & Carlsmith, J. M. Experimentation in social psychology. In G. Lindzey & E. Aronson (Eds.), *The handbook of social psychology* (Vol. 2, 2nd ed.). Reading, Mass.: Addison-Wesley, 1968.

Banks, W. C., McQuater, G. V., & Hubbard, J. L. Toward a reconceptualization of the social-cognitive bases of achievement orientations in blacks. *Review of Educational Research*, 1978, *48*, 381–397.

Barker, R. G., & Wright, H. F. *Midwest and its children*. Evanston, Ill.: Row, Peterson, 1955.

Bass, B. M. *Leadership, psychology, and organizational behavior*. New York: Harper & Row, 1960.

Beck, S. J. The science of personality: Nomothetic or idiographic? *Psychological Review*, 1953, *60*, 353–359.

Bem, D. J., & Allen, A. On predicting some of the people some of the time. The search for cross-situational consistencies in behavior. *Psychological Review*, 1974, *81*, 506–520.

Berg, I. A. (Ed.) *Response set in personality assessment*. Chicago, Ill.: Aldine, 1967.

Bergan, J. R. *Behavioral consultation*. Columbus, Ohio: Charles E. Merrill, 1977.

Bersoff, D. N. Silk purses into sow's ears: The decline of psychological testing and a suggestion for its redemption. *American Psychologist*, 1973, *28*, 892–899.

Bijou, S. W., & Peterson, R. F. The psychological assessment of children: A functional analysis. In P. McReynolds (Ed.), *Advances in psychological assessment* (Vol. 2). Palo Alto, Calif.: Science and Behavior Books, 1971.

Block, J. *The Q-sort method in personality assessment and psychiatric research*. Springfield, Ill.: Charles C Thomas, 1961.

Block, J. *Lives through time*. Berkeley, Calif.: Bancroft Books, 1971.

Bock, R. D., Mislevy, R., & Woodson, C. The next stage in educational assessment. *Educational Researcher*, 1982, *11*(3), 4–16.

Boehm, A. E., & Weinberg, R. A. *The classroom observer: A guide for developing observation skills*. New York: Teachers College Press, 1977.

Bowers, K. S. Situationism in psychology: An analysis and critique. *Psychological Review*, 1973, *80*, 307–336.

Bracht, G. H., & Glass, G. V The external validity of experiments. *American Educational Research Journal*, 1968, *5*, 437–474.

Bradley, R. A. Some statistical methods in taste testing and quality evaluation. *Biometrics*, 1953, *9*, 22–38.

Bradley, R. A., & Terry, M. E. Rank analysis of incomplete block designs. I. The method of paired comparisons. *Biometrika*, 1952, *39*, 324–345.

Brandt, R. M. *Studying behavior in natural settings*. New York: Holt, Rinehart and Winston, 1972.

Brennan, R. L., & Kane, M. T. Generalizability theory: A review. In R. E. Traub (Ed.), *New directions for testing and measurement: Methodological developments*. San Francisco: Jossey-Bass, 1979.

Brogden, H. The Rasch model, the law of comparative judgment and additive conjoint measurement. *Psychometrika*, 1977, *42*, 631–634.

Bronfenbrenner, U. Toward an experimental ecology of human development. *American Psychologist*, 1977, *32*, 513–531.

Burchard, W. W. A study of attitudes towards the use of concealed devices in social science research. *Social Forces*, 1957, *36*, 111.

Burt, C. Test reliability estimated by analysis of variance. *British Journal of Statistical Psychology*, 1955, *8*, 103–118.

Buss, A. R. A multivariate model of quantitative, structural, and quantistructural ontogenetic change. *Developmental Psychology*, 1974, *10*, 190–203.

Campbell, D. T. A typology of tests: Projective and otherwise. *Journal of Consulting Psychology*, 1957, *21*, 207–210.

Campbell, D. T. Systematic error on the part of human links in communication systems. *Information and Control*, 1958, *1*, 297–312.

Campbell, D. T. Recommendations for APA test standards regarding construct, trait or discriminant validity. *American Psychologist*, 1960, *15*, 263–271.

Campbell, D. T., & Fiske, D. W. Convergent and discriminant validation by the multitrait-multimethod matrix. *Psychological Bulletin*, 1959, *56*, 81–105.

Carroll, J. B. On the theory-practice interface in the measurement of intellectual abilities. In P. Suppes (Ed.), *Impact of research on education: Some case studies*. Washington, DC: National Academy of Education, 1978.

Cartwright, C. A., & Cartwright, G. P. *Developing observation skills*. New York: McGraw-Hill, 1974.

Cattell, R. B. Psychological measurement: Normative, ipsative, interactive. *Psychological Review*, 1944, *51*, 292–303.

Cattell, R. B. *The description and measurement of personality*. New York: World Book, 1946.

Cattell, R. B. *Personality and motivation structure and measurement*. New York: Harcourt Brace Jovanovich, 1957.

Cattell, R. B. What is ''objective'' in ''objective

personality tests''? *Journal of Consulting Psychology*, 1958, *5*, 285–289.

Cattell, R. B. Trait-view theory of perturbations in ratings and self ratings (L (BR)- and Q-data): Its application to obtaining pure trait score estimates in questionnaires. *Psychological Review*, 1968, *75*, 96–113.

Cattell, R. B. A more sophisticated look at structure: Perturbation, sampling, role, and observer trait-view theories. In R. B. Cattell & R. M. Dreger (Eds.), *Handbook of modern personality theory.* New York: Wiley, 1977.

Cattell, R. B. *The scientific use of factor analysis in behavioral and life sciences.* New York: Plenum Press, 1978.

Cattell, R. B., & Digman, J. M. A theory of the structure of perturbations in observer ratings and questionnaire data in personality research. *Behavioral Science*, 1964, *9*, 341–358.

Chomsky, N. *Syntactic structures.* S'Gravenhage, Netherlands: Mouton, 1957.

Chomsky, N. *Aspects of the theory of syntax.* Cambridge, Mass.: MIT Press, 1965.

Ciminero, A. R., & Drabman, R. S. Current developments in behavioral assessment of children. In B. B. Lahey & A. E. Kazdin (Eds.), *Advances in clinical child psychology* (Vol. 1). New York: Plenum Press, 1977.

Clarizio, H. F. In defense of the IQ test. *School Psychology Digest*, 1979, *8*, 79–88.

Cole, M., & Bruner, J. S. Cultural differences and inferences about psychological processes. *American Psychologist*, 1971, *26*, 867–876.

Cole, M., Gay, J., Glick, J., & Sharp, D. *The cultural context of learning and thinking.* New York: Basic Books, 1971.

Cronbach, L. J. Coefficient alpha and the internal structure of tests. *Psychometrika*, 1951, *16*, 297–334.

Cronbach, L. J. *Essentials of psychological testing* (3rd ed.). New York: Harper & Row, 1970.

Cronbach, L. J. Test validation. In R. L. Thorndike (Ed.), *Educational measurement* (2nd ed.), Washington, D.C.: American Council on Education, 1971.

Cronbach, L. J., & Gleser, G. C. The signal/noise ratio in the comparison of reliability coefficients. *Educational and Psychological Measurement*, 1964, *24*, 467–480.

Cronbach, L. J., Gleser, G. C., Nanda, H., & Rajaratnam, N. *The dependability of behavioral measurements.* New York: Wiley, 1972.

Cronbach, L. J., Rajaratnam, N., & Gleser, G. C. Theory of generalizability: A liberalization of reliability theory. *British Journal of Statistical Psychology*, 1963, *16*, 137–163.

Cronbach, L. J., & Snow, R. E. *Aptitudes and instructional methods.* New York: Irvington, 1977.

Damarin, F. L., & Messick, S. *Response styles as personality variables: A theoretical integration of multivariate research* (ETS RB 65–10). Princeton, N.J.: Educational Testing Service, 1965.

Dudek, F. J. The continuing misinterpretation of the standard error of measurement. *Psychological Bulletin*, 1979, *86*, 335–337.

Dunnette, M. D. Aptitudes, abilities, and skills. In M. D. Dunnette (Ed.), *Handbook of industrial and organizational psychology.* Chicago: Rand McNally, 1976.

Ebel, R. L. Estimation of reliability of ratings. *Psychometrika*, 1951, *16*, 407–424.

Edwards, A. L. *Manual: Personal Preference Schedule.* New York: Psychological Corporation, 1954.

Edwards, A. L. *The measurement of personality traits by scales and inventories.* New York: Holt, Rinehart and Winston, 1970.

Ekehammar, B. Interactionism in personality from a historical perspective. *Psychological Bulletin*, 1974, *81*, 1026–1048.

Ekman, P., Friesen, W. V., & Ellsworth, P. *Emotion in the human face.* New York: Pergamon, 1972.

Ekman, P., & Oster, H. Facial expressions of emotion. *Annual Review of Psychology*, 1979, *30*, 527–554.

Ellett, C. D., & Bersoff, D. N. An integrated approach to the psychosituational assessment of behavior. *Professional Psychology*, 1976, *7*, 485–494.

Emmerich, W. Personality development and concepts of structure. *Child Development*, 1968, *39*, 671–690.

Emmerich, W. Structure and development of personal-social behaviors in economically disadvantaged preschool children. *Genetic Psychology Monographs*, 1977, *75*, 191–245.

Eysenck, H. J. The science of personality: Nomothetic! *Psychological Review*, 1954, *61*, 339–342.

Eysenck, H. J. *The structure of human personality* (3rd ed.). London: Methuen, 1970.

Eysenck, H. J., & Eysenck, S. B. G. *Personality structure and measurement.* San Diego: Knapp, 1969.

Falk, J. Issues distinguishing idiographic from

nomothetic approaches to personality theory. *Psychological Review,* 1956, *63,* 53–62.

Finlayson, D. S. The reliability of marking essays. *British Journal of Educational Psychology,* 1951, *21,* 126–134.

Flavell, J. H., & Wohlwill, J. F. Formal and functional aspects of cognitive development. In D. Elkin & J. H. Flavell (Eds.), *Studies in cognitive development: Essays in honor of Jean Piaget.* New York: Oxford University Press, 1969.

Galanter, E., & Messick, S. The relation between category and magnitude scales of loudness. *Psychological Review,* 1961, *68,* 363–372.

Glaser, R. Adapting the elementary school curriculum to individual performance. In *Proceedings of the 1967 Invitational Conference on testing problems.* Princeton, N.J.: Educational Testing Service, 1968.

Glaser, R., & Nitko, A. J. Measurement in learning and instruction. In R. L. Thorndike (Ed.), *Educational measurement* (2nd ed.). Washington, D.C.: American Council on Education, 1971.

Gleser, G. C., Cronbach, L. J., & Rajaratnam, N. Generalizability of scores influenced by multiple sources of variance. *Psychometrika,* 1965, *30,* 395–418.

Goldfried, M. R., & D'Zurilla, T. J. A behavioral-analytic model for assessing competence. In C. D. Spielberger (Ed.), *Current topics in clinical and community psychology* (Vol. 1). New York: Academic Press, 1969.

Goode, W. J., & Hatt, P. K. *Methods in social research.* New York: McGraw-Hill, 1952.

Goodenough, F. L. *Mental testing.* New York: Rinehart, 1949.

Goodman, J. F. "Ignorance" versus "stupidity"— the basic disagreement. *School Psychology Digest,* 1979, *8,* 47–62.

Goodwin, W. L., & Driscoll, L. A. *Handbook for measurement and evaluation in early childhood education.* San Francisco: Jossey-Bass, 1980.

Green, D. M., & Swets, J. A. *Signal detection theory and psychophysics.* New York: Wiley, 1966.

Groen, G. J., & Atkinson, R. C. Models for optimizing the learning process. *Psychological Bulletin,* 1966, *66,* 309–320.

Guilford, J. P. *Psychometric methods,* (2nd ed.). New York: McGraw-Hill, 1954.

Guilford, J. P. Creative abilities in the arts. *Psychological Review,* 1957, *64,* 110–118.

Guilford, J. P. *Personality.* New York: McGraw-Hill, 1959.

Gulliksen, H. *Theory of mental tests.* New York: Wiley, 1950.

Guion, R. M. Scoring of content domain samples: The problem of fairness. *Journal of Applied Psychology,* 1978, *63,* 499–506.

Hambleton, R. K. Latent trait models and their applications. In R. E. Traub (Ed.), *New directions for testing and measurement: Methodological developments.* San Francisco: Jossey-Bass, 1979.

Hambleton, R. K., & Cook, L. L. Latent trait models and their use in the analysis of educational test data. *Journal of Educational Measurement,* 1977, *14,* 75–96.

Hambleton, R. K., & Novick, M. R. Toward an integration of theory and method for criterion-referenced tests. *Journal of Educational Measurement,* 1973, *10,* 159–170.

Hambleton, R. K., Swaminathan, H., Cook, L. L., Eignor, D. R., & Gifford, J. A. Developments in latent trait theory: Models, technical issues, and applications. *Review of Educational Research,* 1978, *48,* 467–510.

Hambleton, R. K., & Traub, R. E. Analysis of empirical data using two logistic latent trait models. *British Journal of Mathematical and Statistical Psychology,* 1973, *26,* 195–211.

Hamilton, D. L. Personality attributes associated with extreme response style. *Psychological Bulletin,* 1968, *69,* 192–203.

Hammond, S. B. Personality studied by the method of rating in the life situation. In R. B. Cattell & R. M. Dreger (Eds.), *Handbook of modern personality theory.* New York: Wiley, 1977.

Hertzig, M. E., Birch, H. G., Thomas, A., & Mendez, O. A. Class and ethnic differences in the responsiveness of preschool children to cognitive demands. *Monographs of the Society for Research in Child Development,* 1968, *33,* (1, Serial No. 117).

Heyns, R. W., & Lippitt, R. Systematic observational technique. In G. Lindzey (Ed.), *Handbook of social psychology* (Vol. 1). Cambridge, Mass.: Addison-Wesley, 1954.

Holt, R. R. Individuality and generalization in the psychology of personality: An evaluation. *Journal of Personality,* 1962, *30,* 377–402.

Hoyt, C. Test reliability estimated by analysis of variance. *Psychometrika,* 1941, *6,* 153–160.

Hundleby, J. D., Pawlik, K., & Cattell, R. B. *Personality factors in objective devices: A critical integration of a century's research.* San Diego: Knapp, 1965.

Ishikawa, A. Trait description and measurement through discovered structure in objective tests (T Data). In R. B. Cattell & R. M. Dreger (Eds.),

Handbook of modern personality theory. New York: Wiley, 1977.

Jackson, D. N., & Messick, S. Content and style in personality assessment. *Psychological Bulletin,* 1958, *55,* 243–252.

Jackson, D. N., & Paunonen, S. V. Personality structure and assessment. *Annual Review of Psychology,* 1980, *31,* 503–551.

Jackson, P. W., & Messick, S. The person, the product, and the response: Conceptual problems in the assessment of creativity. *Journal of Personality,* 1965, *33,* 309–329.

Jackson, R. W. B. Reliability of mental tests. *British Journal of Psychology,* 1939, *29,* 267–287.

Jöreskog, K. G., & Sörbom, D. *Advances in factor analysis and structural equation model.* Cambridge, Mass.: Abt, 1979.

Kane, M. T. A sampling model for validity. *Applied Psychological Measurement,* 1982, *6,* 125–160.

Kanfer, F. H., & Saslow, G. Behavioral diagnosis. In C. M. Franks (Ed.), *Behavior therapy: Appraisal and status.* New York: McGraw-Hill, 1969.

Katz, I., Atchison, R., Epps, E., & Roberts, S. Race of evaluator, race of norm, and expectancy as determinants of black performance. *Journal of Experimental Social Psychology,* 1972, *8,* 1–15.

Katz, I., Henchy, T., & Allen, H. Effects of race of tester, approval-disapproval, and need on negro children's learning. *Journal of Personality and Social Psychology,* 1968, *18,* 38–42.

Kelly, G. A. *The psychology of personal constructs* (Vol. 1). New York: Norton, 1955.

Kogan, N. Educational implications of cognitive styles. In G. S. Lesser (Ed.), *Psychology and educational practice.* Glenview, Ill.: Scott, Foresman, 1971.

Kogan, N. *Cognitive styles in infancy and early childhood.* Hillsdale, N.J.: Erlbaum, 1976.

Kenrick, D. T., & Stringfield, D. O. Personality traits and the eye of the beholder: Crossing some traditional philosophical boundaries in the search for consistency in all of the people. *Psychological Review,* 1980, *87,* 88–104.

Lambert, W. W. Interpersonal behavior. In P. H. Mussen (Ed.), *Handbook of research methods in child development.* New York: Wiley, 1960.

Lamiell, J. T. Toward an idiothetic psychology of personality. *American Psychologist,* 1981, *36,* 276–289.

Lazarsfeld, P. F. Latent structure analysis. In S. Koch (Ed.), *Psychology: A study of a science* (Vol. 3). New York: McGraw-Hill, 1959.

Lazarsfeld, P. F. Latent structure analysis and test theory. In H. Gulliksen & S. Messick (Eds.), *Psychological scaling: Theory and applications.* New York: Wiley, 1960.

Levine, M. V., & Rubin, D. B. Measuring the appropriateness of multiple-choice test scores. *Journal of Educational Statistics,* 1980, *4,* 269–290.

Lindquist, E. F. *Design and analysis of experiments in psychology and education.* Boston: Houghton-Mifflin, 1953.

Loevinger, J. Some principles of personality measurement. *Educational and Psychological Measurement,* 1955, *15,* 3–17.

Loevinger, J. Objective tests as instruments of psychological theory. *Psychological Reports,* 1957, *3,* 635–694 (Monograph Supplement 9).

Lord, F. M. An application of confidence intervals and of maximum likelihood to the estimation of an examinee's ability. *Psychometrika,* 1953, *18,* 57–77.

Lord, F. M. Estimating test reliability. *Educational and Psychological Measurement,* 1955, *15,* 324–336. (a)

Lord, F. M. Sampling fluctuations resulting from the sampling of test items. *Psychometrika,* 1955, *20,* 1–22. (b)

Lord, F. M. *Applications of item response theory to practical testing problems.* Hillsdale, N.J.: Erlbaum, 1980.

Lord, F. M., & Novick, M. R. *Statistical theories of mental test scores.* Reading, Mass.: Addison-Wesley, 1968.

Luce, R. D. *Individual choice behavior: A theoretical analysis.* New York: Wiley, 1959.

Lumsden, J. Test theory. *Annual Review of Psychology,* 1976, *27,* 254–280.

Lumsden, J. Variations on a theme by Thurstone. *Applied Psychological Measurement,* 1980, *4,* 1–7.

Mendinnus, G. R. *Child study and observation guide.* New York: Wiley, 1976.

Medley, D. M., & Mitzel, H. E. Measuring classroom behavior by systematic observation. In N. L. Gage (Ed.), *Handbook of research on teaching.* Chicago: Rand McNally, 1963.

Meehl, P. E. *Clinical versus statistical prediction: A theoretical analysis and a review of the evidence.* Minneapolis, Minn.: University of Minnesota Press, 1954.

Mercer, J. R. *System of multicultural pluralistic assessment (SOMPA) technical manual.* New York: Psychological Corporation, 1979.

Mercer, J. R., & Lewis, J. F. *System of multicultural pluralistic assessment: Parent interview manual.* New York: Psychological Corporation, 1977.

Mercer, J. R., & Lewis, J. F. *System of multicultural pluralistic assessment: Student assessment manual.* New York: Psychological Corporation, 1978.

Messick, S. Personality structure. *Annual Review of Psychology,* 1961, *12,* 93–128.

Messick, S. Response sets. In D. L. Sills (Ed.), *International encyclopedia of the social sciences.* New York: Macmillan and Free Press, 1968.

Messick, S. The criterion problem in the evaluation of instruction: Assessing possible, not just intended outcomes. In M. C. Wittrock & D. E. Wiley (Eds.), *The evaluation of instruction: Issues and problems.* New York: Holt, Rinehart and Winston, 1970. (a)

Messick, S. Evaluation of educational programs as research on the educational process. In F. F. Korten, S. W. Cook, & J. I. Lacey (Eds.), *Psychology and the problems of society.* Washington, D.C.: American Psychological Association, 1970. (b).

Messick, S. The standard problem: Meaning and values in measurement and evaluation. *American Psychologist,* 1975, *30,* 955–966.

Messick, S. Personality consistencies in cognition and creativity. In S. Messick (Ed.), *Individuality in learning: Implications of cognitive styles and creativity for human development.* San Francisco: Jossey-Bass, 1976.

Messick, S. Test validity and the ethics of assessment. *American Psychologist,* 1980, *35,* 1012–1027.

Messick, S. Constructs and their vicissitudes. *Psychological Bulletin,* 1981, *89,* 575–588. (a)

Messick, S. Evidence and ethics in the evaluation of tests. *Educational Researcher,* 1981, *10,* 9–20. (b).

Messick, S. *Cognitive styles in educational practice.* (ETS RR 82–13). Princeton: N.J.: Educational Testing Service, 1982. (*Educational Psychologist,* in press.) (a)

Messick, S. Developing abilities and knowledge: Style in the interplay of structure and process. *Educational Analysis,* 1982, *4*(2), 105–121. (b)

Messick, S., & Barrows, T. S. Strategies for research and evaluation in early childhood education. In I. J. Gordon (Ed.), *Early childhood education: The seventy-first yearbook of the National Society for the Study of Education.* Chicago: University of Chicago Press, 1972.

Mischel, W. *Personality and assessment.* New York: Wiley, 1968.

Mosier, C. I. Psychophysics and mental test theory: Fundamental postulates and elementary theorems. *Psychological Review,* 1940, *47,* 355–366.

Mosier, C. I. Psychophysics and mental test theory II: The constant process. *Psychological Review,* 1941, *48,* 235–249.

Murray, H. A. *Explorations in personality.* New York: Oxford University Press, 1938.

Murray, H. A. (Ed.). *Assessment of men.* New York: Holt, Rinehart and Winston, 1948.

Nesselroade, J. R., & Bartsch, T. W. Multivariate perspectives on the construct validity of the trait-state distinction. In R. B. Cattell & R. M. Dreger (Eds.), *Handbook of modern personality theory.* New York: Wiley, 1977.

Nunnally, J. *Psychometric theory.* New York: McGraw-Hill, 1967.

Orne, M. T. On the social psychology of the psychological experiment, with particular reference to demand characteristics and their implications. *American Psychologist,* 1962, *17,* 776–783.

Overton, W. F., & Newman, J. L. Cognitive development: A competence/utilization approach. In T. Field, A. Houston, H. Quay, L. Troll, & G. Finley (Eds.), *Review of human development.* New York: Wiley, 1982.

Patterson, G. R., & Bechtel, G. G. Formulating the situational environment in relation to states and traits. In R. B. Cattell & R. M. Dreger (Eds.), *Handbook of modern personality theory.* New York: Wiley, 1977.

Pilliner, A. E. G. The application of analysis of variance to problems of correlation. *British Journal of Psychology,* 1952, *5,* 31–38.

Radcliffe, J. A. Some properties of ipsative score matrices and their relevance for some current interest tests. *Australian Journal of Psychology,* 1963, *15,* 1–11.

Rapaport, D. The structure of psychoanalytic theory: A systematizing attempt. In S. Koch (Ed.), *Psychology: A study of a science—Formulations of the person and the social context* (Vol. 3). New York: McGraw-Hill, 1959.

Rasch, G. *Probabilistic models for some intelligence and attainment tests.* Copenhagen, Denmark: Danmarks Paedogogiske Institute, 1960.

Rasch, G. An item analysis which takes individual differences into account. *British Journal of Mathematical and Statistical Psychology,* 1966, *19,* 49–57.

Riesman, D., & Watson, J. The sociability project: A chronicle of frustration and achievement. In P.

E. Hammond (Ed.), *Sociologists at work*. New York: Basic Books, 1964.

Rosenthal, R. *Experimenter effects in behavioral research*. New York: Appleton-Century-Crofts, 1966.

Ross, J. The relation between test and person factors. *Psychological Review*, 1963, *70*, 432–443.

Santayana, G. *The sense of beauty*. New York: Scribner's, 1896.

Sattler, J. M. Racial "experimenter effects" in experimentation, testing, interviewing, and psychotherapy. *Psychological Bulletin*, 1970, *73*, 137–160.

Sattler, J. M. *Assessment of children's intelligence and special abilities* (2nd ed.). Boston: Allyn and Bacon, 1982.

Scriven, M. Student values as educational objectives. *Proceedings of the 1965 Invetational Conference on Testing Problems*. Princeton, N.J.: Educational Testing Service, 1966.

Scriven, M. The methodology of evaluation. *Perspectives of curriculum evaluation*. (American Educational Research Association Monograph Series on Curriculum Evaluation). Chicago: Rand McNally, 1967.

Selltiz, C., Jahoda, M., Deutsch, M., & Cook, S. W. *Research methods in social relations*. New York: Holt, 1959.

Selltiz, C., Wrightsman, L. S., & Cook, S. W. (Eds.), *Research methods in social relations* (3rd ed.). New York: Holt, Rinehart and Winston, 1976.

Shavelson, R. J., & Webb, N. M. Generalizability theory: 1973–1980. *British Journal of Mathematical and Statistical Psychology*, 1981, *34*, 133–166.

Shulman, L. S. Reconstruction of educational research. *Review of Educational Research*, 1970, *40*, 371–396.

Sigel, I. E. When do we know what a child knows? *Human Development*, 1974, *17*, 201–217.

Skinner, B. F. *The behavior of organisms*. New York: Appleton-Century-Crofts, 1938.

Skinner, B. F. *Science and human behavior*. New York: Macmillan, 1953.

Skinner, B. F. *Beyond freedom and dignity*. New York: Knopf, 1971.

Snedecor, G. W. *Statistical methods* (5th ed.). Ames, Iowa: Iowa State College Press, 1956.

Spearman, C. The proof and measurement of association between two things. *American Journal of Psychology*, 1904, *15*, 72–101.

Spearman, C. Correlation calculated from faulty data. *British Journal of Psychology*, 1910, *3*, 271–295.

Stallings, J. A. *Learning to look: A handbook on classroom observations and teaching models*. Belmont, Calif.: Wadsworth, 1977.

Stanley, J. C. K-R-20 as the stepped-up mean item intercorrelation. *14th Yearbook of the National Council on Measurement in Education*, 1957, 78–92.

Stanley, J. C. Analysis of unreflected three-way classifications with applications to rater bias and treatment independence. *Psychometrika*, 1961, *26*, 205–219.

Stanley, J. C. Reliability. In R. L. Thorndike (Ed.), *Educational measurement* (2nd ed.). Washington, D.C.: American Council on Education, 1971.

Stephenson, W. *The study of behavior*. Chicago: University of Chicago Press, 1953.

Stevens, S. S., & Galanter, E. H. Ratio scales and category scales for a dozen perceptual continua. *Journal of Experimental Psychology*, 1957, *54*, 377–411.

Stocking, M. L., & Lord, F. M. Developing a common metric in item response theory. *Applied Psychological Measurement*, in press.

Straus, M. A. Measuring families. In H. T. Christensen (Ed.), *Handbook of marriage and the family*. Chicago: Rand McNally, 1964.

Thorndike, R. L. Reliability. In E. F. Lindquist (Ed.), *Educational measurement*. Washington, D.C.: American Council on Education, 1951.

Thorndike, R. L. Reliability. In *Proceedings of the 1963 Invitational Conference on Testing Problems*. Princeton, N.J.: Educational Testing Service, 1964.

Thorndike, R. L. (Ed.). *Educational measurement* (2nd ed.). Washington, D.C.: American Council on Education, 1971.

Thurstone, L. L. The stimulus-response fallacy in psychology. *Psychological Review*, 1923, *30*, 354–369.

Thurstone, L. L. *The nature of intelligence*. Westport, Conn.: Greenwood, 1924.

Thurstone, L. L. A law of comparative judgment. *Psychological Review*, 1927, *34*, 273–286.

Torgerson, W. S. *Theory and methods of scaling*. New York: Wiley, 1958.

Tryon, R. C. Reliability and behavior domain validity: Reformulation and historical critique. *Psychological Bulletin*, 1957, *54*, 229–249.

Tryon, W. W. The test-trait fallacy. *American Psychologist*, 1979, *34*, 402–406.

Tucker, L. R A level of proficiency scale for a unidimensional skill. *American Psychologist*, 1952,

7, 408.

Voyce, C. D., & Jackson, D. N. An evaluation of a threshold theory for personality assessment. *Educational and Psychological Measurement,* 1977, *37,* 383–408.

Walker, D. K. *Socioemotional measures for preschool and kindergarten children.* San Francisco: Jossey-Bass, 1973.

Webb, E. J., Campbell, D. T., Schwartz, R. D., & Sechrest, L. *Unobtrusvie measures: A survey of non-reactive research in social science.* Chicago: Rand McNally, 1966.

Wechsler, D. *Manual for the Wechsler Intelligence Scale for Children—Revised.* New York: Psychological Corporation, 1974.

Weick, K. E. Systematic observational methods. In G. Lindzey & E. Aronson (Eds.), *The handbook of social psychology* (Vol. II, 2nd ed.). Reading, Mass.: Addison-Wesley, 1968.

Whitely, S. E. Estimating measurement error on highly speeded tests. *Applied Psychological Measurement,* 1979, *3,* 141–154.

Whitely, S. E. Latent trait models in the study of intelligence. *Intelligence,* 1980, *4,* 97–132.

Wiggins, J. S. *Personality and prediction: Principles of personality assessment.* Reading, Mass.: Addison-Wesley, 1973.

Wilde, G. J. S. Trait description and measurement by personality questionnaires. In R. B. Cattell & R. M. Dreger (Eds.), *Handbook of modern personality theory.* New York: Wiley, 1977.

Winne, P. H., & Belfry, M. J. Interpretive problems when correcting for attenuation. *Journal of Educational Measurement,* 1982, *19,* 125–134.

Wright, B. D. Solving measurement problems with the Rasch model. *Journal of Educational Measurement,* 1977, *14,* 97–116.

Wright, H. F. Observational child study. In P. H. Mussen (Ed.), *Handbook of research methods in child development.* New York: Wiley, 1960.

Wright, H. F. *Recording and analyzing child behavior.* New York: Harper & Row, 1967.

Wohlwill, J. F. *The study of behavioral development.* New York: Academic Press, 1973.

Zuckerman, M. Traits, states, situations, and uncertainty. *Journal of Behavioral Assessment,* 1979, *1,* 43–54.

EPILOGUE

CLASSIFICATIONS OF THE CHILD*

JEROME KAGAN, *Harvard University*

CHAPTER CONTENTS

There is a tendency to forget that all science is bound up with human culture in general, and that scientific findings, even those which at the moment appear the most advanced and esoteric and difficult to grasp, are meaningless outside their cultural context. (W. Heisenberg, 1952)

DESCRIPTION IN THE SCIENCES

All science relies on descriptions of phenomena that function either as incentives for inferential propositions or affirmations of deductive ones. Although

*Preparation of this chapter was supported in part by Grant HD10094 from the National Institute of Child Health and Human Development, National Institutes of Health, U. S. Public Health Service, and by grants to the Center for Advanced Study in the Behavioral Sciences, BNS 78–24671 from the National Science Foundation and Grant 2T32 MH 14581–04 from the National Institute of Mental Health.

philosophers have always warned of the potential distortion that perception and language can impose on real events, it was not until the late nineteenth century that a serious skepticism about our ability to know the world in its natural state pervaded both the natural and the cultural sciences (Hughes, 1958). The initial reaction to this threat to established procedures was the argument, promoted especially by historians and sociologists, that there was a major difference between the natural sciences and the disciplines that study history and human nature. That first defense was followed, two to three decades later, by three major intellectual movements that attempted to cope with the crisis of certainty. These included a harder line toward meaningful propositions, a flight from objectivity to a celebration of intuition and subjectivity, and a pragmatism that permitted consequences of belief and action to decide issues of meaning and truth. Even though contemporary natural science recognizes the arbitrariness of the division between the observing agent and the observed (D'Espagnat, 1979), it manages to contain the distortion through the use of machines and elegant deductive sequences that stipulate the relation between the signs generated by the apparatus and the phenomena of interest.

But the social sciences are generally without such advantages. Observer bias, which looms large for anthropology, sociology, and psychology, affects both the language of description and the constructs of explanation. Developmental psychology is especially vulnerable because such a large proportion of empirical work involves observations of children in natural contexts or laboratories. Descriptions of play with objects, interactions with peers and adults, and changes in posture and facial expression—all of which are central to modern theory—permit the observer's suppositions to exaggerate some of what happened, ignore most of what happened, and occasionally invent phenomena that never happened.

THE MIND OF THE CLASSIFIER

The purpose of this chapter is to consider historical trends in the suppositions that influenced the constructs and descriptors used to classify children and their behavior, and to show that the choices made reflect unproven assumptions held by the classifier and, by inference, latent in his society. These influences—Bacon's ''Idols of the Theatre''—reveal themselves in four ways: the dimensions chosen for descriptive classification, the constructs invented to name correlations between events, the mechanisms of change postulated to account for growth, and, finally, the telos of development.

Consider a concrete example of a change in explanatory categories which reflects a change in presuppositions. Sixteenth century English scholars classified poor, disadvantaged children who were vagrants as belonging to one of four different categories: (1) those who lost their parents through death or desertion, (2) those who had physical handicaps or serious mental retardation, (3) those who were born into a large family, and (4) those who had idle parents (Pinchbeck & Hewitt, 1969, 1973). None of these classifications implicates either genetic taint or the child's character or motivation. The adolescent was seen as a passive victim of chance, illness, or parental character. The educated citizens of sixteenth-century England assumed children were malleable and the most effective rehabilitation for their disadvantaged state was education. Classifications of comparable classes of children in England and the United States today note explicitly the adolescent's motivations, conflicts, and expectancies (Conger,

1977) and, on occasion, link the child's inheritance to his behavior. The modern categories reflect historical changes in our views regarding the influence on action of both intrapsychic processes and biology.

Many philosophers have written more cogent defenses of the position argued here. Hanson (1961) invented a telling example of the effect of theory on observation when he asked if Tycho Brahe and Johannes Kepler would have seen the same event (and, we add, written similar descriptions) if they had been standing together on the same hill at the same time watching the sun rise. The name or predicate appended to a real event, ''is not determined by the intrinsic quality of whatever sensation happens to prompt its observational use, but by the network of assumptions/beliefs/principles in which it figures'' (Churchland, 1979, p. 15).

As we shall see in our survey of nineteenth-century essays and texts, the terms chosen to classify children were more likely to be inventions than names for behavioral events. The early authors rarely said that the baby cried, flexed his hand, or smiled. Rather they were apt to say the child showed *will* or a *voluntary response*. The constructs used by nineteenth-century writers most often dealt with the relation between a child's internal state and a highly inclusive, relatively nonspecific set of behaviors. Far less frequently did the constructs tie specific prior events to particular actions. But after 1920, following the replacement of instincts with habits, the most popular constructs united prior learning experiences, rather than current psychological states, with observed behavior.

Piaget's writing is intermediate between the two eras. Piaget describes 1-year-olds as being in the sensorimotor stage. The prior events are hypothetical chains of action sequences. The subsequent events are relatively nonspecific categories of acts, not particular actions, for the meaning of the action always depends on the age of the child. The principle that the significance of an action depends on the stage, age, or prior experience of the child moves an observer away from naming specific acts in a descriptive mode and toward the use of terms that imply a particular cause.

The heavy use of constructs rather than descriptors by both nineteenth- and twentieth-century observers seems to have been guided by an unconscious appreciation that the meaning of a response is ambiguous unless antecedent causes can be named. Although operationalism prevented glib guesses as to cause, it led to descriptions of behavioral events with equivocal meaning and encouraged investigators to pool events which probably had different meanings for the child.

The Bases for Classification

An observer categorizing actions under a common name has three choices. In the first place, he or she can group reactions on the basis of similar antecedent events (brain state, external incentive, prior history). Grouping diverse responses under the category "indexes of deprivation" is one example. Or the observer can categorize actions on the basis of similar outcomes, as when "aggression" is applied to all acts that injure another person. Finally, the observer can categorize on the basis of similarity in physical features of the response; the descriptors "cry" or "laugh" are appropriate examples. Because mechanical constraints restrict the number of possible actions to a value far less than the number of possible psychological states, grouping actions solely on the basis of physical similarity is apt to be misleading. One must also include a reference to antecedent events. Consider the following three statements: (1) "These children are in Stage 1 of language acquisition"; (2) "These children are attached"; (3) "These children are adjusted." Although these propositions appear to be similar, they are not. The statement, "These children are in Stage 1 of language acquisition" is based on similarity in behavioral events (i.e., utterances with particular morphemic characteristics). There is no assumption of common prior events or future outcomes. The statement, "These children are attached," however, is not based on behavioral similarities for it refers to acts like running to the caretaker when anxious, being placated easily by the caretaker, crying when the caretaker leaves, and lifting one's hands to the caretaker after she returns following a separation. The classification involves a presumption of particular prior interactions with the caretaker. The statement, "These children are adjusted" is based on similarity in outcomes; especially successful mastery of local challenges in the society. Categorizations based only on similarity in outcome ignore the form of the reaction or the incentive and, therefore, are likely to be influenced by the presuppositions of the classifier. This pragmatic approach to categorization is likely to disguise and distort the prior history of a response, which is at the heart of explanation.

The Selection of Events

There are at least four different factors that influence the phenomena the classifier chooses to describe. The first two are largely tacit; the second pair is more explicit. The first influence consists of a tacit hypothesis as to the primary causes or consequences of an observed event, for most classifications involve an inference as to origin and future state. If the classifier believes in the primacy of a certain cause for a behavior, he or she tends to focus on those phenomena that affirm the classifier's belief. For example, Tiedemann (1897) believed that maximizing pleasure was the primary incentive for action in the infant. Thus, when he looked at his newborn son he noted first that the boy turned to a light and added that the sensations that resulted from this action were pleasurable (actually, he used the word "agreeable"). Millicent Shinn (1907) shared that perspective, for the first description of the infant she summarized in her full diary was, "The child that I observed seemed for the first hour to feel a mild light agreeably" (p. 21). By contrast, Darwin's (1877) first diary descriptions dealt with his child's reflexes (yawning, stretching, and sucking) because Darwin believed the major causes of behavior resided in phylogenetic adaptation. Today's observers of infants are more likely to regard structural maturation of the central nervous system as a major basis for behavior; hence, they describe responses that they believe reflect the structural integrity of the brain. They more frequently note the child's pursuit of a moving light or the placing response, rather than a turning to a light or facial grimaces.

Another tacit hypothesis held by early and modern observers is the belief in a connection between early and later behaviors. This prejudice led theorists to pay special attention to those responses they believed had derivatives in the future; responses that were preserved, although often transformed. Children's play was described by almost all early observers because they believed such action was necessary for future adaptation—in play the child practiced actions he would need in perfected form when he was older. Contemporary observers believe that the attachment of the infant to adults reflects an emotional disposition that is preserved; hence, clinging to the mother, crying at separation, vocalizing on reunion with a caretaker attract as much space as did discussions of play a half-century ago. A belief in connectivity—the future consequences of a behavioral event—need not be the only basis for selecting continuing properties for empirical study. Scientists who study the sleep behavior of infants over the first two years do so in order to make statements about the maturation of the central nervous system. I do not oppose the selection of qualities that have a life beyond the moment of observation, but merely point out that this belief has guided a great deal of observation.

An observer too easily projects onto an event both its prior antecedents and future consequences. Rarely does an observer perceive and name an event as it happens in the contemporaneous present. For example, a child who has spilled some glue on a table "runs to his mother and kisses her." The act of kissing the parent is an event that, only with difficulty, can be viewed as an isolated touching of lip to cheek. It takes effort for the observer to resist assigning to the child internal states that follow the spilling of the glue or changes in state after the act of kissing. Both intrusions color the perception of the event. Film can capture a splash of water frozen in space and time; such perceptions are difficult for human beings. A belief in connectivity leads an observer to emphasize the contributions of the observed phenomenon to the future. If the observer believes the event makes no such contribution, it is usually ignored.

A second influence on classification, also often unconscious, is the disposition to classify an event as similar to or different from some referent. Tiedemann, for instance, wanted to maximize the differences between human beings and animals and so described actions that exaggerated the differences between infant and animal. Darwin, on the other hand, wanted to minimize these differences and so described the infant reflexes that were most similar to those displayed by animals.

The second pair of influences constitute the more conscious agenda of the scientist. The most central is the articulated hypothesis of the investigator. Bernfeld (1929), who promoted psychoanalytic ideas, wished to prove that sensory processes were pleasant. Hence he devoted a great deal of attention to the smiling and cooing of babies while they were looking at interesting events.

The second influence derives from the fact that apparatus directs classifications. For example, the observer with a polygraph will describe heart and breathing rates; the investigator with a computer of average transients will describe the amplitude of the wave forms of an evoked potential; the investigator with a camera will describe small muscular changes in the baby's face. The importance of the relation between the procedures used to generate observations and the descriptors or constructs applied to those observations is better appreciated by physical than by social scientists. When chemists report the acidity, pressure, or temperature of a solution, their colleagues know and approve of the methods used and have articulated the relation between each of these methods and the descriptive statements. Social scientists are more indifferent to method and too often treat statements about a person's self-concept, motivation to achieve, or level of anxiety as being equivalent, even though some descriptions are based on answers to interviews, others on stories to pictures, and still others on autonomic reactions to electric shock.

The meaning of every scientific classification depends upon its procedural origin. When a person says a flower is red we assume he is looking at the flower, not touching or smelling it. When an observer says a person's heart rate is 135 beats per minute, we assume he is looking at the record of a cardiotachometer, not the color of the person's face or his respiratory rate. But when an observer says that a 1-year-old is attached to the mother, it is not always clear what method was used—reunion behavior in the Ainsworth Strange Situation, crying upon separation from the mother in the home, clinging to the mother in a waiting room, or smiling when the mother picks up the child. Because each source of information lends a different meaning to the statement, "This child is attached", each descriptive classification is, in fact, a classification-cum-method unit.

This problem is of particular relevance to developmental psychology because it is in transition from a tradition characterized by almost total dependence on observations of molar behavior in natural contexts to the use of experimental procedures that generate data not observable without a special intervention. When nineteenth-century scholars used classifications like "intelligent" or "moral," they used different procedures than those we employ today, but we continue to use these same words. When Preyer said his son was emotionally labile, his readers knew that this classification was based on watching his son's behavior in the home. When a modern observer makes the same statement, we must be told if the source is the mother's answers to a questionnaire, variability in heart rate, changes in an electroencephalogram, or a microanalysis of film recordings of the child's facial expressions. The meaning of the statement, "The child is emotionally labile" varies with the method used.

The psychologist's indifference to the methodological source of his statements has created serious problems. One investigator uses a paper-and-pencil questionnaire in a classroom to evaluate a child's self-concept and concludes that poor black children have a positive self-concept. Another observer interviews the same children in their homes over a period of 8 weeks and concludes that these children have fragile self-concepts. Because the evidential source of a classification is part of its meaning, classifications of human qualities should note explicitly the method employed. Put in plainest form, the statement, ''The child is anxious'' has as many meanings as sources of observation.

As a science matures, the two more conscious influences—articulated hypotheses and apparatus—dominate the less conscious forces—suppositions as to origin, consequence, and primary referent—but never completely. (For a historical review of more technical sources, see Sears, 1975). It is unlikely that an a priori hypothesis will violate a presupposition as to the cause of an event. Most modern observers do not believe, for example, that infants have ways of representing ''right'' and ''wrong.'' Hence, they would not present an infant with visual stimuli depicting social and antisocial actions in order to see if the infant's reactions are different to the two classes of stimuli, although this experiment might have been performed by nineteenth-century psychologists.

Three Perspectives in Classification

One basis for the disparity in classifications of the infant is the fact that classifiers assume different referents when using descriptors that are comparative, and often evaluative, in meaning. Rarely does the classifier specify the referent and, as a result, the descriptors can be ambiguous. One of three possible referents is available, and each provides a unique perspective.

From the perspective of *individual differences* the referent is children of the same age. Descriptions like ''irritable,'' ''easy to placate,'' and ''securely attached'' are usually intended to differentiate among infants, not between infants and older children or between infants and animals. The second perspective is *developmental;* the implied referent is children of a different age or adults. Descriptive terms like ''undifferentiated,'' ''helpless,'' ''dependent,'' and ''asymbolic'' are usually intended to compare infants with older members of the species. The third perspective is *comparative.* Its implied referent is animals other than *Homo sapiens*—terms like ''linguistic,'' ''social,'' ''symbolic,'' and ''moral'' are intended to differentiate children from animals—or in the nineteenth and early twentieth centuries—infants from savages, a referent that is absent today.

Nineteenth-century writers, who were under the influence of Darwinian theory, typically used terms that assumed animals to be the comparison class (Fiske, 1909); two very popular descriptions were *volitional* and *possessing consciousness.* Twentieth-century writers are more likely to assume an individual difference perspective. But note how ambiguous the statement, ''Infants have no sense of self'' can be if the referent is not given. The sentence has one meaning if other mammals are the referent, but quite another if 3-year-olds are the referent.

THE CHILD AS CLASSIFIED: THE LAST 100 YEARS

The principal purpose of this chapter is to describe the similarities and differences in the prose that psychologists have composed about children over the last century. It is not a history of child psychology, but an essay on the history of ideas. Its evidence includes some major diaries of young children and a small number of significant books on children intended for professionals or educated parents. But, in the main, its domain is textbooks on child psychology written for students, rather than the popular literature that appeared in magazines or sermons on children delivered in churches, schools, and town halls. The intent is to detect the themes and suppositions that were common across the century, as well as those that changed, and to account for the changes in thought that occurred during the second decade of this century. The changes in descriptions of the child took one of three forms.

The most concrete changes involved the introduction of new words to describe the child as a whole, or to name particular behaviors, as well as constructs used to unite coherences. For example, most nineteenth-century writers classified the onset of reliable imitation in the infant (at 8 to 10 months of age) as a sign that the child was now capable of volitional action. Many twentieth-century observers use the same event to index the emergence of social behavior. It is likely that this change in categorization is due, in part, to the increasing importance assigned to social interaction by modern observers. Some classification terms were simply dropped from discussion (''religious ideation,'' for example, is not discussed in modern texts, while ''creativity'' does not appear in the earlier ones). Other terms underwent a transformation. ''Will,'' which was a popular construct in older texts, was replaced by ''motivation'' after 1930.

The second form of change is found in the order in which ideas are discussed and the amount of space devoted to each, assuming that these properties reflect the author's attitudes about the relative importance of these processes. For example, prior to the turn of the century, sensory and motor functioning were usually discussed before learning. After 1920, the child's capacity for learning was given priority. Only recently, due to Piaget's popularity, is sensorimotor functioning discussed, occasionally before conditioning (Gardner, 1978). In older texts, if the author considered language at all, it was always in a late chapter; and emotions were almost always considered after intellect. In time, the chapters on language moved up in the table of contents; now some modern authors consider emotion before cognition.

The third, least obvious form of change is in the sets of presuppositions authors believe they share with their readers, most of which are either unproven or difficult to refute with empirical data.

We begin by considering the presuppositions shared by most authors throughout the period of study. We are not judging the validity of these ideas, some of which may turn out eventually to be theoretically useful and empirically reliable. But at the time the authors were writing none of these tacit hypothesis or accompanying constructs had commanding empirical support. Thier source was intuition, and we wish to track the historical changes in the intuitions about children while attempting to understand them.

Shared Conceptions of Human Development

Five presuppositions that are common to both the early and modern books might be called (1) gradual change, (2) connectivity between phases of development, (3) internalization of external events, (4) the law of effect as the primary mechanism of growth, and (5) freedom as the ideal state of the child and a criterion for developmental maturity.

Gradualism

Most authors assumed that the development of new attributes is gradual, without sudden disruption of habits or internal qualities. James Mark Baldwin (1895) asserted, "In the first place we can fix no absolute time in the history of the mind at which a certain mental function takes its rise" (p. 10). The French psychologist Compayré (1914) applied the essence of the idea behind "the great chain of being" to the growth of the child's mind. "Nothing is formed all of a sudden, by a miracle of nature. . . . From the unconscious to the conscious, from an automatic state to a voluntary state, from diffuse scattered impressions to the concentration of all the states of consciousness around a unified,

identical ego, there is a multitude of insensible transitions and of little successive advances" (Compayré, 1914, p. 276). Modern authors continue to affirm gradual growth, "Attachment does not develop suddenly and unheralded, but emerges in a consistent series of steps in the first six months of life" (Hetherington and Parke, 1979, p. 222).

Faith in slow change, which was also a basic tenet in the "Origin of Species," serves mechanism. Darwin recognized that one basis for resistance to suddenness of change was the strong desire among Enlightenment scholars to designate the mechanisms that mediate a new form. As a result, he and they dismissed descriptions in which a great many intermediate steps are not obvious. "But the chief cause of our natural unwillingness to admit that one species has given birth to other and distinct species, is that we are always slow in admitting great changes of which we do not see the steps" (Darwin, [1859] 1872, p. 180).

If a new property emerges through gradations, scientists feel more certain that they can specify the intermediate steps and meet the aesthetic requirements of a satisfying explanation. The nineteenth-century observer believed that, if new properties emerge suddenly, predictability and specification of intermediate events becomes more difficult. Perhaps that is why Leibniz insisted, "Now this is the axiom which I utilize, namely, that no event can take place by a leap. . . . A body in order to go from one place to another must pass through definite intermediate places" (cited in Lovejoy, 1936, p. 145).

Connectivity

Few authors fail to assume a structural connection between the phases of development, as biologists assumed a link between primitive man and *Homo sapiens*. They wrote in affirmation of Russell's bold assertion, "The chain of causation can be traced by the inquiring mind from any given point backward to the creation of the world," (cited in Hanson, 1961, p. 50). The essence of a connected conception of development is captured by James Mark Baldwin (1895), "Every adaptation rises right out of the bosom of old processes and is filled with old matter" (p. 218).

Piaget's celebration of connectivity is syntactically more complex but identical in connotation. "Thus, when we studied the beginnings of intelligence we were forced to go as far back as the reflex in order to trace the cause of the assimilating activity which finally leads to the construction of adaptive schemas, for it is only by a principle of functional continuity that the indefinite variety of structures can be explained" (Piaget, 1951, p. 6).

Piaget's views are echoed by Jonas Langer (1980), who has recently argued that the origins of adult logic can be traced to the simple object manipulations of 6-month-old infants. Many investigators went so far as to imply that no part of the past could ever be lost. Every psychological property in the adult potentially could be traced to the deep past.

But there seems to be no manner of doubt, among those whose studies have best qualified them to speak with authority, that the mind of any person, child or adult, is made up of the sum total of all of the experiences through which he has passed since birth, plus every impression that has ever touched him in passing, no matter how fleeting and transitory some of these may have seemed. That is to say, that every thought, feeling, experience, or image that has ever impinged upon one's consciousness becomes, once and for all, a component part of a great, constantly growing, indestructible body, his mind—which is to say, his real self. (Richardson, 1926, pp. 33–34)

Bernfeld (1929) believed that all adult cognition had its origin in early infancy. "The powerful significance of the intellectual processes—perception, phantasy, thinking and their social results in science, art, and philosophy in the human being—have their first roots in this specifically human mental structure of the 3 month old child" (p. 138). "Historically all phenomena of adult mental life must be traceable to birth" (p. 213).

Even authors uncommitted to a single theoretical view disseminated this catechism. Tracy and Stimpfl (1909) stated casually that the proprietary instinct grows out of the grasp reflect of the infant, and Rand, Sweeny, and Vincent (1930) believed that the adult's sense of the aesthetic grew out of infant experiences. "General opinion agrees that aesthetic taste can be influenced even at such an early age. It is probably not desirable, then, to give him ugly toys which he may come to love because of the associations with them" (p. 260).

The introduction of psychoanalytic theory enhanced the nineteenth-century fear of the long-term consequences of overstimulation. (Note the contrast with today's apprehension that a baby might be stimulus deprived.) Going to the cinema, for example, was a particularly dangerous experience.

Nor should the young child be taken to public entertainments of any sort. It is not only the ignorant who take their babies to moving picture shows or other entertainments, they may be found at concerts and lectures which draw their audiences from the most cultured. The baby may show no signs of restlessness and be as good as you please, or may make up for lost sleep by an extra nap the next day, and yet be harmed thereby. No serious immediate symptoms of nervous overstimulation may appear, but some day the accounting must come—it may be 20 or even 40 years later before it is paid in full, but paid it will be. (Fenton, 1925, pp. 293–294)

About a half-century later Mussen, Conger, and Kagan (1969) suggested that harsh toilet-training during the second year may have equally dangerous consequences for the adult.

Connectivity is implied not only by asserting that the dispositions shaped during the early years will be preserved, but also, in indirect form, by labeling behaviors in infants with names that are more appropriate for those in adults. Arlitt (1928) posited six instincts in the infant, five of which were more applicable to adults than to infants. They were: self-assertion, to do as others do, to be uncomfortable at the sight of suffering, play, sex, and gregariousness. For example, the infant's tendency to stop crying when he is with a familiar person is treated as a sign of gregariousness; the tendency to cry when another baby does is indicative of the instinct to "do as others do." The reason why these declarations did not strike Arlitt or her audience as odd is that both she and her readers assumed connectivity. Adult behavior had its origins in infancy; therefore, if one saw a response that might be an origin of a later disposition, both author and audience were receptive to the assumption that it was.

A third source of evidence for the belief in connectivity is the awarding of primacy to the affects that appear early in development. Because crying (indicative of fear), motor discharge (indicative of rage), and babbling while being touched (indicative of love) are seen during the first year, while signs of shame, guilt, and pride are not, Arlitt wrote that the latter three can not be basic emotions. The doctrine of connectivity implied for her that the earlier a disposition appears, the more significant it is for development; those that occur later are probably derivatives of earlier processes.

Each historical period looks for the origins of those adult qualities that are of general societal concern or dominate scientific debate. The nineteenth century was concerned with the child's asocial behavior and searched for the origins of jealousy, aggression, and possessiveness in the acts of the infant. After World War I, when Freudian influence was becoming ascendant, observers looked for the origins of adult emotion, especially anxiety, in the infant's repertoire. Currently, the writings of Piaget (1951), Chomsky (1972), and Simon (1969) are dominant, and scholars are preoccupied with how cognitive competences are acquired. Thus the observation of an 8-month-old squeezing a favorite blanket has been regarded, depending upon the historical period, as an early form of aggression, a defense against anxiety, or a logical transformation.

Both gradualism and connectivity are remnants of the growth of historicism that was ascendant during the nineteenth century. This view, as Mandelbaum (1971) notes, was a reaction to the mechanical picture of human beings held by eighteenth-century philosophers. Enlightenment scholars believed that in order to understand a phenomenon one must know its complete history and that the growth of plants and animals is the model for change in humanity and society. In order to understand the appearance of the first blossom in May, or a revolution, one needs complete knowledge of the continuous and connected events from origin to the phenomenon of interest, which is linear and progressive. Although this view of the history of civilizations became far less popular among twentieth-century historians, it remains regnant in developmental psychology.

There are good reasons why there is resistance to positing discontinuities in growth and the emergence of novel structures with short histories. First, the doctrine of connectedness makes original forms useful. If the origin of important adult properties occurs during later childhood or adolescence, the first years of life will then appear to have no future purpose, much like the embryonic notochord that vanishes after its mission is completed. The possibility that the products of an era of development might be temporary or transitional is bothersome to many who want to believe that all psychological products are permanent and that "everything we learn is permanently stored in the mind" (Loftus & Loftus, 1980, p. 410).

Further, arguments for connectivity have the illusion of being mechanistic. When each new function is preceded by another that makes a substantial contribution to it, one is better able to state the cause-and-effect sequence than if a function emerges relatively rapidly as a result of a new endogenous change. In the second instance, the mind is left with an explanatory gap. Scholars invent ideas to fill that gap and lend an illusion of fullness to the epoch of change.

There may be a third source of the persuasiveness of connectivity. During each historical period there is a dominant philosophical view that most scholars avoid confronting—an intellectual electric fence. From the Renaissance to the nineteenth century, philosophers and scientists were reluctant to infer or deduce propositions that would refute or contradict Biblical statements on humankind and nature. Although few contemporary scientists worry about the implications of their work for Christian teaching, many are concerned, often unconsciously, about the implications of their data and ideas for the ethic of egalitarianism. The attacks on Arthur Jensen, Richard Herrnstein, and E. O. Wilson, among others, have less to do with data than with the implications of their writings for the doctrine of equality.

The assumption of connectedness in growth of human characteristics is in accord with egalitarian principles. The discontinuities that appear in early development are likely to be attributable to maturational changes in the central nervous system. But to emphasize the role of structural changes in the brain is to imply that an individual's biology has formative force. Since each person is biologically unique (except for one-egg twins), we are led inevitably to infer different rates of psychological growth, which in turn have their roots in differences in biological processes. However, that conclusion is regarded by some as inconsistent with egalitarian premises. By contrast, positing continuous development implies uniform experiences that gradually establish new properties. Because the experiences of children are potentially controllable, the connected view implies, but does not prove, that one can arrange similar growth-enhancing experiences for all infants. Although developmental psychologists favor a connected and continuist interpretation of change, the most revolutionary, scientific ideas during the last 75 years have been discontinuist in their essence. The photon has replaced the wave, the discrete gene has replaced the continuous effects of climate, diet, and environmental challenge; the possible disintegration of protons replaced steady-state theories of the universe and implied an end, far, far in the future, of what we would like to regard as a continuous cosmos.

Internalization as a Mechanism of Growth

A supposition less obvious than the first two we choose to call the "internalization of external events." The essence of this assumption is that all mental structures (knowledge, self-consciousness, schemas of action) result from the processing of sensory information and the repetition of actions. If the child repeats an action frequently enough, important changes in internal organization will follow. James Mark Baldwin (1895) argued that the disposition to imitate was a derivative of the repetition of simpler actions and not a novel psychological function.

In his second major book, *Social and Ethical Interpretations in Mental Development,* Baldwin (1897) suggested that self-consciousness was a product of the incorporation of the action of others. What a person calls himself, "is in large measure an incorporation of elements that, at an earlier period of his thought of personality, he called someone else" (p. 10). "My sense of self grows by imitation of you and my sense of yourself grows in terms of my sense of myself. Both ego and alter are thus essentially social; each is a *socius* and each is an imitative creation" (p. 9).

Contemporary writers continue to use the principle of internalization. After summarizing persuasive data indicating that the infant shows signs of recognition of the self during the second half of the second year, Lewis and Brooks-Gunn (1979) suggest that this competence "has as its source the interaction of the young organism with others—both people and objects. The implication of this is that action within the interaction of the organism and its environment precedes knowledge. Indeed, it is from action that knowledge develops" (p. 241).

Piaget is most explicit on the process of internalization—what he calls interiorization—as a mechanism of growth, even though he insists that environmental experience alone is insufficient to produce cognitive change. In the section of *Play, Dreams, and Imitation in Childhood* (1951) where he is describing the stages of imitation during the sensorimotor period, Piaget states that the child's behavioral "experimentation is interiorised and coordination takes place before there is external adjustment" (p. 62). A few pages later, when discussing the role of the mental image in imitation, Piaget asks, "Why should it, therefore, not be the product of the interiorisation of imitation once this has reached its full development, just as interior language is both the draft of words to come and the interiorisation of acquired exterior language?" (p. 70).

Piaget is reluctant to assume that some new psychological functions, like imagery and imitation, may appear as the result of lawful, but emergent, changes in the central nervous system. By assuming that knowledge, imagery, reasoning, and consciousness are partly derivative from, and, therefore, partly dependent upon, prior actions and sensory experiences, the theorist can be faithful to the scientific demand that constructs be tied to observable events. The same cultural forces that led Mach and Wittgenstein to reject constructs that were refractory to

quantification or specification may have tempted observers of children to posit internalization. The major alternative is to postulate autochthonous but unspecifiable changes in the brain as contributory to the appearance of new behaviors. But if we can only know as real what we can sense, and all else is regarded as nonsense, then to suggest, as Preyer (1888–1889) did, that the child will become aware of himself, imitate his parents, speak, and image because these competences are part of our species is to yield to a form of occultism. Those who wish to join the scientific enterprise must avoid such forms of explanation. This attitude was, of course, bolstered by Pavlov's famous experiments and the dogmatism of John Watson. "There are no instincts. We build in at an early age everything that is later to appear" (Watson, 1928, p. 38).

The renaissance of the maturational view in modern psychology must be due, in some measure, to the advances in modern biology and molecular genetics. Biologists now show us photographs of the sudden duplication of chromosomes and provide data that require us to assume that the DNA produces, autochthonously, RNA. An inner executive is necessary in the modern theory of the cell, and it would be impossible for anyone to suggest today that all the events in the cell's nucleus are the transformed results of events in the cytoplasm. But during the early decades of this century it was possible to hold that much of what was inside was originally produced by what was outside.

The Law of Effect and the Pleasure/Pain Principle

All observers want to know why the child acts and most expect both a mechanical and purposive answer. Bernfeld (1929), who admitted to being puzzled by the infant's laughter because he could not discern its purpose, finally suggested, "The child's laughter is an activity of love; it aims to arouse and obtain love by its laughter" (p. 109).

There was resistance to the possibility that the energy involved in an action may be expended without some future goal. An action does not mean a twitch of a limb or a brief facial grimace, but a coordinated action that appears to be directed toward a particular state of affairs and is terminated on attaining that state. Birds fly from one branch to another; babies kick the sides of their cribs. Three answers were proposed for those types of behavior:

1. The child acts to maximize pleasure and minimize pain.

2. The child acts in the service of habits established by observation or conditioning and, therefore, through the original operation of the pleasure/pain principle.

3. The child acts because structures in the central nervous system release the action to selected incentives.

Darwin (1871), like modern ethologists, insisted that hedonism is not the only reason for action. "In many instances, however, it is probable that instincts are followed from the mere force of inheritance, without the stimulus of either pleasure or pain. A young pointer when it first scents game apparently cannot help pointing. . . . Hence the common assumption that men must be impelled to every action by experiencing some pleasure or pain may be erroneous" (p. 76).

But as the nineteenth century came to a close, Darwin's view became a minority position; most observers put their faith in the first two principles. Few authors failed to declare loyalty to the law of effect; namely, the consequences of an action influence the future occasions of that action. And most were faithful to Bentham and Locke in positing that the most significant consequences of an action are increases in pleasure and decreases in pain or what Locke called "uneasiness." The eventual victory of the pleasure/pain principle came only after a debate between those who wished to make pleasure and pain primary, like James Mill and Locke, and those, like John Stuart Mill, who thought the pleasures of mind were more important than the sensory pleasures of sexuality, warmth, and food, or the more extreme position of the eighteenth-century philosopher, Johann Fichte, who saw morality, not pleasure, as the basis of action. "far from being true that man is determined to moral goodness by the desire for happiness, the idea of happiness itself and the desire for it, rather arise in the first place out of the moral nature of man. Not, *That which produces happiness is good;—but, that only which is good produces happiness*" (cited in Mandelbaum, 1971, p. 216).

James Mark Baldwin's first major book on the growth of the child, (1895) awarded pleasure and pain a central position in the attempt to explain how the child acquired new behavioral adaptations.

This process is—to state my point before discussing it—the neurological analogue of the hedonic consciousness; and the two aspects in which the happy variation shows itself in the consciousness of the higher organisms are pleasure and pain. These points may be summed up for discussion in

the general proposition: the life history of organisms involves from the start the presence of the organic analogue of the hedonic consciousness. (pp. 176–177)

Pleasure accompanies normal psychophysical process, or its advancement by new stimulations which are vitually good; and second, pain accompanies abnormal psychophysical process or the anticipation of its being brought about by new stimulations which are vitally bad. (p. 177)

But two years later in *Social and Ethical Interpretations in Mental Development* (1897), Baldwin suggested that what he called the hedonistic sanction is only ascendant during infancy—the time when the child is most similar to animals. As the child grows, the moral sanction takes precedence. For the infant, "The stimulus arising from an object becomes the stimulation of a pleasurable or painful object" (p. 369); but later, "The sanction of right tends to supercede the earlier sanctions" (p. 396). "What ought I to do? becomes the mind's spontaneous response both to the demands of impulse and to the attractions of success. . . . The result then is this: that all action which is in any sense interested is ethical; and upon it falls the ethical sanction, after the person has once entered the ethical epoch of growth" (p. 401).

This more cognitive interpretation of what prompted behavior was lost after the turn of the century because, I believe, positivism crushed its metaphysical flavor. Scientists believed they could measure pleasure and pain because the words referred to sensory events. Few believed they could measure a sense of moral obligation. Thus goodness gave way to happiness as the canon of objectivity ran roughshod over philosophy and more and more observers emphasized the sensory consequences of behavior. For Bernard Perez (1900) "pleasant sensations" were central in an infant's life:

A child of 6 months spends at least half of his waking hours exercising the organs which afford him pleasant sensations—visual, auditory, tactile and muscular. . . . The tendency to enjoy pleasant sensations and to repeat them over and over again for their own sake is the dominant instinct at this period. (p. 51)

For Emma Marwedel (1889) pain was the mechanism by which the sense of self emerged.

Before a child learns that the several members of its body are part of itself, it must pass through many experiences, most of them more or less painful. My own child was 408 days old when, standing in its bed, it bit its own arm until it screamed. (p. 541).

Modern texts continue to utilize the language of pleasure/pain. Mussen, Conger, and Kagan (1974) state that the states of discomfort experienced by the infant are ''important psychologically for they force the infant to do something in order to alleviate the discomfort'' (p. 132). ''The caretaking adult typically provides pleasant experiences and reduces the infant's pain and stress. As a result the infant becomes attached to its caretakers'' (p. 227).

It is possible that the Freudian hypothesis of erogeneous zones is an extension of the pleasure/pain principle to sensory functions. If actions that are followed by pleasure are repeated (the law of effect), and experiences of pleasure/pain are the primary bases for consciousness, why not extend the significance of pleasure to sensory function and assume that taste, touch, sight, and hearing, although not skeletal, are also accompanied by pleasure? That idea is central to the concept of erogenous zones. Bernfeld (1929), who was strongly influenced by Freud, states that the baby looks and listens in order to experience pleasure.

The eye is from birth very sensitive to light and moderate light stimuli release manifold reactions of pleasure: opening the eyes wide, turning the head toward objects, the breathing and pulse curves, are all more of the pleasure than of the pain type. (p. 64)

No observer has neglected to mention the high pleasure tone, the great joy, and loud cooing of the child which occurred not only at the first seeing or during the first successful stage of the act of seeing, but which accompany seeing in general and which are especially gleeful and continuous during the first three months. (p. 68)

The need for seeing is so closely related to pleasure, that one very unwillingly accepts the reversal of the relationship that results from the theory of interest. On this theory the biologically adequate interest, when exercised, produces pleasure. The need to see comes from the common perceptive interest; this interest is of biological advantage; it is therefore combined with pleasure. It seems to me simpler to think of the reverse: the need to see is an instance of a general desire for pleasure. Because seeing brings pleasure it is exercised, and so intensely used, that it appears as if a need to see existed. . . . Thus,

seeing is simply an activity, whose purpose is pleasure gain. (p. 70)

Although the law of effect, with pleasure and pain as primary consequences, is central in all texts throughout the past century, there has been a subtle but detectable shift in the source of agency. The nineteenth-century author writes about the child behaving ''in order to gain pleasure.'' The twentieth-century author says that ''acts'' which are followed by positive consequences are repeated and ''acts'' followed by negative consequences are inhibited or not repeated. These sentences may appear to be equivalent, but they have different connotations. In the first, the child is the agent who initiates acts volitionally as a result of the generation of private intentions. In modern texts, however, the notion of the volitional agent is missing, and the system is both more mechanical and deterministic. It is responses that are automatically repeated if they have been followed by pleasant consequences. A baby's vocalization is modified through operant conditioning; the child does not decide to vocalize. The preference for the mechanical view, which eliminates volition, appears after 1910, coincident with the dissemination of the writings of Pavlov, Watson, and Freud and with the more complete commitment by psychologists to the new philosophy of explanation promoted by the Vienna circle.

Freedom as Ideal and Natural State

Perhaps the most profound and, at the same time, the most disguised premise in most texts is that the child naturally enjoys freedom, an affirmation of Locke's declaration that ''Children love liberty and therefore they should be brought to do the things that are fit for them, without feeling any restraint laid upon them'' (Locke, [1693] 1892, p. 83). Even though all children must be socialized, their personal liberty is the most important inherent property to nurture. This idea is hidden in psychological propositions about play, private conscience, independence, and autonomy.

Freedom has at least two major meanings, one political and one psychological. The political definition refers to a society that awards its citizens as much permissiveness in matters of action and belief as it can without infringing on the actions and beliefs of others. There is no guarantee that each citizen will be able to exploit the freedom of belief and action a particular government permits. From a psychological perspective freedom refers to a *belief* that one is able to act in accord with privately generated goals with minimal external coercion. This private belief is abstract, and, we suspect, does not exist in children before early adolesence. Therefore observers who use the term freedom to describe the state of the child are, we submit, unconsciously confusing the political and psychological definitions.

In discussing the growth of the child's sense of agency, Baldwin (1895) noted that the child "begins to grow capricious himself and to feel that he can be so whenever he likes. Suggestion begins to lose the regularity of its working; or to become negative and contrary in its effects. At this period it is that obedience begins to grow hard, and its meaning begins to dawn upon the child as the great reality. It means the subjection of his own agency, his own liberty to be capricious, to the agency and liberty of someone else" (p. 125).

Sully (1896) suggested that the infant's protest to the removal of the feeding bottle before full satisfaction had been obtained is "the first rude germ of that defiance of control and of authority of which I shall have to say more by and by" (p. 231). But Sully is not bothered by these rebellious tendencies; he celebrates them. "We should not care to see a child give up his inclinations at another's bidding without some little show of resistance. These conflicts are frequent and sharp in proportion to the sanity and vigor of the child. The best children, best from a biological point of view, have, I think, most of the rebel in them" (p. 269). Indeed, the natural child resents restriction of his liberty because, Sully declares, freedom is a natural desire. "So strong and deep reaching is this antagonism to law and its restraints apt to be that the childish longing to be big, is I believe, grounded on the expectation of liberty" (p. 277).

Mumford (1925) urges parents to make the child "feel that the only obedience worthy of the name is that of the free man, who chooses to obey because he understands the law. The forced obedience of the slave, whose business is not to understand but merely to obey, who dares not disobey from fear of punishment, is unworthy of him" (p. 123). In a text that purports to be more scientific, Rand, Sweeny, and Vincent (1930) assert the same philosophy.

The whole process of the child's development has as its goal its emancipation from the parents, so that its own life may be free to develop to the fullest without the hindrances that are inevitable if there continues an attachment to the home . . . free development of the personality is only possible if it is free from crippling dependence of any sort. . . . Therefore, parents who are wise will grant freedom gradually and increasingly and will welcome rather than resent signs of a desire for independence on the child's part. (pp. 351–352)

Even John Watson, who prided himself on being scientifically objective, tells parents that if they treat their children properly, "the end result is a happy child free as air because he has mastered the stupidly simple demands society makes upon him" (1928, p. 150).

Play as a State of Freedom

The context of maximal freedom occurs when the child is playing. The behavioral category *play* appears in almost every textbook we consulted, but the fuzzy quality of its definition leads one to suspect that its popularity rests upon a deep presupposition. It is possible that play is regarded as a celebration of freedom. Most definitions of the child's acts (crying, hitting) or states (fear, hostility) are defined in terms that refer to real events. There is little ambiguity regarding the physical actions or phenomena to which the descriptive term applies. But this is less true for the category of play where there is no clear guide one can use to diagnose a response as an instance of play. Play is defined neither in terms of antecedent conditions nor observable reactions, but as a special state. Few major descriptive terms for the child or his properties are treated this way. Since this class of definition is both unusual and ambiguous, one would have thought that it would have a short life. But the category persists, we believe, because it is filling a vital function. The early definitions of play reveal one reason for its persistence.

"It is in play that [the child] gives free scope to all his aptitudes" (Compayré, 1914, p. 143). William Stern (1930) declared that no child can play under the yoke of necessity, "only that being can play whose consciousness is not quite subjugated under the yoke of necessity, under the stress of the struggle for existence . . . play is neither demanded nor imposed, but bubbles up spontaneously from the individual's deepest craving for action and its nature, form, and duration are determined by the player himself" (p. 307). Piaget, too, emphasizes the freedom in play. "Imaginary play is a symbolic transposition which subjects things to the child's activity without rules or limitations" (Piaget, 1951, p. 87).

The least ambiguous statement is found not in a textbook, but in a book on play directed to the general public—A Philosophy of Play—written by Luther Gulick (1920), a leader in developing recreational opportunities for youth and a founder of the Playground and Recreation Association of America. "Play is what we do when we are free to do what we will" (p. 267). "Play as free expression of the self, as the pursuit of the ideal, has direct bearing on the ultimate questions of reality and worth. The spirit of play has value as a philosophy of life'' (p. 11). Play is necessary for America, Gulick declares, because ''the type of freedom found in play is the type of freedom on which democracy rests'' (p. 261).

The words ''subjugated,'' ''yoke of necessity,'' ''compulsion,'' ''freedom,'' ''rules and limitations,'' which are used frequently in descriptions to play, have political connotations. The popularity of play as a scientific category for children may originate, in part, in the deep concern that adults feel about restrictions on their individual liberty and in the devotion they show, at least in the West, to freedom as a cherished state that must be worked for and maintained.[1]

There are other terms an observer might apply to the acts that are now classified as play. When a 1-year-old is building a tower with five blocks (a sequence always treated as play) it is not unreasonable to call that event an instance of morality. The child generates a standard (the idea of a five-block tower as a goal to be reached) and feels compelled to persist until he meets that standard. One might even argue that while the child is building the tower he is anything but free. The rough-and-tumble bodily encounters of 4-year-old boys could be classified as an example of ''healthy behavior,'' ''hostility,'' ''anxiety reduction,'' or even ''sexuality.'' There is so little resemblance between a 1-year-old building a block tower and 4-year-olds wrestling, it is surprising that so many observers have insisted on calling these activities by the same name.

I am not persuaded that individual freedom is one of the hidden purposes in ontogeny. Reproduction, coordination of limbs, and reflective thought may be biologically adaptive teloi, but freedom is a metaphysical ideal. That does not mean it is less significant, only that the statement ''children should be free'' has no firm home either in psychological theory or empirical fact, but is based on political philosophy. The fact that political ideology slips into the descriptions of children's psychological attributes illustrates the major theme of this chapter; our wisest observers have permitted their views about individual liberty to affect their classification of children's actions.

CHANGES IN DESCRIPTIVE TERMS AND CONSTRUCTS

Between 1910 and 1930, there occurred—coincident with the dissemination of both behaviorism and psychoanalytic theory—a coherent set of changes that involved an emphasis on interactive experience in the family, the introduction of motivational language, and a concern with individual differences in adjustment. Although our evidence comes primarily from textbooks and works intended for the professional and educated citizen rather than popular literature and technical papers, some of the changes that occurred in texts around 1920 were also reflected in magazines and professional journals.

From Biological Universals to Acquired Individual Differences

The Role of Interactive Social Experience

A major correlate of the new classificatory terms was a shift in interest from psychological attributes that would become part of every child's repertoire to differences among children in qualities that were less inevitable and more relativistic, especially independence, a sense of emotional security, and a high IQ. Differences among children in the degree of adjustment to society replaced the development of absolute character traits as the seminal puzzle to be solved.

Nineteenth-century observers wanted to know how infants become adults; they were less curious about differences in children's rate of progress toward maturity or the possibility that several adult profiles were possible and acceptable. But these are precisely the puzzles that more modern observers ponder. More importantly, modern writers are persuaded that interactive social experience, especially in the home, is the central reason for the development of these qualities as well as their extraordinary variation. ''Each individual personality is to a large degree a reflection of the personalities with whom he has interaction. . . . His personality grows as he shares life with others and they with him'' (Chave, 1937, p. 1). Some contemporary theorists emphasize not the interactive experience per se but the child's private interpretations. In both cases, direct encounters with others are the important incentives for change. (Davis & Havighurst, 1947; Kagan, 1979.)

A corollary of the new emphasis on direct parent/child interaction is a greater receptivity to conscious intervention in the life of the child. The blunt statements of John Watson, combined with the warnings implicit in Freud's writings, led psychologists to urge self-conscious control and manipulation of the child not only to tame disobedience and aggression (which nineteenth-century parents always did) but to sculpt a keener intelligence, earlier autonomy, and a belief in one's value.

Adults should therefore not only refrain when possible from helping the child who is facing a problem which has arisen naturally; but they should create new ones, when the child is ready for them, not only by implanting new motives, but by pointing out obstacles or difficulties of which the child alone would not have been aware. Only by so doing can they help the young child out of that egocentric self-confidence, which prevents the development of clear understanding and really effective thought and action (Curti, 1932, p. 314).

Essays of advice in magazines intended for well-educated audiences implied that raising children was a technical skill. E. R. Groves (1925) bemoaned immature parents who needed special training to avoid showing off to the child, losing their temper, disparaging the child, or behaving in a tyrannical manner. Even Bertrand Russell (1927) was seduced by the invitation to share his wisdom with the public. Russell admitted to his intellectual attraction to the tenets of behaviorism, affirming Watson's belief that "infancy is of paramount importance to the education of character" (p. 315). However, like most counselors, Russell, too, projected his own desires on to the child: "A child needs to grow like a tree, quietly, in one spot, at his own pace, and in his own manner" (p. 319).

The tenets of behaviorism provided the rational foundation for the assumption that the conditioning of habits in the context of social interaction was the primary mechanism for growth as well as the cause of individual variation. Although Watson's famous 1913 statement in the *Psychological Review*— "Psychology as the Behaviorist Views It"—was essentially a plea for psychology to become an experimental, natural science with social value to the community (not an explanation of differences in human behavior), his later popular writings are more explicit. In a 1926 essay published in *Harper's*, Watson announces the power of social conditioning to shape the child's psychological growth. "We can build any man, starting at birth, into any kind of social or a-social being upon order" (p. 728). "The home (mother, father, brother, sister, relations) is responsible for what the child becomes. Nurture—not nature—is responsible" (p. 729).

So quickly did the popularity of behavioristic assumptions grow that thirty years later the eminent anthropologist Geoffrey Gorer was able to state unabashedly that a unified theory of social science rested on twelve postulates. The second postulate was:

Human behavior is predominantly learned. Although the human infant may be born with some instincts and is born with some basic drives whose satisfaction is necessary to its survival, it is the treatment which the infant undergoes from the other members of the society into which it is born and its experiences in its environment which are of importance in molding adult behavior.

The fifth and sixth postulates were consistent with the second.

Habits are established by differential reward and punishment, chiefly meted out by other members of the society. . . . The habits established early in life of the individual influence all subsequent learning, and, therefore, the experiences of early childhood are of predominant importance. (Gorer, 1955, pp. 31–32.)

It should be pointed out that the commitment to growth through interactive experience promoted by American and British social scientists was less completely accepted by continental Europeans. Educated parents in Germany continued to believe that the mother's behavior as a role model was more important than the profile of rewards and punishments she dispensed (Métraux, 1955). These mothers, like Japanese mothers, did not regard the infant as totally plastic; each child was born with a temperamental disposition—an inner essence—that training could not easily alter. As one popular German author put it, "The mother is a gardener, she is not God" (Plattner, 1951, p. 65).

The Importance of Intrafamilial Interaction

The major source of variation in interactive experience was, of course, the family, and the difference between early and later texts in the amount of space devoted to the family was striking. Prior to 1910, it was unusual for a text to devote more than a few paragraphs to the direct influence of the family on the child. After 1920, it was impossible to find a text that did not devote a long section or whole chapters to parents, siblings, and the social class of the family as formative factors. However, although texts published prior to 1910 ignored the mother's behavior with the child, the popular literature of the mid-nineteenth century often emphasized the mother's role, especially with respect to the moral upbringing of the child. Why, then, were early textbook writers indifferent to the popular belief? (Sunley, 1955).

Forbush (1915) provides a clue. He notes that

because children's moral habits are learned through imitation (by "imitation" he means observation of adults), the actions of parents as role models are more important than their verbal admonishments or the behaviors they direct at the child. "The ideals, which in childhood are formed almost entirely through imitation, must be created largely in the home," (p. 19). "Her [the mother's] moral influence, too, must ultimately rest in what she is and not in what she adjures her children to be" (p. 24).

Because most early writers believed a parent's basic personality can not be changed very easily, it was reasonable to ignore discussion of parental rewards and punishments intended to have direct effects on the growing child. In addition, the authors of texts probably felt that because they were writing science, they could dismiss popular magazine articles and general books on the role of the mother as unsubstantiated folk belief.

Further, there was an obvious diversity of opinion as to which practices mothers should implement. Journalists who supported a Calvinist ideology told mothers that children were untamed and parents were to socialize their child's innate wildness through strict and consistent discipline. Writers who took Rousseau's philosophy as oracular advised mothers to harden the child by natural means—cold baths and cold bedrooms were to constitute the regimen, not harsh punishment. Finally, those who believed in Locke's philosophy urged mothers to be permissive and to socialize by gentler practices. The obvious inconsistency in these manuals of advice, which presented no evidence for their assertions, might have led the authors of the first scientifically oriented textbooks to ignore discussions of parental behavior. Finally, Darwinian theory, which was the leading paradigm for nineteenth-century writers, did not award an essential role to parental actions. It was only when Pavlovian and Freudian ideas replaced the evolutionary model and the advice to parents appeared to flow deductively from theoretical assumptions and the facts of conditioning—all after 1915—that textbook authors began to emphasize what the larger culture had been prepared to believe a century earlier.

The Interest in Infant Attachment and Parental Love

As the child's mutual relationships within the family became a more central theme, descriptions of infants made them more social in their basic propensities. The nineteenth-century author rarely used terms that denoted an inclination to establish an affective relation with adult caretakers. Mothers had intense, unrestrained affection for their babies, but babies did not necessarily reciprocate.

Elizabeth Evans (1875) asserted that "The strongest human tie is, understandably, that which binds a mother to her child" (p. 7), but nowhere in this 129-page essay on maternity does she ever say that the infant naturally binds itself to the mother. Stern (1930), too, does not regard the infant's attachment as very strong. "How quickly the little child gets used to a new nurse, even when it had great affection for her predecessor; how little the child misses—perhaps after short pain at parting—its parents when they leave home or a favorite animal" (p. 531).

Indeed, one author (Fiske, [1883] 1909) suggested that the function of infant helplessness was not to encourage the infant's attachment to the mother but rather to facilitate the emotional bond between the two parents. The cooperativeness necessary to nurture several children through adolescence would inevitably strengthen the emotional tie between the parents and keep them together.

To the nineteenth-century observer the infant was, first, a collection of reflexes, instincts, and sensory capacities which developed a sense of self and a burgeoning morality by acting in the natural world. These properties were established through individual action, not mutual interaction and dependence upon parents. But by the late 1920s—and with increasing regularity after Freud's writing became popular—attachment, trust, and dependence became major descriptive terms for the infant and young child. And this concern was accompanied by more explicit preaching about the importance of the proper amount of parental love. Frank Richardson (1926), a physician who tried to disseminate the implications of Freudian theory for parents, opened the first chapter of his book with the simple declaration, "Love is the greatest thing in the world," (p. 3), and warned parents of the dangers of too little or too much affection for their infants. Too little could cause "a definite injury, whose results, may, and probably will, last as long as the life of the individual" (p. 18). Too much love might cripple a child and produce "unfortunate individuals [who] present a sorry sight 10 or 12 years later. They are irritable, dissatisfied, wholly incapacitated for happy middle-age or later life" (p. 22).

Mussen, Conger, and Kagan (1974) wrote, "Mature, competent and independent pre-school children have parents who are highly consistent, warm, loving, and secure" (p. 414), and Gardner

(1978), who made the infant's attachment the theme of the opening chapter of his text wrote, ''Those who develop the feeling of trust have a good chance of negotiating subsequent crises and of realizing effective interpersonal relations throughout life. Those who fail to develop a trusting relationship with their caretakers and their environment will be perennially plagued by doubt, mistrust, and difficulty in finding a niche within their community'' (Gardner, 1978, p. 56).

Perhaps one of the strongest statements on the significance of the love relation between child and parent is to be found in the final volume of John Bowlby's ambitious trilogy on attachment and loss (Bowlby, 1980). Bowlby begins the monograph on *Loss* with a conclusion that would be difficult to find in a scholarly essay on human experience prior to 1800: ''Loss of a loved person is one of the most intensely painful experiences any human being can suffer'' (p. 7). Bowlby argues that an attachment to another person is instinctive, endures from infancy to adulthood, and, most important, an insecure attachment during infancy is likely to have a permanent affect on future vulnerability to psychopathology. On the final page Bowlby celebrates the centrality of affectional relationships. ''Intimate attachments to other human beings are the hub around which a person's life revolves, not only when he is an infant or a toddler but throughout his adolescence and his years of maturity as well and on into old age'' (p. 442).

This bold hypothesis could not have been written by Erasmus or Montaigne because they did not regard infancy as a formative period and because intimate social relationships were not the major source of gratification or virtue. Although many nineteenth-century observers would have understood and probably agreed with Bowlby, few would have written three books on this theme because, like the blue of the sky, the idea was too obviously true. Bowlby's conclusions are newsworthy in the last half of the twentieth century because historical events have led many citizens to question the inevitability of maternal devotion to the child and the child's love for his family. Parental abuse, neglect, and adolescent attacks on parents have undermined the nineteenth-century faith in the naturalness of familial love. As Shakespeare noted, strong pronouncements usually reflect doubt over the theme of the declaration. Modern citizens have begun to question the universal power of love between adults as well as between parents and children, are saddened by the products of their inquiry, and, therefore, are eager to hear a wise commentator on human nature

assert that love between child and parent is requisite for psychological health.

Interest in the child's interactive social experience was extended to other children and to the child's involvement with peer groups, topics missing from nineteenth-century texts but salient in modern studies of the child. Large cities with large schools create large peer groups that form referents for children and influence them in ways that would be unthinkable to nineteenth-century rural Americans. Discussions of the effects of radio, movies, television, and (more recently) computer games on cognition, morality, and behavior have become more frequent. The message in these discussions is that social events are the major incentives for change, and the foundations for the preservation of habits. This position is to be contrasted with the nineteenth-century view of a more isolated child growing according to a natural plan. At times it seems as if the objects of investigation are two different species—the nineteenth-century observer is describing bears; the twentieth-century scientist is discussing bees.

We can partially understand the change from an isolated child to a social one if we remember that there was a change in perspective over this period. The nineteenth-century author, who took a comparative perspective, regarded the infant as a transition between primates and the human adult and assumed the infant is closer to the former than to the latter. That is why the infant was described in terms one would apply to an animal: untamed, wild, and excitable.

This class of descriptors was replaced by terms that gentled the infant and construed him as dependent, relative to older children. The texts after 1970 inserted a new set of descriptors that took historically earlier statements about the child as its referent. Since 1960, researchers have shown that the baby is more sensitive to sights and sounds than observers previously believed. So, modern writers now declare that the infant is intellectually competent. (A rich volume on the infant, published by Joseph Stone and his colleagues in 1973, is entitled, *The Competent Infant*.) Once again, as in the nineteenth-century, the infant is given innate dispositions and freed from dependence upon others for cognitive growth.

From the Maturation of a Moral Sense to the Acquisition of Values

All reflective citizens are concerned with the conditions that threaten the maintenance of a harmonious society. Modern scholars worry about the danger of excessive variation in values and acquired skills, which is inevitable in a pluralistic society. Nineteenth-century authors, who were less tolerant, were convinced that children had to develop the same virtues for social harmony to be maintained. The nineteenth-century observers believed they could tame the variety in standards of conduct because they thought they knew what was morally proper for all citizens, and because they believed that morality was inevitable once *will* emerged in the second year and the child learned how to distinguish right from wrong.

Nineteenth-century theorists regarded a disposition to morality as partially innate and the primary developmental goal to be achieved, and made the uniform emergence of will and self-consciousness the mechanism of its actualization. James Sully (1896) wrote: "The facts here briefly illustrated seem to me to show that there is in the child from the first rudiment a true law abidingness" (p. 289), a "consciousness of violated instincts" (p. 279), and an "inbred respect for what is customary and wears the appearance of a rule of life" (p. 280). "The day when the child first becomes capable of this putting himself into his mother's place and realizing, if only for an instant, the trouble he has brought on her, is an all-important one in his moral development" (p. 290).

Sully believed all children must, because they were human, realize that causing pain to another is immoral. Such knowledge could never be lost, regardless of any subsequent cruelty the child may have experienced. Therefore, the child does not have to learn that hurting others is bad; it is an insight that accompanies growth.

James Mark Baldwin devoted the first half of his book on mental development (1897) to the growth of morality and tried to explain how the innate predisposition to imitate would lead a child who was exposed to moral adults to acquire a private conscience. "The origin of the moral sense shows it to be an imitative function. We do right by habitually imitating a larger self whose injunctions run counter to the tendencies of our partial selves" (p. 55).

Some texts written just prior to the transition in paradigm after World War I modulated a nineteenth-century emphasis on the maturation of a moral attitude and awarded greater potency, but not yet total power, to specific experiences with adults. For example, Gabriel Compayré, Rector of the University of Lyons, published a two-volume treatise on the infant (1914). He argued that although the inherited disposition of imitation is the basis for the socialization of values, the adults to whom the child is exposed are relevant because they determine what responses the child will imitate and acquire. More important, Compayré anticipated future writers by rejecting the older assumption that a moral sense is innate. In his view morality is acquired gradually, with pleasure and pain as the necessary catalysts.

This is why it is not an anachronism to think from the cradle of the responsibility, the moral obligations, that will one day rest on the head of the little child, smiling now in his unconscious innocence, his ideas and his feeling only the reflections of those of his parents; just as his left cheek or his right cheek, when he has finished nursing, like one side of a peach gilded by the sun, remains very red for several minutes, warmed as it is by the touch of the mother's breast. (Compayré, 1914, p. 185)

Other authors writing just before World War I agreed that although the content of a child's morality is determined by experience, rather than by nature, the child does inherit a disposition to adopt moral values. "The moral tendency to conform to law and to act for the good of others as well as self" (p. 61), is one of the two major instincts of man. "This instinct gives rise to feelings that one ought to act in conformity with certain laws fixed by the experience of the race or by customs and habits of groups of individuals" (Kirkpatrick, 1910, p. 61).

By the 1930s, however, morality was seen as an uncertain outcome unless parents train properly: "Unless a good many habit systems are gradually built into a child's conduct he cannot be expected to operate with any large degree of judgment and freedom" (Chave, 1937, p. 164). "Moral behavior . . . is not an innate tendency . . . it is a by-product of social living" (Chave, 1937, p. 202). And by the 1950s, the commitment to social conditioning was so complete that most writers rejected the notion that all children must be moral. All moral values, as well as the disposition to act morally, are learned. The modern conception of psychopathy assumes it is possible for a human being to be without a moral sense. "Each culture has its own typical personality—a particular pattern of motives, goals, ideals and values which is characteristic of and valued by that culture and which most children growing up in that culture acquire" (Mussen, Conger, and Kagan, 1974, p. 365). Only recently have theorists like Kohlberg returned to the hypothesis of an innate core to moral development; but this time the essential theme is cognitive rather than behavioral.

The commitment after World War I to the position that morality is acquired led naturally to an explanation that leans heavily on the law of effect. The canon of pleasure/pain, emphasized by the behaviorists, was consonant with the Freudian principle that the child wants the love of the mother. So, the loss of parental love, that modern exemplar of pain, became the primary incentive for adopting moral standards.

We are now able to summarize the motives which push the child to learn social controls. Certainly by the time the child is five or six years old, his desire to gain the approval of his parents is the chief motive for his accepting their cultural demands. . . . The desire to win the social acceptance from his parents and older brothers and sisters (and very soon from his teachers and his playmates) becomes a major drive of his behavior. This drive is really a form of adaptive anxiety. It makes him anxious, first, to avoid punishment and, second, to win that approval which leads to social reward (Davis & Havighurst, 1947, p. 38).

Modern texts continue this theme. In their section on the mechanisms of socialization, Mussen, Conger, and Kagan (1969) describe the silent bargain struck between parents and child:

By the end of the first year, the child appears to be highly motivated to please parents and thus insure continued affection and acceptance and, in addition, and related to this, to avoid the unpleasant feelings generated by punishment or rejection. . . . In a sense successful socialization involves an exchange in which the child gives up his desire to do as he pleases in return for the continued love and affection of his mother and father. (p. 260)

All authors are talking about the same set of events. A child washes his hands before dinner; brushes his teeth before bedtime; and refrains, when angry, from swearing, from throwing a plate at the wall, or from hitting his sister. It is not obvious that the reliability of these inhibitions is traceable to, and only maintained by, the fear of loss of love. As we indicated in a recent monograph on the second year (Kagan, 1981), the 2-year-old is bothered by a great many events that have as their central dimension the fact that the integrity of an object had been flawed: a crack in a plastic toy telephone, a chair that is missing an upholstery button. It is possible that the child's emotional distress to these events is not due only to a fear of anticipated loss of love. The nine-

teenth-century authors may have been correct when they guessed that the child may be biologically prepared for adopting moral standards.

From Will to Motive

All texts are concerned in a major way with the forces that determine the child's behavior. In those published before 1920, *will* bears the burden of explaining the acts chosen by the child; in modern texts, *motivation* assumes that responsibility. Listen to the nineteenth-century voice of William Preyer. "It is only through movement that the will directly expresses itself" (1889, p. 193) "All muscular movements of man may, in fact, be distinguished as willed and not willed, voluntary and involuntary" (p. 193). "The development of will . . . and the development of non-willing in the inhibition of frequently repeated movements furnishes the foundation for the formation of character" (p. 195).

Tracy and Stimpfl (1909), who defined will as "the union of desired goal with the action to get it" (p. 96), were most explicit in attempting to explain how will develops as an eventual consequence of action.

It at length comes to pass that movements are performed which are the expression of the conscious self, the index of will in the true and only proper sense of the word, involving a previous representation of the end sought, and (in their earlier stages) of the movements involved in attaining that end, as well as a deliberate forth-putting of the self in conscious effort towards the attainment. (pp. 105–106)

Finally we reach that stage—not necessarily subsequent to all the others, but partially synchronous with them—in which the will rises to its proper place as master of ceremonies, brings into subjection the impulsive and instinctive tendencies of which we have spoken, and assumes control of the child's activities. . . . The will is the person considered as active; and, instead of saying that, with the advent of what we call ideational movements, the will is born, and with that of deliberative movements, is perfected, it would be more correct to say that these movements are the first outward indications that the child is becoming the conscious master of his own activity. (p. 114).

Twenty years later this private executive had been exiled and the child was seen as a collection of habits and motives, "an organism which responds unthinkingly in more or less stereotyped ways to the main features of the environment'' (Curti, 1932, p. 183). *Will* was so central in early twentieth-century texts it was occasionally given a place in the explanatory equation equal to ''heredity'' and ''environment,'' as if it were a special organ every child could use to oppose or enhance the effects of his biology and the conditions created by his family. The seventh chapter of William Forbush's (1915) *Child Study and Child Training,* is entitled ''The Forces That Make a Man.'' The three forces are, in order of their mention, heredity, environment, and will. Forbush intended ''will'' to refer to the child as an actor rather than a passive recipient of heredity or experience.

> In a sense a child chooses his heredity, for while he may not choose any other than his own, he may choose to neglect or improve any part of his own. He may select his noblest competence and let his ignoble ones lie dormant, thus turning capacity into character. So one chooses his environment by making the largest use of his opportunities and ignoring those that would degrade him. Within the limit of his capacity a man may become what he will. (p. 52)

Piaget is an important figure in this story because he effectively compromised the mysterious phenomenon of will with the new language of conditioning. The problem facing any careful observer of young children is to explain intentional behavior. The 1-year-old child imitating his parent or carefully selecting one toy from three attractive alternatives seems to be behaving in a goal-directed way. The nineteenth-century observer explained these events by calling on the unobservable processes of will. The behaviorists strained intuition by suggesting that the imitation and planfulness seen at the end of the first year are conditioned. Piaget struck an attractive middle course. He denied both will and conditioning and posited stages of sensorimotor schemes—an idea that preserves both mechanism and connectivity by permitting intention to grow out of the practice of increasingly complex reflexes. The generality of his description makes it possible for many readers to accept this account or, at least, makes it difficult for them to reject it.

It is useful to focus on the same behaviors and see how pre- and posttransition interpretations differ. Both William Stern (1930) and Robert White (1959) noted that during the second year the child sets himself tasks to master—like the building of a block tower. Stern interpreted this behavior as an index of will. ''One of the earliest signs of awakening spontaneity in will is to be seen in the fact that the child of 15 months will set himself little tasks which he tries to accomplish'' (p. 463). Robert White classified the same event as a sign of the ''motive for effectance.'' The difference in connotation is important. Will connotes freedom of choice and spontaneity in selection. By contrast, Robert White generates the picture of a child impelled by a motive to be effective. The child cannot help building a tower with the blocks in front of him. This different description of the same activity furnishes another example of how the consciousness of a historical period influences the interpretation of the simplest event.

From Moral Choice to Moral Determinism

There is a special component to the construct of will that is missing from the concept of motivation. The former implies freedom of choice; the latter determinism. Nineteenth-century observers believed that punishment for immoral behavior is only possible if one can assume that a person knows right from wrong and can volitionally implement or inhibit an action. Under these conditions, he can be held morally responsible for his behavior. Hence, Preyer and Stern were curious as to when the first signs of this vital competence can be detected; not unlike physicists watching a Wilson cloud chamber and waiting patiently for evidence of the existence of a significant particle predicted by theory.

But by the second decade of the twentieth century, a profound shift in attitude had occurred. Psychologists now assumed that the determinism implicit in physical theory also applies to human action, a view that is temporally linked, not accidentally, to the new data on conditioning. If an adult's behavior is determined by, or is the result of, childhood experiences and the person has no control over those formative experiences, then perhaps we should not hold the person responsible for his immoral acts. This is not an idle controversy.

In a volume of edited essays called *Determinism and Freedom* (Hook, 1958), H. L. A. Hart asserted that one of the basic suppositions in American law is that moral culpability, not the criminal act, is the basis of responsibility in a crime and, therefore, must be the determinant of punishment. Margaret Curti's text on *Child Psychology*, published in 1932, contains a plainer assertion of this principle.

> In the first place, we may assure ourselves that the investigators are on sound ground in assuming that there are, for every delinquent act, antecedent conditions adequate to produce that result. The old doctrines of free choice, of an innate

moral sense, of chance, and of divine intervention have no place in a scientific inquiry into conduct. We must operate on the fundamental assumption of science that every event has a cause, which in psychology may be taken to mean that every act of a human being is a natural response to an adequate stimulating situation. (p. 413)

Although recent texts are not so blunt in challenging the responsibility of the adolescent delinquent, modern books contain that message in subtle form. Hetherington and Parke (1979) reflect the popular view that parental actions like physical punishments predispose a child to aggressive behavior and that "exposure to TV violence can breed indifference to certain individual's plight" (p. 629). This statement is more subtle than Curti's, but the connotation is similar. A child can become a moral or immoral adolescent or adult as a result of experiences over which he has no control. Most authors stop short of posing the dilemma as strikingly as Curti did. They avoid asking if the child is morally responsible for his behaviors; for Western scholars want to believe that poking through the heavy blanket of determinism is a tiny slit of sunlight allowing each person to have a private conscience that is not totally socially conditioned. "If the belief in freedom . . . is a necessary illusion; it is so deep and so pervasive that it is not felt as such" (Berlin, 1954, p. 33). After asserting in the first part of his essay on determinism that, "All our behavior is determined," George Wald finishes by admitting, "I think that we have freedom of will and that it comes out of our uniqueness as individuals, perhaps wholly determined, yet to some degree unpredictable" (Wald, 1965, p. 46).

Why is there such uncertainty surrounding the idea of free will when it is such a phenomenologically compelling experience? What has undermined our intuitions? The implication of determinism in modern physical science is certainly one source of doubt. The nineteenth-century promise of certainty in prediction of physical phenomena has tempted many to abandon the compelling intuition of free will. Both psychoanalytic and behavioral theory supported the determinacy axiom and the usual interpretations of psychological data added that certain events can predispose children to act immorally or incompetently. Parental punishment, insufficient love, foster homes, television, movies, peers, and poverty were all regarded as potentially productive of immoral behavior. And if those events are insufficient, some claimed that genes make a partial contribution to selected behavioral outcomes. The connotations in many chapters suggest that parents want to regard children as helpless victims of events they can not prevent, rather than as agents responsible for their acts of aggression and deceit.

There is, therefore, a serious inconsistency in modern writings on the child. On the one hand, there is a celebration of the competent infant and long chapters devoted to Piagetian principles that make the child active, reflective, inventive, and capable of moral inference and a private conscience. On the other hand, the child is described as a passive, helpless victim of punishment, neglect, indifference and superrealistic films of torture thrown up on 50-foot screens—a Gulliver made impotent by hundreds of thin chains he cannot sever.

We are also uncertain about how much power to award to the group, and how much to the self in situations requiring a moral decision. Western observers tend to regard any person who does not have a private conscience, one who behaves morally only because of concern with the group's reaction, as immature. If group sanctions are to control behavior two conditions must be met. First, there has to be minimal divisiveness among the group with respect to the values being socialized, and, second, the individual has to respect the group that gives or withdraws approval. Neither child nor adult is likely to worry about group disapproval if the "other" is not regarded as virtuous. There is greater heterogeneity of values among class and ethnic groups in Europe and North America than in Japan, and this diversity makes it difficult for the person to gain approval from the many people he or she meets. Indeed, one can count on disapproval of one's values from many individuals encountered during each day. Hence, Catholics, Protestants, Jews, and atheists must be tolerant of one another.

It may be necessary, therefore, that each child and adult become sensitized to the fact that he has a moral choice. Contemporary American parents tell their children not to conform to the peer group, but to decide what they believe and to act in accord with what they believe is proper. By contrast, Japanese parents continually remind their children to avoid behavior that would provoke anger and disapproval from others.[2]

We suggest that these two incentives for socialized behavior may not be part of a hierarchical structure or universal developmental sequence. The desire to avoid group disapproval may not be less mature or ontogenetically less advanced than a private conscience. In our society the former would not work; hence, we must rely on self-governance. To call *shame* less mature than *guilt,* or *anxiety over potential rejection* developmentally more primitive than *conformity to private standards* has an ethnocentric flavor, at least when it refers to adults from different societies, for it declares that one person's source of conscience is superior to another's.

The Stress on Individuality

The need for each individual to select an action based on personal standards has an important corollary. It makes each agent the essential unit of social control. It leads, we believe, to the popular assumption that each person's unique individuality is a gift, one of the sacred qualities of humanness. Geertz (1965) writes, "Being human is being individual" (p. 116); Wald (1965) emphasizes the "extraordinary individuality of living organisms." (I am not certain Wald would have made the unique shape of each snowflake so significant if asked to write an essay on the essential nature of snow.)

Early texts do not waffle in their celebration of individuality. Reflect on the first sentence of Lodge's (1910) book *A Parent and Child.* "The first thing to realize about children is that they are separate individuals, not merely chips off the old block . . . what parents sometimes forget is that they are separate persons, each with a life and destiny of its own" (p. 7). In his (1910) book, Kirkpatrick equates man's instinct for self-preservation with individualism, for he titled his chapter on self-preservation, "Development of the Individualistic Instinct." Kirkpatrick sees a connection among the sucking reflex of the infant in order to get food, the desire for social approval, and the older child's narcissism. He does not condemn these qualities, for they are advantageous instincts. Although "modesty is undoubtedly a most admirable thing in man . . . it is very disadvantageous in a child" (p. 97). "The more pride and ambition a child has . . . the better for his future development" (p. 97). "The first law of life should be one impelling to self-enlargement and development" (p. 97).

In a later chapter, Kirkpatrick explains why individuality is important. It is not, as modern observers may believe, an apology for egalitarianism or a plea for tolerance of minority group values. Rather, Kirkpatrick argues, the celebration of individuality is to permit the more talented in the society to actualize their capacities, as any evolutionist would understand. The children who are innately better adapted to their environment are most likely to be our leaders. Hence, to deny them their unique qualities is to deny society their talents and to fly in the face of evolutionary theory. "To the human race, individuality is even more important, for not only does it favor physical evolution, but also social progress. If there were no persons different from the common mass of mankind to serve as leaders and models for imitation, changes in customs and modes of thinking would be impossible. Progress would come to an eternal standstill" (p. 304).

The fourth edition of this book, published 19 years later (1929), contains no change in either the major themes or the organization. The salient differences reflect the introduction of the writings of Watson and Freud and a greater emphasis on the influence of the environment. There is a new chapter on modification of native endowments, a discussion of the child's need for interaction with other children, and a consideration of conditioning. But there is no evidence that Kirkpatrick thought that either the mother or the family is a primary influence on the child.

THE DETERMINANTS OF CHANGES IN CLASSIFICATION

Although psychological conceptualizations of the child have changed in several dimensions over the last century, I believe that the explicit emphasis on the importance of interactive social experience is the most significant. Although earlier writers acknowledge that stimulation, sensory feedback from action, and proper role models are formative experiences, they provide little or no discussion of the direct effects of the parents' behavior toward the child and almost nothing on the mother's actual caretaking practices. The script for growth describes a biological organism programmed to repeat actions that bring pleasure. Experience is seen as necessary for growth, but no specific contingent interactions between adult and child or between child and child are given any special priority. By 1930, however, this class of experience had become critical, and at a time when interest in the reasons for and, alleviation of, individual differences among children was a focus of concern. Why did this change occur so quickly? Why did it take less than 10 years for Pavlovian and Freudian ideas to enter American textbooks but almost 40 years for Piagetian theory to become as popular? We must assume that many educated Americans were prepared to believe that parental interactions with children, especially the mother's restriction and affection, are of profound significance for development.

Of the many historical events that occurred during the second and third decades of this century, four seem of special significance in contributing to the preoccupation with individual differences in adjustment as acquired through interactive social experience. These four are: (1) the increase in racial and ethnic tension threatening America's egalitarian ethos, (2) the self-consciousness of psychologists regarding the scientific status of their field, (3) the dissemination of conditioning theory, and (4) the growth of pragmatism and a relativistic attitude toward values.

The Threat to Equality

During the years before World War I, there was a serious increase in racial and ethnic tension between the new European immigrant and the urban black populations, on the one hand, and the Caucasian majority, on the other. Cravens (1978) and May (1959), among others, have documented that the increased numbers of European immigrants in the cities produced increased suspicion and hostility between middle-class whites and the minority groups, as well as legislation restricting immigration. This strife was especially strong during the middle of the second decade.

> Part of the reason for increasing tension was, as in earlier crises, economic. The depression of 1914 revived labor's fears of foreign competition and decreased the employer's interest in a steady flow of immigrant workers. Lawrence and Paterson presented to newspaper readers the picture of the dangerous alien immigrant. And everytime anybody, for any reason, worried about the preservation of old ways, he was likely to glance with alarm, at the annual inflow of half a million newcomers. (May, 1959, p, 347)

The highly publicized assumption was that the differences in ability, wealth, status, character, and criminality between native and immigrant groups were essentially biological in origin. Concern with proliferation of a less-advantaged group, which was bound to weaken the capacity of the larger society, led to a national conference on race betterment in 1914. One year later, twelve states had passed sterilization laws. Then, as now, the bias toward blacks centered on intellect. In April 1916 a writer in the *Archives of Psychology* put his conclusions in terms of statistics: "Pure negroes, negroes three-fourths pure, mulattoes, and quadroons have roughly 60, 70, 80 and 90 percent respectively of white intellectual efficiency" (Ferguson, 1916, p. 125, quoted in May, p. 349). And Karl Pearson (1925), who was

uneasy over the consequences of immigration into England wrote, "The whole problem of immigration is fundamental for the rational teaching of national eugenics. What purpose would there be in endeavoring to legislate for a superior breed of men, if at any moment it could be swamped by the influx of immigrants of an inferior race, hastening to profit by the higher civilization of an improved humanity" (cited in Pastore, 1949, p. 7).

The belief that the differences in ethnic and racial habits, styles of interaction, and especially mental abilities were genetic was strengthened when the mental tests administered to recruits as America entered World War I revealed that blacks and ethnic minorities had the lowest scores. The interpretation imposed by Robert Yerkes (1921) and Lewis Terman (1916)—two of the most influential psychologists of the time—was that these differences in mental ability were biologically based.

Sixty-five years later government officials again were worried about the very low scores on army intelligence tests produced by army recruits from minority groups—this time black and Hispanic rather than European. But six decades of history had altered the social consensus regarding the meaning of these scores. Hence, in 1980, the Secretary of the Army, Mr. Alexander, was able to do what his counterpart in 1915 could never have done. He challenged the test, removed the scores from the recruits' files, and insisted that despite their low scores these recruits were as capable as their civilian peers. (*New York Times,* August 10, 1980).

Although Terman softened his views in his later years, the earlier statement was provocative. These objective mental test scores were regarded as an index of a biological quality; hence, a genetic interpretation forced many Americans to confront an idea that was threatening to the national egalitarian ethos. There was good reason to believe that the majority of educated Americans wanted to believe in the ideal of a society in which the poor and disadvantaged could, through effort and motivation, lift themselves to the middle class. This hypothesis, which is essential to our argument, is supported by the fact that many geneticists and social scientists writing during the first two decades of this century—including Cooley, Watson, Boas, and J. B. S. Haldane—explicitly rejected the conclusions of Galton, Pearson, McDougall, and Terman. Hermann Muller (1933), a Nobel Laureate in genetics, wrote: "There is no sufficient basis for the conclusion that the socially lower classes or technically less advanced races, really have a genetically inferior intellectual equipment, since the differences between their averages are, so far as our knowledge goes, to be accounted for fully by the known effects of environment'' (p. 43).

Popular writers also insisted that the low IQ scores of immigrant children were amenable to social engineering. ''When a high level of economic independence and common education has been achieved then also will our tests register a higher level of common attainment'' (Link, 1923, p. 385). Even Arnold Gesell (Gesell & Lord, 1927) was friendly to this idea. He concluded an empirical paper on class differences in the behavior of 3-year-olds with a quotation from a speech that the utopian Robert Owen had given over a century earlier to an audience that included the President and the Congress of the United States.

> External circumstances may be formed as to have an overwhelming and irresistible influence over every infant that comes into existence, either for good or evil. . . . To surround him through life with the most agreeable or disagreeable object [will] . . . make any portion or the whole of the human race poor, ignorant, vicious and wretched, or affluent, intelligent, virtuous and happy. (p. 356)

Henry May (1959) affirms our suggestion that there was a national commitment to egalitarianism. ''The first and central article of faith in the national credo was, as it always had been, the reality, certainty, and eternity of moral values'' (p. 9). In this moral scheme evil was easy to define for ''it was incarnate in extreme inequality, political corruption and ruthless power'' (p. 22). May suggests that a majority of Americans would have been bothered—as Adam Smith and Helvetius would have been two centuries earlier—by any fact that threatened this idea. ''Most of the custodians of culture prophesied that America would prove able to deal with the immigrant flood, the vulgar plutocracy, the rising materialism of the middle-class, the attacks on sound education, and the many incomprehensible vagaries of the youngest generation. With democracy, but under the leadership of its proper guardians, idealism would be strengthened and culture spread through the land'' (p. 51). ''By hard work, most of the newcomers could probably be led toward the light'' (p. 38).

Essays in the *Atlantic Monthly* during the second decade reflected this premise. H. M. Chittenden (1912) asserted his faith in the basic genetic similarity of all humans. ''While human nature is ever the same, the growth and influence of civilization produces from this same nature ever changing re-

sults'' (p. 781). ''What marks us off from our ancestors is a changed environment and not a changed human nature'' (p. 782). Samuel Smith (1912) attacked those who were too quick to argue that genetic taint was the cause of criminal behavior; and William Jewett Tucker (1913) wrote, ''The demand for equality, like the demand for liberty whenever it is serious, takes precedence'' (p. 481).

Some scholars even criticized the institution of science for being too elitist:

> Prizes, honors, badges and degrees—all these have no necessary place in the machinery of higher education. (Speech by David Starr Jordon, cited in MacArthur & MacArthur, 1916, p. 464)

> Prostitution of talent and character, the development of an intellectual aristocracy in a democratic land, and absurd clamoring for petty honors increasing gaps and misunderstandings between classes and professions . . . dependence on reputation rather than on genuine worth . . . the effort to serve two masters—truth and the man immediately above one in rank . . . all of these are evils attendant upon our present system of academic honors and badges. (p. 466)

The objective mental test scores, therefore, posed a potentially serious inconsistency in national philosophy. If poor Italians, Slavs, and Jews were biologically less talented than native Caucasians, individual effort and proper education might not work. The resulting dissonance was as serious a source of unease as E. O. Wilson's suggestion that our moral attitude toward sexuality and aggression should be based on evolutionary facts, or Skinner's claim that each of us is not free because our present behavior is a determined product of past conditioning. It is not surprising that many educated liberals would be eager for any rational weapon that would neutralize the racial inferiority hypothesis.

The Self-Consciousness of Psychology

A second basis for the shift in paradigm lay in the fact that authors of psychological texts trained after 1900 were writing at a time when psychology as a discipline was trying to define itself as an experimental natural science, distinct from philosophy and biology, empirical in character, and pruned of metaphysics. The opening sentence of Watson's 1913 essay in the *Psychological Review* declared: ''Psychology as the behaviorist views it is a purely objective experimental branch of natural science'' (p. 158). Hence, the critique of racial inferiority had to be based on scientific evidence. Pavlov's work, which was made popular by John Watson, was seized on by the new cadre of psychologists. Conditioning was elegant, experimental science and its subject matter and language of description (stimuli, responses, reinforcements) belonged uniquely to the new scientific profession of psychology. In addition, conditioning emphasized the role of experience, not biology, in promoting both change and stability of psychological attributes. By the late 1920s learning had become a key mechanism in all texts, and with that change came longer discussions of the influence of experience, especially experience in the family.

The first empirical paper on the role of conditioning in development to appear in the *Pedagogical Seminary*, the chief organ for dissemination of technical papers on child development, appeared in 1916 when Feingold suggested that the imbecile might be taught to inhibit impulsive action. Five years later George Humphrey (1921) argued that the nineteenth-century assumption that imitation is an innate disposition should be replaced with an explanation that uses conditioning principles. And in 1931, Dorothy Marquis reported the successful conditioning of behavioral signs of ''eating behavior'' in the newborn. Marquis's paper marked the beginning of an increasing number of reports that relied on conditioning explanations of behavior in children. Her final conclusions are worth quoting: ''Systematic training of human infants along social and hygienic lines can be started at birth. Since habit function may begin so early the sharp lines drawn by some writers in their classifications of some acts as instinctive and some acts as learned must be viewed with some hesitation'' (p. 490).

Whether Watson and his colleagues realized it or not, by emphasizing the role of conditioning in development, they supplied the intellectual weapons necessary to defuse the racial inferiority hypothesis. By the 1930s the battle was over, for the hypothesis of innate racial differences was absent from major texts—the change was that rapid and total. Julian Huxley could now write in the *Yale Review* that the eugenicists had been wrong about racial inferiority.

The instinct controversy was all but over in January 1922. It had barely lasted half a dozen years. Before 1917 it was difficult to find any psychologists who questioned the instinct theory. By 1922 it was almost impossible to identify more than a handful of psychologists who still accept-

ed the human instinct theory as a legitimate category of scientific explanation. A similar shift of opinion occurred among social scientists who recognized after 1917 that they must attack the human instinct theory if they were to emancipate the social sciences from the intellectual thralldom of the evolutionary natural sciences. (Cravens, 1978, p. 191)

The ideas of behaviorism were accepted so quickly because there was a fire to put out; the fire was the social danger implied by the hypothesis of racial inferiority promoted during the years before World War I.[3]

The Rise of Pragmatism

The celebration of moral relativism after 1910 was also relevant to changes in the criteria for action and optimal development. The philosophy of pragmatism had been growing for two decades after James had borrowed and popularized Pierce's more abstruse views. Dewey (1910) added more formal and persuasive essays and, as a consequence, the principle that actions and decisions are local to situations became part of normative philosophy. Whatever action suits the situation best is to be the criterion for the morally proper decision. Listen to Dewey.

The abandonment by intelligence of a fixed and static moral end was the necessary precondition of a free and progressive source of both things and morals. (Dewey, quoted in May, p. 148.)

Morality was no longer a fixed unchanging code, but something remarkably like the old code turned up in the particular findings of almost all these transitional thinkers. Progress was no longer a universal single movement, but wherever one looked things were getting better. People no longer needed the old fixities; they could do better without them (and few doubted, at bottom, that they knew what better meant). Repudiate, commanded a generation of relativist thinkers, the outworn notions of universal moral absolutes. When this is done, we will be able to advance toward truth, freedom, and justice. (May, p. 141.)

Pragmatism was seen as an optimistic philosophy that, bolstered by the assumptions of behaviorism and psychoanalysis, ''provides an inspiration and a hope which belief in absolute and unalterable values destroyed. All things are possible provided the will to achieve is present'' (Langdon-Davies, 1926, p. 645).

By 1910 a growing number of scholars were arguing for government interference in the economic affairs of the laissez-faire state in order to protect the less fortunate. Just as the social Darwinian ''philosophy of Spencer had remained supreme in the heroic age of enterprise, so pragmatism, which, in the two decades after 1900, rapidly became the dominant American philosophy, breathed the spirit of the progressive era'' (Hofstadter, [1944] 1959, p. 123).

Between the Spanish-American War and the outbreak of the first World War there was a great restlessness in American society which inevitably affected the patterns of speculative thought. The old scheme of thought was repeatedly assailed by critics who were in sympathy with the new spirit of the progressive era. The intellectual criticism engendered by this discontent fired the energies and released the critical talent of new minds in history, economics, sociology, anthropology, and the law. . . . It is easier to enunciate the achievements of this renaissance than to characterize its intellectual assumptions, but certainly its leading figures did share a common consciousness of society as a collective whole rather than congeries of individual actions . . . the most original thinkers in social science had ceased to make their main aim the justification and perpetuation of existing society and all its details. They were trying to describe it with accuracy, to understand it in new terms and to improve it (pp. 168–169).

Benevolent environmental intervention, which is central to the pragmatic view, is obviously in accord with the central premise of behaviorism.

World War I added the skepticism necessary to make a pragmatic view attractive. The innocence applied in the views of Howells, Taft, and other turn-of-the-century Americans was shattered by the war. If the world is irredeemably evil, then the only reasonable life strategy is to determine what qualities are prized and to get them. Successful adaptation—attaining what is valued—defines moral virtue. If there is no absolute attribute that all children must acquire, but each should develop whatever talents and values befit his time and location, then individual variation in the attainment of the local good is of greater interest than the growth of the species toward some hypothetical terminal state which may not exist. Thus, psychologists turned to

the problem of individual variation in adjustment: how to predict it from behavioral signs in early childhood, its correlated background factors, and, by the 1930s, ways to intervene in order to hasten it.

The acceptance of a relativistic attitude toward morality may have had a profound effect on the dominant mood of the members of our society. Each person must be able to reassure himself of his basic virtue (translate ''goodness,'' if you like). The culture decides on the symbols that define virtue. But of central importance is whether the power of reassurance lies mainly within the person or in the environment. Consider the difference in the definition of virtue between the Puritans and today's middle-class adults. The former followed Locke's declaration that self-denial is the central characteristic of virtue: ''And the great principle and foundation of all virtue and worth is plac'd in this: that a man is able to deny himself his own desires'' (Locke, [1693] 1892, p. 21). Locke implies that if a person temporarily feels he has lost the esteem that conscience awards to self, he can repair that loss by resisting a temptation to excessive power, aggression, money, or love. Aaron Burr's letter to his father-in-law, Jonathan Edwards, captures the ameliorative powers of prudence and restraint: ''From my childhood I used to be under distress of mind'' owing to ''a guilty conscience and the fears of hell; at these times, as I remember, I used to get relief by promises and resolutions. . . . I used to set myself as twere in the presence of God and make over his resolutions which would give me ease'' (cited in Greven, 1977, p. 89).

The evangelical Puritans of the seventeenth and eighteenth centuries, ''often felt themselves to be capable of bringing about their own salvation by the exercise of their own wills and by the power which they felt they had over their own actions and lives'' (Greven, 1977, p. 87). The critical fact is that each person was able to administer this reward autonomously; he did not need help from other people—or chance.

Contrast the Puritan with the contemporary American adult. The relentless seeking of power, fame, wealth, and love have lost their status as sins and, instead, have become the goals to attain. The modern definition of sin is to fail to gain these prizes. Put plainly, it is extremely difficult for an adult who is poor, powerless, anonymous, and lonely to feel virtuous because the person knows he or she has resisted the desires of a corrupt society and an excessive pride in self. In contrast with John Adams and Jonathan Edwards, the modern adult is less able to administer the elixir of worth to the self solely *through his own acts.* He is dependent, to a large degree, on the behaviors and decisions of others, events over which he does not have complete control. That psychological state is likely to generate a mood of anxiety rather than the distress of guilt or conflict characteristic of the Puritans. The search for morality by contemporary adults is a search for a standard of virtue that can be met whenever one chooses, for each person wishes to control the time and occasion of the distribution of moral reassurance.

CHILD PSYCHOLOGY TODAY

I have tried to show that some of the classification terms used for young children and their behaviors are based on historically limited presuppositions about human nature. Some were comparatives whose meaning required specifying the referent. The 3-day-old infant can discriminate red from blue but does not understand the meanings of color terms. This description of real events is of interest and may be used in a future theory of cognitive development. But neither statement implies that the infant is either helpless or competent.

The aim of empirical science is to study regularities in phenomena and to use sentences or mathematical statements to describe and explain them. The empiricist whose work is guided by ideas that do not refer to real events should consider starting with events, rather than words. Newton advised, ''The main business of natural philosophy is to argue from phenomena.'' The modern biologist understands this well, for he does not begin his work by asking about the meaning of life; he searches for relations among real phenomena, or their signs. Social scientists too often begin their inquiry by accepting the reality of a traditional idea whose relation to phenomena is uncertain when it might be more profitable to find first regularities among data. I believe that studies of human development are likely to clarify some of our major problems if more investigators will first gather rich corpora of information on the growing child and to invent classifications a posteriori to explain regularities. I do not favor a rigid avoidance of inventive a priori theorizing. Scientists must continue to make wise guesses about words that may unite real phenomena or guide the gathering of information. But a mood of self-criticism is likely to be helpful during this temporary period of theoretical barrenness.

The Prospect

Although prophecy is rightfully a questionable avocation, a timid form that inquires only a few years into the future does not require excessive originality and probably is not dangerous.

We have suggested, in the body of this chapter, that changes in the presuppositions about the child during the second and third decades of this century were the product of many social forces, including increased ethnic tension, the low IQ scores of World War I recruits, pragmatism, the loss of faith in moral absolutes, and the dissemination of Pavlovian and Freudian theory. But this coherence needed a deeper, unifying assumption—a premise against which to evaluate the social facts. It is likely that the deep premise was a belief in the equality of all citizens and the hypothesis that proper early experiences could attain that desirable goal.

Prediction of the future of developmental psychology cannot be given with complete confidence because it is not possible to know if historical events will threaten this basic premise. A nuclear war, ungovernability, ethnic rebellion, a serious economic depression—each of which is unpredictable—could generate enough unease to alter societal assumptions. I see no reason to doubt that the egalitarian ethic will persist, at least for the next quarter century, and believe that threats to its validity will provoke a reaffirmation of benevolent environments and justice. The alternative is to be persuaded that the fact of biological differences among children implies different privileges and different educational treatments. I do not see America acting on that premise unless civil strife mounts to a point where egalitarianism will be forced to yield to expedience. But assuming the continuity of the present frame, the history of the natural sciences and contemporary trends in psychology provide a useful guide to the likely sources of new constructs and new facts. The two most important influences on future research in developmental psychology are likely to be discoveries in biology and the invention of new methods.

Biology as Guide

When science replaced Christian philosophy as the source of metaphor for man the disciplines that studied human nature looked first to physics for guiding analogies. Enlightenment scholars characterized man in society as machinelike and mechanical, and Saint-Simon tried to establish laws of society that simulated physical laws. Historical change was to obey natural laws in as commanding a way as

Newton's principles. But when biology grew in stature, especially after evolutionary theory, the sciences of man and culture turned to it as sibyl. The ideal of purposive, gradual, connected, and cumulative growth toward a better form emerged, and Herbert Spencer became oracle.

Modern biology, however, contains special facts and suppositions. Until recently, most biologists had not been interested in variations among members of a population. But, advances in biochemistry have led molecular biologists to become more concerned with individual variation. The surprise to many was that although the external characteristics of a species may show little variability, there is often extraordinary variability in their biochemistry. Indeed, it is not unusual to find a dissociation between external and internal properties. Some groups that are morphologically different turn out to be similar biochemically, while groups that have similar external appearances often possess markedly different chemical compositions. Thus, racial groups differing in facial form and body morphology often have similar molecular constituents, while groups with similar morphology have a different biochemistry (Karlin, Kennett, & Bonné-Tamir, 1979). The lack of correlation between external features and internal biochemistry led Kimura (1979) to the controversial suggestion that some biochemical features may have no selective advantage. Some physiological characteristics may emerge and be maintained, despite no adaptive significance, through random drift. It is now possible to entertain the idea that not every genetic change that is maintained over generations is beneficial. Randomness—implied in Monod's *Chance and Necessity* (1971)—is a fact of nature and enduring events that are neither predictable nor beneficial are always a possibility. This notion may make psychologists a bit more receptive to the idea that some behaviors may have no adaptive purpose and occur simply because the conditions that release them persist—the reflex smile of the newborn is one candidate for this class.

The ability of molecular biologists to create in just a few hours new species minimally connected with the past might make developmental psychologists more willing to accept selected discontinuities in psychological growth. The next great developmental theorist may not insist so forcefully that the stages of ontogeny form a seamless story from origin to terminal state.

Perhaps the most significant consequence of the current ascendance of biology is that scholars will once again acknowledge the influence of the maturation of the central nervous system on emerging psychological forms. Investigators will, with increasing frequency, ask about the psychological accompaniments to the growth of the brain. It is likely that the major consequences will involve the enhancement of memory, evaluation, planfulness, inference, and even self-consciousness. For example, the neuronal density in the cortex of the human infant decreases rapidly over the first year and stabilizes in the middle of the second year, a fact that led Rabinowicz (1979) to write "that a very important moment in cortical maturation appears to be the period between 15 and 24 months, a period at which almost all the layers reach, for the first time, a similar rate of maturation" (p. 122).

It is probably not coincidental that this is the same time that Lewis and Brooks-Gunn (1979) report the appearance of self-recognition and when Kagan (1981) finds evidence for the appreciation of standards, distress over not meeting them, and what seems to be an awareness of the self's ability to control the behavior of others. Collaborative studies between neurophysiologists and developmental psychologists are likely to become as frequent and profitable as the cooperation between biochemists and biologists that began over a quarter century ago.

Finally, it is significant that biology deals with organized forms; physics with quantities. Because there exists a more elaborate language for the quantification of discrete entities than there does for the description of forms, psychologists have conceptualized constructs like schema, idea, memory trace, expectancy and motive as continua and arbitrarily assigned numbers on an ordinal scale to different behavioral manifestations of these functions. The invention of new ways to describe the organization of forms will probably facilitate both theorizing and measurement in psychology.

New Methods To Be Tried

A second, more concrete force on the future will be the invention of new methods. A likely consequence of the extraordinary advances in the neurosciences will be the invention of techniques to measure the neural correlates of cognitive functioning using computer analyses of electrocortical recordings—"CAT-scans" for thought. Should such techniques continue to grow in sophistication, study of dynamic cognitive processes like short-term memory, perception, imagery and decision making would become even more central than they are today. Additionally, the growing conviction that the maturation of the central nervous system paces changes in cognition and affective display during the first years of life would be affirmed by the use of such techniques.

Karmel and his colleagues have found a remarkable congruence between the density of contour in a checkerboard pattern on the one hand and both the sensory-evoked potential and duration of behavioral attention in young infants, on the other, which implies an intimate relation between the two dependent variables (Karmel, Hoffman, & Fegy, 1974). Behavioral studies of infants' responses to standardized incentives finds developmental discontinuities at 2, 8, 13, and 21 months (McCall, Eichorn, & Hogarty, 1977). These ages correspond to the times when neurophysiologists have determined new wave forms in brain potentials which imply changes in function and structure (Dreyfus-Brisac, 1979; Emde, Gaensbauer, & Harmon, 1976). I do not interpret these correspondences as indicating that the new physiological functions explain or cause the emergent behavioral events, only that the growth of the brain is one of the many conditions that must be met if the behavior is to occur.

The neurophysiological measures are likely to be helpful in settling issues regarding the state or knowledge structures of the child when the behavioral evidence is ambiguous. One promising phenomenon is the event-related potential. Donchin (1979) has summarized the psychological correlates of the event-related potential. The data are persuasive of the hypothesis that the latency and amplitude of the third positive wave (P_3), and, perhaps, the fourth negative wave (N_4), may be useful parameters. For example, when a subject is exposed to an unexpected event (e.g., a red light after many green ones, or vice versa) a positive wave at about 300 ms appears in the resultant wave form. The amplitude seems to be a function of the surprise value of the event; and the latency to that wave to be a function of how much mental work is necessary to detect the fact that it is discrepant. If these tentative suggestions grow into principles, such techniques will be useful in studying conceptual growth and discrimination. At the present time, investigators working on discrimination and category extraction in infants are dependent upon habituation/dishabituation techniques to infer discriminability or concept acquisition. If the P300 occurred to a stimulus that did not produce dishabituation of attention, investigators would feel more confident about their generalizations regarding the discriminative capacities of infants.

Theory in the cognitive sciences has come to rely on the construct called *speed of information processing* to make inferences about the amount of mental effort required in a specific problem context. The event-related potential is likely to prove useful in providing supplementary evidence regarding the temporal parameter in information processing. A specific illustration of this promise involves the detection of meaning in language. Kutas and Hillyard (1980) have found that when adults read sentences one word at a time that are either true or invalidated on the last word (e.g., "trucks travel on highways" versus "trucks travel on bedspreads"), a negative wave at about 400 ms appears to the false sentences. This fact suggests that recognition of the false quality of the sentences generated the wave, but it took about 400 ms for the brain—or mind—to recognize that fact. An extensive study of dyslexic children found that about one-third of them are very slow in deciding on the validity of propositions as assessed by decision times to oral presentation of sentences. The longer decision times may occur because the dyslexics are slower in retrieving the meaning of the words or because they are slower in evaluating the validity of the sentence (Moore, Kagan, Sahl, & Grant, 1982). If these dyslexic boys showed either the N_4 or the P_3 wave substantially later than normal children, one of the above interpretations would be strengthened considerably and an insight into this syndrome would be gained.

A second methodological advance likely to be helpful to psychologists is use of memory to measure motivational and attitudinal variables. Years ago, Kagan (1967) demonstrated that college women who were more concerned with their grades than with their social relationships recalled more words of a poem they thought was written and read by an achieving college woman than a poem read by a less-achieving woman who was more concerned with affiliation. The opposite result held for women who were more concerned with friendships. Jordan (1973) found that high school adolescents with outstanding grades recalled more words related to power and recognition than adolescents with average or below-average grades. But both groups of children recalled equal numbers of words related to aggression or friendship. Further, Moore, Kagan, and Haith (1978) found that 8-year-old children stated in a recognition memory context that they had heard sentences that were related to their own motivational hierarchy. The children first heard a list of motivationally neutral sentences. Days later, they were read pairs of sentences, both of which contained the same key phrase present in one of the neutral sentences that had been read earlier. However, the two sentences differed in their motivational relevance. For example, one sentence might be,

"John wanted to be with his friends when he went to the aquarium''; the second sentence would be, "John wanted to read a lot of books about fish before he went to the aquarium.'' The phrase "went to the aquarium'' was common to both sentences, but the first had an affiliation content and the second an achievement content. The children whom the teacher said were more concerned with school achievement than with friends chose the second sentence; children whom the teacher said were more concerned with friends than with achievement said they had heard the first sentence. It is reasonable to suppose that the child's hierarchy of concerns will affect the registration and retrieval of information related to those concerns. The child who wants friends and thinks about his lack of friends will be sensitized to information that engages those ideas and, therefore, will register them more clearly. As a result, the child will be more likely to recall such information. Investigators might use differential recognition and recall of information related to a set of motives as a possible index of the child's motive hierarchy.

Similarly, selective recall of information containing references to complementary attitudes might reveal the person's differential commitment to one or the other of the related beliefs. In a recent unpublished study in our laboratory, working- and middle-class mothers of young children first listened to and then recalled a 400-word communication. The brief essay compared the relative desirability of a restrictive socialization regimen that produced a child who would be successful in school and work but afraid of authority, with a permissive regimen that created a less frustrated and less fearful child but one who might become antisocial or reluctant to persist with unpleasant assignments. The working-class mothers recalled more words favoring the permissive regimen; the middle-class mothers recalled more words favoring the restrictive practices. Independent data gathered from interviews with the mothers and home observations of the mother and child suggested that differential recall of the two themes in this communication depended on whether the mother cared more about a child who would be receptive to adopting a posture of reasonable conformity to authority or a child who would not be overly intimidated by authority. Although the use of selective recall to evaluate the position of an attribute in a hierarchy of related beliefs is still a new measurement idea, it seems to be a promising strategy.

Kosslyn's work on imagery also provides a possible basis for studying attitudes and motives. Kosslyn (1980) has found a linear relation between distance separating two elements in an image and the time to traverse mentally the distance between the two elements. This technique might be used to tap how a person implicitly regards others and how he or she regards relationships between people or classes of people. Suppose the investigator wanted to know if a child created an image of the father larger than that of the mother. The child is asked to image the father at a specified distance and then asked to focus mentally on the feet of that person. The subject would then scan the image until he reached the top of the head, and then respond. The time necessary to scan the image presumably reflects the extent scanned over the image and, thus, indexes relative size. It would be interesting to conduct this experiment without requiring that both parents be imaged at the same distance. One might find that subjects seem to image one parent closer than the other (and thus have a greater visual arc to span), which could reflect something about the child's feelings toward the person.

A related phenomenon, called the congruity effect, also might be helpful (Kosslyn, Murphy, Bemesderfer, & Feinstein, 1977). The congruity effect occurs when a subject is asked to compare mentally two entities. If one is asked which of two normally large entities is larger, reaction time is faster than if one is asked which of the two is smaller. The effect is reversed if one is asked about two small entities. Thus people seem to respond more quickly if the question is presented in terms of the pole of the dimension at which they fall. The congruity effect might be used to study motivations and attitudes. The child's attitudes about two individuals could be assessed by asking him or her to image two people or events side by side and decide which is more happy, sad, clean, or better. If the child were asked to evaluate each pair a number of times, each pole of the dimension being used equally often in the question, the differences in response times for the two adjectives presumably would reflect the way in which the child conceived of that pair of people. For example, if a child had an unhappy home life, he or she might require relatively less time to decide which parent was the meaner than which was the nicer one.

The advantage of these techniques is that they circumvent a host of output variables that normally intervene between conception and response. These techniques could be used with children who have difficulty expressing themselves directly or with children who are loathe to discuss emotionally charged topics.

A fourth methodological advance involves multidimensional scaling to assess categories children and adults use to structure experience. It is difficult, if not impossible, to detect those categorical dimensions by interview or other direct methods. For example, consider a child's conceptualization of the peers in his classroom. Third and fourth graders in a public school classroom were told the names of trios of children of the same sex who were in that class, and asked to select the two children who were alike and to eliminate the one who was different. Occasionally, the subject was a member of the trio. When these triad data were submitted to multidimensional scaling, it was found that dominant behavior and academic talent were correlated in some classrooms, and these two attributes were characteristic of the popular children in those classrooms. In other classrooms, academic skill was not correlated with dominance and popularity (Kagan, Hans, Markowitz, Lopez, & Sigal, 1982).

Other investigators are using multidimensional scaling to detect the values, attitudes, and belief systems of parents. Lower middle-class Mexican mothers living in Guadalajara were asked about the desirability of each of 12 psychological attributes for each of five ages and also indicated the degree to which different socialization agents might influence the acquisition of that psychological property. A multidimensional scaling preference analysis revealed that the mothers valued independence in their children but saw themselves as having a relatively small impact on the child's attainment of that quality. However, the mothers believed they did have a serious influence on the child's morality and degree of obedience (Magaña & Magaña, 1980). Investigations of parental attitudes toward children, which now rely on questionnaires and interviews, would be enriched by the use of multidimensional scaling to detect the structure of the parental beliefs, as similar studies of adult conceptualizations of animals have revealed the structure of that semantic space with a sensitivity and power not usually afforded by the direct interview.

Of course, film, telemetry, electromyography, and recordings of heart rate, as well as other new techniques, are likely to continue to be effective. The feature common to the new methodologies is the analytic frame from which they are derived. Although observations of the molar behavior of children and parents have provided the basic material for empirical work in child psychology—as they had to—such observations, like all surface phenomena in nature, are multiply determined and often more ambiguous as to releasing condition than a more elemental component of the subject's repertoire. No science can progress without assessment of both surface and internal properties. A million hours of observation will never reveal, without analysis of body fluid, the fact that there is a hormonal change between 11 and 13 years of age that is accompanied by new psychological profiles. It is important to note that the new methods are indifferent to the content of the construct they serve, for cortical potentials or recall memory can be used to study cognitive, motivational, or affective structures and states. We may see a renewed interest in motivation that will equal the curiosity displayed between the two world wars, a curiosity that waned after 1960 when faith in the extant methodologies was eroded. This writer believes that developmental psychology is about to experience a renaissance as tired dogma is refuted, more sensitive measurement techniques are introduced into the laboratory, and data, rather than sentimental assumptions, provide the ideas for investigations.

NOTES

1. It is likely that another reason for this attitude toward play held by nineteenth-century writers is based on an ambivalence toward economic materialism. A calculating, cost-benefit analysis of major decisions and the conduct of human relations has an emotionally restricting influence on daily life. Such a mood requires acceptance of one's exploitative desires and awards greater salience to man's narcissism and selfishness than to his charitable and cooperative sentiments. Scholars who were friendly to a Romantic conception of human nature were troubled by the demeaning quality of an unrelieved economic rationale for behavior and nostalgic for the innocence of child play, where the act is entered into for its own sake. I am grateful to Isaac Kramnick for this idea.

2. The Japanese view places the individual and society in a more complementary relationship. The individual gains his goals through, and with the help of, the group, without alienation from the group. "What would be strictly a private matter in an individualistic society tends to be a group enterprise in Japan. . . . Collective cooperation is taken so much for granted that a Japanese may not become aware of it until he is displaced from his group." (Lebra, 1976, pp. 25–26). "The Japanese concern for belonging relates to the tendency towards collectivism, which is expressed by an individual's identification with the collective goal of the group to which he belongs. Collectivism thus involves cooperation and solidarity, and the sentimental desire for the warm feeling of *ittaikan* (feeling of oneness) with fellow

members of one's group is widely shared by Japanese,'' (Lebra, 1976, p. 25).

3. It is possible to see analogous historical processes during the last decade. The environmental interpretation of adjustment, which grew steadily more popular from 1930 to the late 1960s, reached a crest in the 1950s when extreme forms of psychopathology—schizophrenia and autism—were regarded as totally environmental in origin. But after the Civil Rights movement and the desegregation of schools, society was led to believe that sufficient expenditure of money and effort to improve the education of minority children would alleviate the gap in wealth and occupational status between the classes. Unfortunately, it did not. The apparent failure, like the test scores of 1917, had to be confronted and reconciled with the unswerving belief in environmentalism. Additionally, scientists had found that schizophrenia had a genetic component and that autism was not simply the product of a harsh mother. The philosophy of extreme environmentalism became suddenly vulnerable at a time when biology was having extraordinary success in demonstrating the brain's inherent properties, including the way human beings perceive the world. Hence, biological explanations of behavior met as receptive an audience as conditioning theory did a half-century earlier, for it seemed to provide a rational explanation for the failings in adjustment of minority groups. But the outcry from those who still believed in the egalitarian ethic was strong. Some of the current arguments against sociobiology often reduce to statements of faith in egalitarianism.

REFERENCES

Arlitt, A. H. *Psychology of infancy and early childhood.* New York: McGraw-Hill, 1928.

Baldwin, J. M. *Mental development in the child and the race.* New York: Macmillan, 1895.

Baldwin, J. M. *Social and ethical interpretations in mental development: A study in social psychology.* New York: Macmillan, 1897.

Berlin, I. *Historical inevitability.* London: Oxford University Press, 1954.

Bernfeld, S. *The psychology of the infant.* New York: Brentano's, 1929.

Bonné-Tamir, B., Karlin, S., & Kennett, R. Analysis of genetic data on Jewish populations, 1. Historical background, Demographic features and genetic markers. *American Journal of Human Genetics,* 1979, *31,* 324–340.

Bowlby, J. *Attachment and loss* (Vol. III, *Loss*). New York: Basic Books, 1980.

Chave, E. J. *Personality development in children.* Chicago: University of Chicago Press, 1937.

Chittenden, H. M. Does human nature change? *The Atlantic Monthly,* 1912, *109,* 777–782.

Chomsky, N. *Language and mind* (2nd ed.), New York: Harcourt Brace Jovanovich, 1972.

Churchland, P. M. *Scientific realism and the plasticity of mind.* Cambridge: Cambridge University Press, 1979.

Compayré, G. *Development of the child in later infancy* (Part 2). New York: D. Appleton, 1914.

Conger, J. *Adolescence and youth* (2nd ed.). New York: Harper & Row, 1977.

Cravens, H. *The triumph of evolution.* Philadelphia: University of Pennsylvania Press, 1978.

Curti, M. W. *Child psychology.* New York: Longmans Green, 1932.

Darwin, C. *Descent of man and selection in relation to sex* (Vol. 1). New York: D. Appleton, 1871.

Darwin, C. *On the origin of species by means of natural selection* (6th ed.). New York and London: Merrill and Baker, 1872. (Originally published, 1859.)

Darwin, C. A biographical sketch of an infant. *Mind,* 1877, *7,* 285–294.

Davis, W. A., & Havighurst, R. J. *The father of the man.* Boston: Houghton-Mifflin, 1947.

D'Espagnat, B. The quantum theory and relativity. *Scientific American,* 1979, *241, 5,* 158–181.

Dewey, J. *The influence of Darwin on philosophy.* New York: Holt, 1910.

Donchin, E. Event-Related Potentials. In H. Begleiter (Ed.), *Evoked potentials in psychiatry.* New York: Plenum, 1979.

Dreyfus-Brisac, C. Ontogenesis of brain bio-electrical activity and sleep organization in neonates and infants. In F. Faulkner and J. M. Tanner (Eds.), *Human Growth* (Vol. 3). New York: Plenum Press, 1979.

Emde, R. N., Gaensbauer, T. J., & Harmon, R. J. *Emotional Expression in Infancy* (Vol. 10, No. 1, Monograph 37). New York: International University Press, 1976.

Evans, E. E. *The abuse of maternity* (Originally published in Philadelphia: Lippincott, 1875). New York: Arno Press, 1975.

Feingold, G. A. The association reflex and moral development. *The Pedagogical Seminary,* 1916, *23,* 468–476.

Fenton, J. C. *A practical psychology of babyhood,* Boston: Houghton, Mifflin, 1925.

Ferguson, G. O. The psychology of the negro. *Archives of Psychology,* 1916, *36.*

Fichte, J. G. *The Science of Knowledge*. London: Trubner, 1889. (Originally published, 1794.)

Fiske, J. *The Meaning of Infancy*. Boston: Houghton-Mifflin, 1909. (Originally published, 1883.)

Forbush, W. B. *Child Study and Child Training*. New York: Scribner's, 1915.

Gardner, H. *Developmental psychology*. Boston: Little-Brown, 1978.

Geertz, C. The impact of the concept of culture on the concept of man. In J. R. Platt (Ed.) *New views of the nature of man*. Chicago: University of Chicago Press, 1965.

Gesell, A., & Lord, E. E. A psychological comparison of nursery school children from homes of low and high economic status. *The Pedagogical Seminary*, 1927, *34*, 339–356.

Gorer, G. Theoretical approaches–1941. In M. Mead & M. Wolfenstein (Eds.), *Children in contemporary cultures*, Chicago: University of Chicago Press, 1955.

Greven, P. *The Protestant temperament*. New York: Knopf, 1977.

Groves, E. R. Parents who haven't grown up. *Harper's Magazine*, 1925, *151*, 571–579.

Gulick, L. *A philosophy of play*. New York: Scribner's, 1920.

Hanson, N. R. *Patterns of discovery*. Cambridge: Cambridge University Press, 1961.

Hart, H. L. A. Legal responsibility and excuses. In S. Hook (Ed.), *Determinism and freedom in the age of modern science*, New York: New York University Press, 1958.

Hetherington, E. M., & Parke, R. *Child psychology* (2nd ed.). Holt Rinehart & Winston, 1979.

Hofstadter, R. *Social Darwinism in American thought* (Rev. ed.). New York: George Braziller, 1959. (Originally published by the University of Pennsylvania Press, 1944).

Hook, S. (Ed.). *Determinism and freedom in the age of modern science*. New York: New York University Press, 1958.

Hughes, H. S. *Consciousness and society*. New York: Vintage Books, 1958.

Humphrey, G. G. Imitation and the conditioned reflex. *The Pedagogical Seminary*, 1921, *28*, 1–21.

Jordan, J. The relationship of sex role orientation to competitive and noncompetitive achievement behaviors. Unpublished doctoral dissertation, Harvard University, 1973.

Kagan, J. On the need for relativism. *American Psychologist*, 1967, *22*, 131–142.

Kagan, J. *Change and continuity in infancy*. New York: John Wiley, 1971.

Kagan, J. Overview: Perspectives on human infancy. In J. Osofsky (Ed.), *Handbook of infant development*. New York: John Wiley, 1979.

Kagan, J. *The second year*. Cambridge, Mass.: Harvard University Press, 1981.

Kagan, J., Hans, S., Markowitz, A., Lopez, D., & Sigal, H. Validity of children's self-reports of psychological qualities. In B. A. Maher and W. B. Maher (Eds.), *Progress in experimental personality research*, vol. 11, New York: Academic Press, 1982, 171–211.

Kagan, J., Linn, S., Mount, R., Reznick, J. S., & Hiatt, S. Asymmetry of inference in the dishabituation paradigm. *Canadian Journal of Psychology*, 1979, 33, 288–305.

Karlin, S. Kennett, R., & Bonné-Tamir, B., Analysis of biochemical data on Jewish populations: 2. Results and interpretations of heterogeneity indices and distant measures with respect to standards. *American Journal of Human Genetics*, 1979, *31*, 341–365.

Karmel, B. Z., Hoffman, R. F., & Fegy, M. J. Processing of contour information by human infants evidenced by pattern-dependent evoked potentials. *Child Development*, 1974, *45*, 39–48.

Kimura, M. The neutral theory of molecular evolution. *Scientific American*, 1979, *241*(5), 98–129.

Kirkpatrick, E. A. *Fundamentals of child study* (Rev. ed.). New York: Macmillan, 1910; 4th ed., 1929.

Kosslyn, S. M. *Image and mind*, Cambridge, Mass.: Harvard University Press, 1980.

Kosslyn, S. M., Murphy G. L., Bemesderfer, M. E., & Feinstein, K. J. Category and continuum in mental comparisons. *Journal of Experimental Psychology: General*, 1977, *106*, 341–375.

Kutas, M., & Hillyard, S. A. Reading senseless sentences: Brain potentials reflect semantic incongruity. *Science*, 1980, *207*, 203–205.

Langdon-Davies, J. The relativity of human nature, *Harper's Magazine*, 1926, *153*, 640–645.

Langer, J. *Logic in the infant*. New York Academic Press, 1980.

Lebra, T. S. *Japanese patterns of behavior*. Honolulu: East-West Press, 1976.

Lewis, M., & Brooks-Gunn, J. *Social cognition and the acquisition of self*. New York: Plenum, 1979.

Link, H. C. What is intelligence? *Atlantic Monthly*, 1923, *132*, 374–381.

Locke, J. *Some thoughts concerning education*. Cambridge: University Press, 1892. (Originally published, 1693.)

Loftus, E. F., & Loftus, G. R. On the permanence of stored information in the human brain. *American Psychologist,* 1980, *35,* 409–420.

Lodge, O. *Parent and child.* New York: Funk & Wagnalls, 1910.

Lovejoy, A. O. *The great chain of being.* Cambridge, Mass.: Harvard University Press, 1936.

MacArthur, C. G., & MacArthur, C. B. The menace of academic distinctions. *The Scientific Monthly* 1916, *2,* 460–466.

Magaña, J. R., & Magaña, H. A. An experimental approach to the study of parental values. (Unpublished manuscript, Harvard University, 1980.)

Mandelbaum, M. *History, man and reason.* Baltimore: The Johns Hopkins University Press, 1971.

Marquis, D. R. Can conditioned responses be established in the newborn infant? *The Pedagogical Seminary,* 1931, *39,* 479–492.

Marwedel, E. *Conscious motherhood* (Part 1). Boston: D. C. Heath, 1889.

May, H. *The end of American innocence.* New York: Knopf, 1959.

McCall, R. B., Eichorn, D. H., & Hogarty, P. Transitions in early mental development. *Monographs of the Society for Research in Child Development,* 1977, *42* (Serial No. 171).

Merry, F. K., & Merry, R. V. *The first two decades of life: A revision and extension of from infancy to adolescence.* New York: Harper & Row, 1950.

Métraux, R. Parents and children: An analysis of contemporary German child-care in youth guidance literature. In M. Mead & M. Wolfenstein (Eds.), *Childhood in contemporary cultures.* Chicago: University of Chicago Press, 1955.

Monod, I. *Chance and Necessity.* New York: Kropf, 1971.

Moore, M. J., Kagan, J., & Haith, M. M. Memory and motives. *Developmental Psychology,* 1978, *14,* 563–564.

Moore, M., Kagan, J., & Sahl, M., & Grant, S. *The study of reading disability. Genetic Psychology Monographs,* 1982, *105,* 41–93.

Muller, H. The dominance of economics over eugenics. *Scientific Monthly.* 1933, *37,* 40–47.

Mumford, E. E. R. *The dawn of character in the mind of the child.* New York: Longmans Green, 1925.

Mussen, P. H., Conger, J. J., & Kagan, J. *Child development and personality* (3rd ed. New York: Harper & Row, 1969.

Mussen, P. H., Conger, J. J., & Kagan, J. *Child development and personality.* (4th ed.). New York: Harper & Row, 1974.

Pastore, N. *The Nature–Nurture Controversy.* New York: King's Crown Press, 1949.

Pearson, K. Problem of alien immigration into Great Britain. *Annals of Eugenics.* 1925, *1,* 5–127.

Perez, B. *The first three years of childhood* (A. M. Christie, Trans.). London: Swann Sonnenschein, 1900.

Piaget, J. *Play, Dreams, and Imitation in Childhood* (C. Gattegno & F. M. Hodgson, Trans.). London: Routledge & Kegan Paul, 1951.

Pinchbeck, I. & Hewitt, M. *Children in English society* (Vols. 1 and 2). London: Routledge & Kegan Paul, 1969, 1973.

Plattner, E. *Die ersten Lebensjahre: Ein Erziehungsbuch.* Heidelberg: Quelle and Meyer, 1951.

Preyer, W. *The mind of the child,* Part I. *The Senses and Will.* New York: Appleton, 1888.

Preyer, W. *The Mind of the Child,* Part II. *The Development of Intellect.* New York: D. Appleton, 1889.

Rabinowicz, T. The differentiate maturation of the human cerebral cortex. In F. Faulkner & J. M. Tanner, *Human Growth* (Vol. 3). New York: Plenum Press, 1979.

Rand, W., Sweeny, M. E., & Vincent, E. L. *Growth and development of the young child.* Philadelphia: W. B. Saunders, 1930.

Richardson, F. H. *Parenthood and the newer psychology,* New York: G. P. Putnam, 1926.

Russell, B. The training of young children. *Harper's Magazine,* 1927, *155,* 313–319.

Sears, R. R. Your ancients revisited. In E. M. Hetherington (Ed.), *Review of Child Development Research* (Vol. 5). Chicago: University of Chicago Press, 1975.

Shinn, M. *Notes on the development of a child* (Vols. 1 and 2, University of California Series, 1893 to 1899). University of California Publications in Education, 1907.

Simon, H. A. *The science of the artificial.* Cambridge, Mass.: MIT Press, 1969.

Smith, S. G. The new science. *The Atlantic Monthly* 1912, *110,* 801–809.

Stern, W. *Psychology of early childhood up to the sixth year of age.* (A. Barwell, Trans.). New York: Holt Rinehart, (6th German ed., 1930).

Stone, L. J., Smith, H. T., & Murphy, L. B. *The competent infant.* New York: Basic Books, 1973.

Sully, J. *Studies of childhood.* New York: D. Appleton, 1896.

Sunley, R. Early 19th-century American literature on child rearing. In M. Mead & M. Wolfenstein (Eds.), *Childhood in contemporary cultures,* Chicago: University of Chicago Press, 1955.

Terman, L. *The measurement of intelligence.* Boston: Houghton Mifflin, 1916.

Tiedemann, D. Beobachtungen über die Entwickelung der Seelenfänigkeiten bei Kindern. Altenburg: Oskar Bonde, 1897.

Tracy, F. & Stimpfl, J. *The psychology of childhood* (7th ed.). Boston: D. C. Heath, 1909.

Tucker, W. J. The goal of equality. *The Atlantic Monthly* 1913, *112,* 480–490.

Wald, G. Determinacy, individuality, and the problem of free will. In J. R. Platt (Ed.), *New views of the nature of man.* Chicago: University of Chi-

cago Press, 1965.

Watson, J. B. Psychology as the behaviorist views it. *Psychological Review,* 1913, *20,* 158–177.

Watson, J. B. The place of the conditioned reflex in psychology. *Psychological Review,* 1916, *23,* 89–116.

Watson, J. B. What is behaviorism? *Harper's Magazine,* 1926, *152,* 723–729.

Watson, J. B. *Psychological care of infant and child.* New York: Norton, 1928.

White, R. W. Motivation reconsidered: The concept of competence. *Psychological Review,* 1959, *66,* 297–333.

Yerkes, R. M. *Psychological examining in the United States Army.* Memoirs of the National Academy of Sciences, Vol. 15. Washington, D.C.: National Academy of Sciences, 1921.

AUTHOR INDEX

SUBJECT INDEX